Creamier

– CONTEMPORARY ART IN CULTURE –

10 international curators visualize the future of contemporary art

A ROUNDTABLE DISCUSSION — *Elena Filipovic, Douglas Fogle, Yukie Kamiya, Inés Katzenstein, Chus Martínez, Kitty Scott, Debra Singer, Adam Szymczyk, Catherine Wood, & Tirdad Zolghadr*

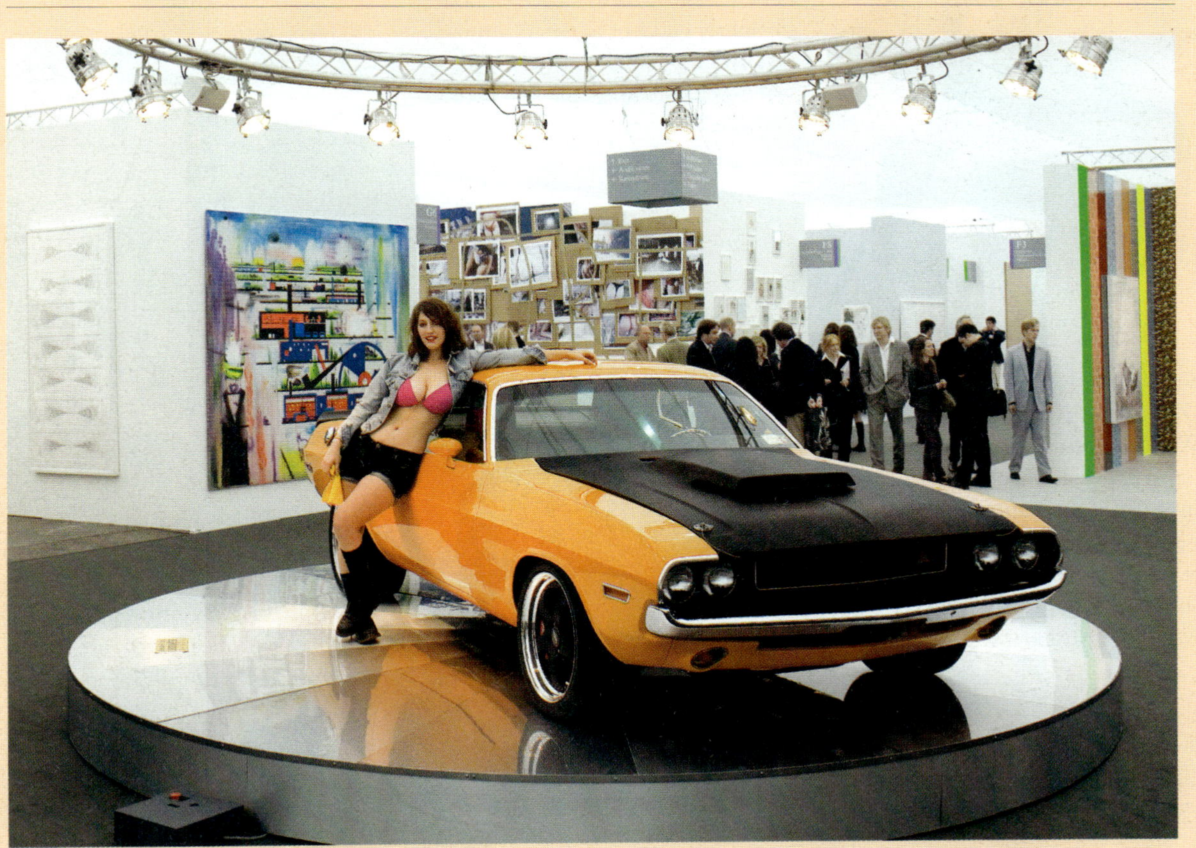
Frieze Art Fair, London, 2007

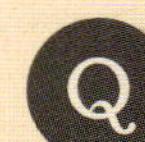

Phaidon

In the autumn of 2007, at London's Frieze Art Fair, the critic Dave Hickey gave a keynote address about the current state of the art world and its market. Referring to the hyper-activity of the fair, he said: 'As exciting as this is, imagine how exciting the collapse will be.' This foreshadowing took place at a moment when the art world was ballooning with hitherto unseen levels of wealth and production. Since then — in a dramatically short space of time — it has felt the reverberations of the current global recession. Undeniably, the art world is experiencing the onset of change due to the economic climate, and many conversations concerning value and content have begun to circulate. As curators working in various cities all over the world in differing curatorial capacities, both independent and institutional, what transformation or adjustments do you see happening in both curatorial and artistic practices?

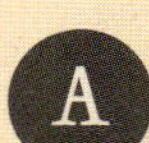

Debra Singer

Historically, moments of economic recession have been extremely interesting times for meaningful art-making, at least in New York. So it's hard not to remain a little bit optimistic that we'll see some important and courageous new work coming down the pike. At an institutional level, the specific financial events of autumn 2008 in New York had a swift and seismic effect, leading to an immediate and significant decline in individual philanthropy throughout the city, which is a mainstay of funding for arts groups here. In this respect, smaller institutions like The Kitchen have probably been weathering the storm a bit more easily than the larger museums. We're perhaps more nimble in our ability to respond quickly to such change. Small non-profit arts institutions

don't have huge endowments, for instance, to rely on for operating funds, so don't suffer from huge fluctuations in those resources. Similarly, for emerging artists in particular, it's not as though the booming go-go days were especially different for them. When you're starting out, resources are always scarce, and you have to be inventive. Going from 'How can we do more with a little?' to 'How can we do more with less?' isn't such a big leap — yet. Obviously, the full effects of this current recession have yet to be felt; let's hope it doesn't go on for too many years.

Inés Katzenstein

In the last years, countries like Argentina, where I work, have enjoyed in a very small way the reverberations of the affluence referred to by Hickey: the small but relevant growth of the local art market, a slow process of professionalization of the art system with some local museums showing international exhibitions. But those reverberations haven't changed the way artists

Undeniably, the art world is experiencing the onset of change due to the economic climate

and the art world operate. Our context is always one of austerity and therefore one in which a sense of permanent construction pervades everything, beyond our financial circumstances.

With this, I'm not suggesting that the global financial circumstances don't affect our work, but rather that a sense of crisis (and a context of financial scarcity) is inherent to the way in which

Continued on page 3

10 Curators

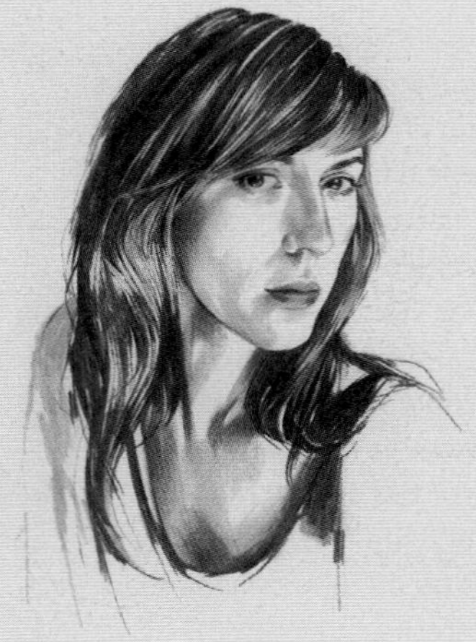

Elena Filipovic
Associate Curator at Wiels Centre d'Art Contemporain, Brussels. She was co-curator of the 5th Berlin Biennial (2008) and co-editor of *The Manifesta Decade: Debates on Contemporary Art Exhibitions and Biennials in Post-Wall Europe* (2006).

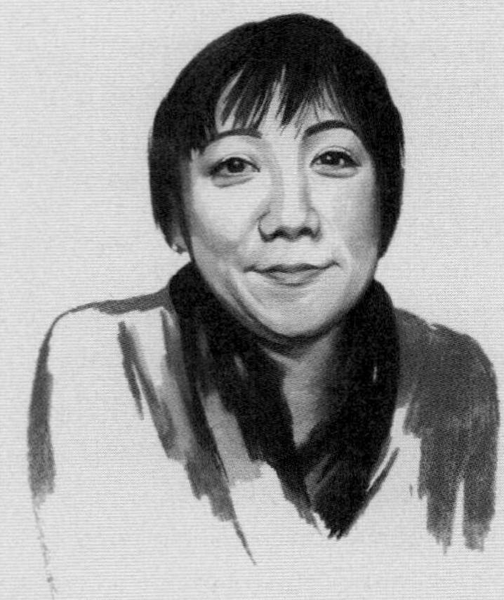

Yukie Kamiya
Chief Curator of the Hiroshima City Museum of Contemporary Art, Japan. She was co-curator of 'Thermocline of Art: New Asian Waves' (2007) at ZKM, Karlsrue, and formerly Adjunct Curator at the New Museum, New York.

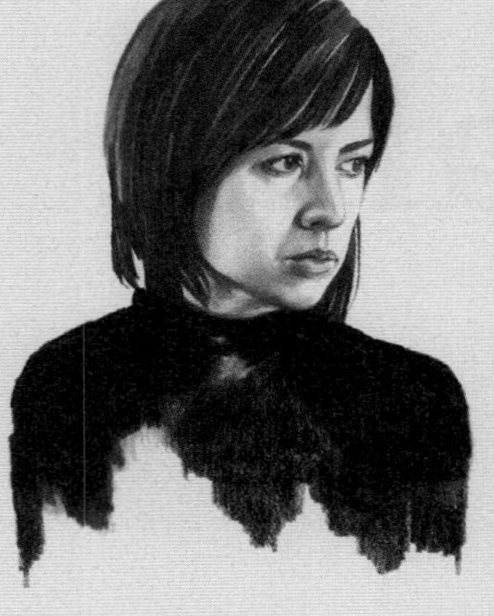

Chus Martínez
Chief Curator of the Museu d'Art Contemporani de Barcelona (MACBA). She is Associate Curator of the 2010 São Paulo Biennial and a former Director of the Frankfurter Kunstverein.

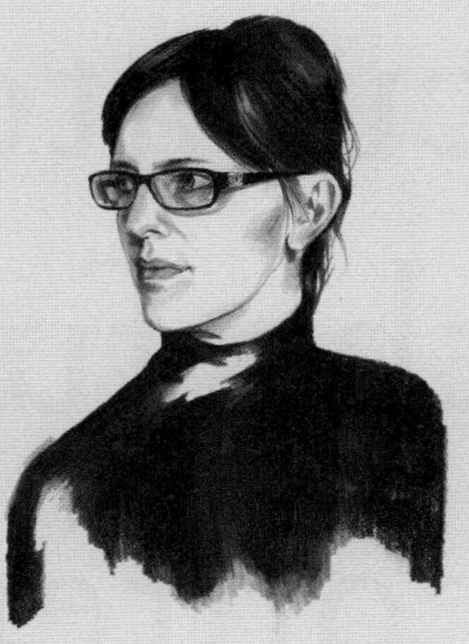

Catherine Wood
Curator of Contemporary Art and Performance at Tate Modern, London, where she co-curated 'Pop Life: Art in a Material World' (2009) and 'The World as a Stage' (2007).

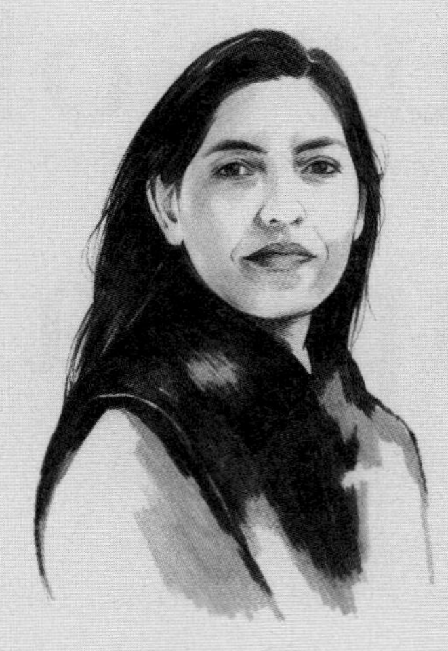

Debra Singer
Director and Chief Curator of The Kitchen, New York. She was formerly Curator at the Whitney Museum of American Art, where she co-curated the 2002 and 2004 Whitney Biennials.

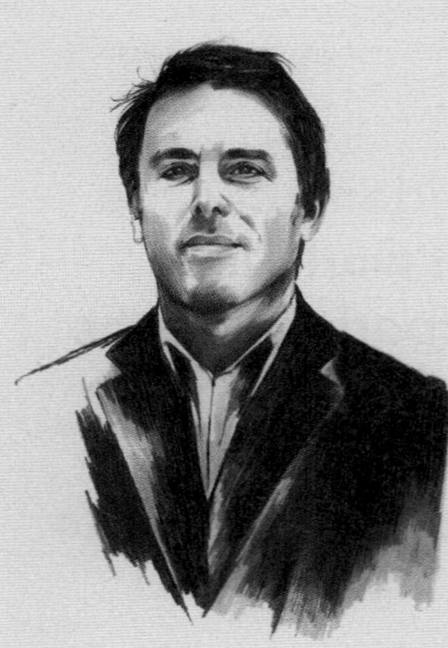

Douglas Fogle
Chief Curator and Deputy Director of Exhibitions and Public Programs at the Hammer Museum, Los Angeles. He was formerly Curator of Contemporary Art at the Carnegie Museum of Art, Pittsburgh.

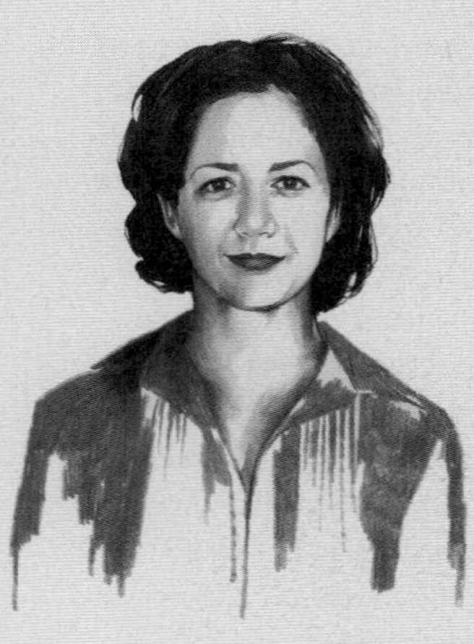

Inés Katzenstein
Independent curator and Director of the Art Department at the Universidad Torcuato Di Tella, Buenos Aires. She was co-curator of the 6th Mercosul Biennial, Brazil, and formerly Curator of the Museo de Arte Latinoamericano de Buenos Aires.

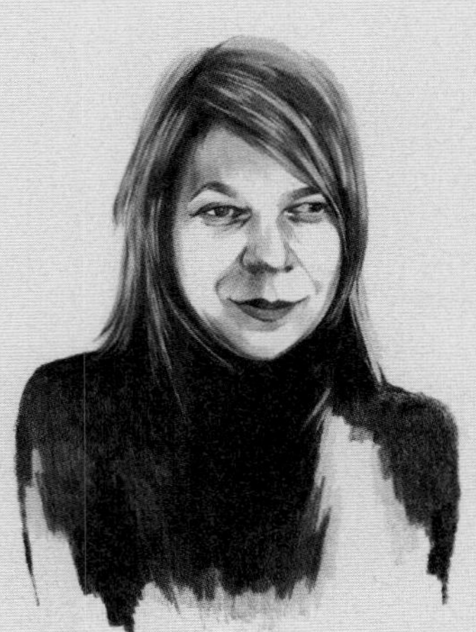

Kitty Scott
Director of Visual Arts at the Walter Phillips Gallery and the Banff International Curatorial Institute at the Banff Centre, Canada. Formerly Chief Curator of the Serpentine Gallery, London, and Curator of Contemporary Art at the National Gallery of Canada, Ottawa.

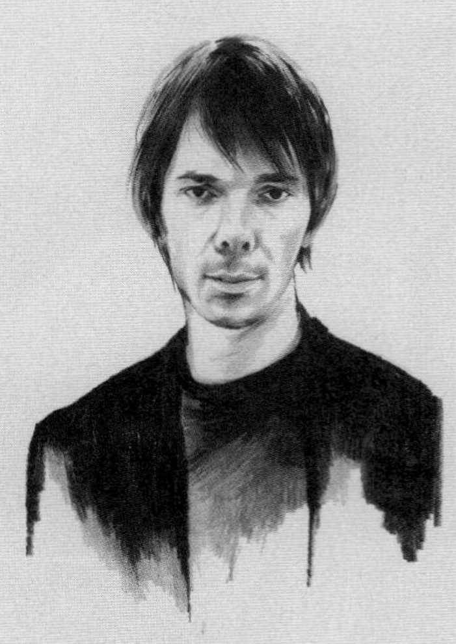

Adam Szymczyk
Director of Kunsthalle Basel. He was co-curator of the 5th Berlin Biennial and formerly Curator of the Foksal Gallery Foundation, Warsaw.

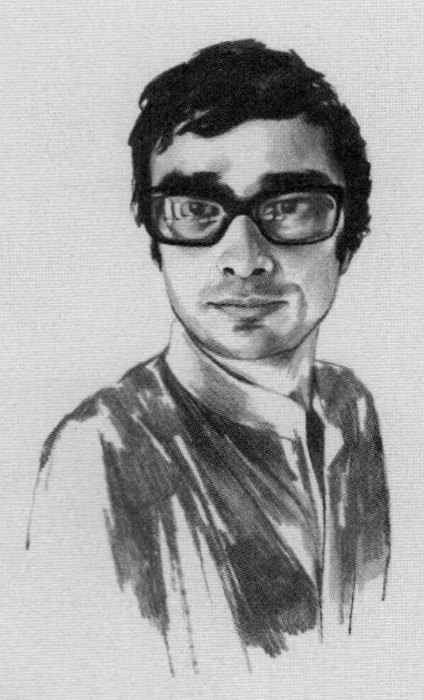

Tirdad Zolghadr
An independent curator and writer based in Berlin. He curated the United Arab Emirates pavilion at the 2009 Venice Biennale and was co-curator of the 2005 Sharjah Biennial.

More and more, the artist's position seems to have become one of responding to demands and fulfilling them to schedule, instead of pursuing aesthetic aims within a practice that sets out its own terms

Continued from page 1

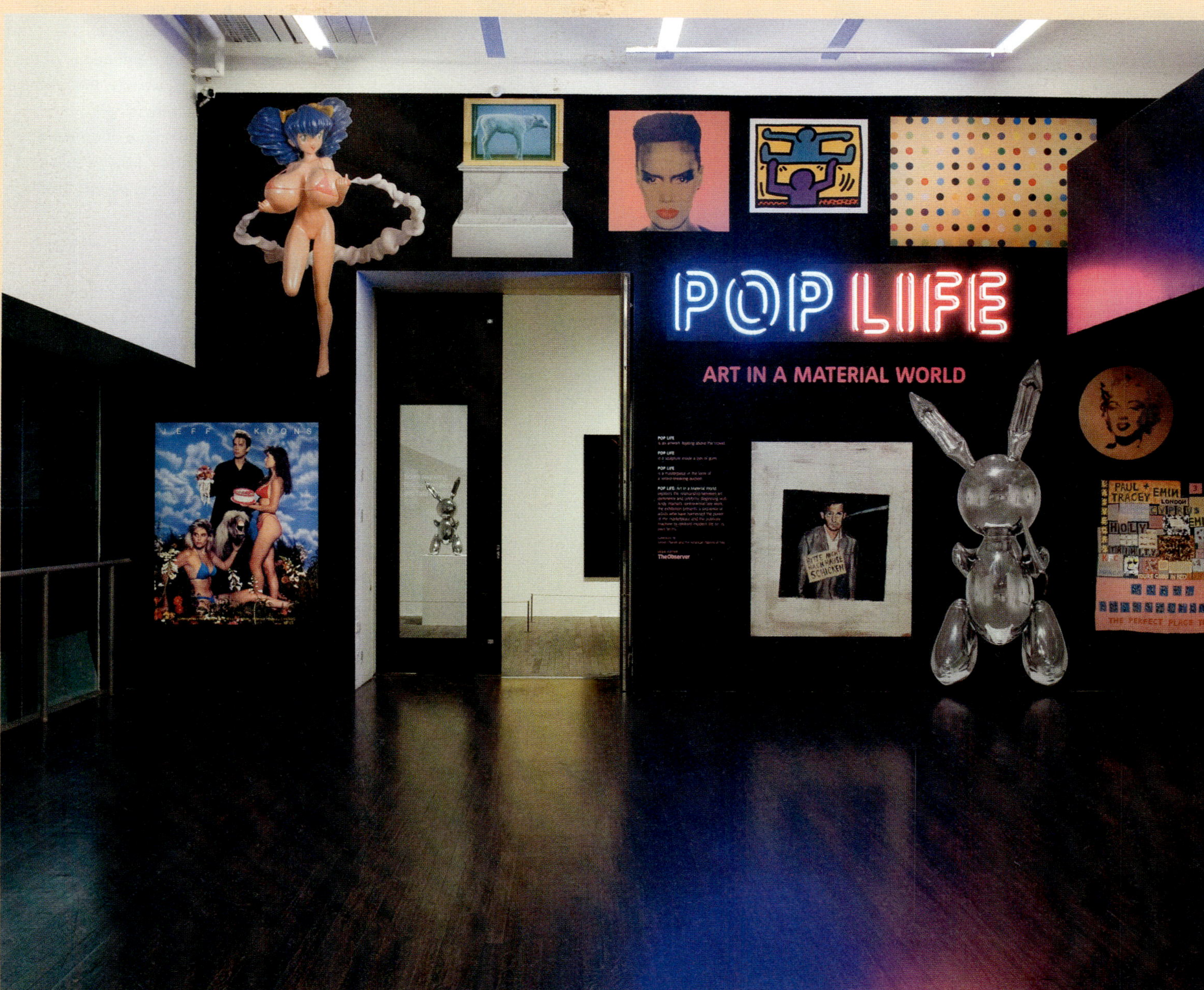

Pop Life, Tate Modern, London, 2009

institutions and artists produce here. Since there was no bubble here (in the sense of a euphoric environment of high prices and affluence), we didn't feel a collapse. But if, as Debra says, the full effects of this crisis have yet to be felt, things might change, and not for the better.

Yukie Kamiya

The unprecedented boom in the art market had a tremendous effect on the art scene in Asia. Starting from an accelerated level of global attention given to Chinese art, it prevailed in other countries, such as India, Korea and here in Japan. In China, many new museums have opened at an amazingly fast pace, almost like the proliferation of Starbucks coffee outlets. But in reality there isn't yet a sufficient variety of infrastructure for art in many Asian countries. That's one reason why the market dominates as a major platform to promote art and artists in Asia.

Not only the blooming of international biennials but also the rise of hyper-active fairs have provided numerous opportunities for exposure to the global art scene for artists working in the local sphere. In this trend, however, artists tend to emphasize stereotypical images of Asia in art that hold a general appeal and repeat a similar or standardized style, technique and subject. The current recession has given us an opportunity to cool down, and we're now able to evaluate artistic practice according to criteria that are different

from the market value, exploring a sustainable system for supporting art. Hopefully, a much greater variety of expression will emerge as a counteraction to the collapse of the art bubble.

In the case of Japan, institutions whose full support comes from public money have been suffering a long recession for the past few years. On top of this, the economic crisis of last year was a hard blow. Under these circumstances, art and artists are being used as a device for revitalizing a city; they are invited to participate in various events and temporary projects in the public space. This is a big concern: that an artistic practice is required to take a specific direction. How does the creative and innovative nature of art survive in such limited conditions? But a ray of hope could be found in the darkness.

Catherine Wood

I've lost count of the number of artists of all persuasions and levels of market success who've told me that they embrace the prospect of a recession. I've felt that it might be a good thing, too. While some artists produce art that suits the rapacious appetite of the market for a consistently high turnover of 'signature' works, many don't, and for the latter I get the strong sense that these last years of increasing globalized demand (via fairs and biennials) have distracted them from the reasons why they set out to make art. More and more, the artist's

position seems to have become one of responding to demands and fulfilling them to schedule, instead of pursuing aesthetic aims within a practice that sets out its own terms. It's true that alongside a collapse of the commercial market comes the withdrawal of philanthropic funding that enables all kinds of presentation formats for art to exist. But the art world has become so vast, so professionalized, such a circus of activity, that perhaps even the corrosion of this situation wouldn't be such a bad thing.

At Tate this past year, I've been working at two very different ends of the spectrum. As a curator specializing in performance, I feel the pinch so far as supplementary funding for this activity goes, which, whilst we recognize it curatorially as a core facet of contemporary practice, is, in funding terms, still deemed to be somewhat 'extracurricular'. At the other end of the spectrum, the exhibition 'Pop Life: Art in a Material World', which I co-curated with Jack Bankowsky and Alison Gingeras, looks specifically at how artists have negotiated their positions as 'workers' vis-à-vis the market, and is presented by the institution as a 'blockbuster'. Whilst performance is generally credited with being antagonistic to the production of valuable objects, it does require substantial resources to put on in a public space. Although the work in 'Pop Life' is popularly understood to be involved with money, and

reliant on it (many people ask whether the show still made sen[se] a recession), in fact, much o[f the] exhibition is concerned with [the] day-to-day survival on a mod[est] (Cosey Fanni Tutti's magazin[e work] or Lucas/Emin's Shop) or wit[h] at the top end of the market [the] re-writing the given commerc[ial] systems in the art world on th[eir] terms, and creatively disrupti[ng] Examples of this would be th[e case] of Andy Warhol selling T-shir[ts for] $100 in the gallery and the sa[me] for $10 in the street, or Dami[en Hirst] gambling on what anyone wo[uld] have told you a year ago was [career] suicide: putting a whole bod[y of] work straight into auction, or [in] the complicated critical loop [made] by Andrea Fraser pre-selling [a video] that documented her having [sex with] the collector who had paid fo[r it].

Maybe a desire for p[eriodic] deprivation is a human tende[ncy], like religious fasting, and ma[ybe] these periods do engender c[reativity]. But perhaps, too, it's danger[ous] to romanticize what the rece[ssion] actually means, which in rea[lity] is bleak unemployment, a sq[ueeze] on public services, the return [of] conservative political values [and the] unglamorous prospect — as [Mark] Leckey recently put it — of '[long] queues at the post office'.

Elena Filipovic

The funny thing (which is to [say not] really funny at all) is that the [market] and the art world have alway[s been] inextricably linked. Whatever

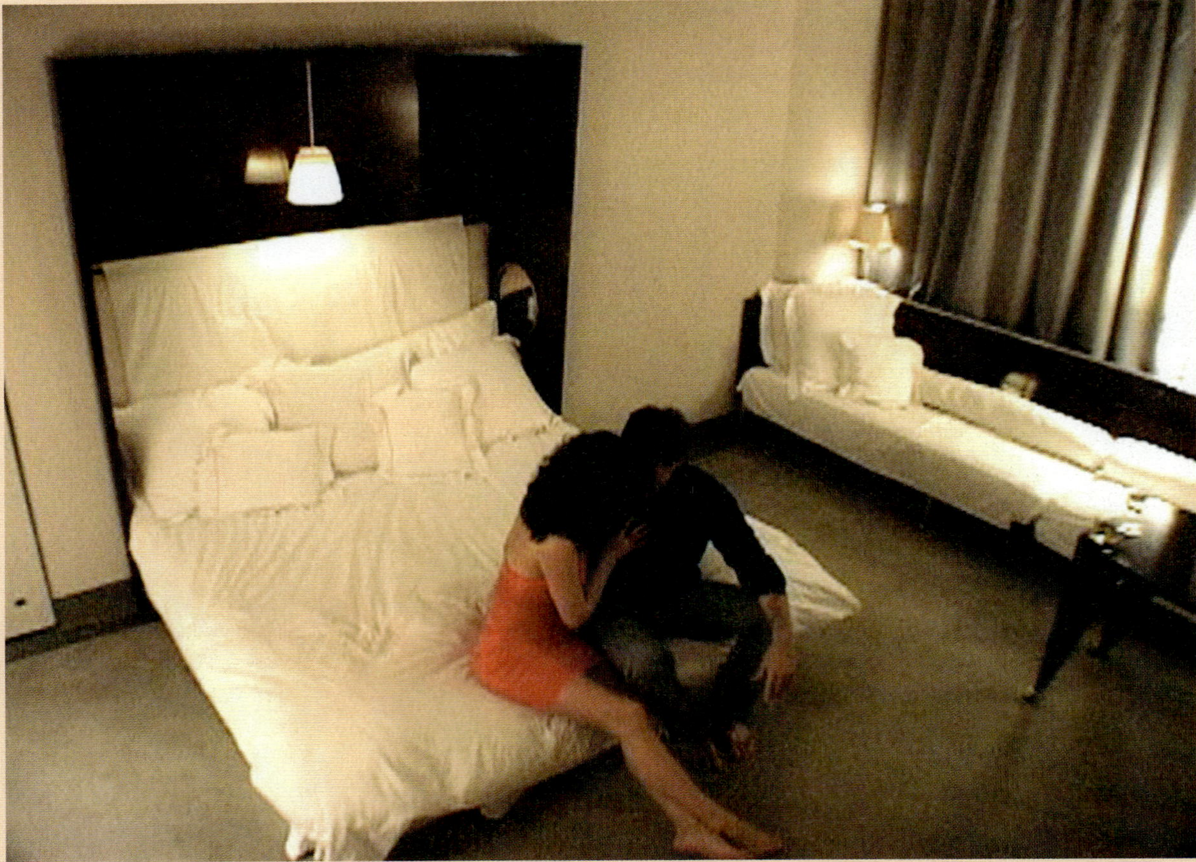

Andrea Fraser. **Untitled**, 2003. DVD, 60 min.

the red iconography was just as routine. What would have been surprising would have been an interrogation of the limitations of the format. Which is, weirdly, the promise of Creamier: a refreshingly unapologetic example of career as exposure as career. Maybe that's where the unpredictable can unfold, particularly in a crisis.

Kitty Scott
Of course, there is less money in the art system, as even the most cursory visit to last summer's Art Basel made clear. But the relevant question for curators working in a Canadian context concerns what we might call our degree of exposure to, or insulation from, that intertwined global network of financial markets and art markets that fuelled the hyper-activity noted above. I, for one, suspect that the Great Recession won't really change the situation for the vast majority of contemporary artists or curators living in Canada, precisely because the art world here is, for the most part, funded by the federal government through the Canada Council.

There is a national market, but it's relatively small, with a concomitantly smaller number of collectors and patrons, and hence it plays a significantly more restricted role in determining what artists make and where they exhibit. This relative insulation from the vicissitudes of the market means that artists can hopefully continue to work on the projects that are of interest to them, regardless of the economic collapse.

Paradoxically, it will be those artists most successfully enmeshed in an international art scene — artists like Jeff Wall, Stan Douglas and Rodney Graham — who potentially face the most dire consequences of the collapse, although one would imagine they've also benefited most from the prior boom. For the majority of Canadian artists, however, this may not mark the watershed that we've come to expect.

This is not to say that no changes are in the air. Federal financing has been cut in one sector in particular, which could have a major impact on Canadian art's visibility on the international stage: funding for international projects such as Canadian participation in the Venice Biennale, the Sydney Biennial and exhibitions such as Documenta 13, as well as cultural tours by international curators. The government has failed to explain its rationale for making these cuts, and I wonder why. Although the cuts represent a significant sum of money for visual artists and international arts organizations, they're still a relatively modest amount with respect to the overall budget, which remains robust compared to that of our neighbour to the south. These changes have placed added responsibilities on curators such as myself; we have become one possible conduit to that larger world, and I've made an effort to keep the programme at the Banff Centre as international as possible.

However there is a larger issue lurking behind the questions

forum for the presentation of art (salon, world's fair, biennial, posh institution, scruffy artist-run space or art fair), the market has always loomed somewhere in the background. This we know. We also know it somehow even when we tend to forget that the beginnings of the Venice Biennale (so often called the 'mother' of all biennials and the model for the formation of the genre) made that explicit, starting off as an unapologetic commercial adventure (an art fair) rather than the public service it now claims to be. In fact, many want to see art as the pure and unspoiled counterpart to the blatantly transactional nature of the art fair. Of course, that's too black and white. It's true and not true at the same time. Art is different from the market, fundamentally and existentially. Otherwise we could all just become bankers or stockbrokers and very likely make a hell of a lot more money for the hours we put in. And yet the art world depends on the market and operates within its reach. (I'm trafficking in clichés, I know; forgive me, but sometimes I think they need to be restated as a way of showing one's cards.) Still, I was a bit surprised when suddenly so many people claimed, as their response to the market crash, that 'content' could finally return. This might also be the subtext to Hickey's comment about how exciting it would be when the bubble bursts. I wonder about this. Sure, I didn't much like the pompousness of previous times and the values they stood for, but, as a curator, I've always been interested in seeking out content and I think I've always found it when I've gone looking, whatever the financial situation of the world. And I have to say that I'm not necessarily finding more now than before the crash.

On the other hand, the recession changes the way in which public art institutions operate, the way they fund their day-to-day operations, and I'm not happy to hear that interesting, dedicated and

engaged institutions that even before the crash barely got by are now finding it necessary to cut back on programming. Just as terrible would be (and we all see it happening) the trend for larger institutions (or more likely their boards or financial advisors) to make visitor numbers or other so-called empirical data count even more than before, so that exhibitions become validated primarily by their potential to draw large crowds, often responding to things like spectacularity, easily digestible themes and lowest-common-denominator equalizing gestures. This would mean that content, at least as it makes its appearance in public institutions, is precisely the thing that risks being the last consideration.

So it seems to me that it's primarily in the galleries and at the art fairs that people are suddenly finding more content, when gallerists decide that if they're going to spend a gazillion dollars to have a booth at Art Basel, for instance, they had better bring out more solid, serious and pedigreed works doubtful investors will more likely buy with their more-precious-than-ever bucks than the newest flash in the pan. I find it odd, though, that so many take the art fair as the primary measure, especially as concerns the presence or absence of content.

Then there are today's biennials, which some want to lump into the same pot as the art fair. Daniel Birnbaum even recently pronounced, 'There can no longer be any doubt: for many the biennial has been eclipsed by the art fair.' I disagree, and the latest Istanbul Biennial, for instance, as well as other predecessors around the world, fortified my belief that the biennial at its best and the serious art exhibition as a genre are, in general, forums for provoking reflection about issues that matter, which art fairs have never yet done for me.

Tirdad Zolghadr
I agree that the crash was romanticized, and that a crisis will rarely benefit the frail. But I have to confess, I was under a similar spell when it kicked off. 'Who knows?', I mumbled into my 1.70 euro Berlin cappuccino. Then again, I don't know enough about the 'crisis' to offer an opinion and keep a straight face while I'm at it. I can barely grasp what I read in the newspapers. But I'm fascinated by the crisis-savvy responses of those who do: how the primary market was quick to distance itself in distinctly moral terms from the secondary one, insisting on proximity to the artist and long-haul careers, condemning the auction fanfare. It casts an interesting light on distinction games in general.

It might be good to trace the role and relevance of us Creamier selectors — visibilizers — in this scheme of things. For example, there was a recent article by Nina Power discussing the difficulties of visualizing the crisis beyond sweaty stockbrokers and empty mom-and-pop stores. This is generally relevant to a field as scopophilic as ours, and particularly relevant to Creamier, which is visibility hyper-commodified, and super-relevant to the market-critical players, for whom the implicit rallying cry is to place people before profit, quality before spectacle, art before exposure, and thus, logically, artworks before hit parades. That's not exactly a Creamy modus operandi. But maybe that's OK? I mean, is it the commercial boom and bust that's the problem? Or is it the boring professionalism evoked in Catherine's contribution? I actually think the last Istanbul Biennial was a political endgame. All those Lenins — like a Checkpoint Charlie souvenir store. Yet the format and the procedure was as conservative as ever. It's hardly surprising that none of the artists were paid, and that the main sponsor has an arm in the defence industries. Meanwhile

posed. Whatever changes are wrought in the art world, the economic collapse is an event with unprecedented and dire consequences across our societies. It's not turning out to be the 'exciting' situation predicted by Hickey in the heady autumn of 2007. Canada, like America, is experiencing a vast restructuring of its economy that will see record unemployment rates and the continued and accelerated erosion of quality of life for the vast majority of its citizens. This is how the economic crisis will ultimately impact the art world — not through a contraction of the marketplace of galleries and collectors, but through the fact that 'our' world is after all part of that larger world.

Debra Singer
Given that we're still in the midst of the recession, I'm wondering how productive a conversation we can have about its impact on the imminent production and presentation of art. In the reflective context of Creamier, it might be more intriguing to discuss what it has meant over the last years to operate within a market frenzy and which aspects of what we do were made more or less difficult by these conditions. For example, one of the parallel developments of the art-market boom that at first seemed unexpected to me — and then seemed to make sense within a systemic logic — was the incredible rise of and renewed interest in performance-based work. Out of

nowhere, my phone just started ringing and didn't stop, with people asking me to recommend artists. The whole art world —from the smallest to the largest of institutions in New York — all of a sudden wanted to produce performances and incorporate experiential time-based work into their programming. And then, within a short timeframe, that was extended to new questions — coming from museum institutions primarily, more than individual collectors — about what it means to purchase and collect 'performance'. Those questions are still being debated in quite lively ways here, especially as a younger generation of artists in particular is contesting issues of what is the 'art' and what is the documentation, and the interesting debates on issues surrounding the re-creation of historical performances. As reflected in a handful of my choices for this book, many exciting artists who have emerged within the last five years have been creating performance-based video and installation work.

Douglas Fogle
I have to say that the question itself seems a bit like disaster porn. We all love to watch a good train wreck, whether it's a metaphorical one, as with Lindsay Lohan, or an actual one such as a car crash. As for Hickey, there seems to be quite a bit of gleeful moral schadenfreude at work in his statement, and we should be careful about that (although who in the non-profit world doesn't enjoy a

bit of schadenfreude once in a while?). The mistake here, though, is to keep on feigning surprise. Anyone in our field with some semblance of a balanced mental portfolio would have seen this coming. It came before (anyone remember the end of the 1980s?), it came last September, and we all know that it will come again. As Mark E. Smith of The Fall croons, 'repetition, repetition, repetition'.

I think that it's important to recognize that the history of the art market precedes the history of the museum by several centuries. It's not a Manichean system. It's not either/or. They're intimately entwined. To which I say, let's acknowledge it, get over it, and do some good, challenging shows. Although one might have taken the Hirst auction as a portent of a coming art apocalypse, I'm of the mind that it somehow signalled the birth (or death?) of an alien, other-artworldly culture, whose most significant artefact was a diamond-encrusted skull, created by a high priest (the artist formerly known as Damien) as a homing beacon for a hedge-fund mother ship that would come to transport the chosen few to heaven, another planet or at least the Hamptons. Did this other parallel art world and its much reported collapse (is it really gone?) truly affect what I could do as a curator at a non-profit contemporary art institution in the United States? Probably not, except to the extent that the upward shift in the market moved many artists' work out of the price range of non-profit

collecting institutions. Budgets have definitely been constricted for exhibitions, but you don't need a huge amount of money to do great shows.

In the US, of course, many of the fallen titans of Wall Street were also some of the biggest collectors. A number of these people were also important supporters of non-profit institutions all over the world and thus enabled both artists and curators to ply their trades. But there are collectors and there are accumulators. Collectors have always been the founders and patrons of great art institutions. Accumulators treat art as a fungible commodity in their portfolios. I'm not sad to see the accumulators go away. However, I've spent the last fifteen years at three institutions founded by individual collectors who wanted to give something back to the world by establishing their museums. My one regret about the most recent bubble is that the same sense of social responsibility was never part of the accumulators' DNA.

As for the artists, I think that many of them were already sensing the seismic shift in the art world (as animals can predict an oncoming earthquake), moving into areas of investigation that eschewed the high gloss while starting to do more with less, all the while emphasizing the ephemeral, the poetic and the performative. Was content dead in the run-up to the global derivatives meltdown? I think not. Was it at times drowned out by the cacophony of

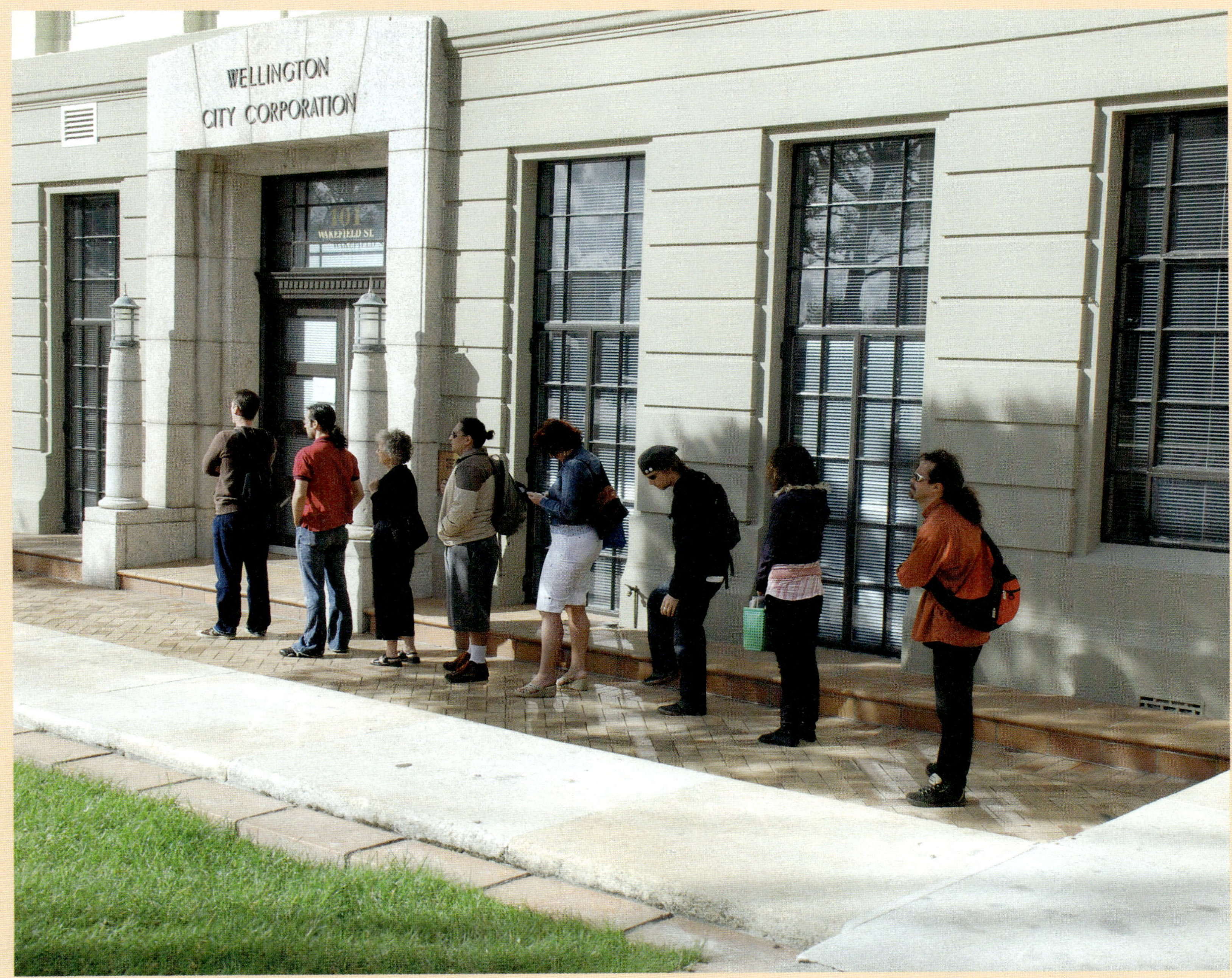

Roman Ondák. **Good Feelings in Good Times**, 2003. Performed in Wellington, New Zealand, March 2008. Presented by Massey University Litmus Research Initiative, 'One Day Sculpture'. Tate Collection, London

the auctioneer's gavel? Perhaps. Maybe the events of the last year have made us able to listen a bit more closely. If so, that could be thought of as a good thing. So here we are after the crash in our postlapsarian fugue state. Has it changed my curatorial practice? A simple answer would be no. Samuel Beckett has a lot to say about our historical moment: 'Go on failing. Go on. Only next time, try to fail better.' That's my curatorial motto for the sub-prime era.

Chus Martinez
It's a moot question whether one should accept the dichotomy between market high and market low as the plus and minus poles of contemporary art production, and whether art (and curating and institutional activity of all stripes) is necessarily predicated on the market. Is the market really the best filter for understanding the interface between art and culture at large? Should it be addressed as the first thing? Why do we need the market to turn into a form of positive knowledge? From a purely pragmatic point of view, the market is a predominant mode of exchange, sure, but that's hardly a revolutionary insight in a world that's politically held together by capital and socially pulled apart by it. Everything is economic because things are in exchange, but the market only operates from one side of this perspective, because it speculates with cash and value. However, should we let this determine thinking and communicative form?

After all, market highs and lows are only the cyclical form of capital that regenerates itself. We could also turn our attention to the fact that our generation has come of age professionally in a cultural climate that has done its utmost to make art and economy indistinguishable through discourses about the 'experience economy', the 'creative industries' and so on — discourses that operationalize art by turning it into a valorizer in a manner that differs from the way in which art was wielded as a symbolic economy in the modernity of the bourgeoisie.

One could also open up the question from a different angle: namely, that it might be worth revisiting various definitions of the market. Hickey's use of the art world and its market is basically (and paradoxically) how both Adam Smith and Karl Marx conceived of the market as a total logic, either in terms of an invisible hand or the exchange of capital. Is there really such a total entity, zone or logic as 'the market'? Isn't there, rather, a multitude of attitudes, entries and exits to the market, a range of various intelligences interacting with it? Nor can the market be reduced to what goes on between buyers and sellers at an art fair. There's also an institutional market, for example. The historian of economics Fernand Braudel proposed a potentially more open-ended definition based on the medieval marketplace — in which producers and consumers link up directly to exchange goods. Gradually, the marketplace is divided into two levels: a lower one that comprises shops and peddlers, and

an upper one that includes fairs and bourses. This development of specialization and hierarchy within and on top of the market is a precondition of capitalism that is thus a different activity from the market economy.

Phaidon
To take up Debra's point about the resurgence of performance-based works, and given that Cream appears once every three years, have you as curators seen a particular kind of work or mode of address developing among emerging artists since the last volume was published?

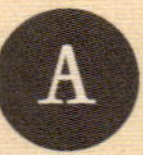

Catherine Wood
I agree with Debra that there has been a rise in performance activity (in London, over the past six to seven years, and still increasing at a rate) and that there's a sudden momentum to discuss 'collecting performance', a topic upon which I'm constantly being asked to comment. At Tate, we've bought several things since 2003, including choreographed actions by Tino Sehgal, Roman Ondák and Tania Bruguera, as well as looking at and collecting video and photography and installation that document or relate to performance (Sanja Ivekovic, Joan Jonas or Ewa Partum, to name just a few). But I think while on one hand the booming market situation has engendered a certain confidence in

collectors to buy into conceptual games with ephemeral actions for sale — in parallel with the performance medium being recognized for its art-historical significance — the wider interest in performance is a bigger issue to do with a highly performative attitude to art production in itself. Recently re-watching John Baldessari's 1971 video I Am Making Art reminded me of the extent to which art production now is more than ever characterized by a self-consciousness about artistic labour and the weighing of an artist's persona against the production of objects themselves. Whether 'producing' oneself as a performing product is a symptom of life in an accelerated, competitive capitalist economy, or whether performance remains as a challenge to the market, is something that is being contested in the work itself. But the idea we inherited from the 1960s and 1970s that performance entirely resists art's commodification doesn't hold true today.

Yukie Kamiya
I'm one of those people who rang Debra and asked for suggestions on performance-based work. This particular interest developed in parallel with the flourishing art market, and it reveals a kind of counteraction to the market that tends to deal in objects without artists. Artists, audiences and curators thirst for the presence of the artist and the one-time-only experience in this era of reproduction. It's not only emerging artists but also artists who've had a career in other forms of artistic

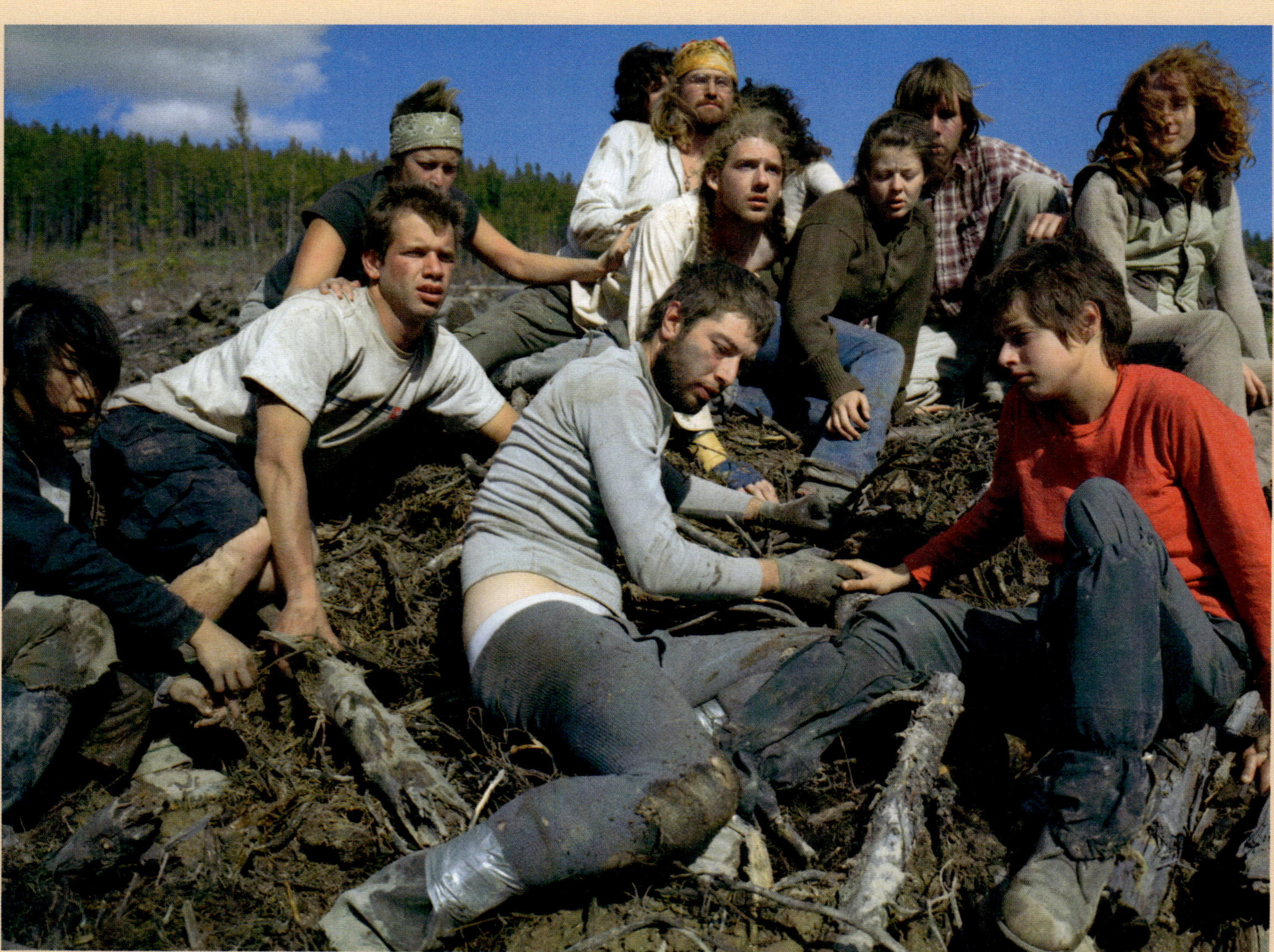

Althea Thauberger. **Northern**, 2005–06. 35mm film with sound transferred to HD video. 8 min.

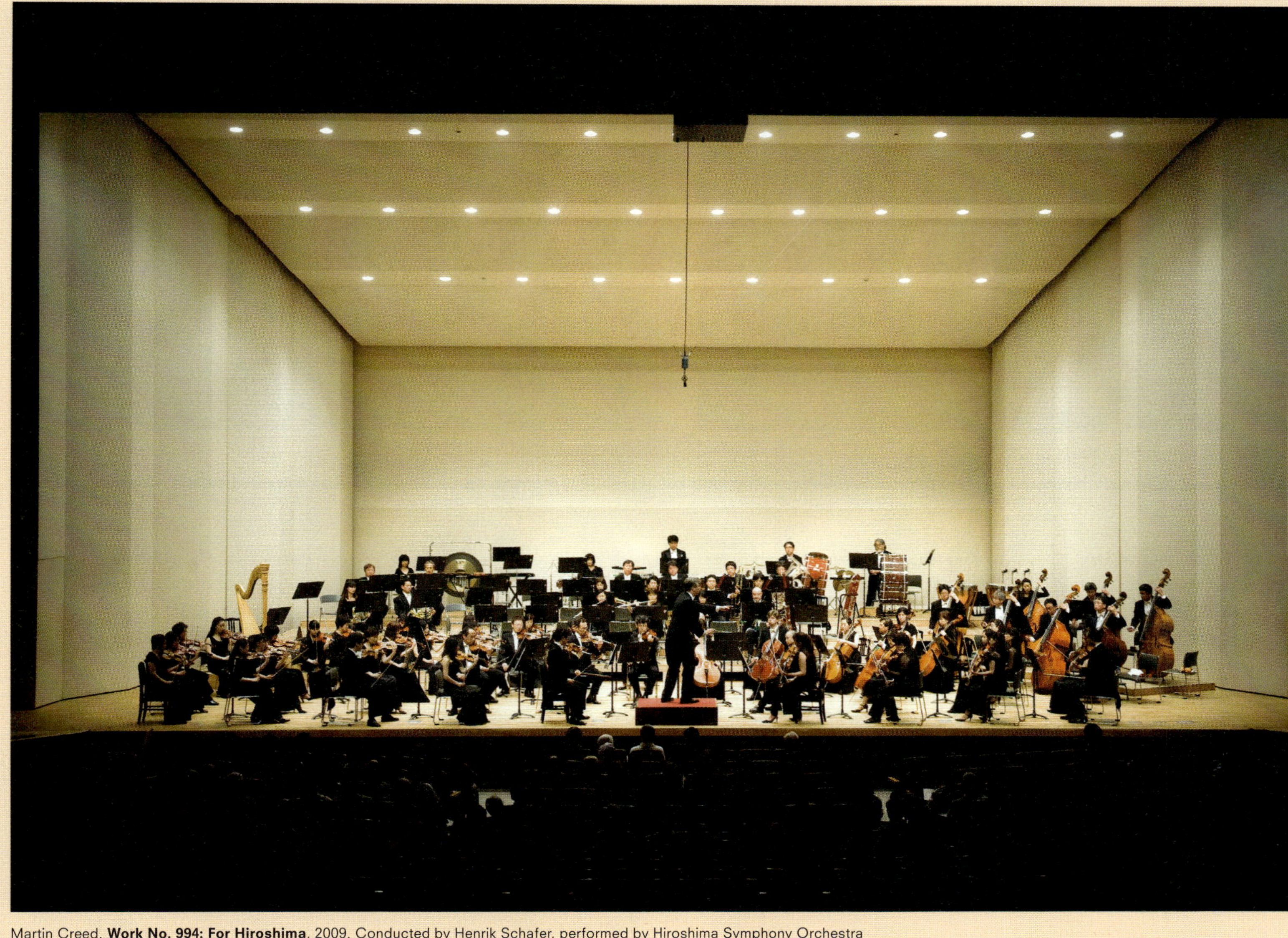

Martin Creed. **Work No. 994: For Hiroshima**, 2009. Conducted by Henrik Schafer, performed by Hiroshima Symphony Orchestra

We could also turn our attention to the fact that our generation has come of age professionally in a cultural climate that has done its utmost to make art and economy indistinguishable through discourses about the 'experience economy', the 'creative industries' and so on

practice who turn their gaze to performance/time-based work as their new artistic venture. I worked with Martin Creed this year to produce his new musical piece dedicated to Hiroshima for an exhibition at Hiroshima MoCA, performed by a hundred-member symphony orchestra. He now choreographs classically trained dancers, developing his interest in performance. Performance-based work takes up a challenge to expand the notion of art and activates the discussion on forms of art. Just as someone like Seth Siegelaub worked with Conceptual artists in the late 1960s and early 1970s to made their work tangible in the form of instructions that he could then distribute through the market and could be collected for future generations, the market works to anchor the recognition and understanding of innovative art forms. From this point of view, the current attention being given to performance and the active market complement each other. For an institution that has the role of providing a stage for artists to present their practices, how to adapt performance as well as experimental time-based work is an exciting, ongoing challenge.

An overview of the practice of emerging artists in Japan, however, shows that painting and drawing are extremely powerful media, encouraged by the success of Takashi Murakami and Yoshitomo Nara, and in reality fulfilling a demand of the market.

Douglas Fogle
The idea of performance goes a long way back in art history. Are more artists crossing the boundaries

between a studio-based practice and a performative practice than ever before? I'm not sure. If so, it might be a function of there simply being more artists in the world. Also, quite a bit of this work was going on at the height of the market and wasn't necessarily a response to the so-called crash. Are these artists who are producing events doing it with an 'anti-market' spirit? I don't find that question interesting or even relevant any more. I have no problem with an artist making a living, whether it's by selling objects or tickets to a performance. Also, if someone's practice is performative, I'm happy if an institution is forward-looking enough to step outside of their painting and sculpture mindset and think about their collecting practice in an expanded field. This is something that was par for the course during my eleven years at the Walker Art Center in Minneapolis as we commissioned, exhibited and collected works by performance-based visual artists. We also had an entire department devoted to the performing arts (an experimental if more traditionally minded programme of events), with which the visual arts curators frequently collaborated. I'd like to think that today it's no longer revolutionary to think about exhibiting or collecting performance-based works.

Adam Szymczyk
Since the economic crisis was announced two years ago and its arrival acknowledged worldwide, those in the upper crust of the art world have been showing visible signs of anxiety: the auction sales have gone down quite a bit and some galleries have had to close their

more exotic franchises and cut jobs, as have some museums, mainly in the US — things unheard of for years and certainly not anticipated by the generation that has grown up during the last decade of continuing prosperity. The PR officers working for art fairs now have the uneasy task of showing the standard optimism while at the same time being forced to develop a completely new vocabulary, insisting on the 'quality' and 'seriousness' of the art offered for sale, and the need for all of us to show 'consideration' and 'solidarity' in order to survive hard times. Looking for safe value, the remaining serious collectors and those secondary-market businessmen who decided to keep investing their clients' money in contemporary art are seeking 'serious' or 'museum-quality' work and buying with caution. What 'serious' means, nobody seems to know in detail or even bother to ask, but instant deals and overspending have gone out of style.

On the other hand, I haven't heard a single artist addressing the current recession as something that has immediately affected their practice or life circumstances in a major way. Perhaps I've happened to work mostly with the artists who, crisis or not, never made a particularly big profit from sales of their work and therefore aren't particularly vulnerable to the current 'adjustment' of prices and dwindling of sales, simply because their financial situation happens to have been constantly fragile, if not in a permanent state of crisis. Perhaps we'll see the effects later. Anyway, it seems that the crisis isn't producing any new type of art, but it may result in shifting the public attention — although probably only for a short

while — away from the art-cele[…] world to the 'core business' of making art and exhibitions. At th[…] same time, as some countries i[…] Central and Eastern Europe see[…] be successfully steering throug[…] crisis (while others collapse ent[…] art from those countries is looke[…] at with relatively more interest, […] it were genetically free from 'bad money', or from money at […]

Elena Filipovic
I want to pick up on something […] Tirdad said, which I think is pert[…] to our discussion and may be […] something many of us have had […] somewhere in the back of our m[…] what does it mean to participat[…] and contribute to the Cream-m[…] (in general, but particularly in th[…] content of crisis)? Tirdad says, […] speaking about a biennial, 'Wha[…] would have been surprising wo[…] have been an interrogation of t[…] limitations of the format. Which[…] weirdly, the promise of Creamie[…] a refreshingly unapologetic exa[…] of career as exposure as caree[…] Maybe that's where the unpredictable can unfold, partic[…] in a crisis context.' None of us […] able to foretell what the econo[…] crisis will actually bring to the a[…] world, not to speak of the worl[…] large, but I can't help thinking c[…] Cream's every-three-year forma[…] loosely replicating (consciously[…] the temporal frequency of the […] biennial, or the fact that it anno[…] itself (unapologetically, as Tirda[…] rightly describes it) as a platfor[…] the presentation of artists who […] 'emerged since 2005' (that was […] of our explicit mandates), whic[…] in many ways also replicates a[…] one of the biennial's unspoken […] mandates, to be a forum for th[…]

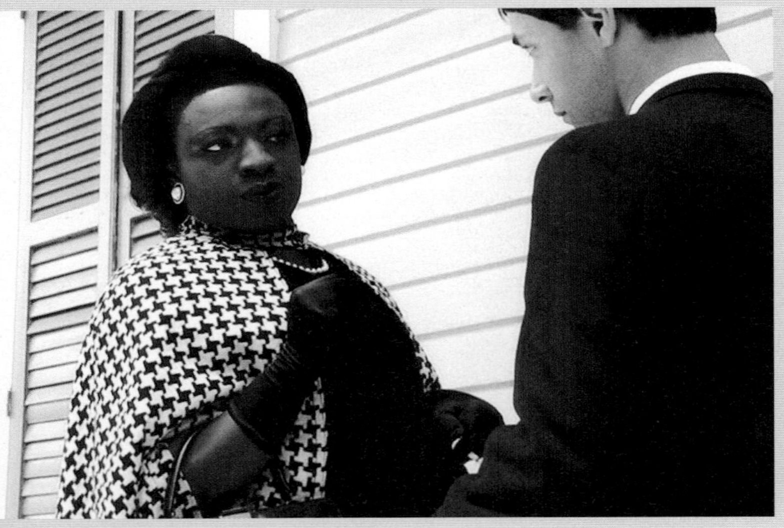
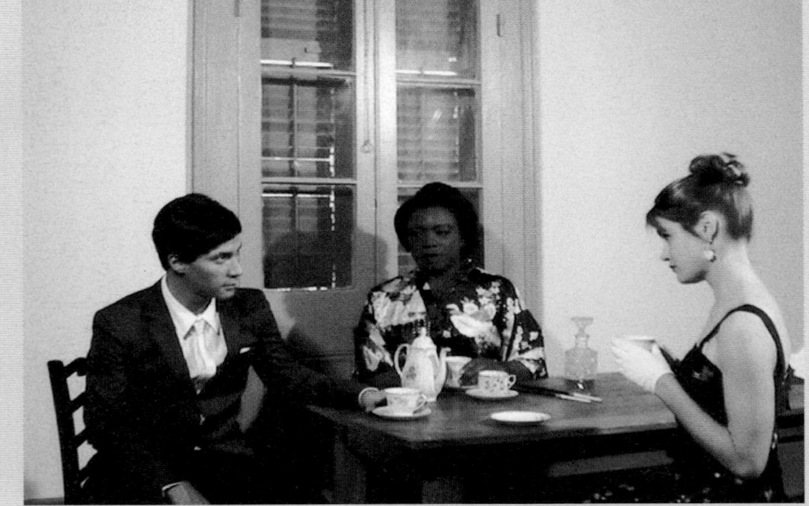

Kalup Linzy. **Keys to Our Heart**, 2008. Video. 24 min.

or 'emerging'. Of course, artists included on these pages are offered no production budget, no artist's fee, and no direct impetus to think about their own work in relation to its presentation with other works in a space as a response to a curatorial engagement or public presentation. And yet we're all aware that it does offer artists a certain kind of visibility (career as exposure as career?), and as curators and critics we're willing to participate, in the belief that this visibility may help them. And we want that for them because we believe in their work. We might also desire it for ourselves (because it would be disingenuous to deny our own potential for visibility in this operation). But all that said, does the Cream series really offer the promise of the unfolding of the 'unpredictable' in its very format? And if it doesn't,

what does it offer, exactly, that other formats (exhibition, biennial, monograph) don't? What makes it something that we're all so willing to contribute to?

Inés Katzenstein
Beyond our possibly shared intellectual resistance to practising curating as the mere manipulation of lists of names, there is a certain relief in such a direct opportunity to give visibility. It has to do with the illusion of acting simply as facilitators of international exposure, which is something we all know brings serious problems, especially when speaking of curators proposing artists from peripheral contexts. There's a real sense of risk in cases where the local scene matters in and of itself — that is, in art scenes that still resist the force of the international, scenes

where it's difficult to understand certain artistic decisions without reference to specific values and myths. Especially in these cases, participating in projects such as Cream entails — as one of the artists whom I chose for the book, Leopoldo Estol told me — a sort of displacement from a local road to the super-highway. That shift is not at all straightforward; it's laden with risks (misunderstanding, indifference, etc). But at the same time, as clichéd as it might sound, we cannot deny that this is, in the end, a space of opportunity.

On the other hand, and considering the current crisis, the title of this edition of the publication, Creamier, sounds, if not ironic, like a manifestation of not wanting to give up on the historical aims of the book project, a sort of raising of the

stakes. I read this less as a simple act of stubbornness than as a way of understanding that exposure and career can mean very different types of achievements in different historical contexts.

Chus Martínez
More than the rise of performance, or any kind of debate on forms and formats, we're fostering a new insight into the meaning of artistic research and how artists shape ideas and develop a kind of language that will contribute to imagining reality anew. We need new logics of thinking to approach artistic production, reception, experience and the role of theory in order to imagine the notion of the political beyond dialectics like sheltering/resisting the mechanisms of the global state of affairs. I see artists increasingly turning towards the

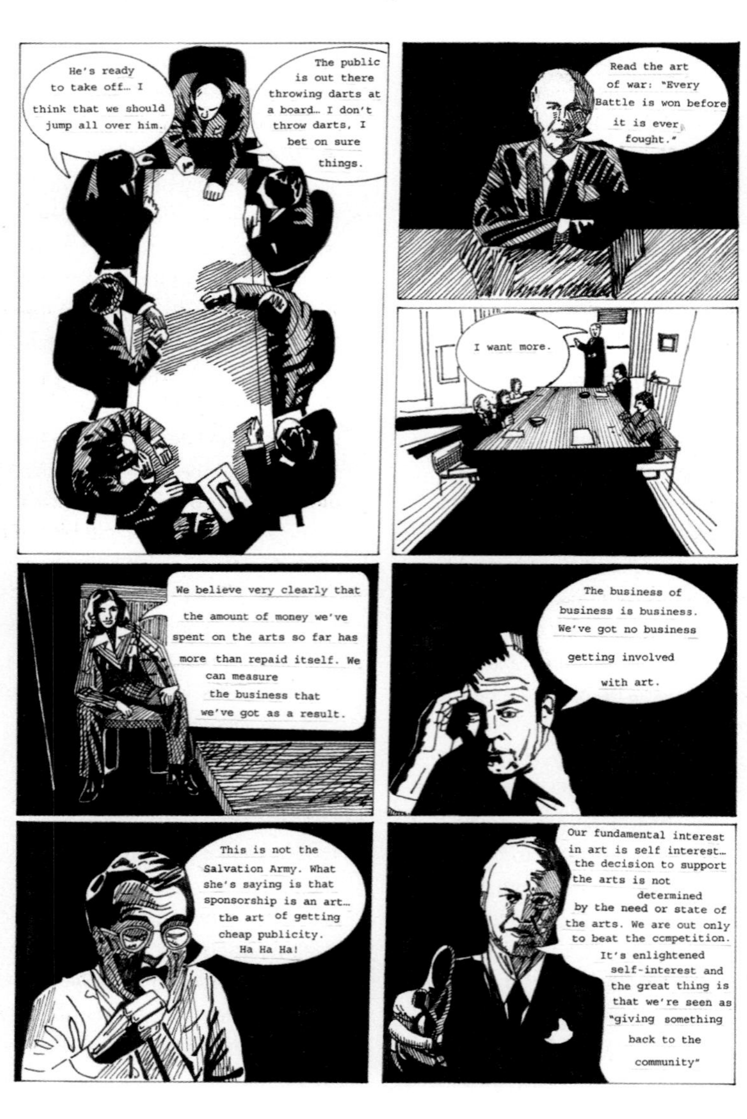

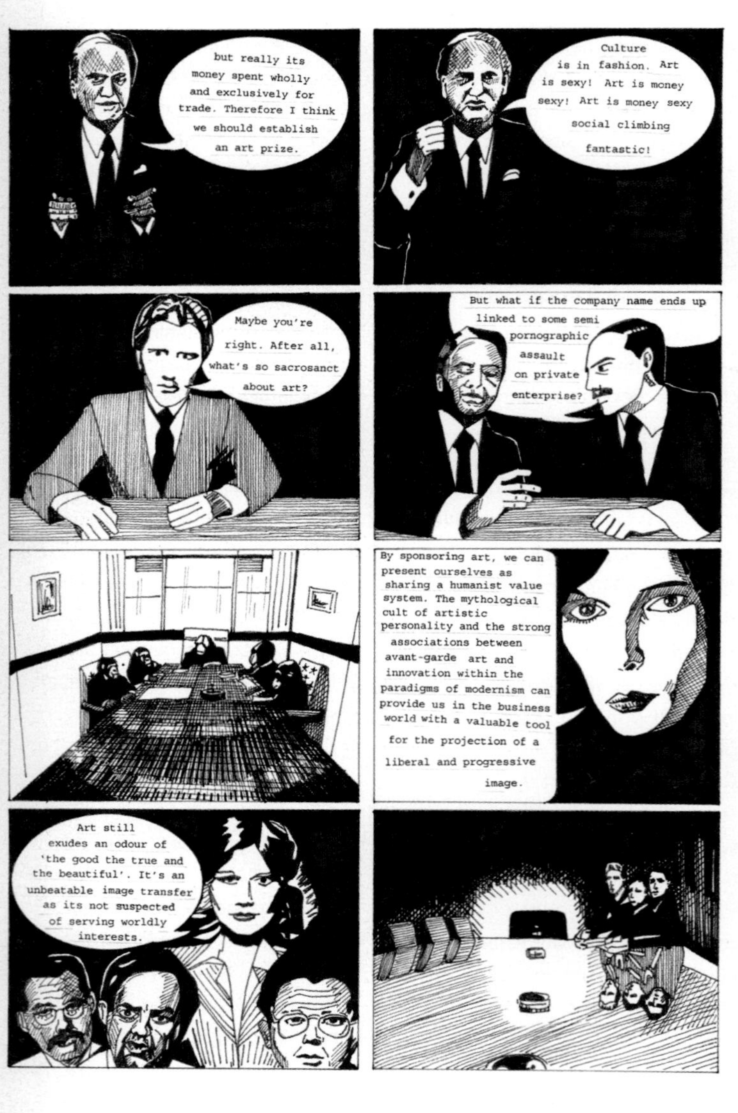

Olivia Plender. **The Masterpiece, no. 5**, 2006. Printed comic book. 40 × 30cm

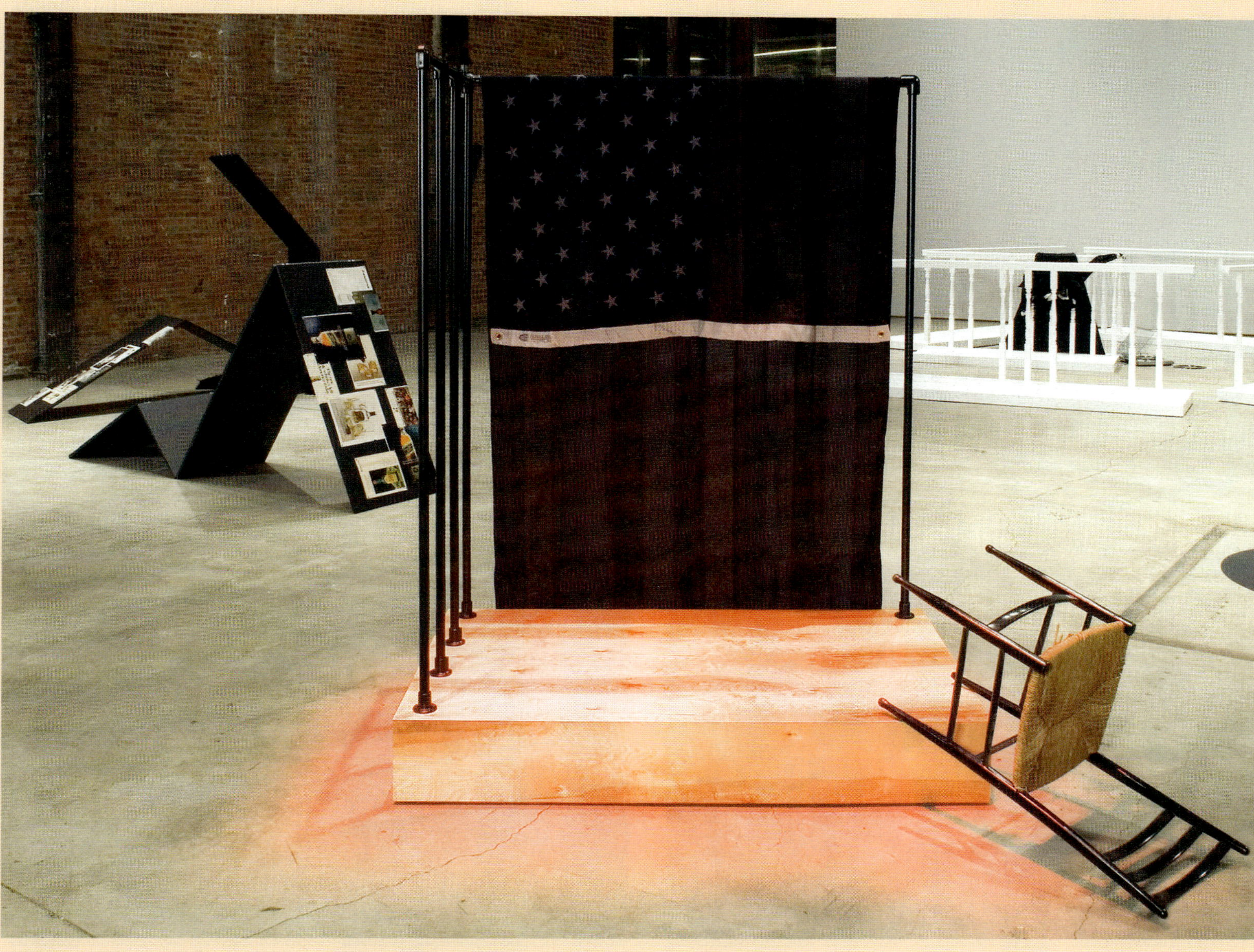

Tom Burr. **Light Cavalry**, 2008, Plywood, aluminium powder coated speedrail, dyed flag, chair. 203 × 163 × 183 cm

specific, paying attention to how works/actions/ideas have the potential for making us think through the artistic material. They're creating a movement that's not afraid of complexity — as sometimes curators and institutions are.

Rhythm is becoming — in my opinion — an important notion again: a notion that helps us to understand time — the time we're in, historical time, the time of globalization — and, at the same time, space, in the sense that rhythm takes place in the quotidian, in the everyday. Artists produce space by making different rhythms appear in the all-encompassing rhythm of the discourse of the crisis.

Phaidon

As both Elena and Inés have said, books such as Creamier fundamentally bring up the notion of 'visibility'. Beyond the 'emerging' remit set forth by this book, what factors did you take into consideration in the selection of your artists?

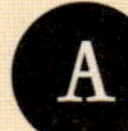

Tirdad Zolghadr

For different reasons, I only nominated artists with whom I've never worked before, the two exceptions being the Jackson Pollock Bar and the Museum of American Art in Berlin. In these cases, I found the uncompromising approach to authorship warranted a different playing field altogether, although I may quite possibly have been wrong.

After all, the issue at hand is quite broad, and so clever ideas on authorship arguably offer no exemption. As suggested elsewhere, the 'visibility' that Elena and Inés are talking about implies that Creamier is a lubricant for artists' careers but also suggests the hyper-visible, unapologetic way in which we curators are asked to play Top Ten jury, like experts, judges, kingmakers, pimps or what have you. The transparency is what I find attractive and weirdly productive here. So, as for my selection criteria, it's not that I'm trying to look like a cleaner kind of juror. Everyone knows that our curatorial choices are always about more than the artwork. Even Clement Greenberg knew that. It ranges from personal likings to institutional liaisons. For one thing, a quick glance at my list will reveal my artists to be extremely simpatico one and all. For another thing, some of them harbour suspiciously close ties to the Center for Curatorial Studies, where I teach. But I did want to offer a gesture, or impose an artificial limit of some sort. At the very least, my criteria pushed me to think beyond my usual suspects. Other criteria: I'm becoming more attentive to artistic reflexivities of various shapes and sizes: a shrewd and maybe humorous feel for the specificities of the exhibition space, the medium, the art — world rituals and pecking orders. I suppose that's visible in my selection of artists like Can Altay, Gerard Byrne, Olivia Plender and others.

Debra Singer

In thinking about my selections, I can't really consider them as one

group. There were several independent factors that seemed to be of equal interest to me, given the context. On the one hand, I wanted to include more than just a few performance-based artists, if only for the fact that they could potentially gain the most from the visibility of the book. They often have very little to sell, so new opportunities to make work and present work live are literally their livelihood. On the other hand, I was also intrigued to include artists whose work reflects in various ways what you might call an updated sense of 'Americana', because work reflecting specific aspects of American cultural history seemed to be oddly lacking in previous volumes. (Perhaps it's because this book circulates more in Europe than in the States? I don't know if this is true or not.) In quite a few other cases, my choices also reflect diverging perspectives toward a highly fluid understanding of gendered indentities; the ways in which, for example, themes of gay identity circulate in the work of Tom Burr, Ryan Trecartin and Kalup Linzy couldn't be more different. (These various points also relate to my choice of Jack Smith's 1963 film Flaming Creatures as a Source work.) Then, there are still others who don't fit neatly into any of the above, but I was excited to have an excuse and an outlet to reflect more closely on their work.

Kitty Scott

I suppose I arrived at my list largely intuitively, composed as it is of artists with whom I've worked or whose work has interested me

recently. I recognize, however, that despite the diversity of their projects, they share a set of common traits. To differing degre[es] each artist engages with a partic[ular] contemporary problem: how to reconcile the critique of representation with a fundamental[ly] affective or emotional aspect of the artwork. This is a broad them[e] that unites the group, and that seems particularly compelling to [me].

The things we may not at [first] recognize as art intrigue me. Somewhere within this, I fall prey [to] what's perhaps an old-fashioned notion of resistance. It plays out i[n] different ways in some of the artist's oeuvres: it lies in the exten[ded] period of time encompassed by Dexter Sinister's Black Whiskey (2009), the potential violence suggested by Claire Fontaine's Change (2006) and the averagene[ss] of Janice Kerbel's Ballgame (2009[)].

There is a national bias in [my] list, with four out of ten artists be[ing] Canadian: Geoffrey Farmer, Jani[ce] Kerbel, Ron Terada and Althea Thauberger. But I'd see it more i[n] terms of a city rather than a cou[ntry] since these are all artists live in o[r] have passed through Vancouver. They've benefited from having gr[eat] teachers and witnessing the brilliance of locals like Ian Wallac[e,] Roy Arden, Stan Douglas, Rodne[y] Graham, Brian Jungen, Tim Lee, [Ken] Lum, Liz Magor, Steven Shearer [and] Jeff Wall. Somewhat perversely, [though] I'm interested in those four preci[sely] because they've turned away fro[m] a specific medium like photograp[hy] which is so predominant or overdetermined in a place such as Vancouver. I had been aware o[f]

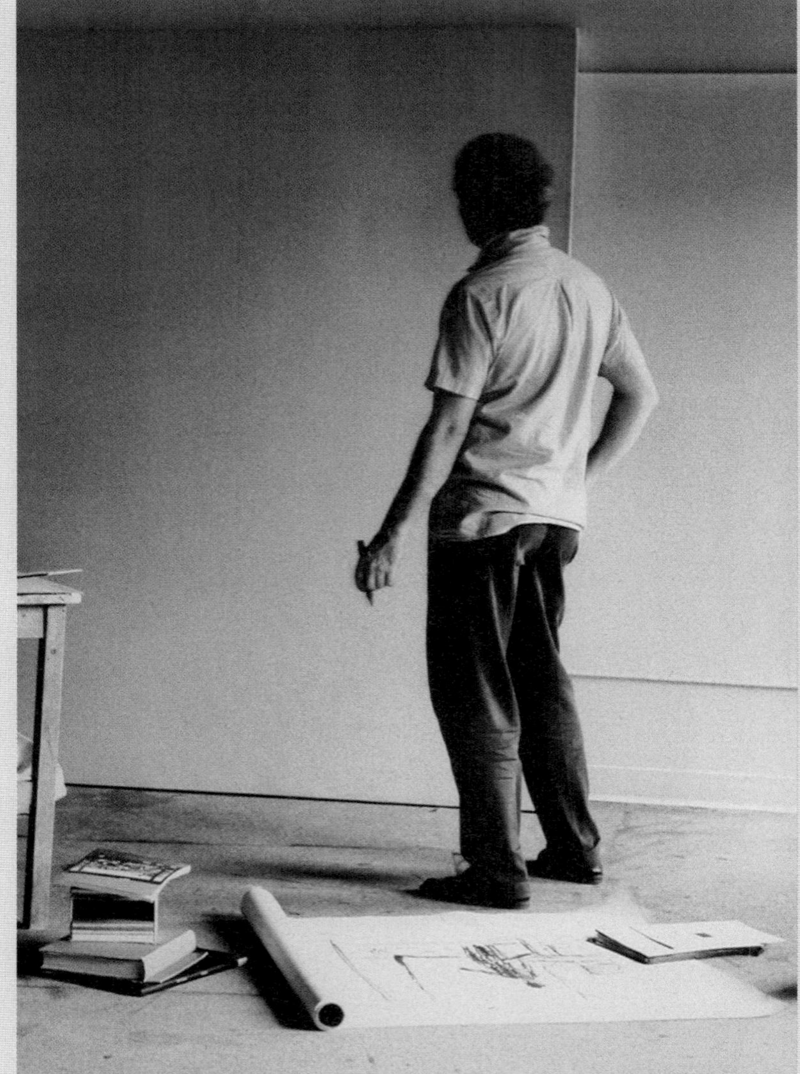 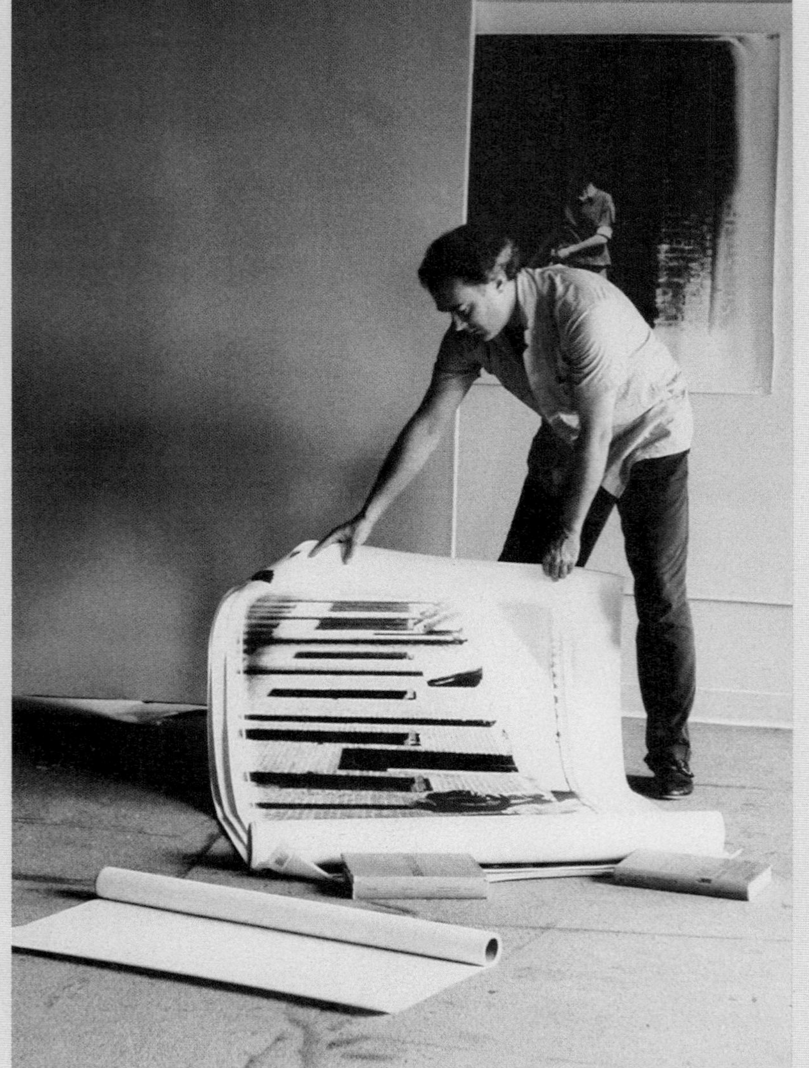

Ian Wallace. **Study for In The Studio 1984**, 1984. 2 black and white photographs. Each 36 × 28 cm

Dexter Sinister before Stuart Bailey spoke at the Banff Centre this past summer, but I was truly captivated by his intelligence. He gave a long lecture on Black Whiskey, a lecture that at first seemed rather dry, focusing as it did on the details of the production announcement and label for an artisanally made whisky which will only be available to drink in 2021. By the end of the talk, however, I was completely convinced of how representative of what they're doing it is, especially with respect to the doubling in the label that refers to the past and present of the bottle itself.

Catherine Wood
I thought of bringing the artists into this book as a way to extend, continue or start a discussion or collaboration. I proposed some artists with whom I've never worked or even met, some whom I've known for a long time, and some with whom I'm currently working on projects. The book is a way of making connections that would be difficult in the real world of exhibitions. But they're mostly artists I've worked with, many of whom are based in London and with whom I have regular dialogue and — to generalize horribly — who make work that in some way examines relations between people via semi-formal strategies: performance, choreography or the idea of a 'script'. These connecting themes relate in different ways to my Source choice of Mike Kelley's early performance (Monkey Island, 1982–83) set in a sculptural installation, and his relationship to artists combining language and action, such as Douglas Huebler or Guy de Cointet.

Yukie Kamiya
Although ten is just a handful, I wanted to celebrate the challenging practices of artists who have an unprejudiced interest in diverse media. I'm always captivated by artists who adapt multiple elements and integrate them into their works — for example, artists like Xijing Men, who have multiple cultural backgrounds sharing a sense of in-between, fluid identity, as well as artists who challengingly broaden their means of expression and naturally integrate them into interdisciplinary, cross-media practices. From their artistic struggles and explorations, innovative creations emerge beyond the classical and overused practice of art. The presence of the body is one of the inspiring elements to me at this moment, to reconsider the uniqueness of an artwork.

Elena Filipovic
I suppose the question of 'visibility' that's at the root of this discussion (how do ten chosen curators choose their ten artists?) should lead to attempts at transparency. But I find it a hopeless task. How to explain why I chose this or that artist? How to draw definitive lines between their (hopefully) disparate practices? And how, implicit in some responses, to justify a selection that can, to my mind, only be partial, arbitrary, personal, and on some level inexplicable, because it speaks for the work of artists whose practice is precisely of interest because it transcends whatever two-line description or definition I can use for all of them together. This is neither a theme show nor a panorama of a zeitgeist; it's a list of 'emerging artists', and that still somewhat

ambiguous and questionable category is what, in fact, is meant to unite them.

I could say that I know some of the artists on my list very well, have worked or am now working with others, and have never met still others, but I wanted, as Adam says, to incite a dialogue that's different from (even if it leads to or from) exhibition-making. But what does all of that actually convey of interest to a public outside of us the selectors? It seems slightly irrelevant to me. I found it interesting and curious that Tirdad announced that he'd never worked with all but two of his selected group. No, it wasn't to proclaim himself a 'cleaner' juror, he said. But the aura of cleanliness stuck just the same. It made me, for an instant, doubt my own selection, as if I shouldn't have named artists with whom I'd already worked or whom I planned to work with in the near future.

What was the unspoken implication there? But in the end, I named those artists because I think they matter and matter now for wildly different reasons. And I hoped to give some visibility and begin a conversation that's different from that of an exhibition or review, some of which I might have already tried out with them. That's not to say that I claim that the ten artists I named (Yukie is right, ten is only a small handful) are the sole ones that matter or even those that matter most, just that they seemed to make the most sense to me at the moment I was asked. And I'm guessing that others did something similar, whatever words we use to say that.

Chus Martínez
I've included those artists who invest in a kind of artistic research concerned with challenging the relations between ideas and things, ideas and ideas, things and things, things and beings, beings and ideas, beings and creatures. They're artists interested in speculation as an economical notion and a concept that relates to other possible ways of imagining the world. They're people who work with the production of the possible, sometimes in a very freaky way.

Douglas Fogle
There wasn't an underlying thematic in my list. I included a mixture of artists with whom I've worked with before (half of my artists) and some that I haven't worked with at all. Having recently moved to Los Angeles to take up a new job as Chief Curator of the Hammer Museum, I also made a conscious effort to select a number of artists from the Los Angeles context (five of my selected artists live here full time; one is European but lives here for the majority of the year). Within the context of a book like this with contributors from all over the world, I thought it was important to represent the city in which I live. On that note, I also chose a particularly Californian entry for my selection for the Source section. Joan Didion's essay 'The White Album' speaks as much to the current state of a culture spinning out of control as it did when it was written. Didion says, 'We tell ourselves stories in order to live.' In the end, isn't that what art is all about?

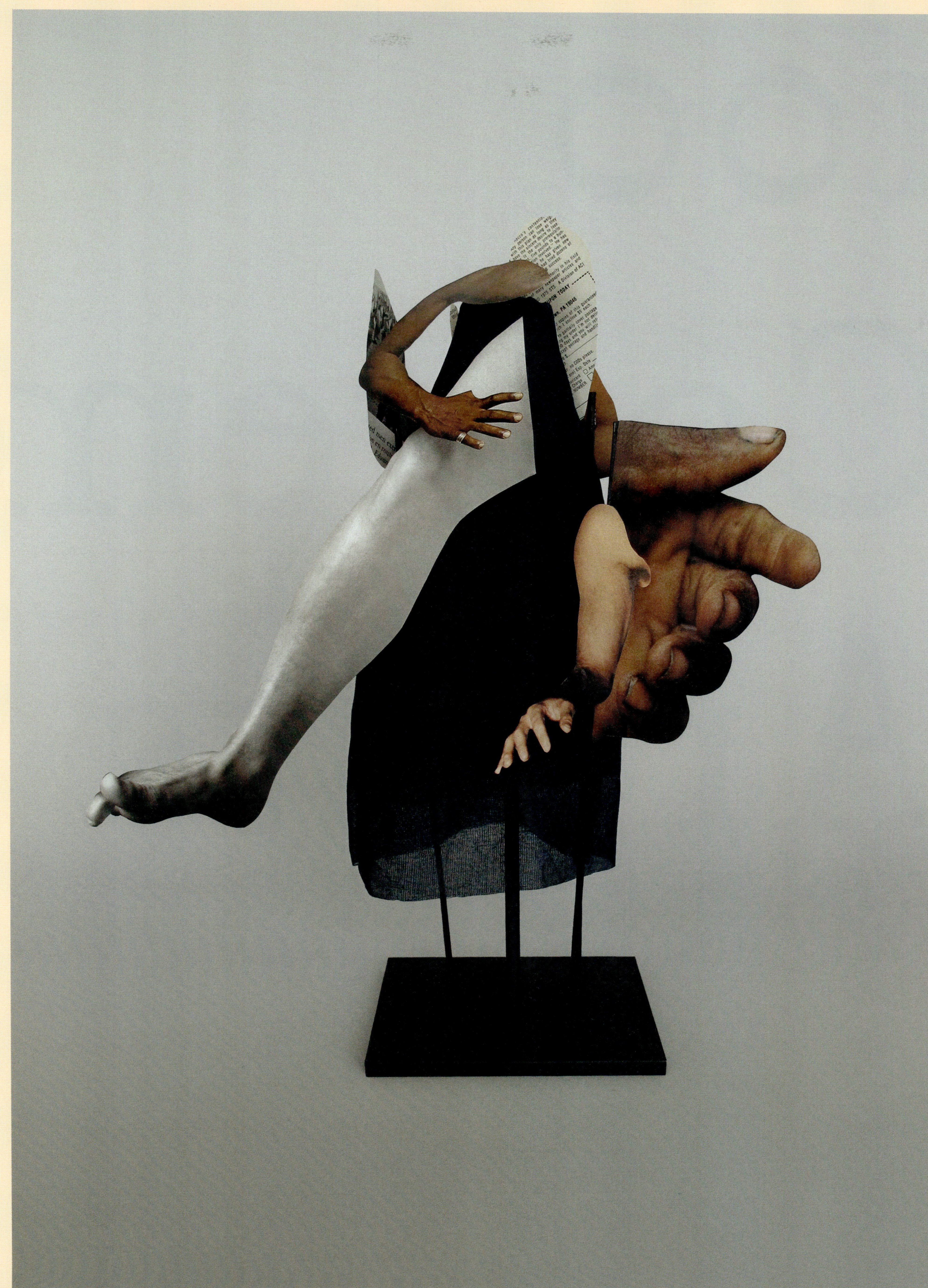

Geoffrey Farmer. **The Surgeon and the Photographer**, 2009. Fabric, paper collage, wood, metal stands. 730 × 450 × 150 cm

100 Contemporary Artists

porary

Gabriel Acevedo Velarde

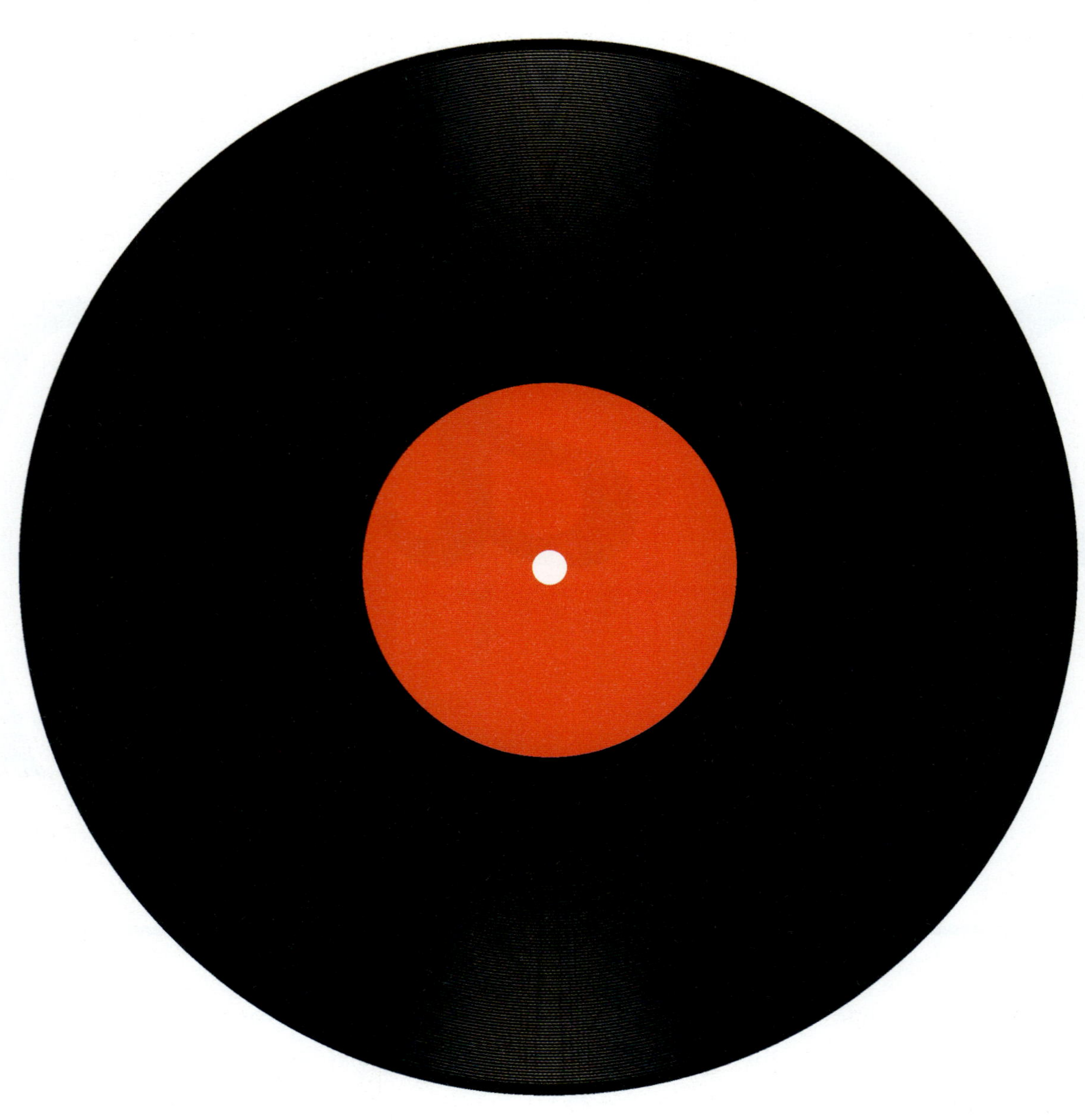

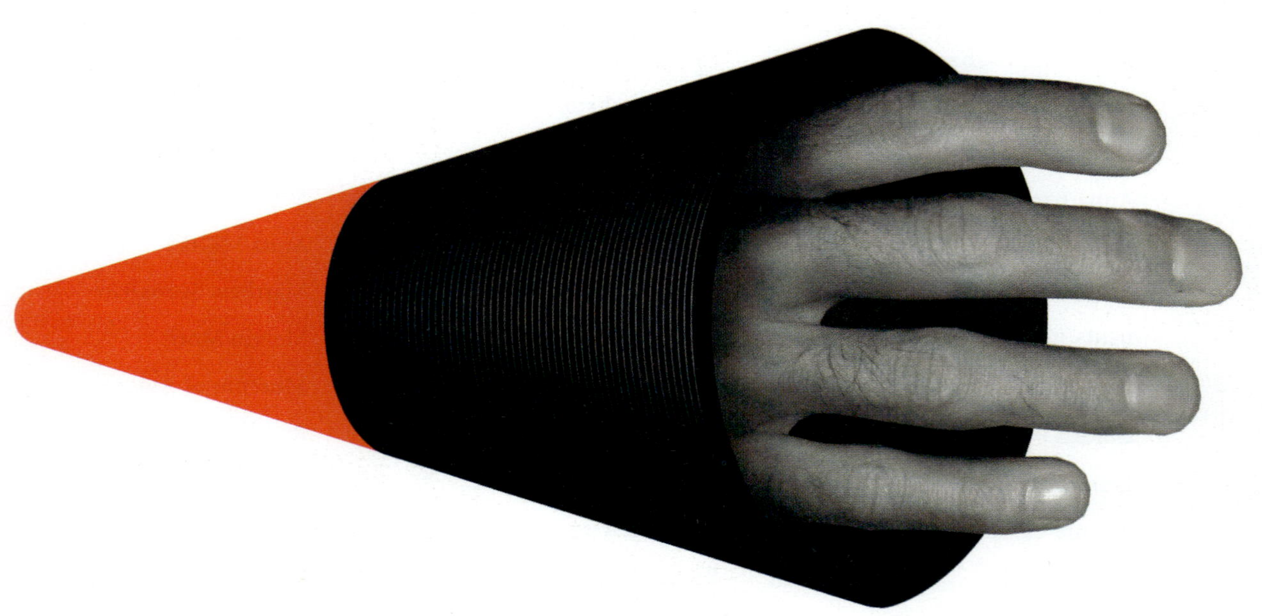

Music cone, 2009. Billboard design for Mercosul Biennial. Dimensions variable

Gabriel Acevedo Velarde's work is not easily summarized or categorized. Born in Peru, trained in Mexico and Brazil and based in Berlin for the last three years, it was originally his drawings and animations that first brought him attention, but nowadays he is focused on researching social fictions through video, music and performance. He continually investigates and opens new paths inspired by various themes, practices and formats — from the

Researching social fictions

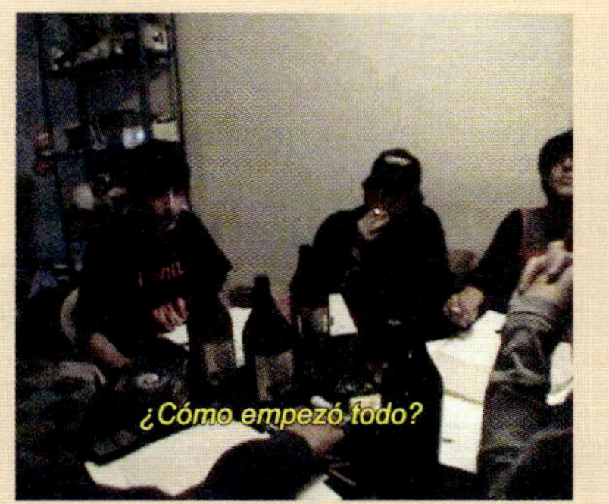
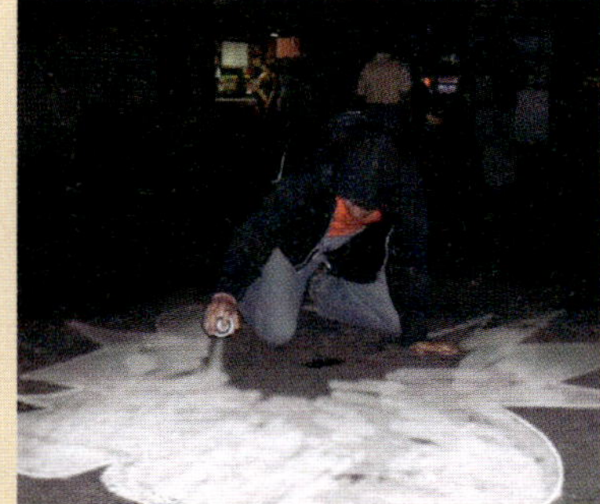
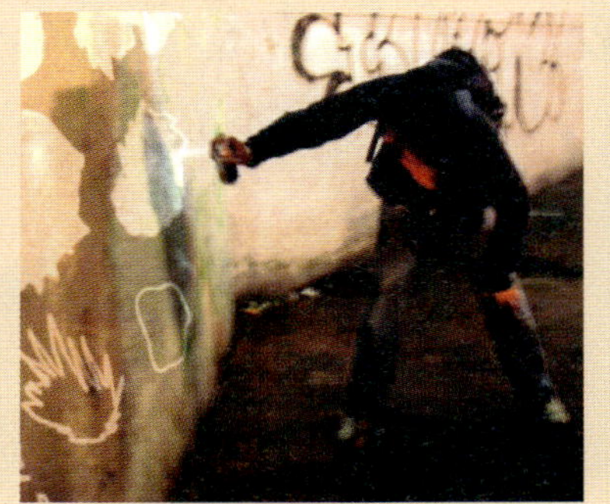
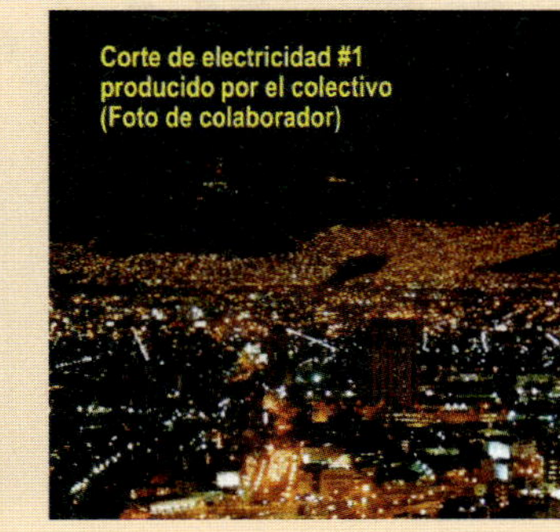

Colectivo Unidad, 2004. Silent video transferred to DVD. 7 min. 20 sec.

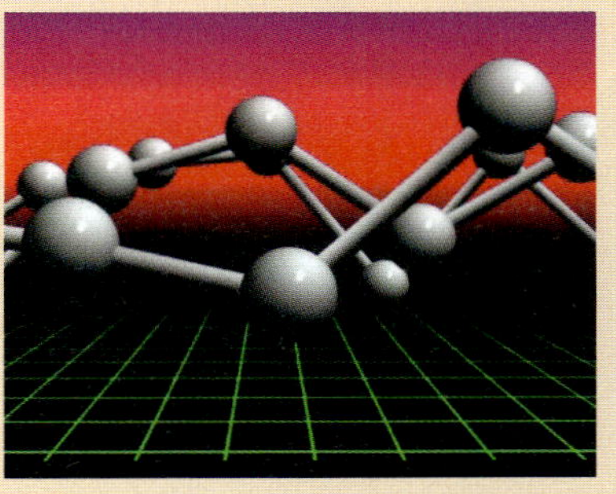
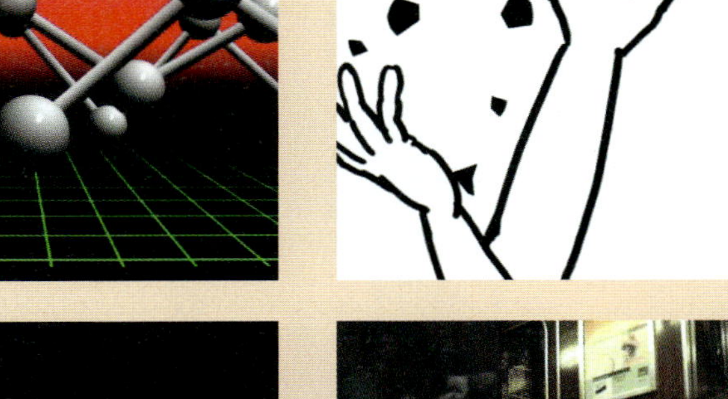
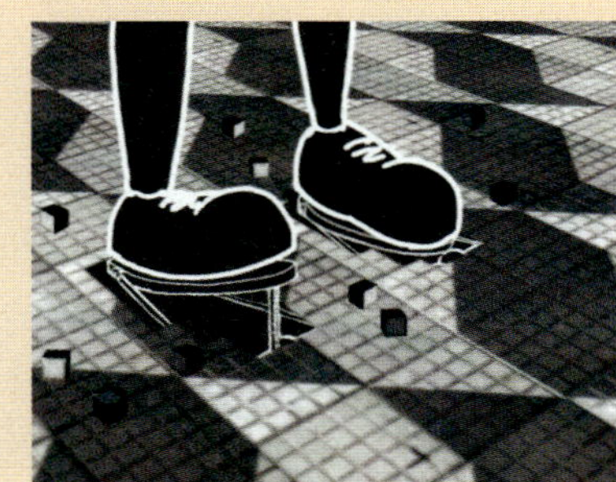
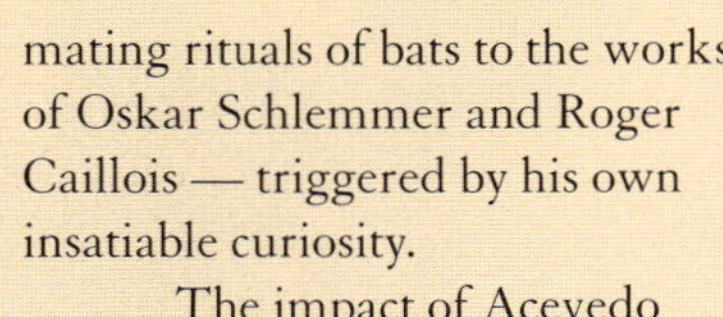
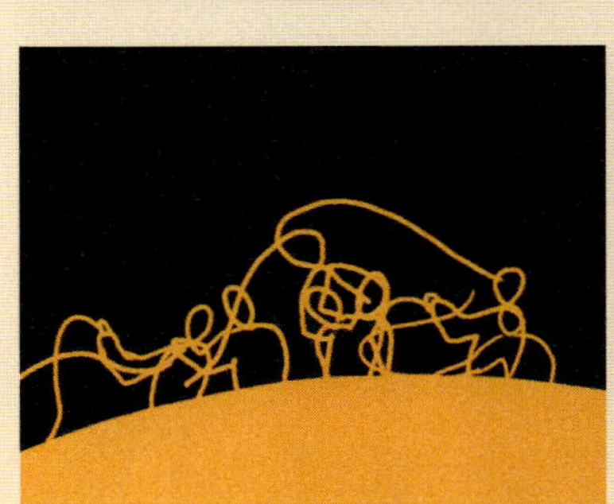
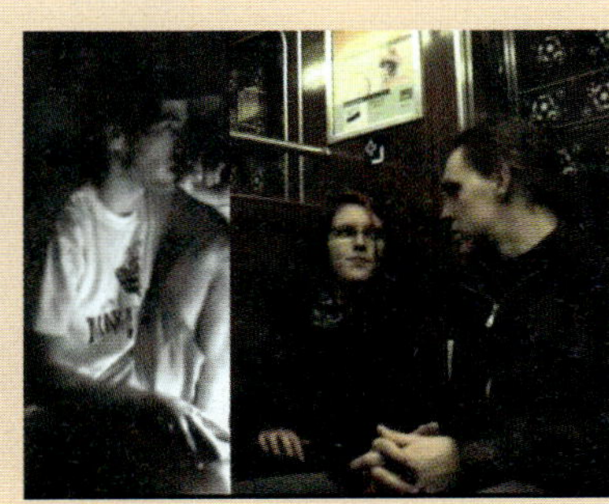
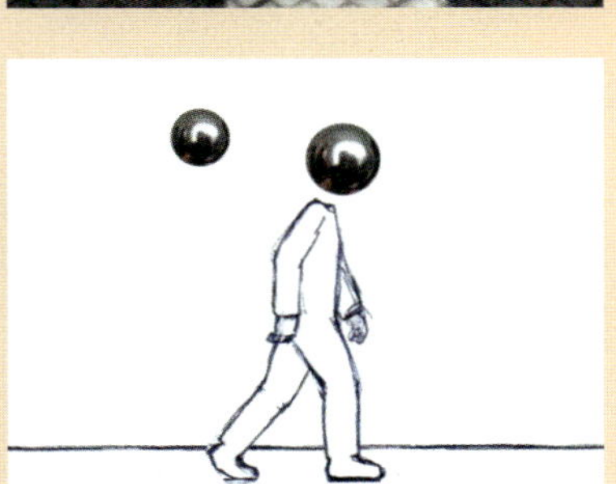
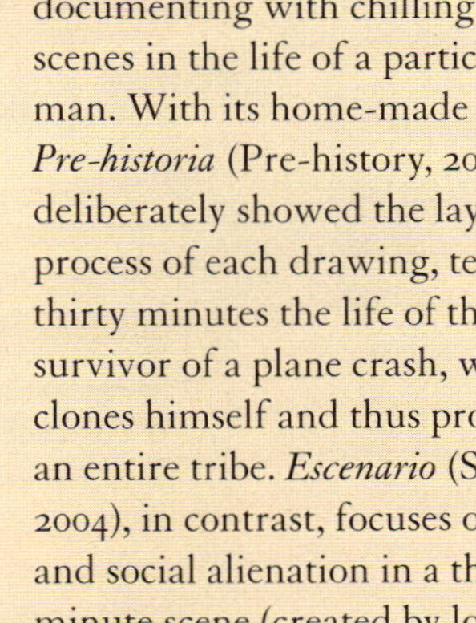
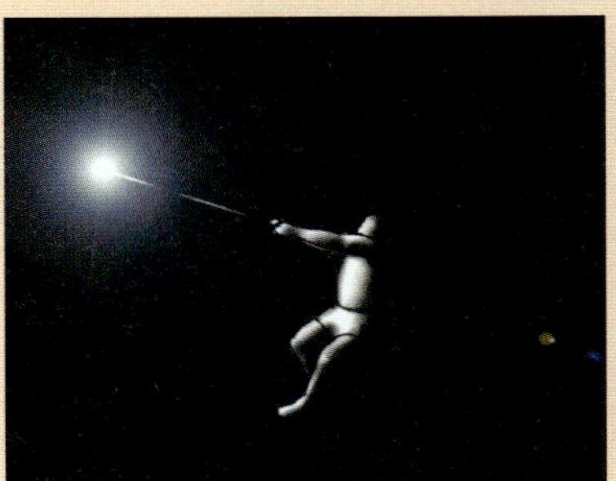
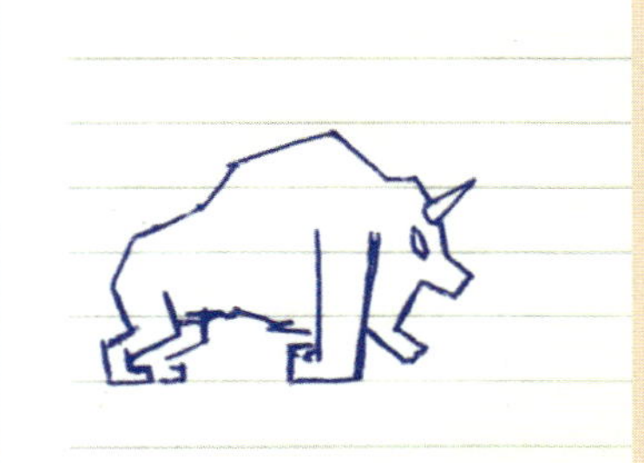
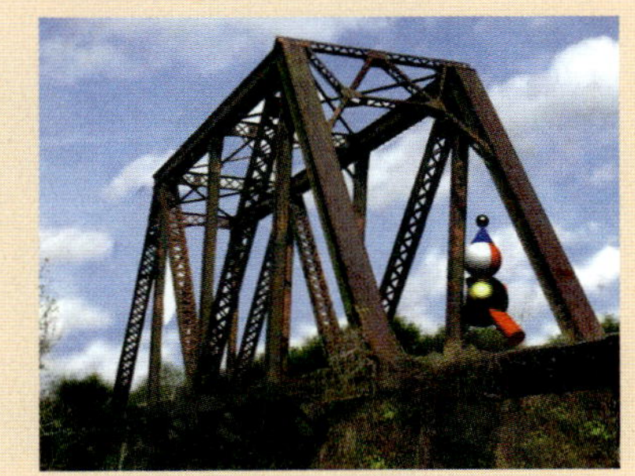

Marathon 1, 2007. Edited video documentation of performance. 26 min.

mating rituals of bats to the works of Oskar Schlemmer and Roger Caillois — triggered by his own insatiable curiosity.

The impact of Acevedo Velarde's first animations was due to the kind of virtuosic social caricature that they conveyed, documenting with chilling humour scenes in the life of a particular little man. With its home-made aesthetic, *Pre-historia* (Pre-history, 2005), deliberately showed the lay-out process of each drawing, telling in thirty minutes the life of the only survivor of a plane crash, who clones himself and thus procreates an entire tribe. *Escenario* (Stage, 2004), in contrast, focuses on vanity and social alienation in a three-minute scene (created by looping a ten-second animation) in which a group of automata are taken one by one on to a stage, where they perform a zombie-like ritual and are hit and thrown on to the ground by a spotlight. With the same corrosive humour and interest in perverted and taboo behaviour

but with even greater abjection, *Exterminio* (Extermination, 200[...]) shows a humanoid couple propelled into the air by their o[wn] horrific copulation, shooting sperm bombs from the sky and destroying cities as they go.

Always motivated by hi[s] own sense of curiosity as opposed to a loyalty to specific materials and forms, Acevedo Velarde's current exploration of different media includes his series of vid[eo] *Quorum Power*, which dubs cas[ual] conversations filmed in the Ber[lin] underground with a soundtrac[k] made up of unbelievable dialog[ue] narrated in the artist's own histrionic voice. Another recent work, *The Hexagonal Hackers*, [is] a lecture-performance about fr[ee] software that takes the form of a political thriller. And for the 2[...] Mercosul Biennial he created *M[...] Cone* (2009), a graphic photo col[lage] for a billboard. In summarizing his work, Acevedo Velarde say[s,] 'In general, all I want is to find my own way of doing politics.'

Home-made aesthetic

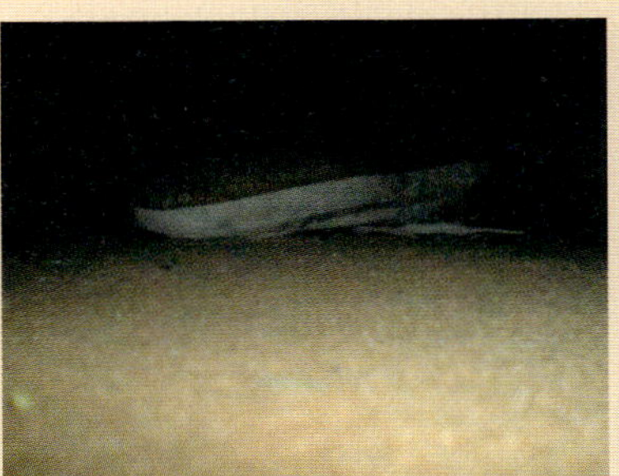
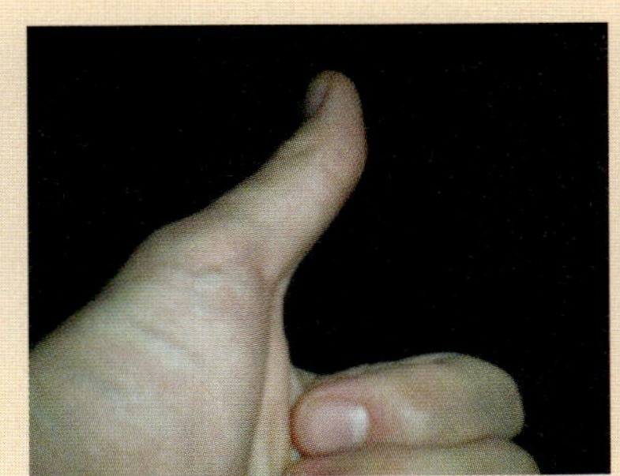
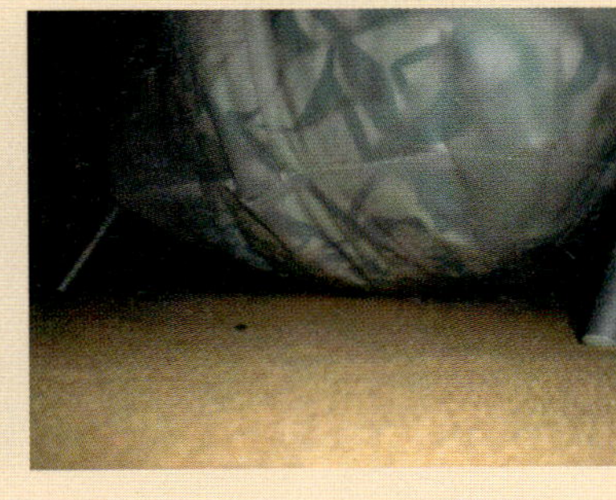
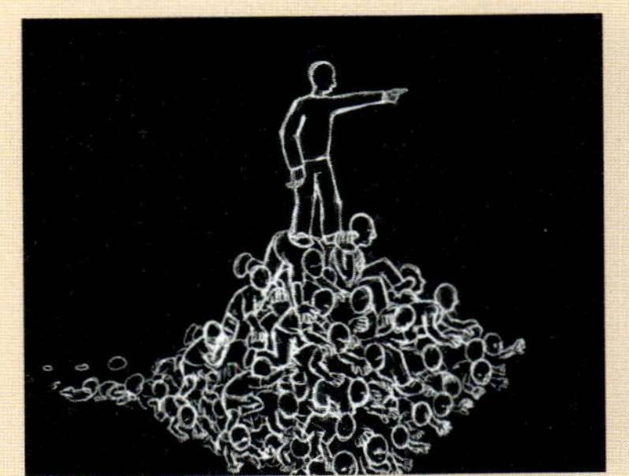
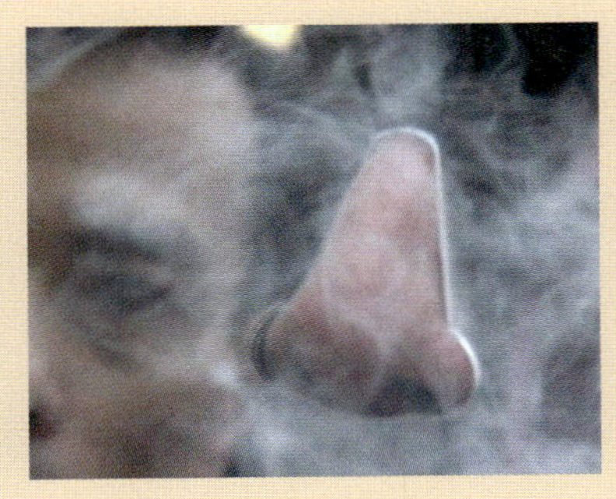
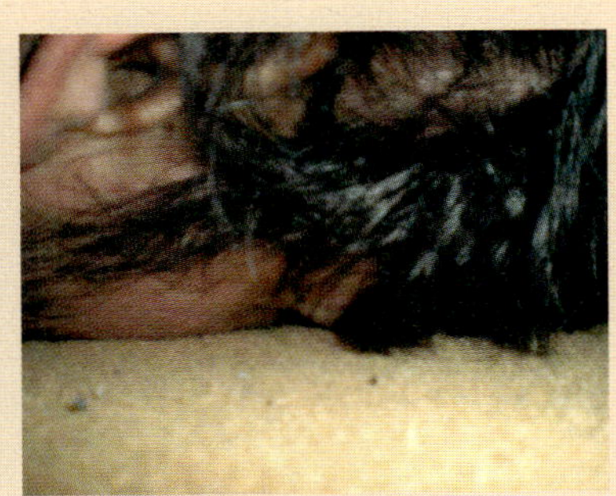
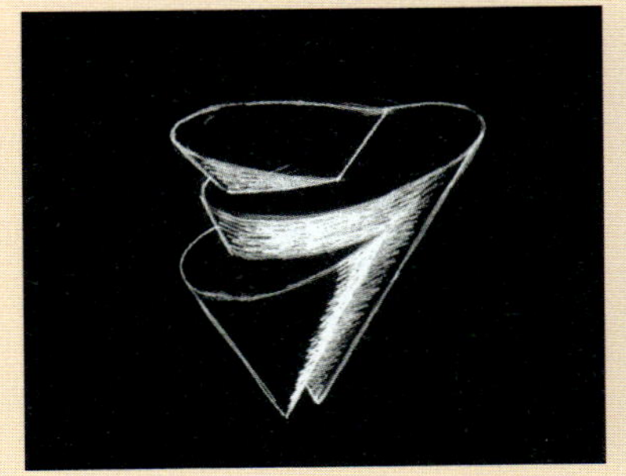
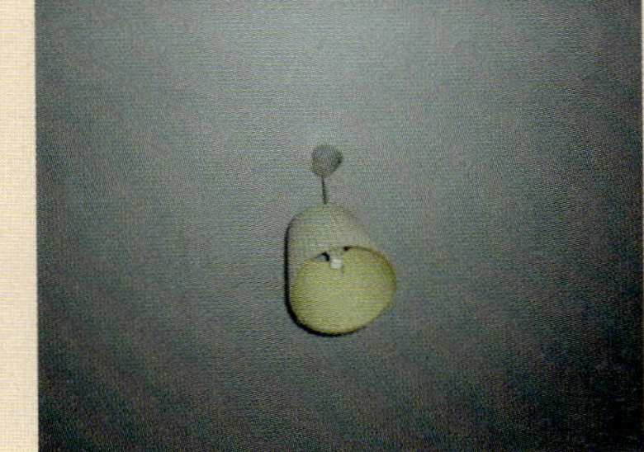
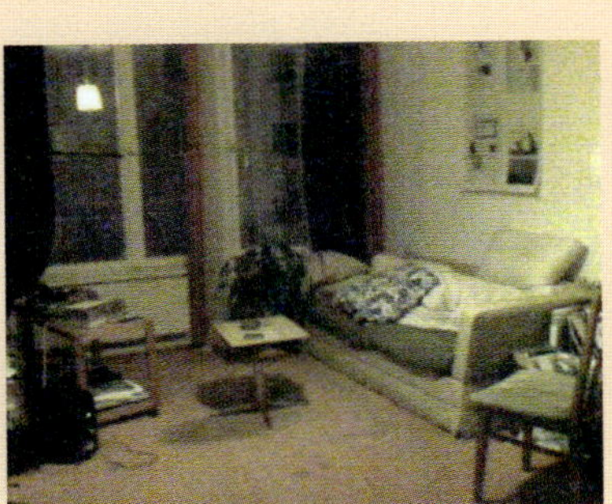

Maratón 2, 2008. Video. 15 min. 20 sec.

Corrosive humour

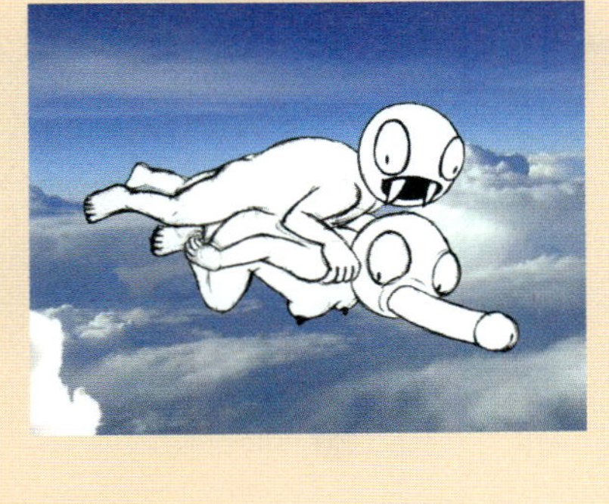
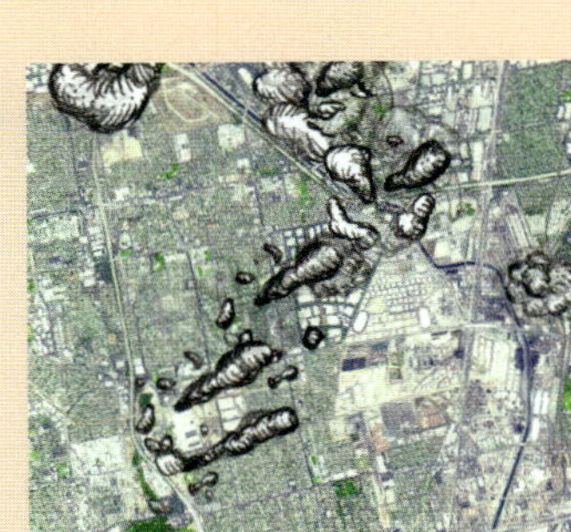
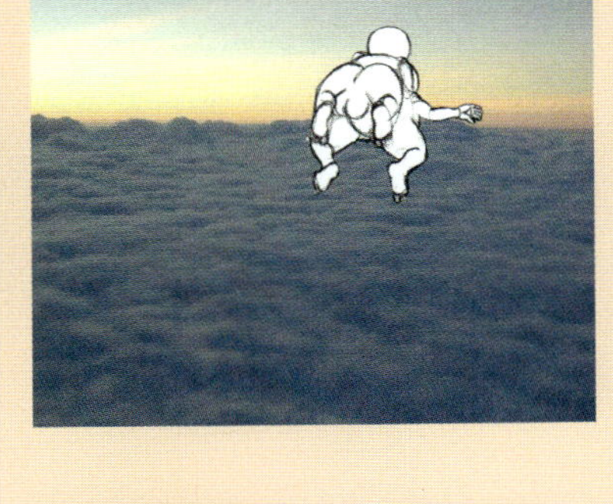
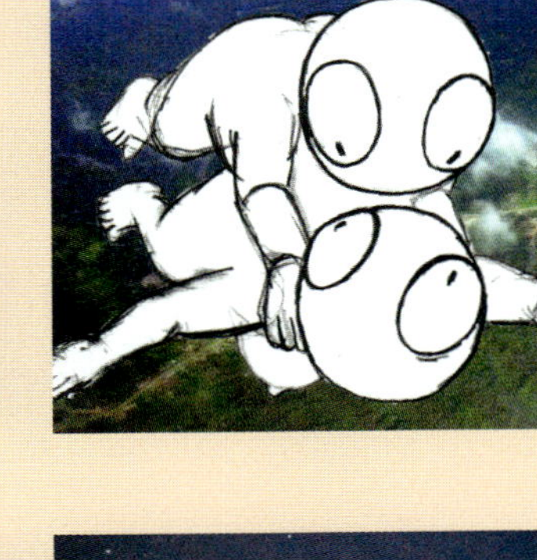
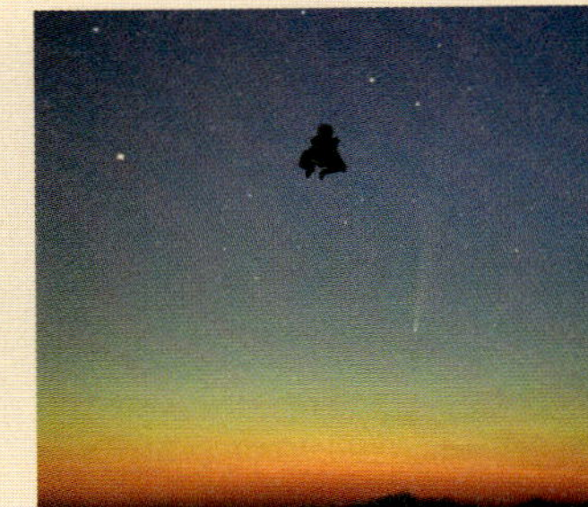

Exterminio, 2006. Animation transferred to DVD. 3 min. loop

Nevin Aladag

The works of Nevin Aladag, a Turkish artist of Kurdish origin who has been living and working in Germany for two decades, can be seen as temporary sculptures dedicated to displaced individuals and social groups, subcultures and exiled people. Frequently, they take the form of collective and individual amateur performances — dancing, singing and music. In this way, Aladag draws our attention to the way in which skills and customs personified by various (migrant) individuals are passed between generations and communities, contributing to the construction of new identities that recall forms of traditional culture while absorbing new influences from their contemporary, globalized and media-saturated context. Freed from the notions of roots and heritage, this new subjectivity is radically heterogeneous.

In her video *Familie Tezcan* (2001), the artist filmed members of a Turkish family in Germany who had mastered break-dancing and other performance skills. Self-consciously staging their artistic expression, they speak, sing and dance in a modest, private setting of a small gym-studio. The presence of the artist recording the scene is discreet and intimate, almost as if the video had been filmed by a member of the family.

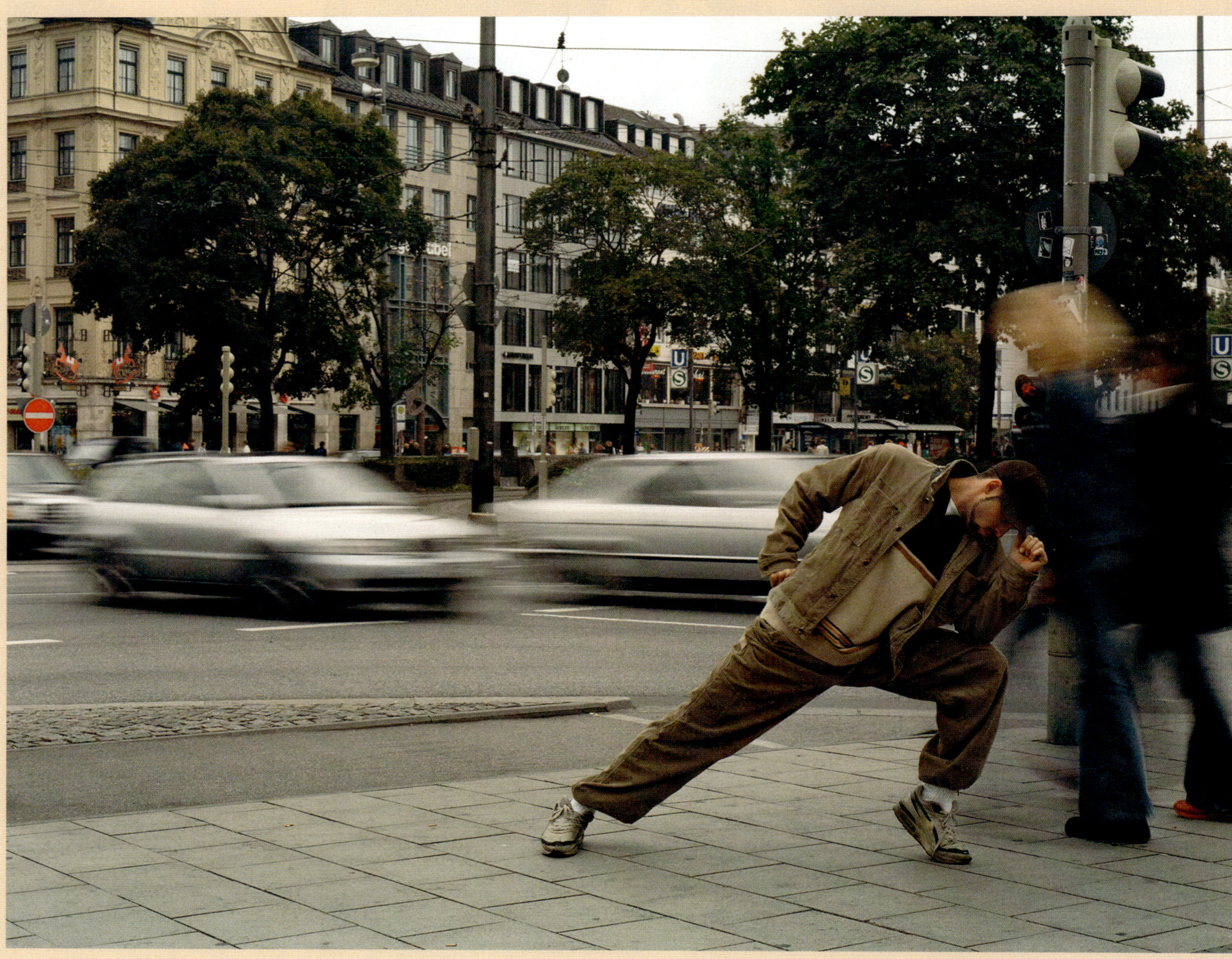

Freeze, 2003. Photographs on aluminium dibond. 11 parts. Each 60 × 80 cm

Temporary sculptures

This unassuming presence, almost a withdrawal of the author, is a trademark of Aladag's anti-spectacular productions.

The series of photographs entitled *Freeze* (2003) portrays break-dancers striking different poses, contorting and 'freezing' for an instant in the midst of city traffic, using the rudimentary infrastructure of roadblocks and pavements instead of pedestals and plinths, which are reserved for permanent official monuments. A complementary series of stickers

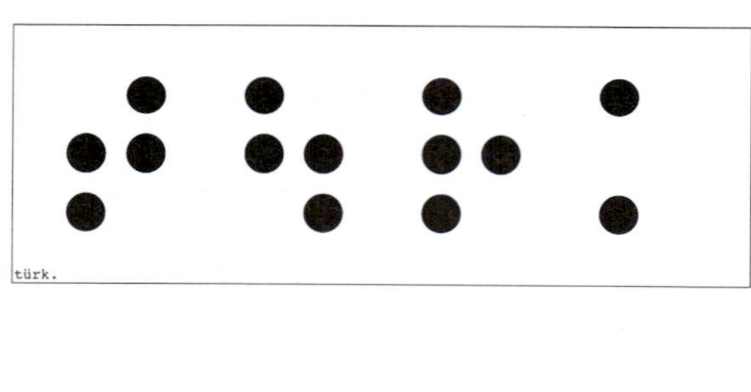

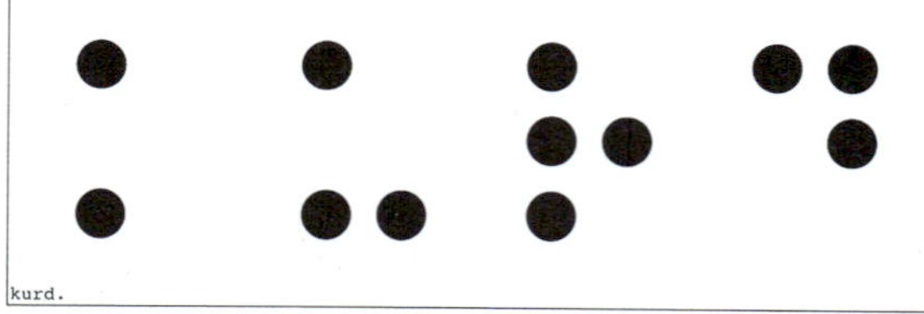

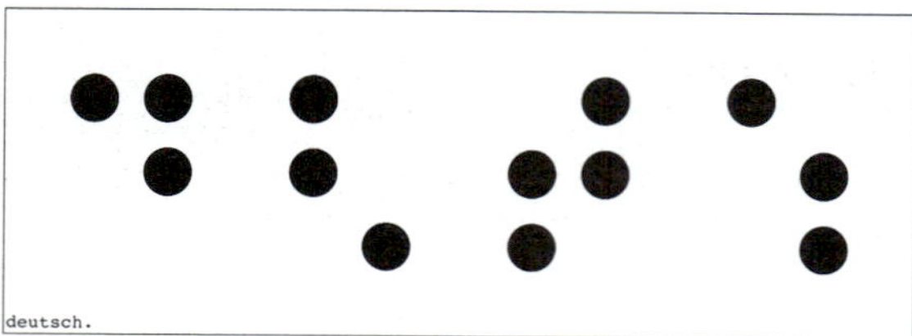

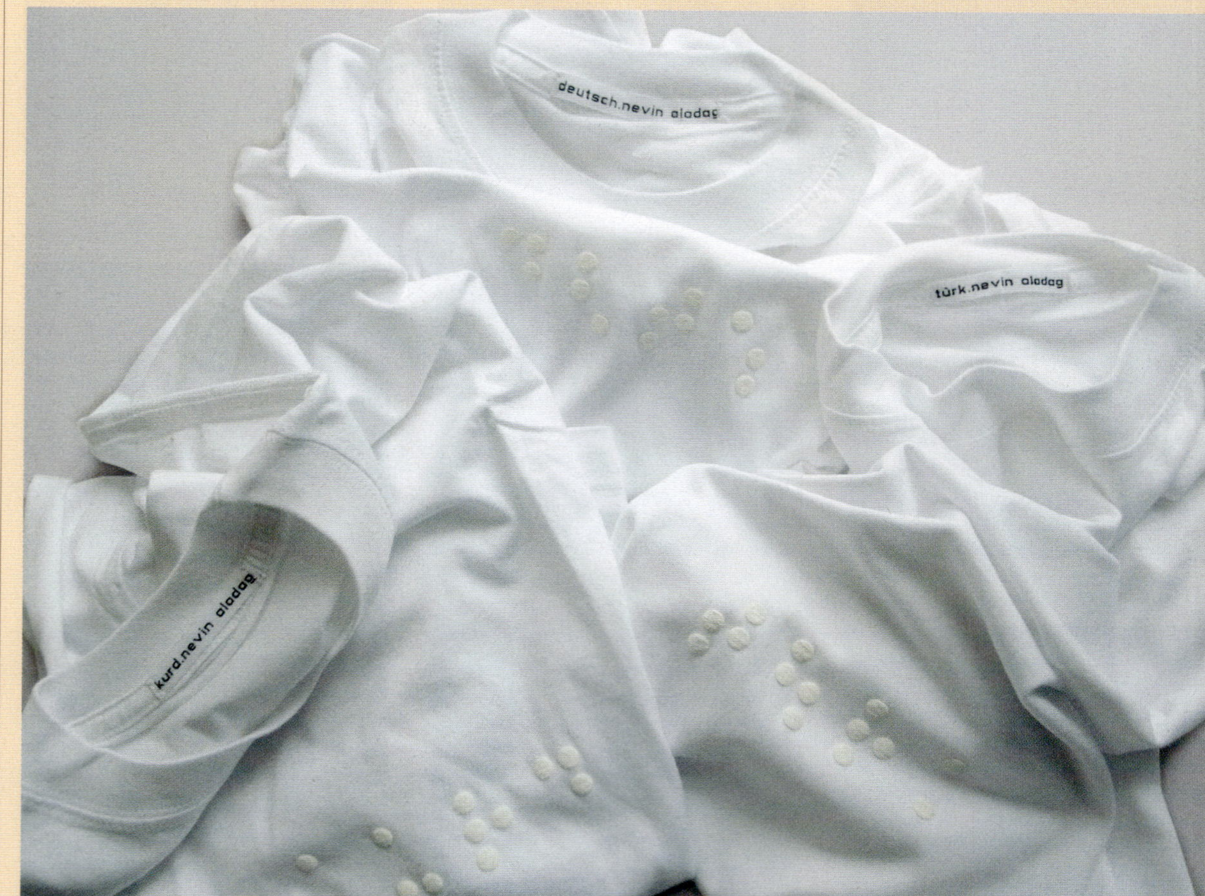

Deutsch. Türk. Kurd., 2003. T–Shirt, edition of 99

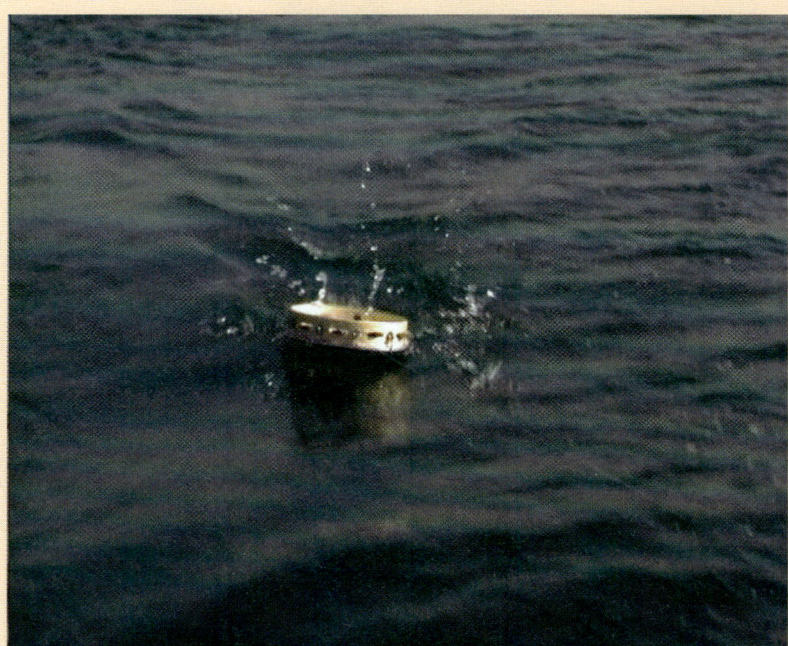

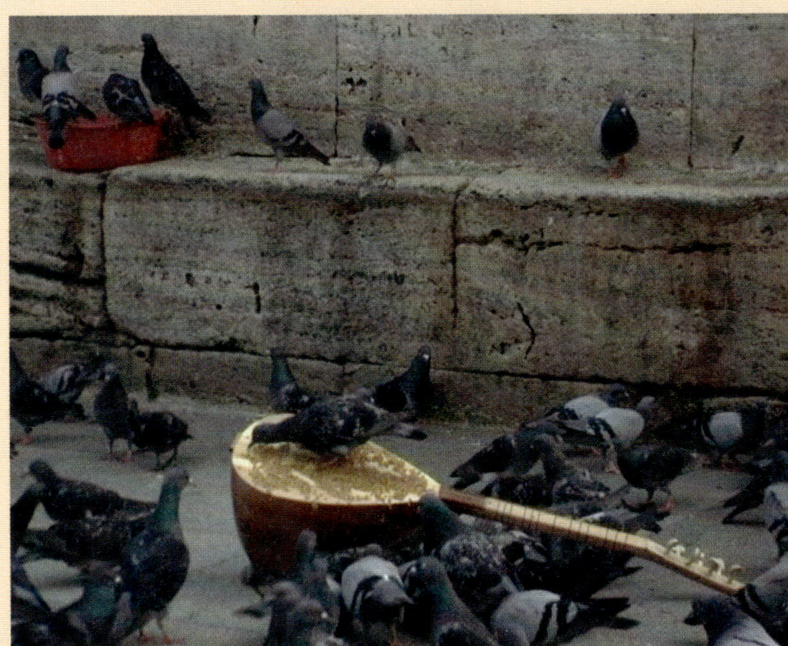

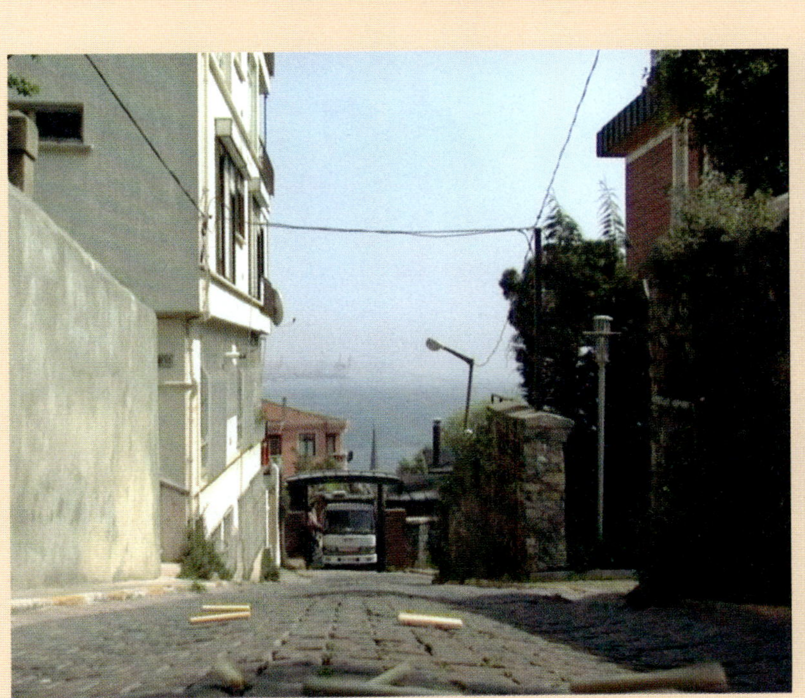

Minor narratives

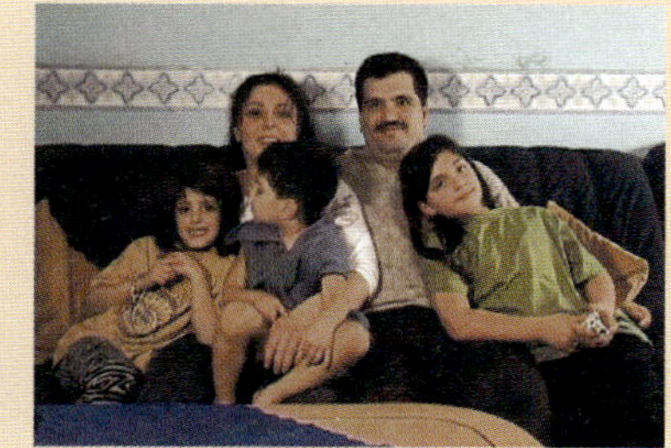 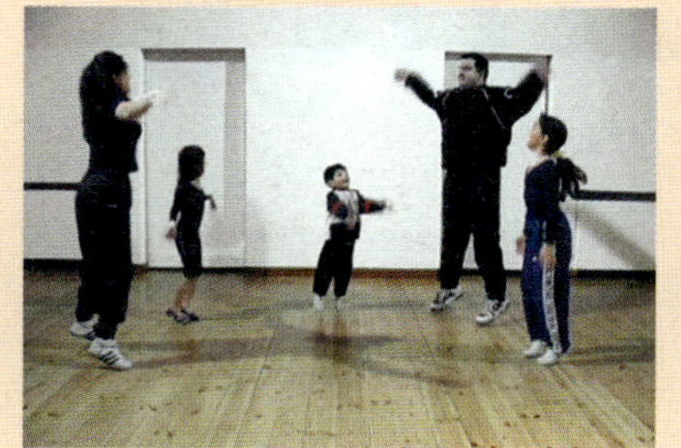 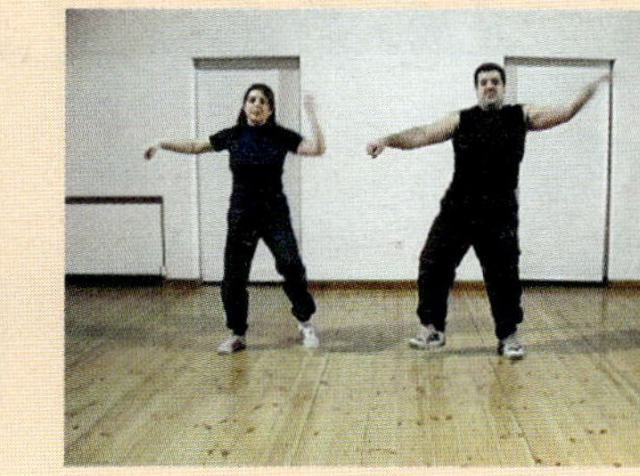

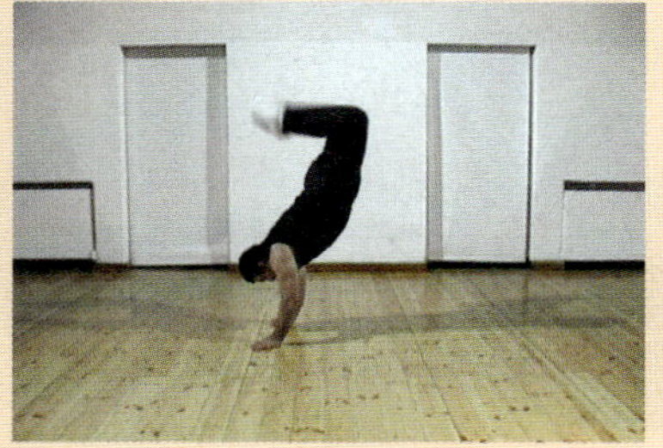 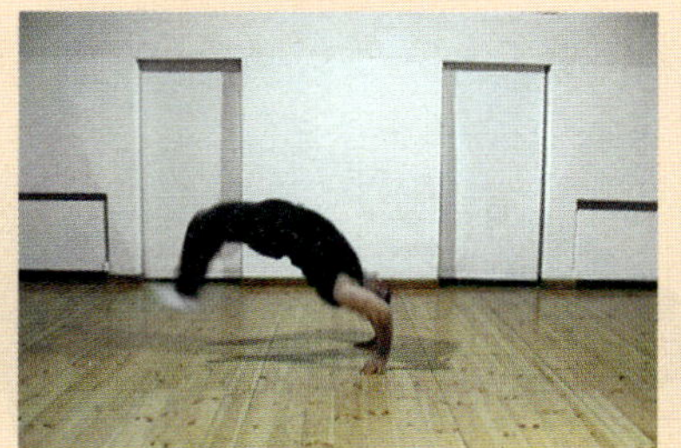 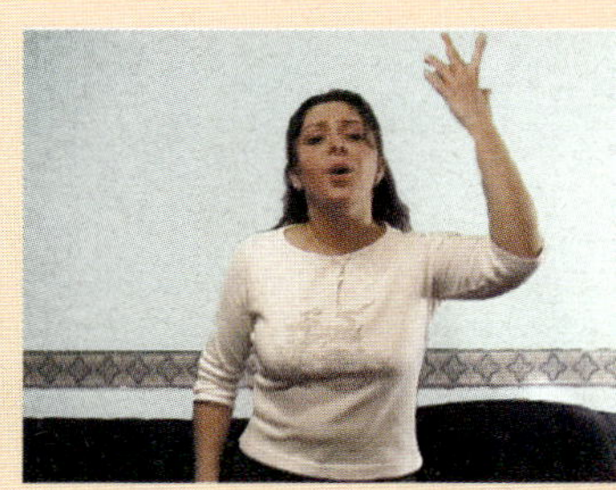

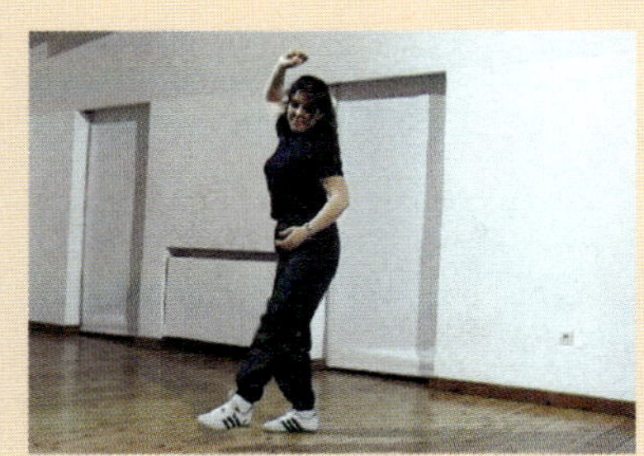 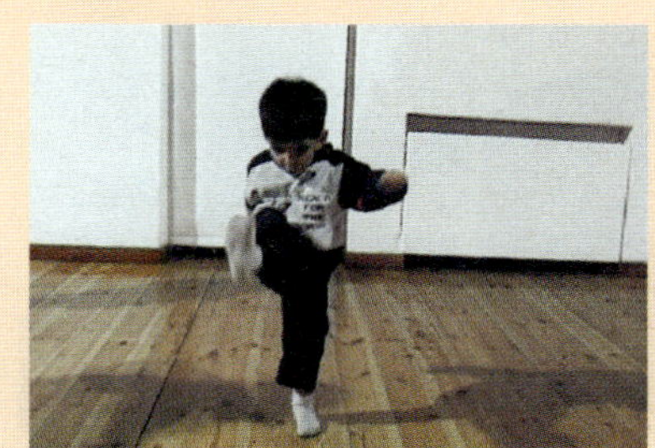 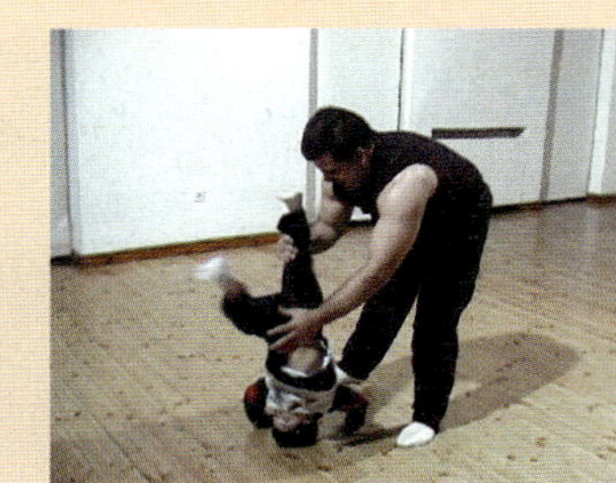

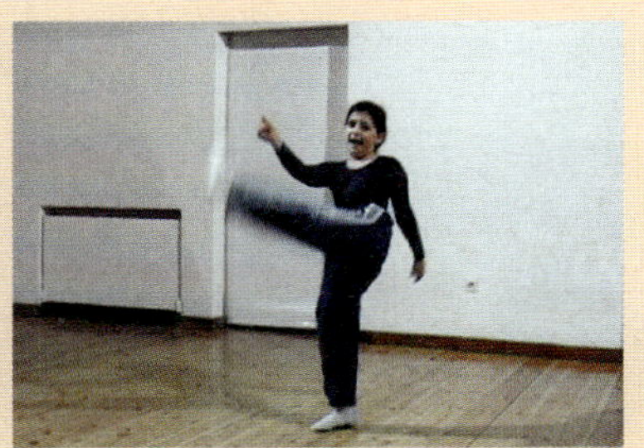 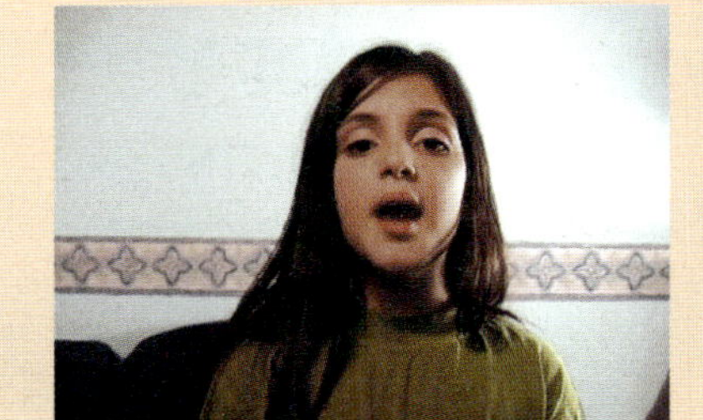 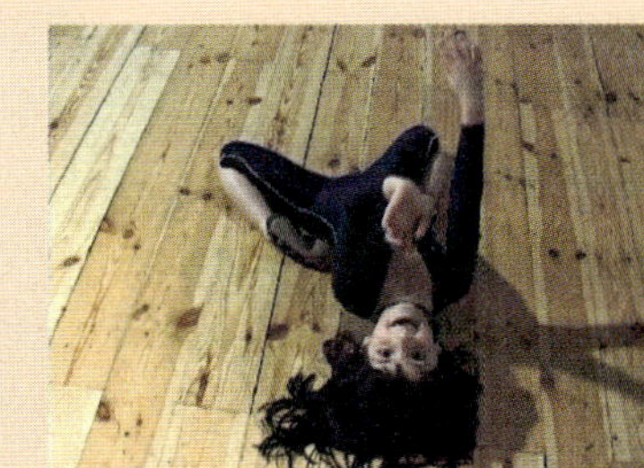

Familie Tezcan, 2001. Video. 6 min. 40 sec.

The works of Nevin Aladag, a Turkish artist of Kurdish origin who has been living and working in Germany for two decades, can be seen as temporary sculptures dedicated to displaced individuals and social groups, subcultures and exiled people. Frequently, they take the form of collective and individual amateur performances — dancing, singing and music. In this way, Aladag draws our attention to the way in which skills and customs personified by various (migrant) individuals are passed between generations and communities, contributing to the construction of new identities that recall forms of traditional culture while absorbing new influences from their contemporary, globalized and media-saturated context. Freed from the notions of roots and heritage, this new subjectivity is radically heterogeneous.

In her video *Familie Tezcan* (2001), the artist filmed members of a Turkish family in Germany who had mastered break-dancing and other performance skills. Self-consciously staging their artistic expression, they speak, sing and dance in a modest, private setting of a small gym-studio. The presence of the artist recording the scene is discreet and intimate,

Withdrawal of the author

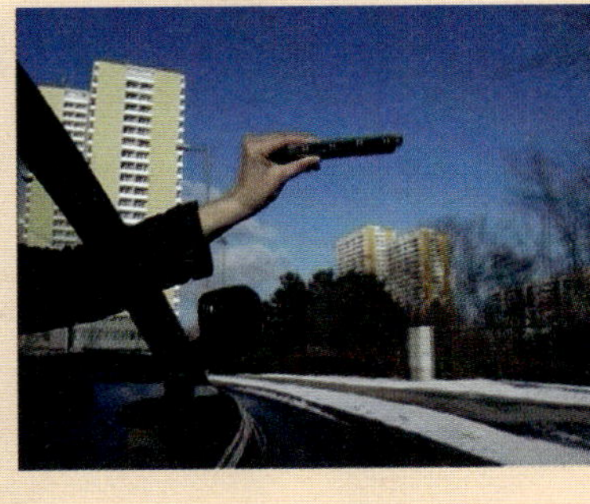

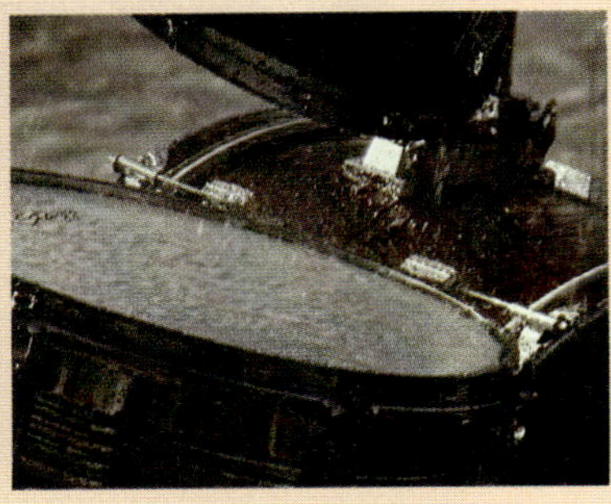

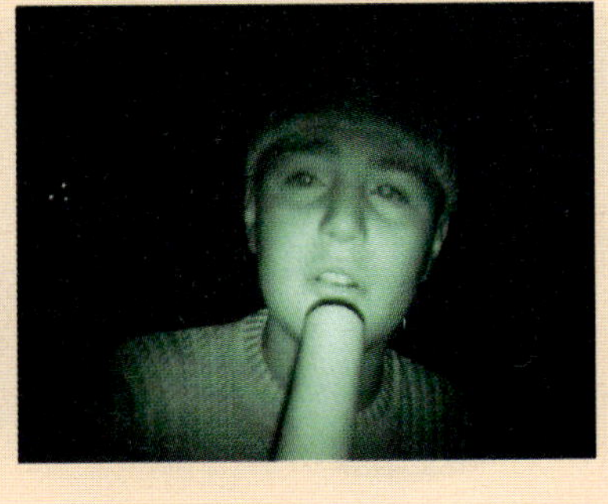

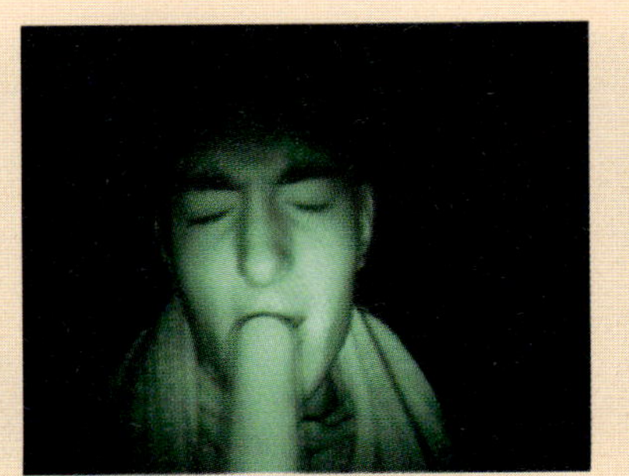

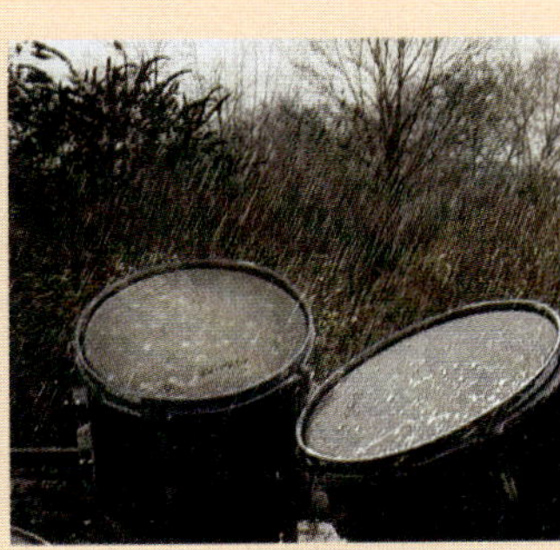

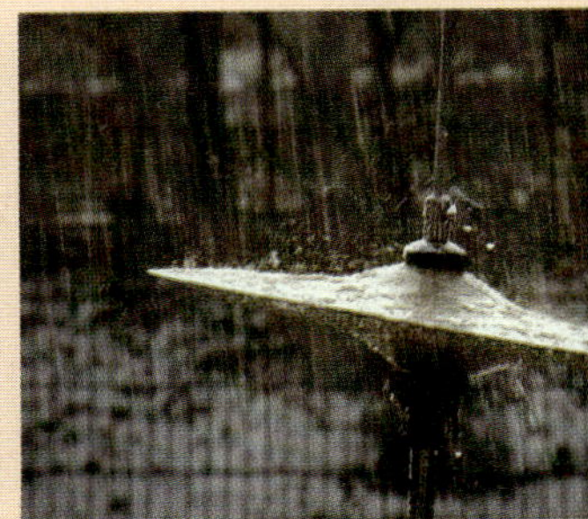

City Language I from the trilogy **City Language I, II, III**, 2009. Video. 5 min.

Voice Over, 2006. DVD. 14 min.

Can Altay

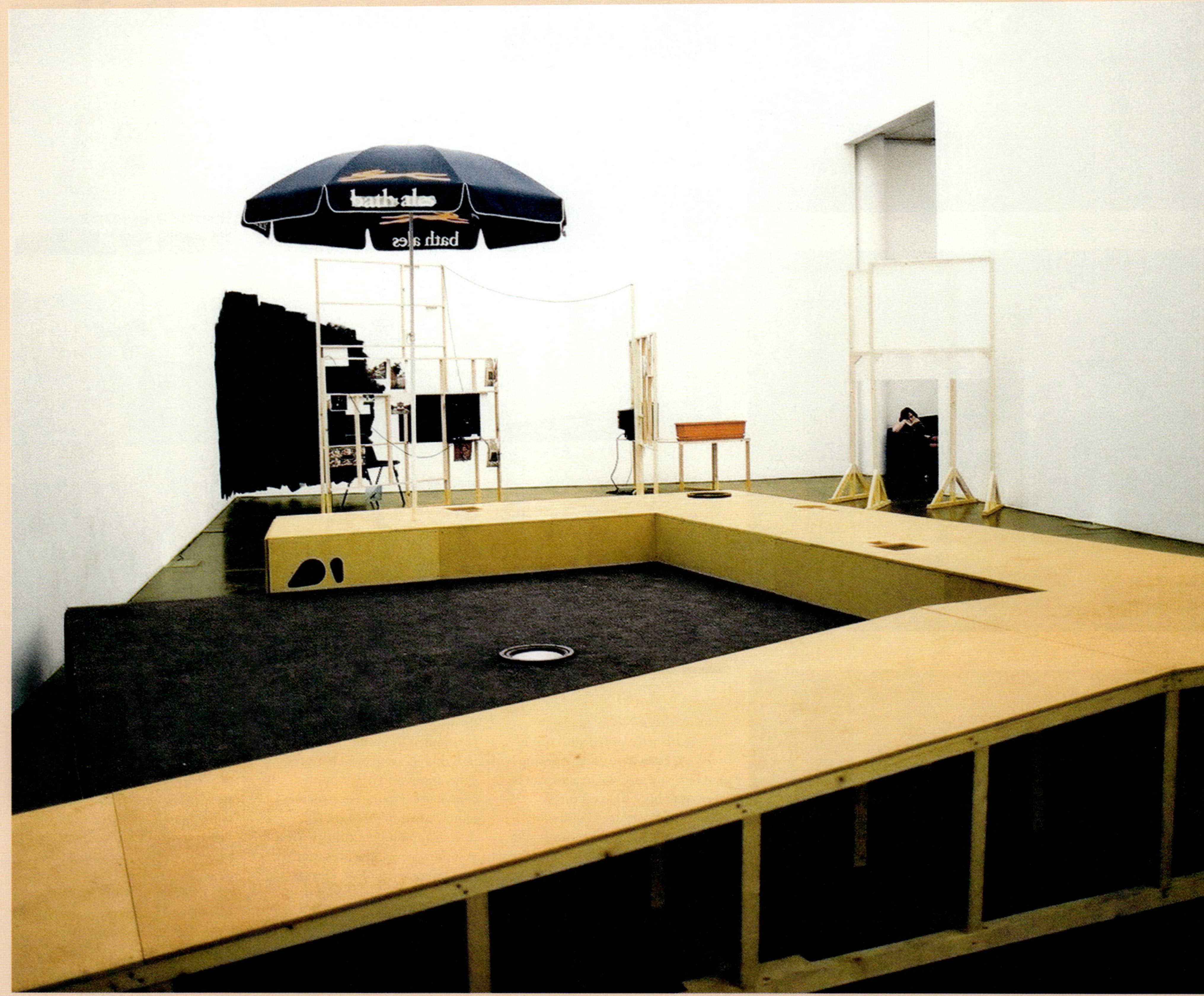

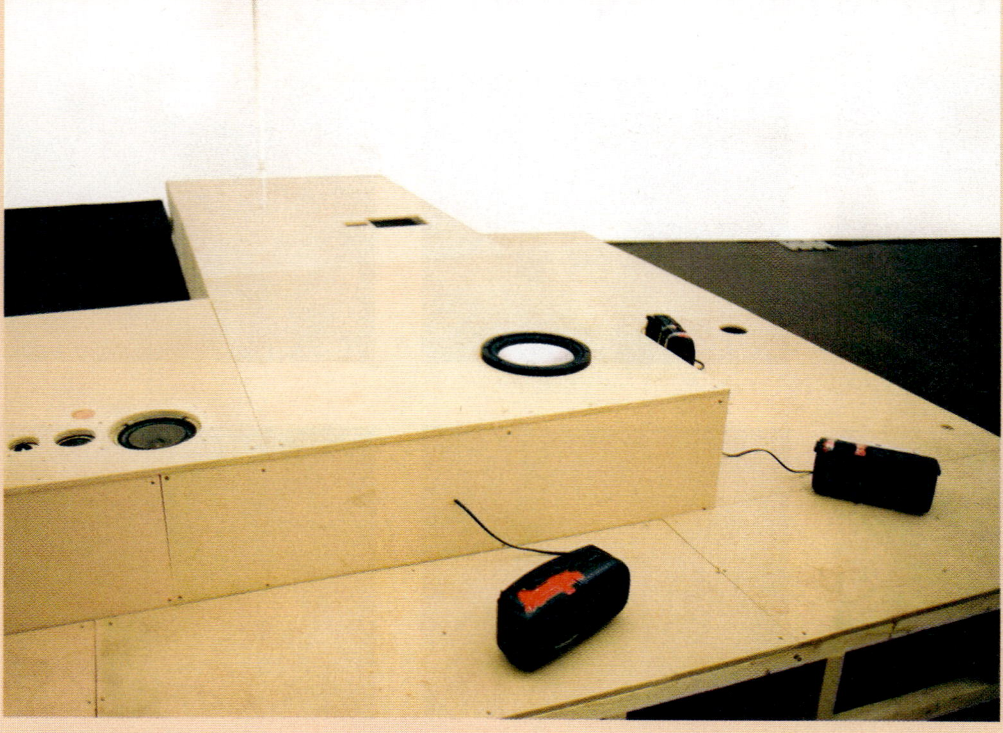

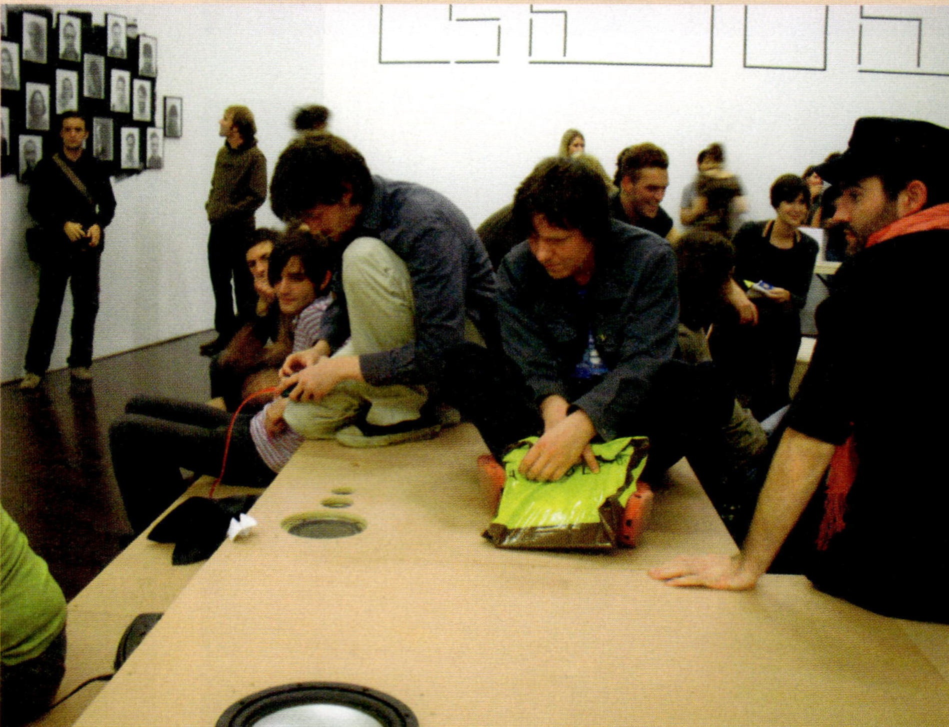

A Damaged Plane (with William Turner Duffin, Barnabas Yianni and Luke Slater), 2007. Wood, MDF, carpets, 12 speakers, 3–channel sound system, used cassette players, pub umbrella. Approx. 350 × 350 × 180 cm

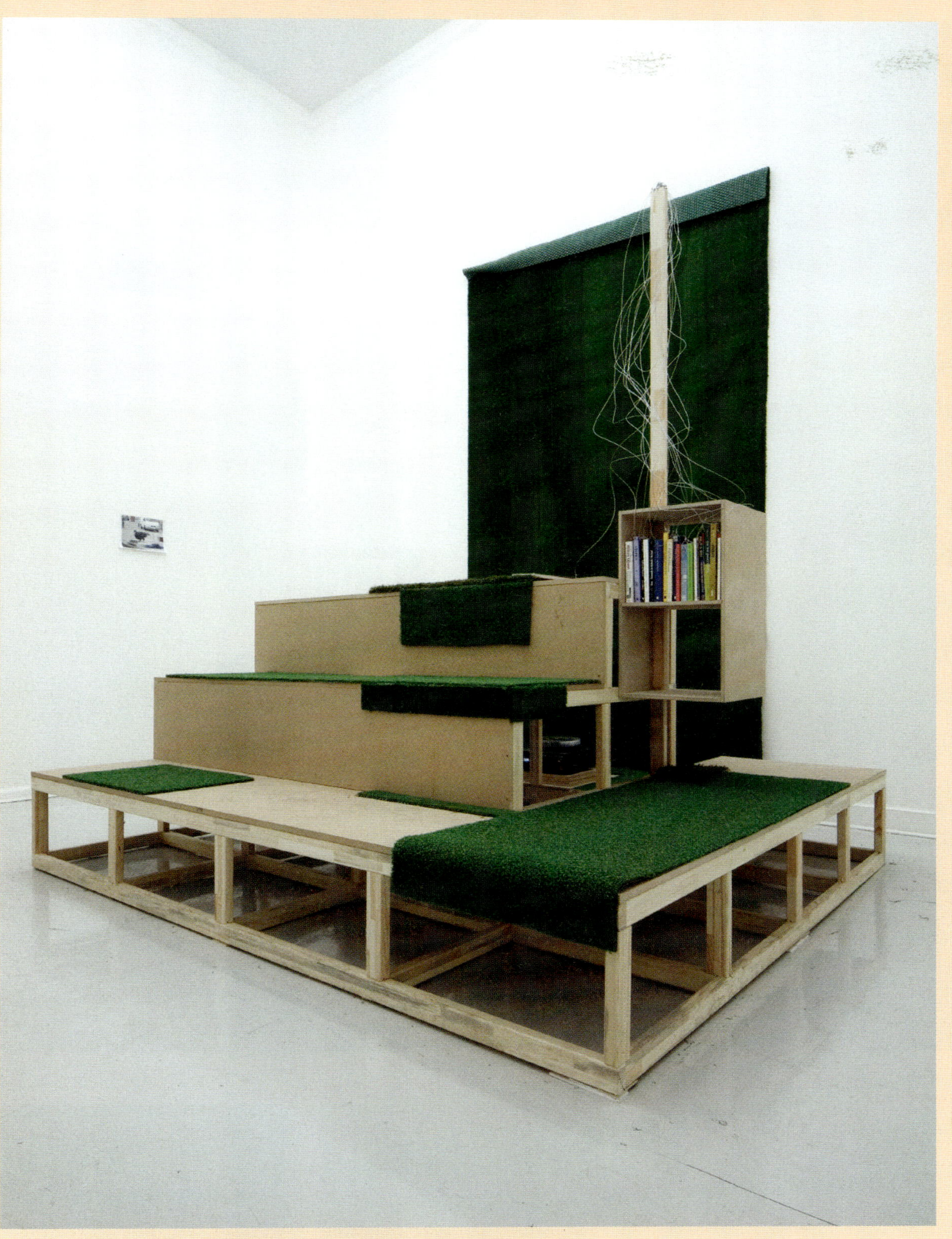

Possibilities of thinking and doing

If the reflexivity of some artists in this selection is that of an aggressive engagement with the unspoken hierarchies inherent in the field of visual art, Can Altay's study of the art world's workings is one of concrete intervention in the material space of the shows in which he partakes. Arguably, since the term 'intervention' implies an element of interruption, intermission and stoppage, something like an epistemic constipator, it is perhaps an inappropriate term here: more than anything else, Altay's contributions enrich the respective possibilities of thinking and doing. Yet the idea of intervention seems the lesser evil when compared to 'contribution', 'installation' or 'sculpture'. The former term is too generic, while the other two are both too self-sustaining, for Altay's work is wonderfully parasitical, in the best sense of the word.

The artist's work in the early 2000s included the much-admired 'Minibar' projects, which documented, by way of various media, the semi-impromptu, nighttime street-corner hangouts of Ankara. They painted a wistful picture of an ephemeral and vibrant community, the kind that the art world always hopes to embody. Our field traditionally prides itself in being unpredictable, flowing, effervescent, when in fact it is as unpredictable, flowing and effervescent as a bingo parlour at best. In later work, Altay often intervenes directly in the exhibition space by way of elements that might be called architectural, scenographic or even infrastructural.

Sometimes he goes a step further, as in the 2005 group show 'Normalization' at Platform Garanti, Istanbul, where he intelligently manipulated the work of other artists by reshaping their pieces over the course of the exhibition. Working in close collaboration, he pushed them to rethink their work and their mode of display, to consider ideas of sampling and documentation, but also to ponder the possibilities of leaving traces in the venue, following the show. Tellingly, for an artist who engages in a sophisticated way with all sorts of divisions of labour, the piece's title is followed by the names of the participating artists, in alphabetical order, followed by the names of those who assisted in the work's execution: *Normalization parts 1 and 2 / Haluk Akakçe, Can Altay, Yetkin Başarır, Cevdet Erek, Leyle Gediz, Hatice Güleryüz, Gülsün Karamustafa, Bülent Şangar, Seçil Yersel, Nerima Polat, Osman Bozkurt, Köken Ergun, Esra Ersen, Erkan Özgen, Şener Özmen / with further contributions Oğuzhan Genç, Aslı Kalınoğlu, Kutlu Gürelli, Sinem Kurultay.*

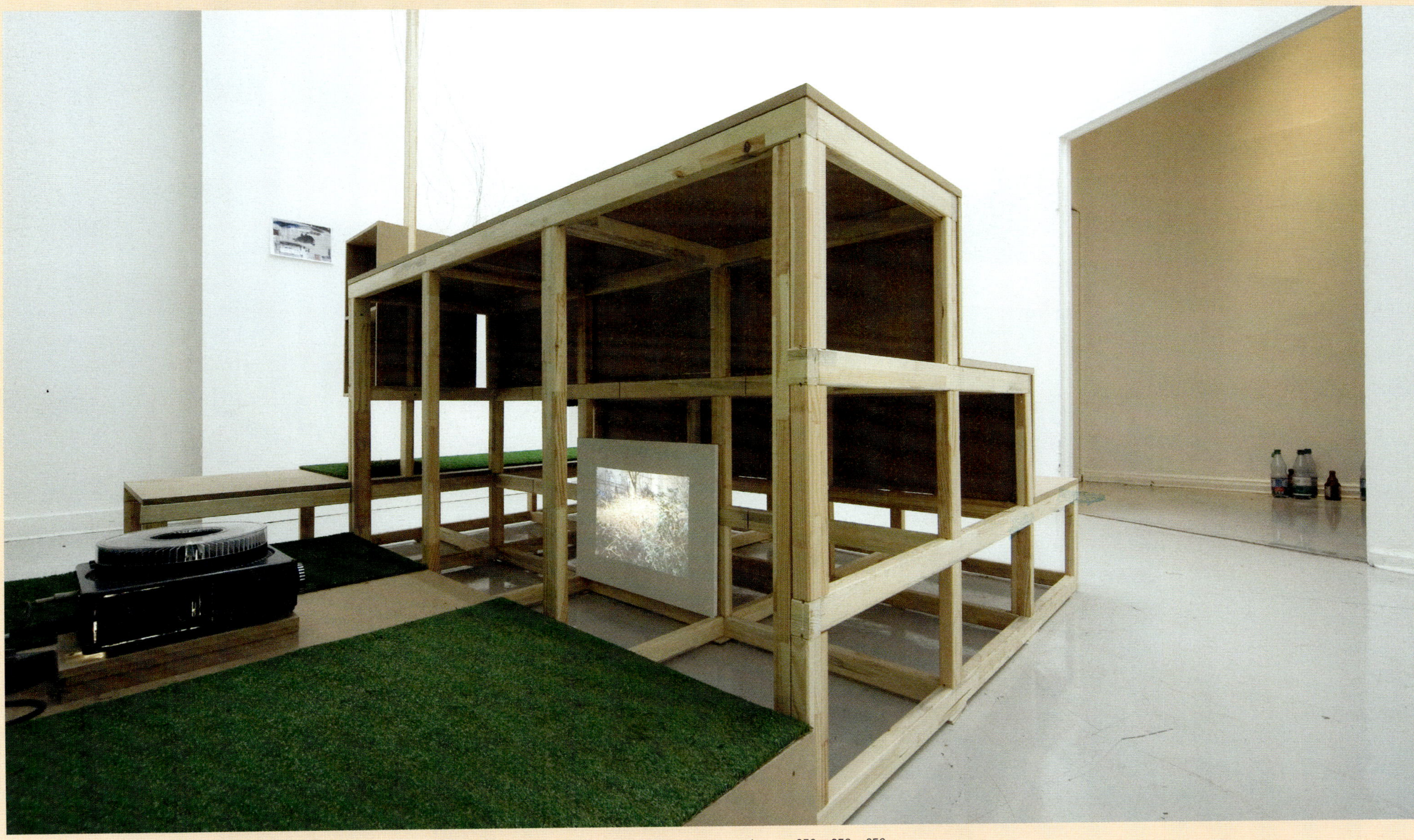

, 2008. Wood, MDF, Astroturf, slide projector, books, metal wire, digital print on paper. Approx. 250 × 250 × 250 cm

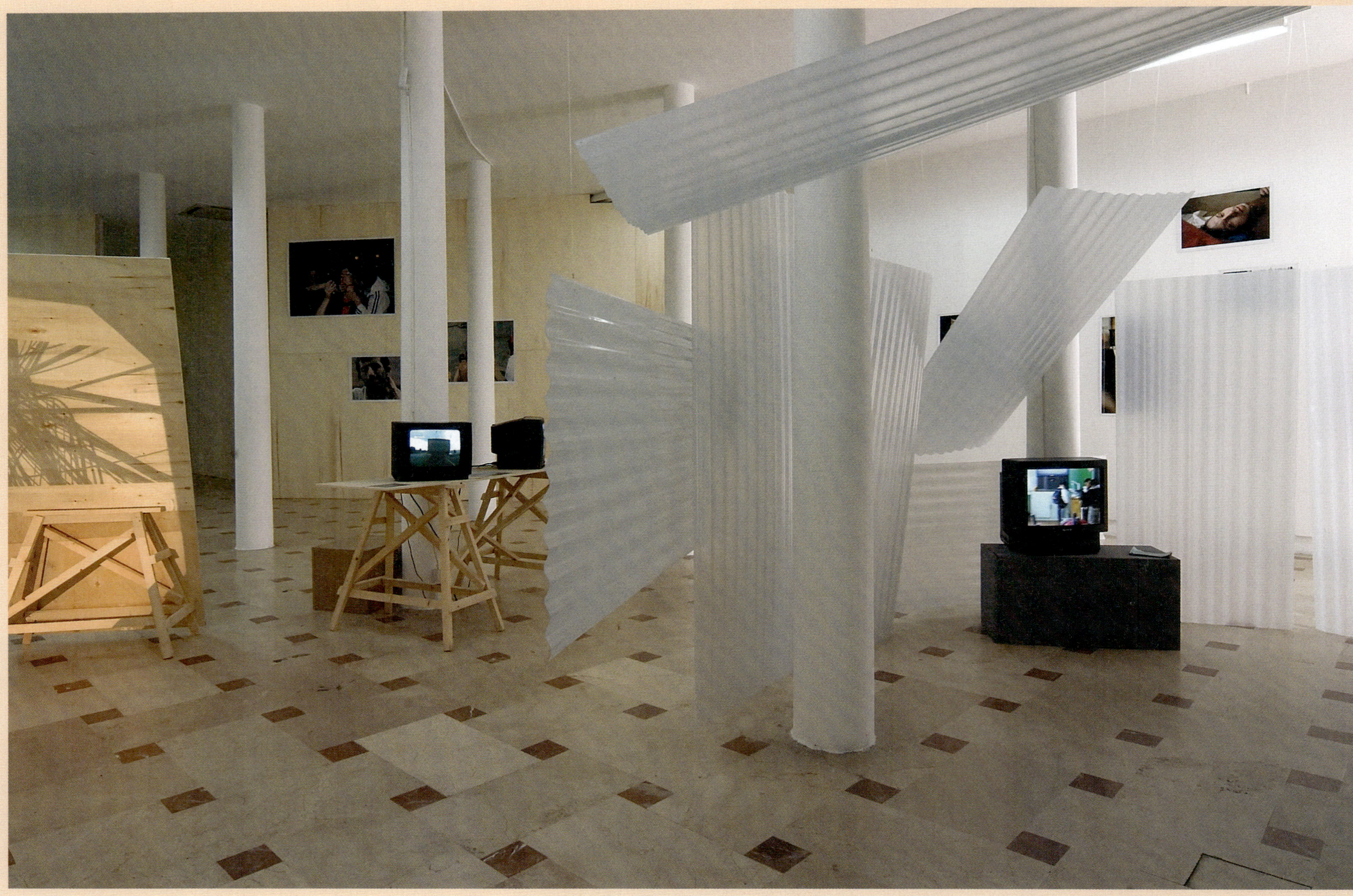

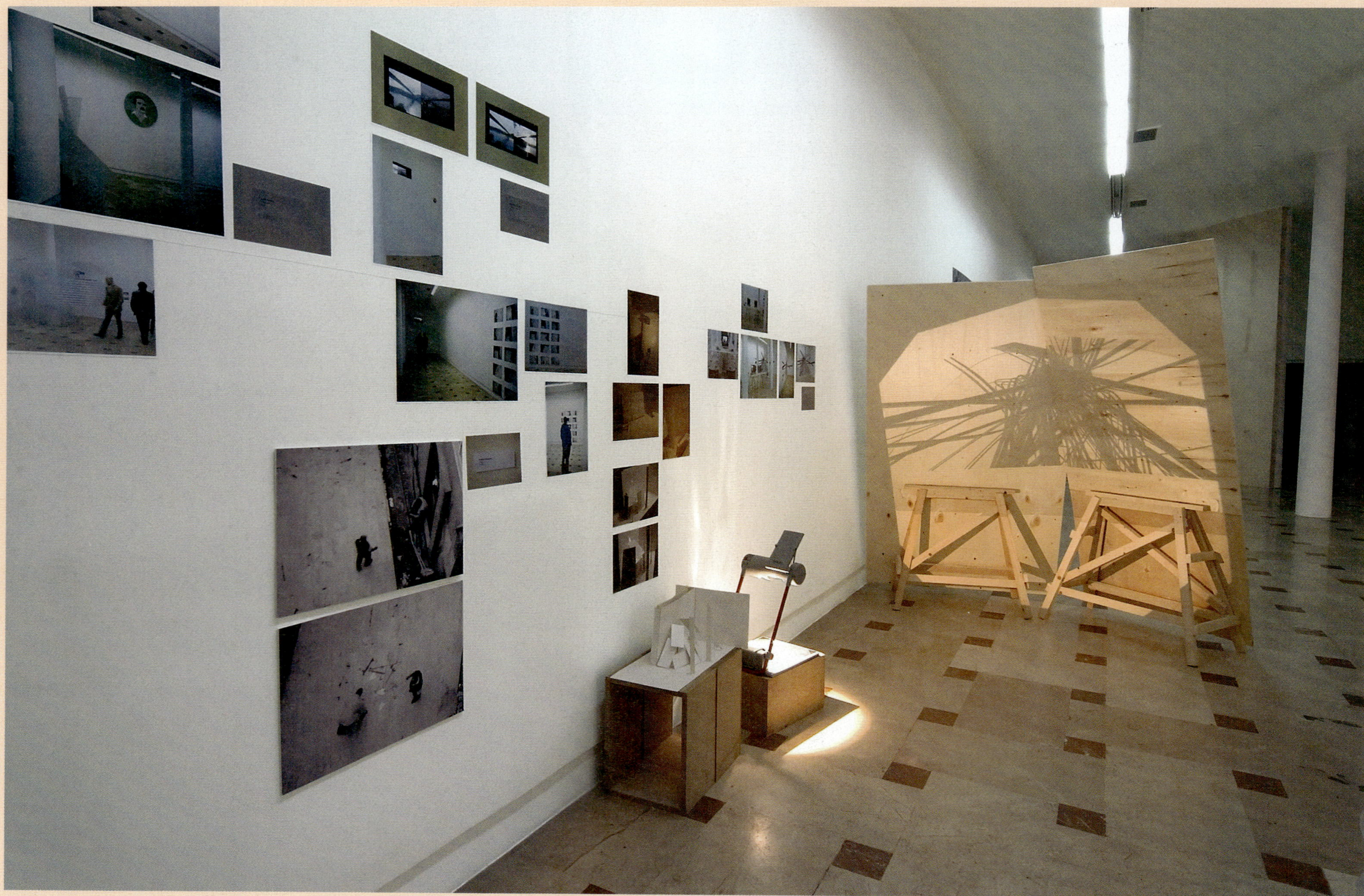

Normalization, parts 1 and 2 (with Haluk Akakçe, Can Altay, Yetkin Başarır, Cevdet Erek, Leyle Gediz, Hatice Güleryüz, Gülsün Karamustafa, Bülent Şangar, Seçil Yersel, Neriman Polat, Osman Bozkurt, Köken Ergun, Esra Ersen, Erkan Özgen, Şener Özmen, Oğuzhan Genç, Aslı Kalınoğlu, Kutlu Gürelli, Sinem Kurultay), 2005. Installation including original artworks by different artists shown previously at Platform Garanti, Istanbul, video, photographic documentation, source material, overhead projector, cardboard model, string, corrugated polycarbonate panels, fishing wire, wood, plywood, furniture. Approx. 600 × 450 × 350 cm. Installation view from 'Normalization', Platform Garanti, Istanbul

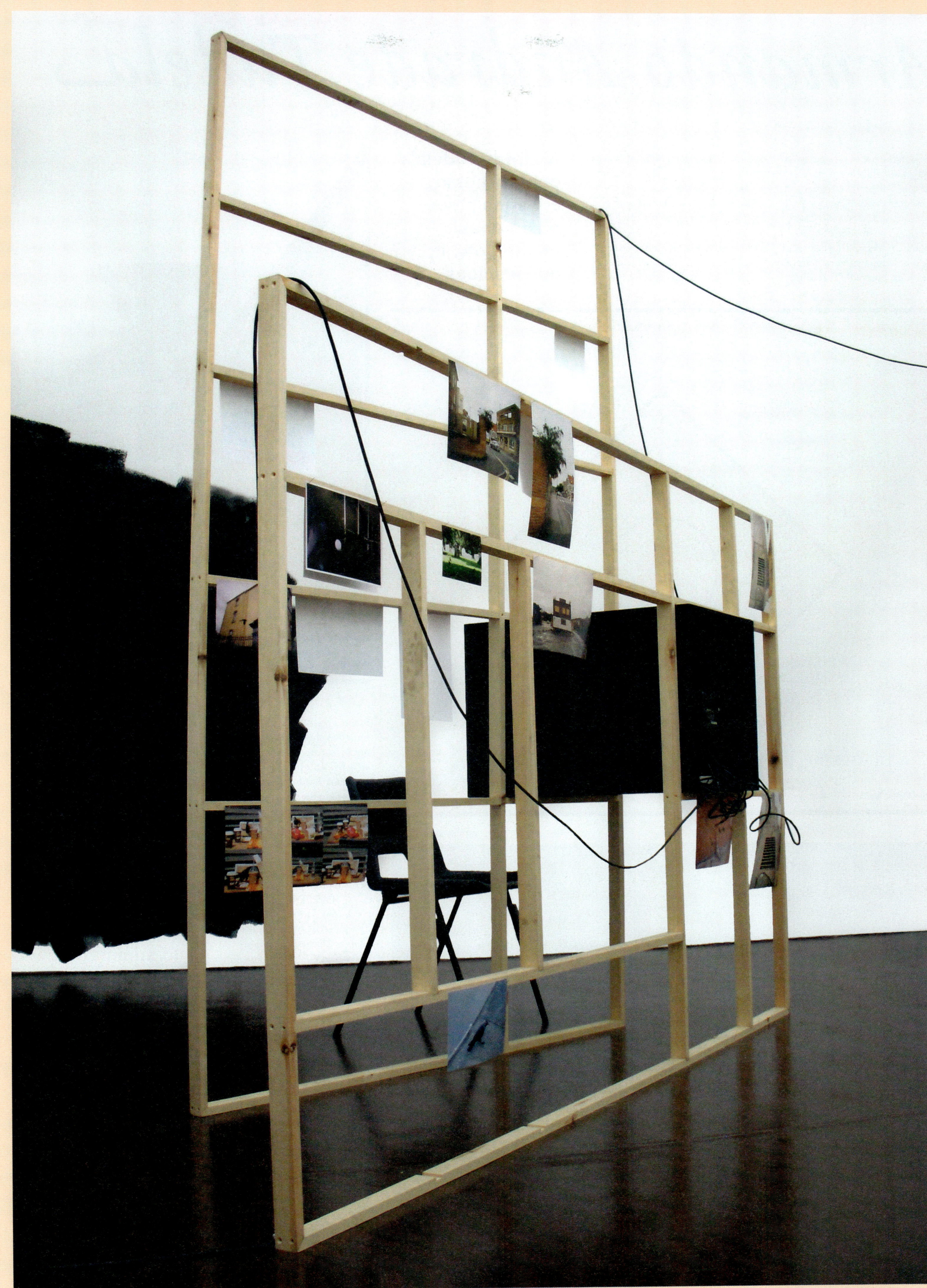

Exercises In Sharing: Aping Me, Aping You, 2007. Unique wooden structure, photographs. Approx. 260 × 260 × 130 cm

Armando Andrade Tudela

Through the use of collage, photography and sculpture Armando Andrade Tudela investigates the difference between legacies of modernity in Europe and Latin America. The 'modernities' to which he refers in his work speak different languages with manifold grammars, especially regarding the use and function of materials. Andrade Tudela's practice seems to prove that there are many ways to process the materials with which culture provides us: asphalt sculptures, a series of pen drawings on paper elaborating the idea of the street corner, collaged images of Eddie Murphy, record

Andrade Tudela's photographic collages place an emphasis on the optical unconscious

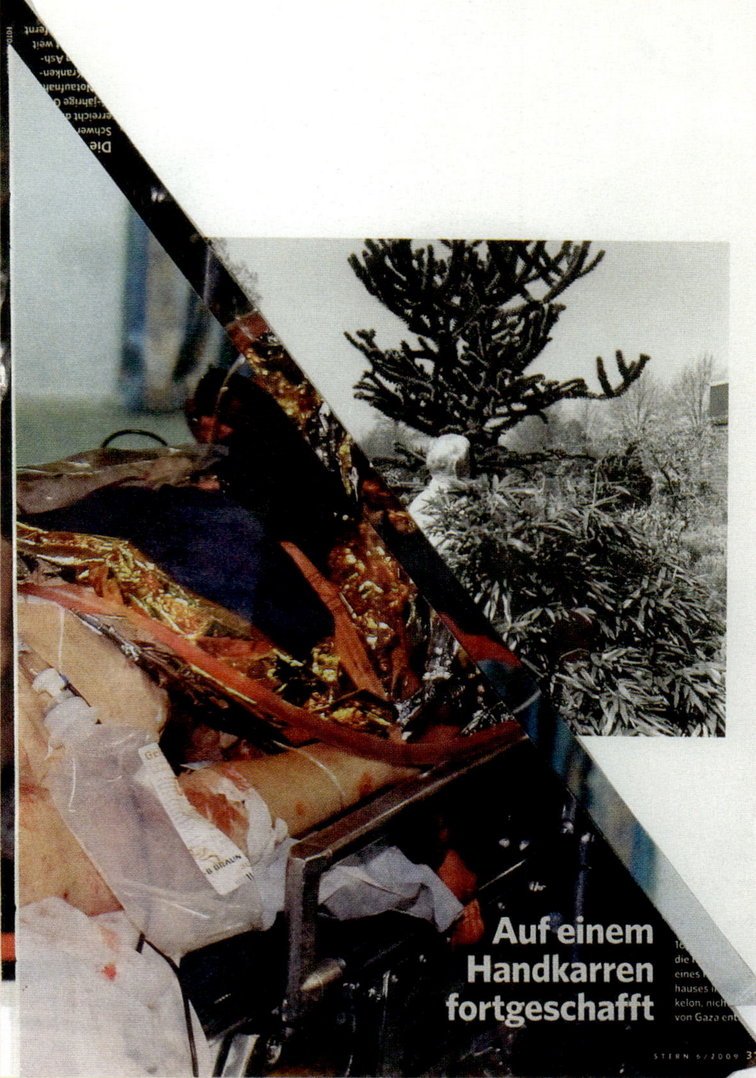

Untitled, 2009. Paper collage. 31 × 24 cm

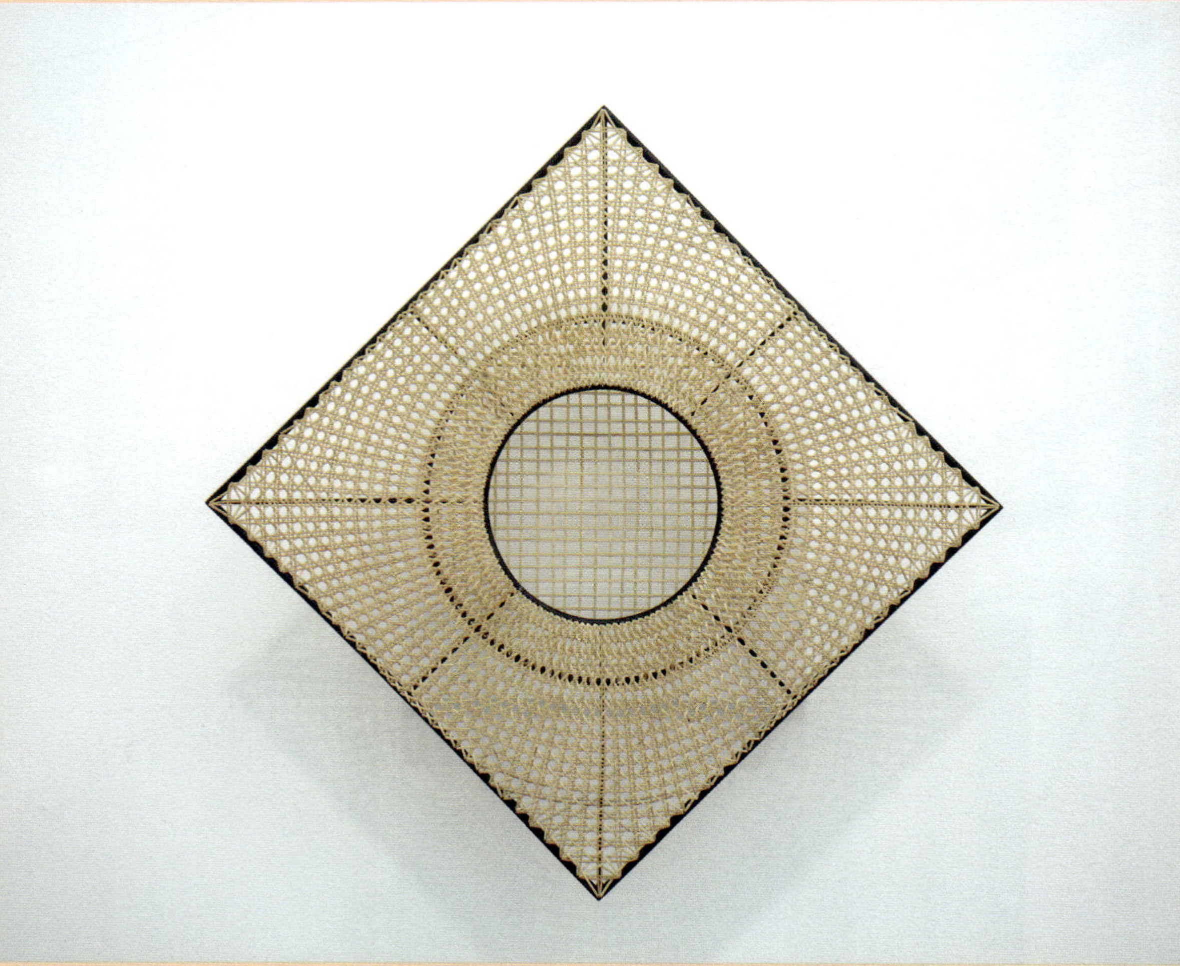

Untitled (Rattan 2), 2008–09. Rattan, wood, metal. 50 × 50 × 20 cm

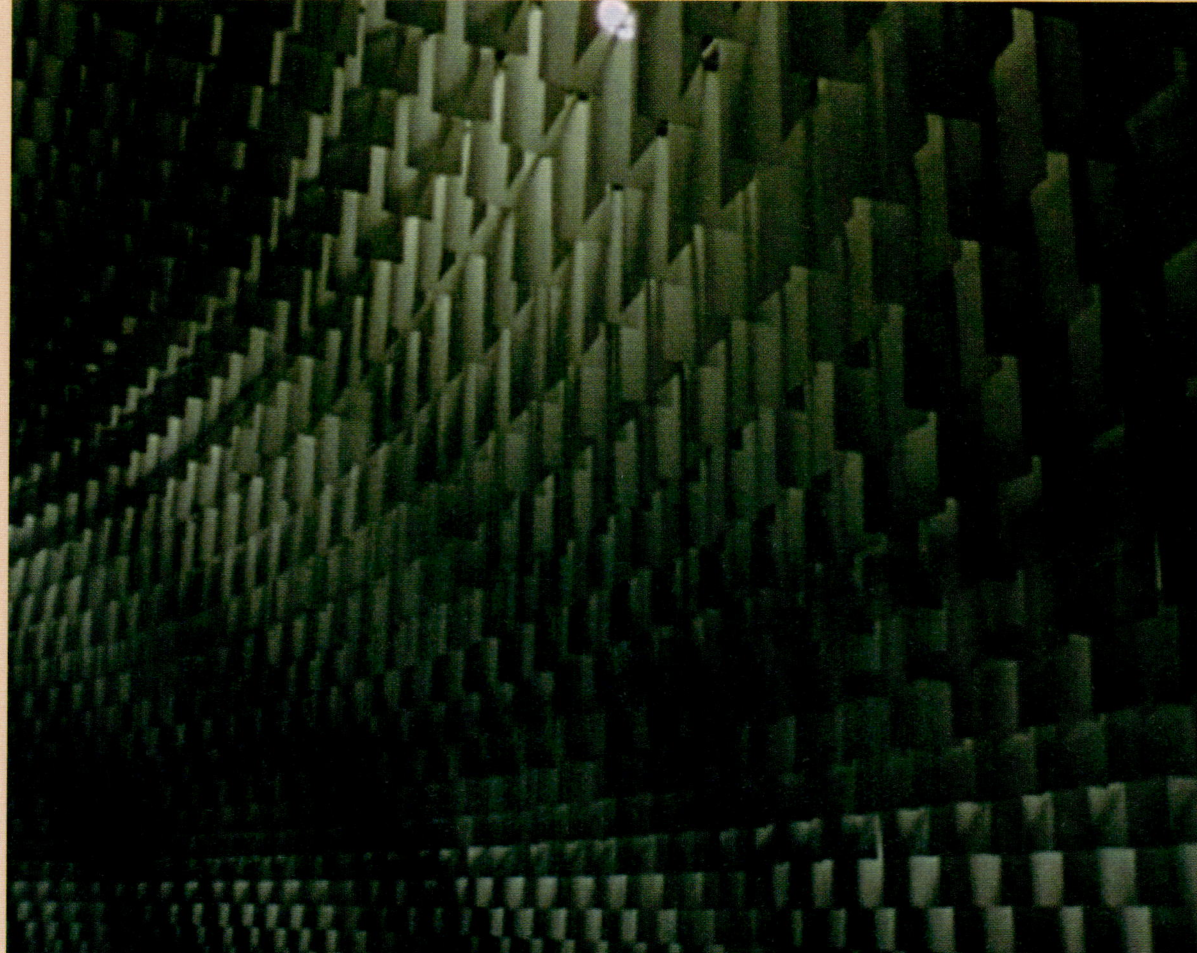

Untitled Film #2 (Espace Niemeyer and Infrared Light), 2007. Double DVD projection. Dimensions variable

covers creating a sculpture, rocks filmed as if they were created not by nature but by the hand of an artist. It is impossible to summarize the works under a common theme, but what they all address is a preoccupation with how we deal with the huge quantity of images, references, cultural narratives, disparate aesthetic qualities that form and deform our living experience.

Part of the new body of work that Andrade Tudela has developed over the last three years is a series of asphalt sculptures. These propose an artistic use of this common material, a semi-solid substance, one of the components of crude petroleum, used to surface highways and roads. In this series, over twenty black, amorphous, opaque figures are combined with folded pieces of transparent Perspex, presented on a low, wide pedestal that they share with printed advertisements for gambling and casinos. The installation is like a strange archaeological site from the future. One cannot help thinking of kryptonite, the only substance that can neutralize the powers of the eponymous hero in the Superman cartoons. The piece also recalls the words of Andre Breton, who wrote in the Manifesto of Surrealism,

'I believe in the future resolution of these two states, dream and reality, which are seemingly so contradictory, into a kind of absolute reality, a surreality, if one may so speak.' Another reference is made to the transparent sculptures of the Brazilian artist Lygia Clark, three-dimensional moveable figures constructed from light and simple materials that

It is impossible to summarize the works under a common theme, but what they all address is a preoccupation with how we deal with the huge quantity of images, references, cultural narratives, disparate aesthetic qualities that form and deform our living experience

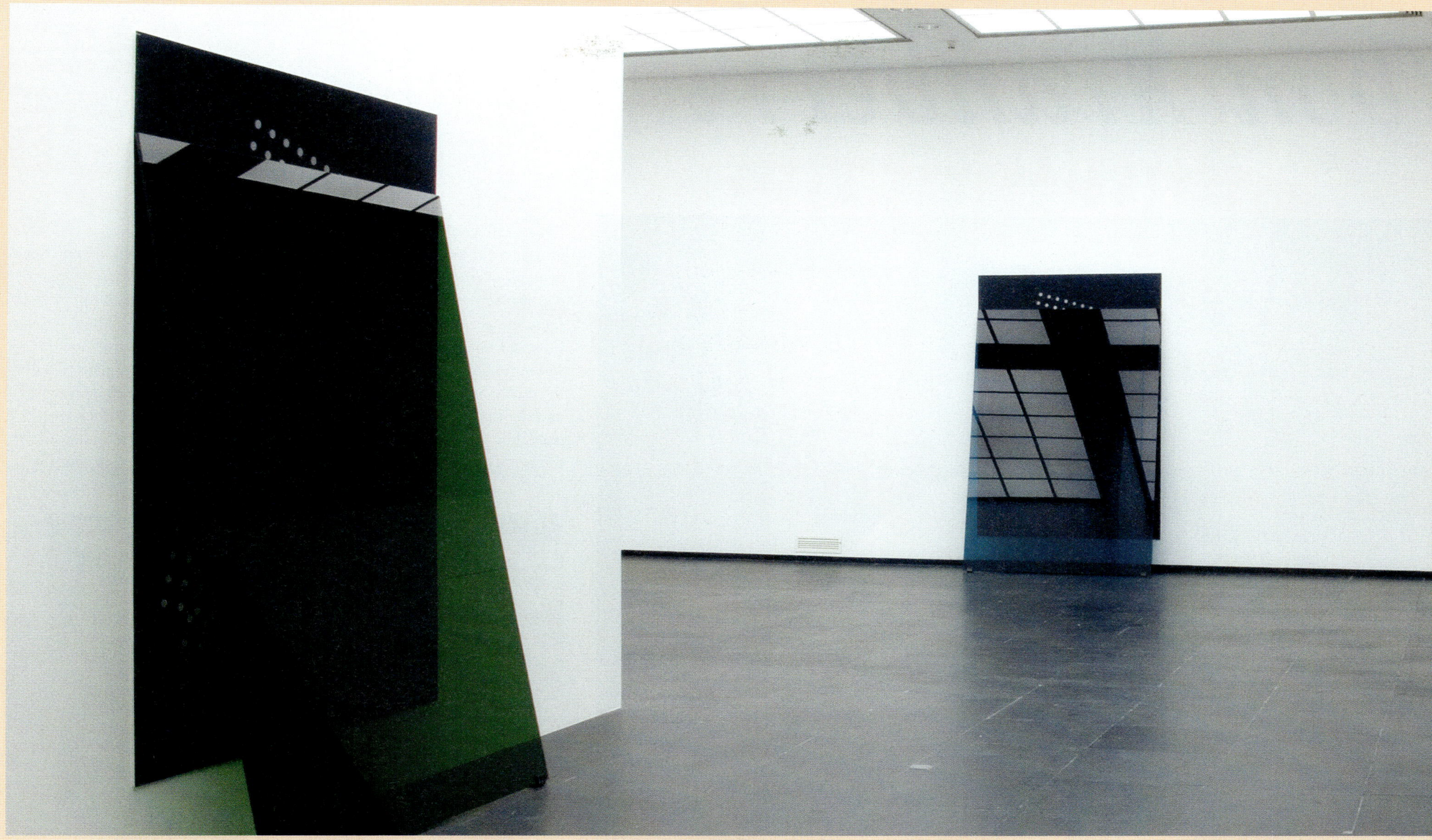

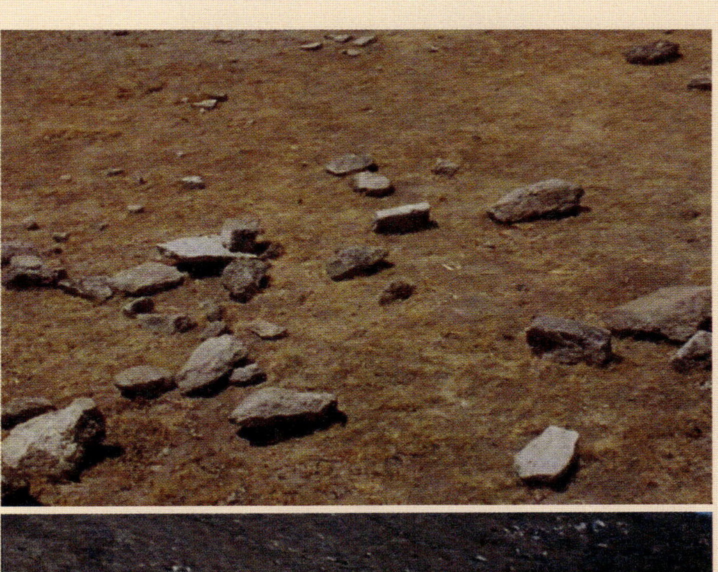

Untitled (Photograph and Glass), 2007–08. 2 of 4 C–type photographs and glass. Each 240 × 170 cm

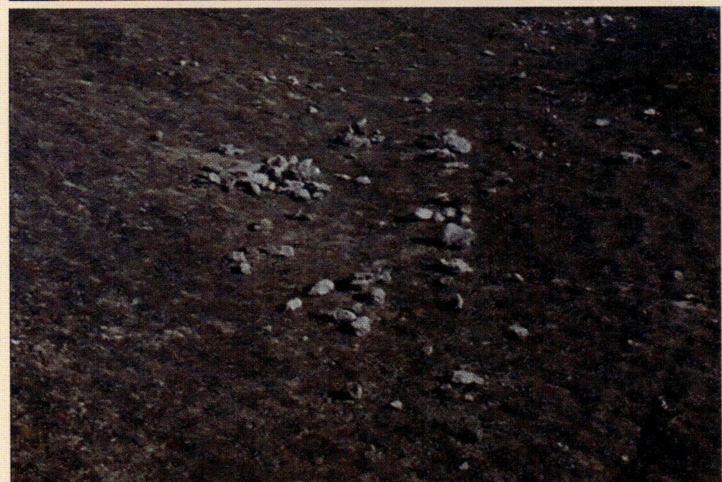

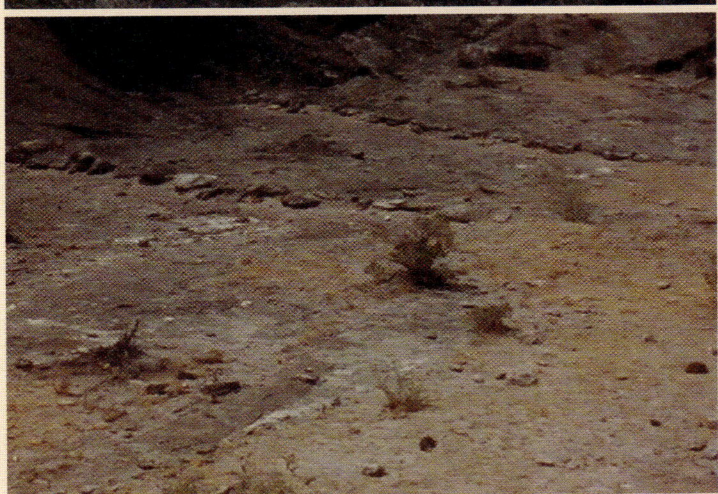

Yesterday, today, tomorrow, tomorrow, yesterday, today, yesterday, tomorrow, today (Film #4), 2009. 16mm film transferred to DVD. Dimensions variable

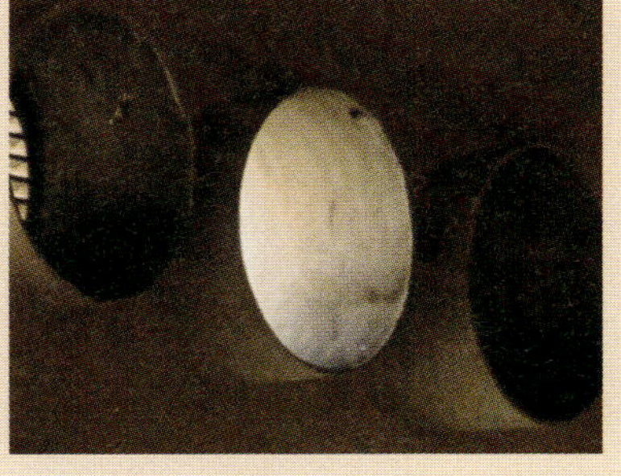

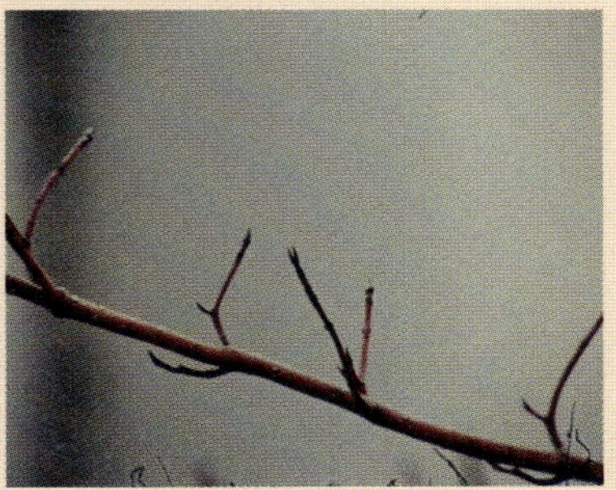

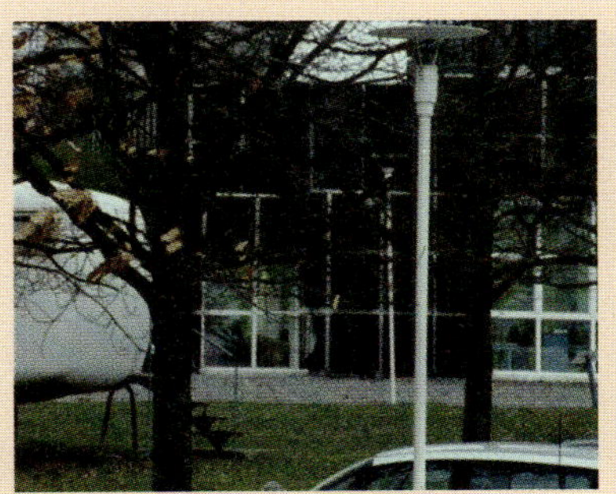

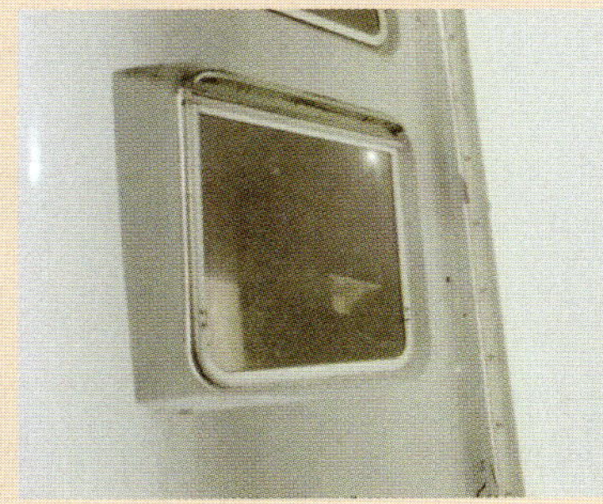

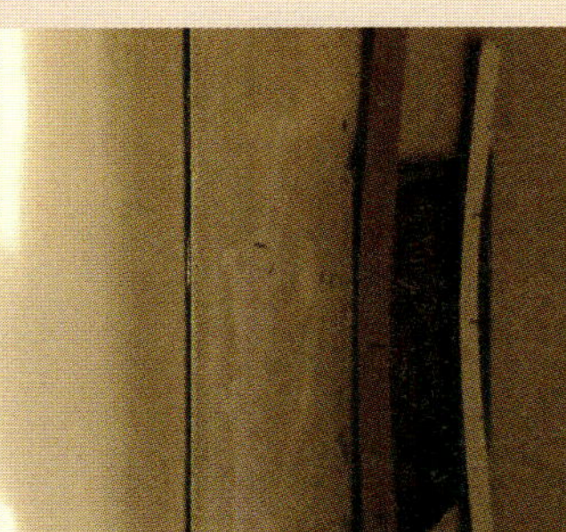

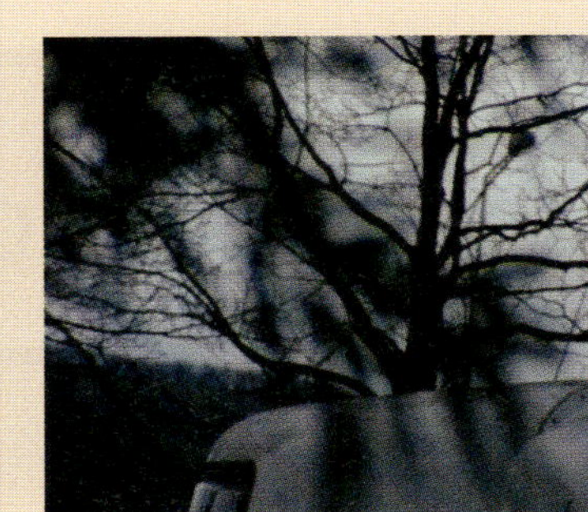

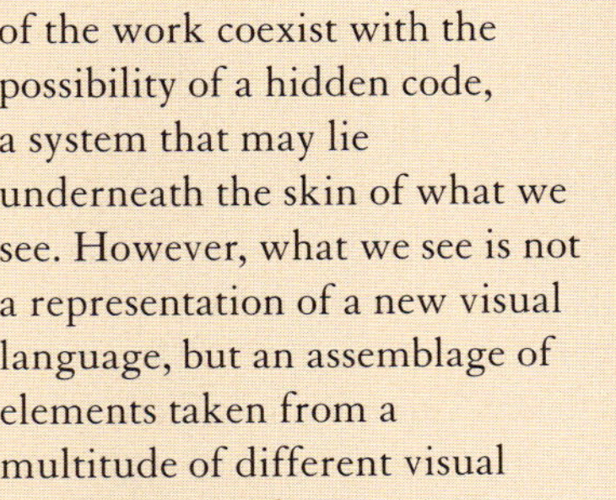

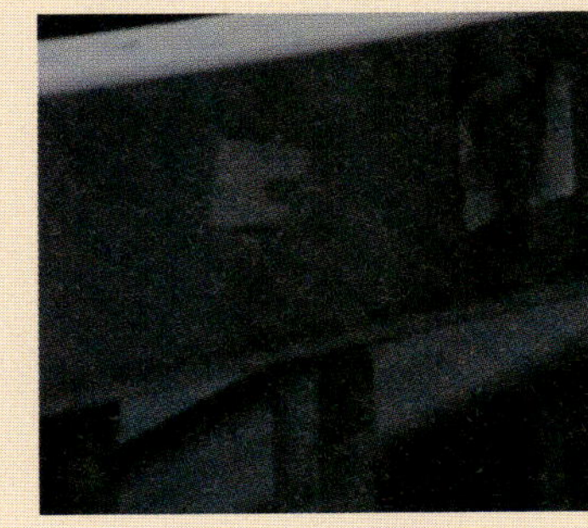

Between legacies of modernity in Europe and Latin America

invite the viewer to interact with them as if part of the work.

Andrade Tudela's photographic collages place an emphasis on the optical unconscious. A simple element — a configuration of dots similar to the Ben-Day dots that appear in Roy Lichtenstein's works — resembles psychedelic patterns. The visual and physical aspects of the work coexist with the possibility of a hidden code, a system that may lie underneath the skin of what we see. However, what we see is not a representation of a new visual language, but an assemblage of elements taken from a multitude of different visual and cultural references in the life of the dot in art history.

Four Descriptions of JB Maneval's Six Sh... Bubble, 2008. 16mm film transferred to DV... Dimensions variable

Ibon Aranberri

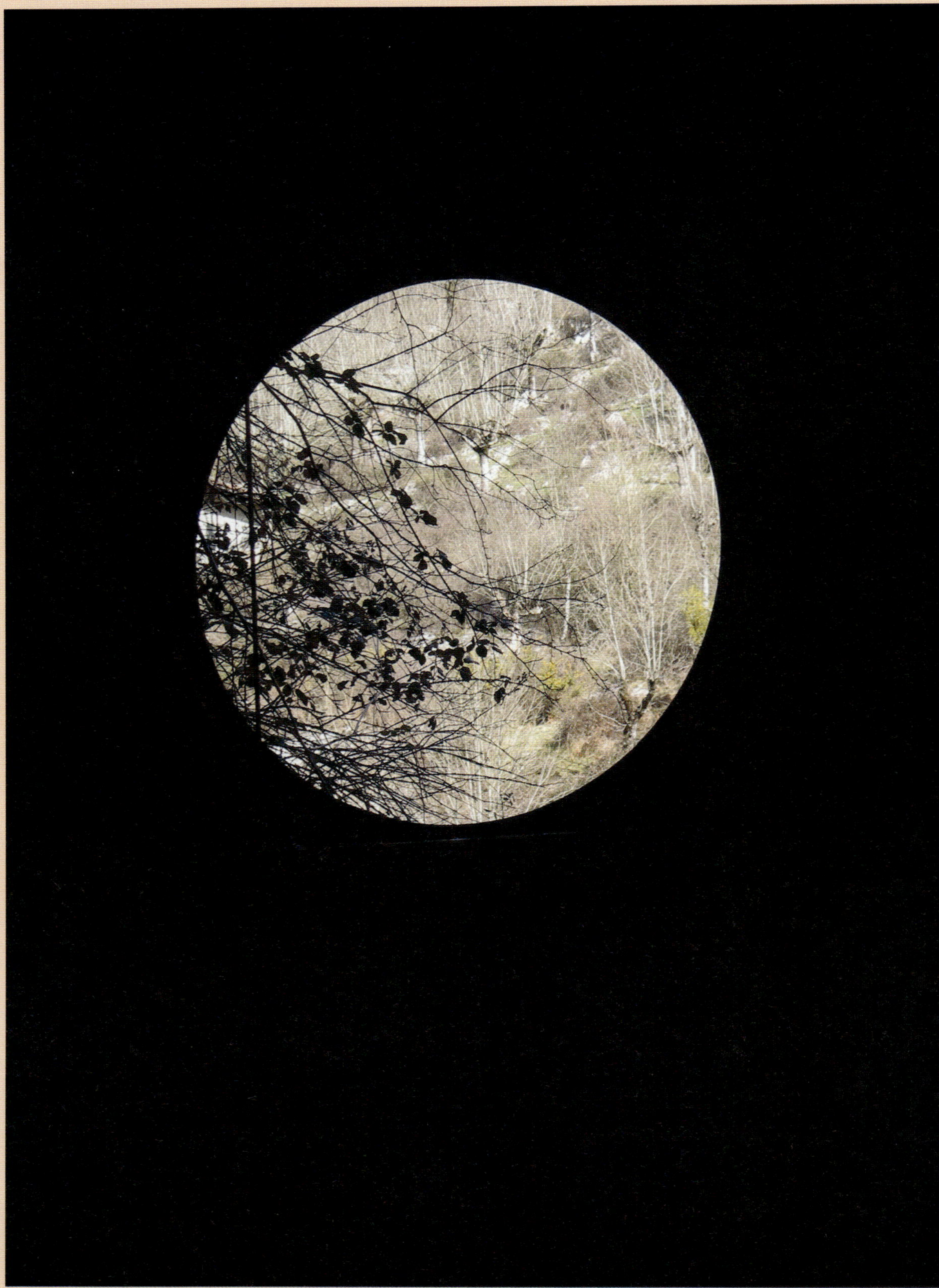

Cave (Ir.T n° 513), 2003–08. 1 of 187 photographs

Ibon Aranberri occupies an idiosyncratic position in the field of contemporary art. It is difficult to classify his work in a regular sense or even to fully understand it. Of importance to Aranberri are signs and objects through which the mechanisms of society and their power structures become clear. His work is integrated into the particularity of context and its specific political conflicts and social relations. Fundamental approaches in Aranberri's work are observation, background research, dialogue and documentation. *Cave (Ir.T n° 513)* (2003) documents a long journey through prehistoric caves in the Basque region, which at first sight seems to be a contemporary version of Land art. A group was invited to visit the

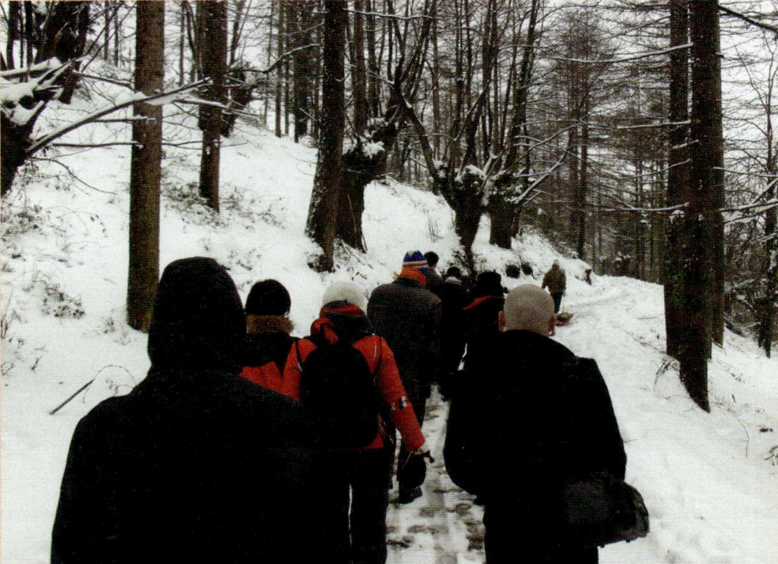

Cave (Ir.T n° 513), 2003–08. 1 of 187 photographs

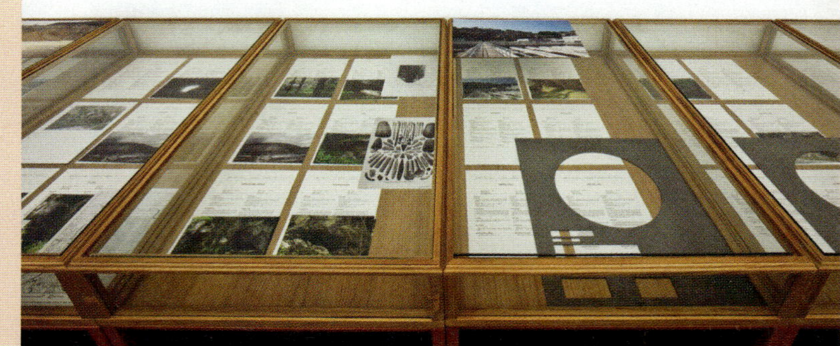

Cave (Ir.T n° 513), 2003–08. 6 vitrines, photographs, documents. 192 × 108 × 86 cm

Traces of power

site of the Iritegi cave, where Aranberri had installed a metal structure over the opening of the cave's mouth. The structure consisted of a door with a lock and key at the base, and a circular opening to allow for the cave's resident bats to come and go. But the fieldwork and the permanent mark that he makes on nature are just part of the overall concept. A more important aspect is the exact documentation of the place, as well as a permanent physical intervention into bureaucratic and administrative systems such as

documentary and geographical notes, maps and archives which thus draw out the invisible political, social and art historical contexts of the site. Aranberri works meticulously, in a fasion comparable to the methods of Conceptual art. A notable part of his documentation is his formal description of how we treat nature, its representation and its inevitable connection with politics. However, he does so without making a specific ethical argument. *Política hidráulica* (2003–07), which was exhibited at Documenta 12,

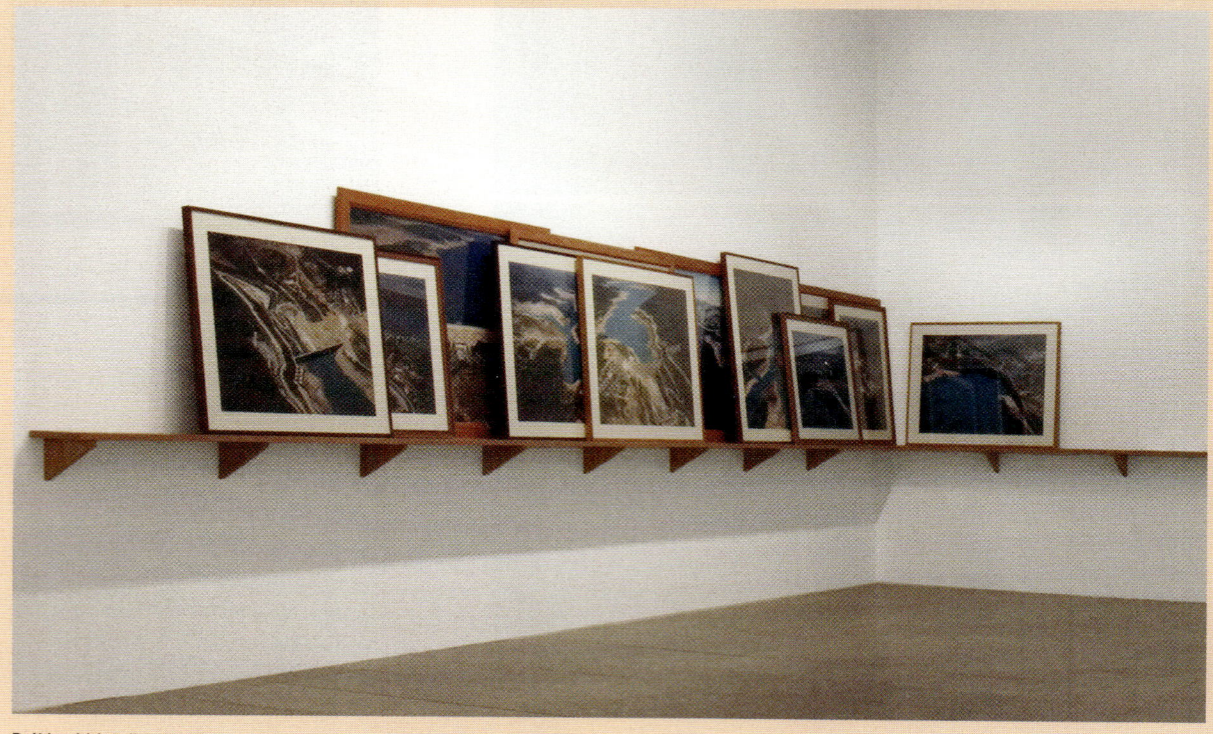

Política hidráulica, 2003–07. 48 framed C-print photographs. Sizes vary from 45 × 60 cm to 150 × 180 cm

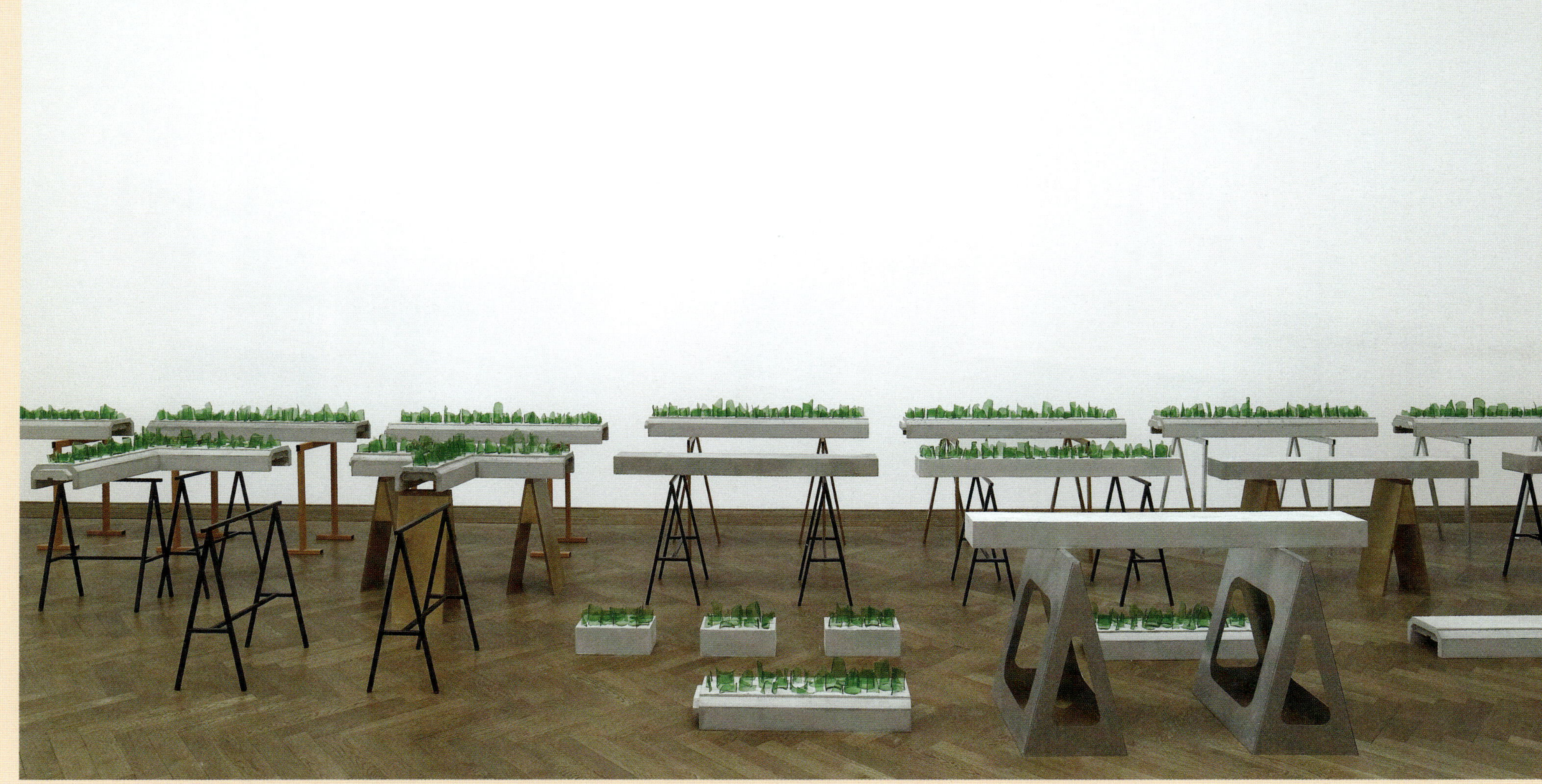

Poetic brutality

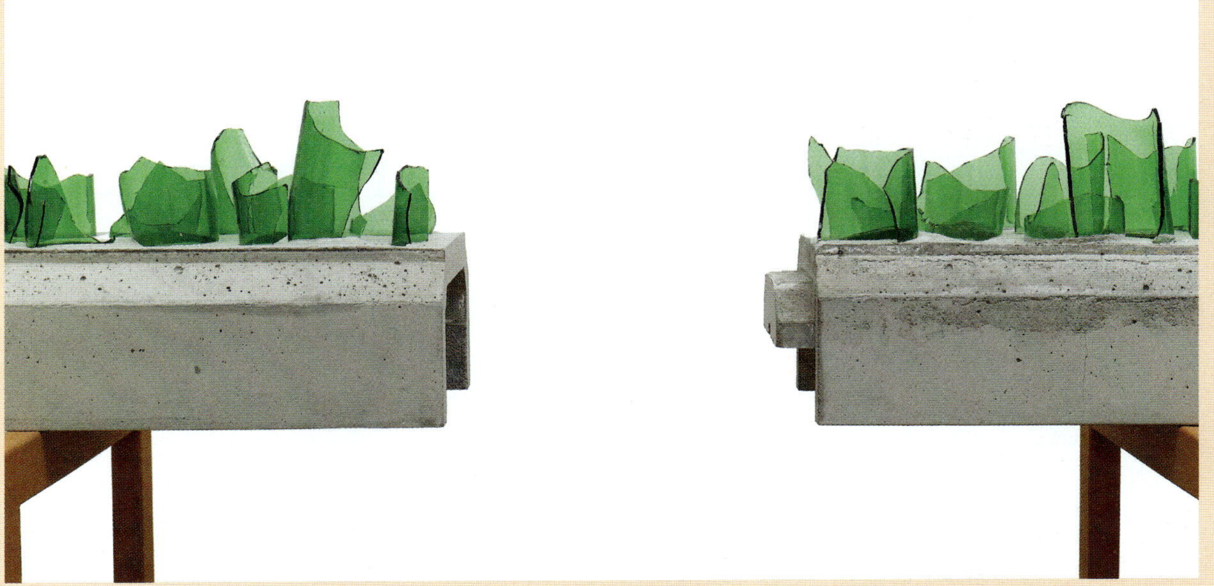

Floating Garden, 2004–07. Concrete modules, broken glass, metal and wooden sawhorses. Dimensions variable

shows the ideological and formal aspects relating to Spanish dam projects since the 1930s. Consisting of a series of aerial photographs commissioned by the artist, which are framed and leaning stacked against the wall as though in storage, he describes with formal soberness how our society and politics can have an effect on nature. He does not openly accuse, but instead lets the content of his work revolve around the traces of power, thrusting them just far enough out of their context to reveal a meta-level. Alongside th work, Aranberri also presented h sculptural installation *Floating Garden* (2004–08). The work consists of series of modules mad of concrete encrusted with broke glass from San Pellegrino water bottles. Alienated from their condition of daily usage, they suggest a prototype for a fictiona architecture of poetic brutality.

Physical intervention

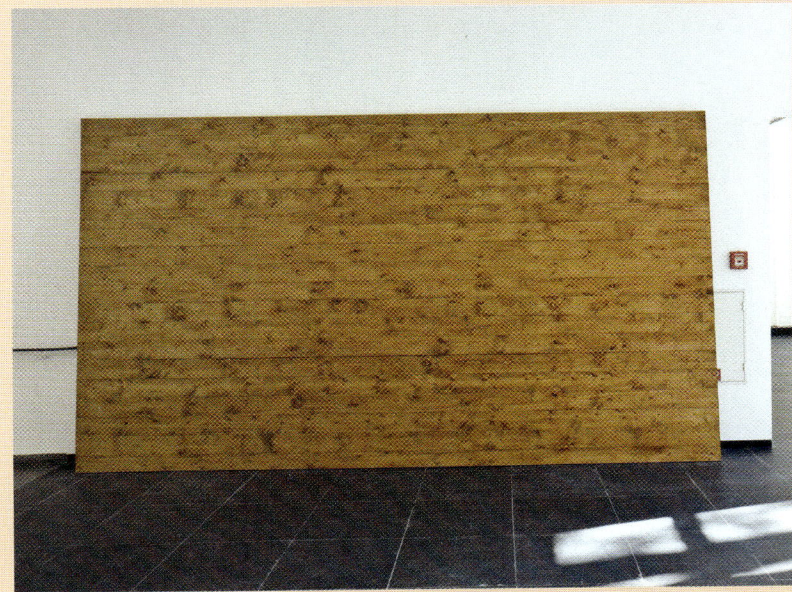

Disorder, 2007. Wooden board. 480 × 260 cm

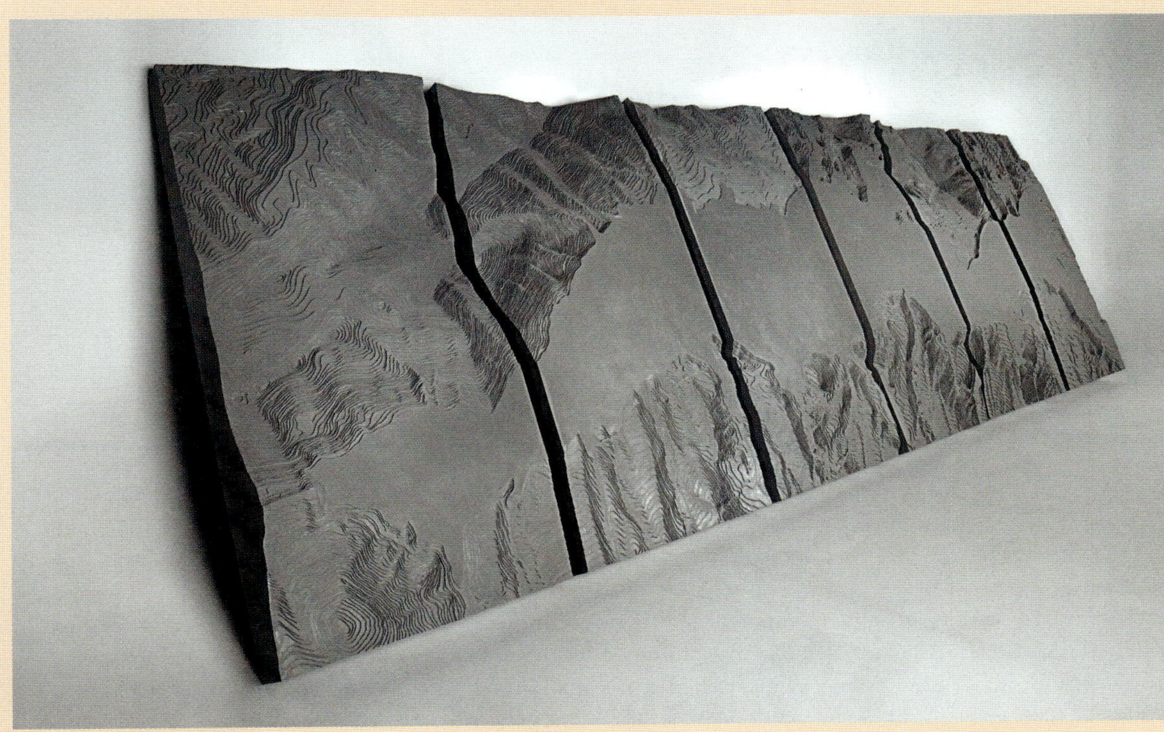

Mar del Pirineo, 2006. Fibreglass-reinforced polyester. 6 parts. Each 28 × 120 × 210 cm

Tonico Lemos Auad

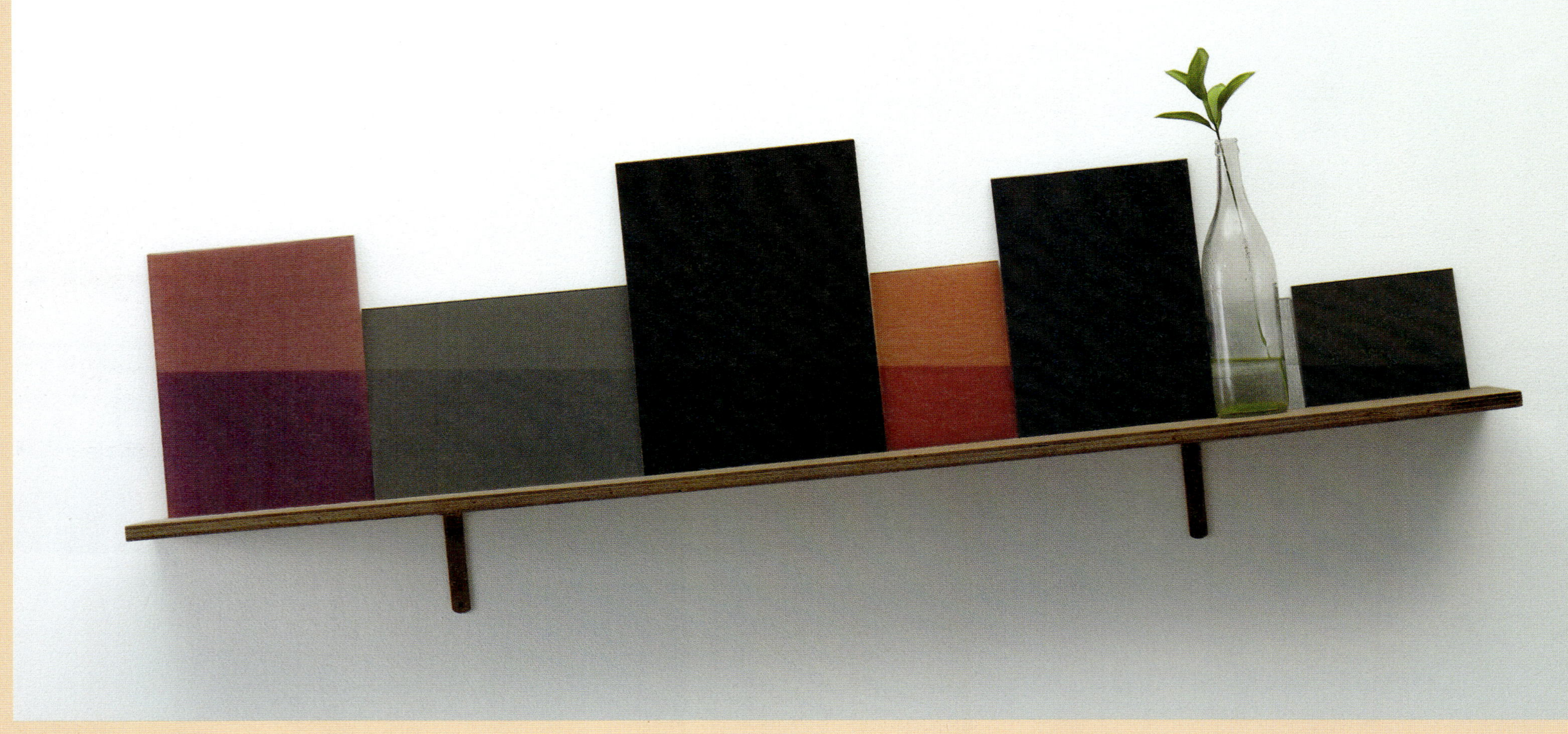

Seven Seas/Night, 2007–09. Paper, glass, wood, water, plant. 60 × 160 × 21 cm

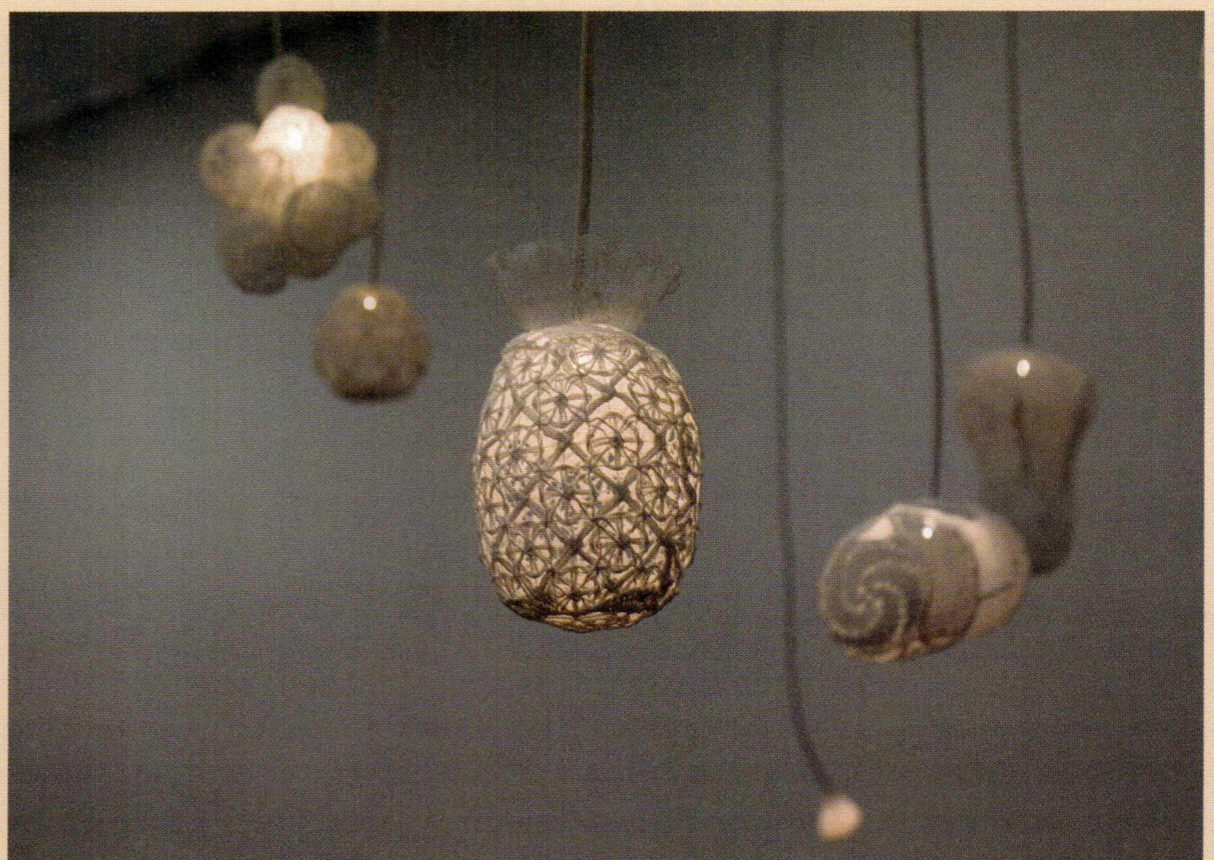

Sleep Walkers, 2009. Brazilian and Belgian lace, electric components. 17 individual hand–sewn lanterns. Dimensions variable

Urbane aesthetic appreciation and wit

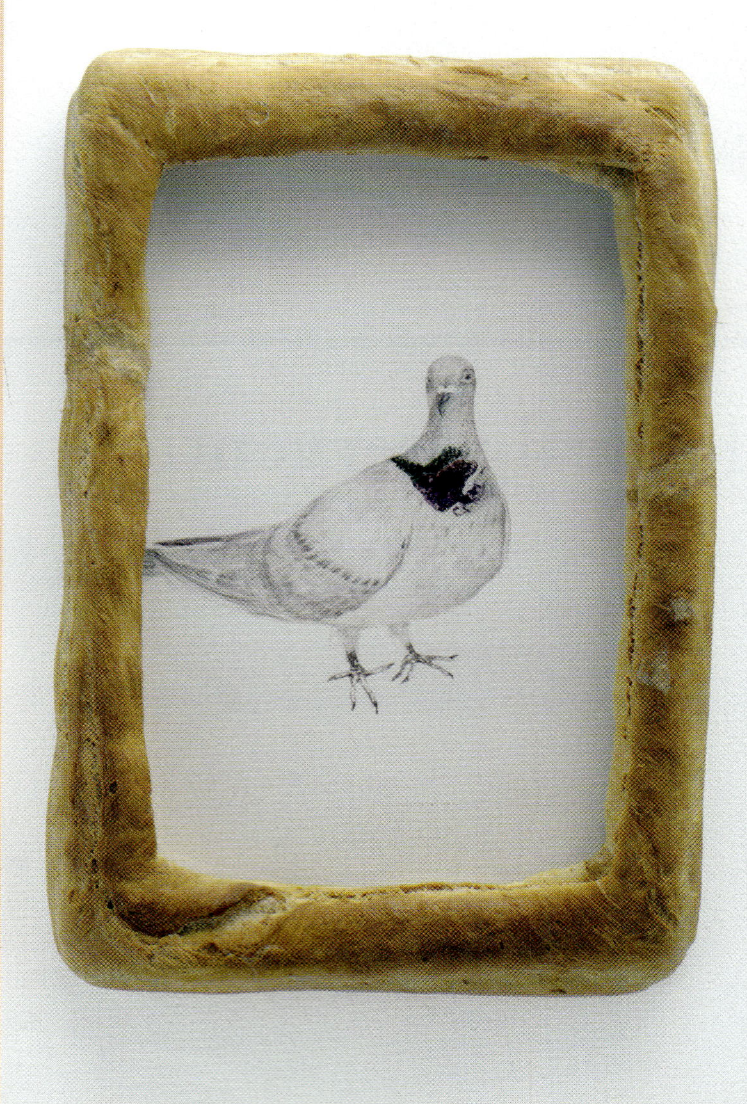

Pigeon Portrait/Amada, 2008. Graphite and foil on paper with bread. 50 × 35 cm

Ritual and legends

Among artists who direct their gaze at the familiar things that comprise our everyday and utilize trifling materials from daily life, Tonico Lemos Auad is conspicuous for his delicate handiwork. His drawings and sculptural pieces are subtle, fragile and ephemeral, presenting themselves to us for just a fleeting moment. Auad's art reminds us that everything under the sun is transient, possesses no fixed form, and will inevitably change.

In his works, Auad takes unexpected materials including objects from nature and household wares, and uses them to create traditional forms of artistic expression such as drawings and sculptures.

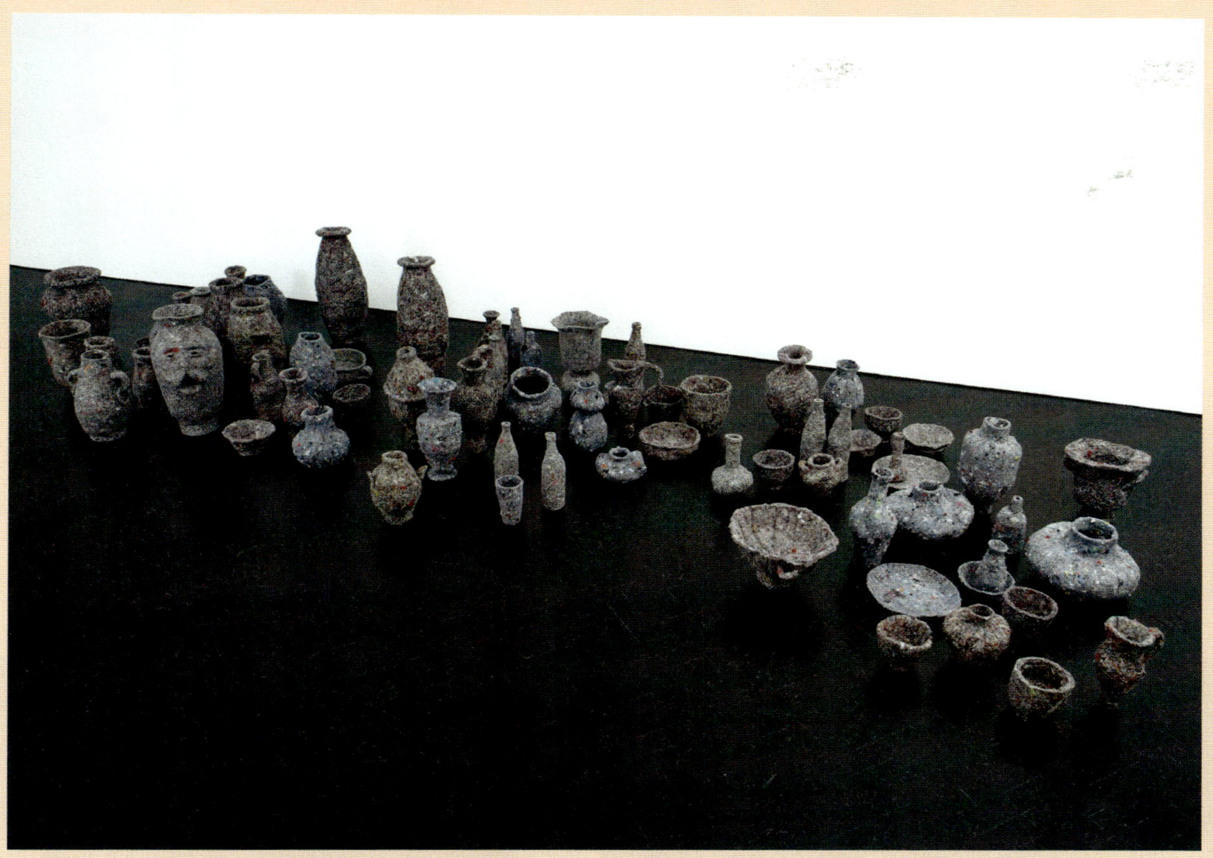

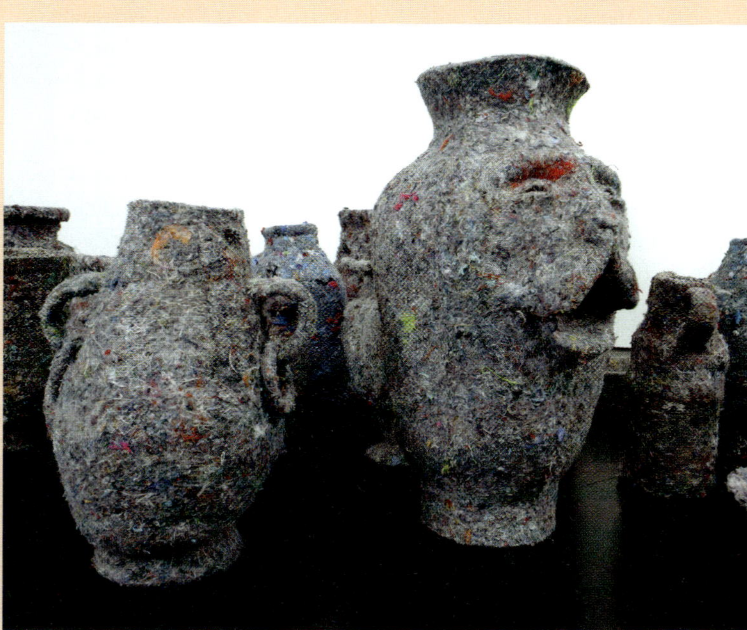

MOUTH, EARS, EYES just like us, 2009. Cloth, thread. 76 parts. Dimensions variable

Profoundly cultural symbolism

This has included pricking a face on a bunch of bananas, making animals from fluff collected off new carpets (an offering nominated for the 2004 Beck's Futures award), making a skull from grape stems, and rendering lines and shapes in fine gold and silver chains. Here a lyricism created through trivial materials, reminiscent of Arte Povera, cohabits with playfulness in a bold challenge to the notion that works of art must always take solid form.

Giving tangible expression to movement and the passing of time, Auad's works appear to be the fruit of moving between two lands: Brazil, where he was born and raised and England where he lives now. While employing the rich cultural assets of Brazilian ritual and legend as the basis of his

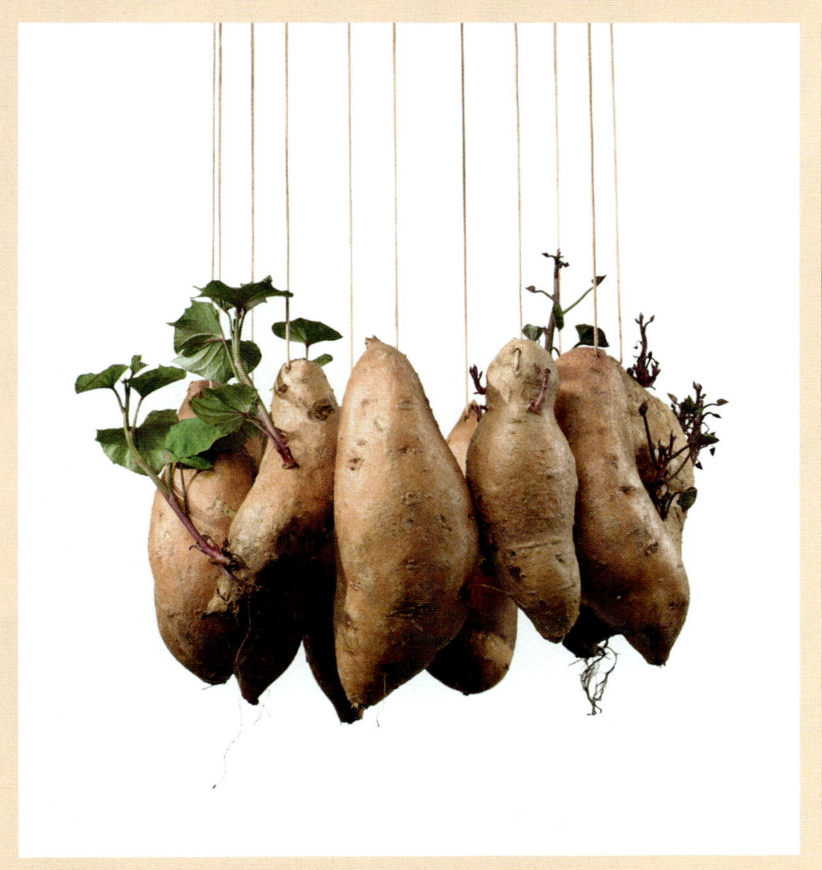

Clairvoyant, 2008. Sweet potatoes, leather. Dimensions variable

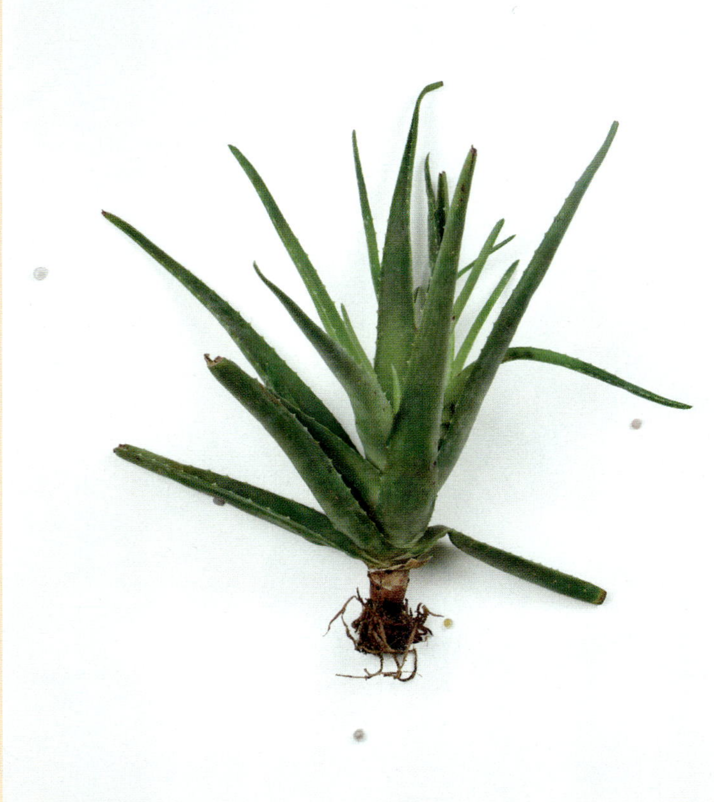

Medusa, 2007. Plant, carved stones. 61 × 53 cm

works, weaving in feelings of attachment to his homeland and the melancholy of being pulled so far from it, he also reflects conceptual ideas brimming with an urbane aesthetic appreciation and wit. *Seven Seas / Night* (2007–09), for example, consists of pieces of paper, partially faded after three years in the summer sun of his native Brazil, arranged on a sloping shelf. Alongside the slanting surface of the water in an accompanying vase, they resurrect, under the leaden skies of London, fragmented memories of sun and sea in the faraway land of Auad's birth. *Reflected Archaeology* (2009) entrusts the drawing process to the audience. Viewers scrape the surface of a silver-covered wallpaper as if it were a scratch card to reveal a collage and drawings beneath. Offerings to

the sea goddess in the Afro-Brazilian religion of Candomble, most prominent in the Bahia region of Brazil, emerge from the watery silver surface.

The hybrid quality cultivated by adapting multiple cultures is also reflected in *Sleep Walkers* (2009). Unveiled in Antwerp, the work consists of lanterns made from Belgian and Brazilian lace and representing Brazilian fruits and vegetables. Using the soft materials that characterized his early works, the lanterns are shaped by weaving together fabrics common to the two countries, highlighting the importance of the trade in textiles shared by both.

Through intricate, painstaking handiwork with an undercurrent of profoundly cultural symbolism, Auad gives temporary shape to mutable things, like tiny whispers of hope.

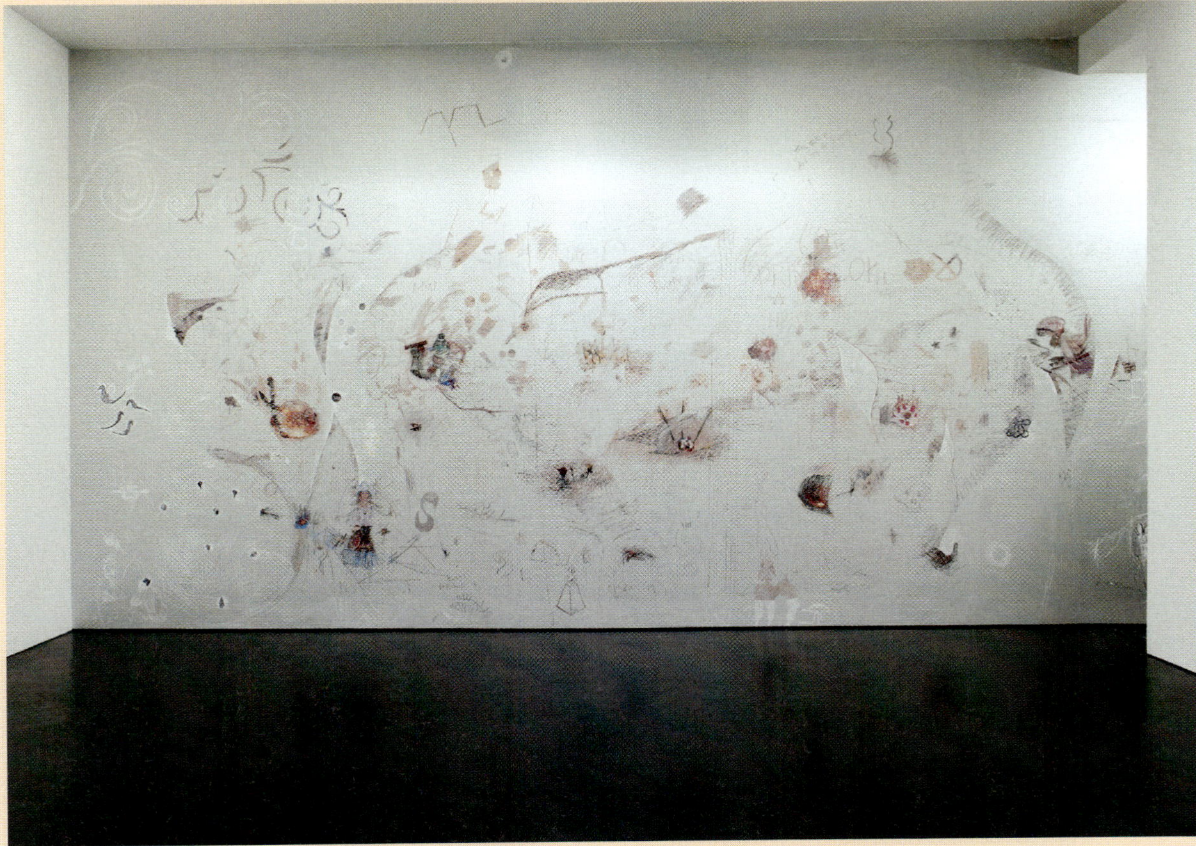

Reflected Archaeology, 2009. Scratch–off silver ink on wallpaper. Dimensions variable

The Los Angeles-based artist Lisa Anne Auerbach stumbled into her artistic calling as an indirect result of completing her degree at the Art Center College of Design in Pasadena in 1994. Trained as a photographer, the artist lost access to the school's dark room once she had graduated. Almost accidentally, she decided to take up knitting as an artistic practice, in part because of her fascination with the self-reliance of DIY culture, but mainly because she loved the custom-knit sweaters worn by Cheap Trick lead guitarist Rick Nielsen during the band's performances. Auerbach wanted to make her own custom-knit sweaters and so taught herself the craft.

One of her first endeavours in this area was *Sandy Koufax Sweater* (1996), a bright blue cardigan with a large white Star of David on the back. Originally inspired by a guy at the gym who sported a Star of David tattoo, the artist realized that she had chosen a yarn the same colour as the Los Angeles Dodgers baseball team uniforms. This sweater quickly became an homage to the Dodgers' star pitcher Sandy Koufax, who was Jewish and refused to play on the Sabbath. Her knitting soon morphed into a medium where politics, humour and a DIY ethos could come together in wearable semi-public art. Her subsequent sweaters, scarves, hats, mittens and dresses take on topical political issues in an ironic and subversively humorous manner. Knitted missives include: 'When there's nothing left to burn, you've got to set yourself on fire', illustrated with a knitted suicide-bomber belt of dynamite; 'We are all heroes'; 'Keep abortion legal'; and jokes like: 'What's your favorite thing about the war on terror? Gives me an excuse not to go to the Frieze Art Fair'; or 'Did you hear what Bush said when asked about Roe vs. Wade? "I don't care how they get out of New Orleans".' All of these works aptly demonstrate the motto of her knitting website stealthissweater.com: 'Get all cozy and radical. Stop making scarves. Start making trouble.'

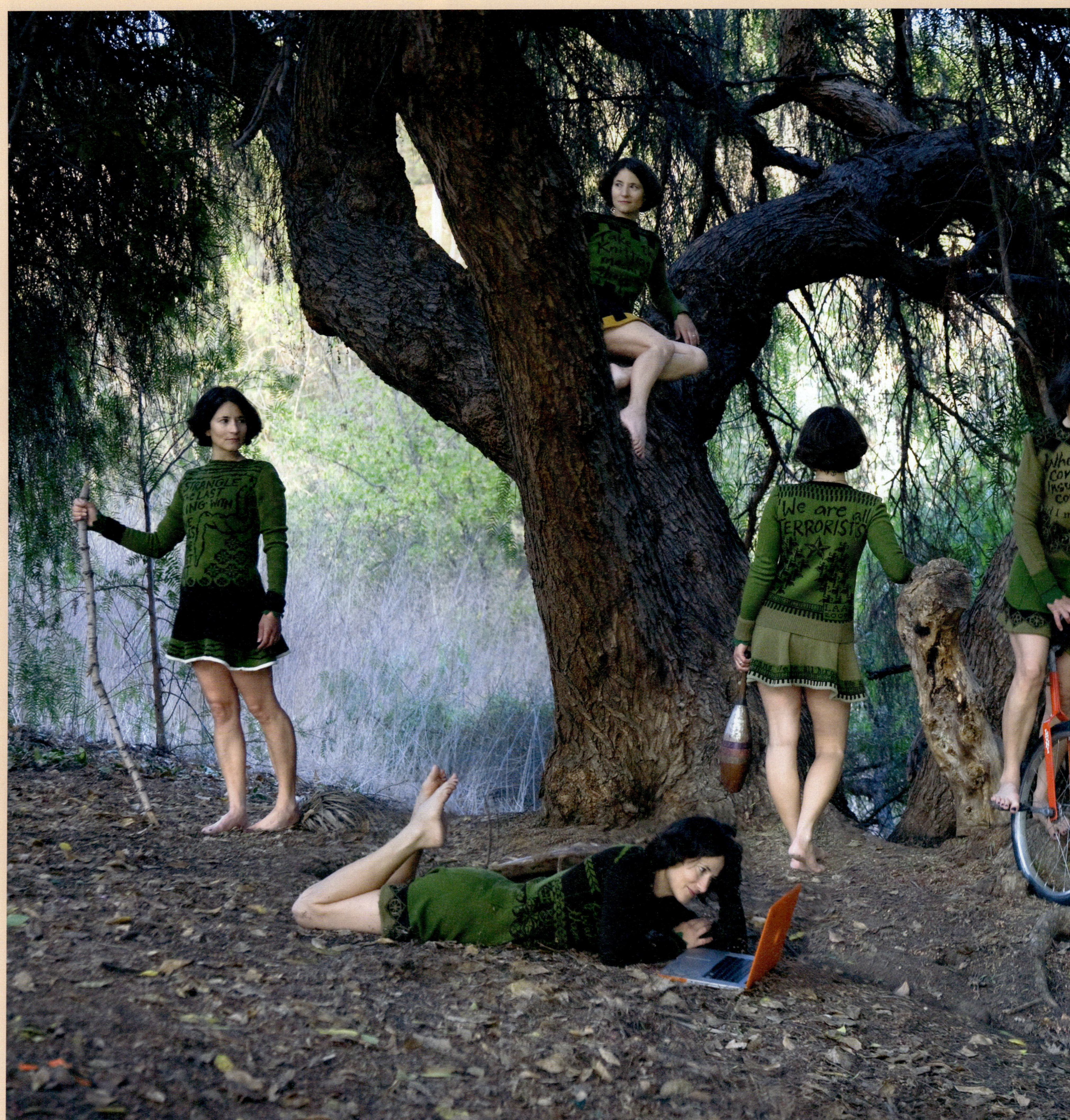

Photomural for Nottingham Contemporary Window Installation, 2009. Colour photograph. 670 × 304 cm

Lisa Anne Auerbach

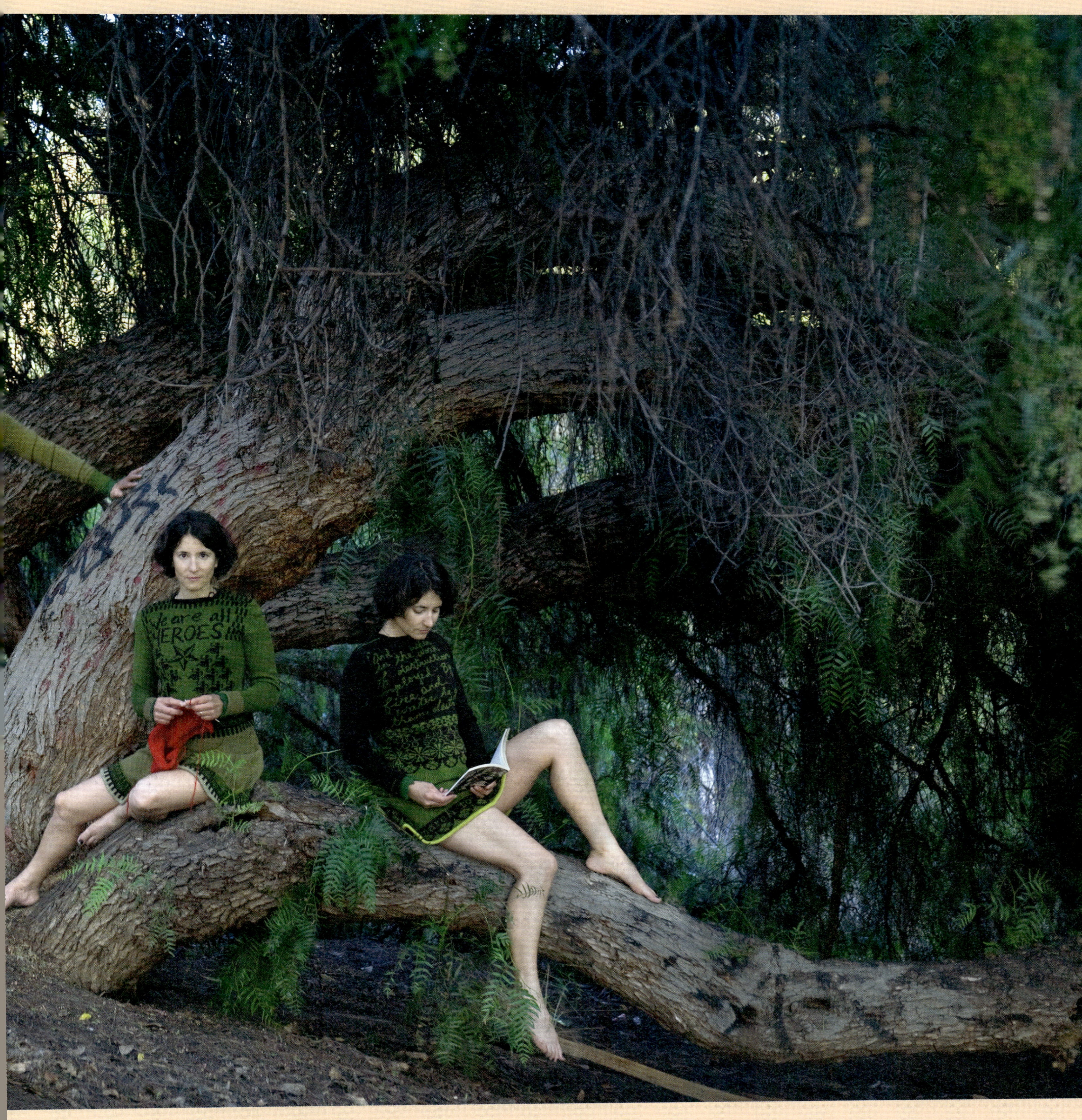

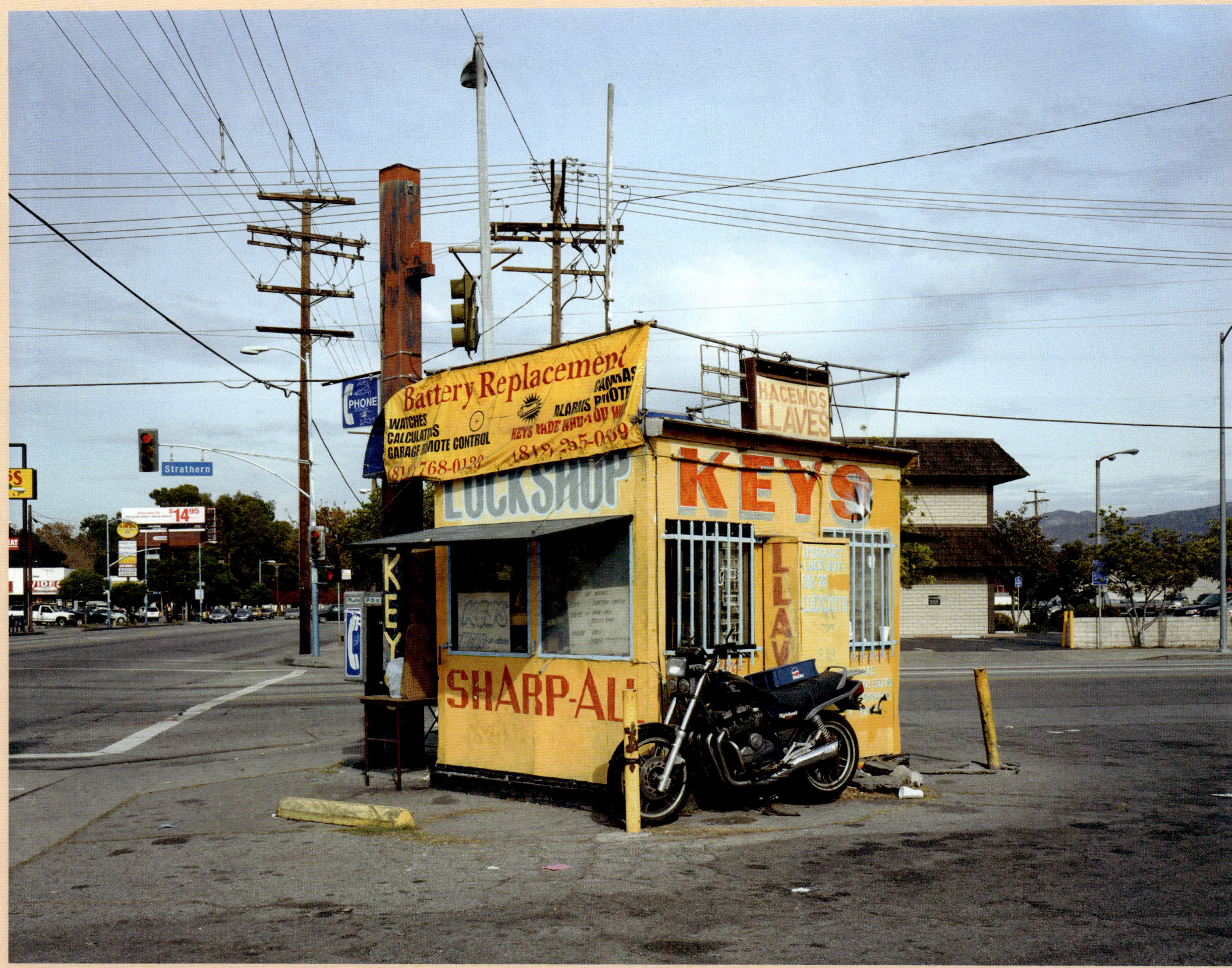

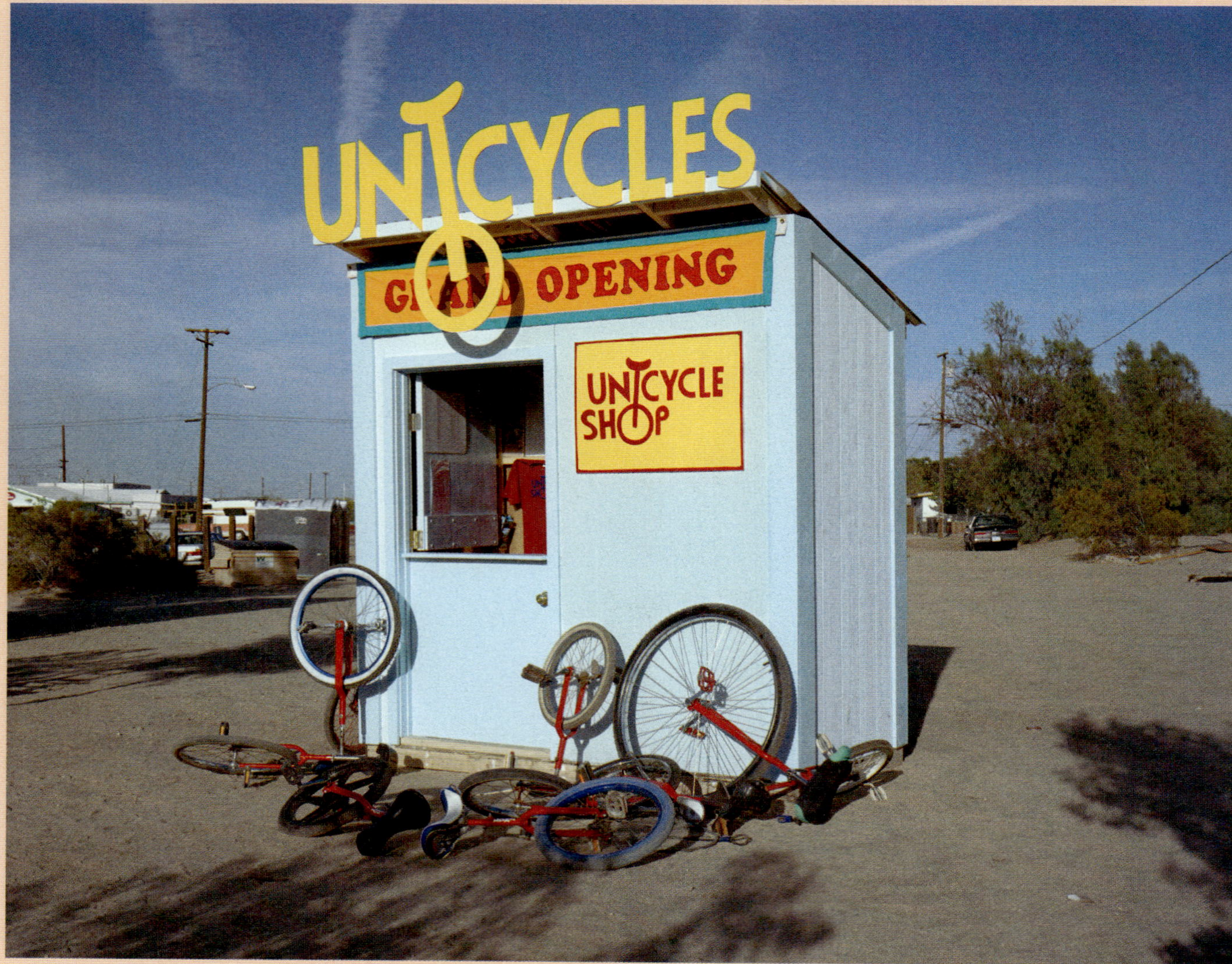

Sharp–All Keys, Pacoima, CA (Small Business Series), 2006. C–print. 76 × 102 cm

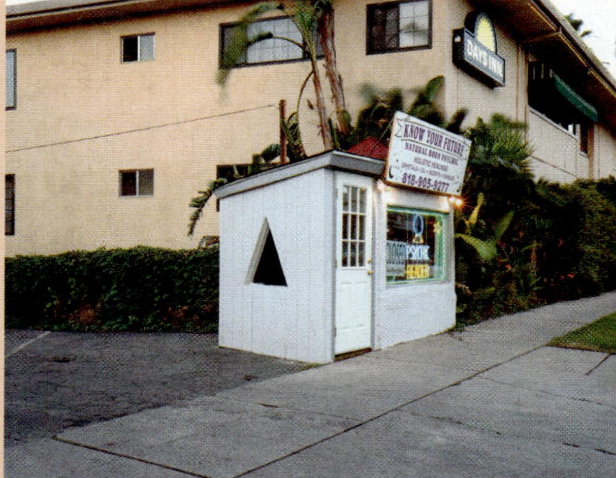

Unicycle Shop, Joshua Tree, CA (Small Business Series), 2007. C–print. 76 × 102 cm

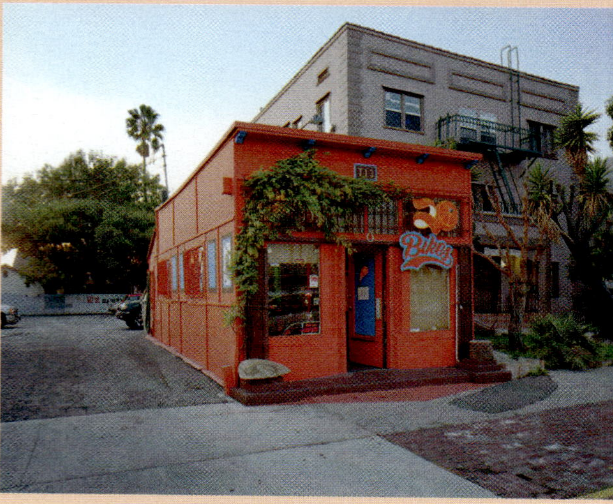

Know Your Future, Los Angeles, CA (Small Business Series), 2003. C–print. 76 × 102 cm

Orange 20 Bikes (Small Business Series), 2008. C–print. 76 × 102 cm

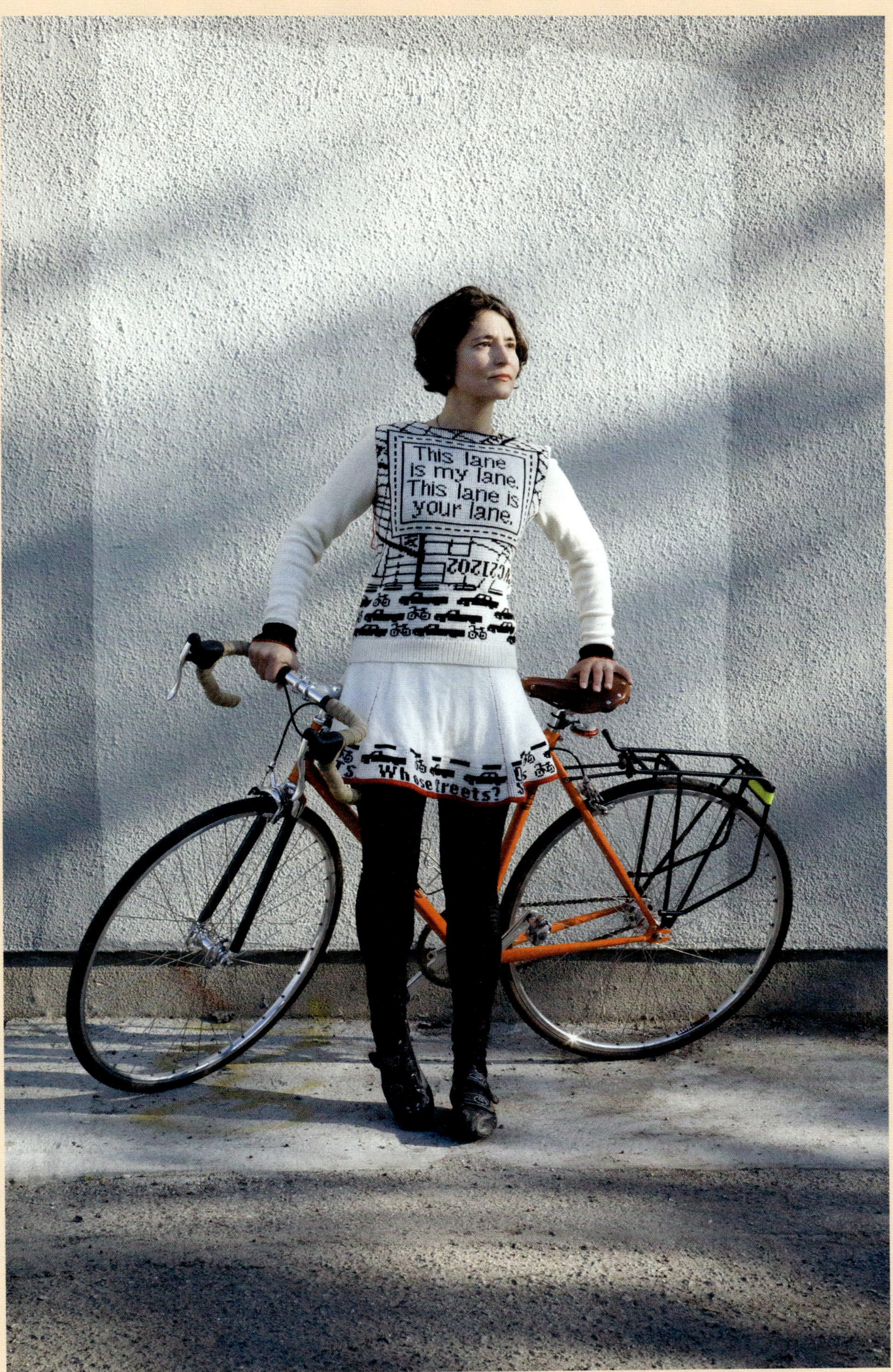

The Tract House, 2008. 63 000 tracts, table, knitted banner. 300 × 370 cm

Subversively humorou

For Auerbach, it's not all about knitting: she is also a bicycle activist, a zine publisher, a writer, a photographer and a model of her own works. In fact, it is the artist's use of her own body in images ranging from classic catalogue fare to slightly more risqué cheesecake pin-ups that makes her subversion of the clichés of advertising so disarming and free of the strident quality of much media critique.

In *Hand Knit Bikini* (2002–08), for example, Auerbach creates a send-up of gun-culture publications in the form of a photograph depicting herself wearing the title object while standing holding an automatic rifle, atop a shot-up car. In other works, her interest in bicycle culture comes to the fore, as can be seen in her humorously 'sexy' photographic self-portraits for the cover of her bicycling zine *Saddlesore*, in which we see her in a post-coital embrace with her cycle, or having fallen off it, wearing stockings and garters with the tag line 'oops I did it again'. Even though Auerbach is politically engaged in her work, its success lies in the fact that it trades-in the tired slogans of the progressive left for a sincere if hilarious alternative

For Auerbach, it's not all about knitting, she is also a bicycle activist, a zine publisher, a writer, a photographer and a model of her own works

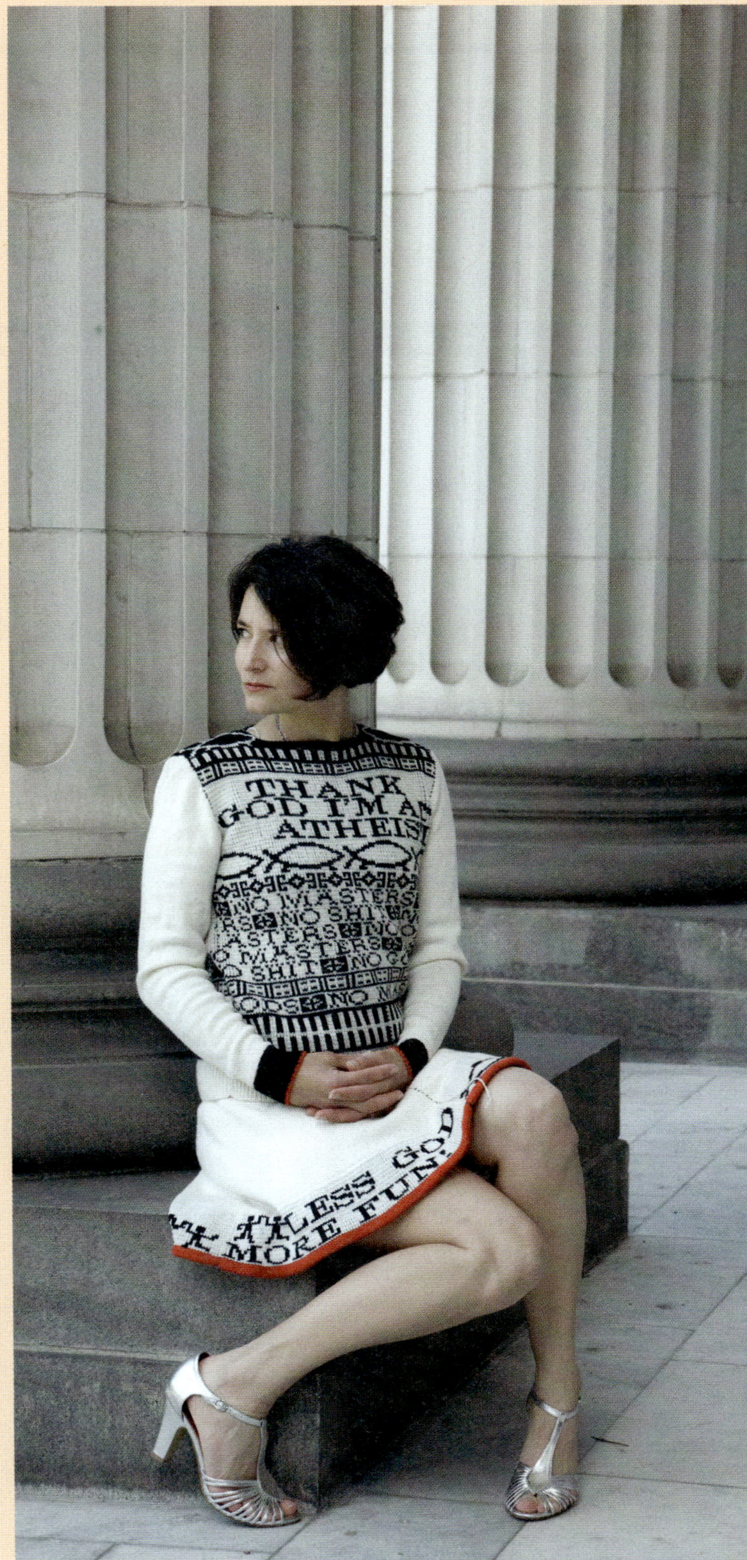

Sharrow Sweater (ghost), 2009. Merino wool. Size medium

Thank God I'm an Atheist (ghost), 2009. Merino wool. Size medium

Sven Augustijnen

Published in 1852, Harriet Beecher Stowe's sentimental abolitionist novel *Uncle Tom's Cabin* provided lasting stereotypes for the representation of black people. The scene in which the runaway black maid Eliza and her child are pursued by dogs while crossing the frozen river provides the inspiration for the white marble sculpture *Nègres marrons surpris par des chiens* (Maroons Surprised by Dogs), conceived by Louis Samain in 1861. It was unveiled in 1895 on Avenue Louise, a Hausmannesque modernist boulevard cutting through the district of Ixelles in Brussels. A contemporary night shot of this academic-sadistic monument that exposes the anonymous fugitive slaves, a man and his child attacked by monstrous dogs, to the gaze of city idlers, is one of the haunting images in Sven Augustijnen's recent project *Les Demoiselles de Bruxelles* (2008).

The picture belongs to a suite of photographs that show black prostitutes posing at night—each one alone—in front of buildings on Avenue Louise. These alternate with other nocturnal images that include a statue dedicated to the 'Colonial Pioneers of Ixelles', a small plaque commemorating Karl Marx's stay at rue d'Orleans (off Avenue Louise) in the years 1846–48, and a close-up of a black female's genitals—a blunt and efficient take on Courbet's portrait of the origin of the (white) world. The photographs were shown as part of an installation that included a reading corner with exotic props—rattan and leather chairs under the leaves of a banana tree growing in a pot. In this inviting setting visitors could study *Spectres*, a book edited by Augustijnen, whose cover layout appropriates Gallimard's classic edition of Jacques Derrida's *Spectres du Marx*, and which includes an essay discussing the aberrant psychology of the Belgian king Leopold II as key to his ruthless exploitation of the Congo. It also features excerpts from the intimate memoirs of Henri Bataille, the king's valet, and Augustijnen's own essay on the nature of 'Historical Coincidences'. The coincidences and cross-readings begin with the installation's title. The statuary poses of Picasso's nameless negroid *Demoiselles d'Avignon* in a non-descript interior with conventional drapes and obligatory still life with fruits, are refuted in this self-confident staging of the *Demoiselles of Brussels*, each portrait titled with the woman's name, and set in a contemporary, historically and politically charged outdoor location.

Augustijnen's work is a concise lesson in political docu-fiction. In an interview with Raimundas Malasauskas, he suggested that the opposition of fact and fiction need not be taken for granted and is a consequence of an even more banal distinction

Fictional plots

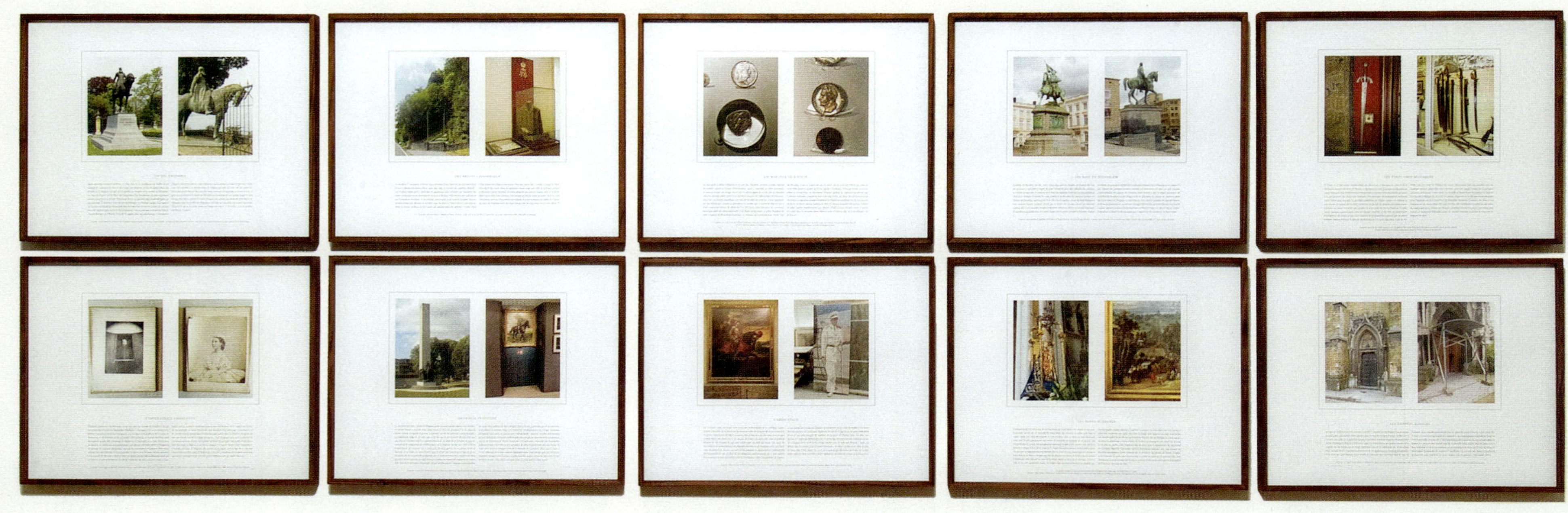

L'Histoire Belge, 2007. 10 offset prints on paper, frames. Each 37 × 48 cm

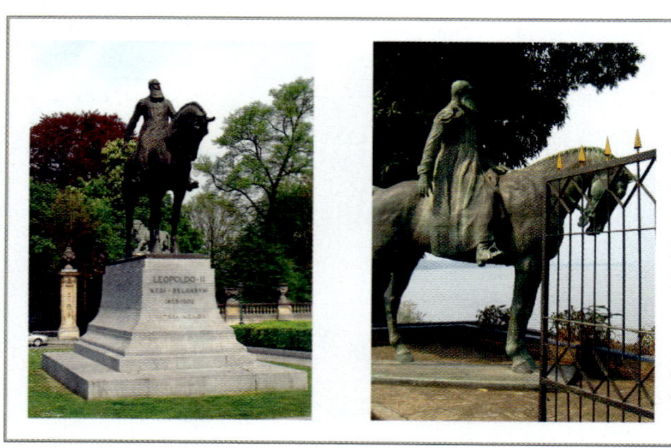

UN BEL ENSEMBLE

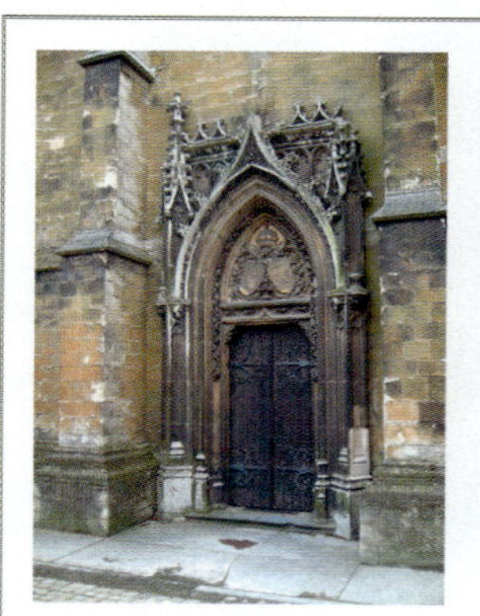

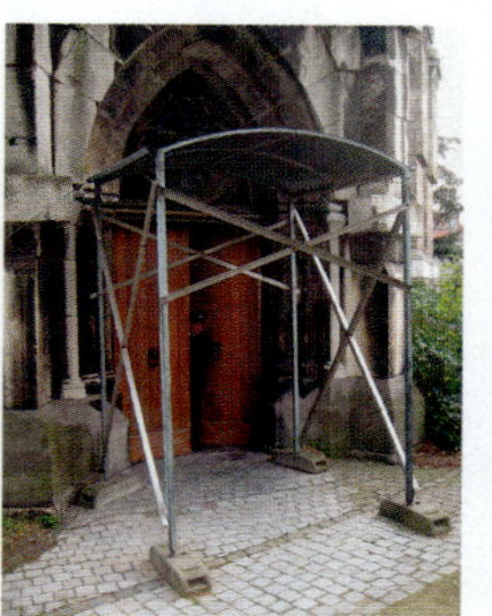

LES CRYPTES ROYALES

L'Histoire Belge, 2007. 2 of 10 offset prints on paper, frames. Each 37 × 48 cm

A concise lesson in political docu-fiction

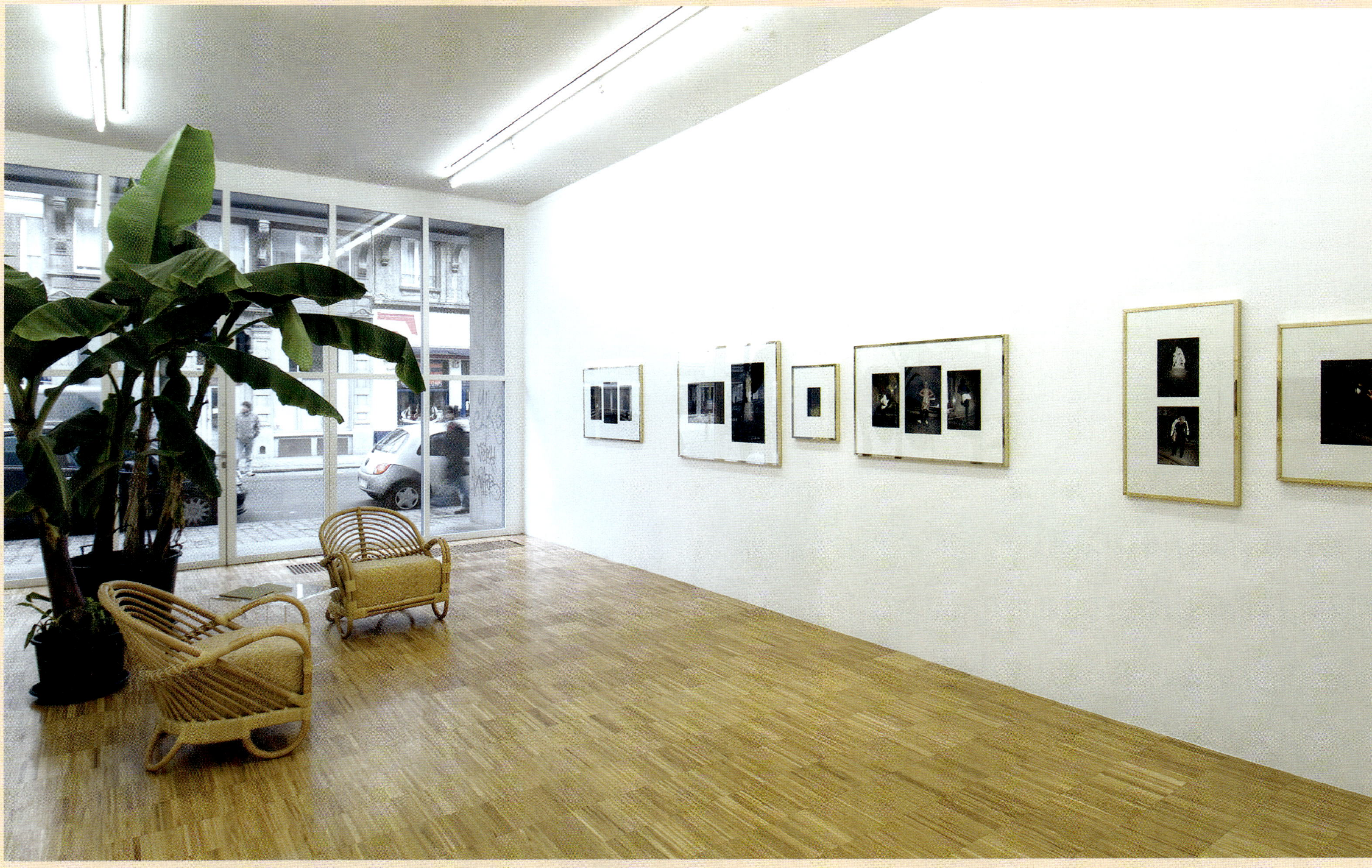

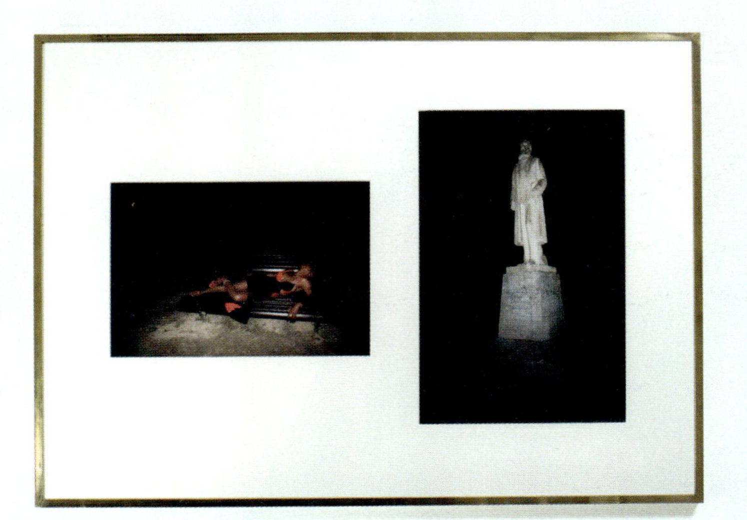

Les Demoiselles de Bruxelles, 2008. Book, 29 lambda prints in 10 brass frames, banana trees, rattan chairs. Dimensions variable

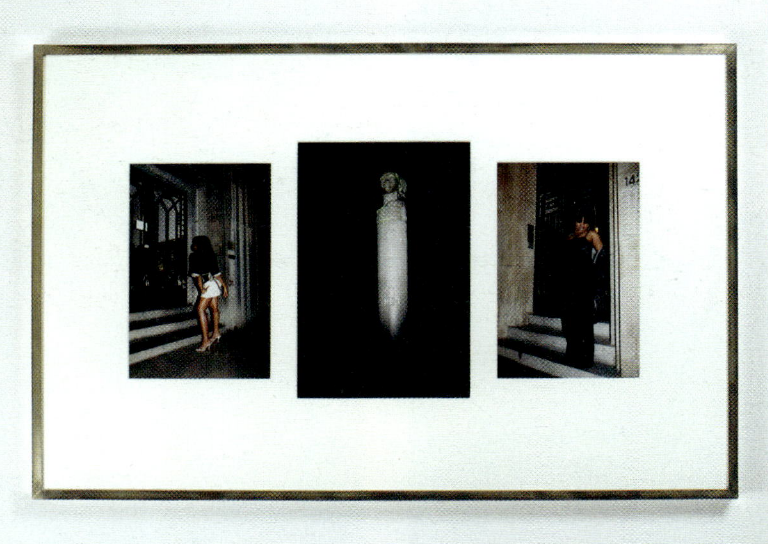

between nature and culture. In his films and works with text and image, Augustijnen seems to be recording a 'real existing history' founded on a plethora of idiosyncratic facts and fictional plots that contradict the monumental history of nations and ideological

The photographs were shown as part of an installation that included a reading corner with exotic props — rattan and leather chairs under the leaves of a banana tree growing in a pot.

formations. History is seen as an active and uncontrollable force constantly invading the present moment, a living resource from which reality constantly borrows, and to which art can give something back. This mutual permeability between history and fiction can be understood and used as a tool for transforming the 'truths' that were once carved in stone.

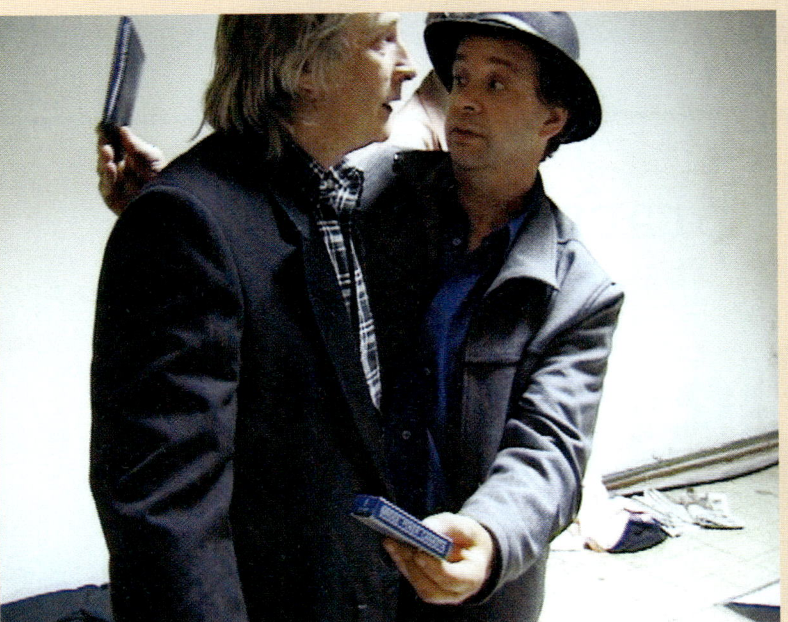

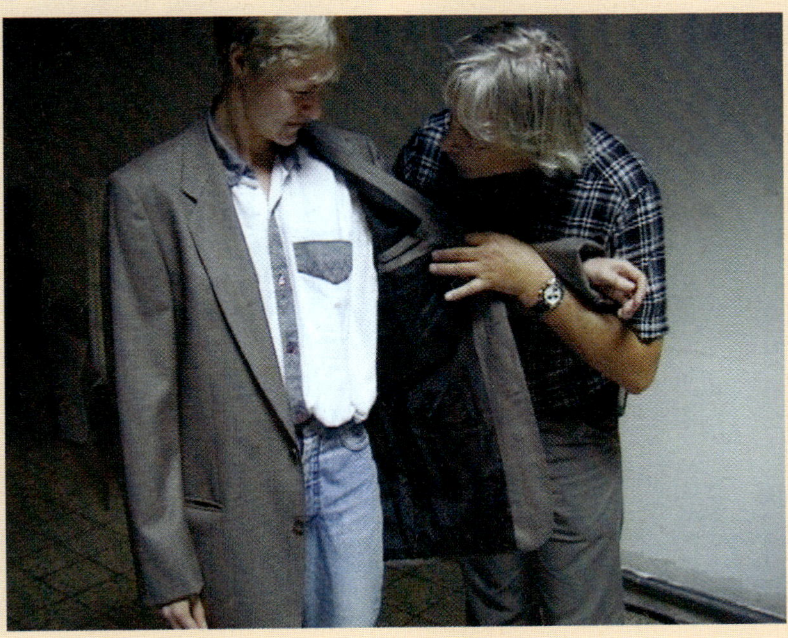

L'école des pickpockets, 2000. Video. 48 min.

Alexandra Bachzetsis

Gestures, social attitudes and language

Alexandra Bachtzetsis sets out on a journey to explore and describe the various forces that shape and mould our society. Through her performative practice she explores the process by which we commodify images, gestures, social attitudes and language and the way in which we use them for the purposes of power. Through the performing body, she shows how we employ forces such as seduction, violence or control to consolidate our position over others. Citing Walter Benjamin, she persuasively alludes to the fact that we are living in a state of alert in a society where a sense of fear predominates over a feeling of possiblity and that this is not an exception but seems to have been the rule in the last decade.

In the performance *Bluff* (2009), for example, three performers appear one after another on an almost empty stage, a black box marked with a small square where the action takes place. They enact

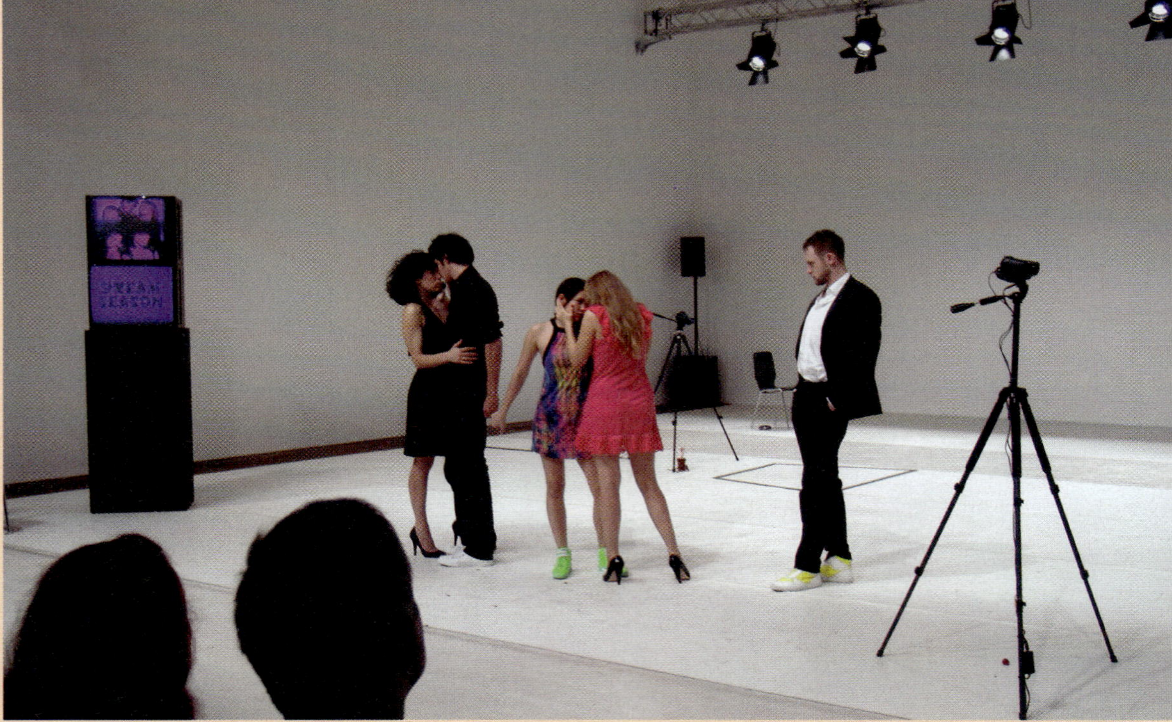

Dream Season, 2008. Performance. 60 min.

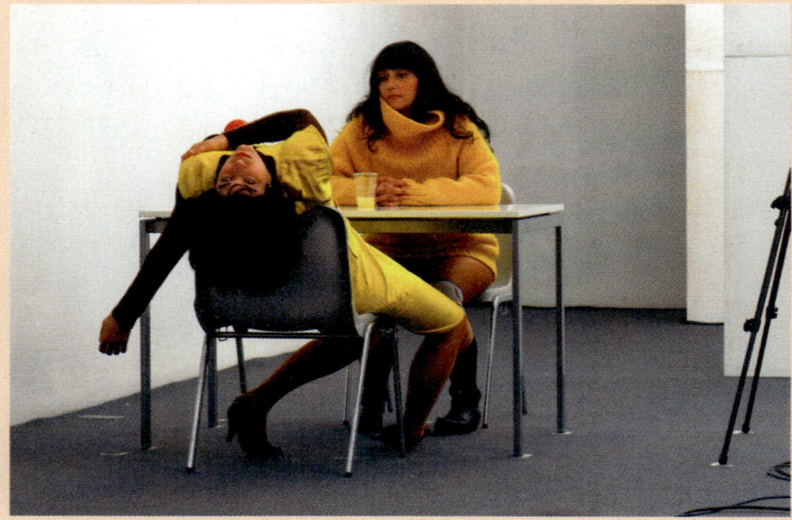

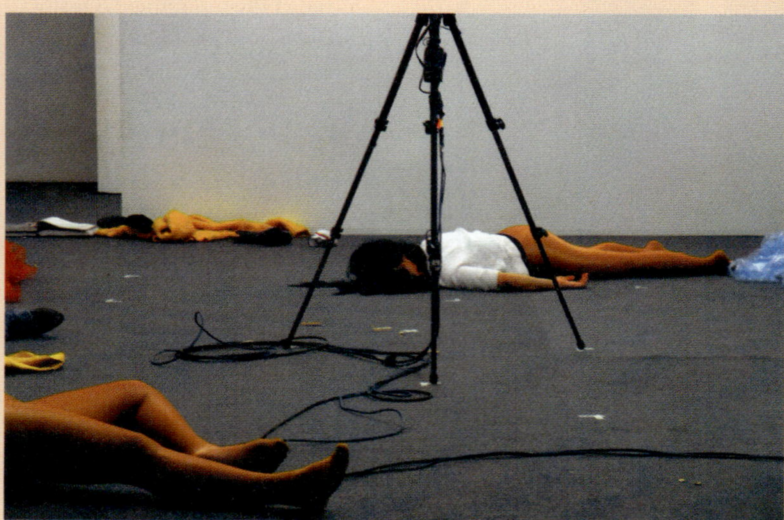

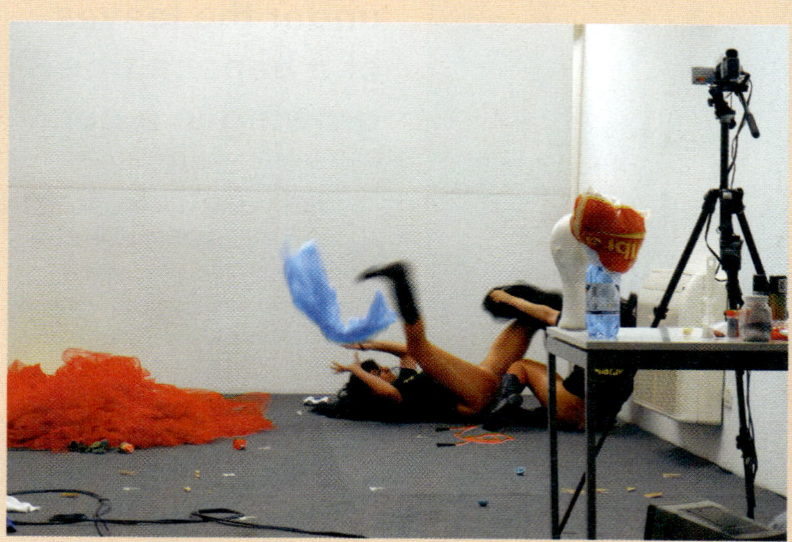

Murder Mysteries, 2004. Performance. 60 min.

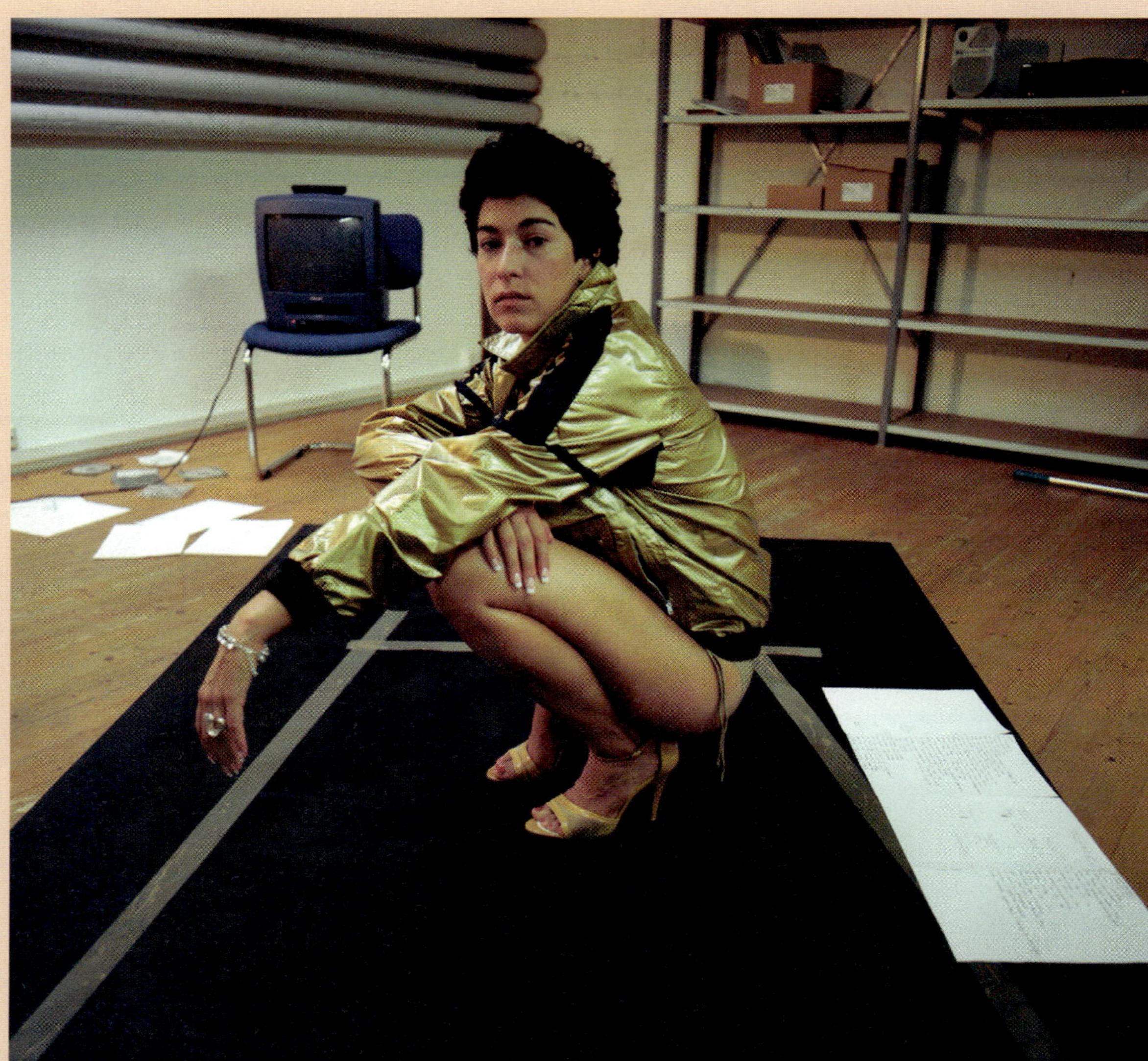

Gold, 2004. Performance. 30 min.

Performative practice

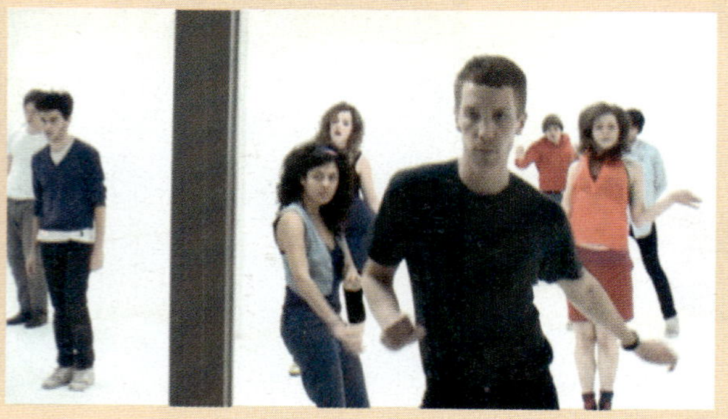

Dancing, 2009. Performance with students of the Gerrit Rietveld Accademie, Amsterdam

Self-control

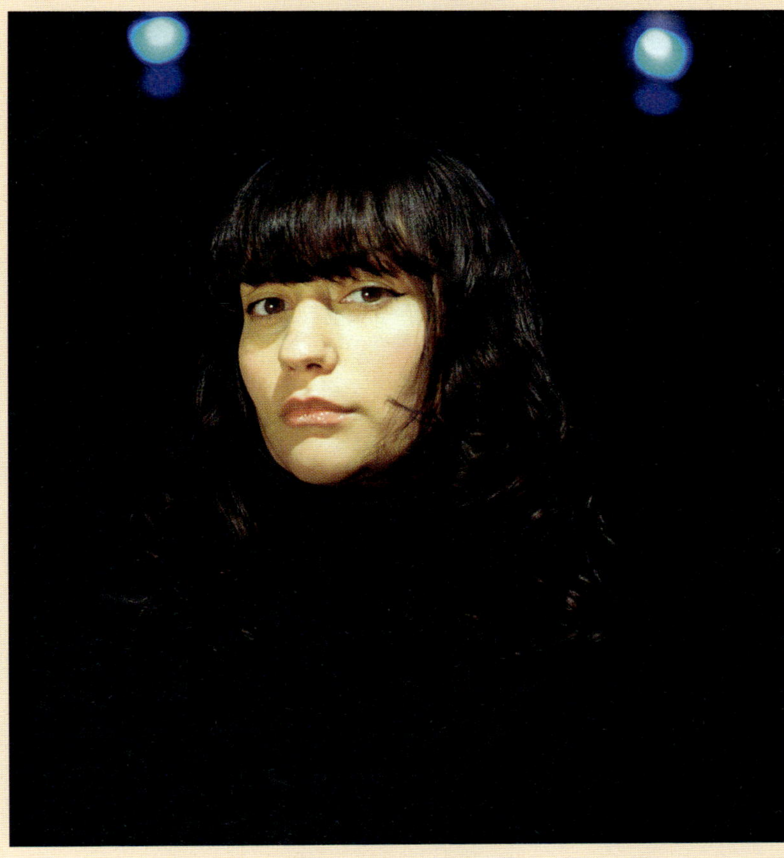

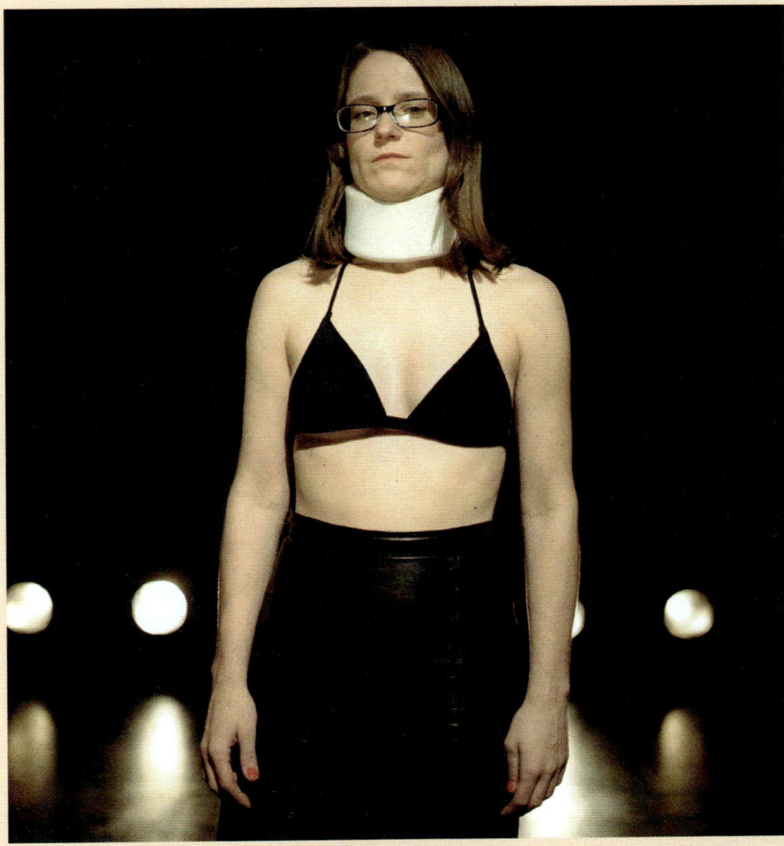

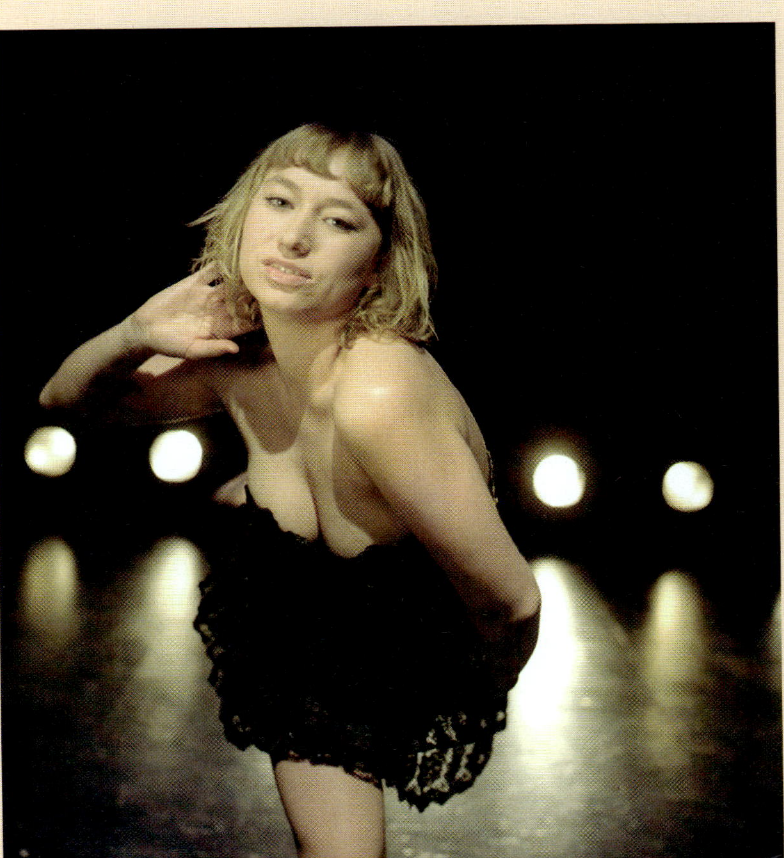

Show Dance, 2004. Performance and party. 60 min

an exchange of gestures that at first seem personal, but then become conventional, repetitive, worn, almost ironical. All of Bachtzetsis's performances depart from very simple situations such as this, paying attention to the basic experiences and codes with which we are all

Through her performative practice she explores the process by which we commodify images, gestures, social attitudes and language

familiar: the particular properties of sight, hearing, movement, touch and even their representation in a performative situation.

Dancing (2009) is another performance piece for fourteen dancers in a white space. The piece begins with a hypnotic staccato sound loop as the background for a sensuous solo by a female dancer. As the music changes into techno beats, a male performer appears in the distance and starts a completely different sequence of extrovert movements, while the girl continues her solo uninterrupted. Various performers and groups enter the stage and leave again in a carefully planned sequence of appearance, like a parade. At the core of this piece are notions of self-control and freedom and their practical application in

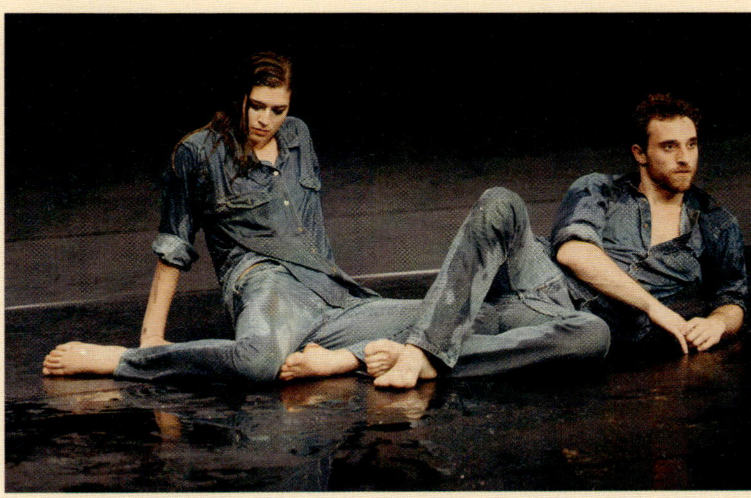

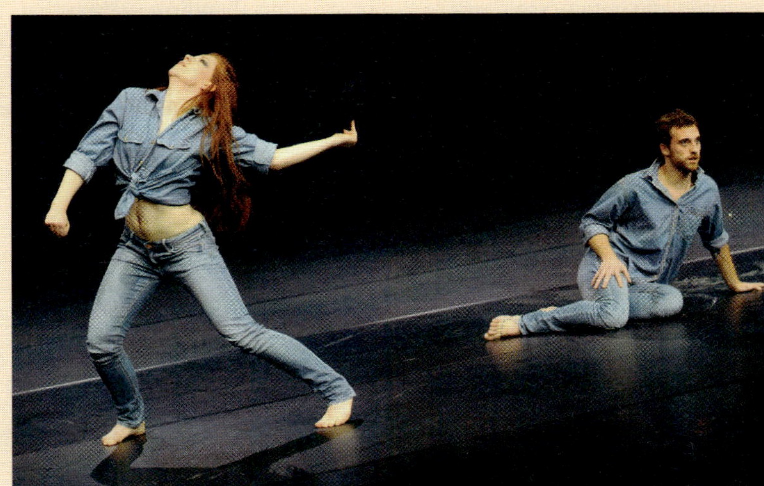

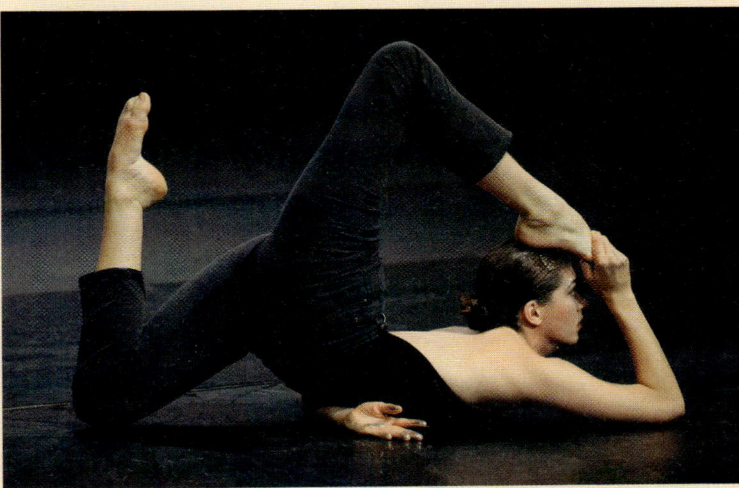

Bluff, 2009. Performance

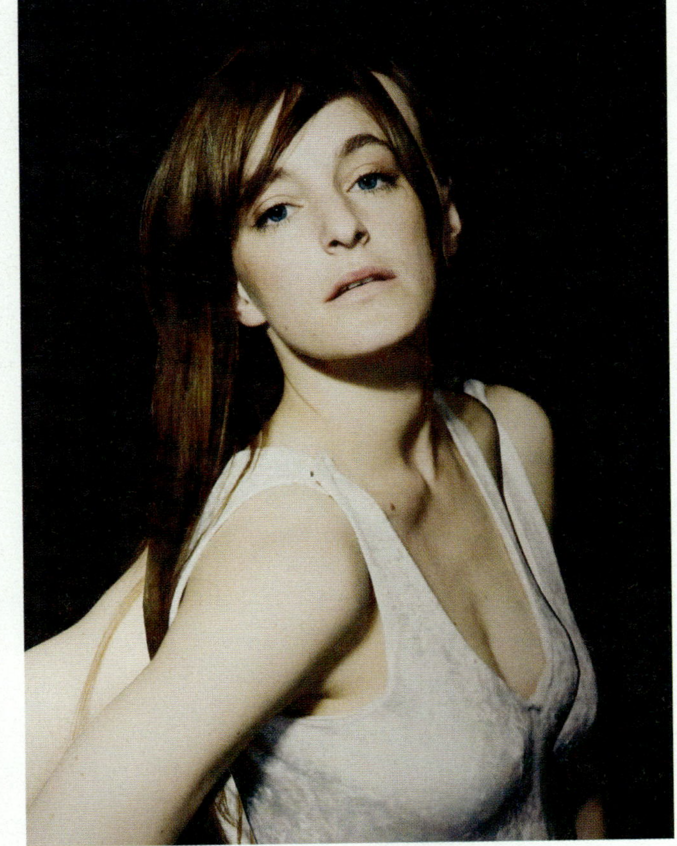

Company is: Alexandra Bachzetsis, Tina Bleuler, Lies Vanborm

Soirée, 2004. Performance and magazine

life itself, through something as simple as dancing, following the music, being part of a group.

'Imagine, for a minute or two, walking into a Helmut Newton photo shoot'— this is the departure point of *Show Dance* (2008), a choreographed parade of 'strong' women, who take turns 'showing off' in front of an audience before finally converging in a dazzling ensemble routine that brings to mind

Bachtzetsis sets out on a journey to explore and describe the various forces that shape and mould our society

both Newton's landmark imagery and Busby Berkeley's kaleidoscopic showgirl choreography. The question that lingers in all these works is how forms of feminine subjectivity are constructed in the elastic world of Bachzetsis.

Nairy Baghramian works mostly with photography and sculpture. Not only does her art reflect an outstanding sense of skill and sheer grace, but it is as compelling to look at as it is challenging to write about. It is the kind of work that leads critics and curators to resort to fluffy attributes such as 'sheer grace', 'absent presence' and 'modernist'. Some artworks lend themselves easily to the linear train of Microsoft Word, others, like Baghramian's, have us scrolling eternally through the thesaurus for the right term. It might be true, for example, that the work has that magnetic, semi-constructivist coolness implied by 'modernist', but the epithet is satisfactory only because it is so damn challenging to find a better one. Critical incommensurability aside, another attractively volatile feature is the work's handling of balance and poise, or more precisely, its handling of the aesthetics thereof.

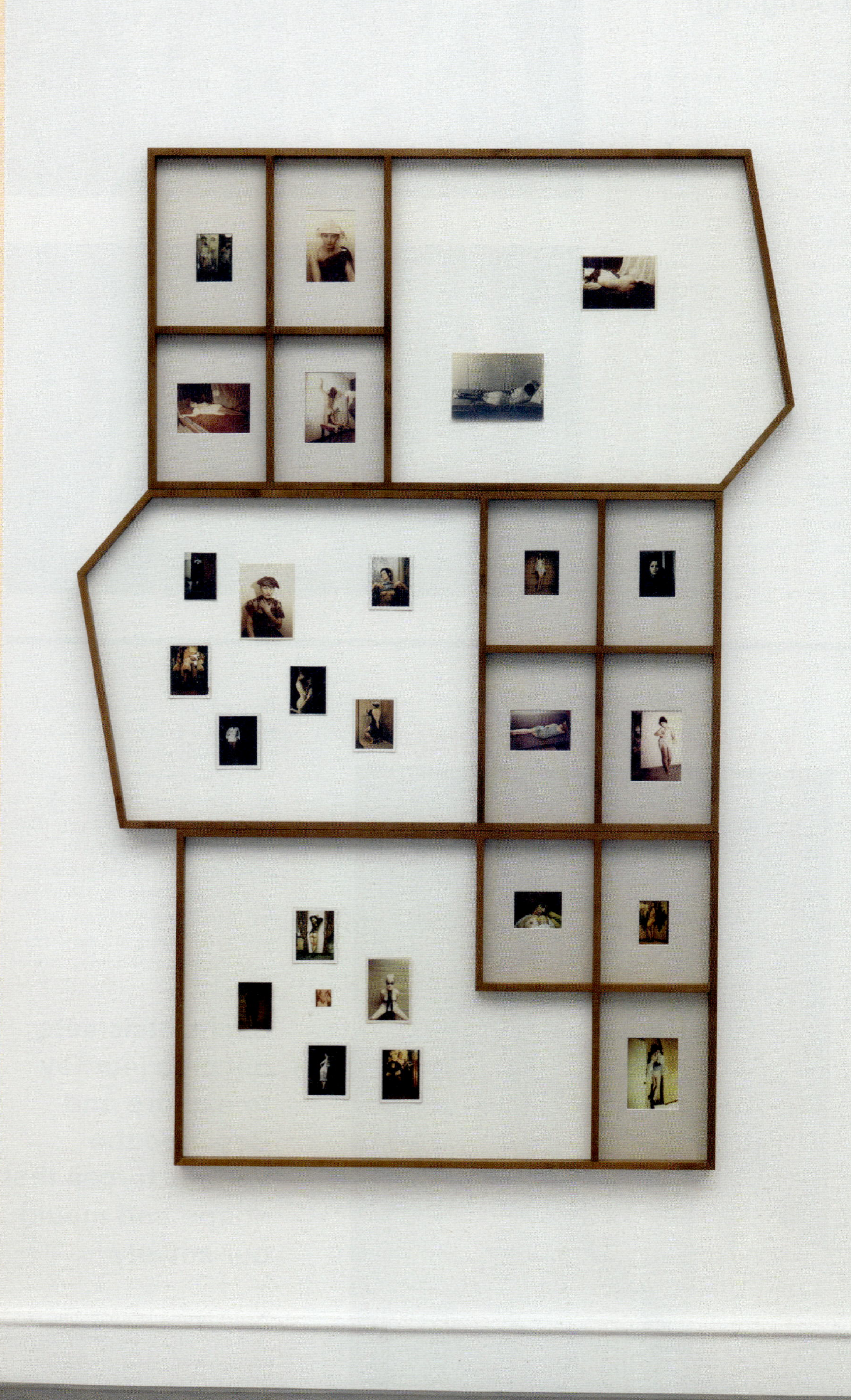

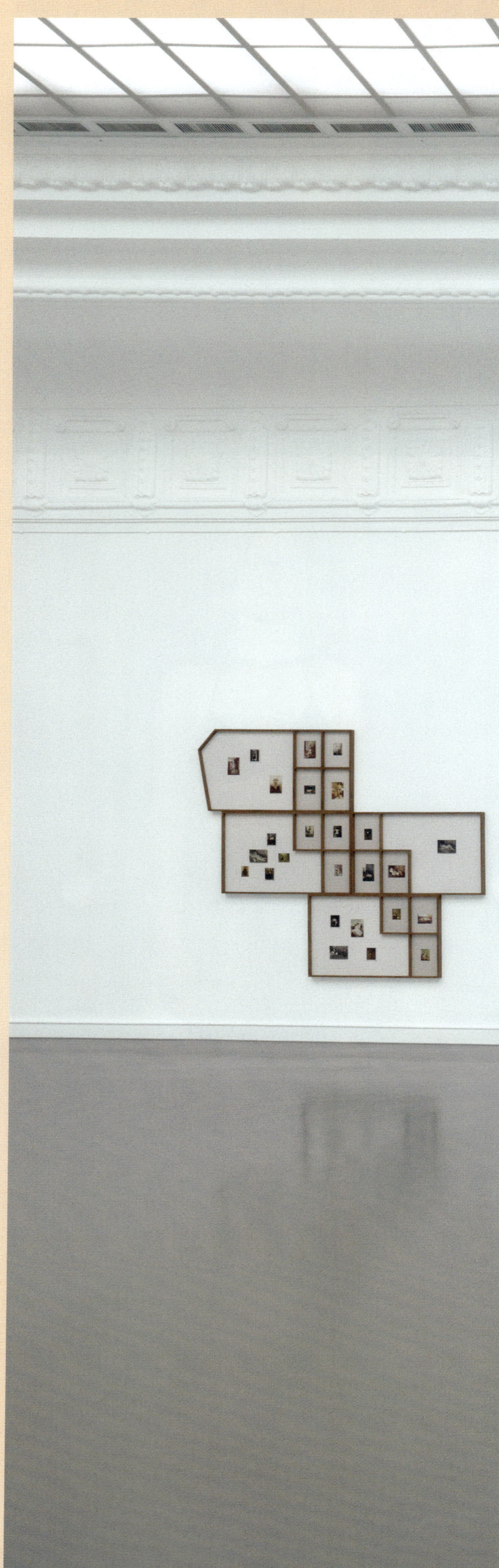

Entre deux actes II (Loge des Comédiennes), 2009. 2 parts: photographs (1940–60) by Carlo Mollino in frames by Nairy Baghramian; reinterpretation of Janette Laverrière's **Entre deux actes (Loge de Comédienne)** (1947). Dimensions variable

Nairy Baghramian

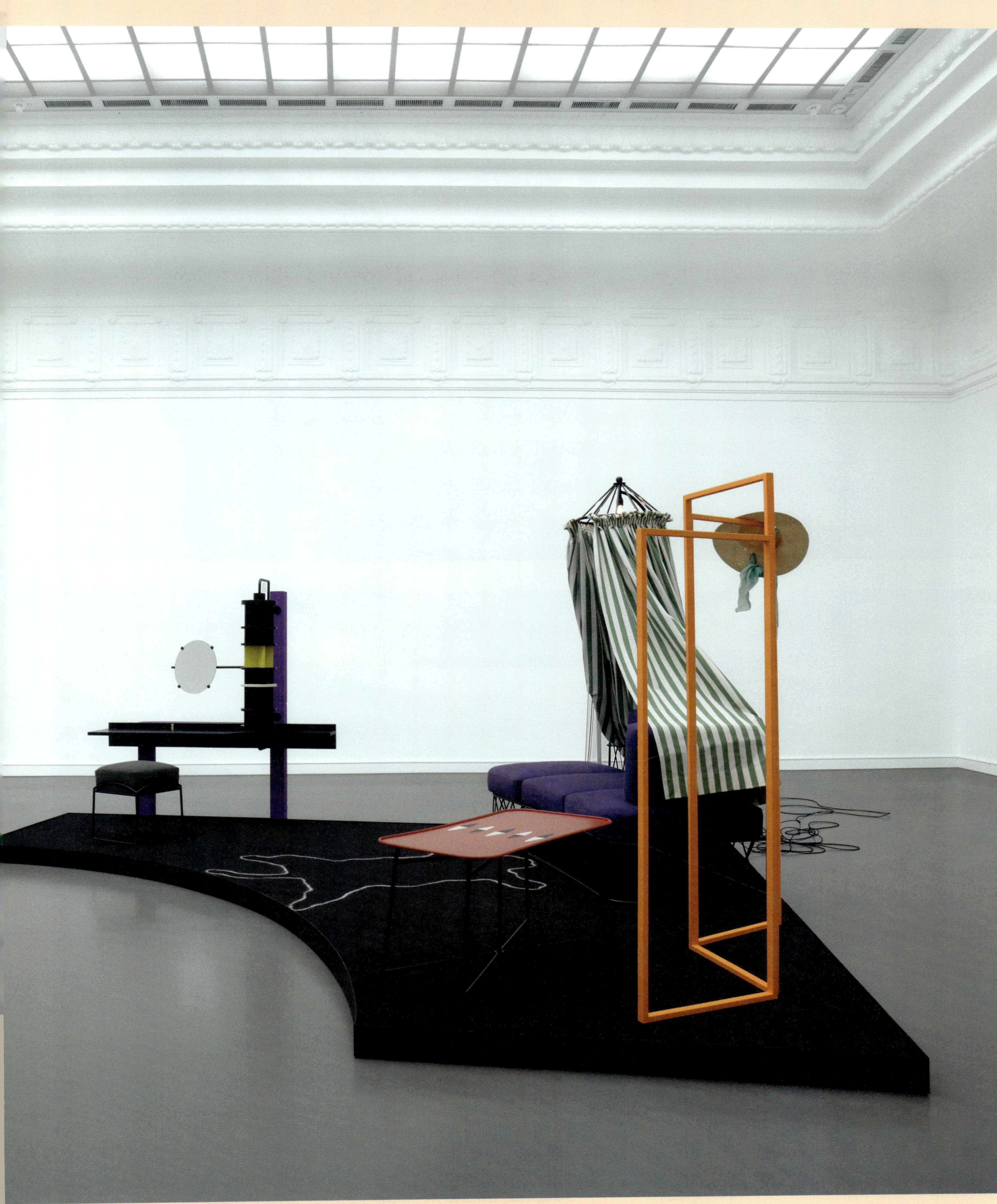

Magnetic, semi-constructivist coolness

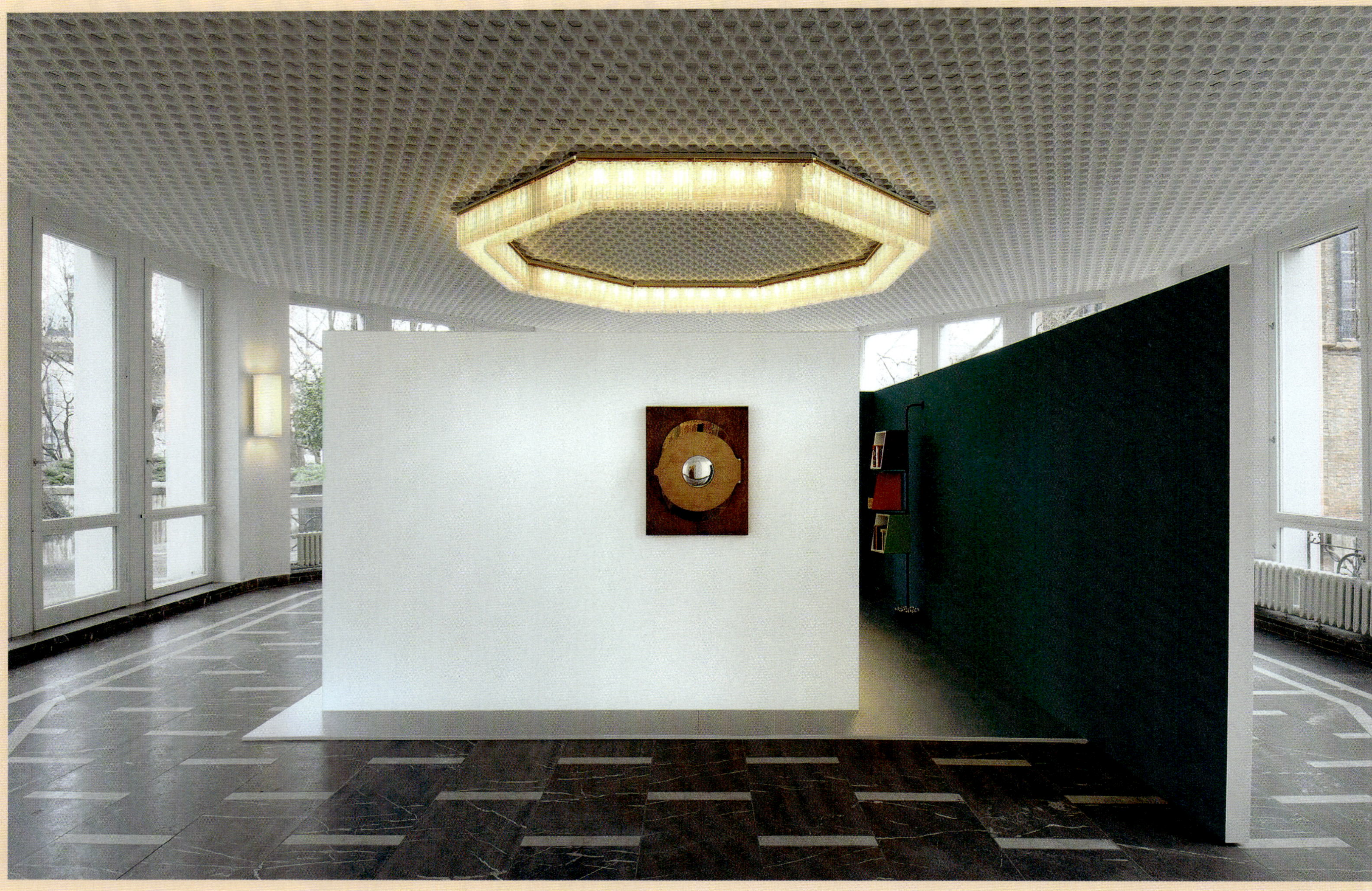

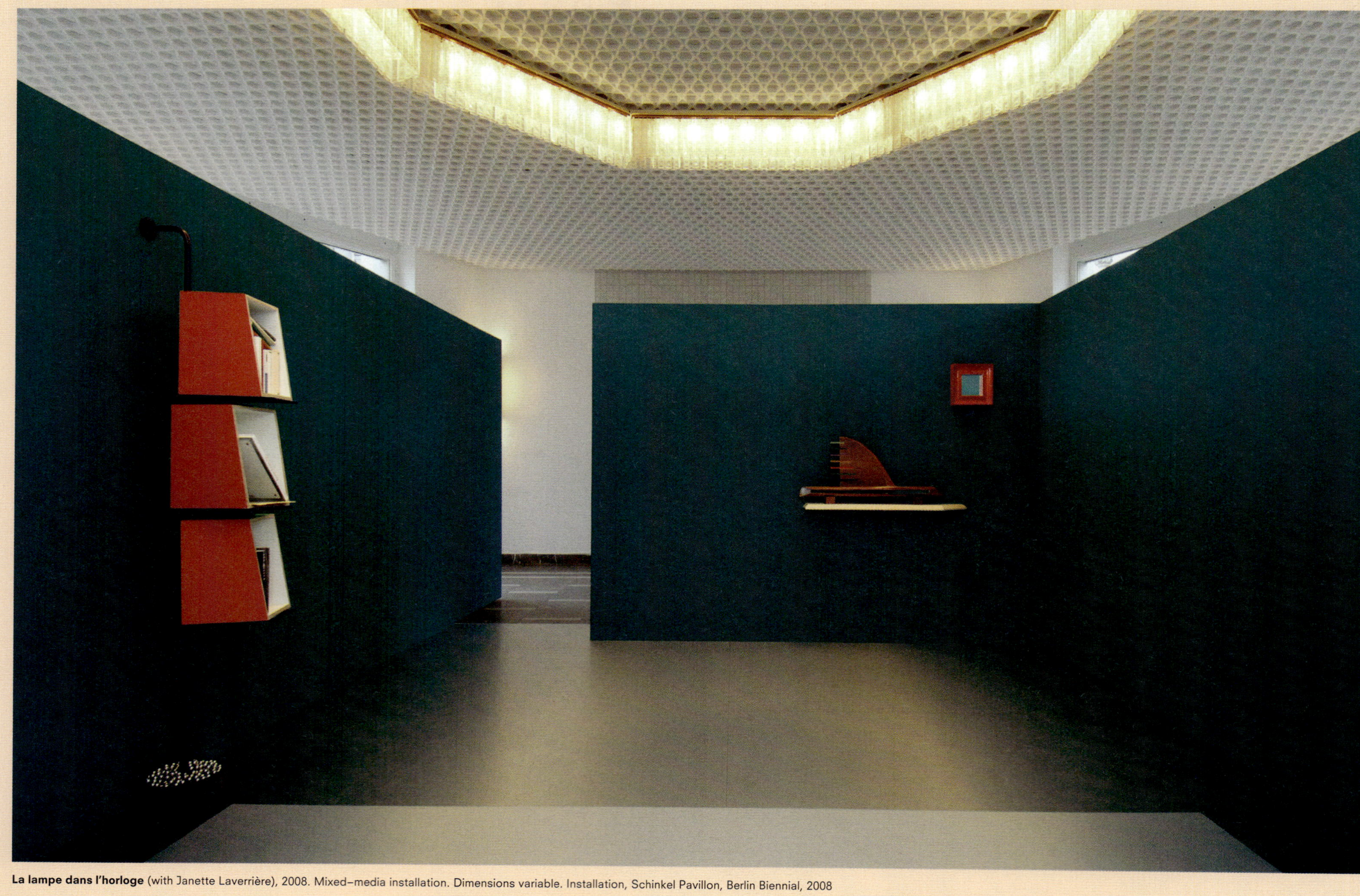

La lampe dans l'horloge (with Janette Laverrière), 2008. Mixed-media installation. Dimensions variable. Installation, Schinkel Pavillon, Berlin Biennial, 2008

Of balance and poise

As other critics have pointed out, structures such as *Vierte Wand / Zwei Protagonistinnen* (Fourth Wall / Two Female Protagonists, 2005) do not seem as sturdy at second glance as they do at first. In time, the structure begins to look precarious, even frail — but importantly, a third glance suggests that it is actually the precariousness that is being feigned here, a fragility flickering between something concealed

It is the kind of work that leads critics and curators to resort to fluffy attributes such as 'sheer grace', 'absent presence' and 'modernist'. Some artworks lend themselves easily to the linear train of Microsoft Word, others, like Baghramian's, have us scrolling eternally through the thesaurus for the right term

and something flaunted. This leaves you wondering what supports structure and which structures support, as writer Bruce Hainley might put it.

At the Berlin Biennial in 2008, Baghramian, whose contribution was far and away the most compelling, worked with designer Janette Laverrière at the Schinkel Pavilion, a sublime yet superbly difficult space in which to work. Baghramian effortlessly devised a perfect setting for Laverrière's work, which ranges from mirror pieces to dressing-room designs. This set the stage for a second partnership in 2009, the exhibition 'Entre deux actes: Loge de comedienne' (Between Two Acts: An Actress' Dressing Room). As it happens, another of Baghramian's pieces, a collaboration with Jan Timme, bears the perfect title *Everlasting layers of ideas, images, feelings, have fallen upon your brain softly as light. Each succession has seemed to bury all that went before. And yet, in reality, not one has been extinguished* (2006). Nothing more to say.

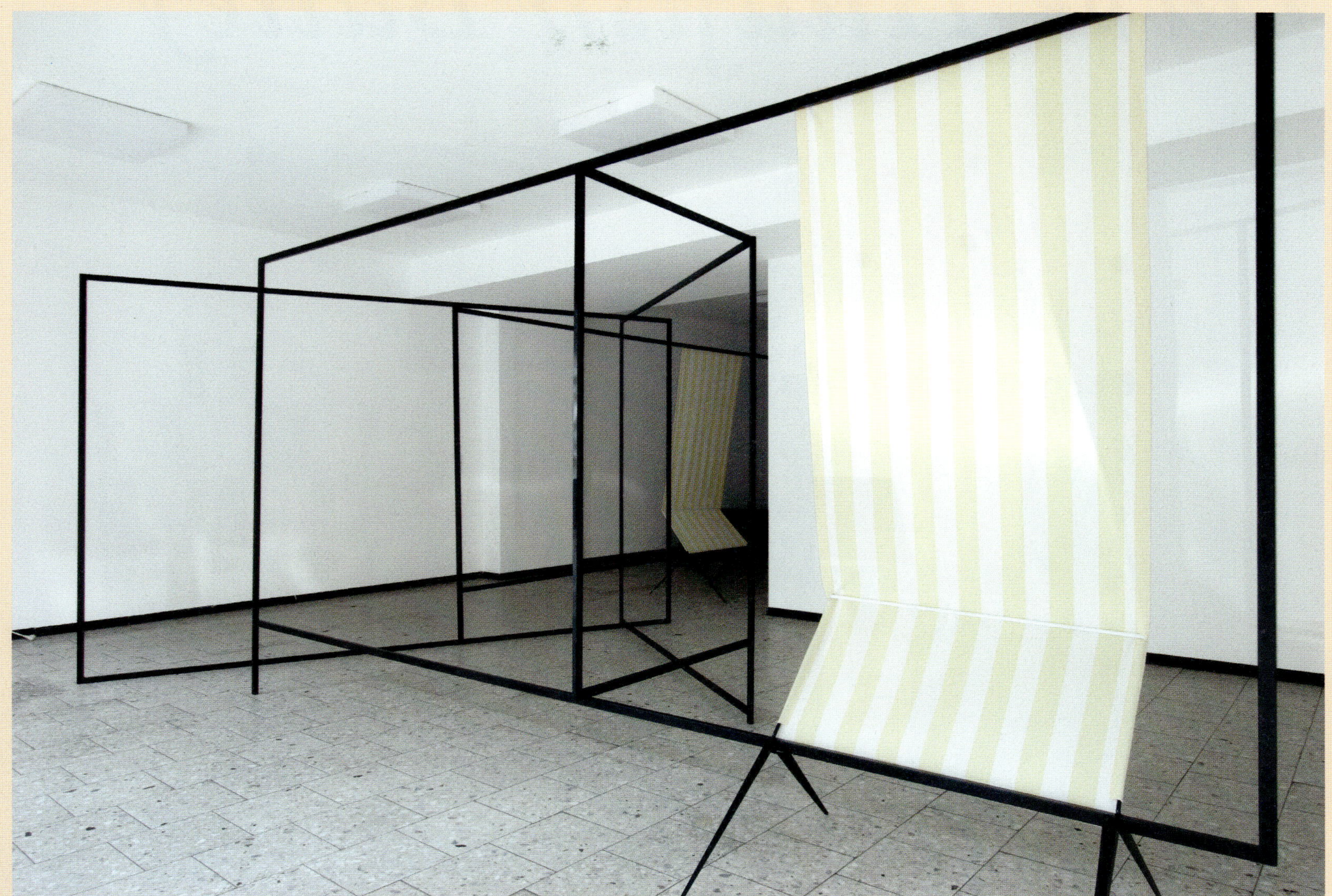

Fourth Wall / Two Female Protagonists, 2005. Painted metal, bleached fabric. 1500 × 230 × 150 cm

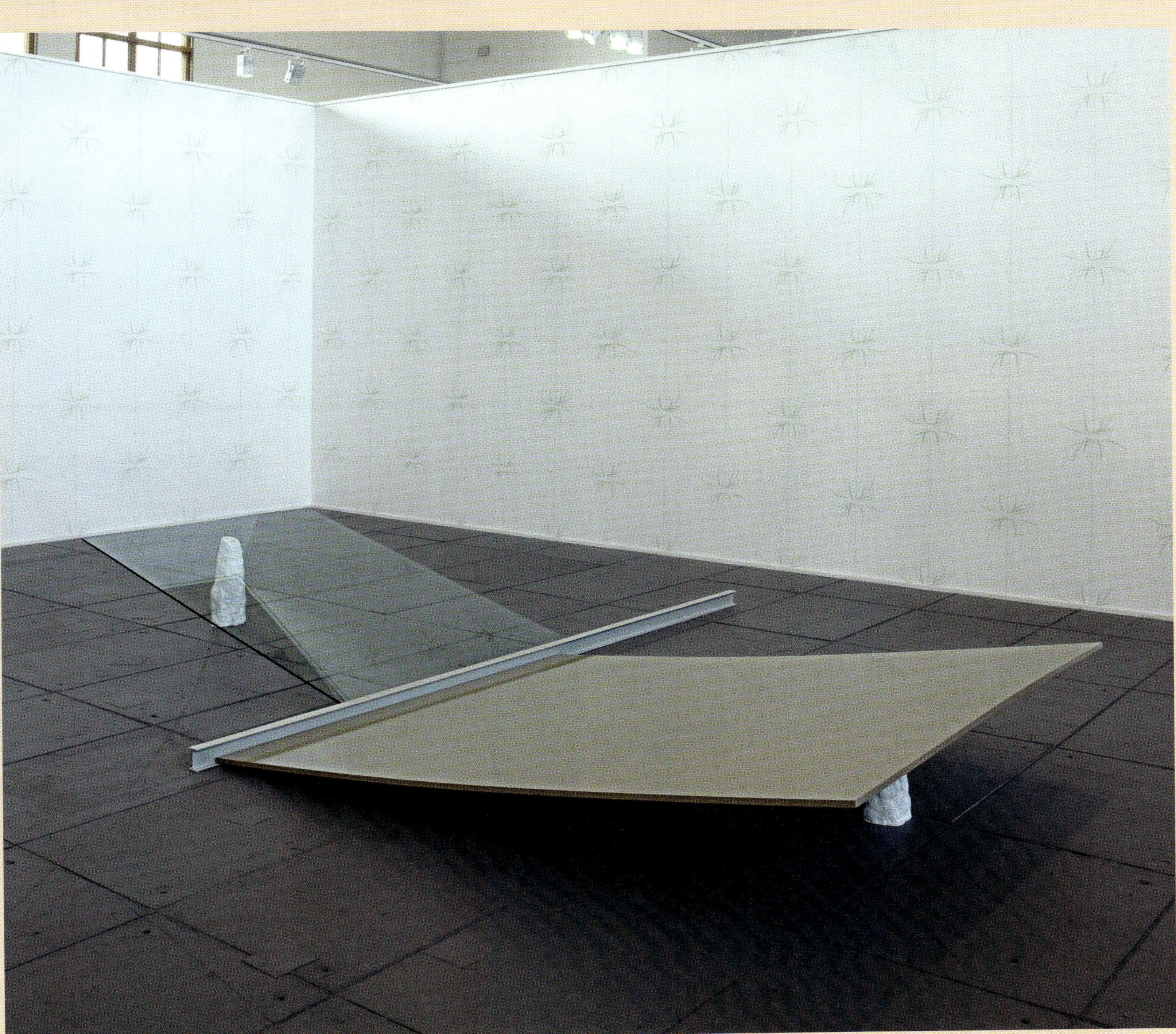

Every lasting layers of ideas, images, feelings, have fallen upon your brain softly as light. Each succession has seemed to bury all that went before. And yet, in reality, not one has been extinguished (with Jan Timme), 2006. Glass, painted double T–girder, painted wood, cast aluminium, silicon, silkscreen. Dimensions variable

Dave Hullfish Bailey

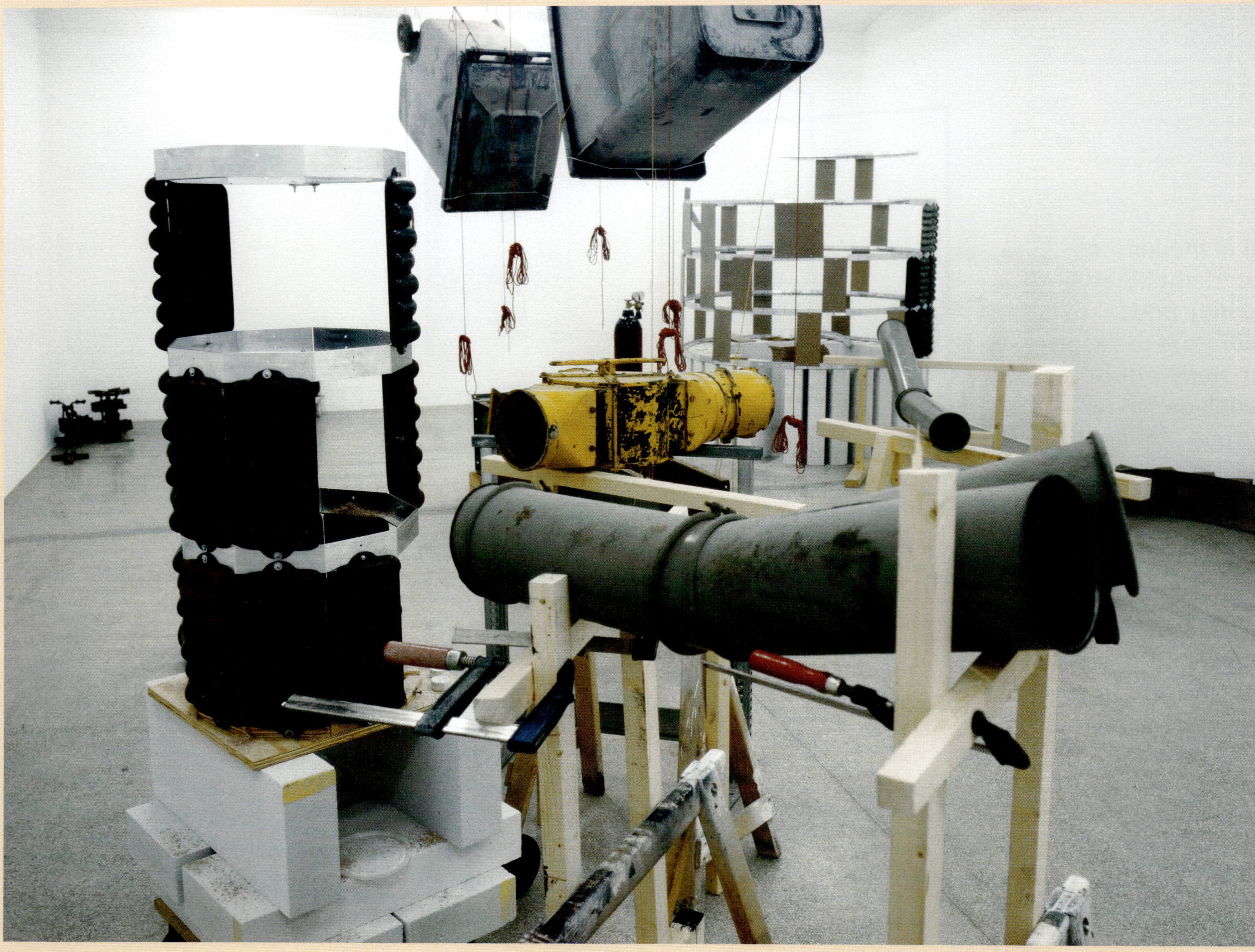

Flour Bomb Werkstatt, 2006. Vintage cast iron cornbread baking pans, vintage grain elevator parts, grain dust, grain dust bins, related materials. Approx. 15 × 6.5 × 3.5 m. From the exhibition 'Elevator', Secession, Vienna

Dave Hullfish Bailey moves with dazzling skill between different systems: the world of materials and their influence on our way of sensing and acting; the realm of objects as already constituted things; and language as our method of describing what we see, feel and think. In his work, Bailey shows the possible interrelations between all these ways of making the world, constructing a universe in which all elements are equally important, and where the material and the immaterial dance together in order to make us reflect on how meaning moves between them. Bailey's research-based approach is inherently experimental and speculative and the material form his work takes is inextricably a part of its conceptual subject.

For his exhibition 'Elevator' at the Secession in Vienna in 2006, Bailey began by researching five state-owned grain elevators built in the 1930s by the Third Reich on the outskirts of Vienna, some of which still move and store grain today. Working heuristically, moving between macro and micro perspectives, Bailey delineated a sculpturally precise yet wholly nonlinear narrative that combined focused local research with a string of lateral displacements. Using photographs, video footage, texts, archival imagery, sculptural objects and functional devices, Bailey framed recognizable questions about the autonomy of individuals and the organization of groups. Familiar symbolic, historical and scientific ways of ordering information about matter, in this case grain, competed with logical machines created through analogy with the material structure and system dynamics of grain as it is churned through the modern elevator. By posing dust explosions as sense-making models as well as possible allegories of bottom-up social transformation, Bailey's project created a bit of speculative distance on the instrumental sorting and categorical binning the elevator was designed to accomplish.

In his recent project commissioned for Raven Row in London, Bailey responded directly to the neighborhood: Spitalfields, a place dense with overlapping histories of immigration, assimilation and exodus, right next to the financial heart of London. Using both conventional and experimental research techniques, he articulated links between seemingly disparate places, events and ideas (from the 'cliff edge' created by the construction of a high-rise dormitory tower on Spitalfield's Frying Pan Alley, to nineteenth-century kindergarten pedagogy, to 1970s utopian communities in the

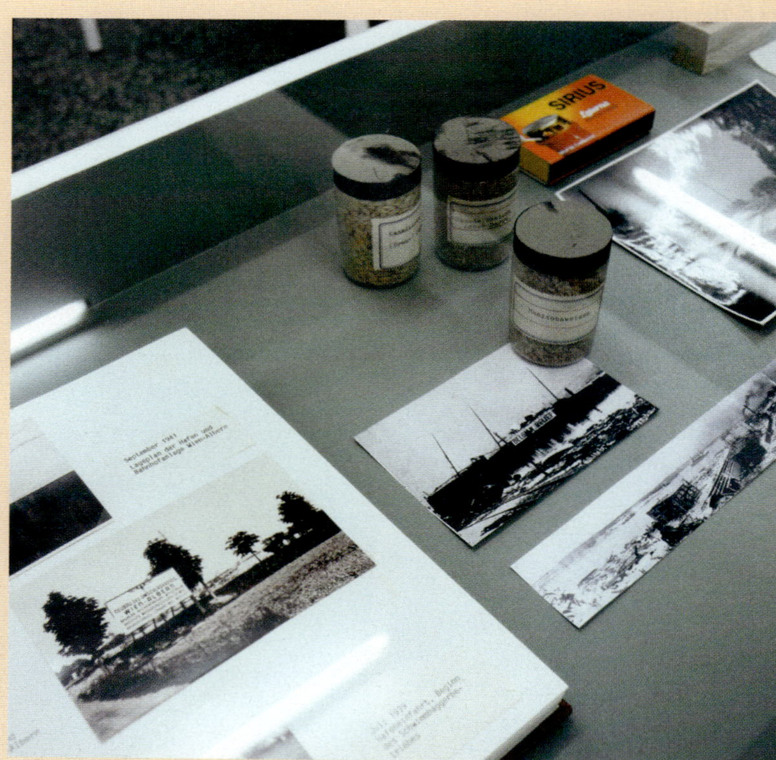

Transient alignment of particles effected by incidental structures found upon their surfaces (detail), 2006. Harbormaster's archive (Albernerhafen, Vienna), archival grain samples, matches, archival photograph, grain dust samples prepared for scanning electron microscope, photocopies, vitrine. Vitrine approx. 150 × 50 × 15 cm. From the exhibition ' Elevator' Secession, Vienna

Various empirical investigations

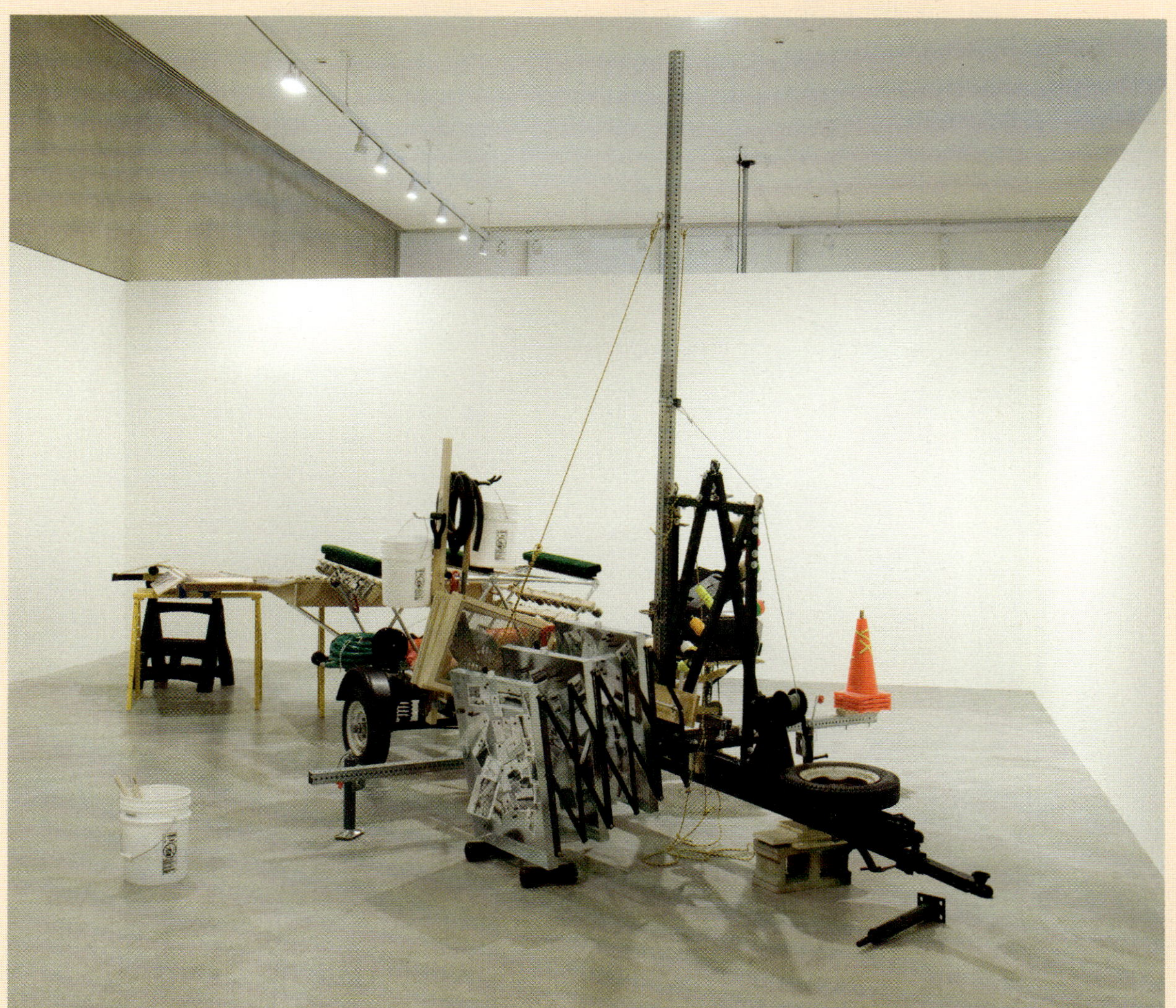

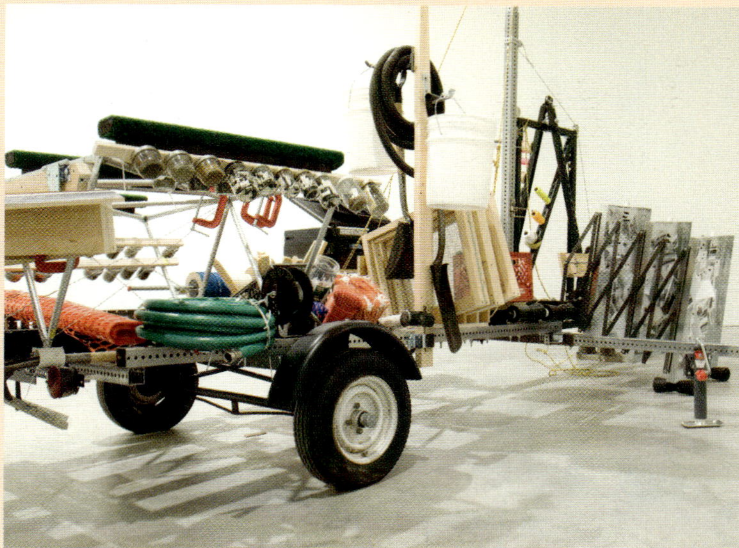

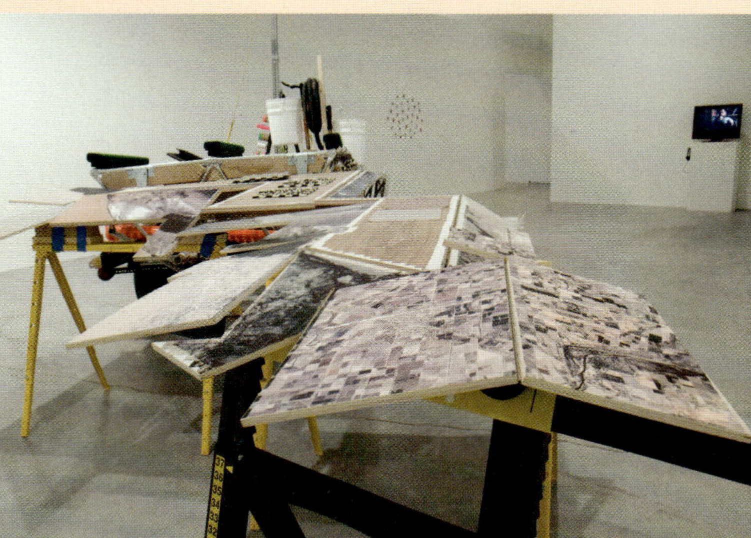

To do with a wide spot along a dusty road crossing a dry channel, somewhere between the old end of Old Red and the dead end of the New West (working prototype), 2009. Modified boat trailer, photocopier, photocopied research materials, Google satellite imagery, soil samples, Lego chess boards and bricks, rope, twine, cable, shovels, sediment screens, traffic cones, galvanized drain pans, water pumps, buckets, hoses, tubing, sandbags, other materials. Approx. 850 × 450 × 375 cm

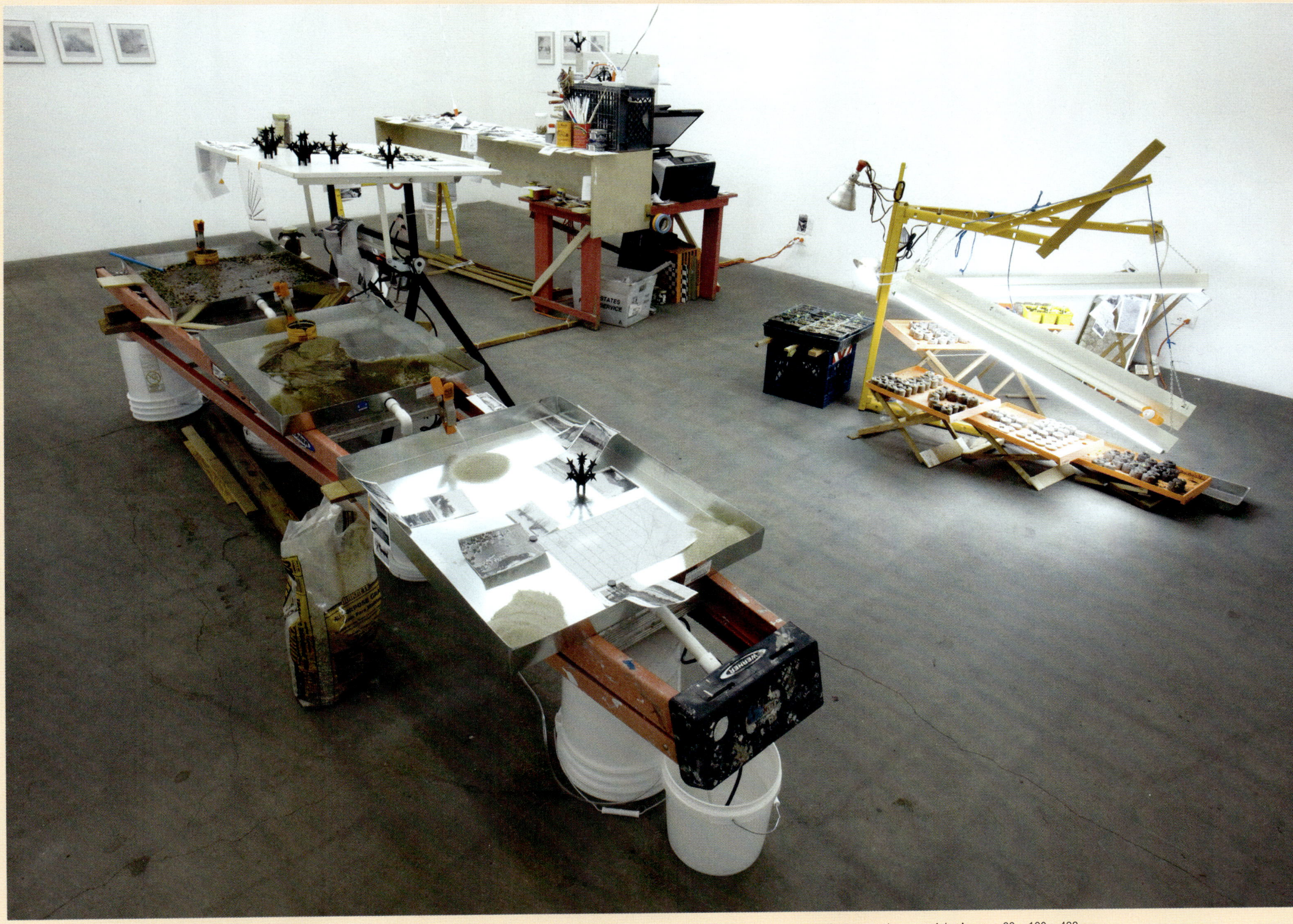

Small changes on plains of various inclinations (Delta Study), 2008. Folding ladder, scrap wood shims, galvanized drain pans, water pumps, buckets, sand, earth, water, other materials. Approx. 60 × 100 × 400 cm

Setting out now, what may become useful, 2008. Folding sawhorse, fluorescent shop lights, found drawers, wood, peat pellets, Palo Verde seeds/seedlings, other materials. Approx. 100 × 120 × 90

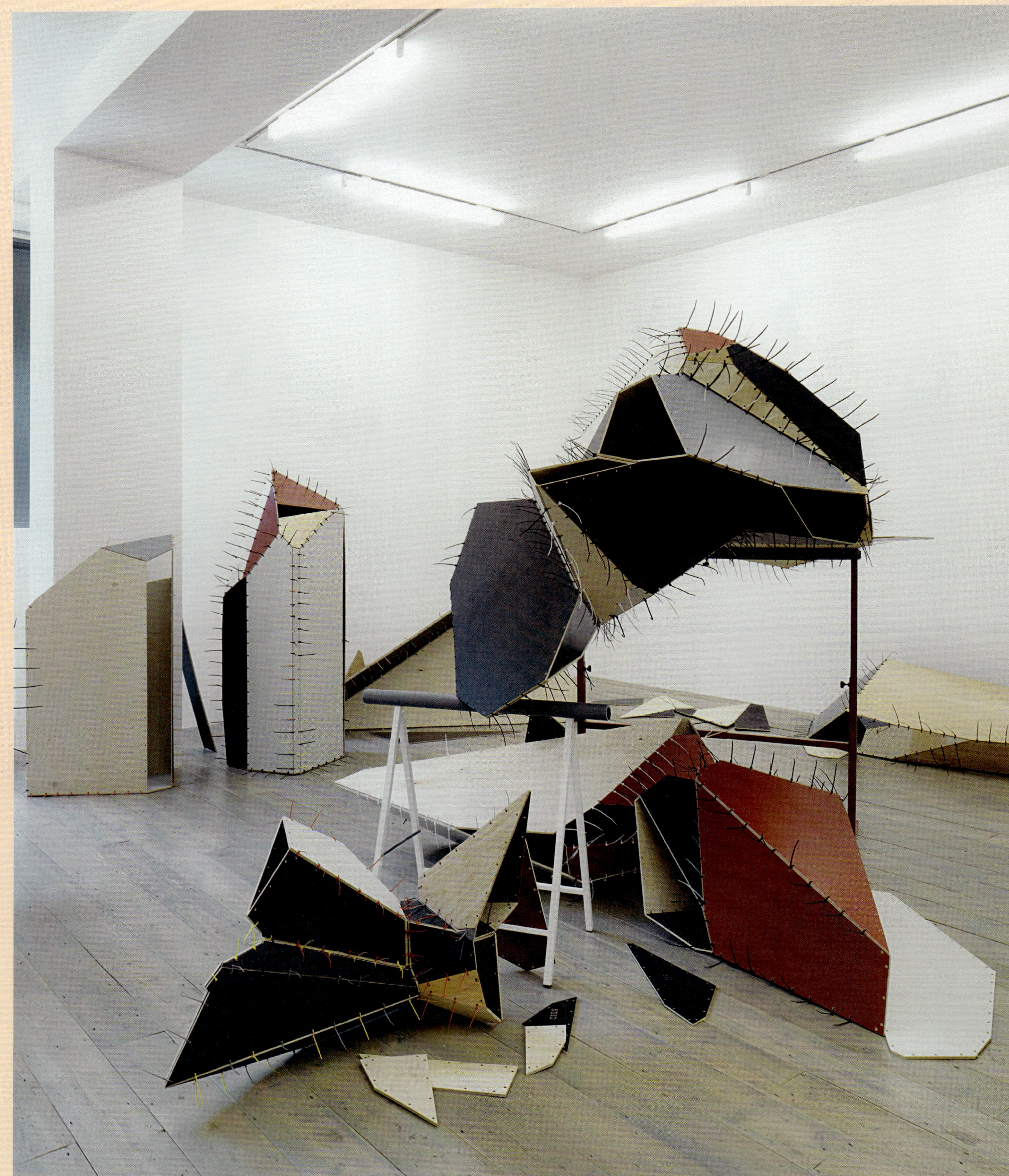

Untitled project (cliff edge), 2009. Detail of initial state. Dimensions variable. Installation, Raven Row, London

American Southwest). Bailey then fed this web of relationships into parametric software that translated it into tessellated polygonal forms. From these abstract spatial mappings he selected several for fabrication, not on the basis of the information they encoded, but rather with an eye toward the functional potentials of their morphologies. Alone and in conjunction with workshop participants, Bailey proposed various empirical investigations and small-scale interventions in the neighborhood, then outfitted the geometric clusters for these purposes.

At first sight, Bailey's works seem disparate: he involves many elements such as different communication codes that encourage the viewer to engage with and interpret them, creating routes that go beyond mere association. His practice is concerned with the way in which very different things can operate together and how this creates a space and a time that is radically different from the information systems, for example, that are created and replicated by the media where communication has turned into a regime that rules our everyday, the rhythm of our lives. With his works Bailey creates a continuum between our here and now, our space and time and the space and time of others.

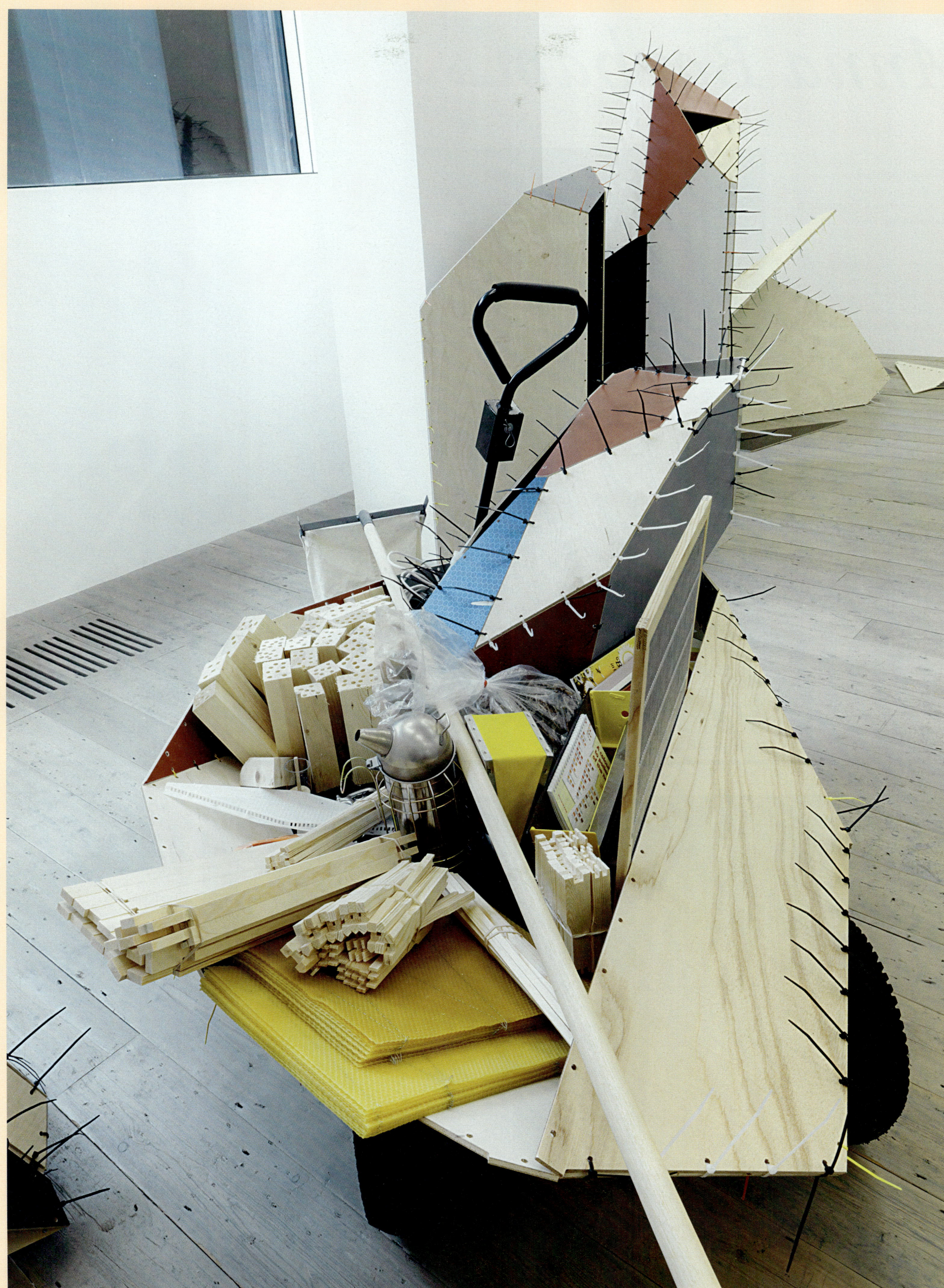

Nido Wagon Cluster (detail), 2009. Plywood, cable ties, wagon chassis, swarm net, bee blocks, smoker, bee tobacco, bee library, pollen collector and colour guide, queen excluder, hive handles, comb foundation, British National Hive frame bars, paint colour samples, other supplies. Dimensions variable. Installation, Raven Row, London

Anna Barham

Whether working in film, sculpture, drawing or performance, Anna Barham often dramatizes the interplay between a system and the paradoxical freedom and potential it engenders. In 2007, she began what has evolved into a sustained investigation into the anagram as a poetic take on this theme. Starting with the name of the ancient Roman city Leptis Magna, she drew long sequences of its two-word anagrams in sprawling biro grids in an attempt to visualize the graphic relation between the words when considered formally as different patterns of letters. The artist's interest did not only lie in the fact that Leptis Magna yielded an unusually high number of permutations ('magenta lips', 'elating amps', 'pliant games', 'plant images'), but that the very concept of the ruined Roman city was conjured as a sculptural equivalent to the idea of letters as building blocks, each sharing a capacity to construct fantastical visions.

This plastic idea of imagination was also present in models that Barham made of the theatre at Leptis Magna, *Pliant Games I — III*. Constructed from discarded packaging and plaster, the models oscillated between illusion and materiality, resembling the crumbled stone of the original while resolutely revealing their constitution from studio detritus.

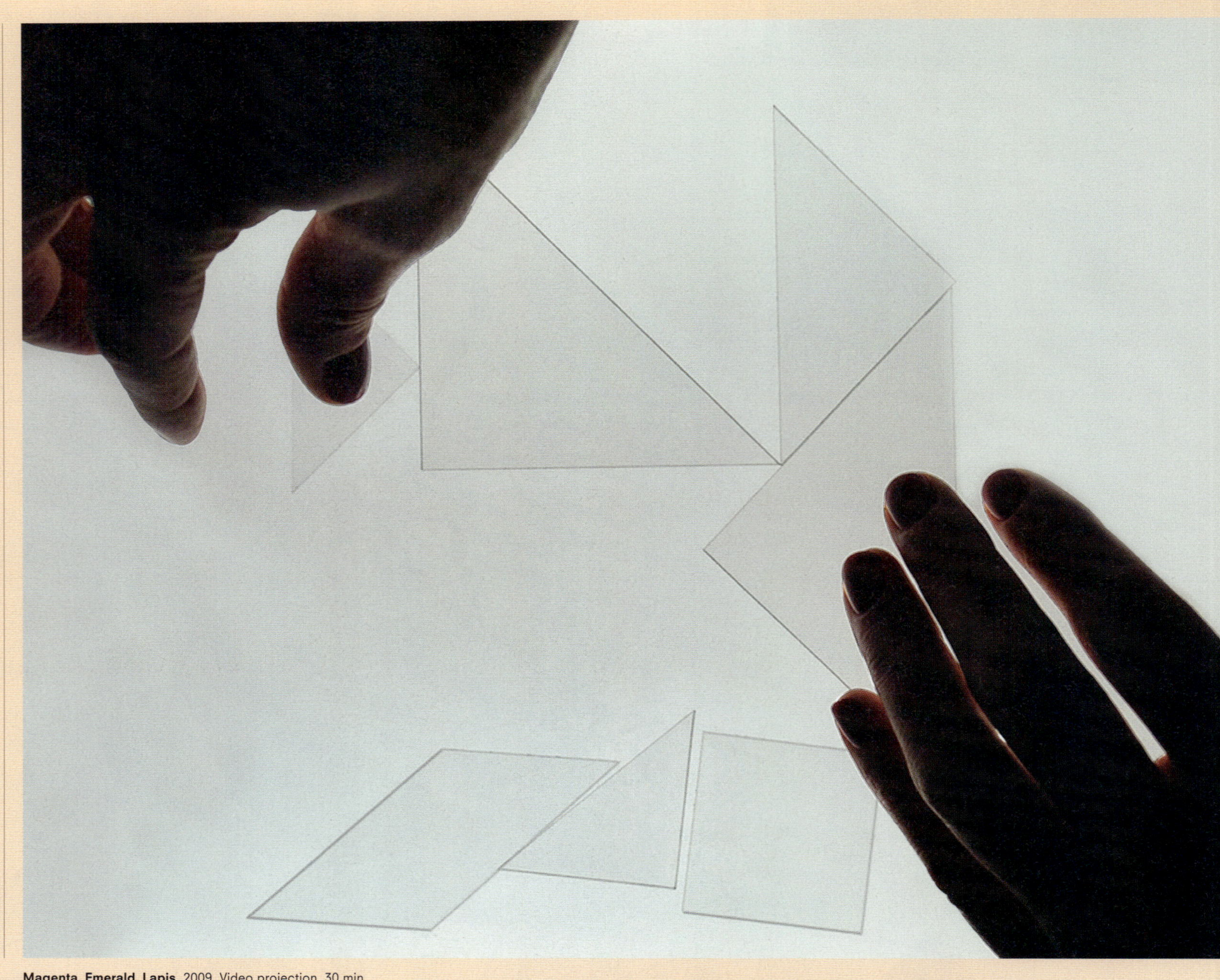

Magenta, Emerald, Lapis, 2009. Video projection. 30 min.

In 2008–09, Barham added four letters to Leptis Magna to create the phrase 'replanted images', from which she generated more than twenty-five new drawings. Rather than ordering words solely according to the contingency of spelling, she began to use the computer as a tool with which to 'mine' sense. From the nearly 67,000 possible three-word anagrams of the phrase, she made deliberate and charged choices, set in sequences that created allusive or rhetorical resonances (SPIE GENTLE DRAMA / SIP ELEGANT DREAM / NEGATE DREAM SLIP / INGEST DREAM LEAP / MAD STEERING LEAP). Barham describes her interest in anagrams as a way of seeking out the 'unconscious' of a word, as though its set form is simply the skin on a teeming proliferation of alternative possibilities that might be conjured if it loses its shape.

In a performance at Arcade, London, in 2009, Barham set up a configuration of sculpture, film, performance and spoken word that brought together the different aspects of her practice in a single event. The space was filled by a multi-level structure

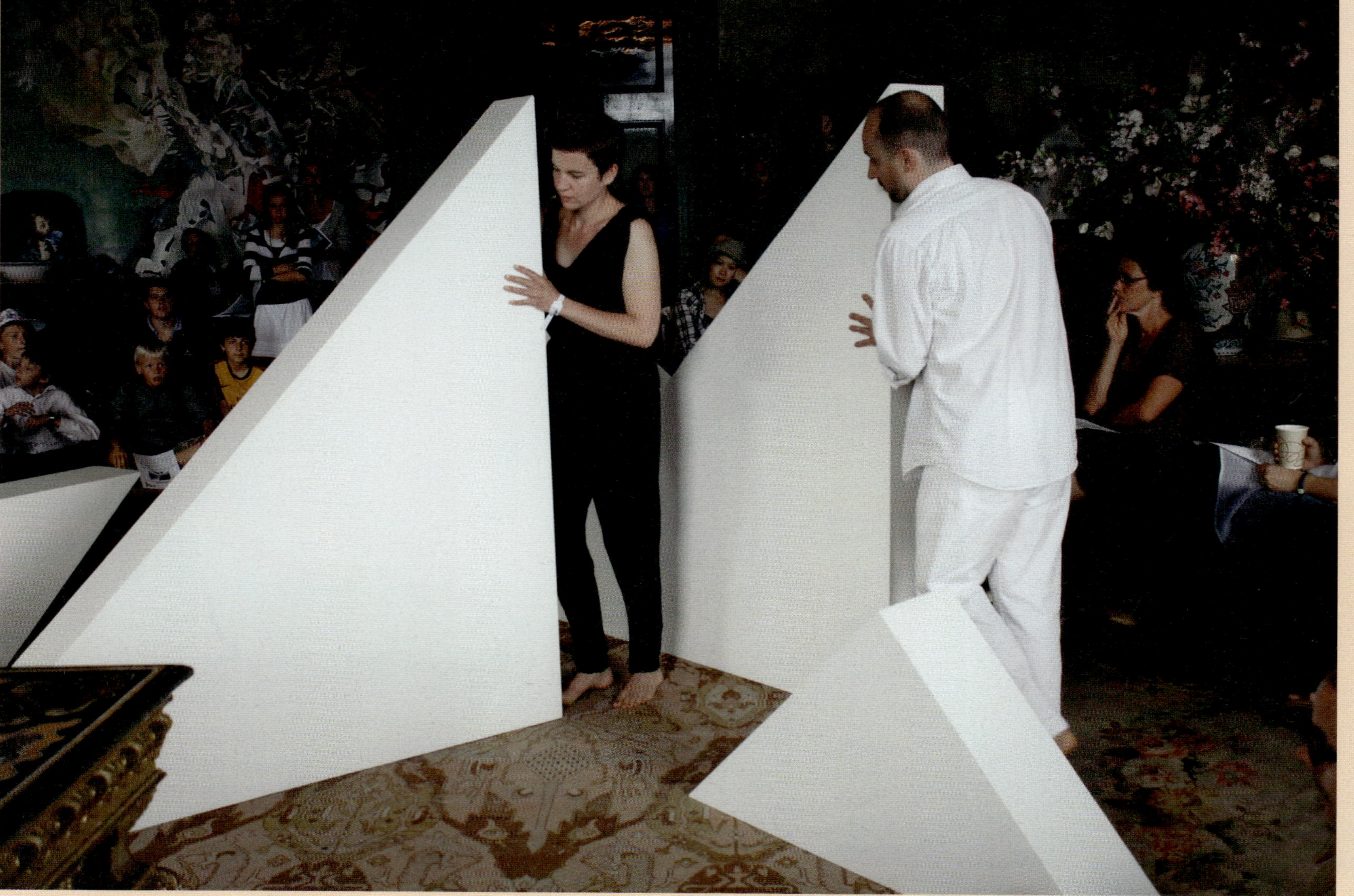

7 (The Round Room), 2009. Performance. 20 min.

A capacity to construct fantastical visions

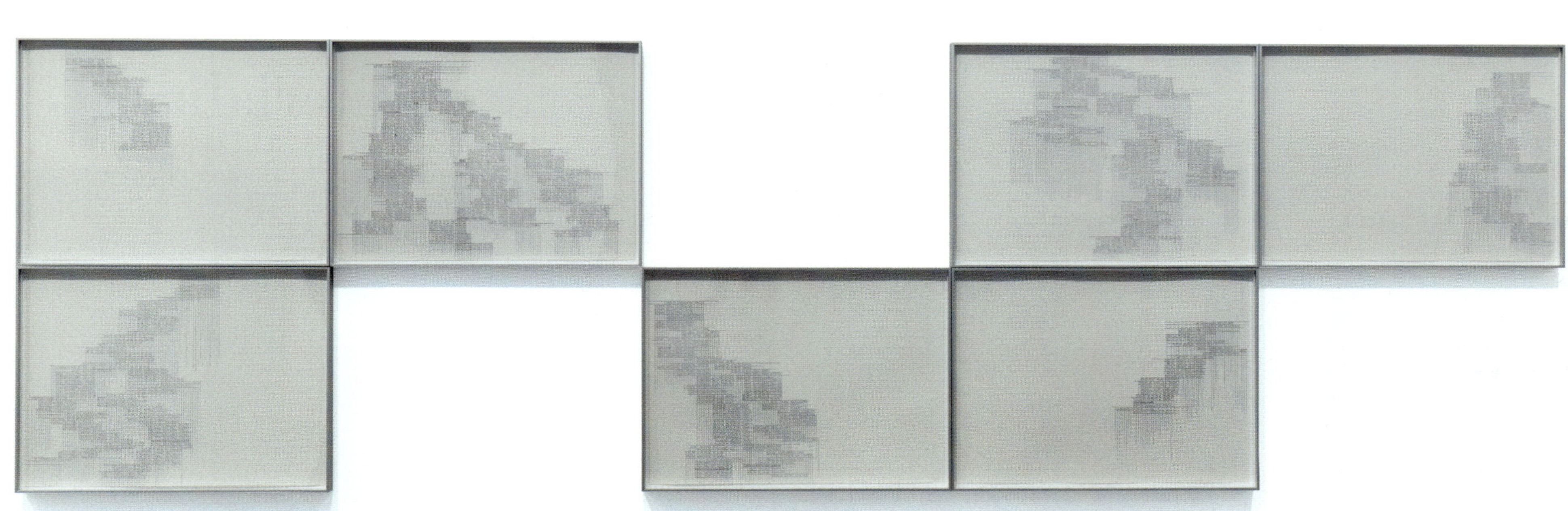

Spied Elegant Arm, 2009. Biro on paper, aluminium frames. 7 parts. Overall 315 × 91 × 4 cm

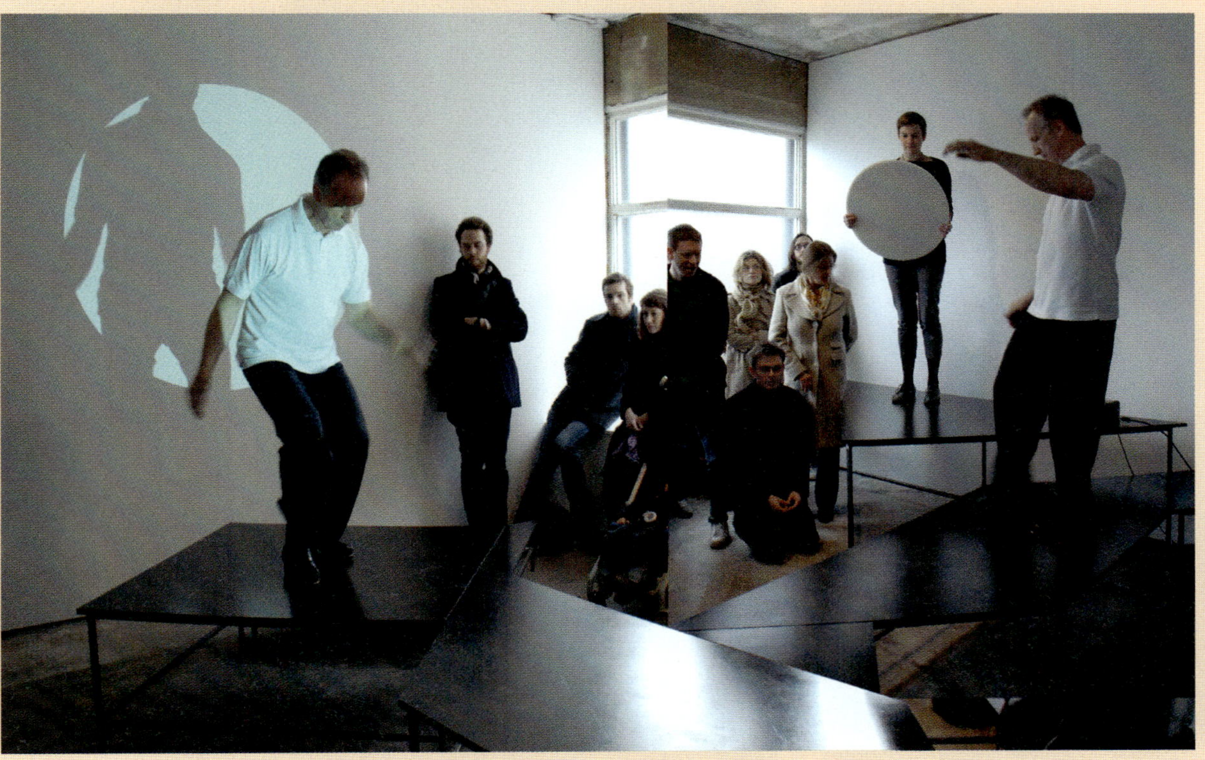

Slick Flection, 2009. Performance with Derek Hartley. 10 min.

Impression of Chance

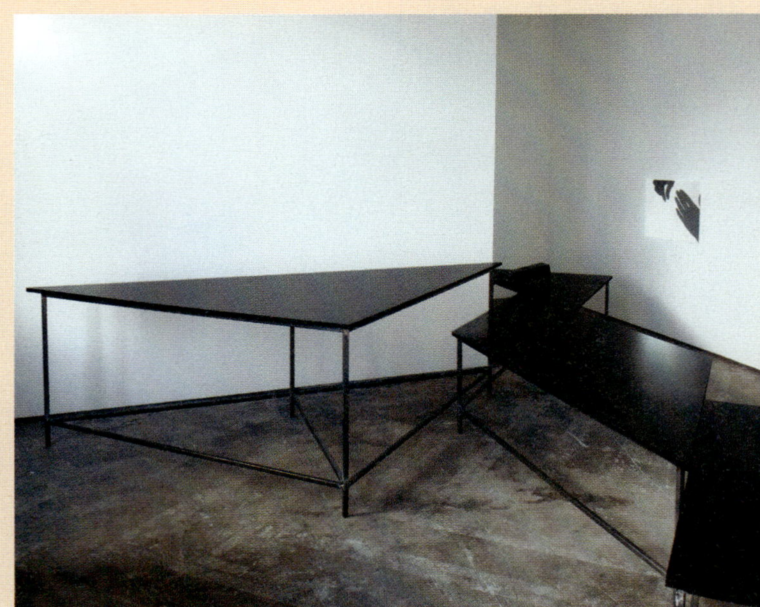

Magenta, Emerald, Lapis, 2009. Mixed-media installation. Dimensions variable

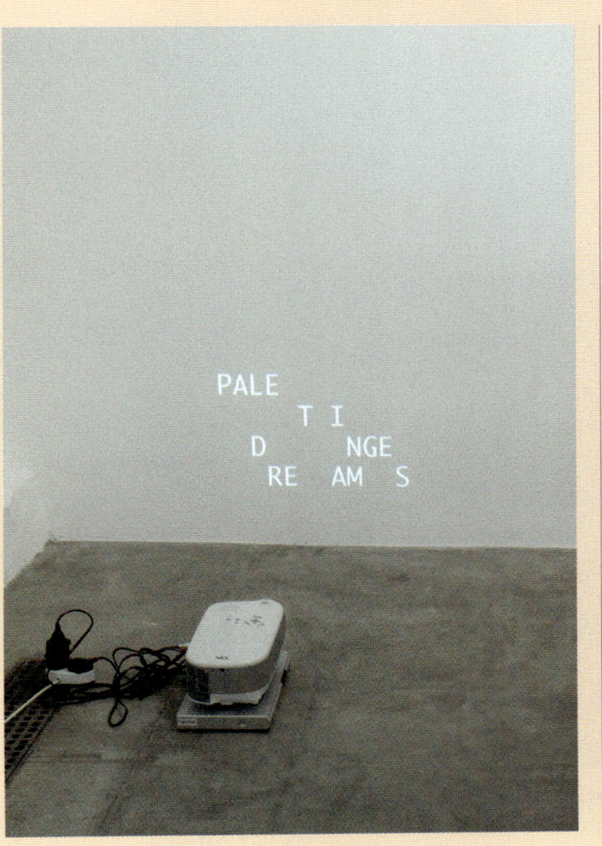

Time Slid Me Again, 2008. Digital projection. 1 minute loop

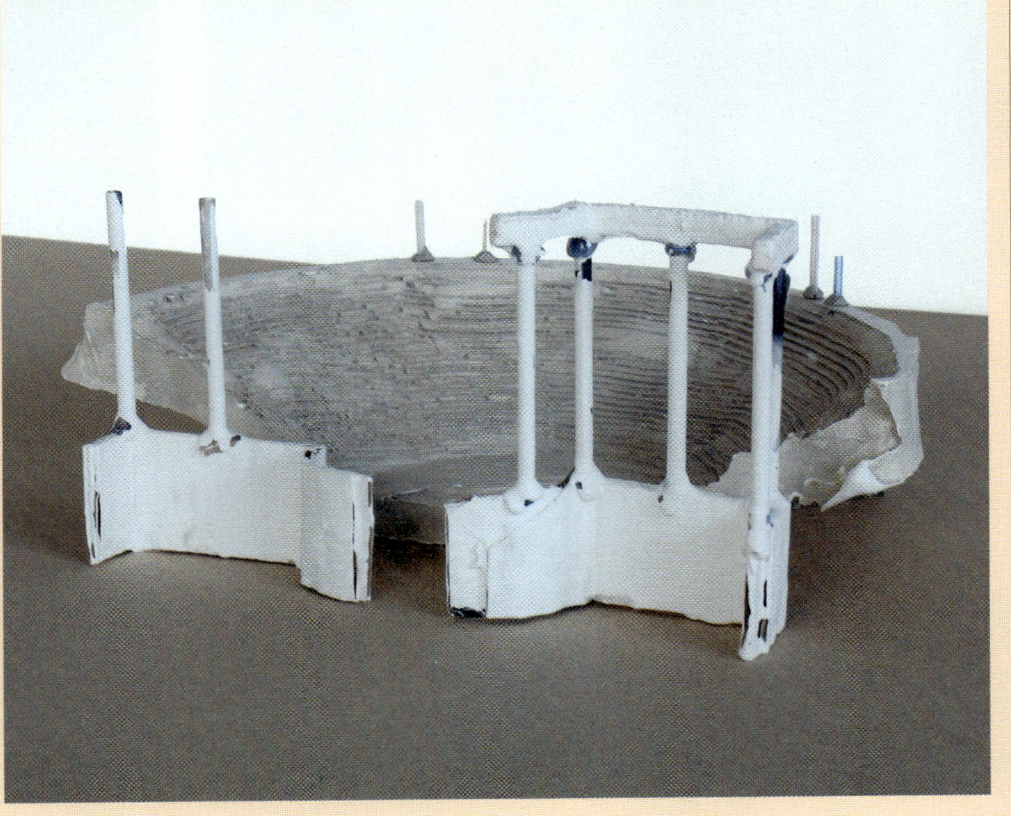

Pliant Games I, 2007. Plaster, clay, cardboard, glue, wood, sellotape, plastic. 40 × 30 × 20 cm

made from tangram shapes, which acted both as sculpture and as seating to view the film *Magenta, Emerald, Lapis*. For the performance, Barham used the construction as a platform, from which she read *Slick Flection*, a text based on tap-dance instructions substituted with other syllables, sometimes making sense and sometimes just creating a rhythm. A projection of a disc of light 'beat' out the original tempo of the instructions as a male tap dancer moved with an insistent but irregular rhythm in and out of the beam of light across the platforms. Typical of Barham's aesthetic investigation, the three systems were choreographed with an impression of chance resonance so that sometimes they were in synch and at other moments obliterated each other.

Walead Beshty

An odd accident sent Los Angeles-based artist Walead Beshty on an exploration of photography's heart of darkness. When returning from a trip abroad, a number of rolls of unexposed film in his luggage were sent through an airport X-ray machine and subsequently damaged. After they were developed, he discovered the chance occurrence of lines and colours that resulted from this unintentional exposure. Once printed, the images (*Travel Pictures*, 2006–07) seemed to represent nothing other than the brute materiality of the photographic process, in which

Brute materiality

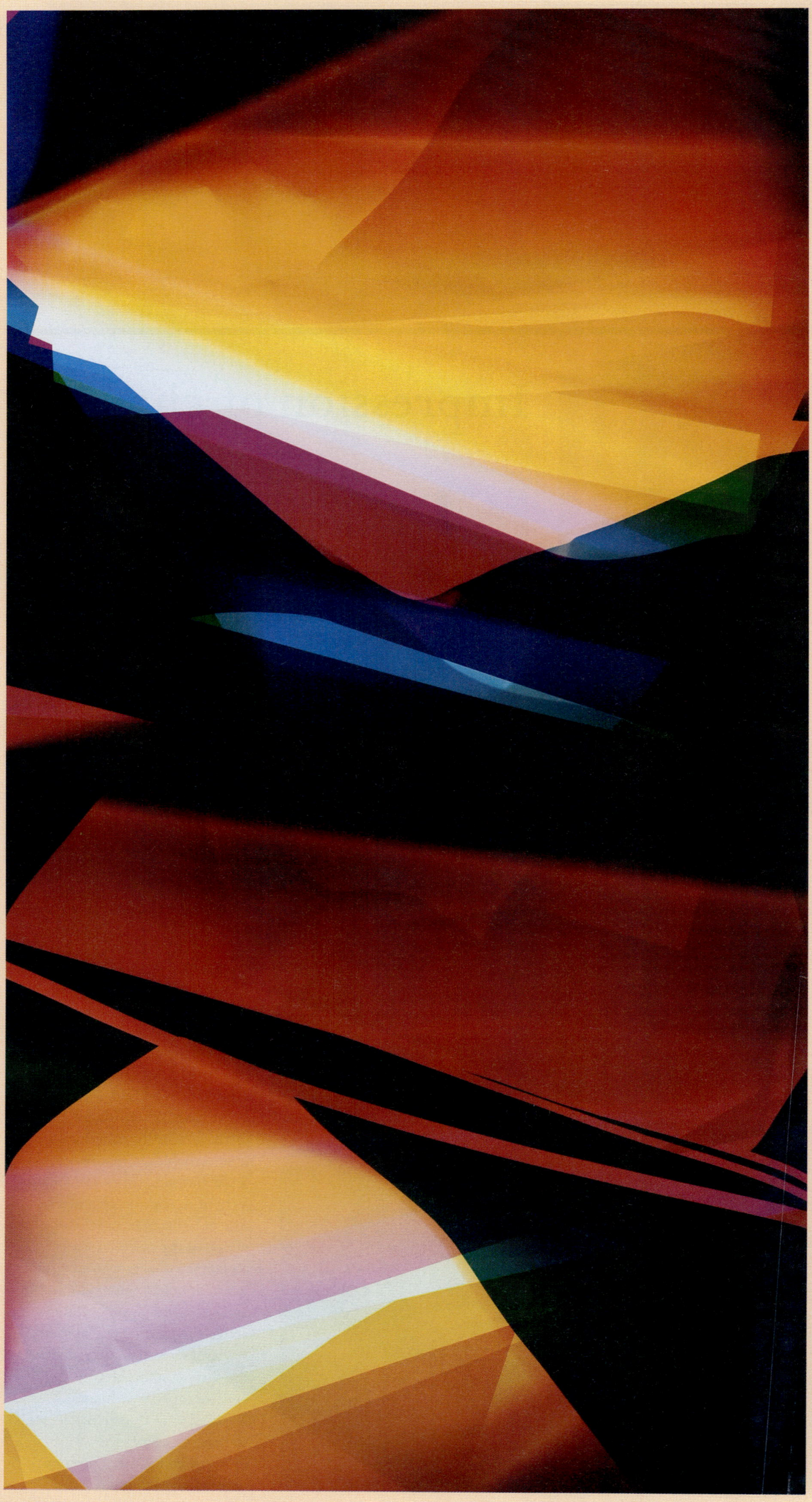

Transparency (Negative) [Kodak NC Color Film: May 8–May 18, 2008 ORD/LHR LHR/IAD IAD/ JFK LGA/DCA DCA/ORD], 2009. Epson Ultrachrome K3 archival ink jet print on Museo Silver Rag paper. 112 × 150 cm

Transparency (Negative) [Kodak NC Color Film: November 4–November 10, 2008 LAX/IAD IAD/BRU BRU/IAD IAD/LAX], 2009. Epson Ultrachrome K3 archival ink jet print on Museo Silver Rag paper. 112 × 150 cm

Six Color Curl (CMMYYC: Irvine, California, July 17th 2008, Fuji Crystal Archive Type C), 2009. Colour photographic paper. 127 × 234 cm

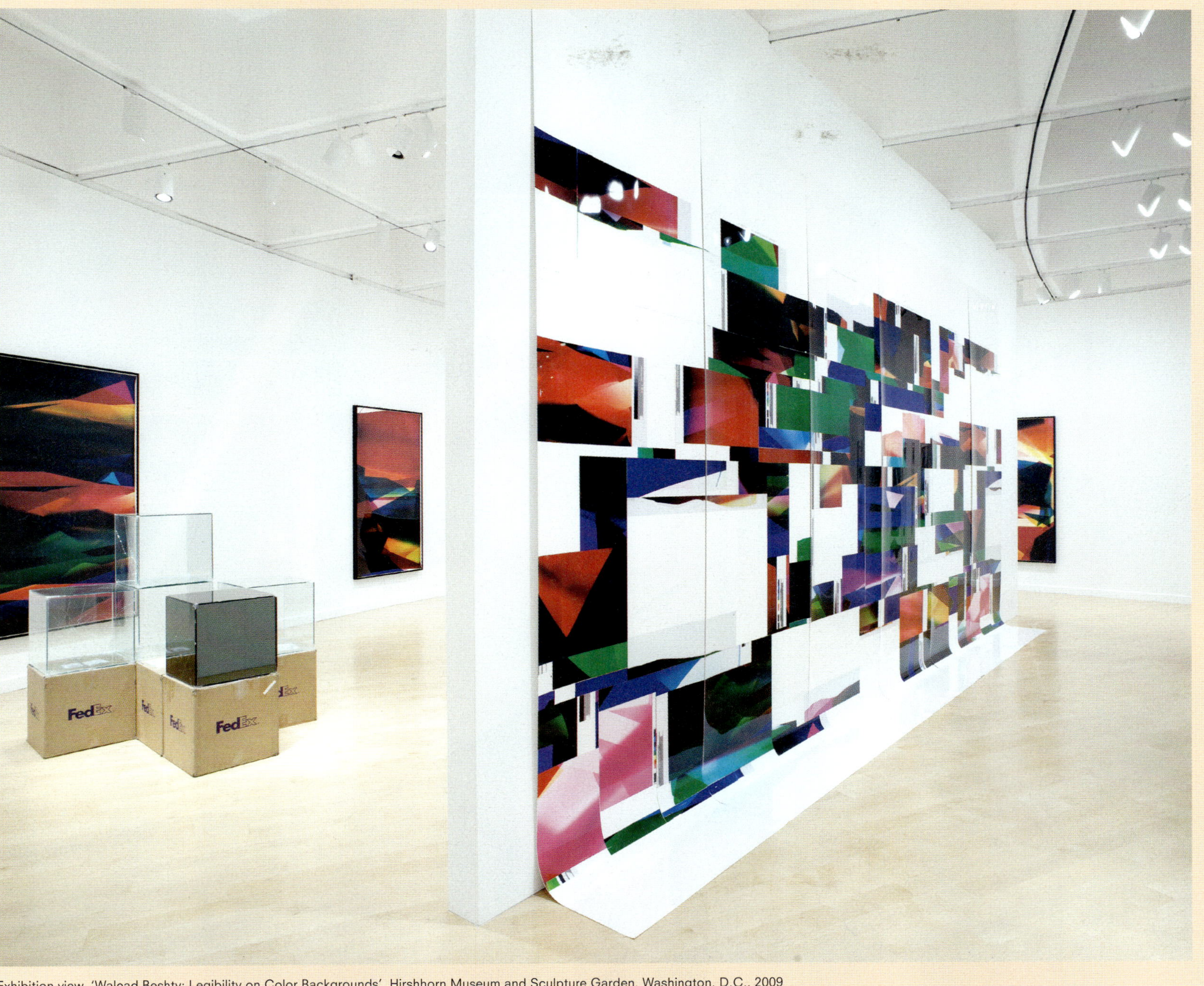

Exhibition view, 'Walead Beshty: Legibility on Color Backgrounds', Hirshhorn Museum and Sculpture Garden, Washington, D.C., 2009

Clockwork-like efficiency

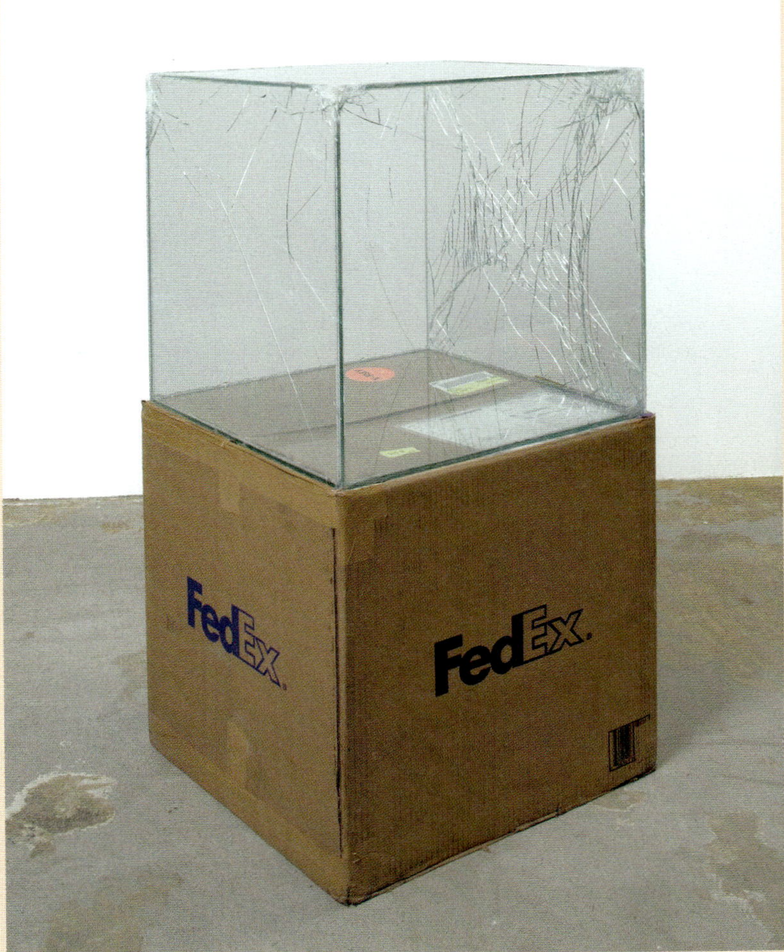

FedEx® Large Kraft Box ©2005 FEDEX 330508, International Priority, Los Angeles–Tijuana
trk# 865282057997 October 28–November 3, 2008, International Priority, Tijuana–Los Angeles
trk# 867279774918 January 2–6, 2009, International Priority, Los Angeles–London
trk# 867279774870 January 14–16, 2009, 2008. FedEx cardboard shipping box, laminated glass, silicone, metal, accrued FedEx shipping and tracking labels. 51 × 51 × 51 cm

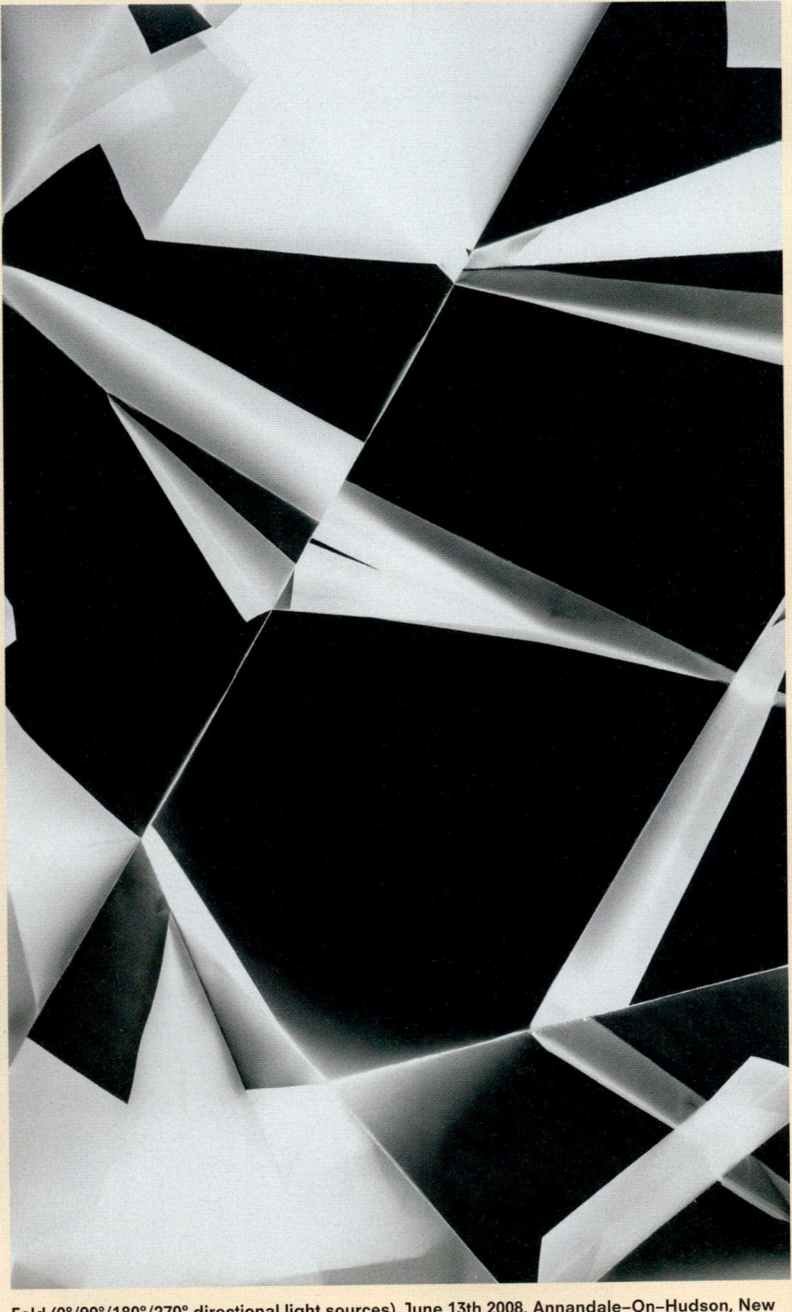

Fold (0°/90°/180°/270° directional light sources), June 13th 2008, Annandale–On–Hudson, New York, Foma Multigrade Fiber, 2008. Black and white fiber based photographic paper. 107 × 176 cm

a chemical emulsion is altered by exposure to a spectrum of radiation. While these aleatory mistakes would seem to be simple chemical traces of the physical world, he quickly realized that they also represented a directly indexical relationship to the social and political world that we inhabit. These were photographs literally inscribed by the security apparatus pervading the post-9/11 netherworld that is the international airport, and so in some sense could be seen as portraits of that system, as well as an embedded memory of the artist's own travels through the world.

A series of Beshty's sculptures further developed his growing fascination with both the idea of 'photographic' indexicality and the strange non-spaces that populate the hyper-connected world that we inhabit. Of particular interest to the artist is the FedEx shipping company, with its clockwork-like post-industrial efficiency in moving objects across national boundaries. Constructing glass vitrines to the exact interior dimensions of standard FedEx shipping boxes, the artist sends these works to their exhibition sites through that now ubiquitous courier system. When unpacked, the glass bears the evidence of its travels through space and time in the form of cracks that record the hidden life of the object on its surface as if they were photographic exposures. These works are not without humour: the FedEx boxes then become the pedestals on which Beshty's Larry Bell-like glass cubes are exhibited in the gallery. The individual titles of the works record the journey taken by the boxes in all their official corporate glory, including the locations, dates and tracking number. In a related series of works, Beshty installs mirrored glass on the floor of the gallery, which similarly cracks as visitors walk across its surface, giving the space itself a patina that develops through multiple uses.

Beshty eschews the suggestion that his photographic works are abstract, insisting instead on their material inscription of the structural conditions and possibilities of the medium. His colour photograms constructed in the darkroom, for example, are akin to language games played with a self-imposed set of rules, having to do with folds or curls in the paper and differing lengths of exposure to light in both the black-and-white and four-colour systems of printing (cyan, magenta, yellow and key black). In the end, whether he is working with the political rules of international travel and shipping or the chemical and physical limits of photography itself, Besthy makes a direct appeal to the viewer to see their interconnected nature as both micro and macro indexical markers of the complicated world that we inhabit.

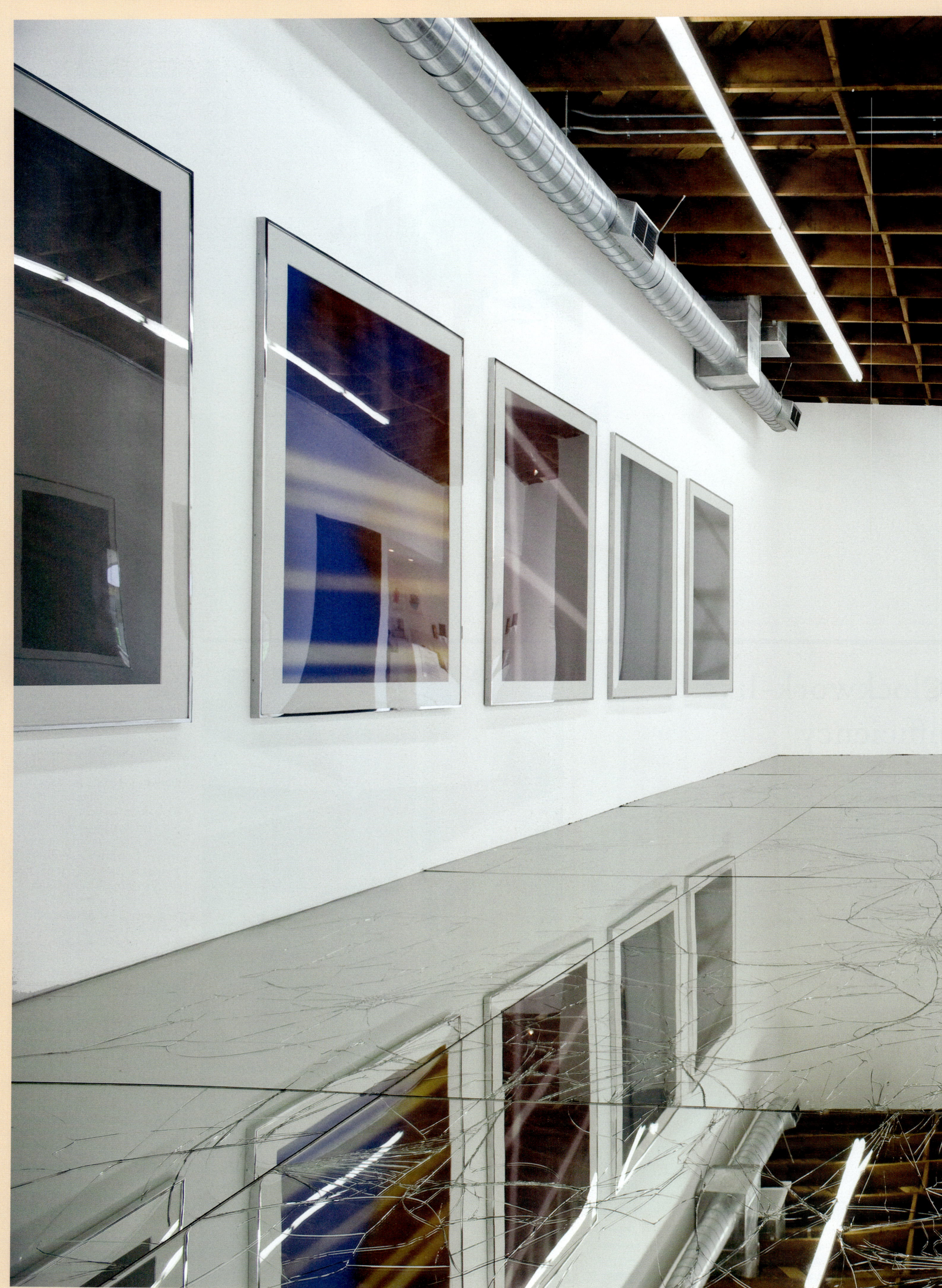

Passages, 2009. Installation view, LA><ART, Los Angeles

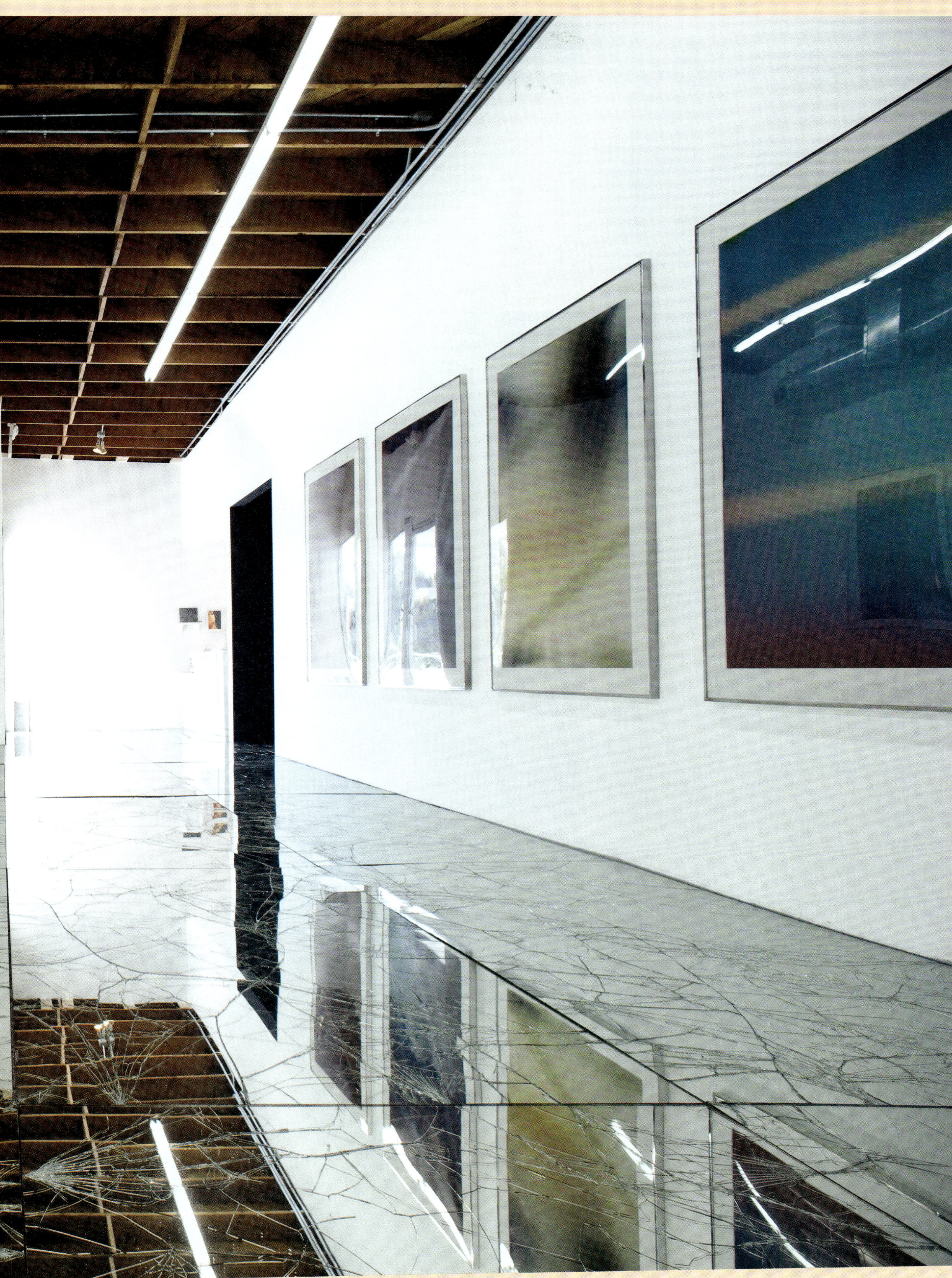

Cezary Bodzianowski

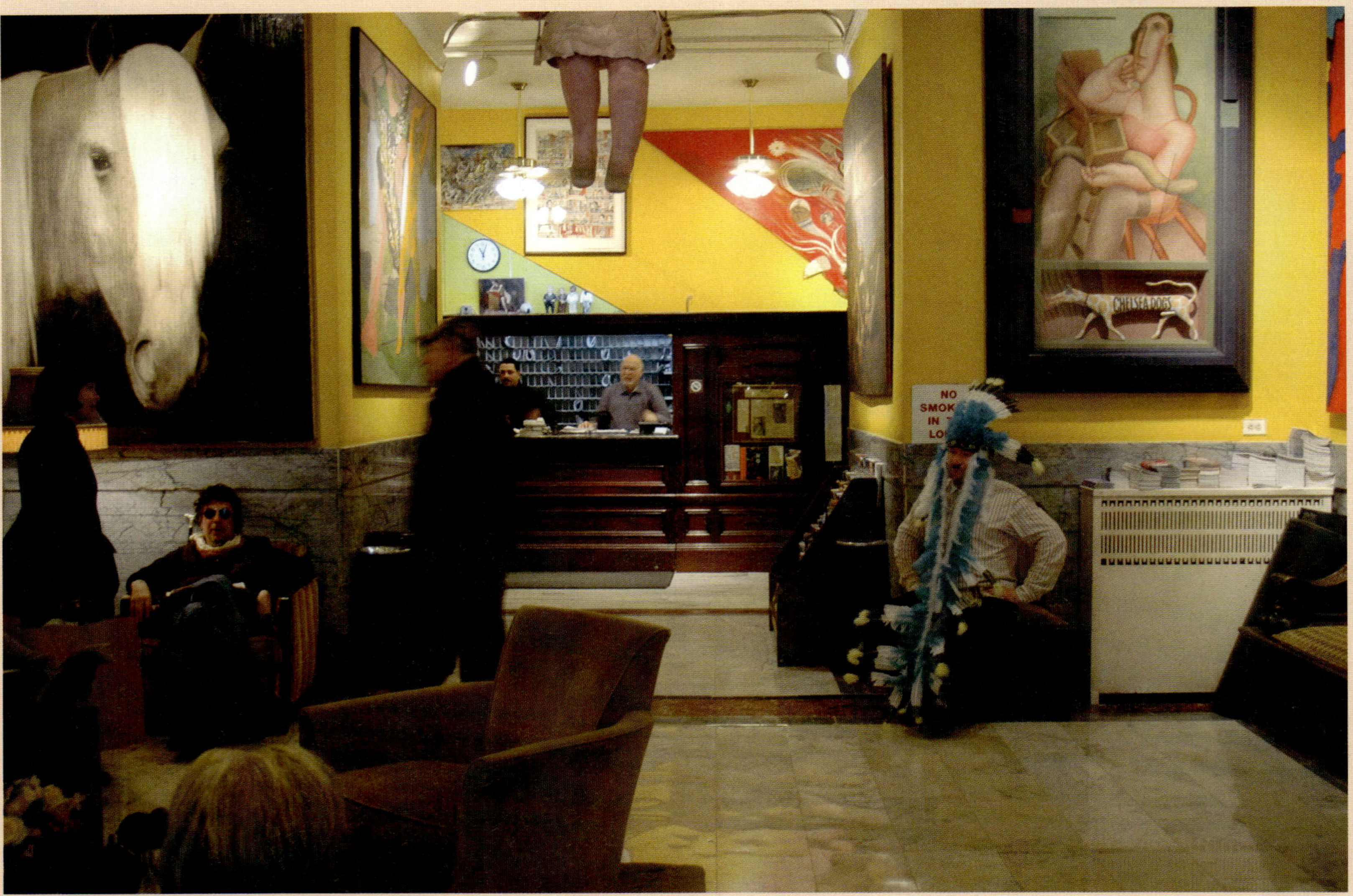

Chelsea, 2006. Performance

Small acts

Cezary Bodzianowski treats the urban environment as a site for his poetic, absurdist performance interventions, akin to Jacques Tati's cityscape in the 1967 film *Playtime*.

But while Tati designed and constructed the elaborate environment for his actors to play in, Bodzianowski wittily 'detourns' existing situations or spaces. Founded upon the freedom offered by the 'think crazy' philosophy of his teacher at the Warsaw academy, Marek Konieczny, and invoking the popular figures of Buster Keaton and Charlie Chaplin, Bodzianowski's work focuses attention on features of the city and its habits that might ordinarily be taken for granted. In collaboration with his wife, Monika Chojnicka, video documentation captures these small acts.

As a part of a piece entitled *4 × Paris* (2004), for example,

Bodzianowski's work focuses attention on features of the city and its habits that might ordinarily be taken for granted

Bodzianowski asked tourists in the French capital to take his photograph in front of the Eiffel tower using what was in fact a toy camera. His piece framed the typical behaviour of the tourist as both poignant and pathetic, since, unbeknown to the people who obliged him, what was being recorded was not a moment in the artist's holiday, but— at a humorous meta-level—the norms of their own behaviour.

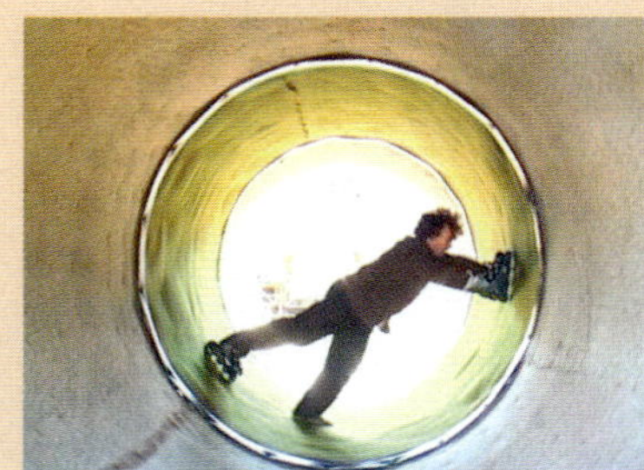

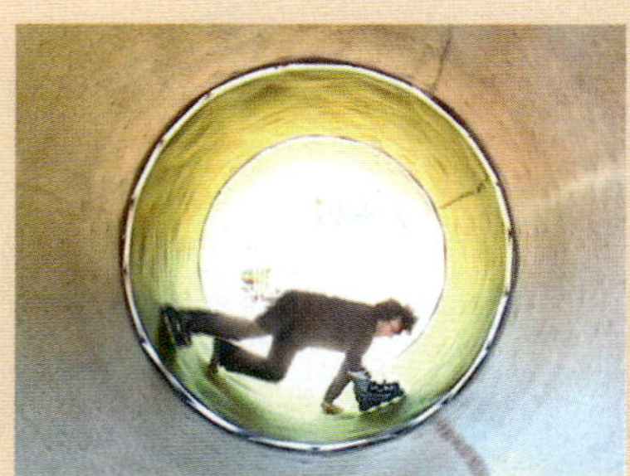

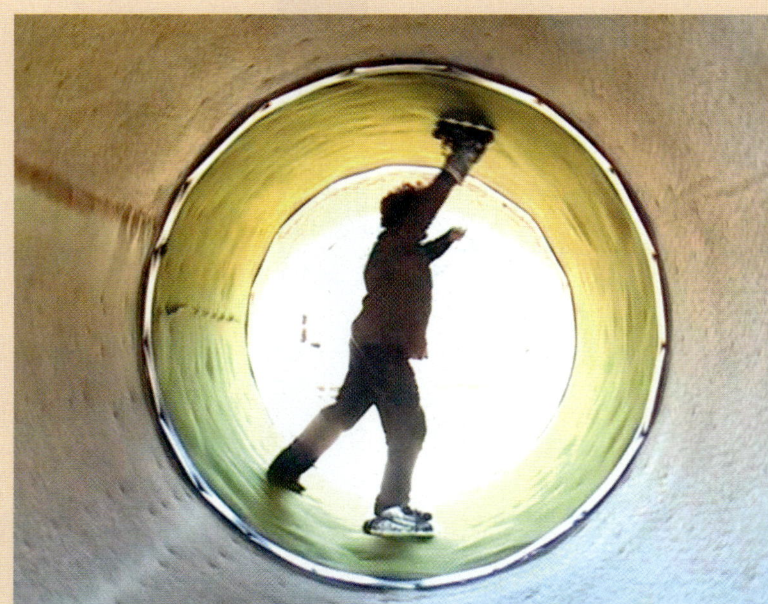

Tourist behaviour

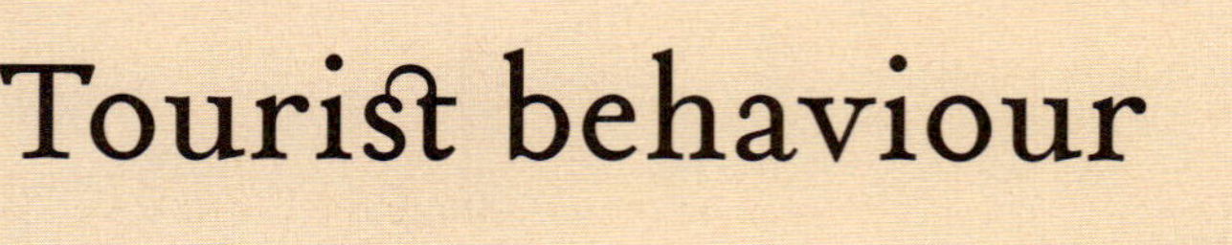

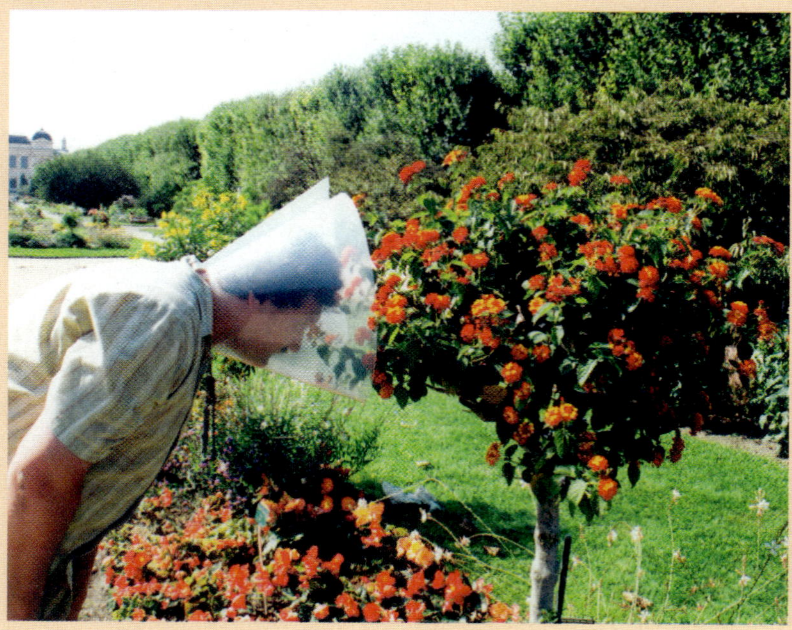

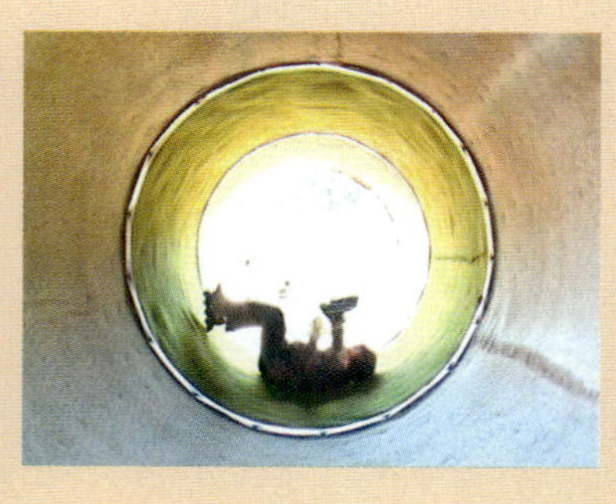

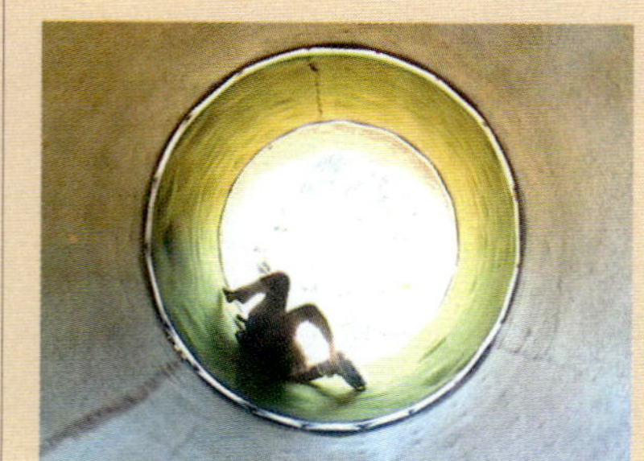

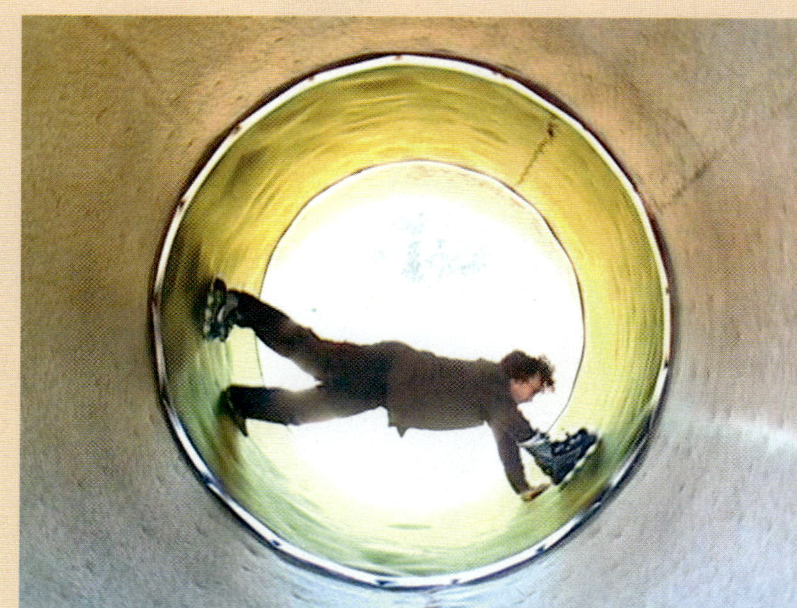

4 × Paris, 2004. Performance

Luna, 2005. DVD. 4 min. 56 sec.

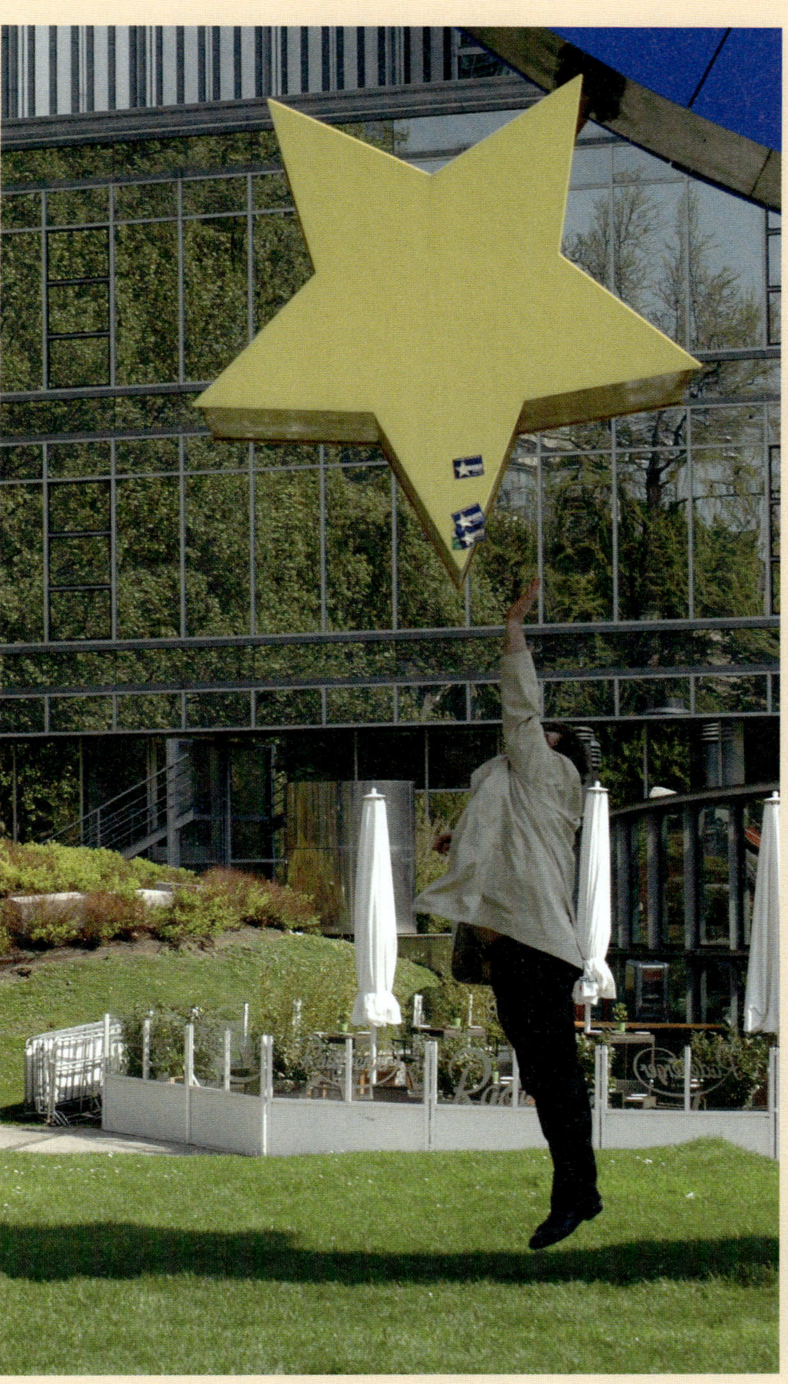

West Point, 2009. Performance

In *Good Morning* (1997), Bodzianowski was lifted up in a crane to the ordinarily inaccessible windows in a high-rise tower block of order to wish the surprised residents good morning. When the exhibition 'From Monet to Gauguin' was showing at the National Museum in Krakow in 2001, there was a huge queue for tickets. Bodzianowski took his place at the end of the line, patiently waiting until he came close to the box-office. He would then ask a person from the end of the queue to take his place, repeating the action many times (*1001 Oddments, 2001*). In *Luna* (2005), Bodzianowski ran like a hamster in a wheel inside a rotating drum while wearing a pair of roller-skates — one on his hand and one on his foot. This action conflated what resembled a bizarre form of exercise at the gym with the myth of Sisyphean endeavour. In Stuntman (2007), the artist climbed on to the top of a building, where there was a vintage neon-tube image of two champagne glasses, formerly advertising

Poetic, absurdist performance

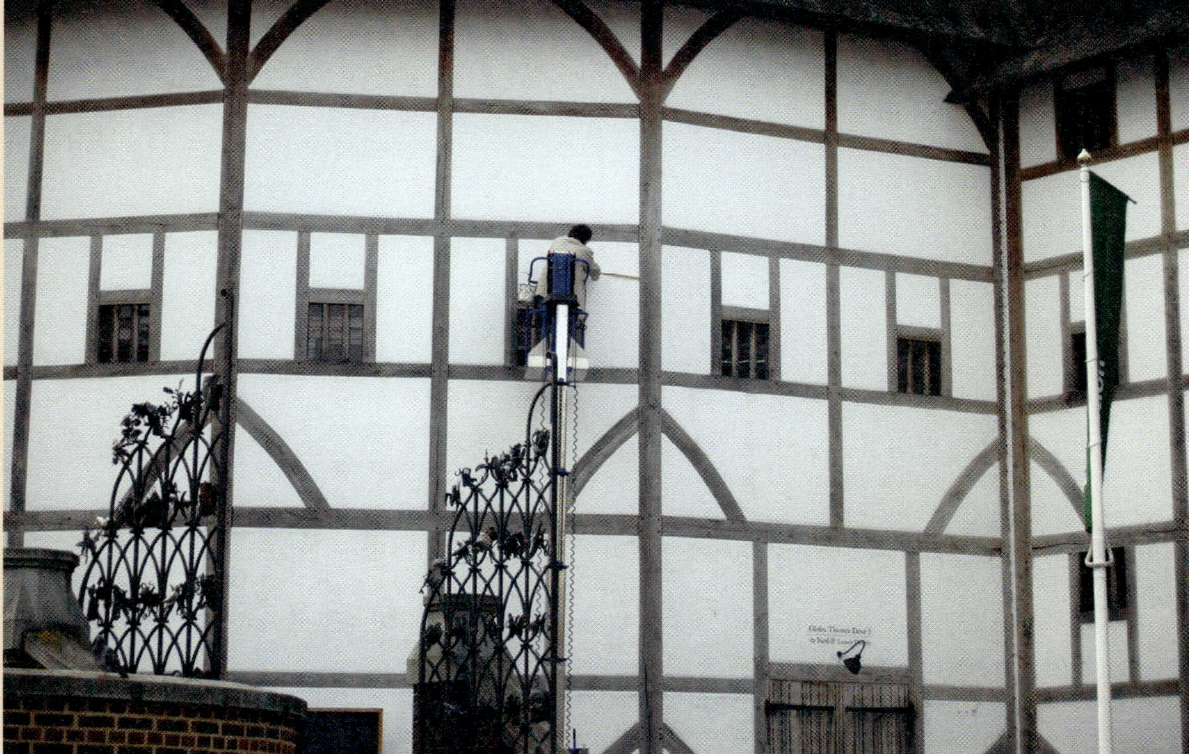

Flying helmet, 2009. Performance

Overlooked features of our daily environment

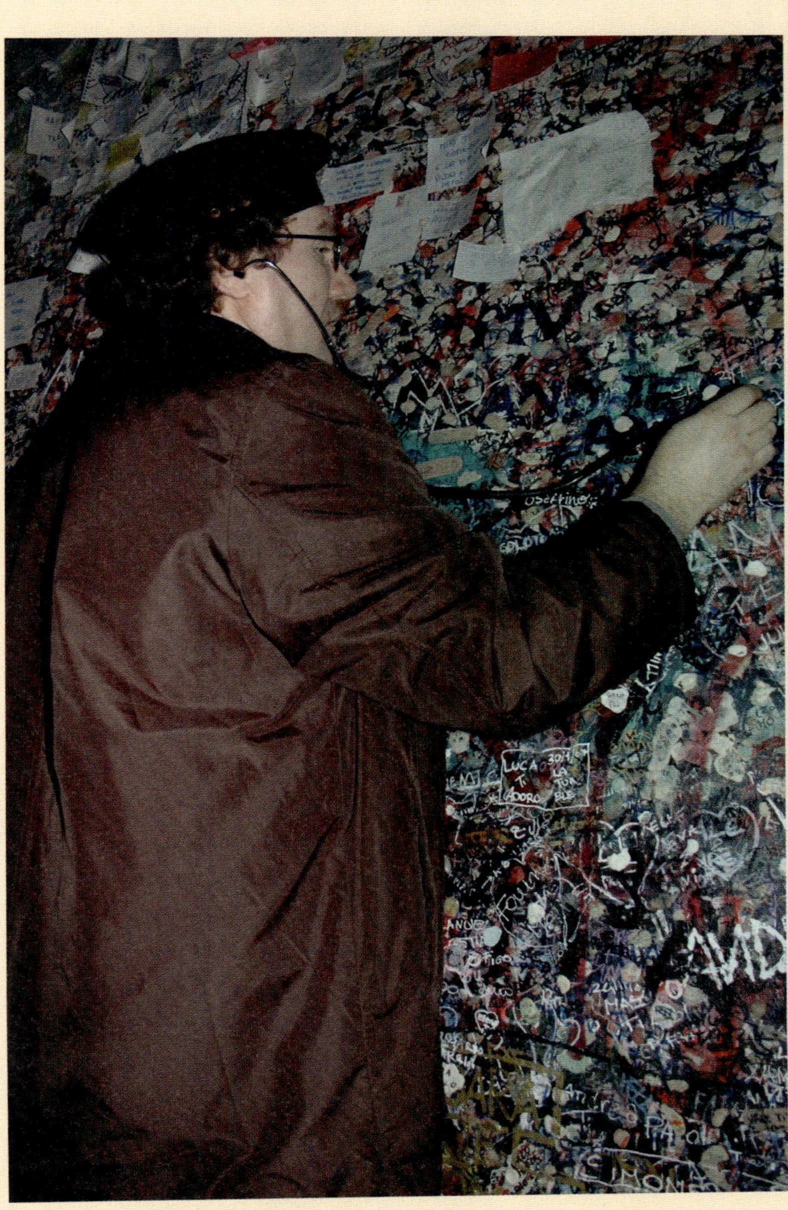

Giulietta project, 2007. Performance

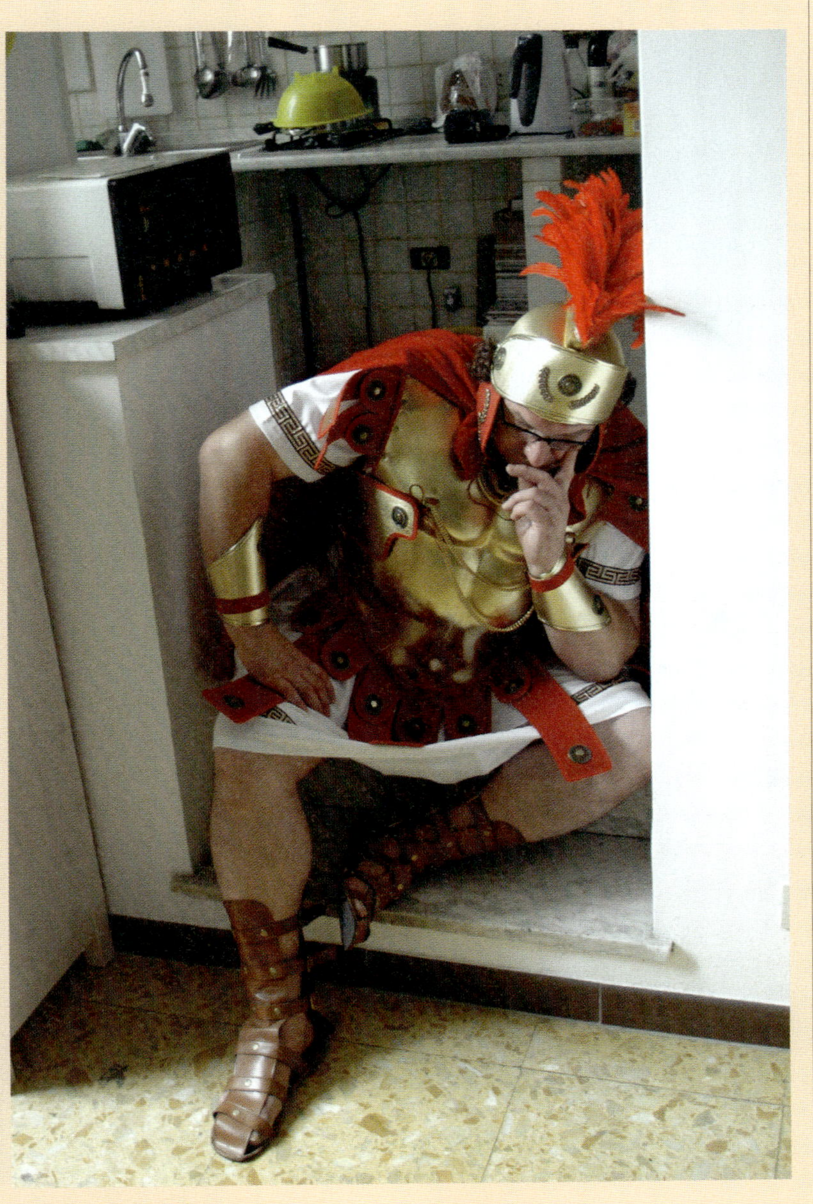

After hours, 2009. Performance

a nightclub. He had taken with him a white hula hoop, which — standing next to the neon sign (now unlit) — he proceeded to throw into the air. The action had the effect of animating the circular rings of neon that stood for bubbles in the representation of the glass, temporarily bringing the sign back to life.

For the project *15:00*, staged by the Cologne Kunstverein in May 2007, Bodzianowski invited his audience to meet at a specified point in the city at 3 pm and to walk to find him in the street. A small crowd gathered around the point at which he was positioned. The artist stood at the side of the road as though about to cross it, but remained completely still. After a while, he began to gaze at the stopped clock on the building opposite — a rudimentary digital one on an obsolete advertising hoarding for a defunct electronics firm. Like Bodzianowski, it did not move forward from 3 pm. Both were temporarily petrified in an extended moment of immobility: in time, and yet outside of it. In this simple act, as with his other actions, Bodzianowski conjured an incongruous yet pathos-filled image that drew attention to the overlooked features of our daily environment through the most economical of means.

Pablo Bronstein

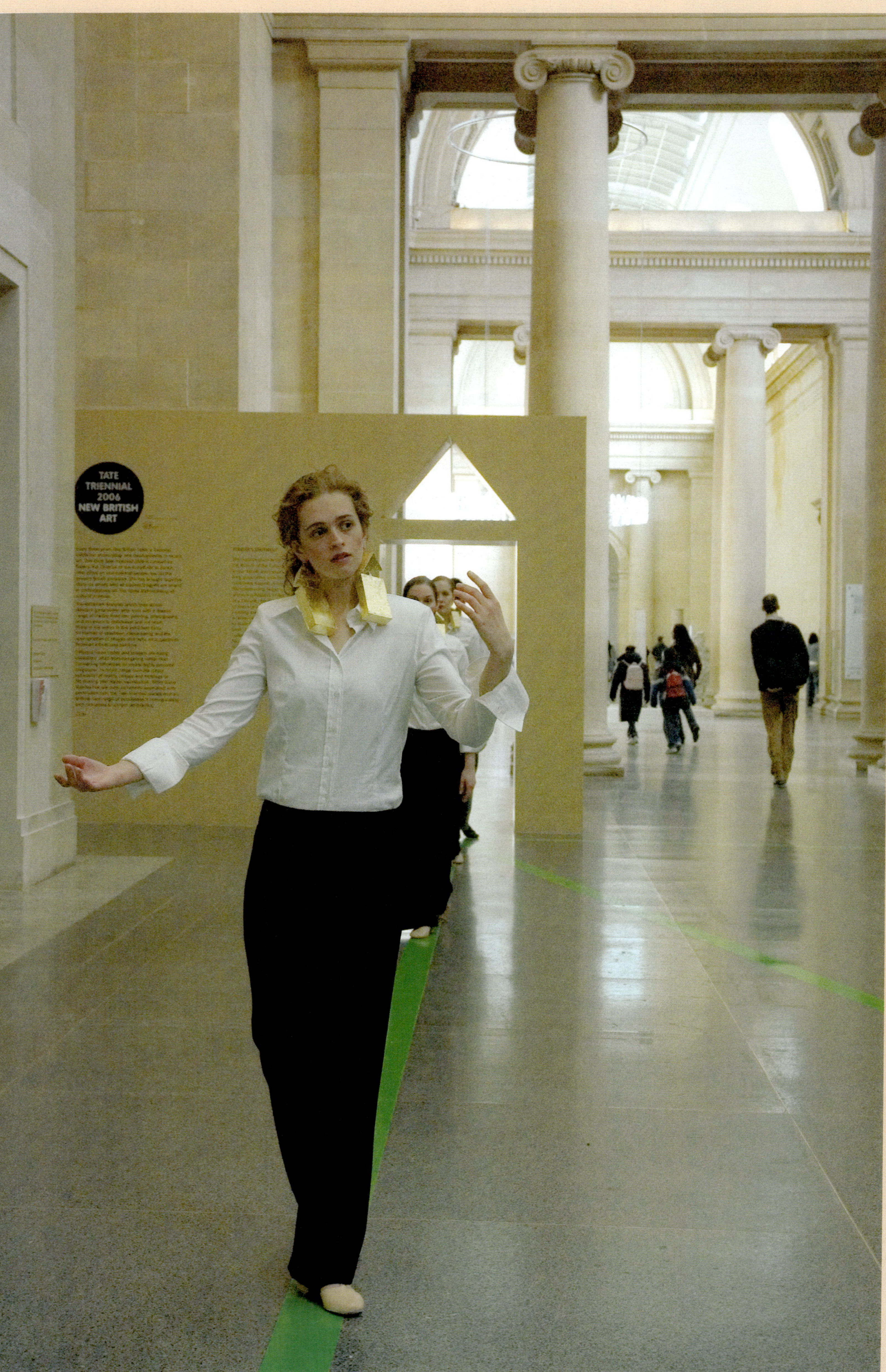

Plaza Minuet, 2006. Installation and performance. Tate Triennial, Tate Britain, London

Pablo Bronstein's practice is rooted in drawing. He focuses on historic architectural subjects and settings ranging from the Baroque era to postmodernism. The drawings are often presented in ways that simulate a kind of period authenticity: they appear in ornate frames that are either antiques or deliberately aged by the artist, which confuses our perception of when they were made. This aspect of masquerade — of 'passing' for

Bronstein focuses on historic architectural subjects and settings ranging from the Baroque to postmodernism

something that they are not — is key to Bronstein's broader project, and relates to his ongoing engagement with dance and theatre. Mediated via the artificial space of the gallery, his practice investigates relations between drawing's capacity for conjuring illusion and the way in which we encounter architecture in everyday life.

In Plaza Minuet, first created for the Tate Triennial 2006 and re-worked for New York's 2007 Performa festival in a sequence of corporate lobbies, Bronstein taped to the floor the 'void' motif that is used in architectural drawings to denote a blank space, creating a temporary stage upon which everyday activity might be disrupted by performance. Upon this marked-out space, he choreographed a group of dancers (at Tate Britain, Baroque dance enthusiasts; in New York, ballet dancers) to perform a succession of tableaux that resembled an ever-changing sequence of architectural 'follies'. Bronstein's 'stage' was deliberately not elevated away from the to-and-fro of pedestrian activity in each space, but formed an emblematic perversion of that activity in movement sequences that were flagrantly aesthetic.

Bronstein's work in recent years has taken on an increasingly political character. As part of Frieze Projects in 2006, he conducted an architectural tour of London that looked at the economic and social interests driving architectural style during the Thatcher years, including buildings by architects such as James Stirling, Leon Krier and Terry Farrell. Bronstein's interest in this architecture is partly to do with its negation, via a sense of humour and fantasy,

Ongoing engagement with dance and theatre

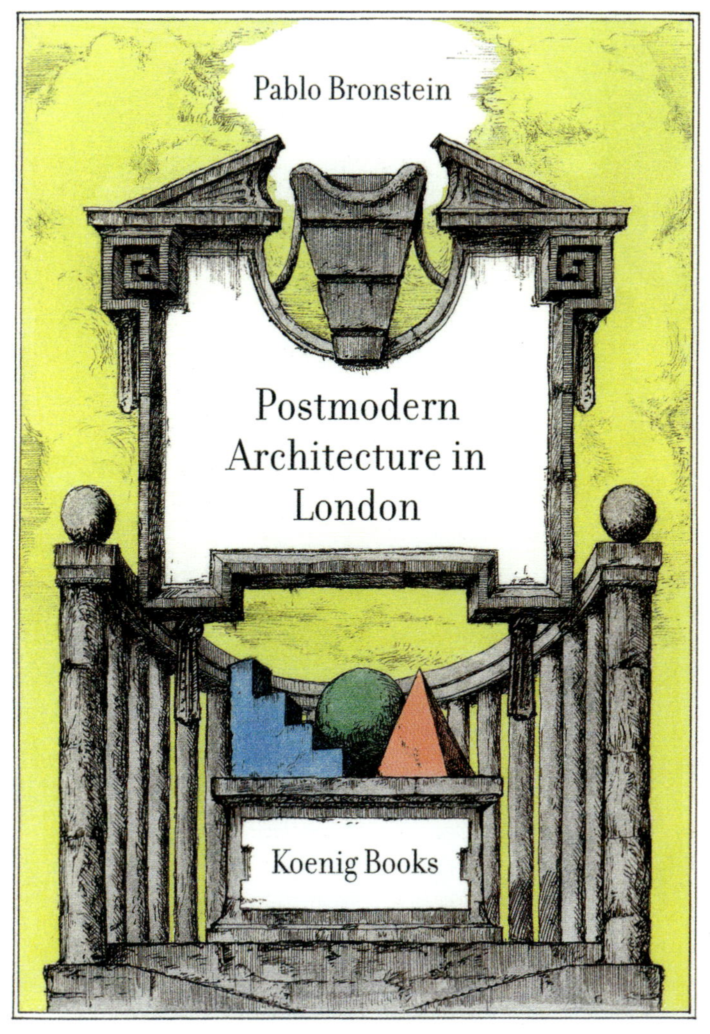

Postmodern Architecture in London, 2007. Book. 88 pages. Walther König, Cologne

Drawing's capacity for conjuring illusion

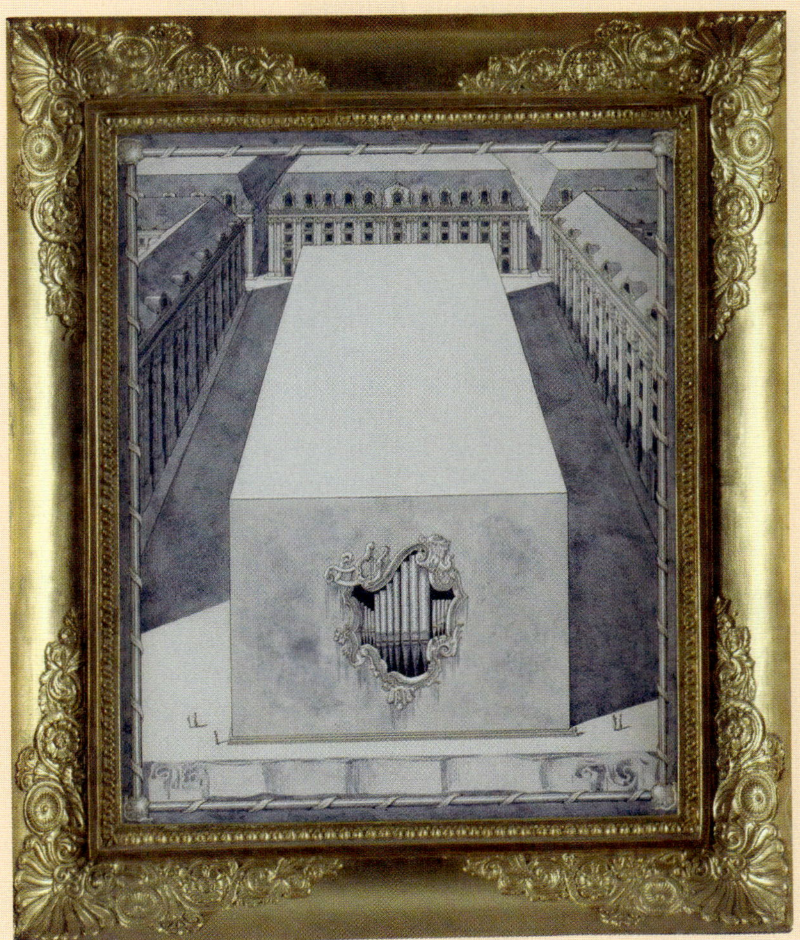

City Monument with Organ Motif, 2006. Ink and gouache on paper in artist's frame. 52 × 46 cm

Performative immersion

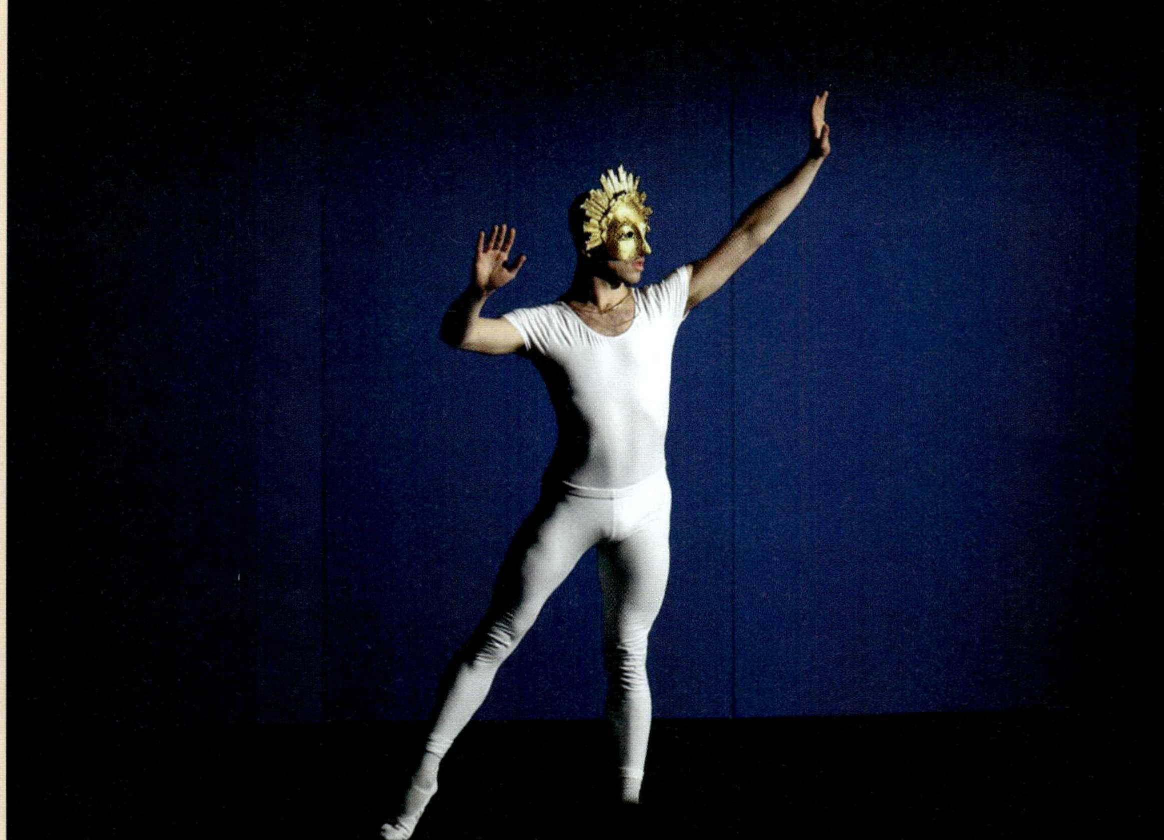

Intermezzo, 2009. Performance. Dancer: Adam Linderman

Between architecture, gesture, gender and subjectivity

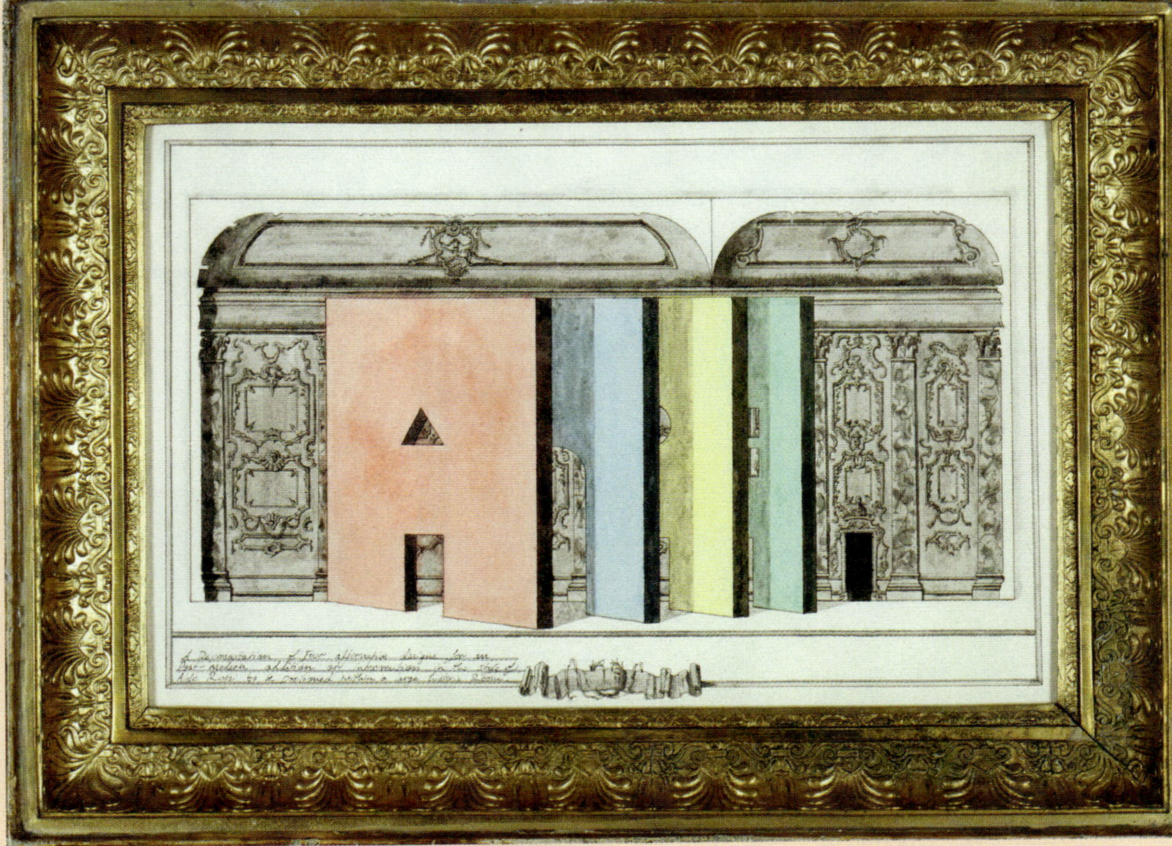

Four Alternate Postmodern Interventions within an Historic Room, 2007. India ink and wash on paper in artist's frame. 46 × 64 cm

of modernist claims of 'truth to materials', but he also considered the way in which spaces such as Paternoster Square mask corporate ownership by performing the language of the historic public square. In 2009, he presented a lecture-performance work at Tate Modern titled *Intermezzo*. He began in the style of an art-historian giving a slide lecture on the work of the sixteenth-century painter Antoine Caron, but as the lecture progressed, Bronstein's narrative about the courtly ceremonial of King Charles ix, depicted in the paintings, was mirrored by a live sequence performed by Bronstein and a professional dancer (Adam Linderman). Wearing gold masks and unitards, they recreated passages from the dances described. In this way, Bronstein effected a transition from what appeared to be a straight lecture to a demonstration of his own performative immersion in his subject. The desire of Charles ix to perform for, and be praised by, his court was echoed in the artist's own exposure of his dancing body, and his potential vulnerability. The lecture also focused on the coded queerness of the king's adopted gestures and how they influenced the evolving language of court etiquette or *sprezzatura*; drawing a line between architecture, gesture, gender and subjectivity.

Tom Burr

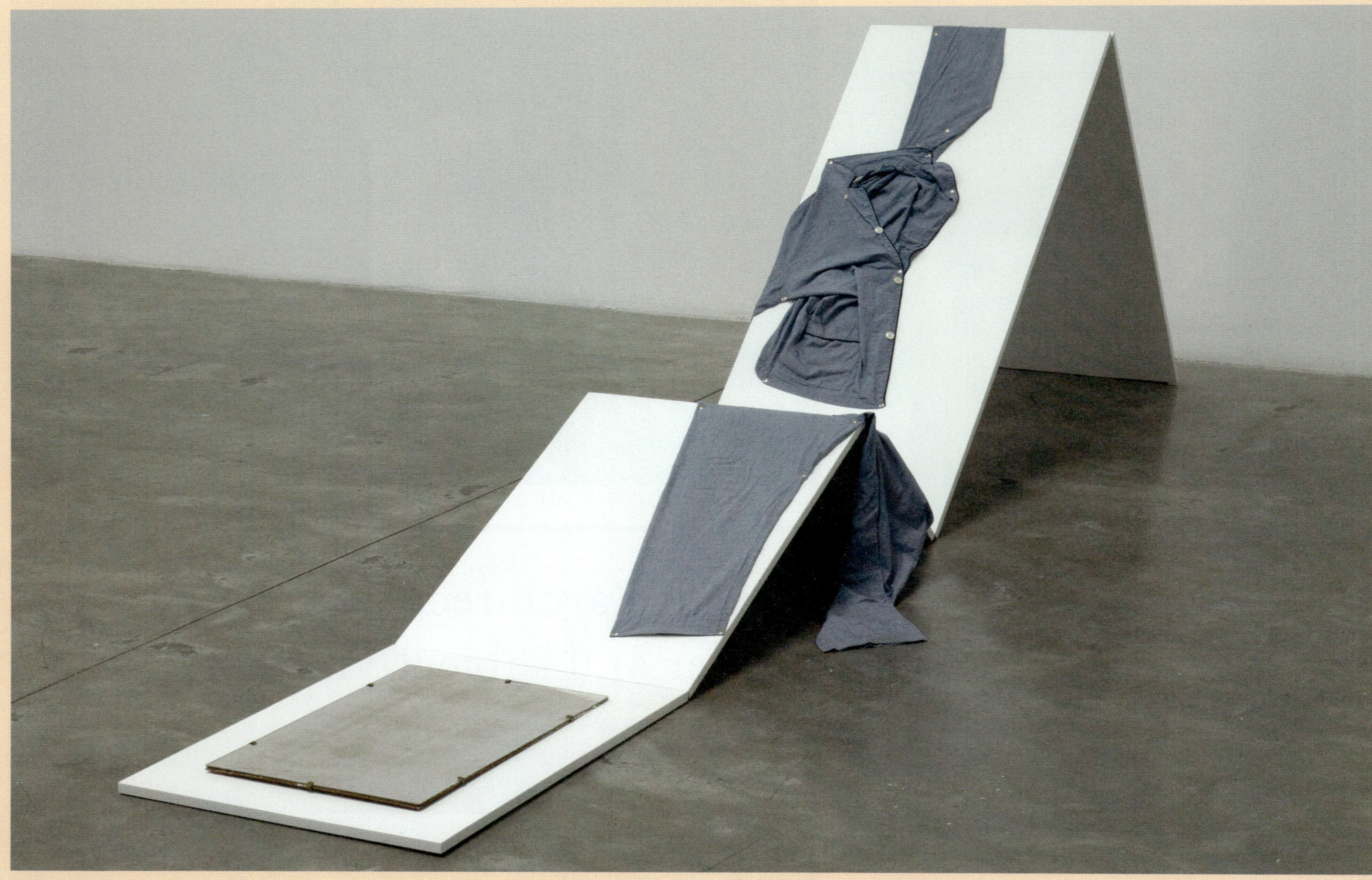

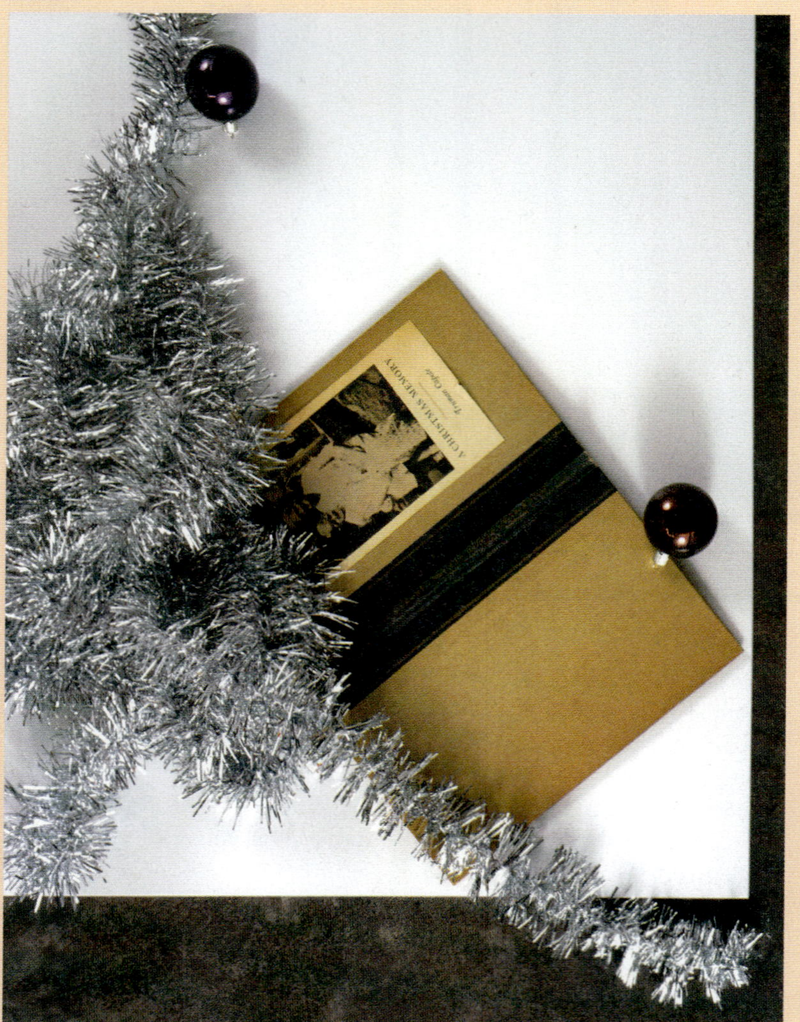

Slumbering object of my sleepless attention, 2009. Wood, white paint, men's pyjamas, antique mirror, push pins. 99 × 61 × 351 cm

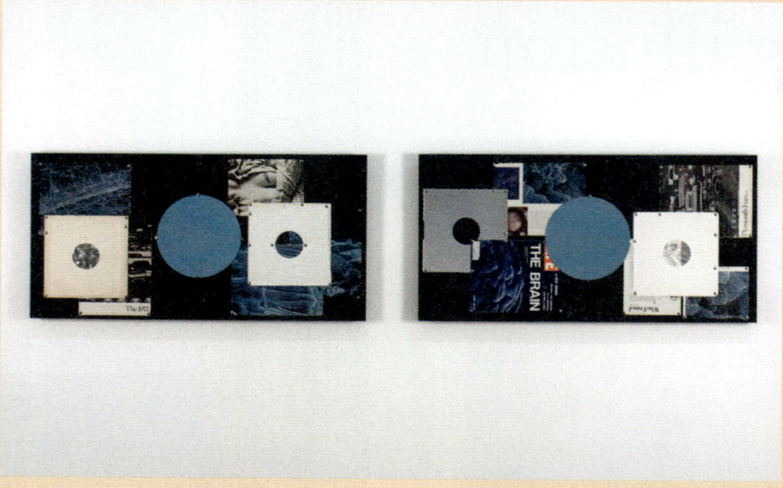

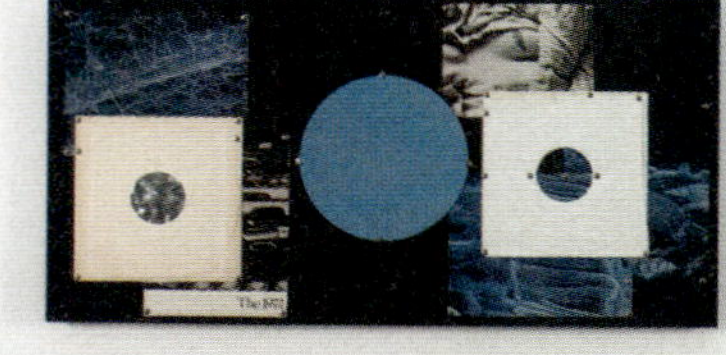

Brain Board, 2008. Stained wood, magazine pages, book pages, thumb tacks, blue mirrored Plexiglas, record sleeves. 61 × 122 × 2 cm

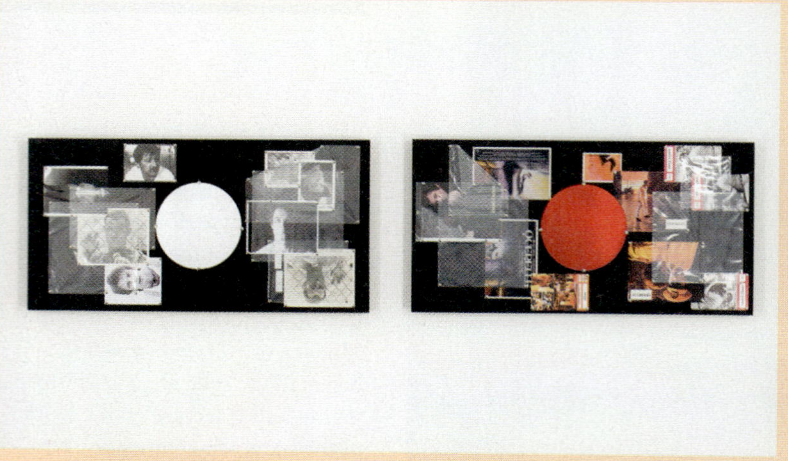

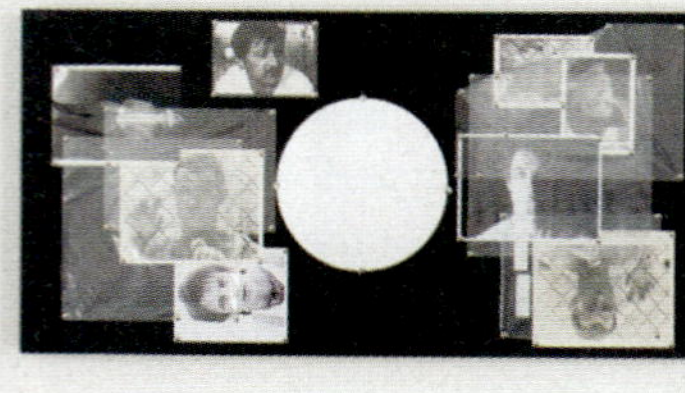

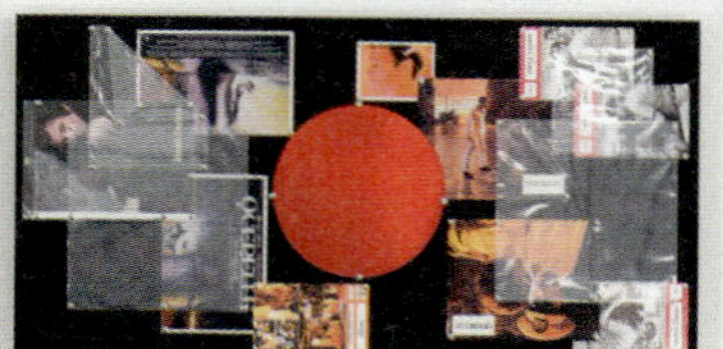

Bad Brad Board 3, 2009. Stained wood, magazine pages, book pages, record, transparent plastic record sleeves, thumb tacks, mirrored Plexiglas. 61 × 122 cm

Tom Burr's finely honed investigations into the fields of sculpture, installation and collage combine built structures that echo Minimalist and post-Minimalist forms through a teasingly mischievous assortment of carefully arranged found elements. Together they evoke open-ended narratives about the elusive flux of memories and identities.

Although much of Burr's early work dealt with how specific tropes in architecture and public space can delimit behavior — most specifically in reference to gay culture and sexuality — his more recent investigations have shifted emphasis and reveal a more personalized aesthetic comprised of ambiguous scenarios within the realm of fictionalized biography. Experimenting with an almost theatrical idea of staging scenes through his sculptures, Burr has described these works as 'captured moments'.

References to particular moments in time circulate in the works, relating to his fascination with twentieth-century culture, from music and art to design and fashion and intermixed with nods

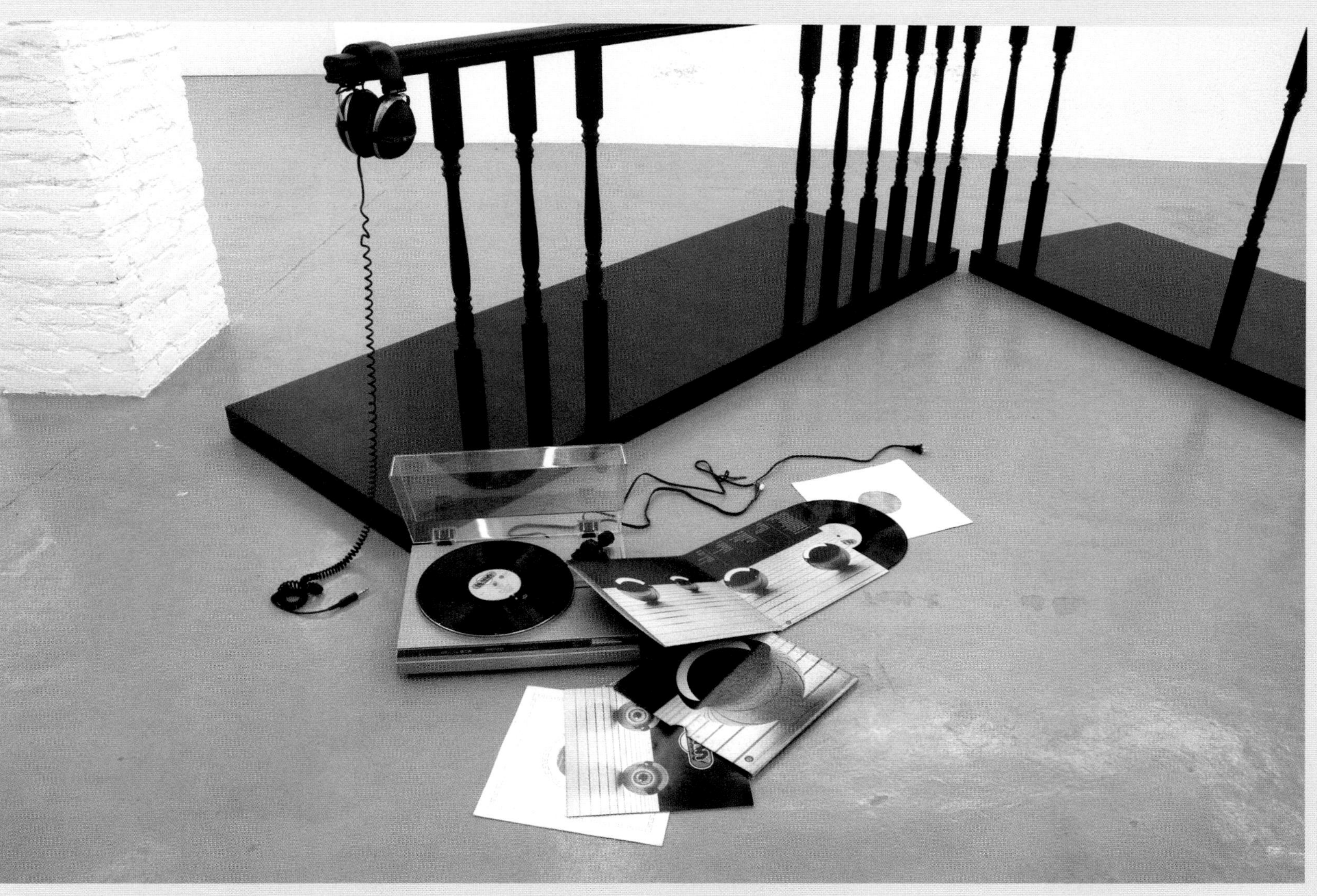

Black Spiral (See Me), 2008. Painted wood, record player, The Who LP, headphones. Dimensions variable

to his own personal biography. Recent works, for example, have been inspired by the lives of such varied figures as Frank O'Hara, Jim Morrison, Truman Capote, John Cage and Kurt Weill.

Burr's fragmentary combinations of fabricated and found elements are lyrically poetic mises-èn-scene whose sensibilities oscillate between elegiac homage and playfully sexy adoration. The works experiment with notions of presence and absence in order to reinvent ideas of portraiture and offer up imagined and partial histories and identities. For Burr, is through the traces and snippets of the past we leave behind that he can effectively examine where we are in the present.

For example, *Black Spiral (See Me)* (2009) is an assemblage-installation based around a black-painted wooden platform and railing that resembles a section of a stage set. Draped nonchalantly over the balustrade is a pair of unplugged headphones, and on the floor beside it sits a turntable and a record by The Who. This casual yet highly stylized scene imparts a sense of anticipation, yet remains

Narratives about the elusive flux of memories and identities

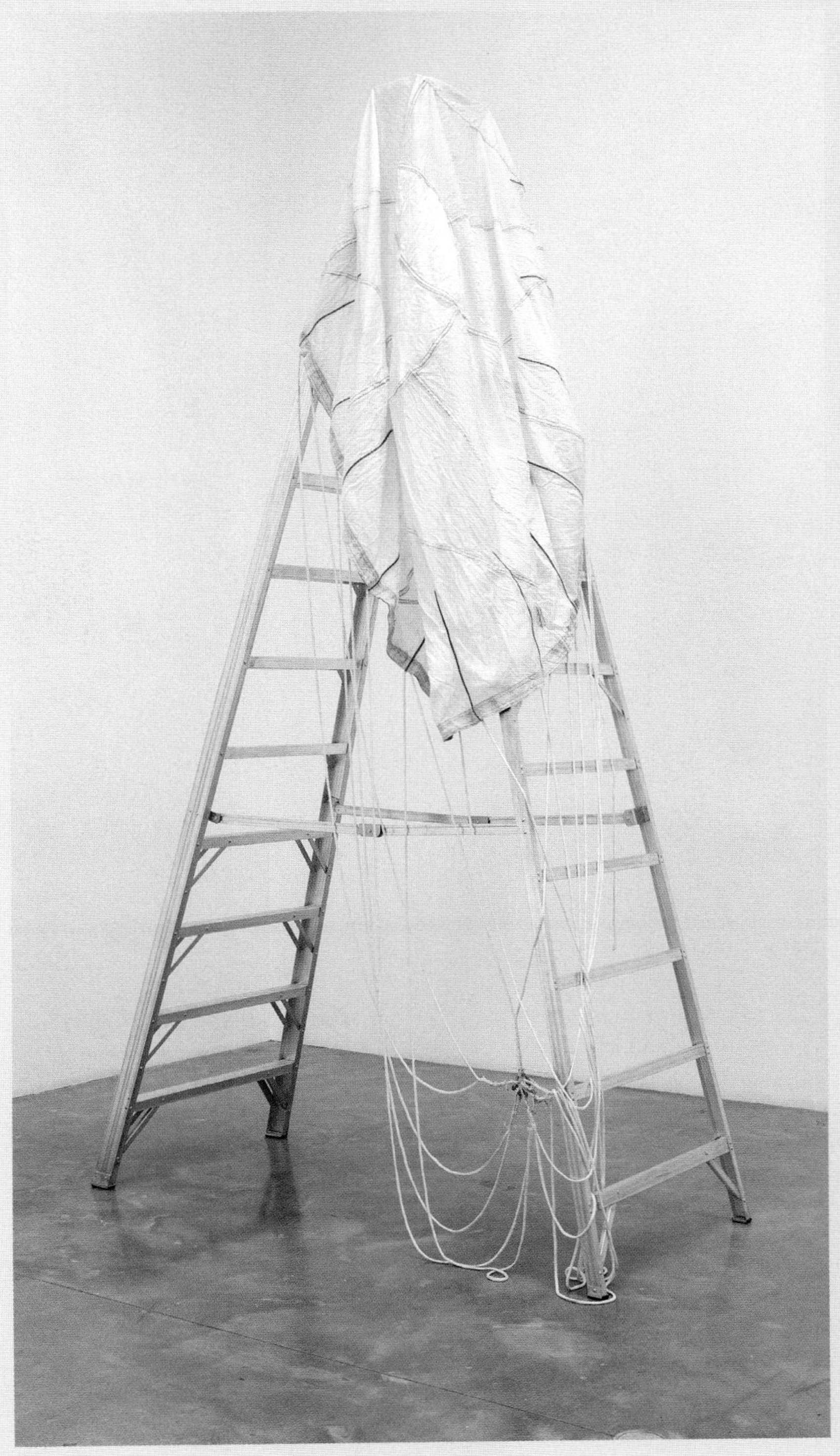

12 Steps to Hell, 2009. Metal ladder, white parachute. Dimensions variable

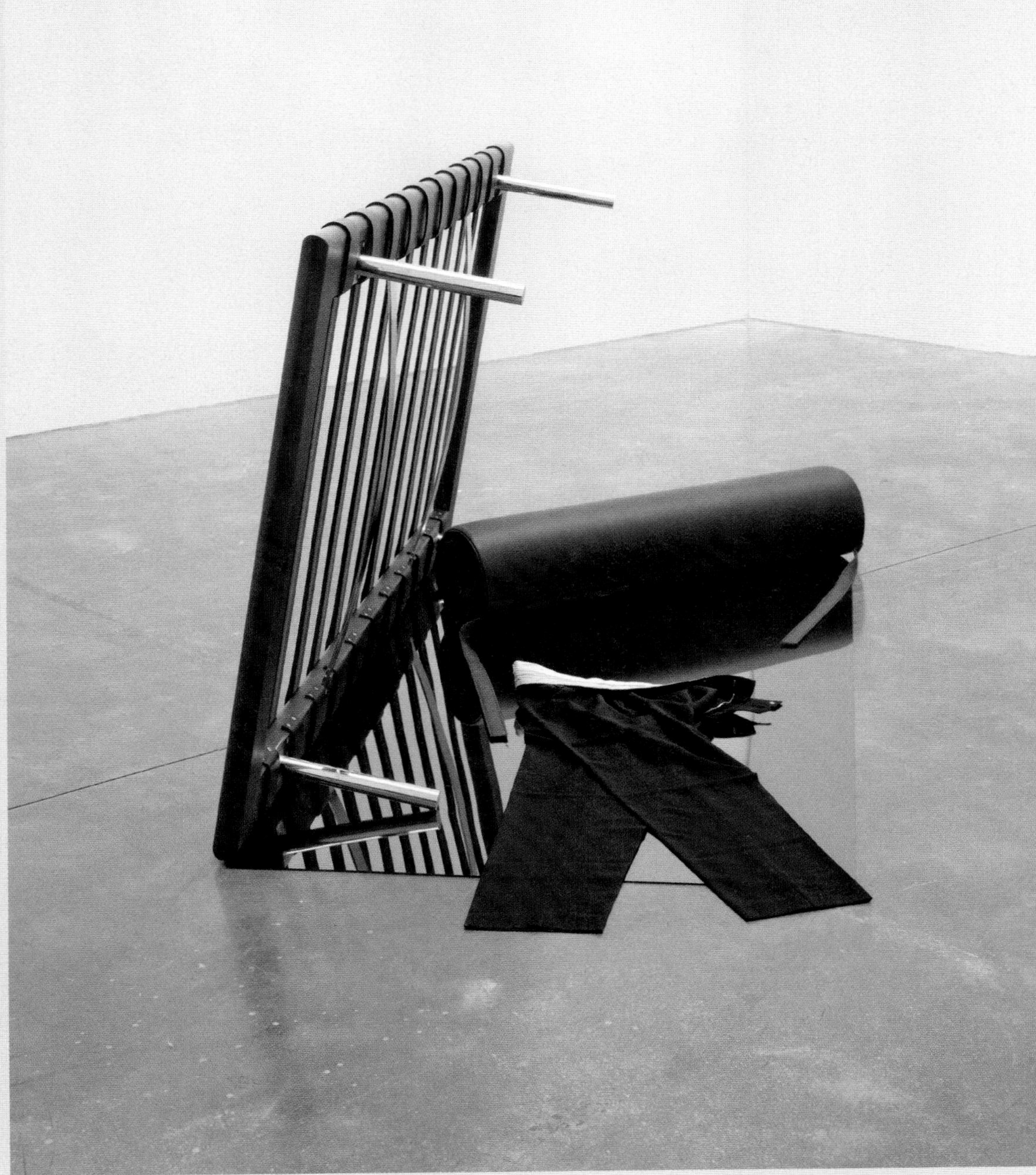

Black Slacks, 2008. Mies van der Rohe Barcelona Daybed, black trousers, smoked mirrored Plexiglas. 98 × 216 × 94 cm

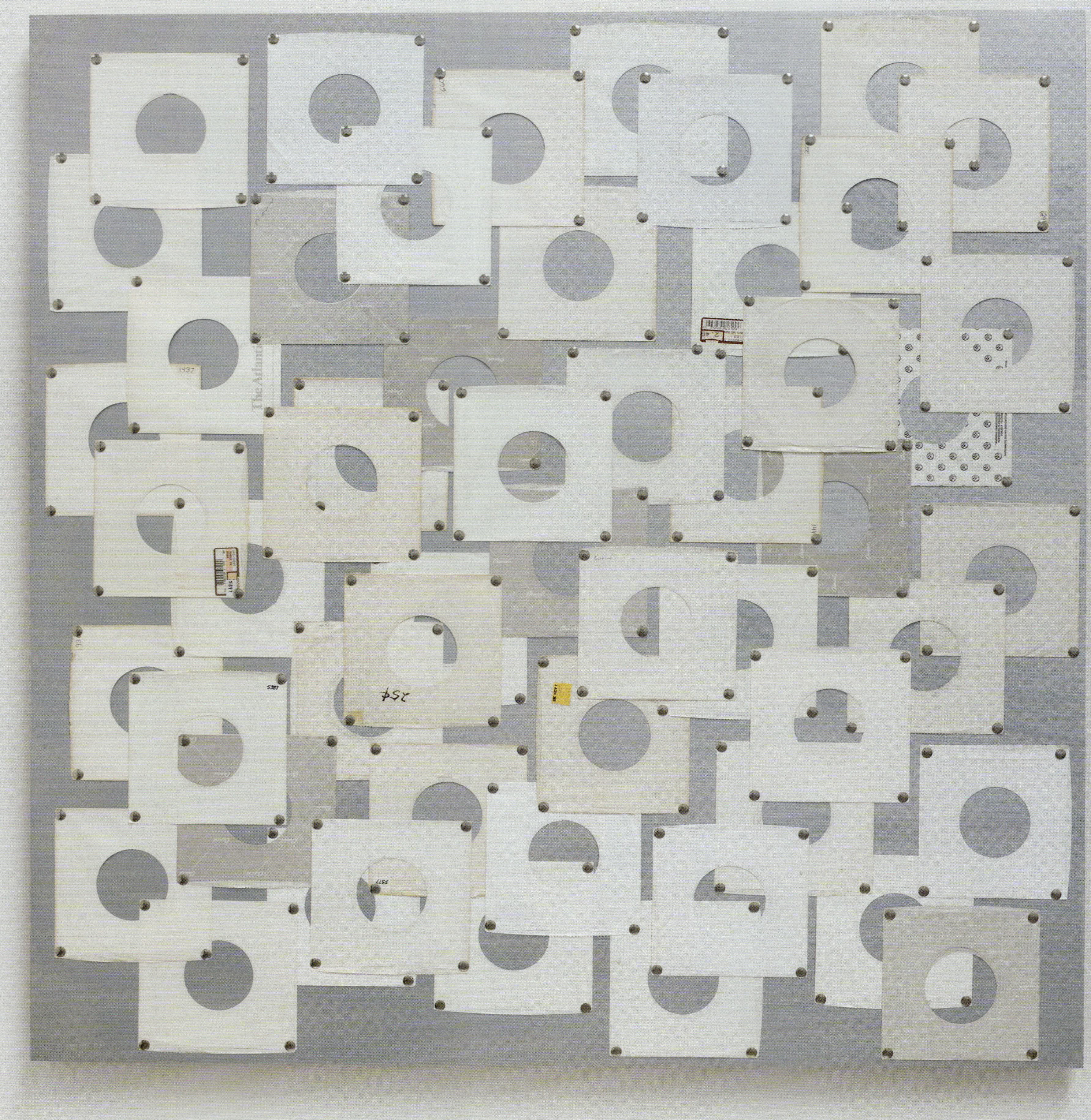

Silver Sleeves (used capital), 2009. Paper, record sleeves, push pins, paint on board. 122 × 122 cm

oblique in its references.
All the objects are outdated, while the railing possesses old-fashioned detailing and exists in a state of partial collapse. Playing with domestic and theatrical codes, the installation is redolent of melancholic potential and anticipation — of a presence come and gone. In this way, Burr sets up specific relations to viewing and spectatorship; viewers must complete the drama on their own, having already arrived late on the scene.

Music as a powerful emotional reminder of particular moments in time has been a recurring motif in many recent works. *Silver Sleeves (used capital)* (2009), is a collage of white 45 record sleeves push-pinned onto a painted board. The stunning simplicity of the abstract geometry possesses its own formal weight, and the empty sleeves conjure up a clear sense of obsolescence and absence.

Ideas of fugitive identities are further suggested in Burr's ongoing series of 'hinged' sculptures, which relate to ideas of the body infused with a ghostly aura. For example, *Slumbering object of my sleepless attention* (2009) is made up of several hinged wooden planks whose undulating contours recall a lounge chair or a reclining figure. On to this support Burr pins articles of clothing (in this case, men's pyjamas) and other elements that can vary from a mirror (as in this example) to photographs or book pages.

Here, the pyjamas suggest the absent body and, as the title indicates, a missing object of desire. The work evokes a sense of emptiness and ephemerality, and while evocative of any number of potential narratives is illustrative of how Burr's work coyly eludes over-determined interpretation.

Through a reinterpreted aesthetic of Minimalism, Burr conjures up imagined encounters with bygone moments and figures. Like abstract, sepulchral surrogates, Burr's dramas are set within minimal sculptural frameworks, which, despite their geometries, are uncannily anthropomorphic. With equal parts of longing, desire and homage, intimations of past existence are transformed into reflective portraits of fluid identities in conversation with their constructed surroundings, leaving us with a lasting sense of bittersweet, tantalizing desire, an endlessly deferred sense of denouement.

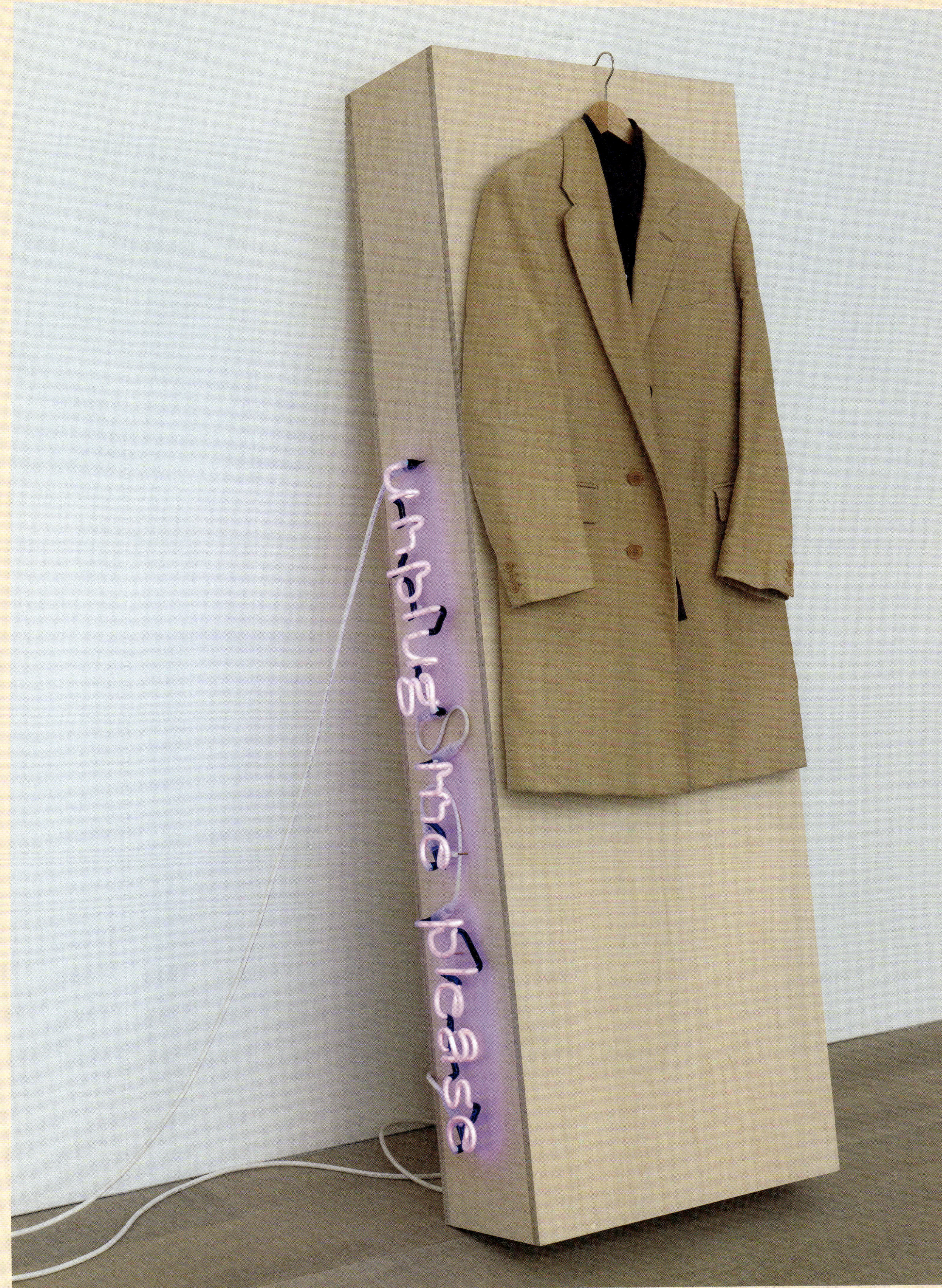

Unplug Me Please (in Purple), 2009. Plywood, neon, coat, shirt, coat hanger. 181 × 195 × 70 cm

Gerard Byrne

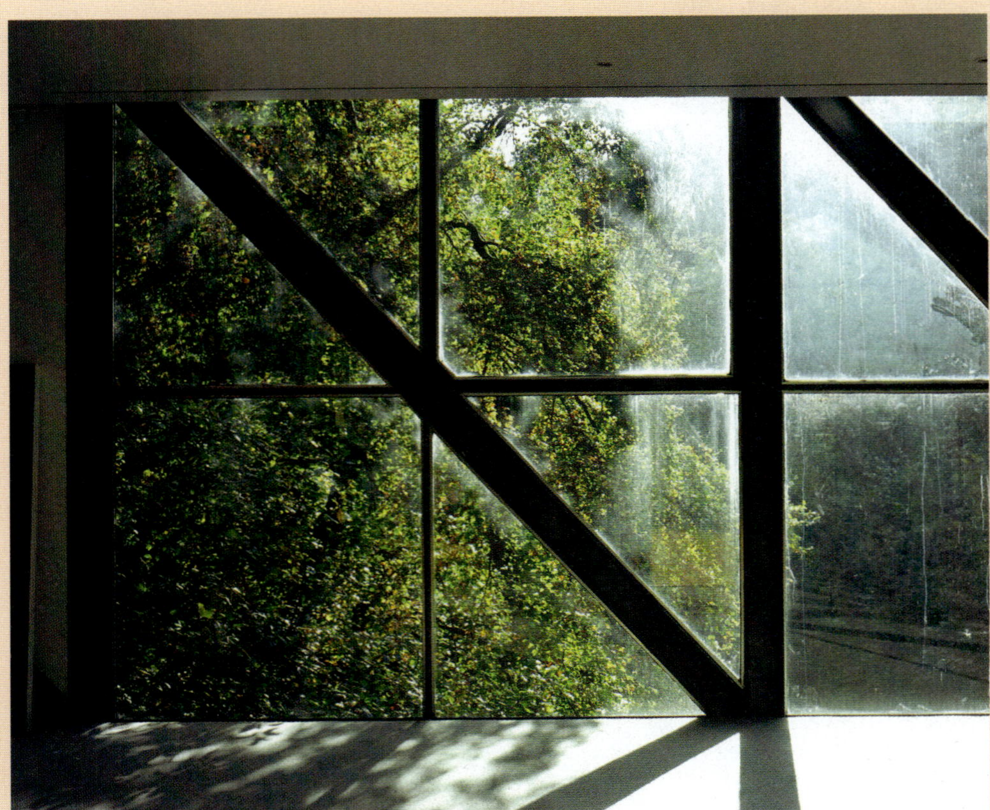
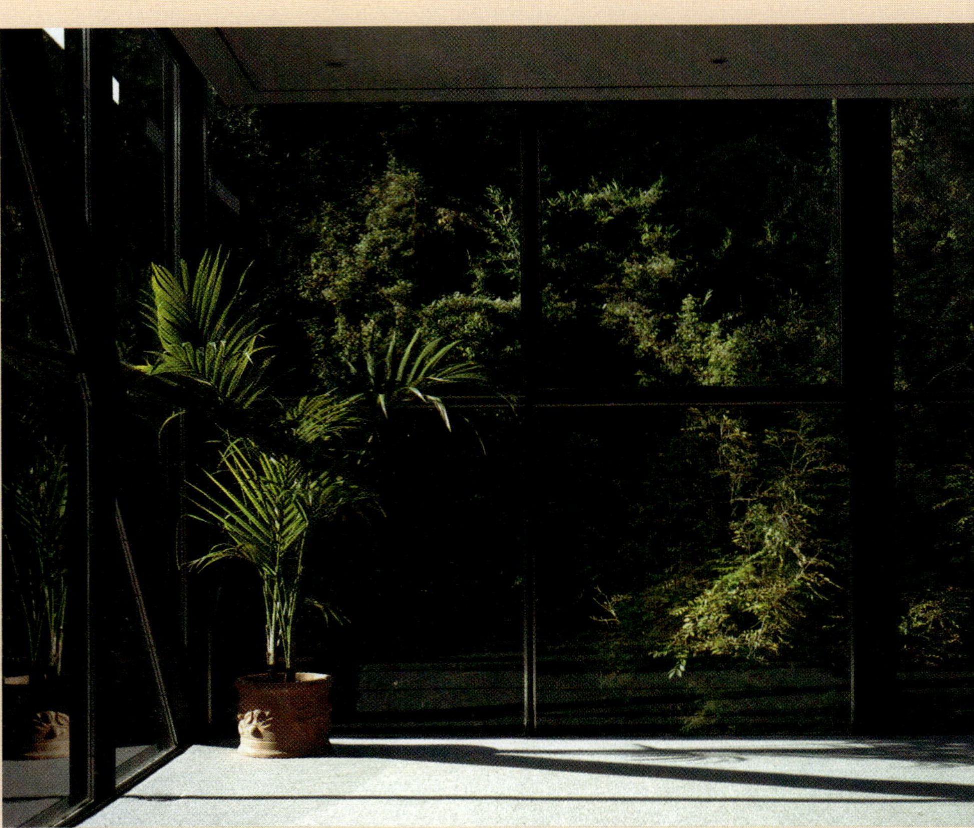

New Sexual Lifestyles, 2003. 3–channel video installation. Non–linear duration (approx. 54 min. total). 7 photographs. Dimensions variable

KMS 1989, a depiction of the reverse of a framed painting, photographed in the Statens Museum, Copenhagen, 348 years after it was painted, and reproduced here at 56.25% of its original size, 2008.
Selenium toned silver gelatin print. 79 × 89 cm

Spectatorship and audience

'Cabin crew, doors to manual and cross check.' Even if you've heard this bizarre phrase a thousand times before, the chances are you won't fully understand it, not even if you're a Gold Card Frequent Flyer. 'Doors to manual' possibly means releasing the doors from lockage, but 'cross check' is inscrutable professional jargon. Interestingly, it is unlikely that anyone has ever felt excluded or belittled by incomprehensible airline lingo; obscure pilot prattle is never as annoying as, say, mysterious art talk. Professional jargon in the arts is frowned upon. It's seen as elitist, exclusivist and worse.

Gerard Byrne, however, who works mainly with photography and video, somehow manages to get away with the difficult, the reflexive and with asking a specifically artistic set of questions. The first reason for this is that his work is never more 'mythifying' or annoying than a simple 'cross check' mumble over the PA: its language is just as deadpan, its tenor almost as technical. An example of this is *KMS 1989, a depiction of the reverse of a framed painting, photographed in the Statens Museum, Copenhagen, 348 years after it was painted, and reproduced here at 56.25% of original size* (2008).

Here, Cornelius Gijsbrecht's seventeenth-century painting *The Reverse of a Framed Painting* is, quite simply, photographed from the back. Meanwhile, in the film piece *68 Mica & Glass (a Demonstration on Camera by Workers from the State Museum)* (2008), two conservators from the Statens Museum Copenhagen work on the 1968 sculpture *Untitled* by Robert Smithson.

Another reason why Byrne gets away with so much self-

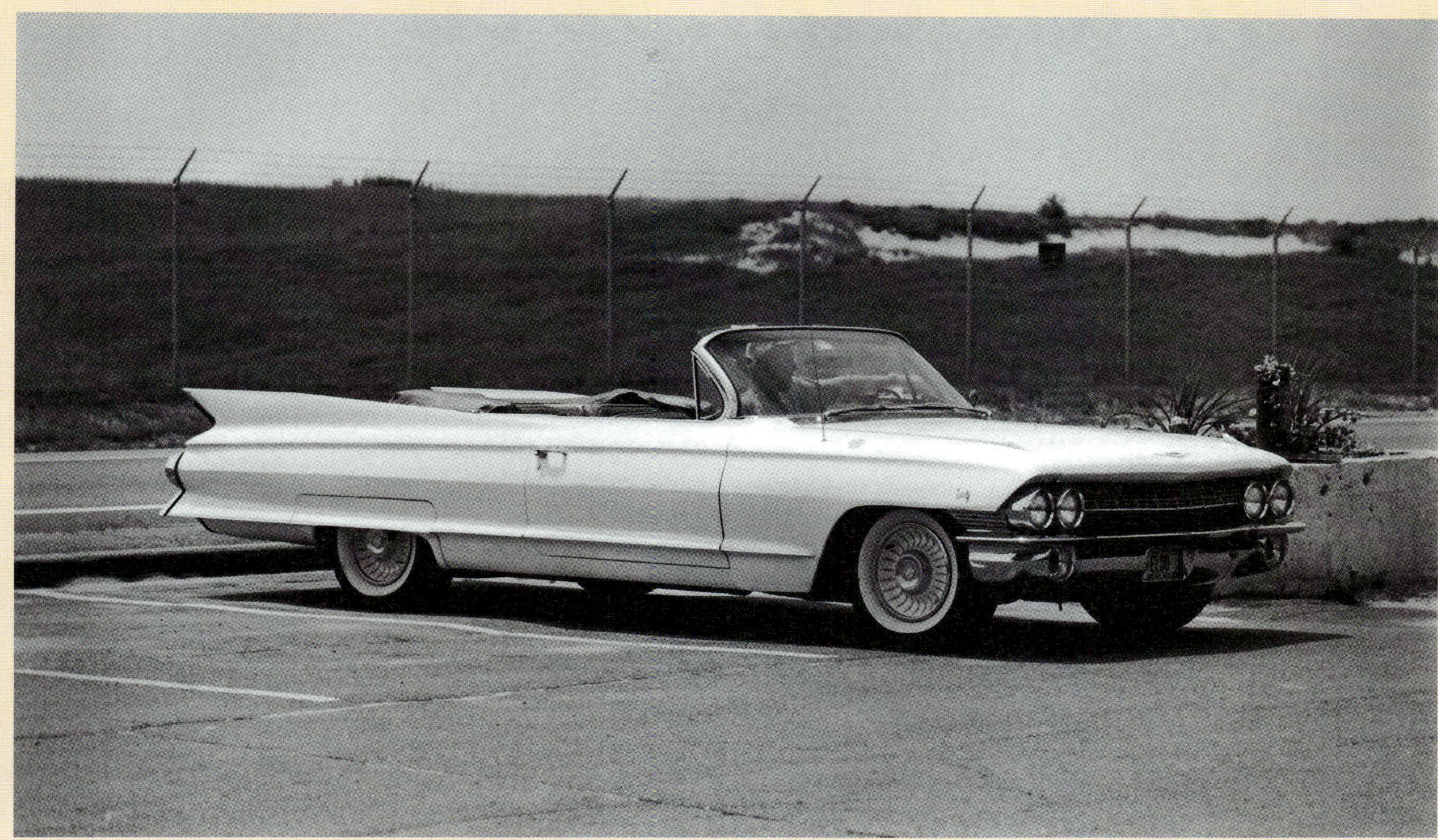

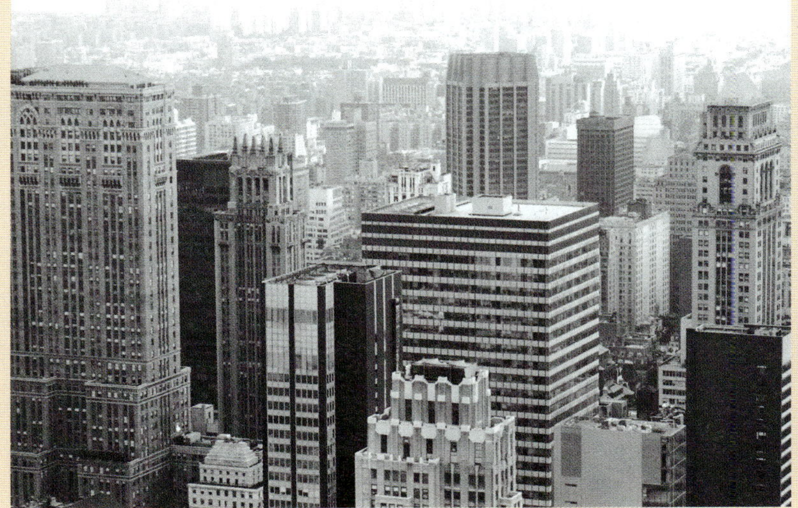

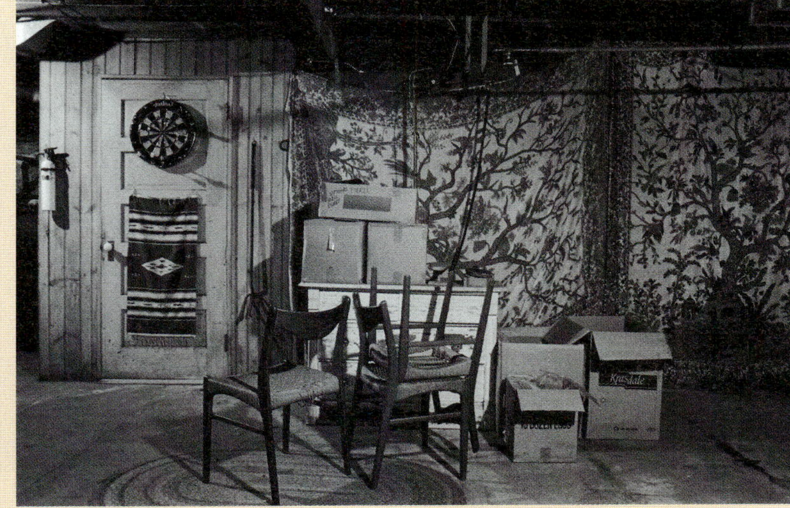

1984 and Beyond, 2005–07. 3–channel video installation, non–linear duration (approx. 60 min. total), twenty black and white photographs. Dimensions variable

From the entertaining to the historiographic

reflection is that he conceives a strain of art that can successfully and effortlessly welcome, even reconcile, a hundred different styles of spectatorship and audience. He's the proof that you can make accessible work without being a one-liner or an idiot, or without creating a great big weather machine. It is therefore interesting that Byrne takes the notion of 'expertise' in and of itself as material for his work. An example is the three-channel video *New Sexual Lifestyles* (2002), in which Byrne has amateur actors reenacting a 1973 Playboy symposium on emerging sexual behaviour patterns.

Here, the specialist know-how is embodied by a porn magazine editor, a porn star, a feminist and others, while in *1984 and Beyond* (2005), a 1963 conversation — again organized by Playboy — between a dozen science-fiction novelists is freely restaged and reinterpreted.

From the entertaining to the historiographic, from the art-reflexive to the theoretically convoluted, a plethora of hermeneutic levels are on offer, all of which are developed and tendered with an equal measure of grace and care.

'68 Mica & Glass (A demonstration on camera by workers from the State Museum), 2008. 16 mm colour film, silent. 8 min. 29 sec

Duncan Campbell

Poetic, formally distinctive films

'Documentary is a peculiar form of fiction', Duncan Campbell once commented, adding, 'It has the appearance of veracity grounded in many of the same formal conventions of fiction — narrative drive, linear plot and closure. Yet the relationship among the author, subject and audience is rarely investigated in the same way as it is in meta-fiction.' It is precisely this knotty problem that is the persistent concern of the Irish-born, Glasgow-based artist: how to reveal the fictive, even illusory, in the documentary genre while simultaneously exposing the interpretative choices, indeed utter subjectivity, of everyone and everything — filmmaker, archival sources, central characters, viewers — involved in any exploration of a 'true story'.

The only plausible response for Campbell in the face of such concerns is what he calls, after Samuel Beckett, 'a form that accommodates the mess'. And a compelling form it is. For, however much the documentary mode in art and filmmaking often prompts the proliferation of dry and apparently 'objective' sameness, Campbell has, over the course of only a few projects, established himself as an inspired maker of poetic, formally distinctive films.

Language (or its failure) frequently drives his films, whether it is the vernacular, stream-of-

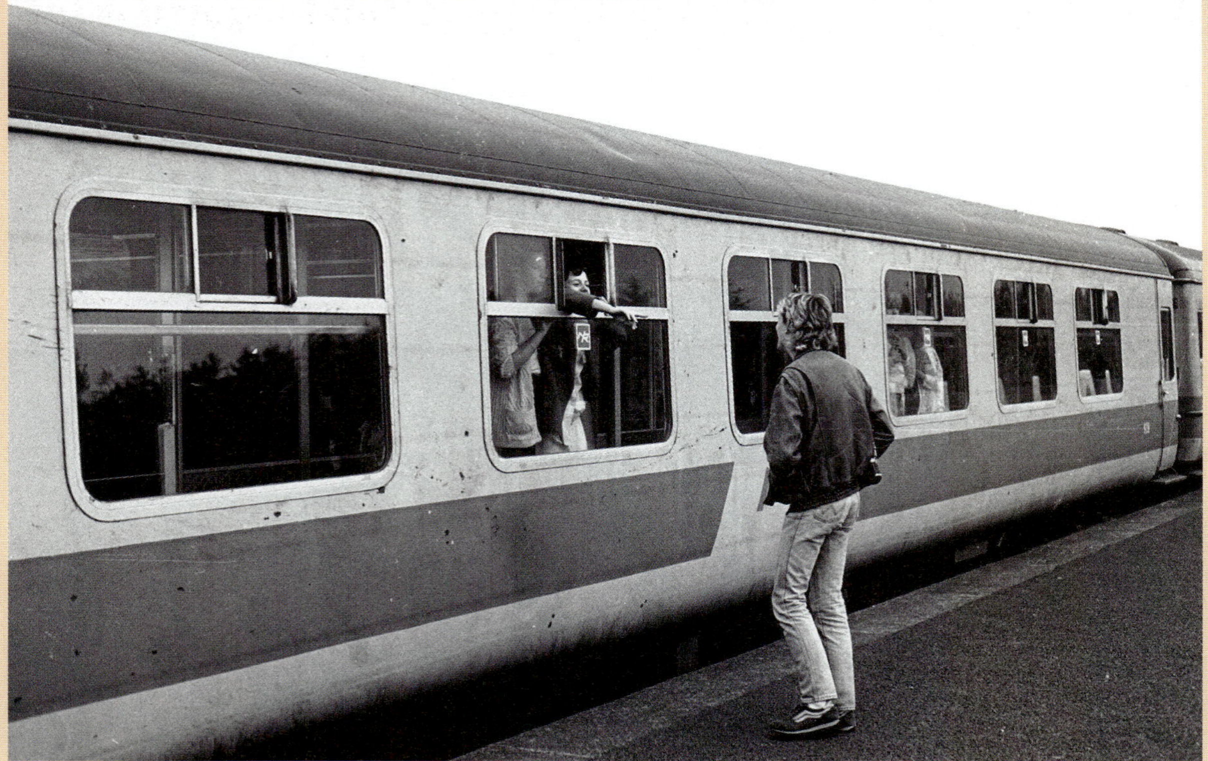

Falls Burns Malone Fiddles, 2003. 35 mm photo negatives, 16mm film, VHS transferred to DVD, 4:3 digital projection. 33 min.

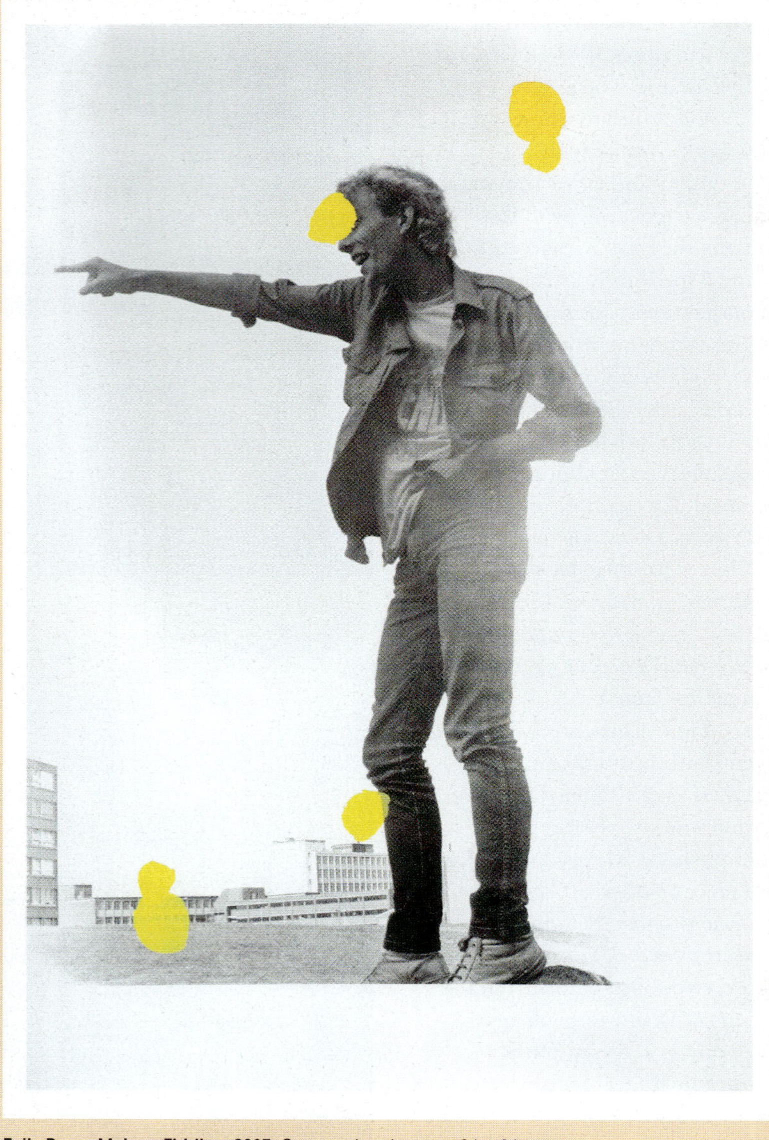

Falls Burns Malone Fiddles, 2007. Screenprinted poster. 94 × 64 cm

consciousness monologue in *Falls Burns Malone Fiddles* (2003), the incomprehensible utterances of *Sigmar* (2008), or the pieced-together snippets of Irish political activist Bernadette Devlin's impassioned oratory in *Bernadette* (2008). But if language propels these films forward, it is also the source of the self-conscious doubt that is central to Campbell's practice. Sometimes this doubt is manifested literally, as in the endlessly uncertain pronouncements of *Falls Burns*'s narrator, at other times metaphorically, as in *Bernadette*, where the occasional sound-image misalignment is so forcefully deployed that any strict realism and the veracity of the document is thrown into question.

Campbell often draws his images from readymade, archival sources. *Falls Burns* is composed from Belfast community photographic archives. Picturing graffiti-lined locales, marked by bleak social conditions, the film is narrated through an existential monologue concerning photography and truth, identity and subjectivity that gives the

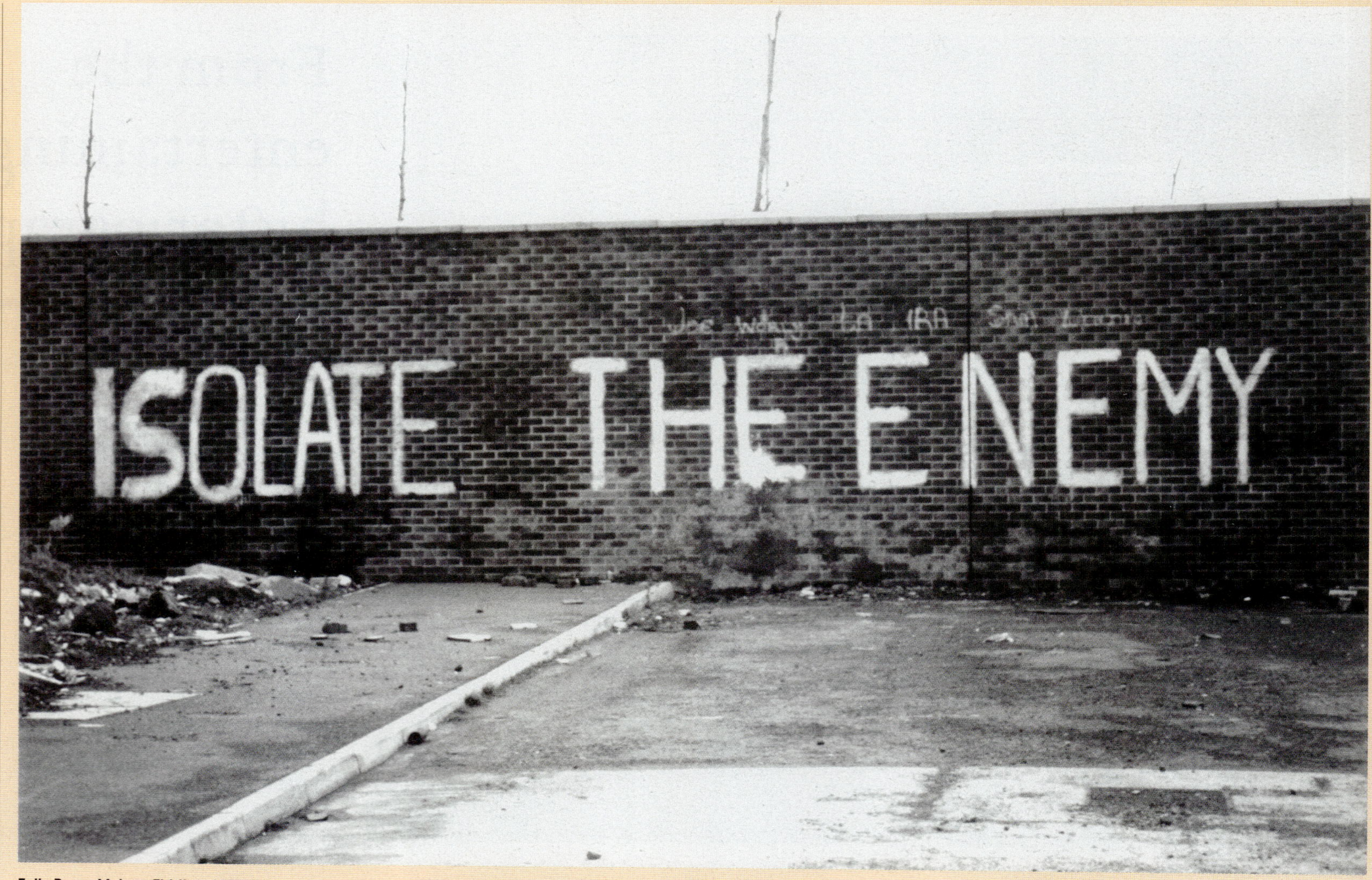

Falls Burns Malone Fiddles, 2003. 35 mm photo negatives, 16mm film, VHS transferred to DVD, 4:3 digital projection. 33 min.

Bernadette

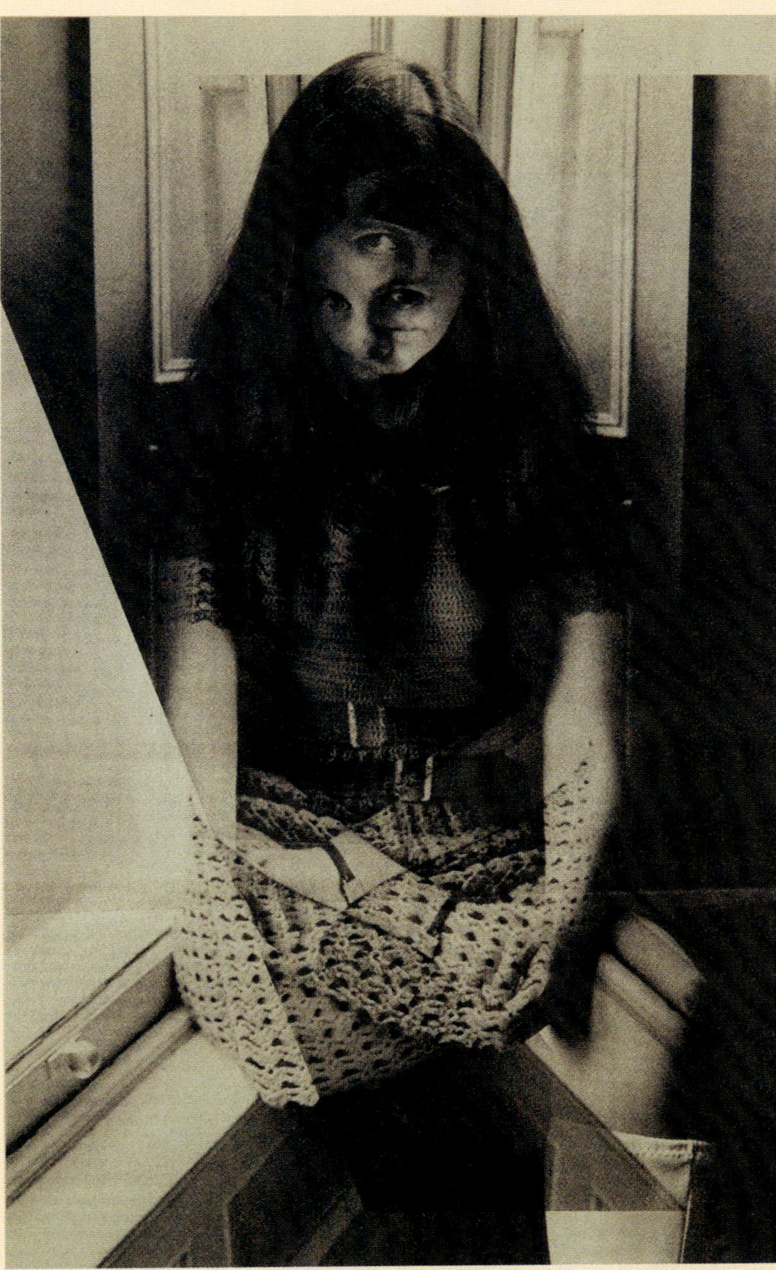

Bernadette, 2008. Screen–printed poster. 90 × 63 cm

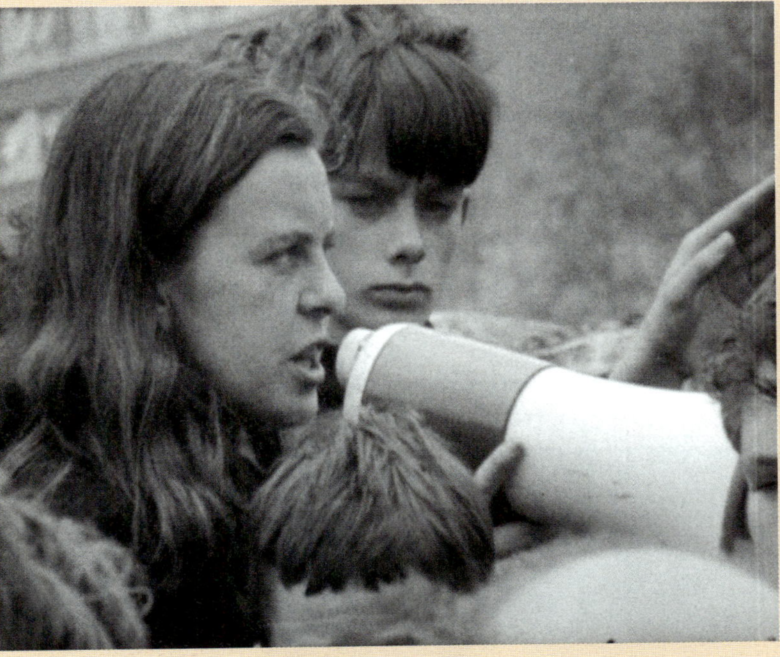

Bernadette, 2008. 16mm film transferred to Digi–beta, 4:3 digital projection. 37 min. 10 sec.

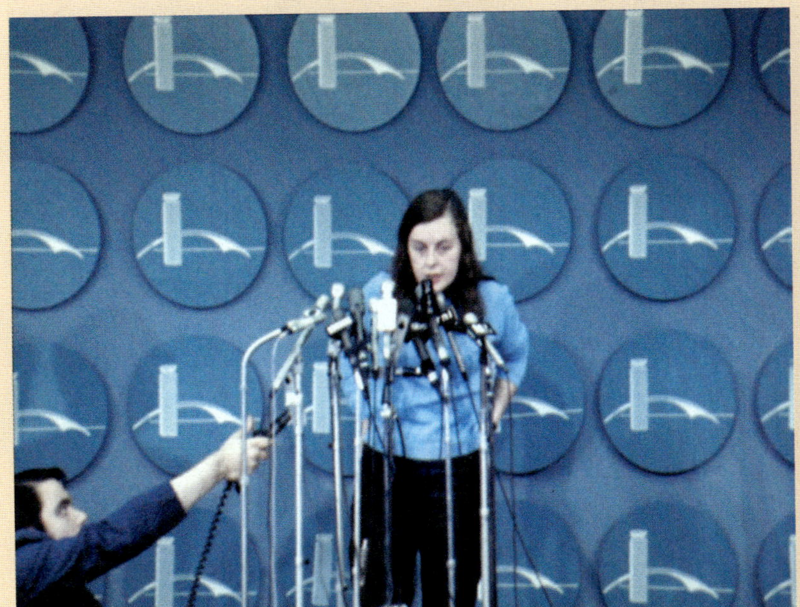

Bernadette, 2008. 16mm film transferred to Digi–beta, 4:3 digital projection. 37 min. 10 sec.

whole a Beckettian magnetism. *Bernadette* is equally comprised of archival material, but in this case, television news sources that already incorporate a will to represent Devlin in a certain way. Campbell makes apparent his act of selection, at times inserting breaks in the images, or his own sounds. This palpable announcement of his position is foretold in the opening shots, filmed in black and white by the artist himself, in which the camera slowly pans across a woman's hands, bare feet and hair as if to declare the utter humanity of his subject against the grain of her media representation.

At a moment when the tag of 'terrorist' has become a convenient and damning category used by those in power, Campbell's portrayal of another side of the Irish troubles — either through his refusal to replicate the media stereotypes of punkish youths hurling petrol bombs at the British Army in *Falls Burns*, or through his homage to the plucky determinism of an activist for the disenfranchised in Northern Ireland in *Bernadette* — suggests that his films have a doggedly political ambition intimately linked to their larger

Sigmar, 2008. Screen–printed poster. 100 × 57 cm

rejection of the pretense of objective truth. His film *Make It New John* (2009) — about the failed car maker John Delorean and the demise of his iconic sports car, which was produced in Northern Ireland — is no different.

Campbell's earliest pieces, made in the wake of art school, include knitted versions of night-club posters. The homey reinterpretations of these found, ephemeral announcements, in which each threaded stitch announces the incalculable distance between itself and the scrap-paper original on which it is based, suggests connec-

'The relationship between the author, subject and audience is rarely investigated in the same way as it is in meta-fiction.' It is precisely this knotty problem that is the persistent concern of the Irish-born, Glasgow-based artist: how to reveal the fictive, even illusory, in the documentary genre.

tions with the artist's revelation of the subjective interpretation of archival materials in his films. Both processes happen through a determination not to assume that the form of the artwork is already and necessarily given by the material on which it is based. Instead, a readiness to question the ultimate authenticity of facts and things is apparent. As the narrator of *Falls Burns Malone Fiddles* says, 'The best thing is not to decide anything in advance.'

Subjective intepretations

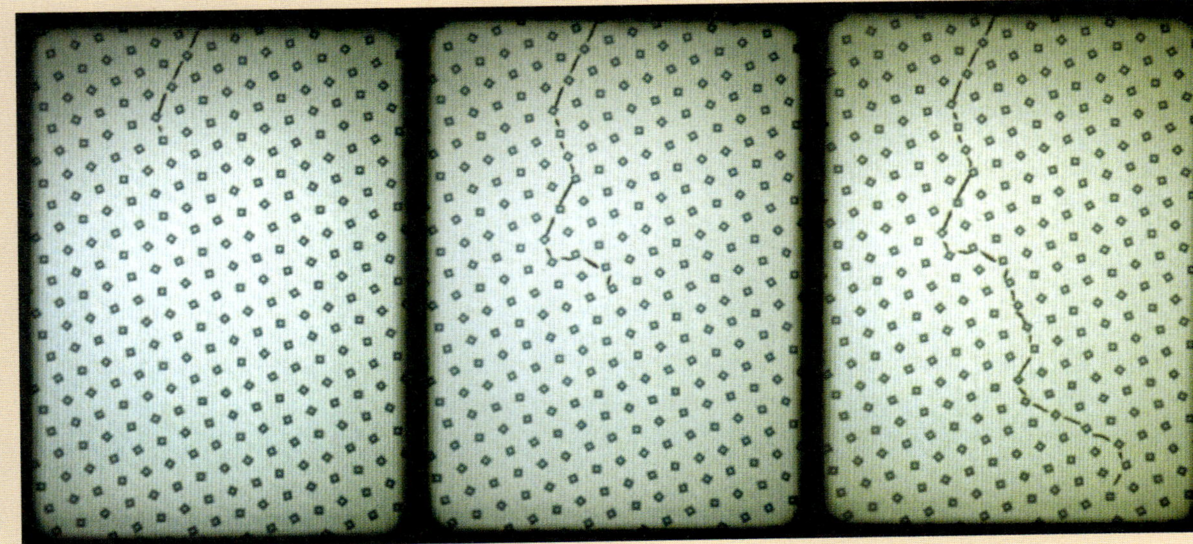

Sigmar, 2008. Super 16mm film. 9 min. 16 sec. loop

Bonnie Camplin

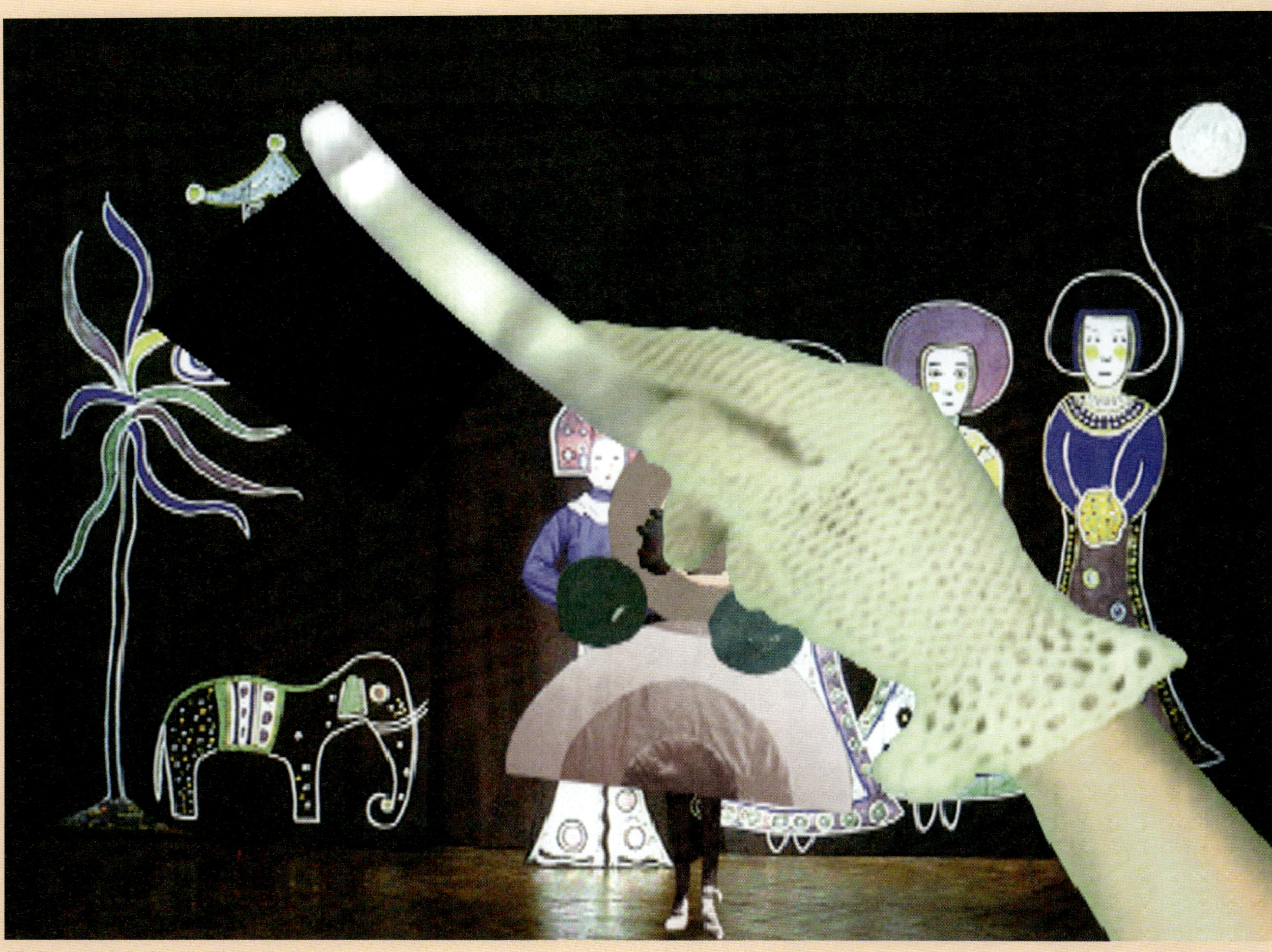

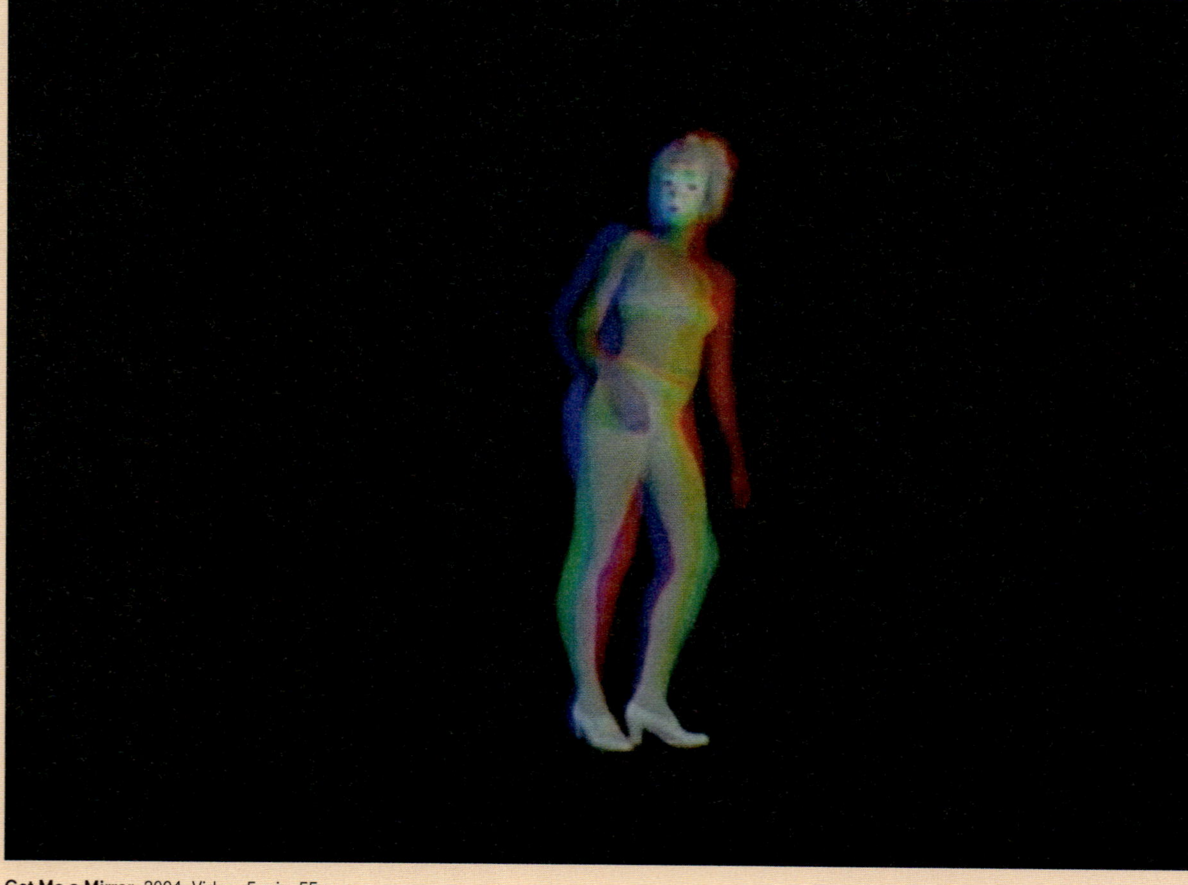

A like Akarova (with Paulina Olowska), 2006. Video. 3 min.

Utilizing low-budget film and music technology, as well as pencil drawing and performance, Bonnie Camplin's work stages an exploration of the rituals and codes of popular culture set against her autobiographical narrative. A close circle of relatives, friends and fellow artists feature both as subjects and collaborators in her works and she employs demotic, readily available means and media — cut-up magazines, home-video editing effects, costumes made from second-hand clothes, or props adapted from found objects — in an improvisational process of making.

From 2002 until 2004, Camplin was a member of Mark Leckey's musical-performance collective DonAteller (described in seductively pop terms in one early flyer as a 'luxury line in performance inspired by the speed, thrill and glamour of contemporary living'). Camplin also co-produced and starred in the video montage *LonDonAteller* (2002), in which she and Ed Laliq inhabited a baroque, self-destructing vision of London — the city as a site for decadent, performative display. DonAteller's theatricalization of mass media's feminized image-realm, as well as Camplin's interests in the self-portrait and in social ritual, have fed into a series of collaborations with the Polish artist Paulina Olowska in works such as *A like Akarova* (2006), *Spectators Only, A Shadow Play* (2007) or *Usher We (Down There)* (2008). Both *A like Akarova* and *Spectators Only* incorporate what the artists have described as their shared political interests not only in feminism but also in the adjectival quality of 'femininity', that is to say, in negotiating the problem of essentialist readings of gender by treating the 'feminine' not as an autonomous quality but as a decorative addition with unique aesthetic capacities that they, as women, can exploit.

Get Me a Mirror, 2004. Video. 5 min. 55 sec.

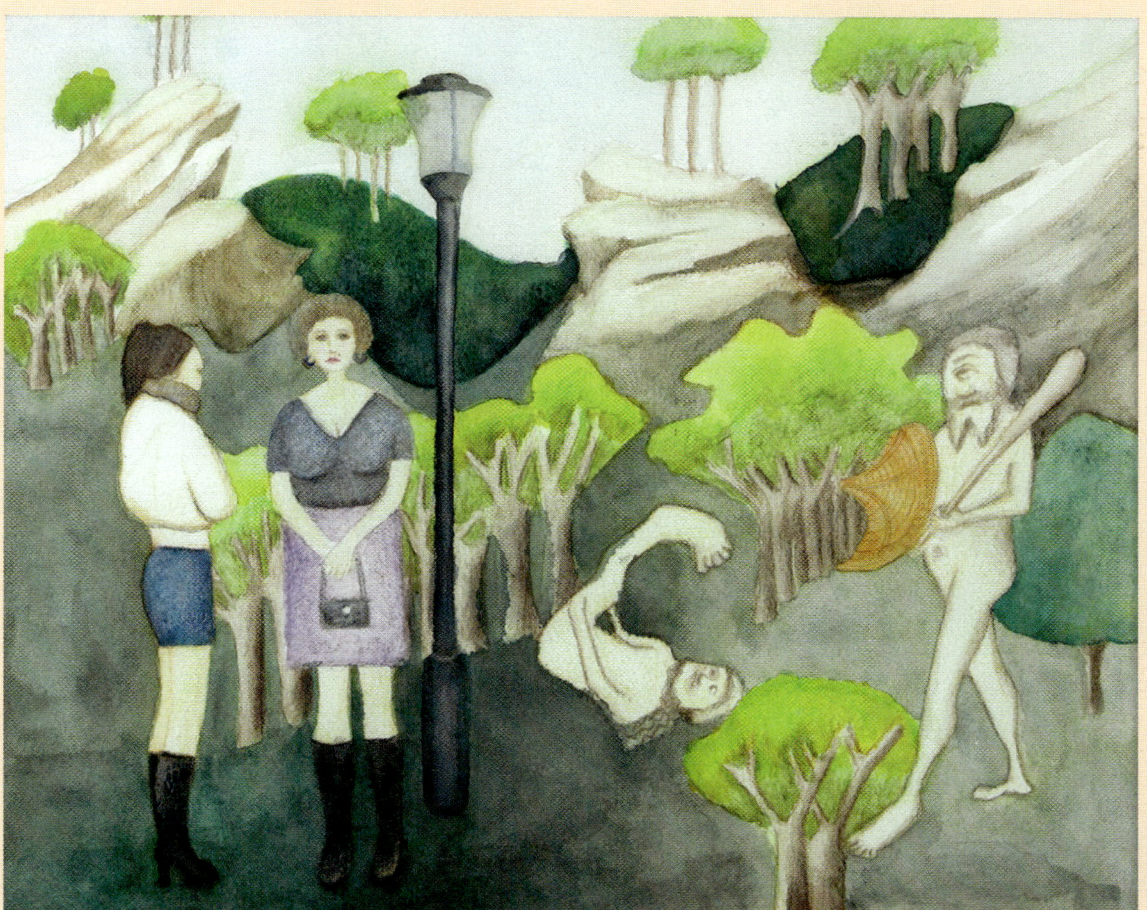

Salty Water/ What of Salty Water (detail), 2006. Watercolour on paper. 33 × 42 cm

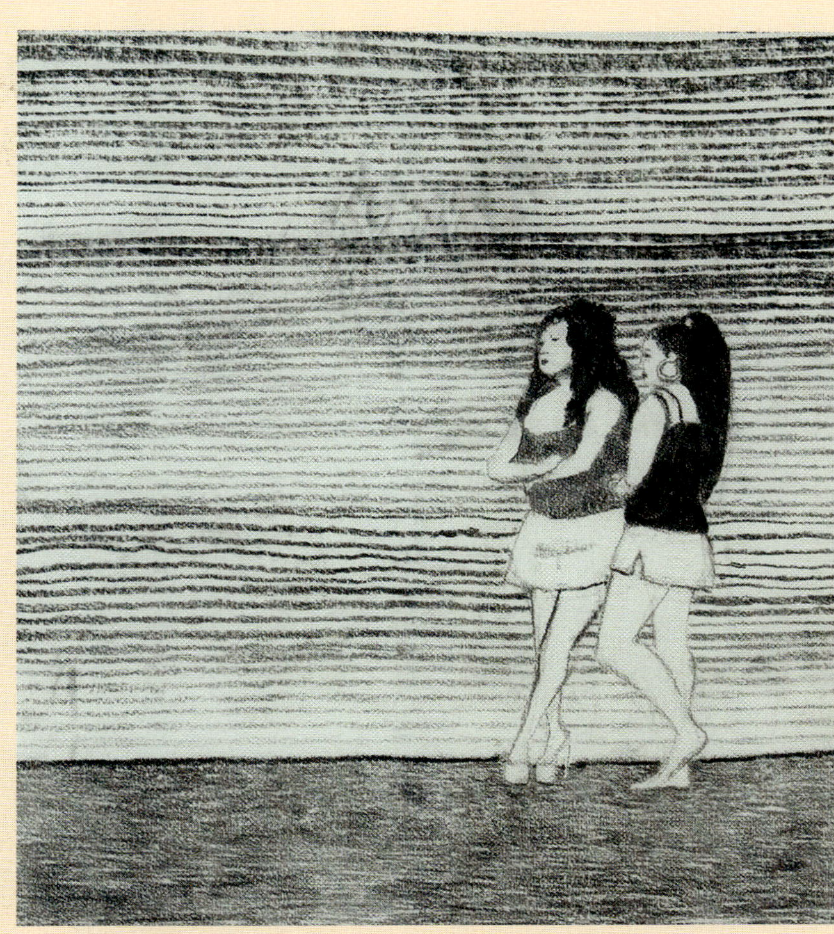

Salty Water/ What of Salty Water (detail), 2006. Charcoal on paper. 39 × 36 cm

The properties of feminine artifice

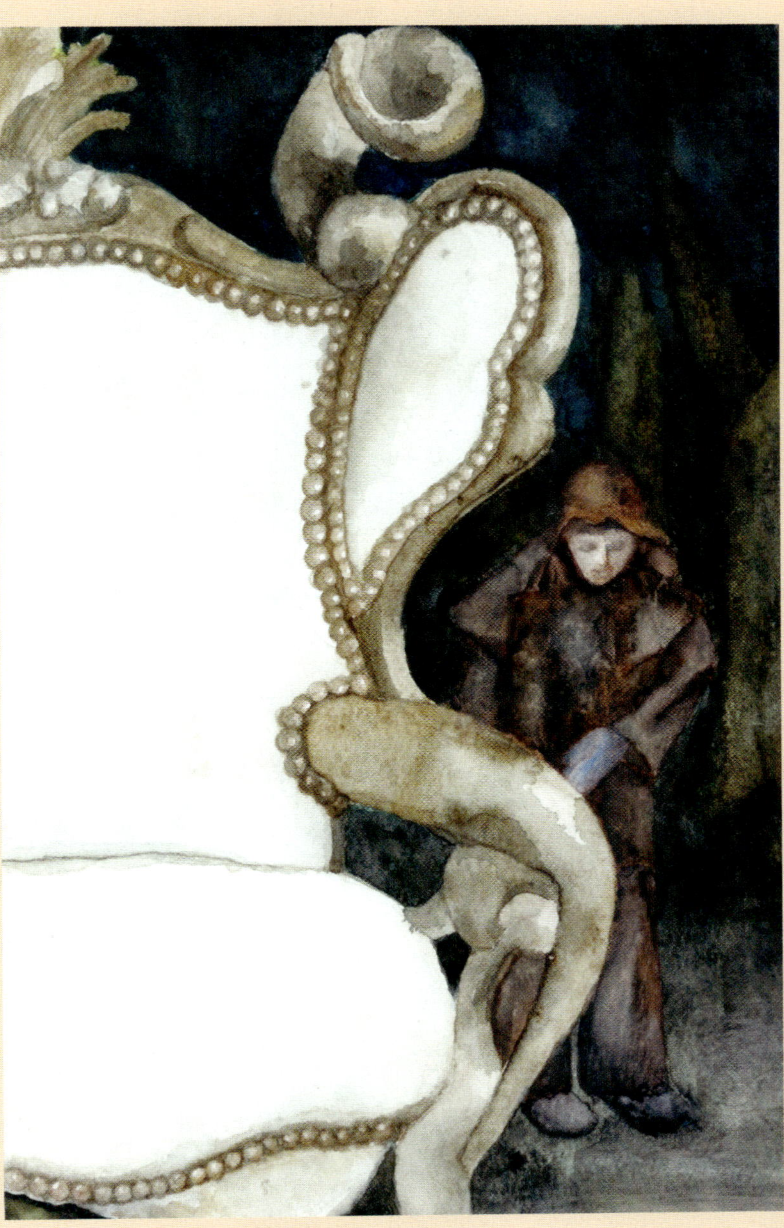

Dog, 2007. Watercolour on paper. 18 × 29 cm

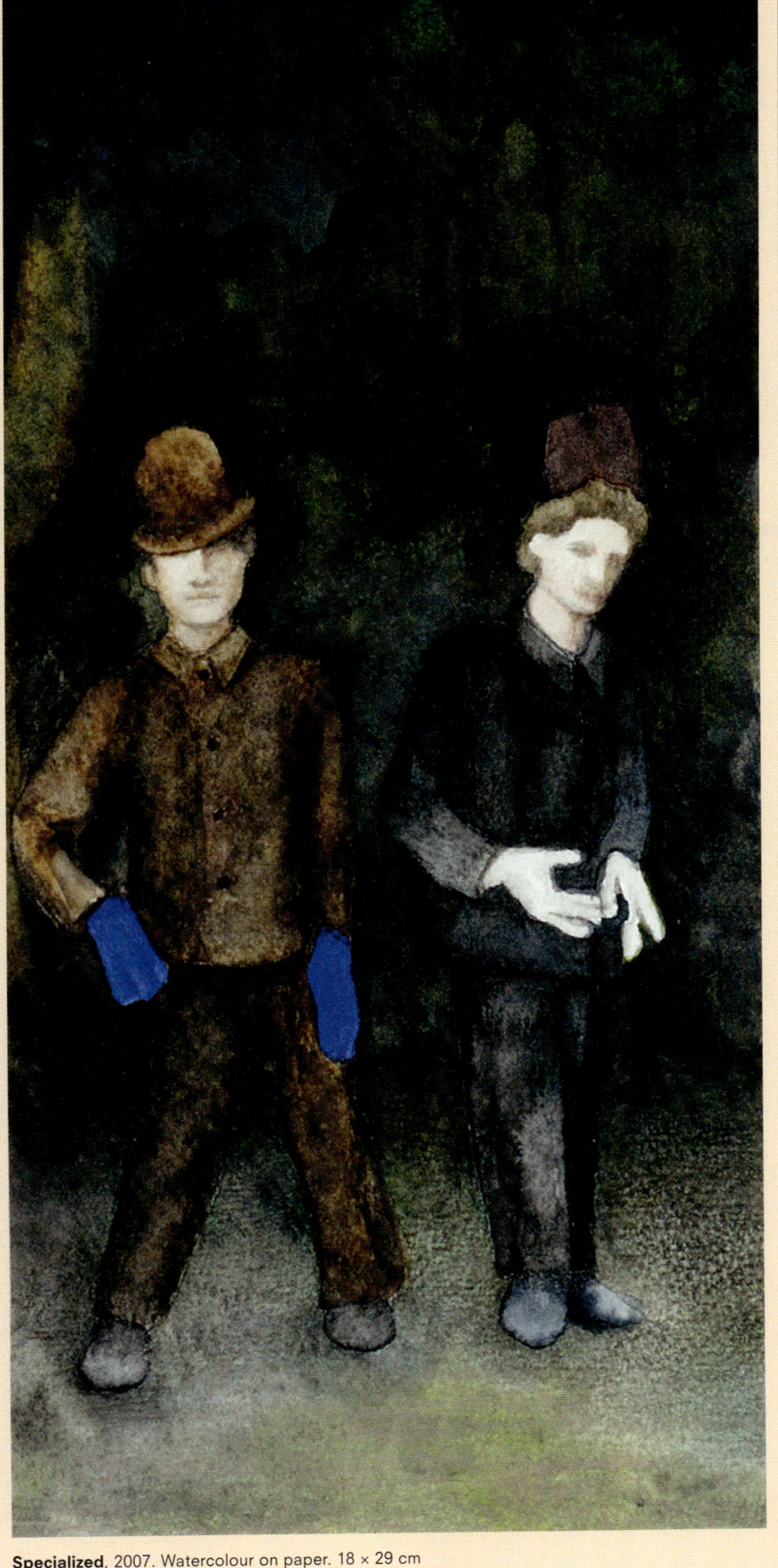

Specialized, 2007. Watercolour on paper. 18 × 29 cm

Camplin's interest in the properties of feminine artifice is mixed with a fascination for witchcraft and the supernatural, qualities that resonate, in turn, with the creative possibilities inherent in the manipulation of film and video. This melding of concerns recalls another vocabulary of symbolic gestures and mythical invocations: that of Joan Jonas. Jonas's alter-ego, the masked 'electronic erotic seductress' Organic Honey, seems to haunt Camplin's 2004 video *Get Me a Mirror*, in which she appears as three simultaneous, monochromatic 'ghosts'—blue, green and red respectively.

Wearing only underwear and a blank mask, the three ghostly components dance in a dark space until gradually they unify into one white whole. Like Jonas, Camplin invokes affinities between the narrative faculties of her medium and the ancient tradition of the female story-teller, a figure brought up to date literally and metaphorically through the exploration of split consciousnesses effected by contemporary technologies.

Sometimes a kind of digital entropy is at play in the work: sound undergoes slurred manipulation; sequences are broken down into stills. In *Cancer* (2004), pixellated disintegrations created with rudimentary video-editing effects parallel the monologue delivered by a male professor, in the style of a public-health broadcast, on the subject of the proliferation of diseased cells. In *When The Wind Blows Up You* at the Chisenhale gallery in 2009, Camplin staged a disorienting, multi-part film and music event that culminated in a theatrical tableau whose liveness was countered by the stills effect of intermittent and localized illumination, its overarching mood evoking the nihilism of the nuclear threat in the 1980s.

Camplin's practice, despite its mercurial nature, is anchored at its core by a stubbornly slow and even times reversed momentum that drags against the urban environment in which she and her characters are embedded. In the case of her large-scale drawings (often based on found photographs or portraits of family members), the laborious industry they require might be seen as a form of resistance to the speed of contemporary life. This resistance is equally pronounced in her film projects. Unafraid of the seductive surface of things, she makes art that is nevertheless haunted by a creeping horror that threatens to eat away at beautiful images.

Nina Canell

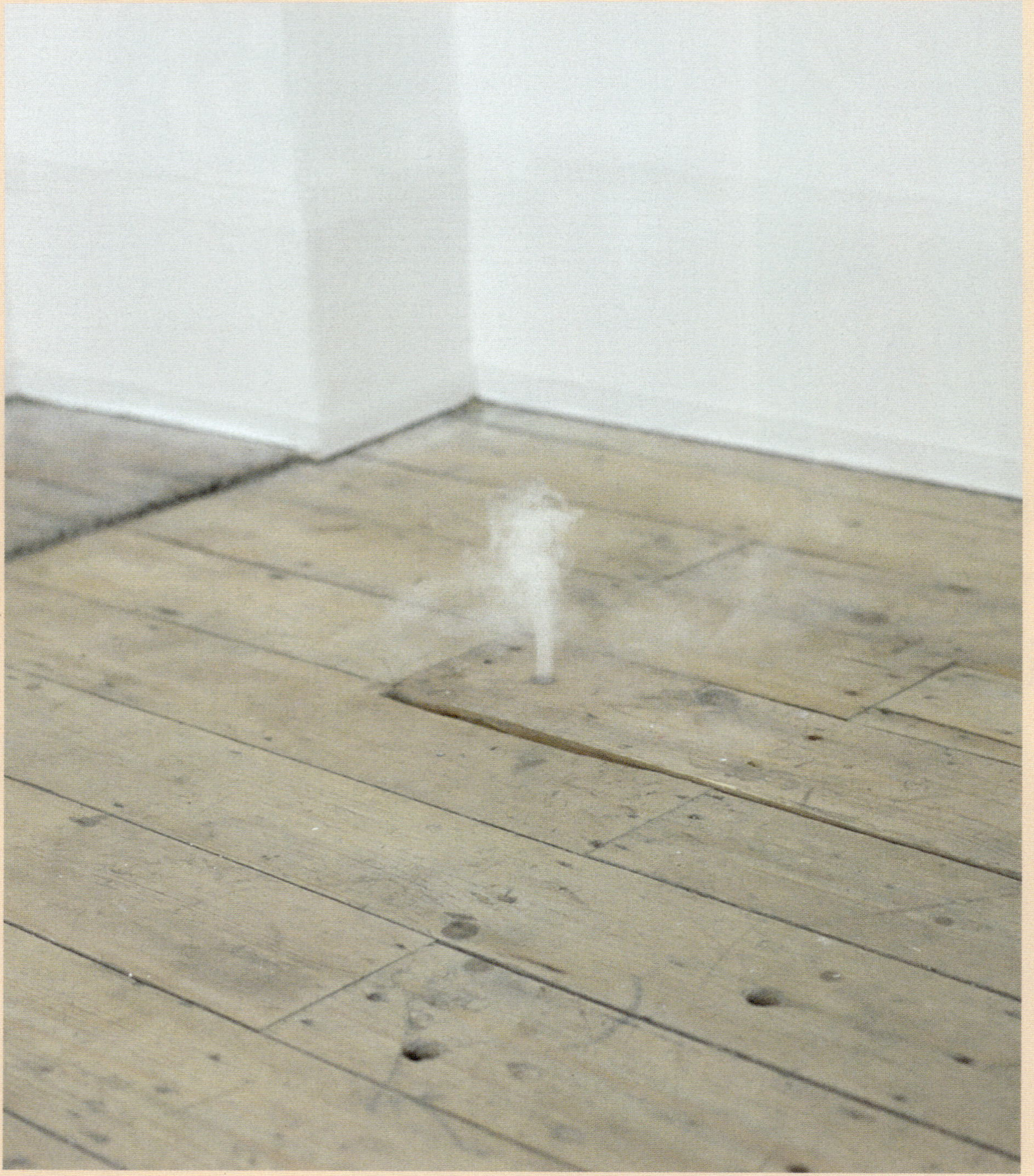

Mist Mouth, 2007. Hole in gallery floor, water, bucket, hose, mist machine, fan. Approx. 20 × 20 × 15 cm

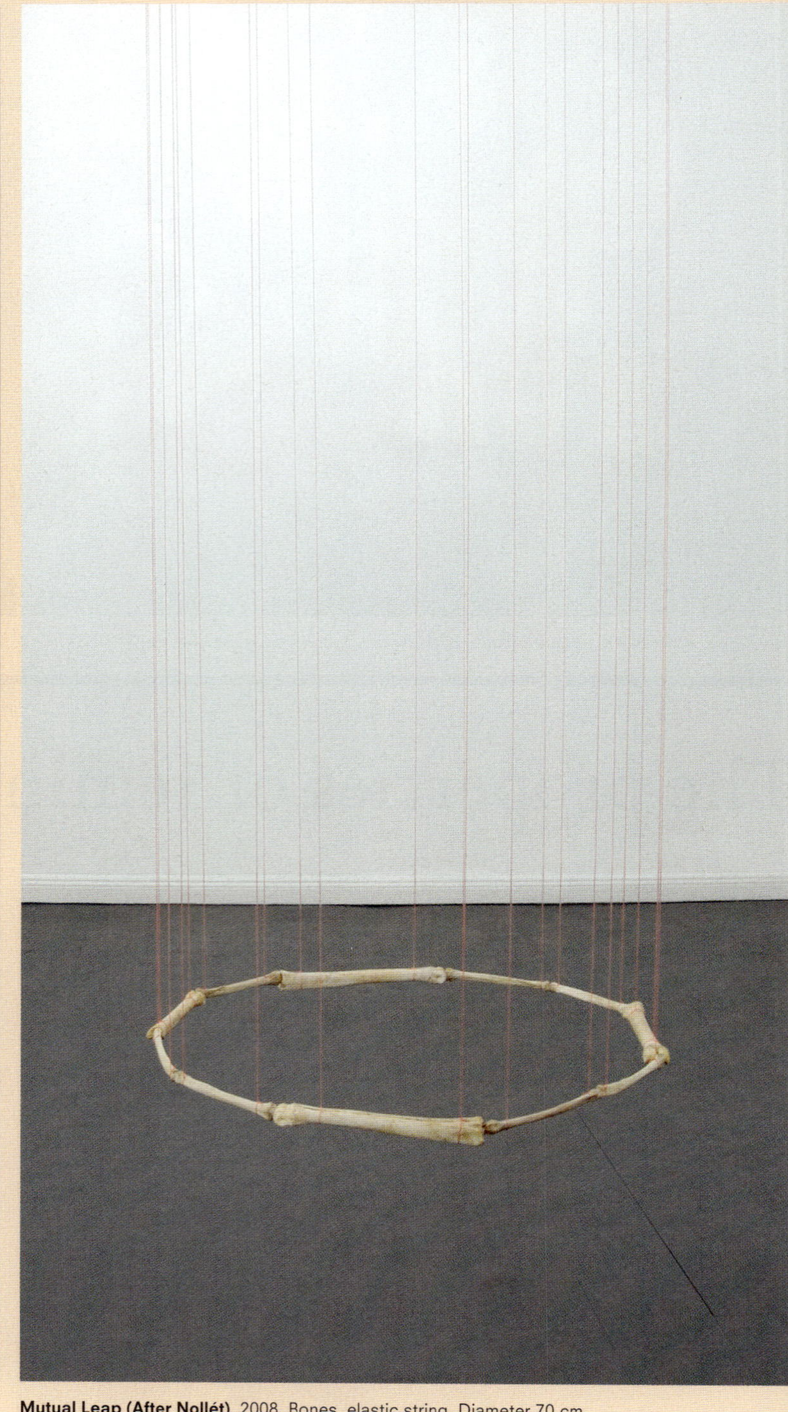

Mutual Leap (After Nollét), 2008. Bones, elastic string. Diameter 70 cm

Arabesques of cables on the floor, obsolete radio equipment and sound-system components, neon tubes creeping languidly over bricks (*Soft Stone*, 2009) or hanging limply on a femur (*Winter Sun, Sleepy Tongue*, 2007), bones joined in a circle suspended from the ceiling (*Mutual Leap (After Nollét)*, 2008), or piled up volcanic stones, lit from within by the red glare of neon (*Bag of Bones*, 2007): Nina Canell's works formalize but at the same time defy the traditional notions of sculpture — a striving for permanence and surrender to gravity — while offering new insights into the repertoire of Minimal art. If, as Lenin once famously claimed, Communism equalled Soviet power plus the electrification of the country, Canell's works enable a gradual awakening of the potential of dead sculptural matter through the application of electricity and sound waves, as well as through invoking physical changes in states of matter. *To Be Hidden And So Invisible (21000 Hz)* (2009), for example, is a 'sublimated watermelon' placed on a wooden shelf next to a speaker and generator of waveforms. In another piece, *Sleep Machine* (2008), a stream of air from a small electric fan fixes a plastic bag to the gallery wall. *Mist Mouth* (2007) is a cloud of steam vaporizing through a hole in the floor.

Canell employs outmoded technical equipment and found objects in her characteristically unassuming low-tech installations. Viewers are invited to witness the ephemeral events in sculpture rather than merely to acknowledge the presence of solid forms. In language, this intermediary caught-in-the-act state of things has an equivalent in poetry, and indeed, Canell's titles are similar to fragments of poems. The dream-like narrative situations that she devises reveal their affinity to language games and literature, while the formal vocabulary is that of the various traditions of modern sculpture.

Precarious combinations

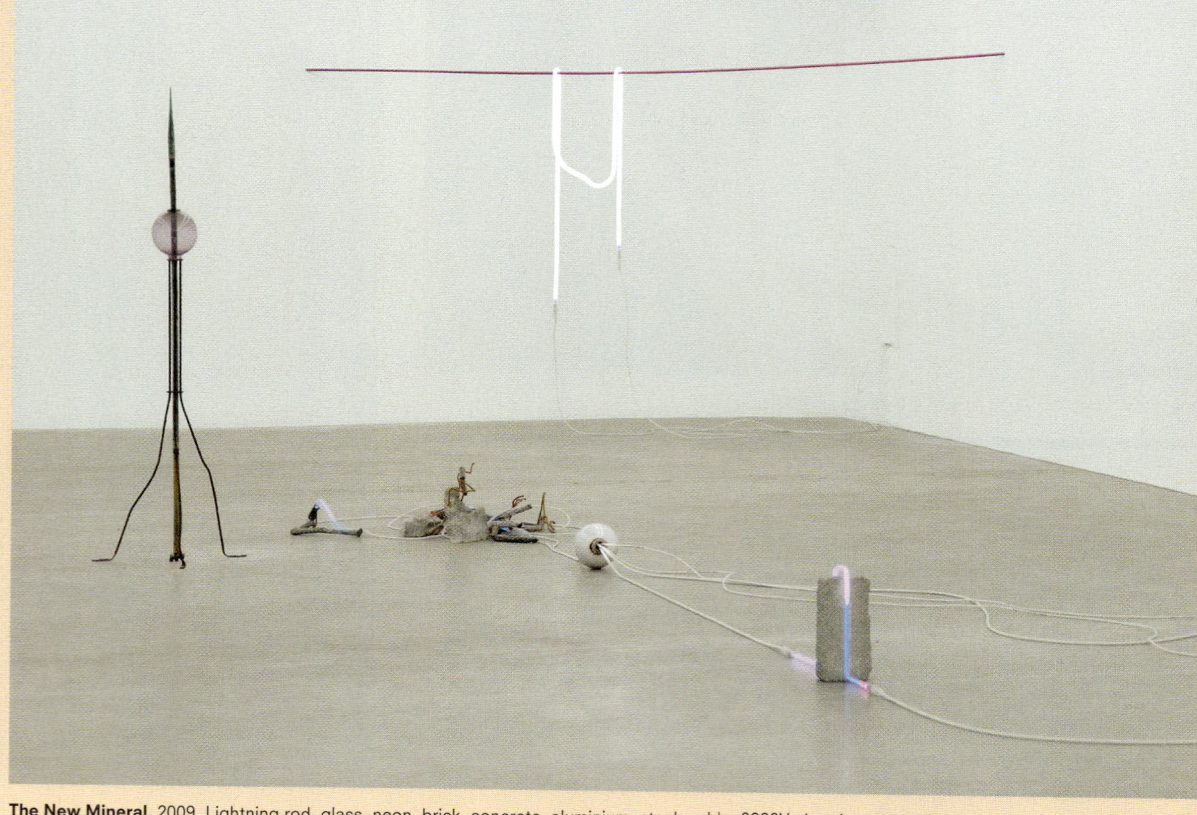

The New Mineral, 2009. Lightning rod, glass, neon, brick, concrete, aluminium, steel, cable, 8000V electric current. Approx. 500 × 700 × 250 cm

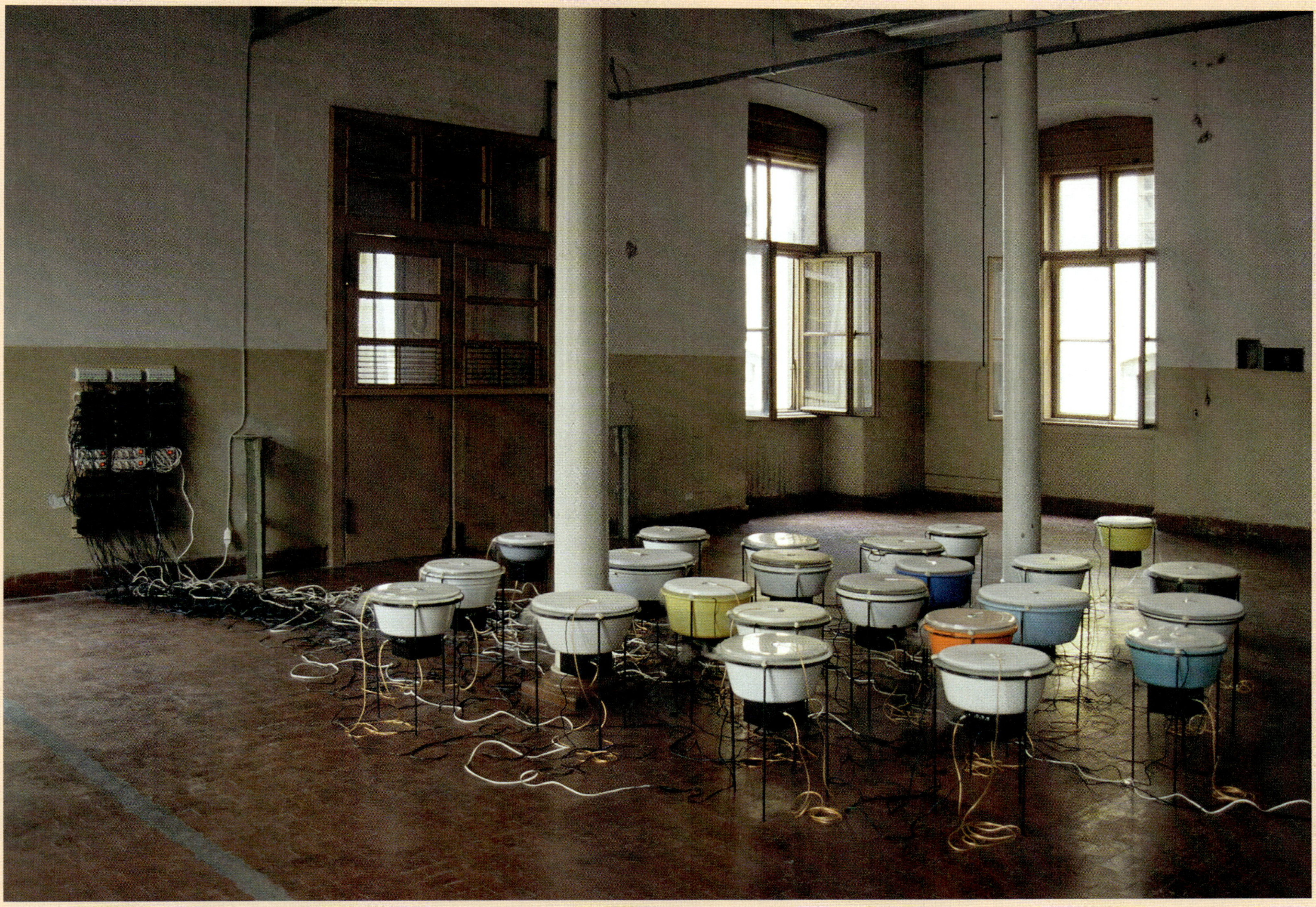

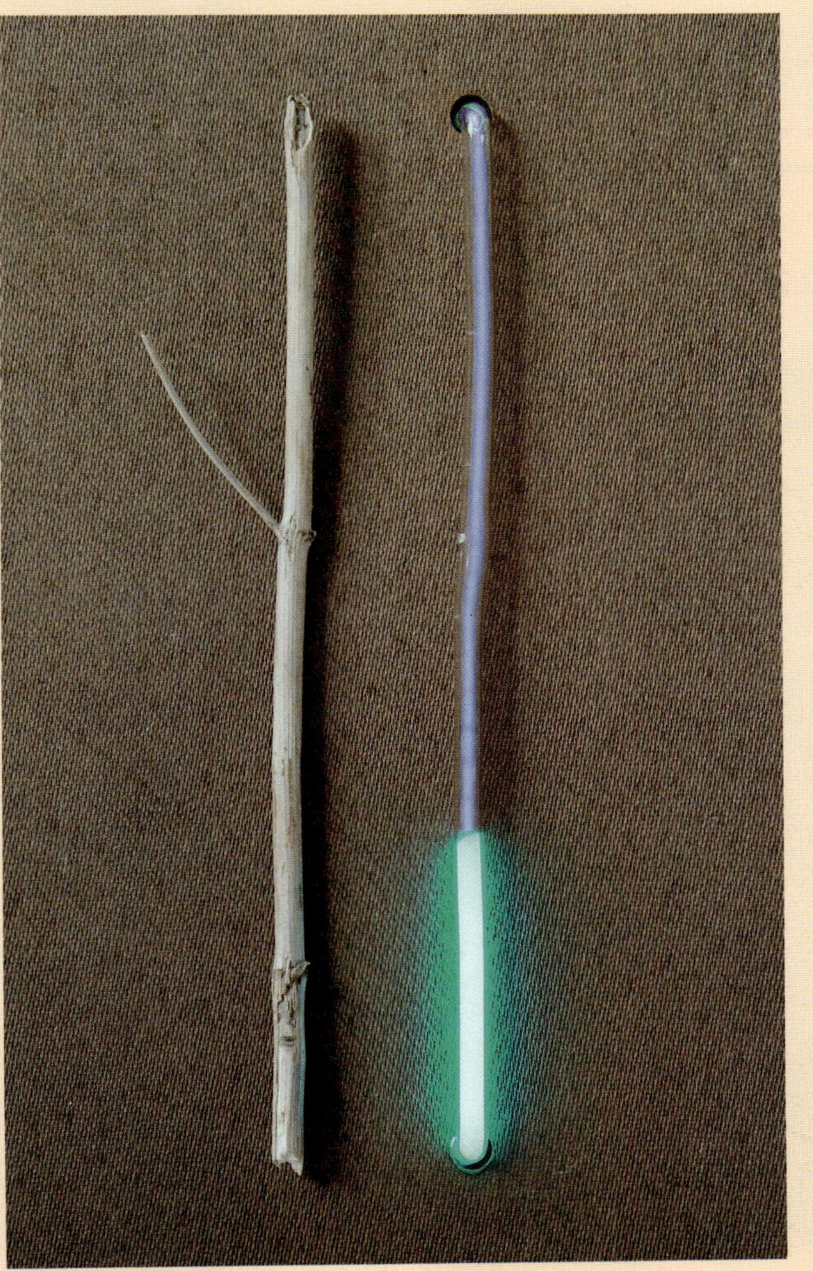

Shedding Skin (Perpetual Current for 24 Buckets), 2008. 240 litres of water, buckets, steel, hydrophones, amplifiers, mist machines, drum skins, clay, relay timers, cable. 500 × 500 × 150 cm

Potential of dead sculptural matter

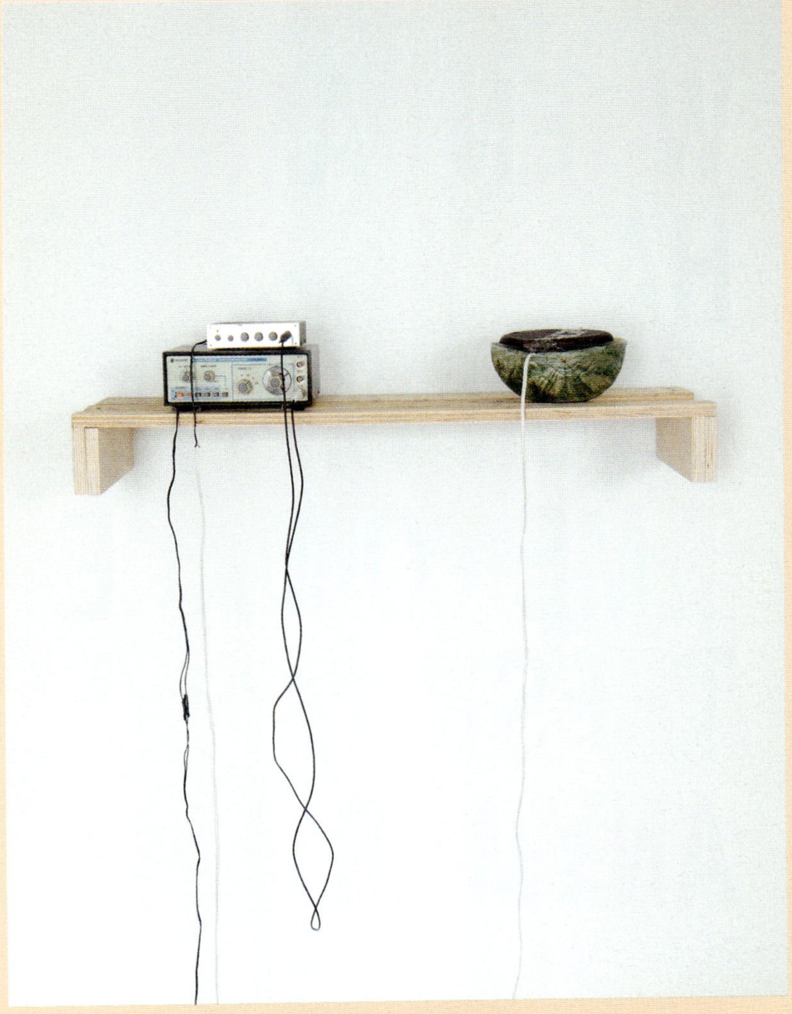

To Be Hidden and So Invisible (21000 Hz), 2009. Sublimated watermelon, function generator, amplifier, speaker, wood, cable. 23 × 92 × 26 cm

Fellow Ribs (detail), 2009. Stick, neon, wood, gypsum, 1000V electric current. 25 × 43 × 15 cm

Endless Column (Alternating Current for Twelve Window Fans) (2009), installed at Konrad Fischer Gallery, points at the avant-garde and mystical origins of Minimalism, conflating a title borrowed from Constantin Brancusi with a structure reminiscent of Donald Judd's stacks. But instead of consisting of twelve galvanized iron boxes attached to the wall, as in Judd's *Untitled (Stack)* of 1967, Canell's work comprises twelve standard-size window fans that produce alternating wind currents and seem to hover above each other in a column extending from floor to ceiling.

Canell juxtaposes man-made and natural things in precarious combinations that point at a state of instability and originate from the contingency inherent to our existence. The basic impulse animating her work seems at least twofold: on the one hand, one might think of Eva Hesse introducing the 'weak' logic of the body into the rigid economy of Minimal art. On the other hand, the performative and temporal components of Canell's practice may be inspired by Bas Jan Ader's refutation of Conceptual art's scholarly stringency in favour of highly personal, narrative and poetic works.

Alejandro Cesarco

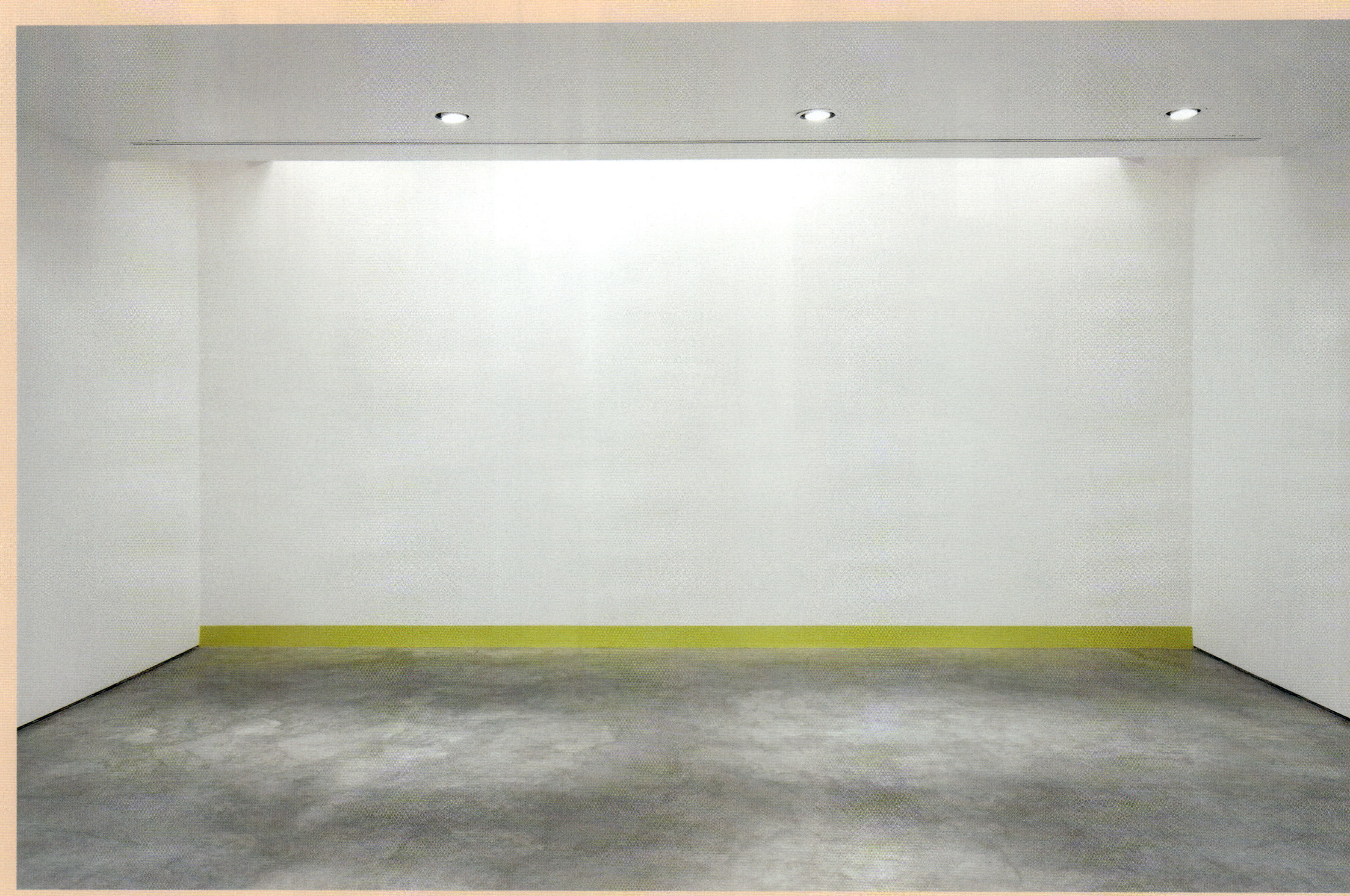

Here Comes the Sun, 2006. Yellow house paint on wall. Dimensions variable

Translation as re-writing

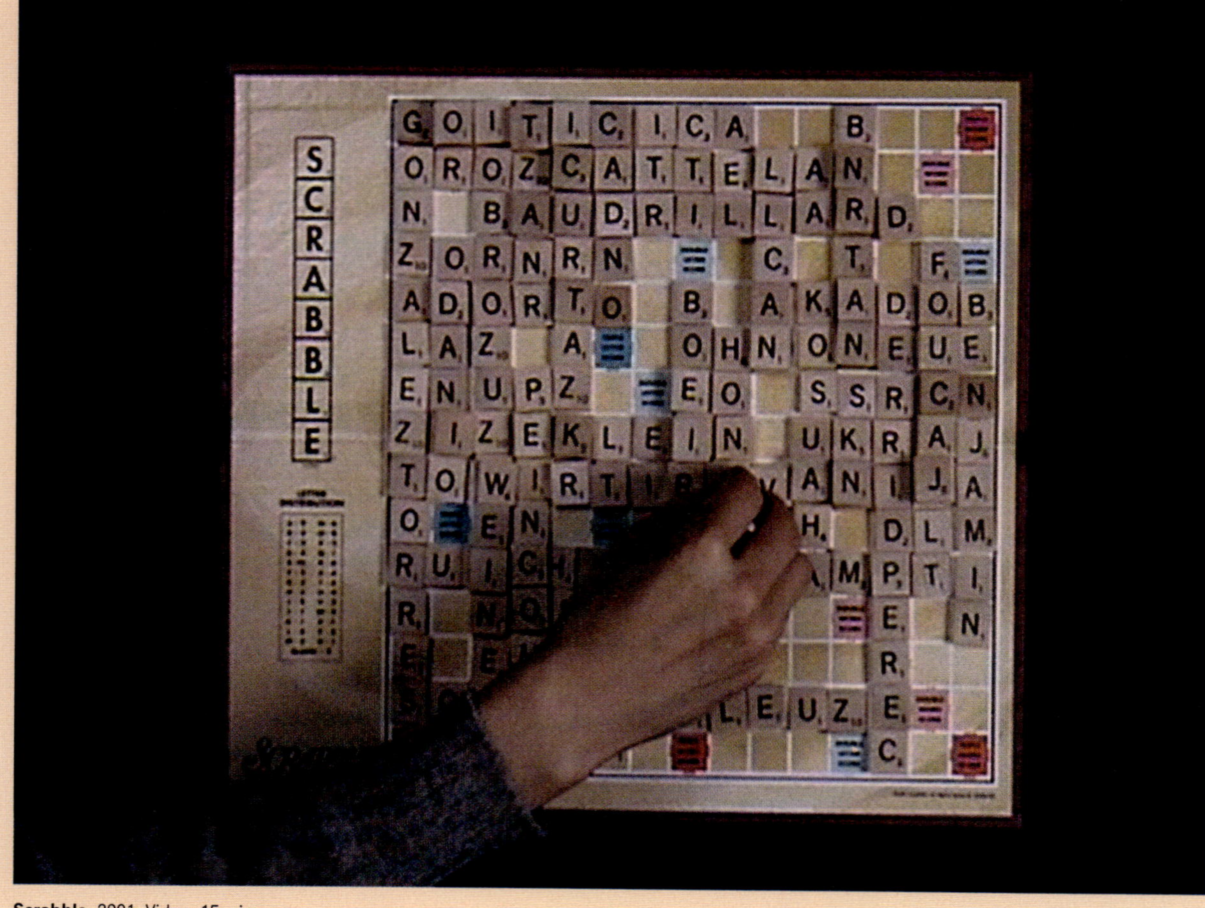

Scrabble, 2001. Video. 15 min.

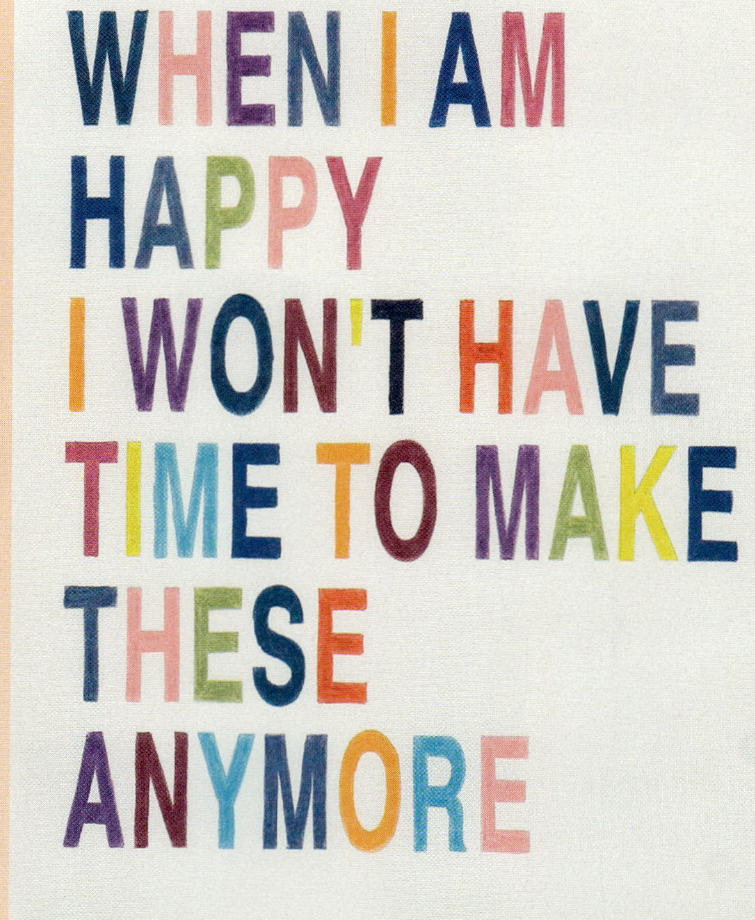

When I am Happy, 2002-present. Coloured pencil on paper. 28 × 23 cm

In conversation with others

Born in Montevideo, Uruguay, Alejandro Cesarco relocated to New York in 1998. Since then he has been defining his role as artist according to his position as a cultural consumer, taking artistic dialogue with those he admires as an essential strategy. His oeuvre, which includes works that are more or less traditional (installations, texts, videos, films), as well as translations, editorial, curatorial and educational projects, began to find its identity through a process of research and identification with his key preferences and influences. At the heart of his project is the history of Conceptual art, while another basic aspect is the melancholic character of his productions, which becomes evident through the inclusion of iconic references to the Romantic tradition—

Stage Direction/Establishing Shot, 2008. Black vinyl. 25 × 15 cm

Picture #8, 2007. C–print. 60 × 77 cm

Platforms for dialogue

always mediated by theory, film or literature.

This cross between sentimentality and the history of Conceptual art is clearly announced in *Index* (2000), twelve pages from a nonexistent book, an index that is 'half biographical and half theoretical text; it is extremely personal, at times even hermetic, yet full of clichés'. Cesarco name-drops Maurice Merleau-Ponty, Jacques Lacan and Louise Lawler, but also the Uruguayan novelist Mario Levrero, his friend the painter López Lage, his 'mamá', as well as Lithuania, where his grandfather was born. As the years pass, this spirit of the good pupil, which was also evident in works such as *Scrabble* (2001), a version of the game in which only influences could be used as words, began to give way to an increasing sophistication in terms of developing his references. If at first, as Luis Camnitzer wrote, 'influences were the work', little by little the idea of apprenticeship that characterized the young artist led to the idea of dialogue as the centre of the work. Now Cesarco does not produce if not in conversation with others, citing, appropriating, circulating information and creating platforms for dialogue. Some examples of this are his series of paperbacks, published through A.R.T. Press, in which he sets up conversations between artists from two generations (Silvia Kolbowski with Walid Raad, Liam Gillick with Lawrence Weiner, Andrea Bowers with Catherine Opie, among others); his participation as co-curator in the 2007 Mercorsul Biennial, in which he conceived of a curatorial methodology based on the conversation between groups of works, selected by the curator and the participating artists as if playing a game; and his exhibition of works produced in collaboration with John Baldessari.

Although he has recently branched into film-making, like any good Conceptualist, Cesarco works fundamentally in text formats: indexes, lists, classifications, footnotes and books. One of his most striking works in book form is *Love Poems* (2004), a translation that he made of *Poemas de amor*, written in 1957 by the Uruguayan poet Idea Vilariño. This project, which he describes as 'a covert form of appropriation that investigates the potential of literal translation as a visual act. Evidence of a construction of self mediated through texts', sums up his preoccupations: the circulation of information between diverse cultural contexts, the artwork as a cultural and therefore political act, writing as image, translation as re-writing, re-writing as appropriation, Conceptual art as Romantic vehicle.

Us, 2008. C–print. 66 × 61 cm

Paul Chan

Who exactly is Paul Chan? Theorist, activist, artist? He is all of these things, and more. He is an artist who uses video to create animations, yet to label him as a video artist would be way off the mark. His works reference a plethora of fields — philosophy, religion, art history, theatre, literature — and while the actions he takes to address political issues may not always be defined as art, for him, art is an arena for pondering the political.

A computer specialist, Chan began drawing vibrantly coloured animations by tweaking software and programmes chosen deliberately for their obsolescence, a process almost akin to making old-fashioned paintings in order to document reality instead of using modern means such as photography and film. His early works included *Happiness (Finally) After 35,000 Years of Civilization (After Henry Darger and Charles Fourier)* (1999–2003), inspired by outsider artist Henry Darger, whose work only became known to the world after his death in the year Chan was born, and nineteenth-century utopian socialist Charles Fourier. *My Birds … Trash … the Future* (2004) featured characters based on rapper Biggie Smalls and the Italian poet and film director Pier Paolo Pasolini, who were both killed by assassins. At first glance these works possess the upbeat playfulness of video games, but what they really portray is an apocalyptic world, a maelstrom of anxiety, senseless violence and promiscuity. In Chan's visual realm, dark shadows lurk. His next offering, *The 7 Lights*

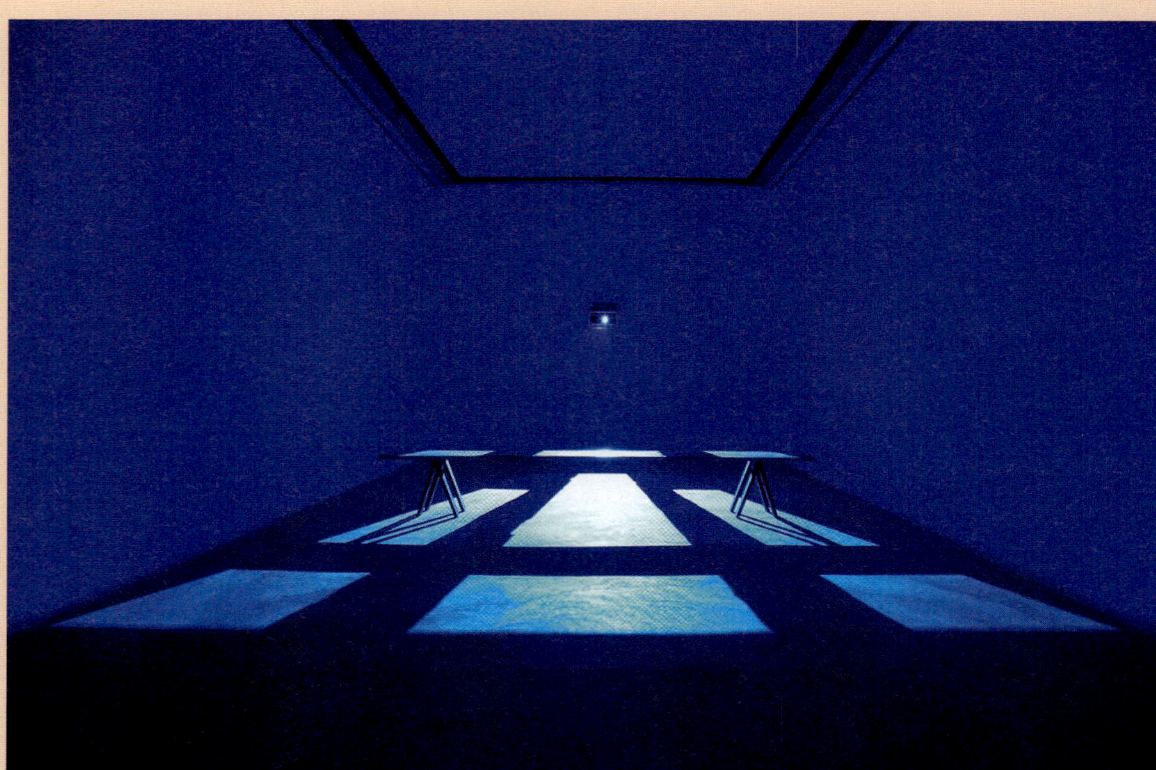

An arena for pondering the politcal

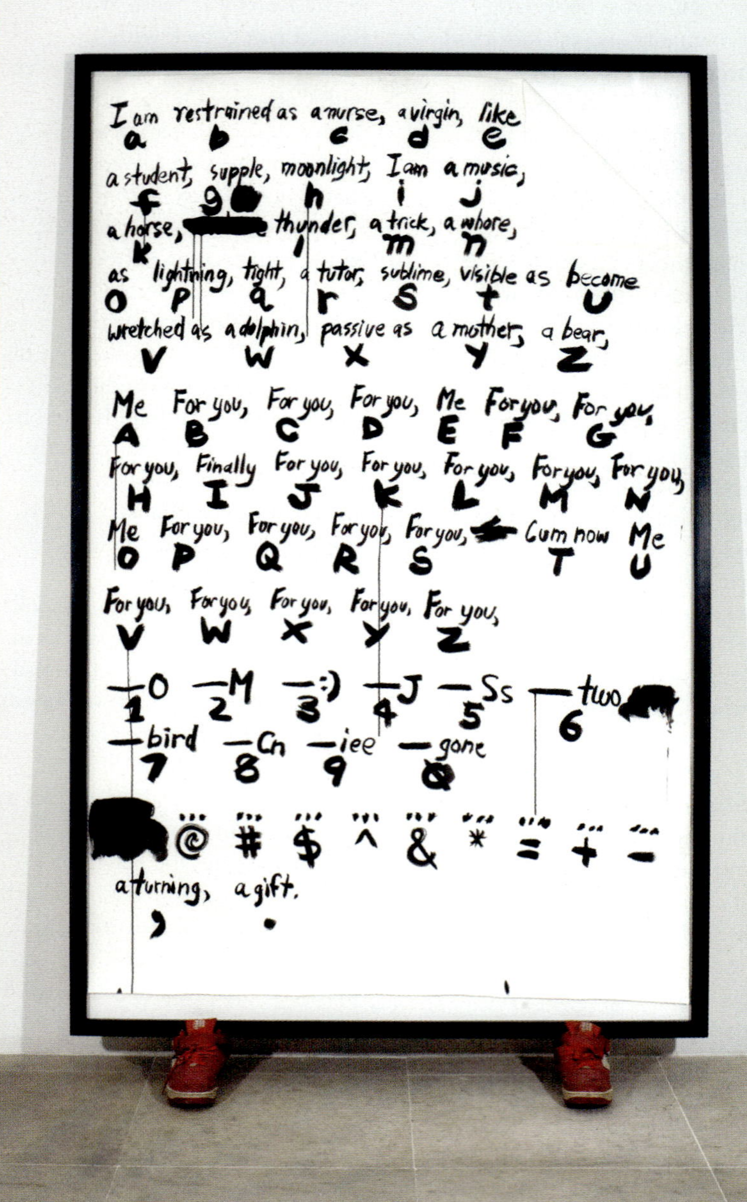

The body of Oh Ho_darlin (truetype font), 2008. Ink on paper, mixed–media. 213 × 137 cm

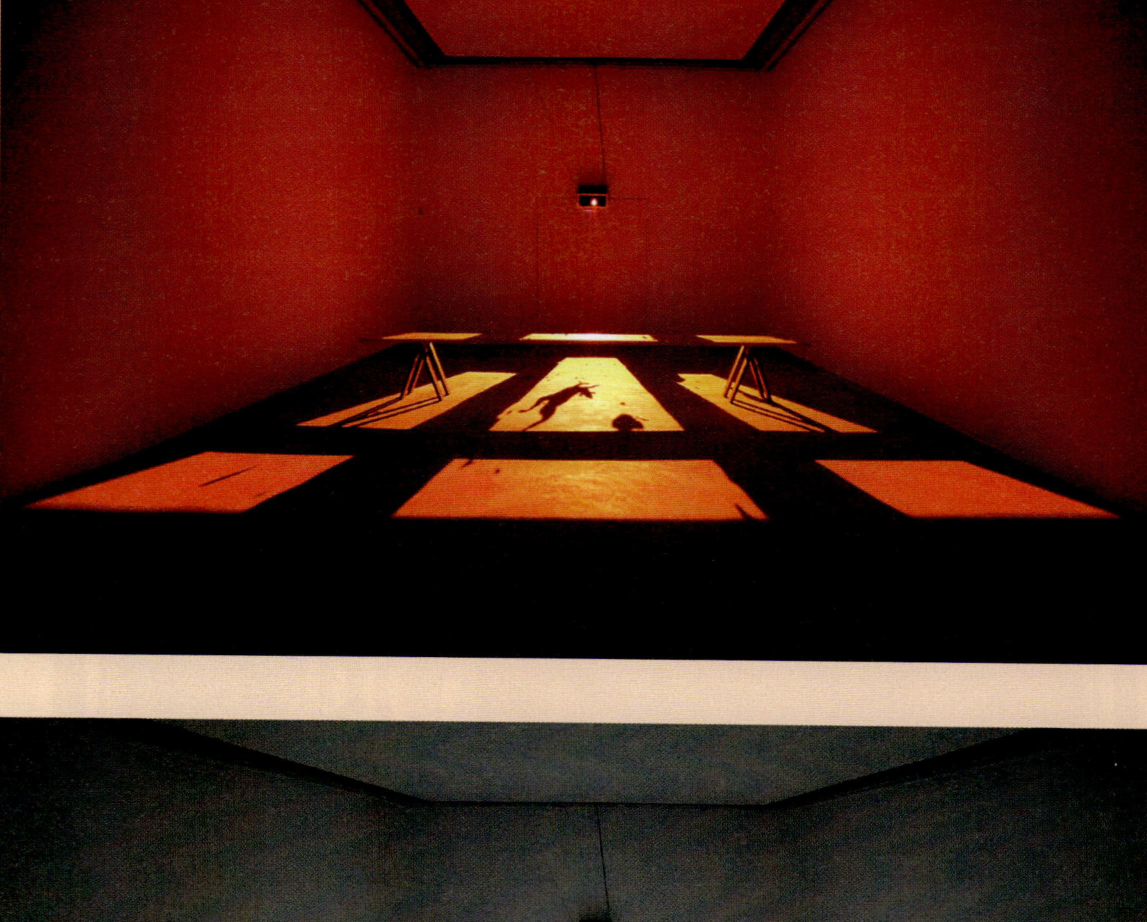

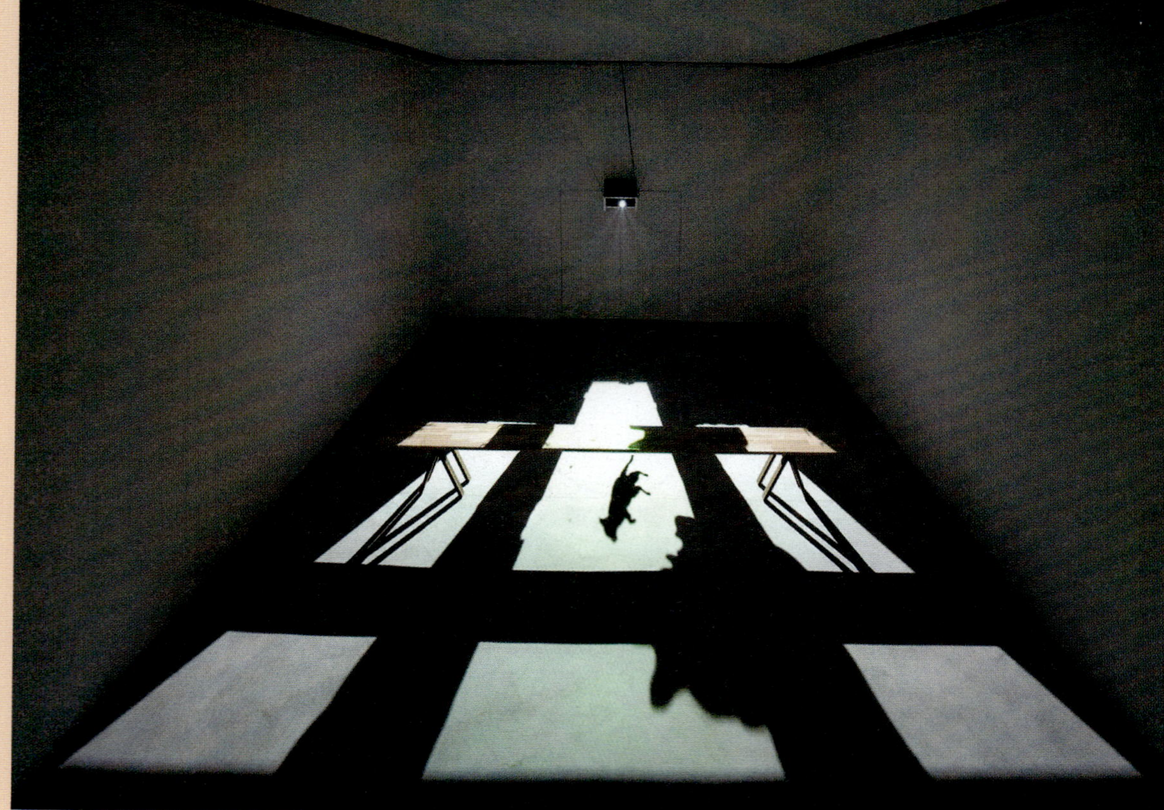

3rd Light, 2006. Digital video projection, table. 14 min. Dimensions variable.

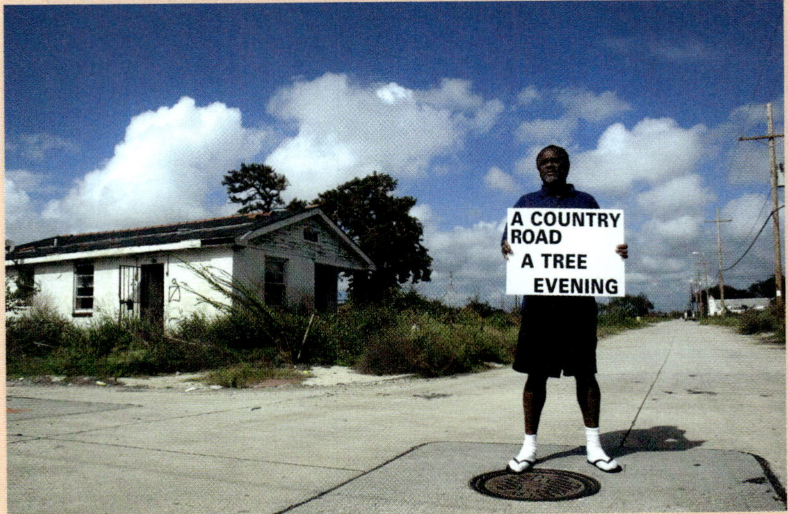
2nd Light, 2006. Digital video projection. 14 min.

Waiting for Godot in New Orleans

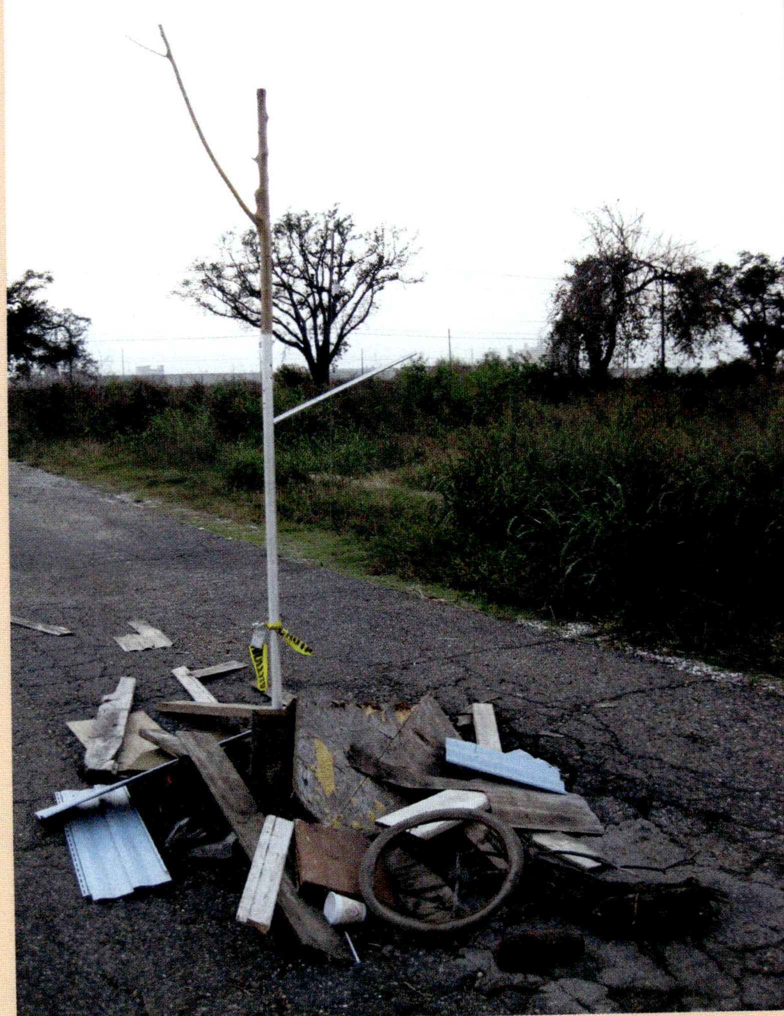

Waiting for Godot in New Orleans, 2007. Play. Actor: Robert Green

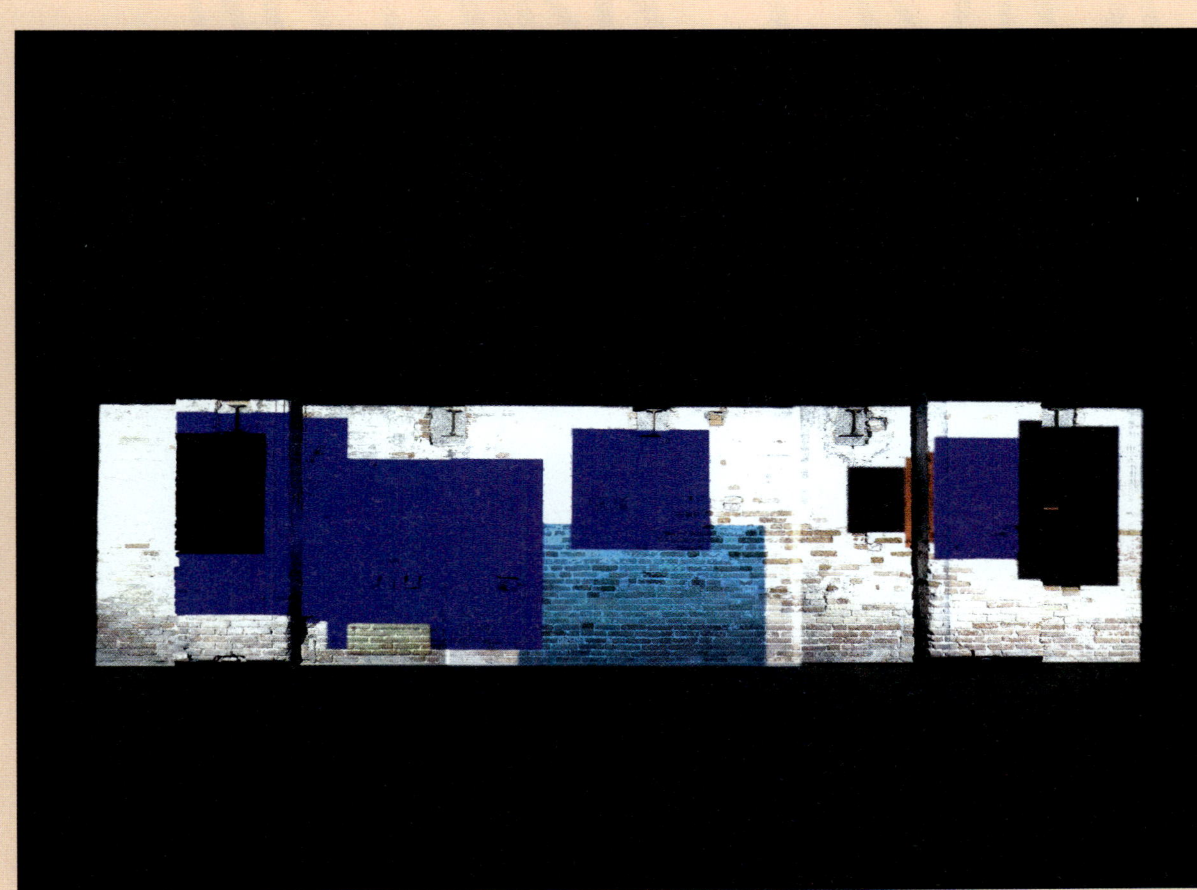
Waiting for Godot in New Orleans, 2007. Play. Detail of set with tree

Politics, philosophy & pornogprahy

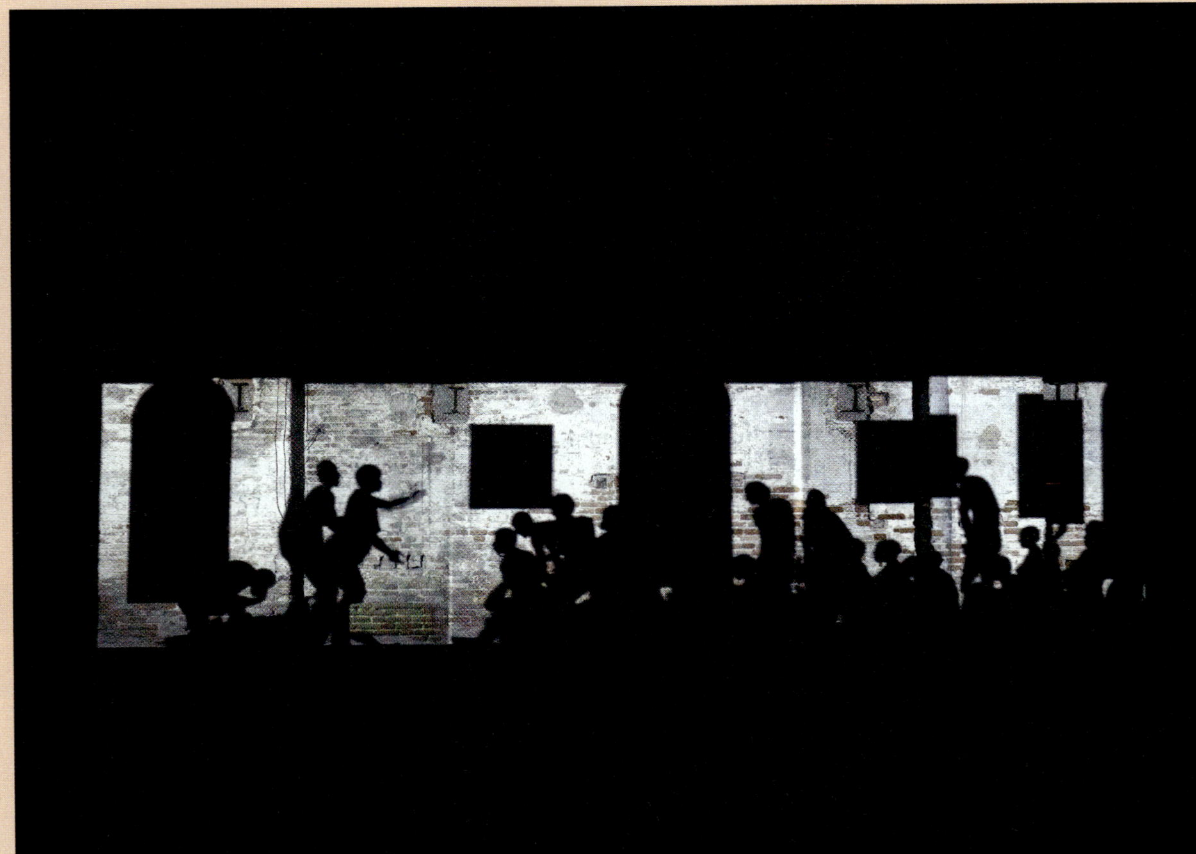
Sade for Sade's sake, 2009. Digital projection. 5 hour 45 min. loop

series (2005–07), consisted of projections that resembles sunlight of constantly changing colour shining in through windows, in which the shadows of all sorts of items found in our materialist society appear and disappear in stately, almost sacred silence. In contrast is the spine-chilling illusion created in some of these works that silhouettes of people are falling to earth. Evoking images of 9/11, they also suggest a last judgement brought down upon humanity.

Chan's new work *Sade for Sade's Sake* (2009) presents, again in silhouette, pornographic scenarios penned by the Marquis du Sade. The three elements of politics, philosophy and pornography, which Chan refers to as the secular trio that freed us from God, combine in a video work with a total running time of close to six hours, projected directly onto the irregular wall of a building. Chan's depiction of human shadows quivering with pleasure and madness in a work drained of colour and impoverished in terms of visual elements, is intended less as a depiction of sex, than as an evocation of the decadence and anarchism of our age.

Chan's ideas are not aired exclusively in the gallery. He also uses his website nationalphilistine. com as an accessible, democratic tool and platform for an ongoing media project. In 2007 he staged a Classical Theatre of Harlem production of Samuel Beckett's *Waiting for Godot* in districts of New Orleans stripped of any vestige of human endeavour by the hurricane, an idea that came to him following his first visit to the city when invited to lecture there. Waiting for Godot had also been staged by Susan Sontag in Sarajevo in 1993, and on both occasions was aimed at people waiting for help in a state of emptiness.

Through his words, actions and ideas, Chan expands the norms, definitions and territory of art. He writes, reads, takes the lectern and responds to interviews, quoting freely from his predecessors. Believing that art is one means of exploring uncharted ideological domains, he is engaged in a quest to find even the smallest ray of light in the hopeless brutality of humanity.

Rosa Chancho

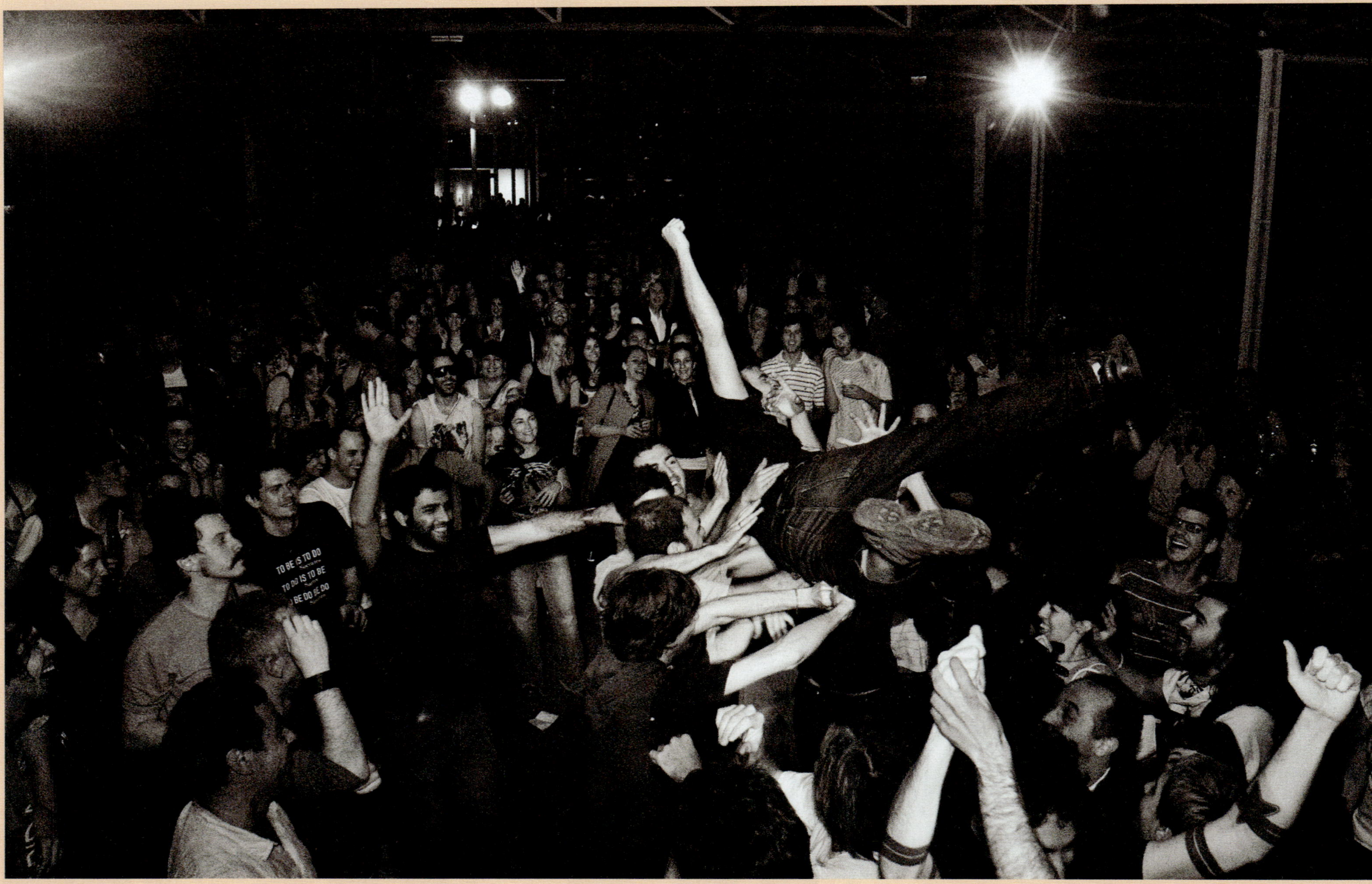

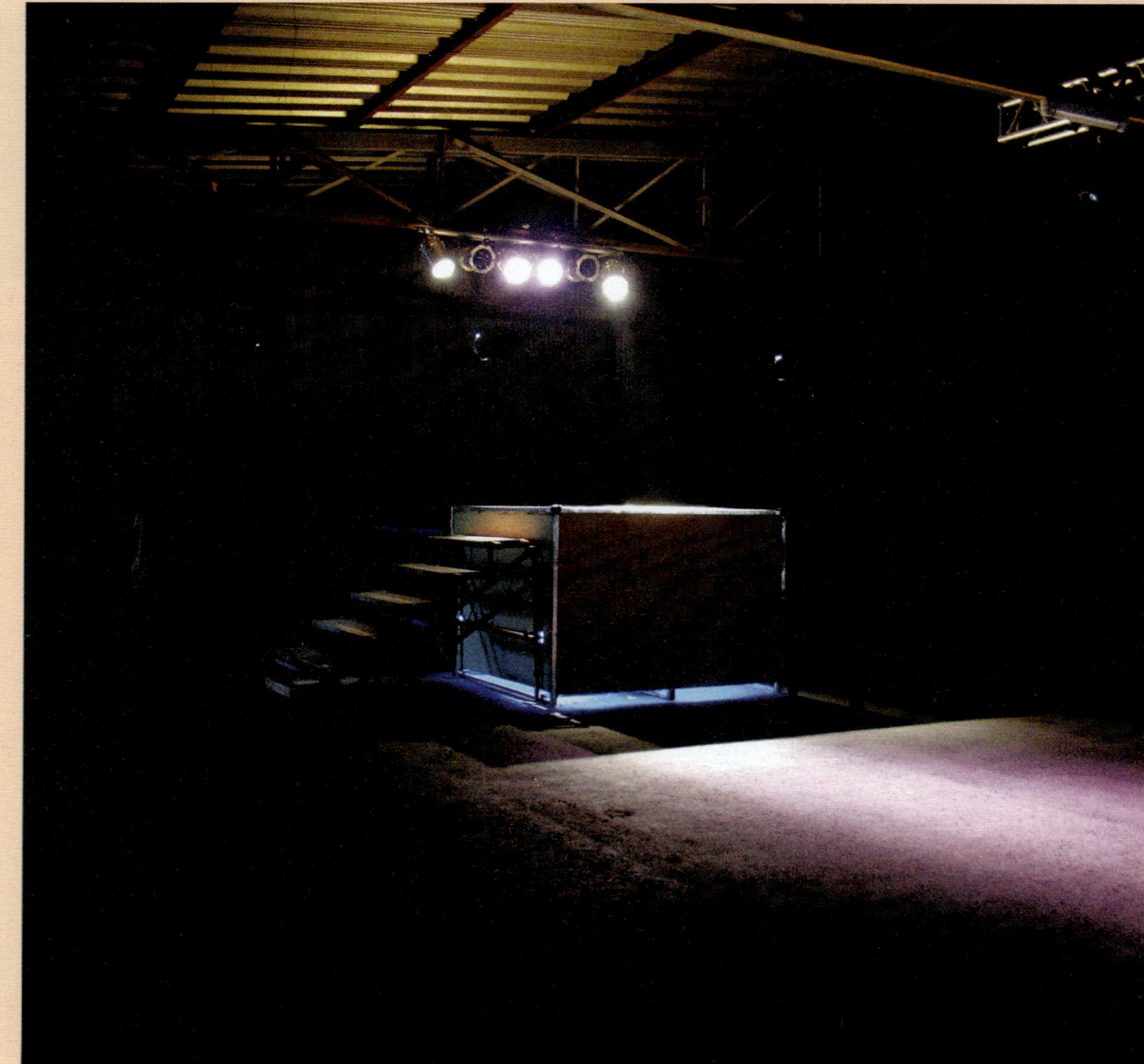

At its inception Rosa Chancho was a gallery venture led by a group of four artists and one critic: Julieta García Vázquez, Mumi, Tomás Lerner, Osías Yanov and Javier Villa. Their gallery operated for a year, from 2006 until 2007, in the Palermo neighbourhood in Buenos Aires, inviting artists to work within specific limitations, experimenting with various exhibition formats and the juxtaposition of projects.

Since then, pushed on by the euphoric condition of the Argentine art world over the last few years, Rosa Chancho has been participating in various events and shows as an artists' collective, under a mutating identity, which has led its participants to take on different roles (artists, curators, collectors, producers and gallerists).

For *Inauguración* (Inauguration, 2006), they built a cubicle at an art fair, where they organized an opening without any actual artworks. With *Hombre obra* (Man Artwork, 2006) they proposed to transform a small-town psychologist into a 'human artwork' which was committed to expert scrutiny to see whether it could be incorporated into the local contemporary art museum's collection. Two years after forming and during their first solo show, they generated their own 'retrospective' (*Retrospectiva*, 2008), imagined as an amusement park, with all new works.

The group is reconfigured in response to institutional invitations, generating works and even its own identity accordingly.

Rosa Chancho's practice is sporadic and reactive. The group is reconfigured in response to institutional invitations, generating works and even its own identity accordingly. Two works exemplify their attitude. *Bola de lodo* (*Mud Ball*, 2007) was their ironic answer to an online project named 'Bola de Nieve' (Snowball) — a virtual network of information on local artists run by the artists themselves.

Untitled (Stage Diving), 2008. 1 DJ, 100 collaborators, 800 people. Platform 200 × 200 × 150 cm

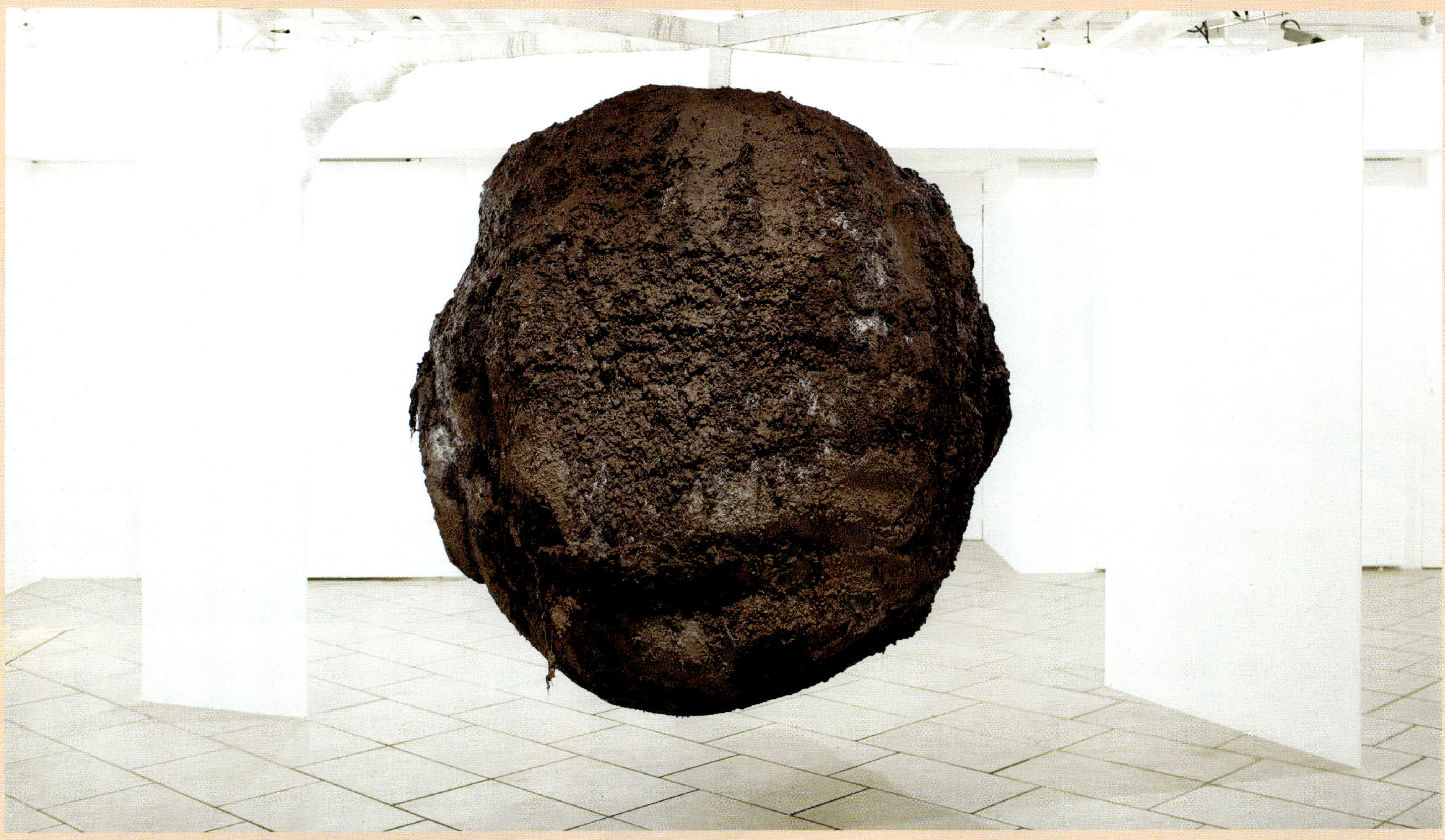

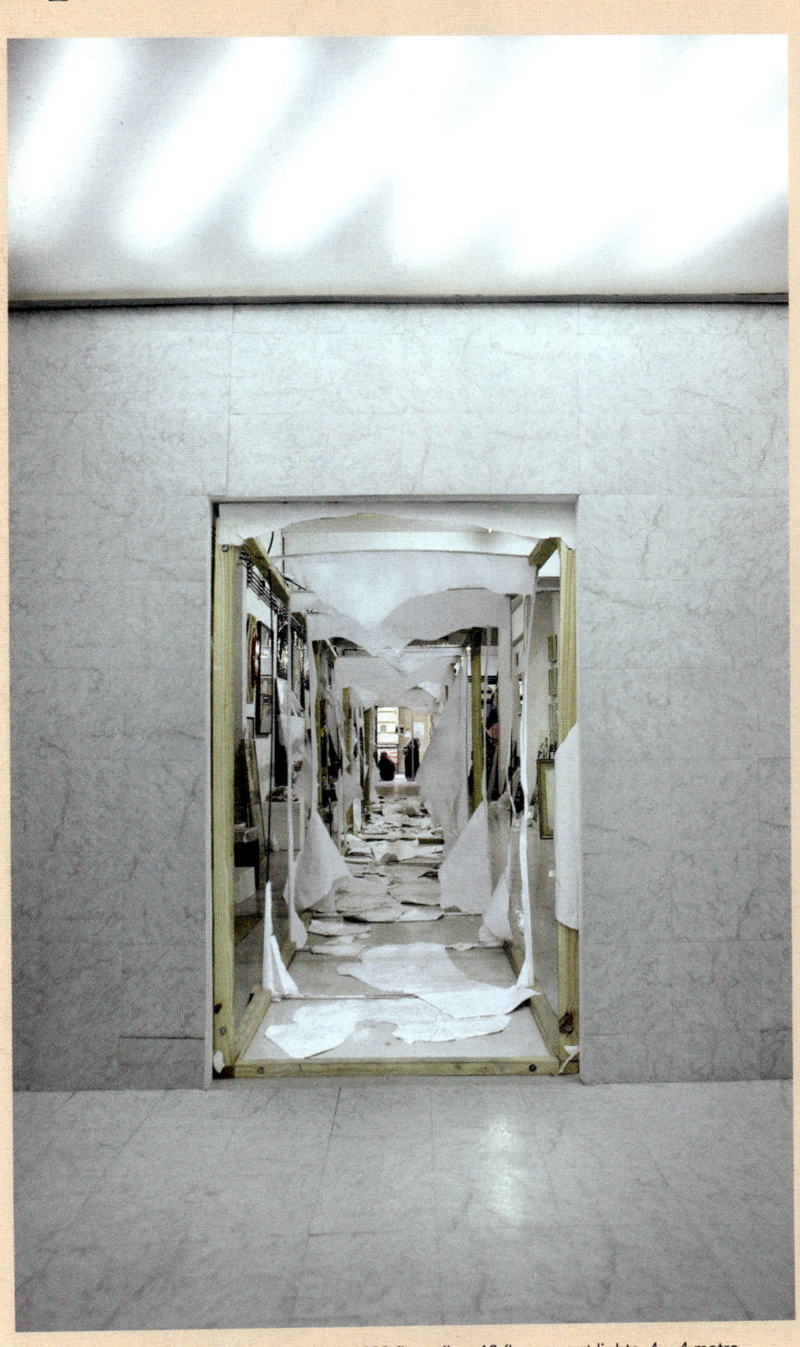

Mud Ball (first stage of work in progress), 2007. Half a ton of soil, water, adhesive. Diameter 2 m

Sporadic and reactive

In response, *Bola de lodo* proposed the creation of a collaborative and accretive work of art, but instead of a virtual 'snowball', they made a gigantic ball of mud in the centre of an exhibition space, working with clay, the most primitive of technologies. In 2008, invited to take part in a performance festival, they invited visitors to give themselves up to the rock-scene practice of 'stage diving' in the corporal action *Untitled (Stage Diving)*.

The group's strength lies in its ability to embed itself in the art world with a critical and humorous sensibility and a feel for the camp, cheap specularity of local TV. According to Javier Villa, the critic in the collective, they differ from the majority of artist groups because they put their 'faith not so much in dialogue-driven potential construction, as more "relational" artist collectives might do, but in the sensorial and emotional power of the group experience'. In this sense, in looking for precedents, Rosa Chancho refers to elements of Argentine art history, such as the artist groups from the Instituto Di Tella and Liliana Maresca's collective projects, whose work lies somewhere between circus and ritual.

Retrospective, 2008. Room panelled with 1220 floor tiles, 18 fluorescent lights, 4 × 4 metre translucent screen, wooden tunnel, steel, 20 sheets of paper. 14 × 2 × 1 m

Humorous sensibility

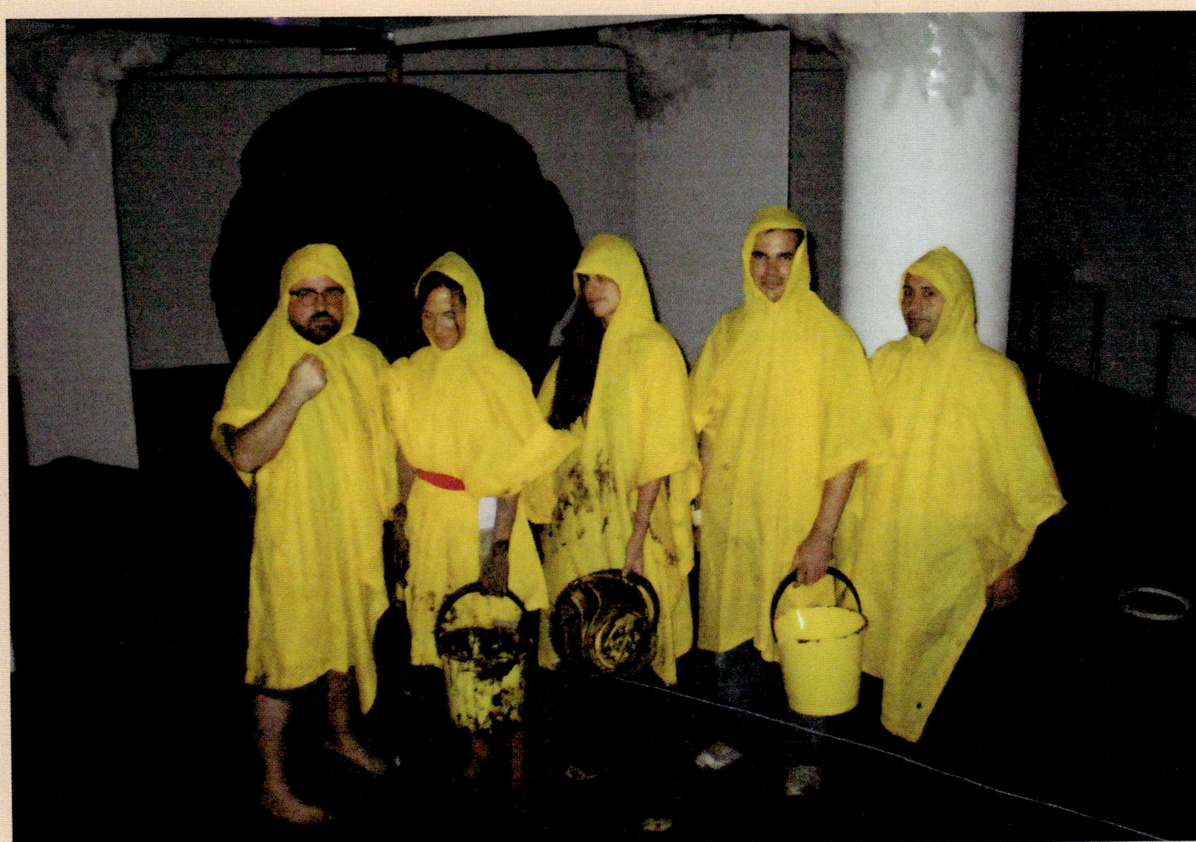

Mud Ball (second stage of work in progress), 2007. Soil, water. Dimensions variable

Spartacus Chetwynd

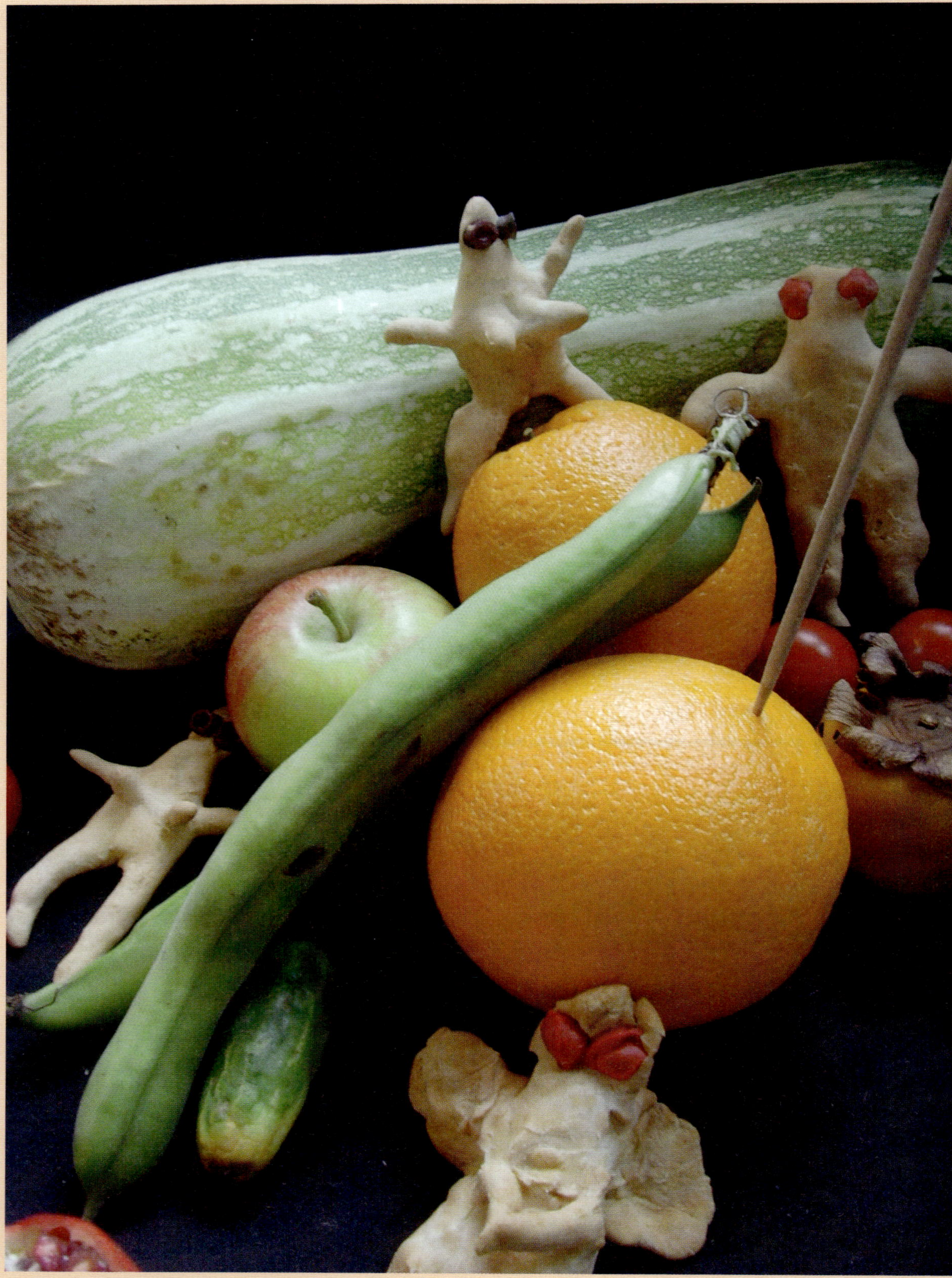

Iron Age Pasta Necklace Workshop, 2009. Performance. Studio Voltaire, London

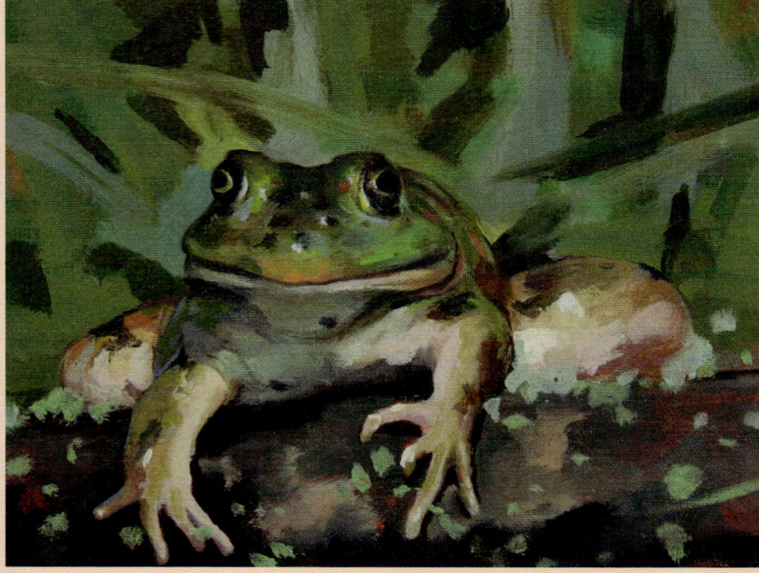

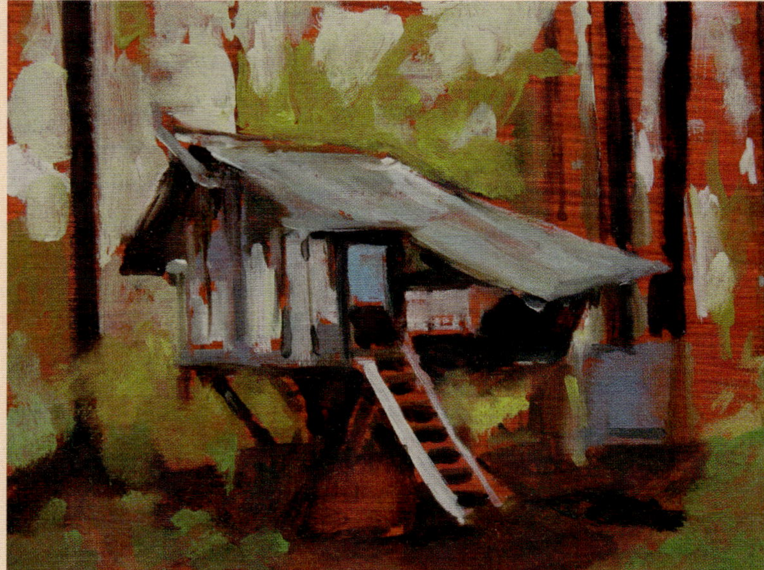

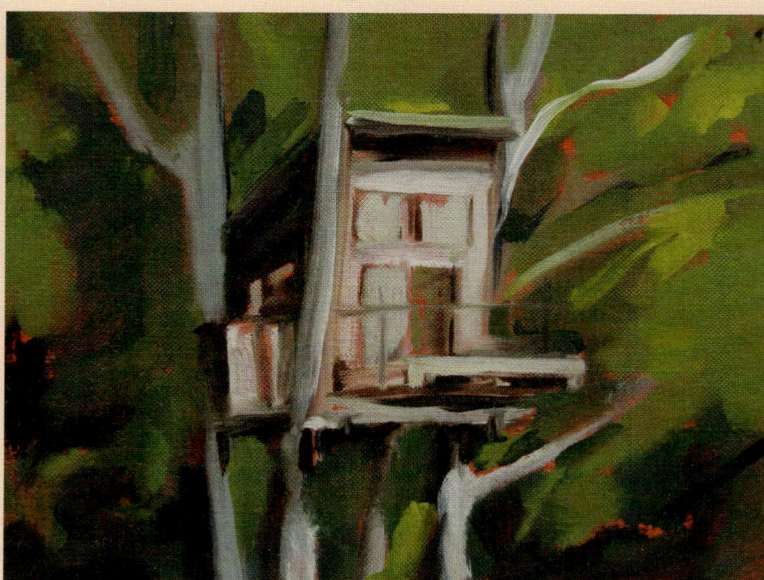

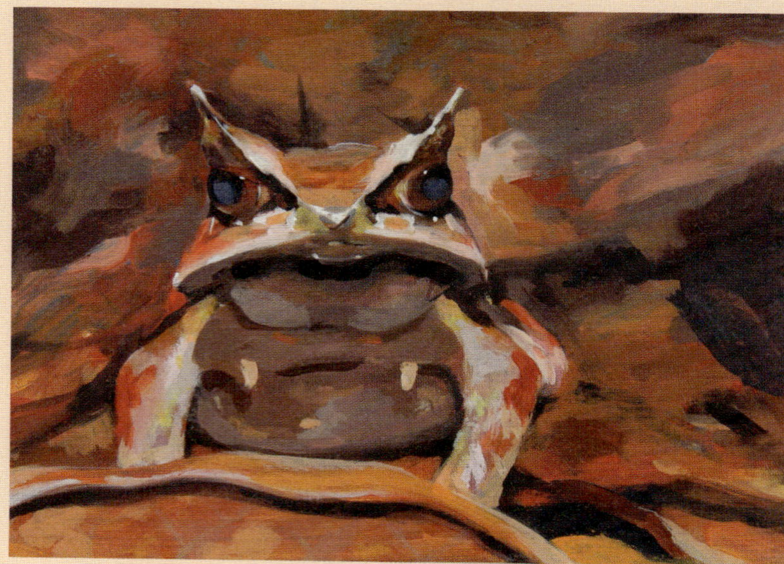

Unique practice rooted in painting and performance

In the past ten years, Spartacus Chetwynd has evolved a unique practice rooted in painting and performance. Her participatory live works have the unruly spirit of the carnival, the circus or a Marx Brothers comedy and exhibit an irreverent, free spirit. Early on, Chetwynd painted miniature pictures on the absurdist theme of the 'bat opera': tiny vignettes of imagined productions. In tandem, she was hand-making props, costumes and scenery for her theatre pieces from a bricolage of discarded materials, including fabric, cardboard and gouache paint.

A proposed equivalence between the possibilities offered by the fantastical space of the stage and the arena of the canvas lies at the root of her project.

The narrative structures on which Chetwynd's performances hinge are often taken from popular sources, usually familiar to the collective imagination. Early works played out crude versions of *The Wicker Man* or *Conan the Barbarian*, as well as a make-shift live version of the ghoulish video for Michael Jackson's 'Thriller', which erupted in the midst of a club night, lasting only for the duration of the song. Later works have evolved into more complex hybrid conceits, including a three-act play accompanied by John Barry's original score for *Born Free* (2004) at Gasworks and the lo-fi sport of *The Snail Race* (2008).

Bat Opera Paintings, 2009. Oil on paper. 20 × 15 cm

Unruly spirit of the carnival

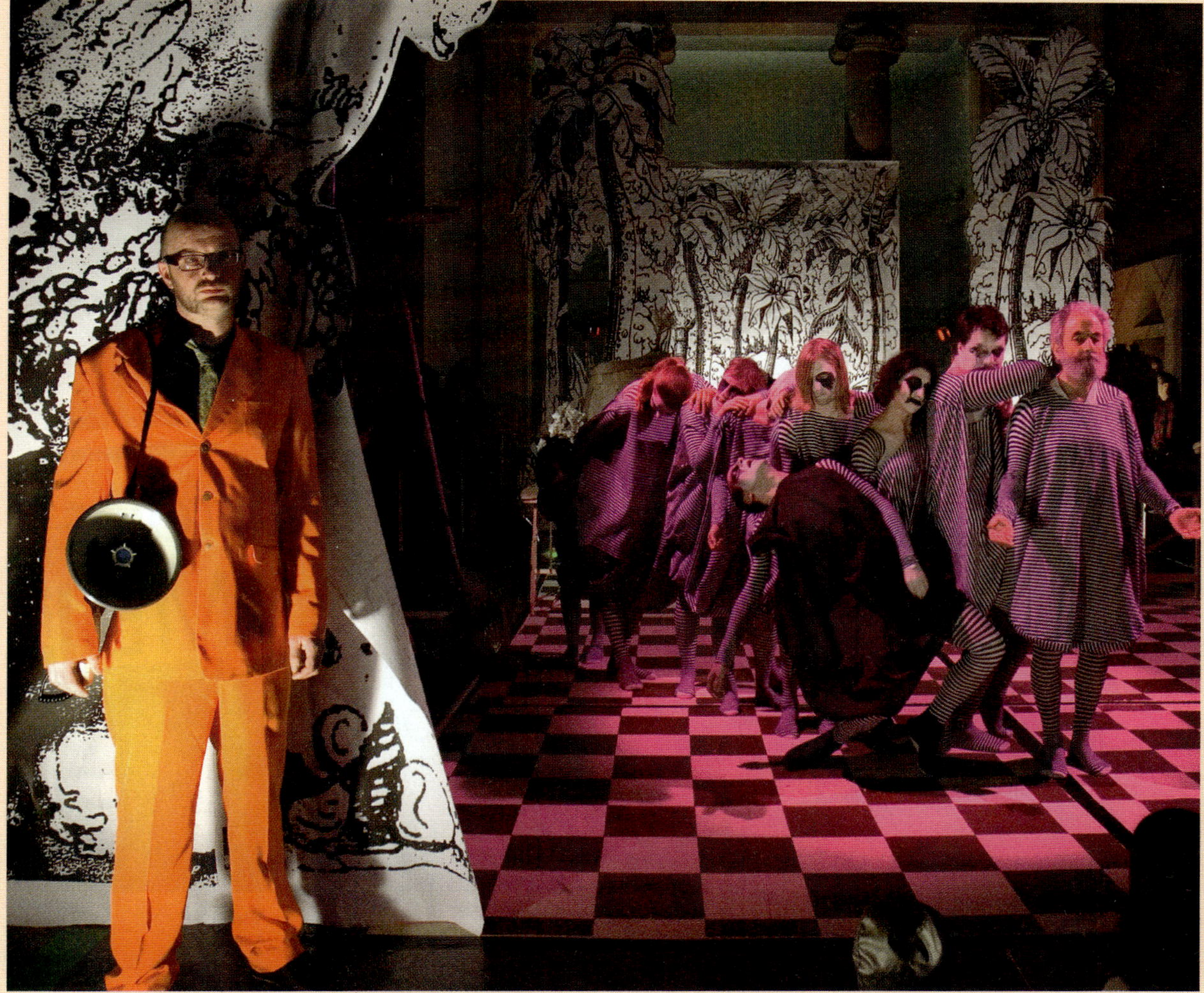

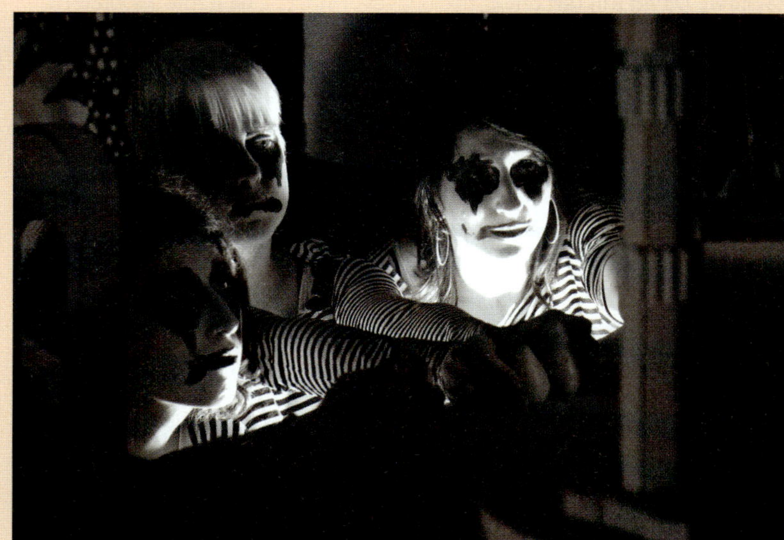

The Fall of Man, 2006. Performance. Tate Triennial, Tate Britain, London

The Walk to Dover (2005) involved the artist and friends playing the role of Victorian street urchins reenacting the walk taken by Dickens's David Copperfield in an adventure that was part living theatre, part survival: they made their way through the countryside eating berries and drinking stream-water, in period costumes and top hats. For the 2006 Tate Triennial she staged *The Fall of Man* as a puppet show in three acts within a divided theatrical space constructed out of cardboard and plumbing pipe, where small groups from within the larger audience were invited to pass under the Proscenium arch into a more intimate seating area where the play would unfold every fifteen minutes. Chetwynd's live work reconsiders the history of performance, especially in regard to post-1970s ideas of body art and communal participation. Her inclusive and exploratory approach to group dynamics prompts her to invite a wide range of friends, acquaintances and family members to feature in her work, making and designing their costumes and props as well as acting. In common with the underground film-maker Jack Smith, Chetwynd's 'found' narratives serve as an exoticized pretext through which she can explore relational interaction. Her approach to participants' involvement registers an attempt to fit her requirements to their own fantasies and desires, under the masquerading cover of a collective suspension of disbelief.

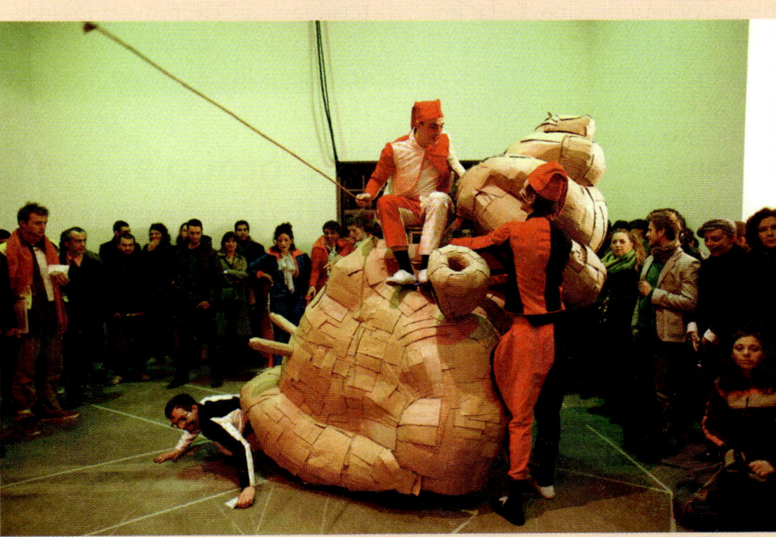

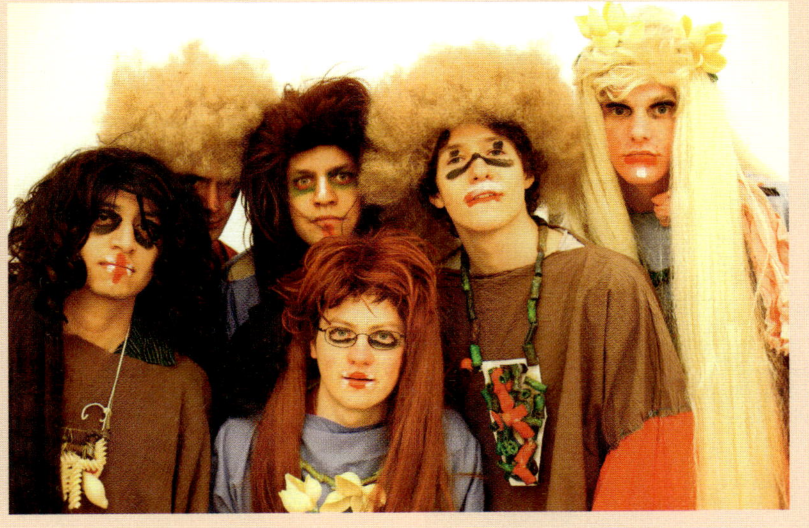

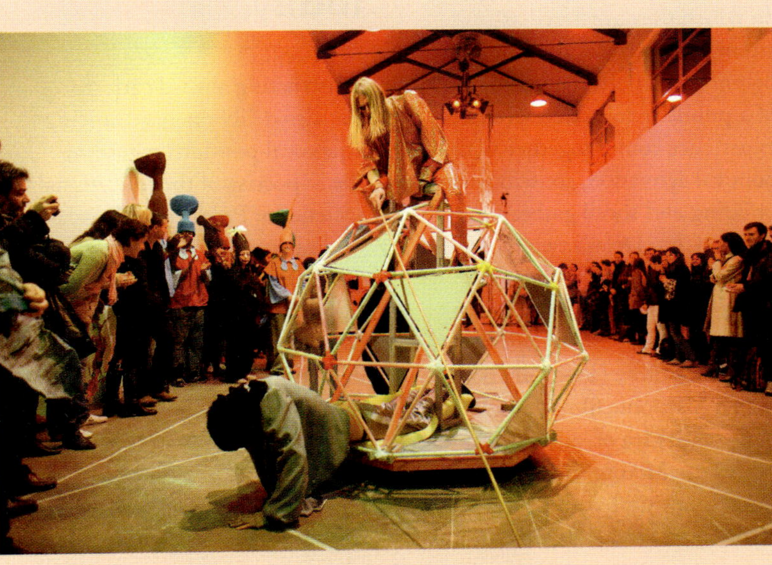

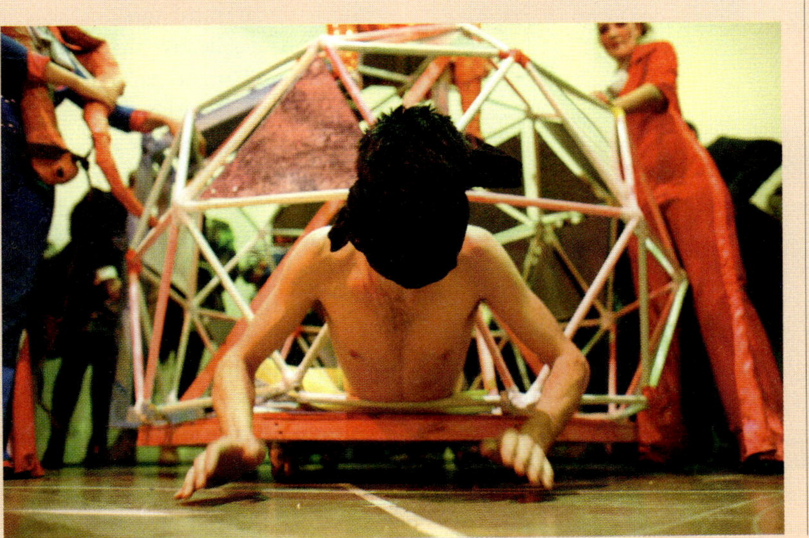

The Snail Race, 2008. Performance. Galleria Massimo De Carlo, Milan

Chetwynd's 'found' narratives serve as an exoticized pretext through which she can explore relational interaction.

In recent work, Chetwynd has evolved the performance format into hybrid educational-cum-entertainment activities. As well as organizing *Sparky Chatroom's Film Club* at Studio Voltaire, her series of *Helmut Newton's Ladies' Nights* at the Royal Academy in 2008–09 combined film, live music, lectures, bingo and dancing to uninhibitedly enjoyable and instructive effect. Her *Iron Age Pasta Necklace Workshop* (2009) expanded the ceremonial elements of her theatrical tableaux into a situation where the audience participants could share in the practice that is key to Chetwynd's art: a primary engagement with the creative transformation of everyday obejcts.

Chto Delat

Chto Delat is:
Olga Egorova/Tsaplya (artist, St Petersburg), Artiom Magun (philosopher, St Petersburg), Nikolay Oleinikov (artist, Moscow), Natalia Pershina-Yakimanskaya/ Glucklya (artist, St Petersburg), Alexei Penzin (philosopher, Moscow), David Riff (art critic, Moscow), Alexander Skidan (poet and critic, St Petersburg), Oxana Timofeeva (philosopher, Moscow) and Dmitry Vilensky (artist, St Petersburg)

For Kant, the question, 'What ought I to do?' was the foundation for thinking about ethical action. For Lenin, some centuries later, the question was formulated differently; his *Chto delat?* (What is to be done?) has been the rallying call for leftist intellectuals ever since. The name adopted by the assembly of artists, critics, philosophers and writers that make up Chto Delat originates from neither, but from a novel by the nineteenth-century Russian author

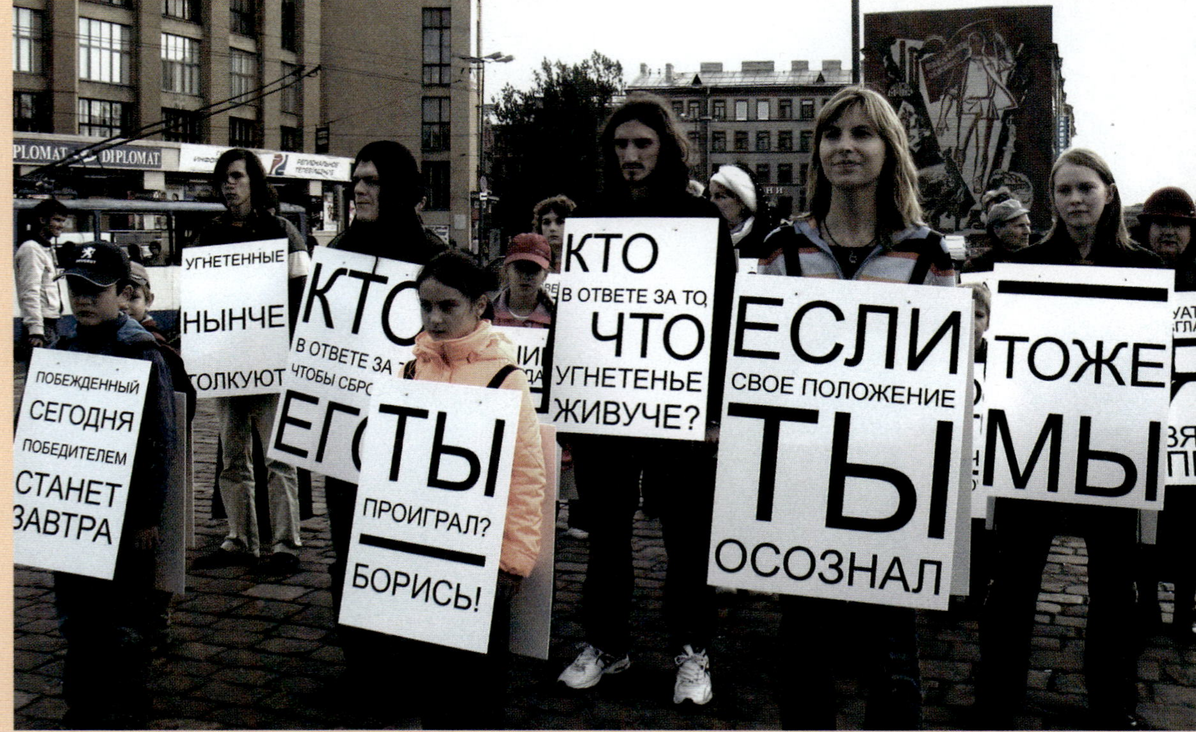

Angry Sandwich people or in a 'Praise of Dialectic', 2005. Video. Realized by Nikolay Oleinikov, Tsaplya and Dmitry Vilensky

Songspiel Cycle

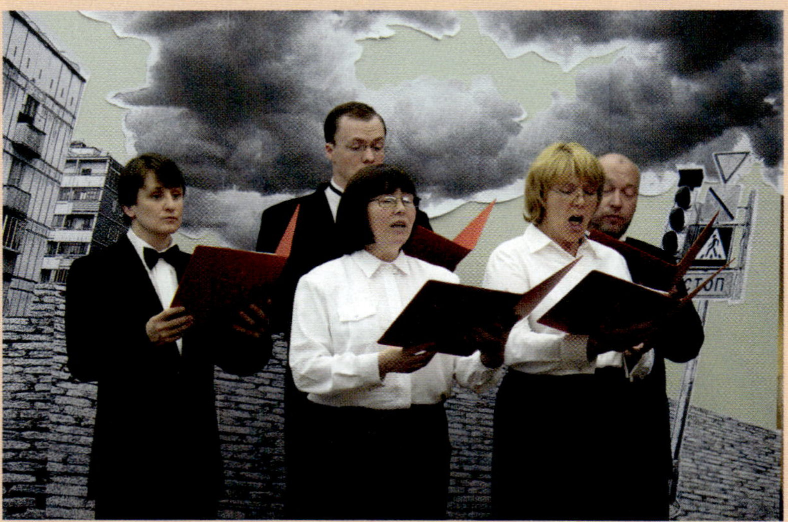

Perestroika Songspiel, 2008. Production still from video. Realized by Gluklya, Vladan Jeremic, Rena Rädle, Tsaplya and Dmitry Vilensky. Composer: Mikhail Krutik

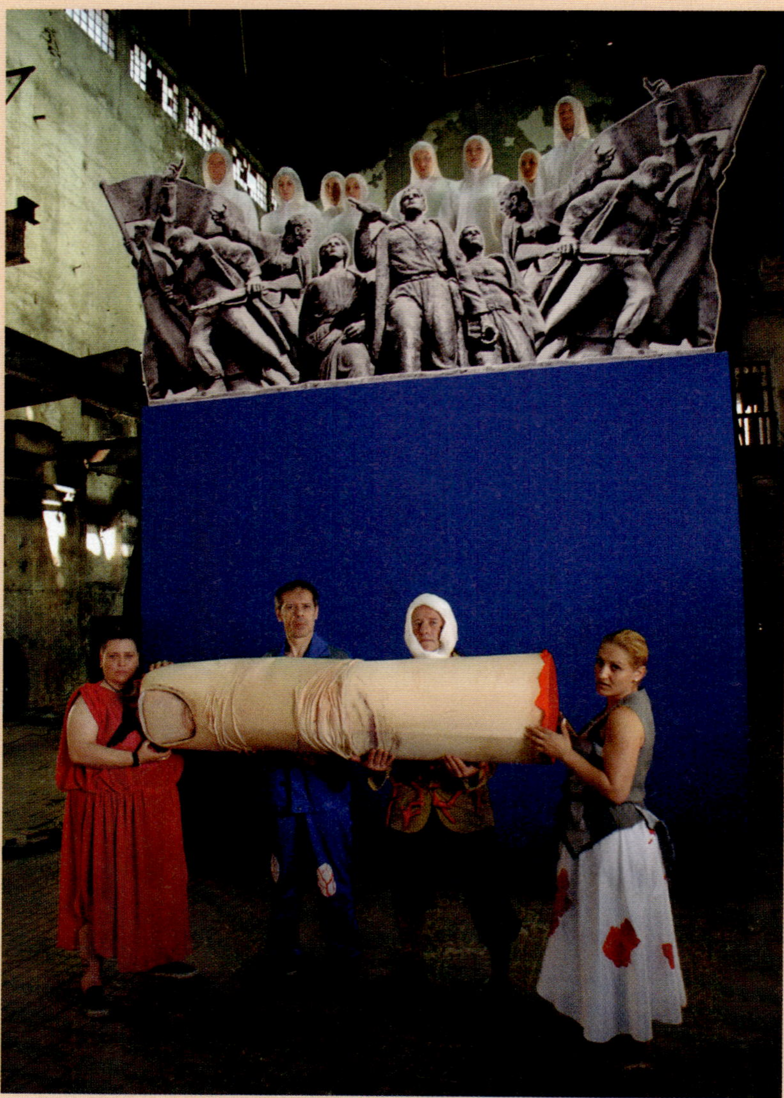

Partisan Songspiel. A Belgrade Story, 2009. Production still from video. Realized by Olga Egorova (Tsaplya), Vladan Jeremic, Rena Rädle, Dmitry Vilensky and Natalya Pershina (Gluklya). Composer: Mikhail Krutik

Redefine the terms of political engagement for cultural practice

Nikolai Chernyshevsky. They first used the title for their newspaper in 2003, when members of the then unnamed group orchestrated an event (somewhere between a demonstration and an art performance) called *The Refoundation of Petersberg*. Chernyshevsky's novel, about the first socialist workers' organizations in Russia, is still read by Russian schoolchildren today, even if it remains largely unknown elsewhere. Of course, Lenin's later and more famous use of the question did not escape the members of Chto Delat, but the fact that they derived their name from a lesser known 'local' story is significant since it hints at the double role that they play: representing a certain history while overcoming common preconceptions in order to act as international translators.

As a collective that vaunts the possibilities and particularities of collaborative authorship, their endeavours bridge art, activism and political theory with a membership that can expand or change depending on the needs of a specific project. Whatever the constellation, the group's defining feature is an intention to think through and redefine the terms of political engagement for cultural practice today. Their publication of an English-Russian newspaper, often produced in the context of art projects or

conferences, but importantly also distributed at social forums, political rallies and demonstrations, remains central to their larger project. But rather than their ideas being hypothesized in a purely discursive way, for Chto Delat it remains crucial that their reflections also take on the concrete form of films, performances or installations, thus engaging with and reactivating the forms and history of the artwork.

Projects such as *Angry Sandwich People or in a 'Praise of Dialectic'* (2005), a protest taking the form of a theatrical happening in an urban space drawn from a Bertolt Brecht poem, or *Activist Club* (2007), modelled on Alexsandr Rodchenko's 1925 prototype for an unrealized 'Worker's Club', are not so much formal replications of the originals on which they are based as attempts to activate their utopian potential: namely, the imagining of a public space where aesthetic experience comes together with political activation, consciousness-building and social gathering.

Chto Delat's two most ambitious projects to date, *Perestroika. Victory Over the Coup* (2008) and *Partisan Songspiel. A Belgrade Story* (2009), are both highly histrionic filmed renderings of Brecht's idea of 'alienation' in theatre. Mixing the genres of the comedy-musical with the classical form of the Greek tragedy,

complete with a chorus and a dramatis personae of certain known 'types' such as the liberal, the nationalist, the intellectual, the corrupted politico, the greed-driven tycoon and the dead revolutionary, the projects explode a bomb of wit, sarcasm and scathing political critique. Not only

The group's defining feature is an intention to think through and redefine the terms of political engagement for cultural practice today.

constructing absurd caricatures but also deliberately advancing equivocal positions regarding the hypocrisy of the transitional societies of Perestroika Russia or post-war Serbia, these, like all Chto Delat's projects so far, speak volumes about the group's playfulness but also about its demand for the audience to take a position. In the process, they manage an exceedingly rare thing: the activation of a more politically engaged public, inside the art world and out.

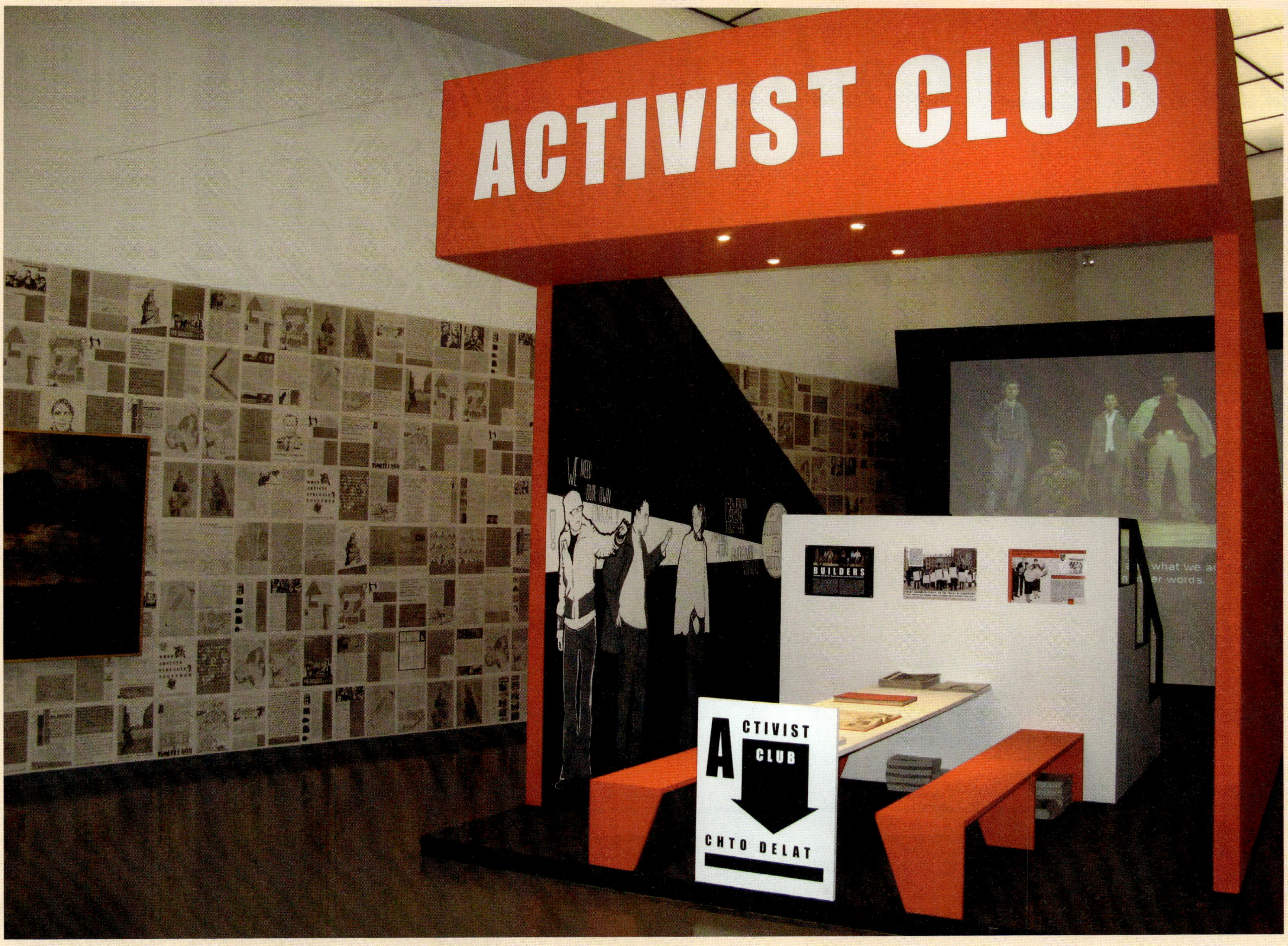

Activist Club, 2009. Site–specific installation, Van Abbe Museum, Eindhoven. Architecture: Dmitry Vilensky. Murals: Nikolay Oleinikov

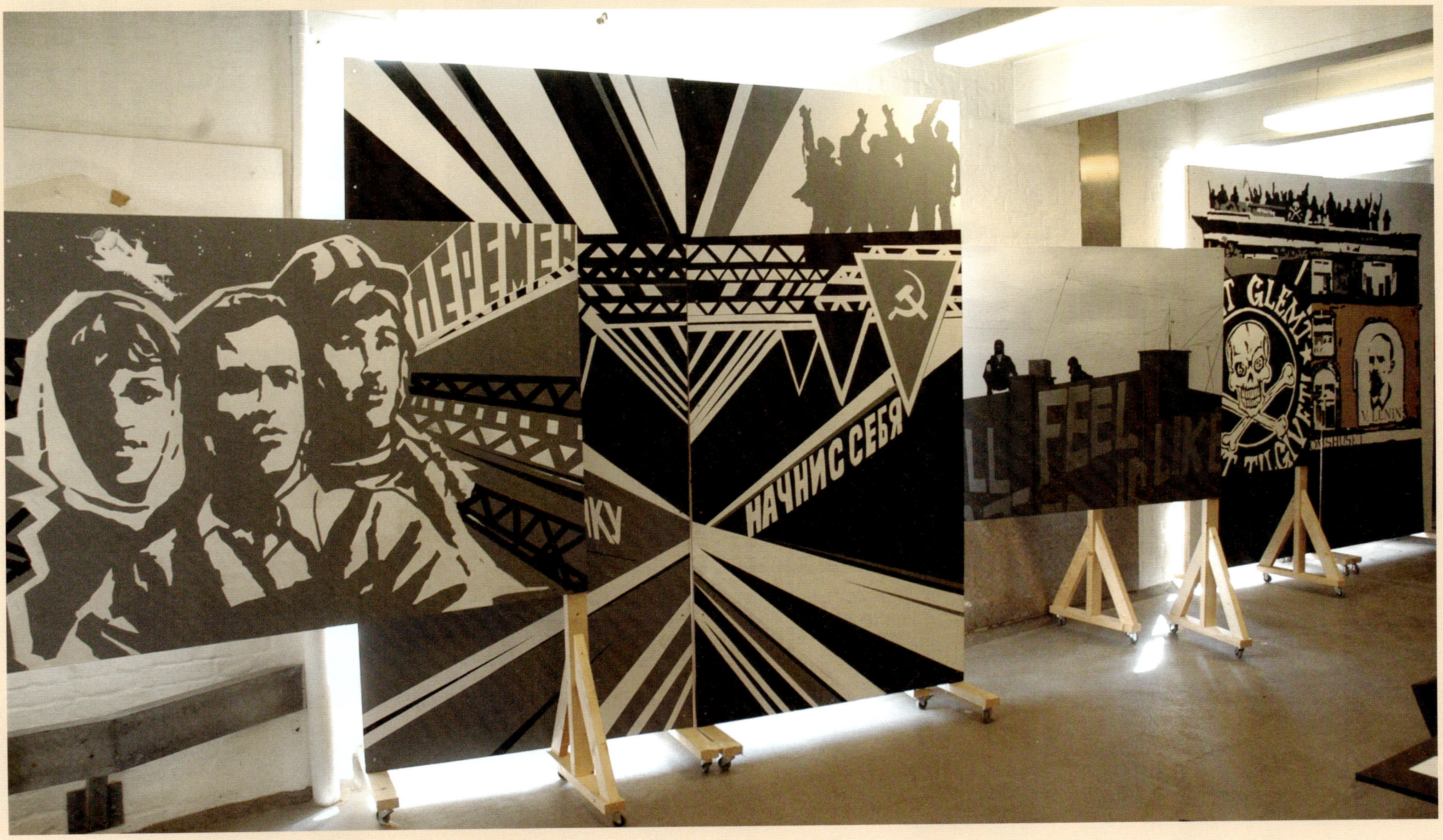

Experiences of Perestroika, 2008. Mixed-media installation. Dimensions variable. Murals: Nikolay Oleinikov

Anne Collier

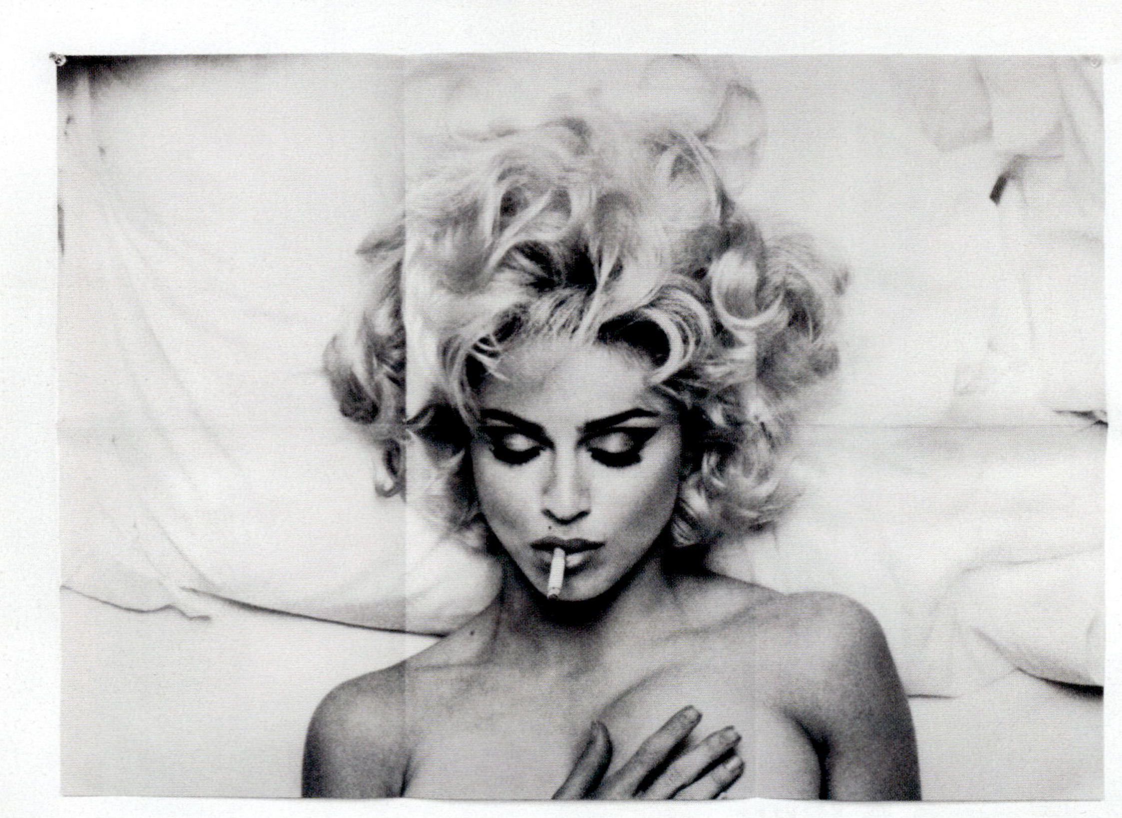

Folded Madonna Poster, 2007. C-print. 127 × 165 cm

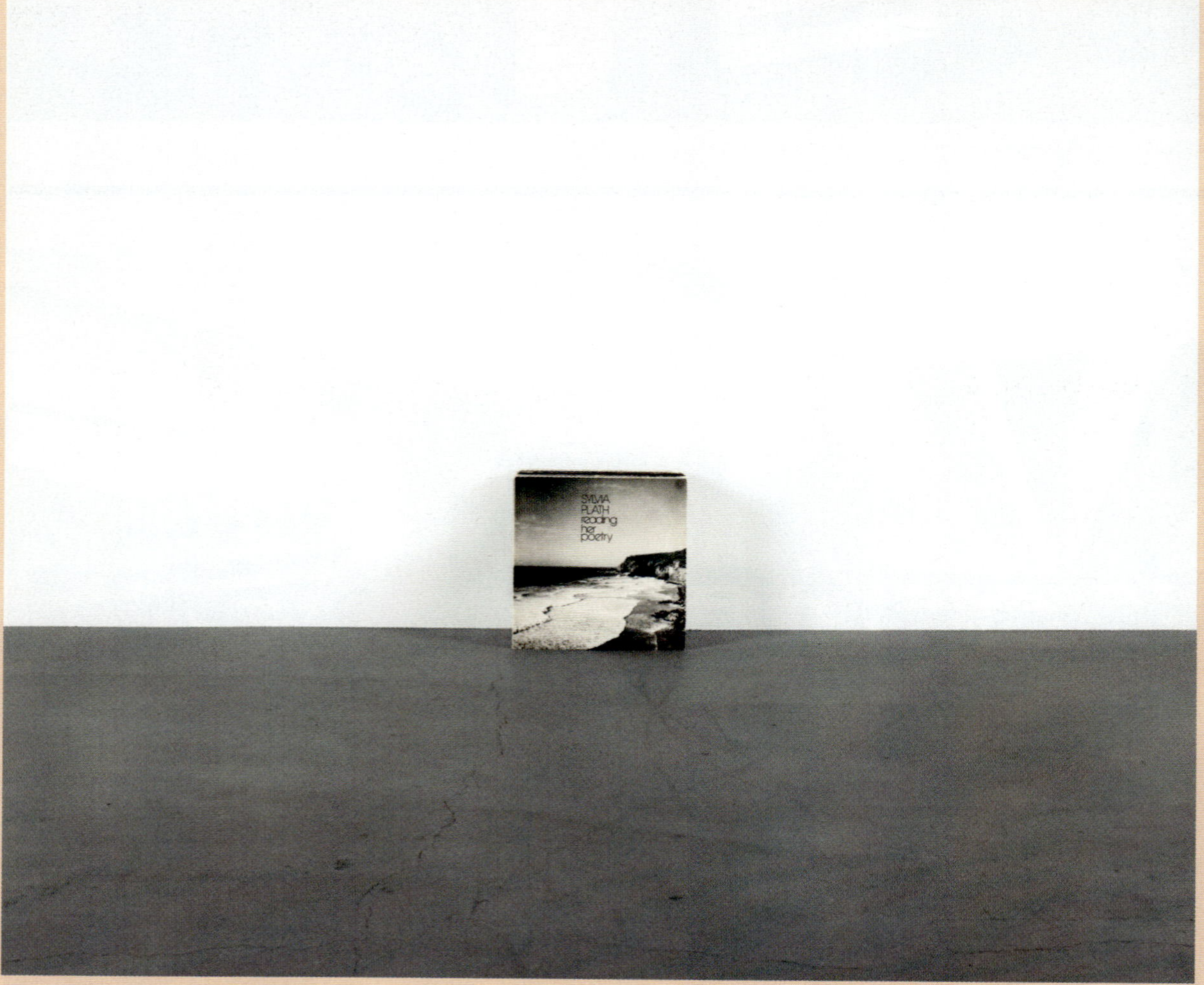

Sylvia Plath, 2008. C-print. 127 × 153 cm

Photographic documentation

simultaneously resist our attempts to ascribe permanent meaning. That ambivalence is only heightened when we learn that these images depict the places where the artist scattered the ashes of her parents.

Sylvia Plath (2008) engages with a similarly unstable emotional intensity. Part of a larger body of work in which Collier photographs the album covers of vintage vinyl against minimal backdrops of floor and wall, it depicts a stack of records, at the front of which is a 1977 release of Plath reading her poetry. The bare décor of grey concrete floor and white wall, along with the rocky beach pictured on the album, recall the format and setting of the *8 × 10* prints of the previous year, and indeed *Sylvia*

Plath evokes a muted melancholy reminiscent of those earlier works. In this case, however, that sentiment is accompanied by a kind of frustration bordering on the comic, since we are denied the satisfaction of hearing the recording and are kept at a resolute distance, forever peering at a scene whose full affective meaning will escape us.

Something of that same impression of the tragicomic is apparent in *My Goals for One Year* (2007), a photograph of a self-help book opened up to two pages encouraging the reader to plan a set of life aims in categories ranging from travel to spirituality. Again and again, Collier has turned to a particular pop-psychological milieu of the 1970s, the decade of her childhood, with

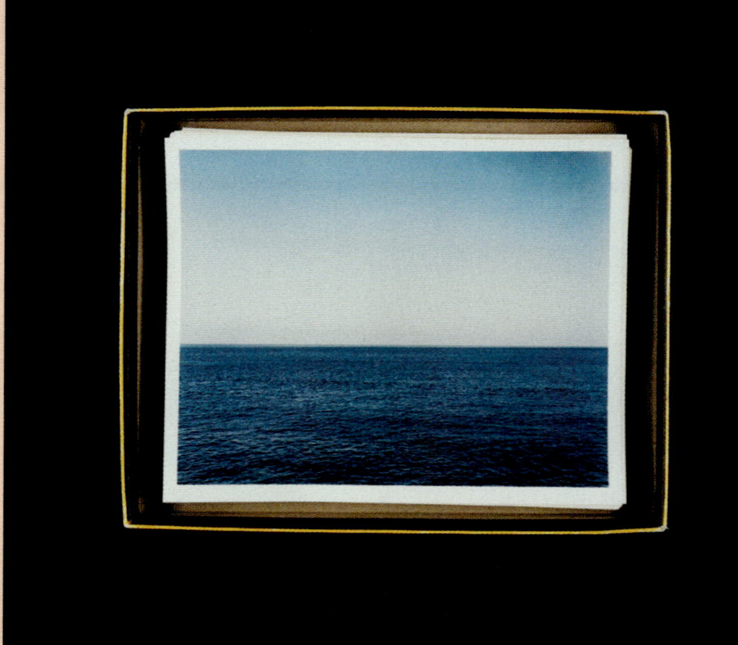

8 × 10 (Jim), 2007. C-print. 75 × 88 cm

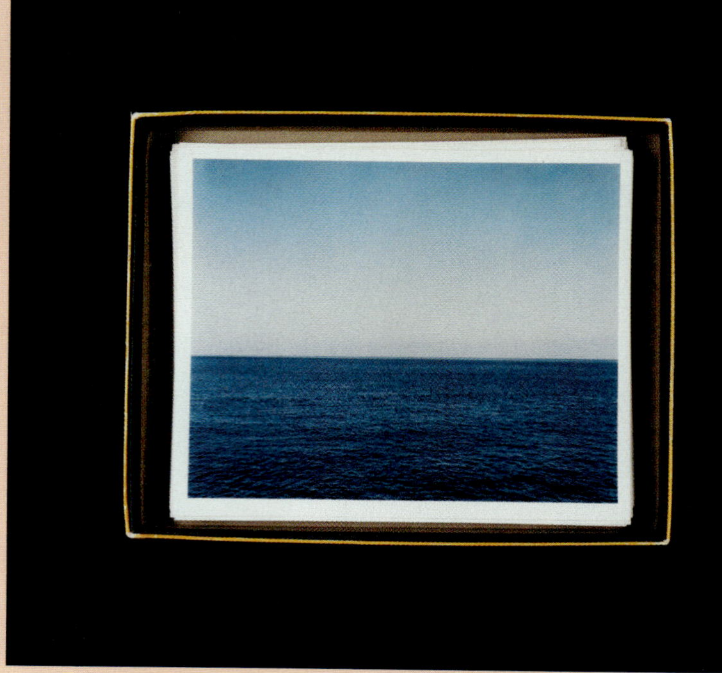

8 × 10 (Lynda), 2007. C-print. 75 × 88 cm

With the historicization of the 'Pictures' generation in full swing, the photography of Anne Collier may at first glance look like a reprise of the cool aesthetics of appropriation associated with artists like Richard Prince or Sherrie Levine. But beneath any surface similarities of technique, Collier's work articulates a singular sensibility in which distance and affectivity are conjoined to produce a unique experience. Take the two related prints, *8 × 10 (Jim)* and *8 × 10 (Lynda)* (both 2007), each of which show a similar photograph of the blue sea reaching out to a cloudless horizon; the photographs rest on the top of piles of prints inside open archival boxes. What are we to make of these blank seascapes, to which names have been appended as if they were portraits? The two photographs solicit our reading into them, while the vacuity of the scene and the very mutability of the ocean

A masked self-portrait

its rather heartbreaking earnestness as well as its commodification of subjectivity. Her deadpan photographic documentation and serial presentation remind us that Conceptual art strategies evolved at the same moment as this pop psychology flourished, and she seems to mine some hidden vein that links the two.

For several years Collier has been rephotographing images of women, most frequently women who have appropriated the traditionally masculine role of looking. *January 1974/January 1981* (2006) shows two stacks of the periodical *ARTnews*; at the top of each is a cover featuring a woman artist, Berenice Abbott and Georgia O'Keeffe. This might appear initially to be a familiar feminist exercise, but the longer we look, the stranger the piece becomes.

We notice the similarity of poses, each with hand on cheek, and the directness of their gazes; we consider the aged features of each, and wonder what private meaning is encoded there for Collier. To some extent we could read this as a masked self-portrait, which is no less true of her extensive ongoing series of rephotographed images entitled *Woman With A Camera* (begun 2006).

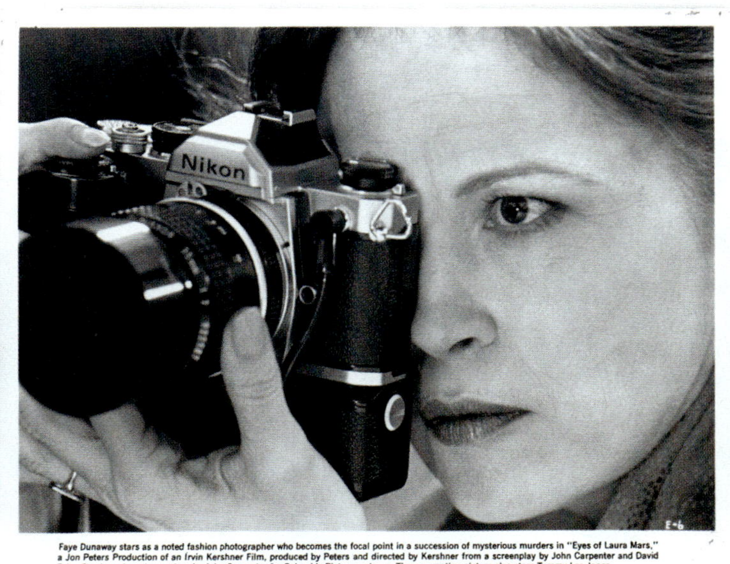

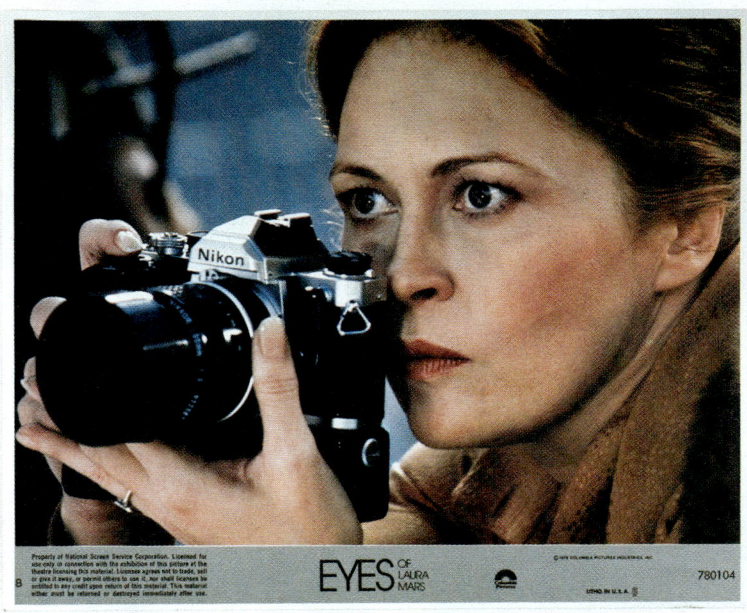

Woman With A Camera (Diptych), 2006. 2 C–prints. Each 136 × 114 cm

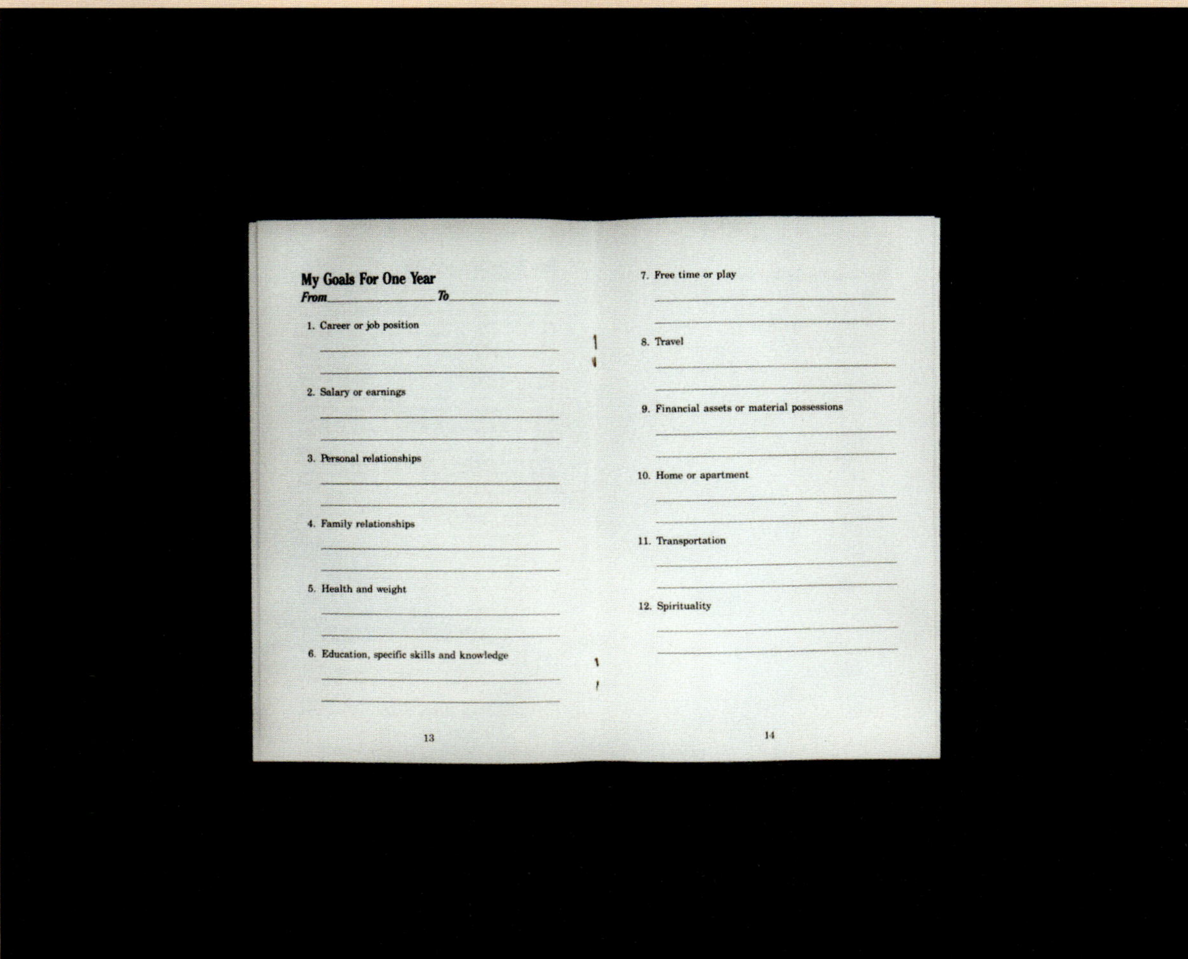

My Goals for One Year, 2007. C–print. 113 × 137 cm

With the historicization of the 'Pictures' generation in full swing, the photography of Anne Collier may at first glance look like a reprise of the cool aesthetics of appropriation associated with names like Richard Prince or Sherrie Levine.

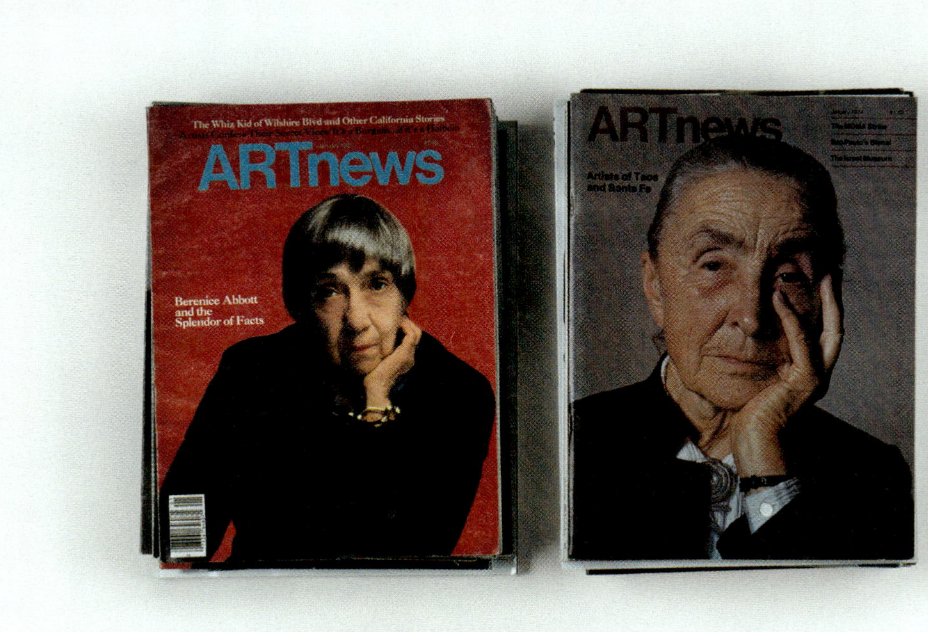

January 1974 / January 1981, 2006. C–print. 89 × 117 cm

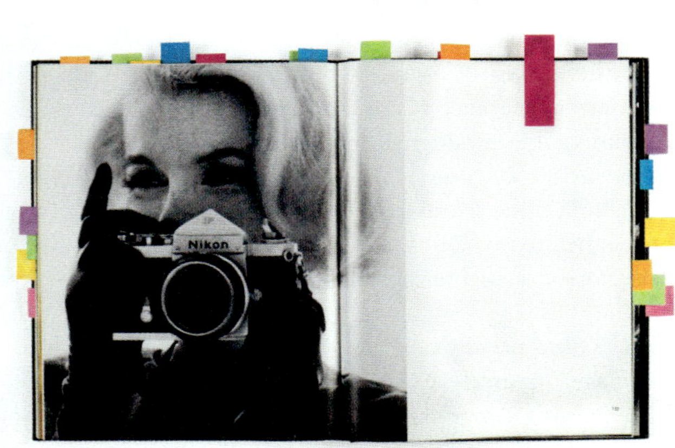

Woman With A Camera (The Last Sitting, Bert Stern), 2009. C–print. 127 × 182 cm

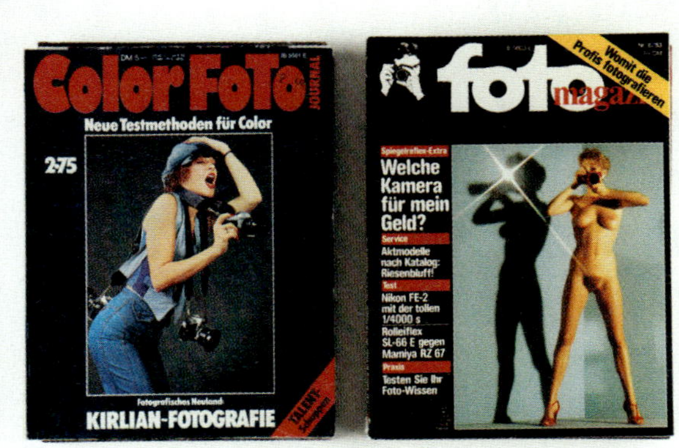

Women With Cameras (German Photography), 2007. C–print. 83 × 108 cm

Keren Cytter

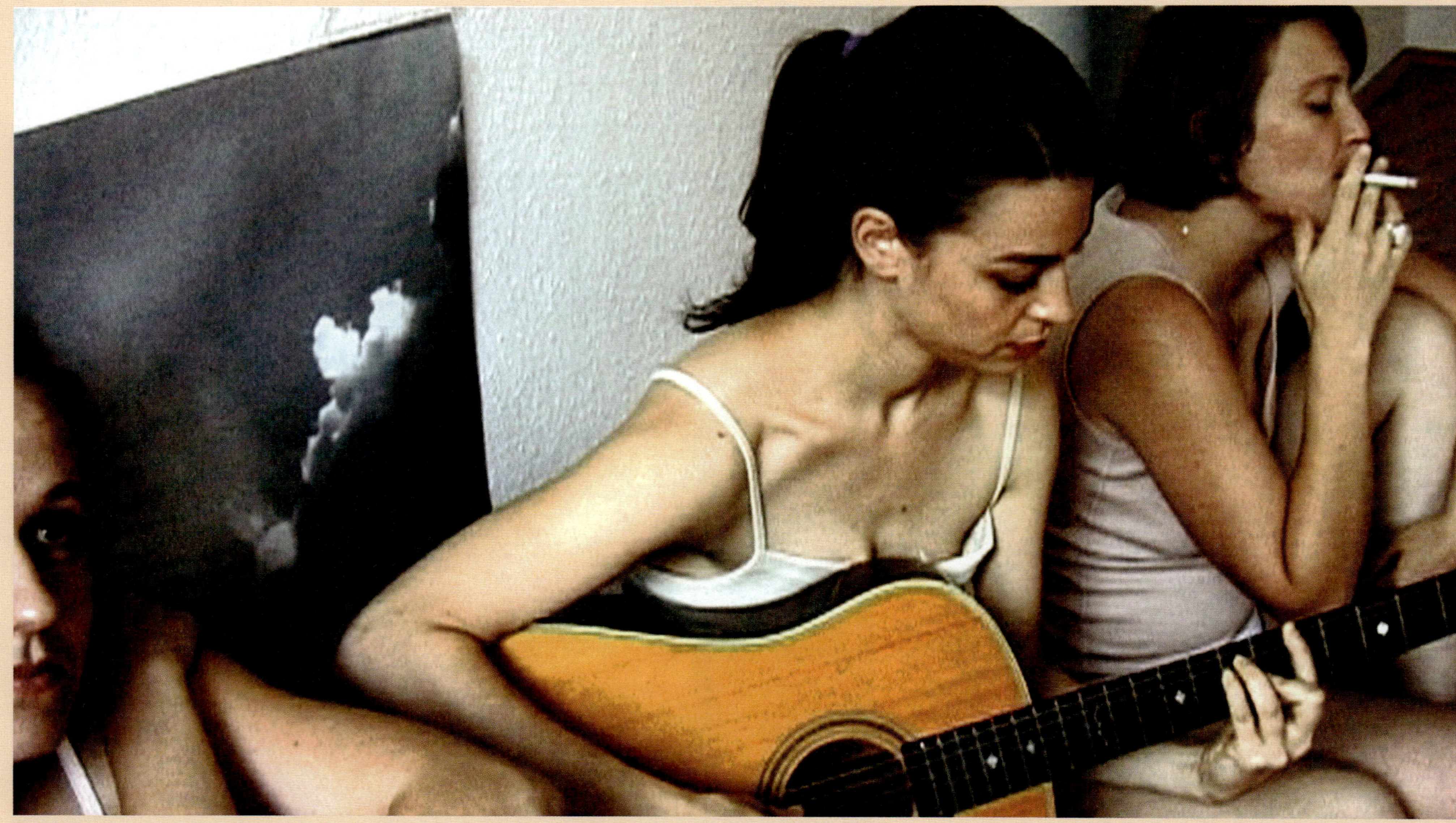

Der Spiegel, 2007. Video. 5 min.

The curious and compelling texture of Keren Cytter's films results, in part, from the way in which she mixes populist cinematic or television cliché with the low-fi aesthetic of early video art. The 'slacker' appearance of the hand-held camera is at productive odds with the artist's shadowy substructure, built upon familiar strategies designed to invoke anticipation, horror, sexual tension or unease.

Cytter's films usually take place in ordinary, if sparsely furnished, domestic settings and are acted by friends, non-actors, in an apparently improvised manner.

Cytter's choreography employs techniques of mirroring, slow motion, shadow theatre and repetition to mimic rudimentary video-editing effects

An echoing, ſlightly out-of-place quality

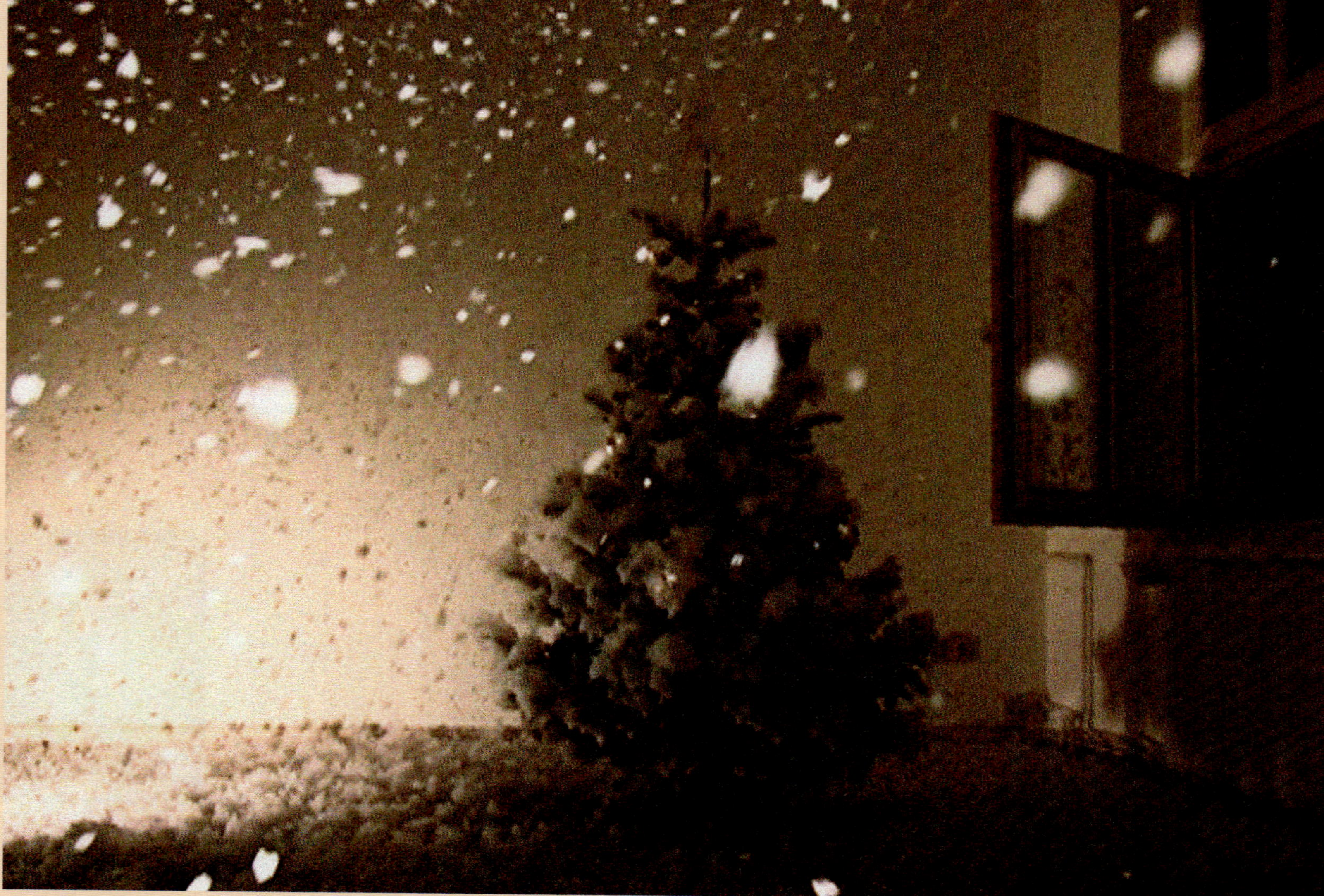

Four Seasons, 2008. Video. 12 min.

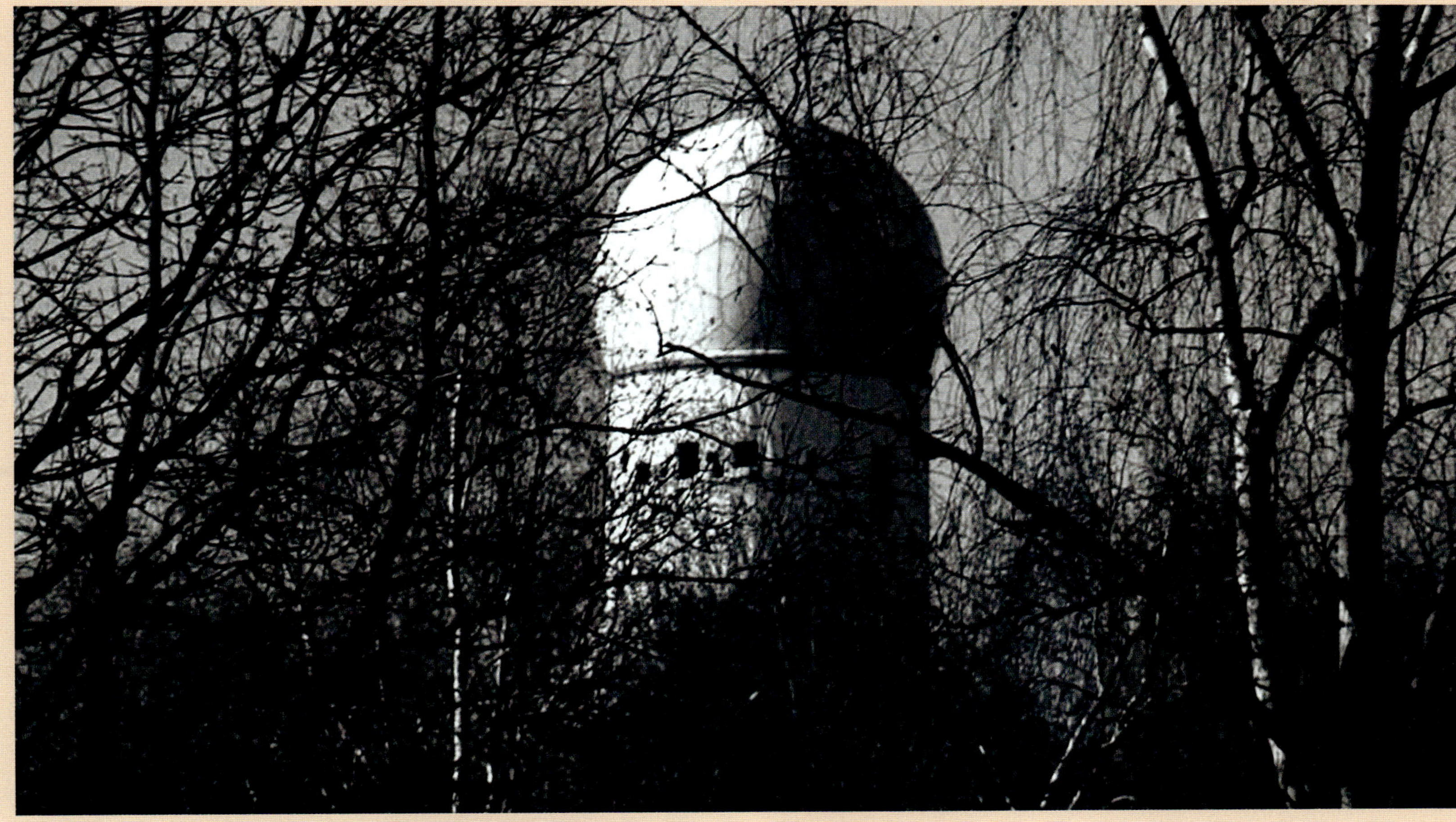

The Great Tale of the Devil's Hill and the Endless Search for Freedom, 2007–09. Video. 75 min.

From soap operas as from theatre history

The characters often speak without dramatic inflection so that the atmosphere within the broken narratives that are played out has the feeling of an interior stream of consciousness that has inadvertently, perhaps abruptly, surfaced prior to being fully 'prepared' for utterance. This impression is made manifest via rudimentary means. The dialogues, cut and spliced between 'acted' speech and voiceover, have an echoing, slightly out-of-place quality, never quite matched to the scenarios in which they are placed.

Nevertheless, Cytter's strong sense of rhythm and the bluntly realist eye of her camera make for a boldly palpable sense of the material and psychological stuff of which her short dramas are made. As Barry Schwabsky observed (*Artforum,* October 2006), in Cytter's hands, 'Inexpressiveness and formal neutrality become a direct way to an almost hysterical intensity.'

Cytter's characters — a shifting cast of men and women in their twenties and thirties who share a similar look (contemporary casual clothes, unmade up, scruffy hair) — verbalize their way through different rituals: eating food, dating, celebrations, betrayals. The styles in which these actions are negotiated and dramatized are drawn equally from soap operas and theatre history, often with a touch of Brechtian alienation and neo noir thrown in, as in her 2008 work *Four Seasons*. She combines seductive trashiness with an art-inflected self-consciousness that lend the films some of the magic of the improvised tableaux of Jack Smith, via the stylized choreographic precision of Catherine Sullivan. In *Der Spiegel* (The Mirror, 2009) a middle-aged woman is taunted by her own mortality and a relentless chorus of younger women, while *Dreamtalk* (2005) and *The Victim* (2006), are both scripted around short narratives, played out in a cyclical manner. The protagonist of *The Victim* has to choose between her son and her lover, who are

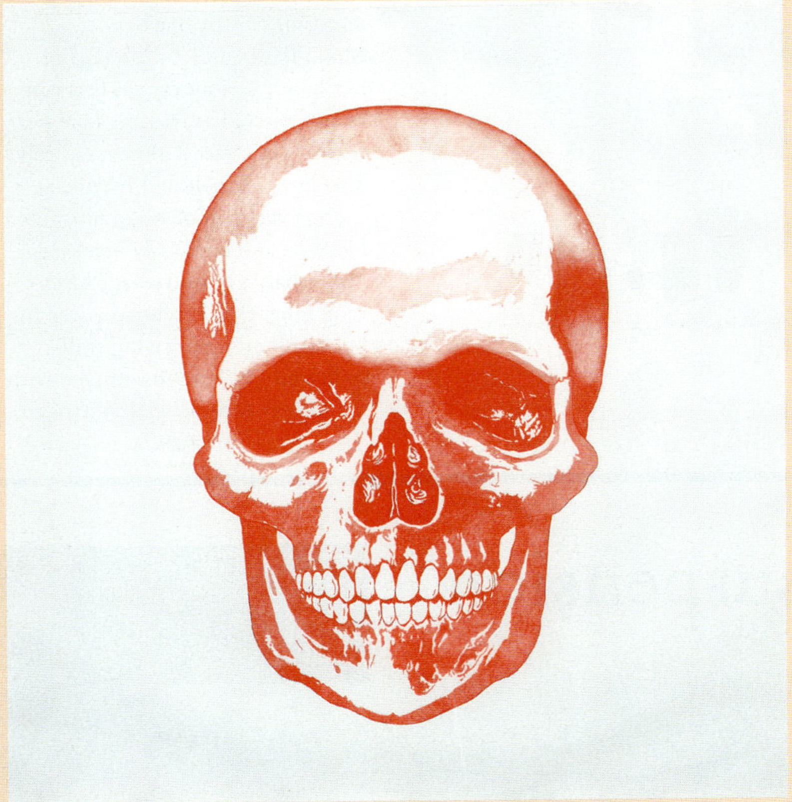

Skull, 2009. Graphite on paper. 150 × 150 cm

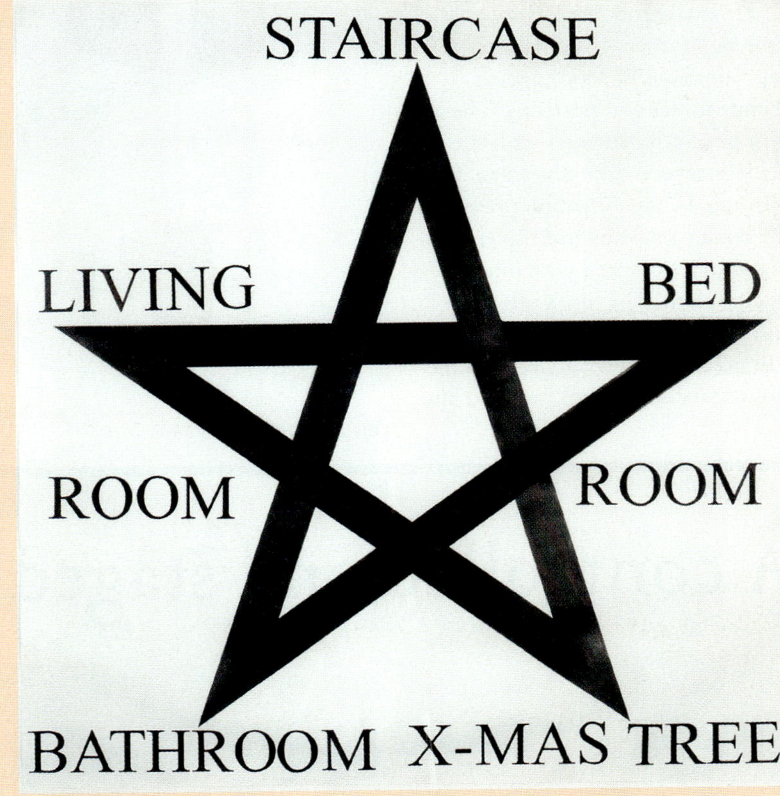

Pentagram, Graphite and pen on paper, 150 × 150 cm

both played by the same actor. The 'acted' nature of the narrative is heightened not only by the looping repetition of the scenario, but by the fact that — as in *Dreamtalk* — the actors visibly read from a script, as though in an endless rehearsal.

Cytter's recent shift to live theatre transposes the palpable materiality of her film and video into three-dimensional space. In collaboration with her provisional dance-theatre group D.I.E. NOW (Dance International Europe NOW), her 2009 production *History in the Making or The Secret Diaries of Linda Schultz* was loosely hinged on the story of a man and a woman who awake to discover that they have each been subject to an unexpected sex change. Cytter's choreography employs techniques of mirroring, slow motion, shadow theatre and repetition to mimic rudimentary video-editing effects, and so the live work performs an explicit relationship to our perception of the world as seen through a lens. Likewise, Cytter's dissections of stage space elaborate on the capacity of a film shot from different camera perspectives. As in her film and video work, the resulting interaction makes anthropological and philosophical observations on the human condition with absurdity and humour. The mood of Cytter's work is always charged with a melancholic sense of her characters dislocation in the present.

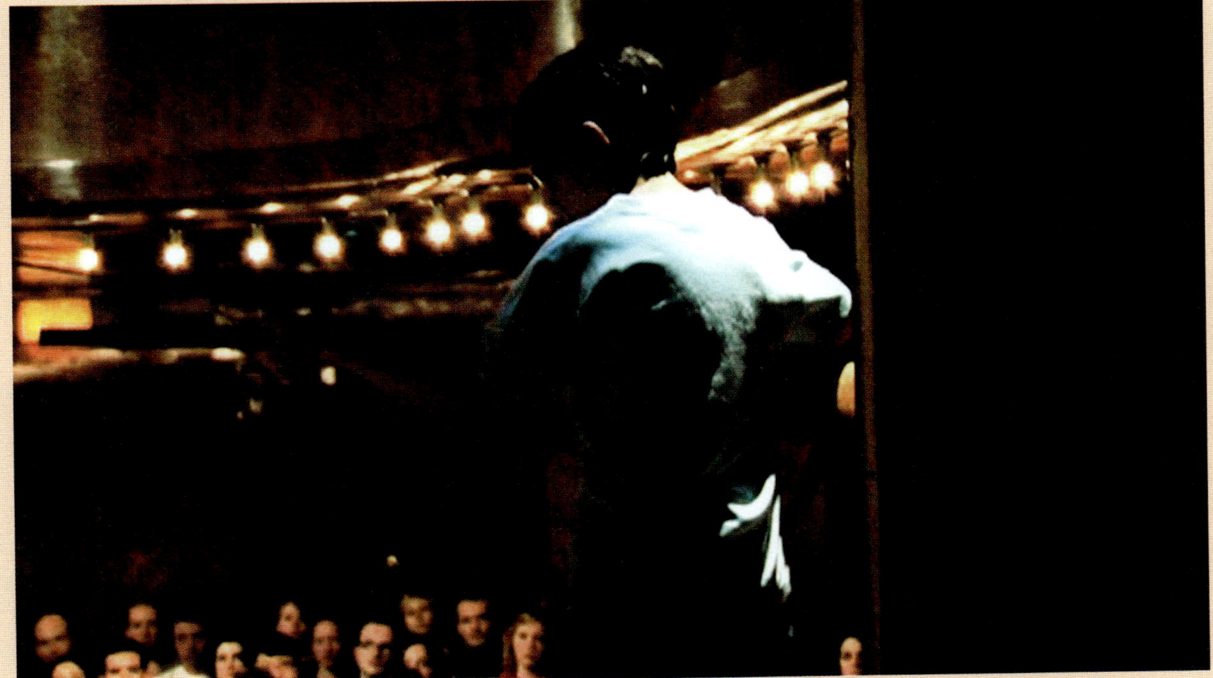

Untitled, 2009. Video. 16 min.

Kate Davis

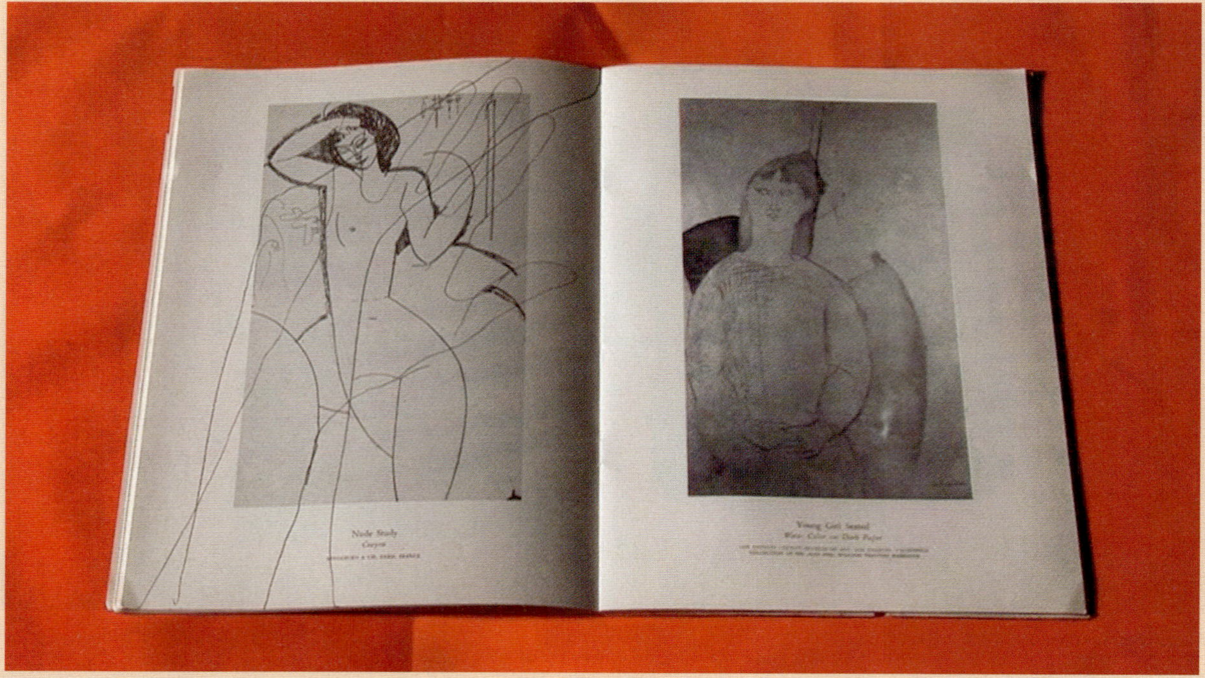

Refusal to compete with the master

Disgrace (2009) is the title of Kate Davis' recent film and accompanying suite of four drawings on pages torn out of a 1972 catalogue *The Drawings of Amedeo Modigliani*, containing reproductions of Modigliani's female nudes and portraits. The film physically engages with the book in several different ways. The opening image of the film presents the book open at its frontispiece, on a surface covered with intensely orange cloth. The film's title and the artist's name, composed of letters cut out, punk-style, from the front cover of the book, are laid out

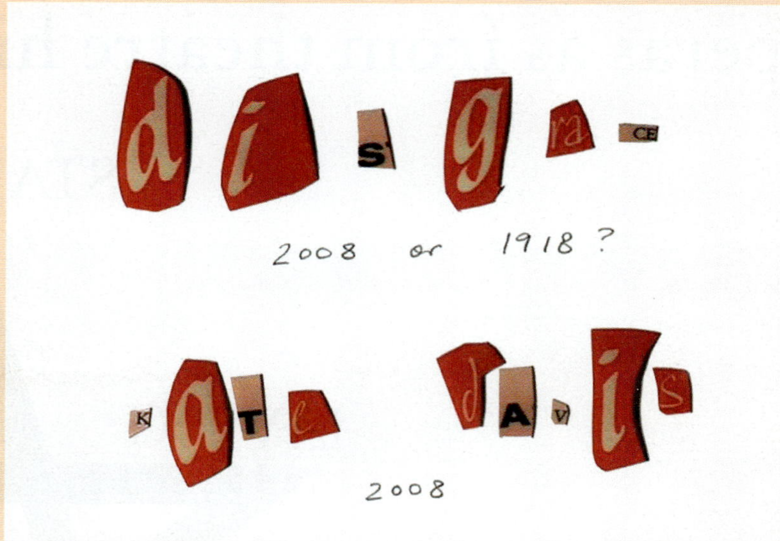

Disgrace, 2009. Video. 9 min

on the inside cover. The subtitle '1918 or 2008?' and the film's date '2008' are handwritten in pencil. A succession of ten-second still frames ensues, all with the book open at the same two-page spread: Modigliani's voluptuous *Nude Study* in crayon appears on one page and the watercolour portrait *Young Girl Seated* (its subject fully dressed and passively looking to one side) on the opposite page. These shots are interspersed with ten-second frames of black, during which the viewer can hear a chorus rhythmically chanting in dismay, 'boo hoo'. In each shot, we see the artist's own drawings amassing one by one over Modigliani's nude — an outline of her hand, various curves that can be interpreted as fragments of her body — to cover it almost entirely. The lines are bold but fragile, as if done very fast or by an untrained hand — and obviously mocking Modigliani's mastery. One has to remember that Davis is known for her outstanding drawing skills, so her refusal here to compete with the master represents a controlled

and staged suspension of her otherwise excellent craftsmanship. The last frame of the film shows the back cover of the book, which was published in the 'Master Draughtsman Series' with its list of other artists in the series — all men, save for Käthe Kollwitz. The 'boo hoo' is now spoken out by a lone female voice.

Davis' performative practice involves both a critical revision of canonical works by male modernist artists and a participatory engagement with the work of feminist artists, with the aim of articulating her own position as female artist working today. To this end, she initiates dialogues and collaborations. Barbara Kruger's iconic 1989 piece *Your Body is a Battleground*, for example, became the subject of Davis's extensive new reading in her 2007 installation *Your Body is a Battleground Still* (2007) at Tate Britain. In *2 or 3 things I know about her* (2009), a collaborative project with Jimmy Robert, Davis made a realistic drawing of Carolee Schneemann performing *Up to and*

A controlled and staged suspension

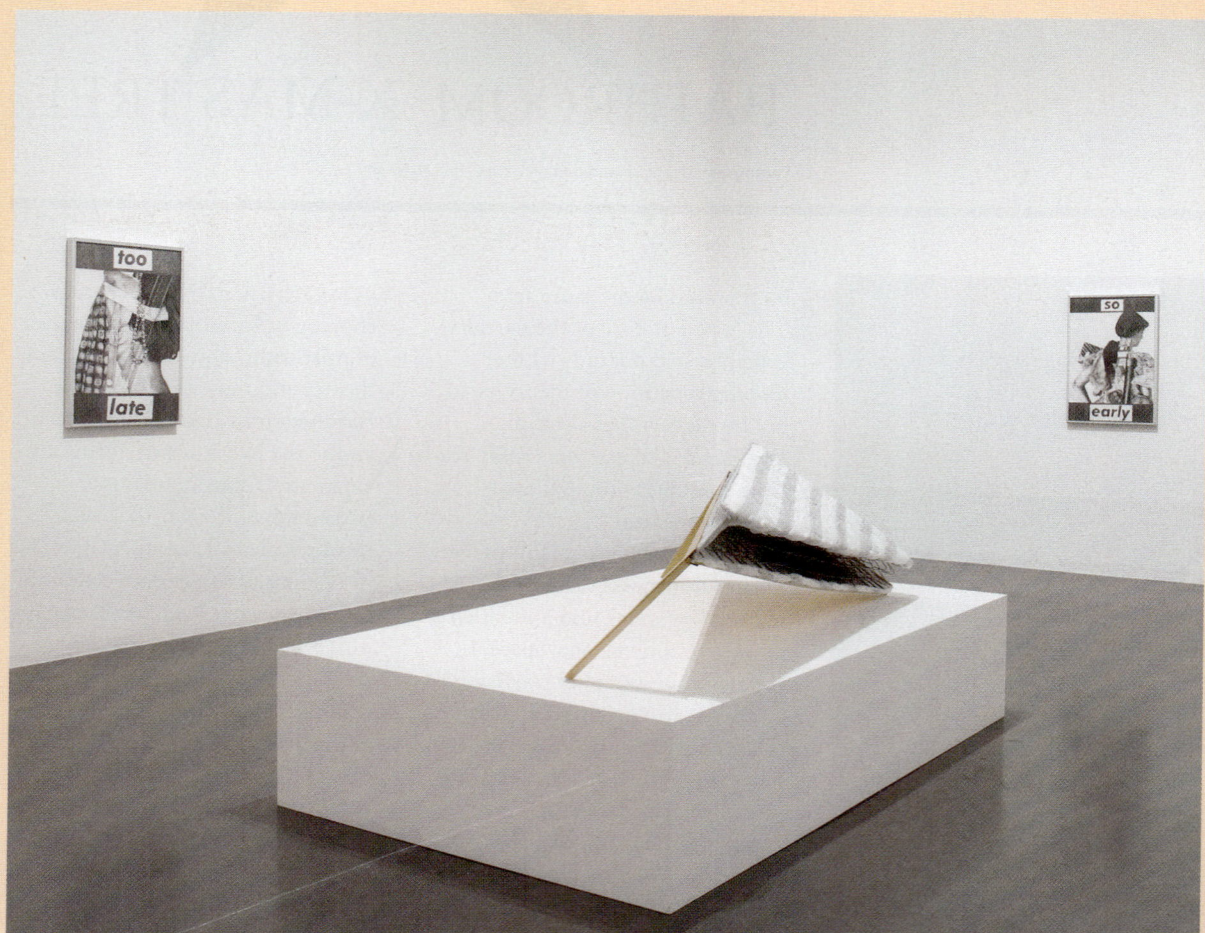

Your Body is a Battleground Still, 2007. Pencil on paper, frame. 2 parts. 100 × 75 cm. Wooden plinth with dissected bed. 250 × 150 × 90 cm

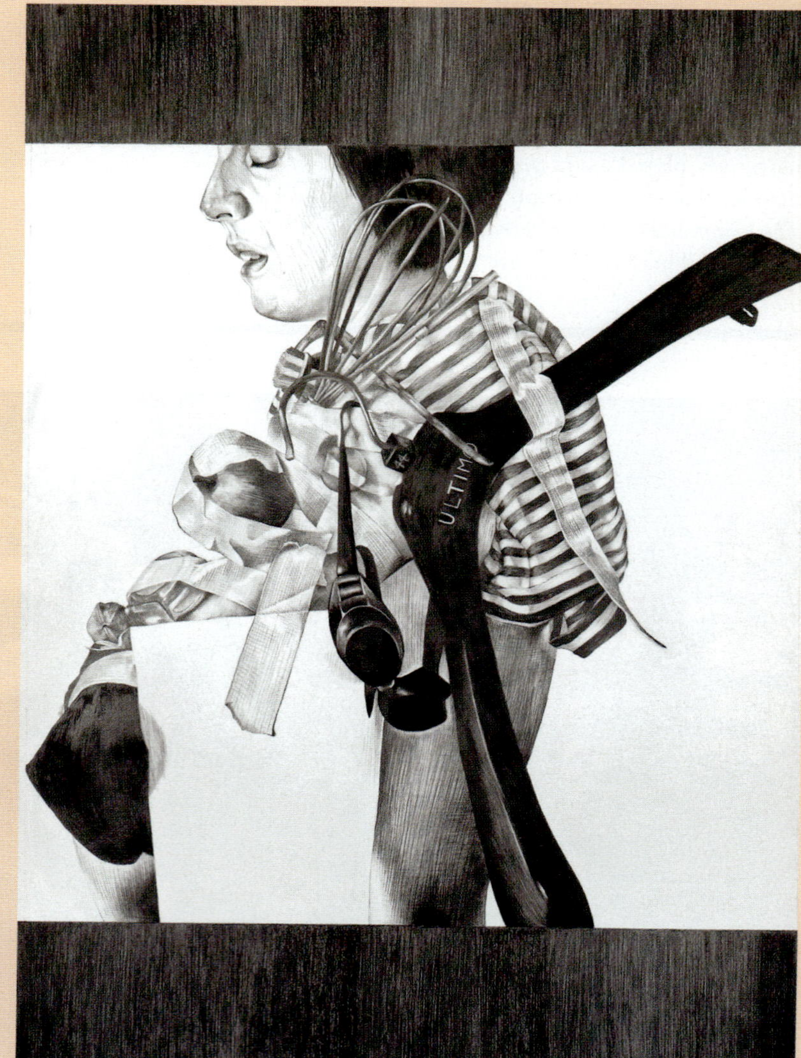

Your Body is a Battleground Still (poster 3), 2007. Pencil on paper. 100 × 75 cm

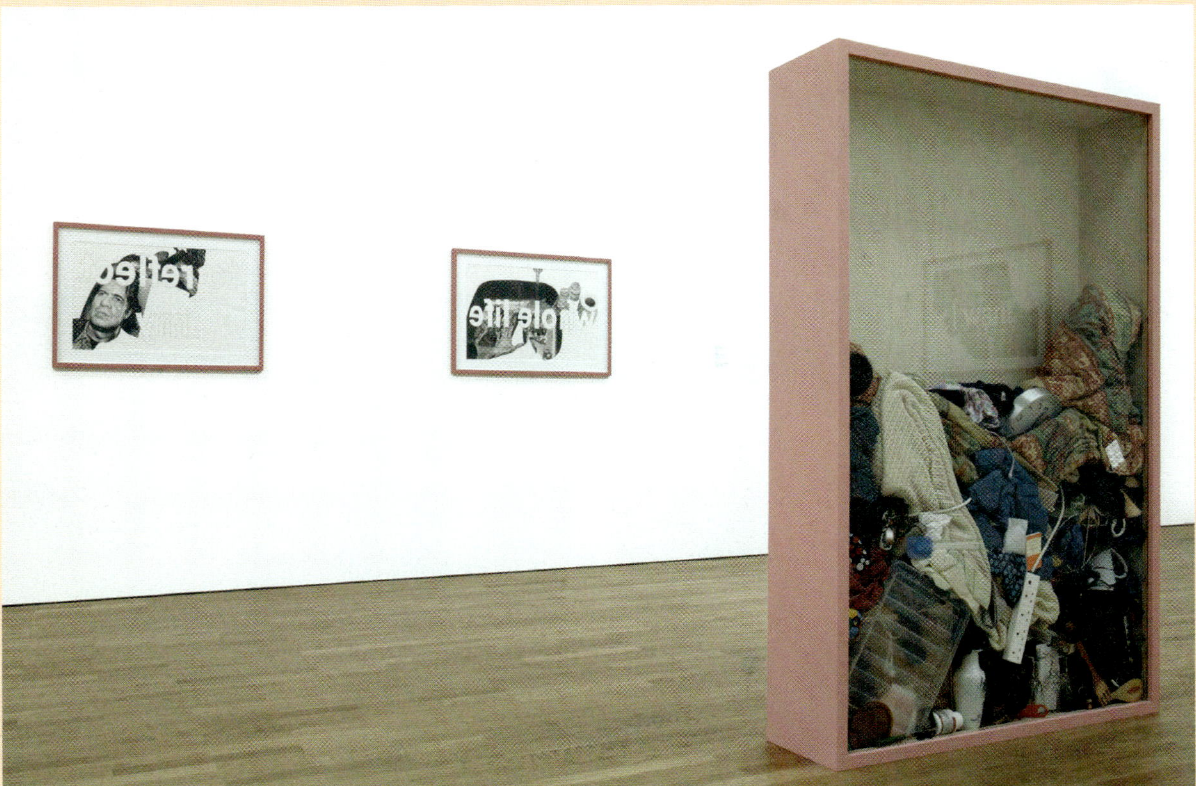

Outsider, 2008. Framed drawings, wooden and glass case containing the artist's possessions. Dimensions variable

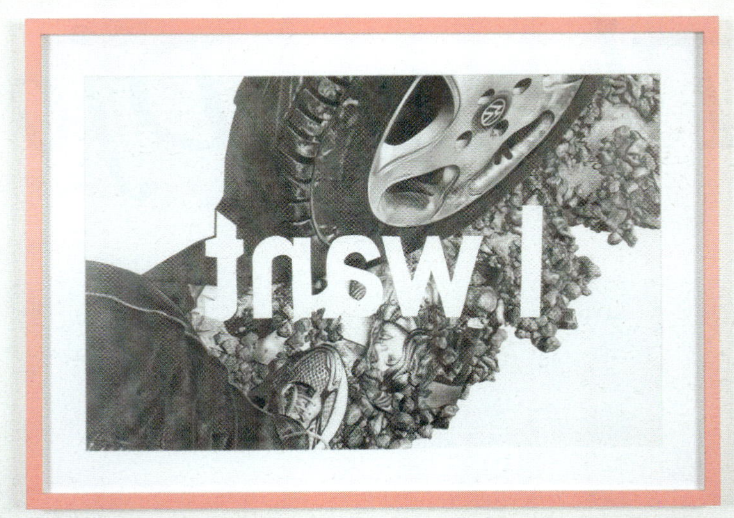

Outsider (I want), 2008. Framed pencil on paper drawing. 69 × 98 cm

Davis' performative practice involves both a critical revision of canonical works by male modernist artists and a participatory engagement with the work of feminist artists, with the aim of articulating her own position as female artist working today. To this end, she initiates dialogues and collaborations.

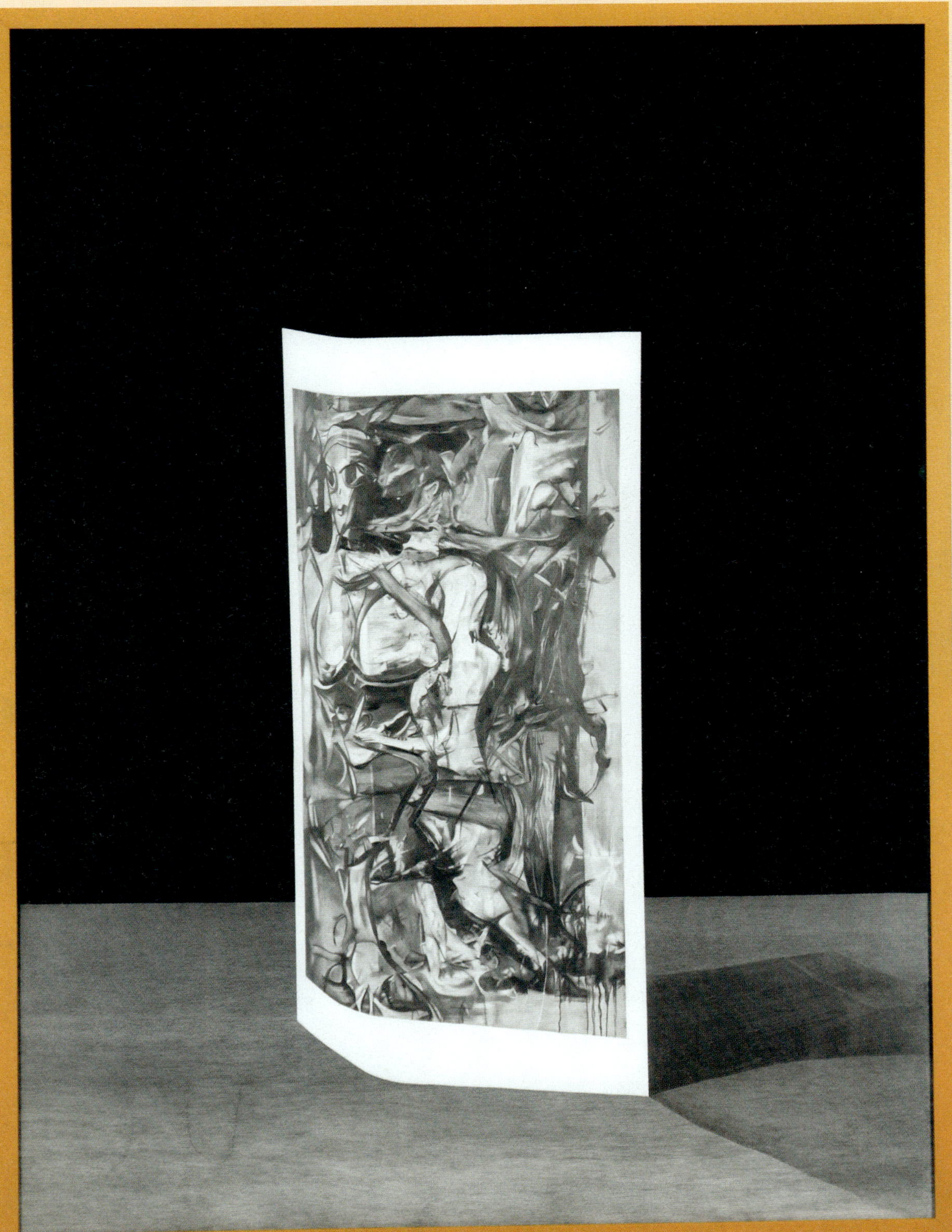

Who is a Woman Now? (II), 2008. Framed screenprint and pencil on paper. 170 × 130 cm

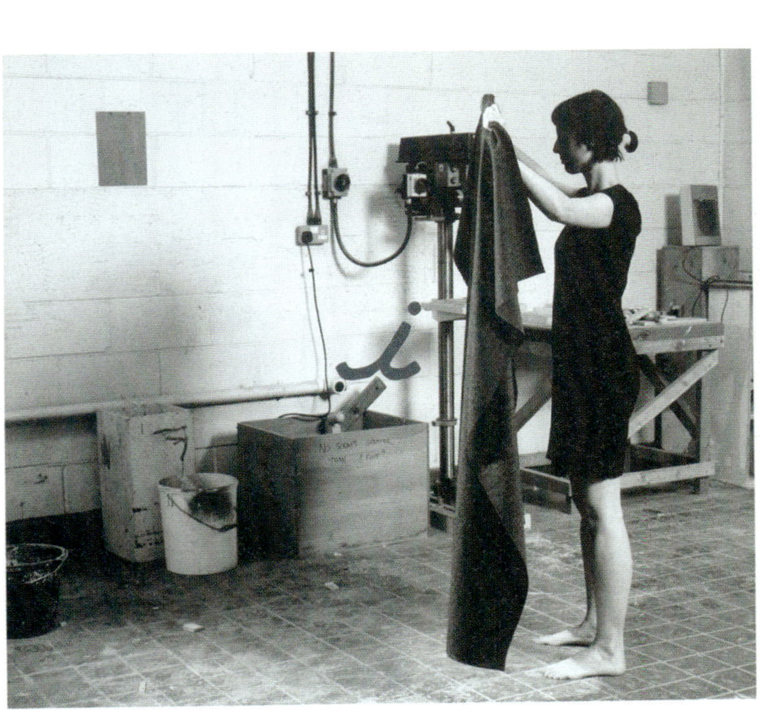

The Clear Stark Vision is Getting Lost Again (I–X), 2007, Screenprint and digital print on wood. 149 × 169 cm

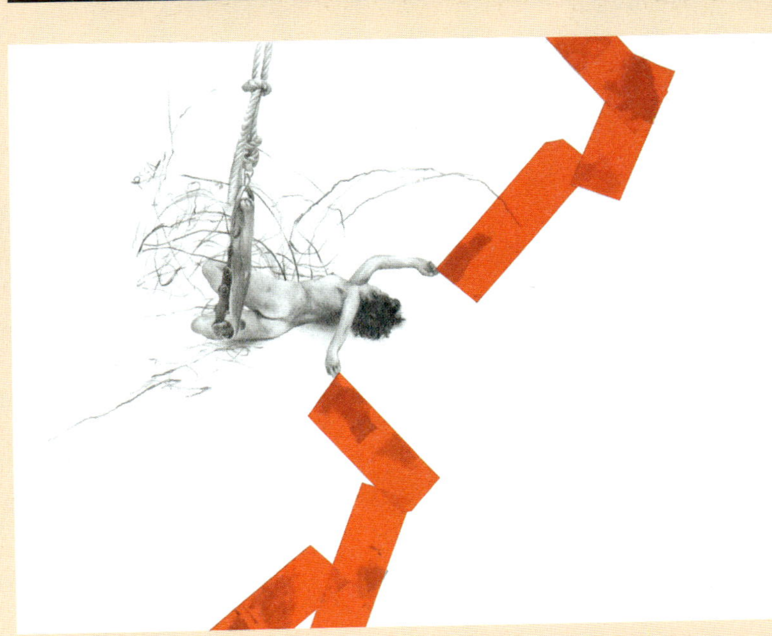

2 or 3 things I know about her (with Jimmy Robert), 2009. Pencil and tape on paper. 27 × 34 cm

Including Her Limits (first realized at The Kitchen, New York, 1973–76), where, suspended naked from a rope in a harness, Schneemann drew freely on the walls of the space around her in a performative act that ecstatically expanded and radicalized Jackson Pollock's action painting into four dimensions. With Faith Wilding, Davis has been working on a project *The Long Loch: How Do We Go On From Here?* (forthcoming in 2010) which will include installations, an online library and a network of reading groups in collaboration with Glasgow Women's Library.

Thea Djordjadze

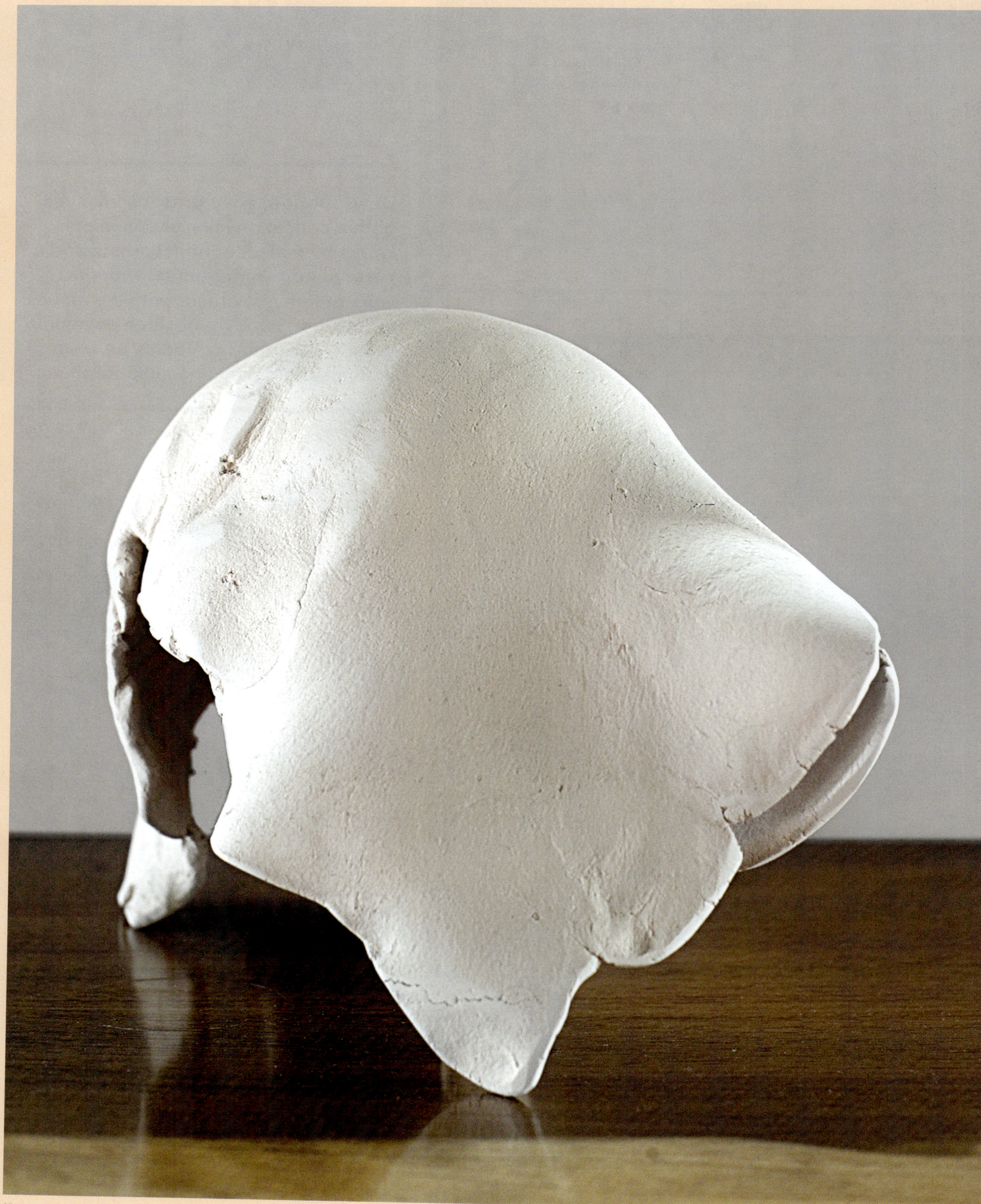

All men are equal but some men are more equal, than others. (Orwell), 2008. Papier–mâché. 18 × 31 × 15 cm

A critic once compared Thea Djordjadze's sculpture to 'calcified doves' wings', a description that captures the frail beauty but also the eerie embodiedness of so many of her emanations. I say 'emanations' because it seems the most appropriate word for the plaster, clay and papier-mâché forms that appear to emerge organically from the Georgian sculptor's hands. The strangely misshapen objects, at once modest, awkward and commanding (that is their paradox), are as much concrete forms in their own right as they are evidence of the gesture and touch that made them: unapologetically showing the stuff of their own making, each piece feels haunted by the ghost of the action as well as of the hands that constructed them.

At times powdered with plaster dust, sitting on salt crystals strewn across the floor, or positioned on traditional rugs made by nomadic tribes in Uzbekistan or Anatolia, Djordjadze's objects seem charged, like props for an archaic ritual, incomprehensible and mysterious. They have been compared to archaeological troves or fossils, and this is in part because they seem decidedly not of our time. Yet where to locate them temporally, historically? Modernist architecture and design is often quietly evoked in her work, but Djordjadze immediately deforms the modernist ideal, abutting its rigidity, its cult of perfection or form-follows-function rationality, with its opposite. Her sculptures sometimes channel geometric lines and a spare architectonics yet, placed next to or around these are craggy, folded forms that are infinitely flawed and wholly human; they sit like vestiges of the past and future, as in *All men are equal but some are more equal, than others (Orwell)* or *Archäology Politik Politik Archäology …* (both 2008). Even though modernism was self-consciously aimed at the transcendent, Djordjadze complicates this notion, since her objects seem to surpass this world and remain decidedly tied to it. It is no coincidence that so many of her pieces lie low to the ground, as if bound by an invisible umbilical cord to the earth beneath: the result propels the viewer to lower his or her body, giving a double sense to her particular base materialism.

For *Deaf and Dumb Universe (Raumgerüst)* (2008), Djordjadze smeared a mix of plaster dust and water onto one window panel of Mies van der Rohe's iconic exercise in absolute symmetry, the Neue Nationalgalerie in Berlin. This messy disruption of the clean modernist minimalism of the site suggests another crucial aspect of her practice: her emphasis on the means of viewing the artwork. In her hands, pedestals become sculpture, perilously encroaching

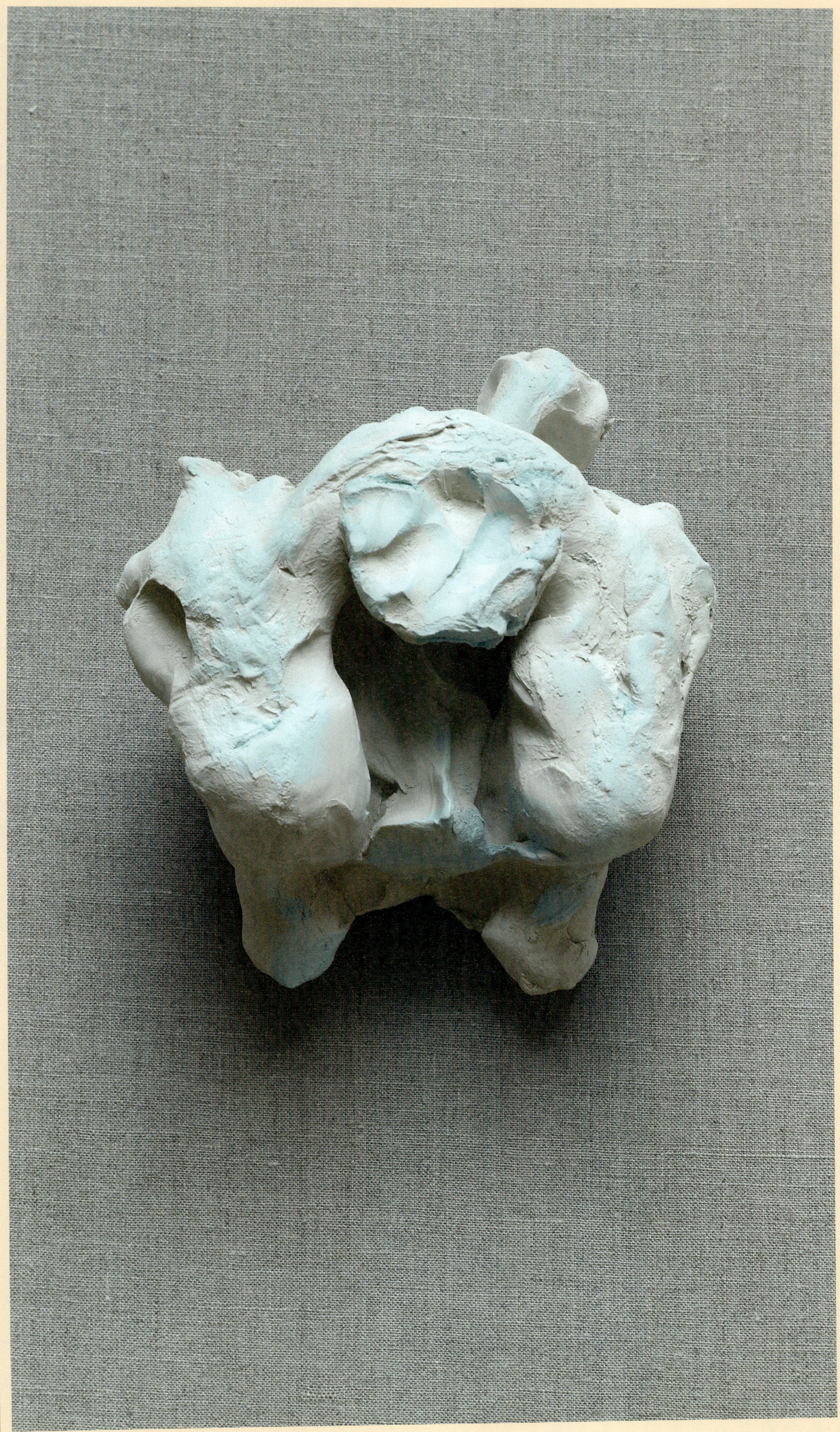

Untitled (detail), 2009. Unfired clay, paint. 188 × 145 × 210 cm

on the status of the objects that they are meant to serve and present. One cannot help but think of Brancusi's radical approach to the plinth, which transformed what had been its secondary and functional role of merely supporting sculpture or constructing a viewing distance for it. Djordjadze emerges from this lineage, extending the idea of the sculpture's base to make it integral and expansive. But if her presentational structures are of the same conceptual order as the objects that she has placed on or near them, rendering ambiguous the boundary between each, she is neither producing pedestals as autonomous objects nor objects that seek out an autonomy distinct from their context. Rather, it is the tension between the two that her work defiantly seeks.

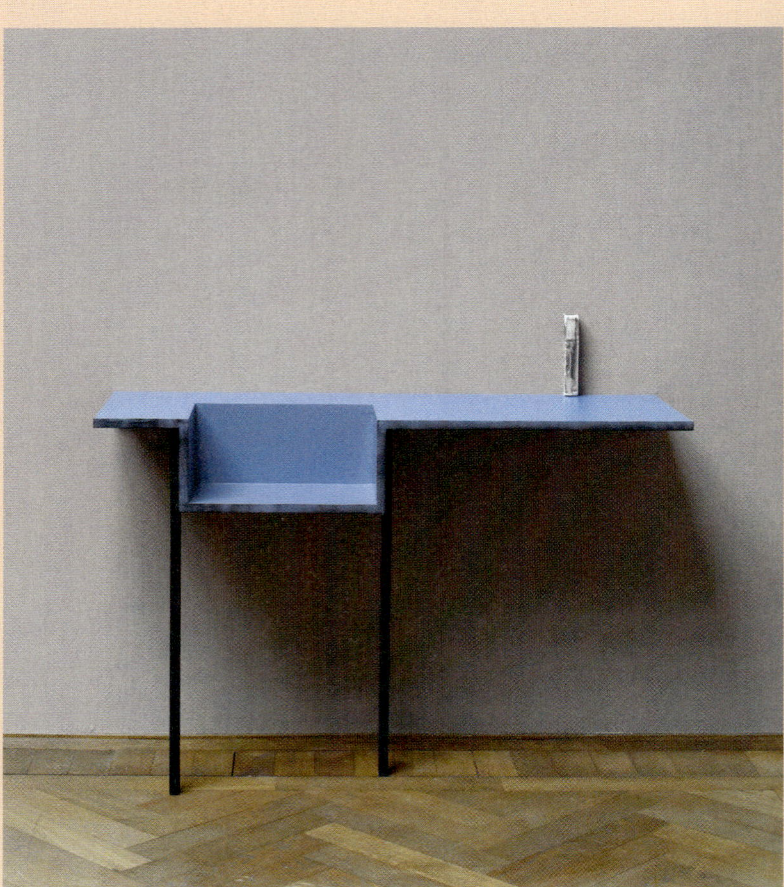

Untitled, 2009. Wood, lacquer, plaster, watercolour. 111 × 140 × 50 cm

Archaic ritual

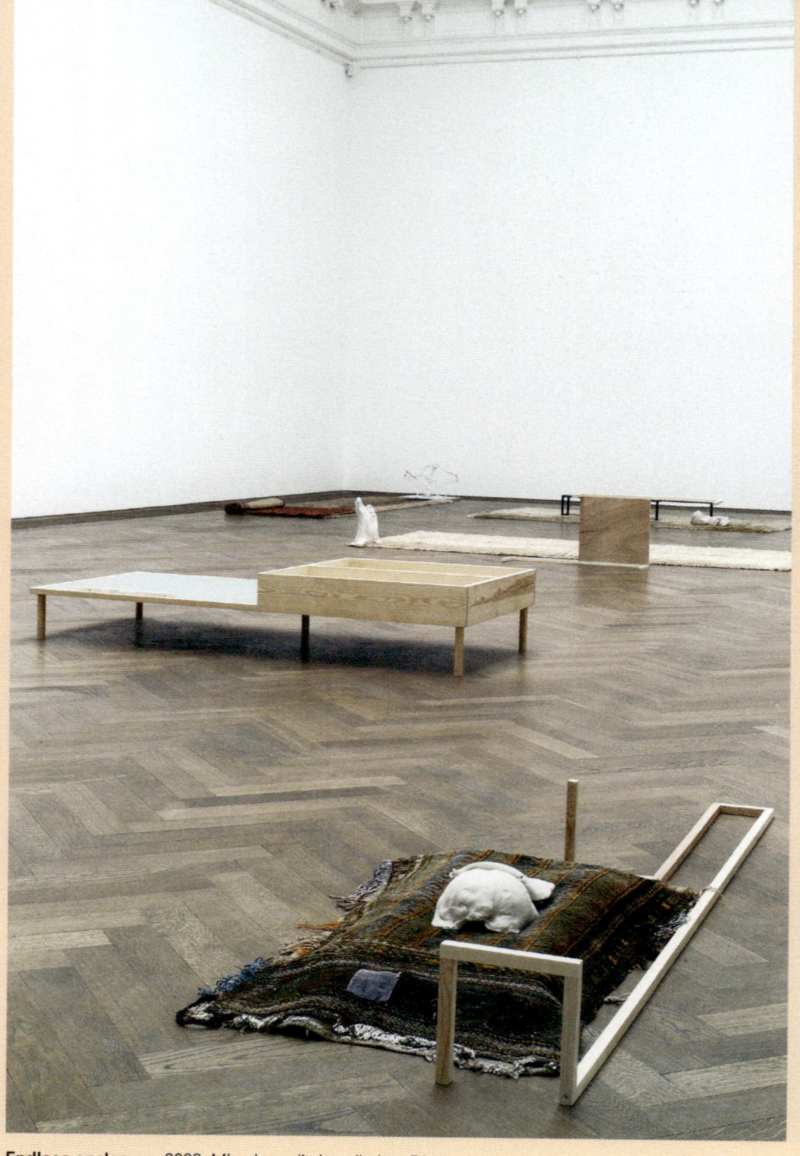

Endless enclosure, 2009. Mixed–media installation. Dimensions variable

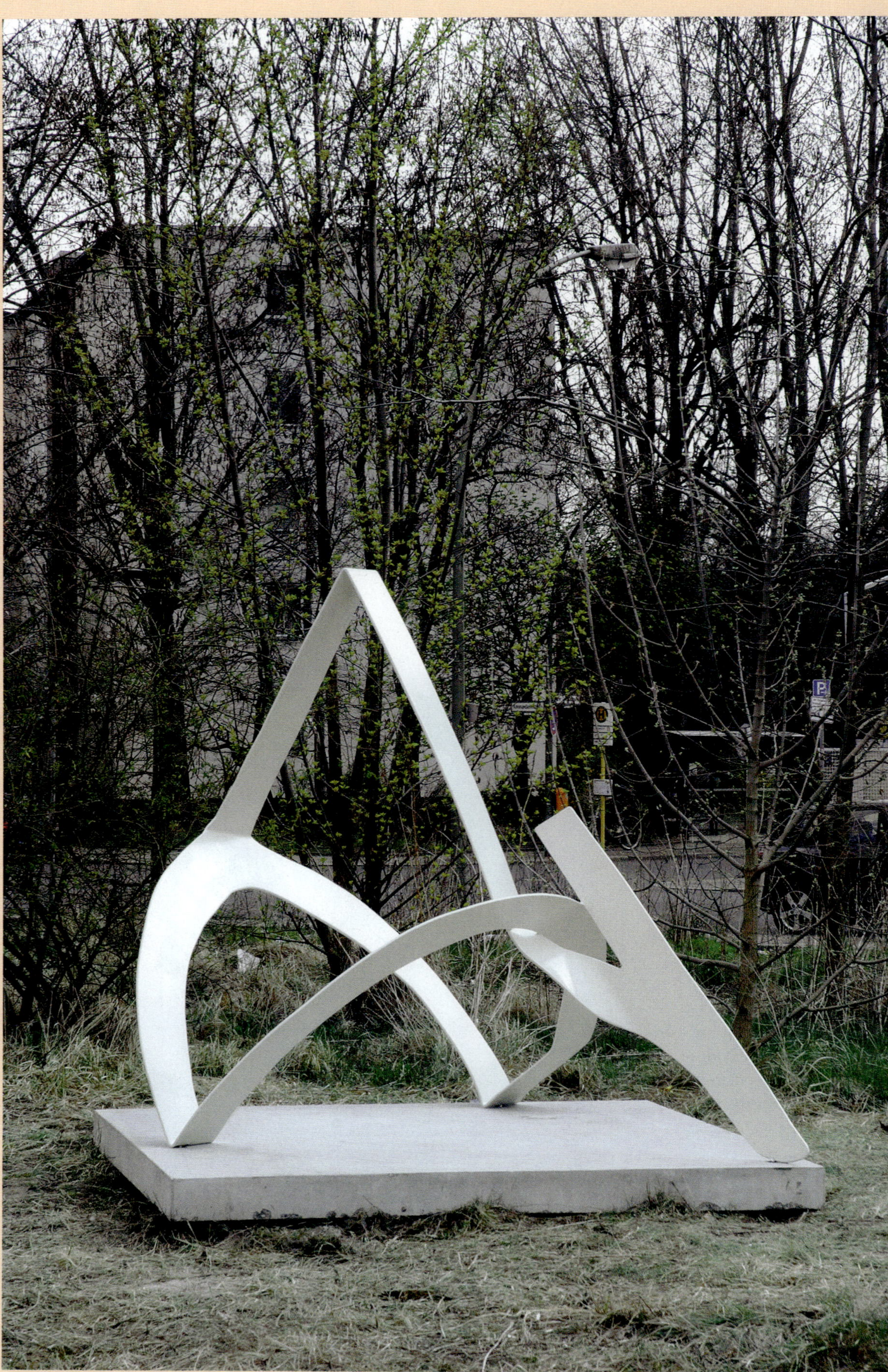

Fold b (large), 2008. Metal, concrete. 250 × 190 × 190 cm. Skulpturenpark, Berlin Biennial

Evidence of the gesture and touch

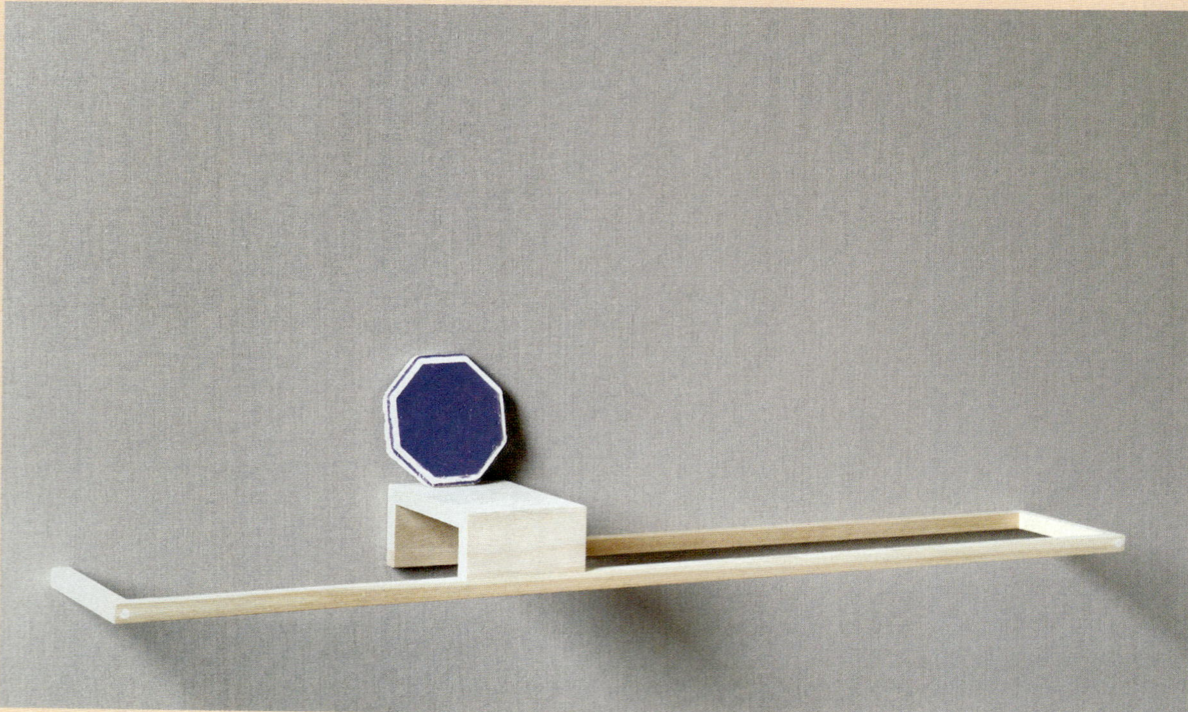

Untitled, 2009. Wood, plaster, paint. 26 × 143 × 22 cm

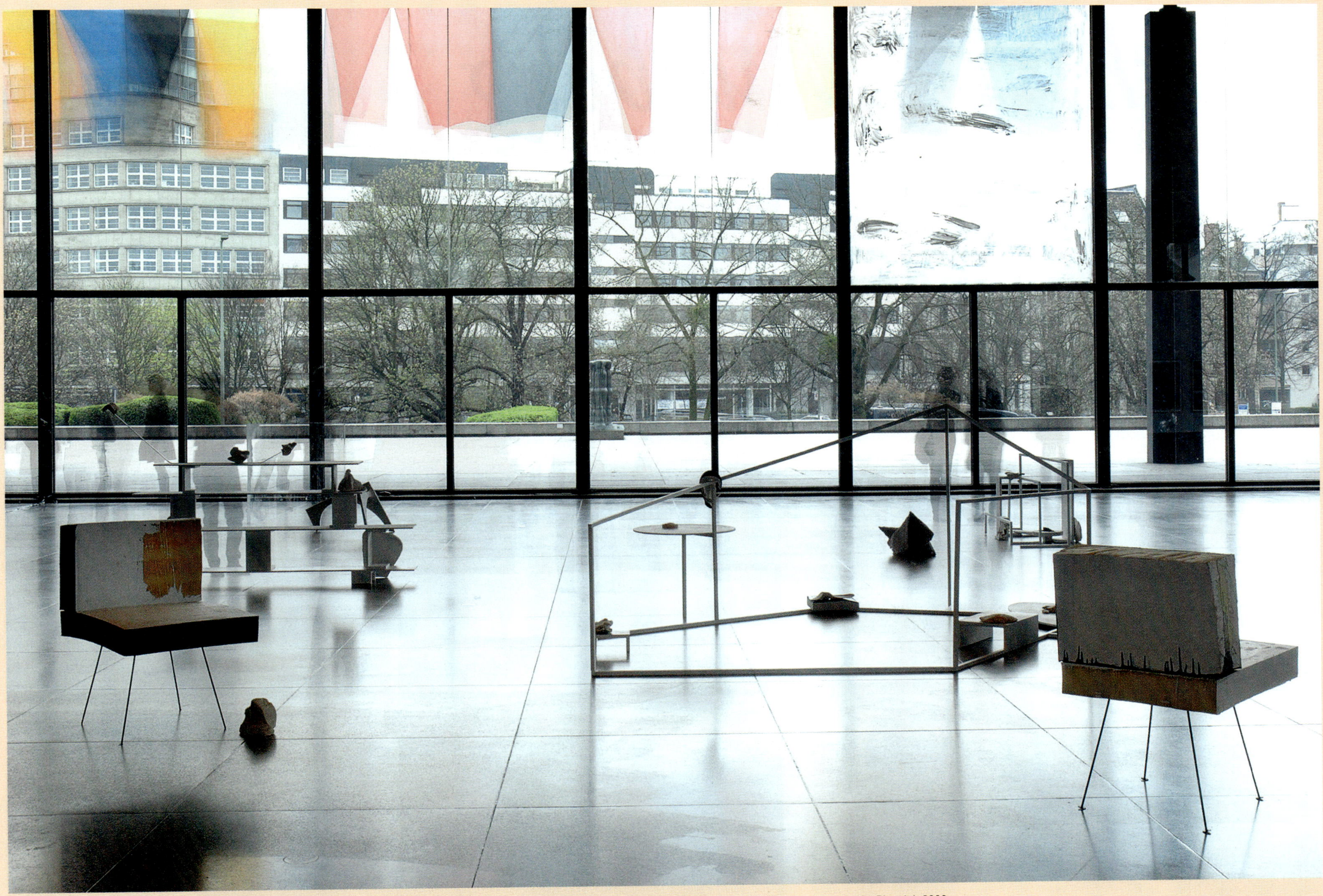

Deaf and dumb universe (Raumgerüst), 2008. Wood, paint, clay, fireclay, papier–mâché, fabric, plaster, silicon, soap. 143 × 260 × 330 cm. Neue Nationalgalerie, Berlin Biennial, 2008

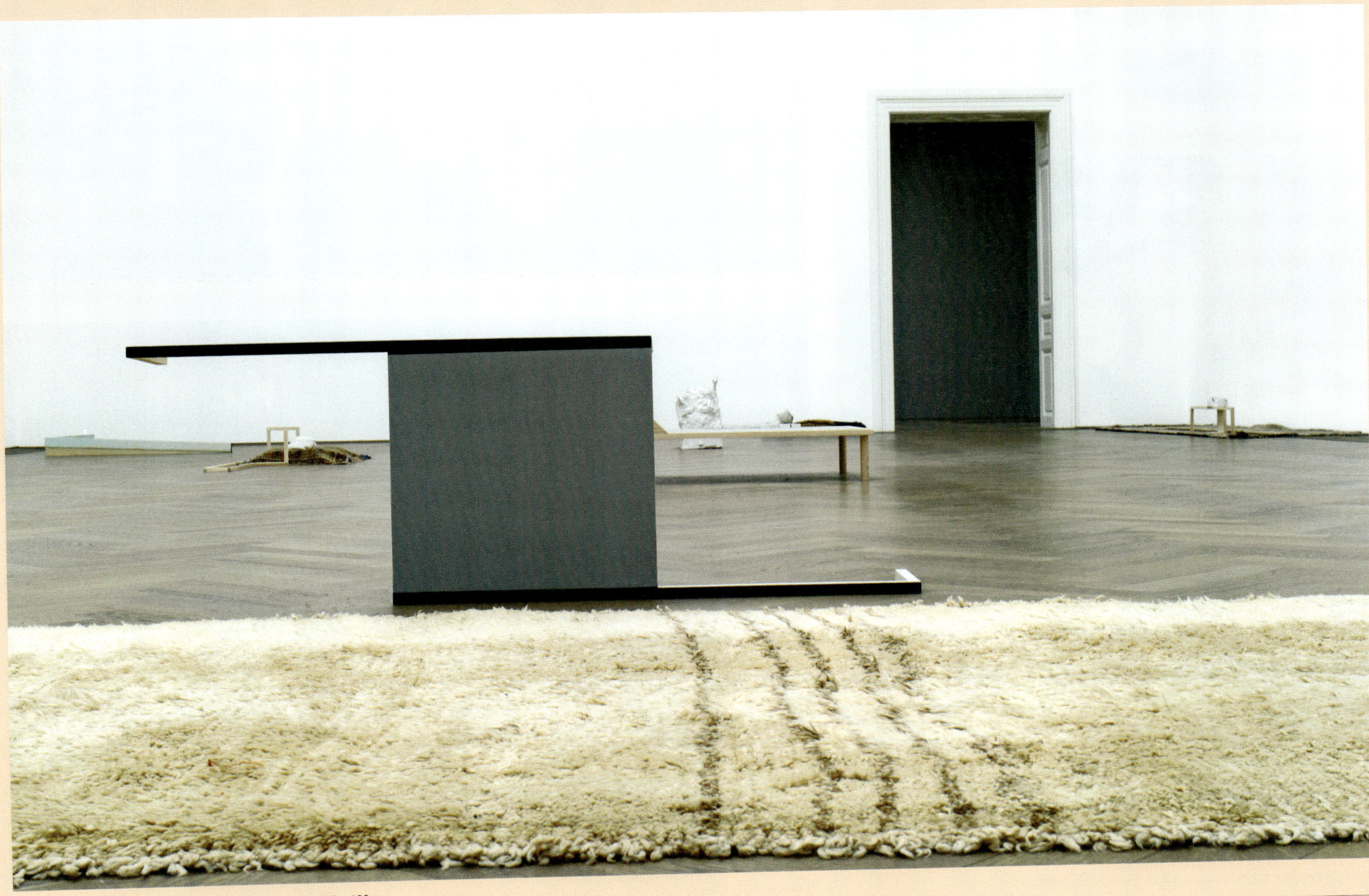

Untitled, 2009. Wood, lacquer, carpet, unfired clay. 22 × 305 × 180 cm

Nathalie Djurberg

Natalie Djurberg's stop-motion claymation videos depict bizarre, dream-like scenarios of repressed sexual desires and violent fantasies. Her candy-coloured fairytale worlds are animated with delicate clay figurines that she creates and manipulates herself. She tells her short stories primarily through actions, accompanied by dramatically suggestive electronic and orchestral musical scores created by her long-standing collaborator Hans Berg. The surreal, sadistic scenes of dismemberment, decomposition and copulation are offset by the playful, let's-pretend, toy-like quality of her vivid, hand-made worlds, which projects an innocence while also revealing clear signs of her role as puppeteer. Such contrasts set up an active tension in her mesmerizing videos between conscious 'proper' behaviour and the uncensored realm of the unconscious, into which Djurberg seems to tap.

The protagonists of her videos tend to be naked women — usually endowed with grotesquely exaggerated physical qualities — who within the same video, due to the malleability of Djurberg's plasticine universe, can transmute from being tortured victim to conquering she-woman, but are often left in more ambiguous positions. For instance, *It's the mother* (2009) revolves around a shapely naked woman surrounded by her five naked children, who one by one decide to return to the womb by climbing back through their mother's vagina and subsequently

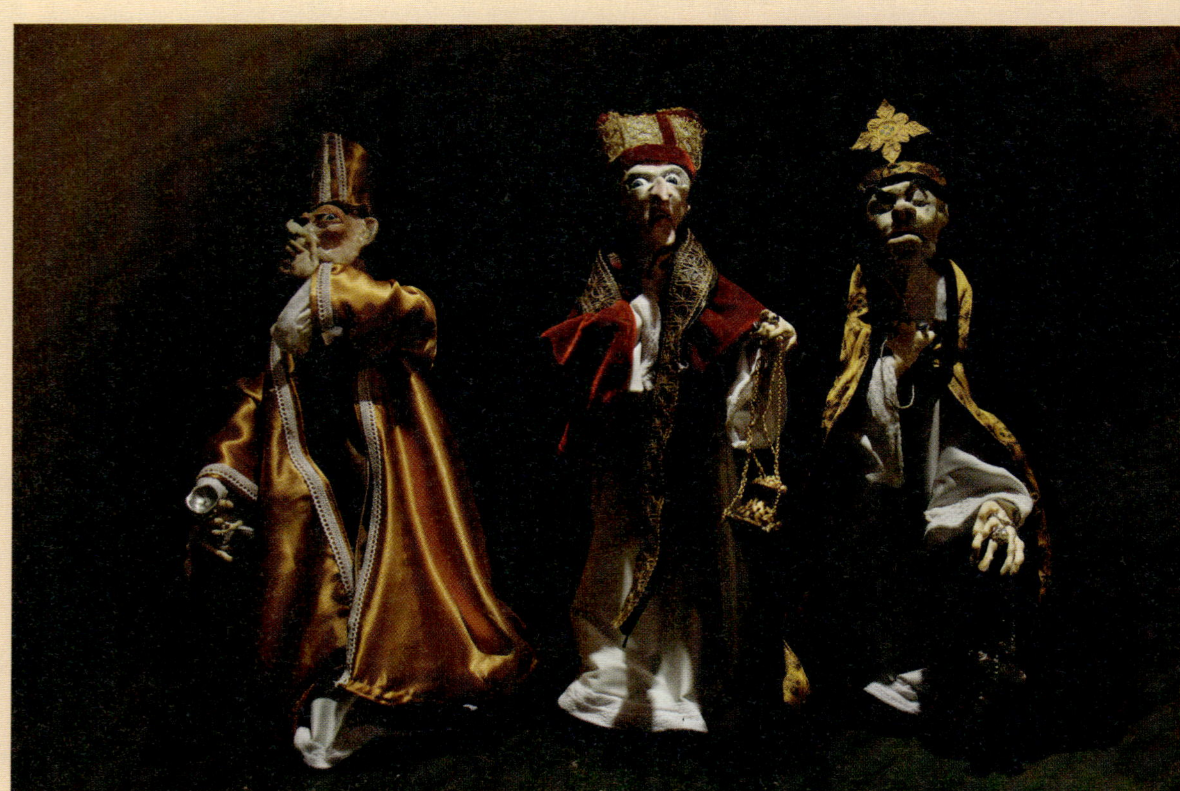

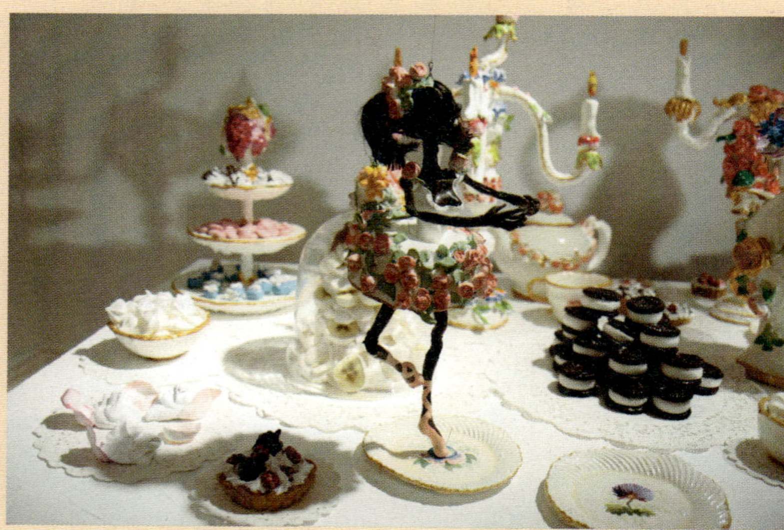

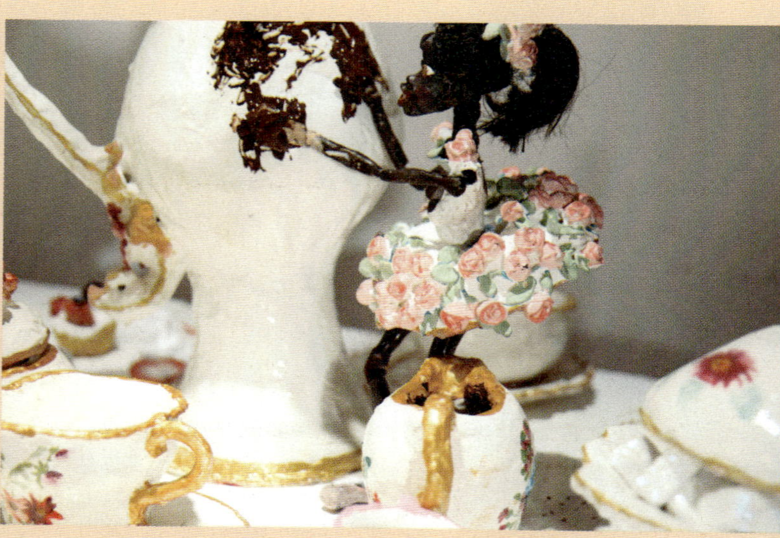

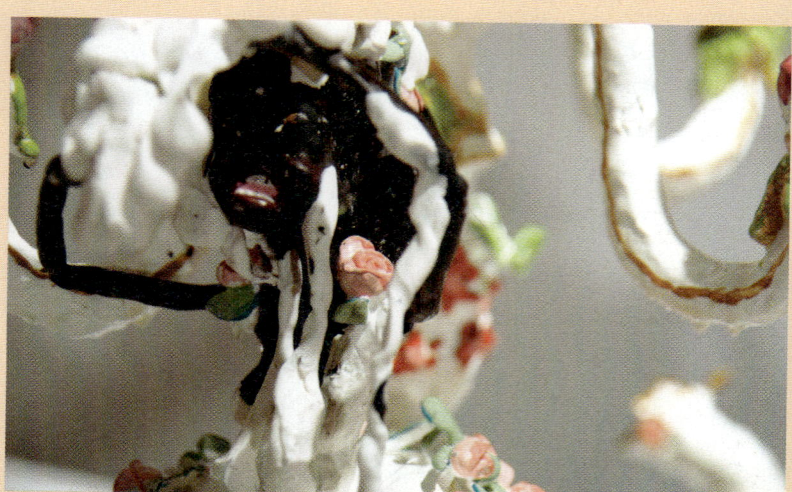

I found myself alone, 2008. Video. 9 min. 45 sec. Music by Hans Berg

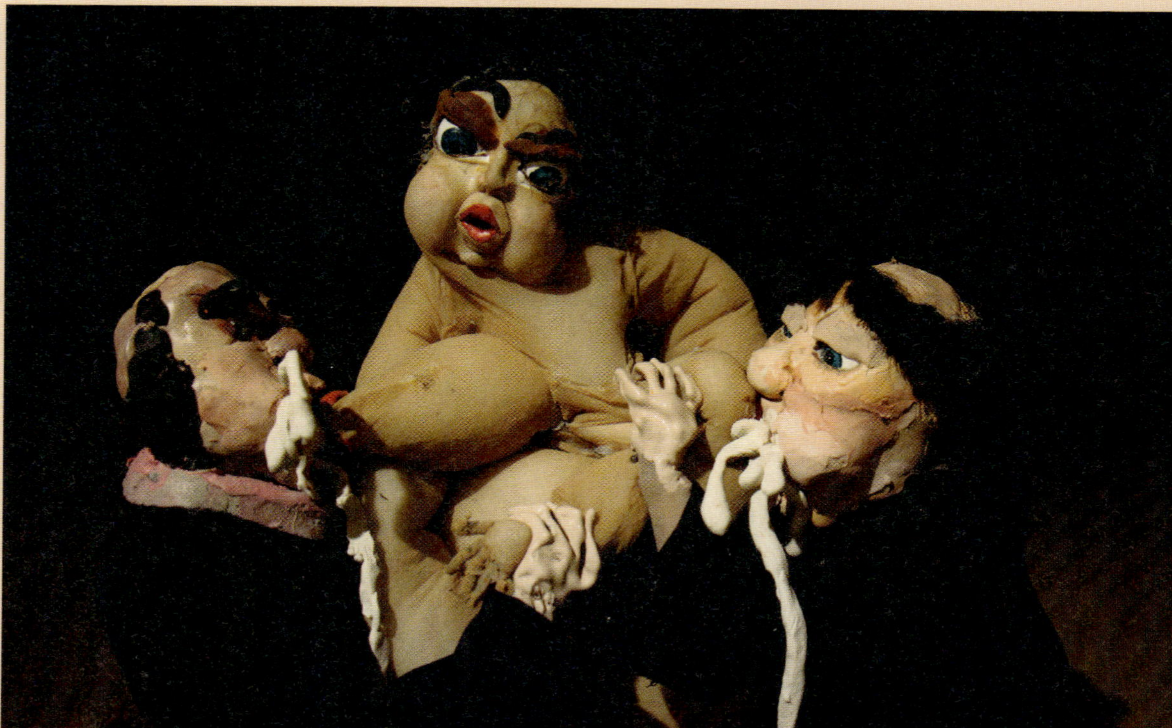

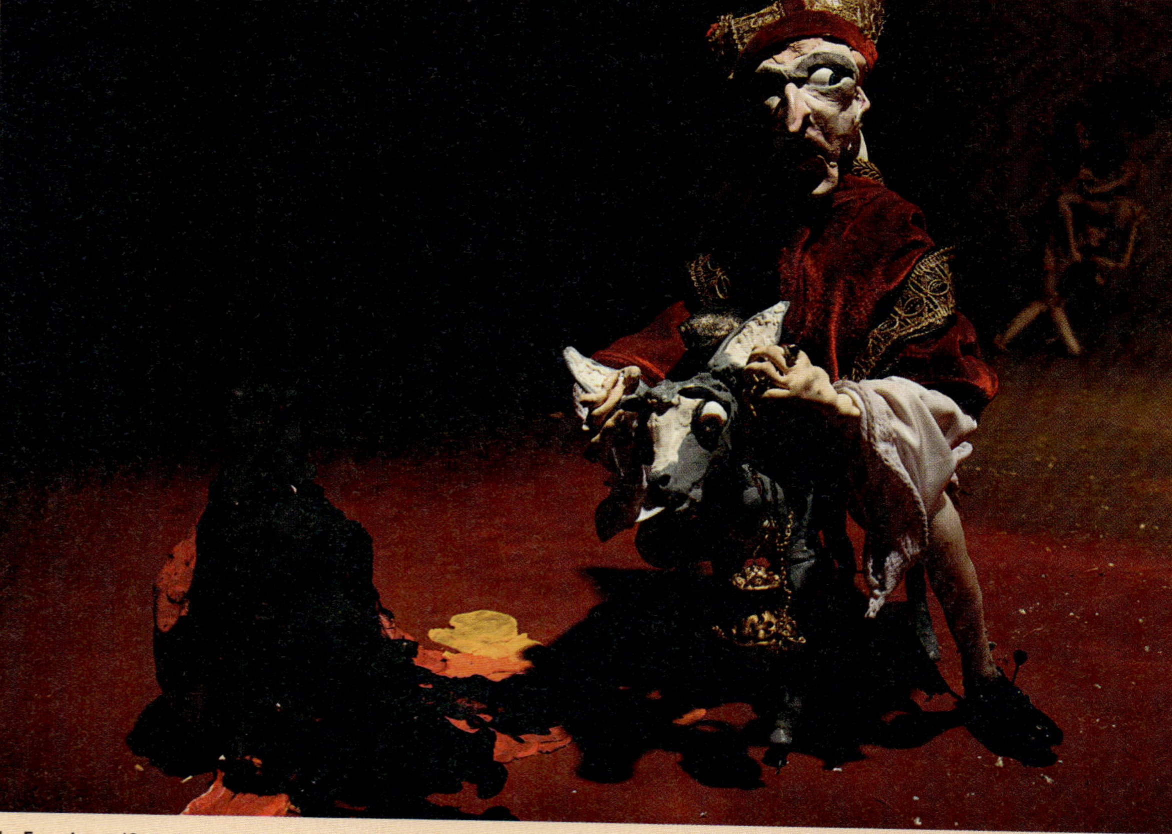

The Experiment (Greed), 2009. Video. 10 min. 45 sec. Music by Hans Berg

reduce her body to chaos. The mother becomes increasingly mortified and blue tears start to stream down her face as she collapses onto the mattress of the Spartan bedroom. Once the last child has clawed its way back into her body, the mother starts to writhe in pain (or pleasure?), and then begins to sprout the arms and legs of the children inside her until she is transformed into a multi-limbed monstrosity, in a dramatic riff on the complexity of motherly love and self-sacrifice.

In *The Experiment (Cave)* (2009), a naked young woman takes up residence in a crystalline cave in which unusual things start to take place. Her limbs are amputated by unknown forces and then begin to take on independent lives as they turn against her, attacking other parts of her torso, or attaching themselves in the wrong configurations and turning her into an amorphous creature. With no outside 'enemy' the video seems to point to our conscious or buried tendencies towards self-destruction.

By contrast, *I found myself alone* (2008) starts off serenely, with disaster striking only at the end. The video focuses on a tiny black ballerina who pirouettes across a tabletop set for high tea with luscious confections and Rococo china. She twirls innocently through the beautiful landscape of sweets until things start to go awry: dripping wax gets in her way, she stumbles on mushy Oreos and melting bananas and cream. At this point, she begins to fight back, smearing the teapots with chocolate sauce, tipping over the milk and building sugar cube staircases from which to witness the destruction. Ultimately, it is a losing battle, and she is finally buried in an avalanche of melting candle wax.

The video is unusual for Djurberg, one of the few that

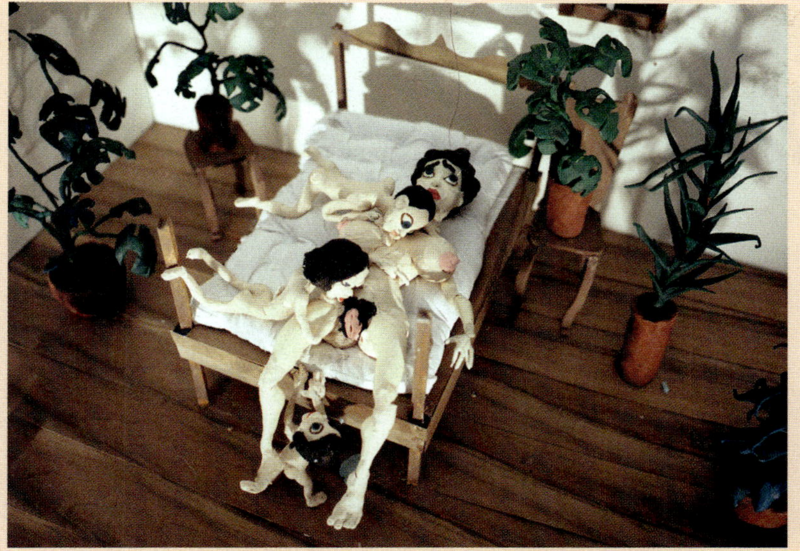

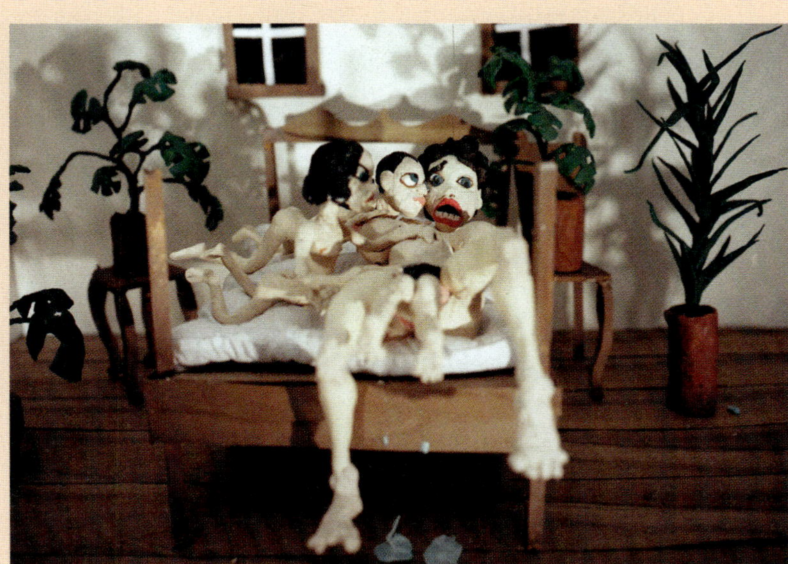

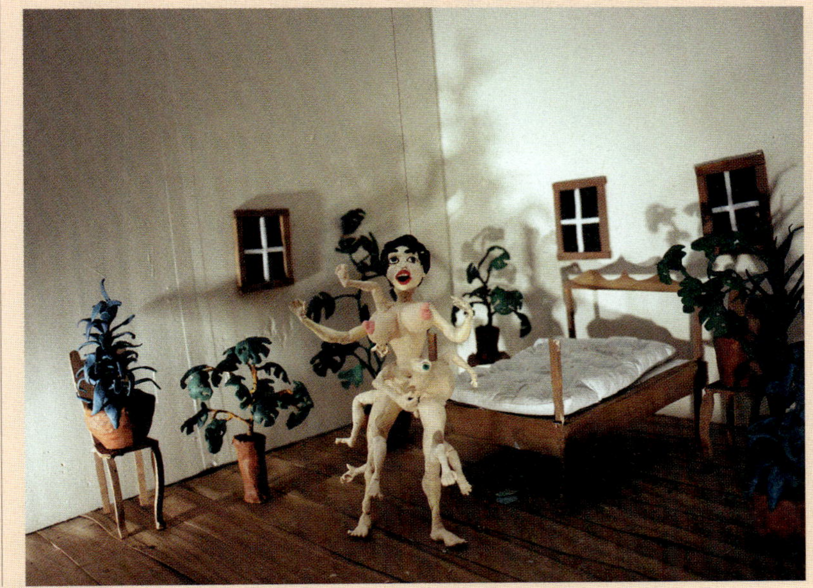

It's the mother, 2008. Video. 6 min. Music by Hans Berg

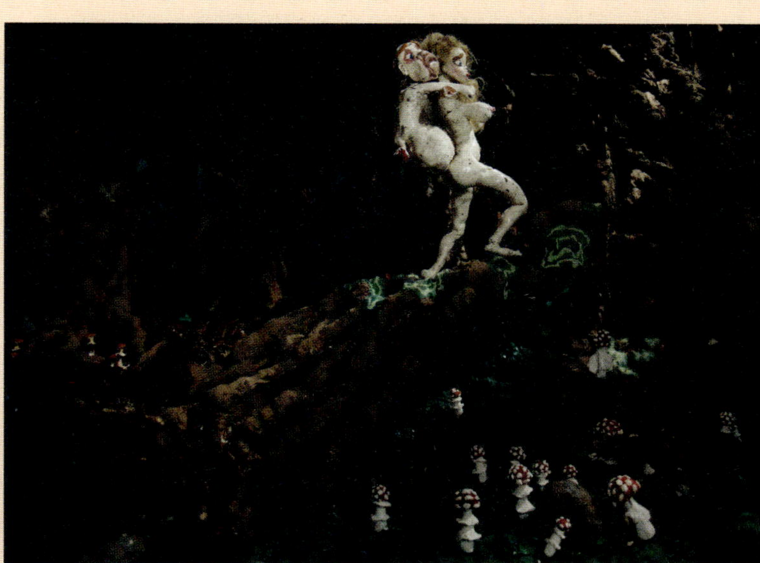

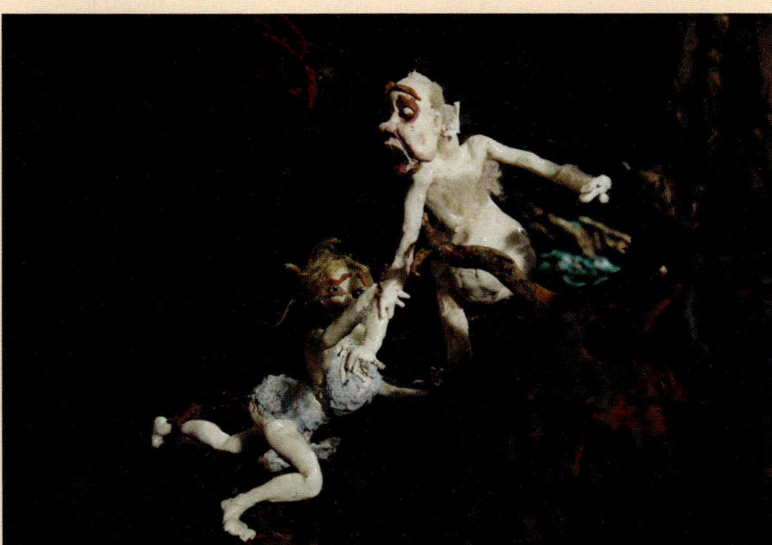

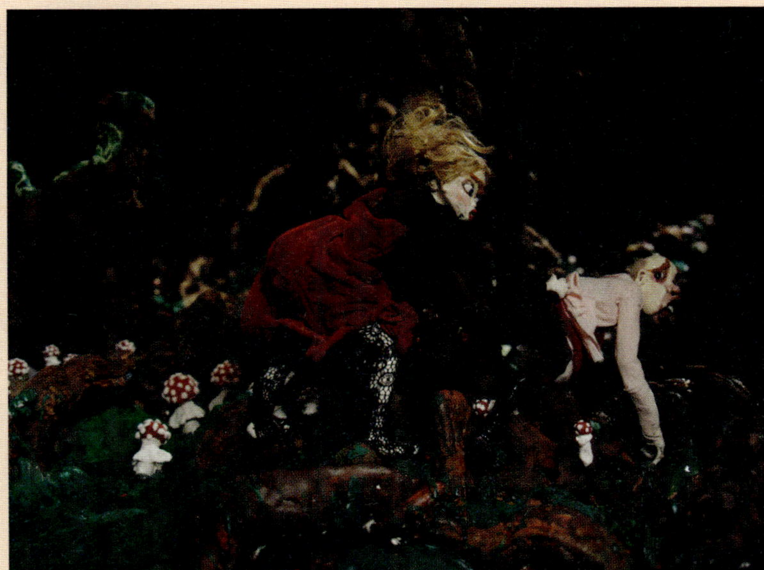

The Experiment (Forest), 2009. Video. 7 min. 27 sec. Music by Hans Berg

Dream-like scenarios

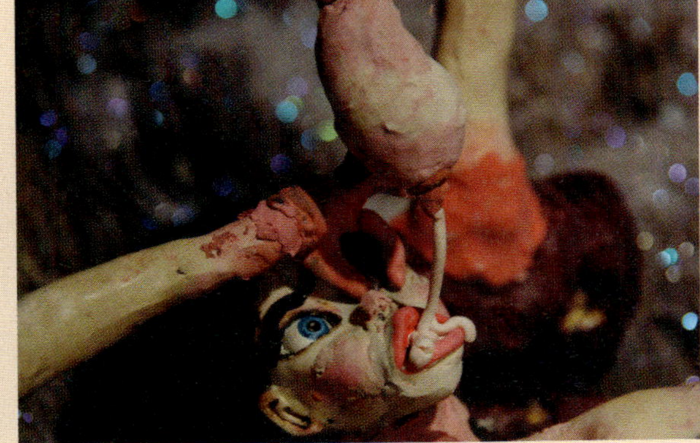

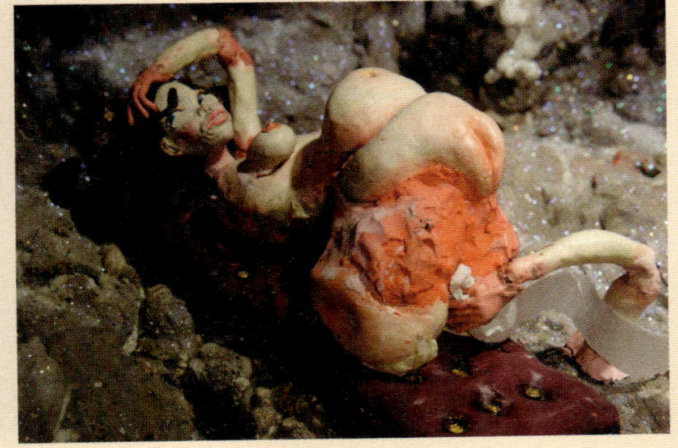

comments primarily on issues of race and legacies of colonialism more than on issues of sex, although desire also plays a key role in this work.

Djurberg's captivating videos explore themes of sexual desire, self-destruction, shame and guilt, creating imagined scenarios that enact the private or subconscious thoughts we would never admit or can never recall. Elements of innocence combine with a world that is ultimately rendered as brutal, revealing contradictions that are irreconcilable when it comes to love, faith and hatred. Mirroring the inexplicable ways in which the unconscious works, Djurberg shies away from any clear resolutions or moralizing judgements; instead, she offers up her charged scenes almost dispassionately, leaving it up to us to make our own endings.

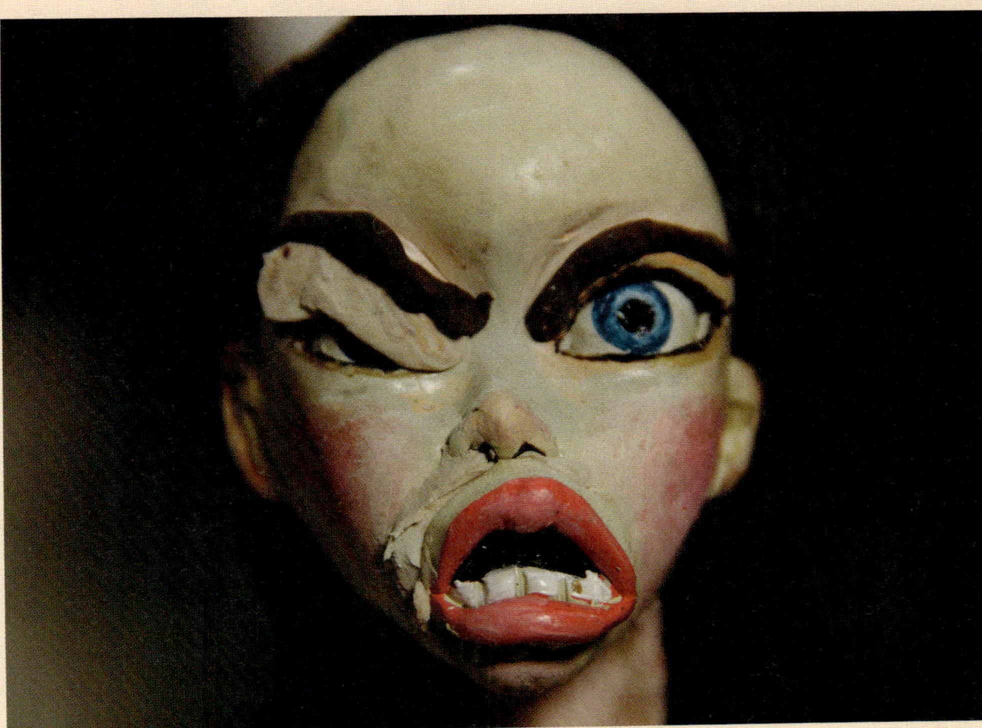

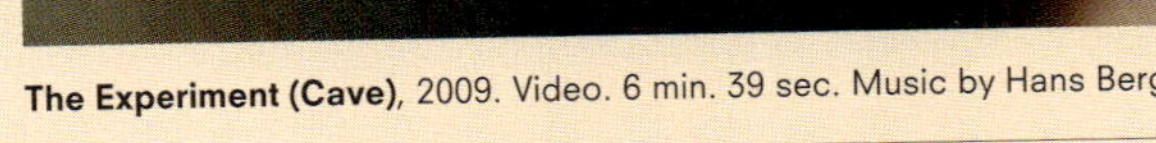

The Experiment (Cave), 2009. Video. 6 min. 39 sec. Music by Hans Berg

Matías Duville

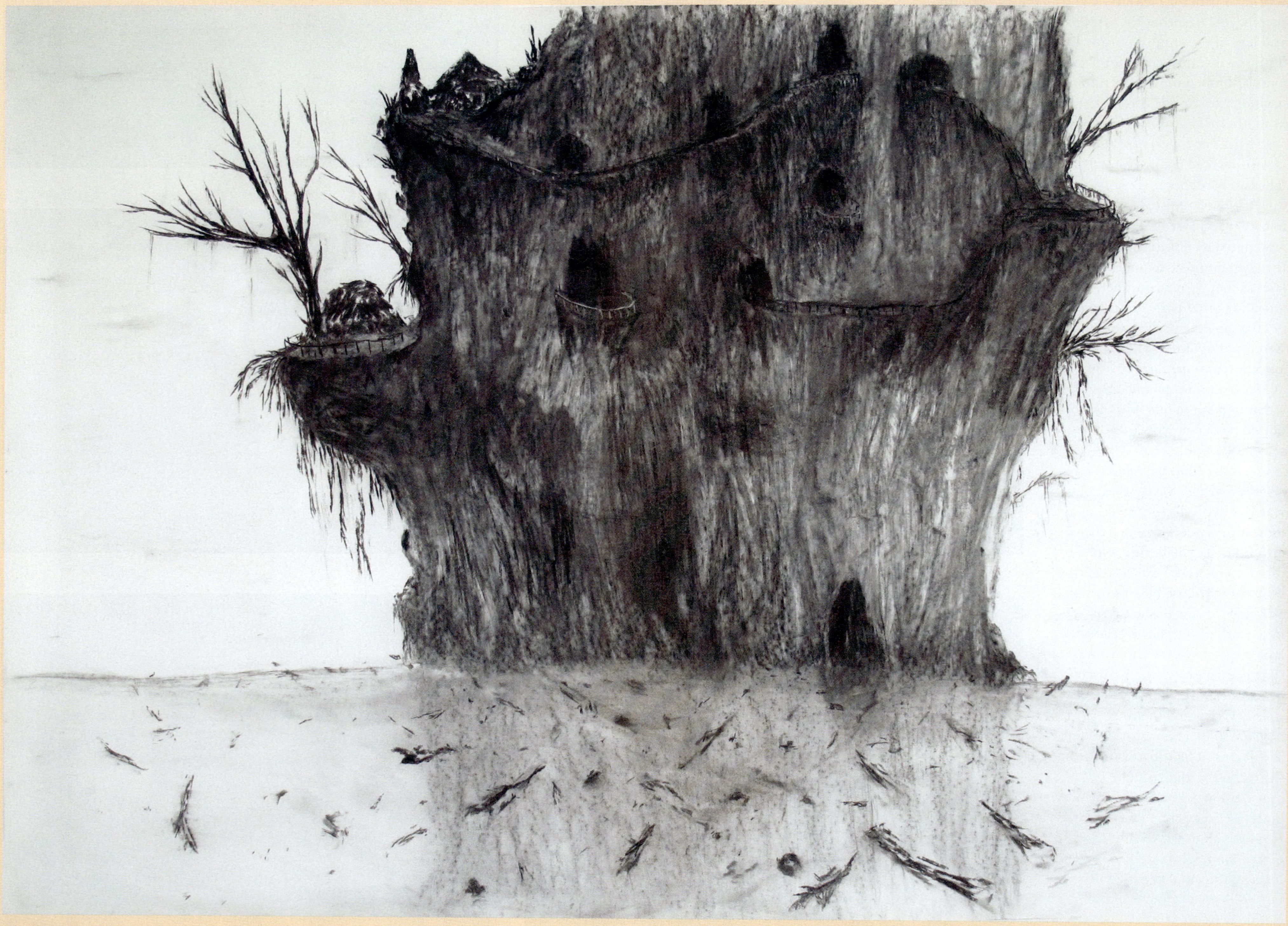

Space echo, 2009. Charcoal on paper. 150 × 250 cm

At the start of his career as an artist in Buenos Aires, Matías Duville decided to do without his undeniable talent as a draughtsman. As a result, he began exploring various types of image supports that would allow him to leave aside his dexterity. For example, drawings he made on swimming pool water filters: once the drawing was completed, Duville would pull out some of the support's silk threads and in this way thin out the image, de-drawing it. There were also drawings done on rugs, which Duville would then shave to generate images of landscapes.

Combining these types of additive and subtractive processes would become one of his strengths: to create a drawing or a painting and then attacking its support until a new image, more unstable than the original, would emerge. His paintings on wood arise from the same process; once a painting is finished,

After spending a few years in a state of prolific experimentation, Duville seems to have found his most successful language in the simplicity of charcoal, whether it is on paper or on a wall.

Duville assaults its support with a hammer, as if the work were being devastated by an out-of-control psychotic.

The feeling of catastrophe, the uncanny or ominous within his imagery — burnt forests,

The uncanny or ominous

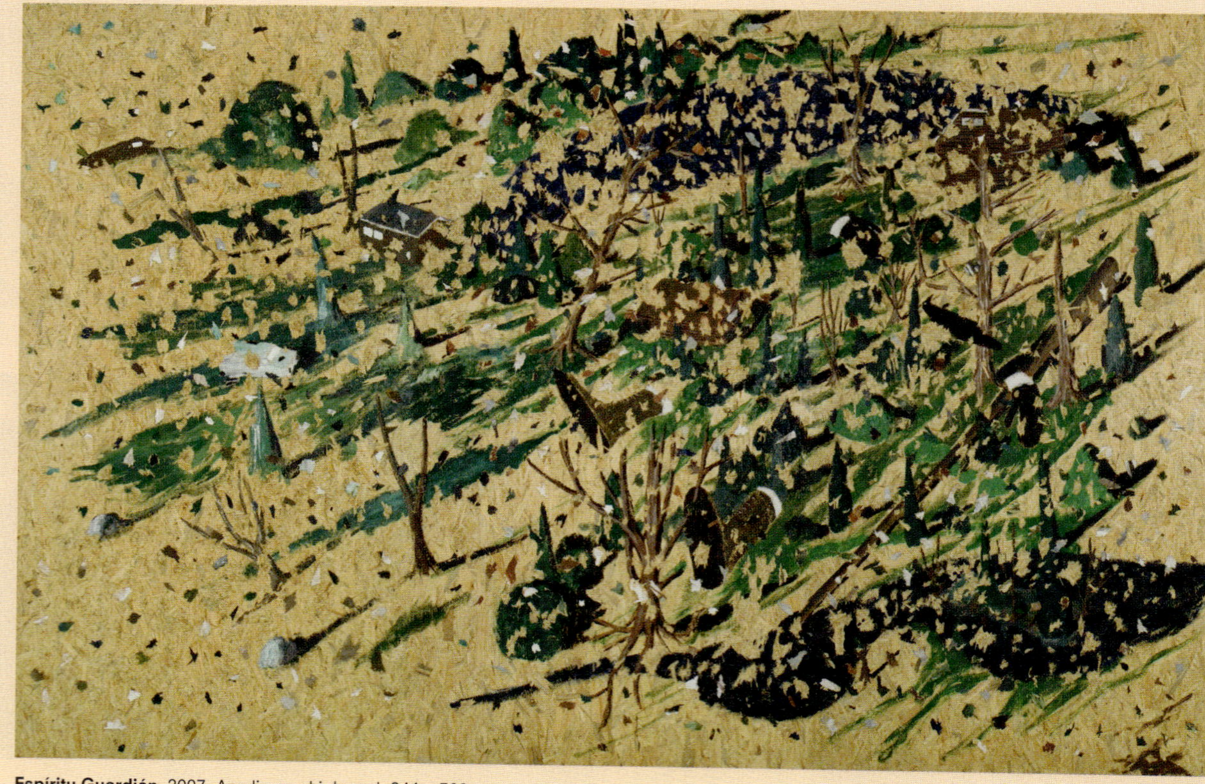

Espíritu Guardián, 2007. Acrylic on chipboard. 244 × 366 cm

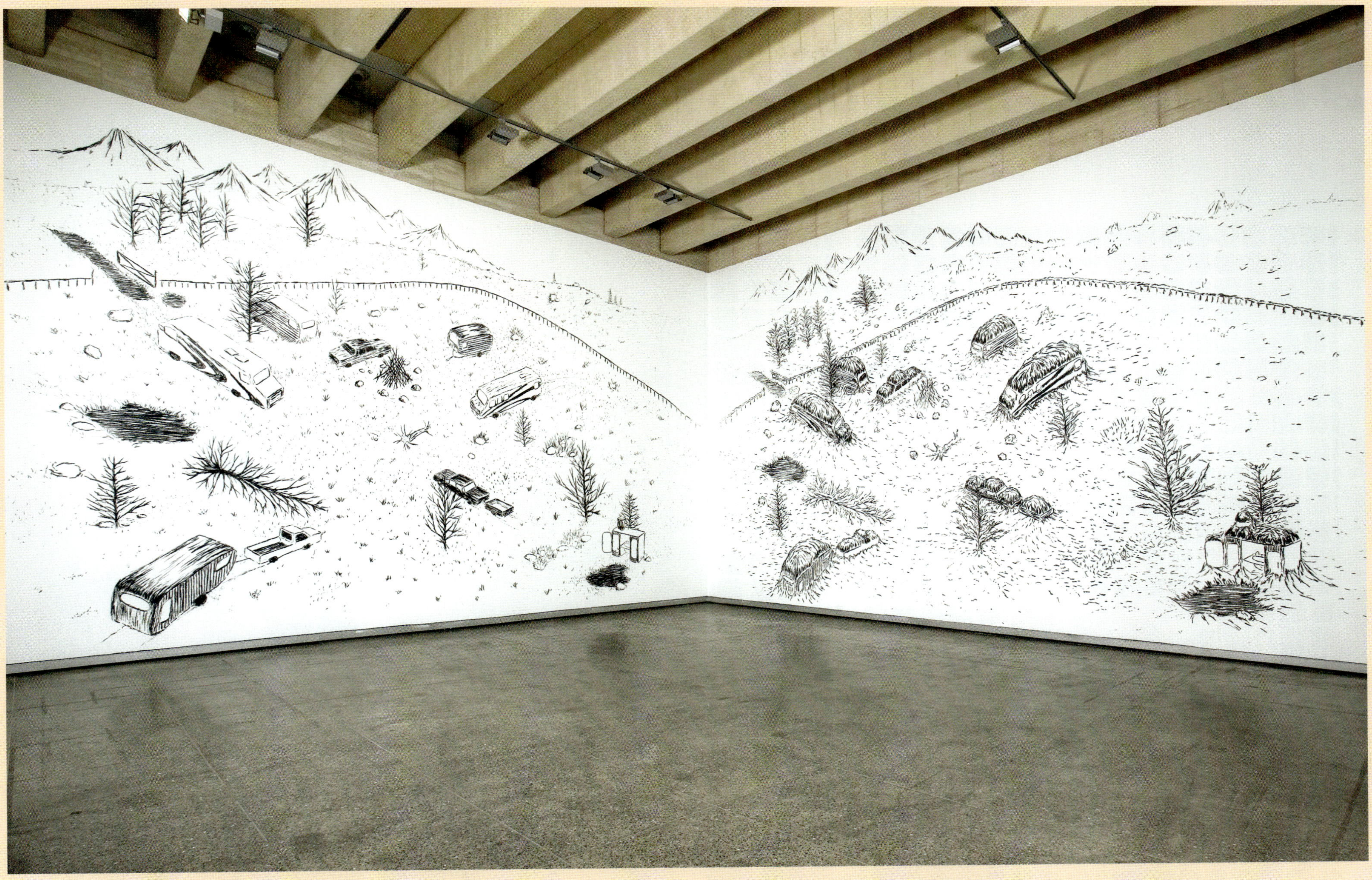

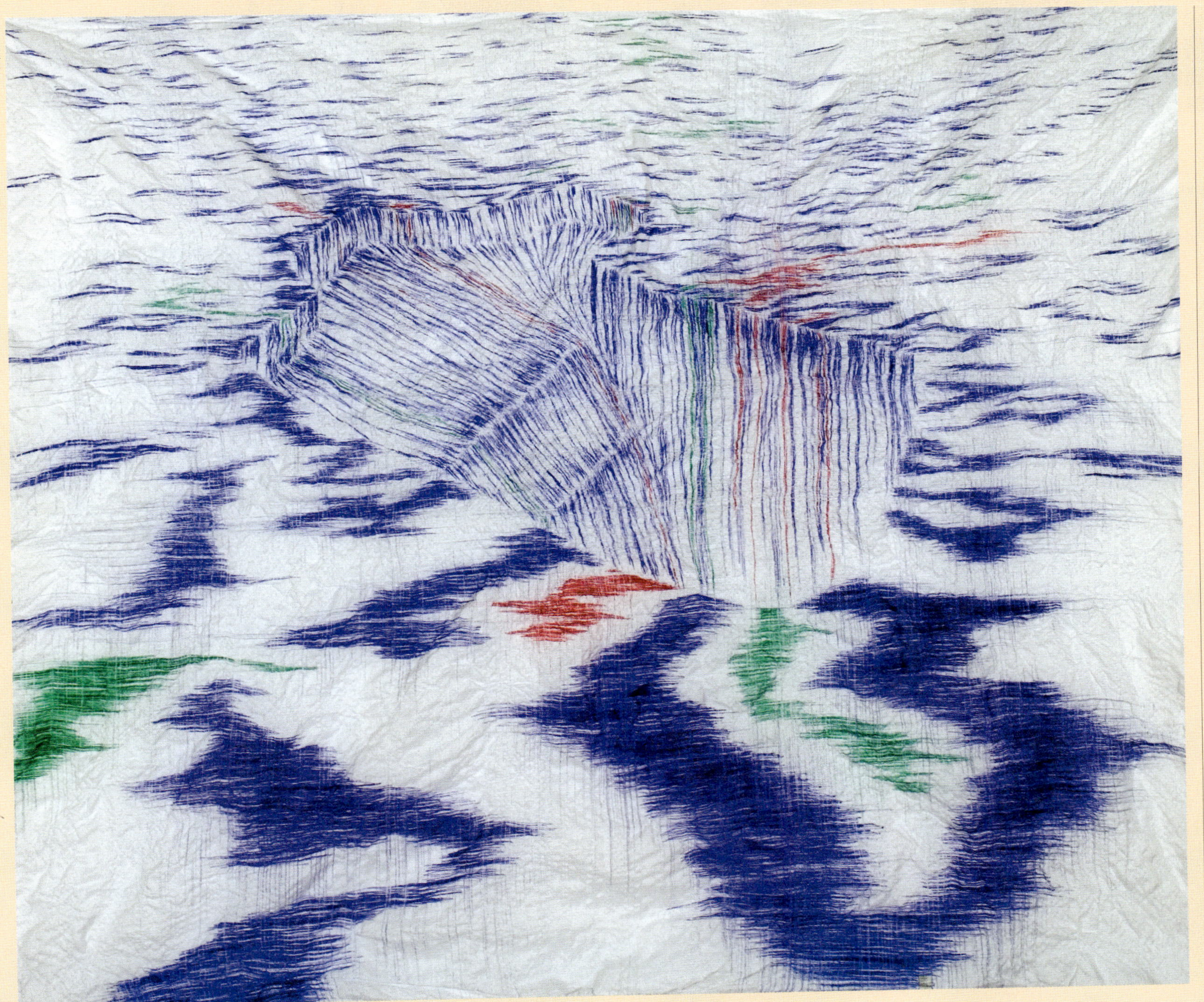

Cover, 2007. Charcoal on wall. 4 × 16 m

Piscina, 2006. Ink on silk. 110 × 120 cm

hurricanes, tidal waves or gigantic burials — is intensified by these destructive processes, which seem physically to drag the work itself through a dark force.

After spending a few years in a state of prolific experimentation, today Duville seems to have found his most successful language in the simplicity of charcoal, whether on paper or on a wall. Now, faithful to the austerity of black on white and to fragmented and violent lines, it is evident that his nightmares have become even more intense. Through this language, he manages to achieve the perfect tension between the silent and tenebrous environments he creates and the performative urgency of his mark-making.

Duville's favourite scenes take place within nature's serenity, but always seem about to veer into disaster. The images in his first shows leaned towards the vertiginous, featuring cars or aeroplanes that were victims of hurricanes or tornadoes. Now his imagery is less realist — 'invented catastrophes' in the artist's own words: seas that due to some impossible freezing process, become forests, caves filled with strange foliage and bonfires in the middle of abandoned grottoes, with everything pointing to a future after the catastrophe, in which there are only fragile traces of solitary survivors.

Shannon Ebner

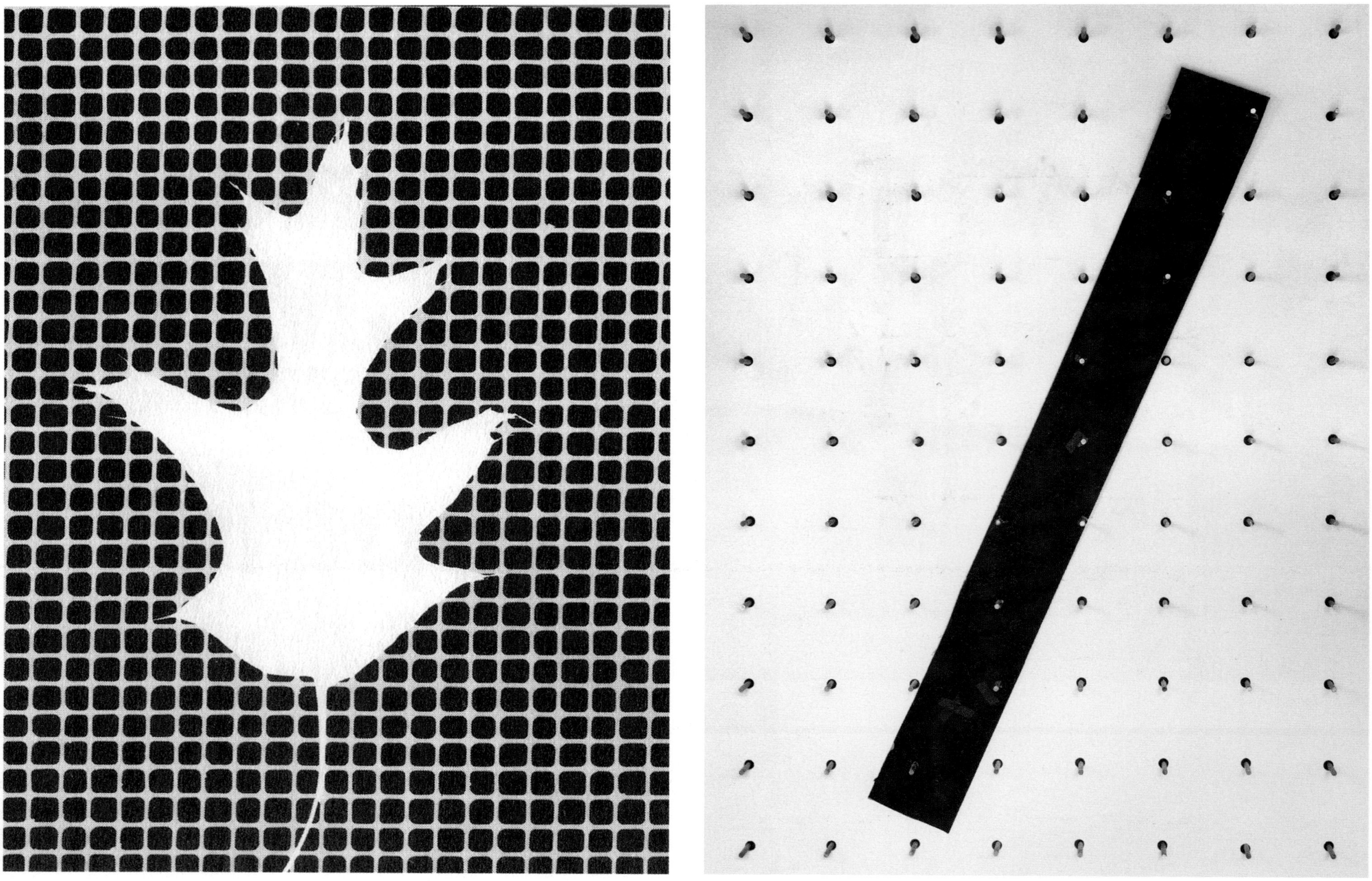

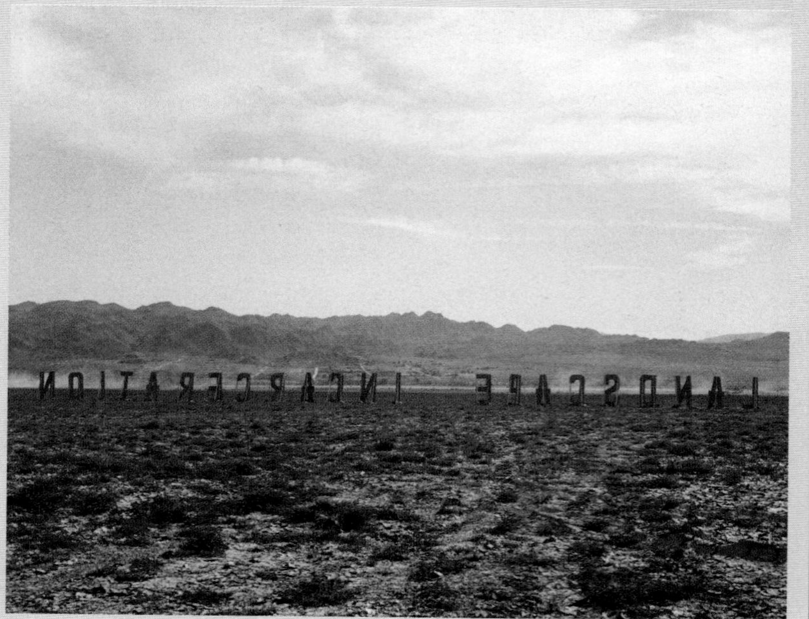

Leaf and Strike, 2009. Chromogenic print. 20 × 31 cm

Over the last seven years, Shannon Ebner has produced one of the most innovative bodies of photographic work in contemporary art, but to say this is already to oversimplify her project, which might better be described as occupying a space where photography, sculpture and language intersect. Working almost exclusively with black and white film, eschewing the high-tech possibilities of her chosen medium, Ebner has explored a photographic dialectic of transience and materiality in rigorous yet frequently playful images.

Early works document words and phrases made from large cardboard letters and placed in various, generally Western American, settings.

Landscape Incarceration, 2003. Chromogenic print. 81 × 103 cm

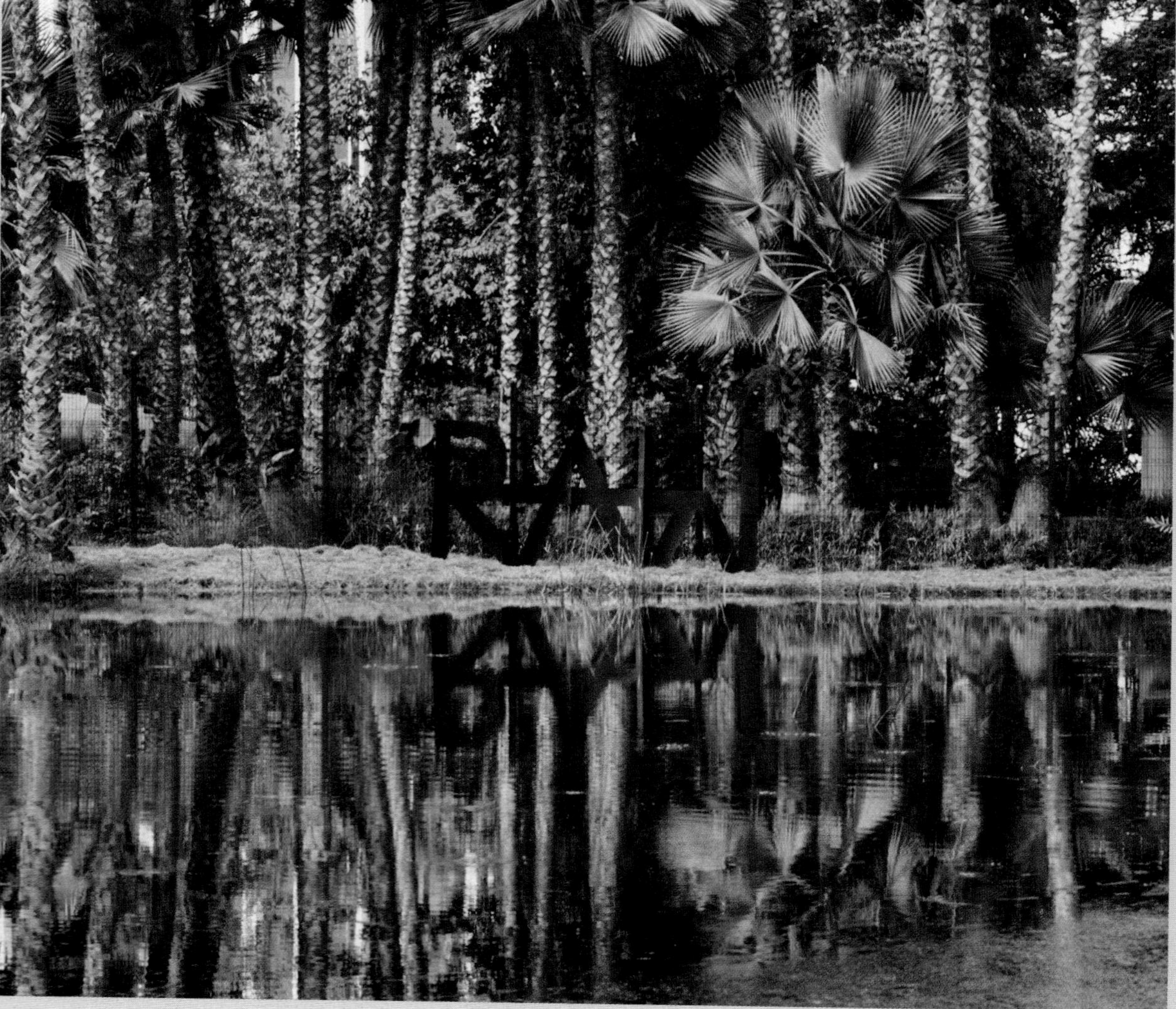

Raw War, 2004. Chromogenic print. 53 × 60 cm

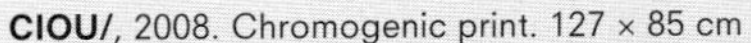

CIOU/, 2008. Chromogenic print. 127 × 85 cm

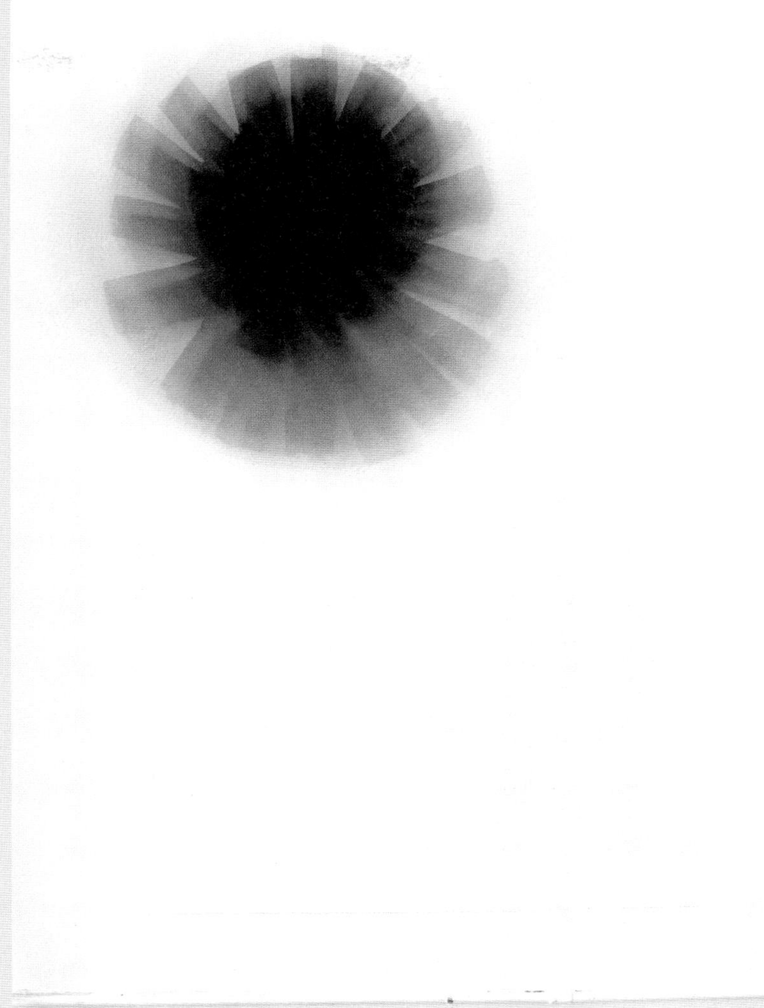

The Sun as Error, 2009. Chromogenic print. 107 × 82 cm

A literal take on concrete poetry

In *Landscape Incarceration* (2003), we see the words of the title from behind, in the middle ground of a vast scrubby desert plain, mountains rising in the distance. The reversal is quite appropriate here, since Ebner's panoramic landscape will always resist 'incarceration', or the attempt to confine it within the norms of aesthetic representation; the distant prospect is only glimpsed across the lettered phrase. In *Raw War* (2004), the conjoined black letters R-A-W are placed against a tropical backdrop of palm trees, at the edge of a murky lake in which the word is reflected upside down.

Critic Todd Alden has characterized Ebner's language in these photographs as 'darkly ambiguous', and *Raw War* in particular seems to partake of the sinister political climate of early twenty-first-century America. However, beyond any topical reference, Ebner taps into an older strain of Los Angeles noir, the underside of the fantasy embodied in the Hollywood sign crowning the city.

Raw War is, of course, also a recreation of Bruce Nauman's 1970 neon of the same name, and Ebner's word play shares his concern with the object-like quality of letters and his fascination with the fluidity of meaning. Ebner has placed herself within a photographic tradition that stretches 'from Atget to Ruscha' — in other words a tradition of documentary, deadpan images — but it would be equally

Fluidity of meaning

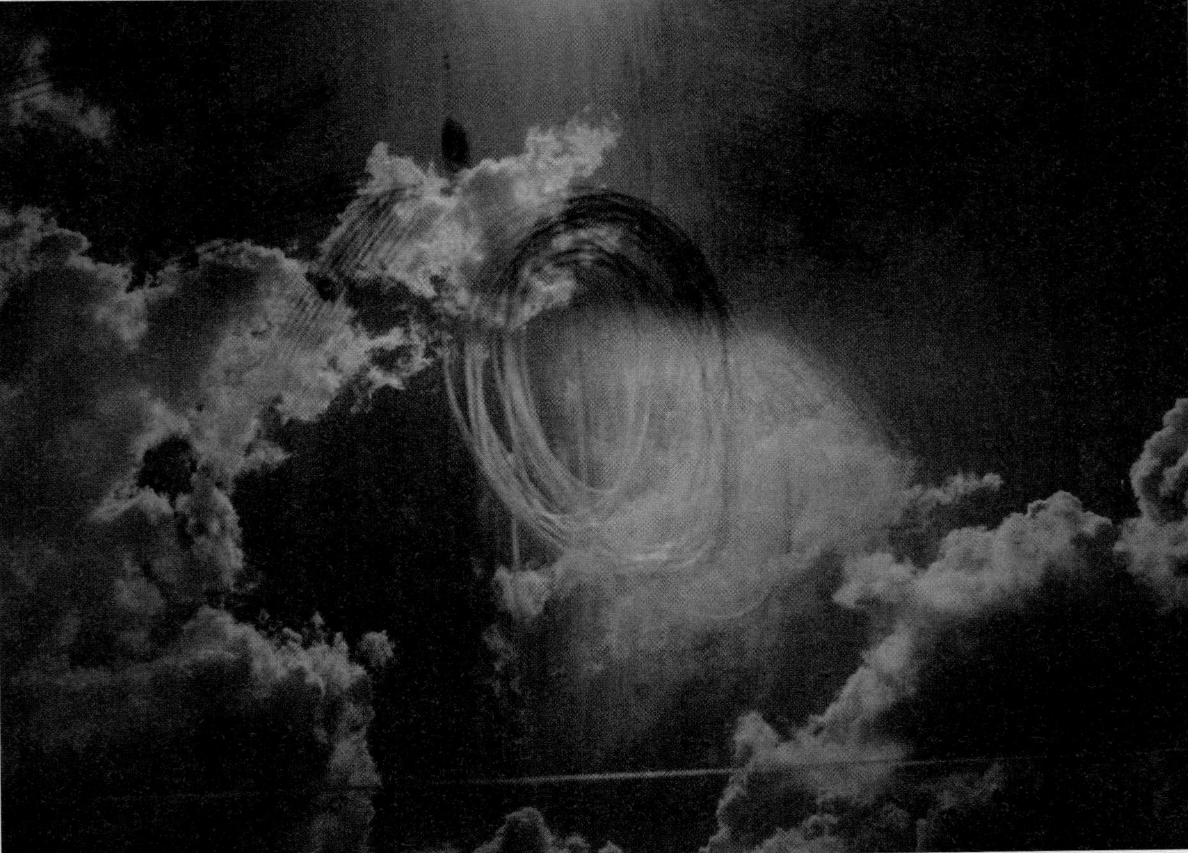

Some Clouds, 2009. Chromogenic print. 80 × 112 cm

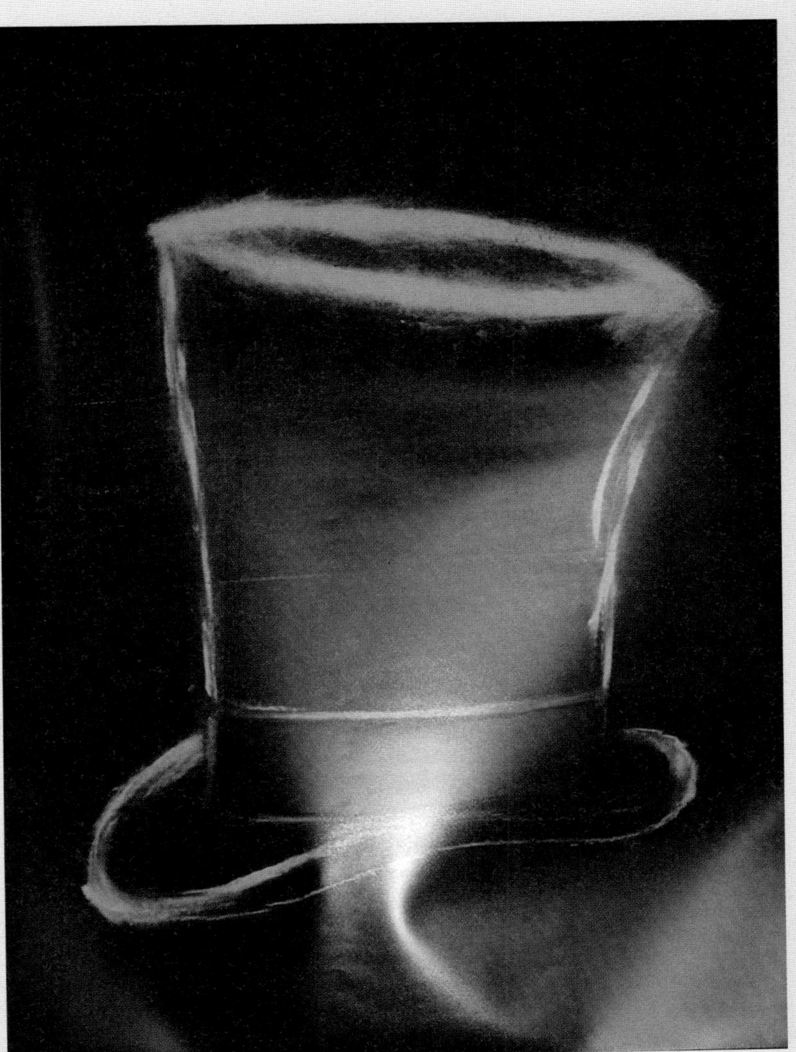

Words Exit Hat, 2009. Chromogenic print. 19 × 14 cm

fair to locate her within a history of materialized language in contemporary art which commences with Nauman and Ruscha and extends through to, say, Christopher Wool. Wool's stencilled canvases of the later 1980s seem a key reference in Ebner's photographs of cinder blocks, configured into letters on a large pegboard, as in *CIOU/* (2008). Seriality and a humorously literal take on concrete poetry are both at work in these images.

Ebner's most recent work seems to recapitulate the history of photography in deceptively modest pictures. *Leaf and Strike* (2009) juxtaposes a photogram of a leaf placed on a grid with a photograph of a backslash fashioned on a gridded pegboard — nature and culture, light and writing, placed side by side. *Some Clouds* (2009) appears like a down-market Alfred Stieglitz photograph, one of his famous *Equivalents* seen through

the cloudy scratched glass of what seems to be a windshield. Here, too, language and natural forms are seen in opposition to each other, since the scratches are barely decipherable letters. From the photographs of her cardboard monuments to these images, Ebner has insisted that our technologies of seeing are never simple mirrors of the world, but are inevitably mediated through the eminently cultural forms of language.

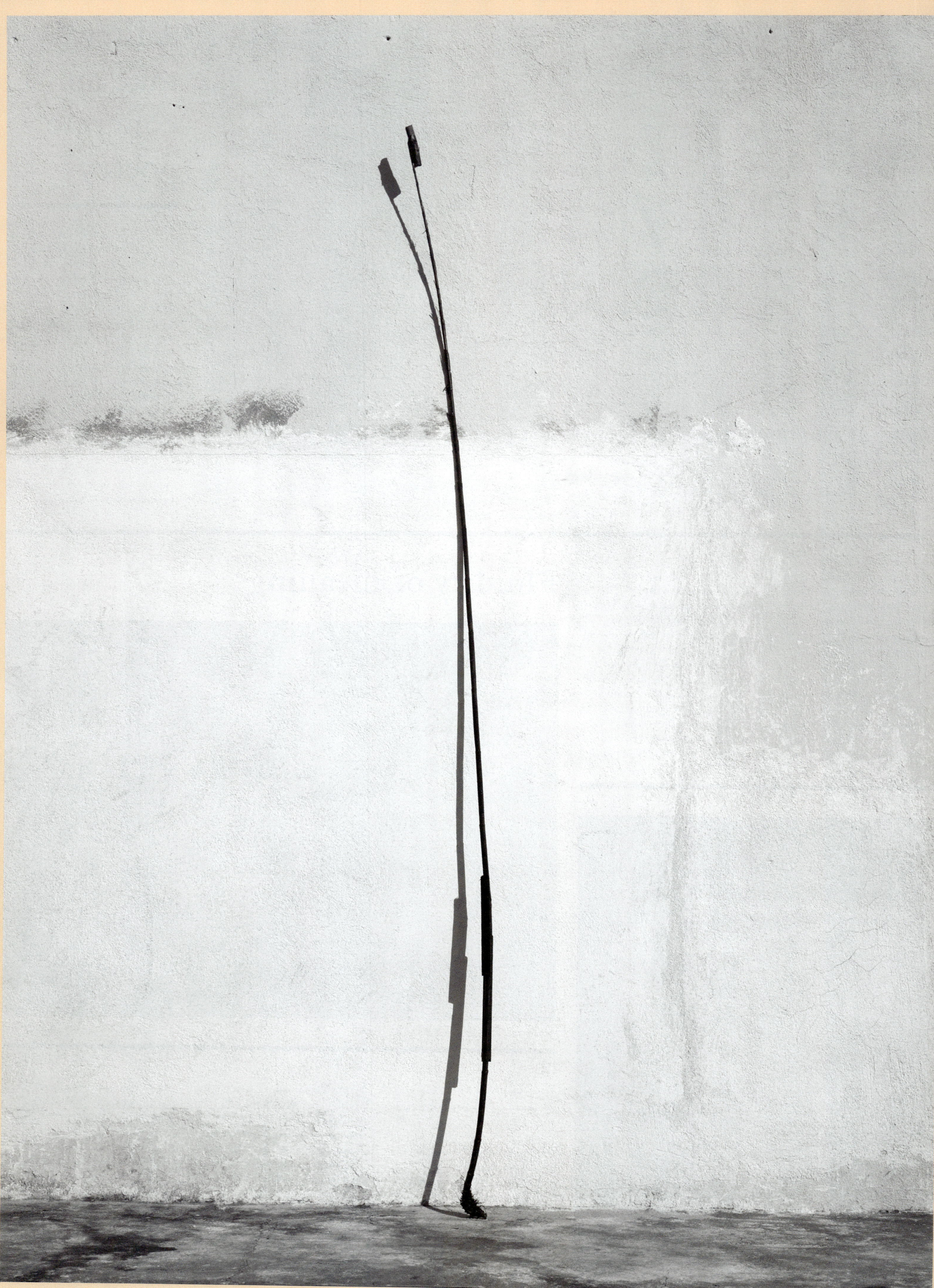

Writing Staff for Middle Ground, 2009. Chromogenic print. 160 × 122 cm

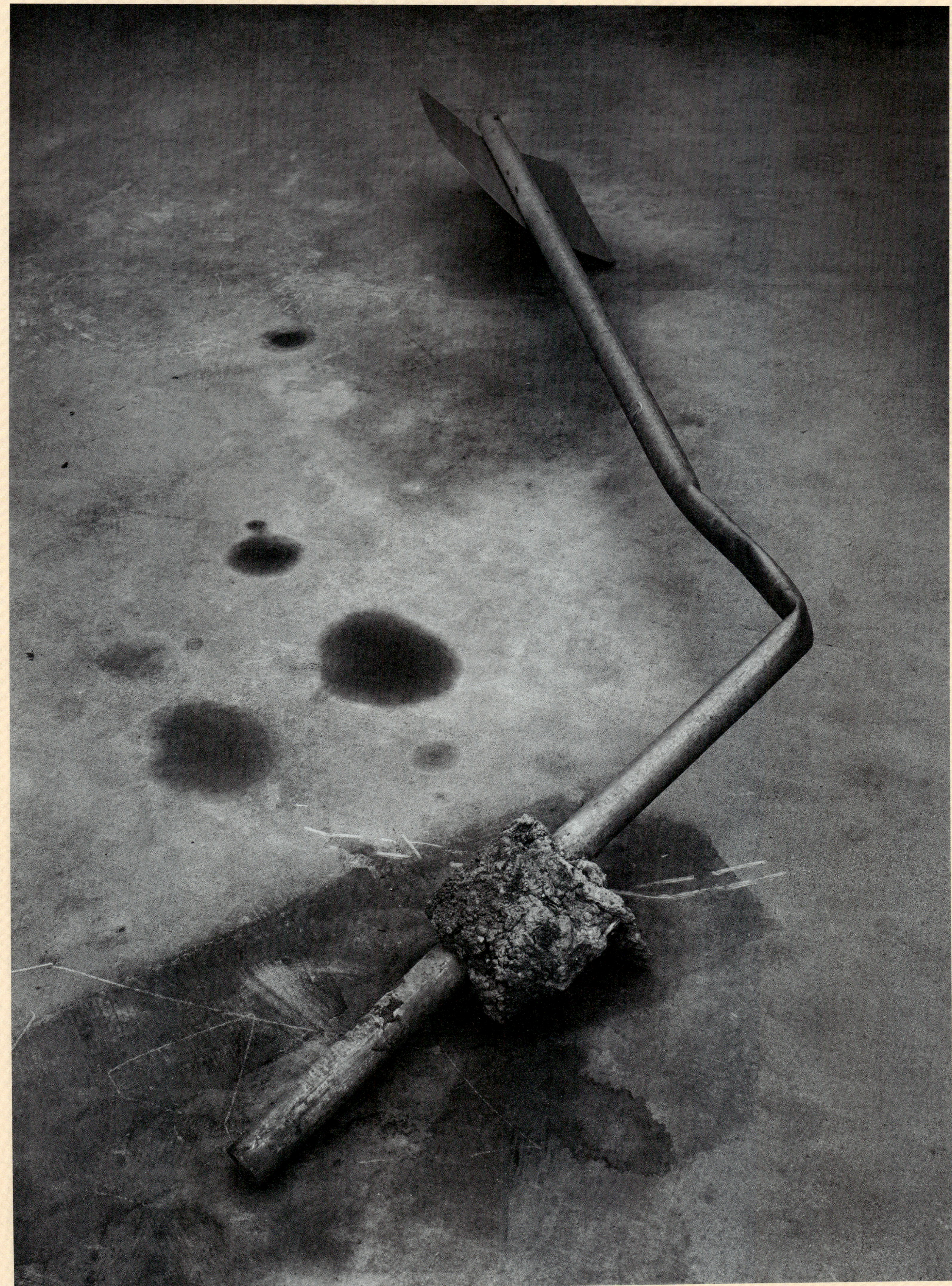

The Crooked Sign, 2006. Chromogenic print. 165 × 119 cm

Sherif El Azma

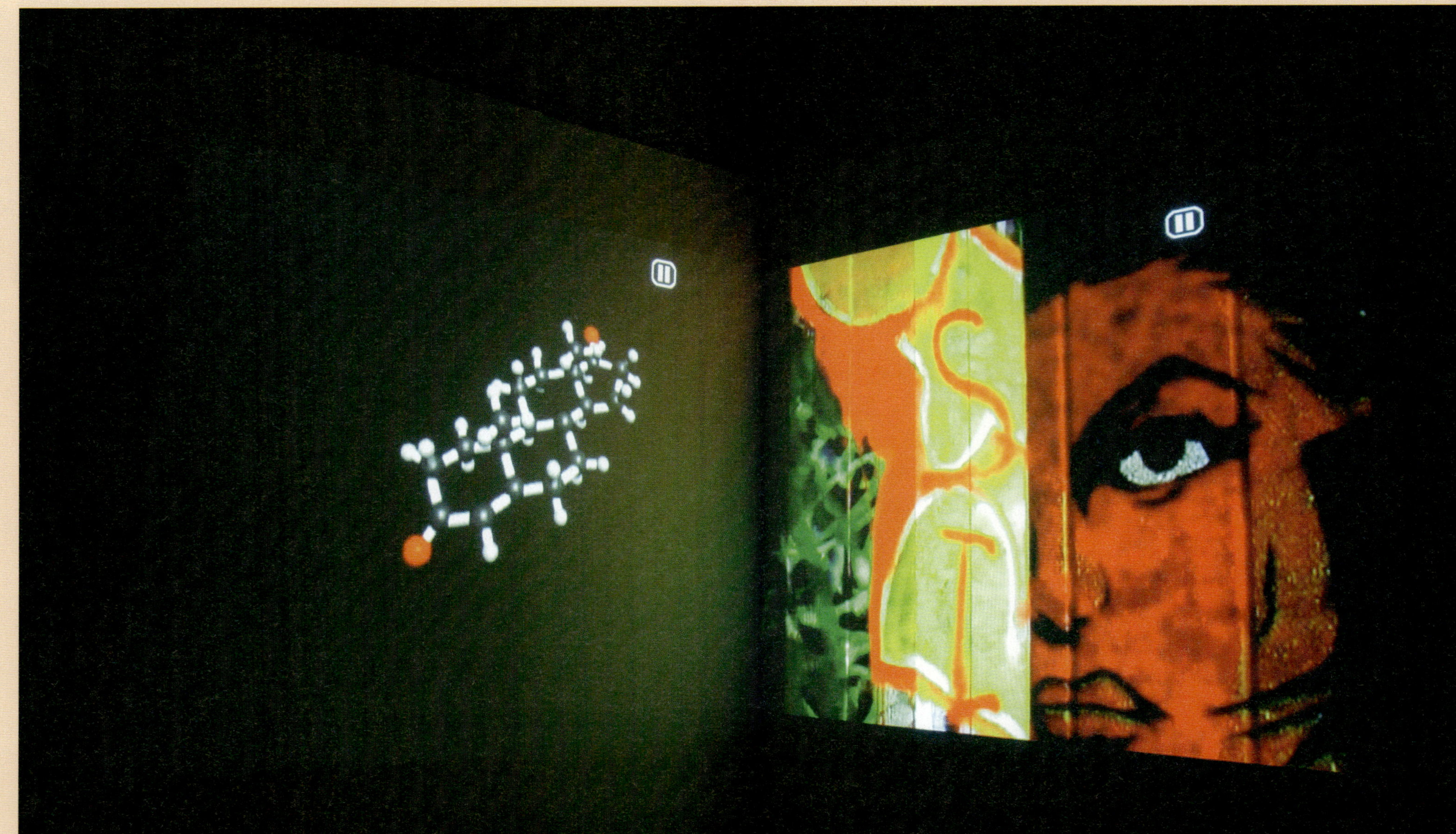

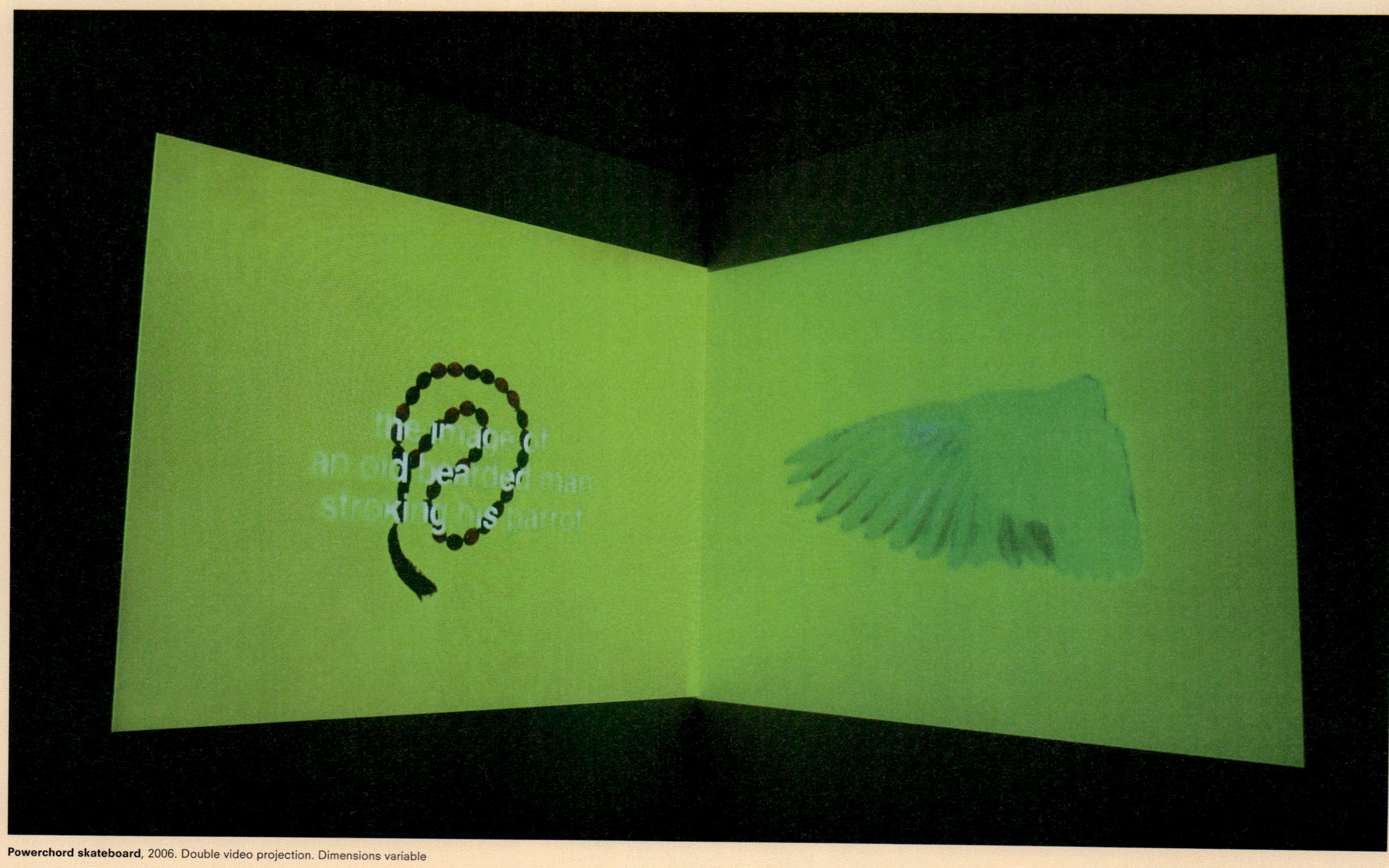

Powerchord skateboard, 2006. Double video projection. Dimensions variable

Pushed to strangely skewed limits

Sherif El Azma works mostly with video. One of his earliest pieces, the rough-and-tumble, crassly edited, documentary-style *Interview with a Housewife* (2001), easily lends a thematic needlepoint of gender politics, autobiographic narrative and cultural capital a significance that is not only novel but also far more complex than what we've generally become accustomed to in the arts.

A few years later, in *Television pilot for an Egyptian air hostess soap opera* (2003), we're told the story of four women hoping for a future within the in-flight service industries, who are undergoing a rather strange training programme. Here, the aesthetics are more haunting and less coarse than *Interview with a housewife* — less 'hand-held video' and more 'studio production' — and the narrative is pushed to strangely skewed limits, arhythmical, counterintuitive and jarring.

A more recent example, the double channel *Powerchord Skateboard* (2007), demonstrates that El Azma's work has become yet more elusive. A quick google will show that it's the kind of piece that drives curators to say tired, desperate things such as, 'the artist constructs a fragmented narrative in which the viewer is given room for their own associations'. Indeed, the artist appears to ditch conventional drives for narrative altogether, offering a string of images — featuring, among many other things, childhood memories, graffiti and former Egyptian President Anwar El Sadat — which are not always easy to comprehend as sequences relating to each other. This is nothing unusual, you might say, in the ADD-riddled field of the arts, but the good news here is that El Azma manages nonetheless to grip and relentlessly maintain the

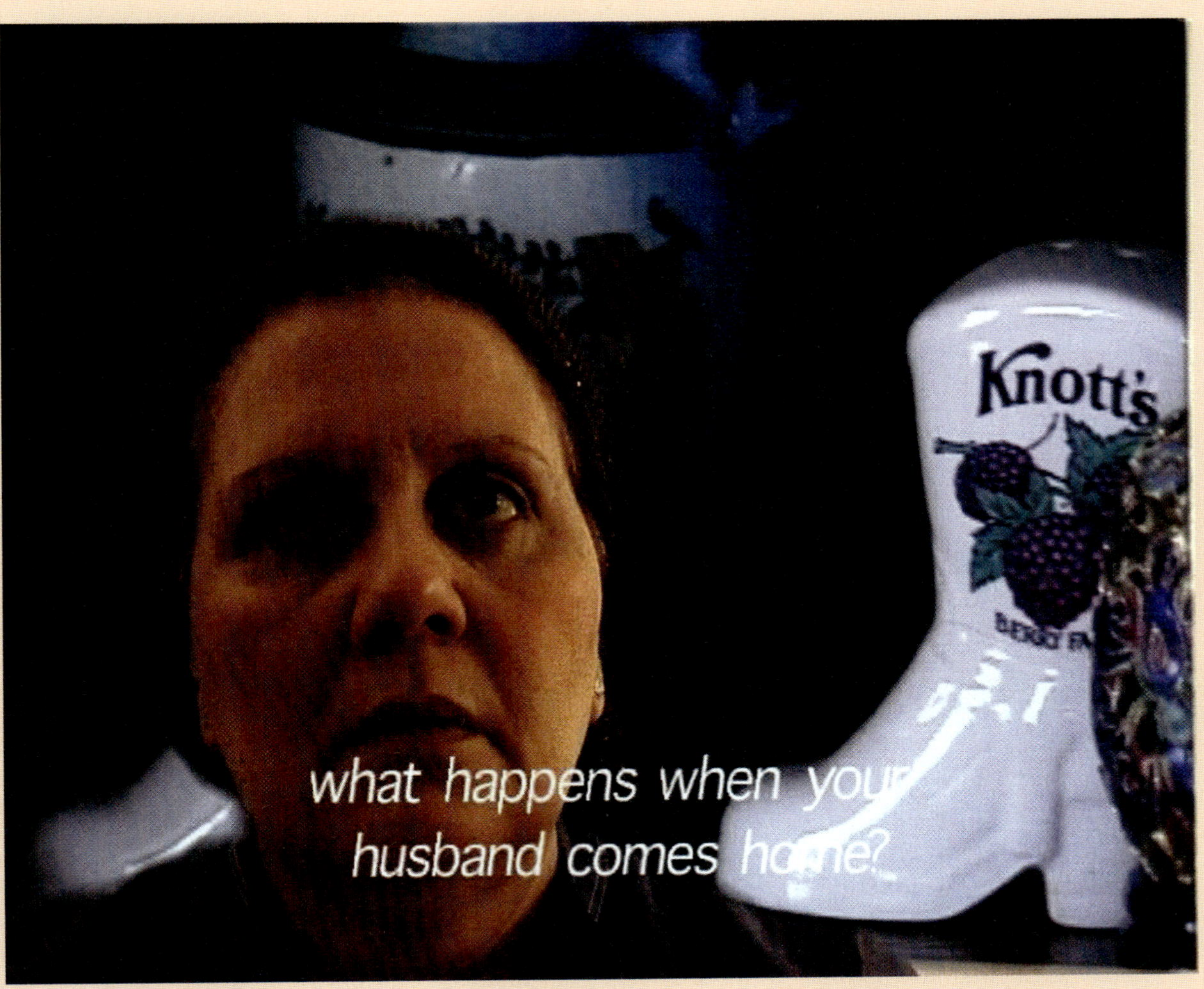

Interview with a housewife, 2001. Video. 7 min.

Arhythmical, counter-intuitive and jarring

viewer's attention throughout. He masters film and video in all its facets, from the script to the directing to the editing and beyond, in a way that makes it seem easy. This kind of panache makes you want to do it yourself, only to find that you would need buckets of talent, technique and determination to achieve the same results.

In his recent book *Nine Lessons Learned from Sherif El Azma* (published by the Contemporary Image Collective, Cairo in 2009), artist Hassan Khan notes some of the lessons he has learned from his friend and collaborator over the years, including how 'everybody is ultimately conservative', how one needs to be 'conscious of the way one loves oneself', how 'the most interesting things are only an easy step away', and that one should 'never trust voiceovers even if one should use them all the time'. I would add that the most efficient way of teaching is when you manage not to give the impression that anything is being taught, and if anyone can pull off that kind of nonchalance, it's El Azma.

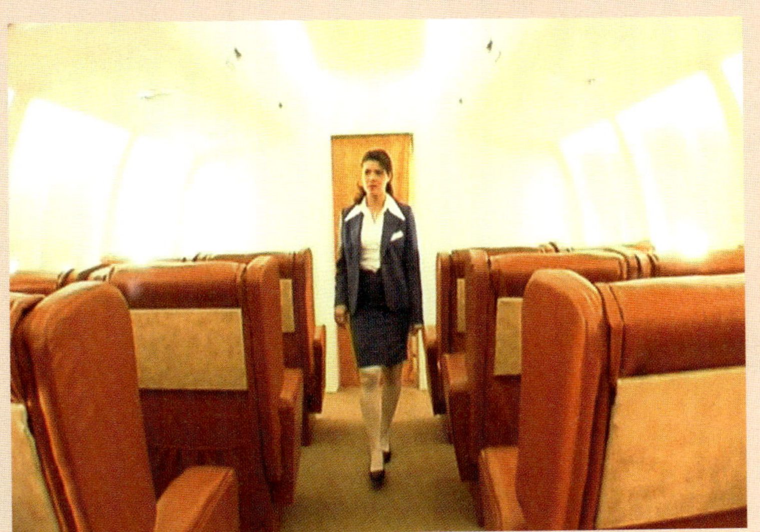

Fragmented narrative

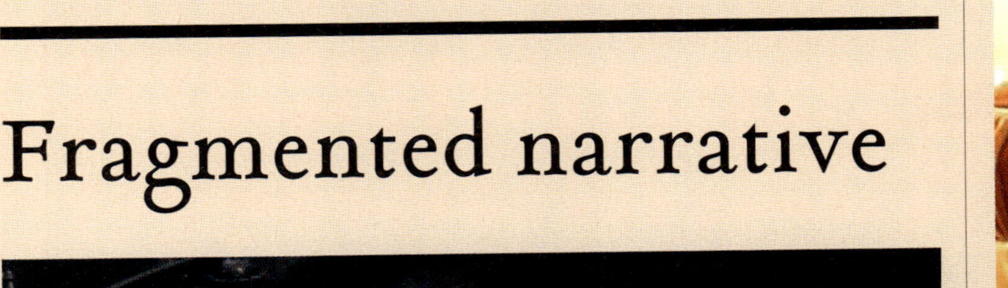

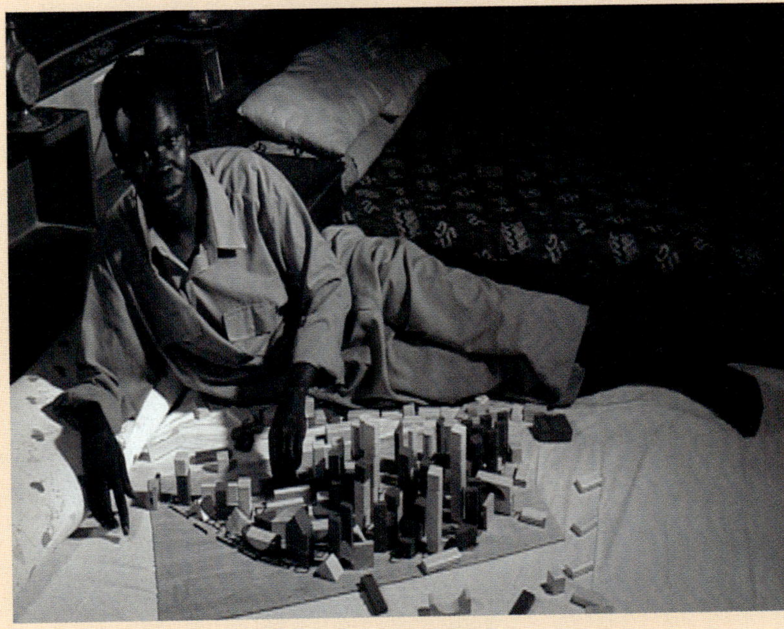

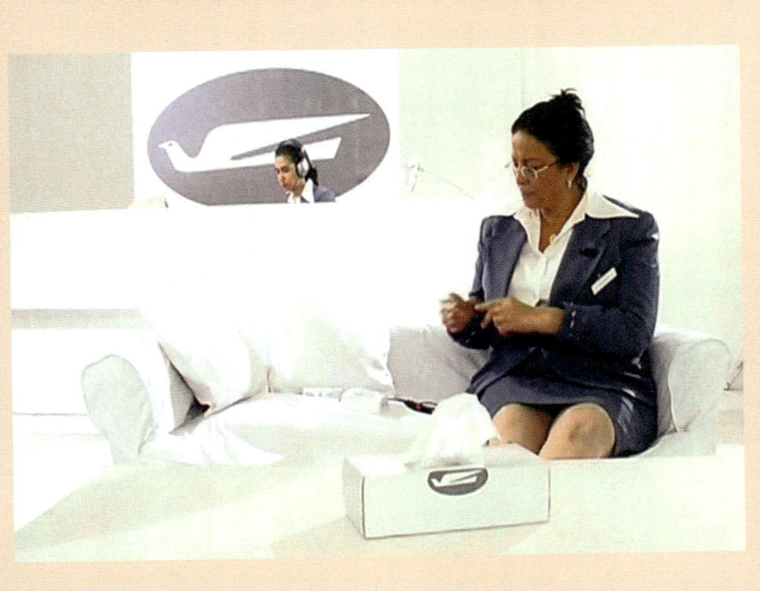

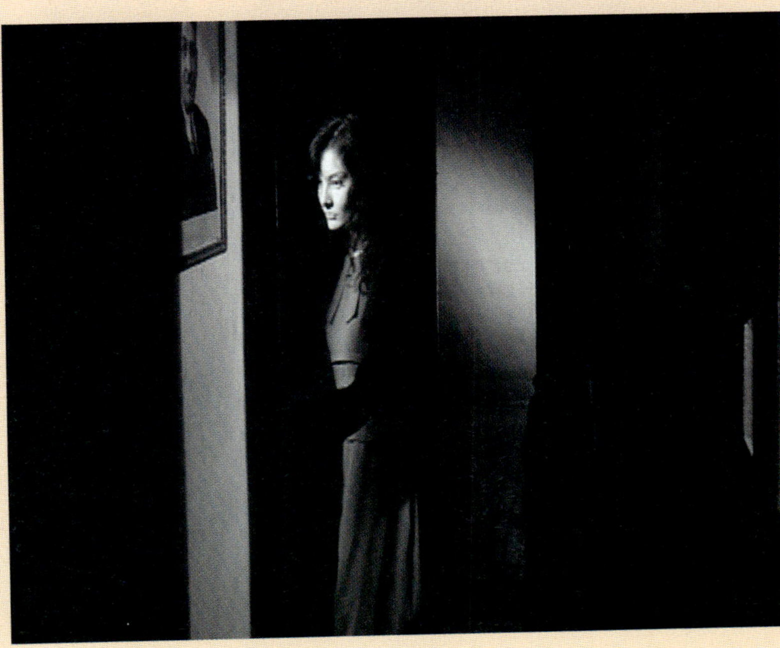

City of rice, 2009. Video.

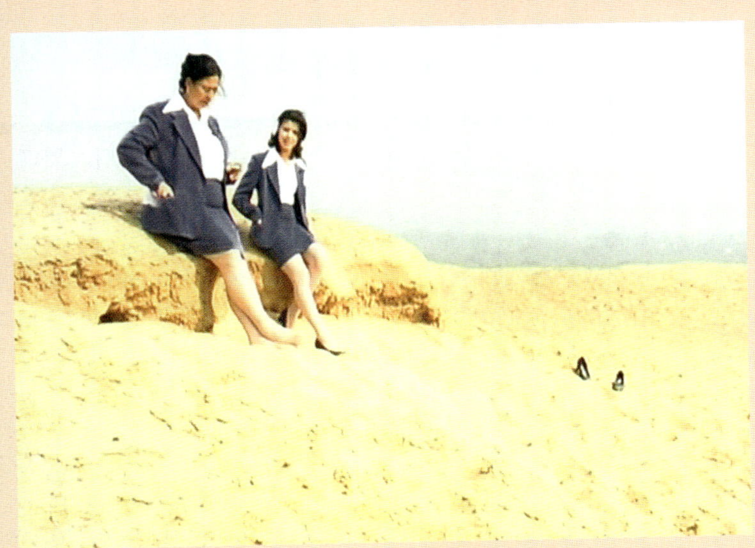

Television pilot for an Egyptian air hostess soap opera, 2003. Video. 58 min.

Haris Epaminonda

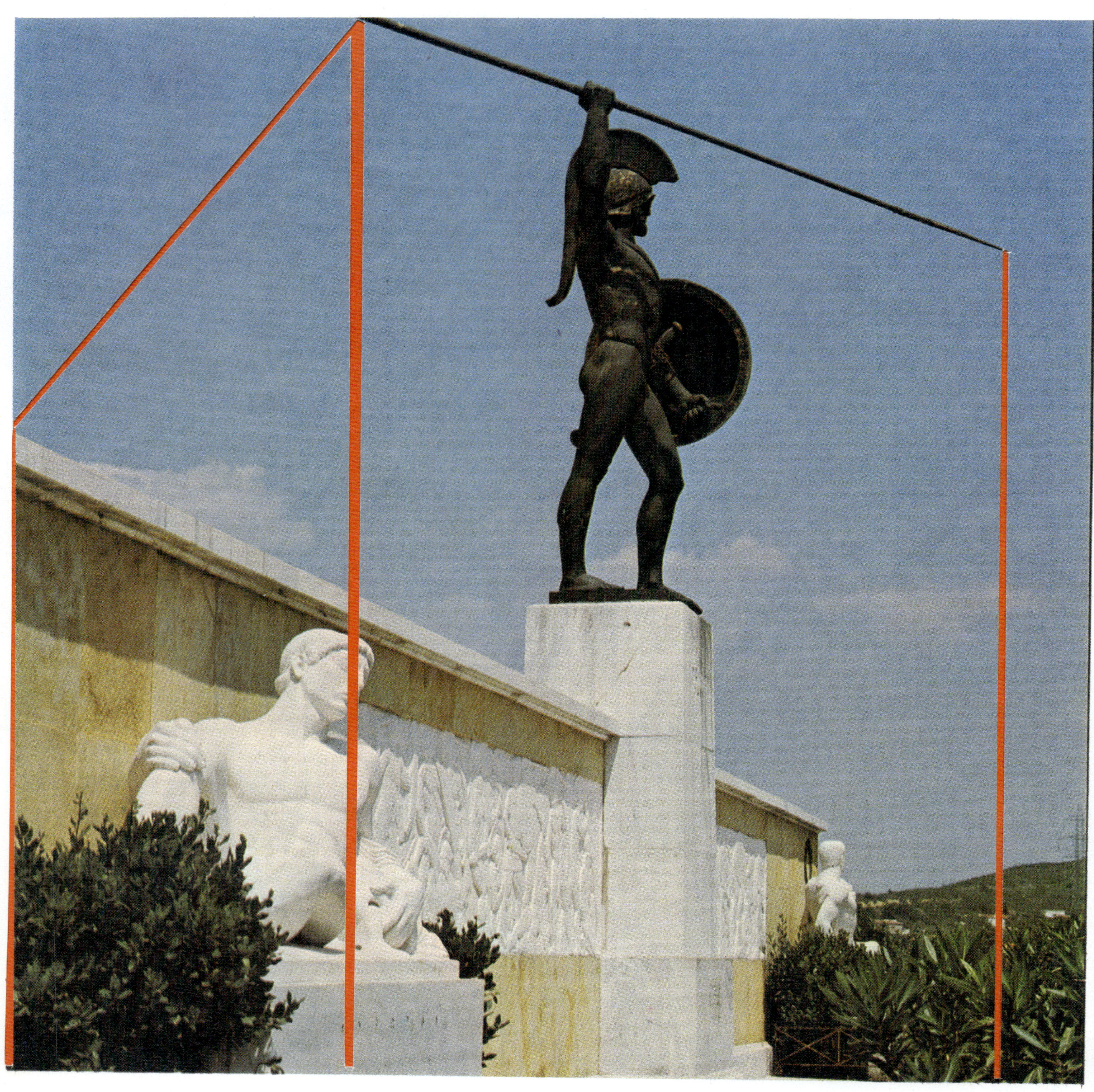

Untitled 0011c/g, 2007. Paper collage. 18 × 17 cm

Haris Epaminonda has always been fascinated by discarded things: televisual imagery from forgotten soap operas, the pages of outdated magazines, old books and artefacts from civilizations she has never known. As a result, the Cypriot artist's work bathes in the auburn haze of the bygone, her films, collages, sculptures and reconstituted books bearing signs that they owe more to the past than to the aesthetics of the present. And yet, it is her acute eye and reconstitution or reassembly of objects and imagery taken from their original context and thrust into the present that gives her work its particular grace.

As critics have noted, Epaminonda's process of editing her short films sourced from found footage is fundamentally related to her composing of collages through the making of decisive cuts. One of her ongoing projects consists of a series of images largely constructed from the pages of 1950s and 60s nature and travel magazines, where her careful incisions are visible due to a layer of coloured paper peeking out from beneath. Each is called *Untitled*, followed by a sequential number and the classification *c/g*, *c/a* or *c/l* giving it the ordered, rational air of an institutional archive. These are not reconstitutions of the commercial image à la Kurt Schwitters or Hannah Hoch. Instead, Epaminonda's cuts suggest a continuation of a secret logic internal to the image, almost as if *it*, not her, had dictated it. Take, for instance, *Untitled 009 c/g* (2007), where an incision runs from the axis of a lone mountaineer's gaze to the pinnacle of a rocky mountain and then to the edges of various rocks, the whole insinuating a Euclidian geometrical form (as if his arrival at that very point was in order to form the pyramid now visible to us).

In *Untitled 012 c/g* (2007), two ancient statues communicate via a jagged-shaped cut which connects them along points that emerge from each figure's own angles and lines.

Epaminonda's attraction to the hidden sense of the world extends to her photographic production, in which she depicts extraordinary phenomena encountered in the everyday: Polaroid photographs of the decapitated heads of Greek statues sitting on a curb, a rainbow stretching across an expansive field, a 'film' consisting of a single, unmoving image of a zebra caught in a psychedelic harness by three men (*Zebra*, 2006). The latter's strange burst of color is nothing more than an optical defect on a slide image, a mistake, but with Epaminonda's insistence that we look at the still picture over time, as a film, the full surreality of the scene becomes apparent.

In recent years, the same juxtaposition and recontextualization found in her collage and filmic work has been brought to the space of display.

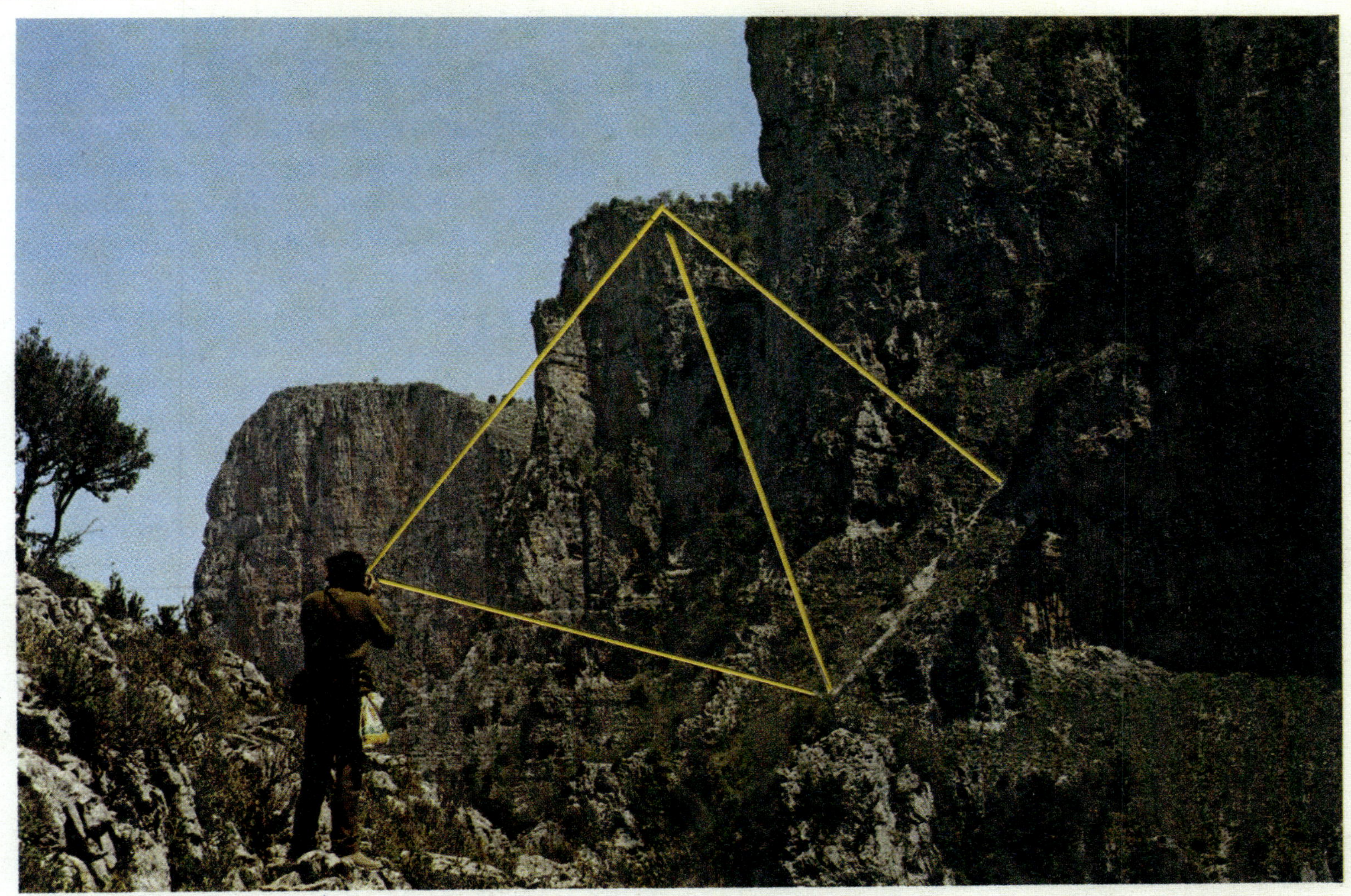

Untitled 009c/g, 2007. Paper collage. 18 × 12 cm

Haze of the bygone

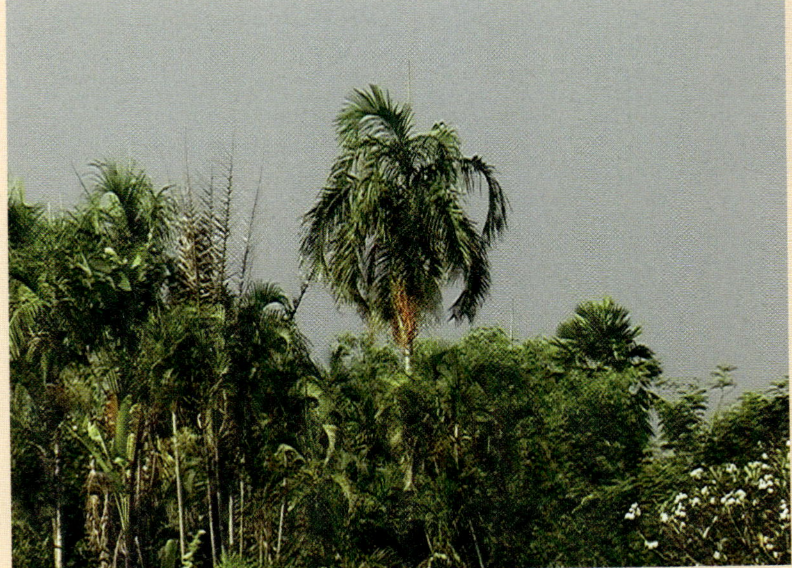

Palm, 2009. Video. 2 min. 34 sec.

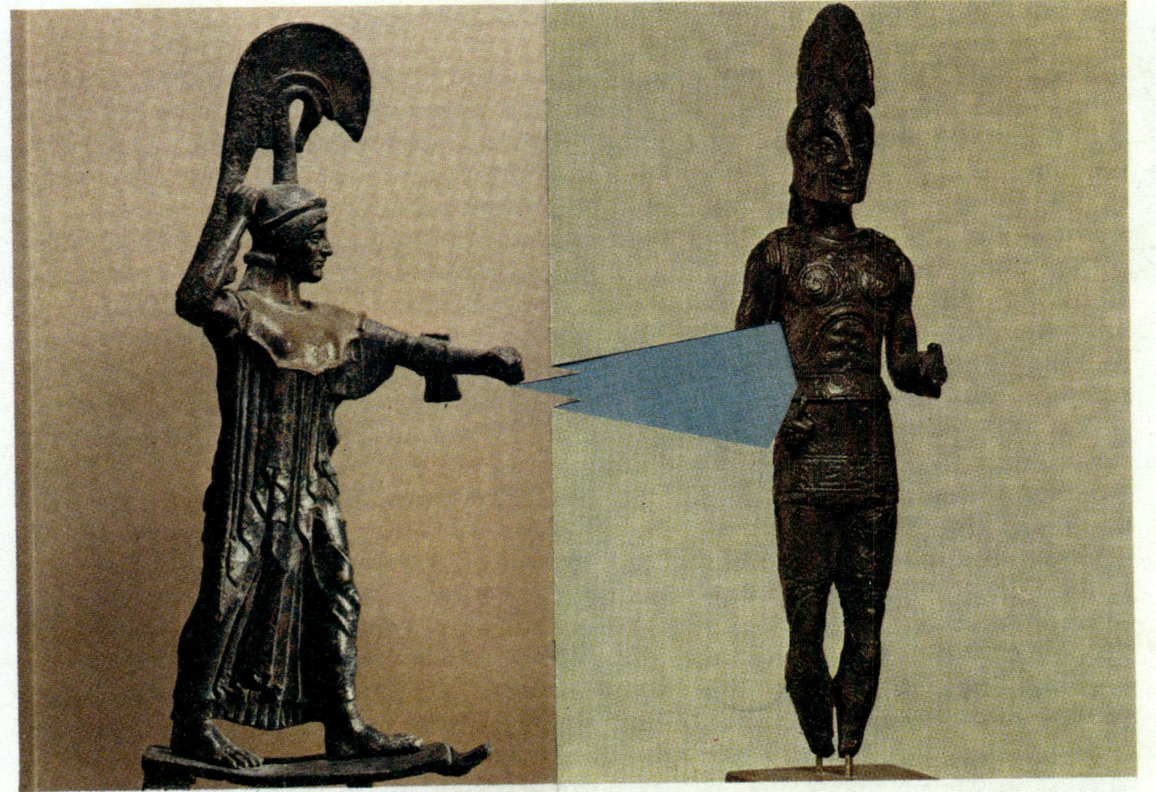

Untitled 0012c/g, 2007. Paper collage. 16 × 12 cm

Careful incisions

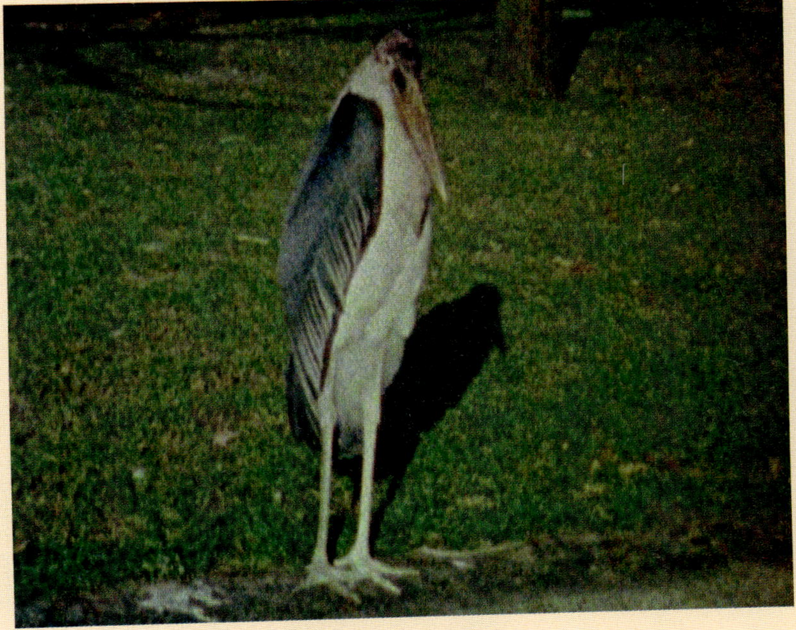

Marabu, 2009. Digitally transferred Super 8 with sound. 52 sec.

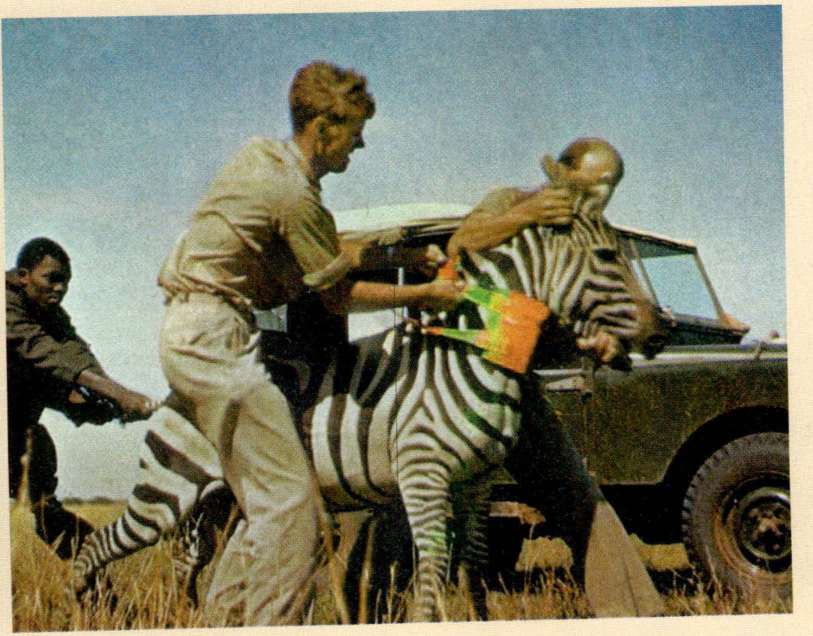

Zebra, 2006. Video. 2 min. 29 sec.

Caught

African tribal statues, Greek figurines, eBay-purchased vases, Giorgio de Chirico-like plinths, even cacti and ostrich eggs reconfigure the white cube into a place of wondrous strangeness. This is achieved through Epaminonda's sensitivity to how their combination with even the simplest of 8mm films of a standing bird (*Marabu*, 2009), or a tree's leaves waving in the wind (*Palm*, 2009), can make the mundane appear scintillating.

Patricia Esquivias

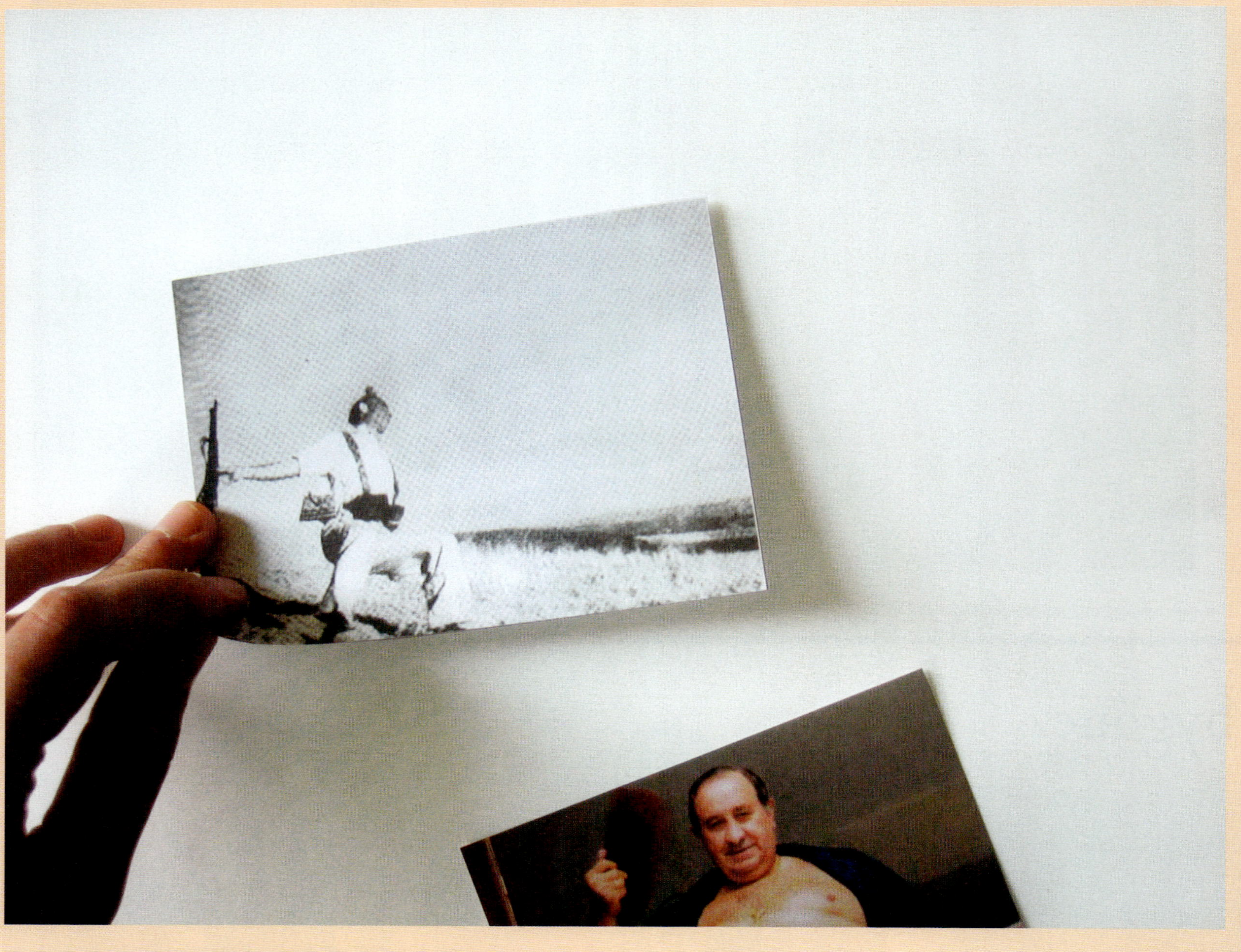

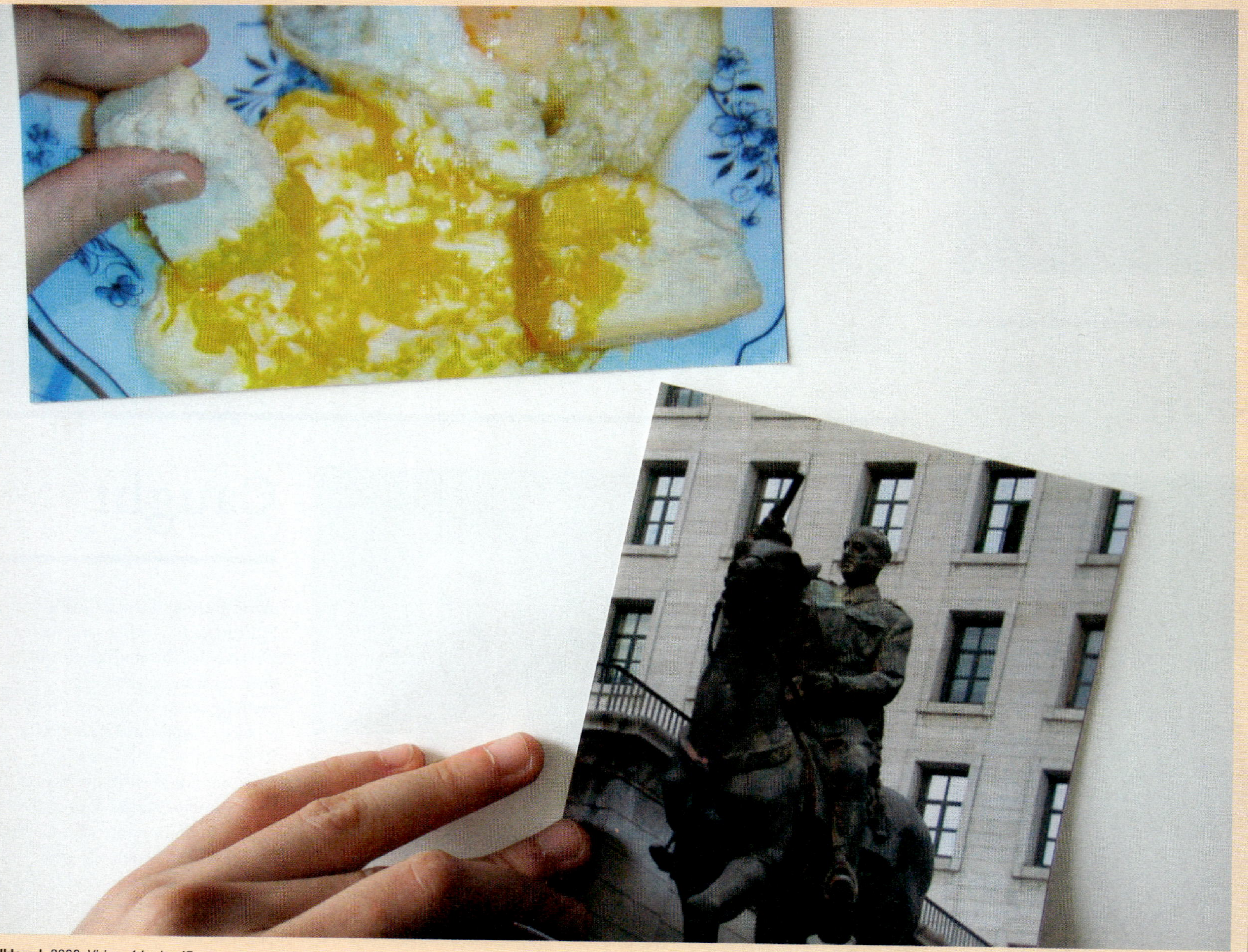

Folklore I, 2006. Video. 14 min. 43 sec.

The themes that preoccupy Patricia Esquivias, as well as her typically casual, elliptical way of narrating stories, are already evident in her early short film *Sped Up Dawn* (2006). Here, we see the accelerated movement of sunlight suddenly fading to black and then returning to illuminate the corner of a museum room, with its static ethnographic display of antique domestic objects — a broom, a bucket, a model ship, a drum and a landscape painting — cozily arranged around a fireplace. On the soundtrack we hear two women speaking off-screen, first the artist, who attempts to describe a work she has seen in a museum: 'In New England, there's a history museum in a 1780s house and they had a work which was *Sped Up Dawn* and … umm… beside it the plaque explained that the dawn had been sped up at the same rate as the United States history is sped up and … umm… it even gave the facts and numbers of how the things had happened there, much faster and bigger than in other places.' The museum director then gives a short explanation that repeats with more authority the same cryptic information that the artist quoted earlier from the plaque and the film ends here, after one minute and thirty-two seconds.

It is unclear whether this story is fictional, or whether we are supposed to believe that such a work exists, or even that the museum itself really existed. The work seems to ask, Who has

Esquivias opts for a dialectical approach, weaving personal, contradictory and parallel narratives

the right to history — not only the history of New England — and who is able to tell it?

Esquivias opts for a dialectical approach, weaving together personal, contradictory and parallel narratives. In the last five years she has made two groups of films: *Folklore I, II and IV* (2005, 2008 and 2009) and *Reads Like the Paper — Group I–IV* (2005–present). *Folklore II* presents a comparative reading of the history of King Phillip II of Spain and Julio Iglesias, the Spanish popstar. These seemingly incommen-surable biographies meet through metaphors of the sun and of gold, which are central to Spain's identity in the past (as a gold-hungry empire) and in the present

Dialectical approach

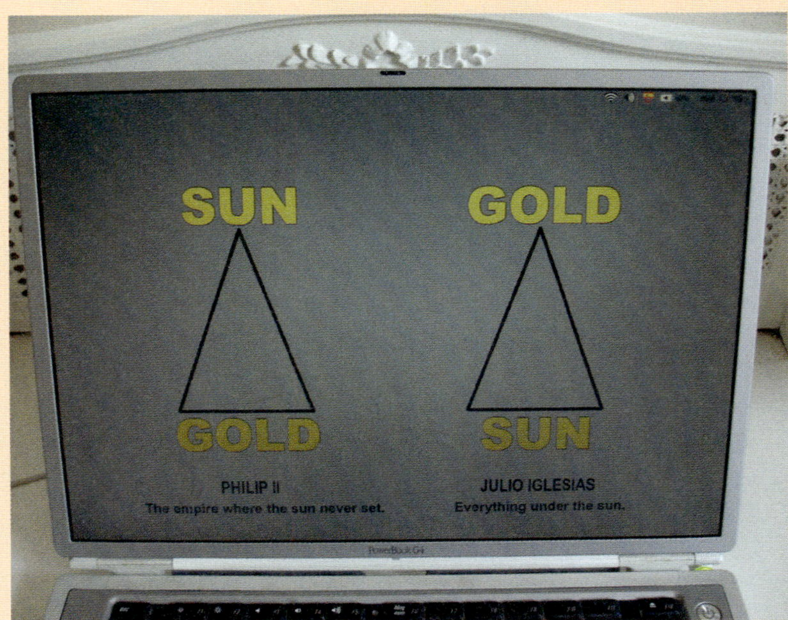

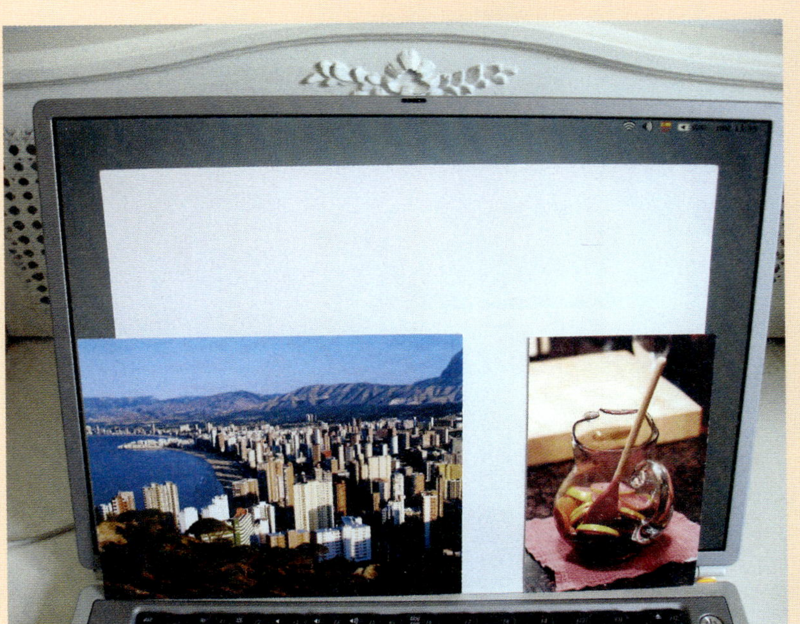

Folklore II, 2008. Video. 13 min. 43 sec.

Ellipitacal way of narrating

(as a sunny tourist destination). Improvised drawings, photographs from family albums, maps, postcards, newspapers, books and web pages are simply moved in front of the camera by the artist's hands in a subversion of modern presentation technologies.
In a similar vein, Esquivias's most recent work, *The Future Was*

When (2009) is a piece of urban archaeology unearthing the work of the artist Susan Brown, who in the 1980s decided to make creative repairs on the deteriorating mosaics in the New York subway, first illegally and then later when commissioned by the authorities in charge of improving the image of the city.

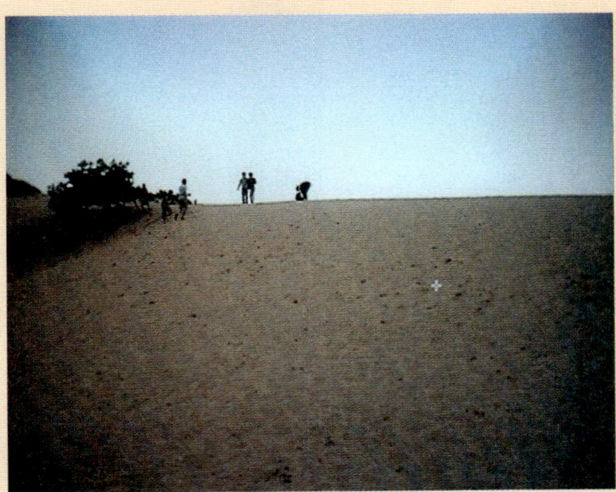

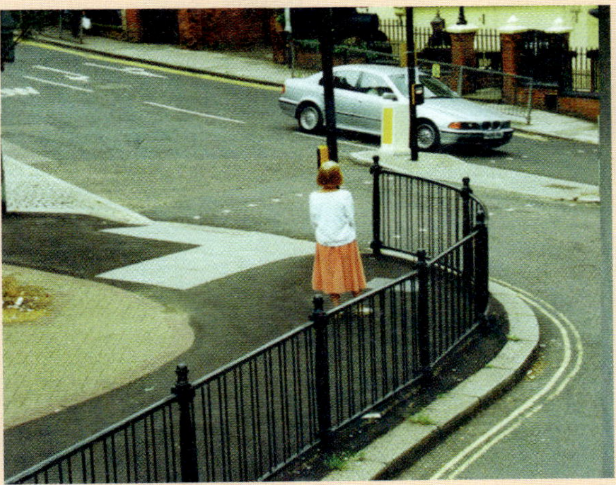

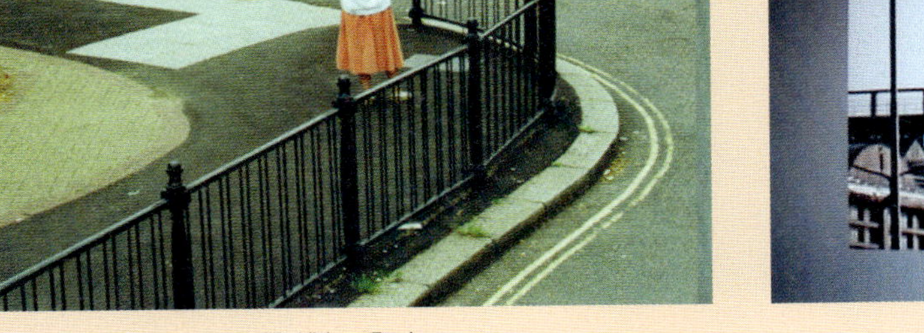

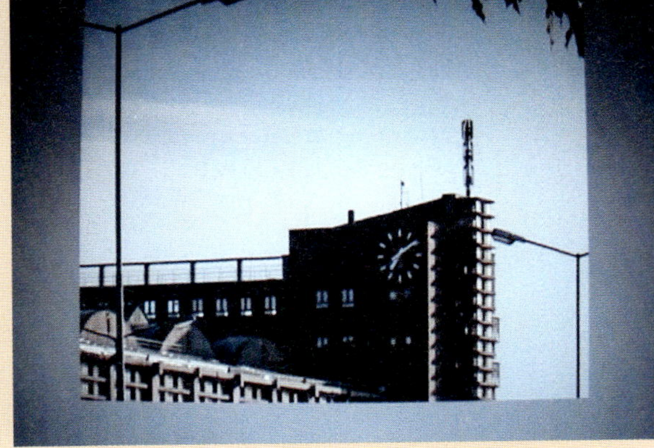

Reads Like the Paper, 2007–08. Video. 3 min.

Analogue documents

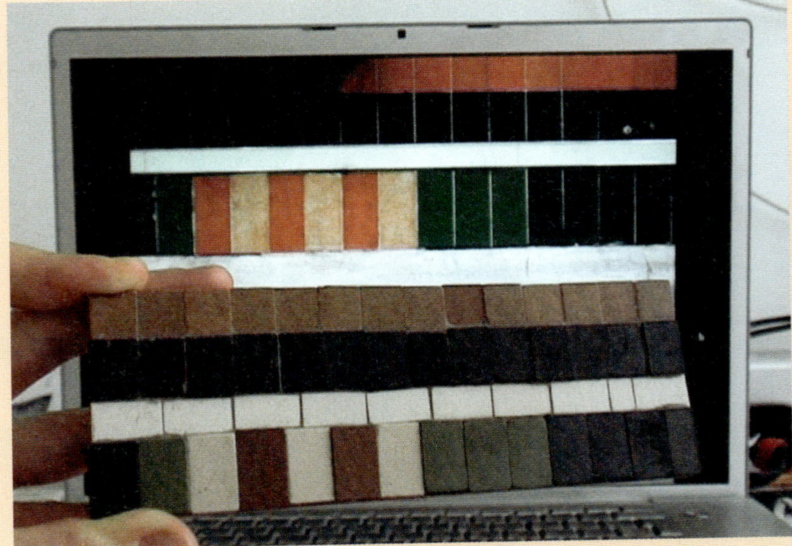

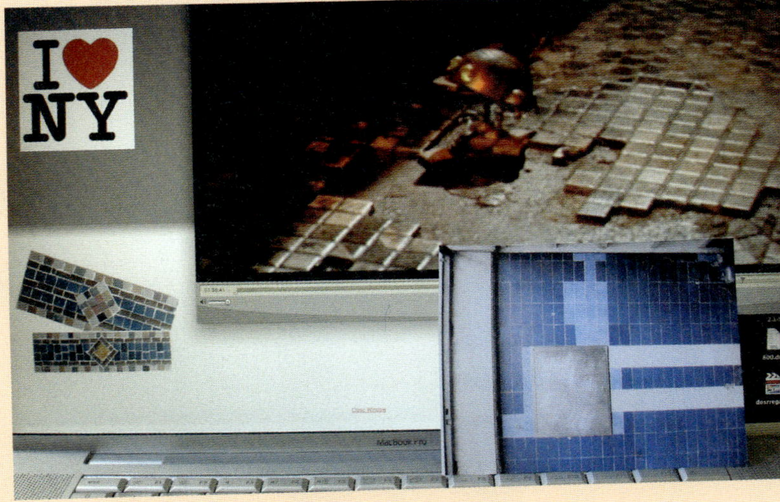

The Future Was When, 2009. Video. 20 min.

Weaving personal, contradictory and parallel narratives

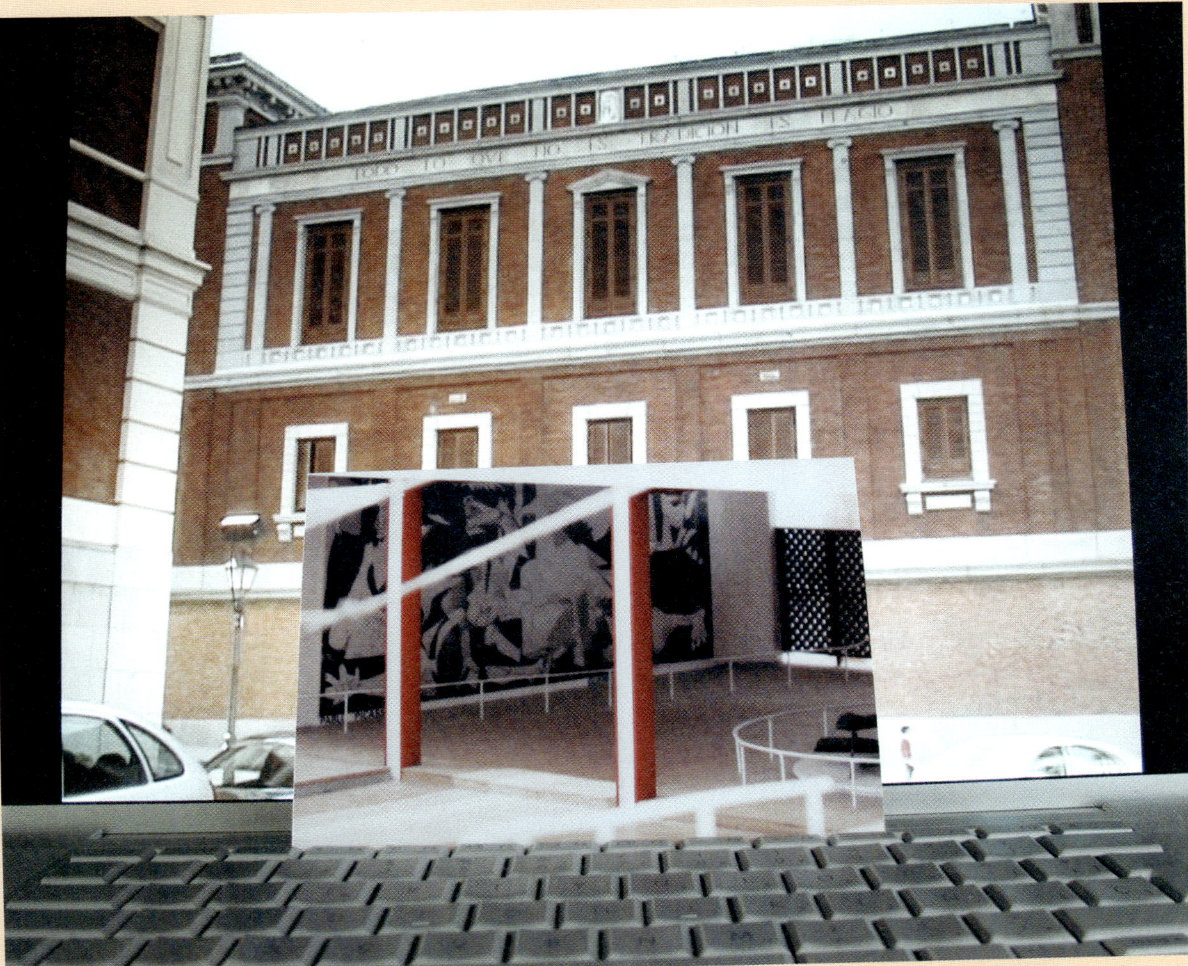

Folklore IV, 2009. Video. 20 min

Leopoldo Estol

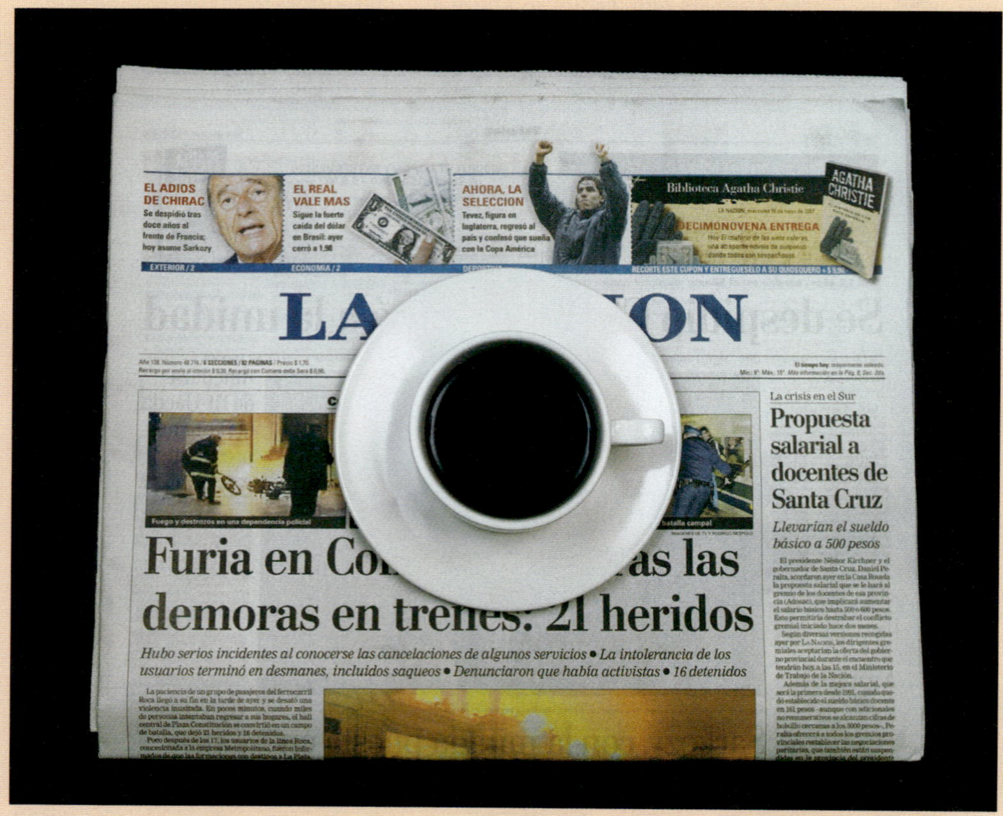

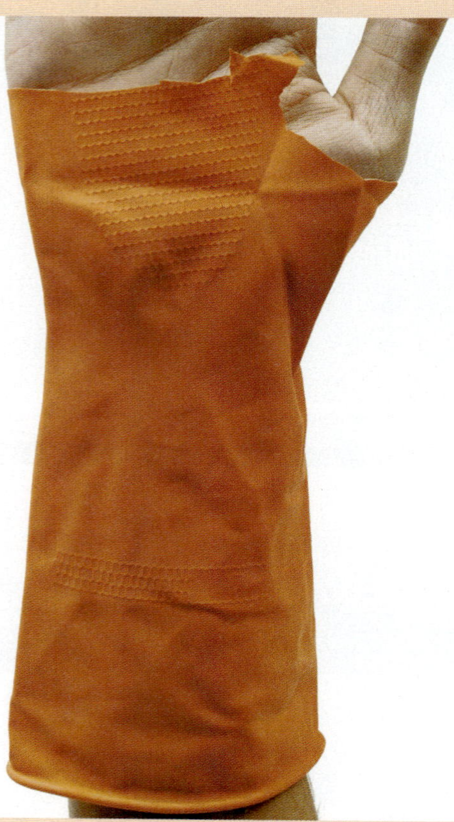

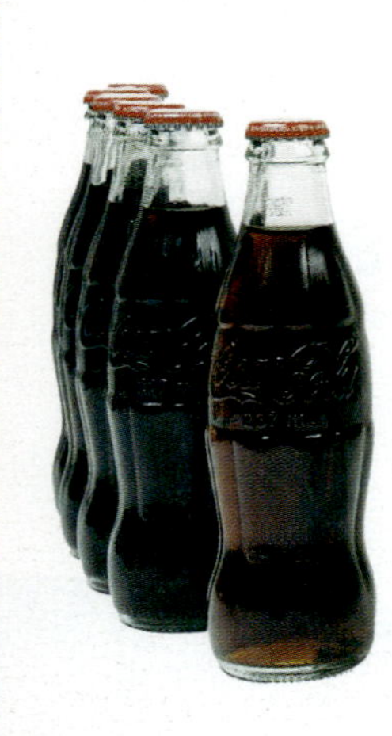

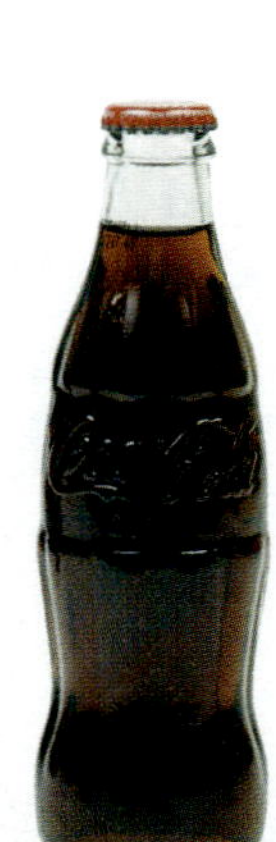

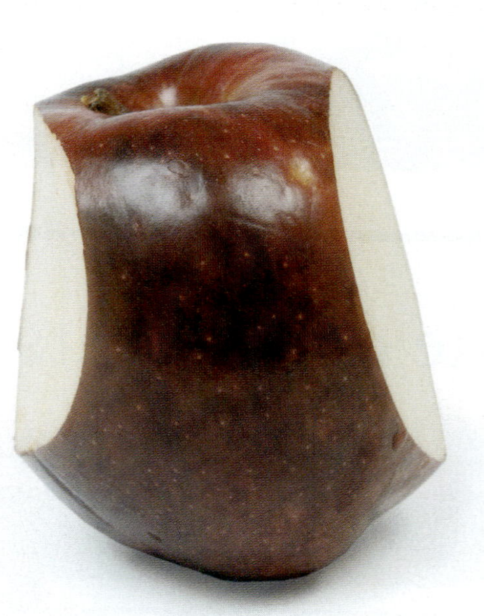

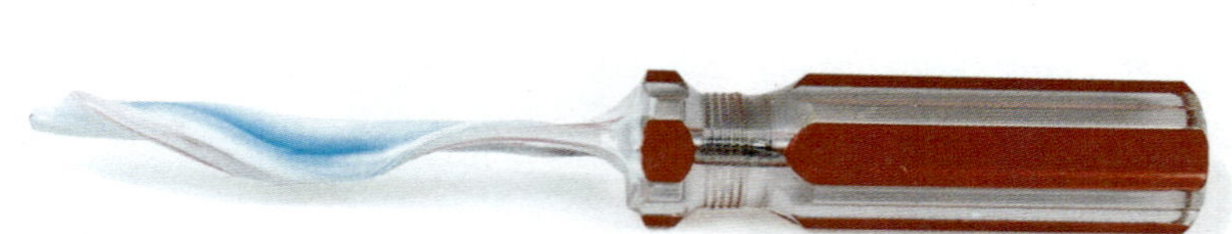

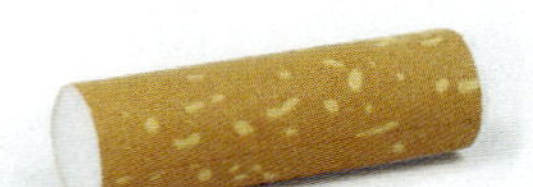

Poxipics: Images from the Turn of the Century (with Marino Balbuena), 2007. 6 of 28 photographs. Each 40 × 50 cm

Intimacy with incisive institutional critique

Leopoldo Estol's journey through the Argentine art world, which up until now has been brief yet intense, traces a path between the clichéd notion of the brilliant and promising young artist and the most unconventional example of a young master. That path started in the early years of the decade, when Estol began producing his first works, largely inspired by the poetics of Gabriel Orozco and the spatial dispersion of contemporary installation art, which have now culminated in their current manifestation: a 'relational art for intimacy', according to his Estol's definition. Through his work he conducts a kind of education of the senses for his contemporaries, in which the affective plays a determining role.

Estol swiftly and deliberately began to distance himself from the usual circuits of an artistic career and the networks in which he had fully participated some years before, not only through his own works but also through his own writing and curatorial activity. He began instead to mix pop and youth culture with art, disseminating his work through

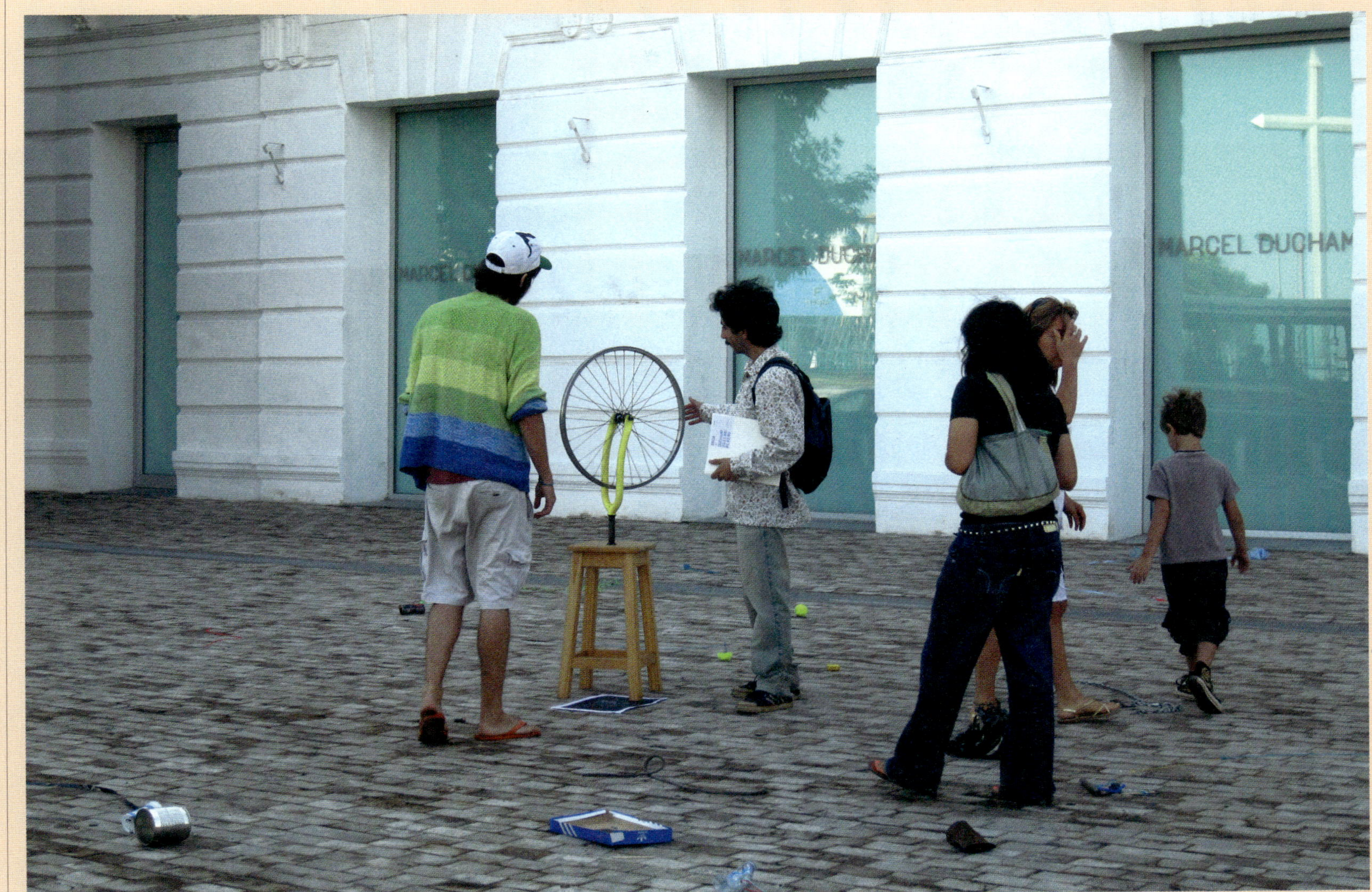

Saying hola to Marcel ongoing wheel, 2009. Performance. Fundación Proa, Buenos Aires

Unexpected juxtapositions

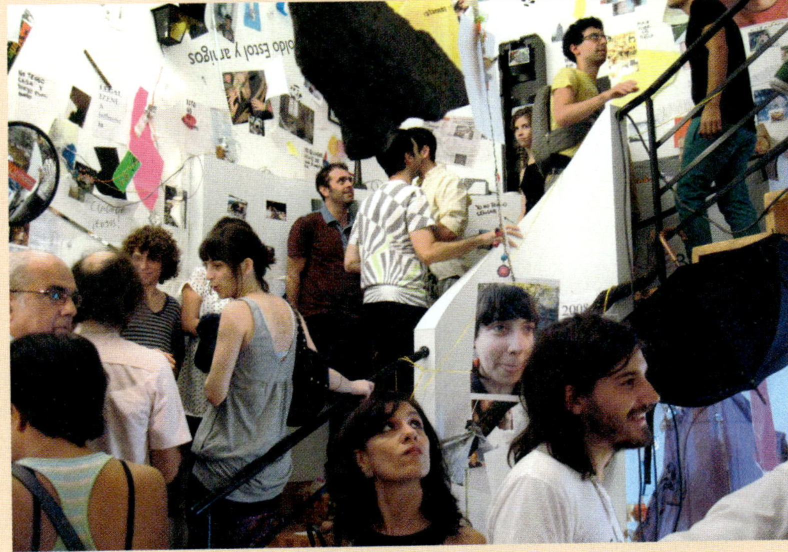

La Mañana del Mundo, 2008. Site–specific installation and collage. Dimensions variable

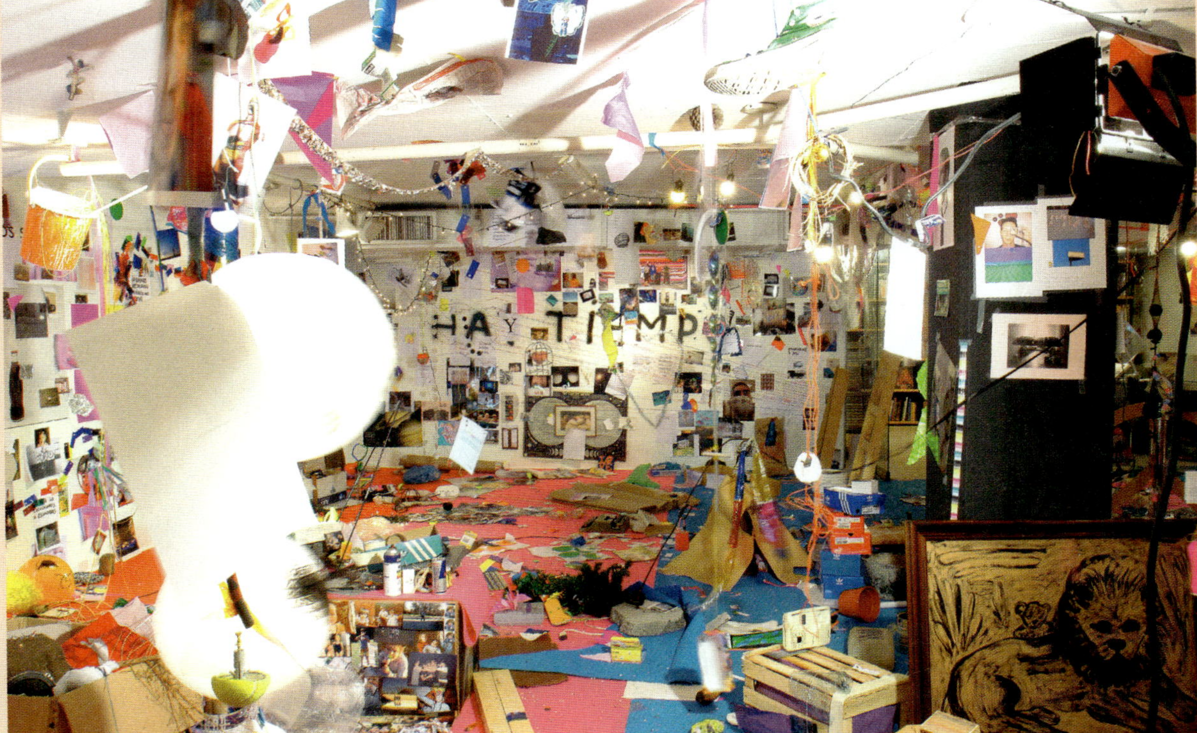

a network that combines intimacy with incisive institutional critique and a playful knowingness with naiveté.

Poxi-pics: Imagenes de Principios de Siglo (Poxi-pics: Images from the Turn of the Century, 2007), for example, is an installation consisting of photographs, objects and newspaper clippings that he presented at the Mercosur Biennial in 2007. In the pictures, anodyne objects appear in unexpected juxtapositions, but nothing could be further from the whimsical than these encounters between things. Instead, his idea was to create allegories of the present from the most common-plage objects — like haikus of contemporary life.

A rolled-up dollar bill inserted into a strongbox, alluding to the rituals of peripheral economies; the brand logo of an aspirin scraped off and replaced with a medical cross; a razor peers from the inside of a passport; a can of the energy drink Speed is used as an ashtray. With these images Estol wished to create a 'temporary museum pointing to relations of objects that are visible and eye-catching at the turn of the century but that, due to the speed established by technological advances and to the insatiability of consumption, can disappear from day to day'.

In a similar spirit, that same year he made *Mi primer escultura* (My first sculpture), which consisted of a large number of used Speed cans, empty Marlboro packages and spent bottles of mineral water scattered on the ground of the space so that spectators could circulate around them. The gesture dispassionately resituated the leftovers of a rave party within the context of the museum. *La mañana del mundo* (The world's morning, 2008) exemplifies a different mood and intentionality. This exhibition resulted from the process of translating the disordered and cumulative logic of the artist's dwelling space into a commercial gallery. Estol made this action jointly with a group of artist friends, with whom he filled the gallery with objects, texts, family photographs, music, videos and furniture.

The result was a light-hearted and optimistic chaos that demonstrated the group's intention with absolute clarity: to compose a space of the greatest sensory intensity possible, as a youthful manifesto and as a safeguard against cynicism — a huge poster on the wall delared 'Hay tiempo' (there is time).

Today, Estol's oeuvre is split between romanticism and professionalism, between a critique of the system and extreme innocence, between hermetism and pedagogy, all of which are consistently developing in new, imaginative and provocative ways.

Roe Ethridge

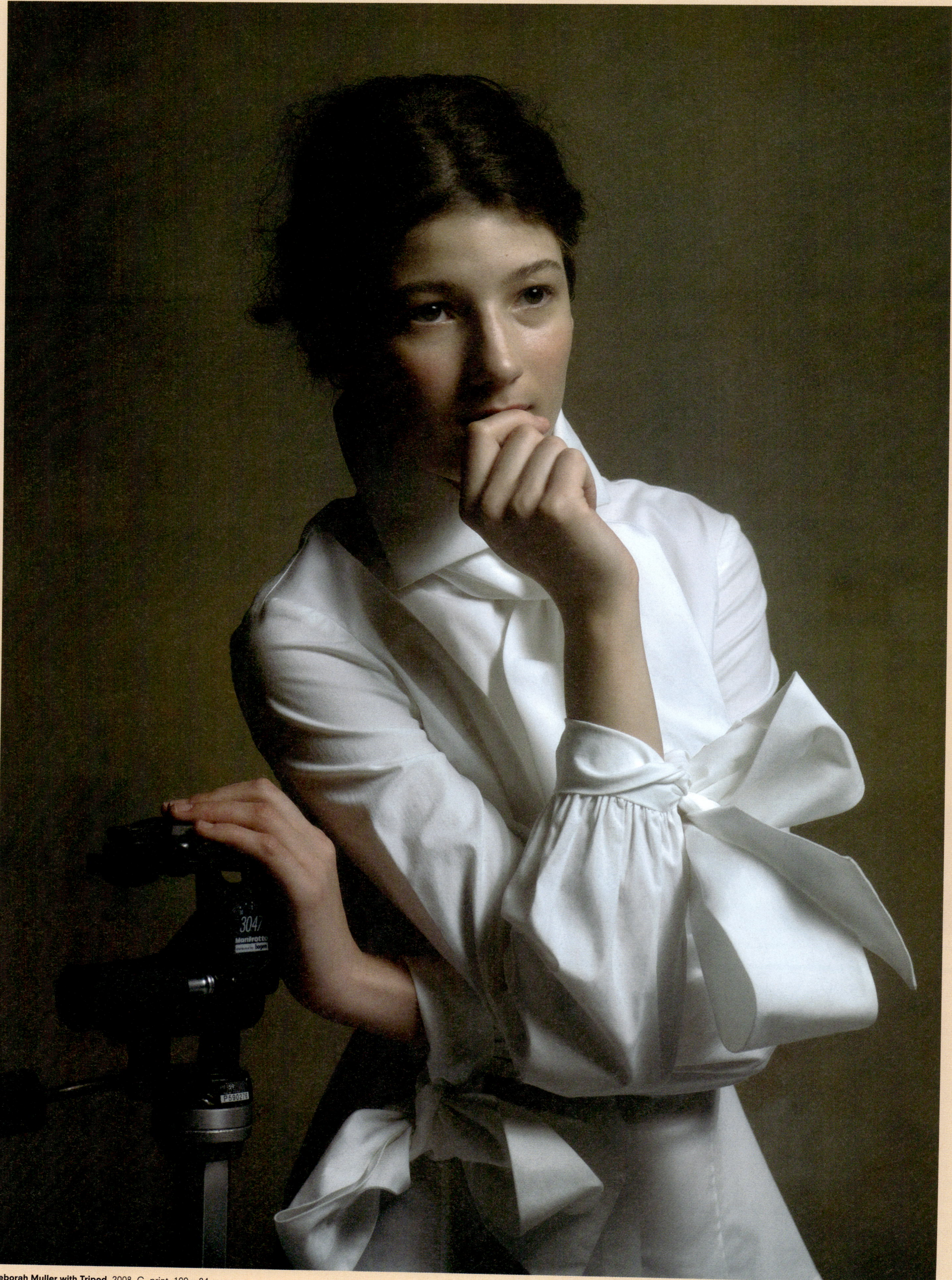

Deborah Muller with Tripod, 2008. C–print. 109 × 84 cm

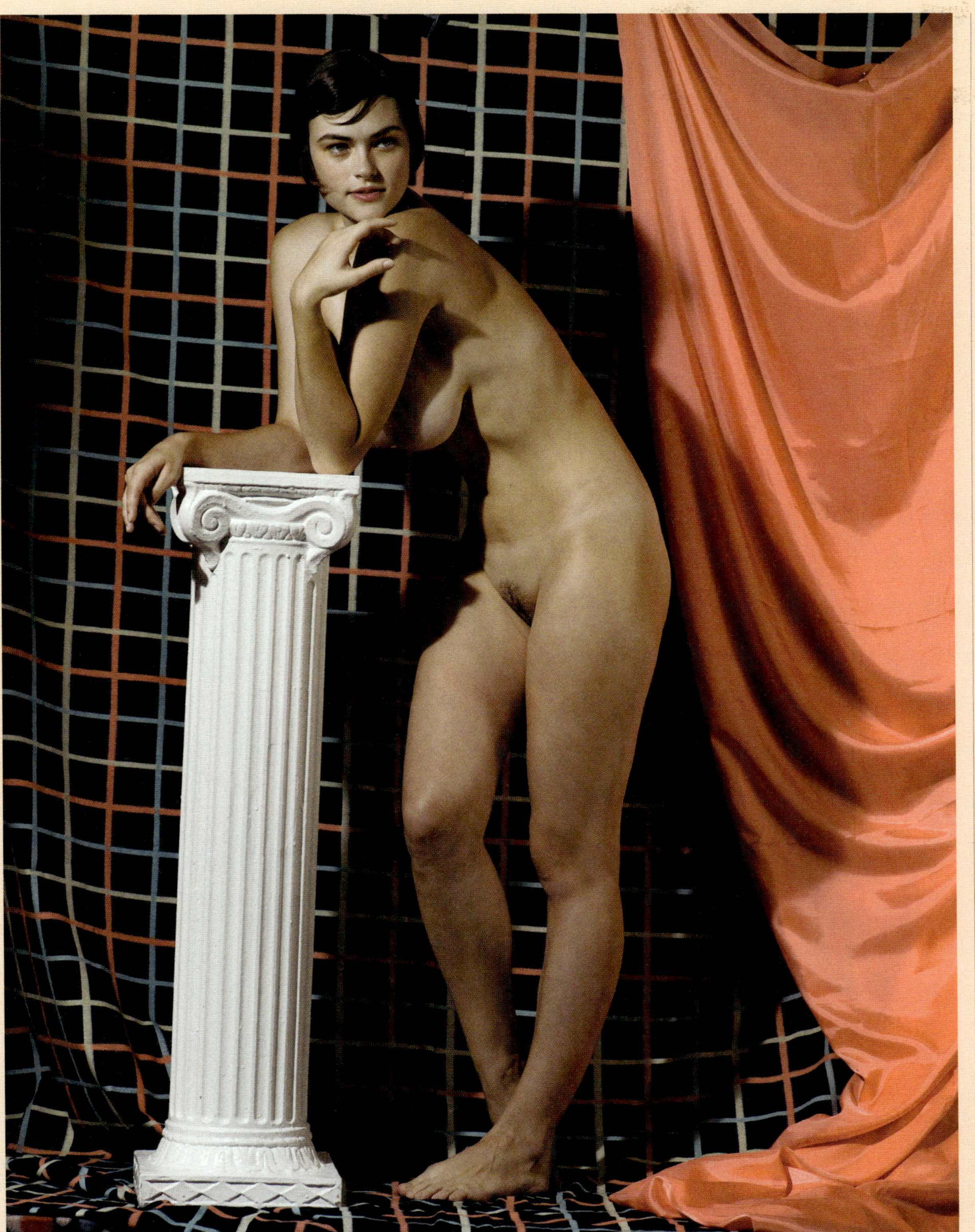

Myla with Column, 2008. C–print. 135 × 102 cm

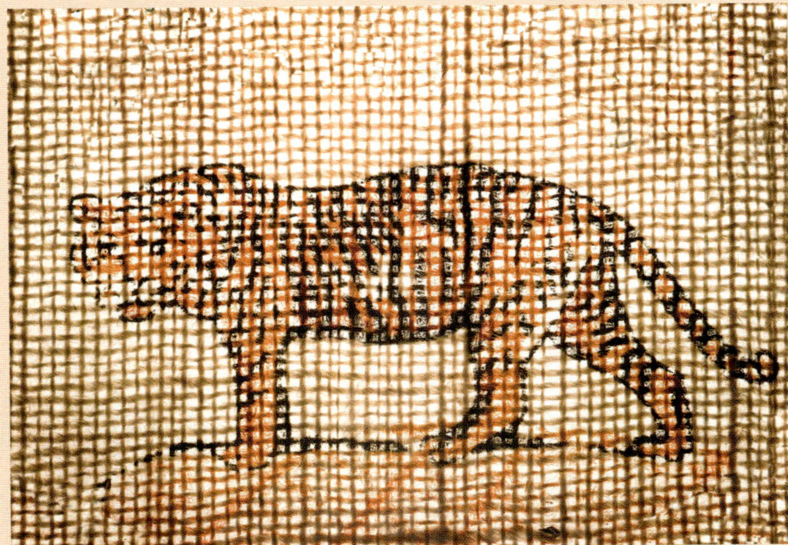

Tiger, 2009. C–print. 102 × 152 cm

At the heart of Roe Ethridge's conceptual approach to photography is a playful attack on the traditions and conventions of photography itself. Spurning the autonomy of any individual image, Ethridge instead makes unexpected juxtapositions of colour photographs, blending the realm of 'art photography' with images more commonly associated with the commercial realm. Sequences of photographs yield different kinds of interstitial and associative meanings, and Ethridge's carefully ordered choices lend his ostensibly mundane images a hyper-real, uncanny edge. Their off-hand sensibility often belies their carefully structured and manufactured origins.

Although Ethridge usually engages in a serial, thematic approach to his practice, the images within any given series can seem almost like random selections from some stock-photography website. The work constructs its meaning more like a photo-essay than as discrete images of individual moments, echoing the editorial format of magazines. Seemingly wide-ranging subjects sit side by side, forcing viewers to grapple with shifts between the worlds of documentary, fashion, advertising, landscape, portrait and catalogue photography. A photographic studio portrait might be presented alongside a postcard-worthy sunset scene or some kitschy still-life arrangement from a gift catalogue.

For example, in Ethridge's recent *Rockaway, New York* series (2007), he explores an ostensibly 'coastal' theme; the images themselves meander promiscuously far afield from his seaside topic, as he dispassionately presents his widely varied subjects as transposable equivalents. Viewers are

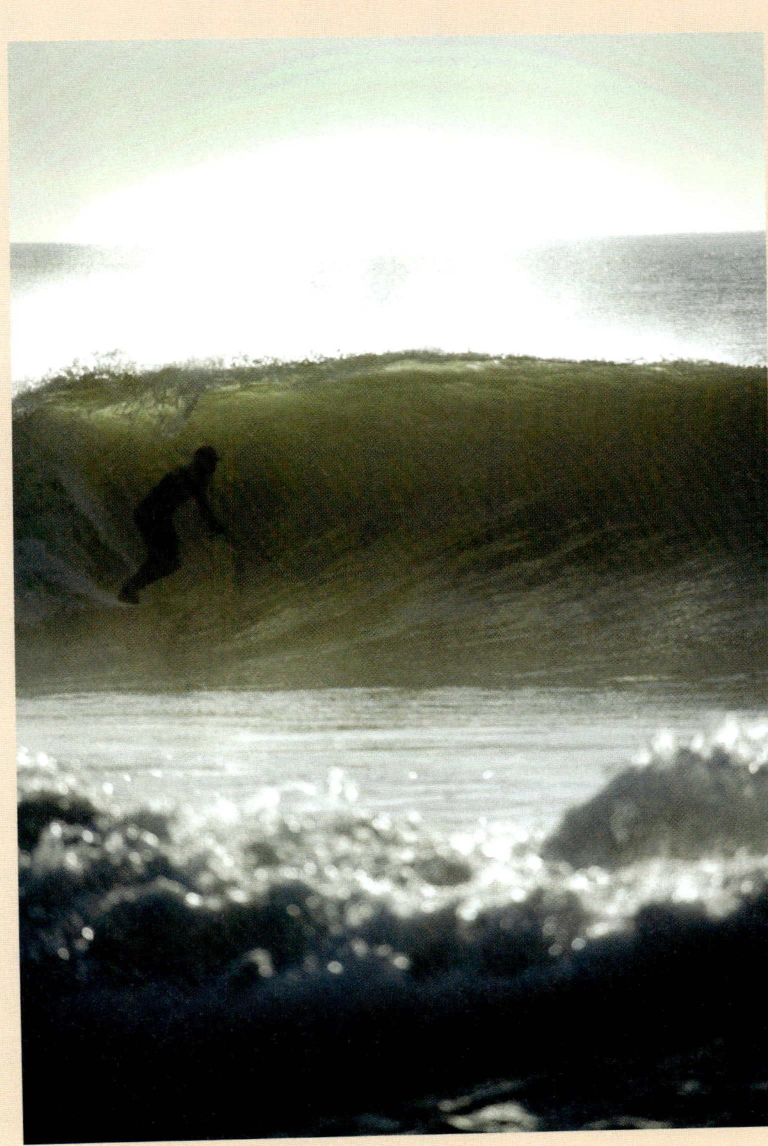

Rockaway (90th Street), 2008. C–print. 152 × 102 cm

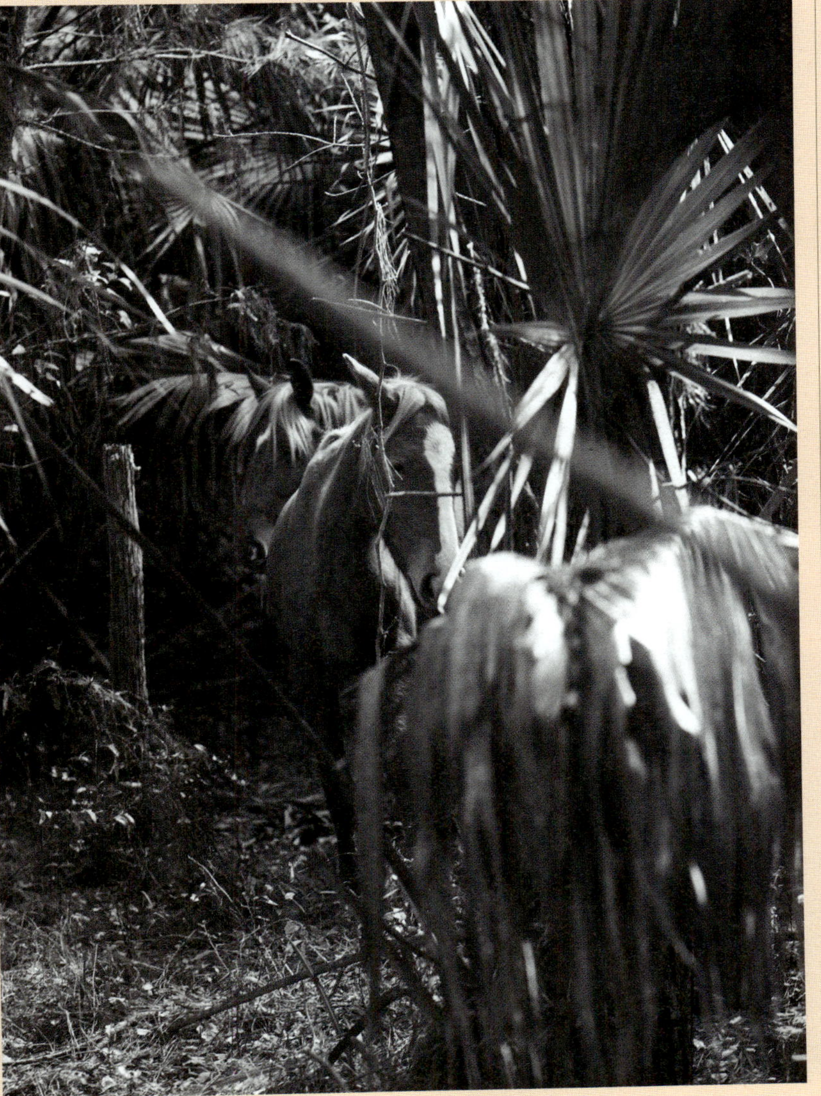

Farewell Horse (In the Woods), 2008. Silver gelatin print. 132 × 102 cm

catapulted from a tongue-in-cheek self-portrait of the artist donning a captain's hat, to surfers riding a wave, to a dreary overcast beach promenade scene, to ferry boats docked in Mumbai, to a glistening plate of oysters on the half shell, to a kitschy studio shot of a model casually untying her red bikini top, to an advertisement for a Harry and David catalogue, to a Caribbean sunset, to technical photographs of the moon. Such idiosyncratic combinations activate a tension, for instance, between the distant stance of documentary photography and the persuasive ambition of advertising photography, or between the flawed studio portrait and the aesthetics of personal snapshots. As the artist explains, he is not attempting to generate a literal construction of a coastal-thematic, but to suggest something more 'fugue-like', with multiple perspectives weaving in and out of the work in a contrapuntal dialogue, indirectly teasing out the issues at hand.

Contextual associations

Deliberate juxtapositions unhinge the photographs from their more familiar contextual associations and synaptic gaps between the images generate new meanings, sensibilities and often a pseudo-narrative arc.

Influenced by the appropriation strategies and conceptual, serial approaches of many artists since the late 1970s and 1980s, such as Richard Prince, Christopher Williams and Thomas Ruff, Ethridge's work relinquishes modernist notions of originality within any given photograph, and embraces a post-appropriative sense of authorship wherein significance is situated at the in-between junctures and within the means and mechanisms of his restagings.

Aided by the advances of digital technologies, which afford ever greater flexibility in manipulating existing imagery, Ethridge is comfortable as an artist working in both the

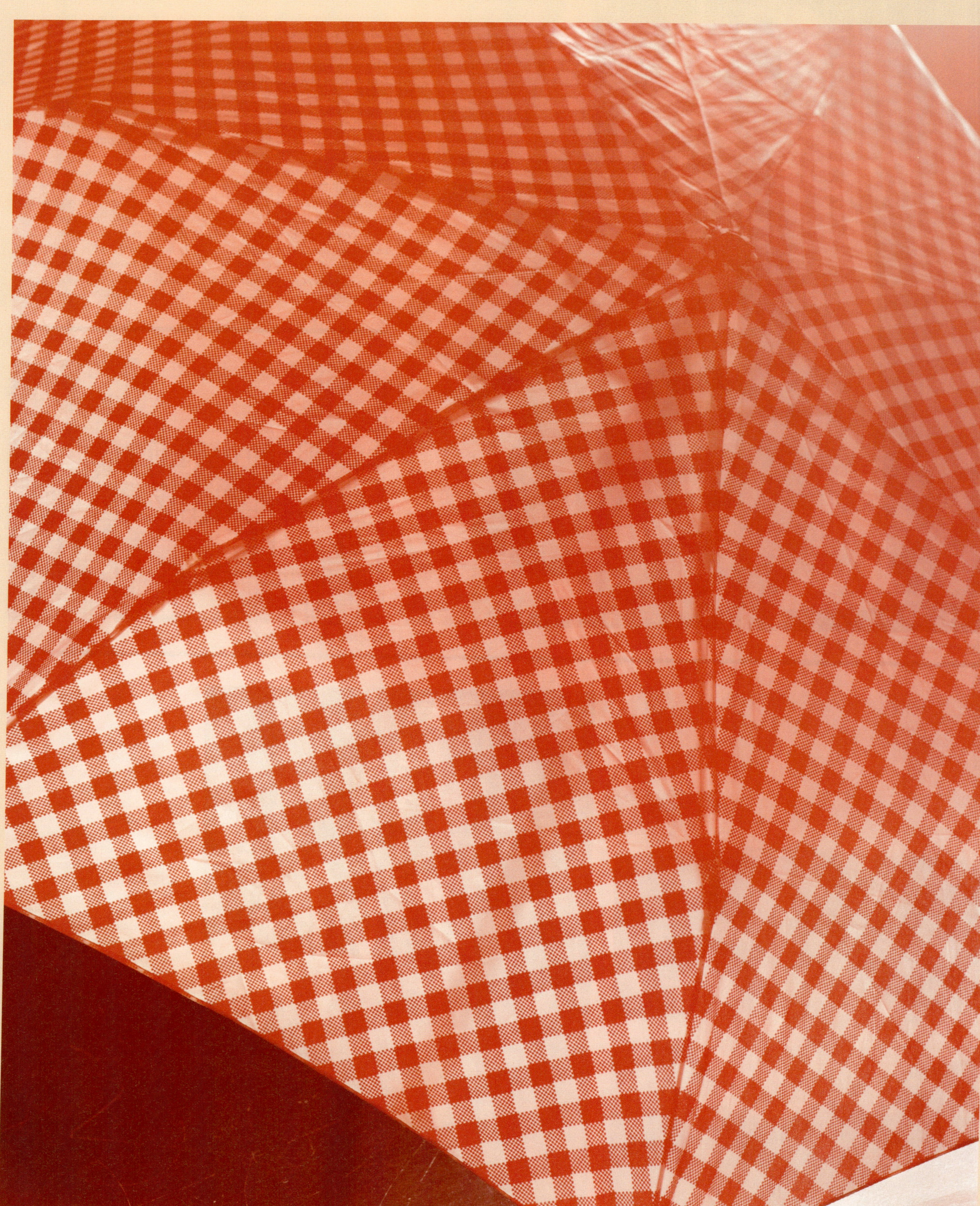

Marc's Umbrella, 2009. C–print. 127 × 102 cm

New sensibilities

commercial and art-photography worlds. This gives him the ability to strategically misrepresent extant photographic topologies and to suggest slippages between them. As Etheridge exhumes and samples the photographic past, he wilfully offers up imperfections rehearsing the histories, genres and styles of photography in order to pit them against one another. In this way, he implies that the various realms of photography —whether 'high' or 'low'— are interchangeable in today's consumer-dominated society. Moreover, his practice reflects the potentially unnerving proposition that any given image — or by extension, any object itself — can be a substitute for another, implying that our contemporary moment may be shaped not so much by the particular objects we consume, but by the delivery systems and modes of distribution that circulate them throughout the world.

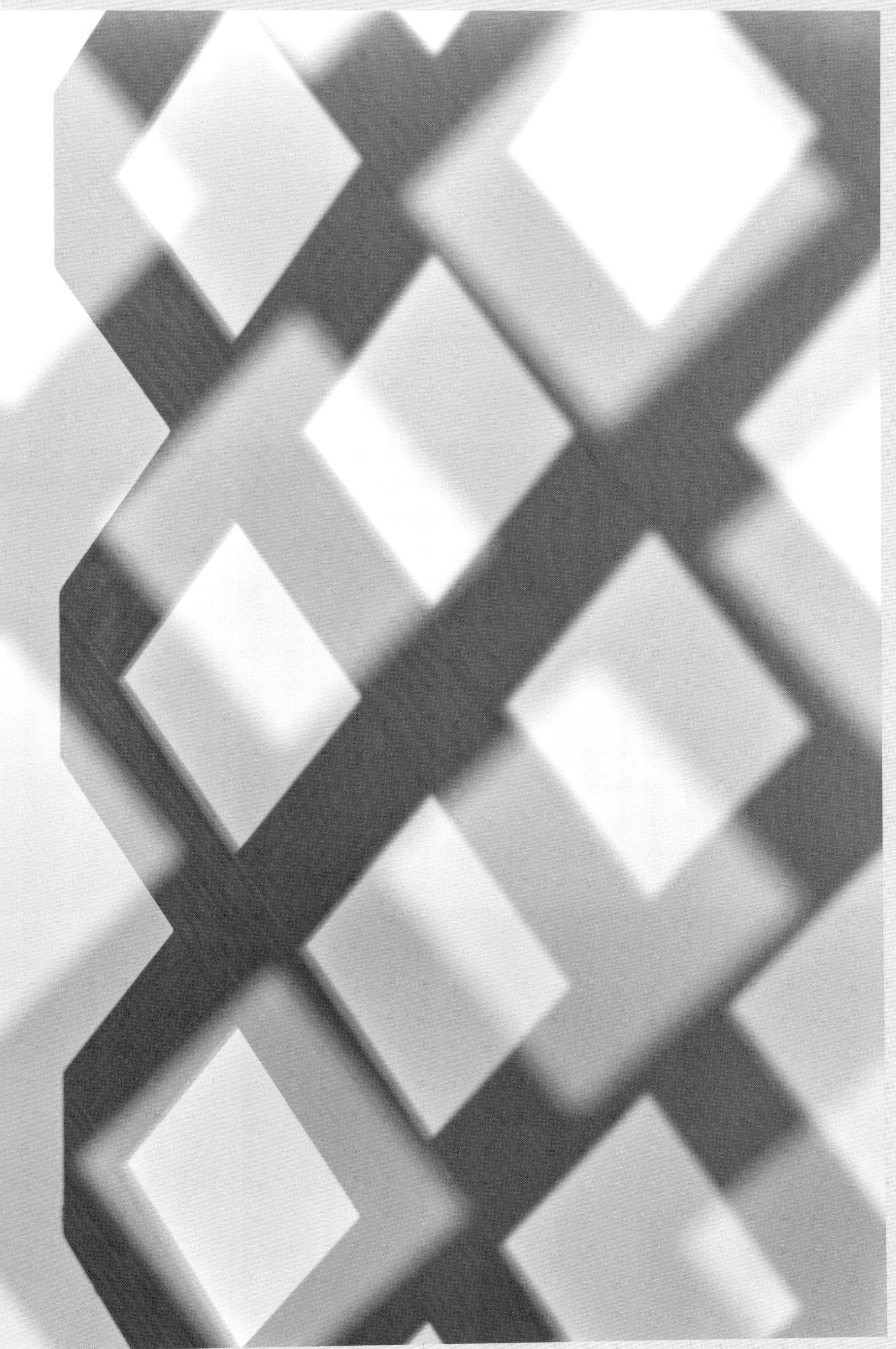

Double Lattice, 2009. C–print. 127 × 102 cm

Geoffrey Farmer

Geoffrey Farmer's works are unpredictable, memorable and rarely, if ever, exhibited in the same way twice. Every exhibition and major work is a temporal event, a theatrical performance intended for a particular time and place, and embedded within this methodology is a form of resistance and social commentary. Farmer uses all media and his process-oriented approach, which is intuitive and research-based, is drawn from philosophy, storytelling, dreams, literature and theatre.

In 2000, Farmer took the text of Victor Hugo's *Notre Dame de Paris* and transformed it into a sculptural object entitled *The Hunchback Kit* (2000), a thirteen-foot metal travelling crate with its width and depth scaled proportionately to the same dimensions as Farmer's edition of the book. The case contains objects collected during his travels, which the artist uses to create installations and actions in an ongoing process that has spanned over ten years. The latest manifestation takes the form of a feeder for a hawk moth that he made with a Quaker community, using melted candies sourced from a work by Felix Gonzales-Torres.

In *The Last Two Million Years* (2007), Farmer cut up a *Reader's Digest* book of the same title from the 1970s and re-introduced the two-dimensional images (drawings and photographs) of this overarching history into a three-dimensional world made up of a series of differently shaped and sized foam-core pedestals. Figures and objects from different cultures and times were displayed together in this mash-up museum. Each was numbered and viewers could find supporting descriptions in a small newsprint book accompanying the

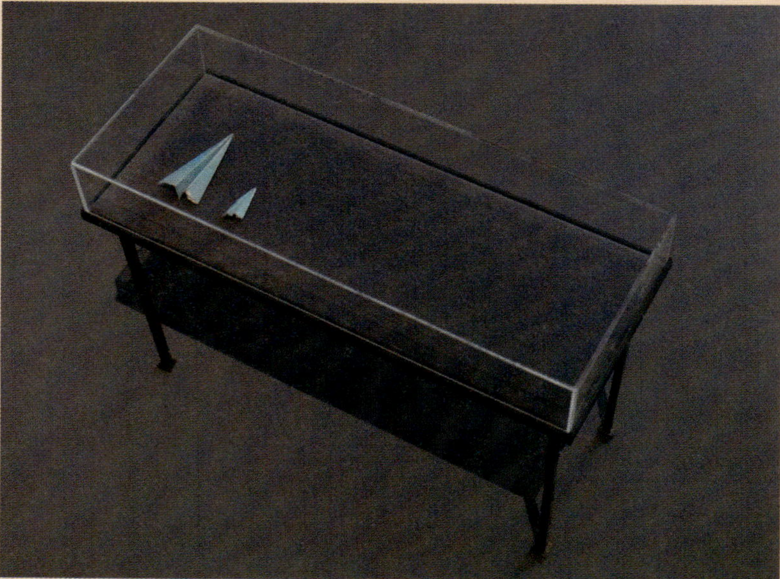

Theatrical performance

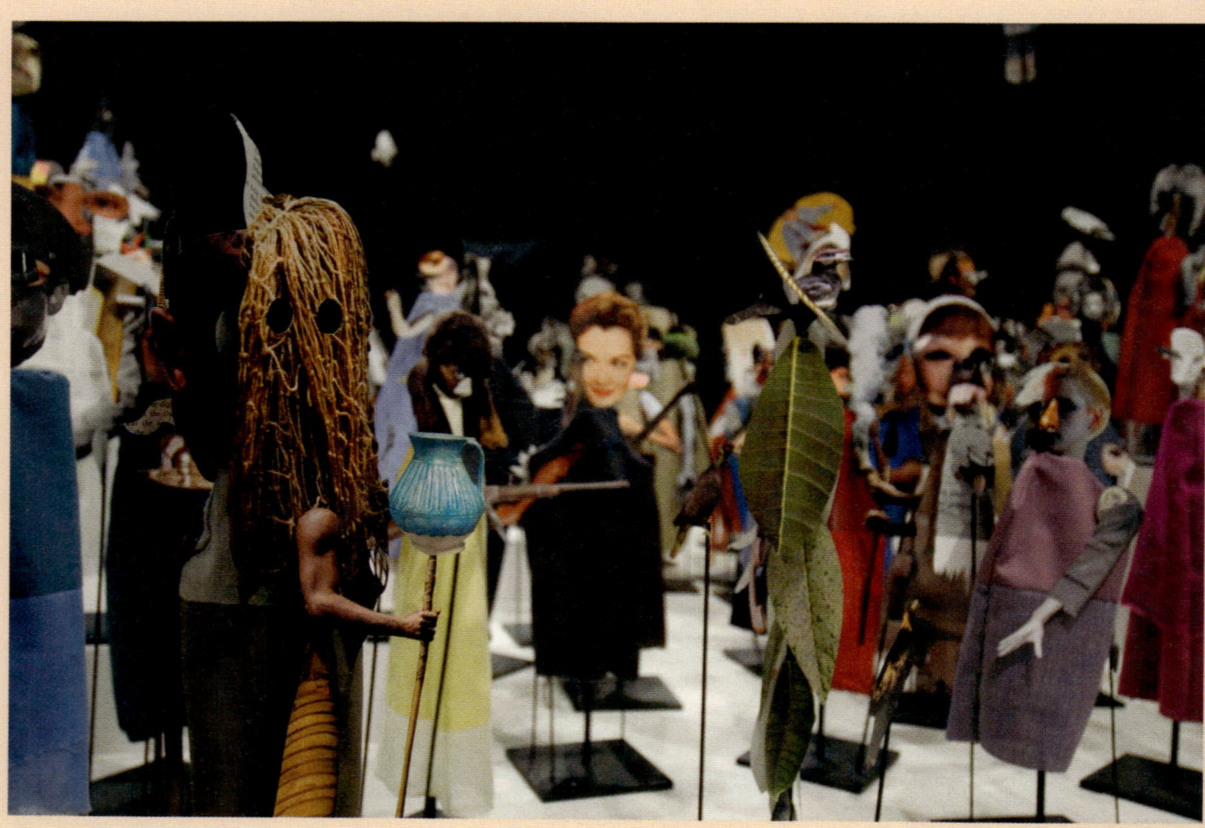

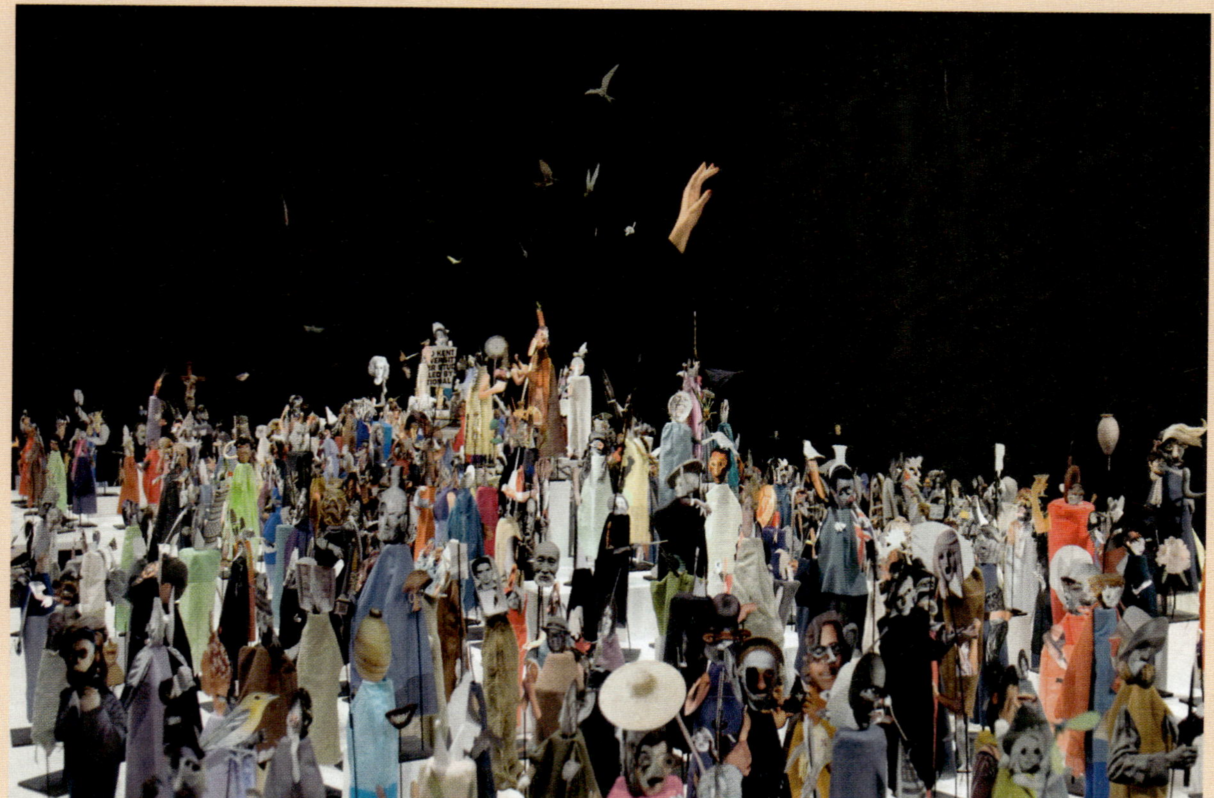

The Surgeon and the Photographer, 2009. Fabric, paper collage, wood, metal stands. 730 × 450 × 150 cm

Forgetting Air (Slow Play), 2008. 767 aeroplane fuselage, airline seats, wooden chairs, pillows, wooden stage, sound system, lights, mirrors, drums, feathers, fabric, costumes, blankets, towel, shoes, string, eggs, tape, projector, video monitors, various display cases. Dimensions variable

piece. The poetic mix of factual and subjective pondering in this miniature publication further extended the potential of the work. Similarly, in *The Surgeon and the Photographer* (2009), Farmer created a calendar of puppet figures, cut up from books he had acquired from a second-hand bookshop that was about to close. The calendar and accompanying film work confound our sense of time and history, and their reliance on the photographic form.

In late 2009 Farmer opened Every Letter in the Alphabet, a Vancouver space that will operate for a year and where he will oversee the development of projects focusing on language in art. A cross between an artist-initiated space, a museum, an archive and a distribution centre, Every Letter in the Alphabet is open to the public, and commissions posters, poetry, writing, banners, billboards and performances. One of the initial projects borrows text from the windows of local shopkeepers who are suffering during the recession and transforms them into large billboards in an effort to advertise and make their services more visible. Every Letter in the Alphabet is actively collecting text works, as well as protest signs, scripts and other ephemera that hold significance for the surrounding community.

When the Musée d'Art Contemporain de Montréal organized a survey in 2007, Farmer reformulated many of his works in a highly theatrical display. For example, the formerly stand-alone wooden replica *Trailer* (2002) was installed with a life-size figurative sculpture of a woman beside it. The night before the opening, Farmer made the connection between a past event and his impulse to create the work. During his time as a student at the San Francisco Art Institute he witnessed a gruesome accident in which an elderly women was flattened by a large white trailer. The next day, before the exhibition was to open, Farmer took apart another work to create a figure in a simple dress and a cardboard mask to accompany the piece. Through this continuous process of re-contextualizing and re-writing the formal elements of his work, Farmer explores the mutability of our personal and social histories.

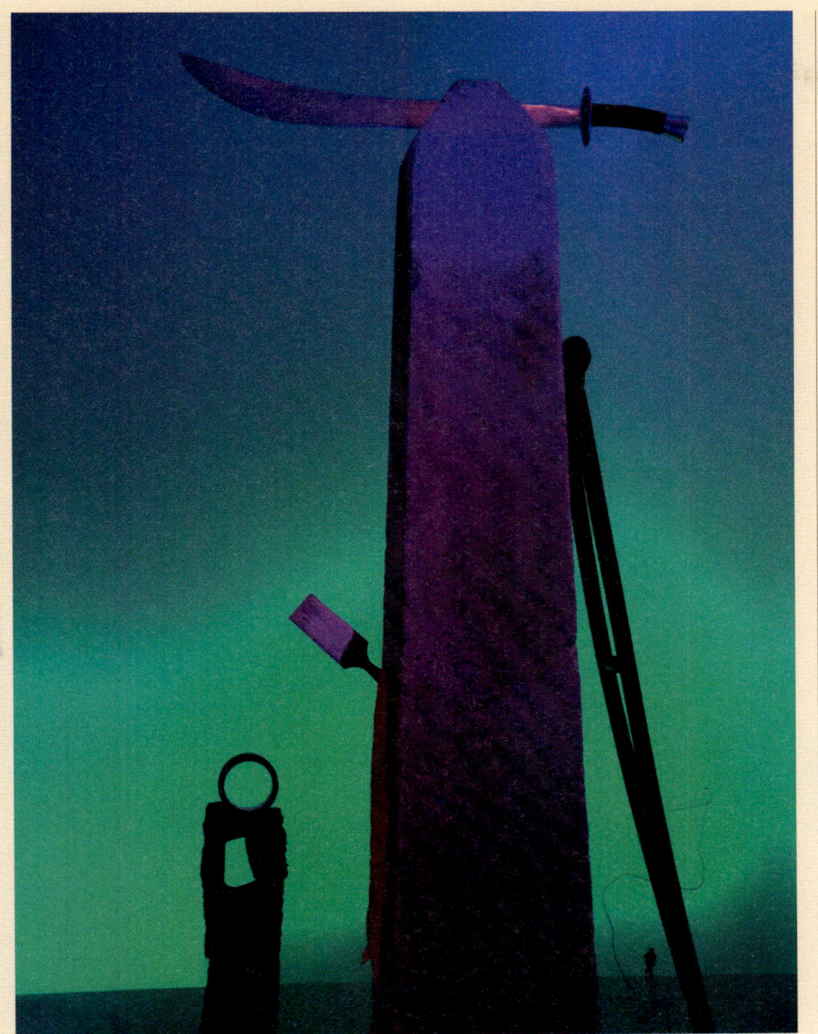

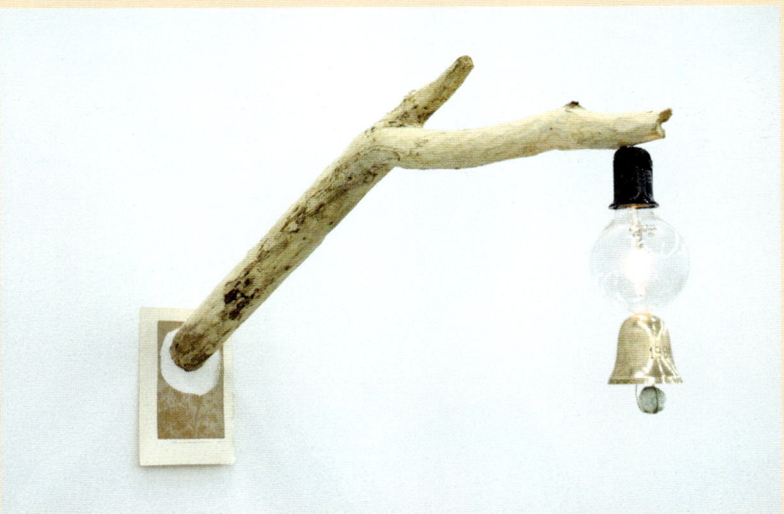

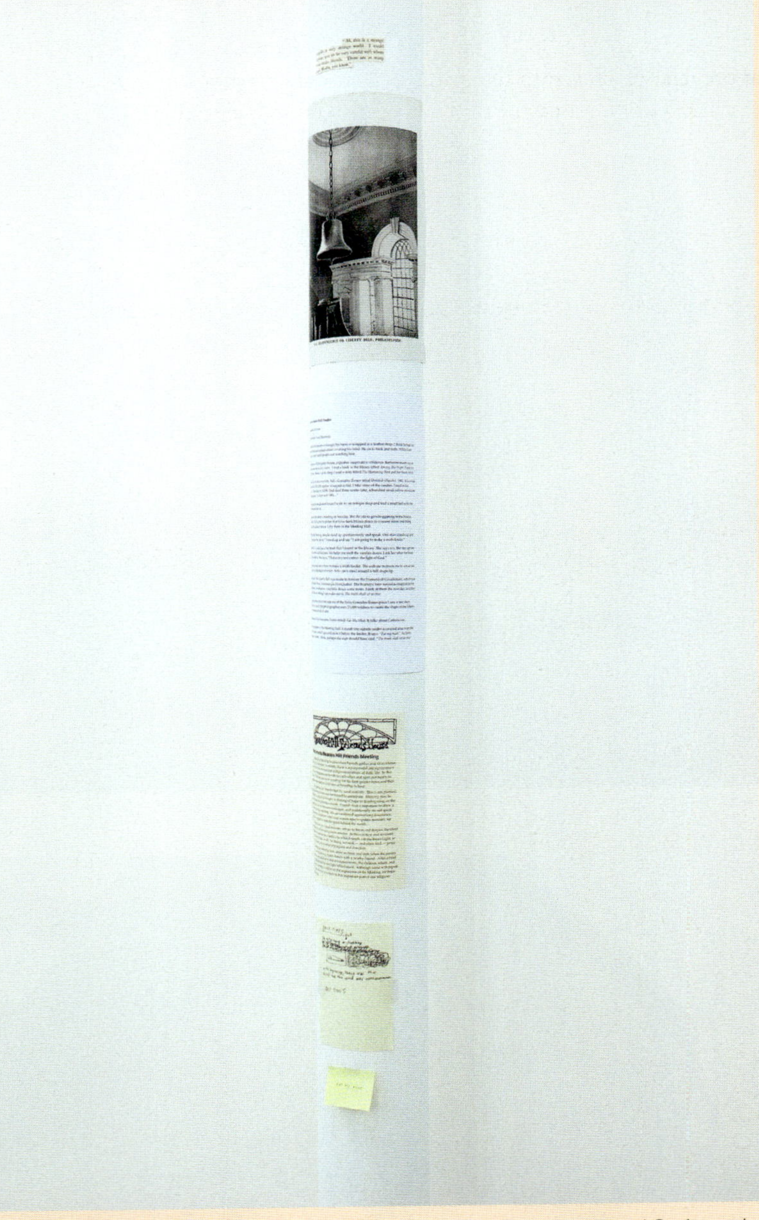

I'm Not Praying I'm Just Stretching... (detail), 2008 – 09. Candle snuffer, abandoned Quaker–style chair taken from the streets of Boston, 'Among The Night People' by Clara D. Pierson, borrowed from the Library of The Beacon Hill Friends House, photograph of The Human Liberty Bell (1918), branch from a tree used for public hangings on the Boston Commons, light socket with the embossed words 'Proclaim Liberty Throughout The Land', found bell inscribed with the date 1991, a bell clapper/moth feeder made from a cotton ball soaked in a solution of sugar derived from a candy taken from a work by Felix Gonzalez–Torres, drinking glass, vase, antique bottle, lights, various notes. Dimensions variable

Ongoing processes

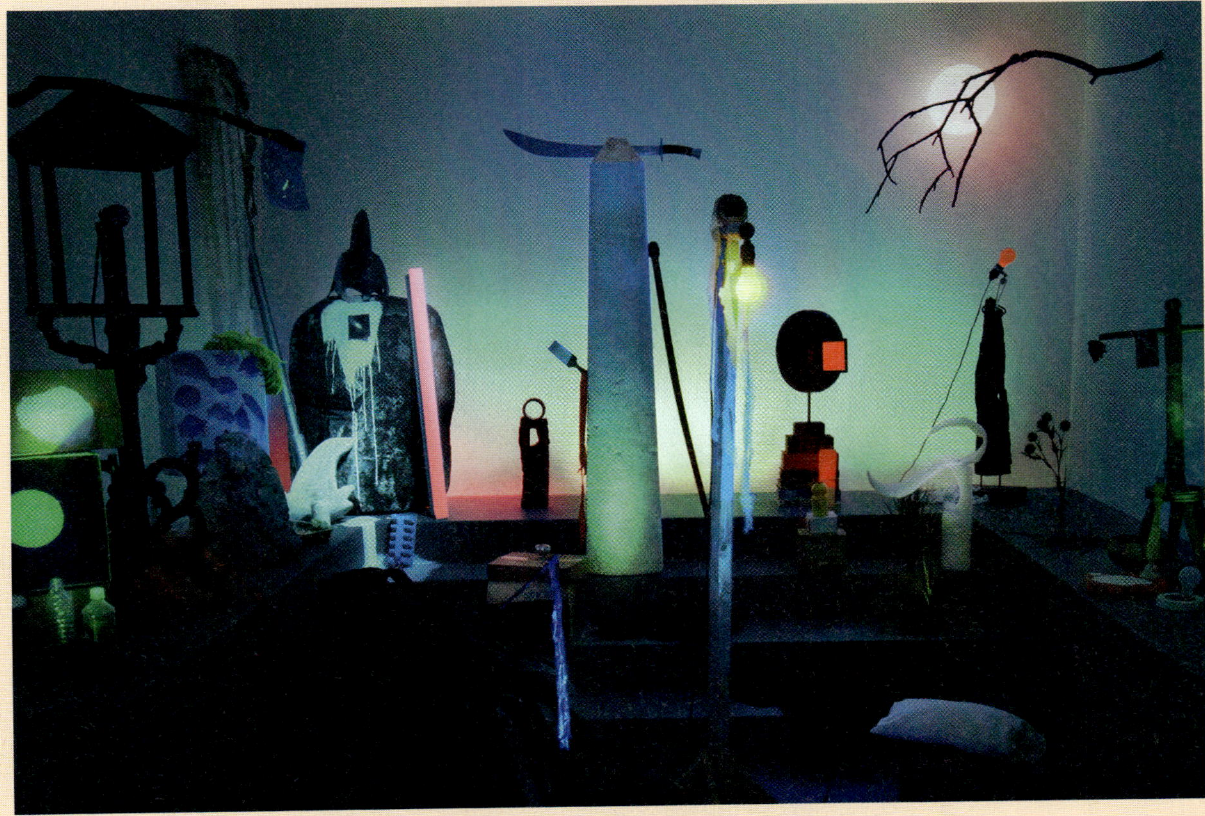

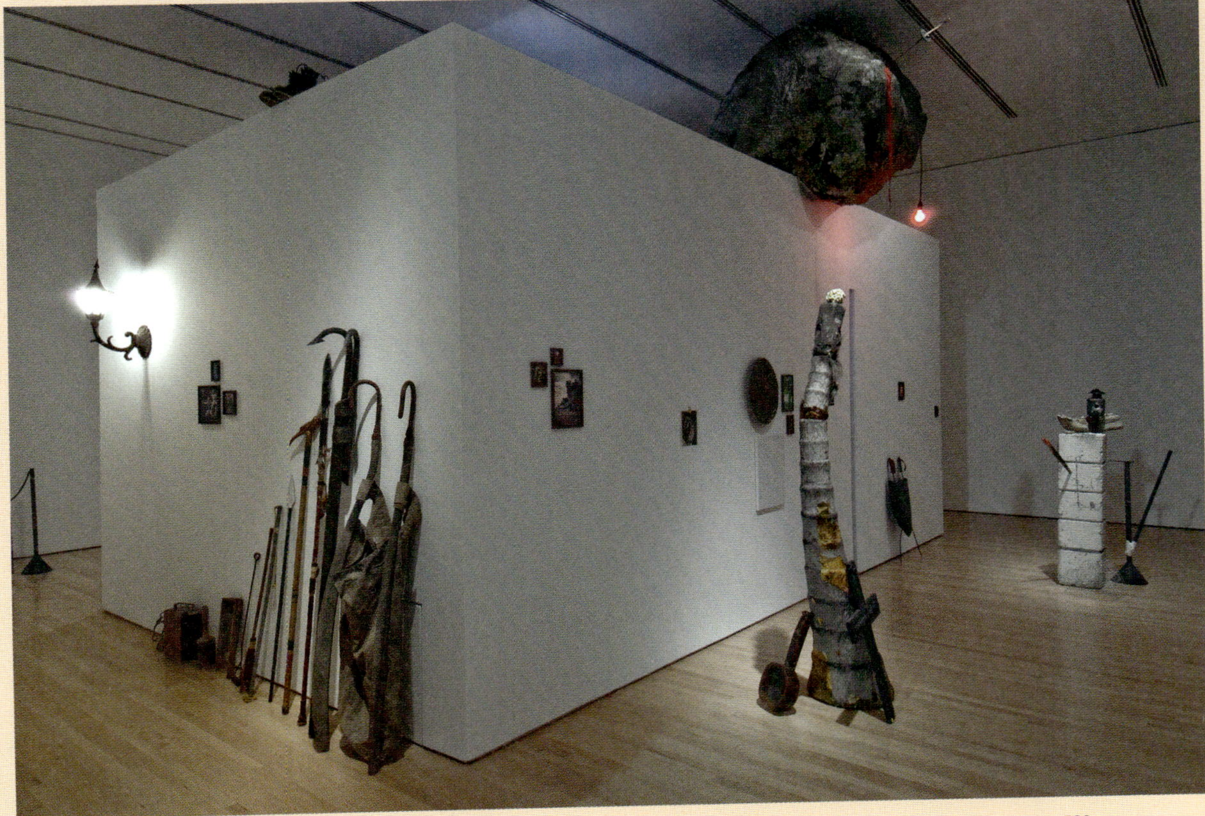

Theatre of Cruelty, 2008. Props, found objects, fabric, computer–controlled LED lighting system, framed photographs. 700 × 420 × 300 cm

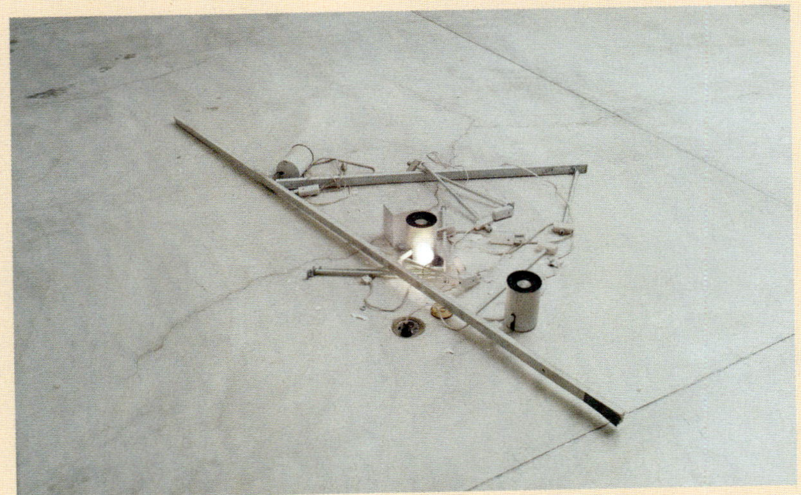

Hunchback Kit (detail), 2005. Custom–built shipping container, fitted foam case liner, pencil, feathers, buttons, sticks, book, bell. Dimensions variable

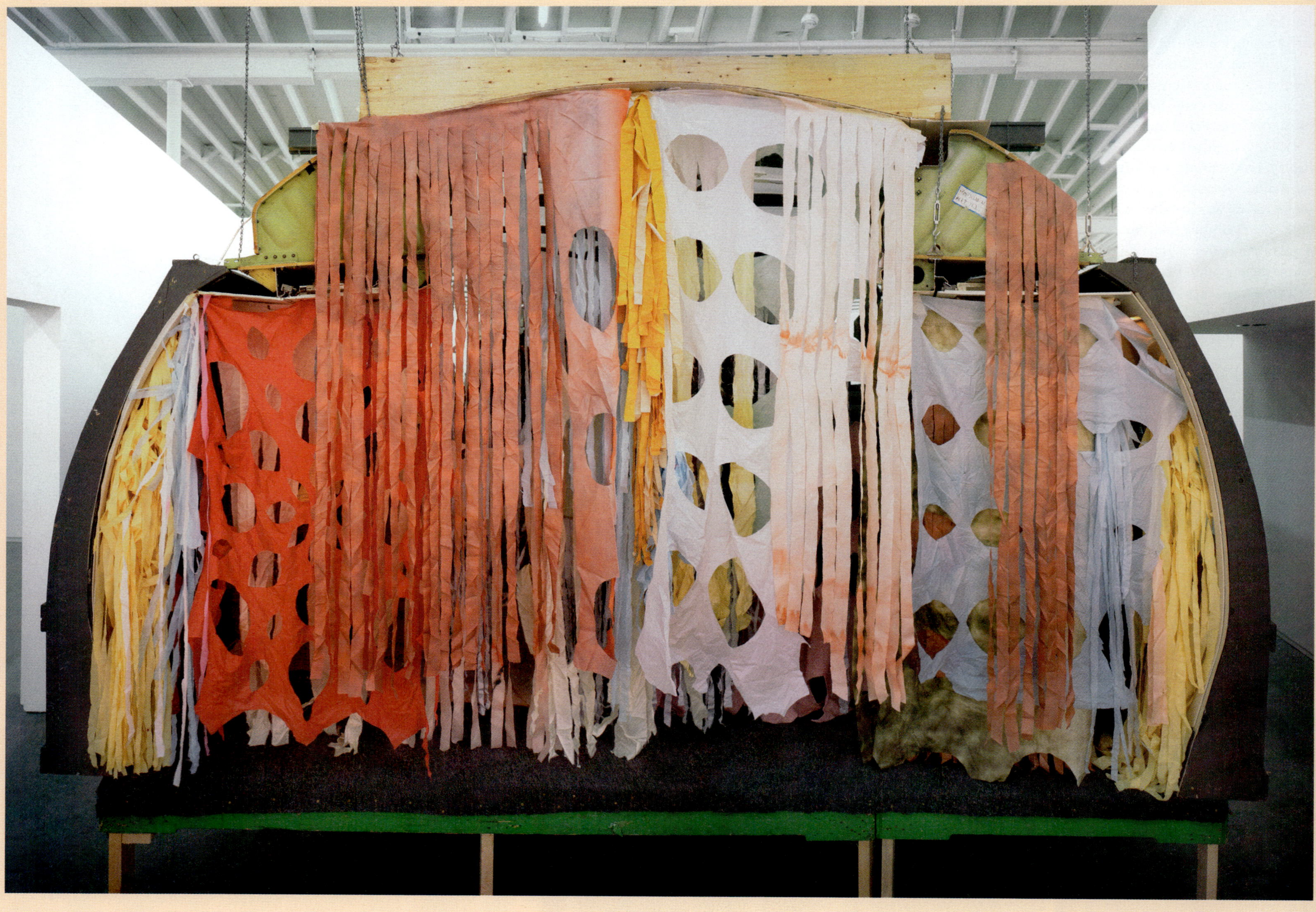

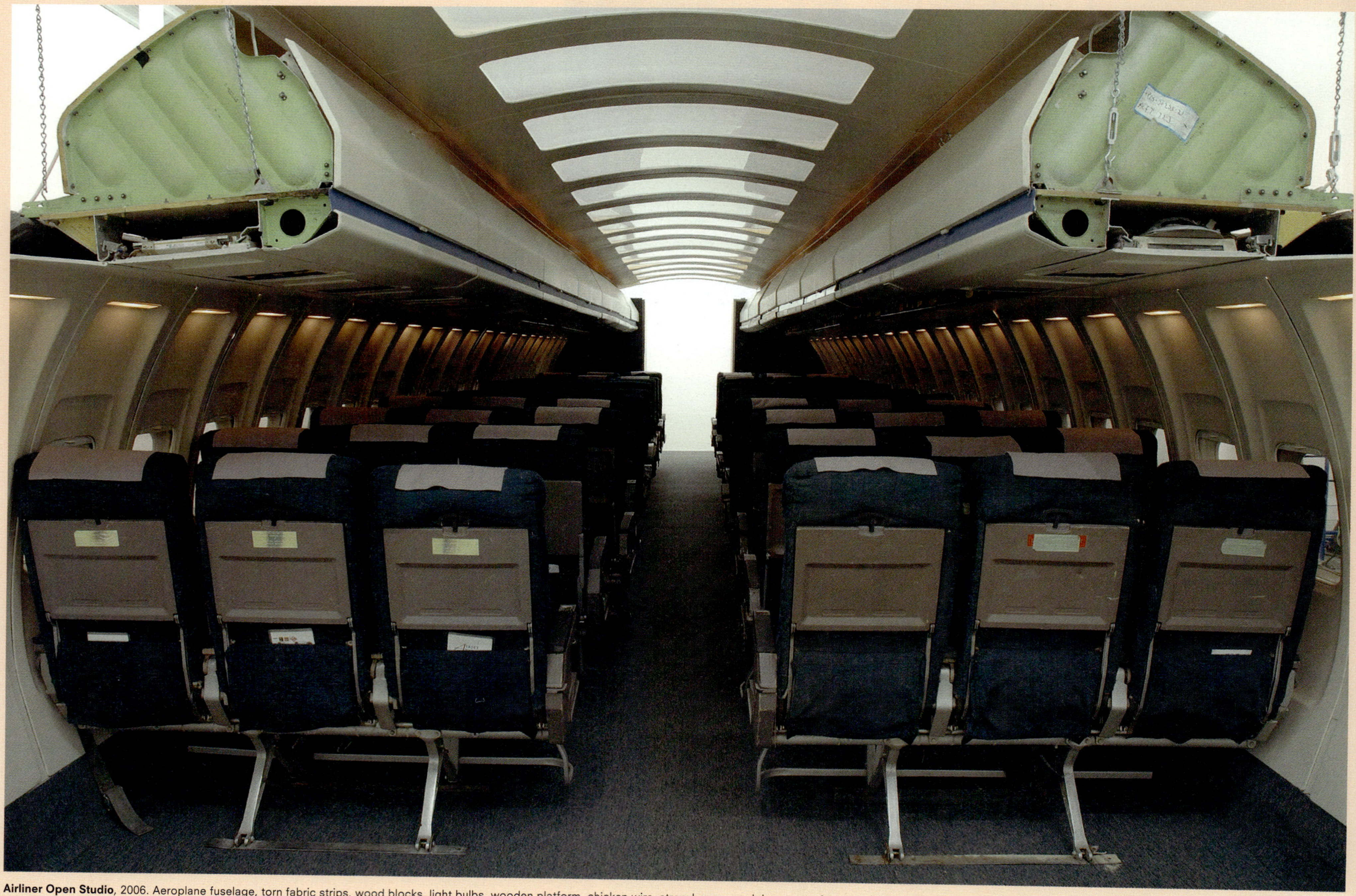

Airliner Open Studio, 2006. Aeroplane fuselage, torn fabric strips, wood blocks, light bulbs, wooden platform, chicken wire, straw broom, push broom, projector, video camera. Dimensions variable

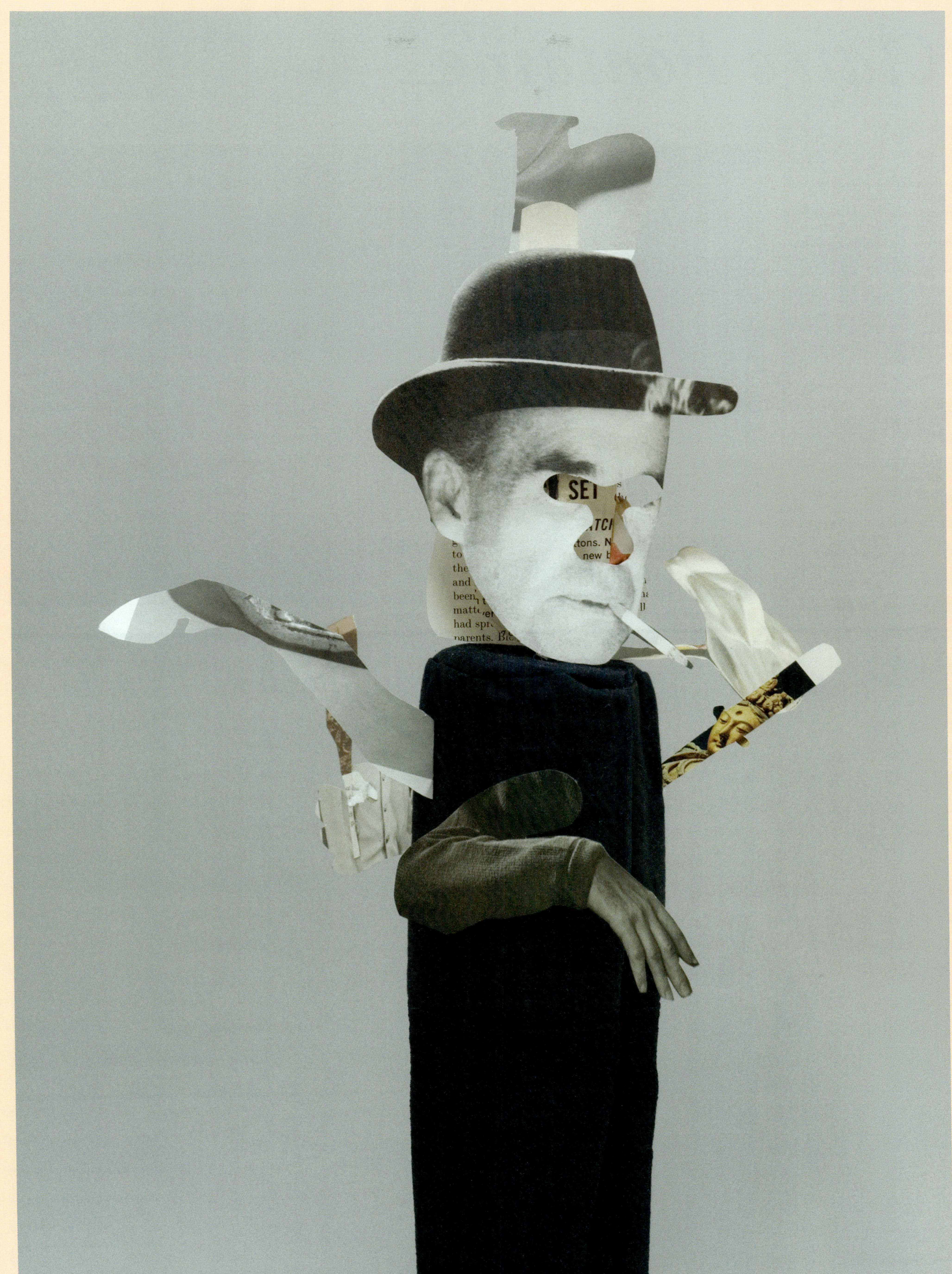

The Surgeon and the Photographer (detail), 2009. Fabric, paper collage, wood, metal stands. 730 × 450 × 150 cm

Claire Fontaine

Claire Fontaine is the 'collective artist' invented in 2004 by Fulvia Carnevale and James Thornhill, under whose name they have produced an extensive body of writing and exhibited a range of objects and installations that explore the intersection of art, politics and economy. The name derives from a popular brand of French notebooks, and points both to their Paris base and to the often highly discursive nature of their work, which stems equally from the artistic training of Thornhill and the philosophical background of Carnevale.

Claire Fontaine's works frequently mimic the forms of classic Conceptual art, as in their *The True Artist* (2004), which takes up the spiralling text of Bruce Nauman's 1967 neon, *The True Artist Helps the World by Revealing Mystic Truths*. Three decades later, it has been reinvented in the highly ephemeral form of a drawing made of smoke, inscribed now on the ceiling rather than hung on a window or a wall. Additionally, Nauman's tongue-in-cheek statement of private conviction has been

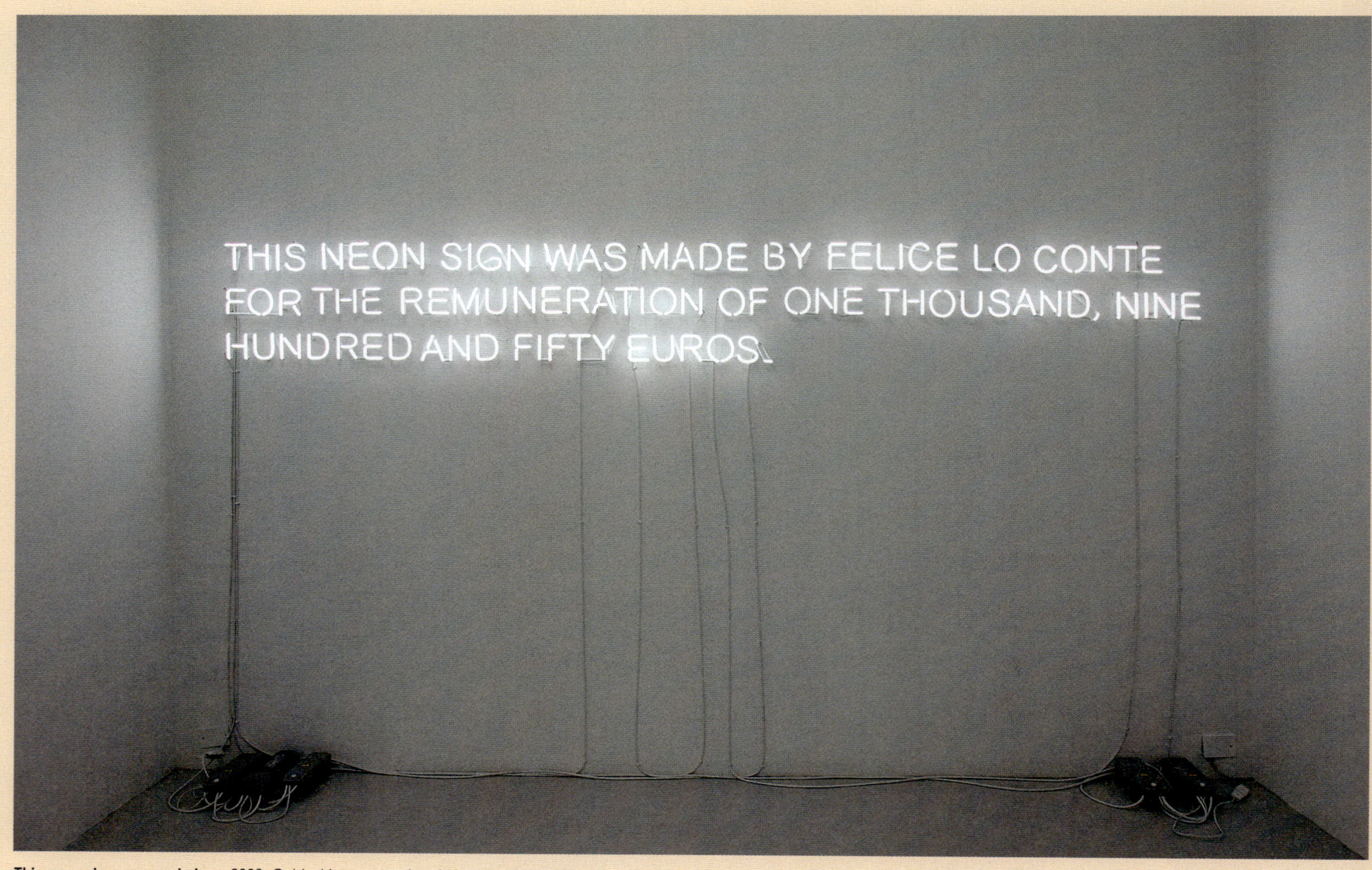

This neon sign was made by..., 2009. Cold white neon, painted glass, cables, fixtures, transformers. Approx. 48 × 300 cm

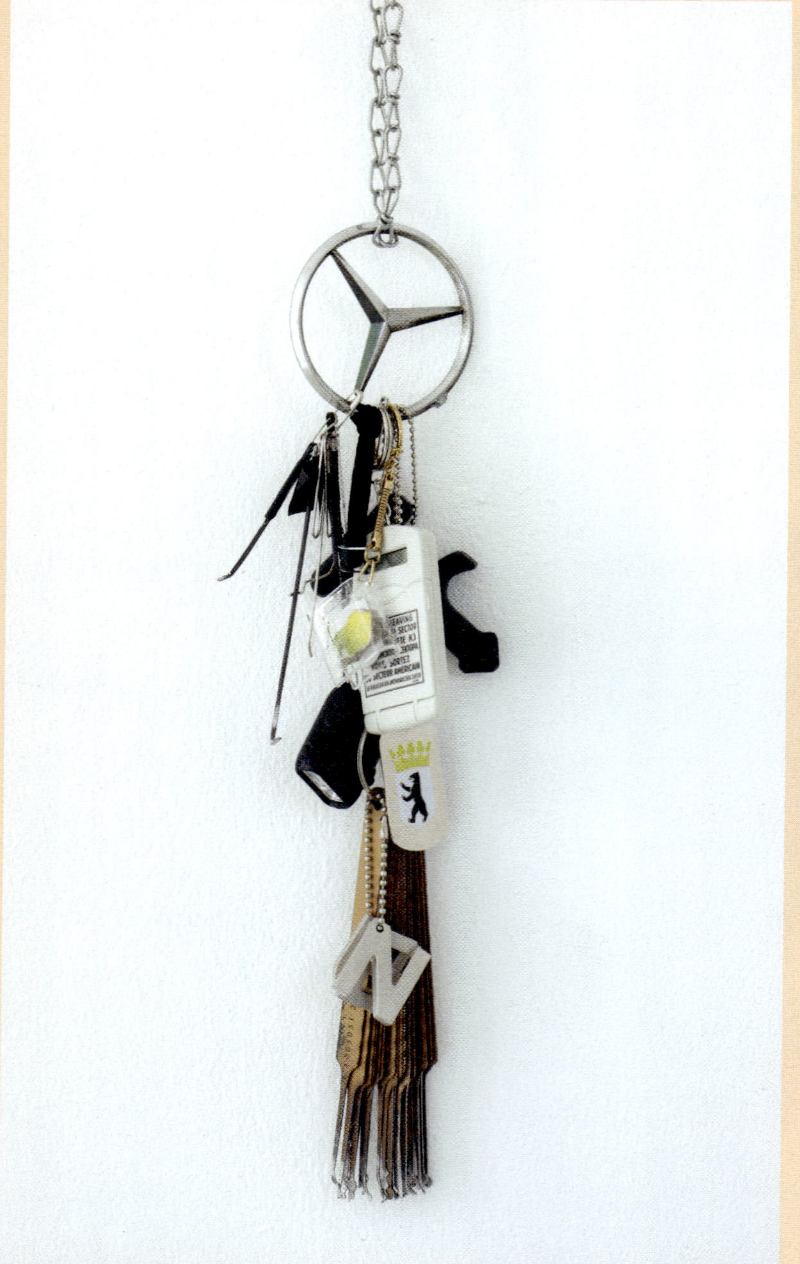

Passe–Partout, (Berlin–Mitte), 2008. Hacksaw blades, bicycle spokes, allen keys, safety pins, hair pins, paperclips, pocket lamp, keyrings, knuckle–duster, electrical tape, chain . Approx. 50 × 5 cm

Flirting with illegality

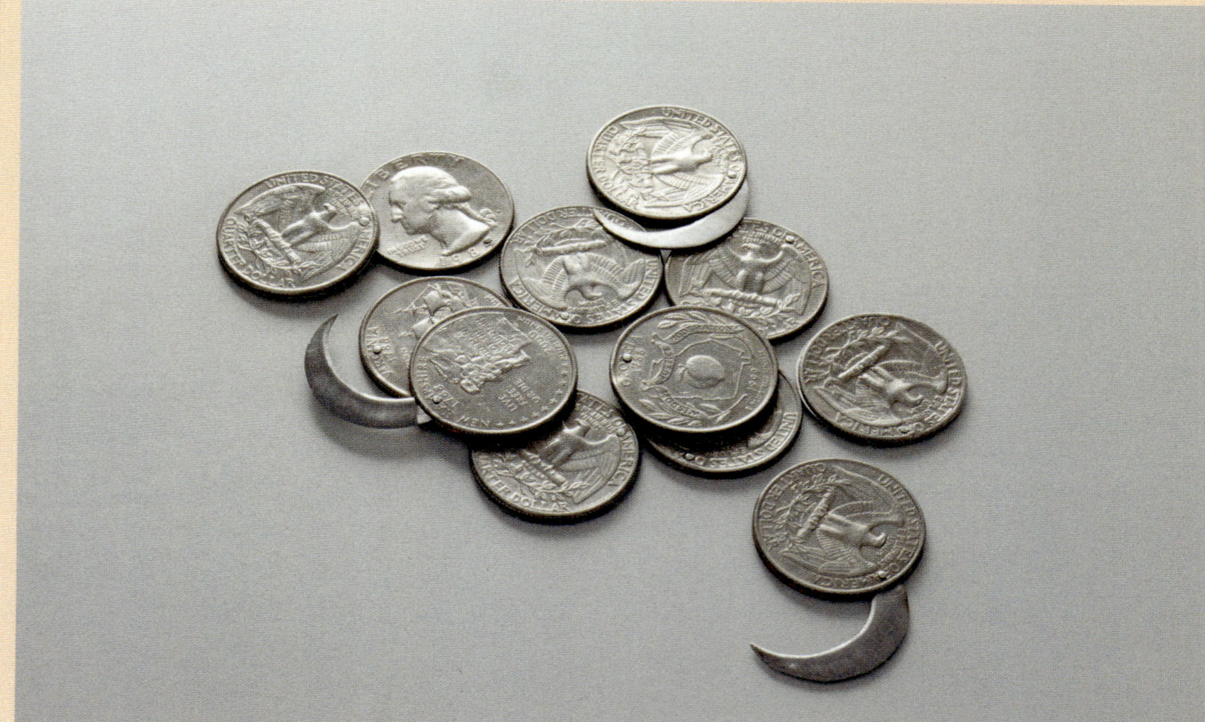

Change, 2006. 12 coins, steel box–cutter blades, solder, rivets. Dimensions variable

altered to one of public declamation: 'The true artist produces the most prestigious commodity'. Similarly, *This neon sign was made by…* (2009) reproduces the look of Joseph Kosuth's white neon statements, but his analytic expressions have been replaced by a simple naming of the fabricator of the piece and how much he or she was remunerated for their labour.

In both cases, Claire Fontaine turns the self-reflexivity of Conceptual art back on the economics of the contemporary artwork itself.

La Société du Spectacle brickbat (2005) wraps the cover of a classic text of 1960s French revolutionary theory by Guy Debord around a brick, conjoining two moments of politico-aesthetic radicalism: the work of the

Situationist International, a group whose writings are seen as crucial precursors to the student unrest of the late 1960s, and the art of Carl Andre, whose Minimalist sculptures frequently made use of simple, repeatable forms such as firebricks. But this is no mere exercise in nostalgia; if on the one hand the work literalizes the militant promise of the book,

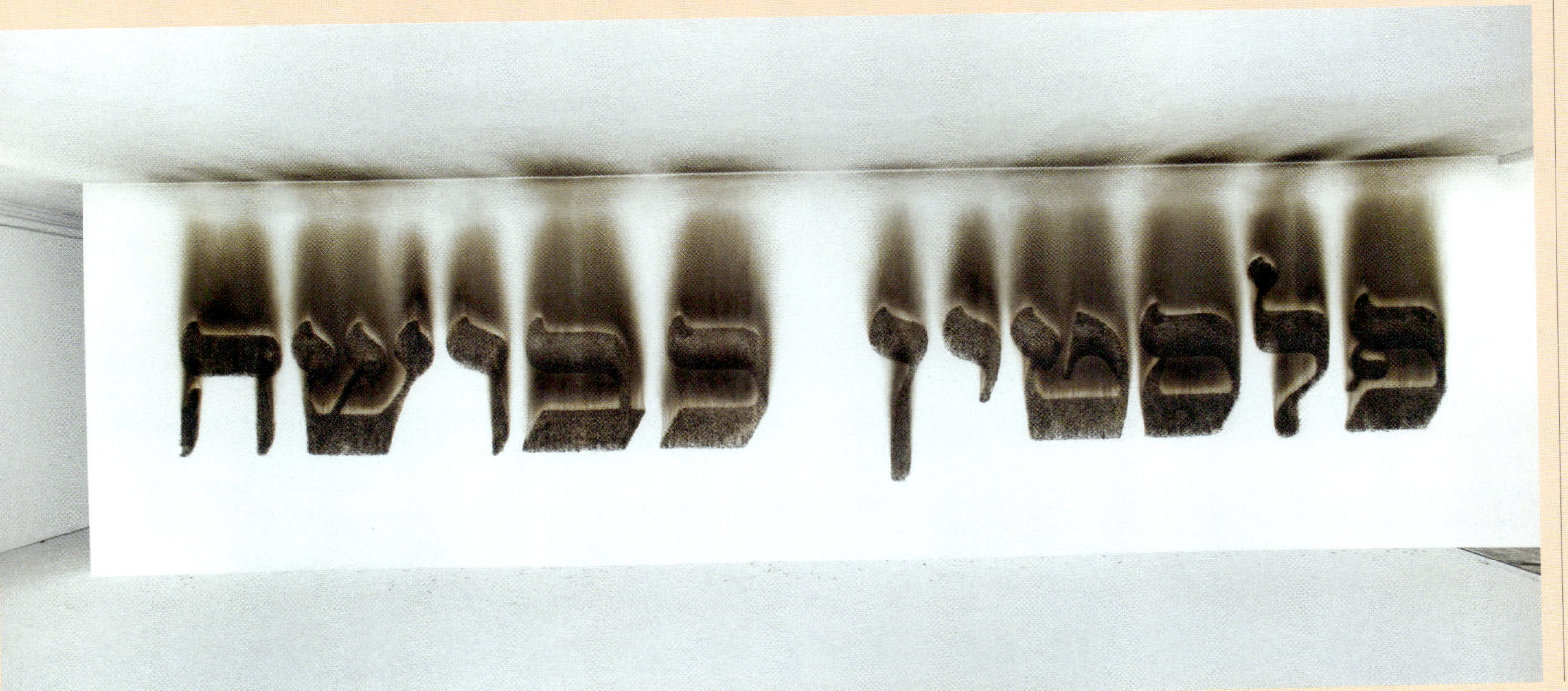

The True Artist (spiral version), 2004. Smoke on ceiling. Approx. 150 × 150 cm

Tool of protest

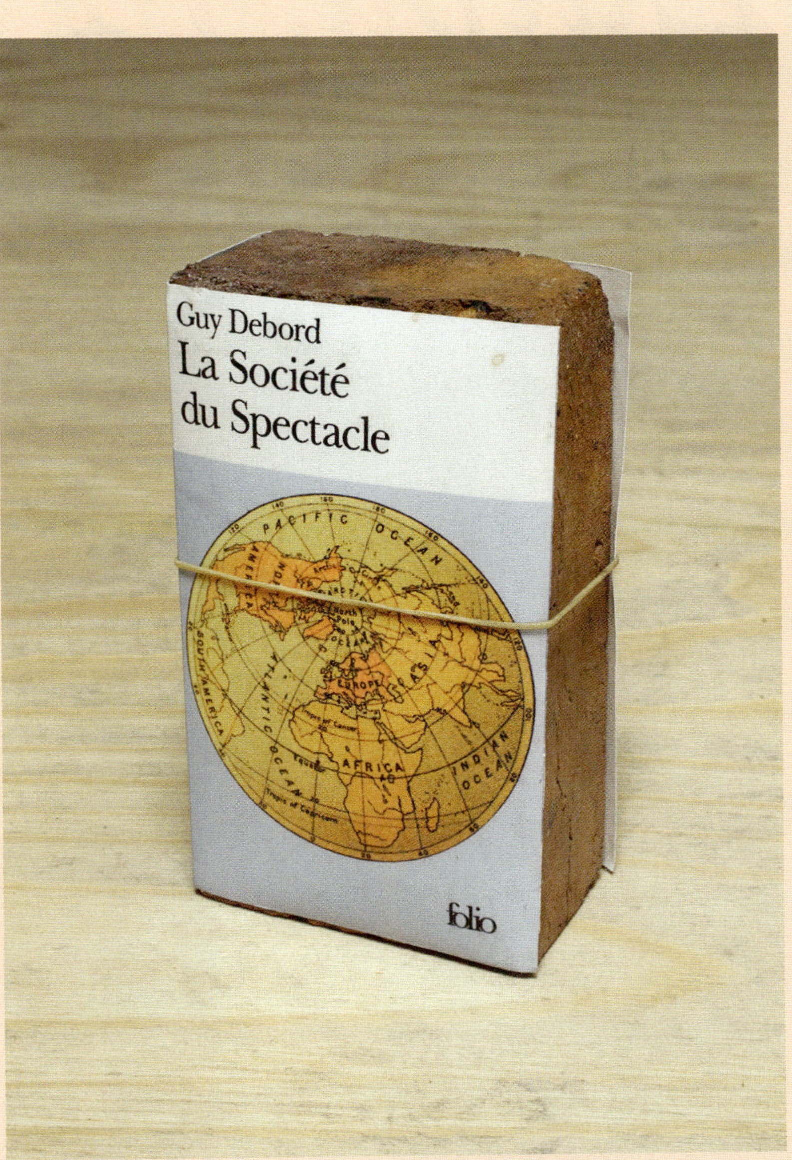

La Société du Spectacle brickbat, 2005. Brick, archival laser print, elastic band. 19 × 12 × 6 cm

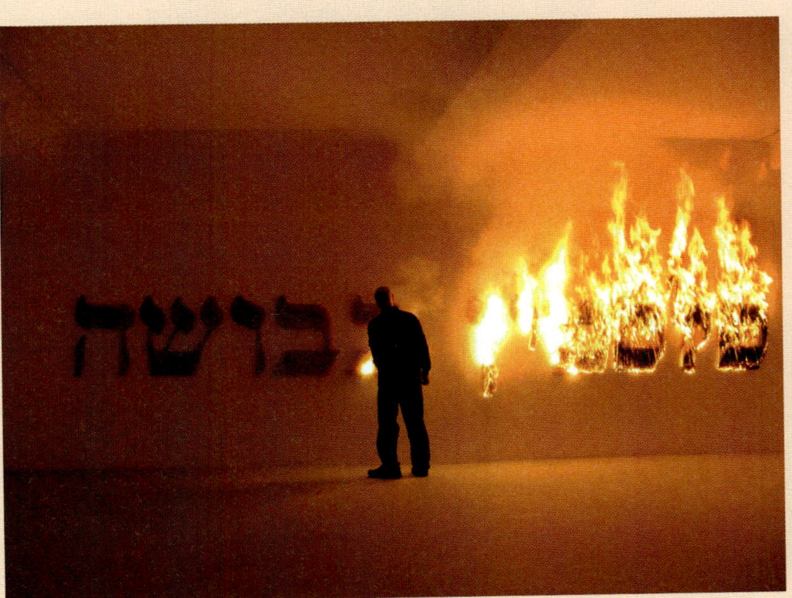

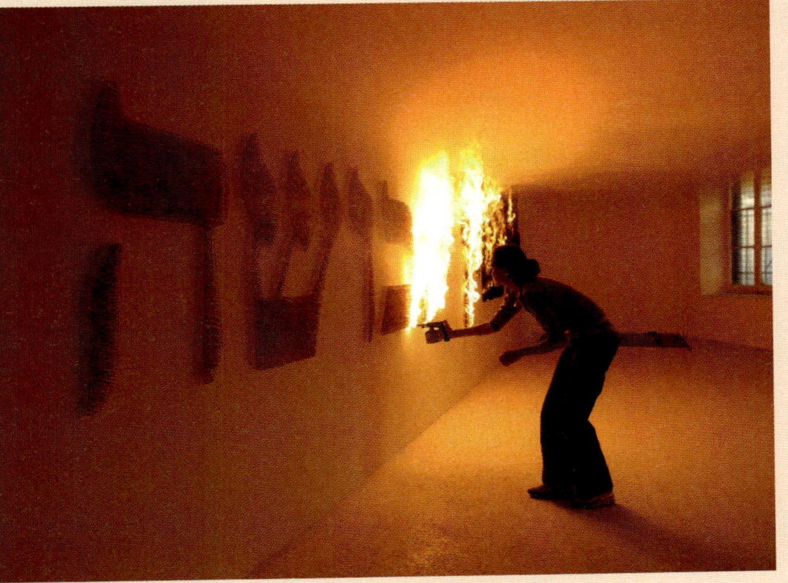

Palestine Occupied, 2008. 45,000 to 60,000 matchsticks, plaster wall and corridor, fire extinguisher, projected digital video. Approx. 12 × 3 × 3 m

so that now it can literally become a tool of protest, ready to be chucked through the nearest window, on the other hand it embodies a more disillusioned view of the legacy of that radicalism. The once-revolutionary text is now published by the most prestigious press in France, and appears here as a commodity as reproducible and devoid of content as the brick it disguises.

Other pieces have further explored the potential use-value of the artwork by flirting with illegality. *Change* (2006) consists of a number of American quarters that have been altered to conceal box-cutters, transforming currency into a potential weapon for future terrorists. The title plays on this duality: made from monetary change, it is also an instrument of change, and, we might add, it names the activity of the artists themselves, which changes an innocuous object into a threatening one. *Change* could be read as a twenty-first-century update of the Situationist practice of *détournement*, the appropriation of objects from the everyday world and their alteration into vehicles of revolutionary action. However *détournement* is also the French term for the hijacking of an airplane, and Claire Fontaine's *Change* acknowledges both connotations of the term, looking back to the 1960s and 9/11. In its attempt to smuggle subversive content in a seemingly innocent guise, it is perhaps an ideal emblem of their practice.

Zachary Formwalt

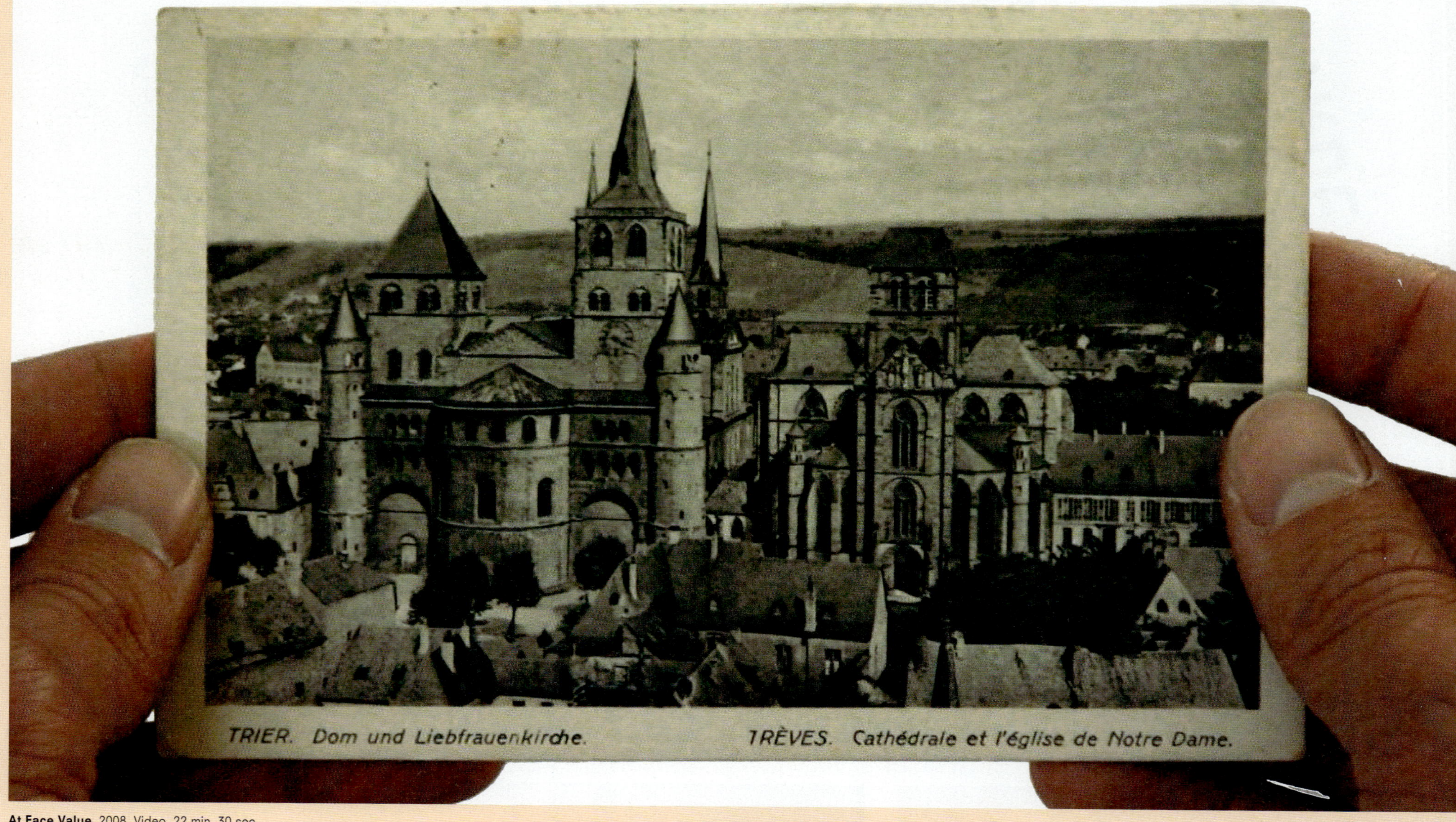

At Face Value, 2008. Video, 22 min. 30 sec.

If art has the capacity to make present what would otherwise remain unnoticed, Zachary Formwalt's work deals with the least visual, most obscure and elusive of processes: the movement of capital.

Formwalt's films and photographs enquire into the nature and origin of still and moving images and their relationship to economic and social history

The unhindered circulation of money between financial markets is one of the basic premises of the global economy and is considered a fundamental freedom in modern democracies. But Formwalt's critical attention to these invisible processes reveals that they are omnipresent forces pervading our everyday lives.

Formwalt's films and photographs enquire into the nature and origin of still and moving images and their relationship to economic and social history. He attempts to capture the immaterial traces of capital and its multitudinous appearances in the material culture of modernity through a focus on specific buildings and documents, objects and iconographic motifs—in short, the presence of capital is recognized in traces that constitute the material culture of modernity. The two major film works that he has made to date are constructed as elaborate visual essays built of sequences filmed in different locations and using a variety of text and image sources that are presented in a matter-of-fact manner, seemingly 'at face value', and supplied with an investigative, critical narrative voiceover.

At Face Value (2008) focuses on a collection of German postage stamps from the 1920s, which illustrate the progress of inflation. The face value of the stamps gets higher and higher in direct correspondence with the unfolding of the economic crisis that took place in Germany a decade before the Great

Obscure and elusive

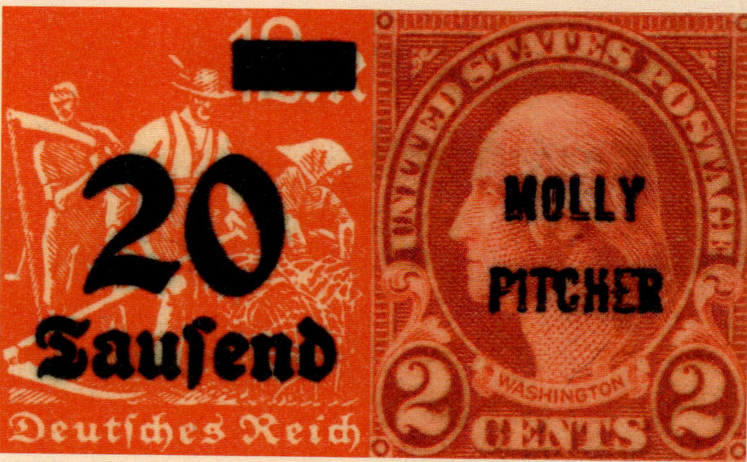

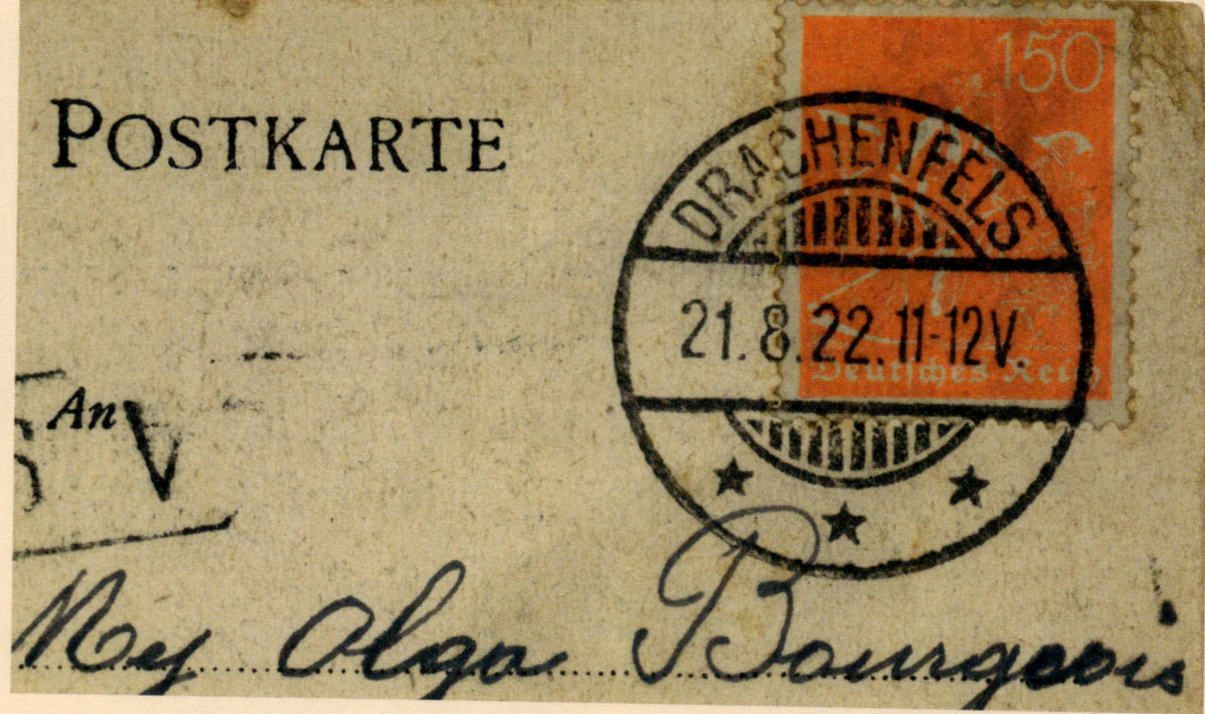

At Face Value, 2008. Production photographs from video

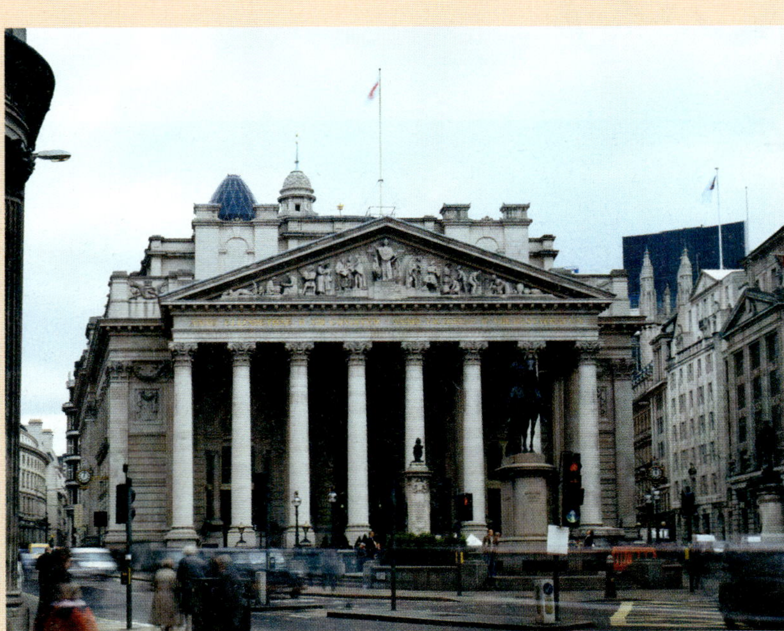

Invisible processes

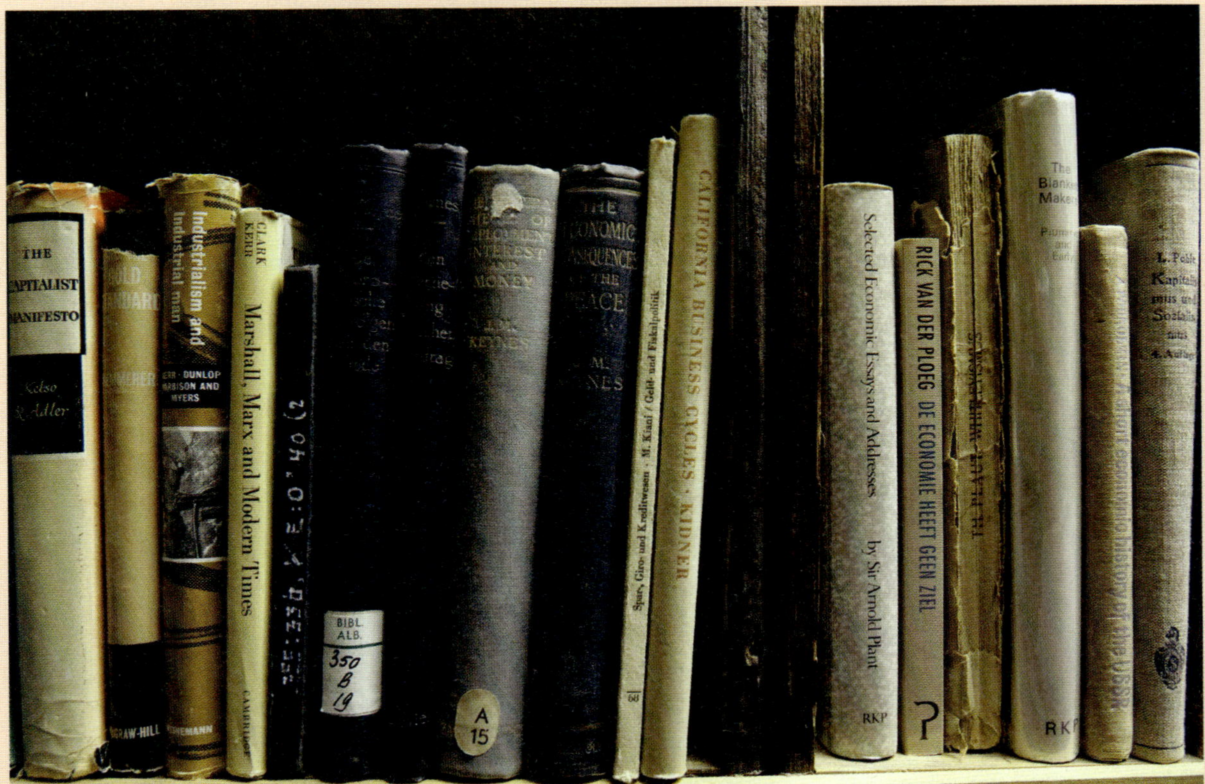

Economic History at the Antiquariat, 2009. Colour photograph. 50 × 34 cm

Traces of capital and its multitudinous appearances in the material culture of modernity

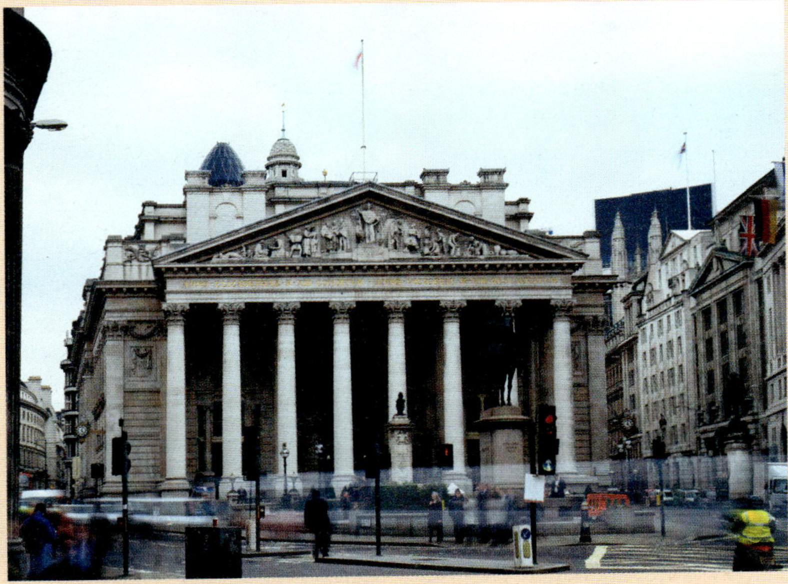

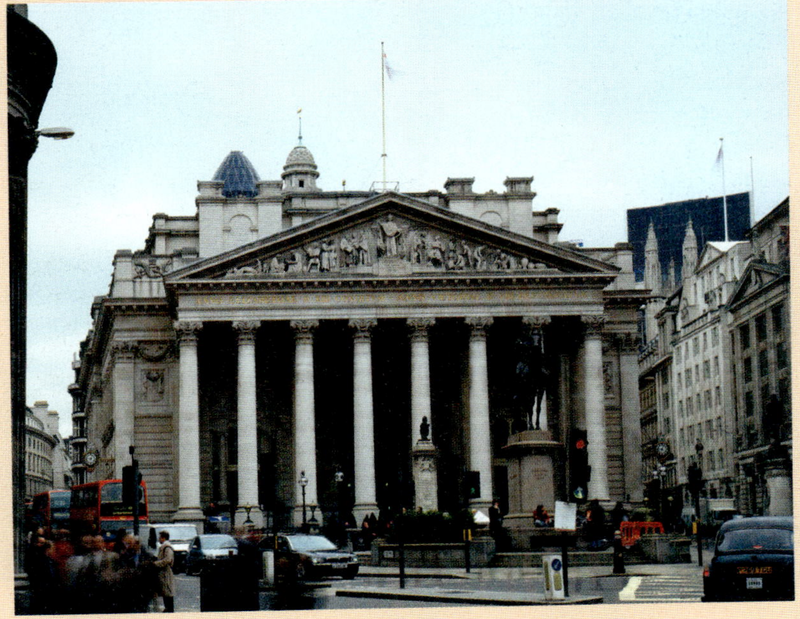

Depression of the early 1930s and the advance of Nazism in Germany. This investigation into symbols that fail adequately to represent real value is further explored in the second film of the ongoing trilogy, *In Place of Capital* (2009). Here, four photographs of the Royal Exchange in London, taken by William Henry Fox Talbot in 1845, after it had been rebuilt in 1844 following a fire, are shown in a sequence that 'animates' them. Due to the long exposure time required, people are not represented in these pictures. This absence, the lack

of human actors in this portrait of the financial institution at the peak of the industrial phase of capitalism, is a telling sign of the ominous work of capital, metaphorically hiding behind the anachronistic classicist facade and felt in the spookily empty square in front of it.

The film is accompanied by a series of four contemporary photographs of the Royal Exchange taken by Formwalt from exactly the same vantage point as Talbot's, with Norman Foster's Gherkin office tower visible behind the temple-like portico.

Formwalt's series of photographs *Economic History at the Antiquariat* (2009) also makes the issue of economy visible as a material thing. It presents frontal views of book spines on the shelves of the economics section in an antiquarian bookshop. Organized alphabetically by author and including both modern and obsolete economic theories, the arrangement is without ideology or hierarchy. Equal value is given to the knowledge contained in all the books—knowledge that is reduced in the shop to a nominal economic value.

The Royal Exchange (after Henry Talbot), 2009. 4 colour photographs. Each 142 × 112 cm

Cyprien Gaillard

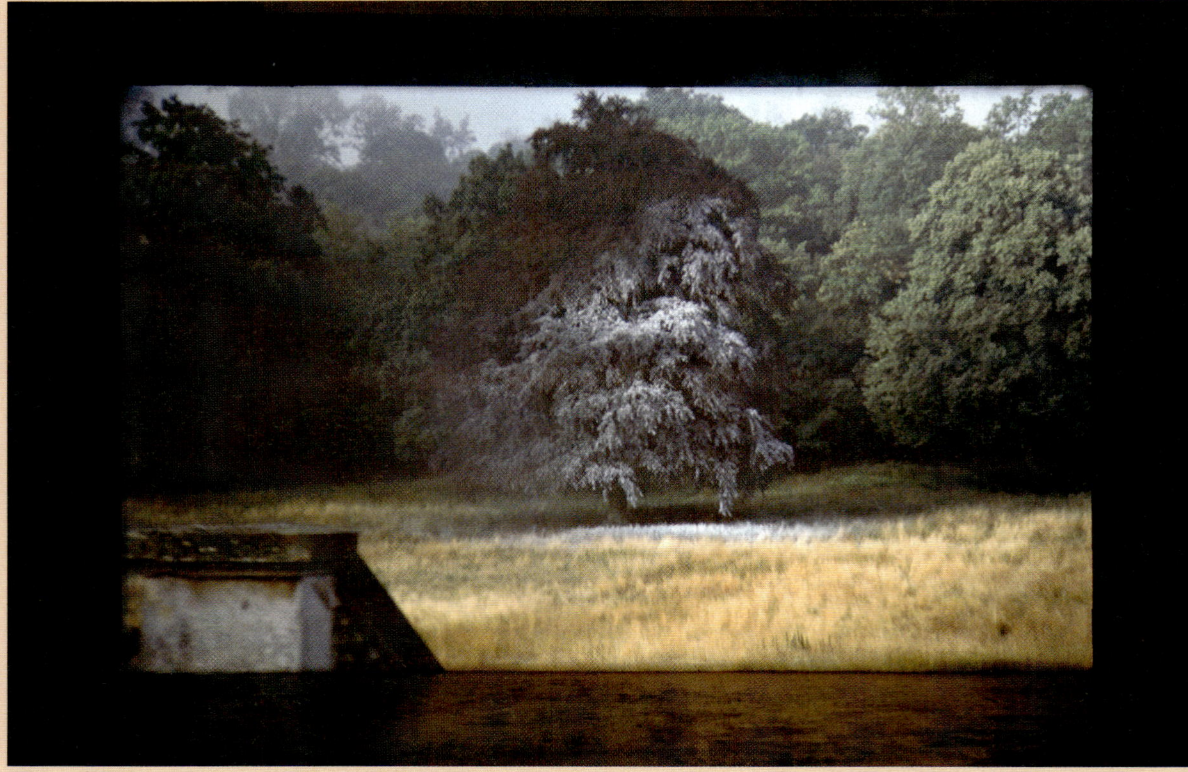

Real Remnants of Fictive Wars (Part V), 2005. 35mm film. 7 min.

Cyprien Gaillard is fascinated by the monuments that link past and present, whether Ancient Egyptian colossi intended to last millennia but then, like the temple Abu Simbel, moved rock by rock to guarantee their preservation, or the concrete high-rise buildings hastily erected in the post-war period and already in the process of decay. His triptych *Desniansky Raion* (2007) opens with the nihilistic spectacle of a violent confrontation between rival gangs in front of a housing complex in Belgrade.

Gaillard cites Robert Smithson's 1966 essay 'Entropy and the New Monuments' as a formative influence on his practice, which grew simultaneously from these archaeological interests and his involvement in hooliganism and graffiti in his youth. 'Instead of causing us to remember the past like the old monuments, the new monuments seem to cause us to forget the future,' Smithson wrote. Since early in this decade, Gaillard has been making images and objects that interrogate, from an abject perspective, the monuments of our built environment in the post-Cold War period, as well as the rituals and narratives that underwrite their mute presence. A recent project for the Hayward Gallery in London involved the making of a Cleopatra's Needle-like monolith from the concrete rubble and detritus of a housing complex in Glasgow whose demolition the artist had witnessed and documented. Rather than occupying a central position, Gaillard's 'new monument' was placed in one of the Southbank

Centre's obscure 'non-spaces': an unusable patch of ground created by the gaps between individual architectural-utopian visions.

While these monuments are fashioned from rubble, found footage and debris, Gaillard's aesthetic is entirely at odds with any ethos of recycling as a progressive activity. His is an ecology of disintegration that results in a form of poetry composed of art objects and actions that provide the material and temporal elements of his oeuvre. This lyric aspect is perhaps what

He stages a collapse of past and future that excavates the archaeology of the present.

distinguishes Gaillard from other Smithson followers, who often view their mentor through an academic lens. In his series *Real Remnants of Fictive Wars* (2004–05), Gaillard created a kind of Land art gesture, effecting the slow obliteration of a sequence of six picturesque landscape views with white vapour from industrial fire extinguishers. One of these actions involved Gaillard and a collaborator effectively vandalizing the site of Smithson's *Spiral Jetty*. A highly provocative acknowledgement of a revered artist's influence, the gesture simultaneously honoured and aggressively erased evidence of Smithson's legacy.

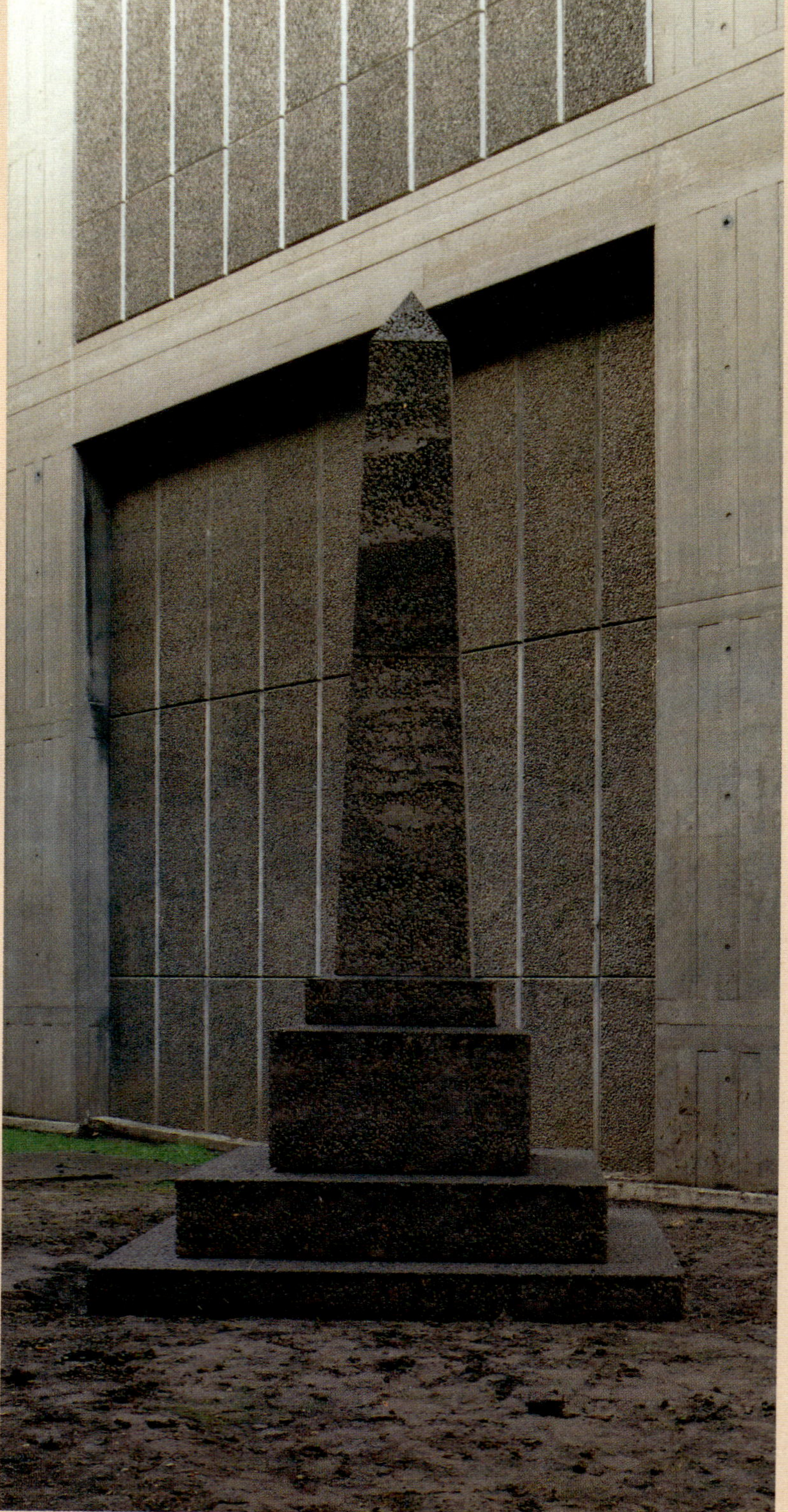

Cenotaph to 12 Riverford Road, Pollockshaws, Glasgow, 2008. Recycled concrete and building detritus from demolished housing estate, cement, steel frame. 4 × 2 × 2 m

Past and present

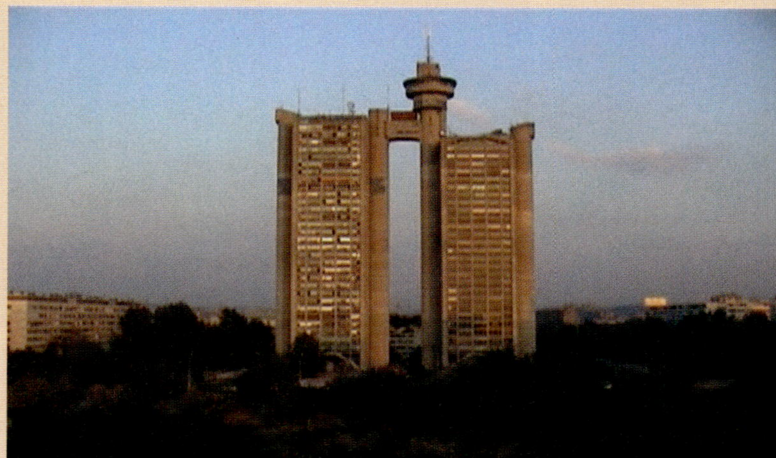

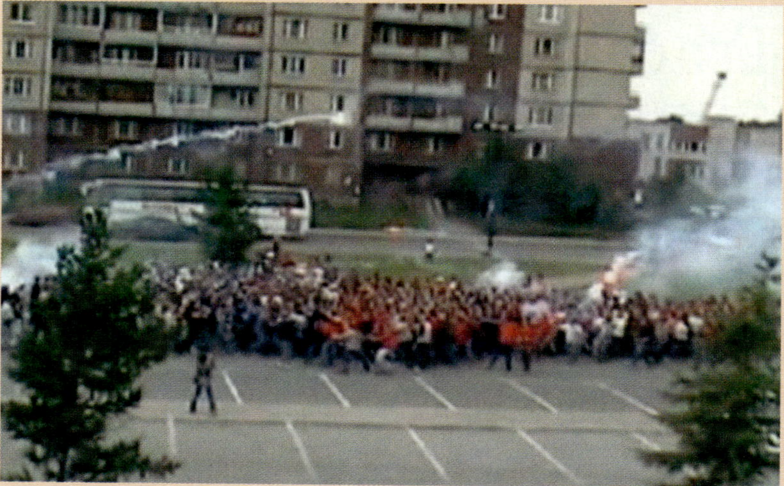

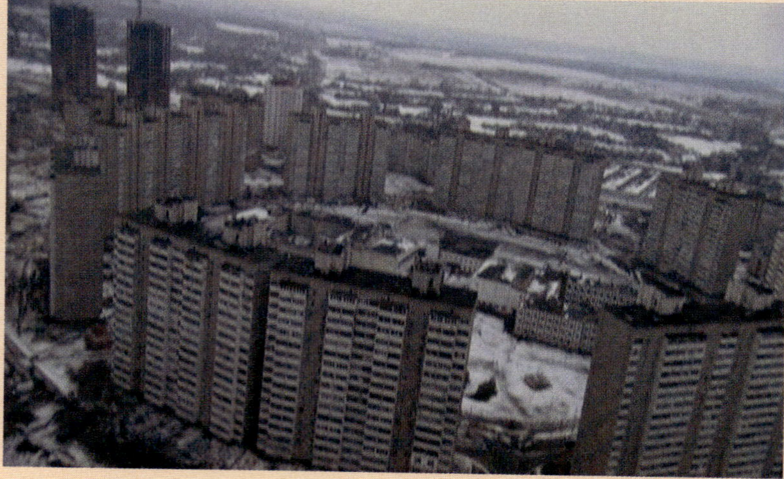

Desniansky Raion, 2007. Video. 29 min.

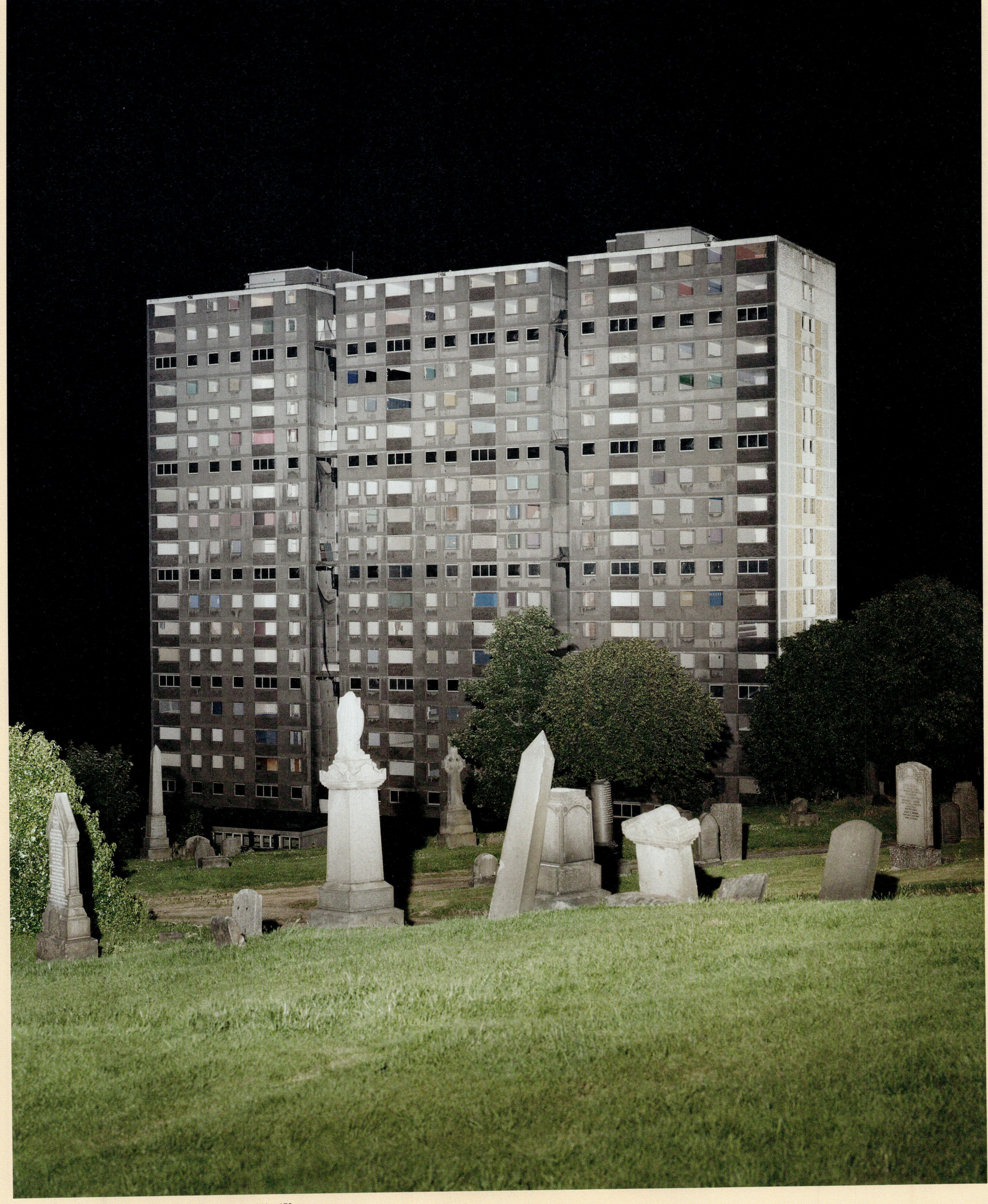

View of Sighthill Cemetery, 2008. C–print mounted to Diasec. 211 × 170 cm

Gaillard's obsession with the concrete 'ruins' of the present and their transmutation — like his parallel preoccupations with the eighteenth-century follies of Romantic landscapes and with the graveyard depicted in *Cairns* (2007) — is perhaps a fascination with marking out indicators of human transience. However, he sets an understanding of that transience in tension with our desire to make things. Recent history, after all, has been characterized by grand narratives of man-made destruction on a mass scale. But Gaillard explores grand attempts at 'relational' counternarratives — from urban planning to communal festivals to public sculptures. In investigating these moments of human agency, he stages a collapse of past and future that excavates the archaeology of the present.

Mario Garcia Torres

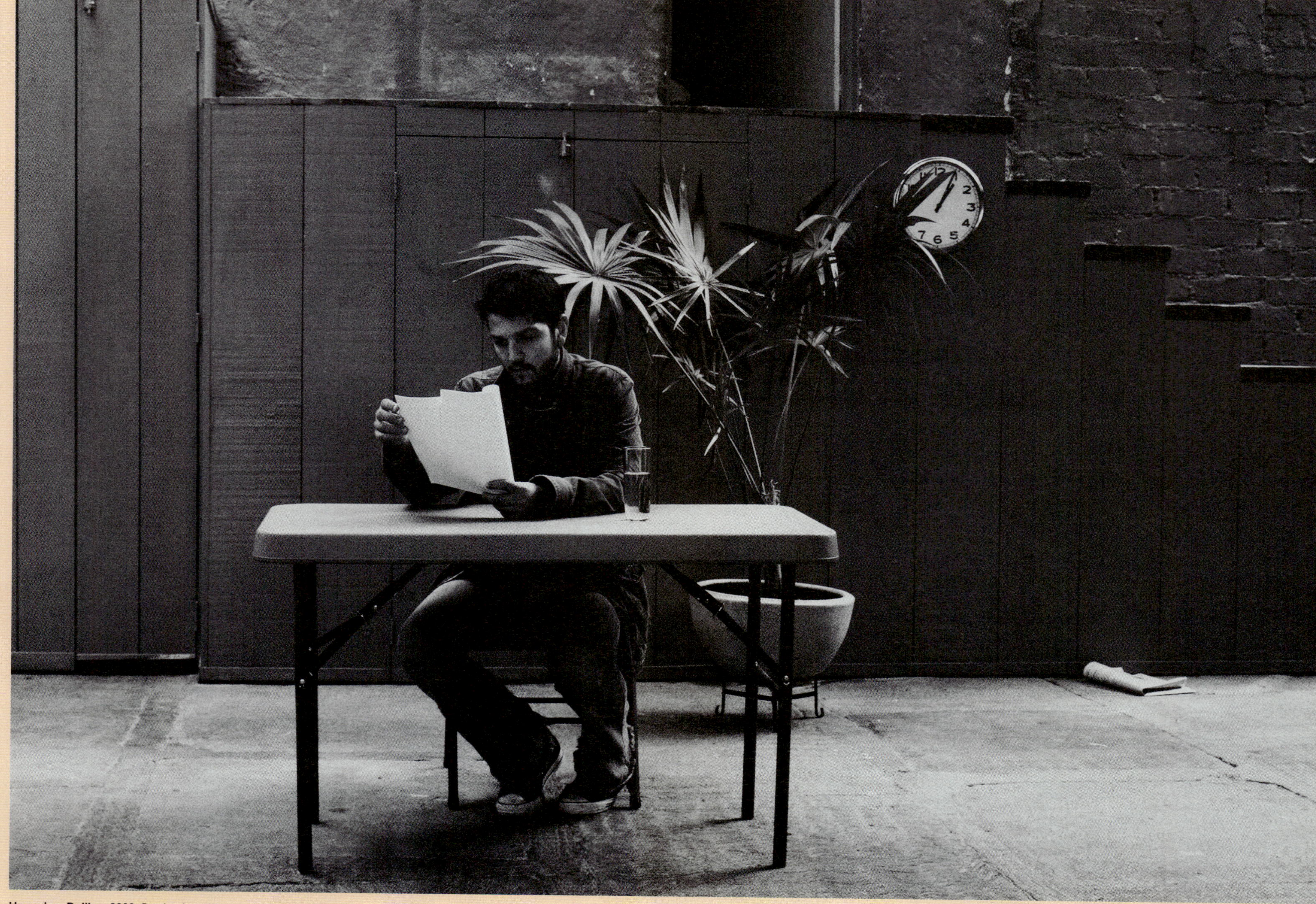

Unspoken Dailies, 2009. Production photograph from a black and white 16mm film. 64 min.

I Promise… , 2004–present. Ink on hotel letterhead paper. A4

Unspoken and forgotten

Mario Garcia Torres's medium is the history of Conceptual art. He revisits projects by artists such as David Askevold, Alighiero Boetti, Daniel Buren, Martin Kippenberger, Robert Morris and Ed Ruscha, remaking them as part of his own history. In this way he attempts to create new, more emotional narratives from his frequently laconic source material, narratives that often investigate contemporary political and social issues.

For example, the photographic documentation of *Today… (News from Kabul)* (2006) shows the artist with his back to us and his body pressed against a wall, his arms fully stretched out as he writes with pencils held in each hand. His action directly quotes Boetti's *Oggi è venerdì ventisette marzo millenovecentosettanta (Today is Friday the nineteenth of March nineteen seventy)*, (1970), a phrase that he wrote on the wall in both regular and mirrored script. Each time Garcia Torres makes his version, he writes a phrase taken from the day's news stories on Kabul, a place that Boetti visited repeatedly. The work has been shown several times since 2006, and Garcia Torres has commented on how the simple action emphasizes the continuing devastation in Afghanistan.

This time-bound performance is prefigured in a work of 2004 in which, following in the footsteps of the artists who have drawn and written on hotel stationery, Garcia Torres began a long-term diaristic project, *I promise…* Each time he stays in a hotel, he writes on its letterhead, 'I promise to do my best as an artist for the next…', followed by a period of time whose length depends on his current mood, before signing and dating it and posting it to the collector who owns the series of works.

Whereas better-known slide works, such as *What Happens in Halifax Stays in Halifax (In 36 slides)* (2004–06) and *What Doesn't Kill You Makes You Stronger* (2007), explore projects by Askevold and Kippenberger, respectively, Garcia Torres's ongoing series *This Painting is Missing / This Painting Has Been Found*, begun in 2006, documents through oil-on-canvas stand-ins the paintings in Ruscha's oeuvre that have been lost and subsequently found.

Set in Mexico City and shot in real time, the film *Unspoken Dailies* (2009) studies actor Diego Luna as he reads a text to himself that the artist wrote for a conference about silence, the unsaid and forgotten in a work of art. At once a portrait of Mexico City and an extended screen test of the actor, the film is also a manifesto for Garcia Torres himself, an artist who has produced a continually surprising and rich body of work from the unspoken and forgotten histories of the recent past.

This Painting Has Been Found, 2006–09. Acrylic on canvas. Number of elements and dimensions variable

Time-bound performance

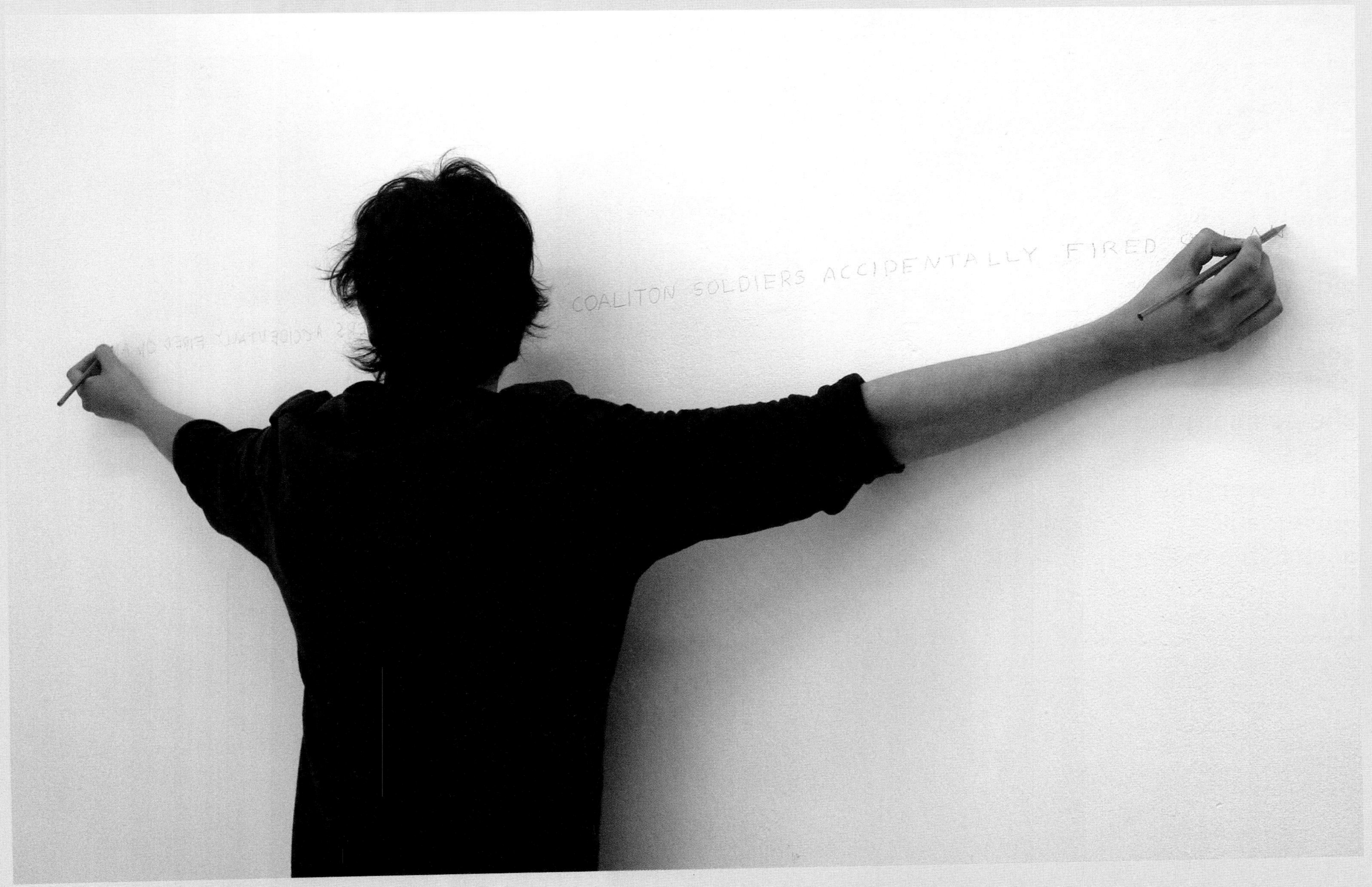

Today (News from Kabul), 2004. Graphite on wall. Approx. 4 × 156 cm

Shilpa Gupta

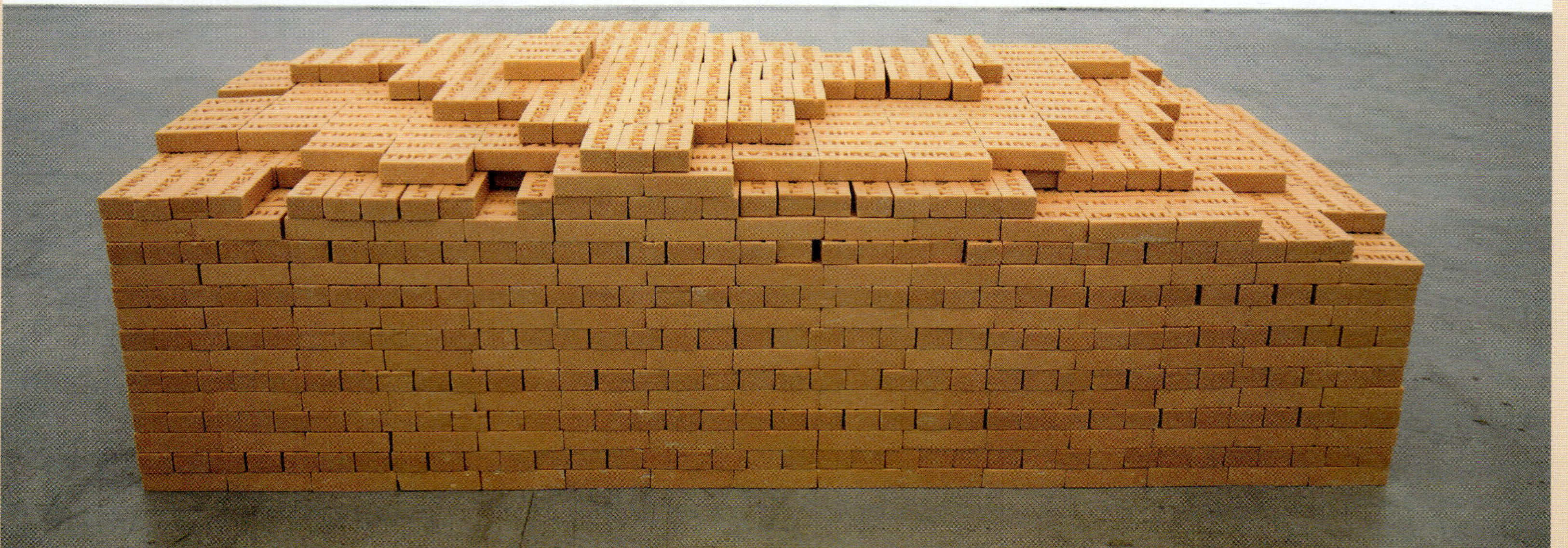

Threat, 2009. 4500 bars of embossed body soap. 72 × 224 × 104 cm

Shilpa Gupta focuses on complex and difficult issues — religion, nation, notions of security and freedom in the realm of global connectivity — with which we are compelled to engage in today's strife-torn world. Through a variety of formats, including video, installation, photography, sound and public performance, Gupta positions her practice in the universally accessible realm of the everday — the lives and lifestyles of ordinary people. To achieve this, she makes use of the technologies that offer people shared platforms. Participation and interactivity are indispensable to any discussion of her work.

Untitled (Shadow) (2006–07) is a series of video installations featuring interactive devices. The silhouette of the visitor on a grey screen, captured on live camera, engages in a mutually responsive manner with a variety of other figures and objects projected on to the screen.

Such play with silhouettes may be fun, but the shadows, with their connotations of the dark and spectral, hint at a more disturbing side. Appearing, then forming pairs with their real-life counterparts, they are an anonymous presence that undermines the uniqeness of the individual. Standing before the work, viewers are drawn into the images on screen regardless of their

Through a variety of formats, including video, installation, photography, sound and public performance, she positions her practice in the everyday, universally accessible realm

wishes; their translation into shadows is analogous to the state of unavoidable involvement in religious and ethnic conflicts.

There Is No Explosive in This (2007) encourages participation in public spaces. People are invited to take a white-covered suitcase or a bag, printed with the words of the title, from a flat in London, and carry it with them along their usual route. Gupta later asks them what

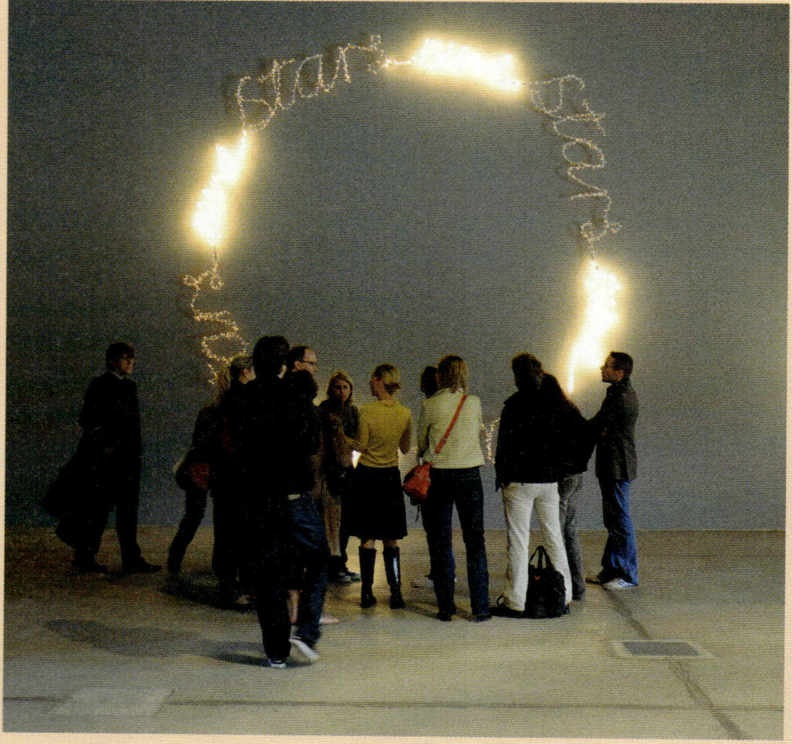

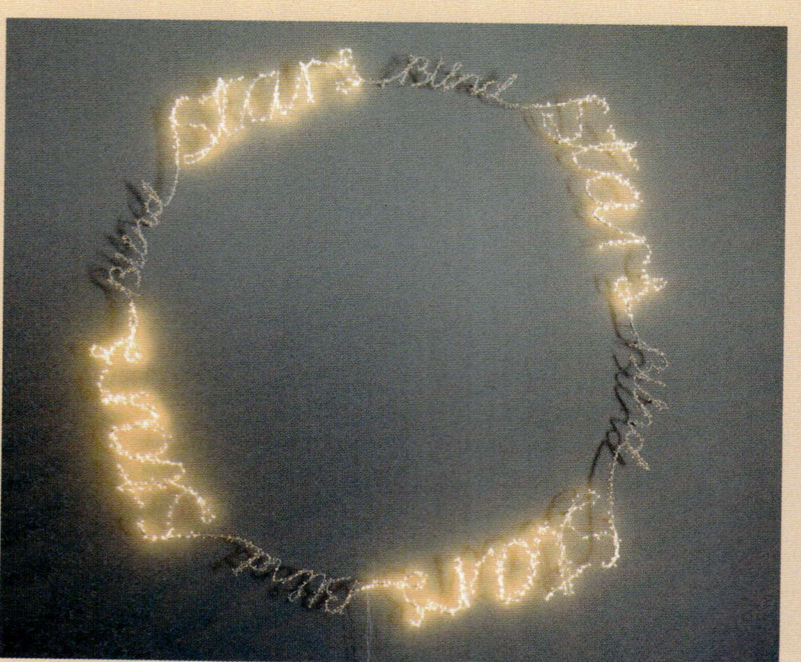

Blind Stars Stars Blind, 2008. Installation with lights. Diameter 457 cm

Particpation and interactivity

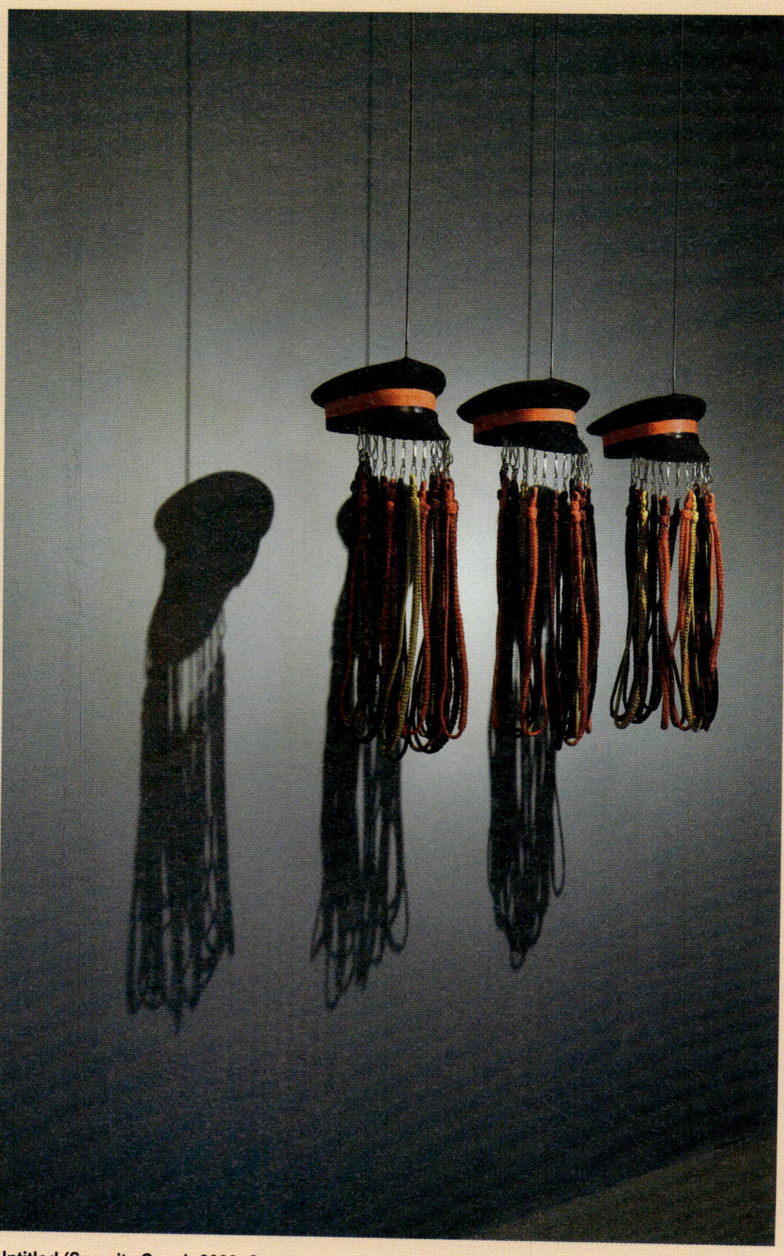

Untitled (Security Caps), 2008. Set of 3 security caps with lanyards. 64 × 30 × 23 cm

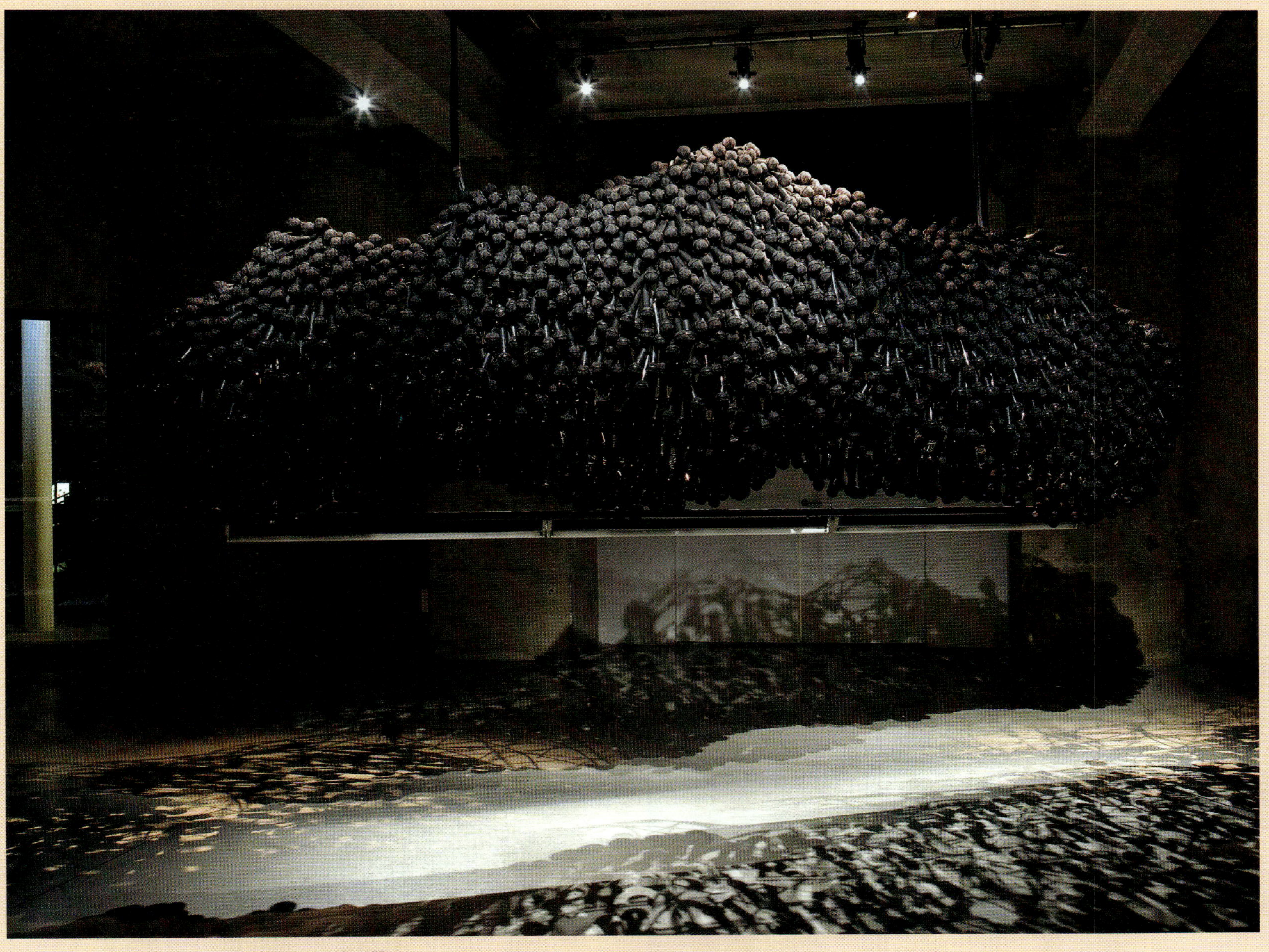

Singing Cloud, 2008–09. Microphones and sound. 400 × 150 cm

they have experienced. Amid today's heightened fear of terrorist activity, everyday acts such as going to cafés, standing at bus stops and travelling on the Tube invite suspicion and generate tension between the carrier of the bag and people on the streets. Using such guerilla-type tactics, Gupta shakes up concepts of security in everyday life, at the same time posing questions about the significance and function of the activity that we call art.

Gupta's recent works comment on the conflict between India and Pakistan over Kashmir, stimulating memory both visually and aurally. *Tryst with Destiny* (2007–08) consists of old-fashioned microphones that seesaw on a stand, emitting speeches made in 1947 on the occasion of independence by Jawaharlal Nehru, India's first prime minister, and founder of Pakistan Muhammad Ali Jinnah. Drawing out collective memory, the words of each turn the listener's thoughts to a conflict that remains unresolved today. Gupta's intellectual, conceptual experiment in combining the visual presence of an object and the universal nature of the media lends a voice to a situation that cannot speak for itself.

Stimulating memory

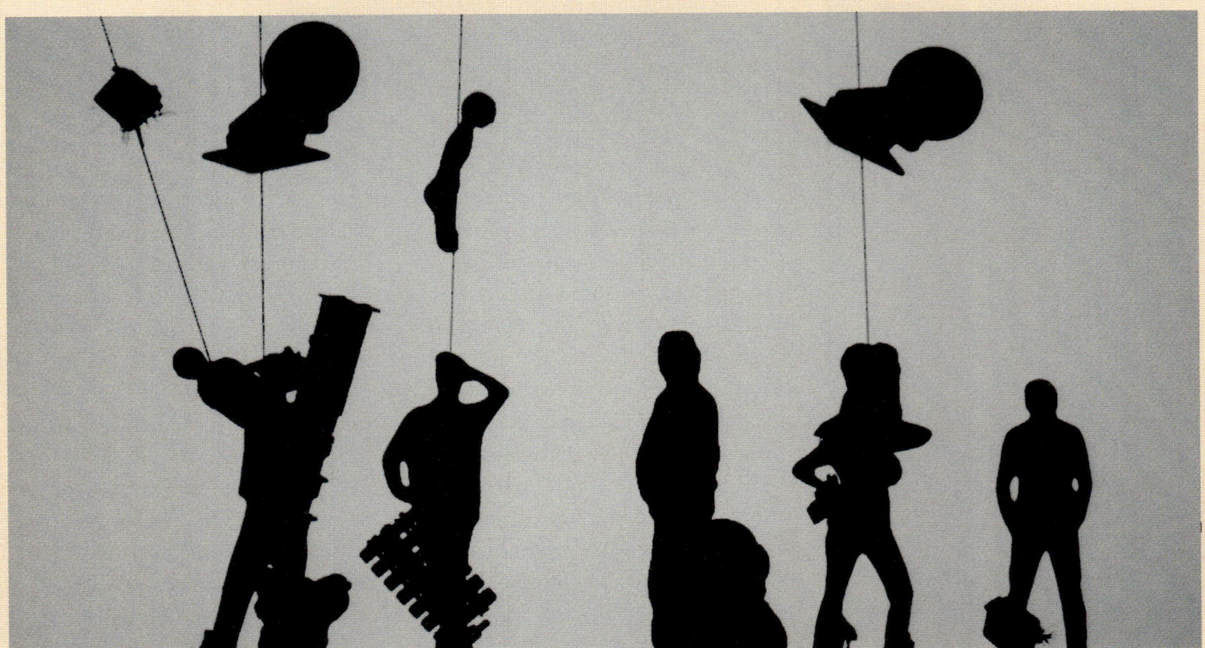

Untitled (Shadow), 2006–07. Interactive video projection. Dimensions variable

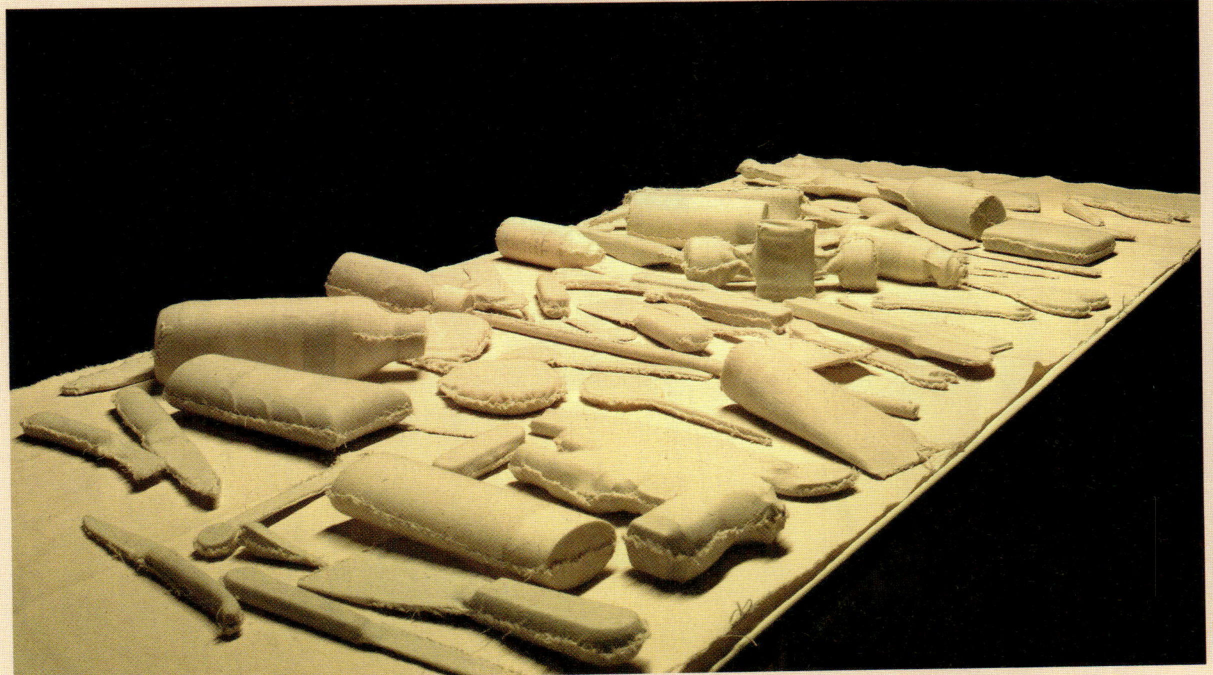

There is no Explosive in this Table II, 2007. 67 confiscated objects from international airports covered with white fabric. 103 × 160 × 65 cm

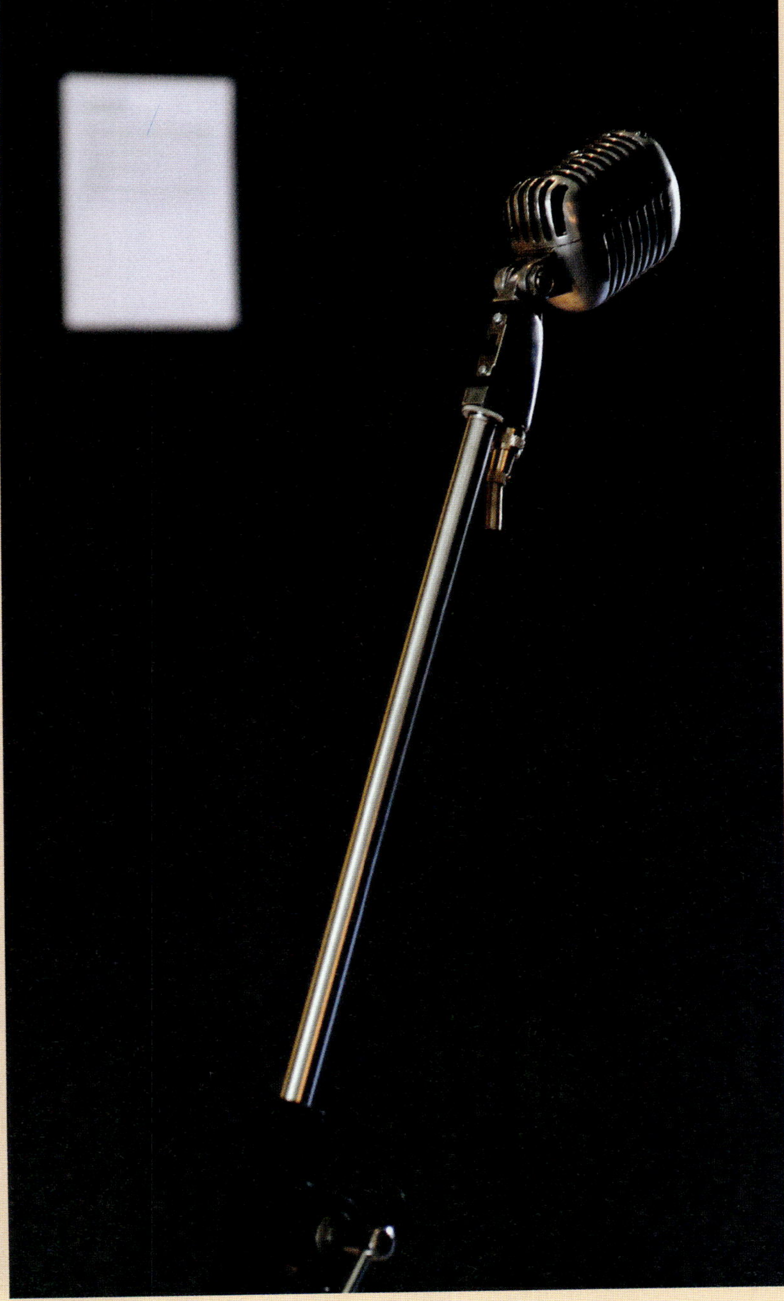

Tryst with Destiny, 2008. Microphone, stand, sound. Dimensions variable

Lasse Schmidt Hansen

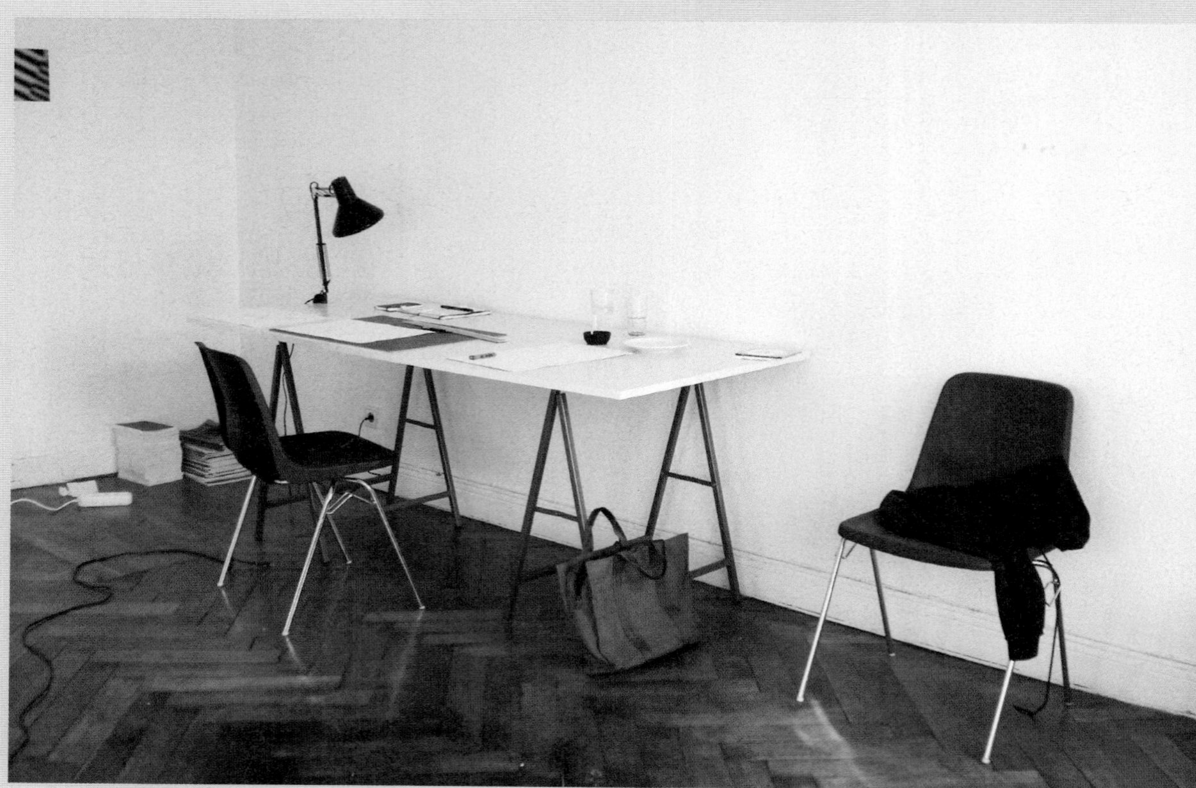

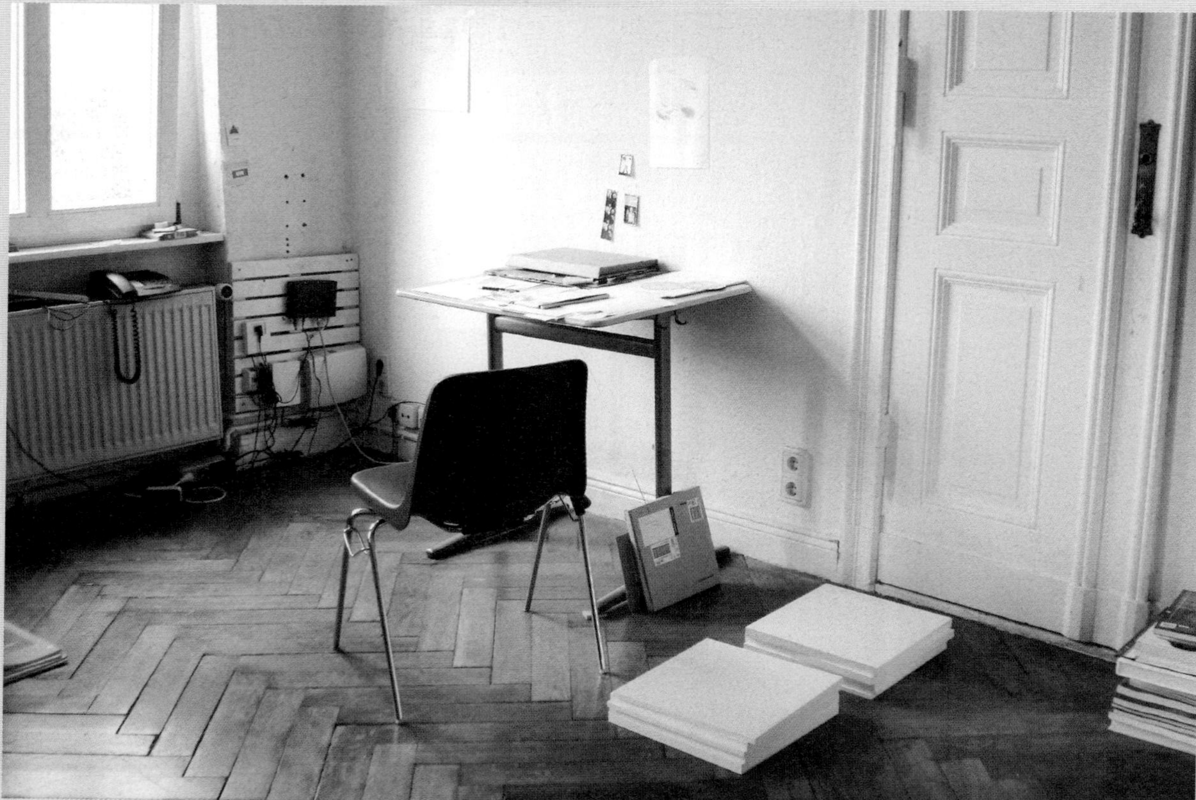

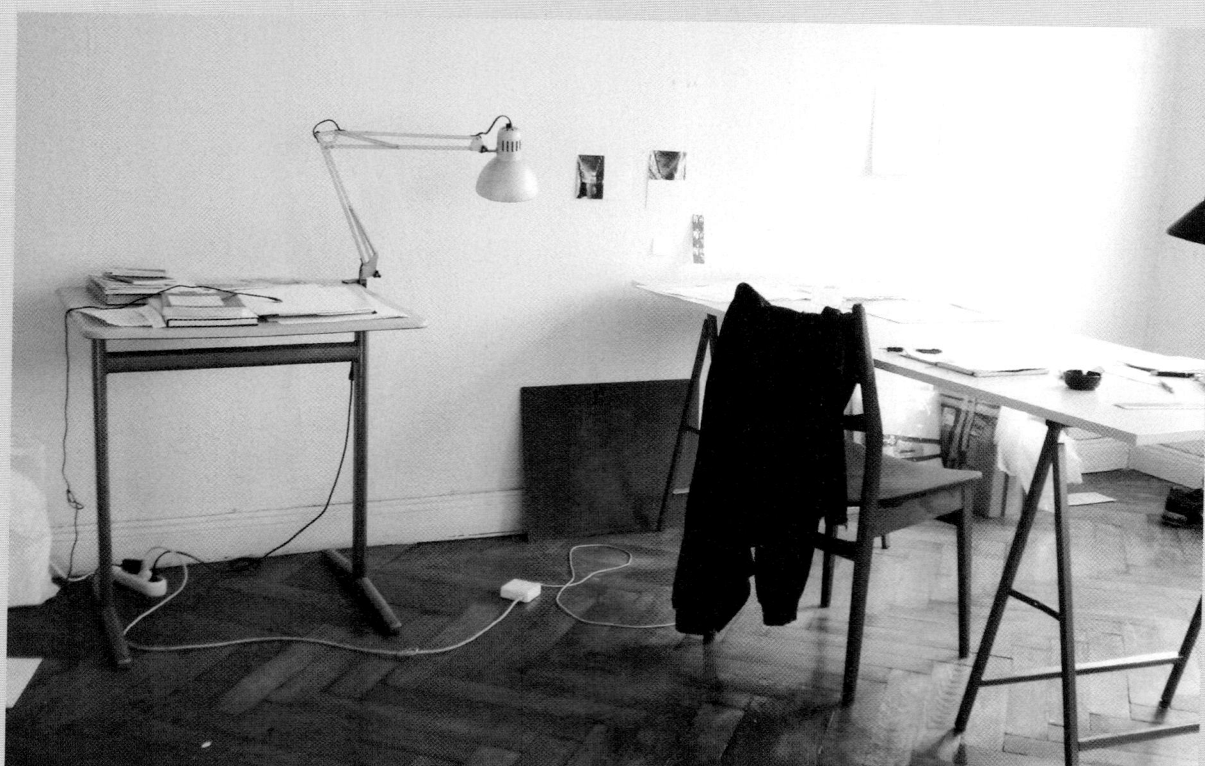

Making Things, 2009. 3 black and white photographs. 3 parts. Each 15 × 25 cm

Lasse Schmidt Hansen's materials comprise the various commonplace objects and elements that shape our world. At first sight, his works suggest an interest in design objects and the way in which they are displayed. Indeed, they do offer an interesting insight into how objects create or dismantle our notion of the space intended for their viewing and interpretation. But Hansen has no rigid formula for the exhibition of his works; even if they are three-dimensional, they are never presented as an installation, and he contests the spectrum of familiar design solutions, referring to the installation only through its absence.

In works such as his series of photographs *Piled up stuff photographed from the front, back, right and left but not necessarily in that order* (2007), objects are reduced to materials for artistic research. Here, stacks of folders, envelopes, papers — quotidian piles that everyone has on their desk — are scrutinized from various angles, none of which reveal their textual content. By composing an image that represents nothing in particular, he revokes the notion of the artwork as an artefact.

855, 3 × 238, 8 × 39, 2 × 110, 2 × 105, 2 × 522, 1 × 29, 2 × 110, 6 × 15 × 54, 2 × 226 (2007) is a nondescript light grey carpet cut to the original floor plan of the gallery floor on which it is laid. In *Uro* (2006), the artist hung white vertical blinds from the ceiling, but by eliminating the standard system by which they are all made to turn in the same direction, he causes them to float freely in the space. In both works he emphasizes the uneventful, the unexceptional and the colourless, showing how these are important elements in understanding the nature of objects and, by extension, the subjects who use them.

The discretion and fragility of Hansen's works radically oppose the bold desire for experimentation that has been crucial in modern times. The artist replaces the dramatic gestures of a self-confident modernist language with one that proposes in a quivering voice the possibility of a formal and aesthetic twist. In this way, Hansen suggests a new way to study our relationship with the production of modern culture and reveals how a combination of the intuitive, the practical and the reflective can produce different tools for the analysis of the real. His work brings theoretical and practical concerns into play through a frail choreography of minimal gestures and interventions, whereby he imports external dialects and styles into his own artistic language to highlight their almost imperceptible differences. Freeing his work from the

Every work he creates is completely different, devoid of any subjective style

phantoms of identity, every work he creates is completely different, devoid of any subjective style. However, what could be perceived as a cold or remote sensibility is neutralized by the delicacy and fragility of the works. The main quality of life — not the life of an individual, but of life itself — is that it is feeble and continually being altered without our noticing it. The objects and the images that Hansen creates are preoccupied with how life is sustained by a logic that surpasses the biographical aspects of the everyday; he makes an effort to capture the vast number of non-events that compose reality.

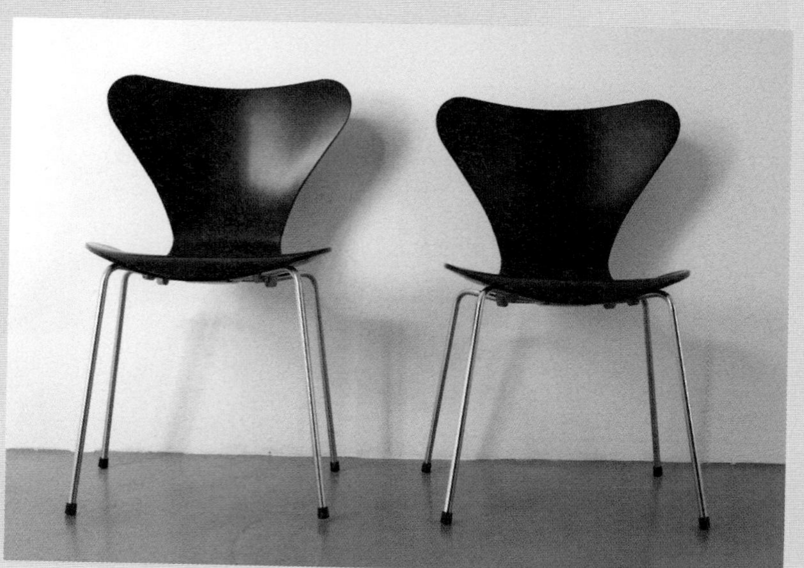

3107/3107, 2008. Painted wood, metal, rubber, plastic. Approx. 85 × 120 × 50 cm

Piled up stuff
photographed from the front, back, right and left but not necessarily in that order

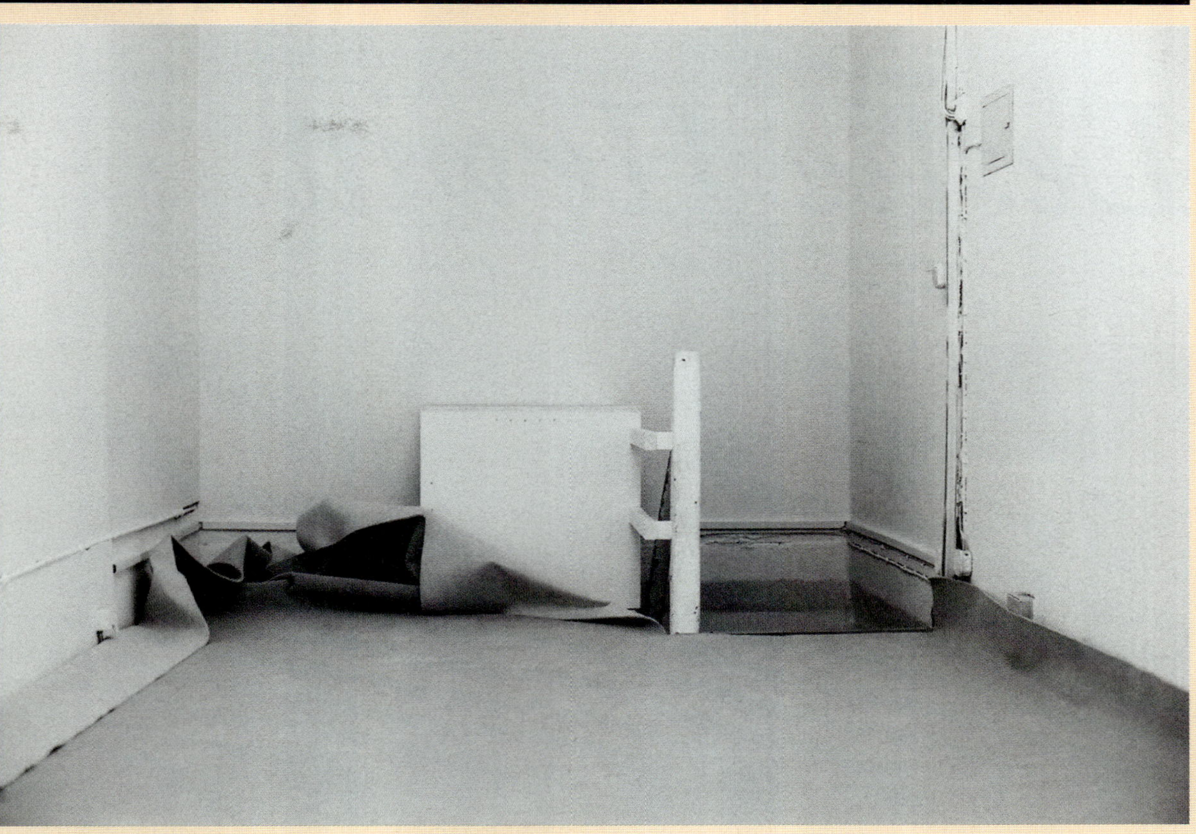

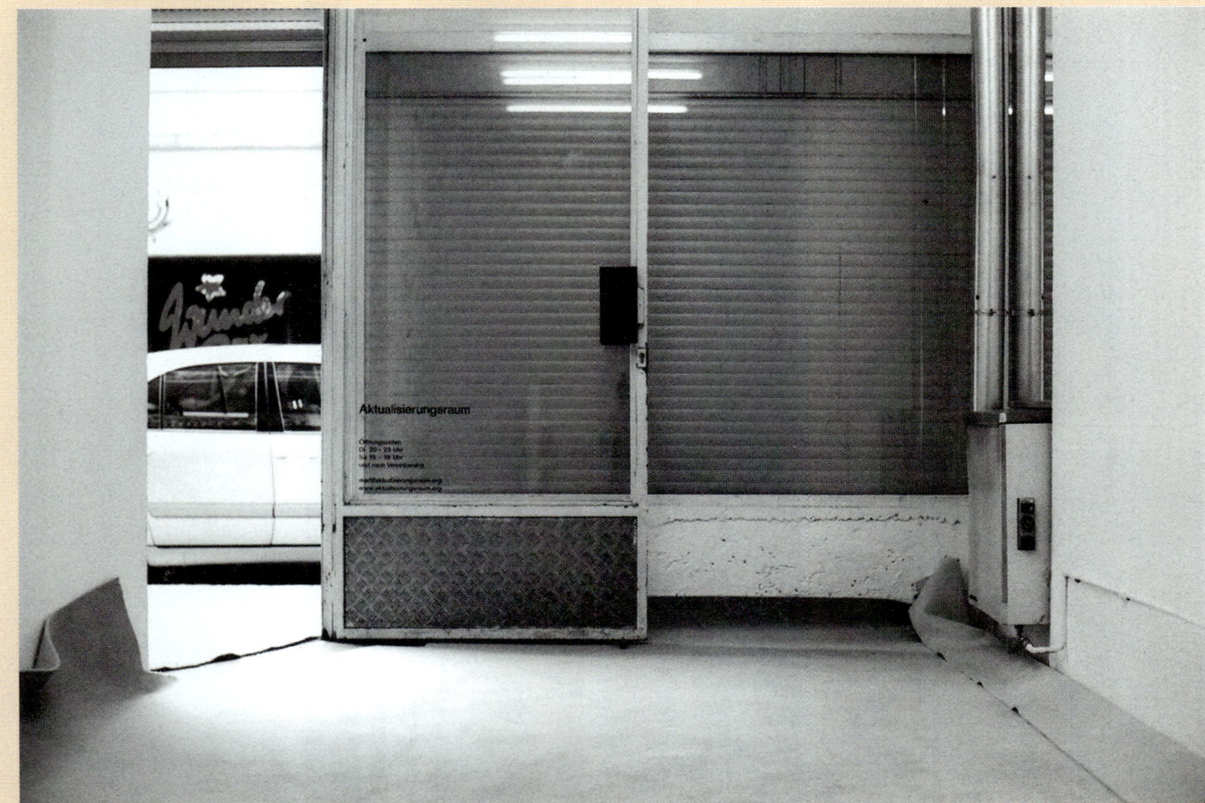

855, 3 × 238, 8 × 39, 2 × 110, 2 × 105, 2 × 522, 1 × 29, 2 × 110, 6 × 15 × 54, 2 × 226, 3, 2007. Carpet. 855 × 454 cm

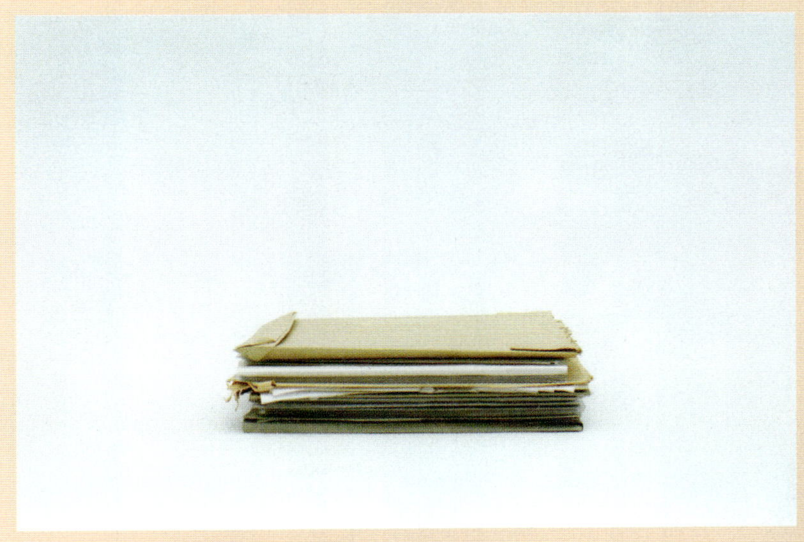

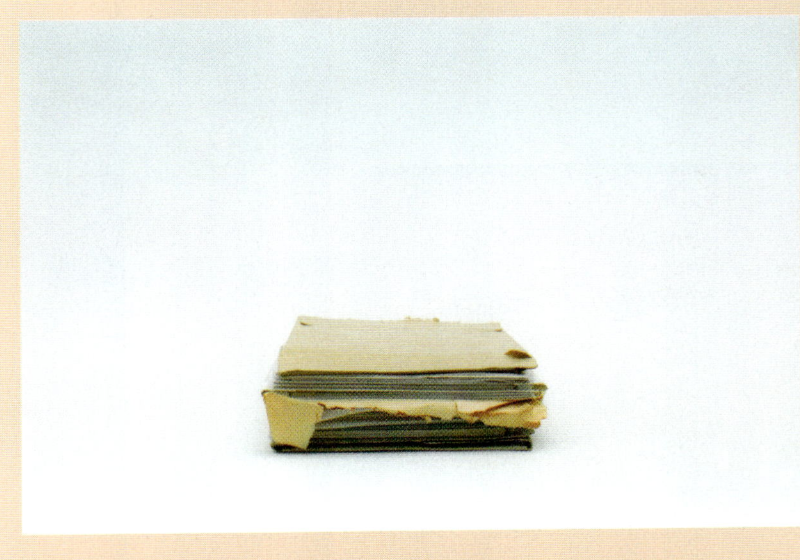

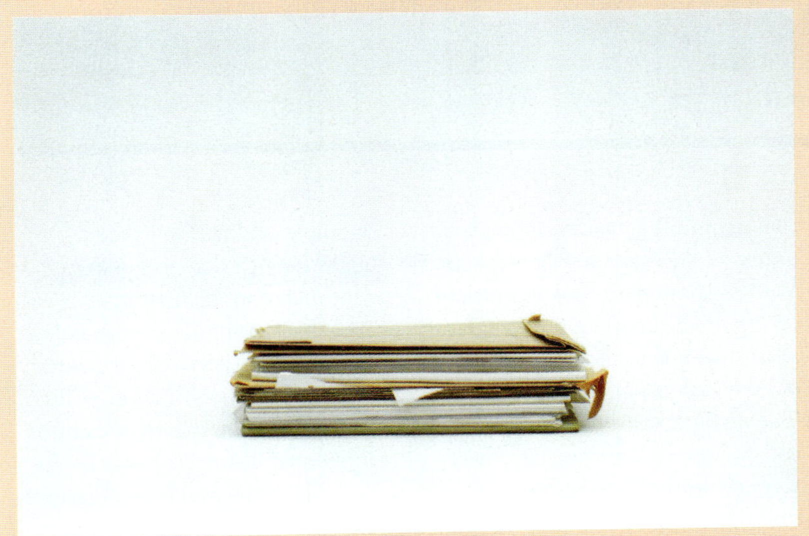

Piled up stuff photographed from the front, back, right and left but not necessarily in that order
2007. 4 C–prints. Each 20 × 30 cm

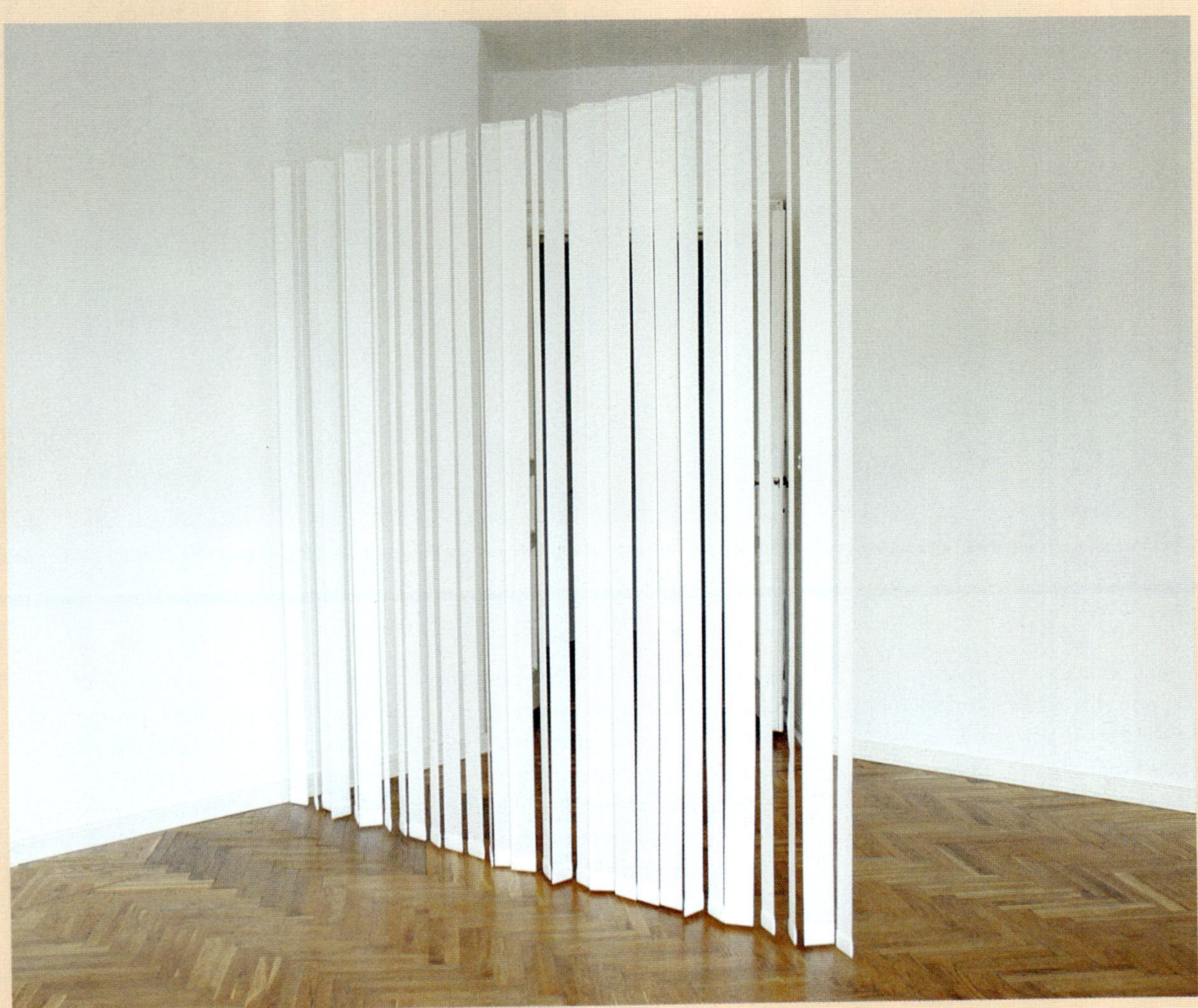

Uro, 2006. Vertical blinds, thread. Approx. 260 × 320 × 10 cm

Leslie Hewitt

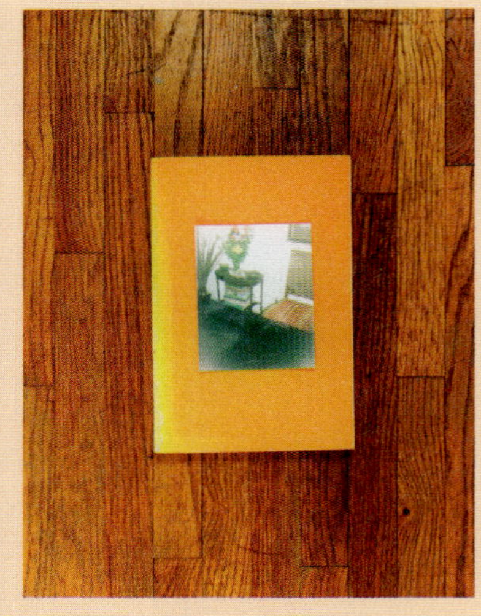
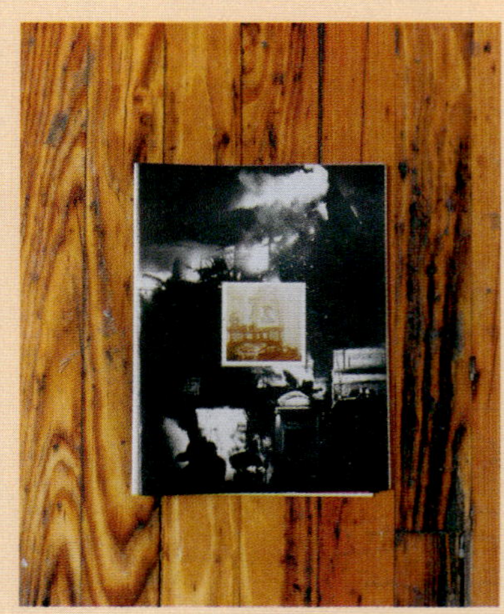
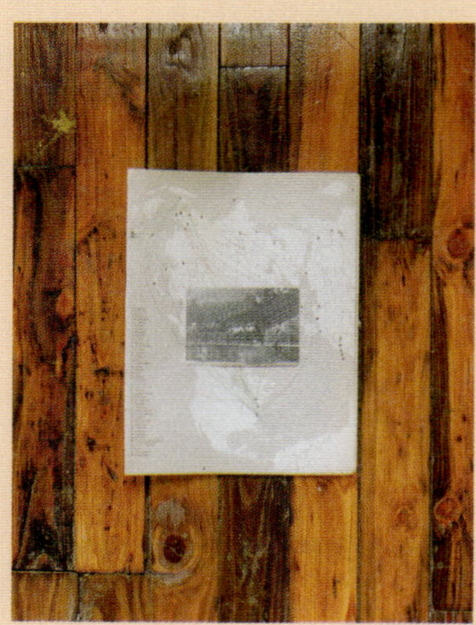
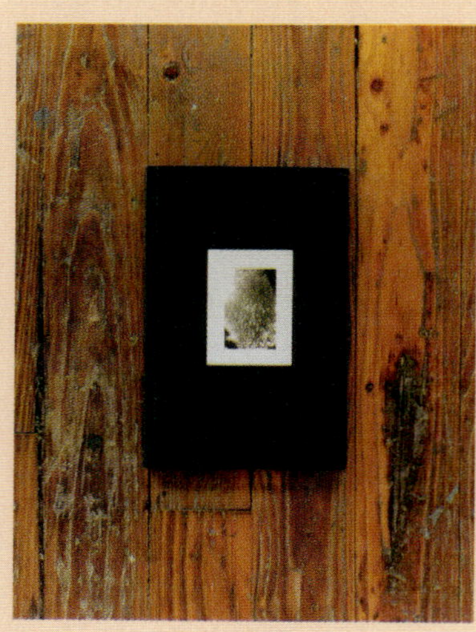

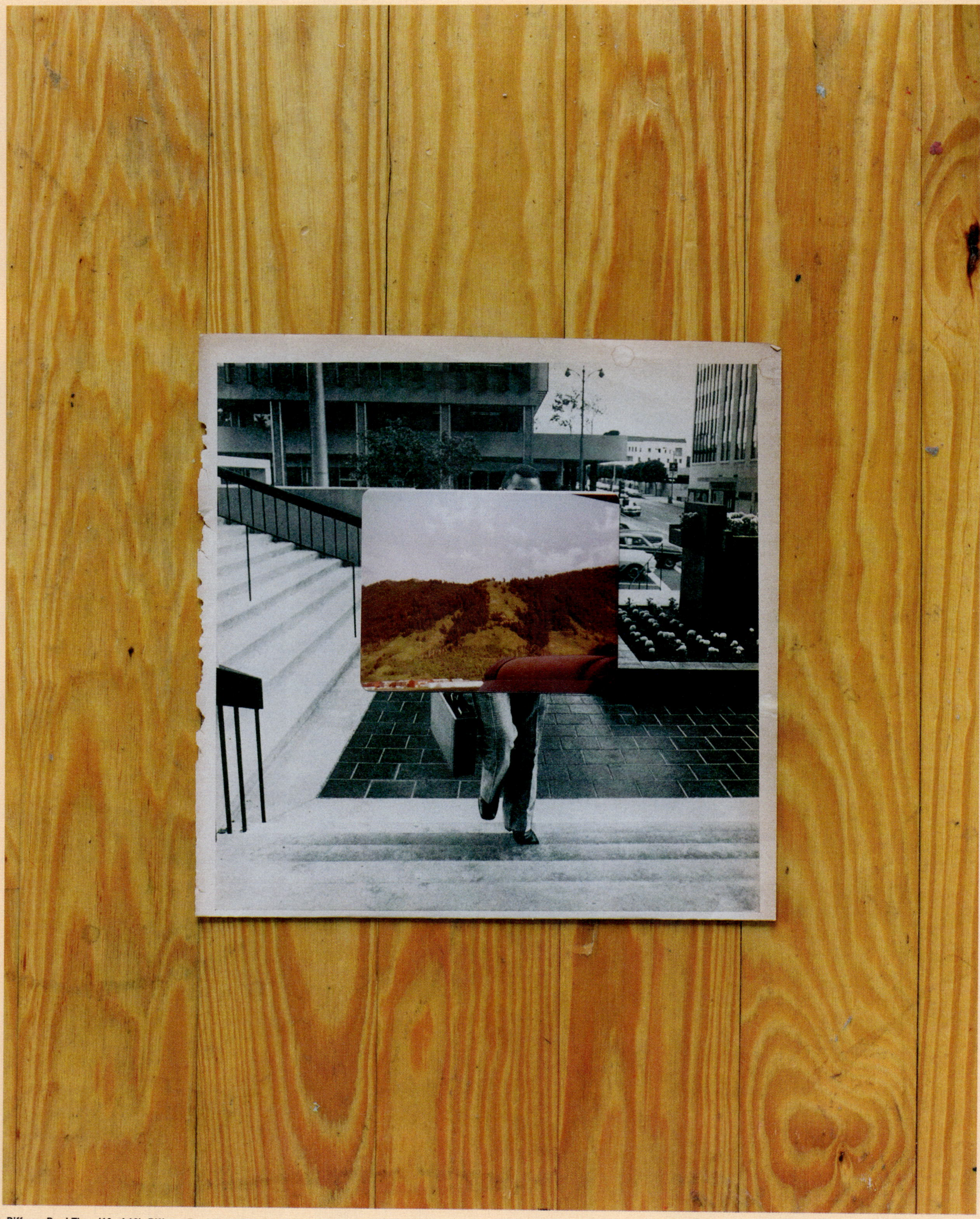

Clockwise from top left: **Riffs on Real Time (1 of 10)**, **Riffs on Real Time (10 of 10)**, **Riffs on Real Time (8 of 10)**, **Riffs on Real Time (7 of 10)**, **Riffs on Real Time (2 of 10)**, 2008. C–prints. Each 102 × 76 cm

In her photographs, photo-sculptural works and installations, Leslie Hewitt reformulates extant materials to tell new stories that draw on the power of individual circumstance and suggest broader collective narratives. Versions of the past are at the heart of her investigations, specifically those relating to African-American history of the 1960s and 1970s, an era filled with a sense of optimism for social change. Embracing photography as a generative rather than a reflective force, Hewitt examines the potential and limits of photographic representation, questioning its critical functions and our expectations of the camera.

Perhaps Hewitt's best-known series to date is *Riffs on Real Time* (2002–05). It was created through her signature style of re-photography. Each photograph was made by carefully layering images — ranging from photographs depicting American landscapes to found family snapshots to book and magazine covers relating to mainstream American culture generally and specifically black culture to texts and press images highlighting civil rights history and socio-political unrest to old school notebook pages. Various combinations were stacked on top of one another, presented against simple backdrops of old wood floors or shag carpets. The final photographs of these collage-assemblages are extremely formal compositions with a distinctly intimate sensibility. Each photograph seems to contain a whole world within it: the suggestion of a domestic setting, as intimated in the floor or carpet background, the personal or individual perspective represented in family snapshots or hand-written scribbles, and the collective realm as represented by magazines or books.

In this way, Hewitt disrupts the visual conventions of mass media through her more personal

Optimism for social Change

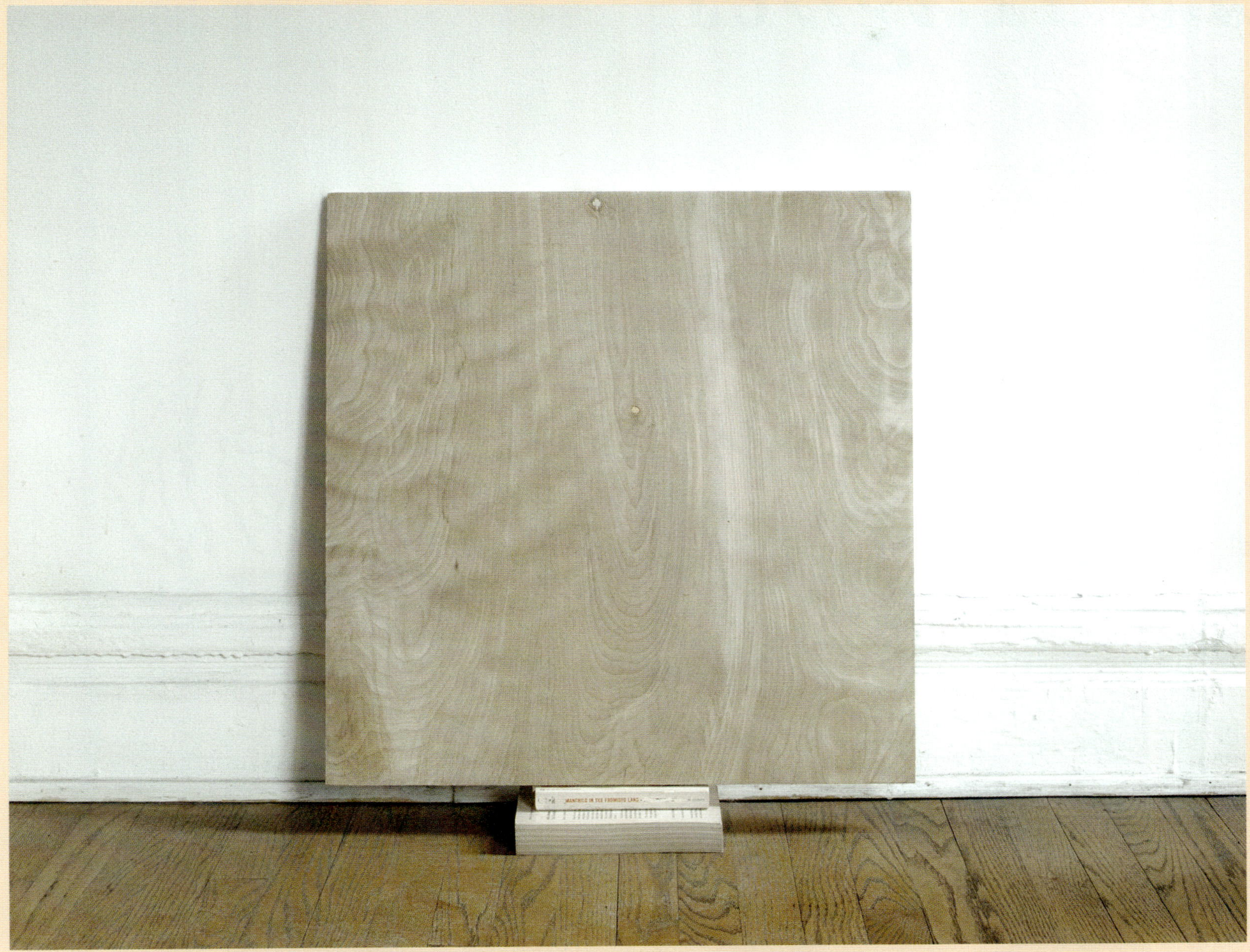

Untitled (Hours) (detail), 2009. Digital C–print in custom maple wood frame. 134 × 159 × 13 cm

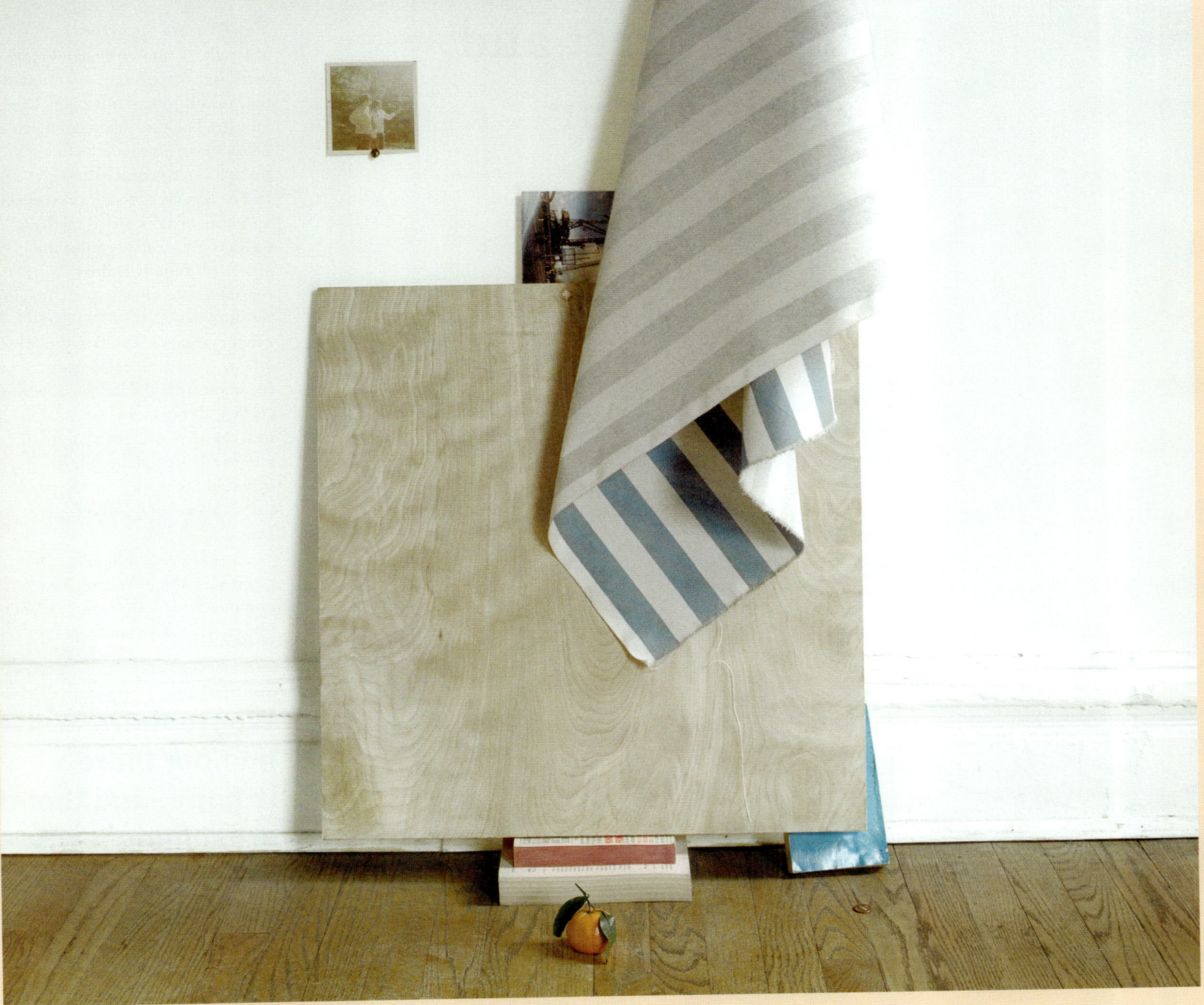

Untitled (Seems To Be Necessary) (detail), 2009. Digital C–print in custom maple wood frame. 134 × 159 × 13 cm

perspectives, which are closer to a family album.

Layering ephemera of the past, Hewitt creates a palimpsest that invites viewers to create their own narratives by projecting their personal associations on to seemingly familiar images. Her technique alludes to the unreliability of memory, to a non-linear approach to the passage of time and to how fragments can build on each other in non-sequential ways to generate many different stories.

Make It Plain (2006) is a series of large-scale photographs that instead of conventionally hanging on the walls, are exhibited on the floor, leaning against gallery walls like sculptural objects. Each work depicts meticulous arrangements of books, photographs and drawings — themselves also leaning against the bare white wall within the pictorial frame of the photograph. The objects in the images alternately reference fragments of African-American literary or civil rights history and other texts that relate to techniques of observation and reproduction such as Eastman Kodak's *How to Make Good Photographs*.

Although using some similar presentation strategies to earlier works, the more recent *Midday* series (2009), by contrast, focuses on the recurring 'character' of a blank plywood square, which is an empty slate or blank canvas. In various works in the series, this central element is then situated on top of books, draped with fabric and presented alongside carefully placed fruit and snapshots pinned to the wall. The austere formal elegance of these works emphasizes the con-structed nature of the photographic image, and resonates with more historical painterly traditions, such as seventeenth-century still-life painting — an important relay point in history for Hewitt as it was an important moment of scientific advancements in optics/techniques of 'seeing' and of intercultural trade and exchange. These works most directly invite the viewer to fill in the blank and bring to the reading of the image their own personal associations.

In both series, Hewitt's recursive sense of space is reflected in the presentation of the photo-graphic work as a sculptural object in the gallery and echoed in the illusionistic pictorial space of the photograph itself. This doubling tactic generates a perceptual distance that seems to foreground a deep ambivalence towards any remnant of photographic 'objectivity' and to question from what kind of past these 'documents' arose. The complexity of Hewitt's temporal-spatial constructions belie their quiet elegance and alacrity, as she proposes new ways of re-presenting historical fragments and symbols in the present day. By bringing together questions of memory, time and space, she shows how existing images accrue different meanings through shifts of context and thereby open up new possibilities for tomorrow.

Richard Hughes

Decay, decadence and the detumescence of post-war utopian social visions are the vectors that transverse the sculptural practice of Richard Hughes. Having grown up in the neglected post-industrial and decaying landscape of the 1980s UK West Midlands, this London-based artist approaches the best intentions of modernist urban planners with the wry intellect and dark humour of a stand-up comedian. His cast and carved resin sculptures of decrepit, discarded everyday objects resemble props for a play based on Cormac McCarthy's *The Road*, albeit a version starring the comedian Andy Kaufman. In *Too Long at the Fair* (2008), the artist has cast an over-sized children's teddy bear that might be a prize at a seedy travelling carnival, only to give it a dark, filthy patina that suggests it has been excavated from an archaeological dig. It is at once a sad and humorous object whose title might stand in as a metaphor for the recent collapse of the global financial markets, suggesting that the party is over and that the world's recent prosperity was never more than a cheap saccharine facade.

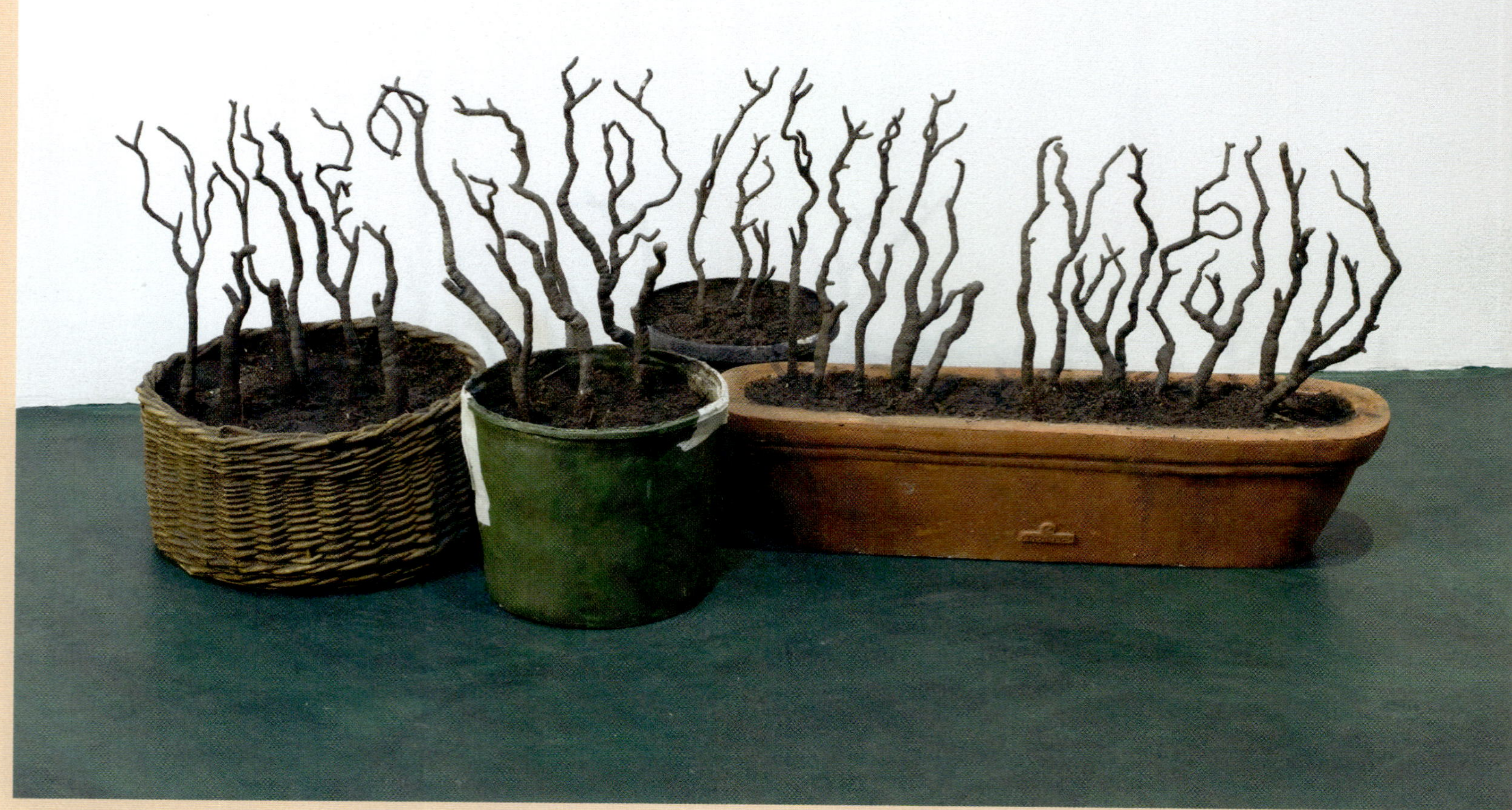

We're all mad (4 cast potted plants), 2008. Polyester resin, jesmonite, modelling putty wire, acrylic paint, dirt. 135 × 41 × 43 cm

Wry intellect and dark humour

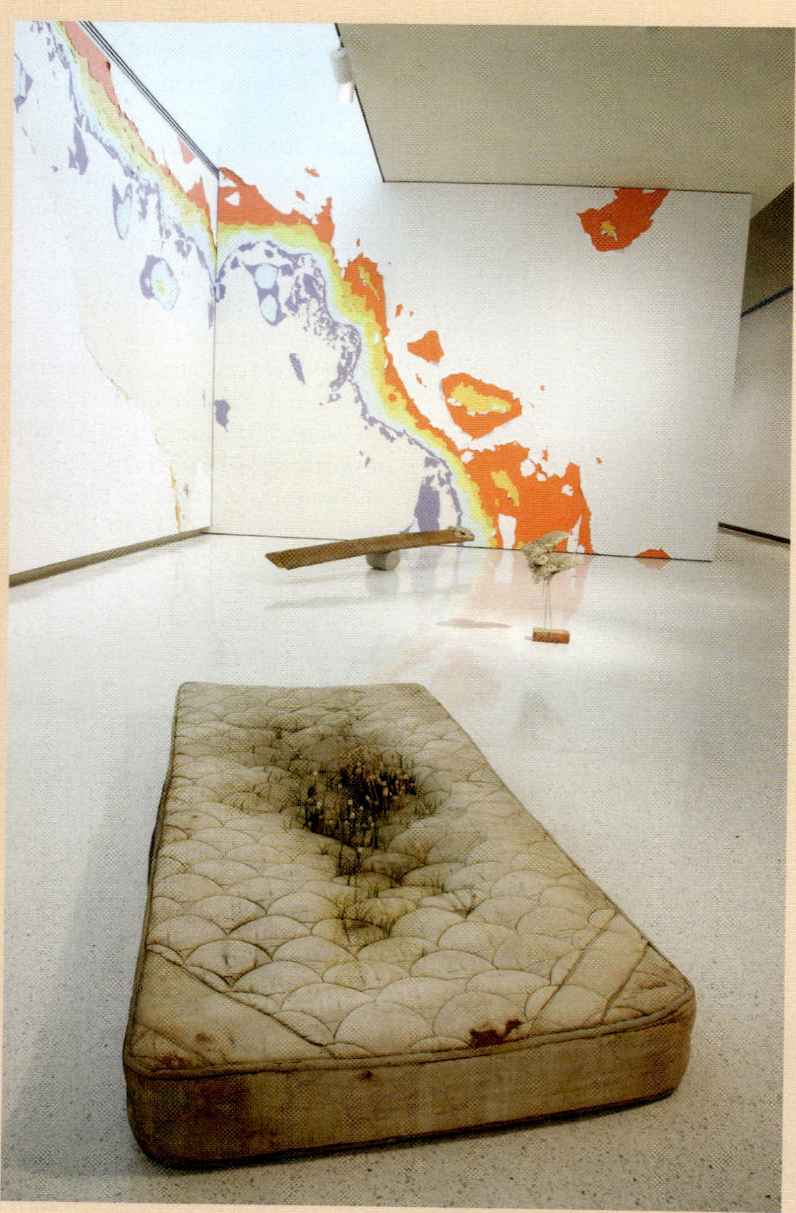

From front: **The Big Sleep**, 2007. Jesmonite, pigment, acrylic paint, modeling putty, plastic. 24 × 191 × 91 cm. **Trip Over**, 2007. Epoxy resin, polyurethane foam, jesemite, steel rod, acrylic paint, shoe laces. 69 × 28 × 15 cm. **The Legendary Chock**, 2007. Cast silicone rubber, stitched canvas, acrylic paint, cast concrete, cast polyurethane. 39 × 282 × 22 cm. On wall: **The Aura of a Savage Man**, 2008. Acrylic paint and emulsion paint on wall. Dimensions variable

One of the ironies of Hughes's rigorously handmade work is his meticulous attention to the faithful reconstruction of industrial objects that seem to have fallen apart; his might be called a trompe l'œil trash aesthetic. In *The Big Sleep* (2007), a cast-resin sculpture of a discarded mattress has become a Petri dish for the artist's exquisitely crafted reproductions of psilocybin 'magic' mushrooms. As its title suggests, Hughes posits a 'world without us', where the organic takes back the night from the industrial realm. Its logical conclusion can be seen in *We're all mad* (2008), a series of sculpted potted plants whose denuded limbs spell out the work's title in a kind of rebellion as seen in *Day of the Triffids*.

Hughes' outlook isn't simply negative, though. Where there is humour there is hope, and the artist finds a wry urban poetry in the

Where there is humour there is hope, and the artist finds a wry urban poetry in the erosion of the industrial everyday

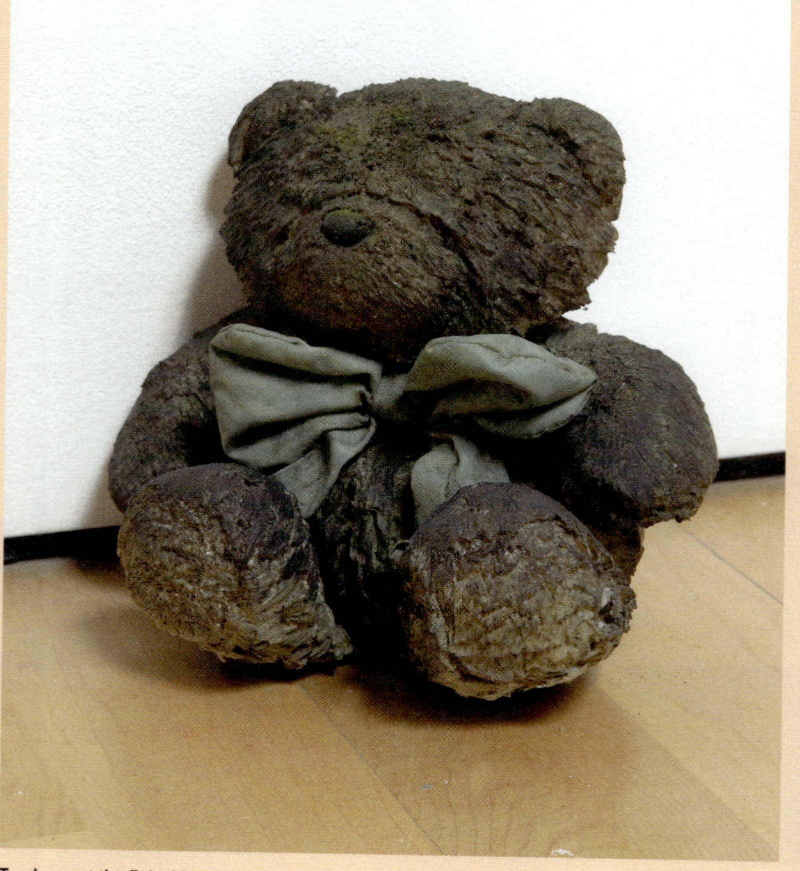

Too Long at the Fair, 2008. Polyester resin, paint. 22 × 22 × 12 cm

The tragic becomes the comic in a sculptural inversion

Hopeful if melancholic

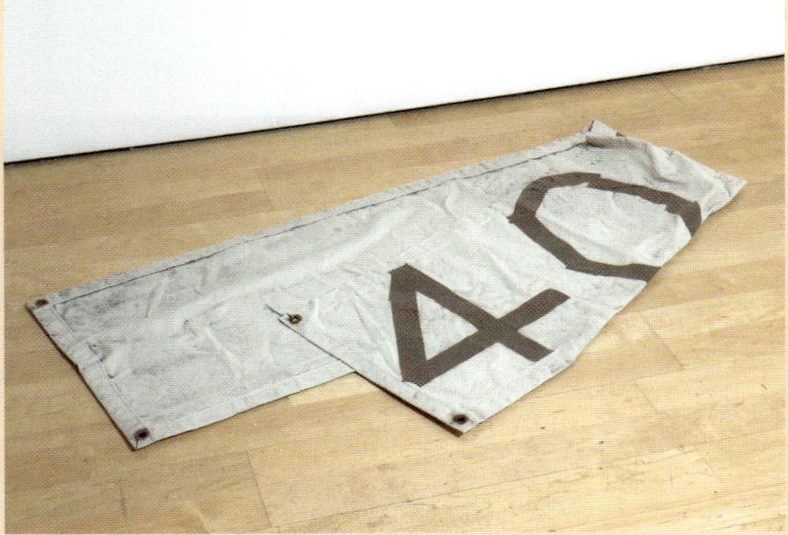

False Start, 2008. Polyester resin, paint. 150 × 77 cm

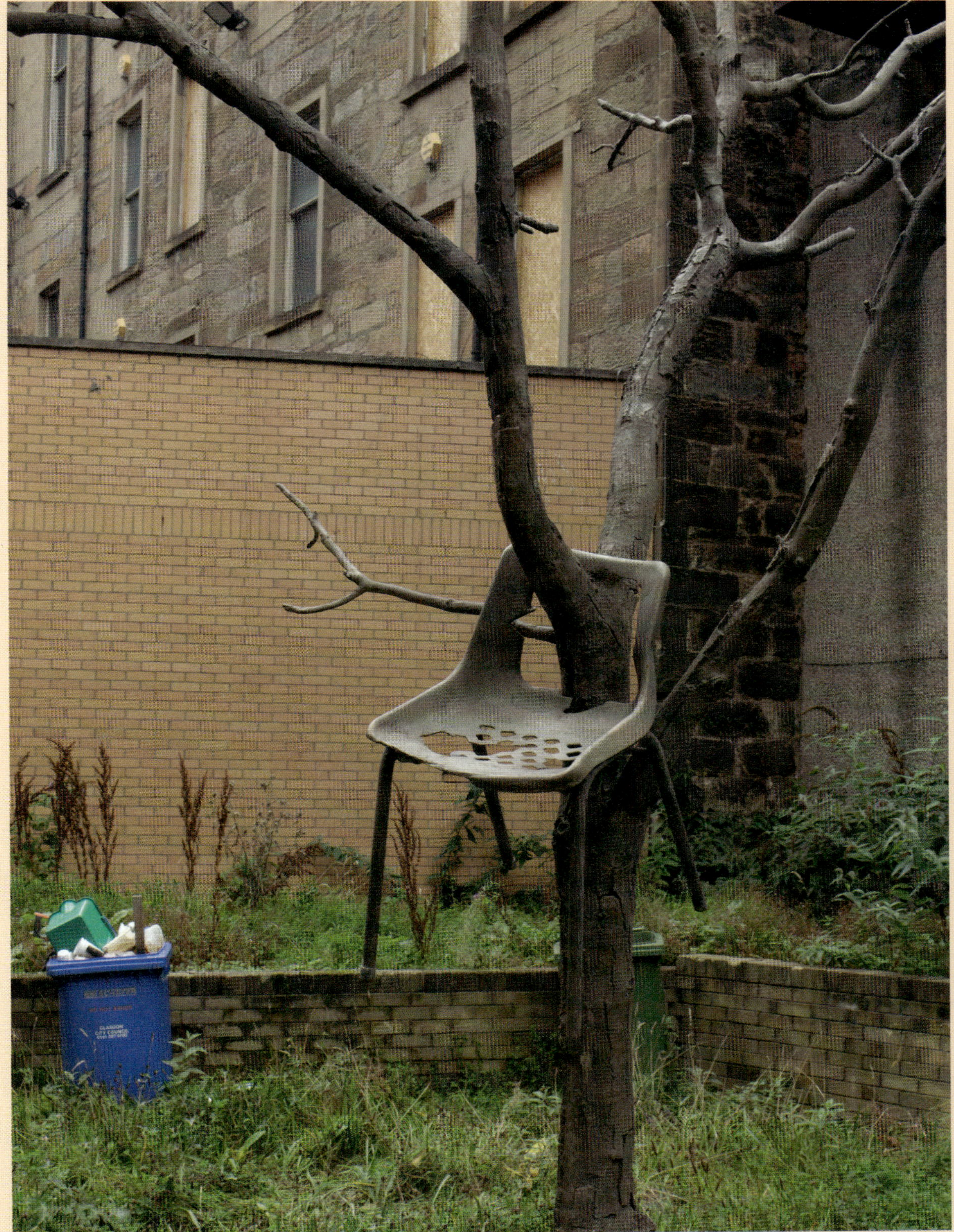

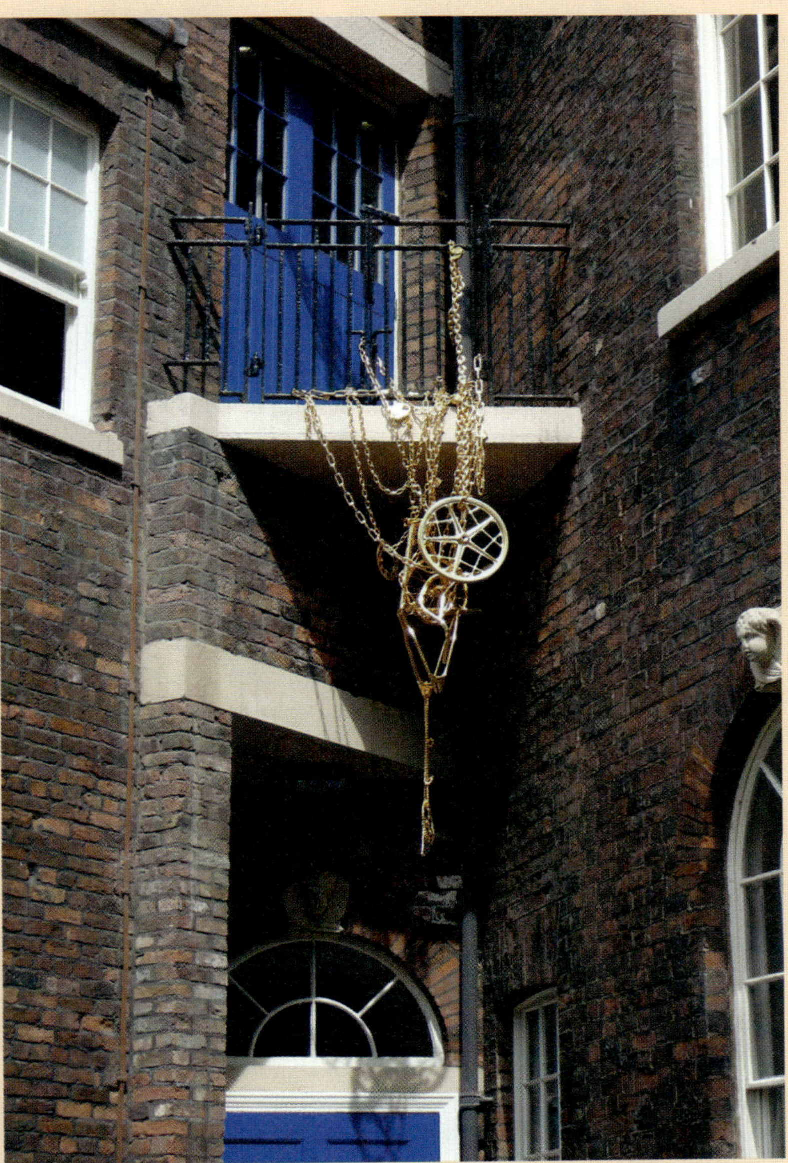

Today and Forever, 2008. Bicycle parts, chains, padlocks, gold plating. Dimensions variable

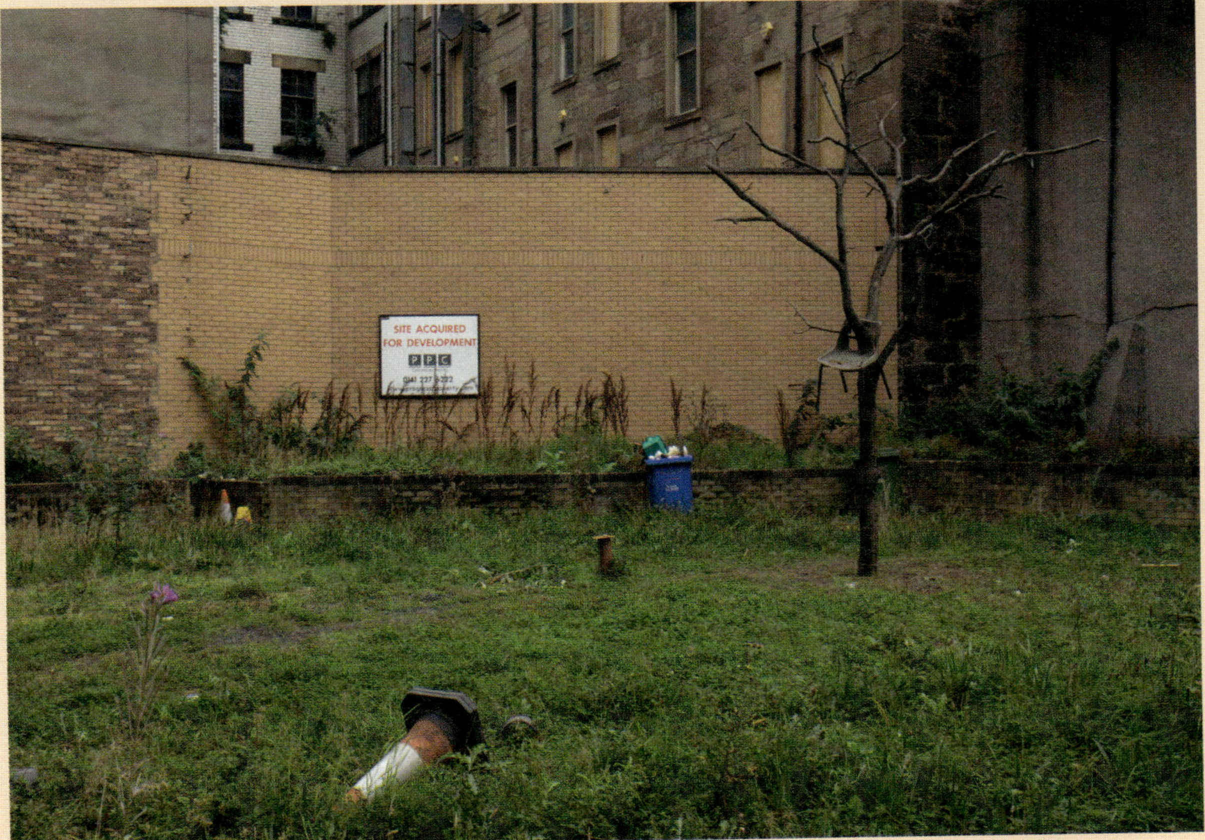

It is Never Too Late To Become What You Might Have Been, 2008. Bronze. 480 × 230 × 210 cm

erosion of the industrial everyday. In *The Aura of a Savage Man* (2008), for example, Hughes attached crumbling layers of acrylic paint to a wall. Each layer was painstakingly applied to sheets of plastic, dried, peeled away, and then sculpturally added to the wall, creating a multihued fresco that negotiates a terrain somewhere between the unkempt pallor of decommissioned public housing and the cave paintings of Lascaux. The tragic becomes the comic in a sculptural inversion as the archaeology of house paint reveals a hope-filled rainbow arching across the horizon of the gallery walls. Whether the savage man is the one who built the ill-conceived public housing or the hunter-gatherer who first scrawled images on a rock wall is not completely clear.

Hughes also offers us a hopeful if melancholic piece of advice in his sculpture *It is Never Too Late to Become What You Might Have Been* (2008), a bronze cast of a broken mass-produced plastic school chair that hangs from the small tree that pierces it. It is as if the tree has grown up through the forlorn chair over the course of many, many years. All the hopes and dreams of youth, as embodied in the school chair, have seemingly been crushed, yet hope remains as organic life goes on.

Jamie Isenstein

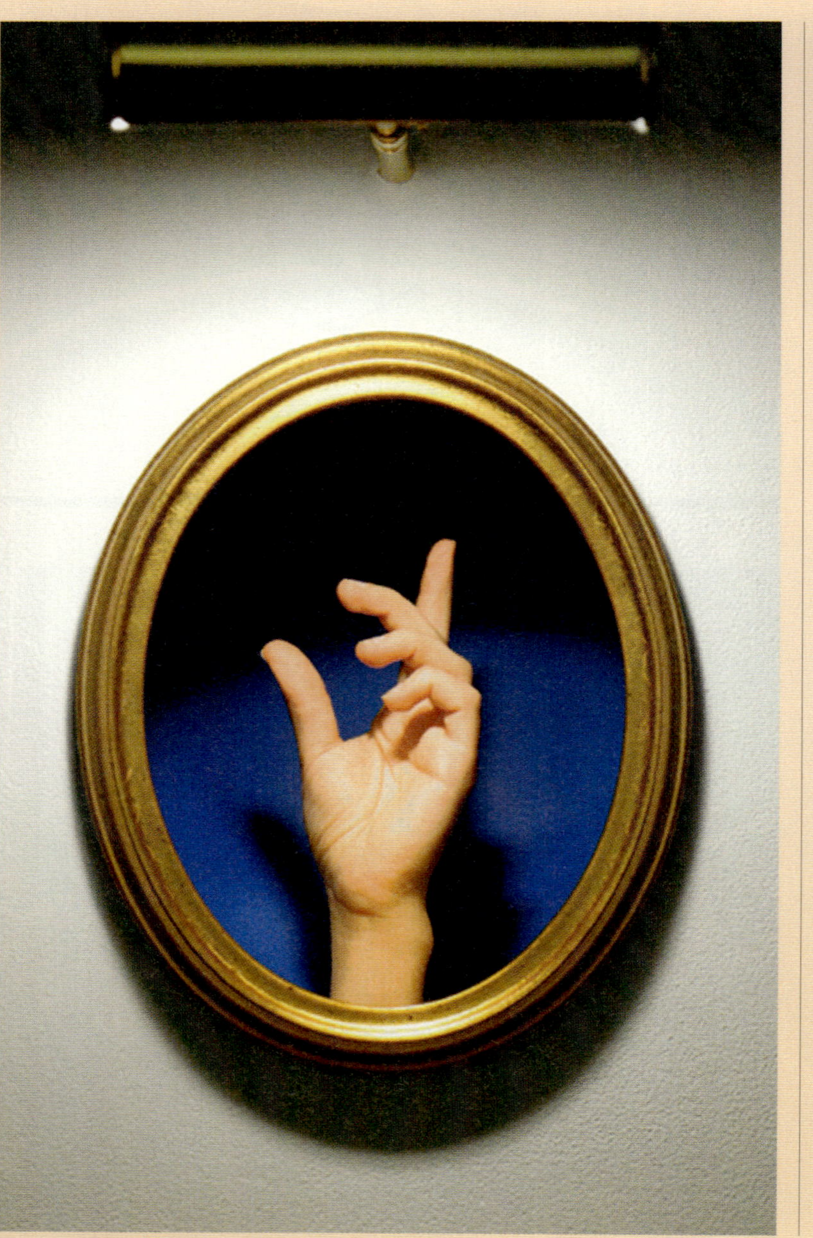

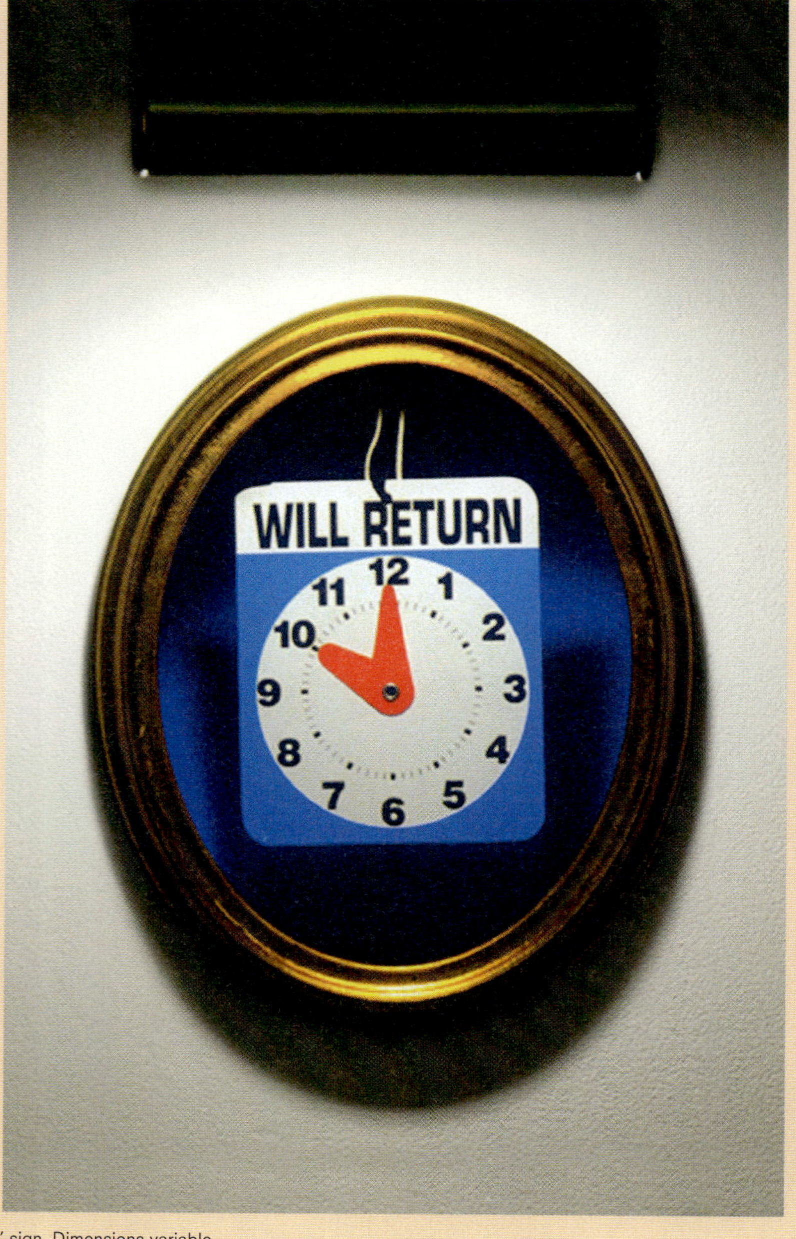

Uncanny hybrids

'If you put a living body into the sculpture, is it still a sculpture, or is it a performance?' This question lies at the crux of much of Jamie Isenstein's work, an improbable blend of endurance-performance art and dark

Isenstein teases out underlying issues of presence and absence with a deadpan wit.

comedy. Her practice turns on this issue as she tries to solve simultaneously problems of performance and of sculpture within a single work. Whether taking the form of sculptural installations or videos, in which she may or may not perform, the visual elements of her work

Unexpected transformation

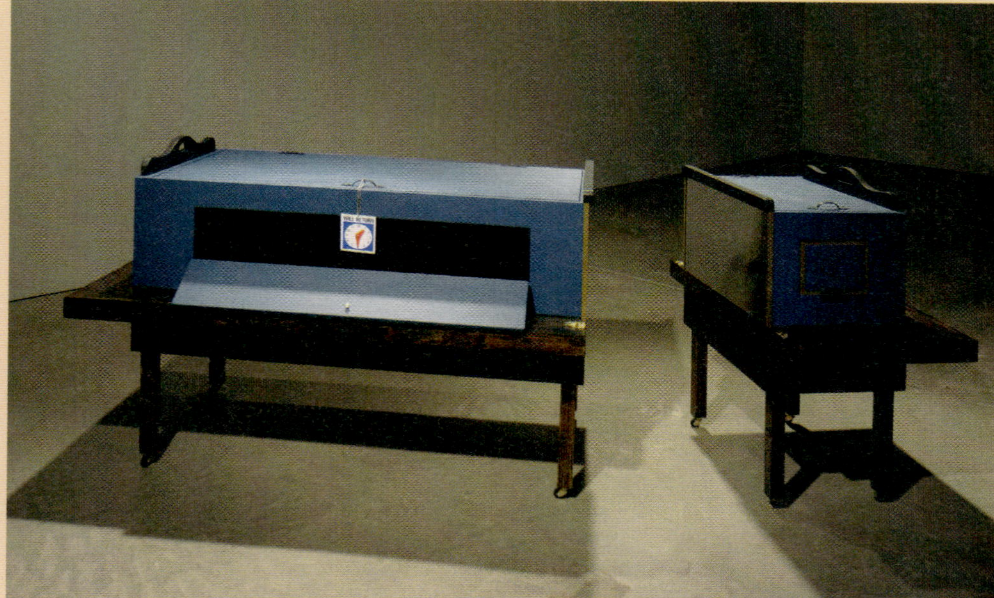

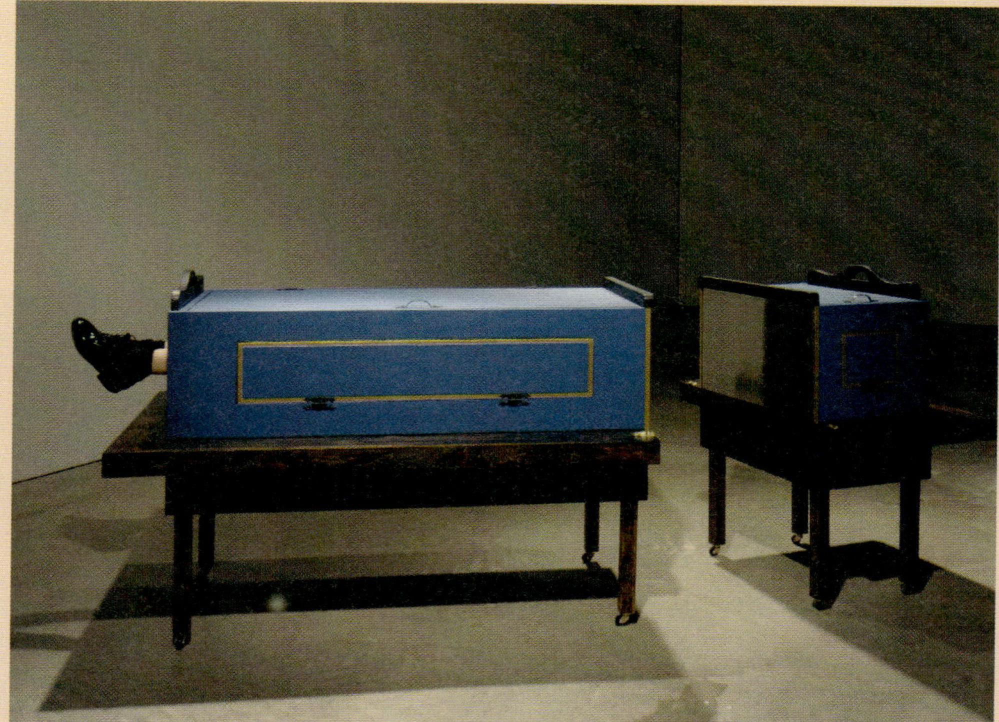

Saw the Lady, 2007. Wood, metal blades, copper hardware, human body or just head and 'Will return' sign. Dimensions variable

draw as much on early twentieth-century entertainment spectacles — vaudeville, circus and magic acts – as they do on the Surrealists' uncanny, idiosyncratic sensibility. Think Buster Keaton meets René Magritte as reimagined by Yves Klein.

As she transforms her body into various sculptures, Isenstein teases out underlying issues of presence and absence with a deadpan wit. In *Magic Fingers* (2003), one of her earliest endurance-performance installations, an empty gilded oval frame is embedded into a false gallery wall. For hours at a time, Isenstein sits behind the wall, with only her hand displayed within the frame, as she slowly cycles through various art-historical hand gestures, like a Renaissance study that has suddenly come to life.

In other works, Isenstein literally animates everyday objects to create uncanny hybrids with her unexpected presence. In *Arm Chair* (2006), she 'wears' a classic wingback armchair — her arms and legs morphing into the arms and legs of the chair. A physically demanding feat, the work requires her to sit perfectly still for many hours, maintaining her composure as viewers respond to this unexpected transformation of an otherwise entirely familiar piece of furniture.

More recently, Isenstein

presented *Rug Rug Rug Rug* (2009) where she lies completely still, splayed out on her stomach in the middle of the gallery floor, sandwiched between a large, stacked-up pile of animal skins with only her hands and feet protruding. Works such as these function like contemporary sculptural extensions of the seventeenth-century Dutch vanitas painting tradition which addressed the ephemerality of life through depictions of death.

Saw the Lady (2007) is a twist on the illusionism of this familiar magician's act. In her version, Isenstein inhabits a magician's box, but is headless rather than cut in half since the 'cut' has been made at the neck. A pair of feet clad in ankle socks and patent leather shoes poke out from the coffin-like case. Such work offers a wry commentary on our own mortality, and also touches on issues of anticipation and spectacle.

These latter themes are also addressed by another important 'performer' in most of Isenstein's projects: a 'Will return' sign, which the artist uses whenever she needs to go on a break. The sign serves an

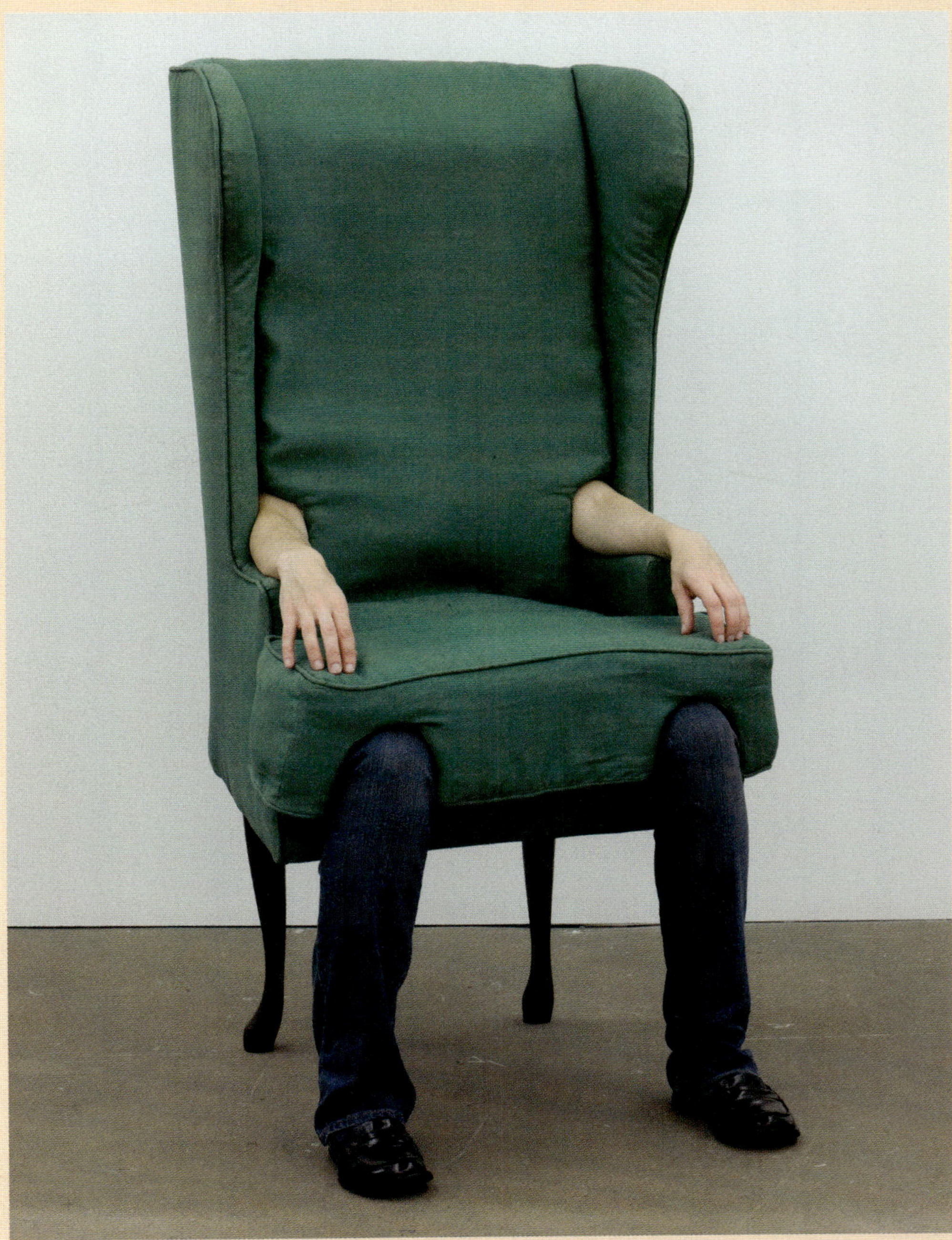

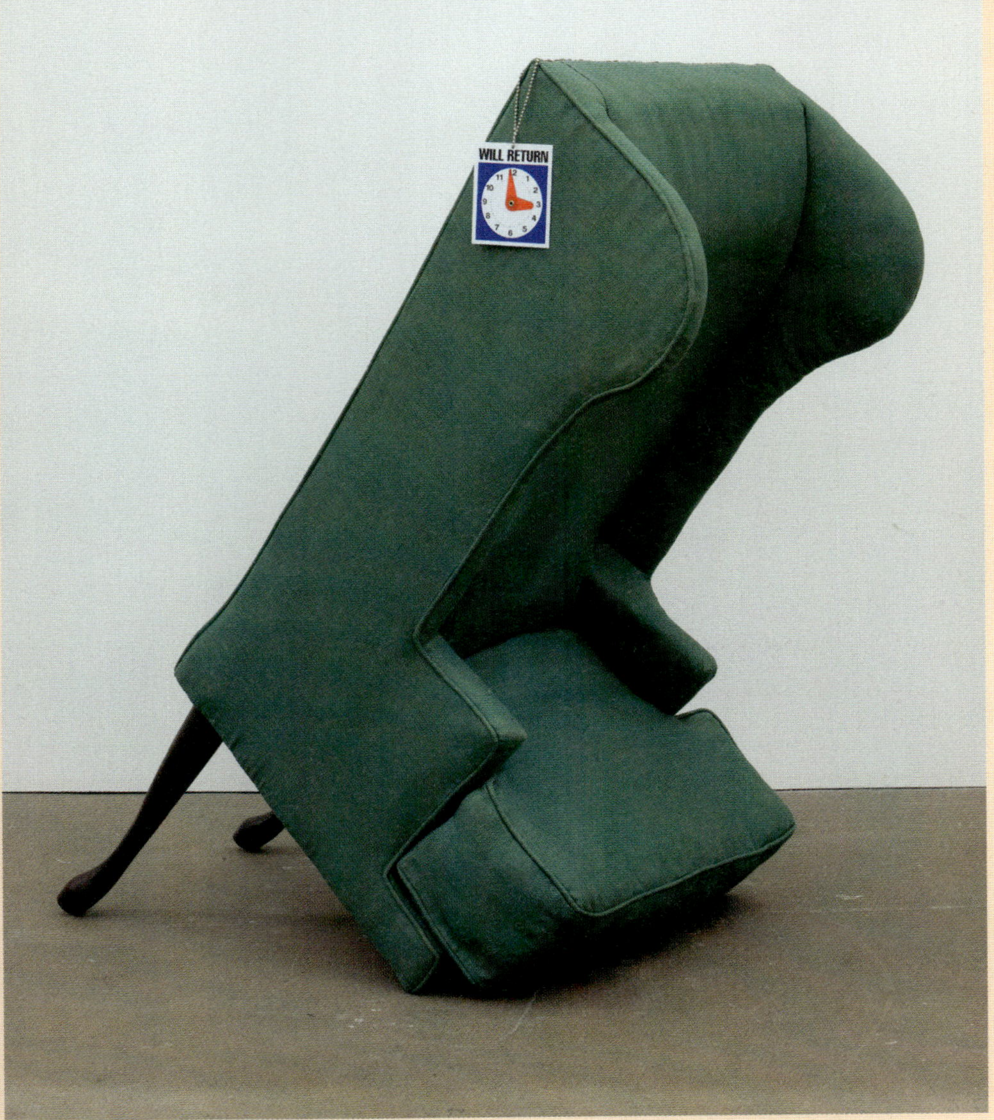

Arm Chair, 2006. Linen, wood, metal, nylon, raw cotton, upholstery foam, human arms and human legs or 'Will return' sign. Dimensions variable

Spectacle

important dual function. On the one hand, it literally indicates when the artist will return to the gallery, but, more metaphorically, it also allows the performance to continue ad infinitum. The sign invites viewers to suspend disbelief, suggesting that the performance does not end, but is merely interrupted temporarily, to be resumed at a future moment.

The ways in which Isenstein questions the limitations of both performance and sculpture also poke fun at the gravitas of much 1970s performance art and the grand narratives of art history. As she transforms herself into an artwork, she extends the life of the work as well as her own. If the problem with performance is that it always ends, Isenstein's work slyly offers up the possibility that the show can go on … and on … and on …

Rug Rug Rug Rug Rug, 2009, Bear rug, sheep rug, wolf rug, human rug or 'Will return' sign, pile rug. Dimensions variable

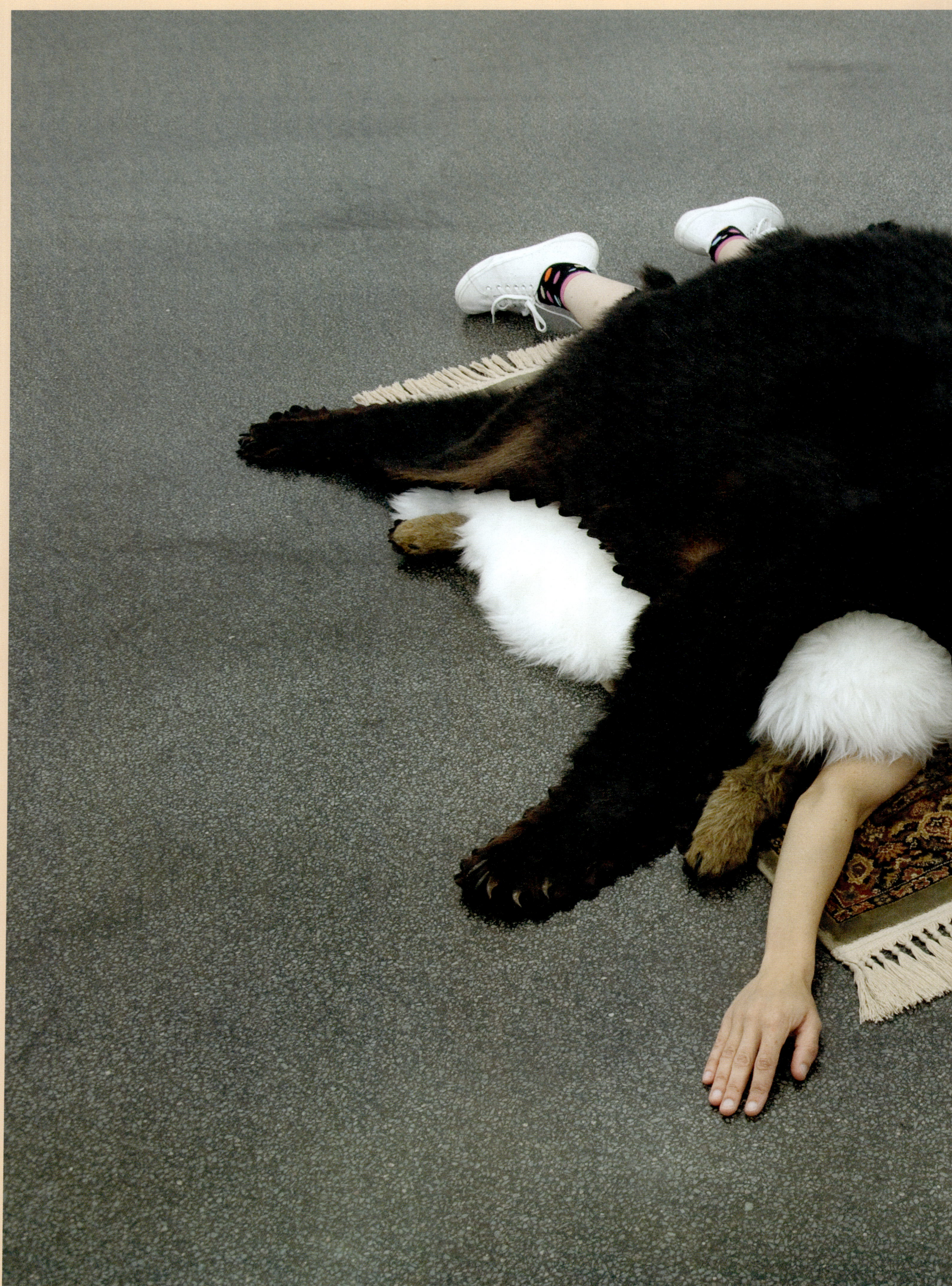

Rug Rug Rug Rug Rug, 2009, Bear rug, sheep rug, wolf rug, human rug or 'Will return' sign, pile rug. Dimensions variable

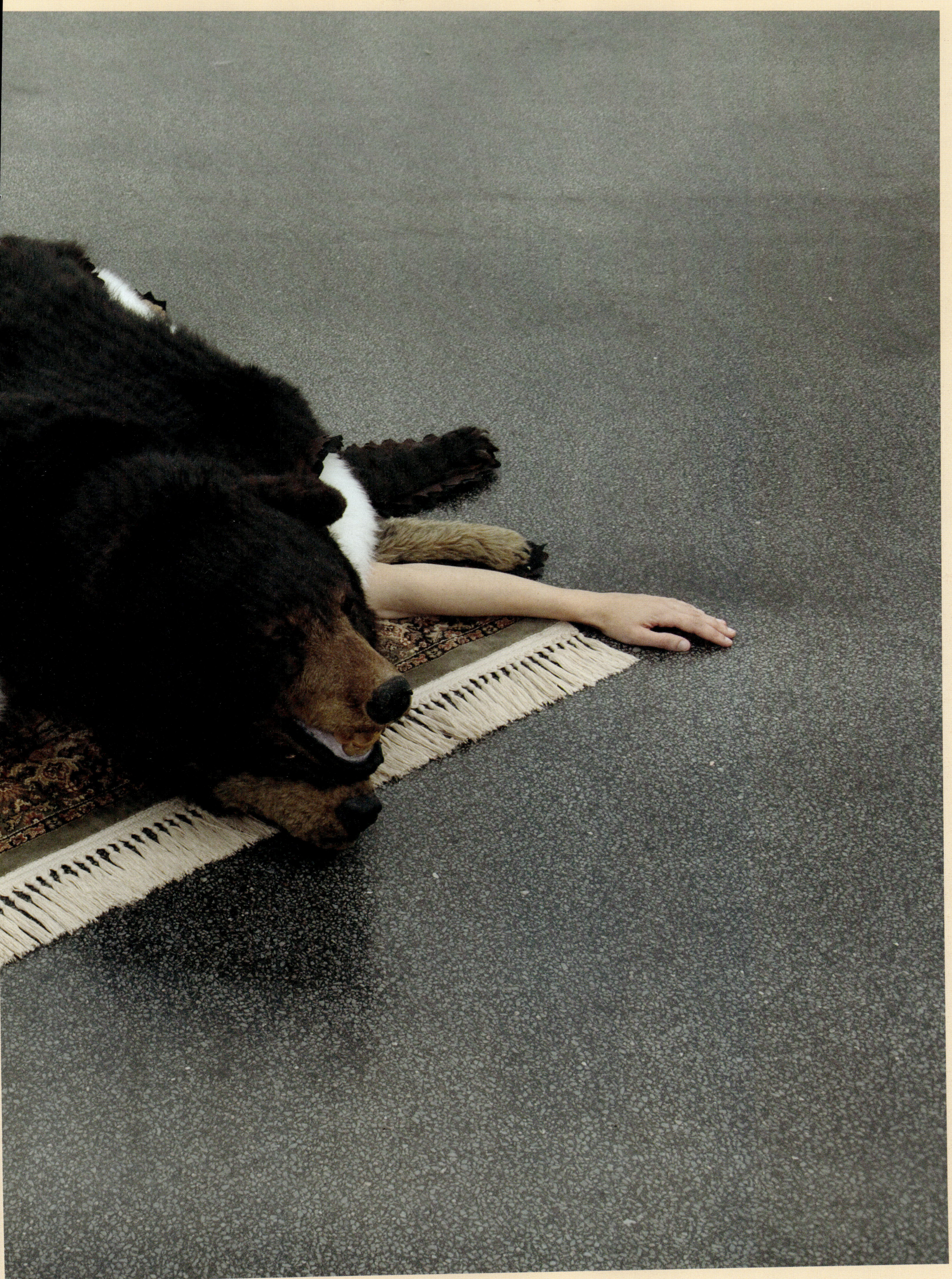

Jackson Pollock Bar

In the spring of 2007, Art & Language held a panel discussion at the unitednationsplaza in Berlin, a one-year project organized by artist Anton Vidokle, where I participated as a co-organizer and advisor. During the panel, as the members of the artist collective drank their mineral water, each and every sip was booming over the sound system with suspicious clarity. So was every watery gulp, and every rustle of paper, or throaty cough. This evening conference was called 'Theses on Feuerbach', and was announced as a project upholding the working premise of 'institutional critique as institution'. Typically for Art & Language, the speedy volley of high theory and critical terminology was such that we could only barely keep up, but as this ruthless density was unleashed upon the fragile minds of my own ADD generation, throughout that hour and a half, everyone made a tremendous effort to follow. You could hear the proverbial pin drop. The reason for this almost obsessive concentration on the speaker's lips was that they were actually actors working with the Jackson Pollock Bar, under the director Christian Matthiessen, who has been reenacting panels and other discursive events for almost twenty years in an impressive range of venues including Documenta x and the Getty Center in Los Angeles.

Matthiessen calls these projects 'playback performances of aesthetic discourse', or 'theory installations'. The Jackson Pollock Bar reconstructs such conferences and lectures by transcribing, editing, and re-recording the events, then re-enacting them on stage — lip-synching to a playback soundtrack. I worked with the Freiburg-based director and his crew on the first national pavilion of the United Arab Emirates in the Arsenale venue of the 2009 Venice Biennale. For this project, Matthiessen collaborated with Dubai-based artists Nanaz Azari and Rodin Hamidi and the journalist and actor Ed Jones, to re-enact the first press conference of our pavilion. This conference was held at the Cartier Dome, Art Basel Miami

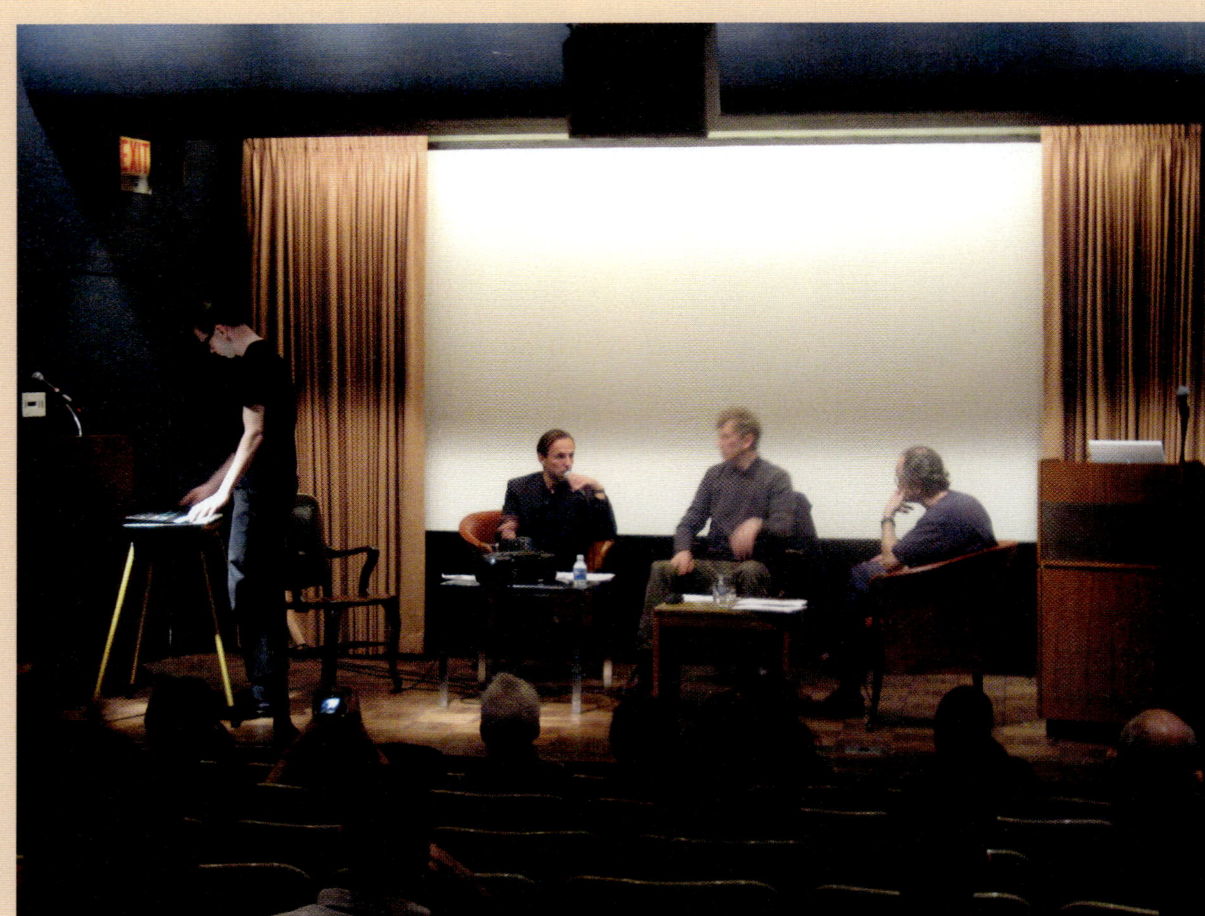

Art & Language Interview with Mayo Thompson installed in the style of the Jackson Pollock Bar, 2009. CD player, loudspeakers, dummy microphones, keyboard, furniture. Re–enactment of Art & Language interview with Mayo Thompson. Actors: Martin Horn, Peter Cieslinski, Gotthard Lange, John Spelman. Soundtrack: Ray Austin, Thomas Douglas, Brad Decker, Jack Jackson. Art Institute of Chicago

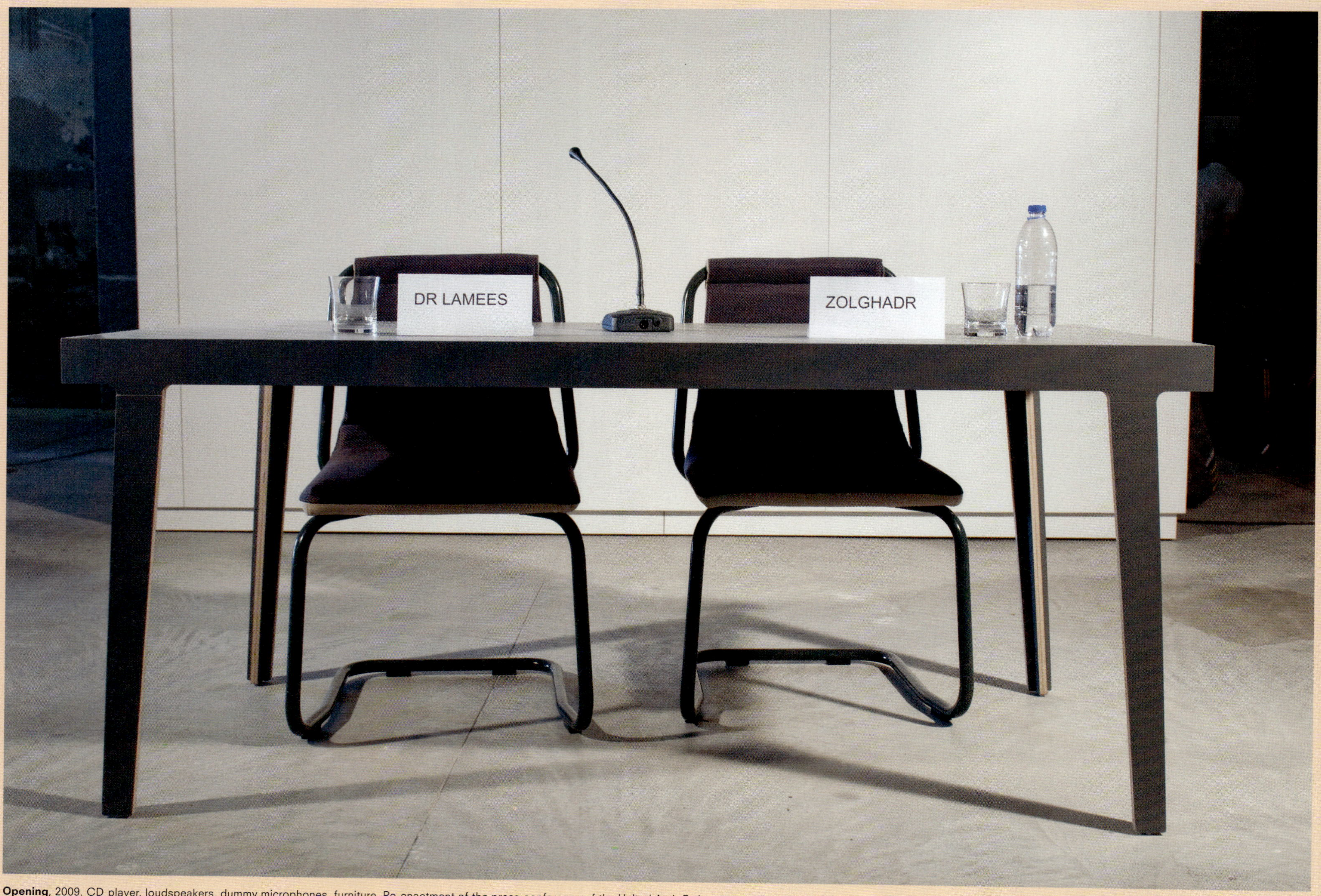

Opening, 2009. CD player, loudspeakers, dummy microphones, furniture. Re-enactment of the press conference of the United Arab Emirates on the occasion of the first UAE pavillion at the Venice Biennale. Actors: Nanaz Azari, Rodin Hamidi, Ed Jones. Soundtrack: Thomas Douglas, Ray Austin, Ann Malcolm

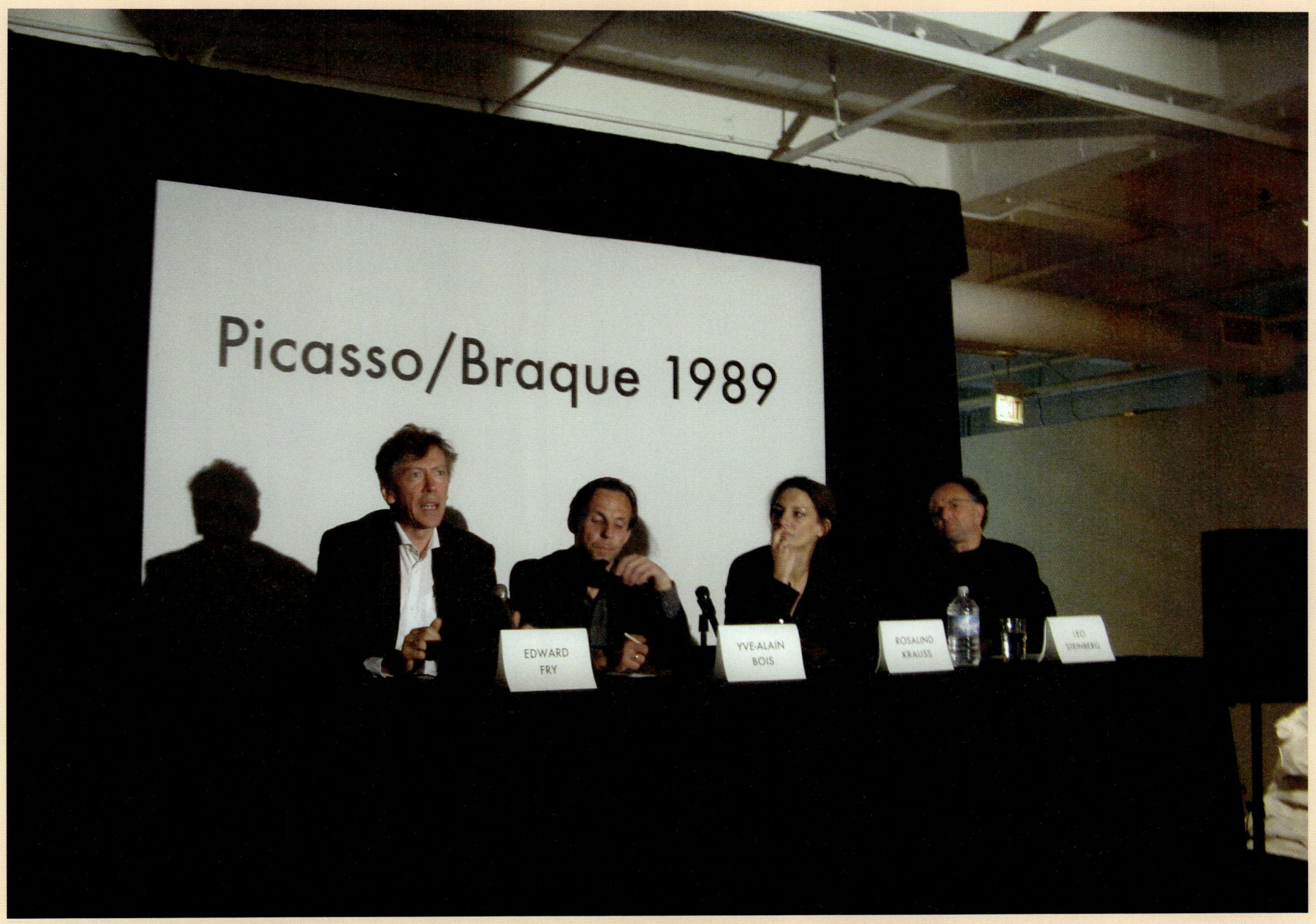

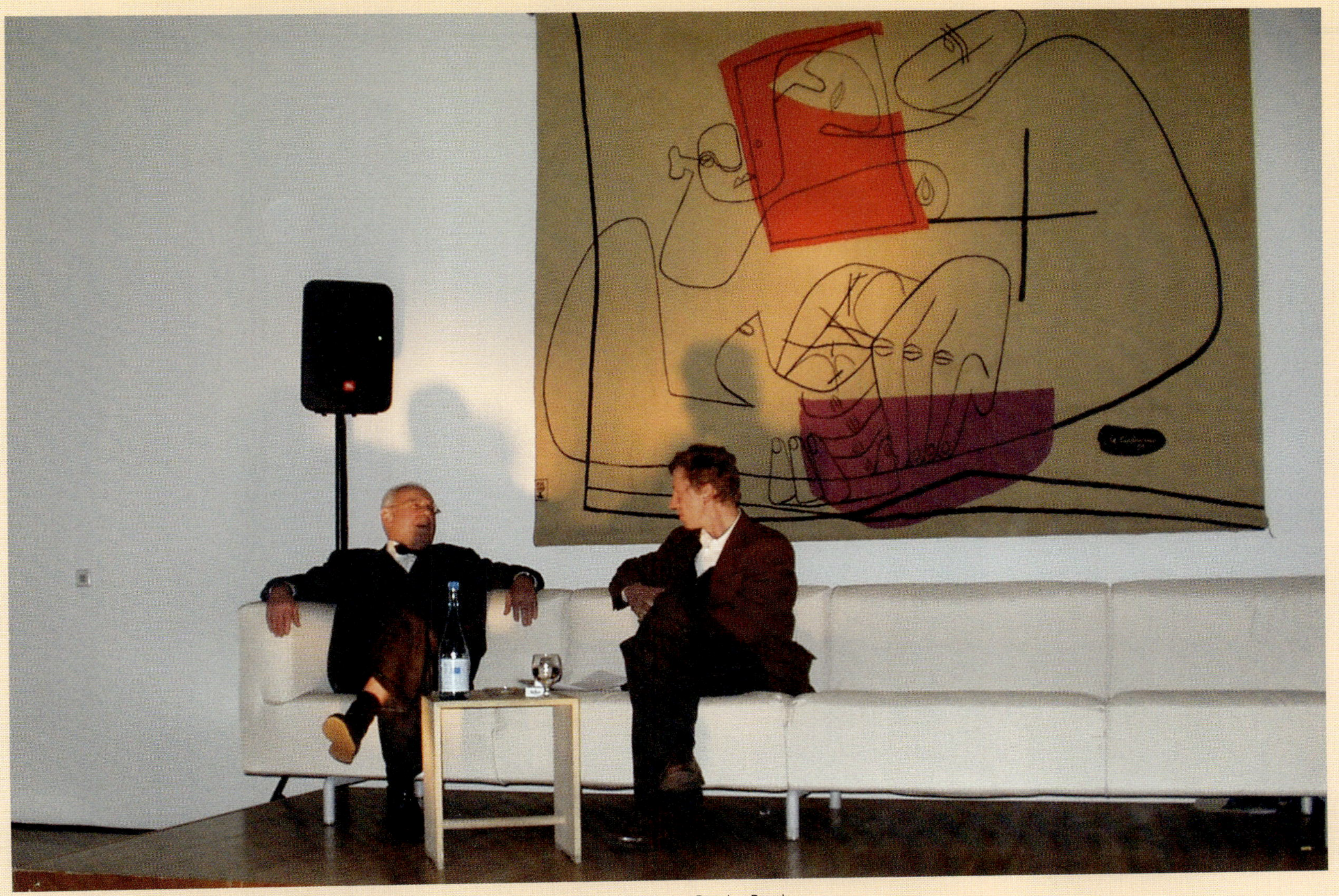

Picasso/Braque 1989, 2009. CD player, loudspeakers, dummy microphones, panel. Re–enactment of panel discussion between Rosalind Krauss, Edward Fry, Yve–Alain Bois, Leo Steinberg. Actors: Gotthard Lange, Martin Horn, Catrin Strieberg, Peter Cieslinski. Soundtrack: Thomas Douglas, Ray Austin, Brad Decker, Ann Malcolm. University of Chicago

Playback performances of aesthetic discourse

John Peter interview with Frank Lloyd Wright, 2006. Actors: Ullo von Peinen and Martin Horn. Fondation Beyeler, Basel

Beach in December 2008, and was duly re-enacted by the actors, first at the Dubai Art Fair (March 2009), and later during the opening week of the Venice Biennale. One of the key perks here, among many, is the dragging of routinely underestimated trappings of the

The artist calls these projects 'playback performances of aesthetic discourse', or theory installations.

arts, from the curatorial statement to the press conference, into a more critical limelight.

To put it crudely and simply, the Jackson Pollock Bar performances usually offer a chronology of preliminary puzzlement (what the fuck is this?), followed by a sheer fascination for the technique of lip-synching (how do they do that?) and, finally, a strange and renewed appreciation of the actual discourse.

Izumi Kato

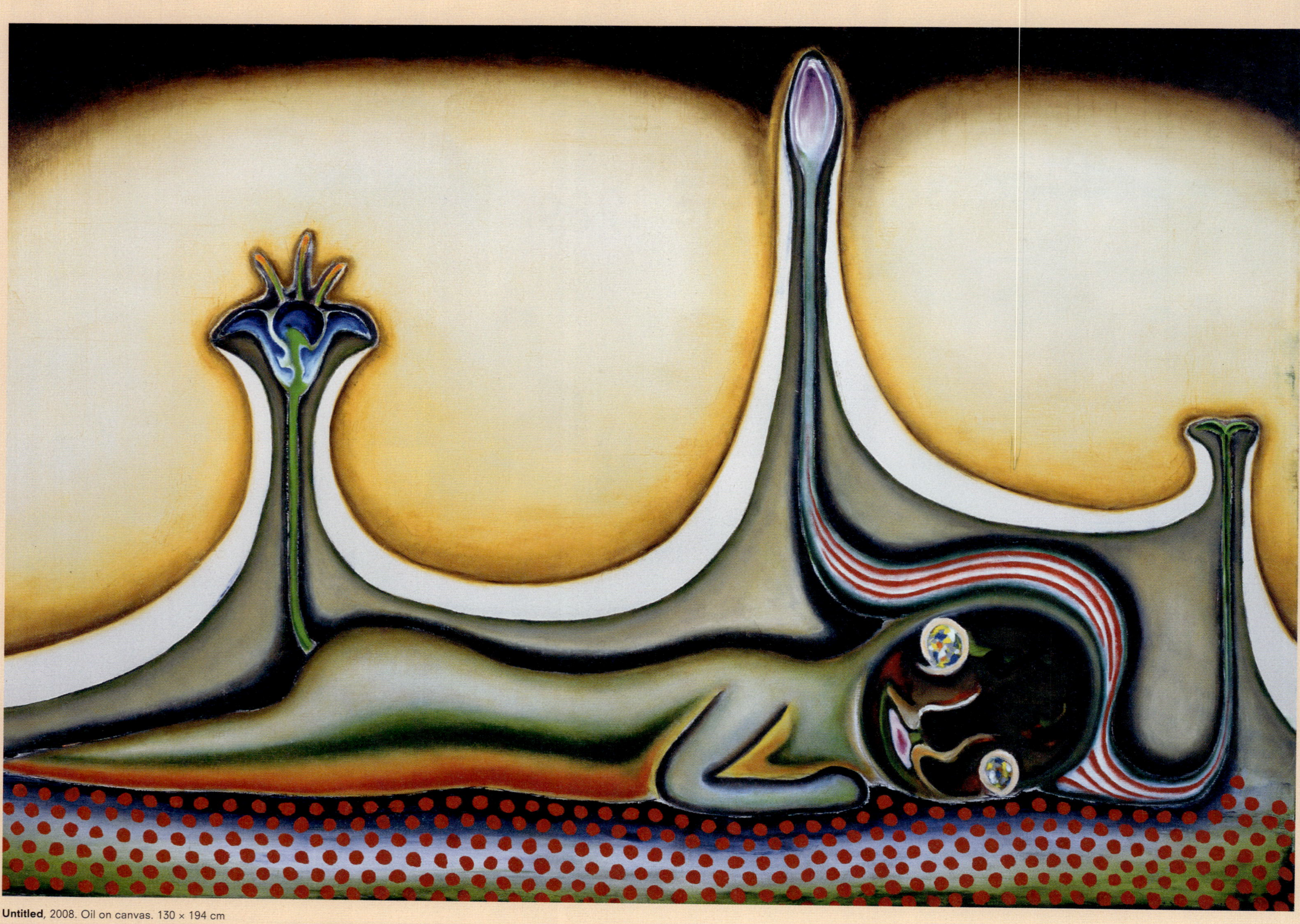

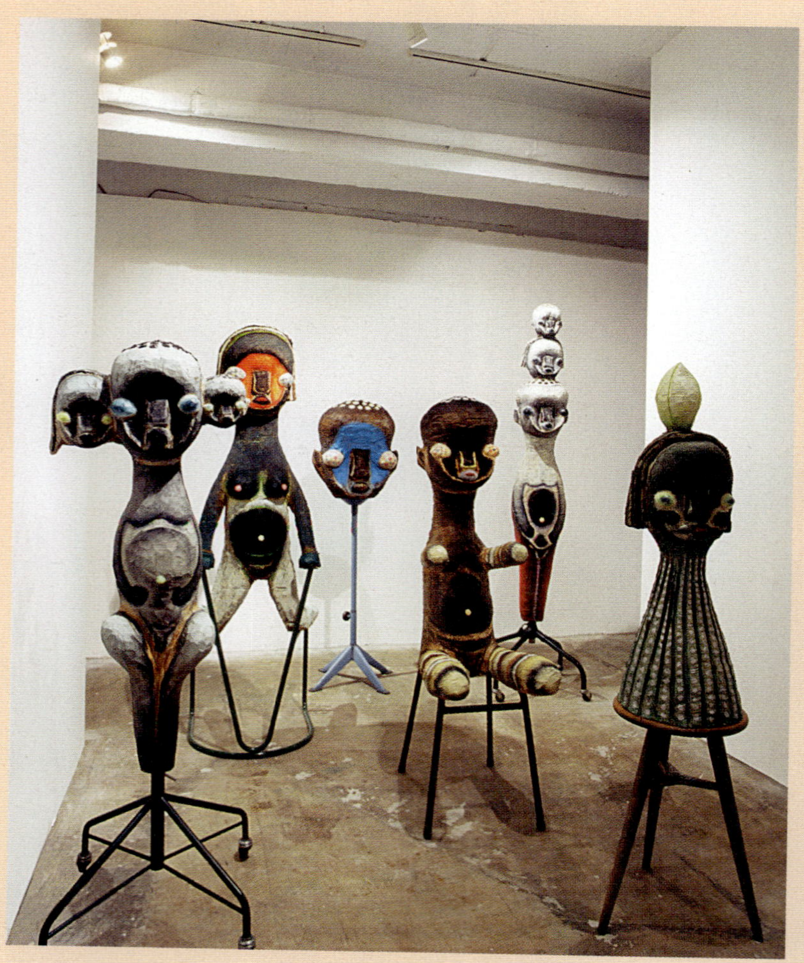

Untitled, 2008. Oil on canvas. 130 × 194 cm

Layer upon layer

Izumi Kato is an artist who began painting after laying down his brush. Eschewing tools, as if to reject any reliance on the flightiness of brushwork, he applies layer upon layer of sombre-hued pigment directly with his hands, not so much to paint as to rub the colour on to the canvas. In this way, he depicts creatures with human contours, two staring eyes, a head, hands and feet. Those bold, forceful curves, throwing into relief the human shape, those organic lines, that distortion and simplification of form, are the products of painting with the hands, and as a result, Kato's works possess a powerful presence that seems to illuminate the core of the human body.

Dear Humans, 2007. Wood, acrylic, charcoal, silicon. From left: 123 × 45 × 45 cm, 144 × 50 × 50 cm, 123 × 47 × 47 cm, 119 × 34 × 55 cm, 168 × 41 × 41 cm, 123 × 32 × 32 cm

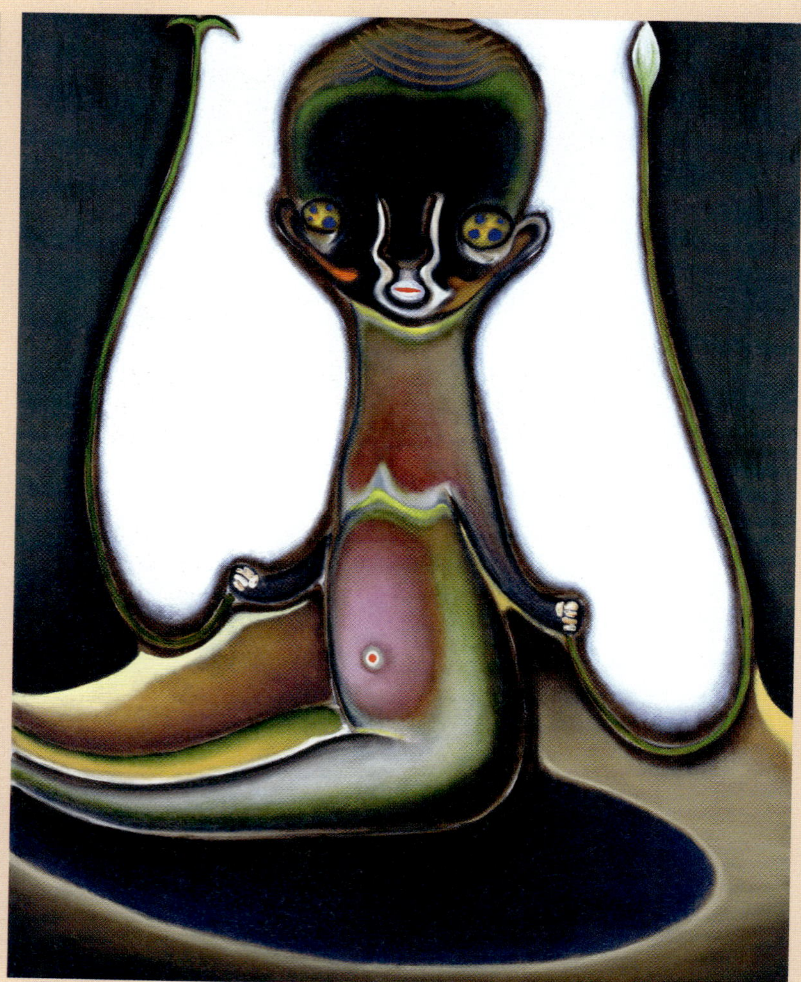

Untitled, 2008. Oil on canvas. 162 × 130 cm

Kato was a relative latecomer to the art world, making his debut at the age of thirty. He had worked as a manual labourer for some years, which left him feeling at one with the world of corporeal achievement, and a humble appreciation of his place as just another creature on this earth. From here he set out on a new journey of engagement with the vast realm of painting. An artist who began with creaing abstract works, he now depicts nothing but human figures.

All Kato's recent works are untitled, and he does not set up any specific model to paint; nor does he draft or sketch. These paintings have no narrative element. They are dialogues, creations arising from a direct, barely suppressible physical urge to touch, a trait given play by humans since the days of prehistoric cave murals. The figures sealed within the frame of the canvas seem to radiate an enigmatic aura, their undifferentiated bodies encased in thin membranes reminiscent of a budding life form in the embrace of its mother's amniotic fluid. Kato performs the act of capturing life through his body.

In 2005 Kato also turned to sculpture. Deliberately avoiding

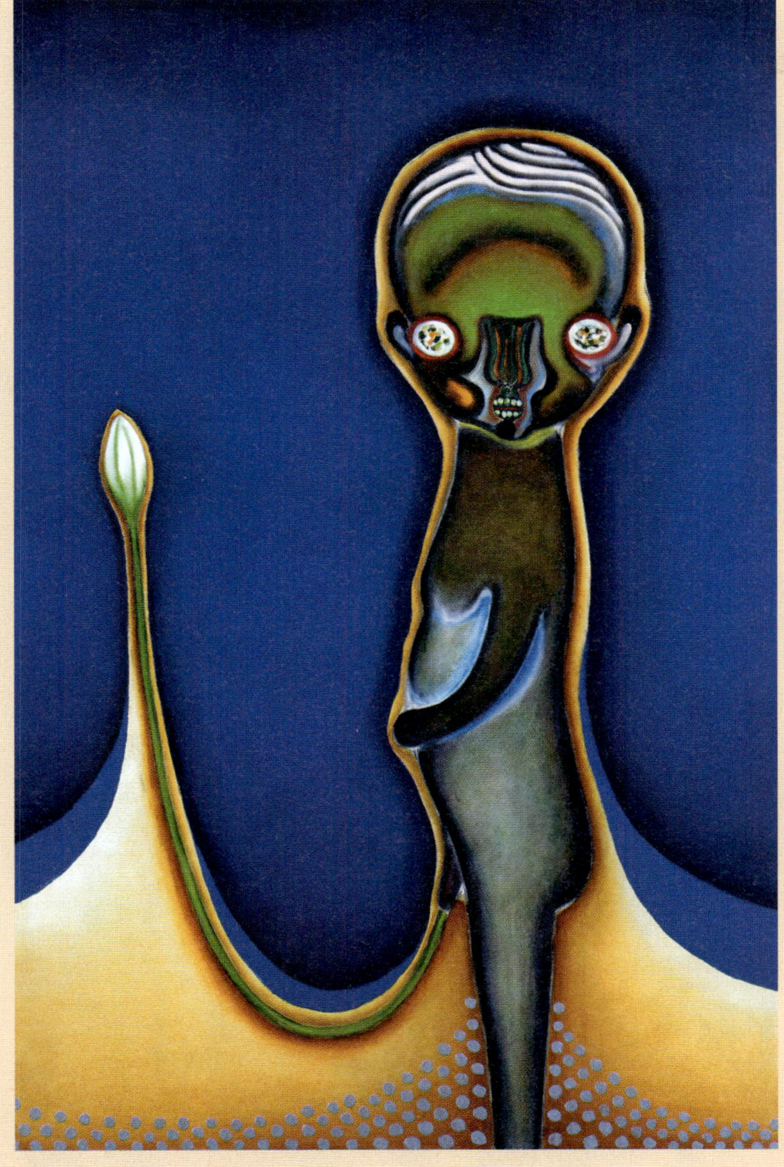
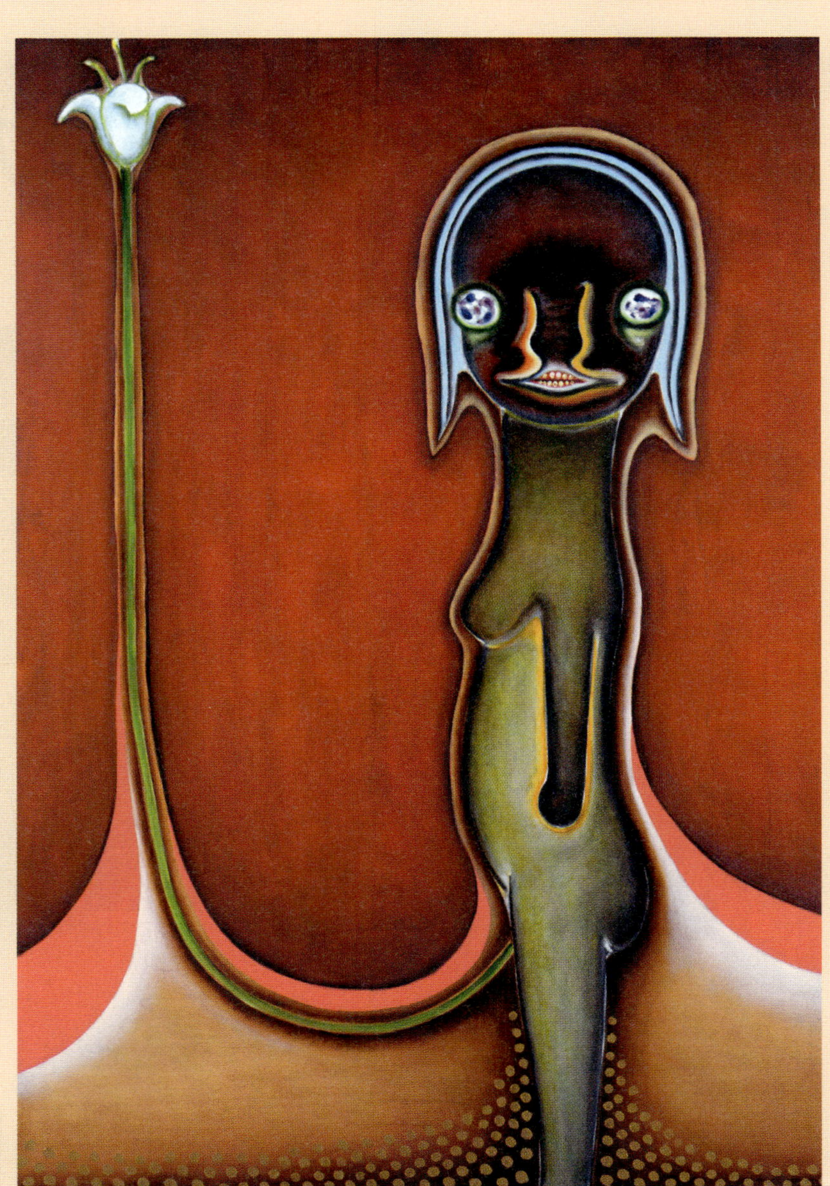

Untitled, 2008. Oil on canvas. 2 of 3 parts. 194 × 130 cm. 227× 162 cm

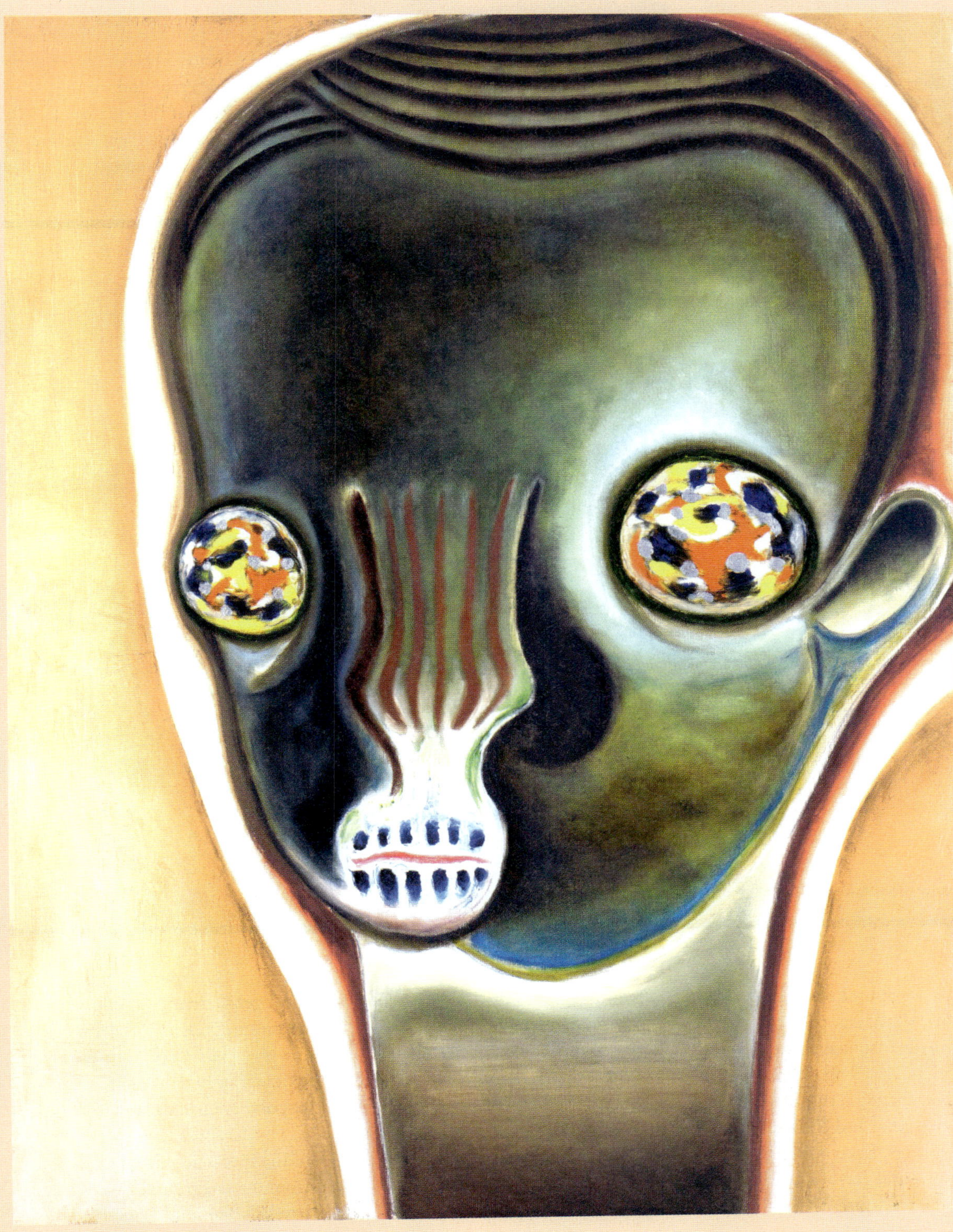

Untitled, 2008. Oil on canvas. 1 of 3 parts. 162 × 130 cm

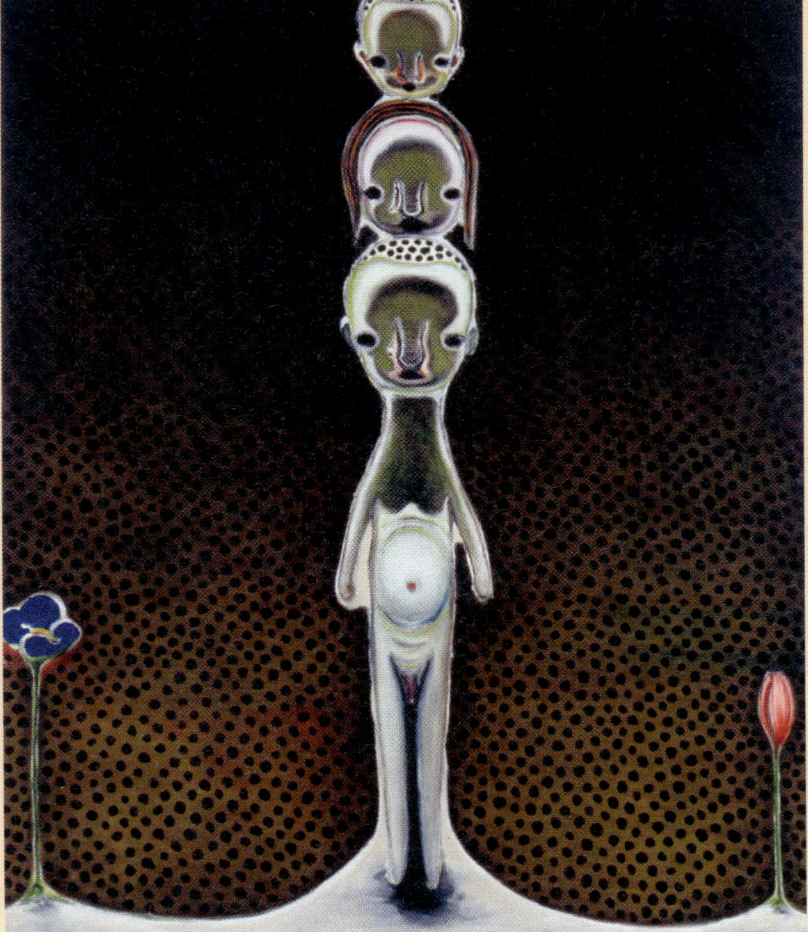

Untitled, 2006. Oil on canvas. 1 of 3 parts. 194 × 162 cm

materials that are easy to mould, such as clay and resin, he works only in wood, carving it directly. Once again he focuses consistently on human figures, chisel marks and cracks left like idiosyncrasies of the flesh. The coloured nature of these roughly hewn bodies indicates that for Kato, they are an extension of his painting. Some of his works are equipped with legs or castors resembling those on desks and chairs.

Echoing Brancusi perhaps, through the pursuit of the substance of things he has arrived at the simplification of form. He also attempts to explore the possibilities in different materials and textures.

Through the classical techniques of painting and sculpture, Kato practises an unrefined yet direct, shareable, real artistic expression in a contemporary world where virtual elements proliferate.

Janice Kerbel

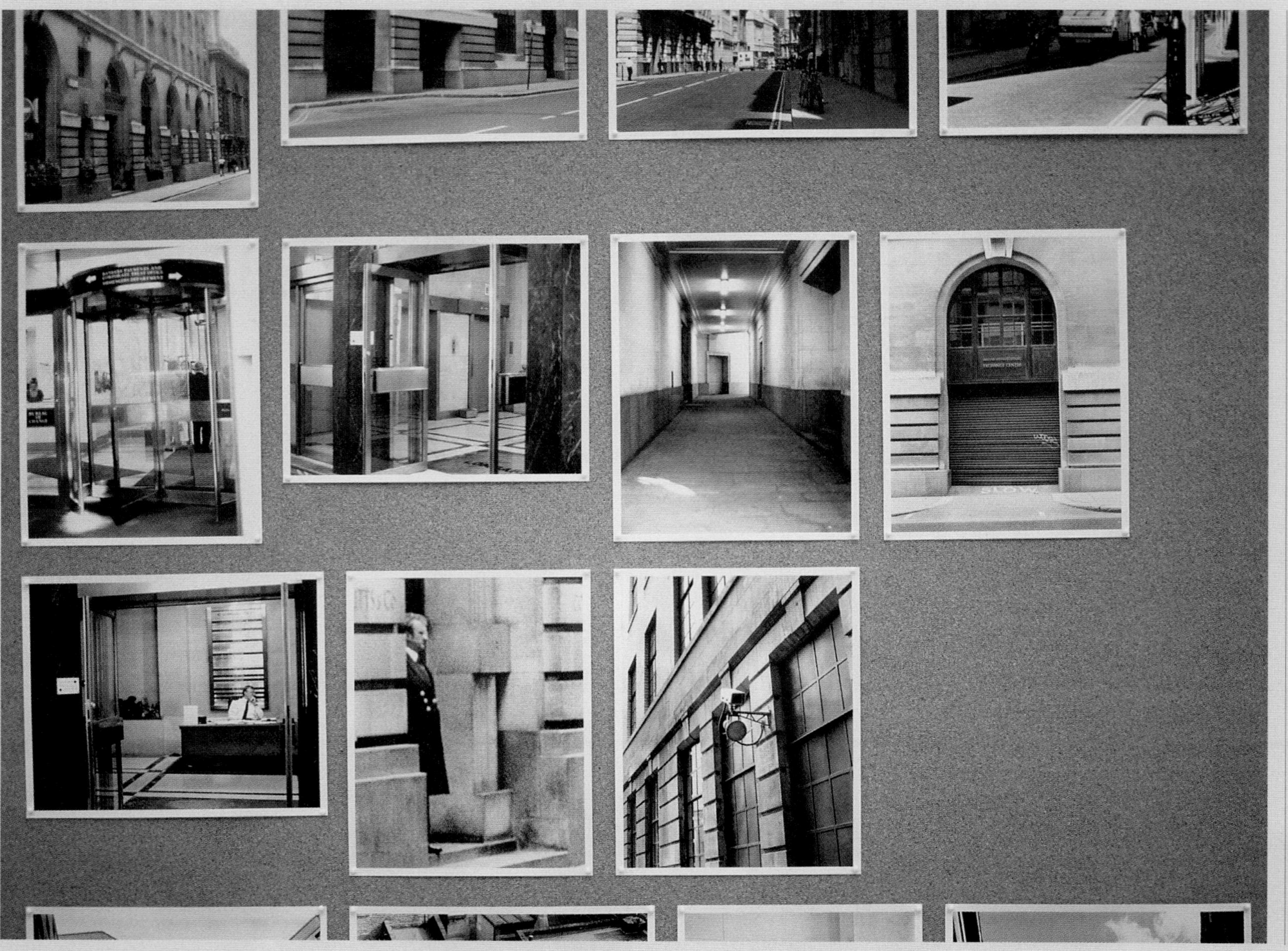

Janice Kerbel is a meticulous and dedicated researcher. Central to her work is the future and its potential. This position is evident in the form her works take: scripts, proposals, plans and promotional materials such as posters and websites. Her early low-key projects were oriented towards stealing, cheating and, more generally, avoiding detection. *Bank Job* (1999) mapped out, through blueprints, photographs and timetables, a way to rob a specific London branch of Coutts & Co. *Three Marked Decks* (1999), if brought into play, would facilitate a dishonest cardplayer's win. The *Home Fittings* (2000–08) series of architectural drawings provided silent and shadow-free passages through various spaces, thereby encouraging deception and concealment.

Underwood (2006) is a series of four beautifully written love letters. Each letter focuses its attention on one of the seasons and uses a digital font that mimics a classic typewriter with a faulty key. Readers engage in a voyeuristic pleasure that is ever so slightly disturbed by the repetitive typographic error and the knowledge that this quaint mistake is lost to us with current technological advances.

Bank Job (detail), 1999. Digital inkjet prints, black and white photographs, aerial photograph, ordnance survey map, blueprint, city map, string, pins, cork, wood. 740 × 120 cm

While working on a garden for insomniacs featuring plants that only bloomed at night-time, Kerbel found that it would be difficult to provide the combination of necessary environmental conditions for the species selected. This inspired *Nick Silver Can't Sleep* (2006), a radio play for insomniacs. While much of Kerbel's work takes the form of plans for unrealised projects, this play was produced live and broadcast on the radio. It enacts a story of unrequited botanical love between a nocturnal subtropical perennial and an exotic climbing perennial in sixteen minutes, the time it takes to drift off to sleep.

Kerbel's *Remarkable* series (2007) also departs from her characteristic tactic of defying the visible.

Fascination with the novel and extraordinary

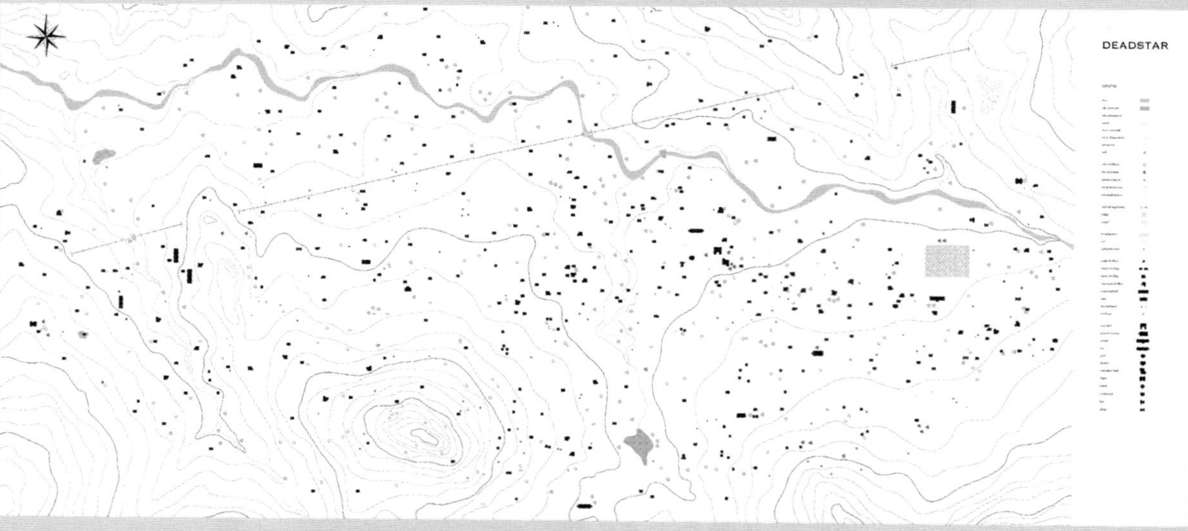

Deadstar (Ghosttown), 2007. Digital copperplate photogravure etching. 140 × 300 cm

These large unique digitally crafted silkscreen posters, originally installed at the Frieze Art Fair, are all about making visible a fictional cast of sensational but marginal and freakish performers. Each poster promoted a fairground act — The Human Firefly, Faintgirl, A One-Eyed Soothsayer and the World's Shyest Person, The Regurgitating Lady and Temperamental Barometric Contortionist — using hyperbolic language and typefaces inspired by the nineteenth-century letterpress. Playing on the art fair's insatiable desire for spectacle, inflation and endless hype, these posters are a gentle reminder of our continuing fascination with the novel and the extraordinary, whether in high culture or popular entertainment.

Kerbel's investigation of the spectacle shifted in 2008 from the fairground to the baseball diamond.

Defying the visible

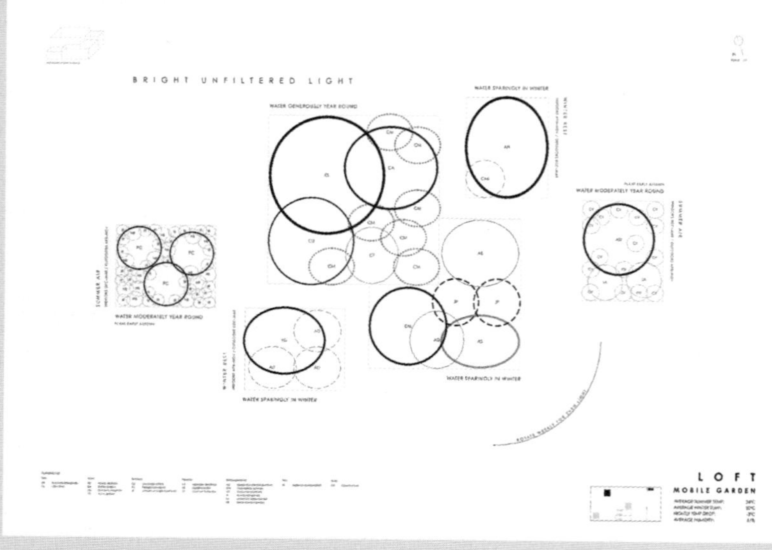

Home Climate Gardens: Loft (Mobile Garden), 2004, Digital inkjet print on paper. 119 × 84 cm

WELCOME

!!TO-NIGHT **ONLY!!**

A GREAT SPECTRAL AND METEORIC WONDER & NEVER BEFORE SEEN

IGGY FATUSE

WILL MAKE A RADIANT APPEARANCE!

THIS EXPLOSIVE BEAUTY,

— "THE HUMAN FIREFLY" —

Bound By Neither **LAWS OF GRAVITY** nor **PRINCIPLES OF THERMOPHOTONICS**

RIGHT BEFORE YOUR VERY EYES

WILL TRANSFORM

RANDOM ENERGY into **VISIBLE LIGHT**

TO RENDER HERSELF AT ONCE

WEIGHTLESS and **LUMINOUS.**

NO ORDINARY ACT OF SPONTANEOUS COMBUSTION!
NO SIMPLE FEAT OF LEVITATIONAL METAMORPHOSIS!
NO MERE TEMPERATURE-GRADIENT INVERSION MIRAGE!

In a Brilliant Aura of Sublime Courage – WITH NO EXTERNAL SOURCE OF IGNITION – This Daring Maverick

WILL ELEVATE TO AN EMINENCE

UPWARDS OF

FORTY-FOUR FEET

8X THE HEIGHT OF THIS POSTER!!

before disappearing into a glowing streak in the sky.

Remarkable: **Iggy Fatuse, The Human Firefly**, 2007. Silkscreen on campaign poster paper. 107 × 157 cm

ON THIS DAY ONLY, Welcome with *Disbelief—*

LIKE THE TRUEST OF SCALES

AND FAIREST OF BEAUTIES,

THIS POLYGRAPHIC WONDER

PERFORMS THE MOST DELICATE BALANCING ACT,

SWOONING

IN THE FACE OF ANY UNTRUTH!

WHITE LIES, BLACK LIES, complex and elaborate LIES – LIES *told to protect,* LIES *told to enchant,*
LIES *told in pursuit* – EVASIONS, EXAGGERATIONS, EQUIVOCATIONS – FALSE MODESTIES, INSINCERITIES, SELF-AGGRANDISEMENTS
– HARMLESS LIES and HURTFUL LIES – LIES *told by omission,* LIES *told to oneself* –

INDEED, ALL forms of FALSEHOOD!

Compensating With EQUAL & OPPOSITE Measure For EACH & EVERY Deception

HER HEARTBEAT SLOWS, HER BREATH SHALLOWS;
HER VISION DIMS, HER PALLOR ASHENS

AND HER DIVINE, SOOTHSAYING BODY
crumples to the ground.

A HEROINE

OF THE SINCEREST BENEVOLENCE AND MOST INFALLIBLE COMPASSION

WITNESS THIS INCREDULOUS SPECTACLE OF STAGGERING

!!EQUILIBRIUM!!

FAINTGIRL

Remarkable: **Faintgirl**, 2007. Silkscreen on campaign poster paper. 107 × 157 cm

Ballgame is a script for a baseball game that uses statistics generated over the last 100 years of the sport to create the perfectly average game. Written in the form of a play-by-play announcement, and still incomplete, the script's early innings have been performed live and presented as an audio piece, via a lone speaker in an empty space. Unlike a game of chess, a baseball game generated through a script is impossible to play, since every game depends on chance. It is not only this impossibility of the narrative that makes the work so compelling, but also its divergence from excitement, extreme feats, crowds, spectacle—almost everything that sport is purported to be.

HOME	AB	R	H	2B	3B	HR	RBI	BB	SO	HBP	SH	SB	CS	AVG	OBP	SLG
White (10), p 6'1", 180lbs.; BR/TR	307	23	52	9	2	1	25	13	69	1	21	2	1	.168	.195	.261
Jones (3), c 6'0", 178lbs.; BR/TR	529	67	143	26	3	14	79	54	48	3	14	4	3	.271	.333	.491
Garcia (35), 1b 6'2", 195lbs.; BR/TR	614	76	177	33	6	20	97	65	71	4	6	12	4	.289	.357	.555
Wright (17), 2b 5'11", 176lbs.; BR/TR	550	77	148	24	5	6	59	60	51	5	14	14	6	.269	.338	.427
Young (16), 3b 6'0", 177lbs.; BR/TR	597	88	166	31	6	16	87	66	72	5	9	9	5	.277	.349	.518
Bell (26), ss 5'9", 163lbs.; BR/TR	605	84	164	28	7	7	63	55	49	4	15	16	6	.272	.330	.447
Davis (7), lf 5'11", 185lbs.; BR/TL	543	84	151	28	6	16	81	64	80	3	6	11	5	.278	.354	.532
Smith (2), cf 6'1", 182lbs.; BL/TL	561	89	162	31	8	13	76	56	56	4	11	15	7	.288	.351	.535
Sullivan (14), rf 6'0", 183lbs.; BR/TR	626	95	183	33	8	14	89	60	66	5	8	12	6	.293	.355	.526

Ballgame: Team Stats (Home), 2009. Silkscreen on paper. 59 × 84 cm

VISITORS	AB	R	H	2B	3B	HR	RBI	BB	SO	HBP	SH	SB	CS	AVG	OBP	SLG
Anderson (12), p 6'3", 212lbs.; BL/TL	273	20	50	6	1	1	20	9	63	1	19	1	0	.183	.198	.252
Clarke (9), c 6'1", 186lbs.; BR/TR	524	59	140	24	4	5	68	38	59	3	7	5	2	.267	.316	.419
Walker (15), 1b 6'1", 198lbs.; BL/TL	560	80	159	30	7	16	88	51	65	6	7	11	3	.284	.346	.542
Wilson (8), 2b 6'1", 198lbs.; BL/TR	586	90	162	29	7	9	71	61	40	2	10	20	6	.276	.341	.472
Brown (4), 3b 5'11", 188lbs.; BL/TR	573	84	157	27	5	13	76	61	54	3	9	12	5	.274	.342	.485
Williams (6), ss 5'10", 172lbs.; BR/TR	588	78	158	27	7	8	58	46	58	3	10	19	3	.266	.319	.450
Martinez (19), lf 6'1", 188lbs.; BL/TL	569	95	166	31	7	23	96	75	74	4	6	17	5	.291	.374	.599
Johnson (2), cf 5'11.5", 179lbs.; BL/TL	567	88	163	25	7	13	63	62	68	3	8	18	5	.288	.355	.504
Baker (22), rf 6'1", 191lbs.; BR/TR	574	84	160	28	11	17	48	48	70	1	20	5	4	.279	.325	.552

Ballgame: Team Stats (Visitors), 2009. Silkscreen on paper. 59 × 84 cm

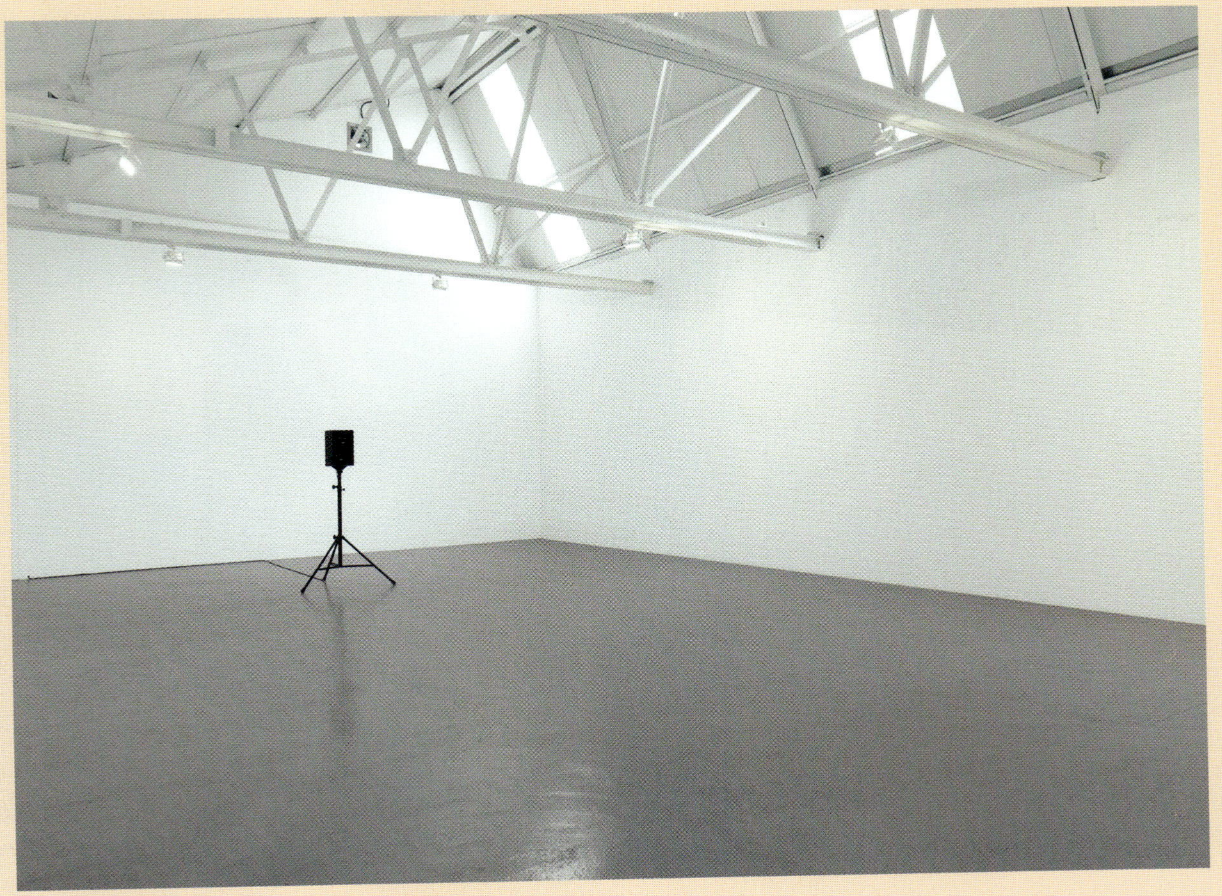

Ballgame (Innings 1–3), 2009. Audio recording, loudspeaker, stand. 74 min.

Hassan Khan

Hassan Khan has developed his work in many directions, using a wide range of media, including video, music, installation, sculpture, performance and writing. Khan has been an active and influential participant in Cairo's cultural life since the mid 1990s both as an artist and as a musician — exhibiting and screening his works as well as publishing, lecturing and performing live concerts in a variety of contexts. His practice concerns the production of space, both conceptually and physically under many different conditions: through words, objects, films, as well as live performance.

'Kompressor (an exhibition based on translating sets of dreams into different forms by the dreamer)' (2006–09) is a series of exhibitions that operate both as discrete spaces and as a totality of shows. In each, a motley group of works that includes photographic prints, animation, books, video and sound pieces, share the space in a precise arrangement. Each piece forms its own unit and the total scenography of the space, a mixture of architecture and sculpture, remains significant. Featured in one show was *stuffedpigfollies* (2007), which consists of six inkjet prints of drawings of cartoon-like pigs in various poses of paranoia, accompanied by a series of enigmatic sentences printed in a font designed by the artist. The series relies on a generic figure, that of the Disney-like humanized pig, but for Khan this is not a 'self-conscious and affected usage of pop icons but rather a rediscovery of generic tropes that are part of my imaginary too'.

Read Fanon you Fucking Bastards (2003–present) is a work that has appeared in many different guises, including text and graphics, email responses to curators of regionally based shows, sentences in fonts designed by the artist, as well as an installation referencing its intentional and self-conscious theft by art students in Vienna. The title is a direct

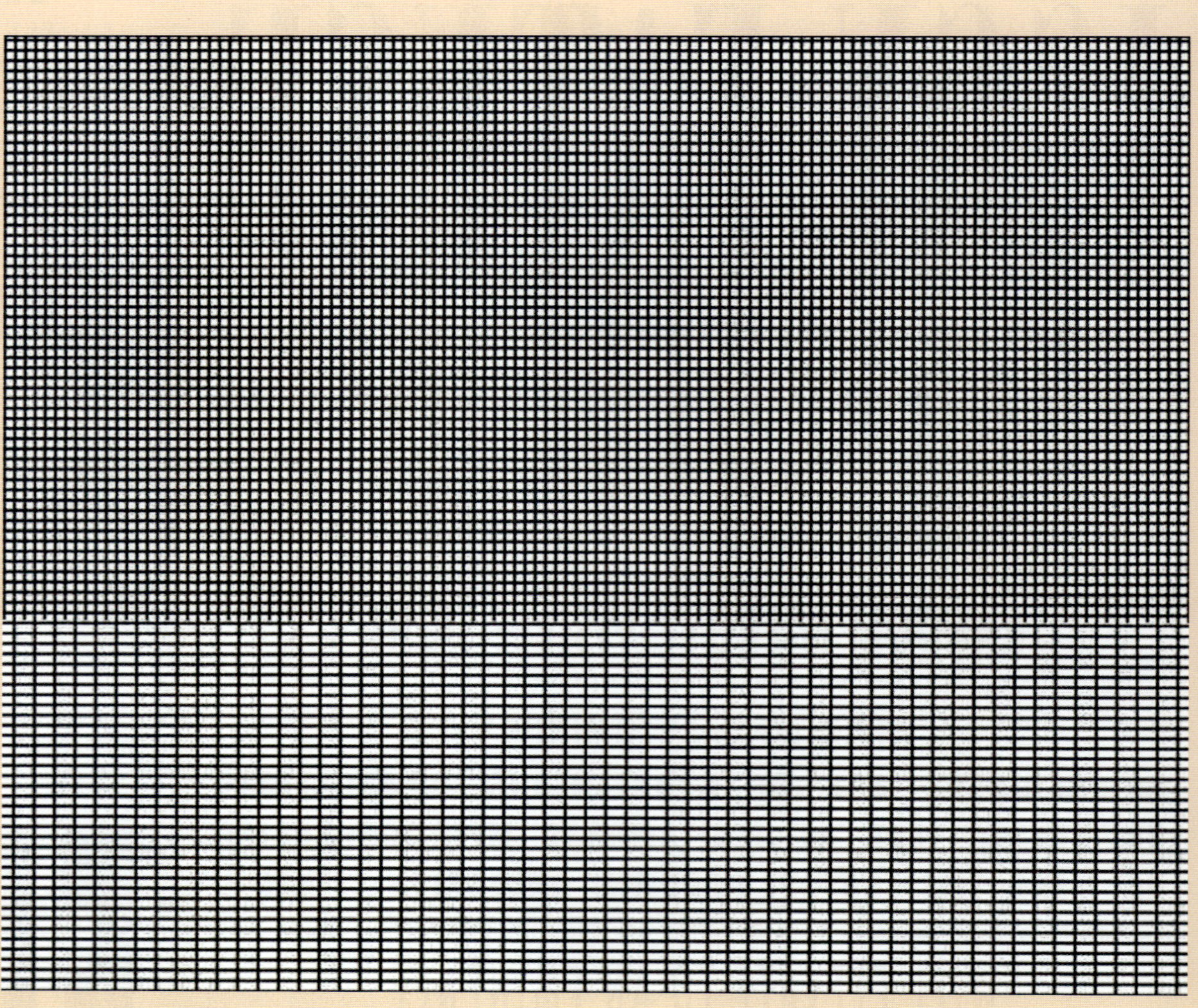

I am not what I am (diagram), 2009. Silent animation. 5 min.

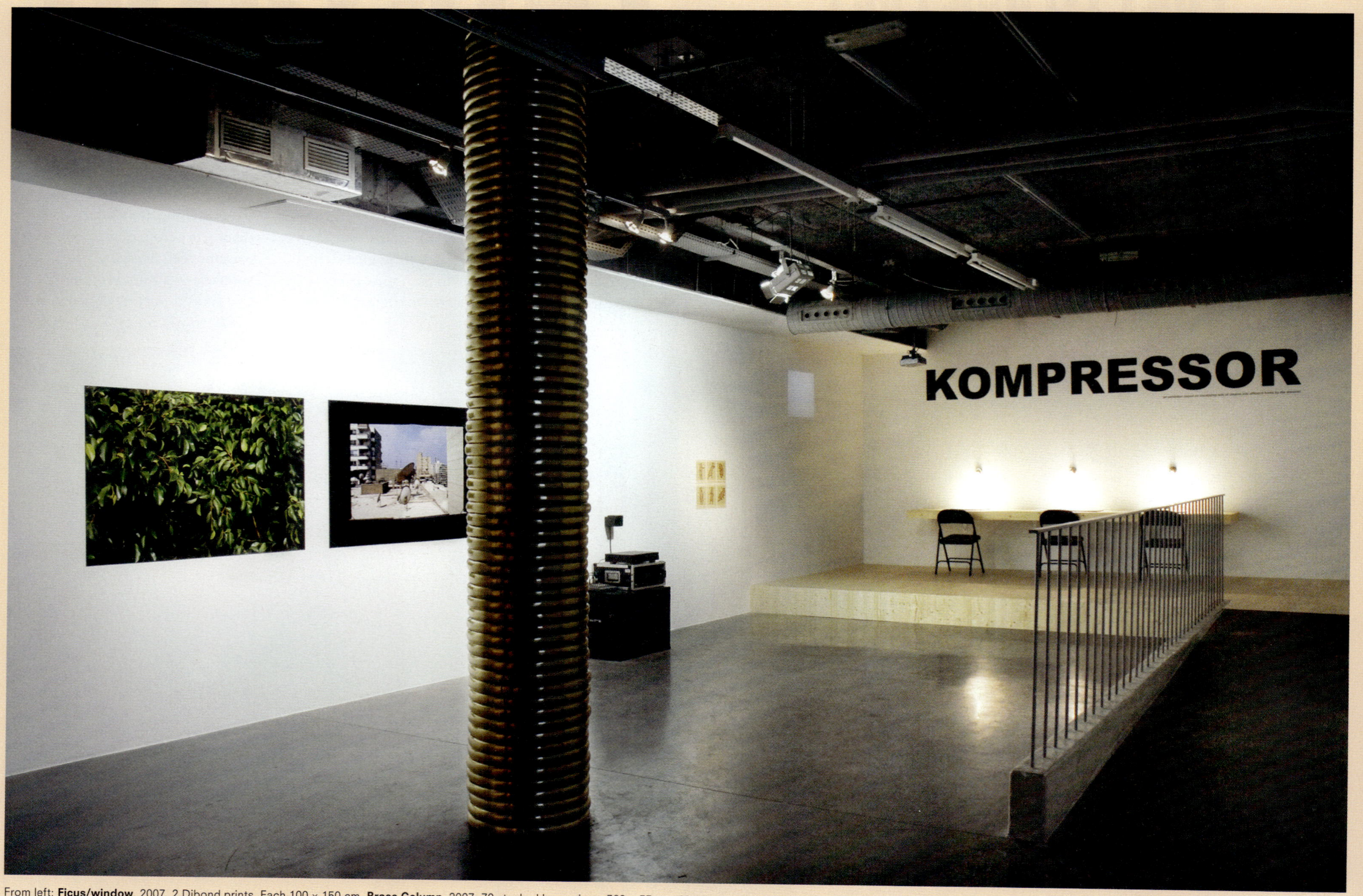

From left: **Ficus/window**, 2007. 2 Dibond prints. Each 100 × 150 cm. **Brass Column**, 2007. 70 stacked brass rings. 360 × 55 cm. **10 1–minute pieces of music based on dreams**, 2006. 10 one–minute music pieces composed and produced by the artist played every 7 minutes. **stuffedpigfollies**, 2007. 6 inkjet print of computer drawings on yellow Canson paper pasted to wall. Each 20 × 25 cm. **Diagrams no.1-6**, 2007. Projected silent animation. 3 min. 24 sec. loop. **The Alphabet Book**, 2006. Artist book. 80 × 40 cm. From the installation **Kompressor (an exhibition based on translating sets of dreams into different forms by the dreamer)**, 2007

Daily concerns of communication

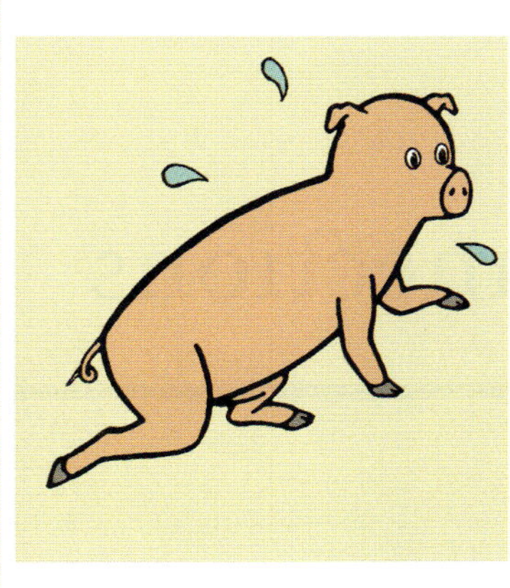

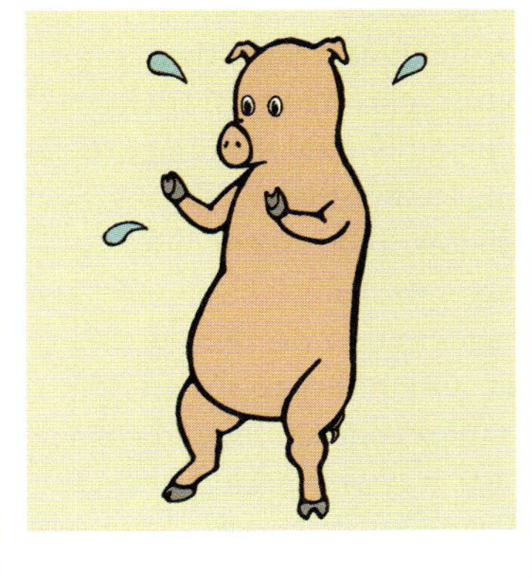

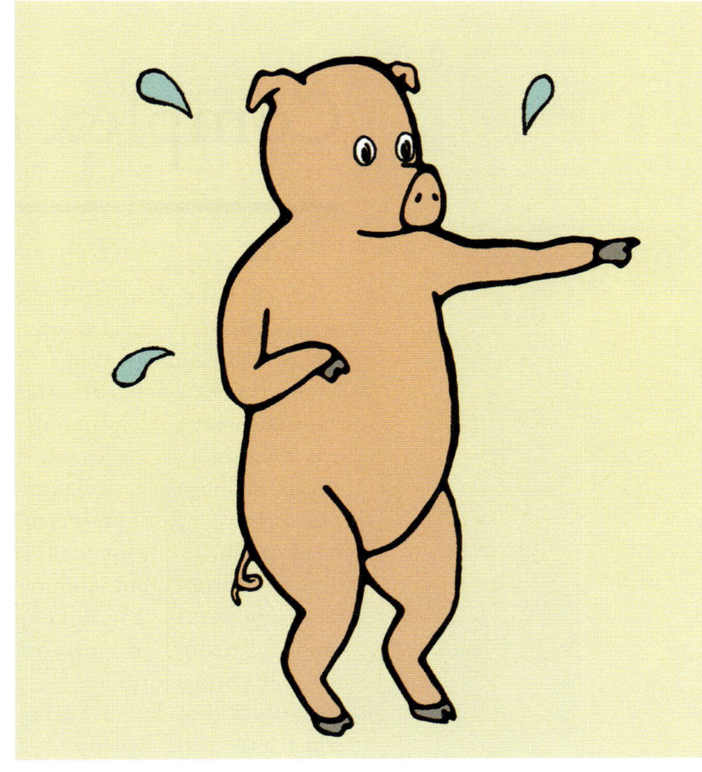

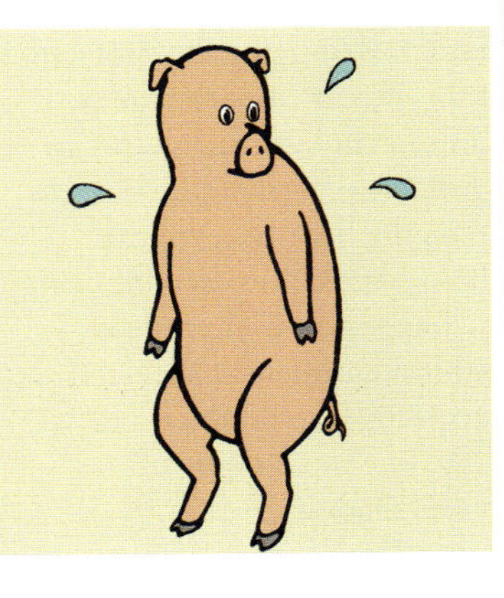

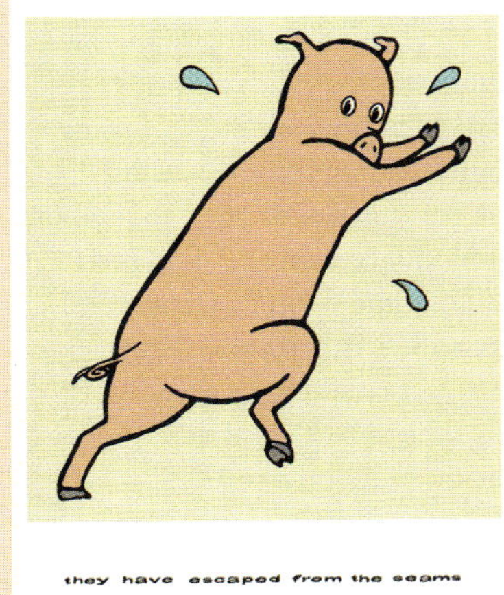

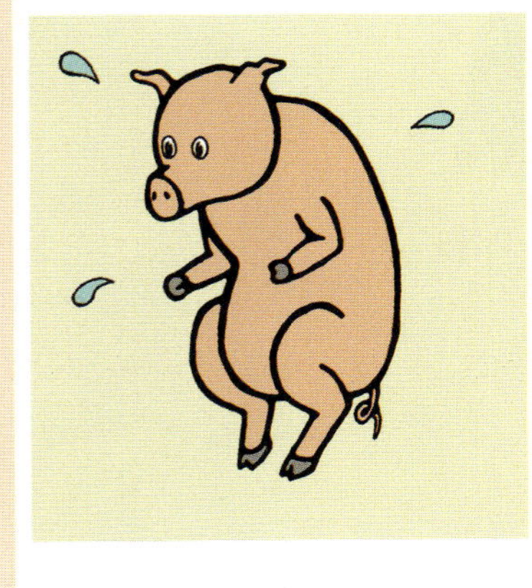

stuffedpigfollies, 2007. 6 inkjet print of computer drawings on yellow Canson paper pasted to wall. Each 20 × 25 cm

response to the reductive demands of the knowledge industry, as well as an attempt to lift the influential philosopher and pioneer of anti-colonialism Franz Fanon out of the academic context and into the vernacular.

For *Decoy* (2008), the art audience that was in attendance for the opening dinner of the exhibition in which the work was included was invited to 'experience an artwork by Hassan Khan'. As well as the invitation, the artist produced a minimalist sculpture composed of stacked wood, which replaced and was cut to the same dimensions as one of the tables in the expensive restaurant where the dinner took place. What was revealed by the end of the dinner was that four of the guests with which the audience had been socializing were actually actors

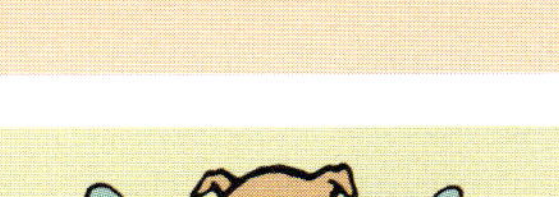

CHAPTER II

He walked up to me. I hadn't seen him for easily eight years. The neighbour, the younger brother of someone I knew very slightly in my childhood. We had always known that he was a bit slow, in the way children sort of always know. As a young boy he played Judo at the comfortably upper-middle class sporting club, and when he grew a bit older he started bodybuilding. He still looks like he is bodybuilding; it still feels like he is a bit slow. He walks up to me- or to be more precise, I suddenly hear a voice from behind my back. He is saying 'can I shake your hands' in his slow smiling way. I turn around and immediately recognize him. I Put down my bag and extend my hand. A hand and a shake. He then starts talking. Chit-chat. My sister approaches- greetings are renewed. His permanent condition is clear to both of us. Something is a bit off. The way he carries himself- the shades he is wearing; perfectly normal on any one else become, on him, a revealing detail of the seriousness of his mental condition. The slow measured pace of his speech, the way he asks about us after all those years. My sister informs him that she is now working as an assistant director. His face momentarily lights up, and he proceeds to tell us about his friend. His friend who is at this very moment flying back to Dubai. His friend who started bodybuilding and then discovered he has special powers. Who can jump from a 30-storey building. Snap a steel rod in two. He addresses my sister- staring at her unblinkingly with an impassive unrevealing smile- it is impossible to understand what is going on behind those eyes. Well my friend wants to make a video, a show of some of his most amazing feats of endurance. My sister states that she can't really help him. He goes on without registering her reaction- do we know Abu-Ghraïb, the prison in Iraq- Abu Ghraib. Yes. Do you remember the torture? He asks. Yes. He wants to make a show on video where he would re-enact the torture of the prisoners in Abu Ghraib, a demonstration of his amazing powers. My sister repeats that she can't really help him. Some people in Germany are interested, he adds, lazily trying to catch her interest. I feel uncomfortable, but at the same time I am purely amazed. I knew that my narrative for the Shedhalle piece was on its way; the striving for a moment, a flicker that takes itself outside of constraints the moment that is beyond translation that lies bey-

54

Modulation no 1, 2007. Fictional text written by the artist printed on vintage paper. 21 × 27 cm

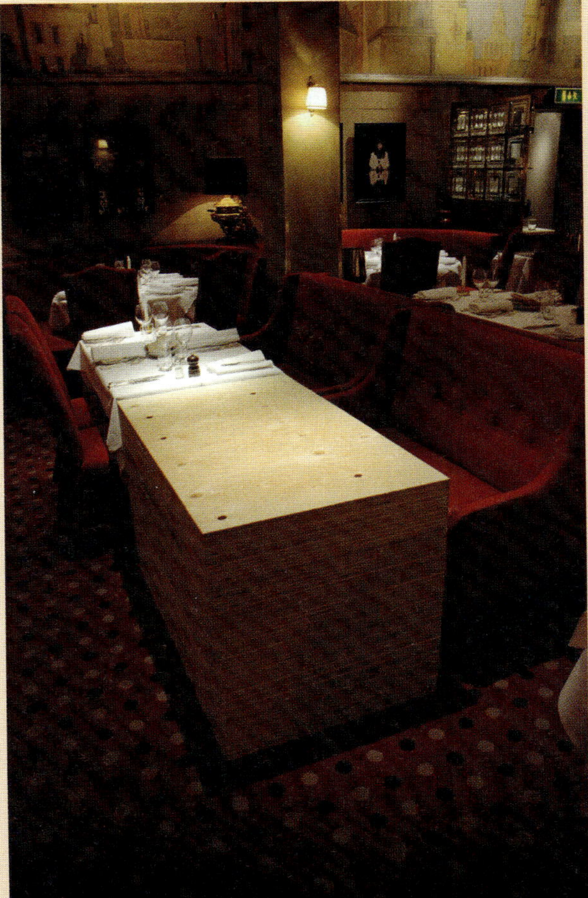

Subtle investigation

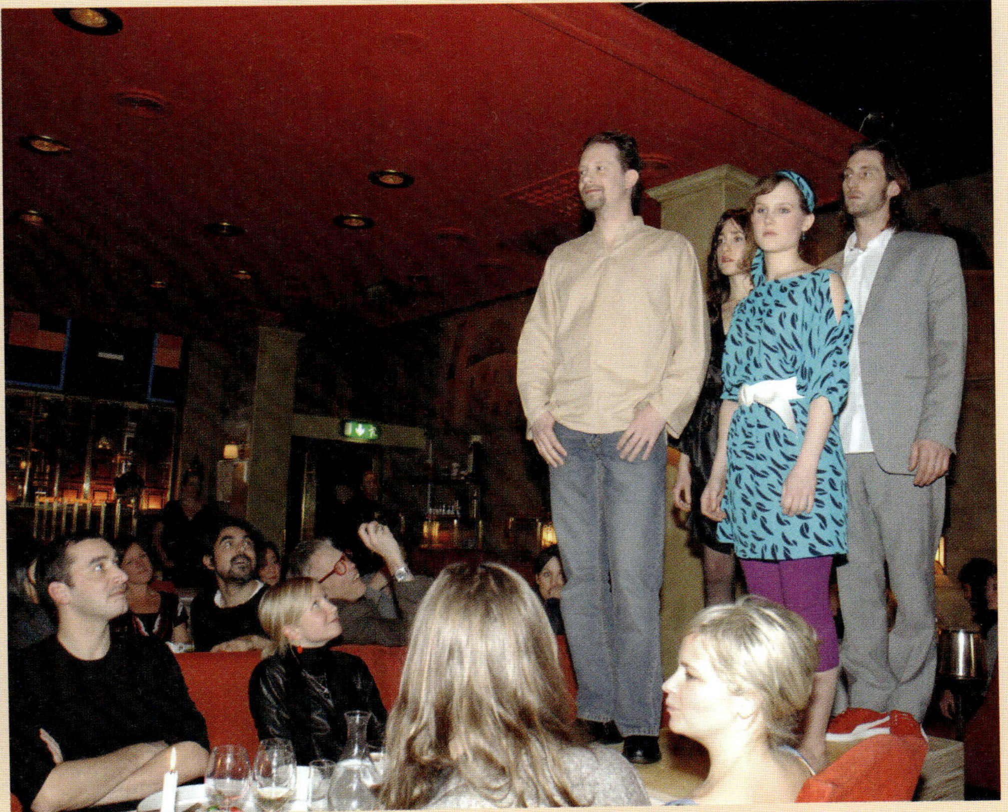

whom the artist had worked with over a long period of time to develop characters, based on art-world stereotypes, specifically for this dinner. The climax was the moment at which the actors, near the end of the dinner, revealed themselves through a series of toasts and counter-toasts running the gamut from embarrassing private confessions to generalized platitudes about art before proceeding to mount the sculpture, thus desacralizing the work of art and transforming it back into a wooden platform. In this work, a subtle investigation of what exactly an art object is in relation to its audience goes head to head with social contexts and the daily concerns of communication.

Whatever medium he works in, for Khan the notions of presence and situation are key, producing new encounters with forms of sociability, as well as making cultural operations the raw material of the work.

Decoy, 2008. 3 course meal for 500 Swedish Kroner, stacked plywood sculpture installed in place of one of the dinner tables at TheaterGrillen Restaurant in Stockholm, unannounced performance by actors

Yuki Kimura

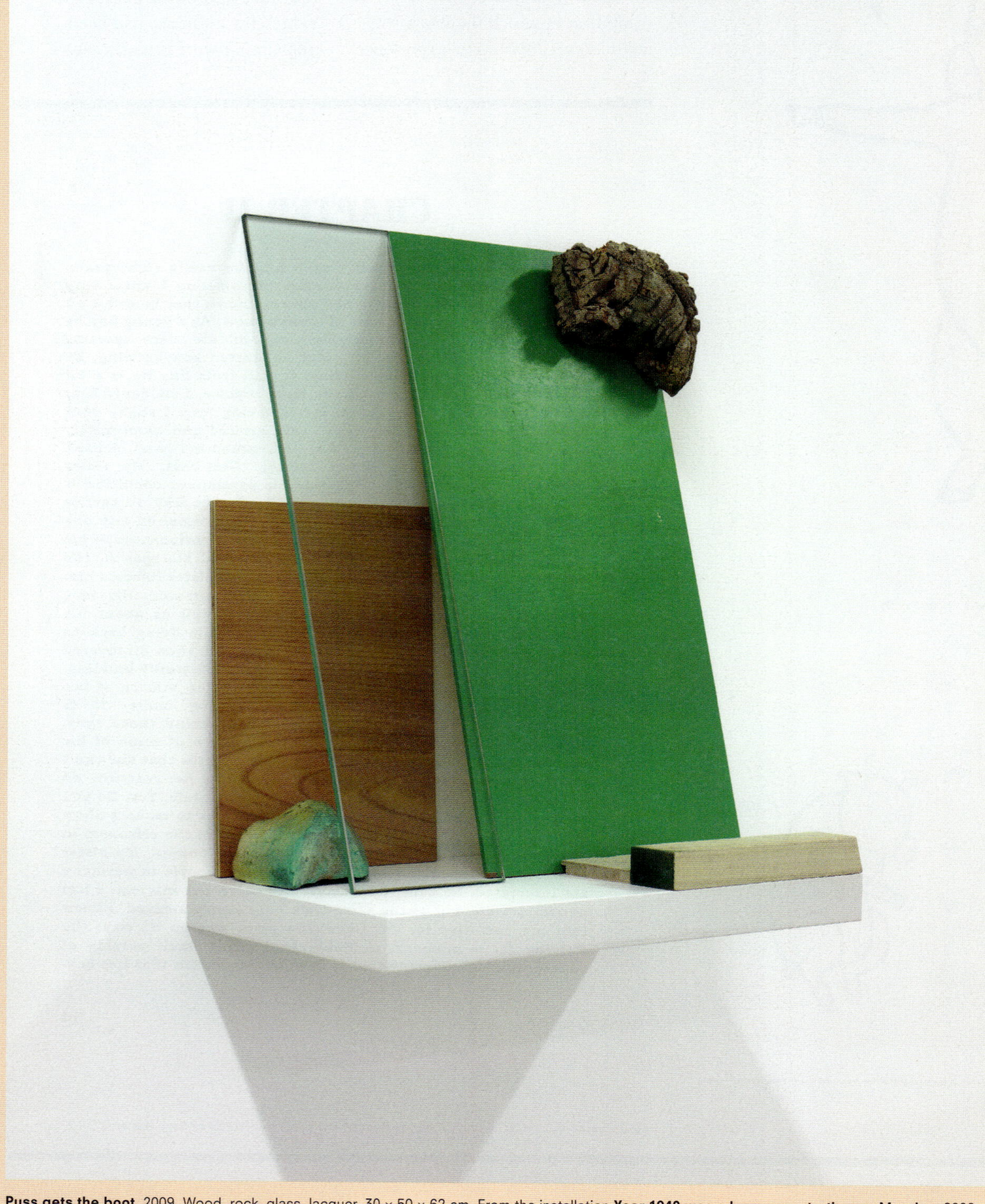

Puss gets the boot, 2009. Wood, rock, glass, lacquer. 30 × 50 × 62 cm. From the installation **Year 1940 was a leap year starting on Monday**, 2009

Complex connections

While choosing photography as her medium, which captures the reality before our eyes, Yuki Kimura endeavours to draw out those elements hidden from the eye, what she calls the 'latent effects' of images—associations that summon up our powers of imagination, leading on to other, derivative images. For Kimura photography is not a means of capturing reality, but a material for giving visual form to conceptual ideas. In her works, which also include video and more recently sculpture and installation, she gathers trifling events and mundane images to entice the viewer into a totally new realm—a construct of her imagination. The experience is akin to entering Alice's wonderland through the looking glass.

Initially taking her own photographs, in 2003 Kimura arrived at the technique of using found photographs. By using the private souvenirs of anonymous individuals, pictures of no special value, come upon by chance and not sufficiently representative of a particular era or set of social customs to be classed as vintage, she conjures up a certain association or fiction that she invites us to interpret as we choose. Rather than placing the image in a frame, she teams it with objects to form sculptures, which she develops into a spatial installation.

To avoid bringing the aura and history of the original into her work, Kimura does not use found photographs in their existing form. She removes part of the image, or makes additions, changes colours, or cuts out fragments and turns them into objects, playing visual tricks by manipulating the image to give wings to her flights of fancy. She recognizes the potential for images to change, or of derivative images to take on a life of their own and in turn to spawn complex connections and changes in her way of thinking as a result of using a computer.

Image and the shadow (st. elmo's fire) (2006) is constructed around fifteen monochrome photographs of a mysterious object found in a Paris flea market. Removing the silhouettes of this model from the images, Kimura cut out their shapes in white Plexiglass and lined them up on the floor beneath the photographs, thus reconfiguring the images from multiple two- and three-dimensional perspectives to produce a new, wave-like topography of 'photo shadows'.

In YOU MAY ATTEND A PARTY WHERE STRANGE CUSTOMS PREVAIL (2006), which takes its title from the message in a fortune cookie, Kimura begins by cutting the arched door from a found photograph of a castle wall, then cuts the same arch shape over and over again from background images in other photographs. In the resulting aggregation, spread around the gallery, connections are forged through this encoded image between fragments of landscape from different, unrelated, locations.

Pictures of a Man (2007) grew out of found photographs of a man with a moustache, a figure with whom Kimura felt a fateful connection. Picking out distinguishing details, such as the wallpaper behind him, his nose and his moustache, she recomposed them in photographic and sculptural forms.

In this way, she makes a playful experiment that tests the notion that photographs are not simply records, but triggers that create memories and wellsprings of the imagination.

Encoded image

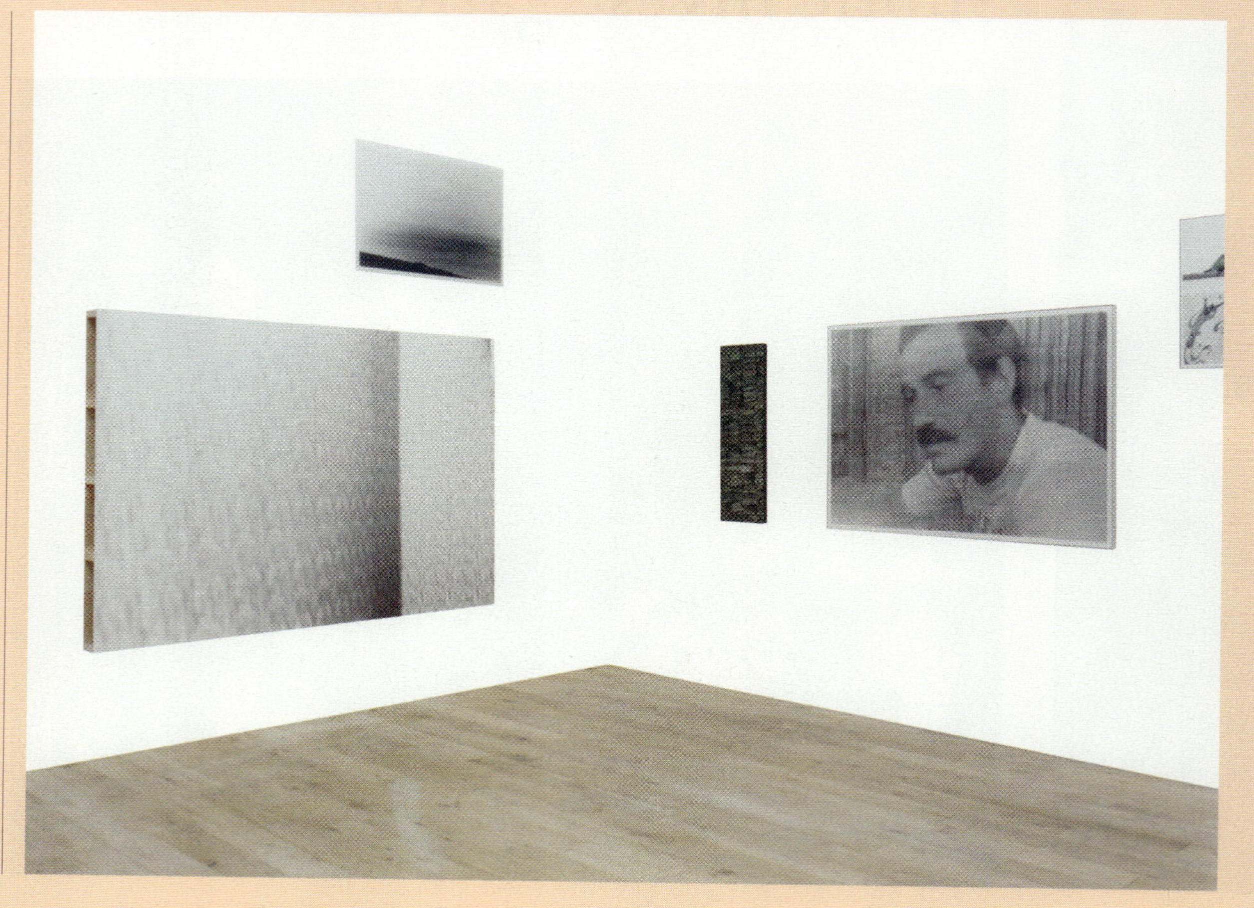

Wall paper, 2007. Lambda print mounted on wood, laminate. 120 × 178 × 10 cm. **Smoked landscape**, 2007. Lambda print mounted on Plexiglas, wood. 56 × 80 × 3 cm. **The pattern**, 2007. Oil on wood. 105 × 25 × 3 cm. **The man**, 2007. Lambda print mounted on alpolic, laminate, frame. 86 × 121 × 3 cm. **Untitled**, 2007. Lambda print mounted on alpolic, laminate, frame. 51 × 37 × 3 cm.

From the installation **Pictures of a Man**, 2007

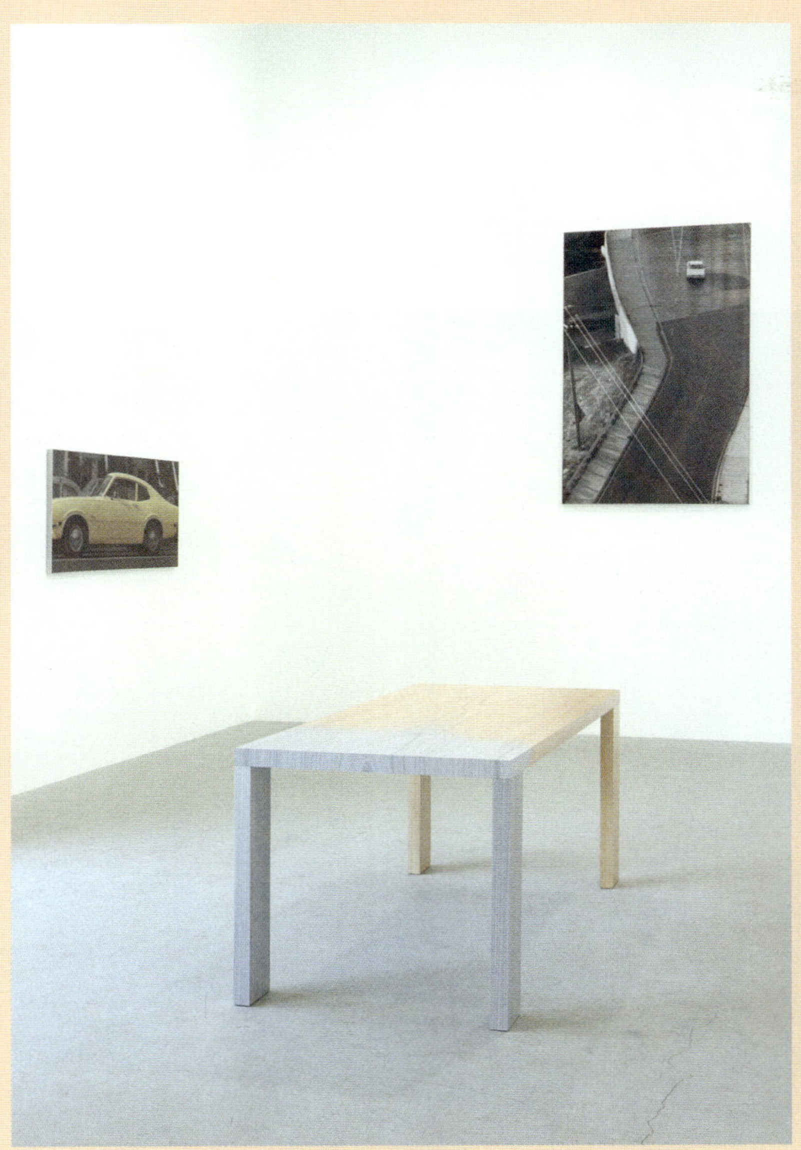

Forgetting Range / yellow, 2009. Lambda print mounted on alpolic, frame. 150 × 64 cm.
Forgetting Range / a table, 2007. Ink jet print on PVC sheet, wood, iron. 72 × 80 × 180 cm. **Forgetting Range / y**, 2009. Lambda print mounted on alpolic, frame. 178 × 120 cm

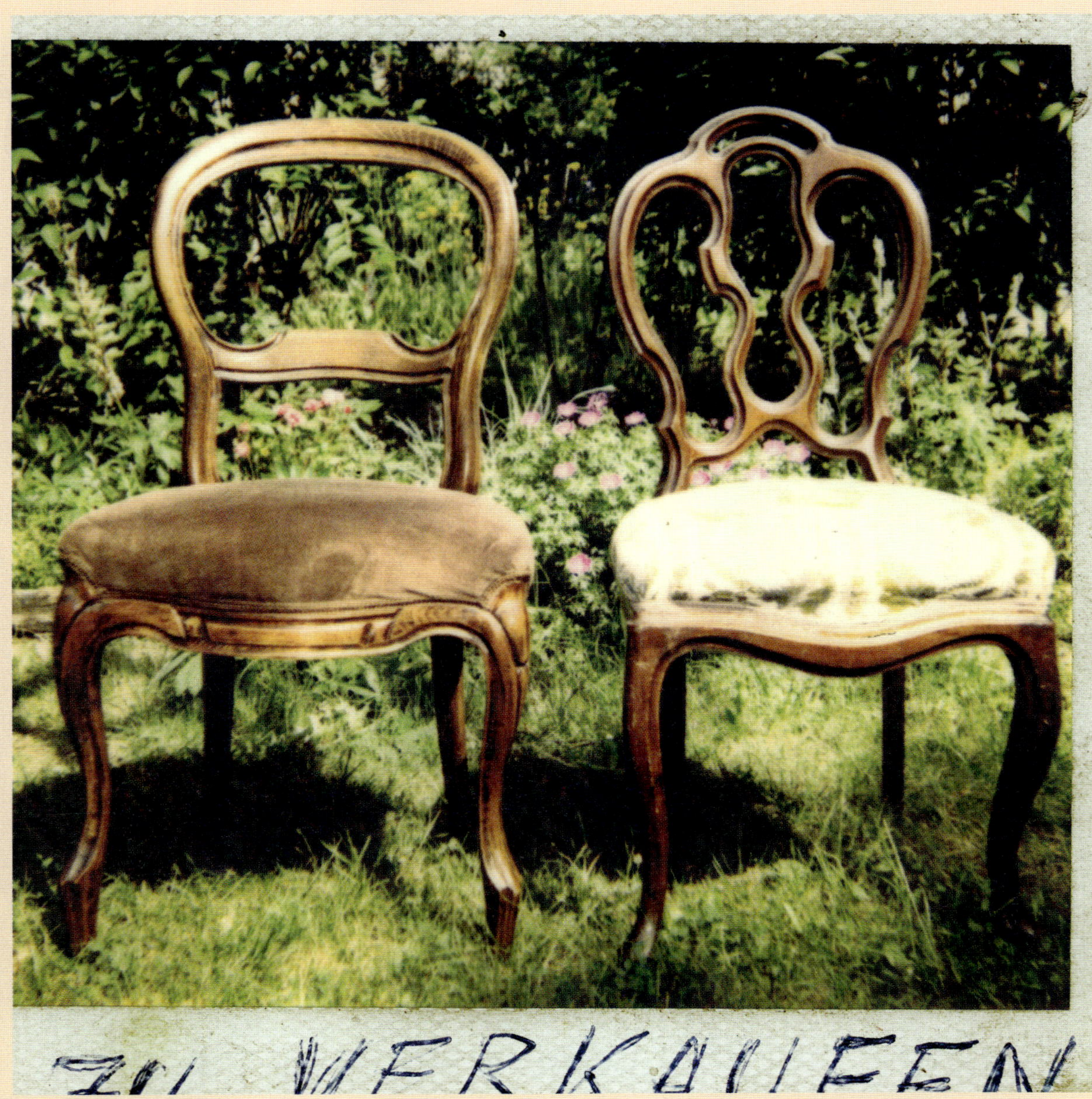

Zuver, 2005. Lambda print mounted on alpolic, frame. 80 × 80 cm

Cylinder shape shadow, 2008. Wood, acrylic colour. 82 × 7 × 7 cm. **White board**, 2008. Wood, oil pastel, lacquer. 77 × 80 × 1 cm. **Records of pray, or play 02**, 2008. Lambda print mounted on alpolic, laminate, frame. 70 × 71 cm. From the installation, **Records of pray, or play**, 2008

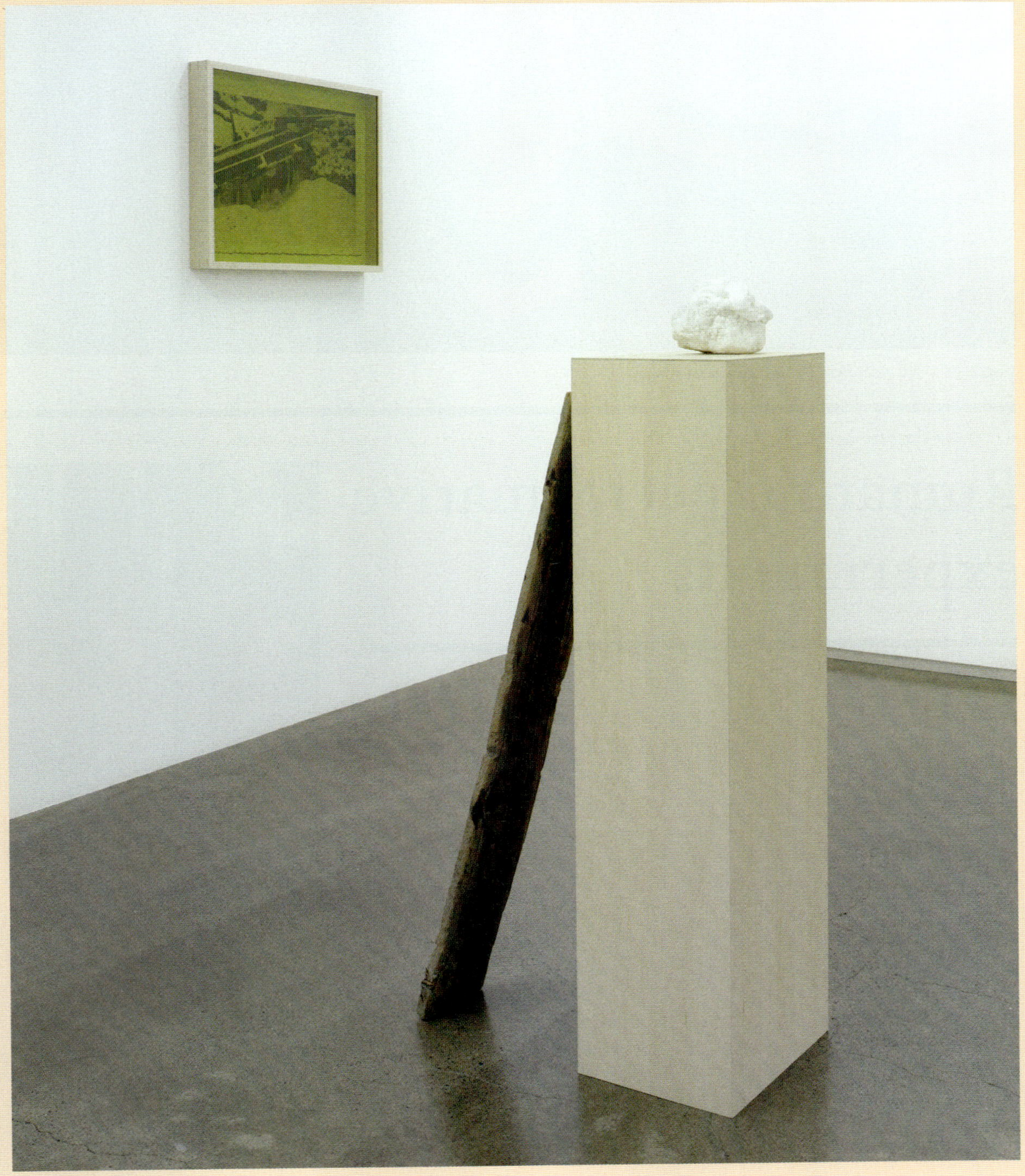

Untitled, 2009. Lambda print mounted on alpolic, coloured plexiglass, frame. 51 × 69 × 7 cm. **Reproduction**, 2009. Wood, rock, plastic clay. 70 × 33 × 118 cm. From the installation **Year 1940 was a leap year starting on Monday**, 2009

Ragnar Kjartansson

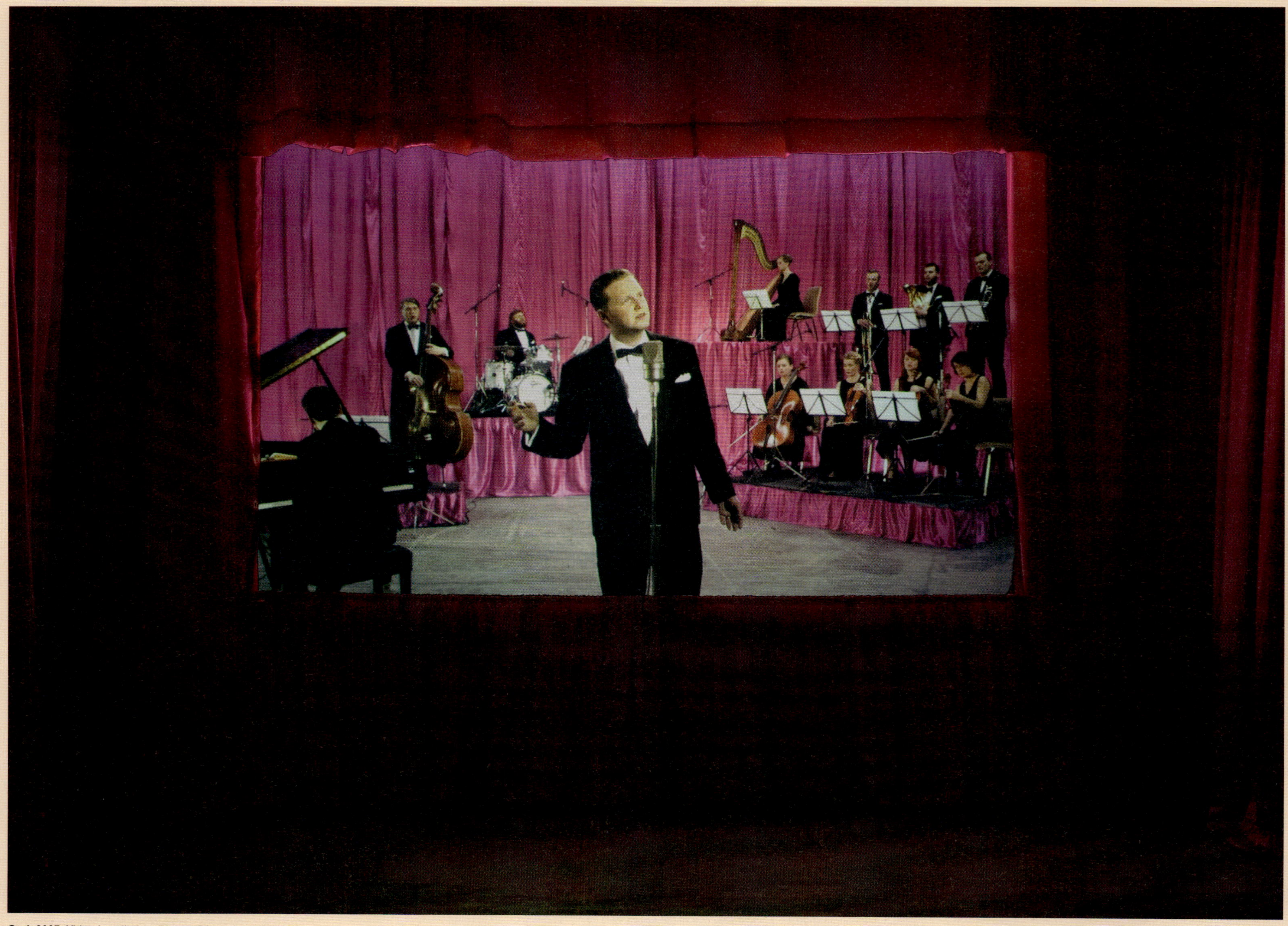

God, 2007. Video installation. 30 min. Dimensions variable

Romantic performative experiments

Ragnar Kjartansson's career to date can be characterized by his repetitive, durational and sometimes romantic performative experiments in the realms of visual art, music and theatre. Like many artists today, he works with whatever medium best suits his needs; while known mostly for his performances, he also makes paintings, videos and drawings. The artist often inhabits musical genres, whether classical, popular and experimental, to explore contradictory emotions: he is attracted to the opposites of sorrow and happiness, horror and beauty, as well as drama and humour.

The large screen video *God* (2007) features Kjartansson dressed in a 1950s-era tuxedo as he repeatedly sings into a microphone, 'Sorrow conquers happiness.' With a shiny, kitsch magenta backdrop and a big band behind him, Kjartansson evokes another era with its attendant emotions of humour, sadness and joy.

For Manifesta 7 Kjartansson performed *Schumann Machine* (2008). He memorized Robert Schumann's *Dichterliebe* and sang the sixteen-song cycle for eight hours a day while his collaborator Davíd Thór Jonsson accompanied him on the piano. Spectators encountered the duo

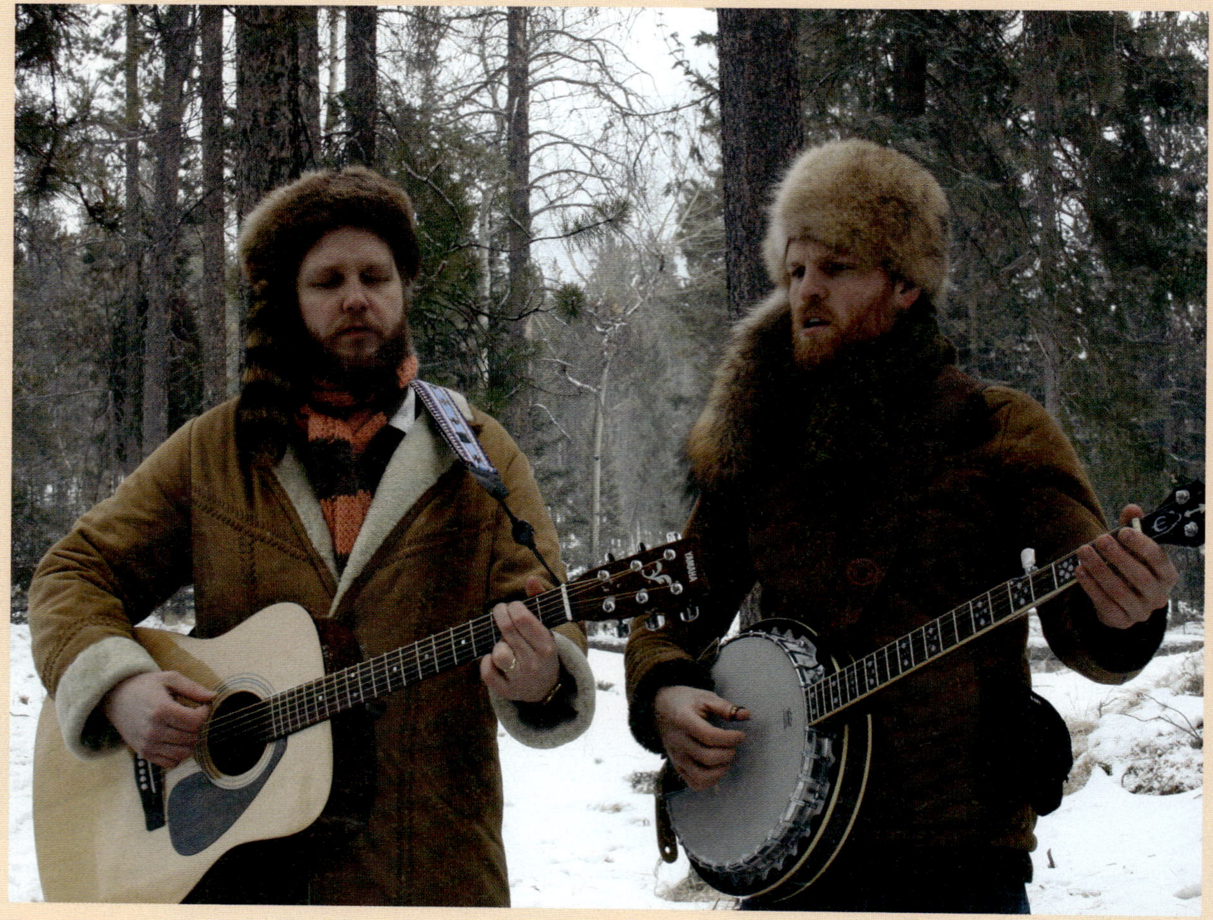
The End — Rocky Mountains, 2009. 5–channel HD video. 30 min. 58 sec.

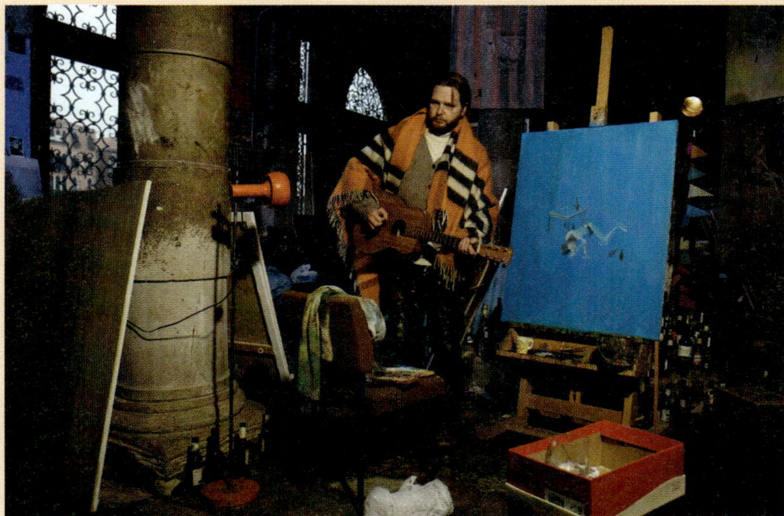

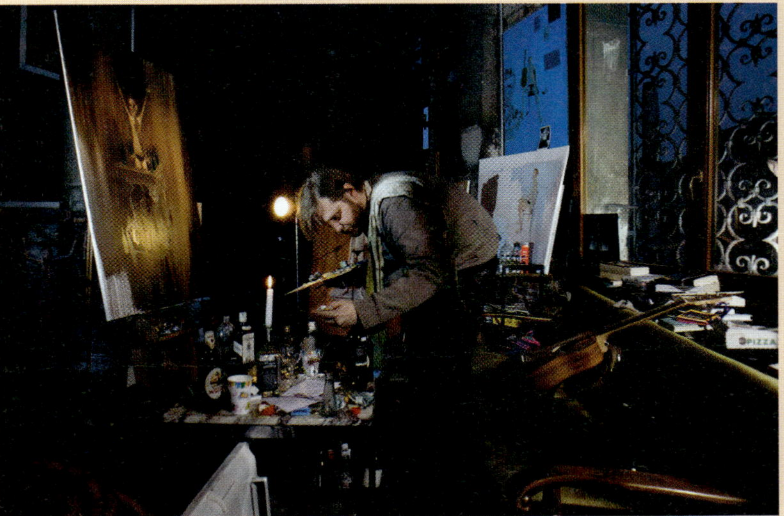

The End — Venice, 2009. Performance installation

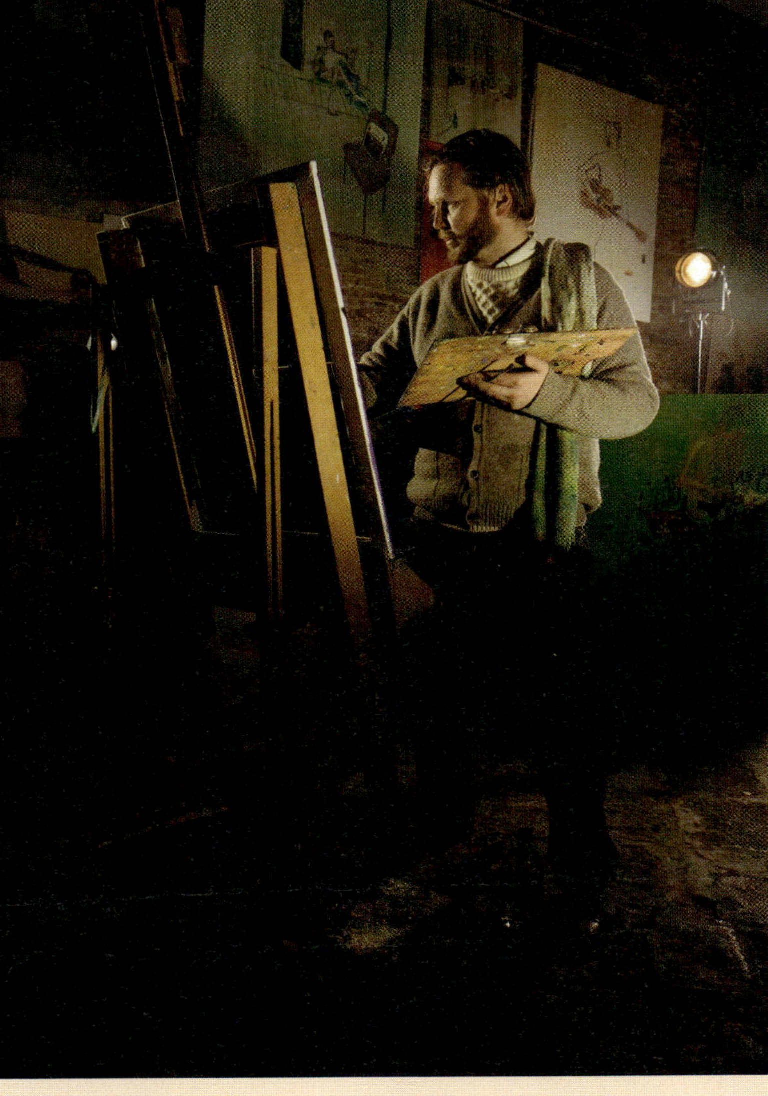

Countless fictions

drinking prosecco and smoking cigars while performing in the courtyard of a toboacco factory in Rovereto, a town in northern Italy.

At the 2009 Venice Biennale, Kjartansson presented two works under the apocalyptic heading *The End*. The central component was a vaguely fin-de-siècle performance that lasted the entire length of the Biennale, for which Kjartansson transformed the ground floor of the fourteenth-century Palazzo Michiel dal Brusà on the Grand Canal near the Rialto into a painter's studio equipped with various props including cigarettes, a record player, bottles of beer and spirits. Every day, with the exception of Mondays, the artist painted his young Speedo-clad model, Haukur Bjornsson, another Icelandic artist, who posed with a beer bottle or played the guitar while day after day

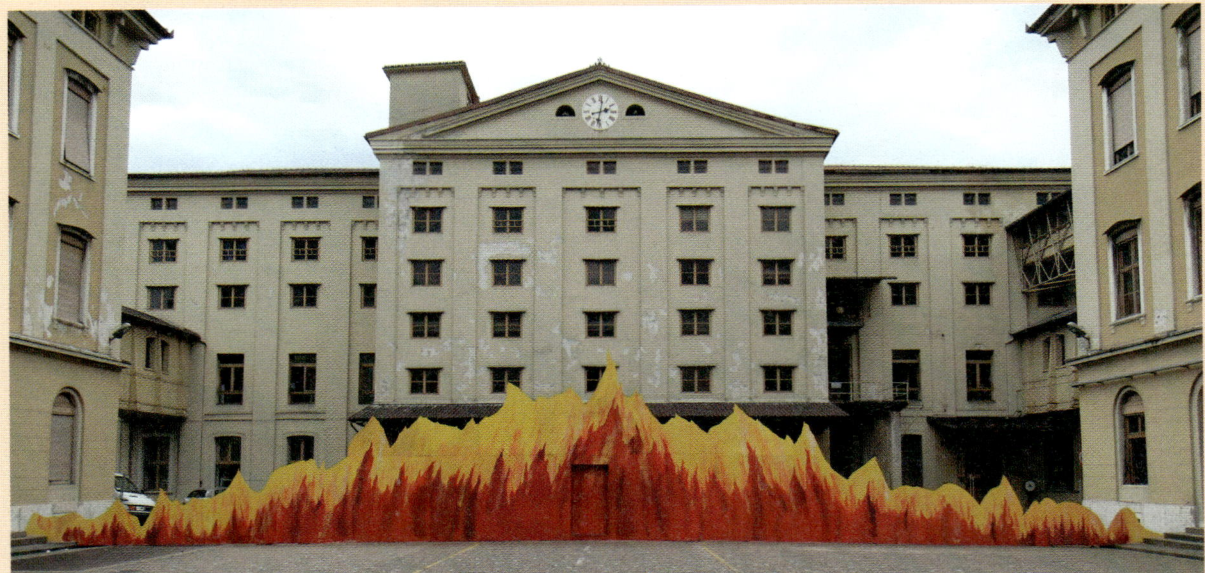

Between parody and sincerity

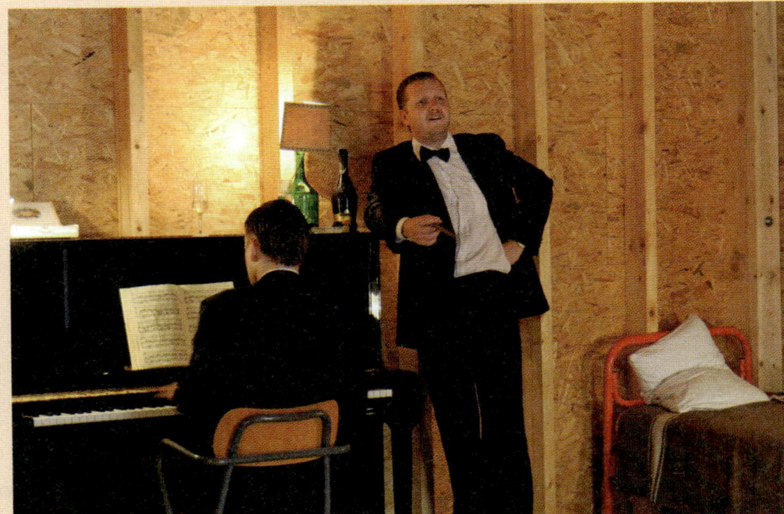

Schumann Machine, 2008. HD video. 52 min.

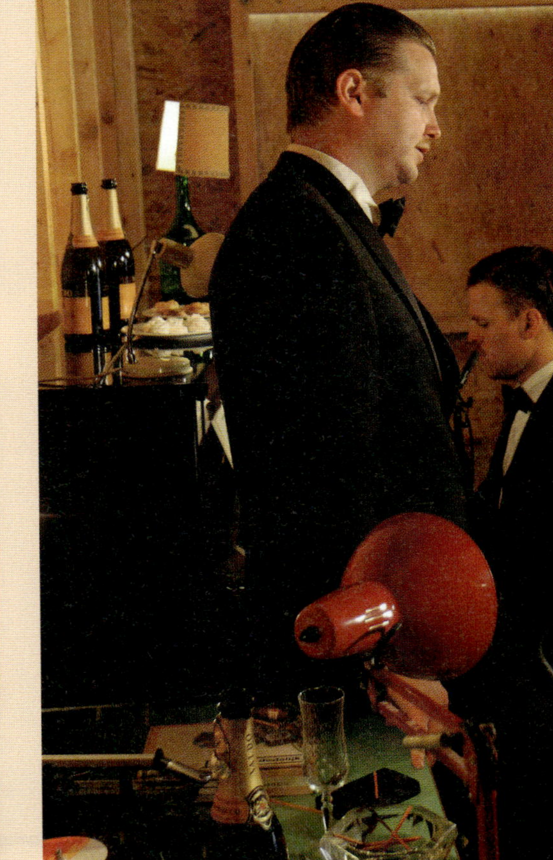

Kjartansson sought to render his form on canvas. The finished paintings were hung all around the space and stacked up against various corners. The absurdity of this spectacle was tempered by the fact that slowly, day-by-day, Kjartansson becomes the performer he is performing.

Installed in another room on the same floor was a compelling five-channel video shot in the Rocky Mountains. It depicts two musicians — Kjartansson and his collaborator Jonsson — playing folk/country-meets-experimental music on a frozen, snowclad lake. Both characters are dressed as Davy Crockett-type frontiersmen, an extreme example of a stereotype that persists and contributes to countless fictions projected on to the Western landscape.

Kjartansson always carries a notebook with him, which he fills with sketches and words. He makes beautiful, delicate and often very funny drawings documenting his daily activities or exploring scenarios for future projects. On a research trip to Venice he covered a page with a gondola; another drawing featured Bob Dylan in one of his mariachi-style suits enthusiastically playing keyboards. These notebooks present another side of Kjartansson, and remind us, as in the dual character of the Venice performance, that his work occupies a space between parody and sincerity.

Friedrich Kunath

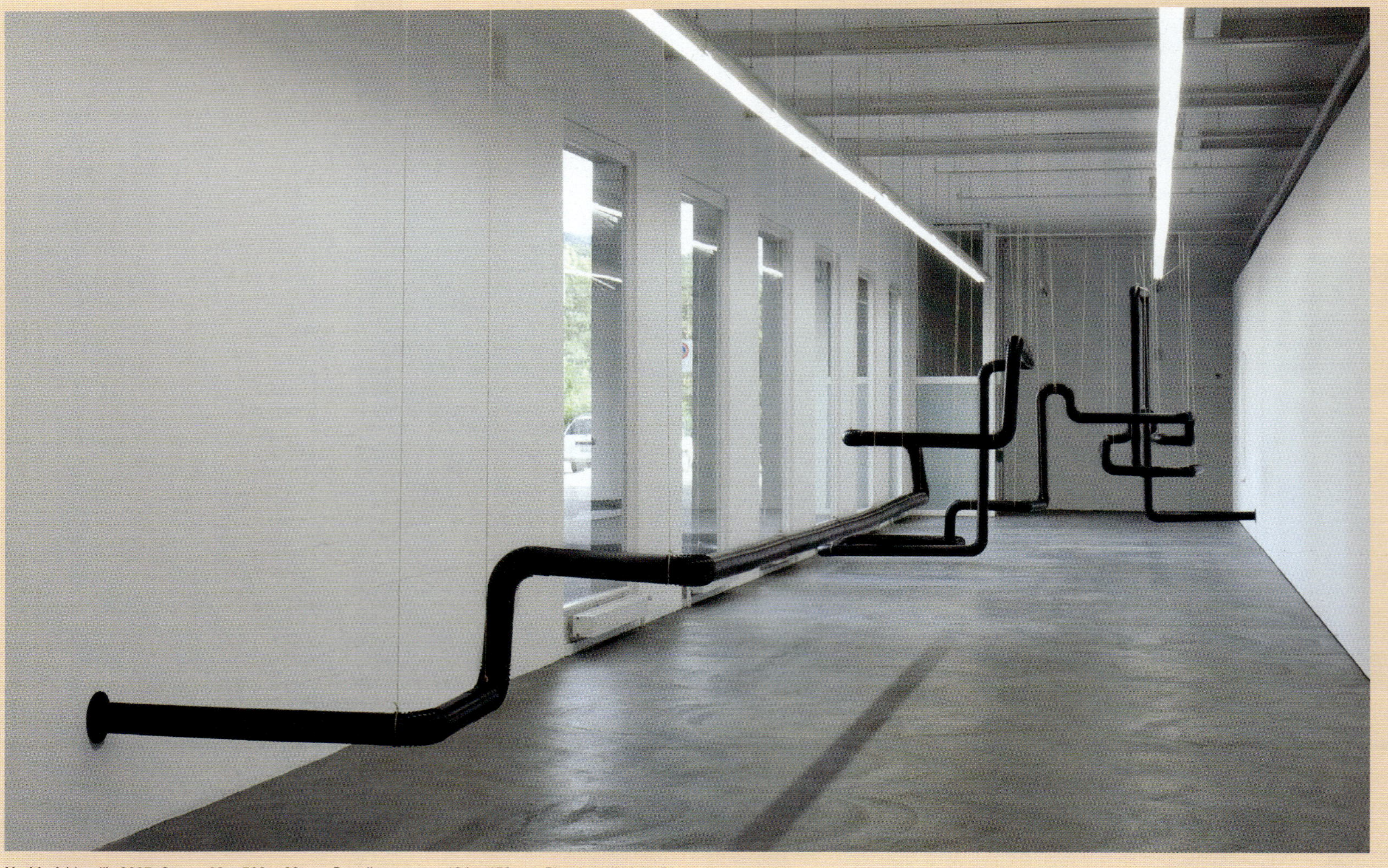

Untitled (detail), 2007. Stove. 62 × 389 × 29 cm. Pencil on paper. 194 × 150 cm. Pipe installation. Dimensions variable

Friedrich Kunath is neither simply a painter nor a sculptor. He is a stand-up comedian, a Romantic, a poet and a shipwrecked sailor. Splitting his time between Cologne and Los Angeles, Kunath works across a wide variety of media, including painting, sculpture, video, installation, drawing, photography and performance. In all of them, what stands out is his ability to express the loneliness of the long-distance runner amidst a pack of alienated fellow travellers. Kunath is an emotional lone gunman, stranded on a sea of indifference. While he treats all of his chosen media equally, one gets a sense that he is grounded by his prolific production of paintings. These works range in scale from the intimate to the monumental, but in each case they demonstrate a penchant for the fragile and fleeting character of existence, while channelling his heartbreaking penchant for slapstick melancholia.

Combining a light painterly touch with a psychedelic, stained and dripping palate,

Kunath occupies a space somewhere between figuration and abstraction, while constantly grounding his work in the emotional here and now of love, loss and lamentation.

A small painting by Kunath, *One Day Goodbye will be Farewell* (2009), speaks to these core concerns, as a multi-hued sun vanishes into a vaporous haze. The sun sets every day anew, but love does not last. In other paintings, we see examples of Kunath's use of appropriated text and iconography to further his existential quest. In *Hourace 2* (2009), for example, the artist applies to his canvas a hand-lettered poem by the nineteenth-century American educational reformer Horace Mann that laments the fleeting nature of time. In an earlier work, *It seems as men get older they turn towards the water* (2007), the artist depicts a giant blue gouache tsunami that is about to crash down on an empty lone skiff, its anchor having become dangerously unmoored from the ocean floor. As the blue water comes to its crescendo on the surface of the canvas, we are left wondering if the captain of the ship has been swept out of his now empty boat by a previous wave and dragged down to a watery grave. In many of Kunath's paintings, the artist seems to be clinging to the hope of some sort of emotional rescue.

In other works, painting becomes a slapstick metaphor for profound existential questions. An untitled series of photographs from 2008 depicts the artist completely dressed in black applying black paint to a white canvas. By the last photograph, as the painter completes his work, he has both literally and metaphorically painted himself out of the picture. Dressed in black

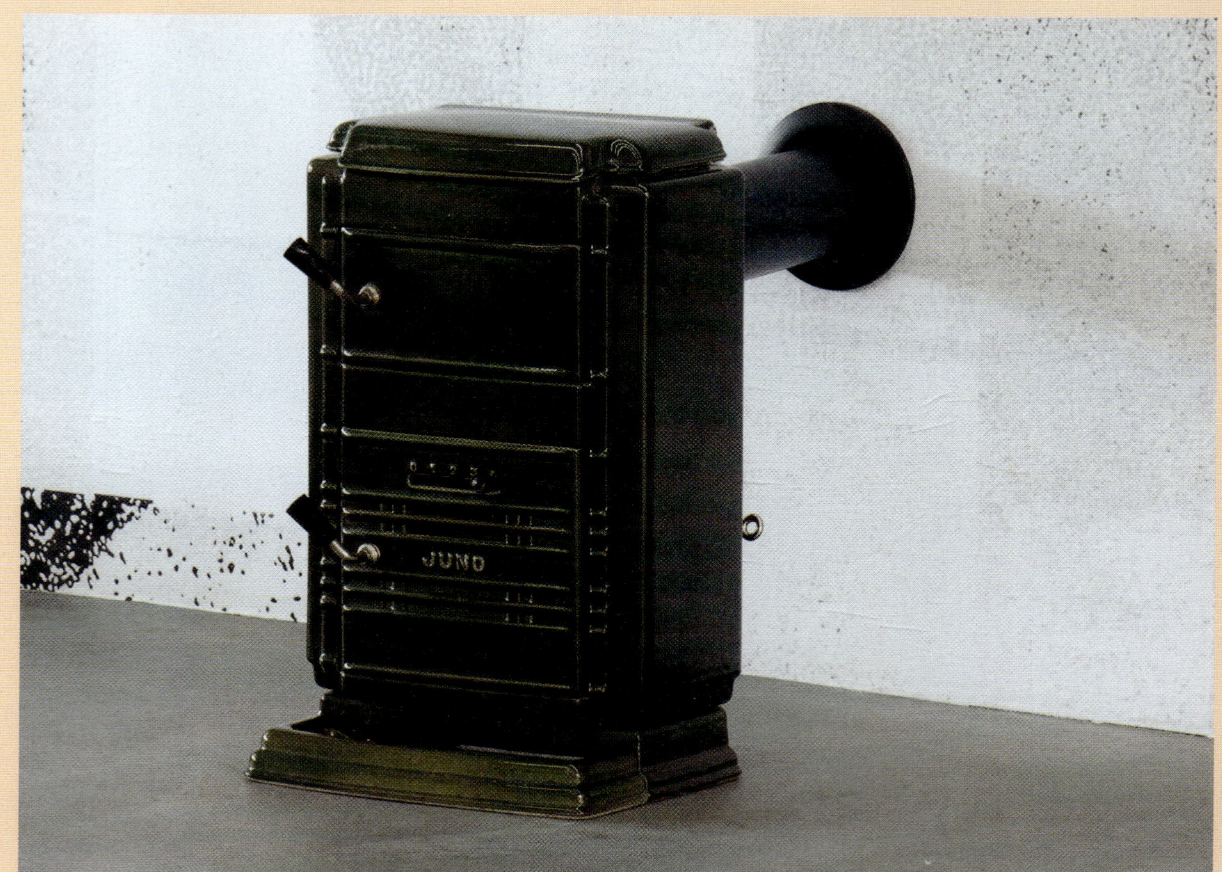

Untitled (detail), 2007. Stove. 62 × 389 × 29 cm. Pencil on paper. 194 × 150 cm. Pipe installation. Dimensions variable

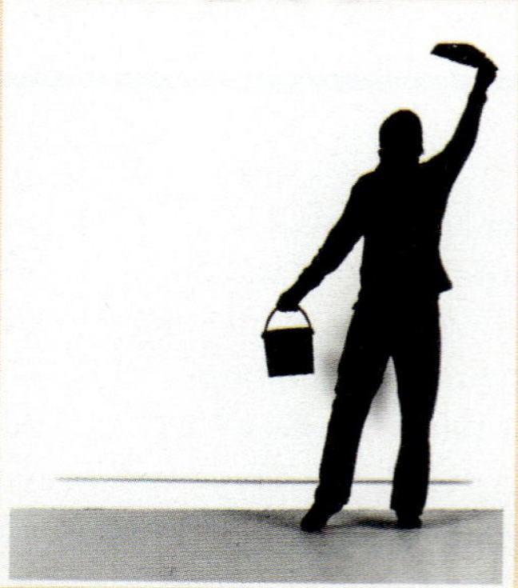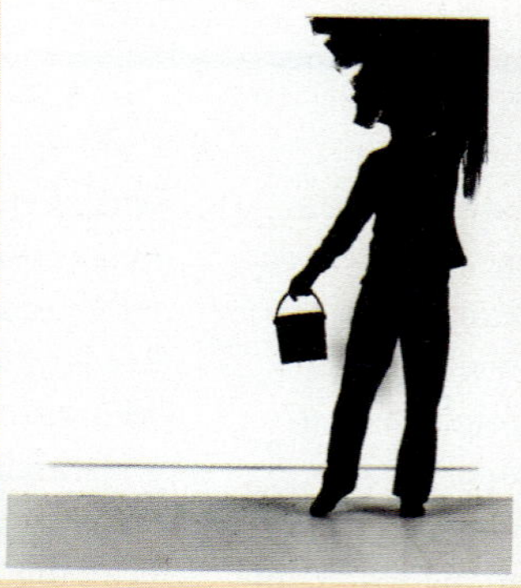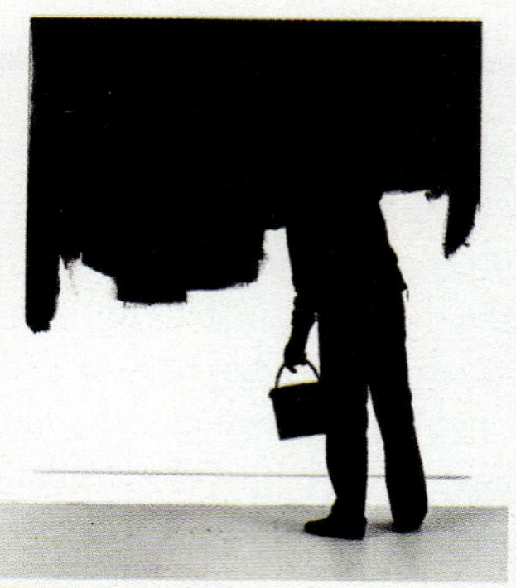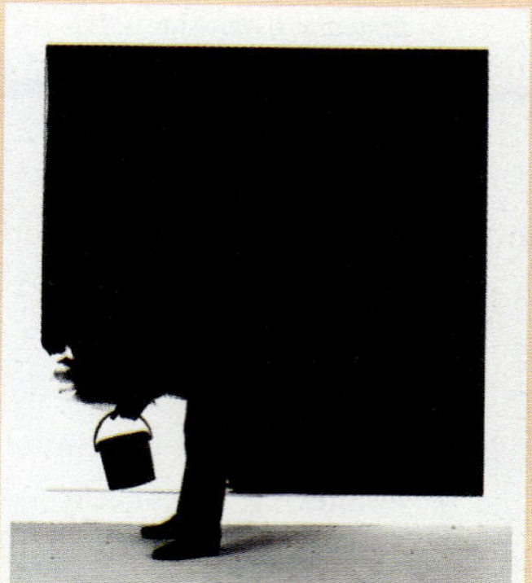

Untitled, 2008. 6 of 8 black and white photographs. Each 44 × 39 cm

A penchant for the fragile and fleeting

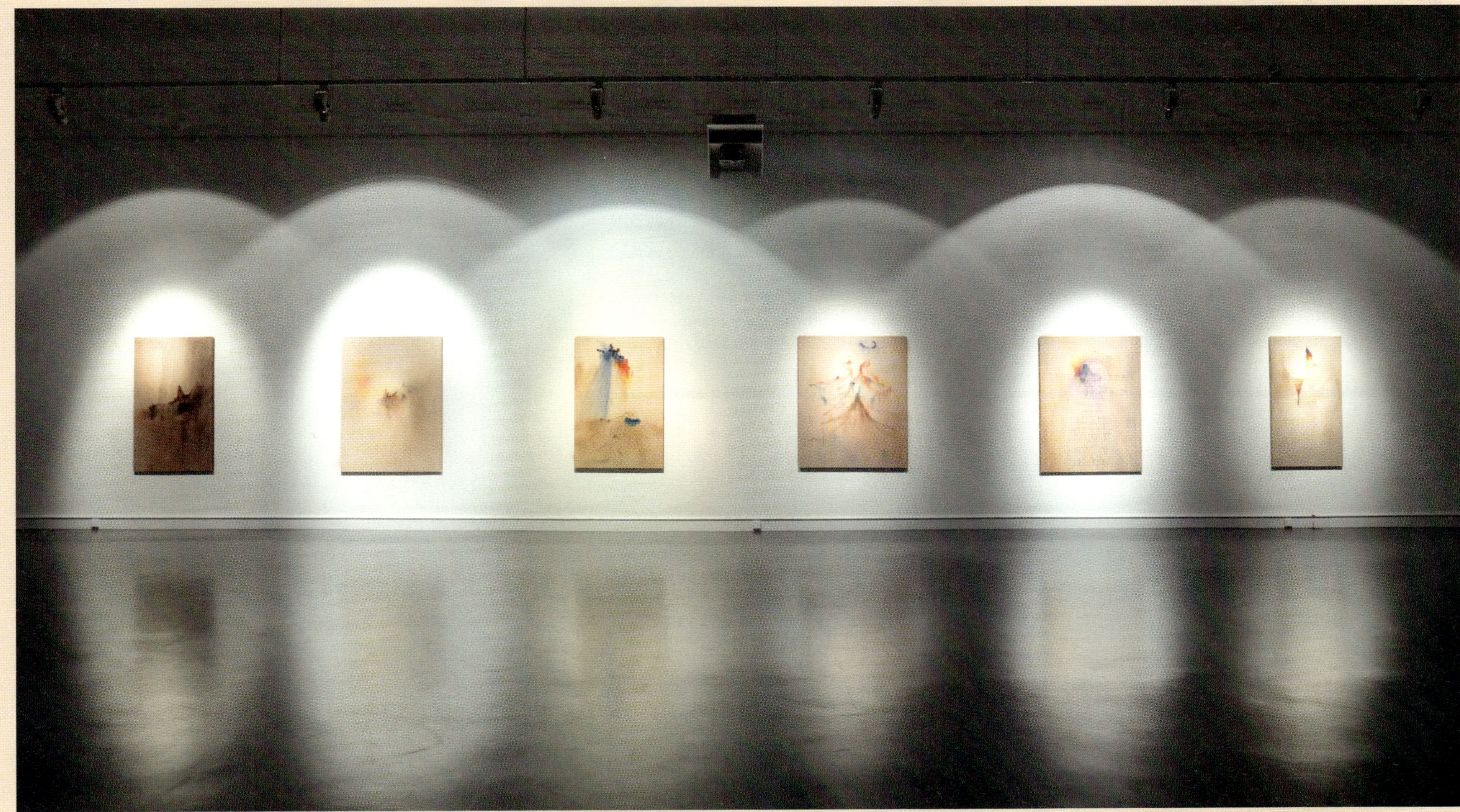

Always Further, 2009 Watercolour, gouache, lacquer on canvas. 140 × 85 cm. **Regrets**, 2009. Watercolour, lacquer on canvas. 140 × 105 cm. **The Artist in His Time**, 2009. Watercolour, lacquer on canvas. 135 × 90 cm. **Please Stay**, 2009. Watercolour and lacquer on canvas. 135 × 110 cm. **Horace 2**, 2009. Silkscreen print, gouache, lacquer on canvas. 140 × 105 cm. **Death and Life**, 2009. Watercolour on canvas. 135 × 75 cm

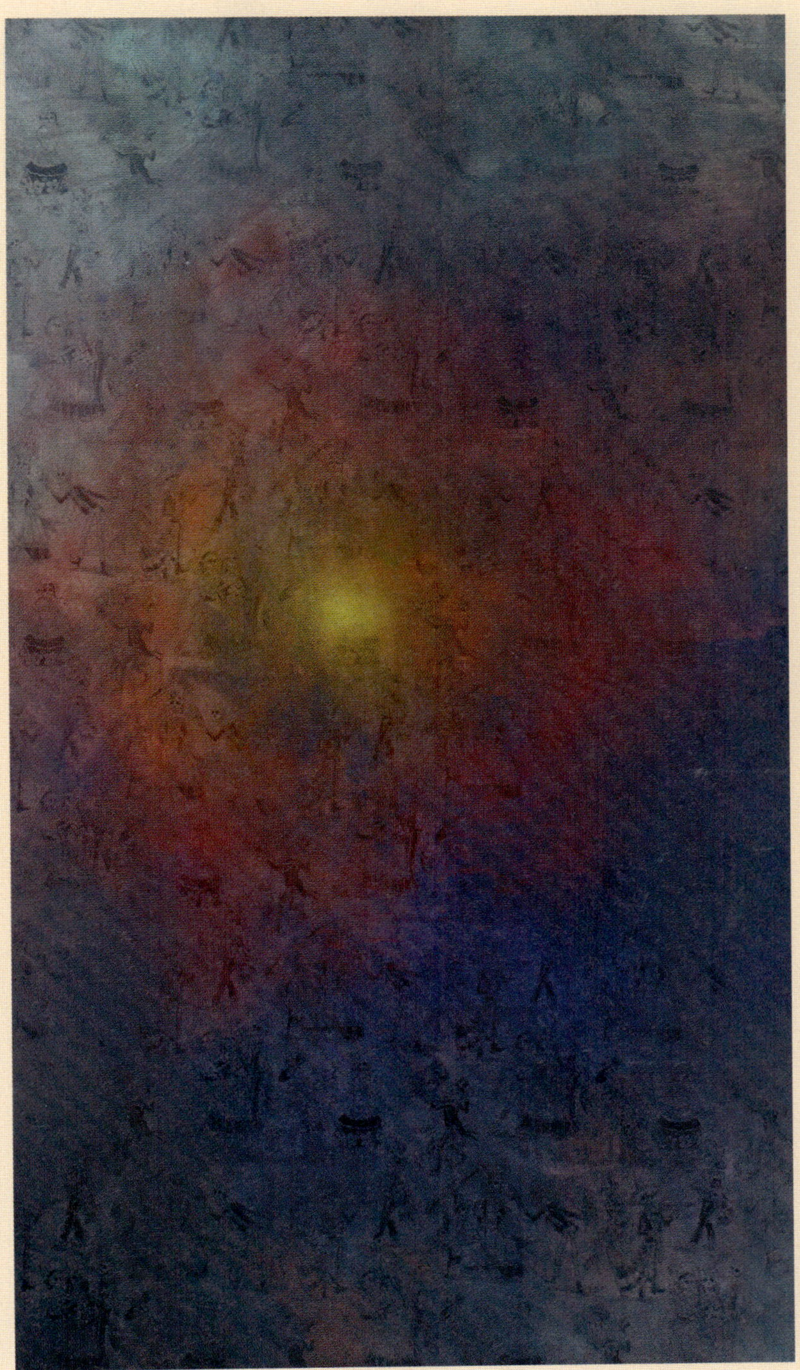

One Day Goodbye Will Be Farewell, 2009. Mixed media on patterned fabric 175 × 101 cm

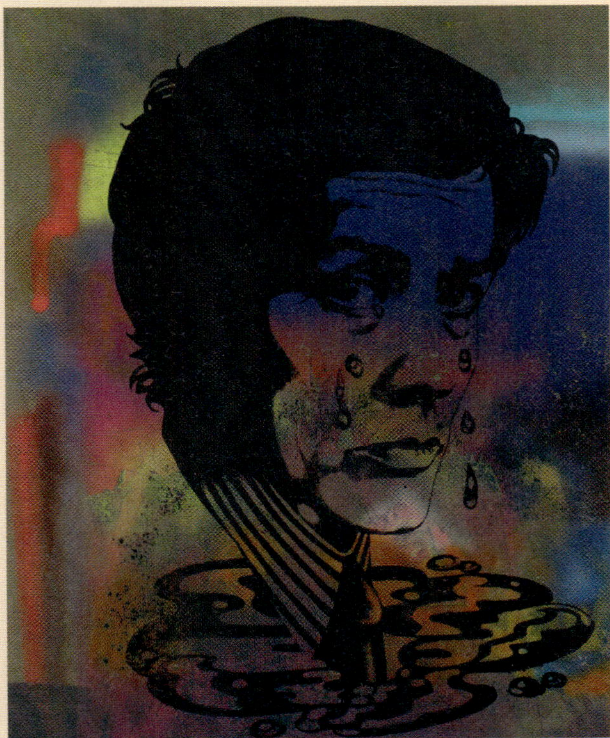

Alain Curtis (Disco), 2009. Mixed–media, silkscreen print on paper. 125 × 104 cm

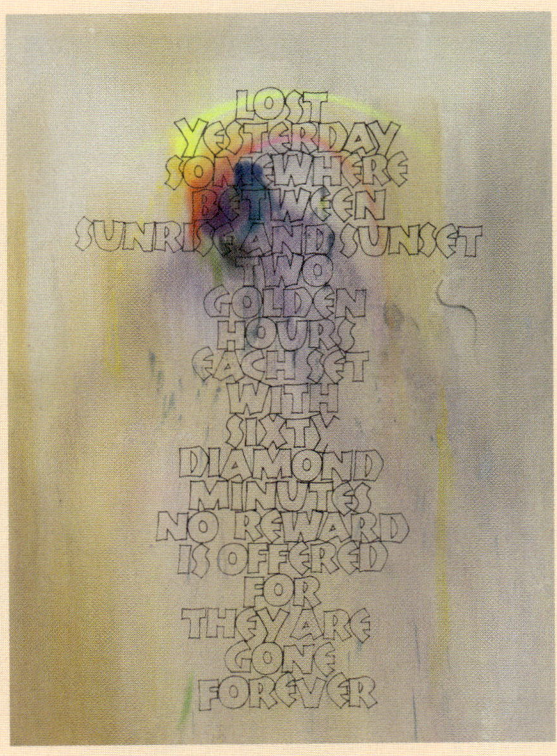

Horace 2, 2009. Silkscreen print, gouache, lacquer on canvas. 140 × 105 cm

and working with black paint, he becomes an anti-mime, silently giving the monochrome a much more humorous and yet somehow sadder meaning altogether.

Kunath is not simply a painter, however; he takes his sculptural practice equally seriously. A recent installation, *Failed Melancholy* (2009), sums up many of his concerns. A silent homage to the work of Caspar David Friedrich, the work is a room-sized sculpture of an exploded house. In this ship-wrecked home, splintered wooden siding, walls and door frames mingle with tchotchkes and other trappings of domesticity. Standing alone as the sole survivor of this disaster is a taxidermy fox encased in a Plexiglas box. Finding some shelter from the storm, the fox seems neither sad nor melancholic, just eager to get home. In the end, homesickness is at the centre of much of Kunath's work. Like everyone else, he just wants to get home safely.

Friedrich Kunath occupies a space somewhere between figuration and abstraction, while constantly grounding his work in the emotional here and now

Ignacio Lang

The absurdity and violence inherent in both human nature and identity construction might be said to lie at the centre of Ignacio Lang's practice. The most direct exploration of this can be found in his series of works based on the ceremonial outfits of the Ku Klux Klan (KKK). The Puerto Rico-born artist's *Reconquista* (2006) was his first to use the robe, mask and conical hat that are characteristic of the American secret society, long devoted to establishing white supremacy through violence and intimidation. Taking the iconic outfits as readymades upon which sewn interventions add further signification and transform them into 'sculptures', Lang explores the potential aggression but also the identity-shifting nature of something as seemingly innocuous as a combination of cloth and stitching.

Originally founded in the aftermath of the American Civil War, but still alive and active today, the KKK's contemporary resurgence and shift of emphasis

Idiosyncrasy of human nature

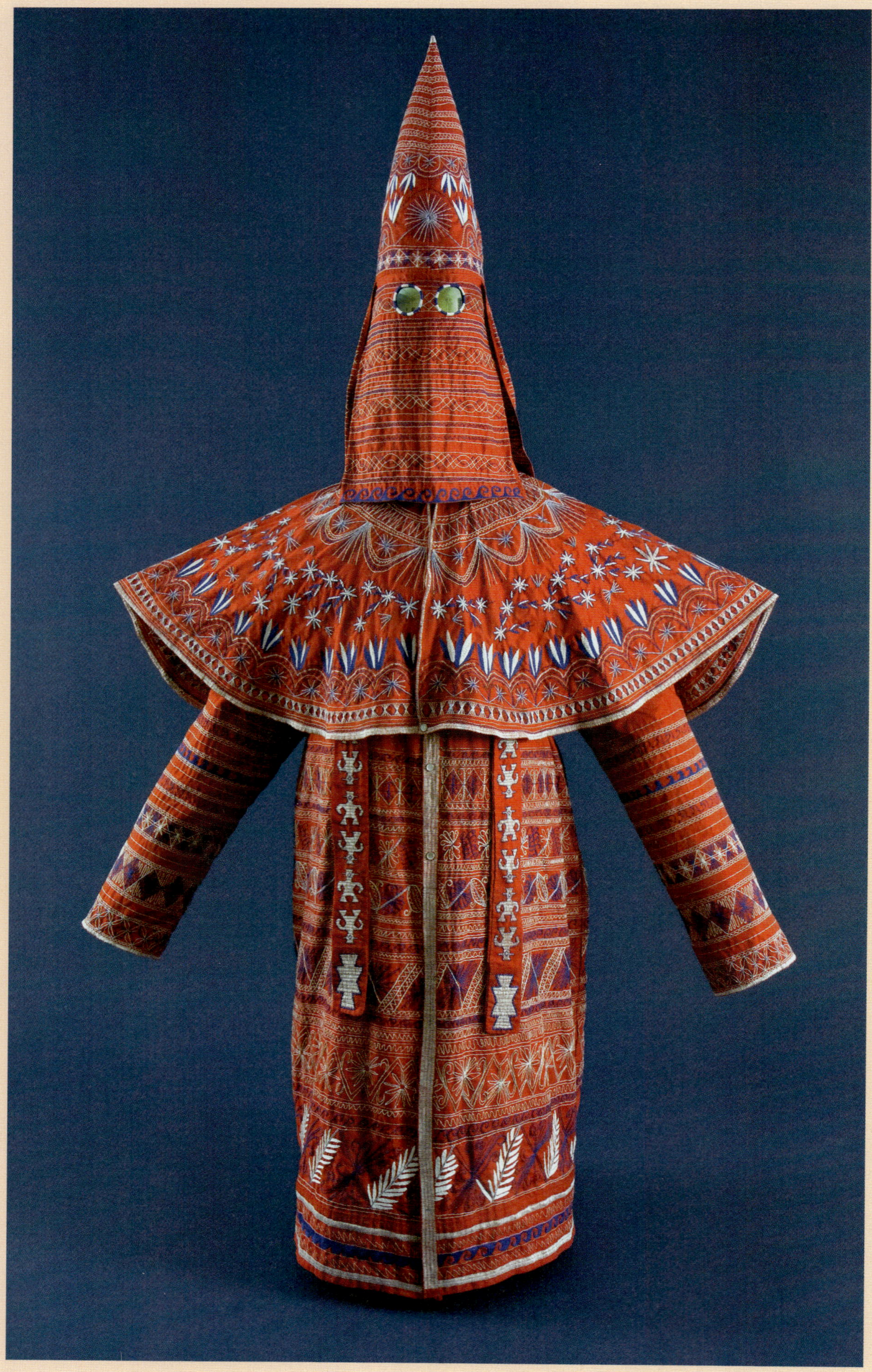

Kueens, 2009. Cotton KKK robe, white and blue cotton thread, iridium lenses, body form. 163 × 122 × 66 cm

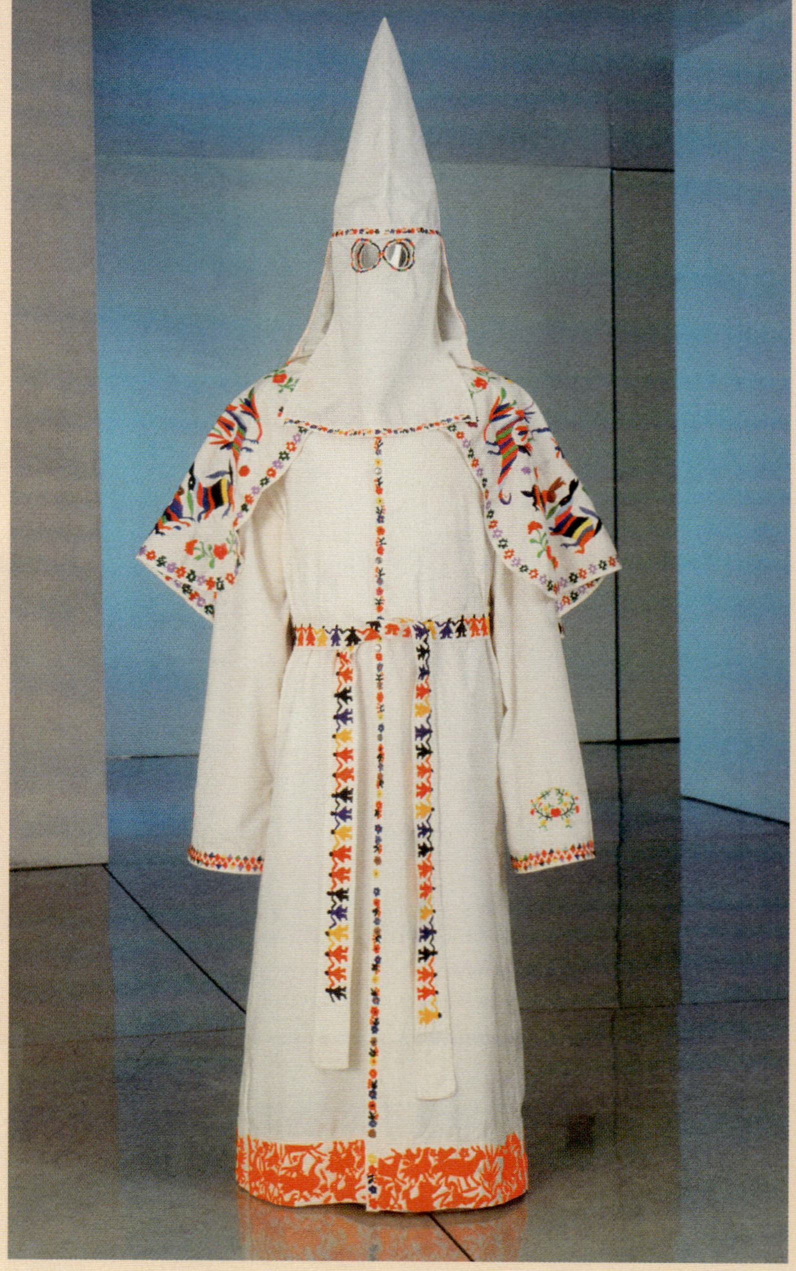

Reconquista, 2006. Cotton KKK robe, acrylic thread, mirror mask, modified mannequin. 160 × 90 × 60 cm

interests the artist; hostility towards blacks and Jews has been, in recent years, largely redirected towards illegal immigrants from Mexico. While the KKK's masks and robes were originally meant to hide the identities of the Klansmen operating in small towns and rural areas, where people knew each other's faces, they were also integral to the construction of another identity: that of the group, in which a historic lineage (to the Scottish Highlands) and medieval armour is self-consciously evoked. The artist purchased the robe used in *Reconquista* at an auction in southern Texas and sent it to Mexicali, the northernmost city in Latin America, where local artisans working with indigenous Otomi textile motifs embroidered the robe. 'Reconquista' is a term denoting the potential re-conquest by Mexicans of the Southwestern United States, once a Mexican province, in a reversal nineteenth-century history when the massive influx of illegal white settlers led to the United States overtaking the area. *Reconquista* thus points to the historical contradictions in the question of who is a native or an immigrant, with reference to the border-making, border-blurring and border-crossing between the United States and Mexico.

A second version, *Kueens* (2009), uses a robe purchased online from a Louisiana woman who sews the ceremonial hoods and tunics for KKK members from her home. It was then sent by Lang to be embroidered by an illegal immigrant residing in Queens, New York, who has used motifs that are central to the identity of the native American peoples. In so doing, the artist builds a bridge of labour between the two women whose businesses operate in a parallel economy or black market in which all laws of commerce, taxation and regulations of trade are sidestepped. In uniting these two forms of craftsmanship that have been passed down from generation to generation, Lang reveals the connections between two irreconcilable ideological and cultural positions and

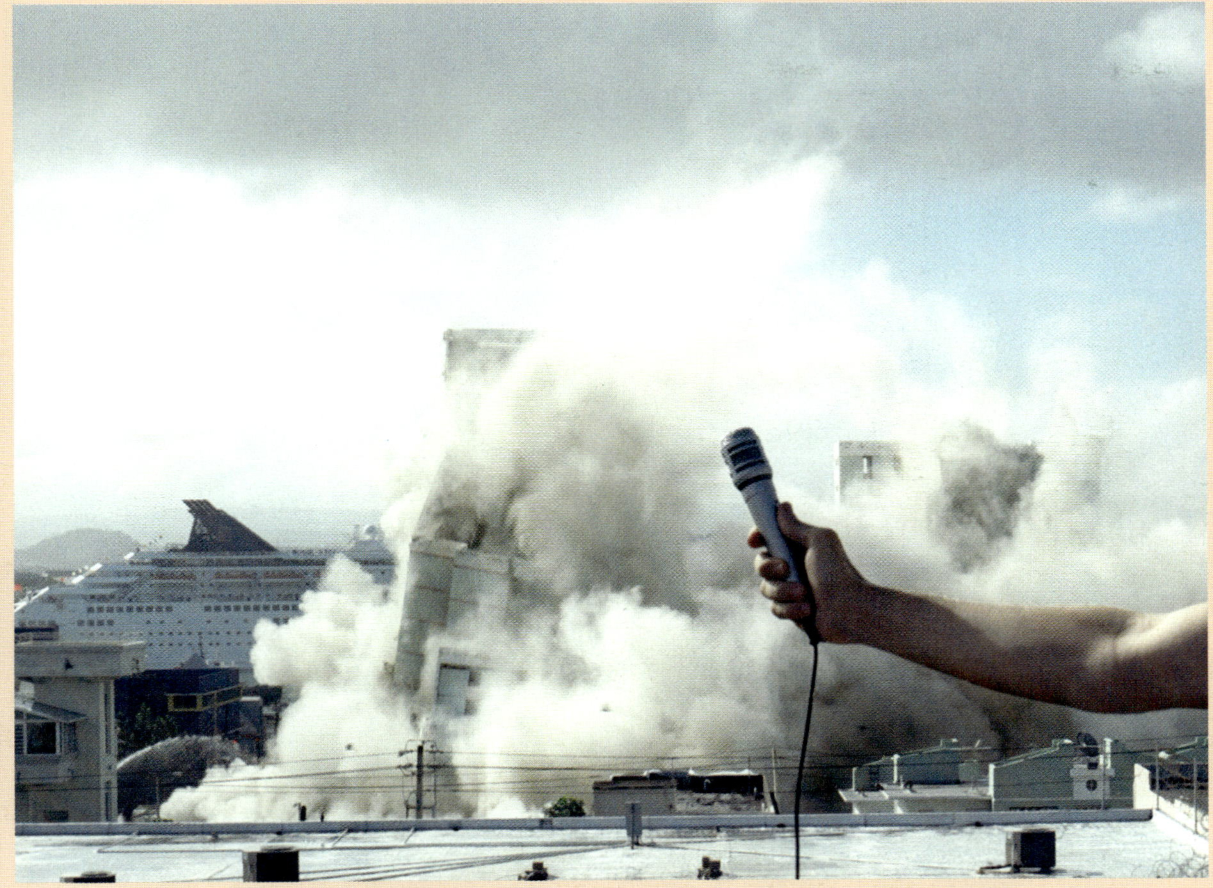

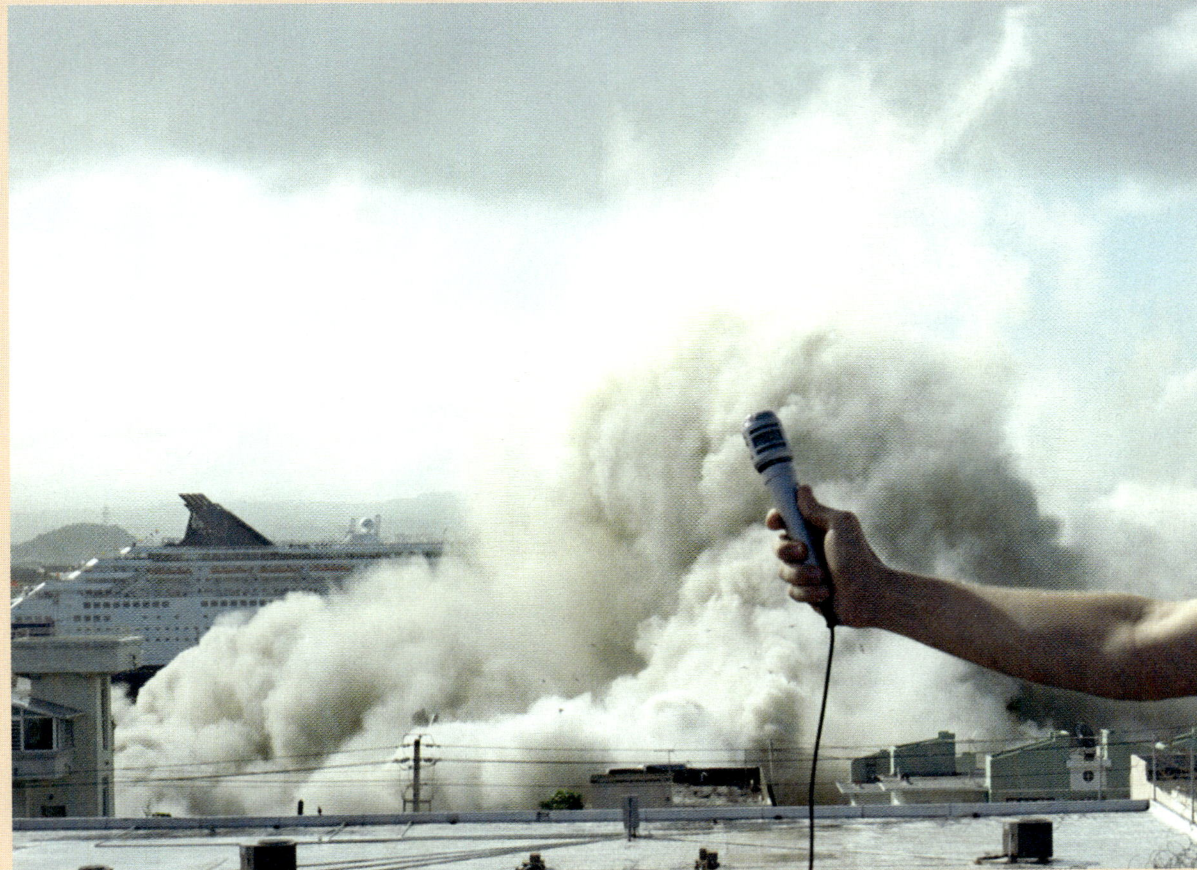

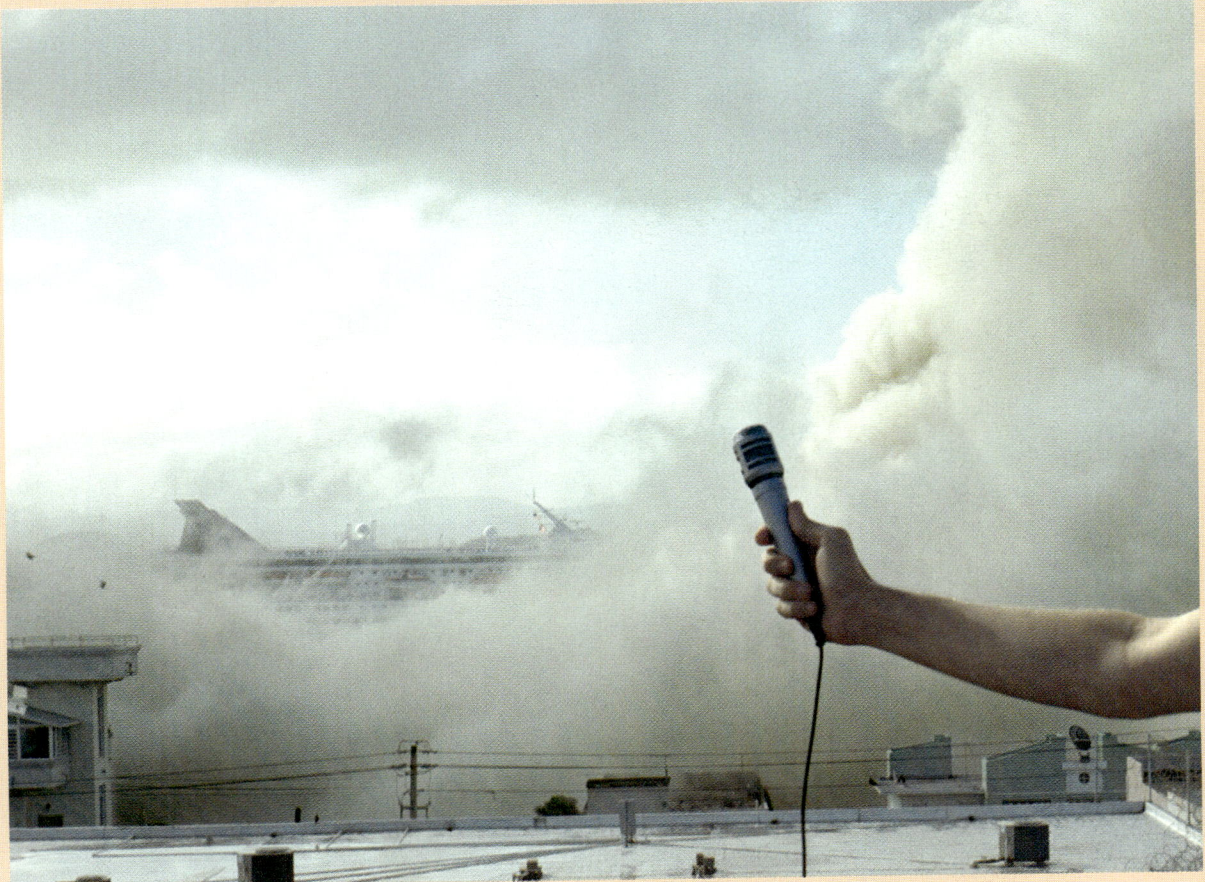

Las Acacias, 2000. 3 C-prints. Each 101 × 152 cm

their respective symbolizations of societal belonging.

No less concerned with the ways in which the idiosyncrasy of human nature reveals itself, *Analfabeto* (2004–present) is a work in progress, thus far consisting of nearly 6,000 newspaper clippings collected in the last few years from *The New York Post*, *The New York Times* and *El Vocero*. Lang pairs the anecdotes detailed in the clippings, united by their 'strange but true' character, with images, imparting a visual identity to the found text. Variously poignant, comical, disturbing or political, the accumulated marginal histories create a vast index about the peculiarities of our contemporary civilization. Like Lang's work with readymade robes, *Analfabeto* suggests that the stuff of art might be found in the circulation of objects and forms through which societies represent themselves.

Marginal histories

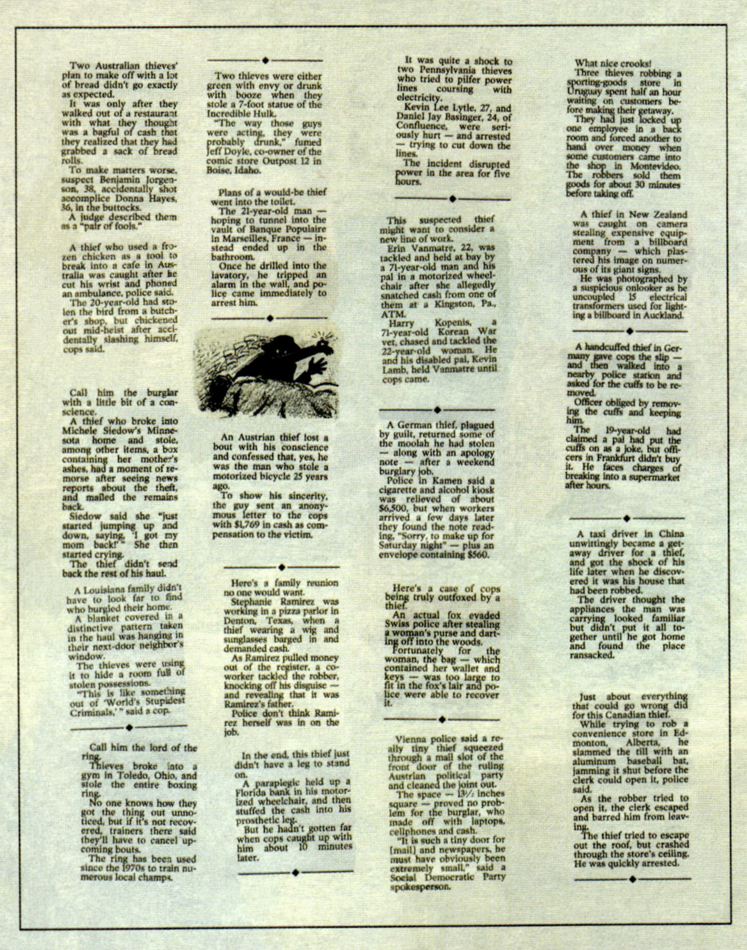

Analfabeto (Thiefs), 2004–09. Newspaper clippings. 20 × 25 cm

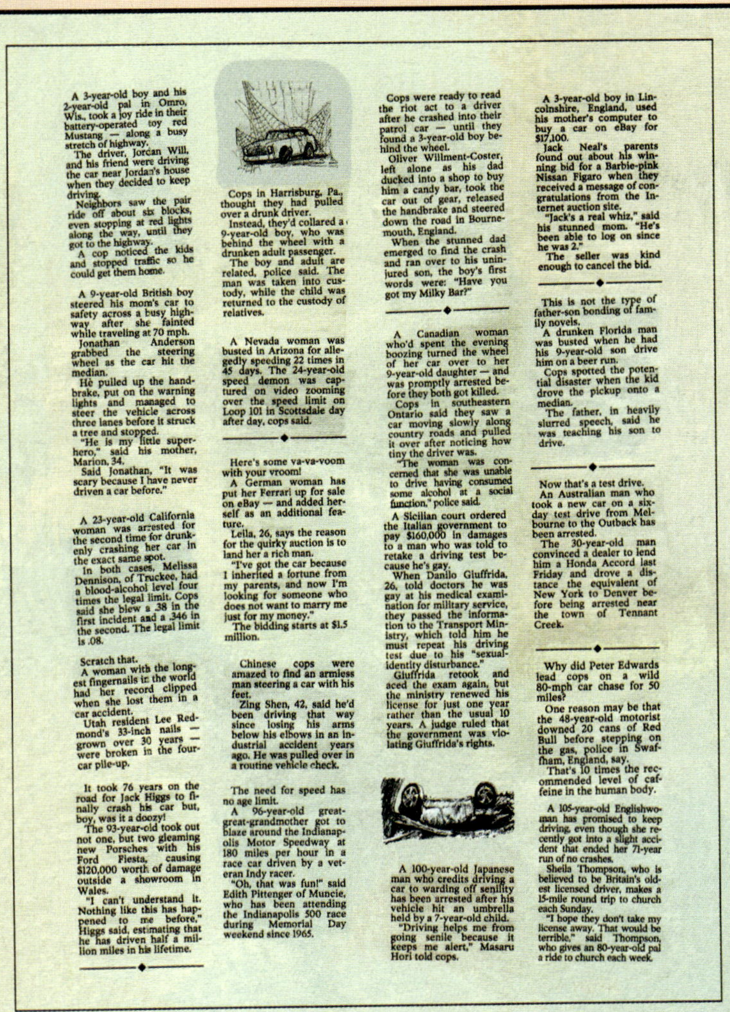

Analfabeto (Cars), 2004–09. Newspaper clippings. 25 × 20 cm

Valentina Liernur

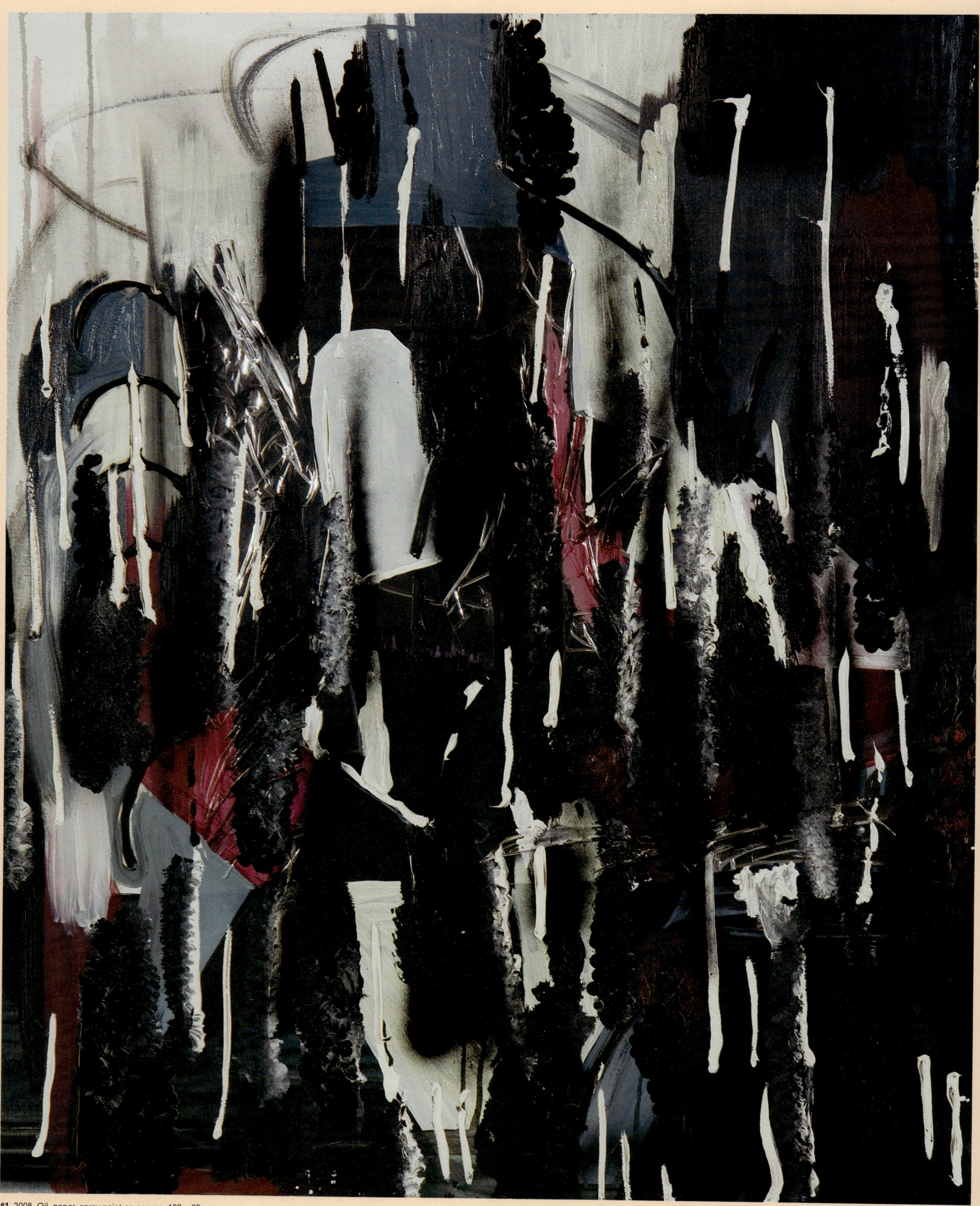

#1, 2008. Oil, paper, spray paint on canvas. 102 × 85 cm

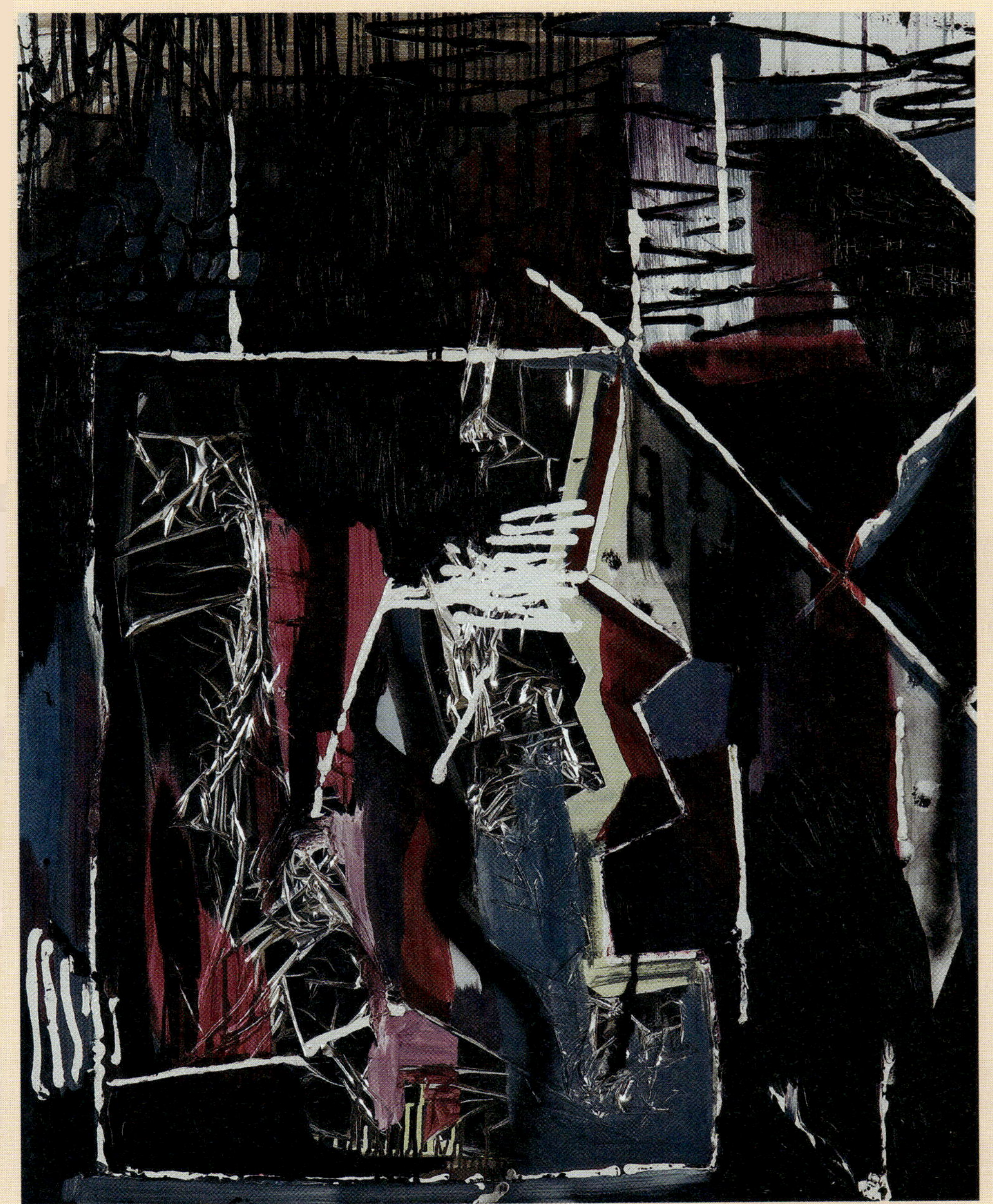

#2, 2008. Oil, paper, spray paint on canvas. 102 × 85 cm

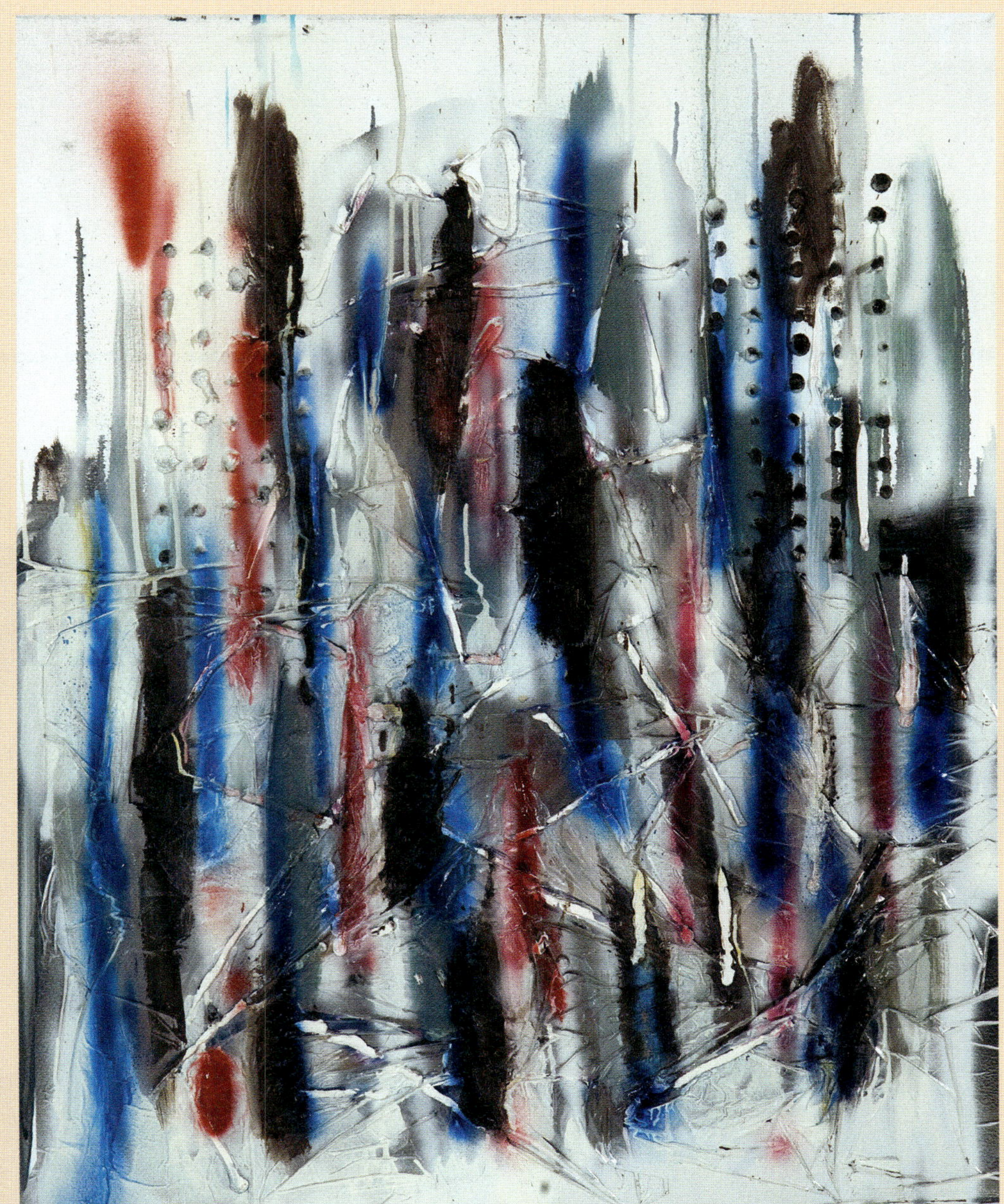

#3, 2008. Oil, paper, spray paint on canvas. 102 × 85 cm

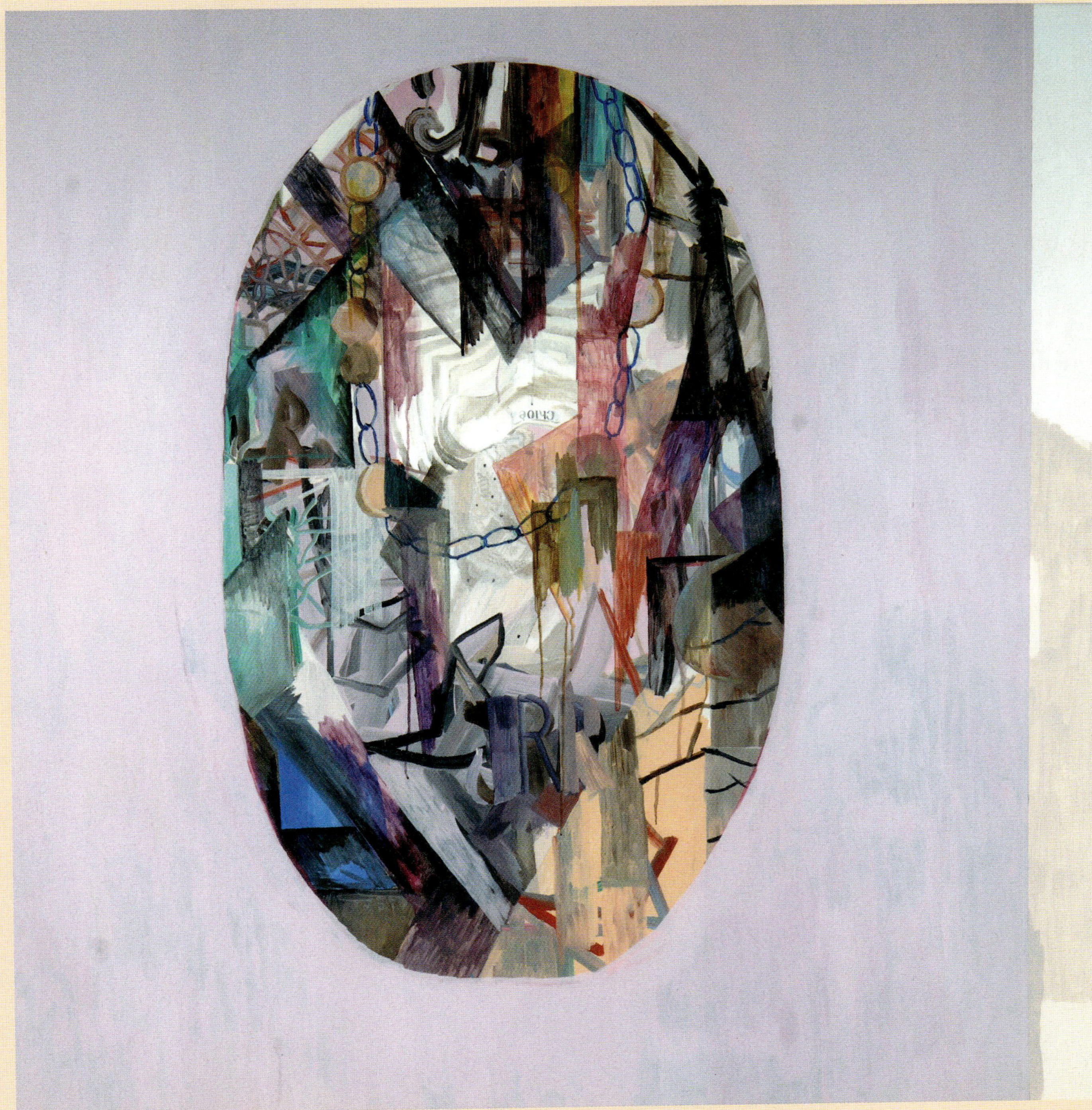

Huevo Cubista, 2006. Acrylic on canvas. 175 × 208 cm

Always provisional

Valentina Liernur's training as an actor and playwright, as well as a painter, still marks her current work, as she has always felt uncomfortable with the kind of exclusive attention that painting usually demands. The way she was able to confront this anxiety was to build up a complex relationship between painting and theatre, where painting, and specifically style, could be utilized performatively in relation to different circumstances in a focused and resolute way that is indicative of a constantly shifting identity that is unfixed and always provisional.

Nowadays Liernur defines herself as a 'hysteric subject' whose work not only courses through various art-historical styles, but also mixes those references with elements taken from fashion, using it as an almost subliminal strategy of seduction and thus escaping any historicist solemnity. Her paintings arise from heroic moments in the history of painting, especially Cubism but also Lucio Fontana's Spatialism and certain aspects of 1980s painting.

However, Liernur paints her versions of them as if unable to get rid of a dark and capricious rebelliousness, executed with a fatally contemporary speed. A compulsive browser of fashion magazines, Liernur renders a Cubist painting as if it were a design for a scarf or handkerchief, and when she attempts a destructive unfolding à la Fontana she does so with the visual elements of graffiti and punk. In this way, the mood of her work swings between the fetishism of the fashion industry and a sentimental identification with the avant-garde's utopian ideals. But for Liernur quotation never works like a collage of heterogeneous fragments. Rather, each of her series is dedicated to one period or image in particular, something concrete upon which she attempts to concentrate for a specific length of time. 'In this sense', she says, 'some kind of belief and value scale more modernist than pastiche is established'.

Besides her paintings, Liernur has made a series of performances. *Aquello que finalmente uno cree que no es tan determinante que los demás sepan sobre las propias ideas* (That which in the end one believes is not as necessary as others know about our own ideas, 2008) was a collaborative long-distance project with a dancer and a lighting technician for a live show in a performance festival. Directed from Europe by Liernur, the group made a performance in Buenos Aires that interpreted a list of topics proposed by the artist through a series of light signs and movements, among which were 'Arm suprematism', 'Balenciaga and M. Margiela's fantastic shoulder cut', 'Envy', 'Constructivism', 'Drum', 'Airport', 'Telepathy' amongst many others.

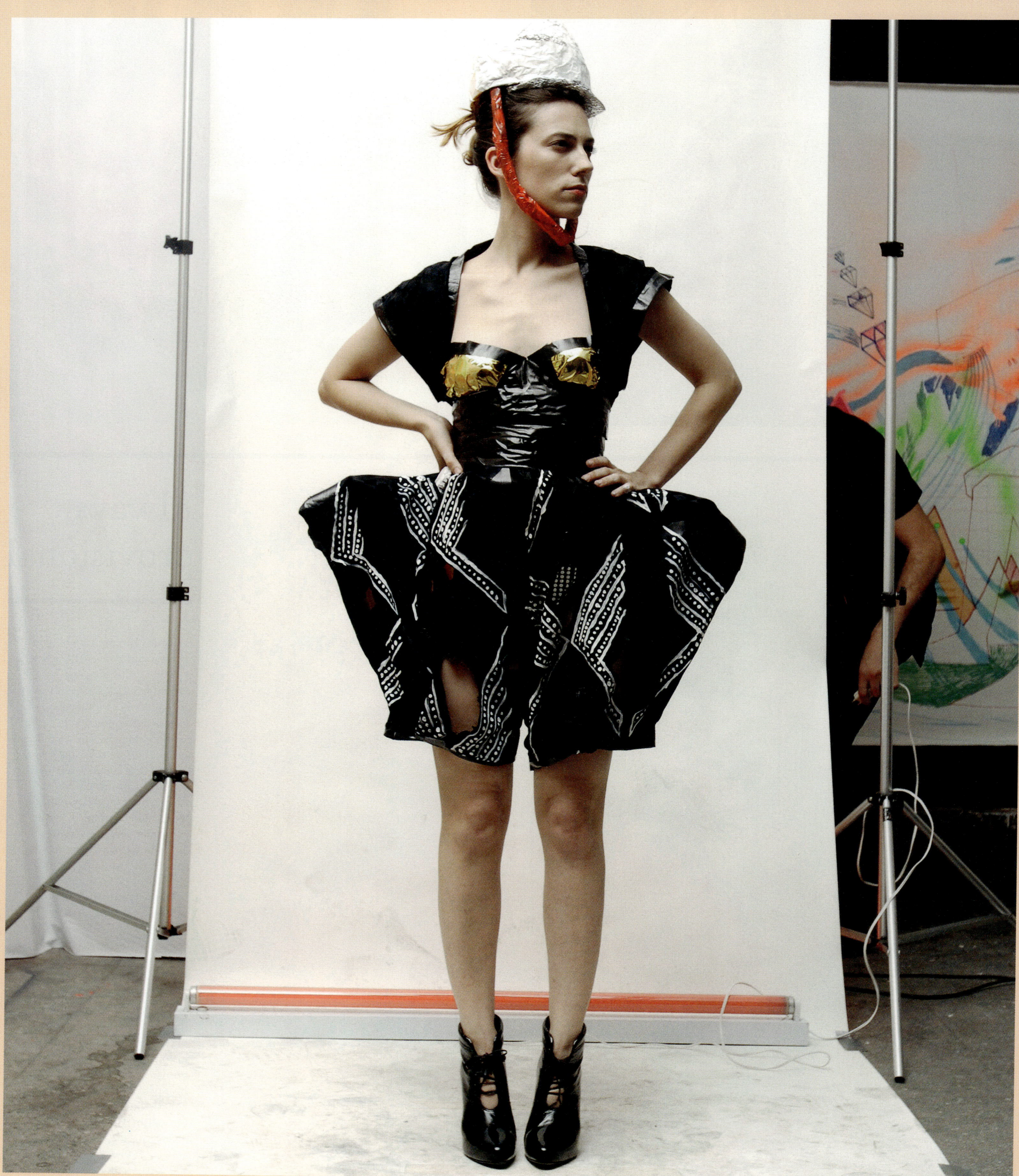

DiasDorados, 2007. Performance. 3 hours

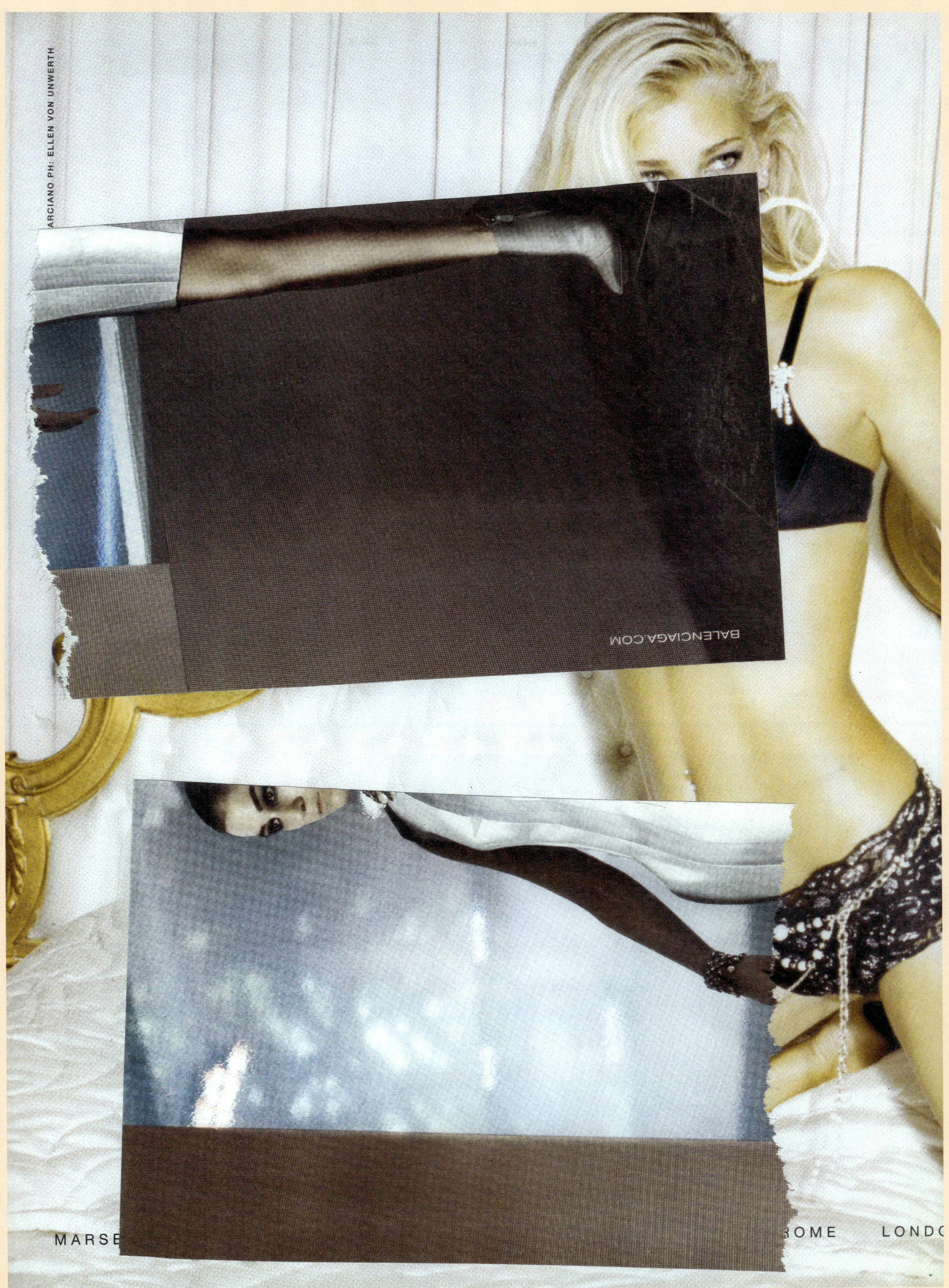

Collage #34, 2009. Paper collage. 30 × 22 cm

Kalup Linzy

Kalup Linzy's videos and live performances are a campy, theatrical blend of raunchy humour, sexual intrigue, art-world satire, identity politics and poignant social commentary. Through them, Linzy concocts his own alternative televisual world, inspired by personal events and the daytime television soap operas with which he was obsessed in his youth. He inflects the convoluted melodrama and artificial style of soaps with an unusual combination of outrageous humour and touching sincerity, replacing the predominantly white, heterosexual characters with a cast of protagonists more relevant to his own life as a Southern, black, gay man.

Linzy's intimate personal dramas are all conveyed through his distinctive low-tech production style, DIY aesthetic and methods, in which he serves as the writer, director, cinematographer and editor, while also playing multiple roles, both male and female. Artist friends typically make up his casts, but Linzy usually dubs his own voice over theirs, using software to shift the pitch and timbre into variations on his own reinvented black vernacular, characterized by double entendres, meaningful slang and a pronounced Southern drawl.

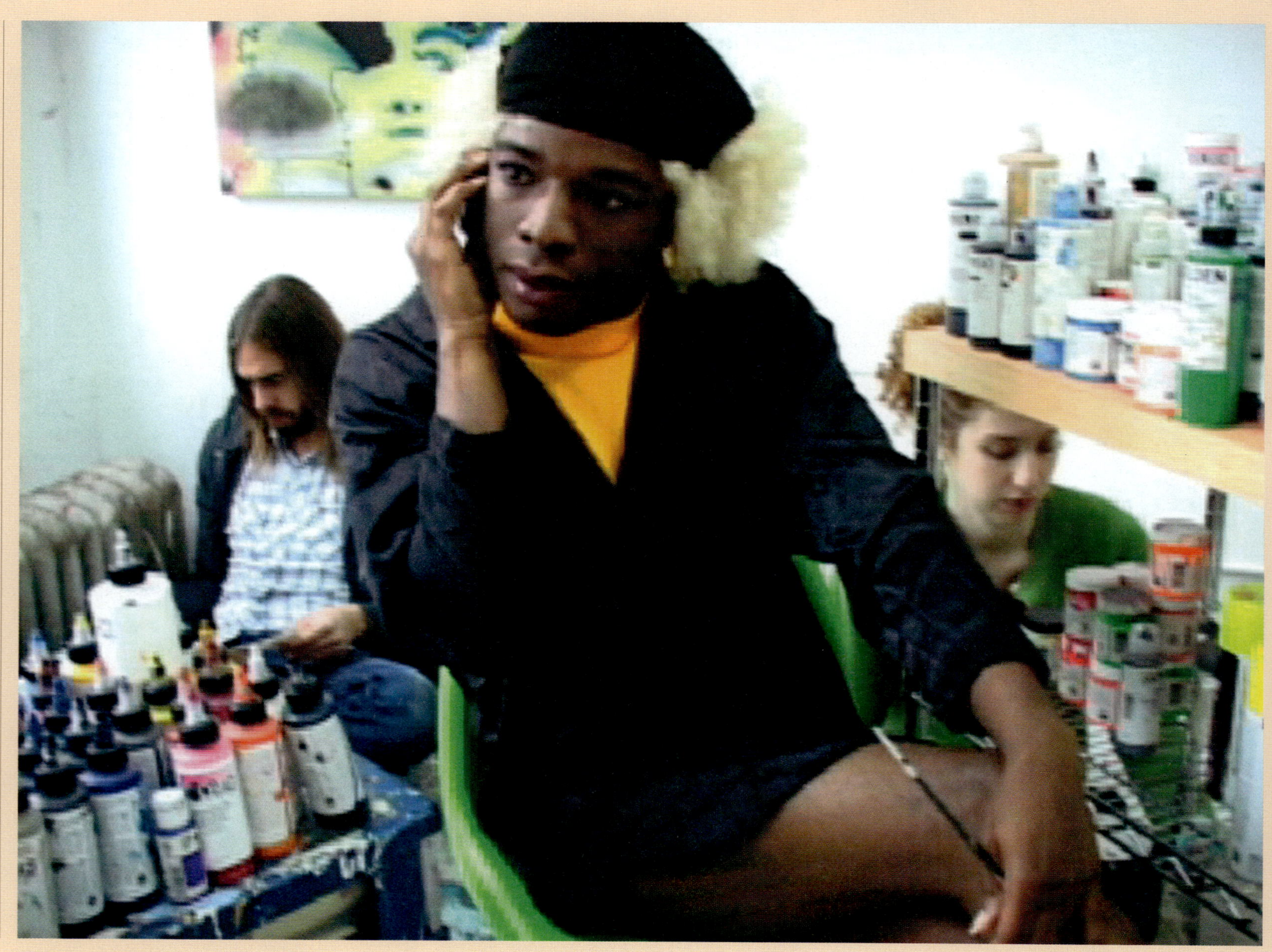

KK Queens Survey, 2005. Video. 7 min. 20 sec.

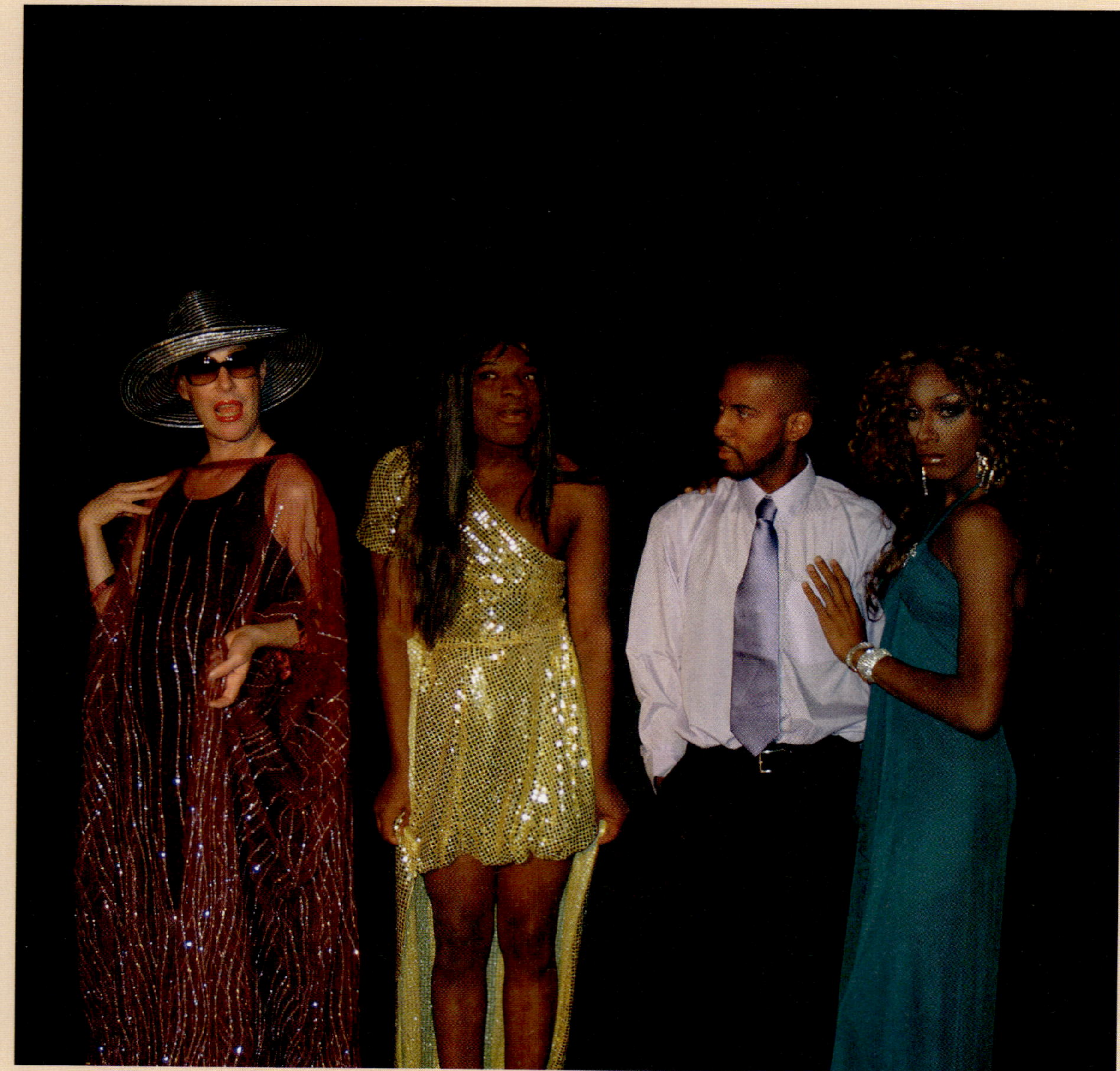

Melody Set Me Free, 2007. Video. 15 min. 19 sec.

Endless parodic relay

Most often, men play women, and occasionally women play men, with the characters decked out in over-the-top comic drag. Donning unconvincing wigs and ill-fitting dresses, they perform an endless parodic relay that disrupts and undermines conventional categories of gender, sexuality and race.

Linzy cites as early influences Keenen Ivory Wayans's 1990s sketch comedy show 'In Living Color' and the performances of drag queen RuPaul, as well as early John Waters films. More recently, he has combined styles of gay club culture and pop videos with those from early black-and-white-films. Citations from Italian Renaissance and nineteenth-century French painting traditions are thrown into the mix. His complex, stylized expressiveness, cross-dressing antics and critical use of humour also reference the specific histories of African-American minstrelsy as well as performances on the Chitlin Circuit (the network of venues in segregated America where black theatrical acts performed for mostly black audiences), in addition to contemporary black comedians like Eddie Murphy or Martin Lawrence.

Combining all of these influences seamlessly into his work, Linzy tells stories of family sagas, unrequited love and sexual longing. *Keys to Our Heart* (2008), for example, is presented with the look of a 1940s black-and-white film and revolves around a love triangle between a man and two women that unfolds with a lesbian twist at the end. These themes are intertwined with aspirations to fame and money circulating around the powerful worlds of contemporary art and pop music. Earlier works such as *KK Queens Survey* (2005) are blistering lampoons of art-world power dynamics. In *Melody Set Me Free* (2007) the story unfolds around an aspiring pop singer played by a cross-dressing Linzy, sending up contemporary reality-TV talent shows.

Intimate personal dramas

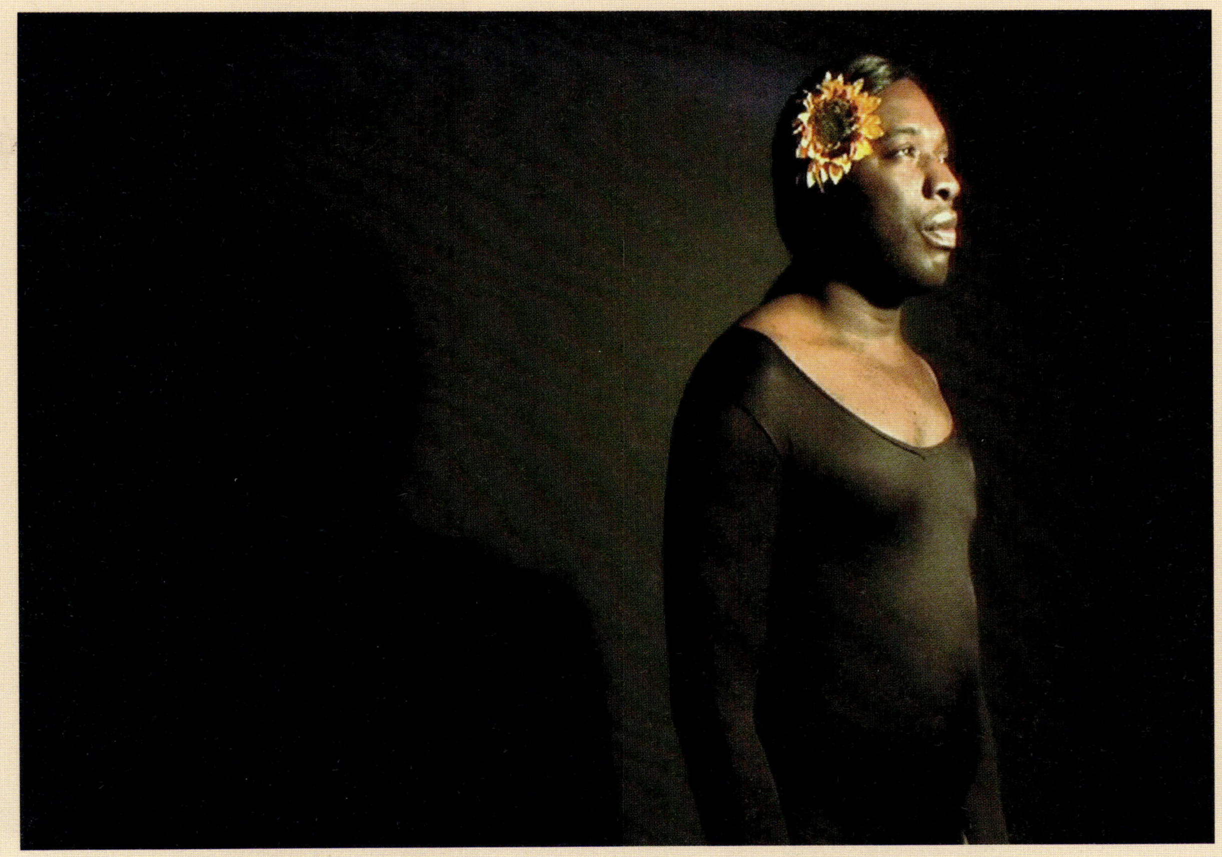

Conversations wit de Churen (2002–present) is Linzy's most elaborate project to date: multiple interrelated installments made over six years that centre on the travails of the Braswells, a Southern, black, small-town family.

In *Conversations wit de Churen III: Da Young and Da Mess* (2005), drag queen and aspiring singer Taiwan receives a marriage proposal from his rich and handsome boyfriend, Harry. Taiwan plunges into an emotional crisis as he tries to decide whether to make a public commitment to Harry and thereby risk losing the security of his family and church relationships. Played by Linzy with compassion and comic aplomb, Taiwan emerges as an empathetic character with an agonizing dilemma. In Linzy's universe, campy irony doubles back on itself, turning into irresistible sincerity.

Emphasizing the constructed multiplicity of gendered, sexual and racial identities, Linzy's works tease out what makes each of us individual, while also underscoring connections that we all share. His compelling combination of witty camp and poignant drama transcend the limits of satire and allows his works to function as affirmations of black and gay identities and as sincere, astute social observation about empathy, love, friendship and family.

Kalup Linzy's videos and live performances are a campy, theatrical blend of raunchy humour, sexual intrigue, art-world satire, identity politics and poignant social commentary.

Distinctive lo-tech production

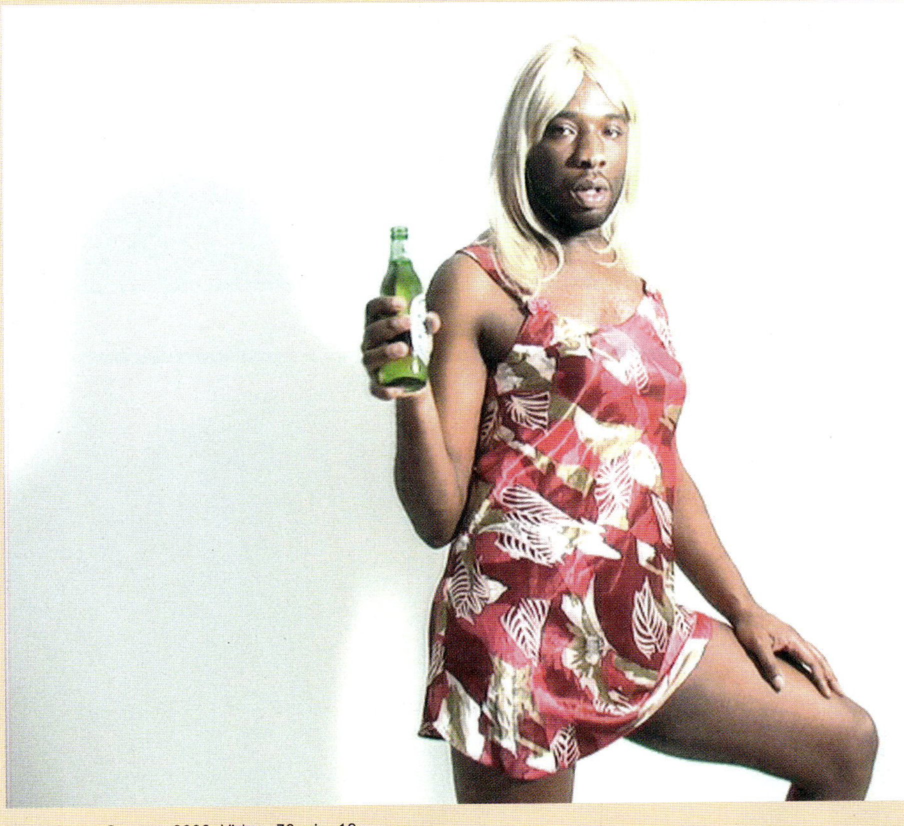

Sweetberry Sonnet, 2008. Video. 38 min. 12 sec.

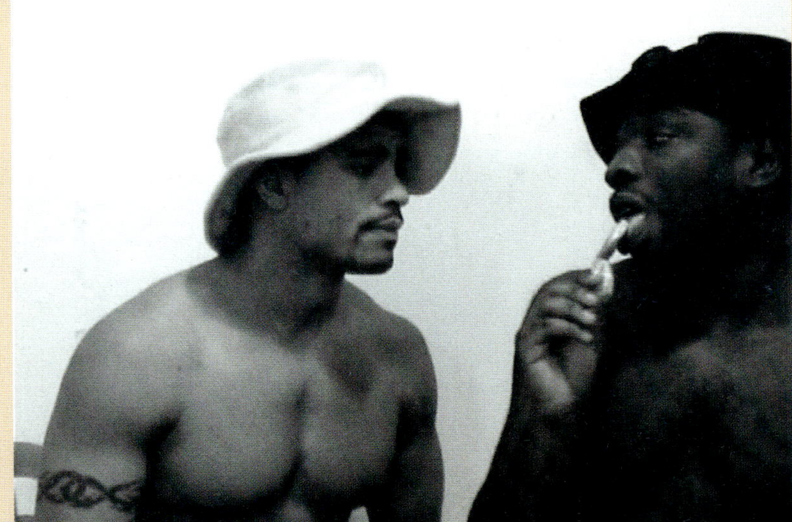

Lollypop, 2006. Black and white digital video. 3 min. 24 sec.

His own alternate televisual world

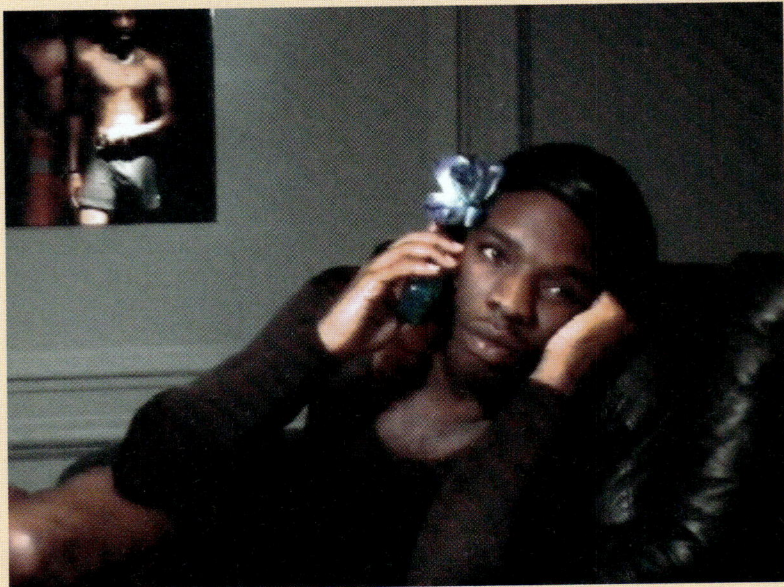

Conversations wit de Churen II: All My Churen, 2003. Video. 29 min. 14 sec.

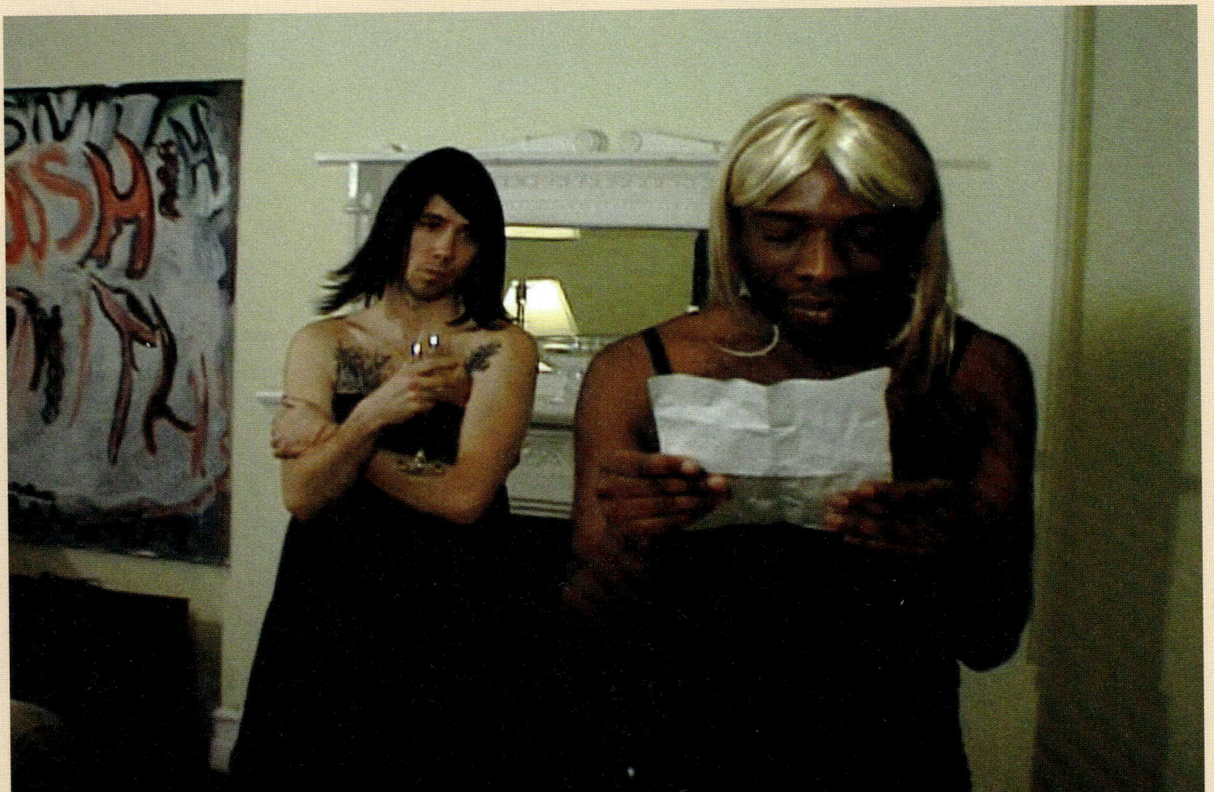

Conversations wit de Churen V: As da Art World Might Turn, 2006. Video. 12 min. 9 sec.

Hilary Lloyd

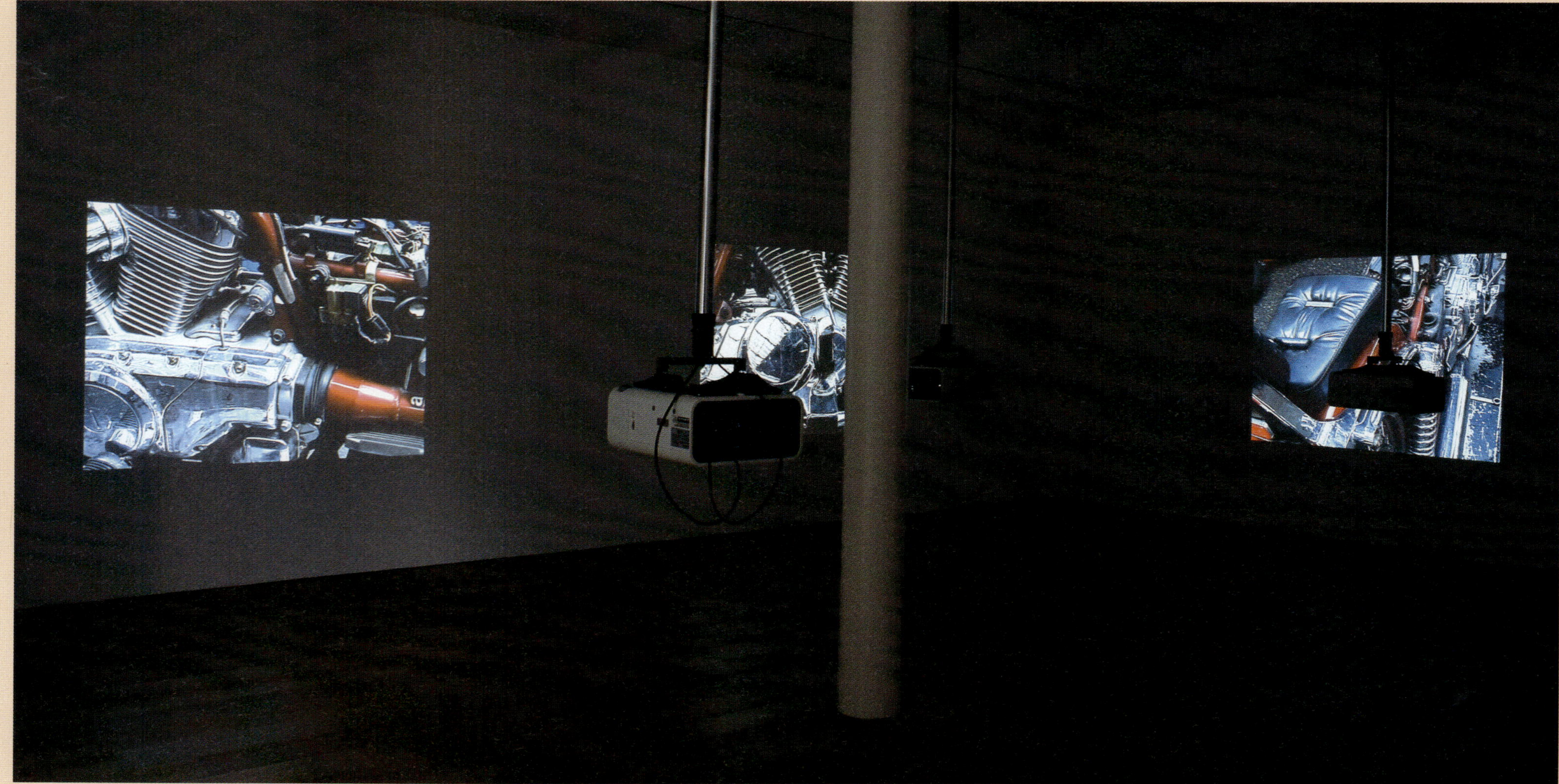

Motorcycles, 2008. 3 Sanyo PLC–XP100 projectors, 3 Pioneer DVD–V7300D players, 3 Cambridge audio A5 amplifiers, 9 Unicol suspension units, JBL Control 23 speakers. Dimensions variable

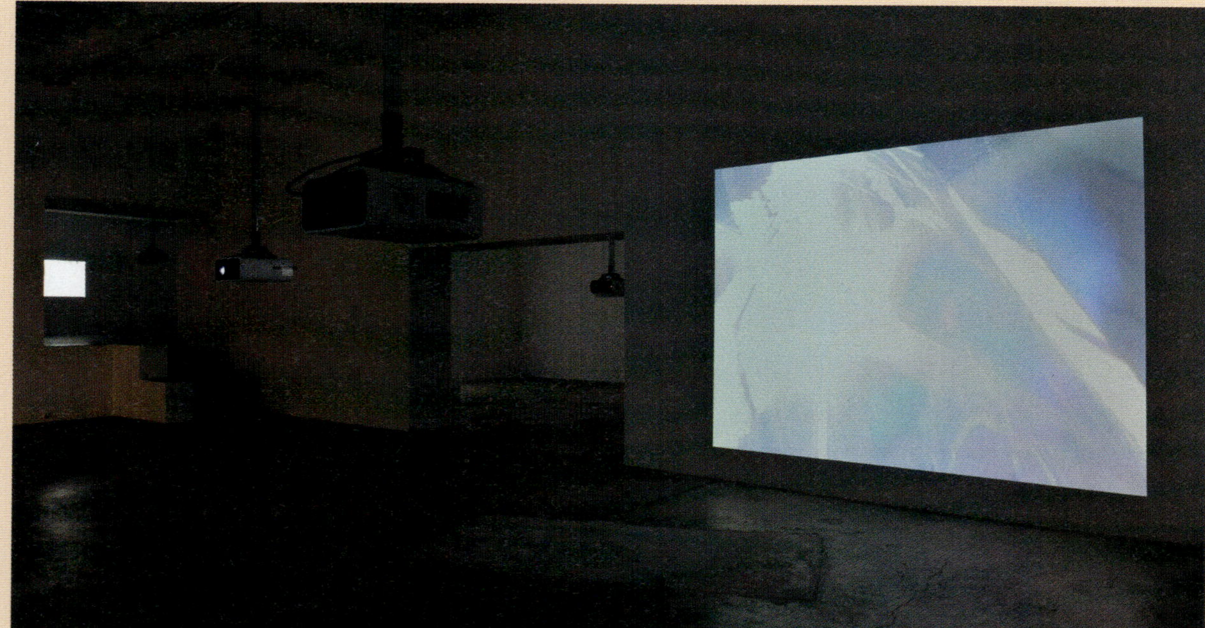

Studio #2, 2009. 7 Sanyo PLC-XP100 projectors, 7 Pioneer DVD-V7300D players, 14 Unicol suspension units. Dimensions variable

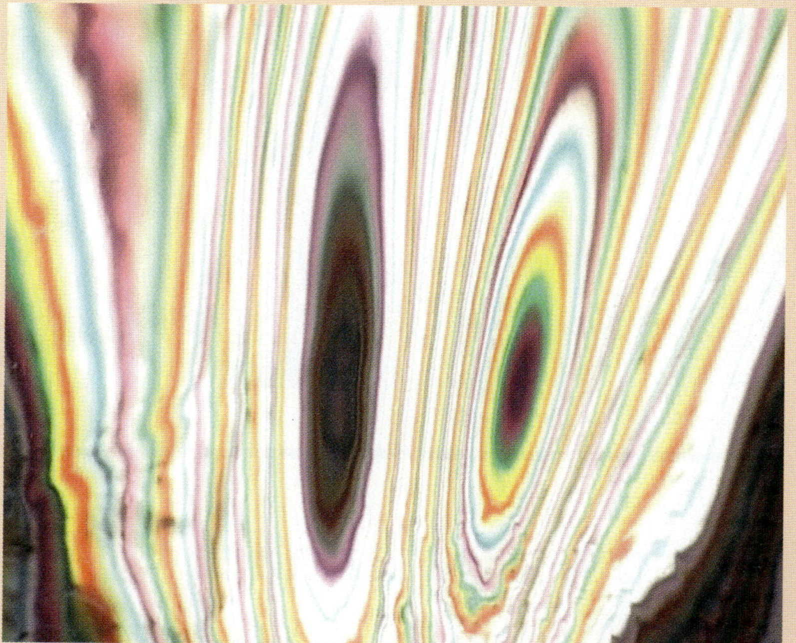

Plane of vision

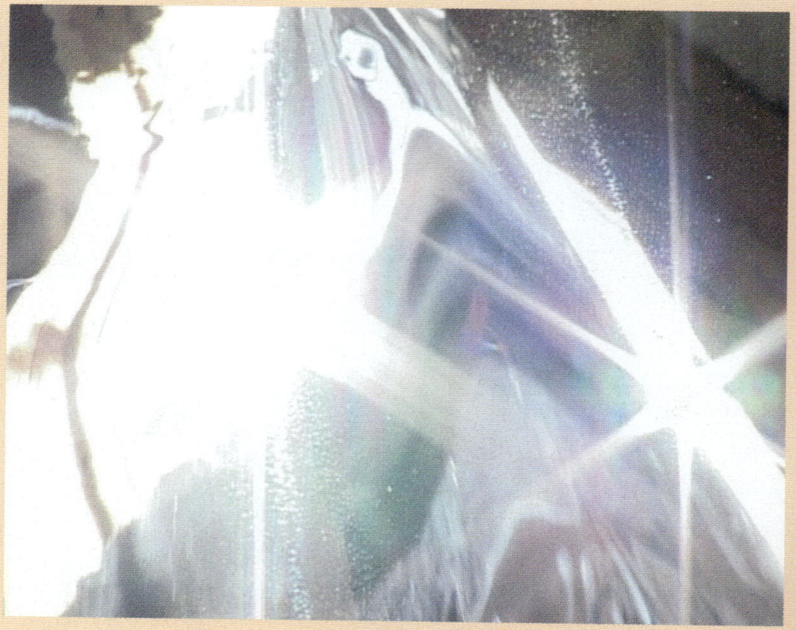

Hilary Lloyd's videos, 35mm-slide and 8mm-film installations often document everyday behaviour — ordinary activities such as walking in the street, waiting tables, or washing a car — but if her work has its roots in the 'pedestrian' aesthetic of 1960s Minimalist choreography, its charged, voyeuristic aspect separates it from such practice. The relations between observer and observed in Vito Acconci's 1969 *Following Piece* might be invoked as a more relevant precedent. In her early work, Lloyd often explored 'found' choreographies, staged with the participation of passers-by whom she persuaded to collaborate with her: a group of builders on scaffolding, a woman repeatedly building a house of cards, skateboarders performing tricks. The artist exhibits a Warholian fascination with the desire to be looked at and filmed: even in the most mundane everyday situation, she uses her position behind the camera to tap into her subjects' latent exhibitionism, and to reveal it to the viewer.

Lloyd balances this intense scrutiny of individuals with an impression of abstraction: movements are often presented as sculptural rhythms. This sense is

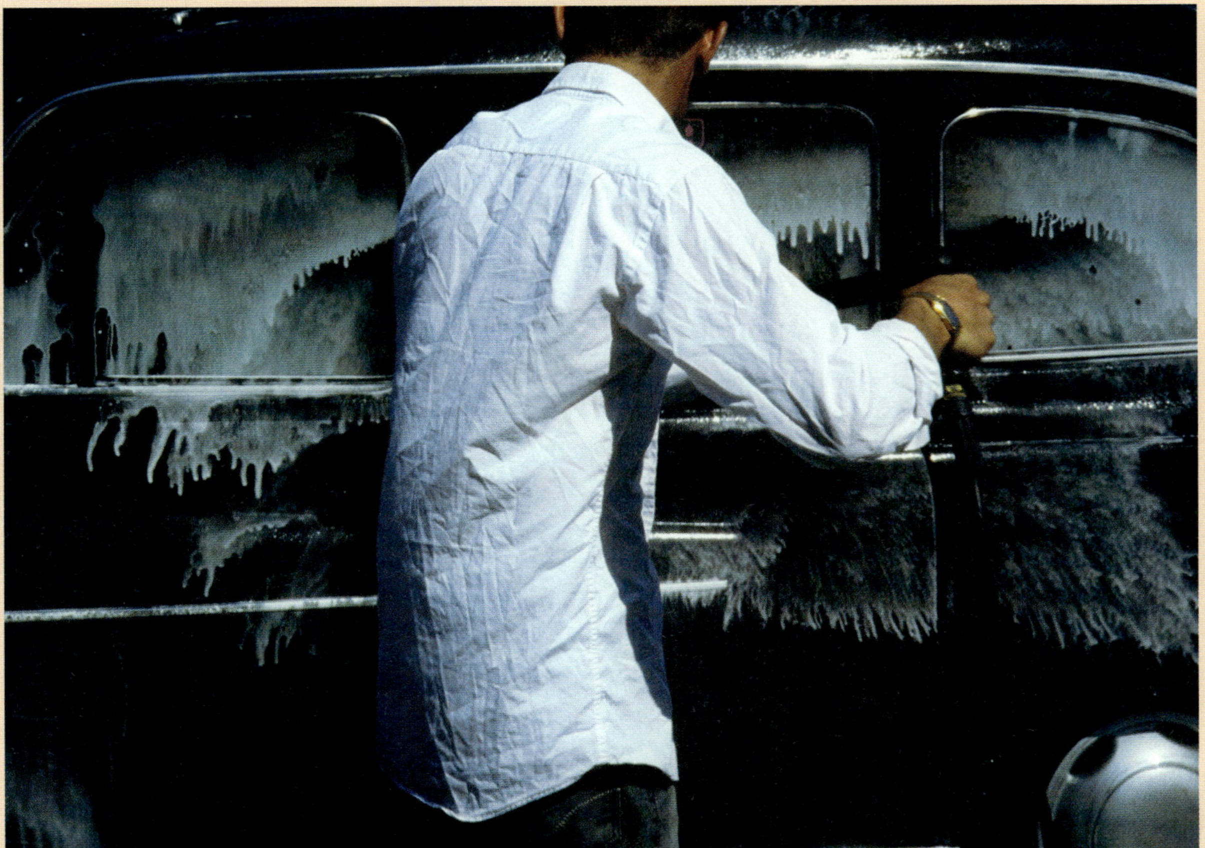

Car Wash, 2005. 320 slides, 4 Kodak Ektapro 9020 slide projectors, 4 Unicol projector stands. Dimensions variable

Latent exhibitionism

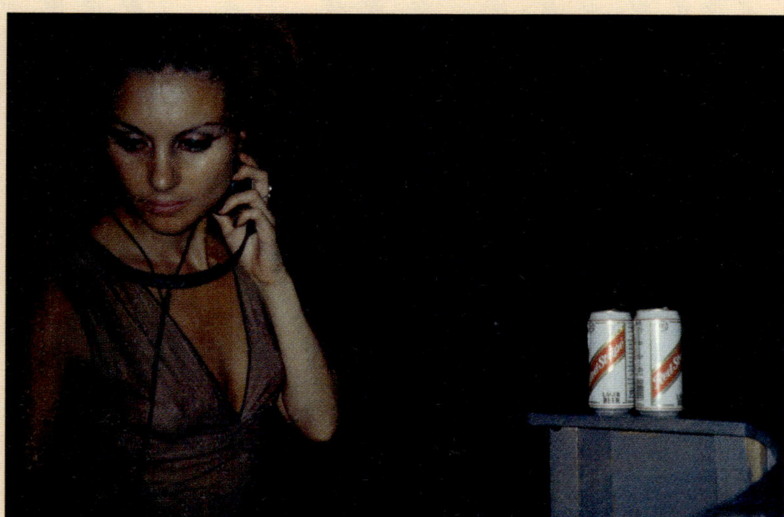

Princess Julia, 1997. 80 slides, Kodak Ektapro 5020 slide projector, Unicol projector stand. Dimensions variable

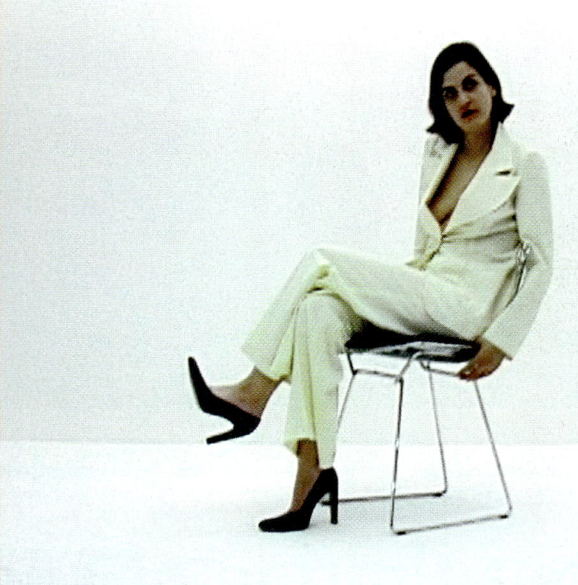

Dawn, 1999. Sony PVM–14N5E video monitor, Sony SVP–9020 SVHS videocassette player, flight cases, Unicol single column television stand. Dimensions variable

emphasized by her means of installation, via the choreographic manner in which she sets out her monitors and projections in architectural space, and through her emphasis on the supporting technology (her choice of particular monitors, projector supports and screens, with visible brand names), which are foregrounded rather than concealed or treated as transparent. These specific choices regarding technology acknowledge her media as part of the urban, technological landscape out of which the work is born. Their command of the total space of encounter also exacerbates a sense of suffocating closeness to the subjects depicted.

Lloyd's disparate themes and narratives are anchored throughout her practice by a stop-and-start rhythm that creates—from a variety of urban vistas—a sense of the multiplicity of the city as a body of people carrying out various activities. In *Princess Julia Slide Projection* (1997) Lloyd sequenced the moments and gestures performed by a DJ in a slideshow of eighty images, drawing our attention to the performance implicit in her behavioural patterns. Other rituals that Lloyd captures might be as mundane as four men washing a car in a garage in Sheffield (*Car Wash*, 2005)—a slide-show piece projected on four walls that captures a rough but lyrical found choreography—or *Motorcycles* (2008), a series of close-up shots of revving motorbikes that fetishistically reveal glimpses of the hands of the mechanics repairing them. Both works become arenas for the performance of masculinity. More recent work has transposed this scopophilic intensity of focus on interpersonal relations to abstract surfaces: *Studio* (2007) traces the paint marks found on the artist's studio floor with myopic intensity, as though forensically tracking their genesis over time. *Studio #2*, a four-screen installation made in 2009, warps and distorts the viewer's plane of vision by capturing the shifting colours and reflections of refracted light on contorted pieces of mylar and plastic.

Maria Loboda

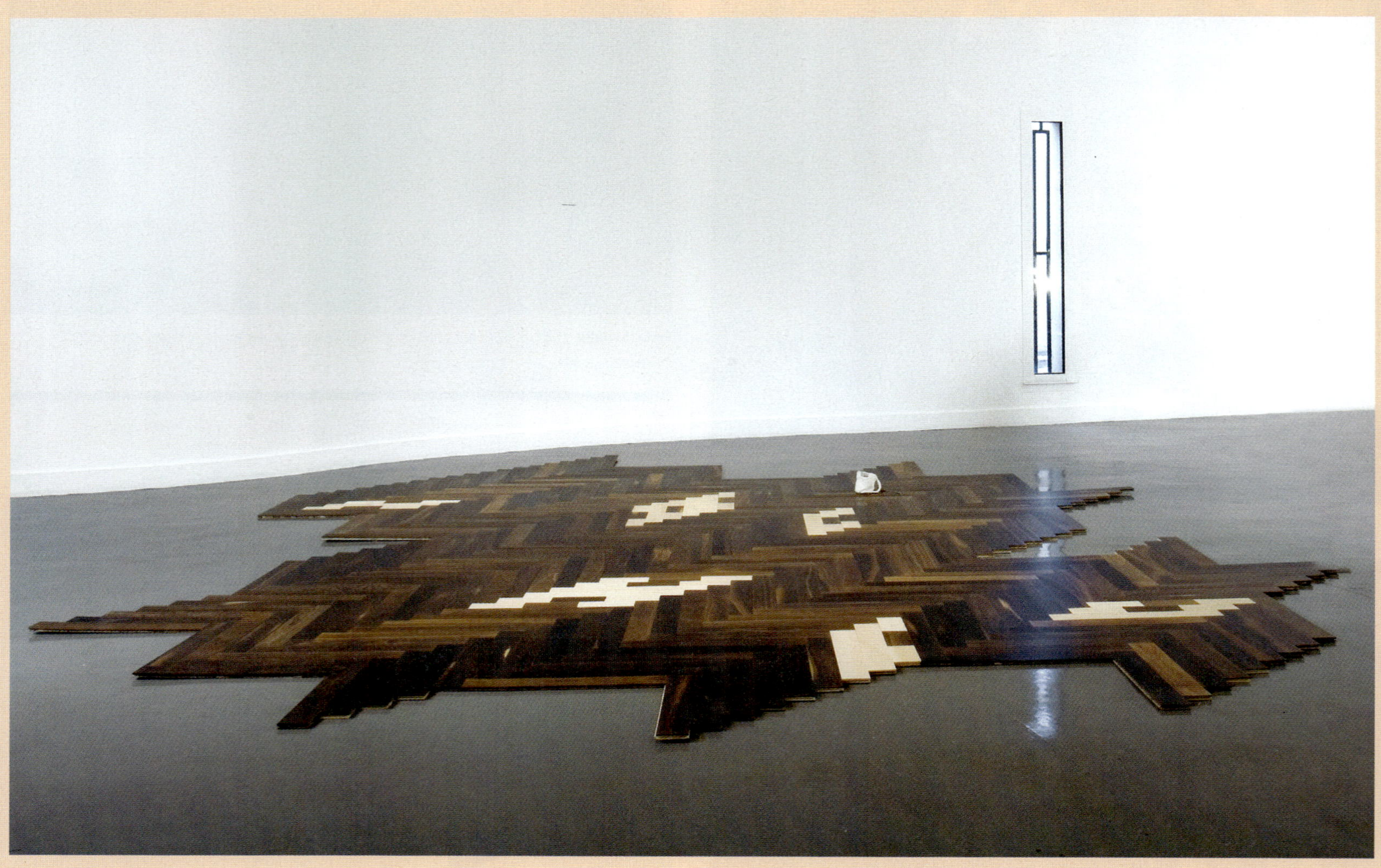

What will happen?, 2007. Parquet floor. Dimensions variable

With delicious anarchy, the work of Maria Loboda investigates the trafficking between the object and the spirit, rationality and magic. Her method is to trace knowledge through a study of the tension between *res* and *deus*, thing and God — with God understood here as the symbol of Order.

In the installation *What will happen?* (2007), the artist consults the *I-Ching* — the ancient book of divination — with the question 'What will happen?' each time she realizes the work. She lays out the answer, encrypted within the angles of the contrasting shades of a parquet floor. This process of encryption and abstraction, obtained via the consultation of ancient spiritual and esoteric sources, lies at the heart of Loboda's practice. Her works pay much attention to obscure codified systems, such as the Victorian language of flowers, which she used to create seemingly benign bouquets that actually express insults (*A guide to insults and misanthropy*, 2006).

The consultation of ancient spiritual and esoteric sources

Process of encryption and abstraction

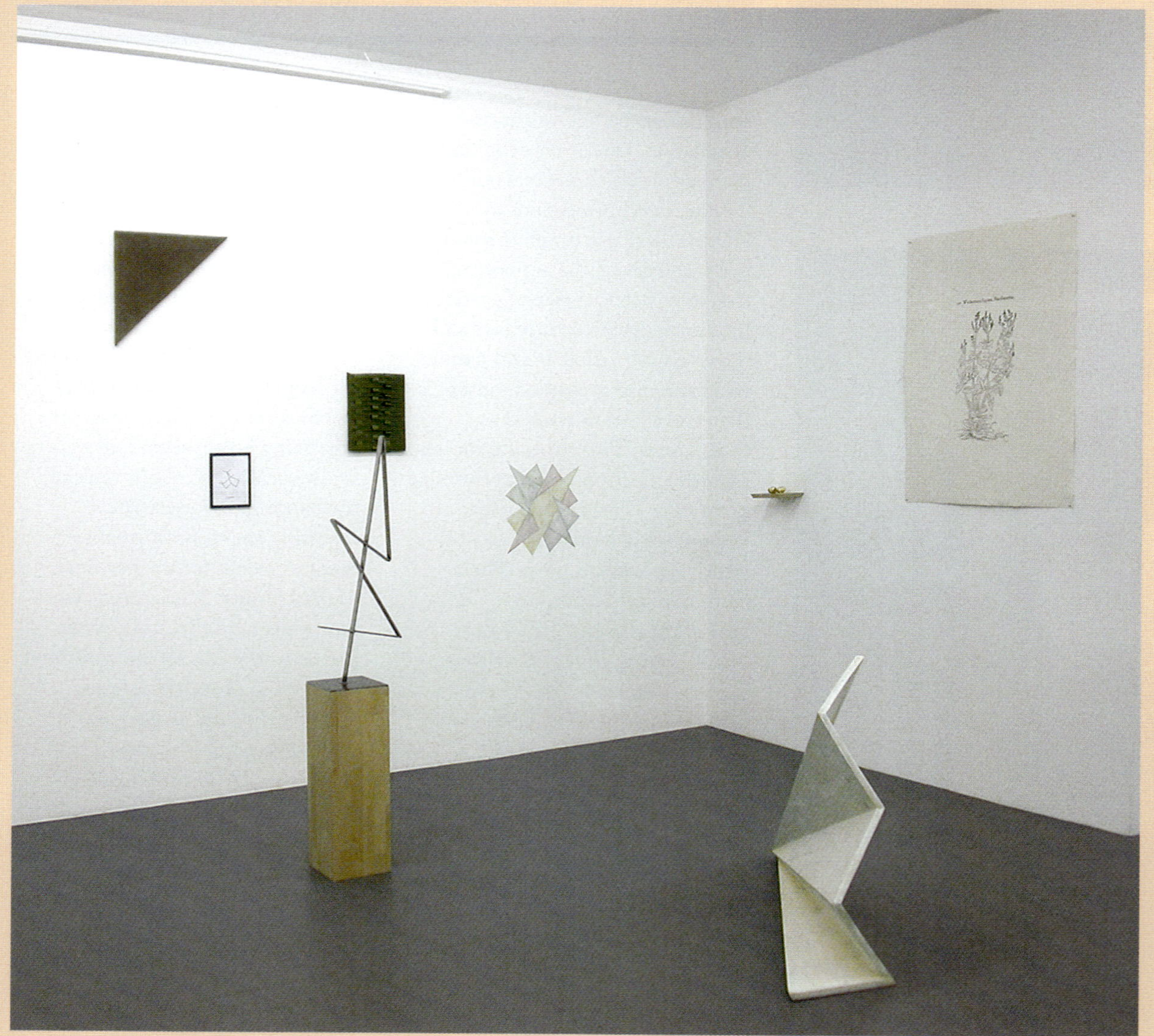

The grand conjuration of Lucifuge Rofocale, 2005. Fine steel, white wood, brandy, verbena, green ribbon, goat skin, camphor, half gold–plated walnut. Dimensions variable

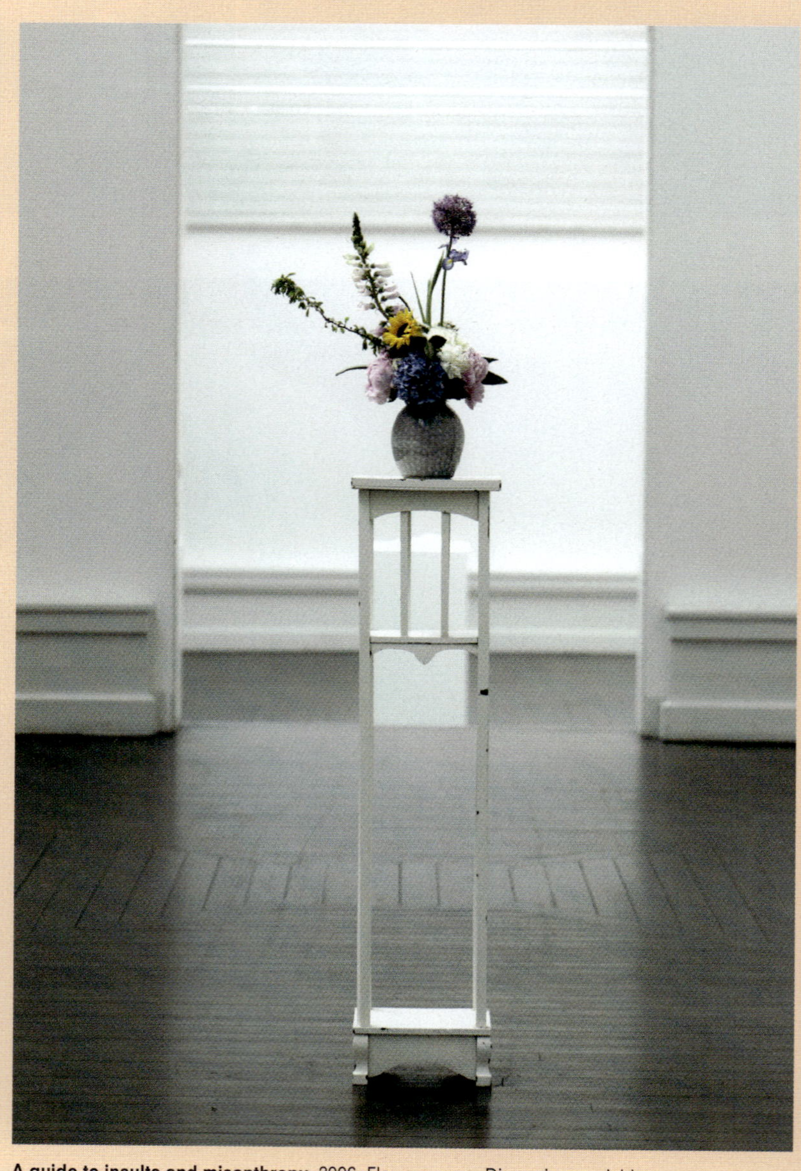

A guide to insults and misanthropy, 2006. Flowers, vase. Dimensions variable

An unhinged and discordant conversation with time

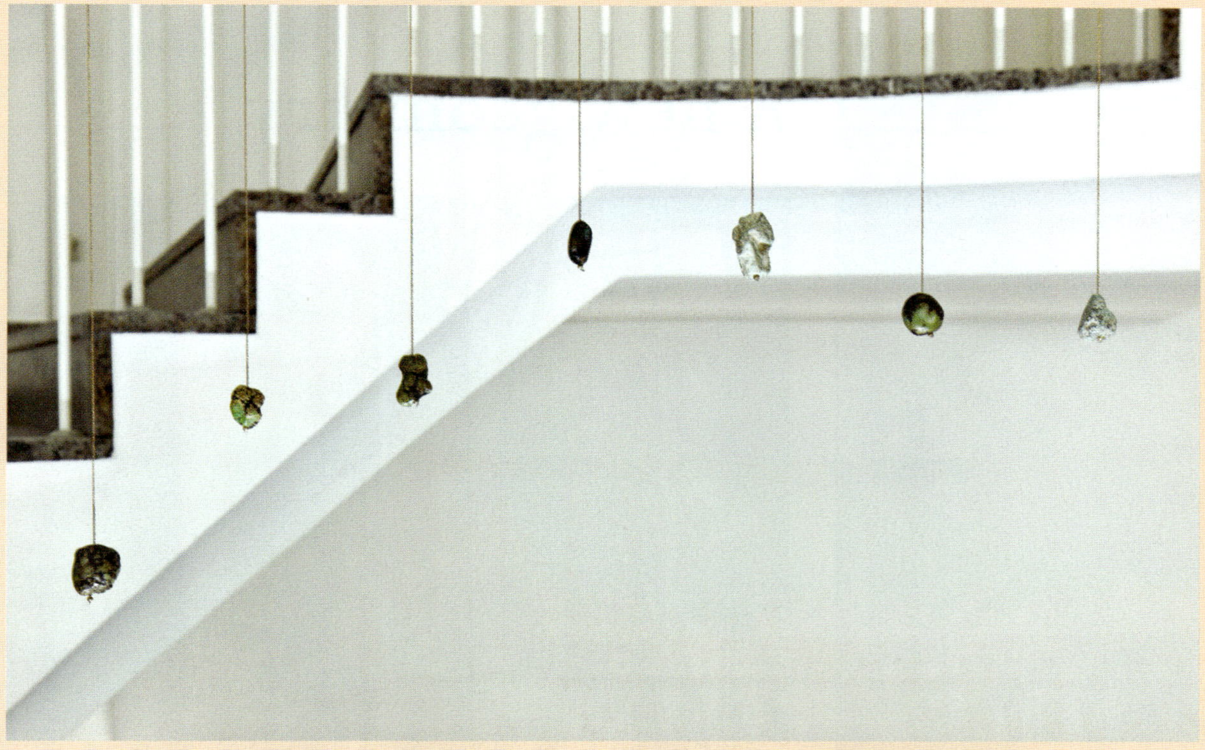

The Moral Antithesis of the Perfect Consonance, 2008. Rough turquoises, copper, wire. Dimensions variable

Similarly, in *The grand conjuration of Lucifuge Rofocle* (2005), Loboda created a suite of works based on a Satanist anti-love spell from the fourteenth century that together contain the potential to break apart a pair of lovers. The materials required for the spell came disguised in an apparently innocuous arrangement of modernist sculpture and drawing, their malevolent capacity kept hidden through their form as artworks.

Loboda's investigation into subjects related to the magical suggests a fascination with transformation. The elements she places in front of our eyes are quite simple: wood, cloth, paper, light; there is nothing produced or manufactured in her installations. They are concrete things, but their meaning is created through their interconnection. The whole is more than the sum of its parts, and this is what enables Loboda's works to transcend the neutrality of their materials, transfiguring their banality.

In *The Moral Antithesis of the Perfect Consonance* (2008) unpolished turquoise stones hang from lengths of copper wire positioned in space as an index for the first notes of Camille de Saint-Saëns's cello work 'Danse Macabre'. Loboda chose these notes because they form a tritone interval, also known as the 'Devils Chord' banned in the Middle Ages for its latently evil properties. In *A room as a word* (2009), Loboda created a constellation of works based on the twelve letters of the word 'conversation', referring to Joseph Haydn's description of chamber music as a 'conversational style of composition'. Each letter abstrusely manifested through abstract sculptural forms, allowing viewers to find the word as they moved through the space.

Loboda's works engage in an unhinged and discordant conversation with time and history. They do not seem to belong to the present, but are difficult to place in the past or the future. They generate a sense of movement

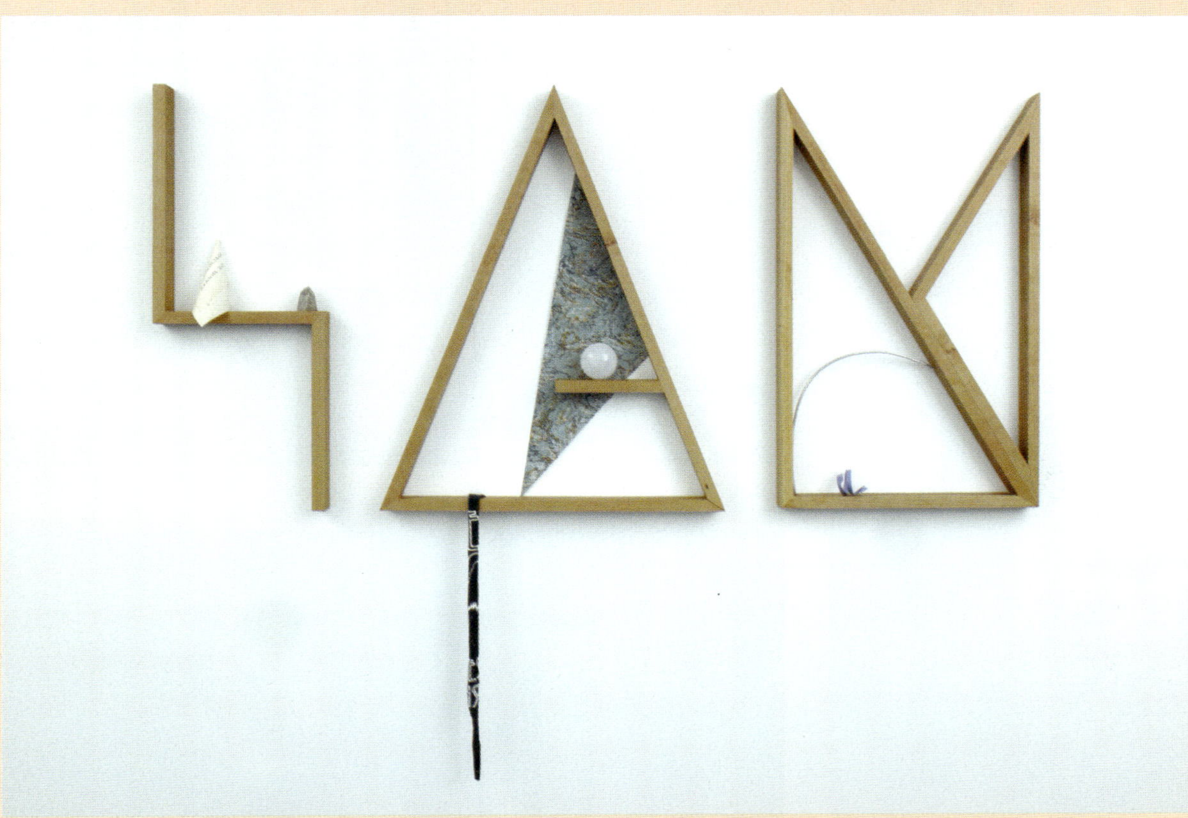

Sphere, cone, rod, crystalline form, plate strip, 2008. Milk glass, paper, aluminium, quartz, crystal, shirt, book page, wood. 124 × 158 × 7 cm

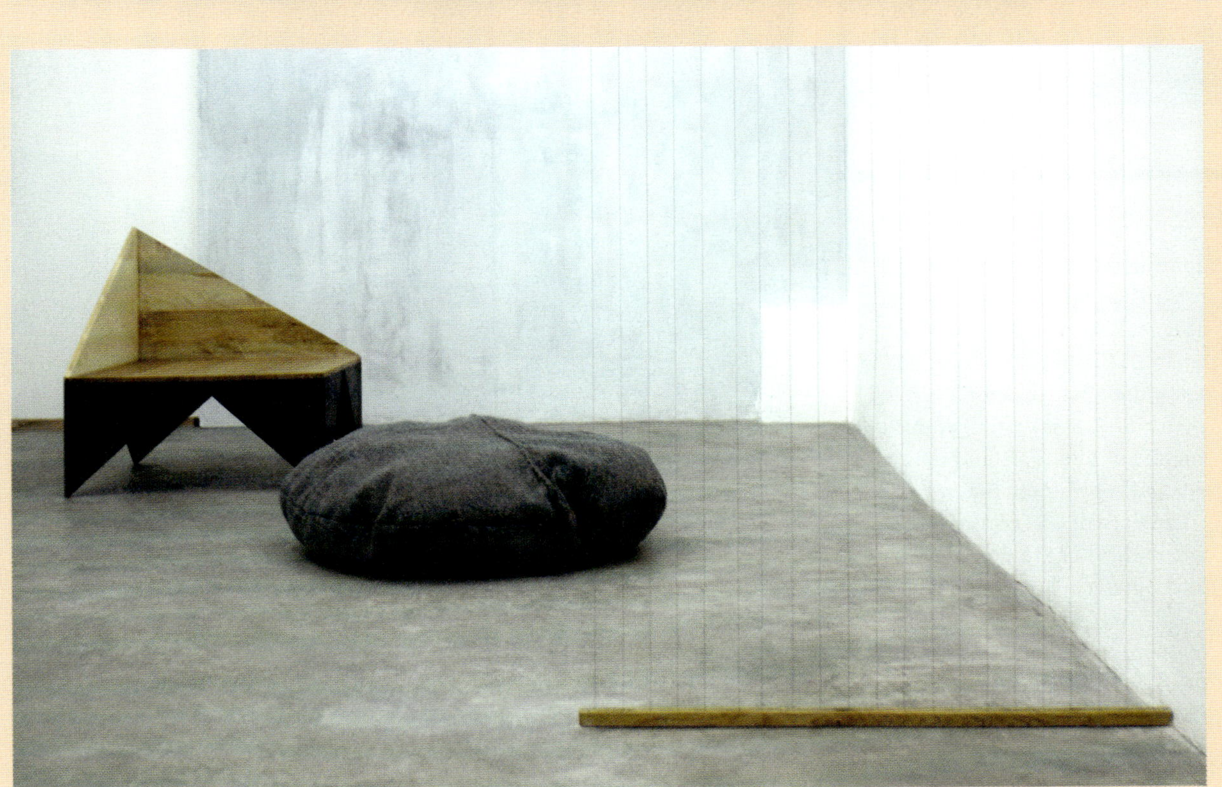

A room as a song, 2009. Materials for a harpsichord: oak, maple, walnut, ayous, steel, strings, felt. Dimensions variable

Material capacity kept hidden

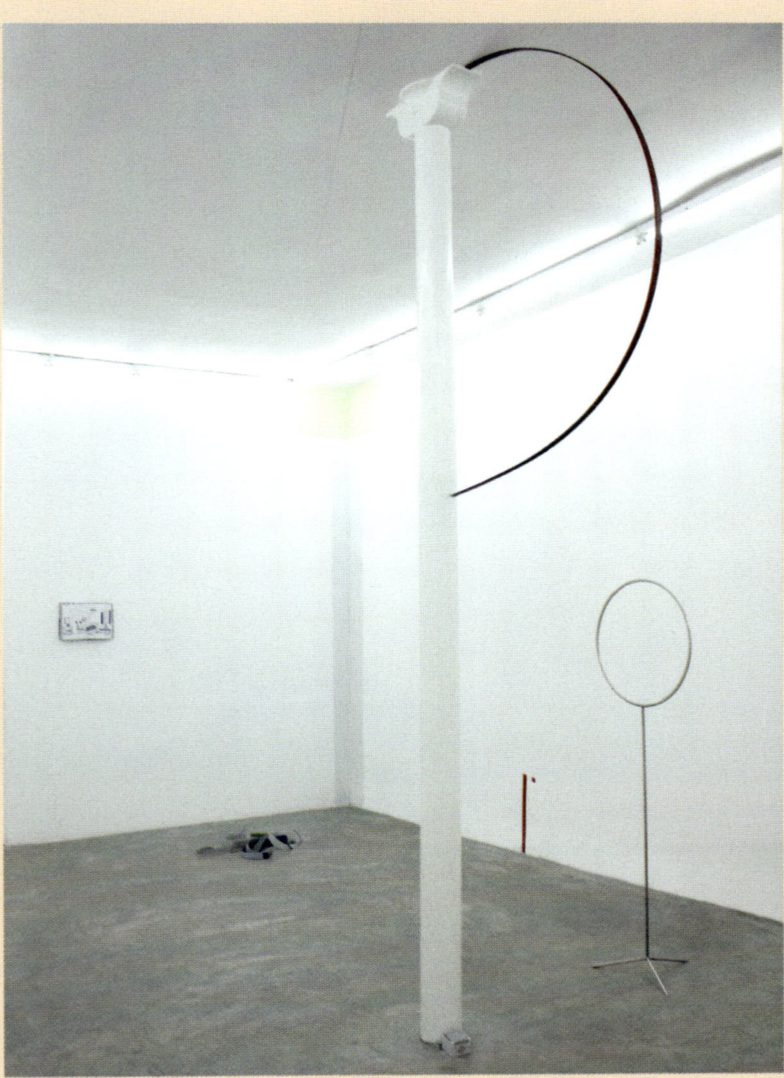

A Room as a word, 2009. Wood, paint, paper, book, framed picture, rope, fabric, steel. Dimensions variable

between all three temporalities, but at the same time cannot be described simply as anachronistic. They elude the contemporary and are not made in response to any topical reality. Gilles Deleuze wrote that in the paradox of eluding the present is the paradox of infinite identity. Lodoba's works, neither exactly modern sculpture nor contemporary installation, embody an infinite connection to history, as clouds do to the sky.

Renata Lucas

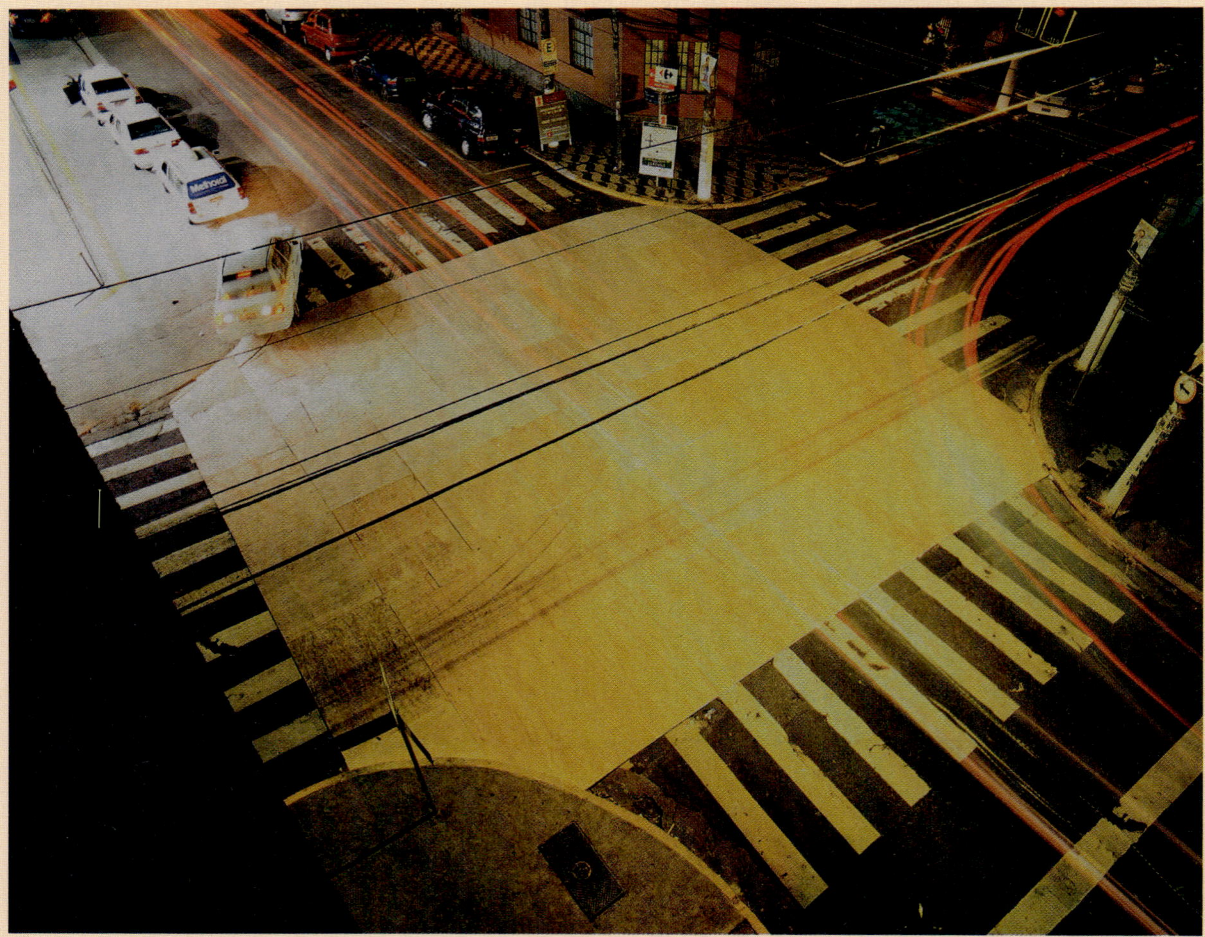

Cruzamento, 2004. Plywood. Approx. 15 × 16 m. São Paulo

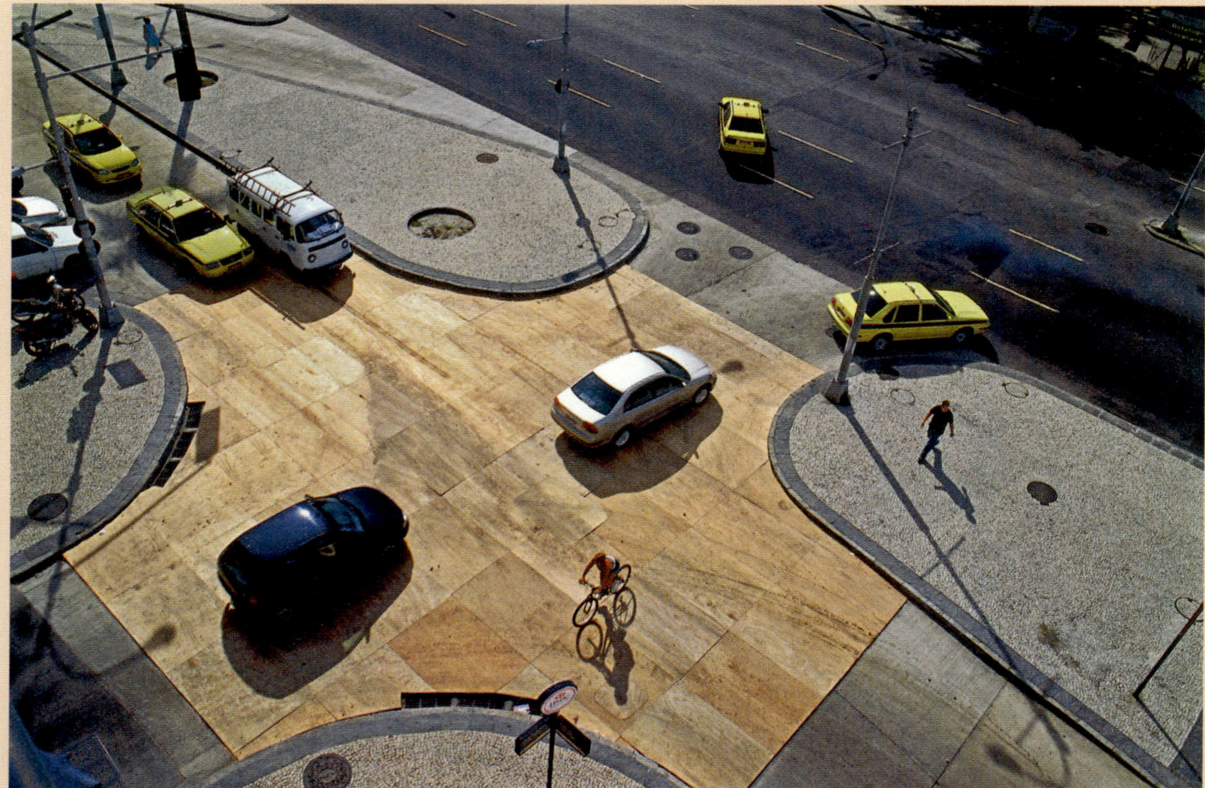

Cruzamento, 2003. Plywood. Approx. 17 × 18 m. Rio de Janeiro

A new geometry

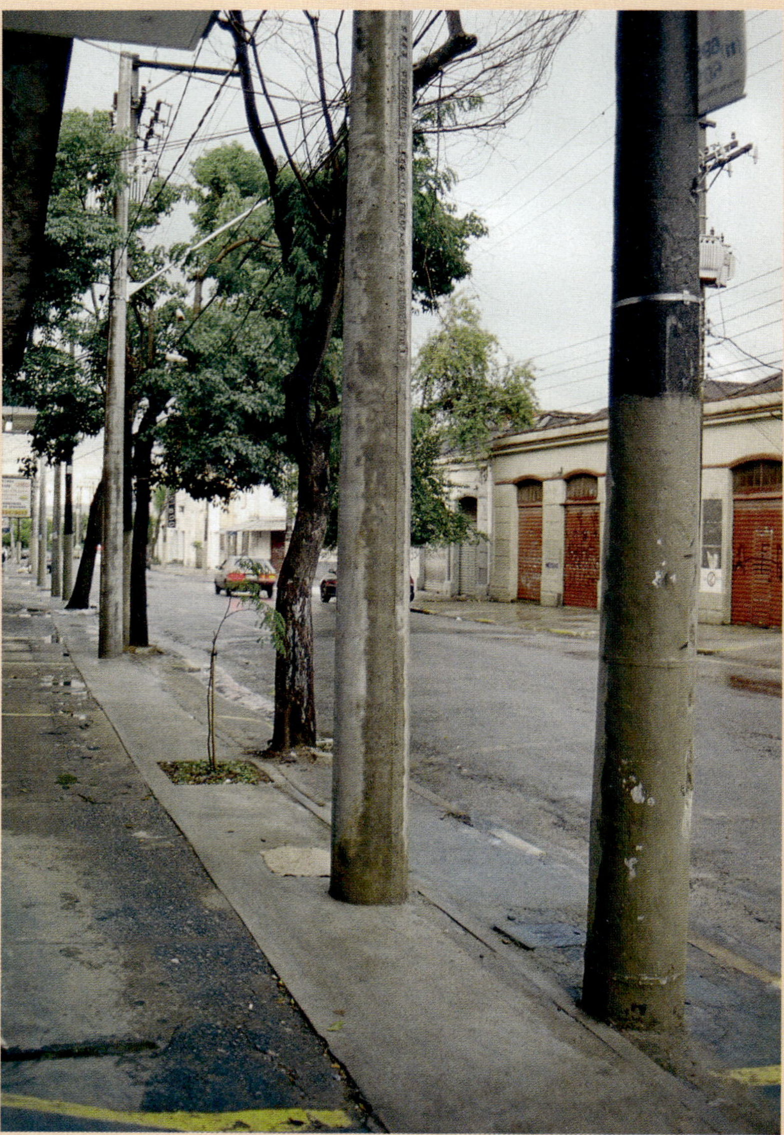

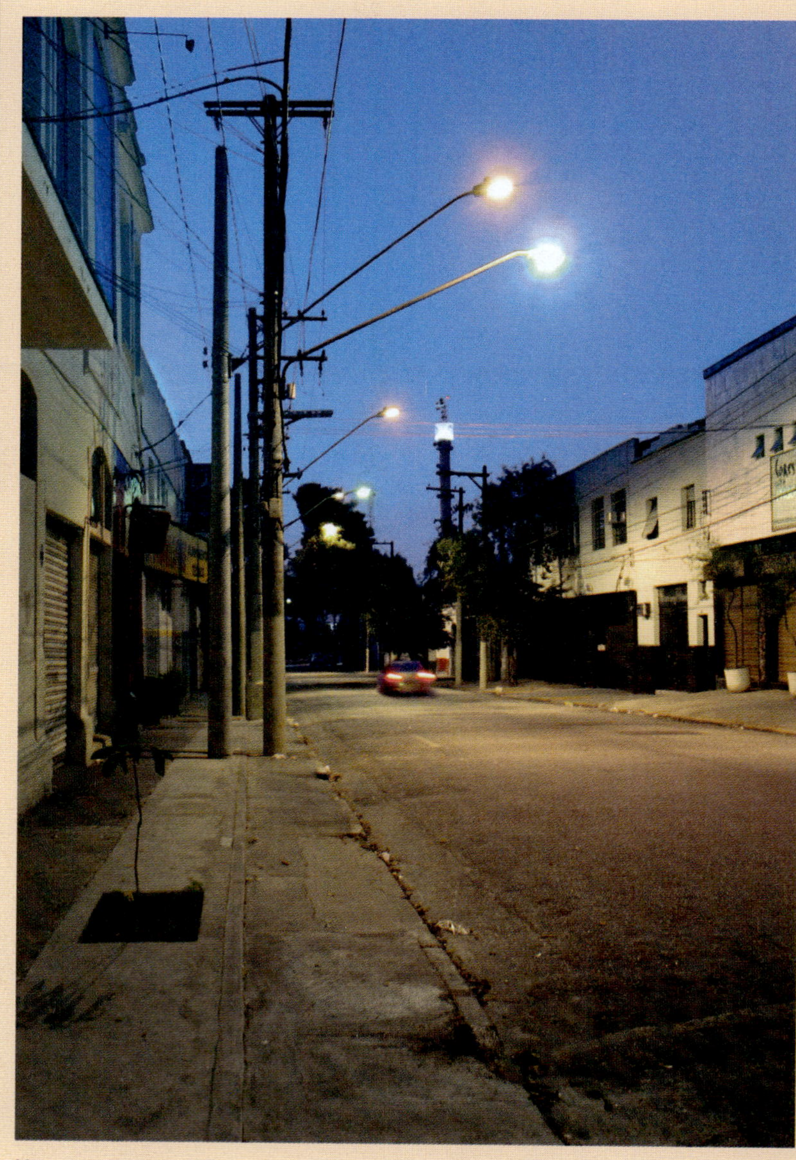

Matemática Rápida, 2006. Duplicate concrete sidewalk, including lampposts, tree planters, kerbstone. Dimensions variable. São Paulo

The Brazilian artist Renata Lucas attempts to introduce a new vocabulary into site-specific practice by exploring the critical implications of reciprocity as a quality of the built environment.

In 2003, Lucas realized *Cruzamento* (Crossing) in Rio de Janeiro, at the crossing of Praia do Flamengo with Dois de Dezembro. She repeated the work a year later in São Paulo, at the corner of Padre Joao Manuel and Oscar Freire. *Cruzamento* consisted of repaving the intersection with plywood. In doing so, a curious geometric form appears — a cross with rounded arms, emerging from the street like a relief or a second skin imposed upon the surface. The colour and texture of the new material interrupts the linear reading of the street, claiming a new geometry. By projecting this imaginary situation upon a real one, *Cruzamento* embodies the ultimate contradiction of representational form. This new territory in the middle of the road becomes a spatial segment capable of establishing communication between heterogeneous elements and scales (passers-by, cars, architecture). Lucas's delimited zone inserts another rhythm into urban time by functioning as a stage. Like a stage, the work creates a discontinuity as a separate space upon which actors can perform. In this way, *Cruzamento* enables us to understand the city not as a continuum, but as a sequence of co-existing spaces where different functions and phenomena are inseparably linked.

Matemática rápida (Quick mathematics, 2006), conceived for the 2006 São Paulo Biennial, elaborates upon Lucas's exploration of twinned realities and the realm of the in-between.

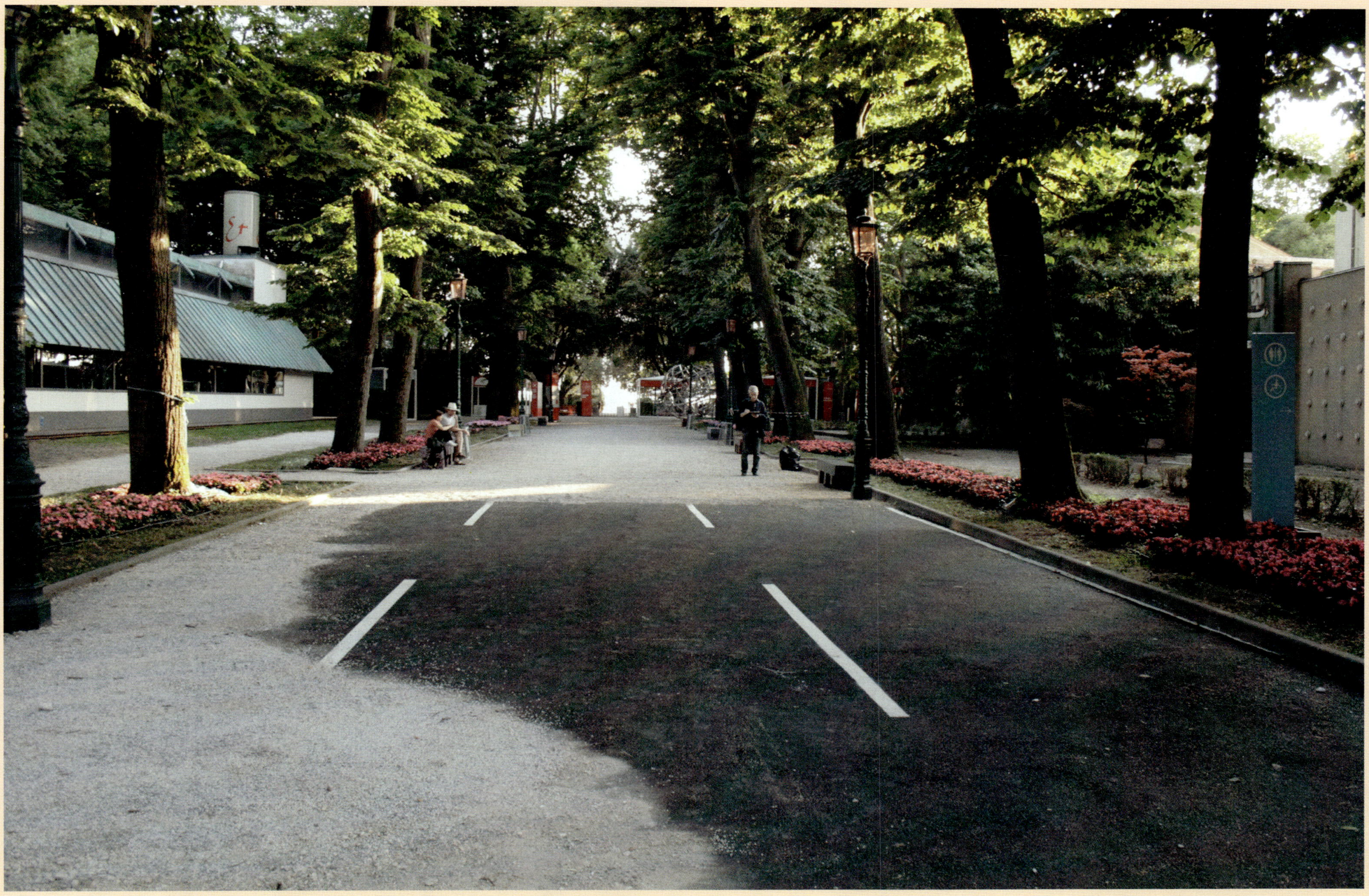

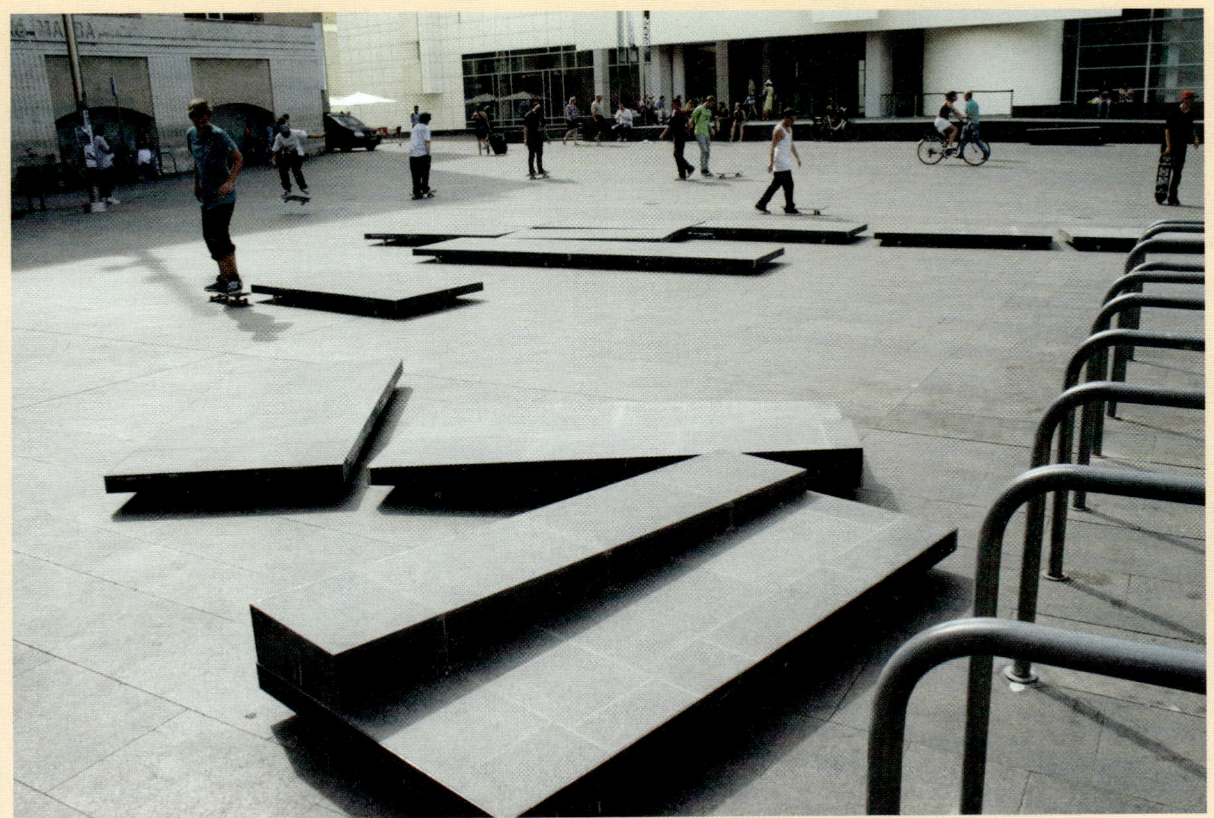

Venice suitcase, 2009. Asphalt, paint. Dimensions variable

Intimate spaces

The fact that town planning is arbitrarily split into two disciplines — architecture and urbanism — demonstrates that the way in which our cities are devised has not yet opened up to the necessity of transforming the mechanisms of the design process. *Matemática rápida* productively interprets the notion of these false alternatives in urban planning, and in our way of reading the city space, by simply replicating a basic element of urban planning: a sidewalk. Instead of rendering the intervention more visible by creating an oppositional or negative element or form, as in *Cruzamento*, she simply built a new footpath over the existing one on Rua Brigadeiro Galvão in the Barra Funda neighbourhood, duplicating lamp-posts, trees and flowerbeds.

In these two public interventions, Lucas seems to aim towards more intimate spaces within the city. This is not to imply any Romantic conception of human scale versus architecture or the monument, but the possibility of a break with the idea of spatial continuity and the tendency to erase every articulation between spaces, between outside and inside, one space and the next. Instead, she suggests that the idea of articulation, of defined in-between places, will induce awareness of what is significant on either side.

Lucas's works, intervening inside or outside the gallery space, operate on the law of reflection, a particular dialectics of how one becomes two in order to produce a 'third way'. It would be wrong to read her interventions as being simply about the generic relationships that we establish with space and its architectural dimension. Instead, they provide a ground on which to investigate the relationship between language, image and behaviour in the context of a given situation — or, to use Hélio Oiticica's term, an 'acting field'. Her work provides a temporary stage for alternative action while also creating an awareness of the specific conditions that determine our interpretation of the built environment.

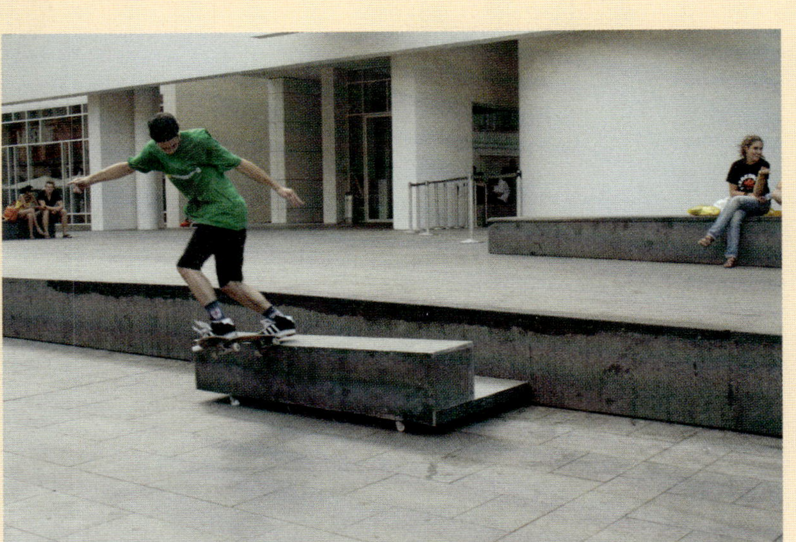

A temporary stage for alternate action

Prototype for a Sliding Ground, 2009. 15 granite slabs mounted on wheels. Each 1 × 2 m

Goshka Macuga

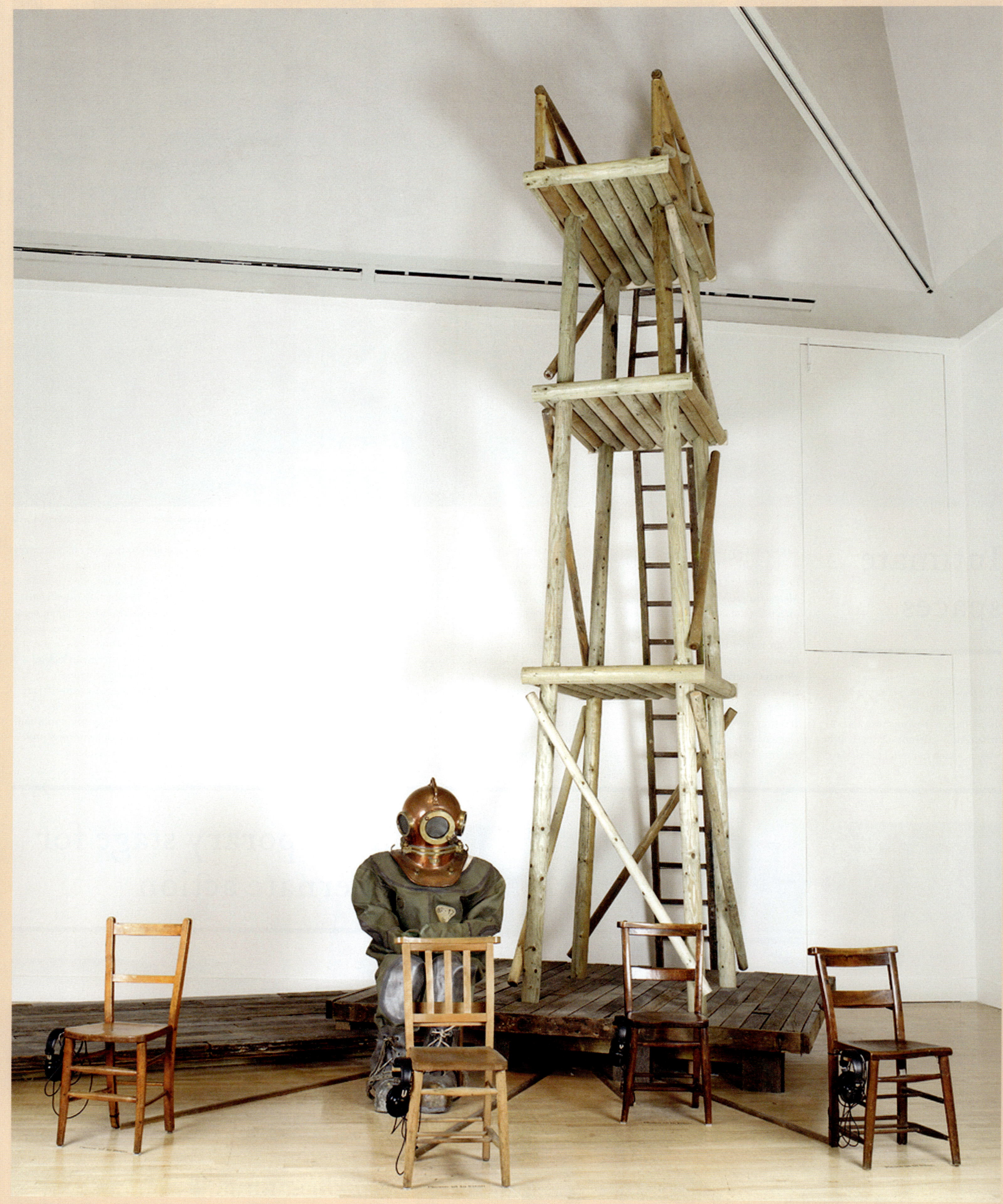

The Diving Stage (1928) after Paul Nash, 2007. Wooden diving stage, 4 chairs, headphones, Russian diving suit, audio (excerpts from Herbert Read, 'The Freedom of the artist'; Paul Élouard, 'Poetic Evidence'; André Breton, 'Limits Not Frontiers of Surrealism'; unknown, 'The Situation in England, the intellectual position with regard to Surrealism, the formation of an English group, immediate activities' from The International Surrealist Bulletin, no. 4, September 1936). Dimensions variable.

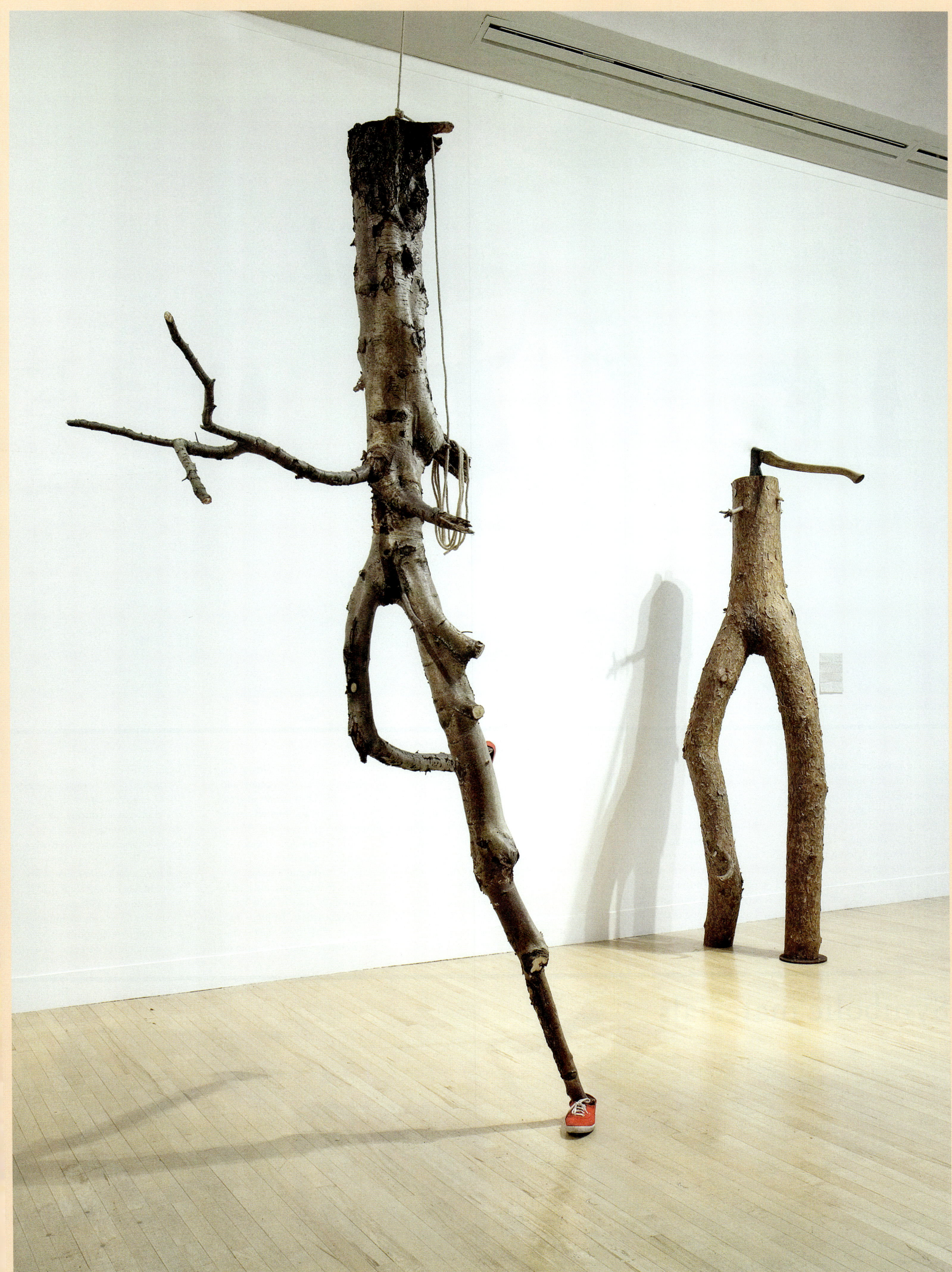

Boy, 2007. Wood, plimsolls, rope. 332 × 186 × 170 cm. **Girl**, 2007. Wood, axe. 315 × 145 × 63 cm.

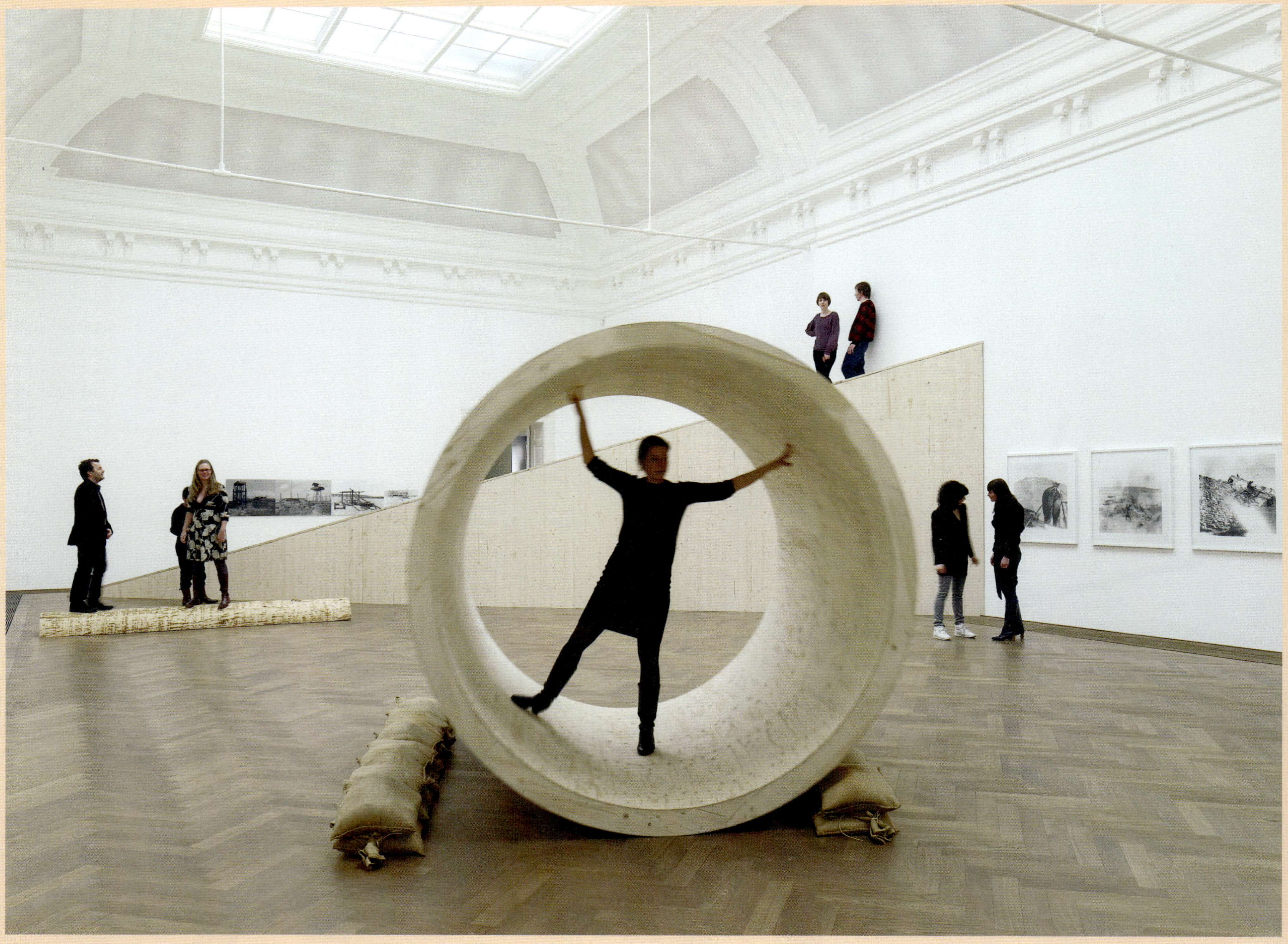

I Am Become Death, 2009. Mixed–media installation. Dimensions variable.

Amateur collectors, curators and artists all share a similar curiosity and passion for art, despite their differing reasons and motivations. The least specifically defined approach — that of an artist who not only contemplates things that others make but also gets involved in the making — sums up the multi-faceted practice of Goshka Macuga, who has defined herself as a 'guest in the past'. Macuga has assumed the role of a historian, a skilful mediator between opposing genres and professions, a curator and occasional collector of contemporary and historical artefacts.

Employing an impressive variety of formats to organize her displays of artworks, material objects and documents, Macuga critiques the art-historical narratives and the ideologies that support them. In her installation at Tate Britain in 2008, she studied the museum's archives in search of images and texts relating to British Surrealism and abstraction of the 1930s, including the work of Eileen Agar, Paul Nash and his ephemeral Unit One group. The installation, which expanded over an entire gallery, was an immersive environment, an idiosyncratic assemblage that seemed as carefully orchestrated as Macuga's new works in the genre of collage. Among the unusual inventory was an ancient diver's costume (*The Diving Stage (1928) after Paul Nash*, 2007) and the raw, symbolic materials of art and magic: rocks and human-shaped tree trunks (*Boy*, 2007; *Girl*, 2007).

Certain elements of Macuga's vocabulary recur in her various works and the scope of her interest changes constantly. In her recent show at Kunsthalle Basel (2009), the visit to the Hopi Indians made in 1895–96 by the German art historian Aby Warburg in order to study the ritual known as the 'Serpent's Dance' became a pretext for Macuga's own travel to the United States during the 2008 presidential campaign. Macuga made a documentary that partly retraced Warburg steps and partly followed a path of her own. This brought her, among other places, to the house of a Vietnam War veteran, who made his private archive of photographs from the war available for Macuga's project.

Symbolic materials

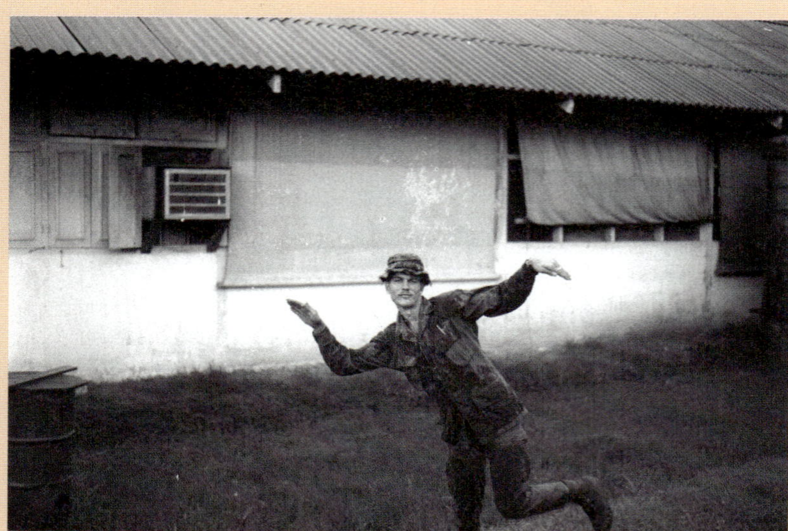

Triptych, 2008. 1 of 3 C–prints purchashed by the artist. 95 × 129 cm

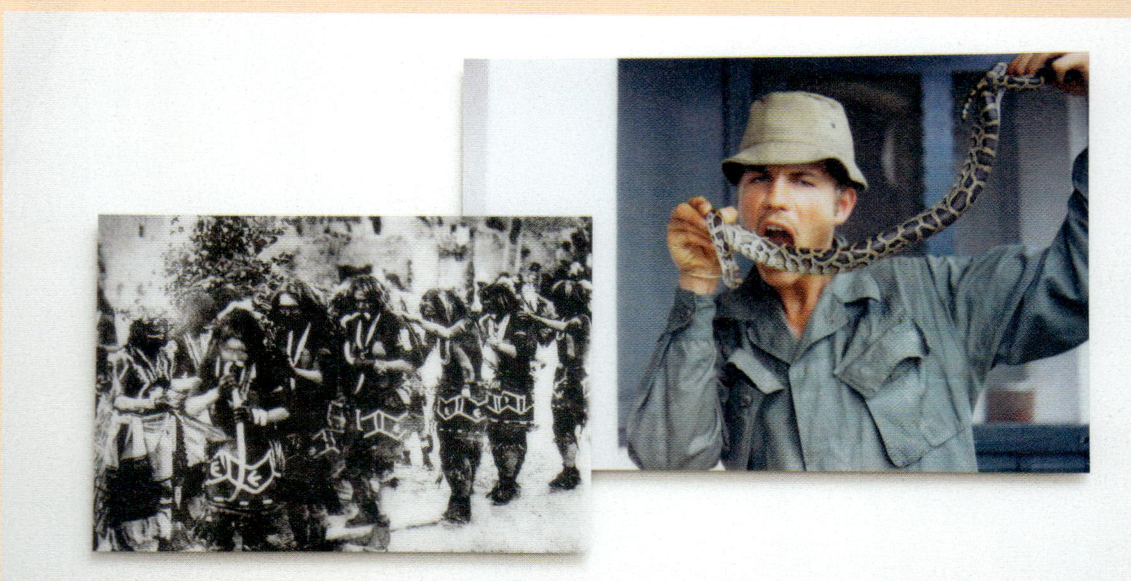

Untitled, 2009. 2 C–prints mounted on Diasec. Left: image purchased by Aby Warburg. Right: image purchased by the artist.
122 × 183 cm, 99 × 147 cm

Guest in the past

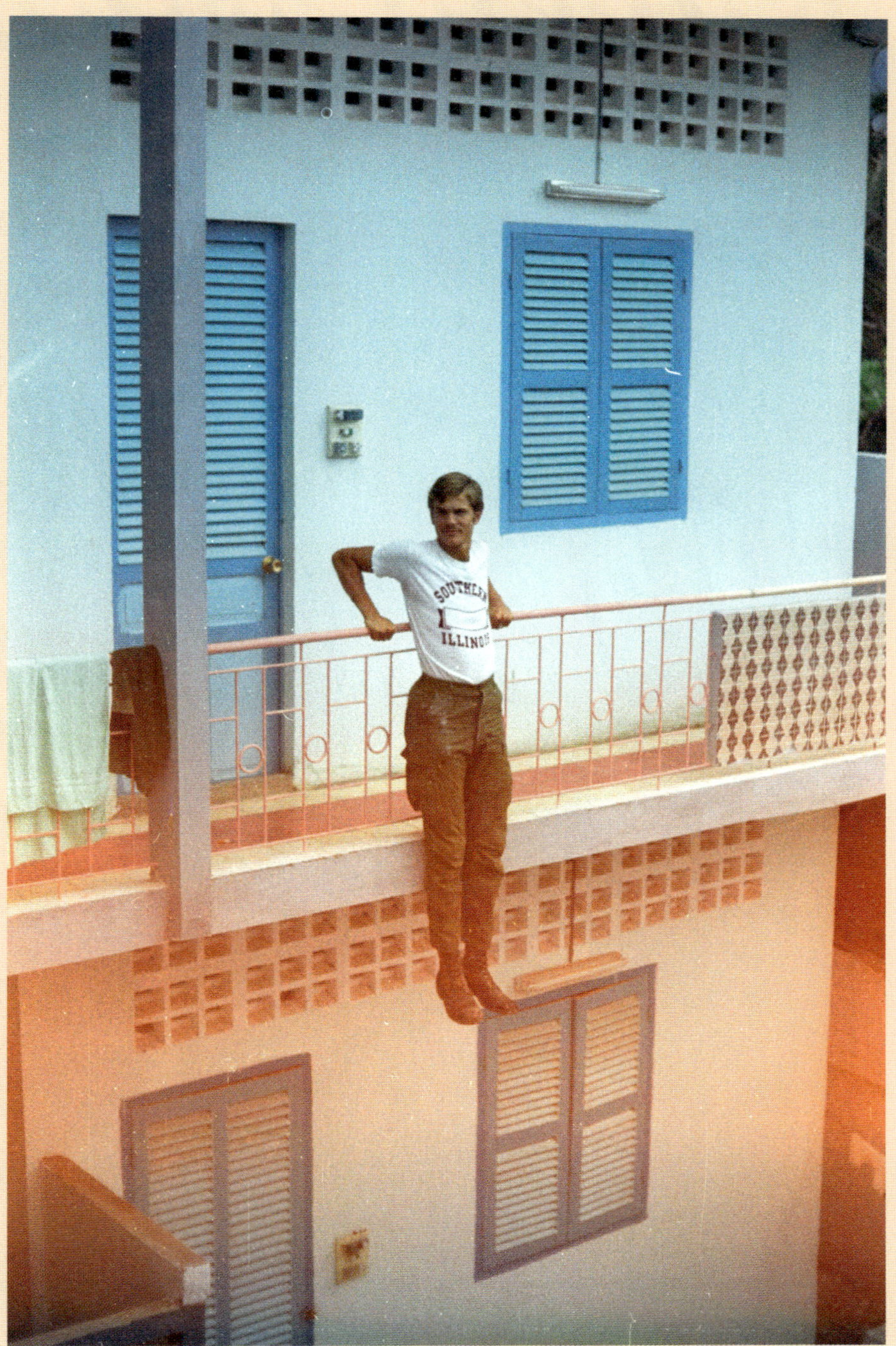

Objects In Relation, 2007. Mixed–media installation. Dimensions variable. Installation view, Tate Britain, London

Balcony, 2008. C–print. Image purchased by the artist. 210 × 140 cm

Historical panorama

The exhibition took the shape of a landscape of sculptural forms, a take on Robert Morris's 1971 'interactive' installation at the Tate Gallery, which was closed after some days due to the risk of injuries to which it exposed visitors. In Macuga's interpretation, the large wooden ramp looming over the main room offered viewers a historical panorama, and the works in the show addressed an array of dramatic events: the disappearance of Native American culture at the end of the nineteenth century, epitomized by Warburg, and the last phase of the Vietnam War, which coincided with Morris's 'participatory' exhibition. A quote from the Hindu scripture *Bhagavad Gita*, uttered by J. Robert Oppenheimer (director of the US atomic programme in 1942–45) when he saw the effect of the first nuclear explosion, gave Macuga's exhibition its apocalyptic title 'I Am Become Death'.

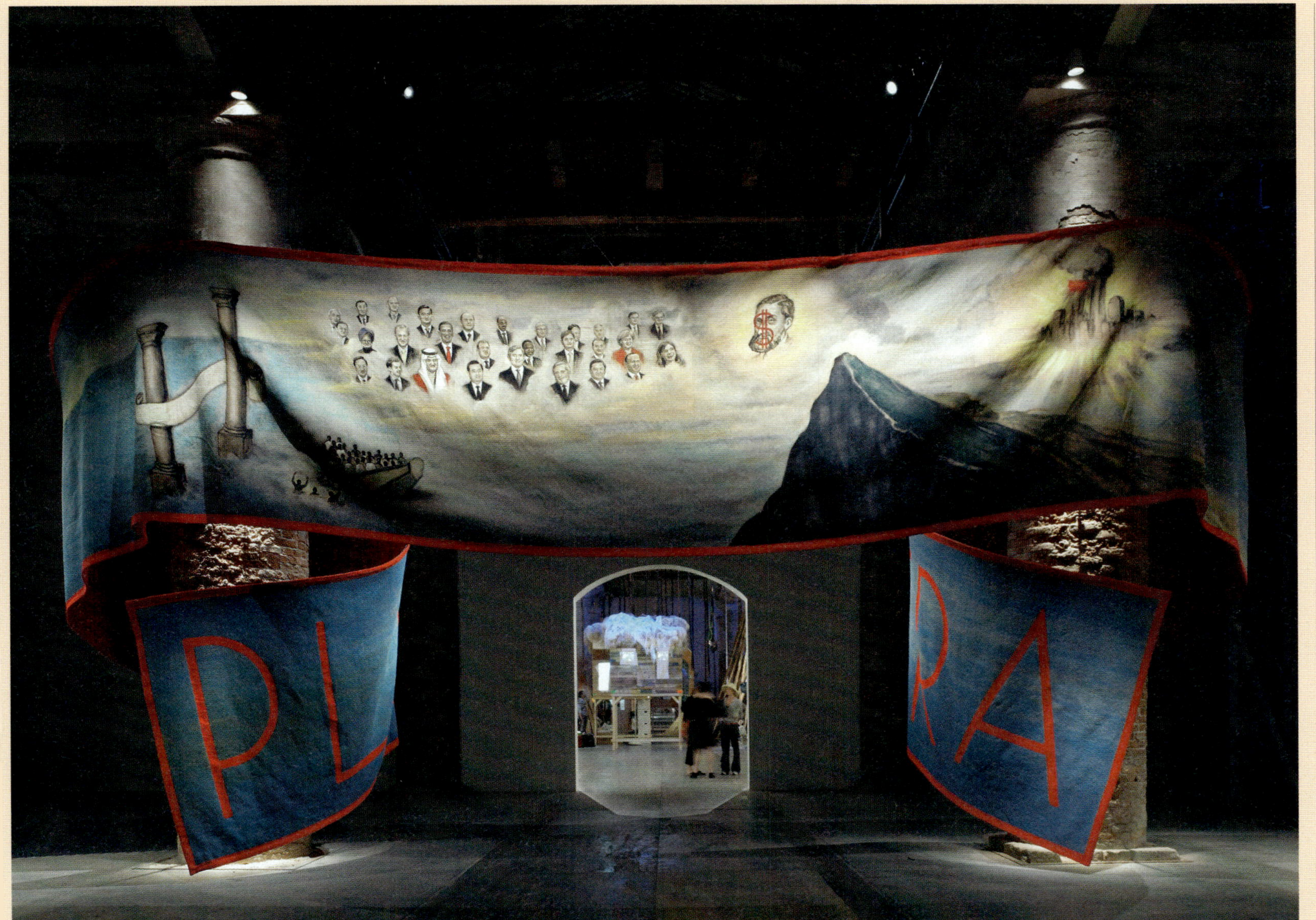

Plus Ultra, 2009. Woven tapestry. Dimensions variable. Installation view, 53rd Venice Biennale, 2009

Rubens Mano

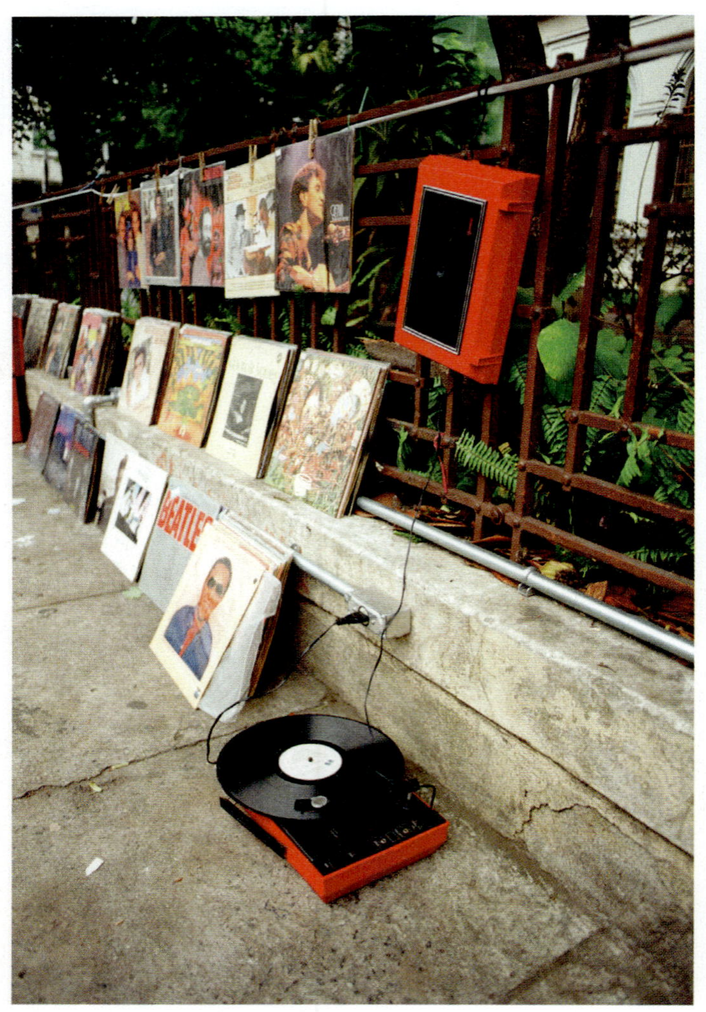

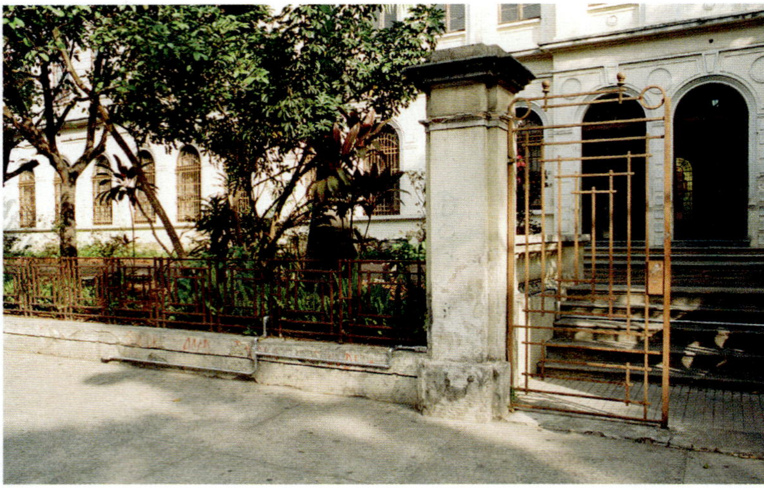

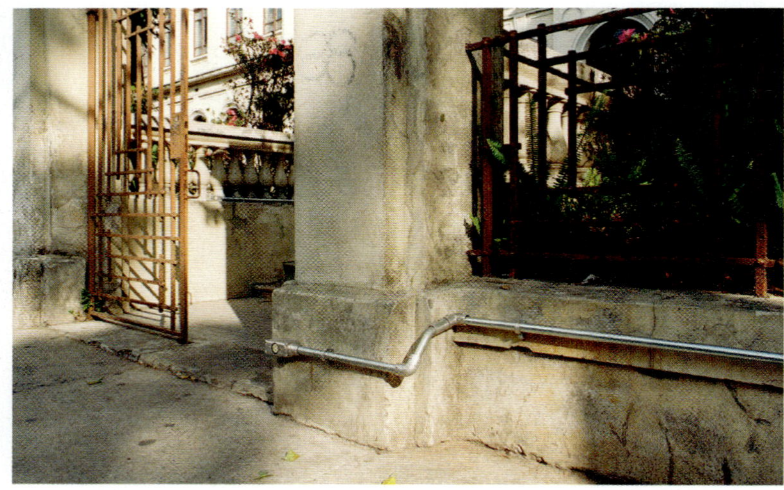

Calçada, 1999. Iron conduits, power sockets, electric power. Dimensions variable. Oswald de Andrade Cultural Centre, São Paulo

Silent language

Made specifically for the 2002 São Paulo Biennial, *Vazadores* (Leakers) perfectly sums up the questioning of public and institutional space that since the mid-1990s has preoccupied Brazilian artist Rubens Mano. Using a characteristically clean, precise and silent language, the work comprised a corridor connecting the interior of the pavilion to its exterior, identical to the design of the facade of Oscar Niemeyer's emblematic Biennial building. Camouflaged as such, the piece was not identifiable as an authored piece, but instead looked like an anomaly in Niemeyer's original design. The corridor acted as a passage, allowing free entry to the interior of the pavilion for those who discovered it. In this way, Mano's subtle intervention in the building — a barely perceptible architectural modification — provoked a leakage beyond the normal security limitations

of the event. This opened up a series of political and institutional debates about the relationship between art and the public sphere, all of which lie at the heart of Mano's practice.

Ever since his urban intervention *Detector of Absences* (1994), Mano, who trained in architecture and photography, has developed his works in the field of site-specificity, making spatial alterations in order to subvert the operative conditions of the art system. With *Calçada* (Sidewalk, 1999), he made another simple, almost invisible alteration to a pre-existing structure in order to open up, discreetly and literally, a resource usually not available to the public. Invited by the Oswald de Andrade Cultural Centre to make a work on its premises, Mano extended the electrics of the centre to the street by placing sockets on the external wall of the office. This free electricity was available and used by street vendors and any passers-by who decided to make use of it.

Mano combines his interest in creating critical infiltrations of this kind with making other more phenomenological and metaphorical works, as in his *Contemplaçao Suspensa* (Suspended Contemplation, 2008), a hanging structure that he placed at the highest point of the central atrium of the São Paulo Pinacoteca, or the hermetic and solemn images included in his exhibition 'Let's Play' (2008).

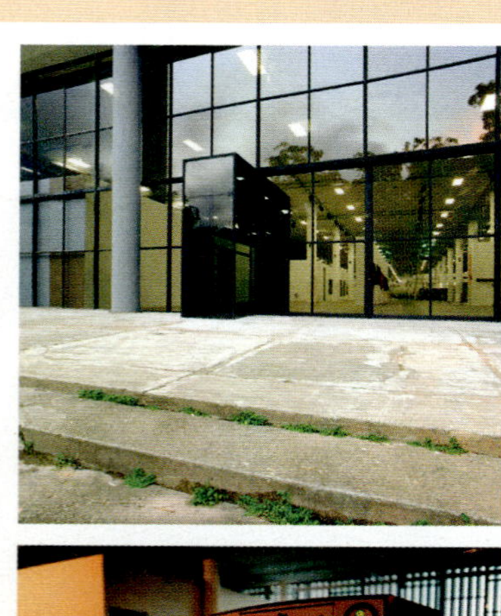

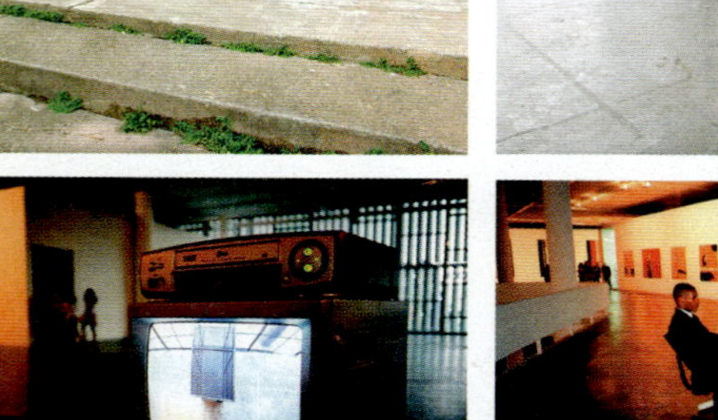

Vazadores, 2002. Glass, iron, security camera, monitor, VHS recorder, table, two chairs and security guard. Dimensions variable. Ciccillo Matarazzo Pavilion, São Paulo Biennial

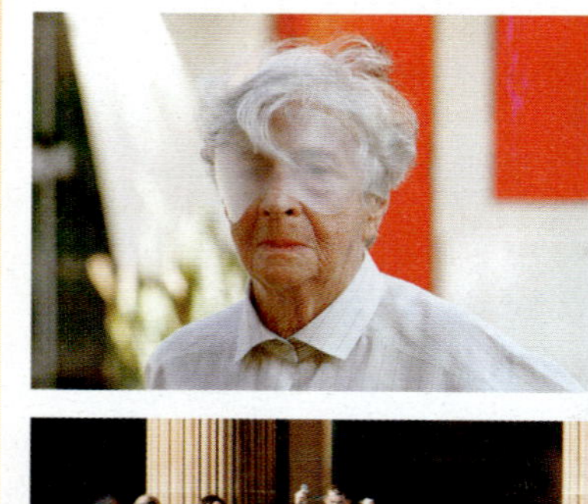

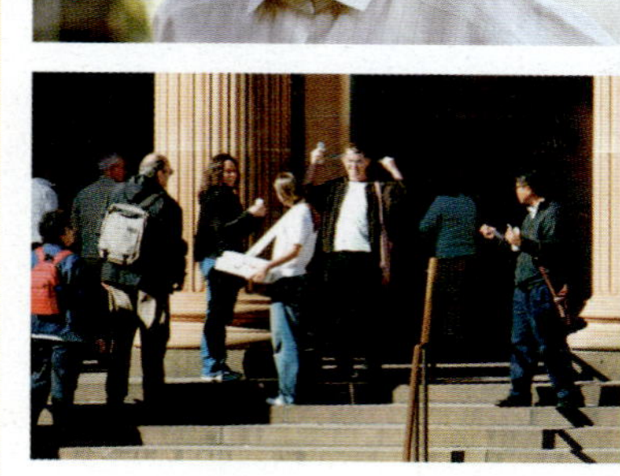

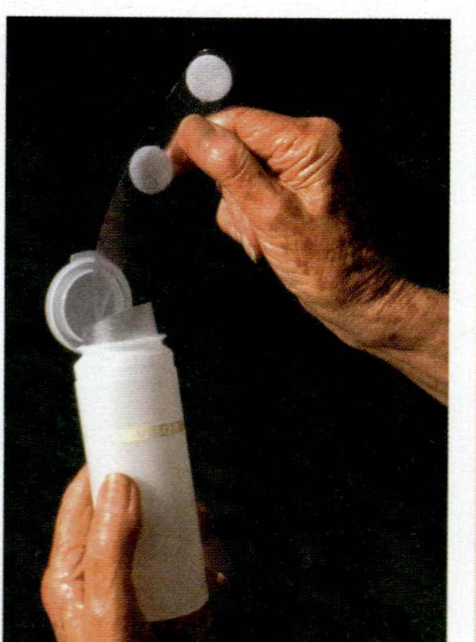

Visor, 2004. PVC masks, polyethylene bottles, wood table, photograph. Dimensions variable

Critical infiltrations

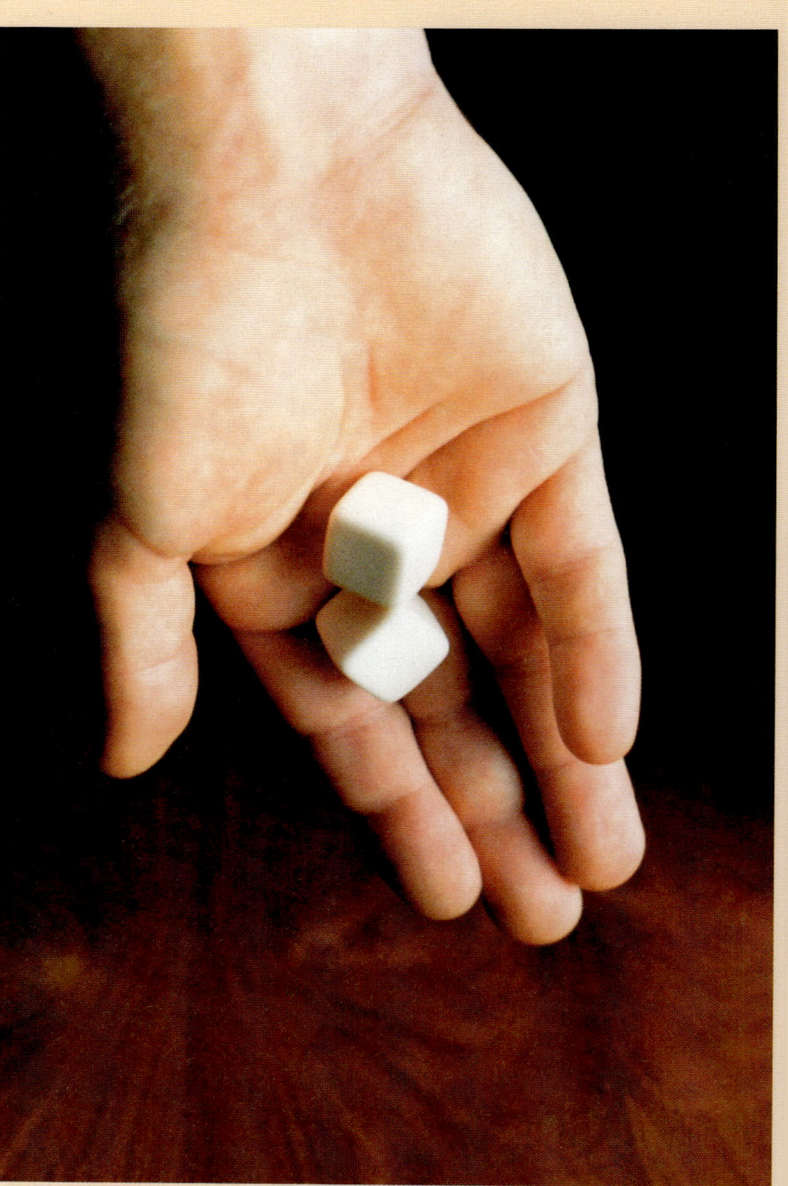

Let's Play, 2008. Photograph. 105 × 71 cm

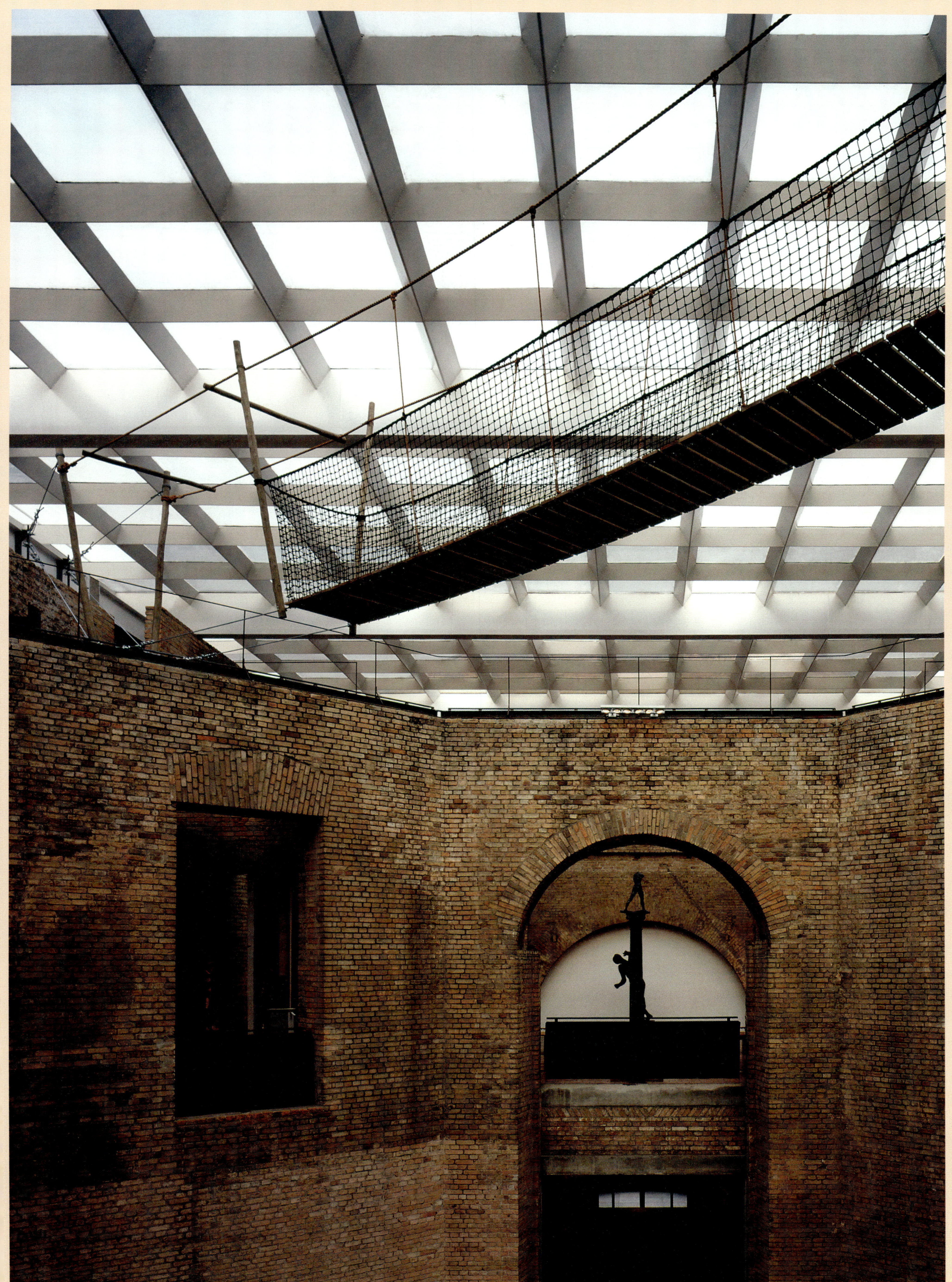

Contemplação Suspensa, 2008. Wood, rope, metal, steel cables, HD televsion. Dimensions variable. Installation, Pinacoteca do Estado, São Paulo

Josephine Meckseper

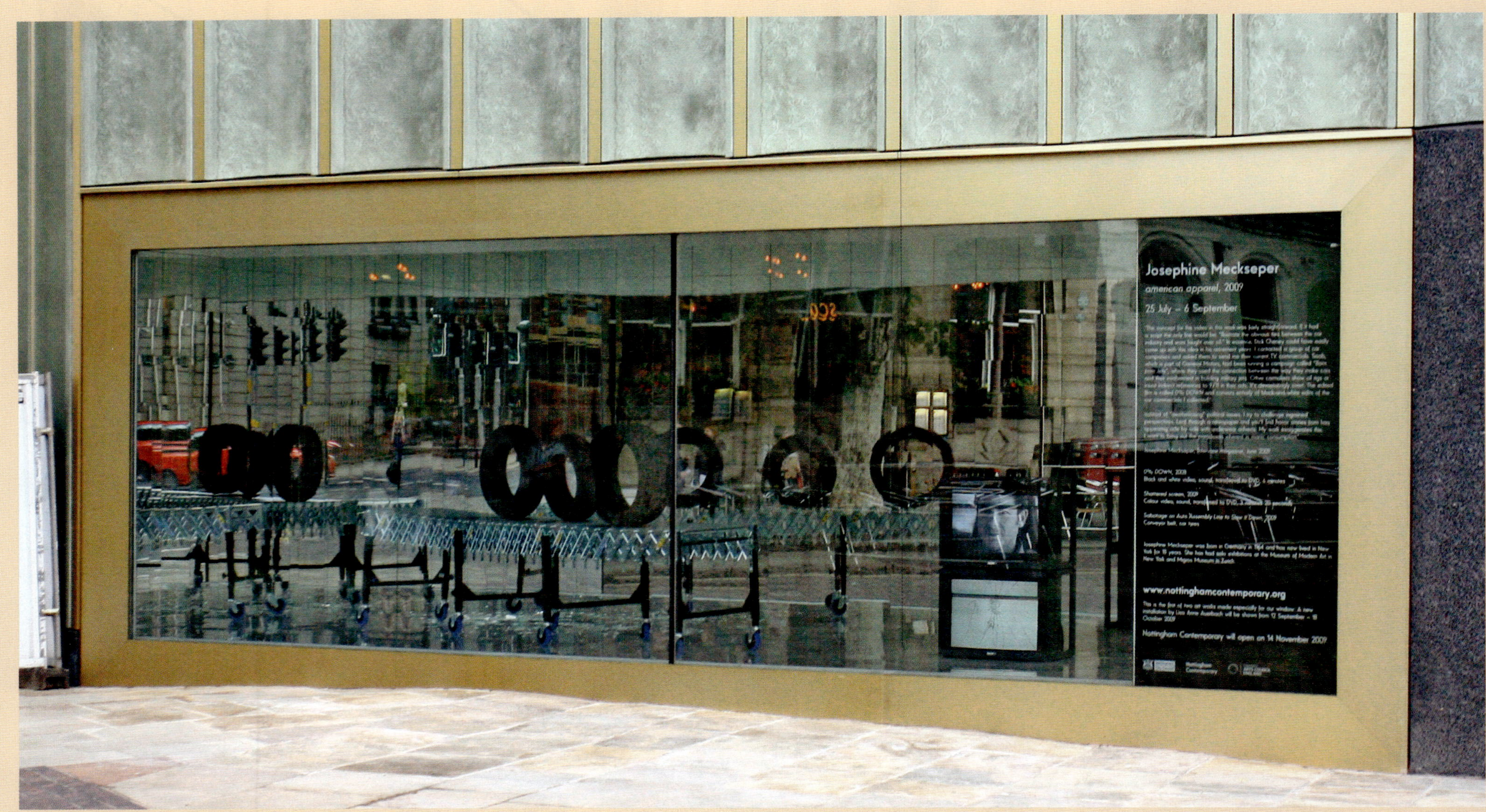

Sabotage on Auto Assembly Line to Slow it Down, 2009. Conveyor belt, car tyres. Dimensions variable. **0% Down**, 2008. Black and white video transferred to DVD with sound. 6 min. 2 sec. **Shattered Screen**, 2009. Black and white video transferred to DVD with sound. 3 min. 22 sec. Installation view, 'american apparel', Nottingham Contemporary, 2009

Constrasting philosophies underlying the text and objects

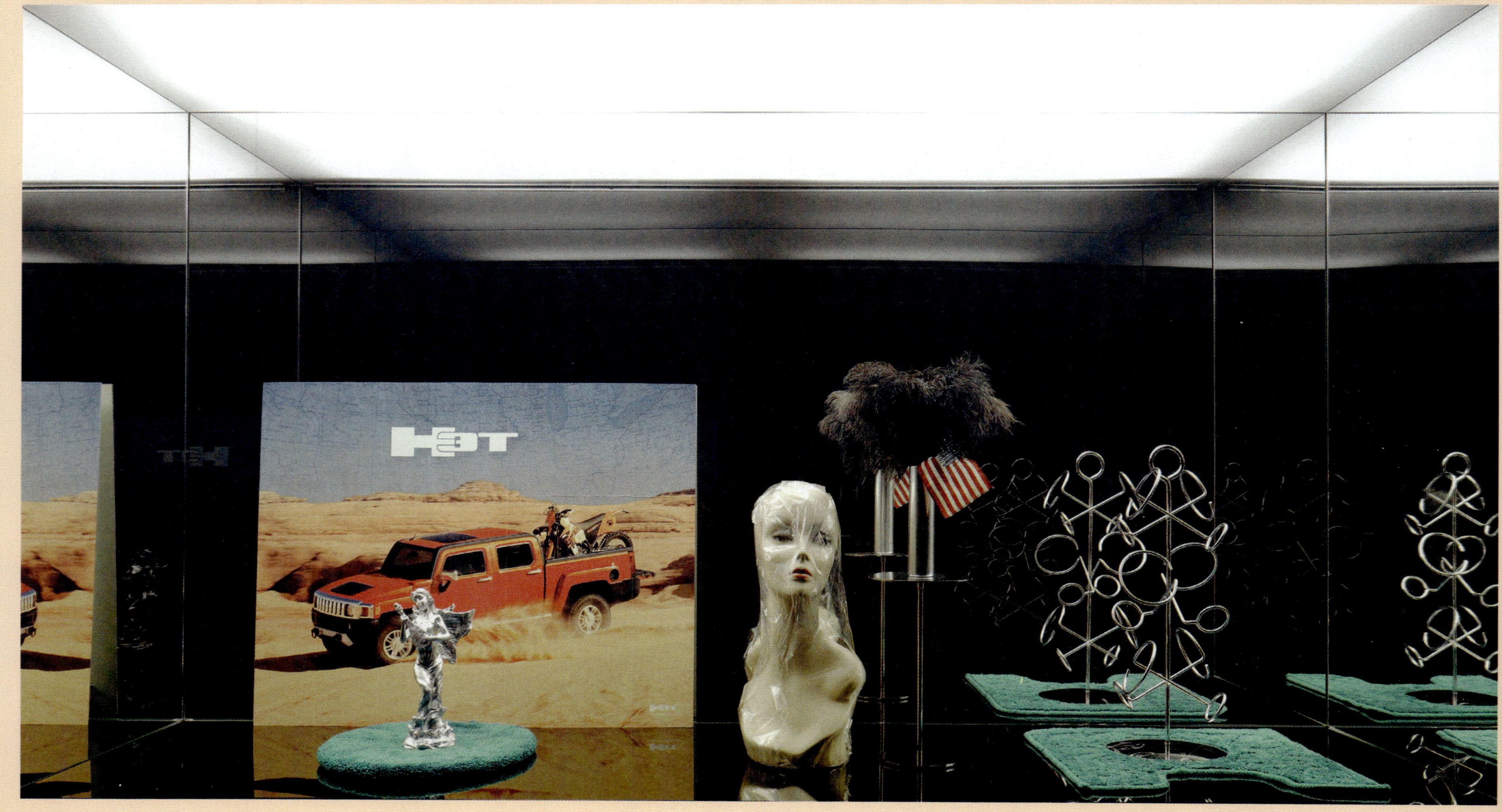

Fall of the Empire, 2008. Mannequin head, metal wine rack, feather duster, metal display stand, small flag, bath mats, mounted poster, small statue, vase. 125 × 232 × 63 cm

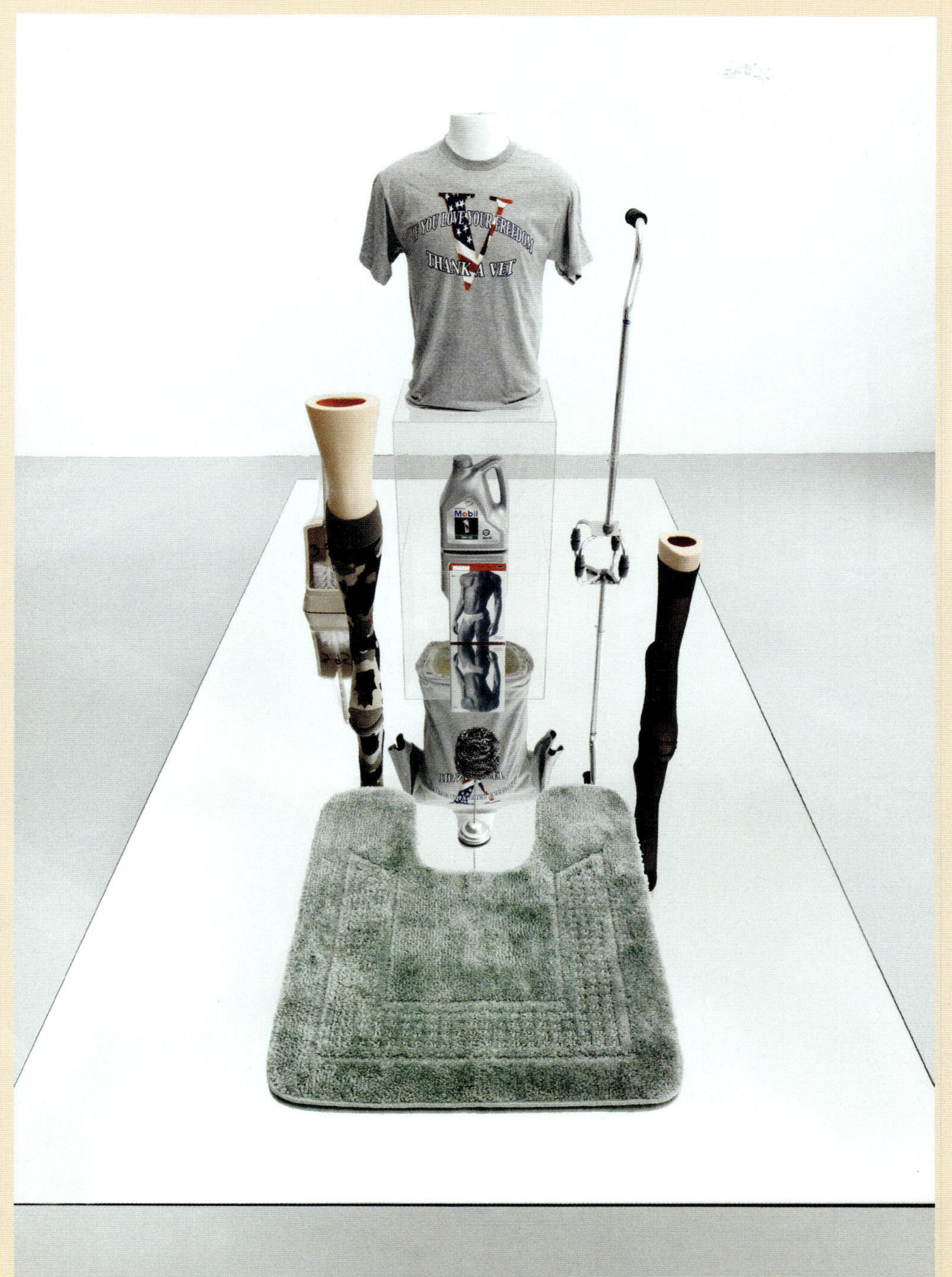

Thank a Vet, 2008. Walker, mannequin legs, socks, toilet mat, metal clip stand, steel wool, box of underwear, toilet brush, mannequin chest, T–shirt, motor oil container, Plexiglas cube. 183 × 240 × 120 cm

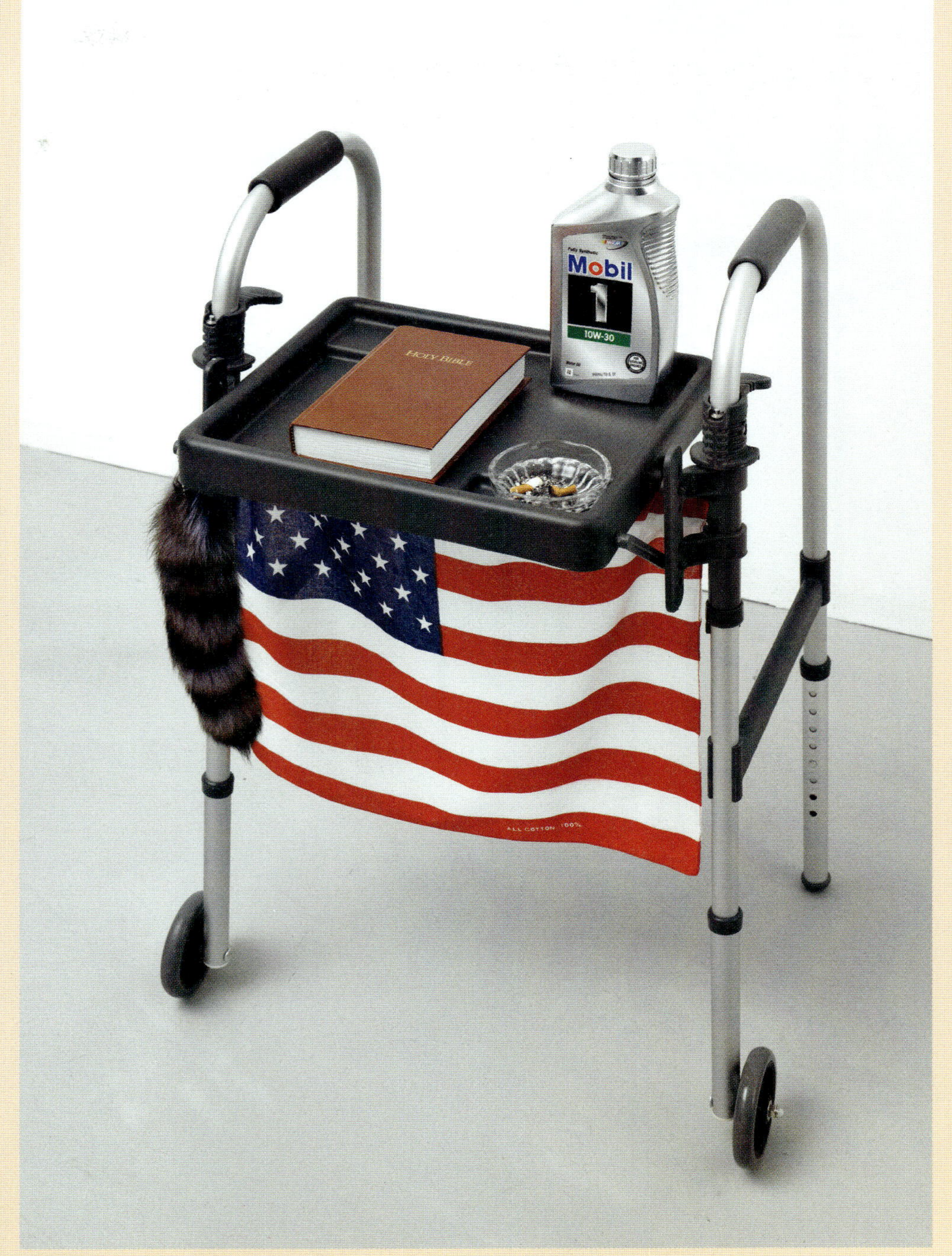

Unable Bodies, 2008. Walker, Bible, flag, fur tail, ashtray, motor oil container. 102 × 61 × 38 cm

Mining the increasingly overlapping domains of politics, war, corporate interest and consumerism, Josephine Meckseper creates installations, sculptures, videos and photographic collages that juxtapose incongruous commercial and household items with references to the aesthetics and issues of 1960s countercultural movements and their contemporary corollaries, such as America's recent war with Iraq and the earlier Gulf War. Her work critiques and challenges the celebratory triumph of Western capitalism reflected in the everyday experience of mass media, focusing on the intersection of the military-industrial complex and the persuasive corporate advertising that drives consumer culture.

Meckseper's installations often take the form of sleek commercial window and shelf displays, levelling objects and ideas so that sink plungers are on par with perfume bottles and fashion ads with revolutionary manifestos and Marxist texts. Glossy black Plexiglas shelves and mirrored surfaces hold neatly arranged items that might include mannequin body parts, sparkling crystal fragments, snippets of lace and toilet brushes — all set alongside books, quotations and pages from Marx, E. M. Cioran, The Angry Brigade and other authors whose

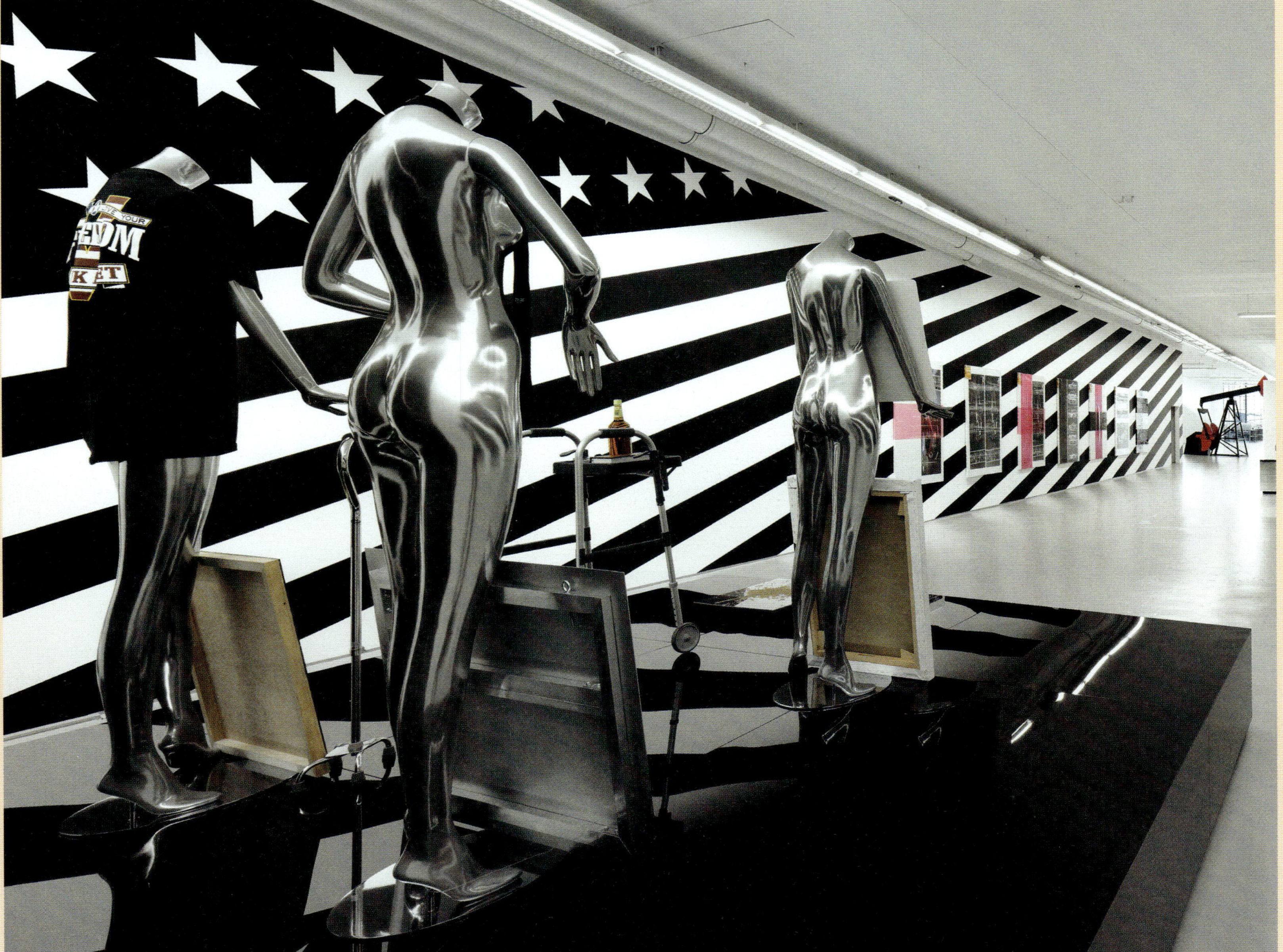

Exhibition view, 'Josephine Meckseper', Migros Museum für Gegenwartskunst, Zurich, 2009

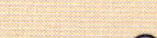

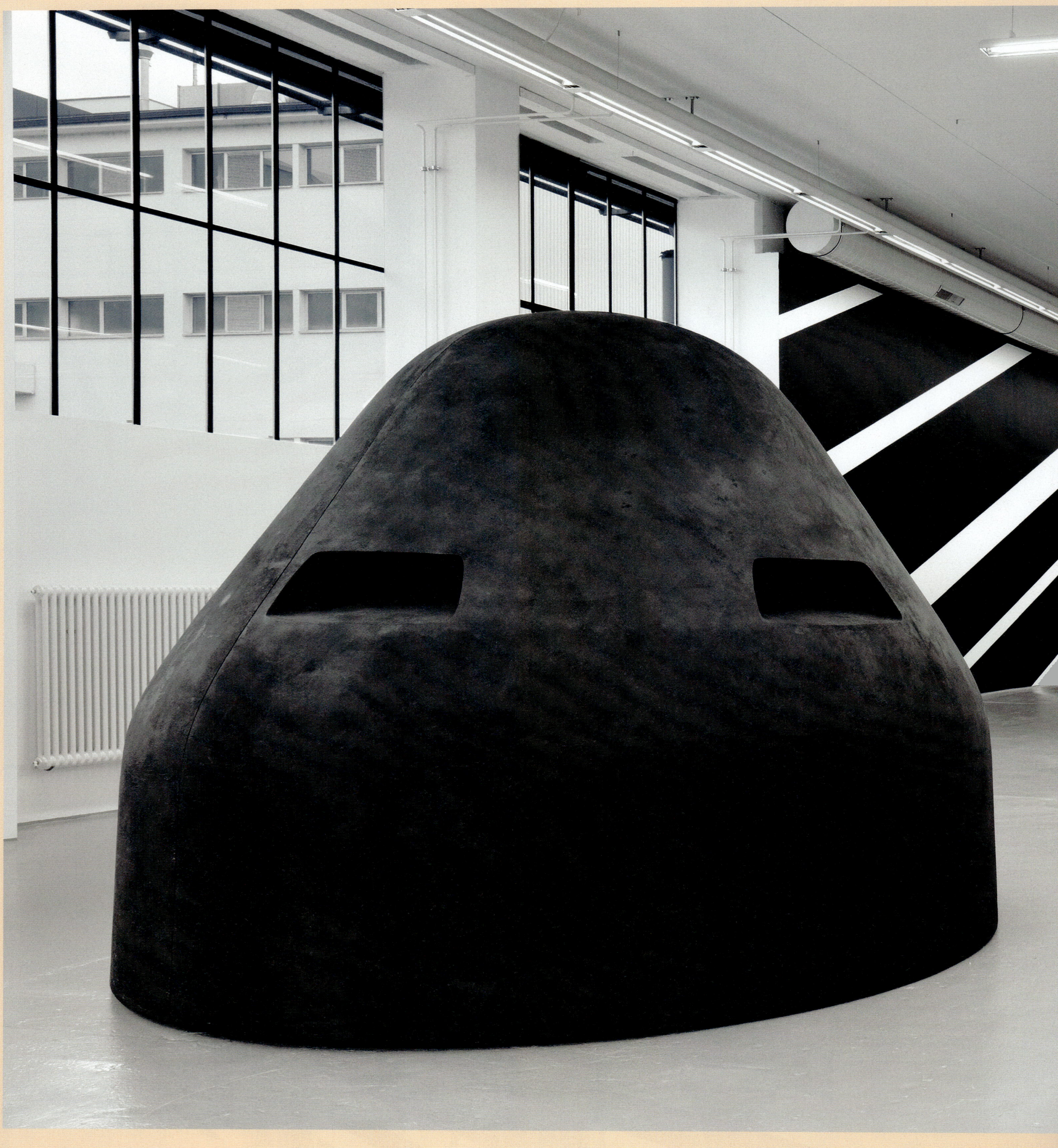

Untitled (Bunker), 2009. Chipboard, polystyrene foam, glue, foam spray, acrylic plaster, fibreglass, sand, acrylic paint, metallic spray. 220 × 289 × 289 cm. **Untitled (Black and White Wall)**, 2007. Black paint on white wall. Dimensions variable. **Untitled (Oil Rig No. 1)**, 2009. Paint, iron, wood. Approx. 400 × 133 × 497 cm. **Fall of the Empire**, 2008. Mannequin head, metal wine rack, feather duster, metal display stand, small flag, bath mats, mounted poster, small statue, vase. 126 × 232 × 64 cm. **Untitled (Oil Rig No. 2)**, 2009. Paint, iron, wood. Approx. 363 × 133 × 497 cm

works contain utopian or dystopian commentaries on society's prospects. Together, the contrasting philosophies underlying the texts and objects work in concert to evoke a sense of uncertainty, undermining the reassurance of the 'promise' of the consumer items and intimating the possibility of their future undoing.

Fall of the Empire (2008) continues Meckseper's investigation into connections between American consumption, nationalism and war. The large-scale installation is a cross between a museum presentation and a boutique window display with assorted objects carefully presented, as the artist humorously equates the material desire for expensive follies with commonplace household needs. The work brings an advertisement for a gigantic gas-guzzling luxury truck together with a female mannequin bust wrapped in plastic, in an almost violent act of suffocation. A kitschy silver angel figurine playing a lute sits atop a shaggy teal bath mat, while a feather duster sprouts out of a silver display stand, alongside a small American flag in which a barcode stands in for the proper stars, like bizarre accoutrements for some unidentified parade. A send-up of patriotic zeal, it is a darkly absurd proposition implicating our consumption patterns in recent American drives towards war.

Other recent works similarly play with linkages between American commerce, military power and the oil industry. In a recent solo exhibition, a replica of an oil rig (*Untitled (Oil Rig, No. 1)*, 2009) sat next to a mock armored bunker (*Untitled (Bunker)*, 2009) that was juxtaposed against an immense black and white backdrop of the American flag's

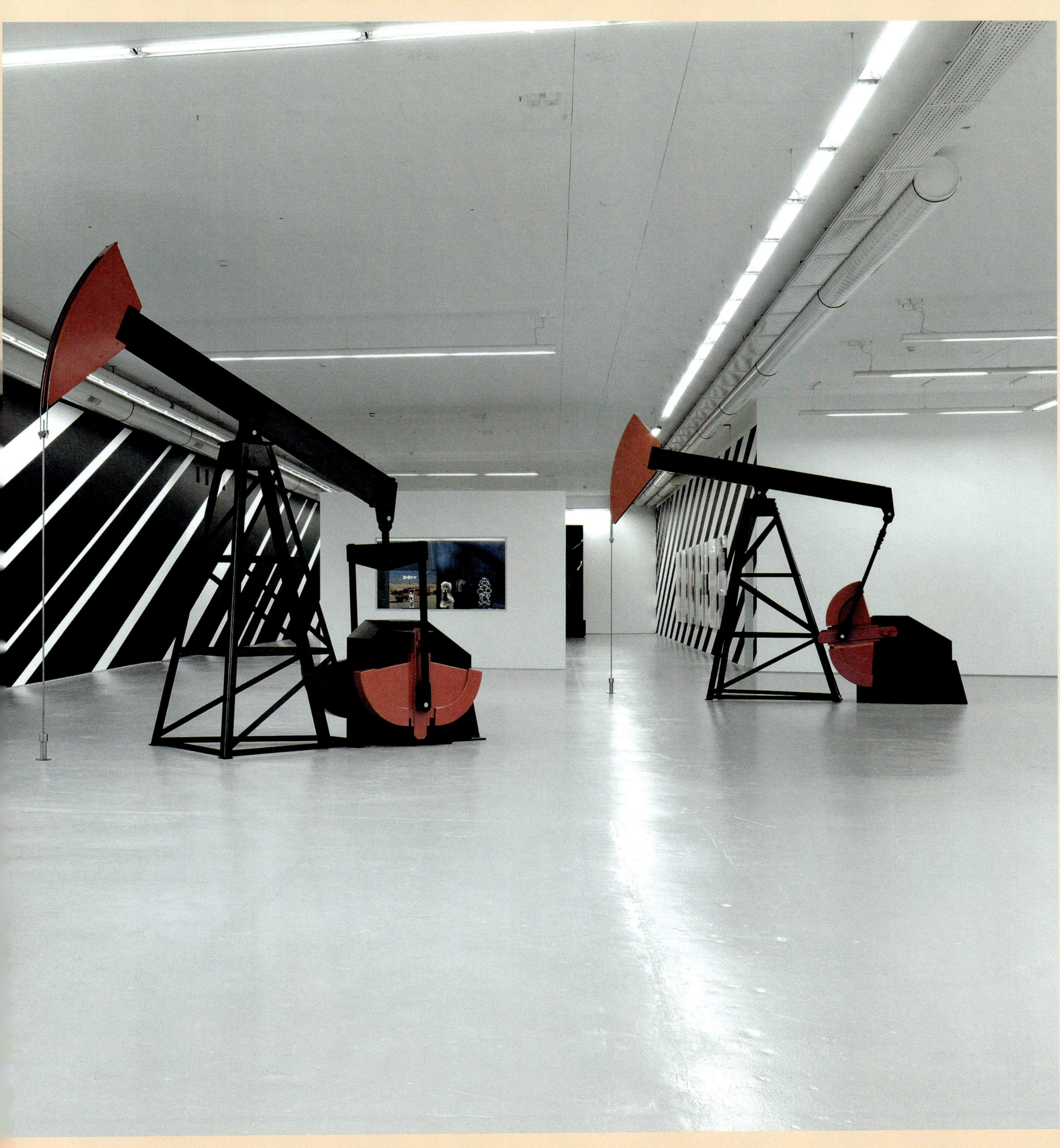

Meckseper's installations often take the form of sleek commercial window and shelf displays, levelling objects and ideas so that toilet plungers are on par with perfume bottles and fashion ads with revolutionary manifestos and Marxist texts.

stars and stripes (*Untitled (Black and White Wall)*, 2007), bathroom rugs, shrink-wrapped posters of shiny new Mustang muscle cars and chrome car hubcap rims — all of which were situated in a gallery space dolled up to resemble a brightly lit, glossy, high-end showroom. Meckseper takes these ideas to a more personal level with her assemblage sculpture *Unable Bodies* (2008). In this work, a medical walker is festooned with a raccoon's tail and American flag, while on top of the walker's tray sits a bible, an ashtray with cigarette butts, and a bottle of 10W-30 oil. A grim commentary on the physical human toll of war, the work questions America's motives for waging war and alludes to how religious motivations or corporate interests influence policy decisions. At the same time, it points to the questionable treatment of veterans returning home.

Meckseper's lexicon of objects forms a vocabulary that draws attention to how extravagant consumption has acquired its own kind of reigning global hegemony. Mining the dark underbelly of consumerist materialism to reveal complex underlying connections, she ultimately comments on how everything is exchangeable, not least art itself, which — like so many other luxury commodities — carries a lofty price tag.

Miguel Mitlag

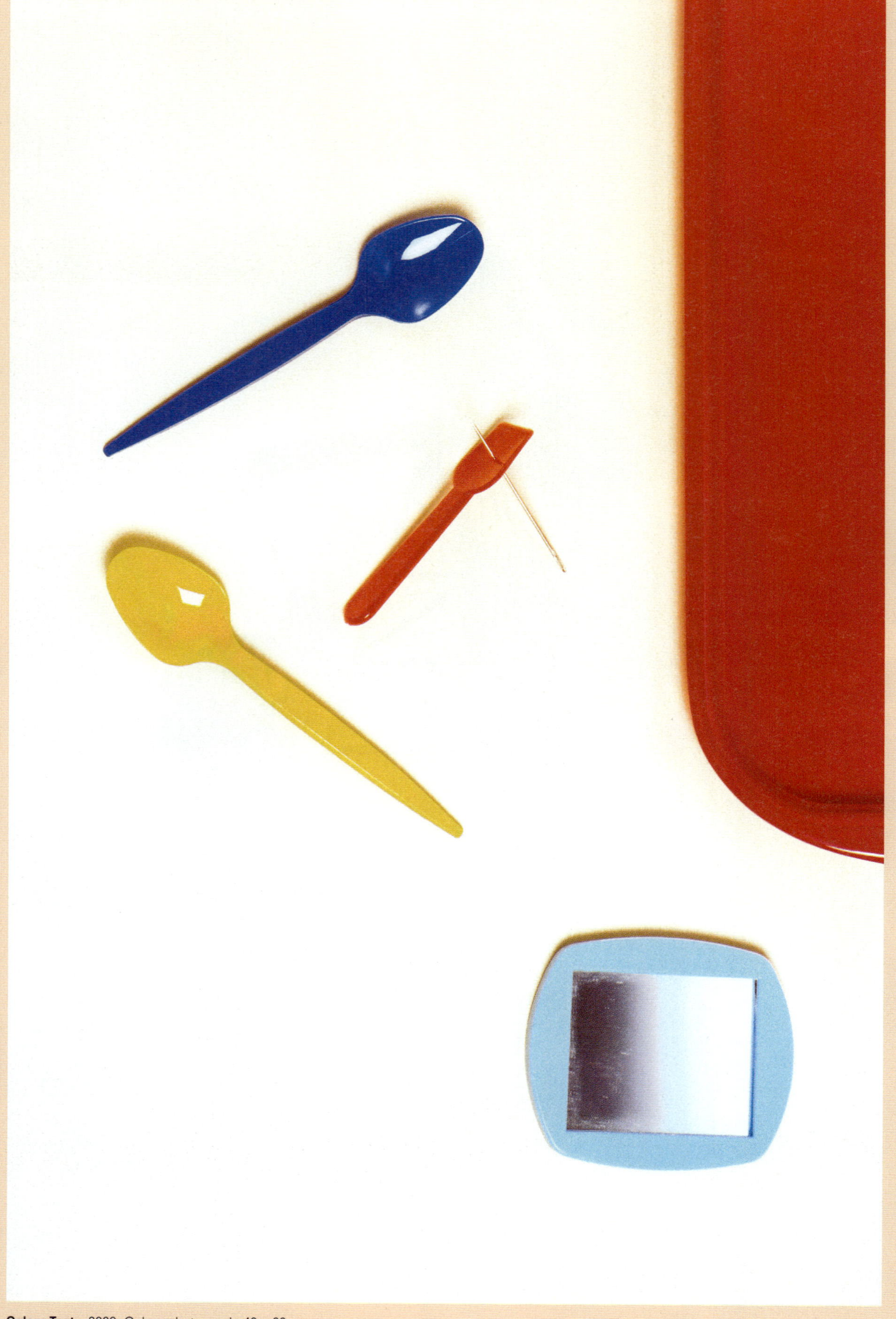

Colour Tests, 2009. Colour photograph. 40 × 60 cm

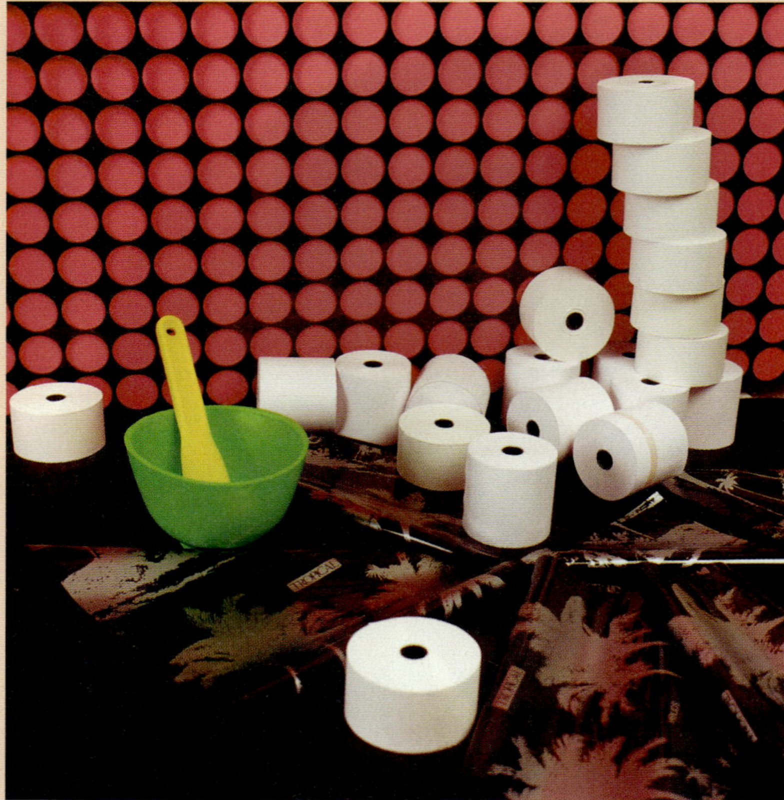

Tropical Afternoon Experiment, 2009. Colour photograph. 90 × 90 cm

Formal concentration

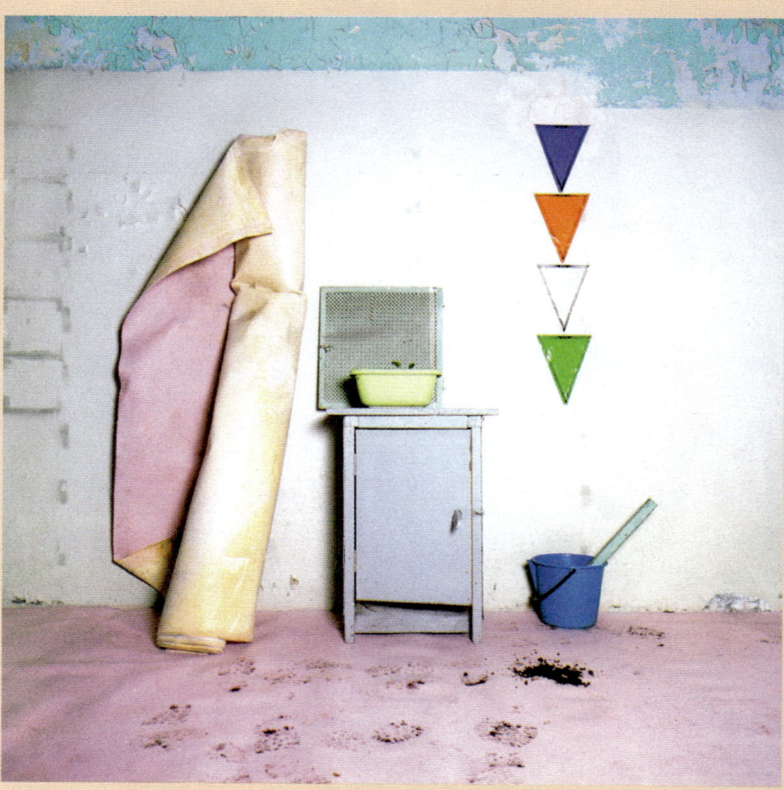

Experimental Vehicle, 2004. Colour photograph. 60 × 60 cm

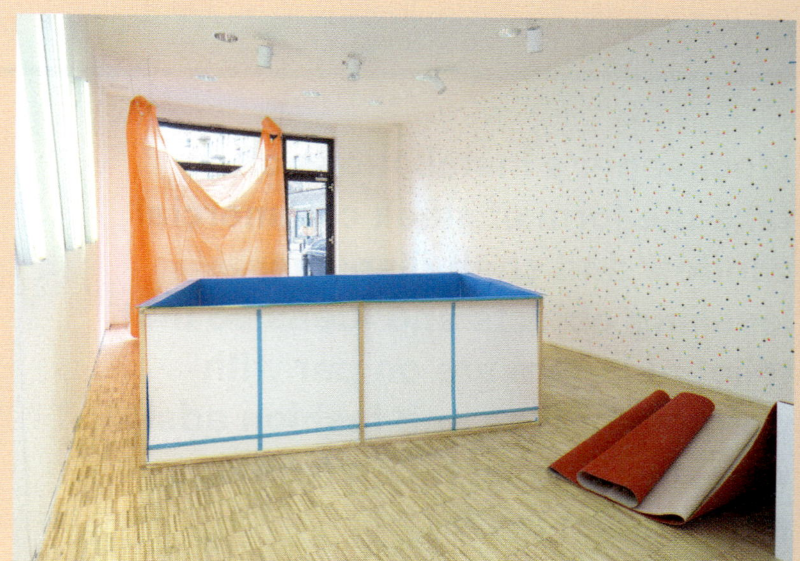

Holiay, 2008. Mixed–media installation. 780 × 470 × 360 cm

Scenarios for leisure
activities or for secret vices,
places where one imagines
subjects enjoying solitary rituals

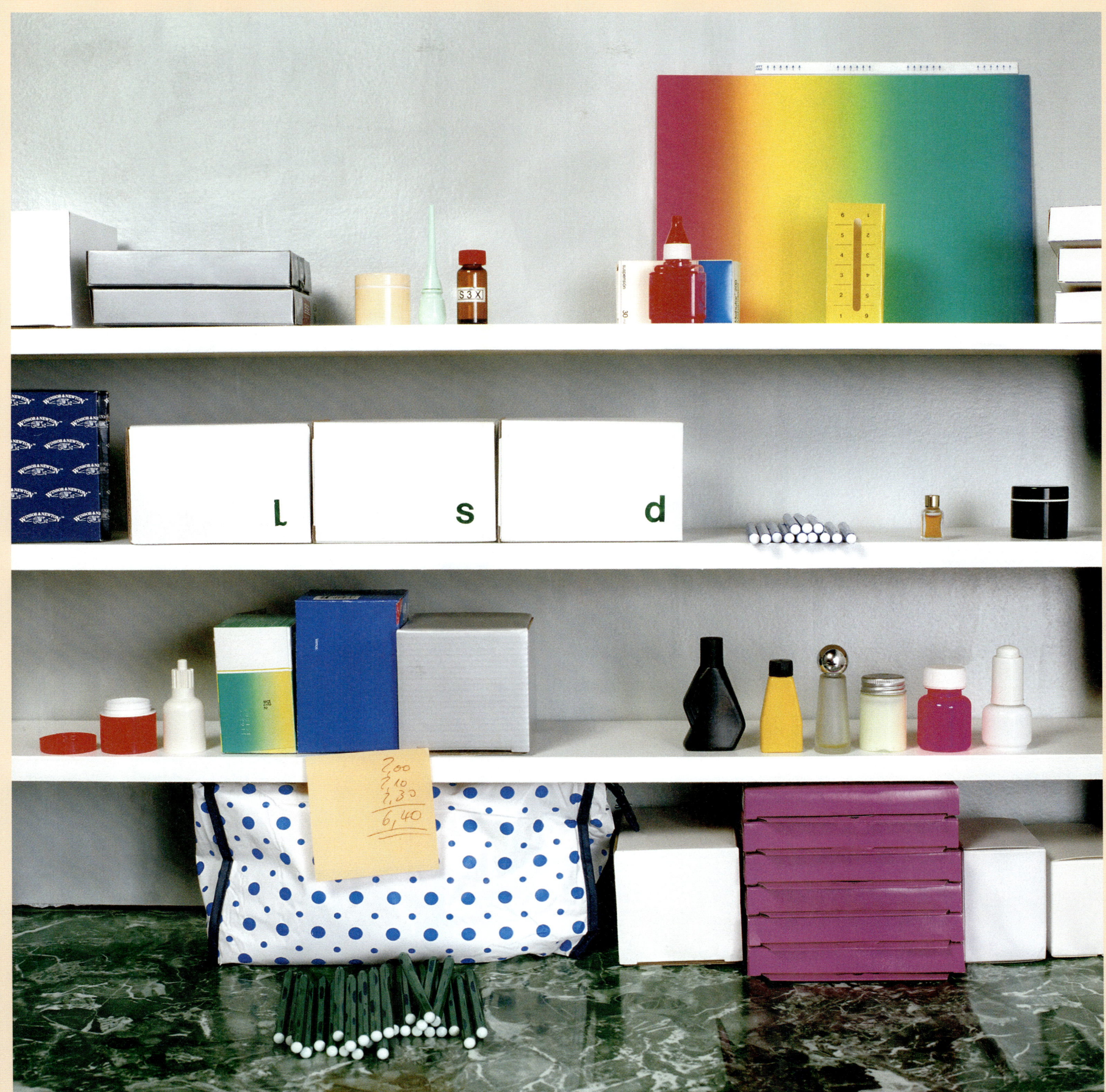

Minilab, 2009. Colour photograph. 100 × 100 cm

Photographer and sculptor Miguel Mitlag is an artist who imbues his constructions with high levels of formal concentration and conceptual hermeticism. Concise in his choice of materials, motifs and colours, Mitlag frankly declares that 'things don't move me much'. Thus he aims not for the spectacle or the unfolding of metaphor, but to provoke experiences of subtle perceptual transformation.

Mitlag is a committed formalist, totally distanced from the idea of the decorative unless it is to imbue a scene with a specific atmosphere and artificiality.

His photographic compositions and spatial constructions project a cryptic philosophy about the world around us — the tools, designs and spaces that we see in the everyday environment. These works leap towards a visual hypothesis that, from a deliberately toned-down, barely-there perspective, forces us to challenge the domestication of our gaze.

Thus, for example, his photographs present scenarios for leisure activities or for secret vices. These works present tableaus of places where one imagines subjects enjoying solitary rituals, assisted by objects, chairs, pillows, rugs and carefully selected coloured objects that distil an atmosphere of hedonism and perversion.

Mitlag's sculptures and installations are also highly detailed and extremely controlled in their facture; in *Plataforma Striper* (2006), the artist constructed a stripper's platform made out of Formica as a plastic monument to eroticism. In another sculptural work a money exchange booth functioned as an invitation to trespass an uncertain threshold (*Codex Platino*, 2007), or the prototype for an Adidas shoebox made on a 10:1 scale as a provocation to question the viewers own sense of perception. There is no room for chance here, but it is not possible to speak of realism or simulation. Instead Mitlag refers to his works as 'pseudo realist'. He is searching for verisimilitude while at the same time making the construction of the set obvious, so that his works may be viewed as maquettes or prototypes of reality.

Mitlag has also occasionally delved into film. Among other projects, his extraordinary documentary *Una Historia del Trash Rococó* (A Story of Trash Rococo, 2009) courses through the life of the Argentine cult artist Sergio De Loof while revealing Mitlag's sophisticated outlook on the world.

Mitlag's sculptures and installations are also highly detailed and extremely controlled

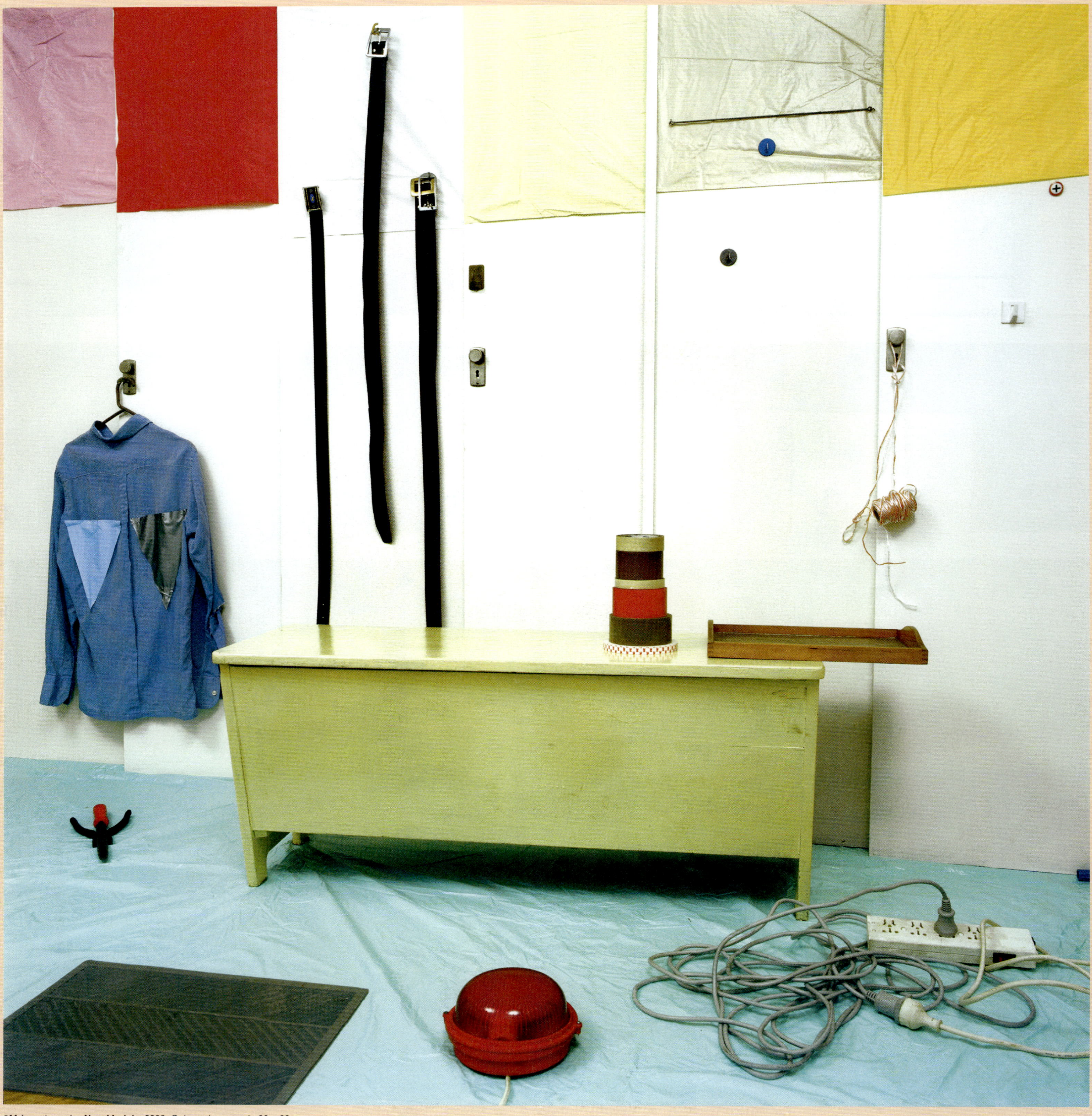

#11 from the series **New Models**, 2006. Colour photograph. 90 × 90 cm

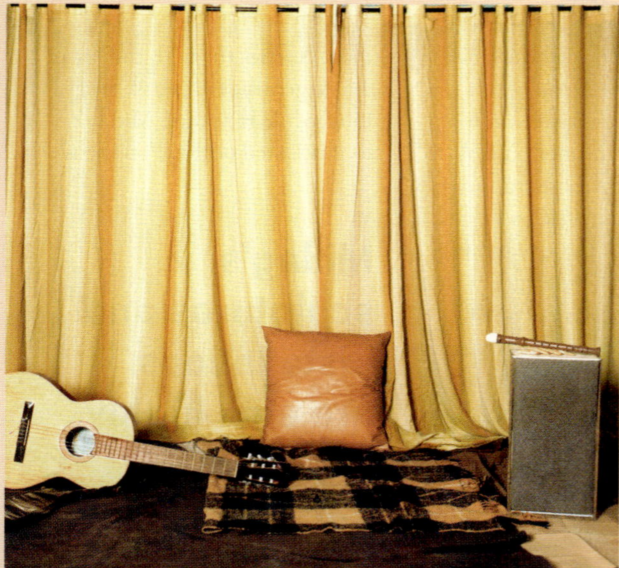

Brown Monument, 2004. Colour photograph. 68 × 60 cm

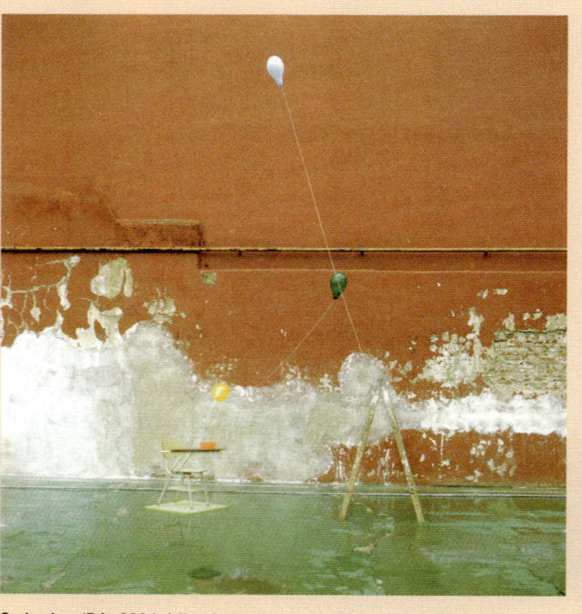

Swinging 'BA, 2004. Mixed–media installation. 400 × 600 × 400 cm

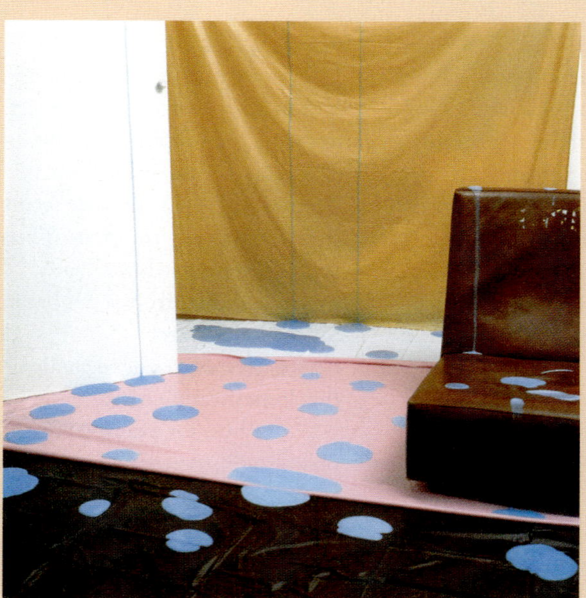

#08 from the series **New Models**, 2006. Colour photograph. 110 × 110 cm

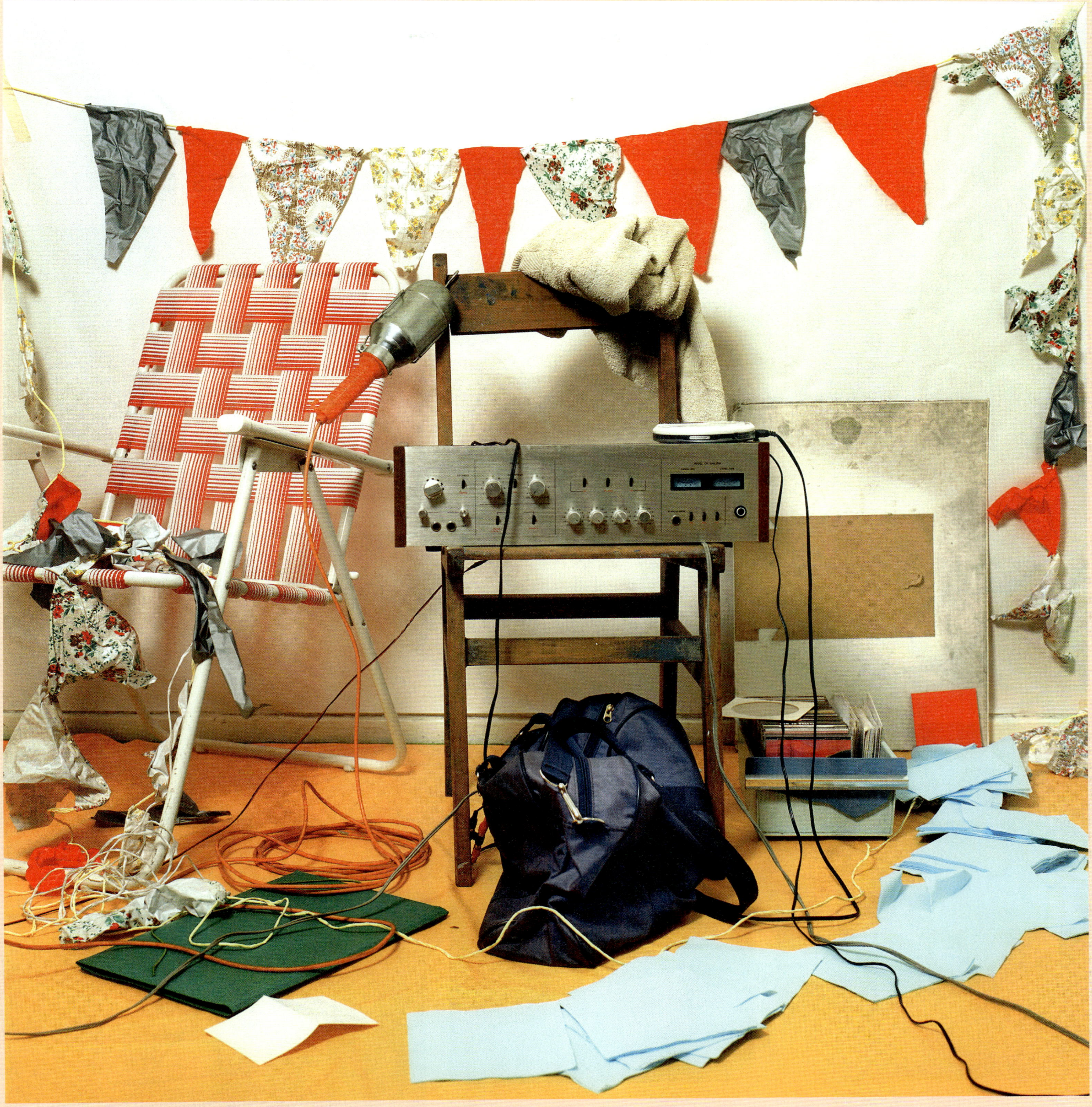

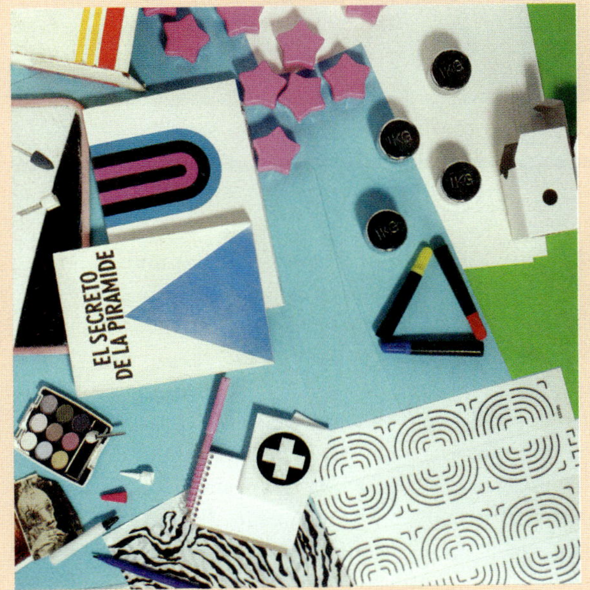

#04 — Litio, 2005. Colour photograph. 110 × 110 cm

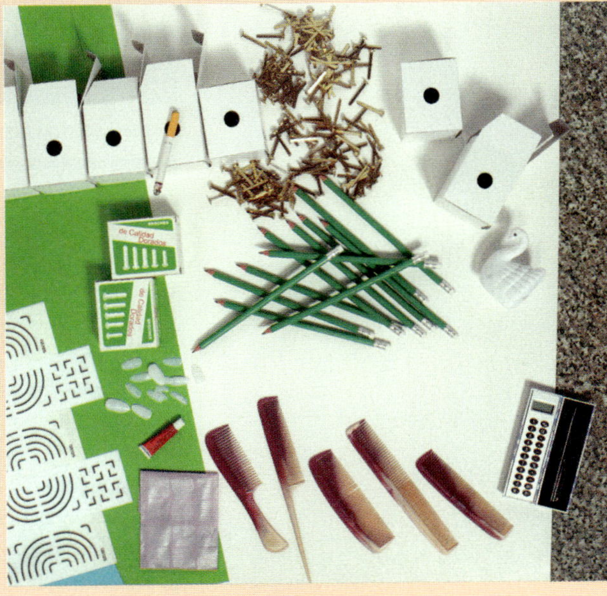
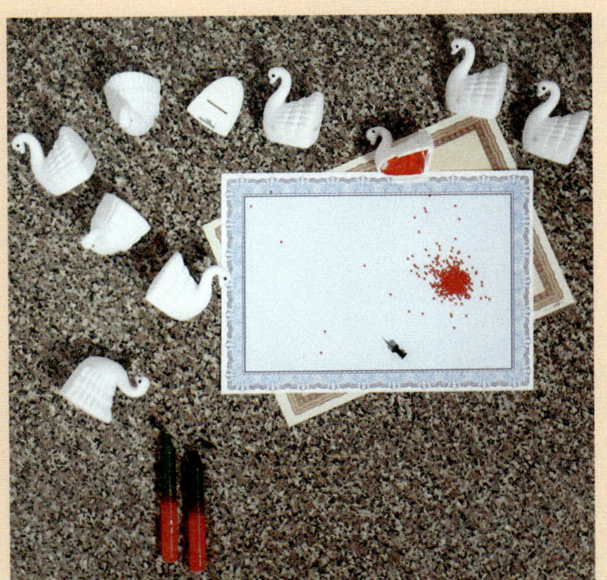

Office jobs, 2009. 3 Colour photographs. Overall 260 × 80 cm

Anna Molska

In the 1990s, Poland's leap into the market economy was accompanied by a rise of conservative ideas on morality, family, religion and politics. Artists clashed with reactionary attitudes in society and came under fire from right-wing politicians. This state of affairs was aptly defined by the artist Zbigniew Libera as a 'cold war between artists and society'. The artists won the battle for a new generation, who now face a different set of problems. Anna Molska belongs to this younger generation, and her films address the complex post-political environment of today's Poland: the shift in the working world from production to services and from the hard power of politicians to the soft talk of 'experts'.

The titles of the two films in Molska's double video projection *W = F*S (Work)* and *P=W:T (Power)* (2007–08) constitute a pair of basic physics equations — work equals force times displacement,

Basic physics equations

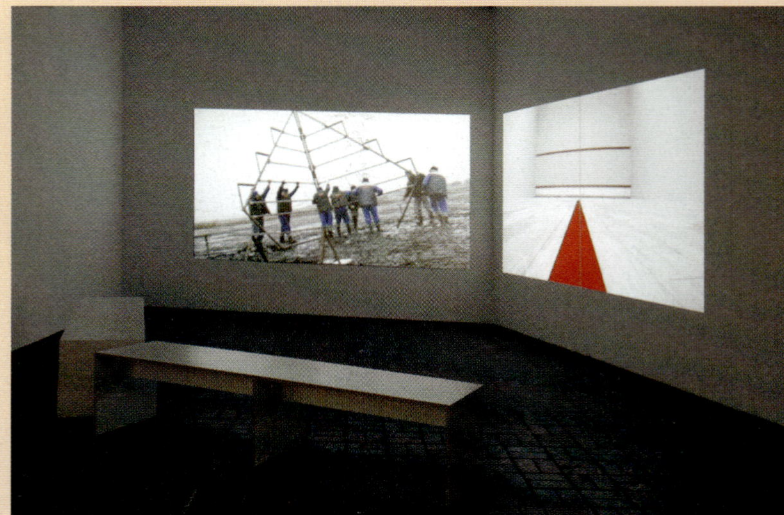

W=F*S (Work) and **P=W:T (Power)**, 2007–08. 2–channel video installation

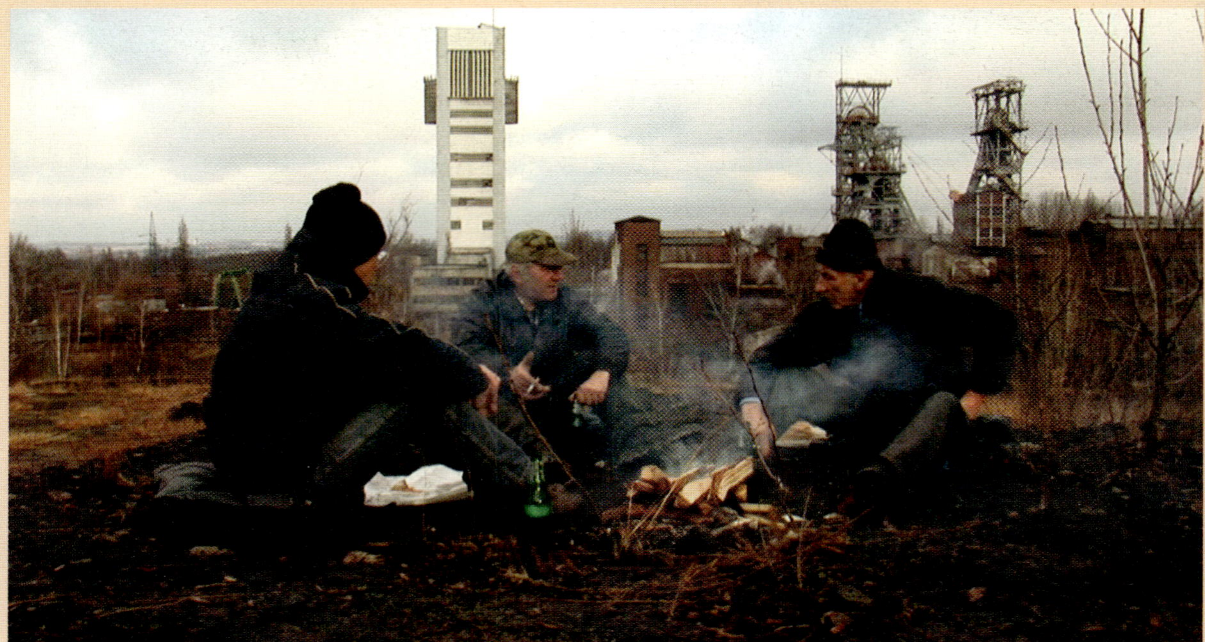

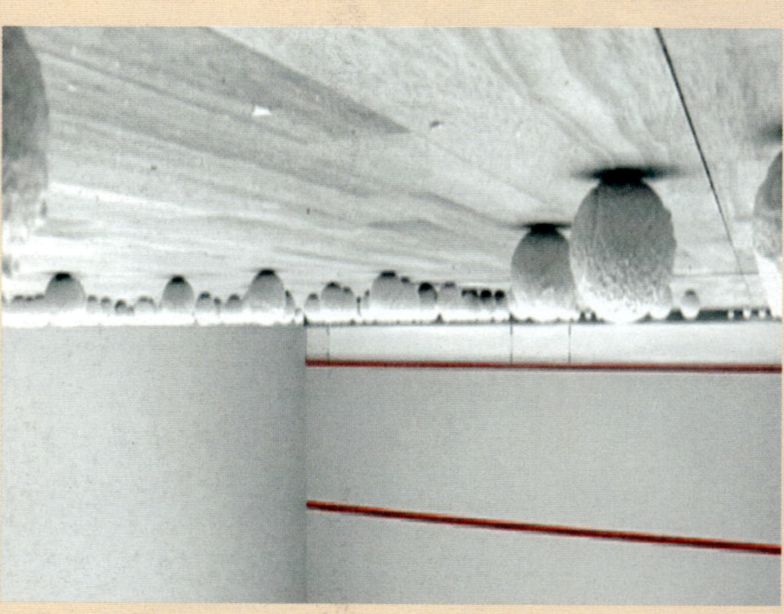

W=F*S (Work), 2008. Video. 9 min.

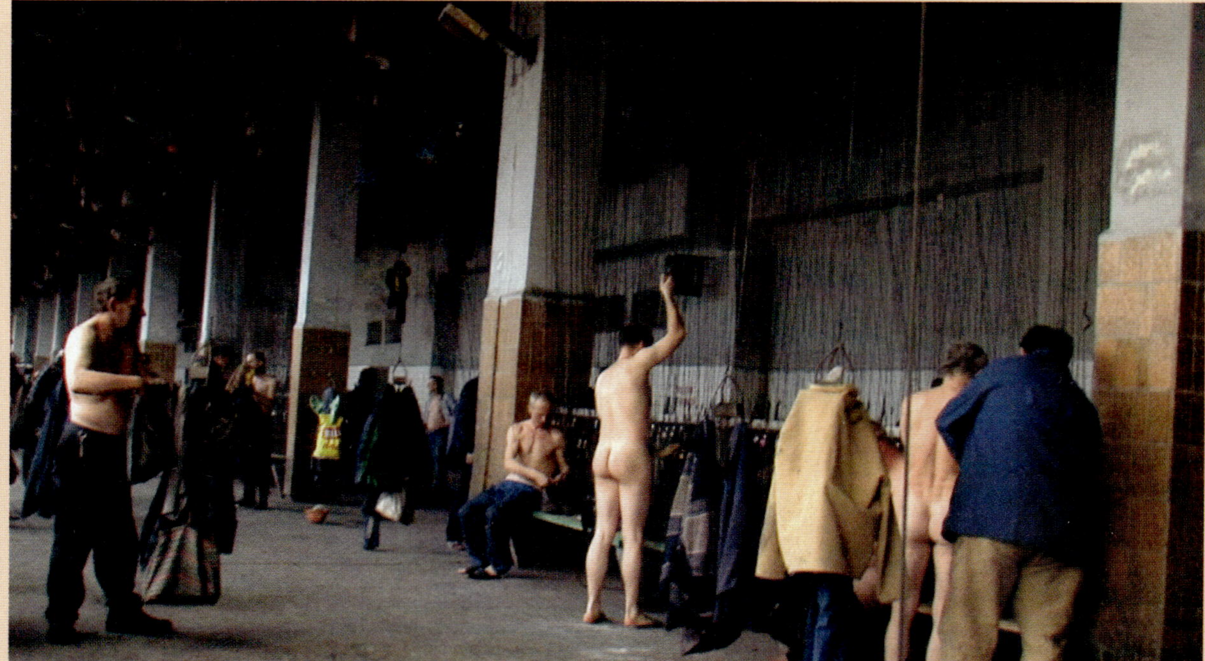

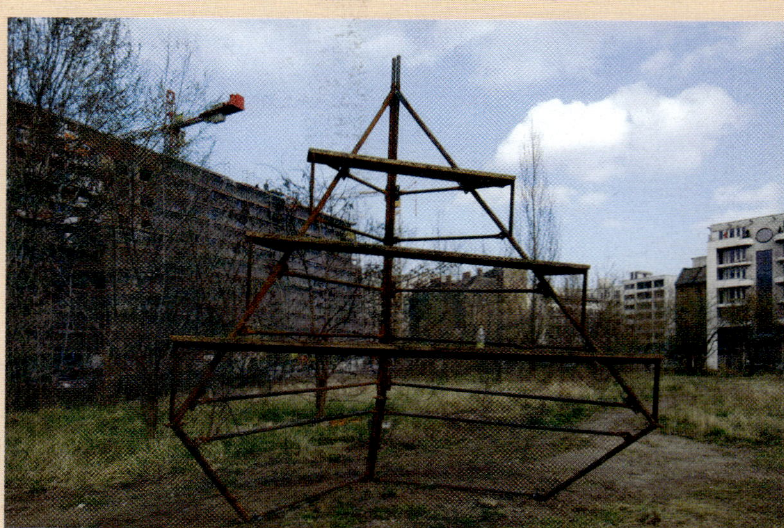

Untitled, 2008. Metal, wood. 600 × 500 × 340 cm. Skulpturenpark, Berlin Biennial

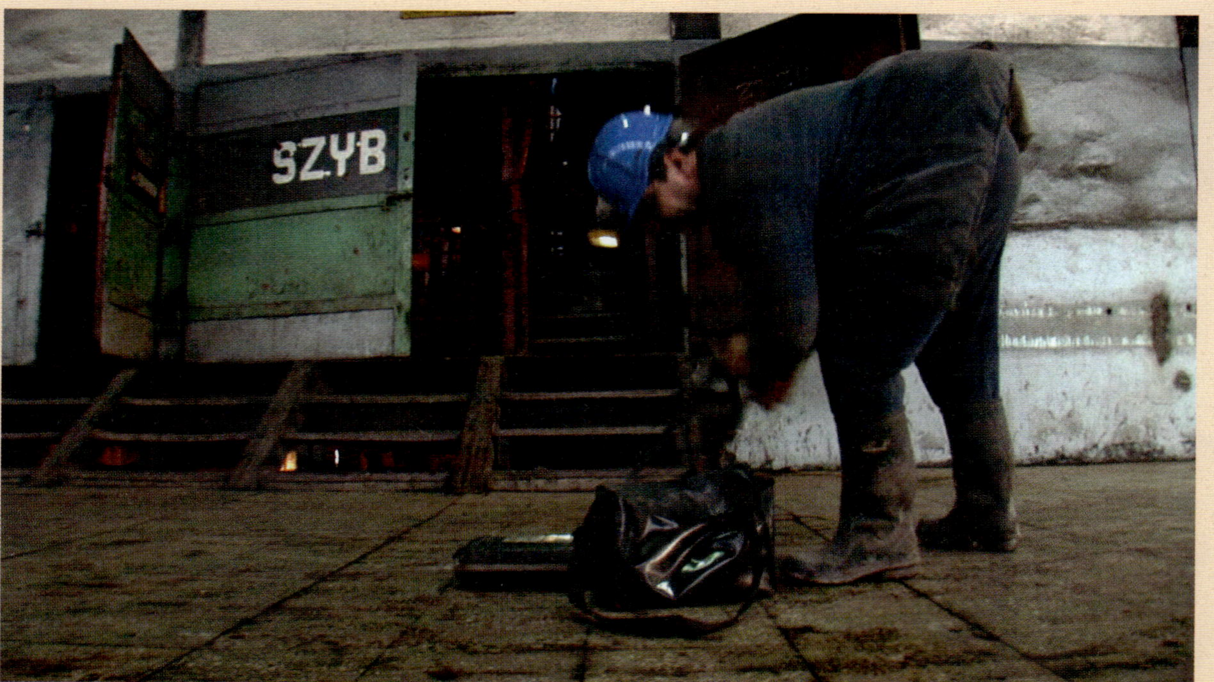

The Weavers, 2009. Video. 12 min.

power equals work divided by time — that, in relation to the images, assume a political significance. *W = F*S (Work)* documents the assembly of scaffolding pipes into a triangular construction. The process is carried out on a cold day in a muddy field by a group of men wearing blue work clothes and boots, who arrive at this entropic landscape on a small tractor. Slowly and with few words exchanged, without a leader or any visible rules, the men build the unmonumental piece of architecture and then clumsily climb it to strike poses, as if parodying the Soviet gymnasts immortalized by Aleksandr Rodchenko in the 1930s. The men seem alienated and exposed by the very structure that gives them a temporary feeling of

Complex post-political environment

belonging and employment. Then, as if attempting to turn the human mass into a group of individual subjects, they shout out their familiar diminutive names one by one. *P=W:t (Power)* shows an empty indoor squash court marked with red lines, recalling an abstract composition. A hail of white balls shoots into the image at accelerating speed, accompanied by a loud banging sound. Work equals force times displacement, power equals work divided by time — the neutral terms of physics read as political statements when applied to the useless structure built by the blue-collar workers made redundant by the collapse of collective farms in rural Poland, and to new forms of leisure cultivated as status symbols by social-climbing business managers and employees of the creative industries.

Molska's recent piece *The Weavers* (2009) features a group of coal miners barbecuing food on a slag heap and exchanging phrases adapted from Gerhart Hauptmann's naturalistic play *The Weavers*. Hauptmann's drama about the revolt of Silesian weavers in 1844 lends its language to a powerful depiction of today's decline in the coal mining industry, which has resulted in the destruction of traditional social structures and a redefinition of values. Molska's staging of the scenes may be unassuming, but her position as a female director of actors in the male-only world of labour is anything but neutral.

Tanagram, 2006–07. Video. 5 min. 10 sec.

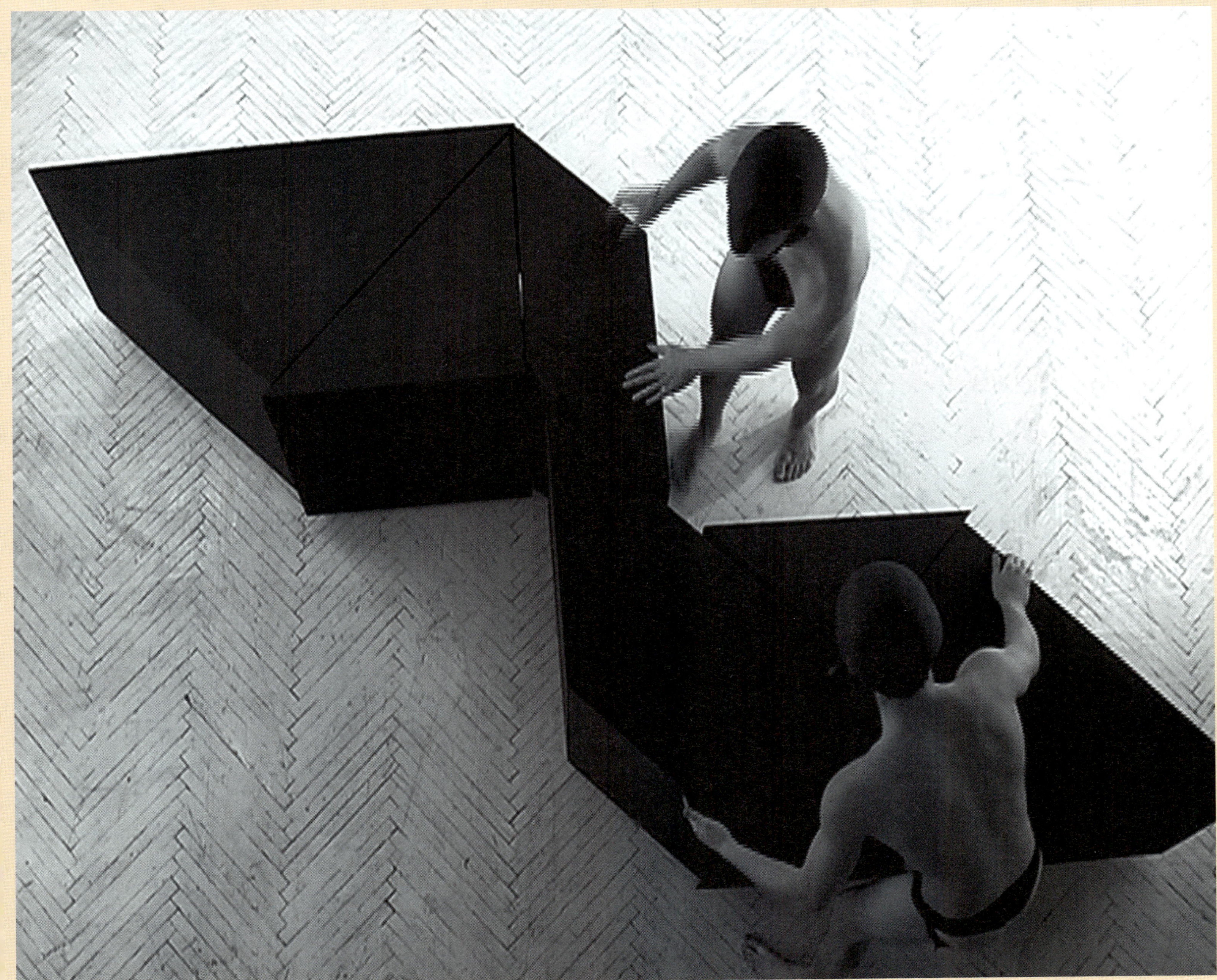

Tanagram, 2006–07. Video. 5 min. 10 sec.

Matthew Monahan

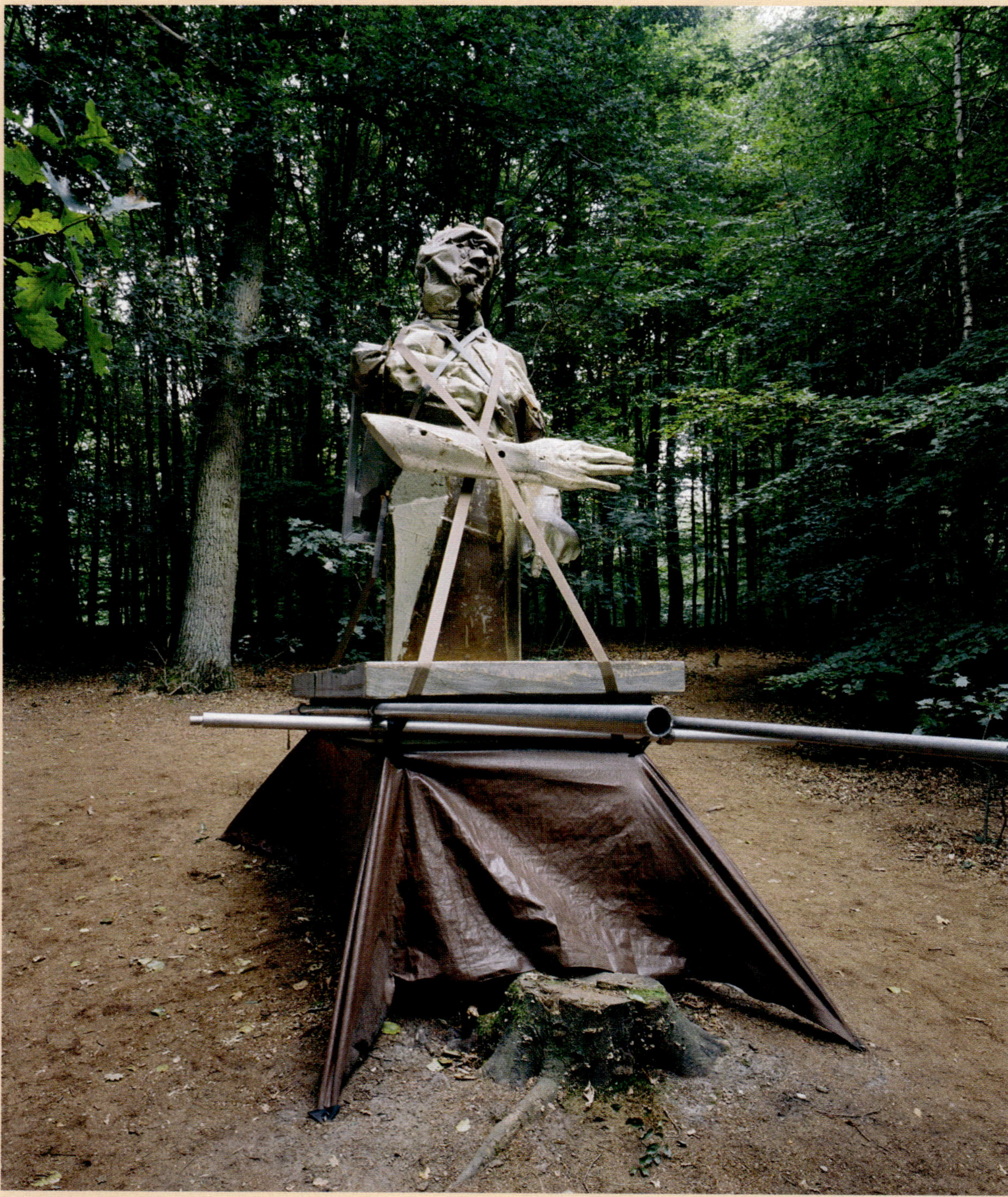

Ornamental Hermit, 2008. Mixed media. 300 × 200 × 300 cm

In his 1951 book *The Voices of Silence* André Malraux speaks of a 'museum without walls' afforded to us by photographic reproductions through which objects and works of art from a multitude of different places and times can be brought together into intimate if virtual proximity. Matthew Monahan's sculptures and drawings present us with a physically concrete version of Malraux's museum as he plunders his imagined history of the human form. Made from malleable materials ranging from beeswax to paper to floral foam, Monahan's sculptures affect a kind of cabinet of curiosities on speed, whose elements are brought together into often disturbing and paradoxically intoxicating promiscuity. The result of his explorations is an almost alchemical invocation of the figure who attempted to breathe life into his these inanimate sculptural forms as if they were secular golems.

But while a concern with the multitude of possible representations of the human form is at the heart of Monahan's work, none of his sculptures attempt any kind of faithful or realistic depiction of the body. Instead, his figures come off as ad-hoc reconstructions of imaginary heroes and deities from unknown worlds and past eras, including fallen crusaders, beatific reliquaries, unknown religious icons and shamanistic totems. One sees echoes of Egyptian mummies, terracotta Han warriors, the Moai monoliths of Easter Island, as well as Babylonian, Roman and Greek antiquities. Each of Monahan's figures appears to have been carefully reassembled by a team of forensic archaeologists working without a blueprint.
Spliced, taped, glued, nailed and even bound together with shipping straps, their raw, fragmented materiality speaks more of poetry than of pottery. It is in fact precisely the poetic imagination that comes to mind when looking at these works.

His imagined history

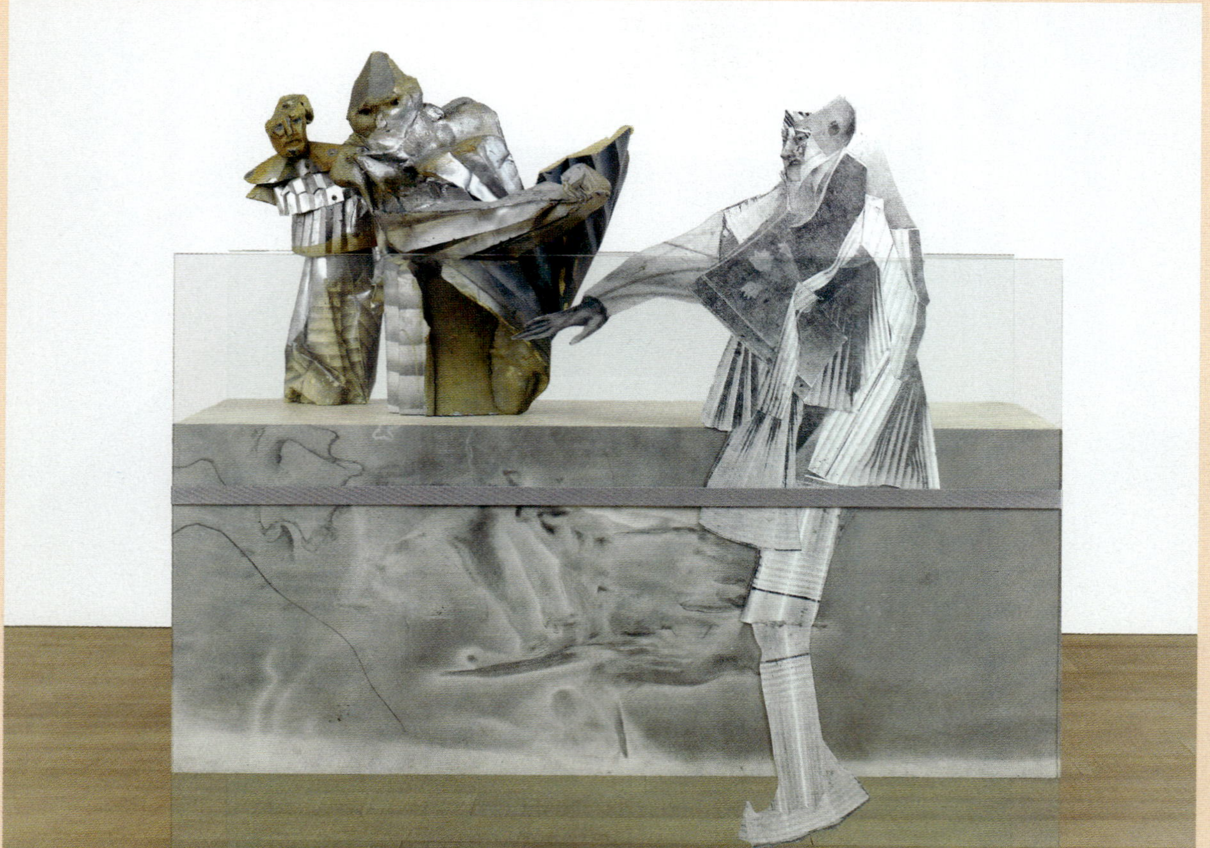

Squint Spirits, 2009. Polyurethane foam, wax, epoxy resin, photocopy and charcoal on paper, aluminium, paint, pigment, metal leaf, glitter, glass, ratchet strap. 154 × 152 × 68 cm

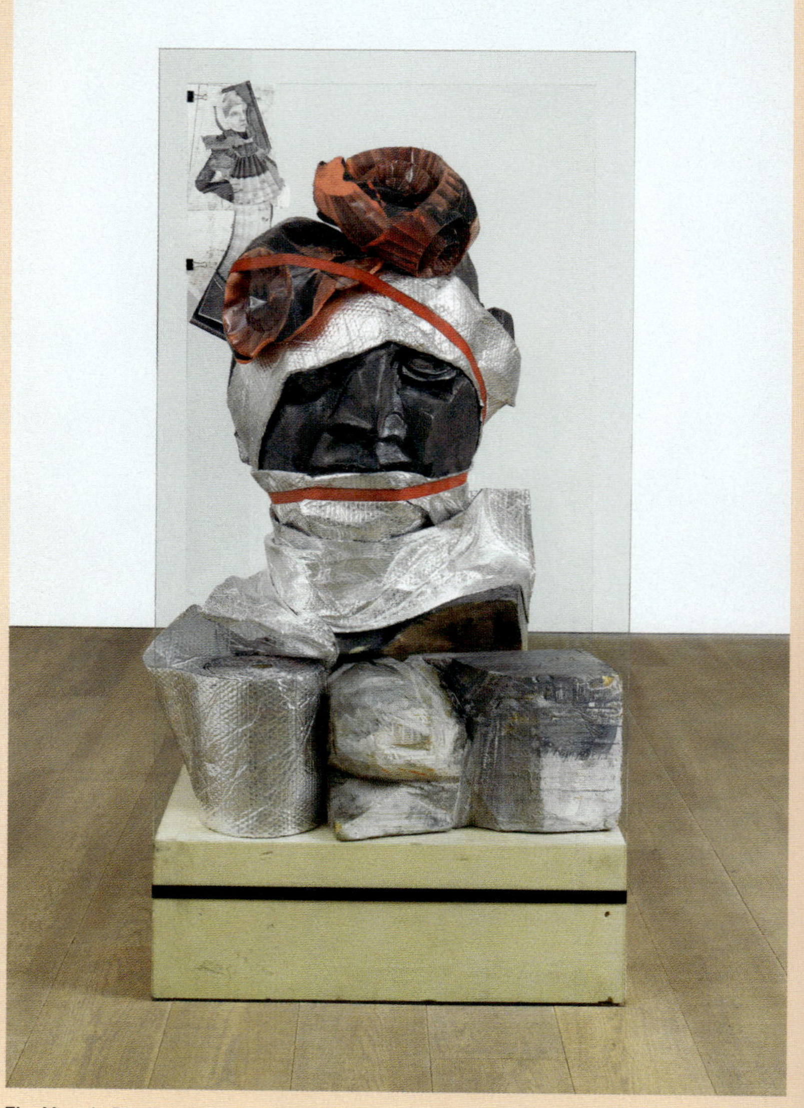

The Magpie Dirge, 2009. Polyurethane foam, wax, epoxy resin, graphite powder, photocopy collage with graphite on paper, clips, pigment, insulating bubble wrap, glass, ratchet strap. 183 × 91 × 65 cm

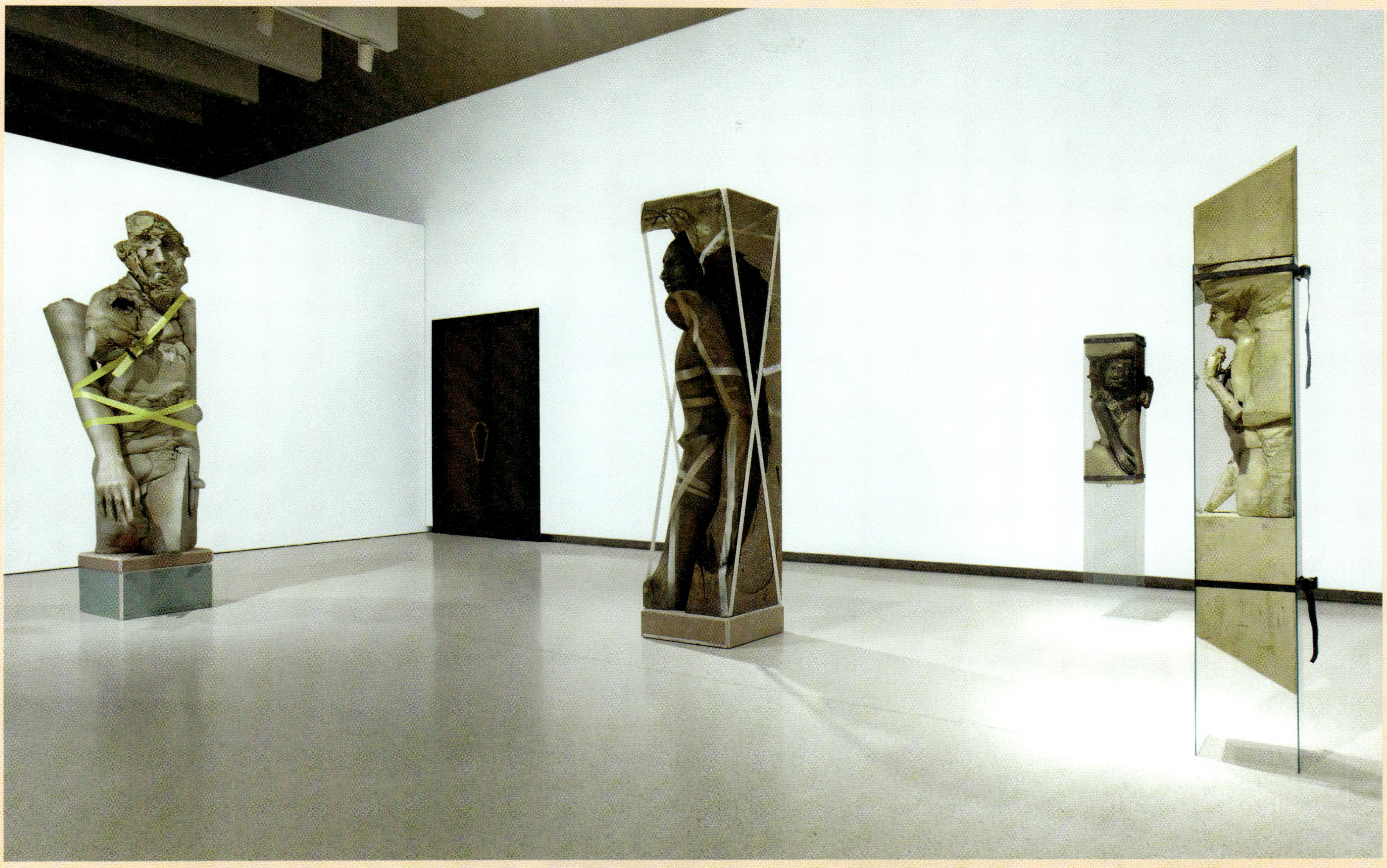

Phantom Limb, 2008. Foam, resin, paint, nylon, metal, drywall. 282 × 61 × 61 cm. **Youth Fenced In**, 2008. Foam, resin, paint, nylon, metal, drywall. 259 × 61 × 61 cm. **The Feral**, 2007. Foam, wax, paint, resin, chalk, strap, glass. 183 × 30 × 30 cm. **The Apprentice**, 2007. Foam, wax, pigment, resin, graphite, brass, copper, strap, glass. 221 × 30 × 30 cm

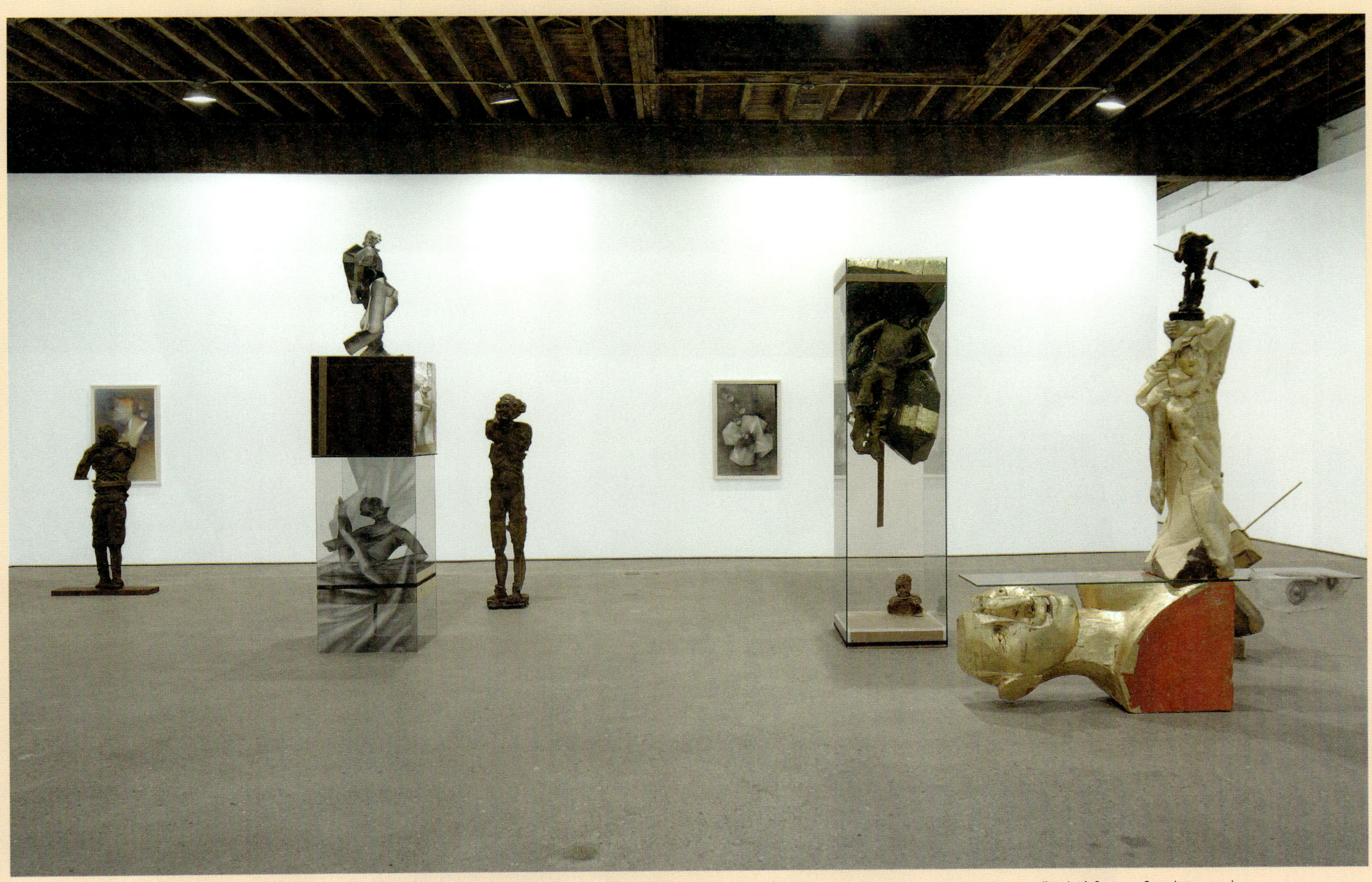

Leshko on A, 2008. Foam, pigment, wood. 149 × 84 × 28 cm. **Recordings (B)**, 2008. Spray paint on paper. 99 × 34 cm. **Chamber Command**, 2008. Glass, foam, plastic, charcoal on paper, wax, silver leaf, 2 straps, 2 ratchets, wood. 271 × 35 × 52 cm. **Untitled**, 2008. Foam, pigment. 168 × 38 × 29 cm. **Recordings (C)**, 2008. Spray paint on paper. 99 × 64 cm. **Gone to See the River, Man,** 2008. Glass, foam, wax, pigment, 2 straps, 2 ratchets, drywall. **Scale of Orange**, 1994–2008. Glass, foam, wax, pigment, metal, charcoal on paper, glitter. 223 × 30 × 183 cm

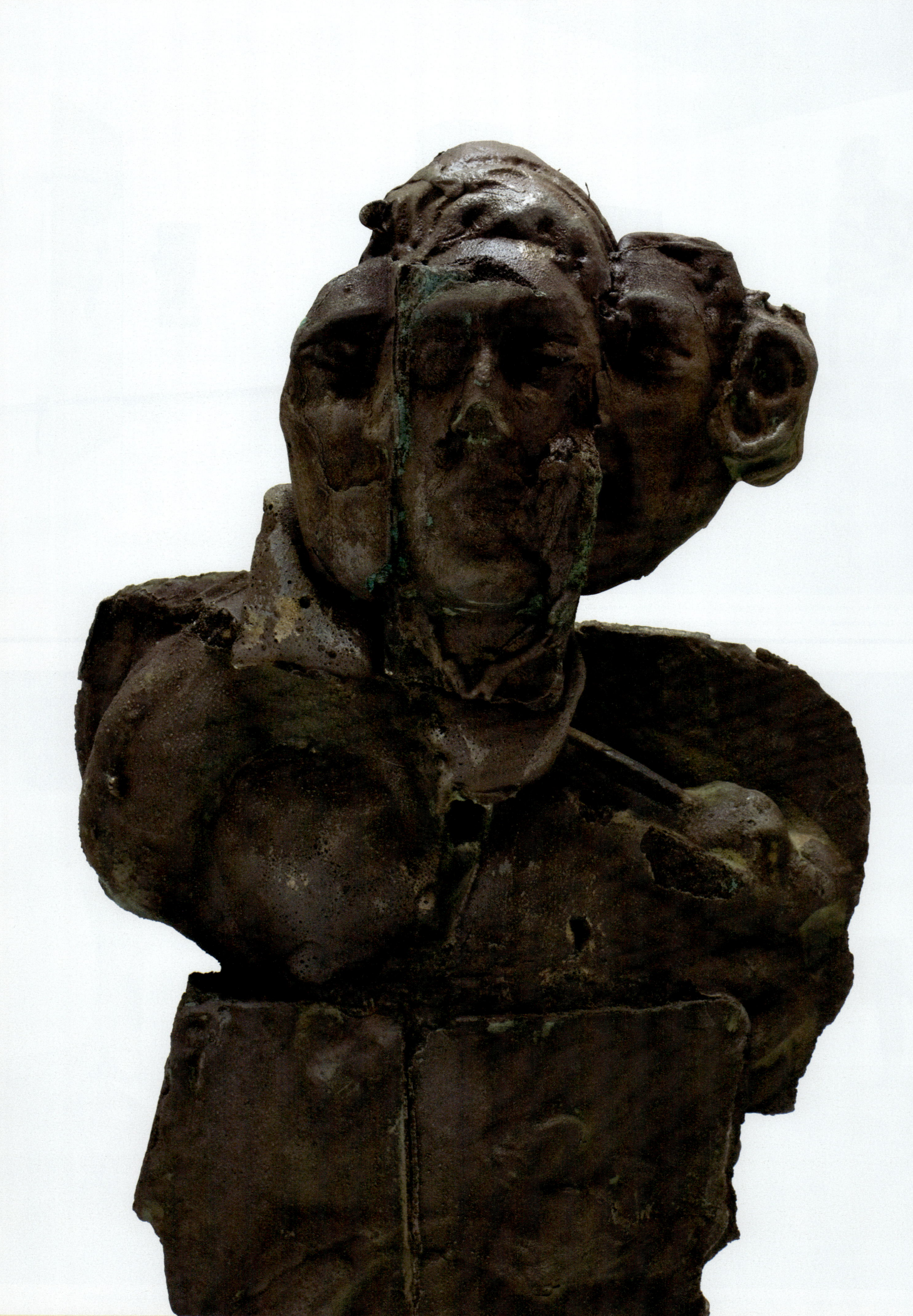

Untitled (detail), 2008. Foam, pigment. 168 × 38 × 29 cm

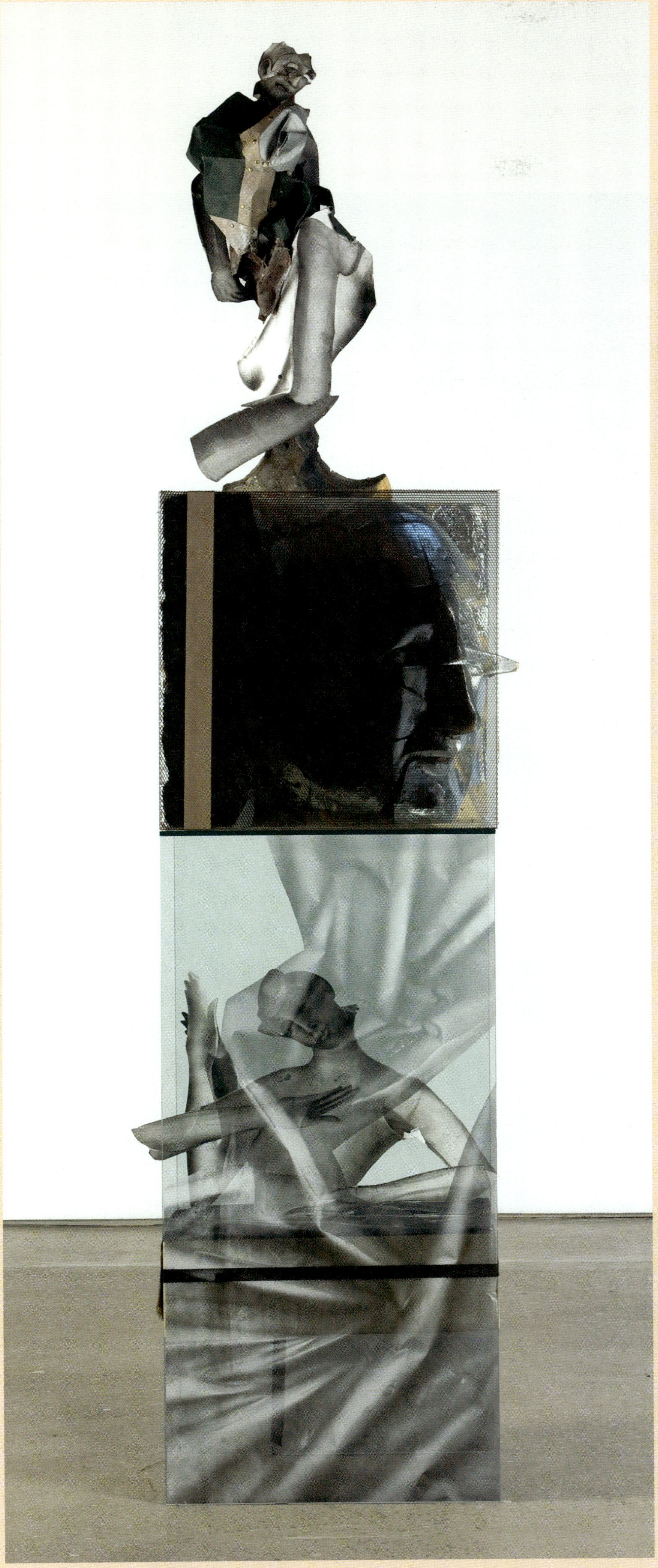

Chamber Command, 2008. Glass, foam, plastic, charcoal on paper, wax, silver leaf, 2 straps, 2 ratchets, wood. 270 × 65 × 51 cm

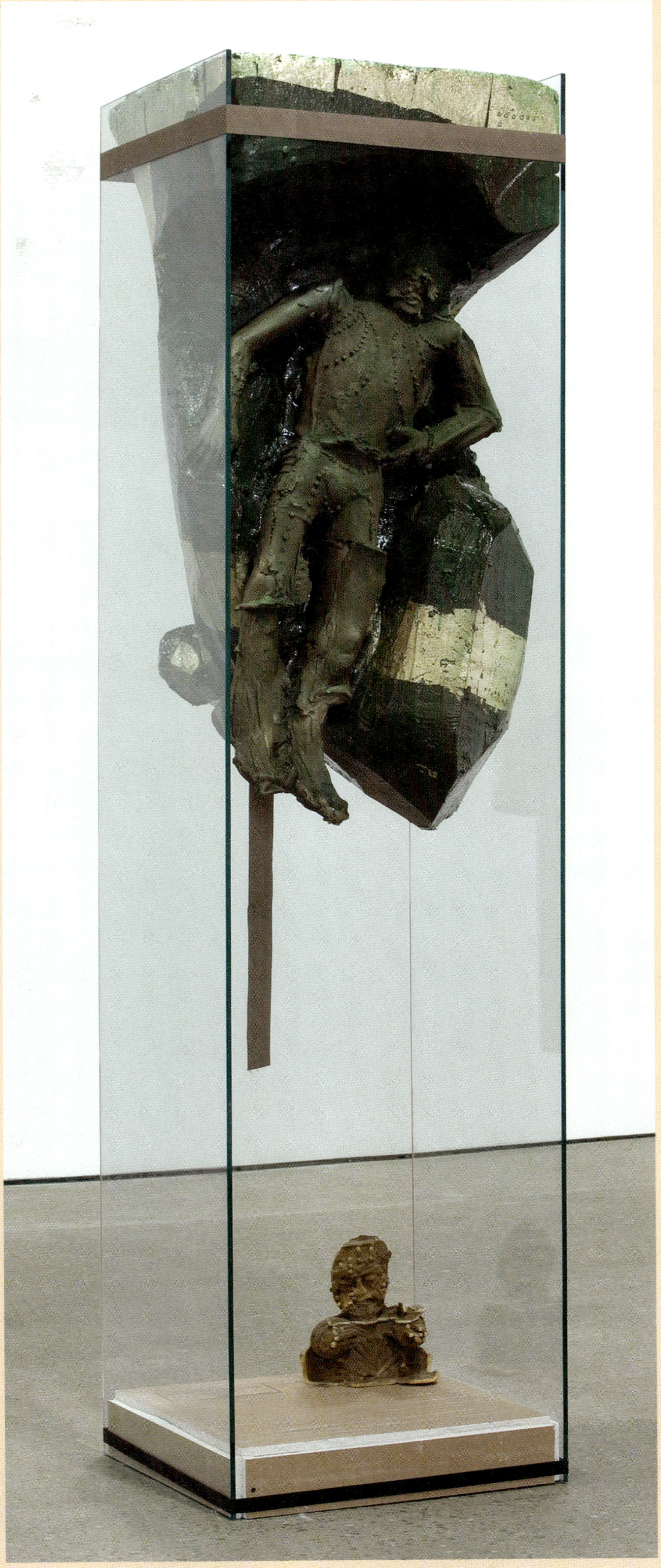

Gone to See the River Man, 2008. Glass, foam, wax, pigment, 2 straps, 2 ratchets, drywall. 243 × 59 × 62 cm

Conjured as they are from the recesses of the artist's (and perhaps our own) collective unconscious, Monahan's works result from materials forced together in a productive collision of opposites that generates a friction akin to that found between words in a poem, perhaps suggesting a new interpretation of the words 'concrete poetry'.

These figures do not stand on their own, however. A central part of Monahan's sculptural practice is his evocation of museological systems of display that both contain and morph into the figures that they hold. Composed of raw pieces of drywall, plate glass and wood, these improvised vitrines and plinths speak as much to Minimalist forms as they do to museum practices. They are the makeshift containers of Monahan's museum without walls, the equally provisional containers of his cabinet of curiosities. In the end, these glass vitrines take on another more poetic quality. They present themselves less as museum furniture and more as space capsules conveying time travellers that have been frozen in suspended animation somewhere between yesterday and tomorrow. Caught in this chronotopic amber, Monahan's figures are at once iconic survivors of some long-gone imaginary world and iconoclastic forays into the history of sculptural figuration.

Melvin Moti

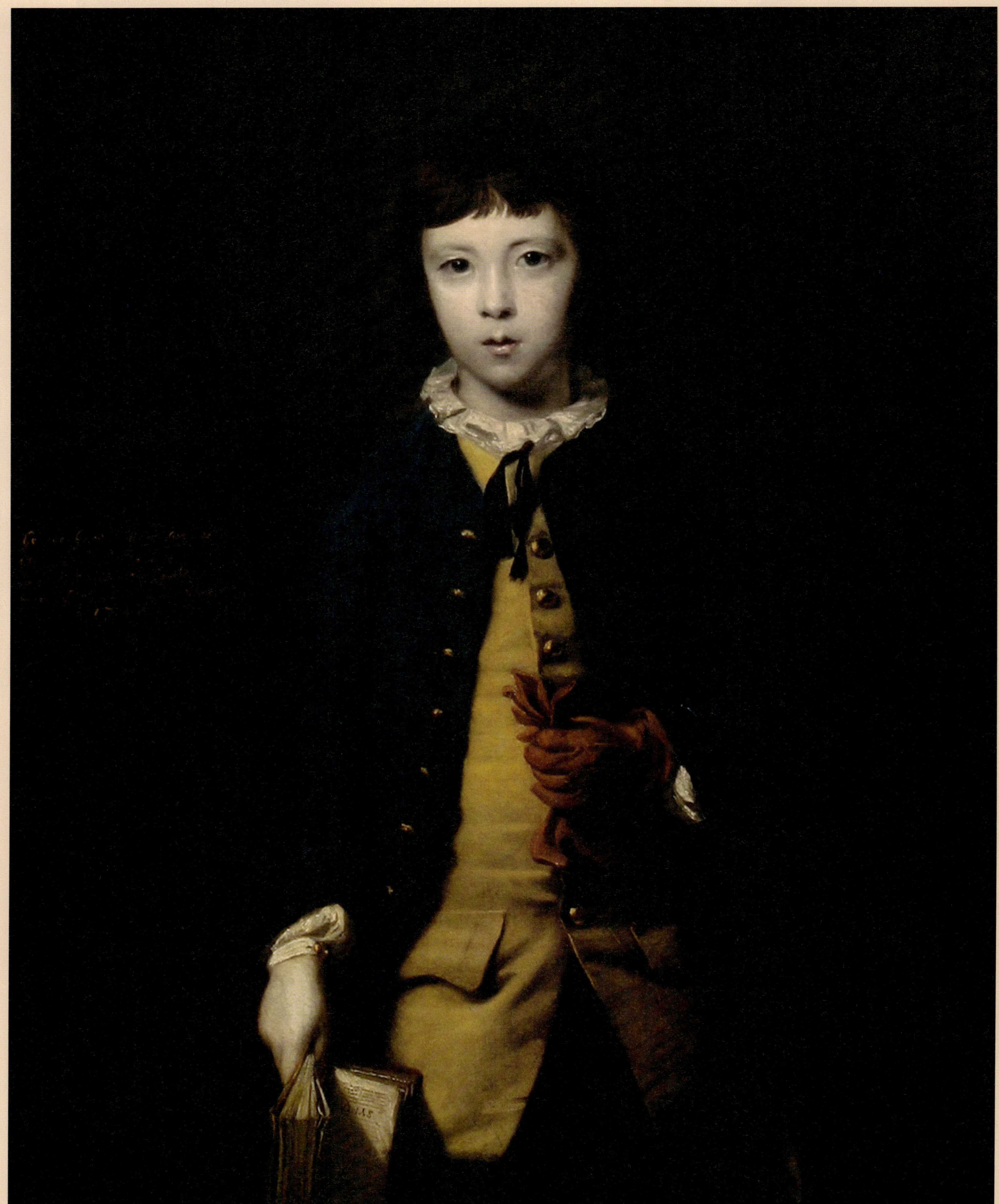

Damask of the Dead, 2009. Painting, 4000–word text. 91 × 71 cm

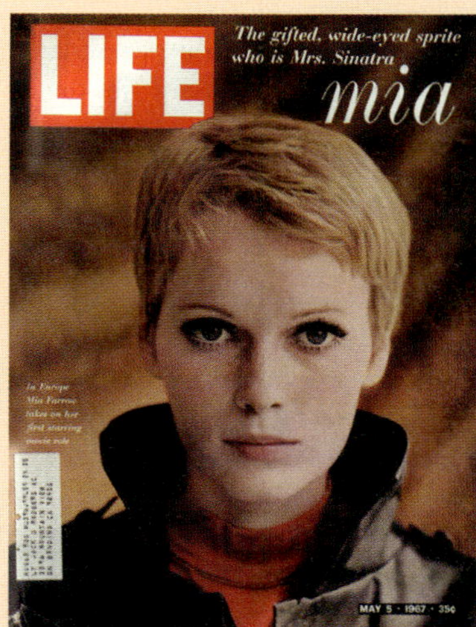

Miamalism, 2008. 2000–word text, magazine.
50 × 40 cm

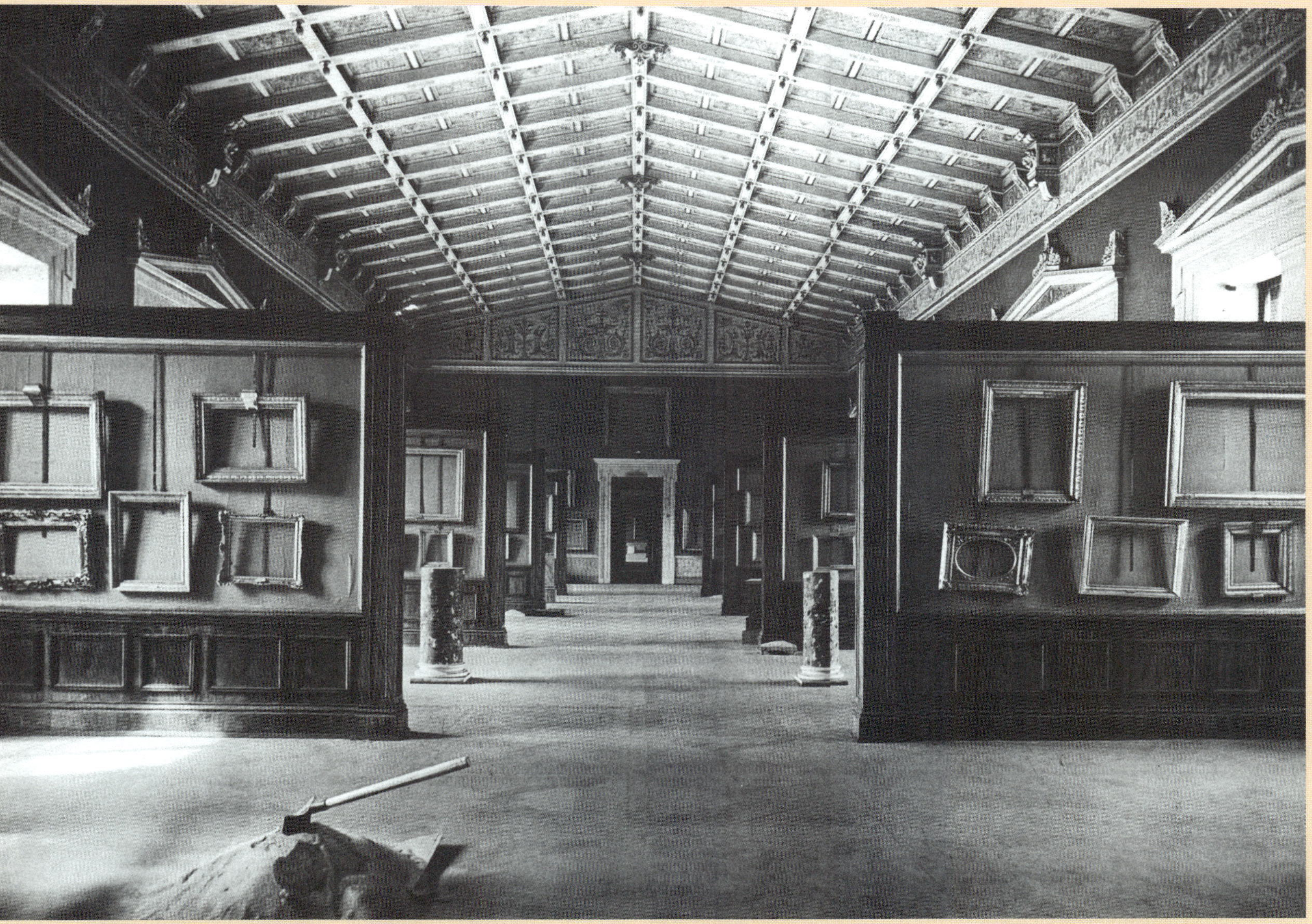

No Show, 2004. 16mm film transferred to DVD. 24 min.

On the surface, the following is not untrue: Dutch artist Melvin Moti primarily makes 35mm films, often accompanied by photographs, objects and book works. His penchant for that near-obsolete medium of celluloid and flickering light is not negligible, since its materiality provides both the hypnotic sensuousness and fragility that characterizes his films. But there is something else, beyond medium and form that is crucial to his work—an element that gleefully resists articulation. It is

Between lucidity and consciousness

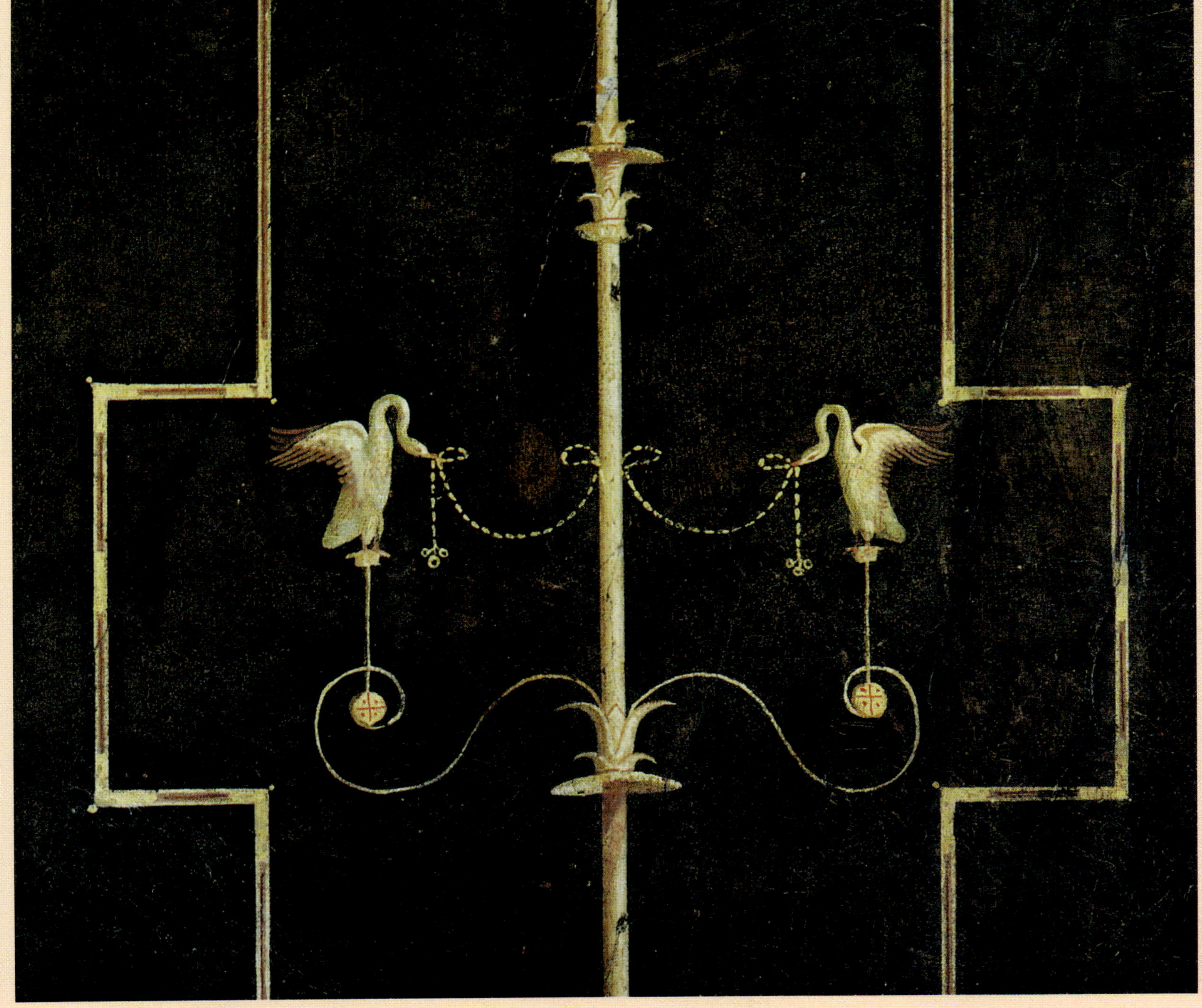

The Black Room, 2005. 16mm film transferred to DVD. 25 min.

perfectly appropriate, therefore, to speak of Moti's work as something that eludes (definition, time, the viewer, even perhaps its explicit subject). This is precisely the terrain with which he is most preoccupied: the distance between the visible and the invisible, between the factual and the unbelievable, and between lucidity and unconsciousness.

Even Moti's subjects could be described as hallucinatory, from Katie King, one of the nineteenth century's most famous 'spectres' (in the series of photographs and documents entitled *The Biography of a Phantom*, 2005) to the writings of J.W. Dunne, who could dream the events of the future (in the film *E.S.P,* 2007), and from the mental wanderings of French Surrealist poet Robert Desnos (in the film *The Black Room,* 2005) to the organizational patterns of that most fleeting of microscopic particles, dust *(Dust,* 2010). Yet if this willed elusiveness permeates his work, he nevertheless aims at reconstructing these 'radical histories' with the eye of an amateur detective-historian and with an intensity and slowness that is rare among artists of his generation. In this way, Moti gives form to these obscure anecdotes, incidents and individuals — 'black holes' that, as he says, 'haven't been contextualized by official historiography'.

But Moti eschews simply or blindly filling in these black holes. The studied reduction in his art is so acute that there are very few concrete images even in the films, which can range from eleven to twenty minutes in duration. *Prisoner's Cinema* (2008),

Obscure anecdotes, incidents and individuals

for example, which concerns the neurological effects of visual deprivation, is comprised of a mere few rays of light streaming through a stained-glass window. *The Black Room* pans with an almost imperceptible slowness over the ruined black frescoed walls of the Roman Villa Agrippa. *No Show* (2004) features a single, almost immobile shot of an empty room;

E.S.P. fills the screen with the explosion of a translucent bubble slowed down from 0.8 seconds to eighteen minutes. Yet in each, the precise articulation of the voiceover, which sometimes seems at odds with the images shown, provides a new mental image for the viewer. It is this construction of images through something that is not a visual image that endows

Moti's works with their particular power. For, like any ghost-hunter, he knows that visual representation is essentially volatile; in his hands it shows itself to be inadequate and partial. The combination of text and image that he produces questions its own authority and incites viewers to take an active part in the imaginative phantasmagoria he presents.

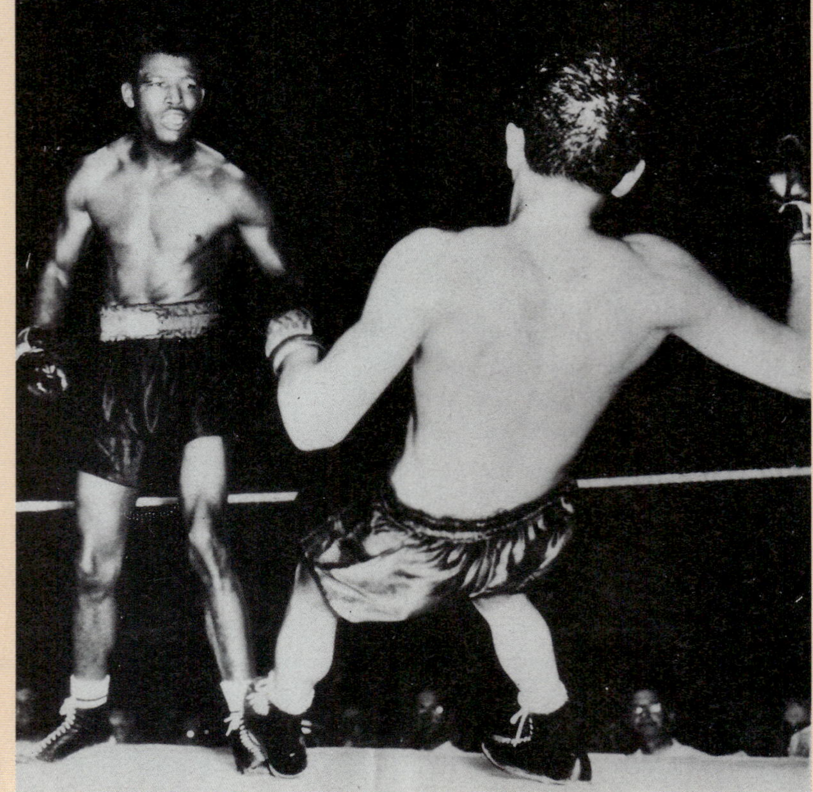

E.S.P. (K.O. Mortel), 2007. Black–and–white photograph. 150 × 150 cm

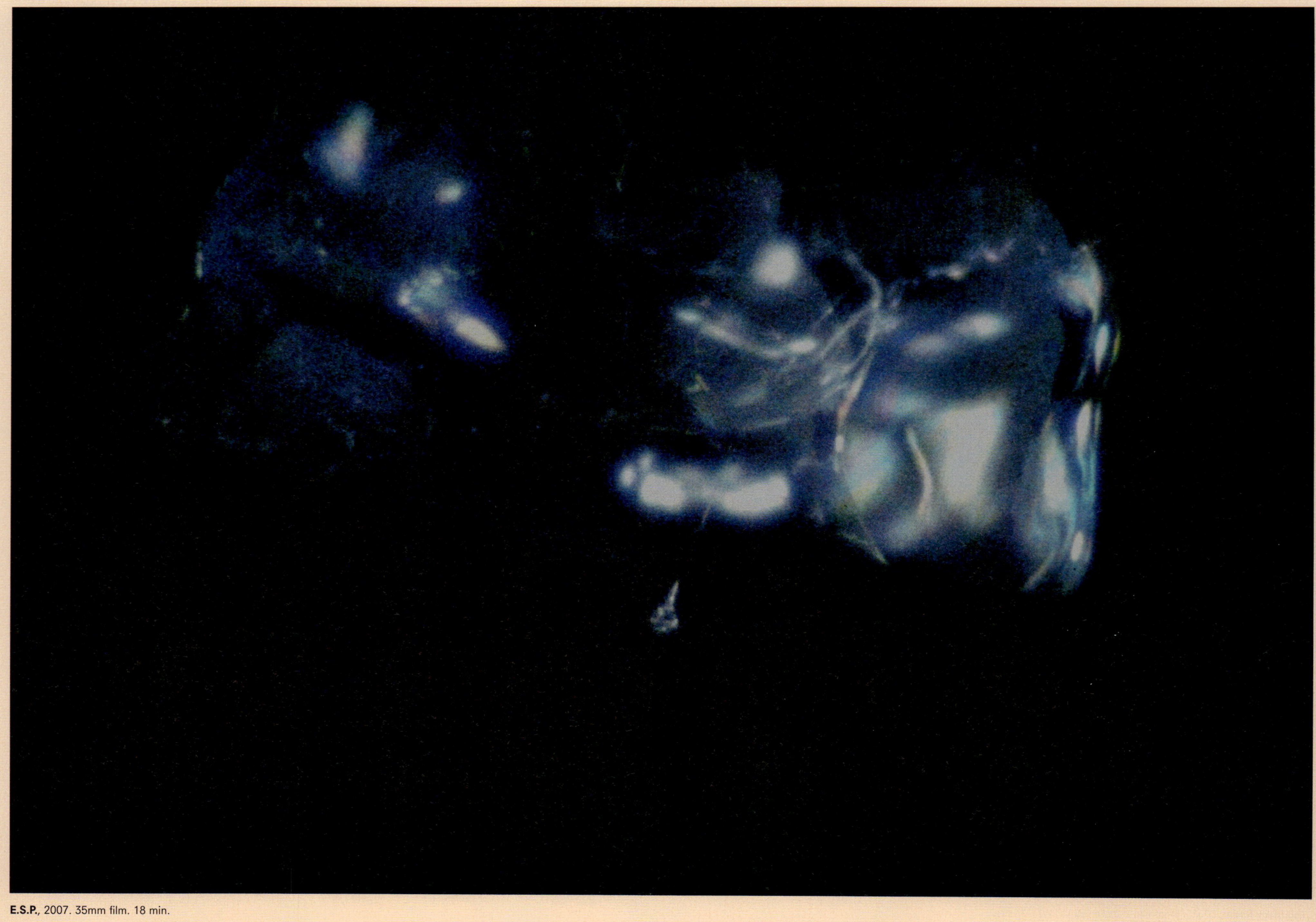

E.S.P., 2007. 35mm film. 18 min.

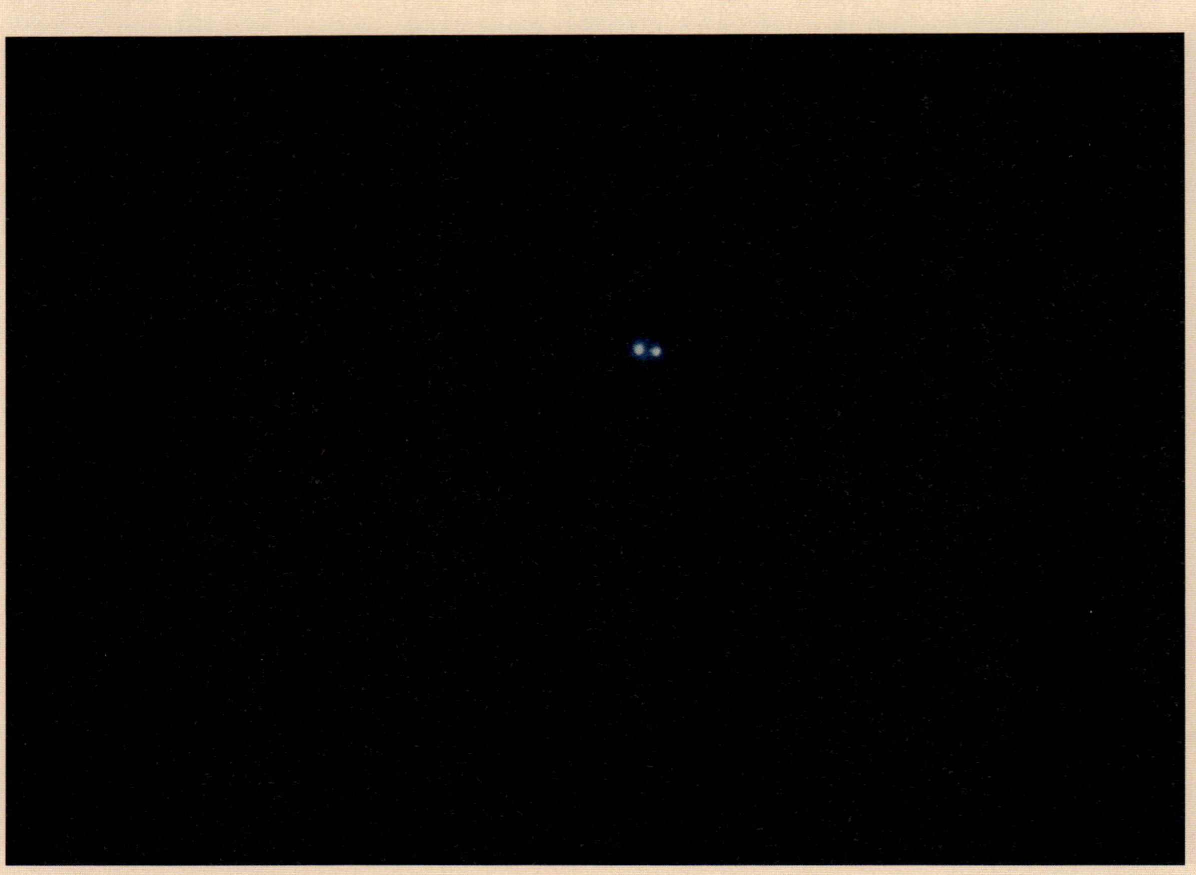

E.S.P., 2007. 35mm film. 18 min.

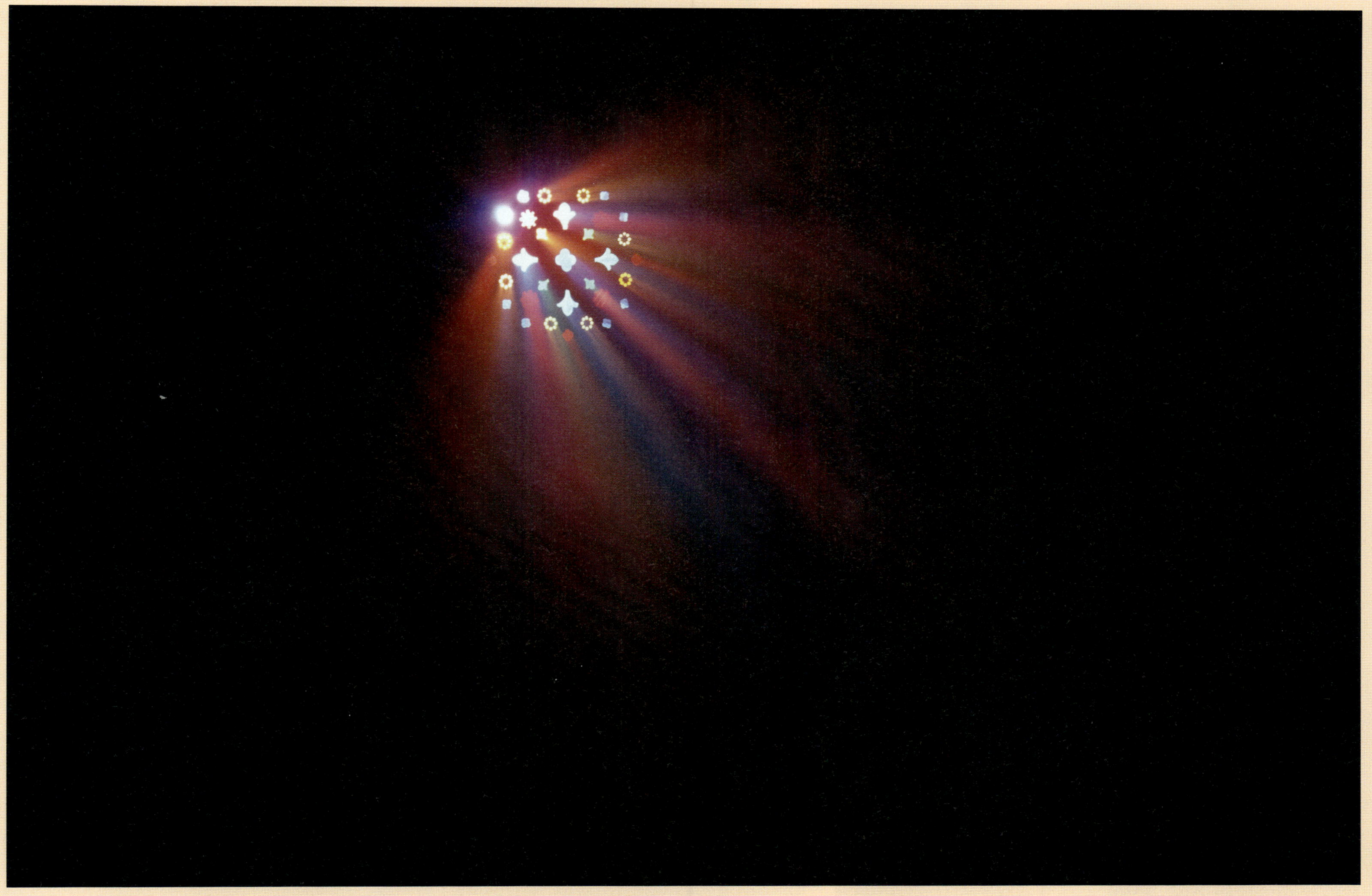

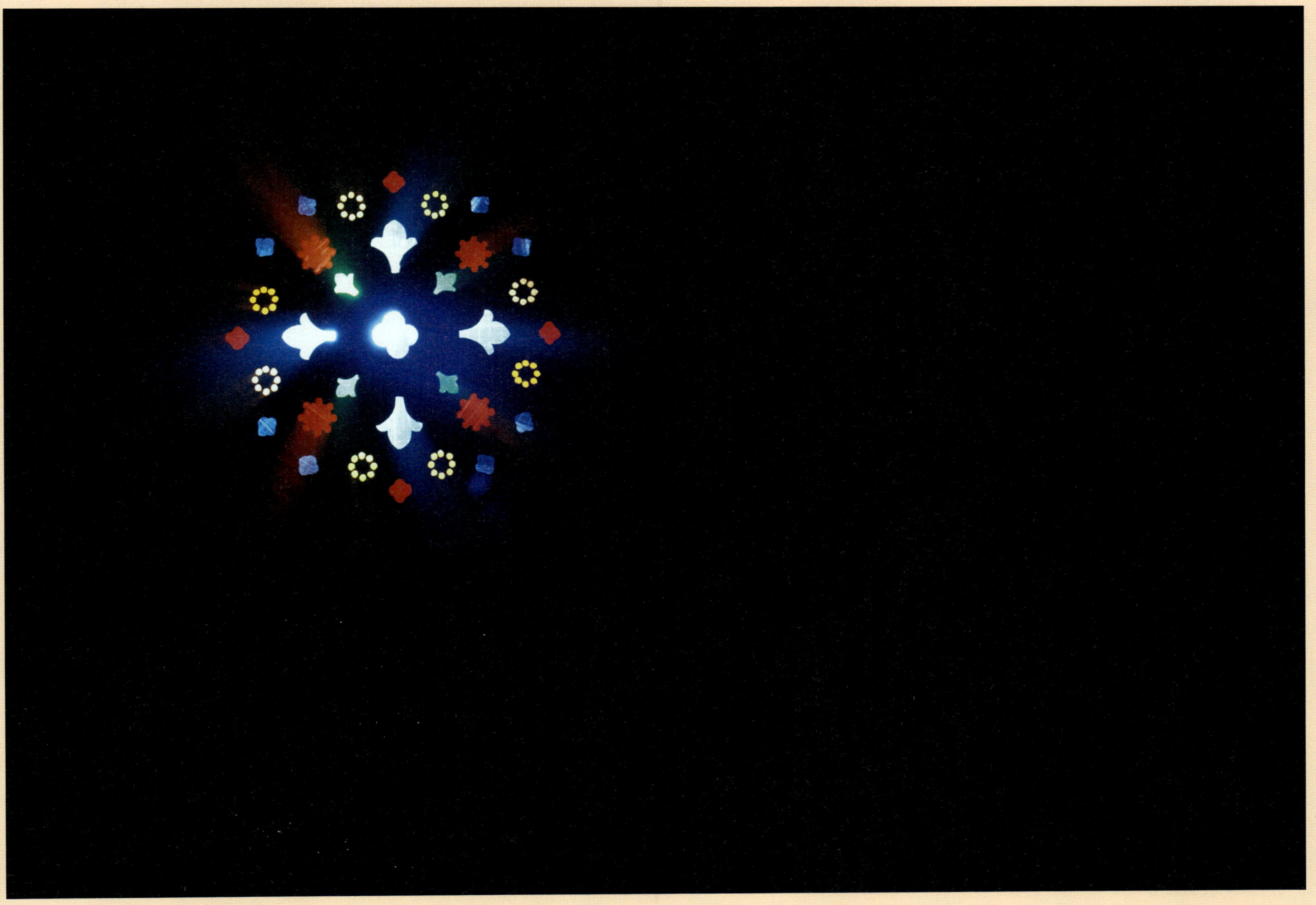

The Prisoner's Cinema, 2008. 35mm film. 22 min.

Museum of American Art

Aura, history and reception

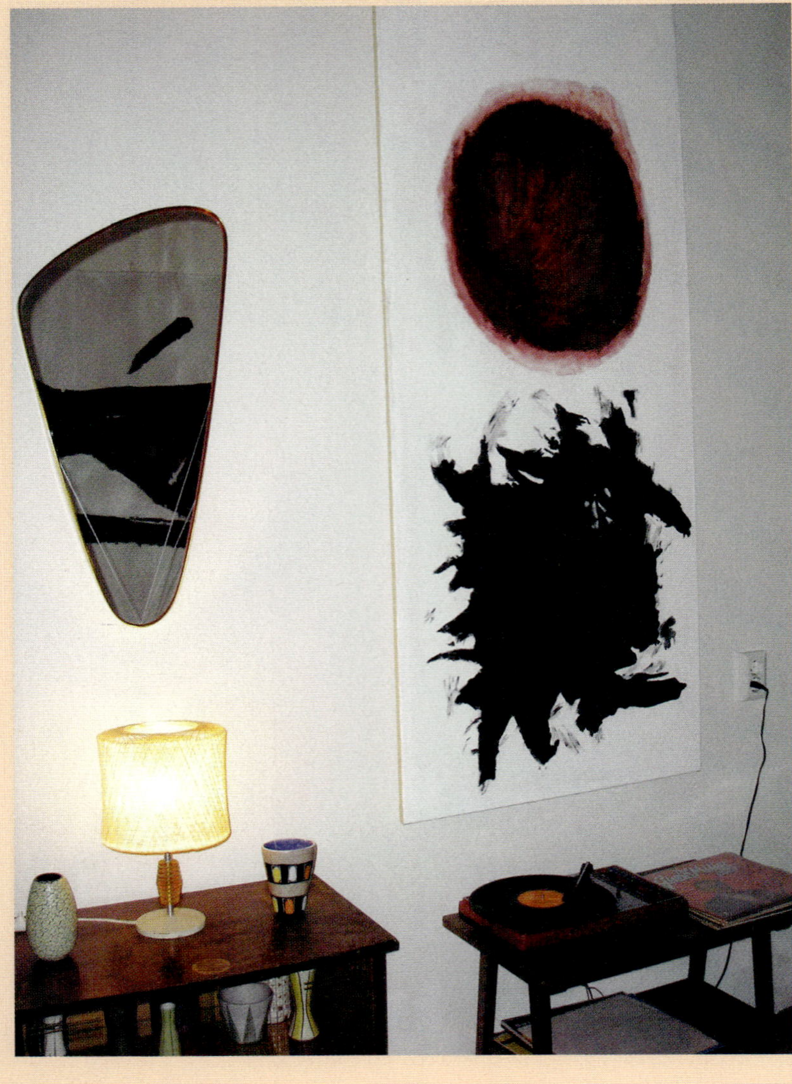

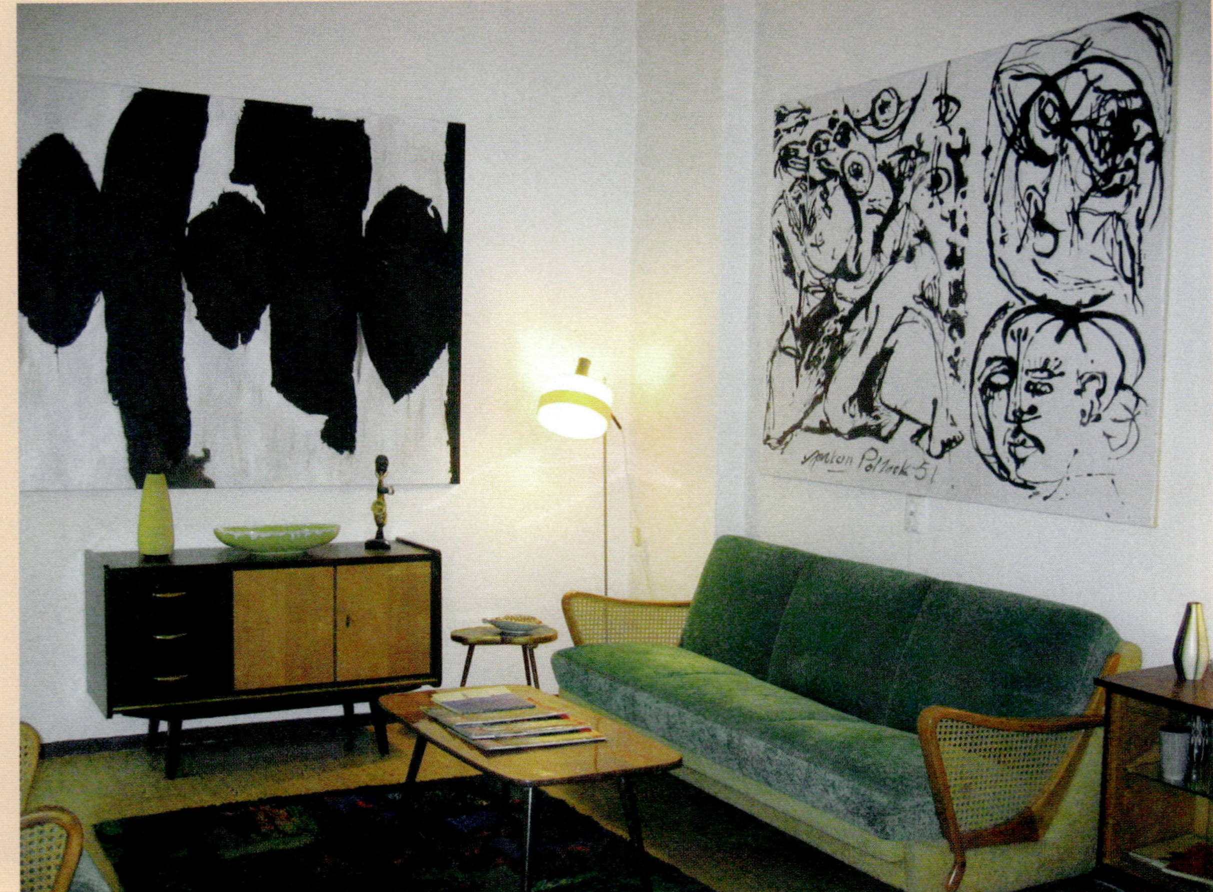

The New American Painting, Dorothy Miller Gallery, 1958. Paintings on canvas. 600 × 400 × 300 cm

Workings of art history

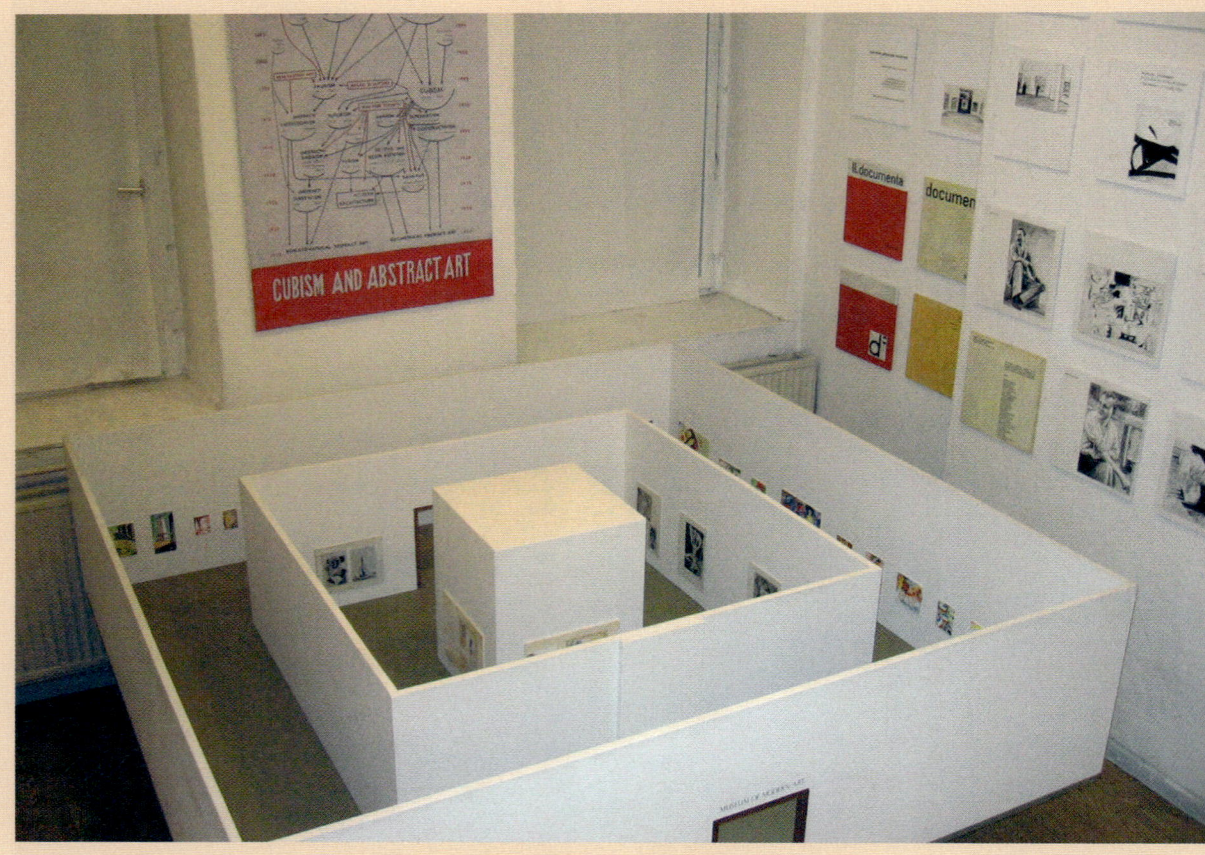

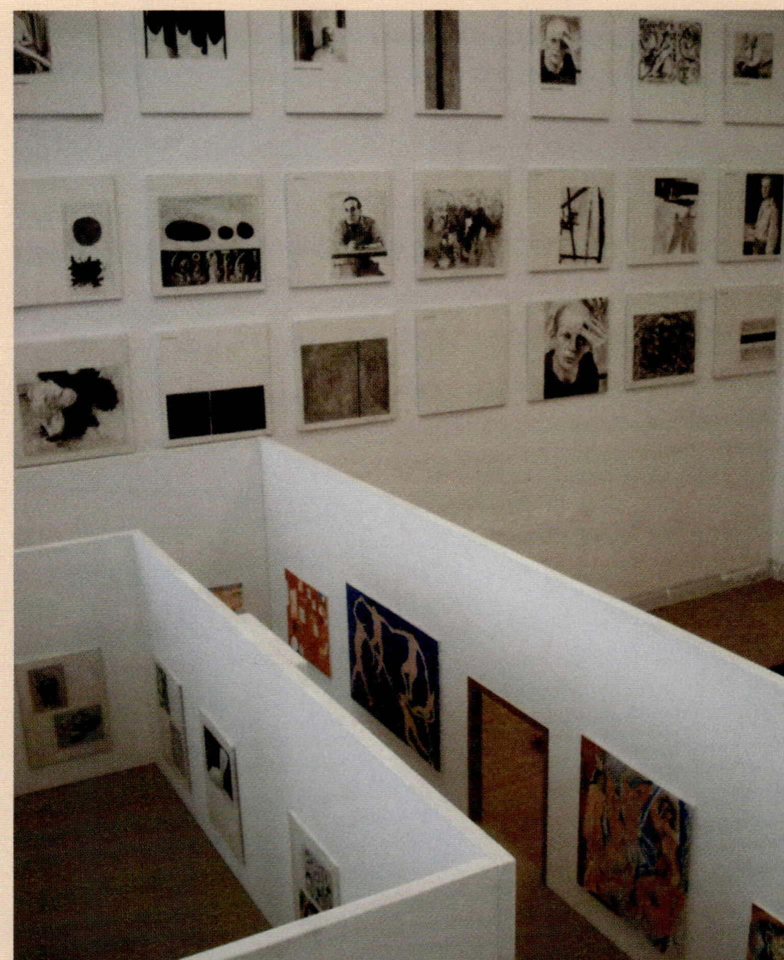

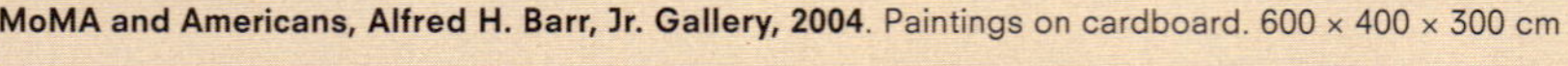

MoMA and Americans, Alfred H. Barr, Jr. Gallery, 2004. Paintings on cardboard. 600 × 400 × 300 cm

The Museum of American Art has been responsible for a variety of projects over the years, including the Salon de Fleurus in Manhattan, the *International Exhibition of Modern Art / Associate of American Painters and Sculptors* as a guest of the Serbia & Montenegro Pavilion at the Venice Biennale in 2003, and a weird but terrific 1987 film entitled *Mondrian '63–'96, lecture, 1986.* Apart from certain thematic commonalities, what these endeavours share is a tendency to produce subtle misunderstandings regarding their authorship.

The 1987 film/lecture, for example, is attributed to a certain 'Walter Benjamin', who uses the example of Mondrian to deliver a lengthy, detailed discussion of matters related to aura, history and reception. Moreover, neither the *International Exhibition of Modern Art / Associate of American Painters and Sculptors* nor the Salon de Fleurus —an artist's reconstruction of Gertrude Stein's famous private collection — offered any clear indication as to who the author

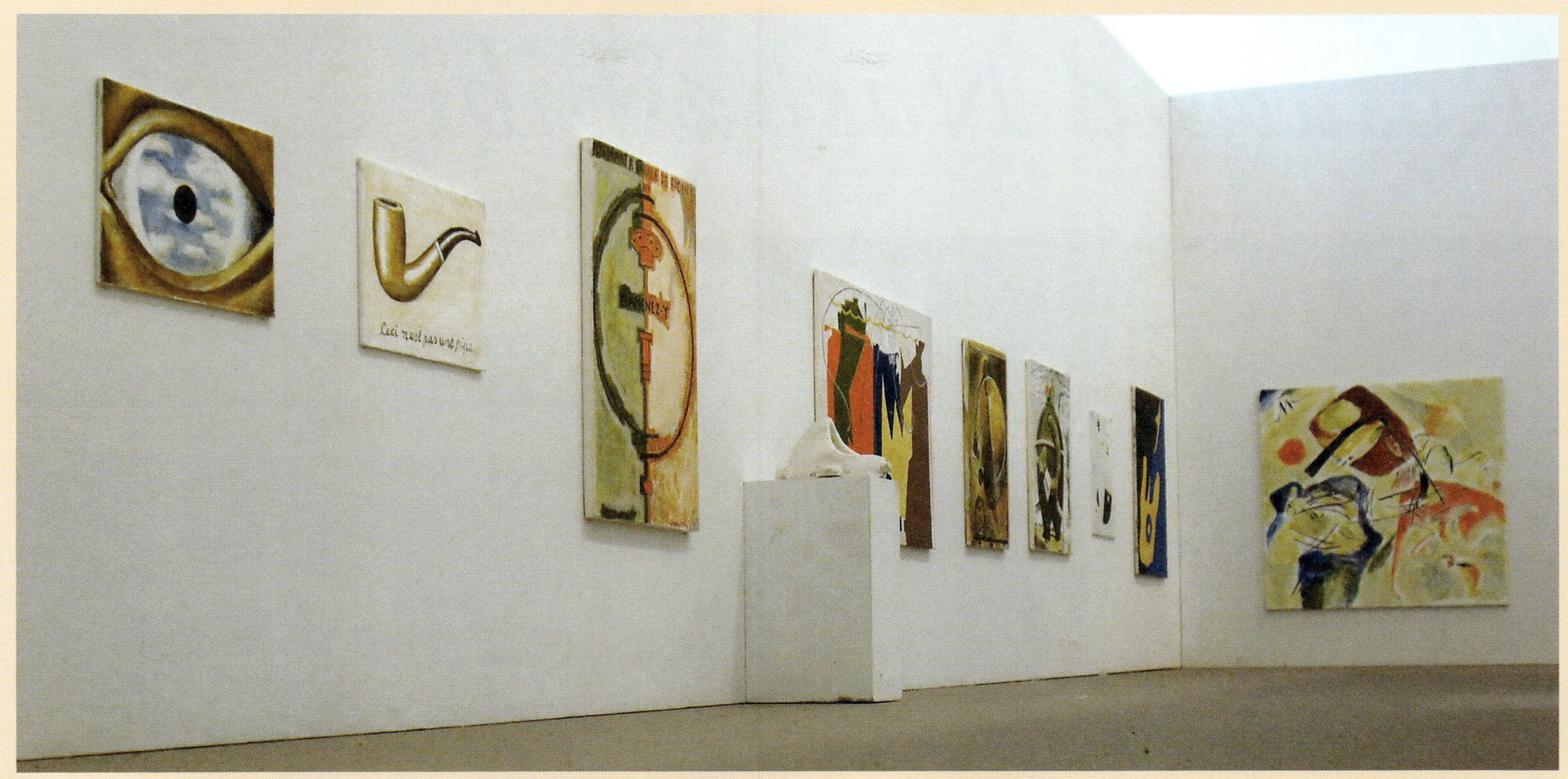

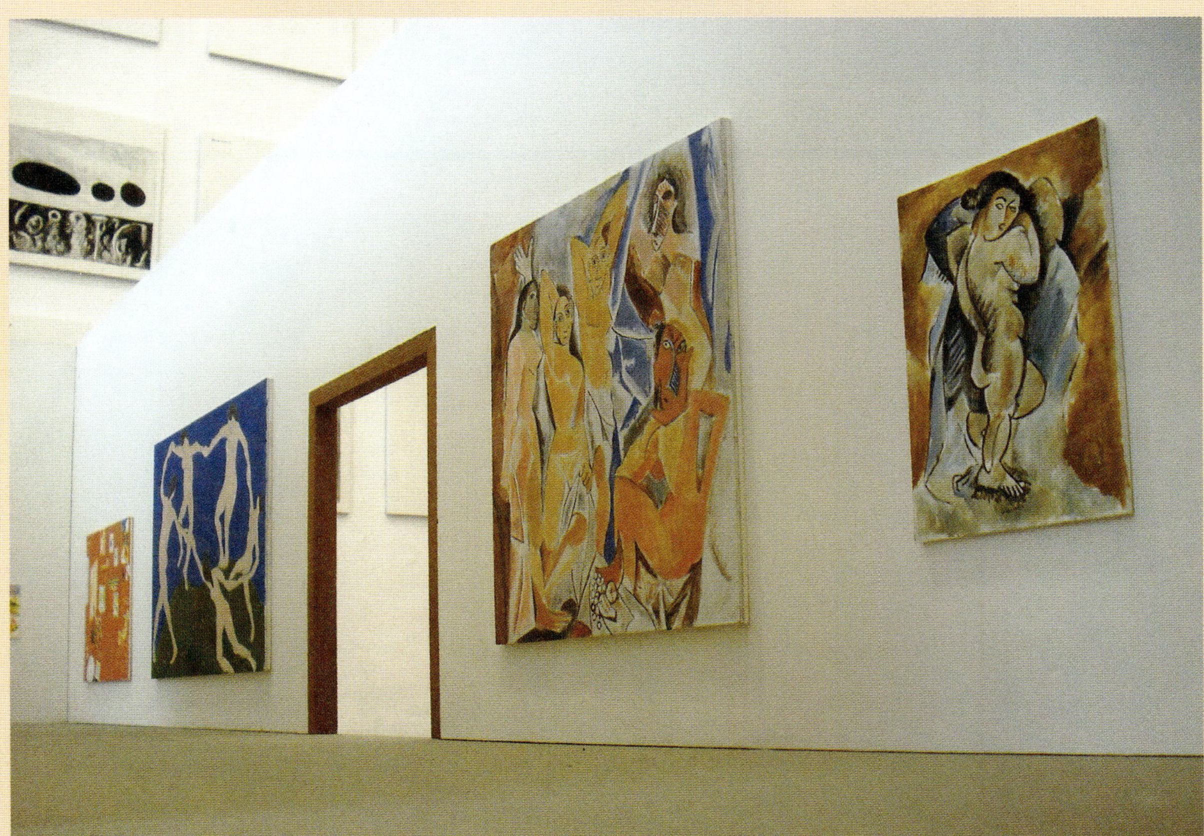

or producer might be. When I collaborated with the Museum of American Art in 2007 as a minor curatorial participant in the Lyon Biennial, *Frieze* magazine assumed that I myself was the artist.

A visit to the Museum itself, though highly recommended, may only serve to befuddle the viewer further. You're treated to a marvellous assemblage of paintings and drawings pertaining to the collection of Alfred H. Barr Jr., founder of The Museum of Modern Art in New York. If you're lucky, the museum attendant will make tea, play some LPs, and share a thought or two on the intricate workings of art history in the United States in the first half of the twentieth century. During the course of this conversation, you may be reminded of Katherine S. Dreier's Société Anonyme, or of more recent artists who have dealt with questions of authorship, such as the appropriation artists of the late 1970s. This is not an exercise in nostalgia so much as a study and critique of certain fundamentals, particularly a confused idea of internationalism, which were defined by the institutional decision-makers of the 1930s and still pervade the art world today. The discussion encourages you to reconsider the traditional assumptions of historical authority and authorship as part of a new and wider set of questions. It would be unfair to suggest that all artists challenging the politics of authorship need to remain anonymous to be credible, but it's encouraging to see that some artists do draw radical conclusions from their critical engagements.

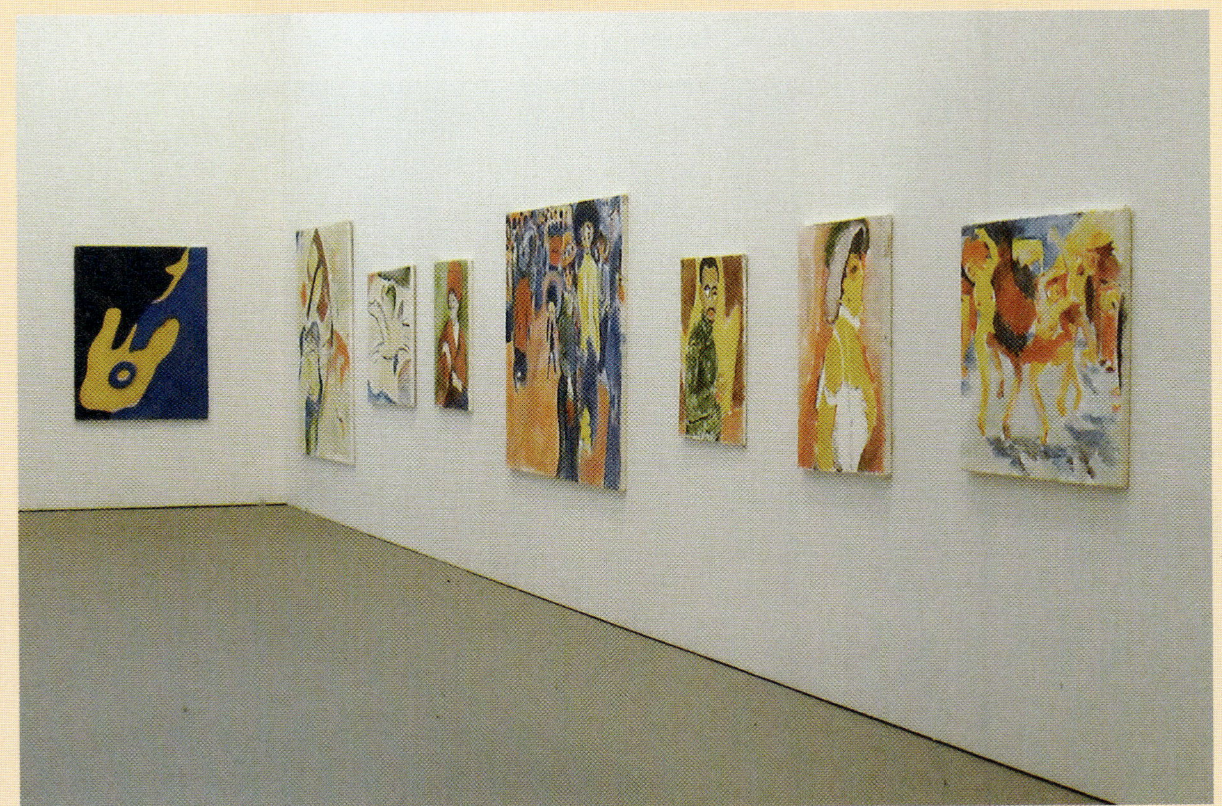

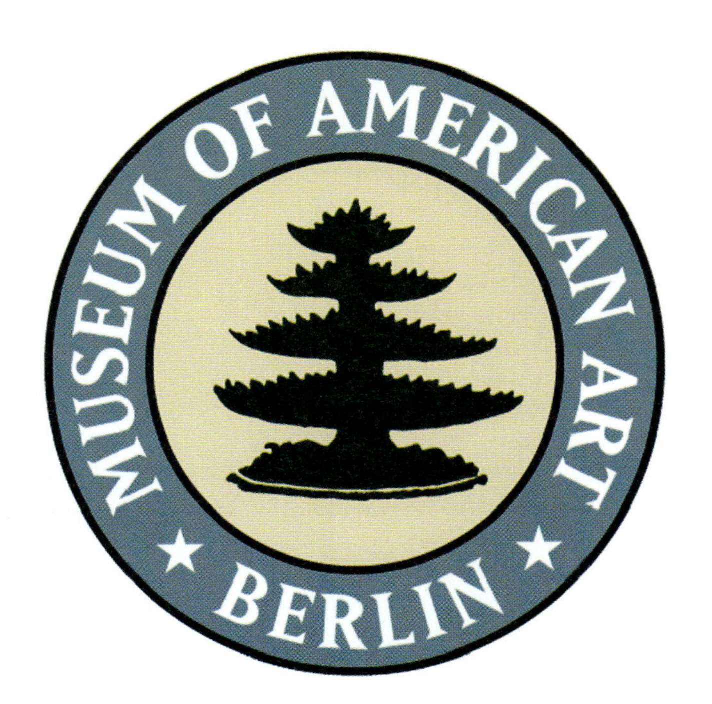

MoMA and Americans, Alfred H. Barr, Jr. Gallery, 1936. Paintings on cardboard. 200 × 200 × 50 cm

Museum of American Art, Berlin, 2004

Rosalind Nashashibi

Erratic nocturnal tour

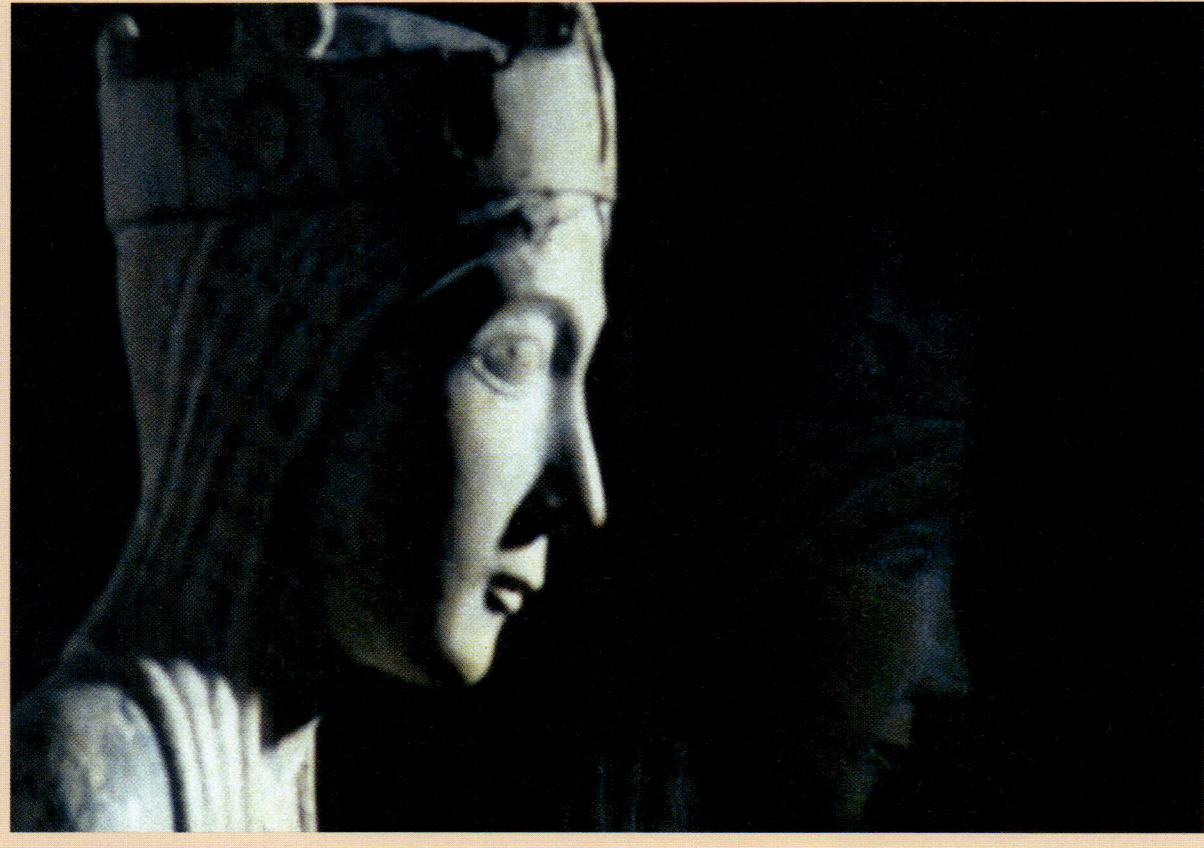

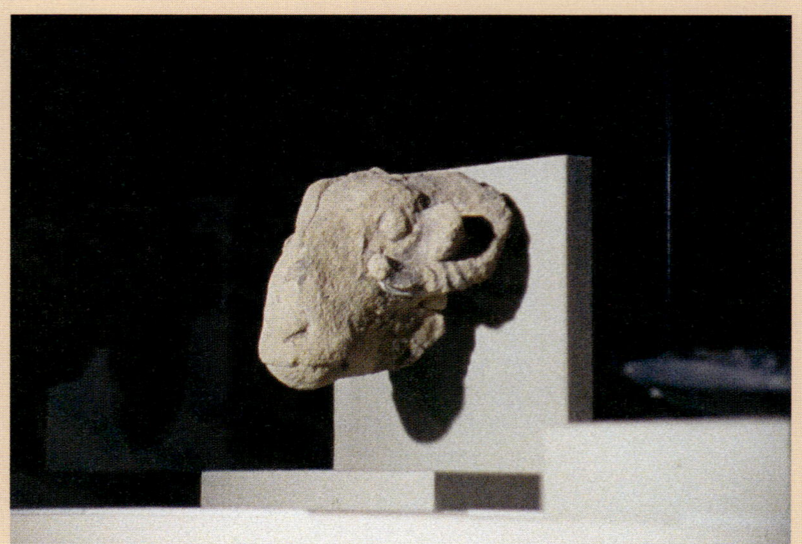

Flash in the Metropolitan (with Lucy Skaer), 2006. 16mm film. 3 min. 25 sec.

A stone, a wooden table, a book cover, relic displayed in a museum or an electric socket that has the shape of a face — these objects, indifferent and opaque, stand motionless before the anthropomorphic eye of the camera, a mechanical Cyclops of a kind. In the 16 mm film *Flash in the Metropolitan* (2006), realized by Rosalind Nashashibi in collaboration with the artist Lucy Skaer, viewers are taken on an erratic nocturnal tour through the collections of the Metropolitan Museum in New York. Flashes of white strobe illuminate the artefacts at brief intervals. The sculptures, vessels and other fine examples of material culture seem to look back at the viewer as if suddenly awoken from a deep sleep, caught by surprise outside the museum's opening hours.

Nashashibi's films are exploratory journeys into a world where inanimate objects and living human beings exist on the same level with neither of these categorically different species taking the upper hand. The films often feel as if they have been produced with a hidden camera, since their protagonists appear unmoved by the filmmaker's presence, busying themselves with daily chores or whiling away the hours, like animals in a wildlife film. In the aptly titled *Eyeballing* (2005), NYPD officers chat, smoke and look around, loitering in front of a police station in Tribeca. In *Midwest* (2002), workers meet over a meal at Gaby's Café, while in *Midwest: Field* (2002), a group of men fly model aeroplanes. All the films capture moments of serene

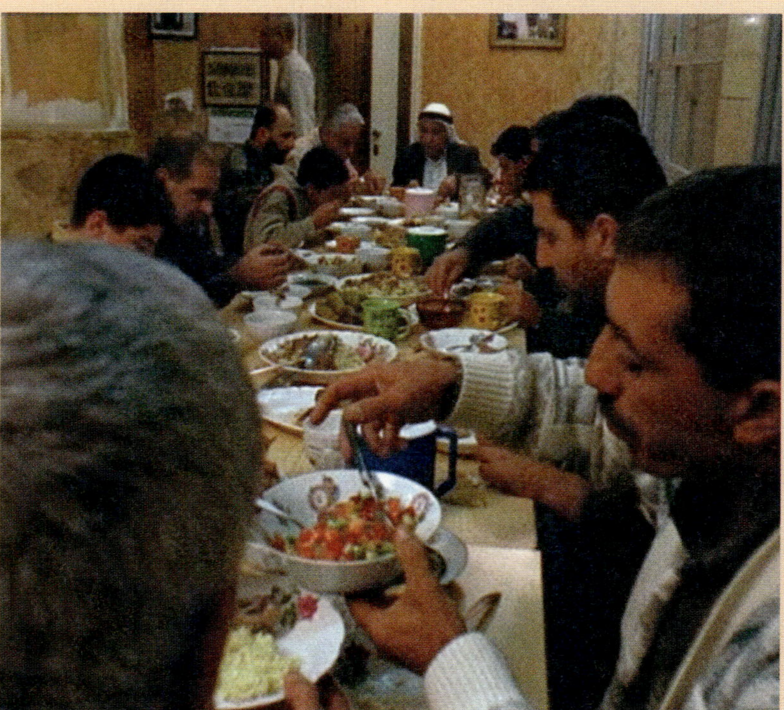

Hreash House, 2004. DVD projection. 20 min.

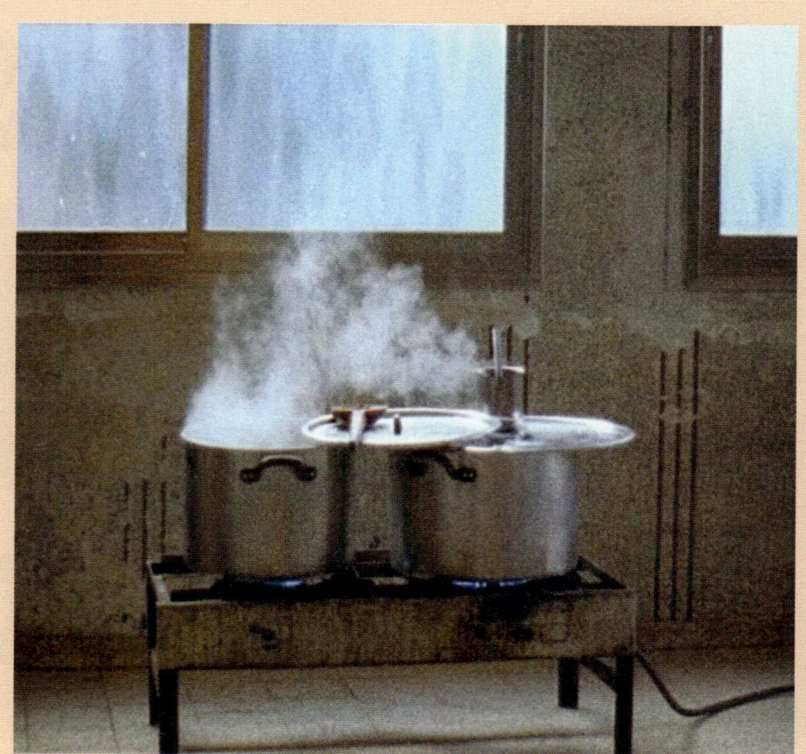

Hreash House, 2004. DVD projection. 20 min.

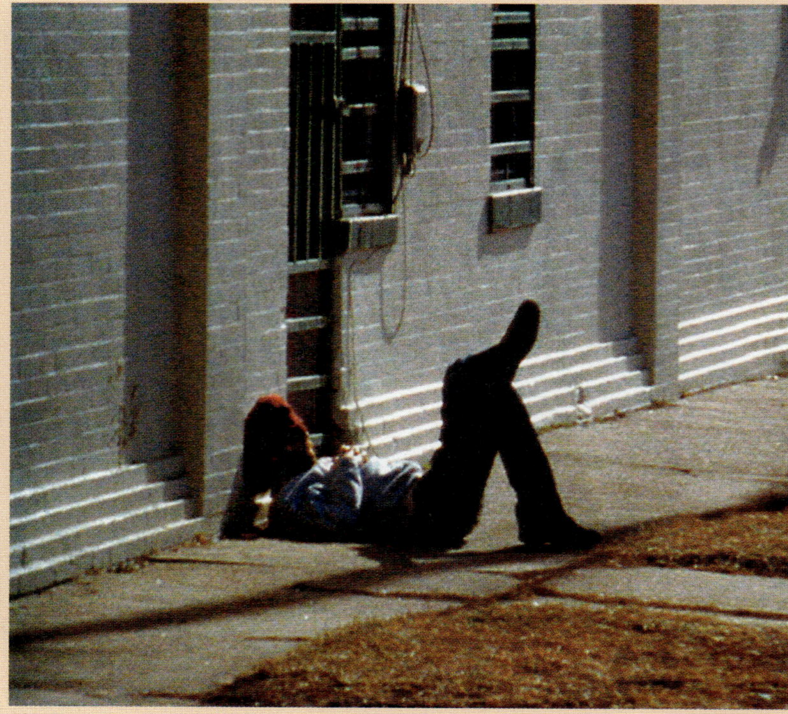

Midwest, 2002. 16mm colour film transferred to BetaSP. 12 min.

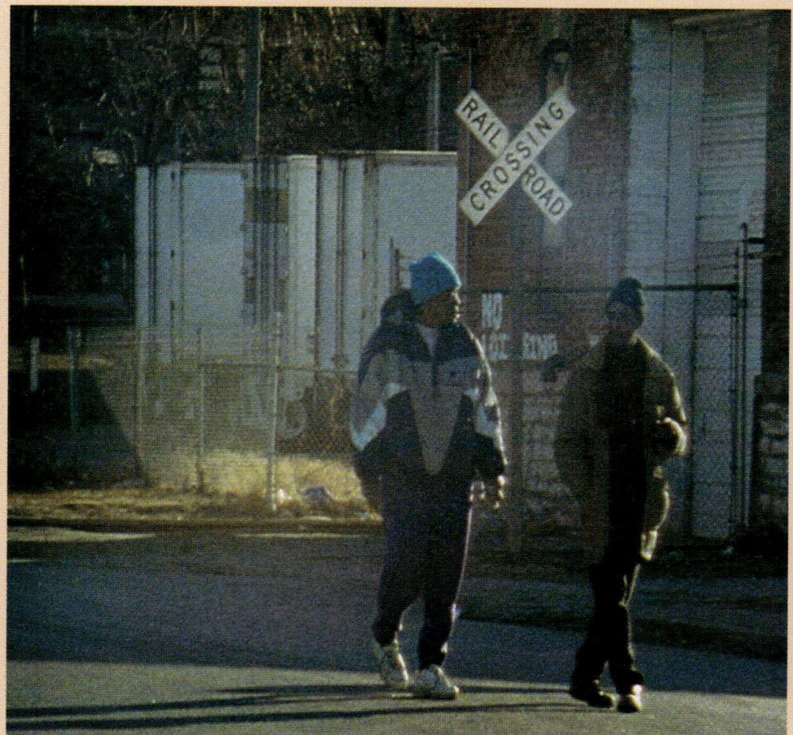

Midwest, 2002. 16mm colour film transferred to BetaSP. 12 min.

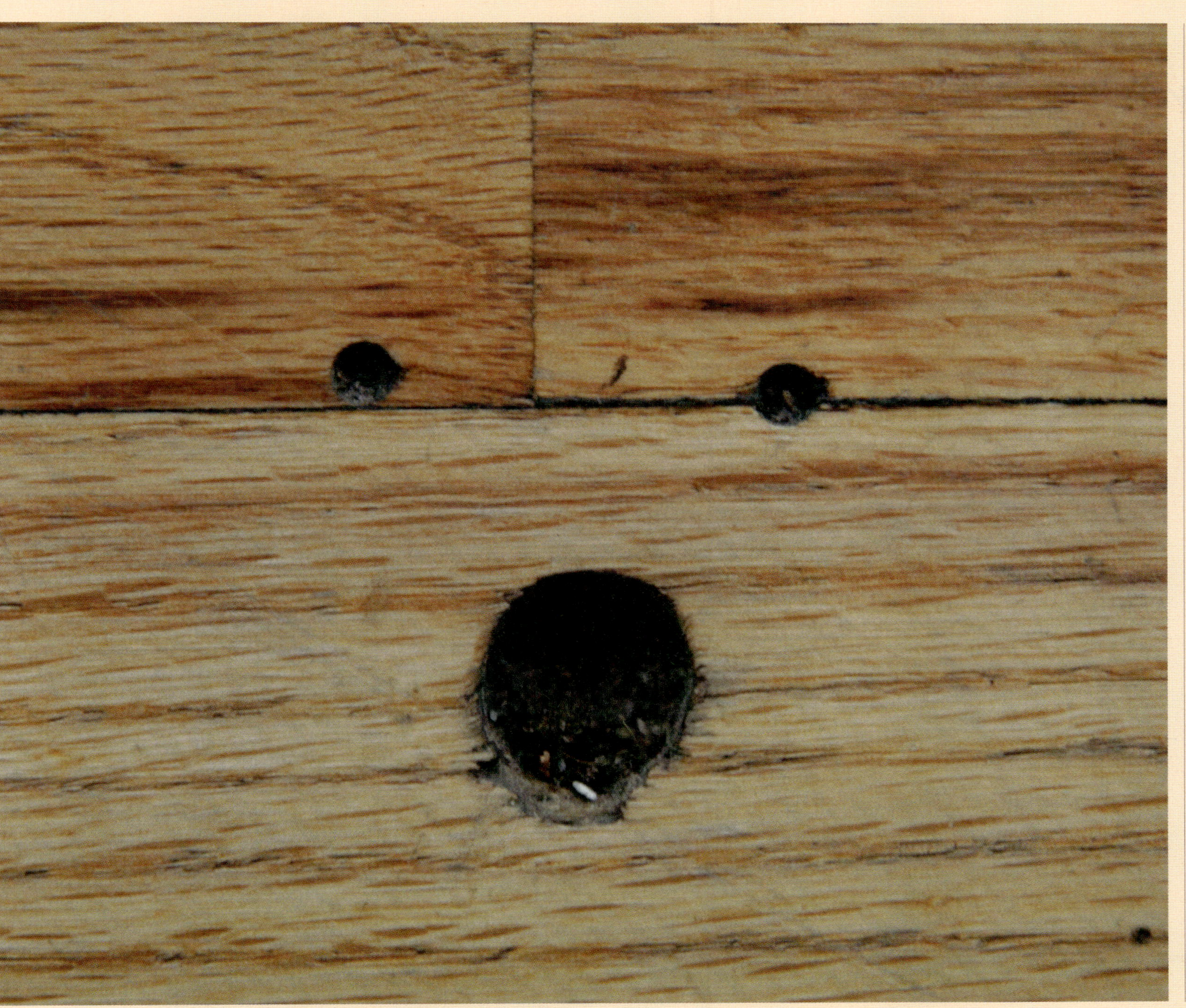

passivity in the restless flow of everyday life. They seem to point to some constant, almost archetypal element of human nature concerned with the fullness of being in the moment and not with the anxiety of becoming. When members of society no longer have a role in production, killing time becomes a strategic issue. The main concern in the northern hemisphere is not work, but the organization of leisure time.

However it is perhaps Nashashibi's films shot in various locations in the Middle East that establish the way of looking at things that is typical of her work. Her attention is directed towards the quotidian aspects of existence — the tranquil rhythm of daily life in *Dahiet Al Bareed* (2002) — a district in East Jerusalem designed by the artist's father — or the recurring domestic rituals in *Hreash House* (2004). The artist is also drawn to minor protagonists who do not usually earn a mention in historical narratives, such as the visitors to a jumble sale depicted in the *The States of Things* (2000), a modest black-and-white film that features a soundtrack that lends it an epic dimension — the passionate, melancholic song of Egyptian diva Oum Khaltoum. *Humaniora* (2003) focuses on the coming and going of ambulance cars outside hospital buildings. Our human share in the world is made visible by bringing the marginalia to light.

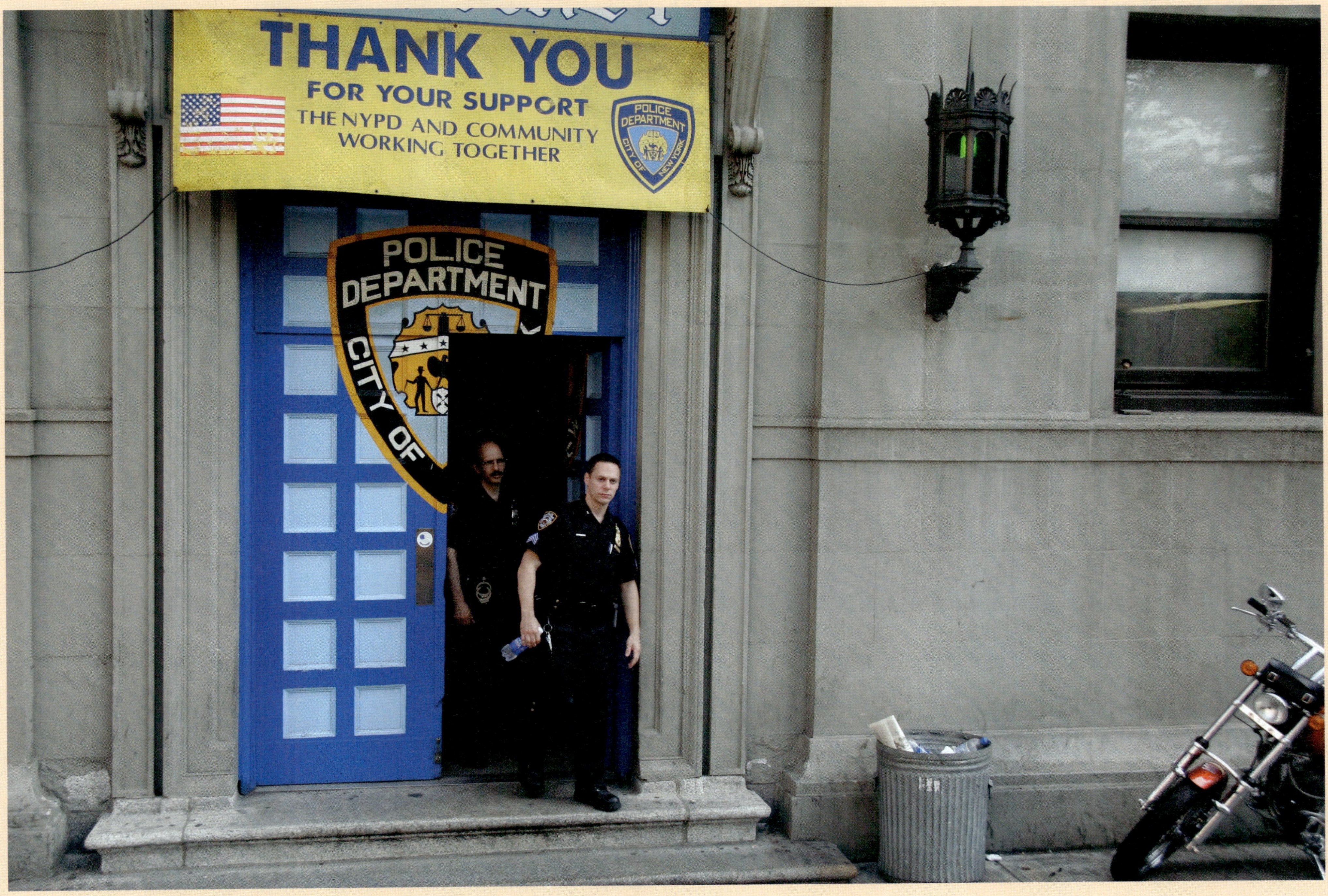

Eyeballing, 2005. 16mm film. 10 min.

Eduardo Navarro

Despite being comfortably embedded within the latest contemporary art trends, Eduardo Navarro's oeuvre evades simplistic classification. There is something excessively precise yet absurd in each of his projects, which at first appear to stem from a strategic and even political intentionality, but ultimately function with an unusual degree of ambiguity and humour.

Navarro's fundamental artistic strategy can be defined as the interruption of the normative contexts in which he chooses to work, through the production of experimental situations within pre-existing structures and social codes of behaviour. As he himself declares, he makes 'half absurd sculptures of reality', striking mimicries of life produced with the intention of provoking an uncanny tension for the viewer.

In order to achieve this, Navarro takes subjects such as religion, self-help, the esoteric, psychology or economics as the nuclei of his work, and proceeds to recontextualize them with absolute conviction.

His work *Colleagues* (2006) made at the Skowhegan School of Painting in Maine, stood as a paradigm of such, as the piece transformed a workshop in an artists' rural residency programme into a psychoanalyst's consulting room solely for the community of resident artists. Appointments had to be paid for with works of art, all of which were shown in the psychoanalyst's office at the end of the project. This type of exchange between spaces and their function was further explored in the clandestine pudding factory that Navarro constructed in a rented space within the most commercial neighbourhood in Buenos Aires (*Fabricantes Unidos*, 2008). It could also be seen in *Arts Centre Chapel* (2008), for which the Frankfurter

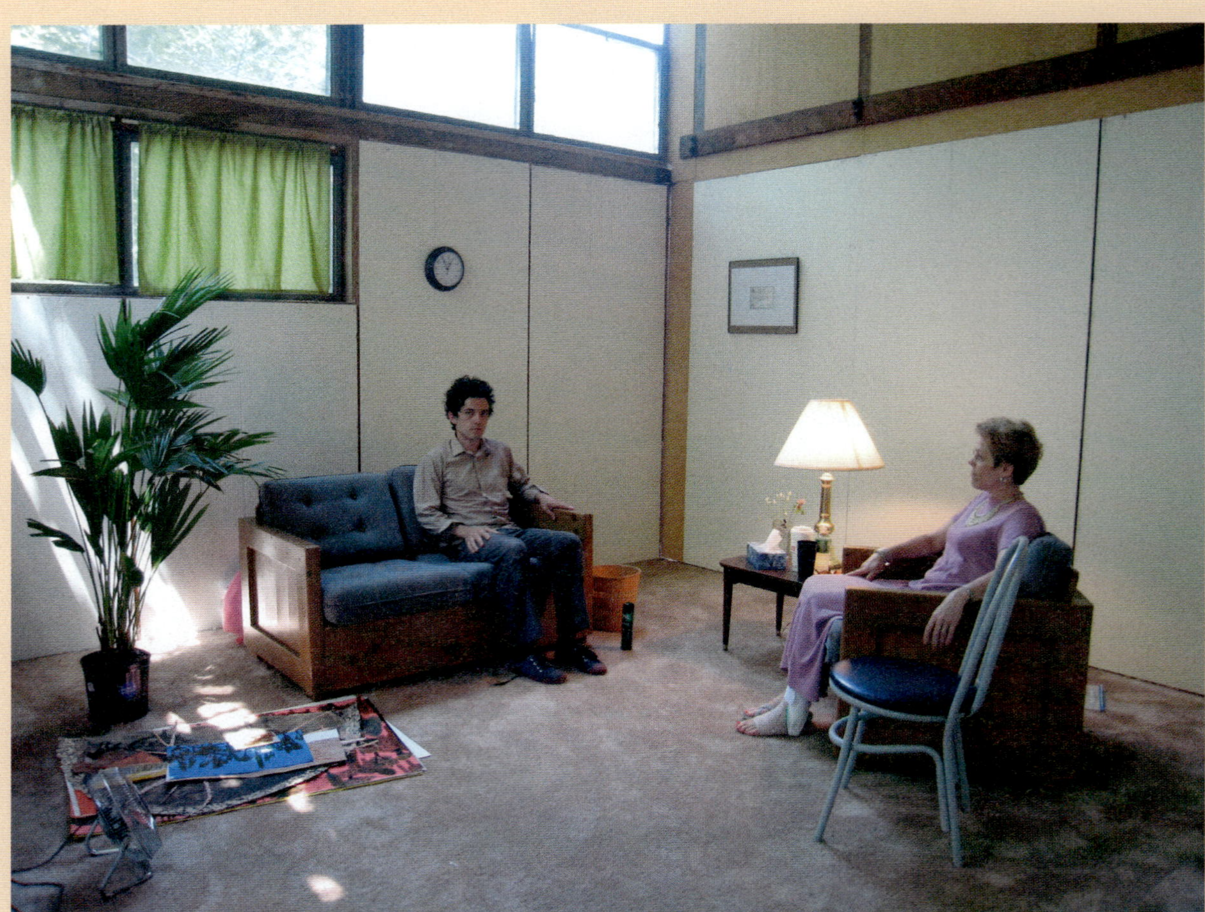

Colleagues (with Dr. Lee Haskell), 2006. Photograph of Santiago Paoli, a resident artist attending a session at a studio transformed into a therapist's counseling office at the Skowhegan School of Painting residency

Excessively precise yet absurd

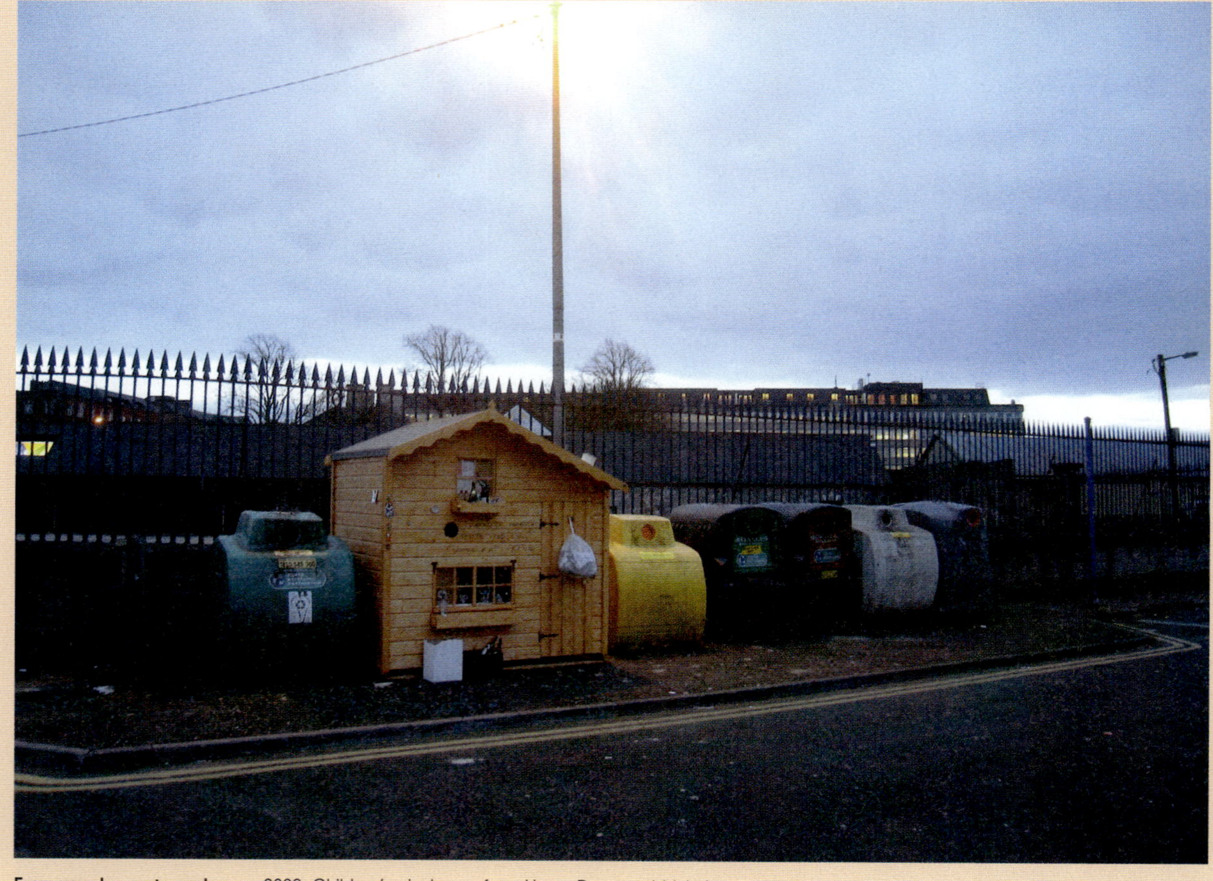

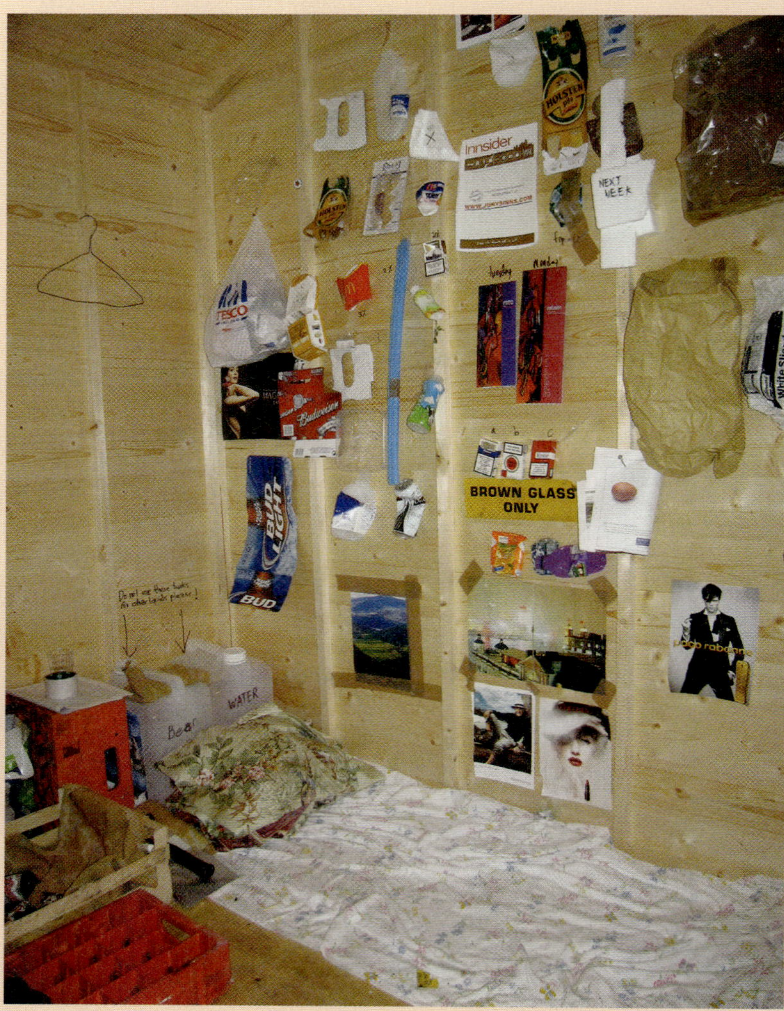

From your house to my house, 2009. Children's playhouse from Home Depot, rubbish, hammer, nails, hot–glue gun, blanket, found objects. 300 × 300 × 220 cm

Kunstverein was transformed into a consecrated chapel where mass was held for a group of art devotees. Similarly, for a project made in Limerick, Ireland, in 2009 (*From your house to my house*), a wooden children's playhouse was installed in the street alongside rubbish and recycling bins. The artist placed small biomorphic sculptures made of trash in the doll's house windows, which thus became a rubbish skip itself, although one that progressively gave back artworks to the community.

In all these instances, Navarro appropriates the typologies and architectural styles of each place (church, consulting room, factory), in order to intensify the feeling of realism and the resoluteness of his engagement with these sites of social and economic exchange. Through these processes, he satisfies his own curiosity about communities, beliefs, practices and social conventions that appear exotic to him, while restraining the illusion of empathy or communion. All of his projects gain both their critical and humorous character through acknowledging, from their inception, the enormous distance that separates certain artists' practices from the diversity of the social world. In this aspect, Navarro's work is not a sculpture built out of an idealism of the social, but rather a practice that provokes from and despite of, a position of political disenchantment.

Striking mimicries

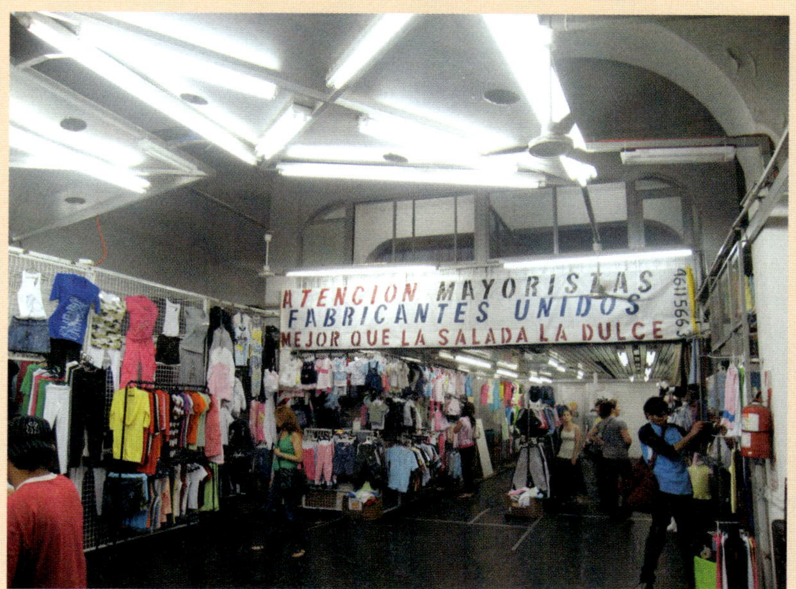

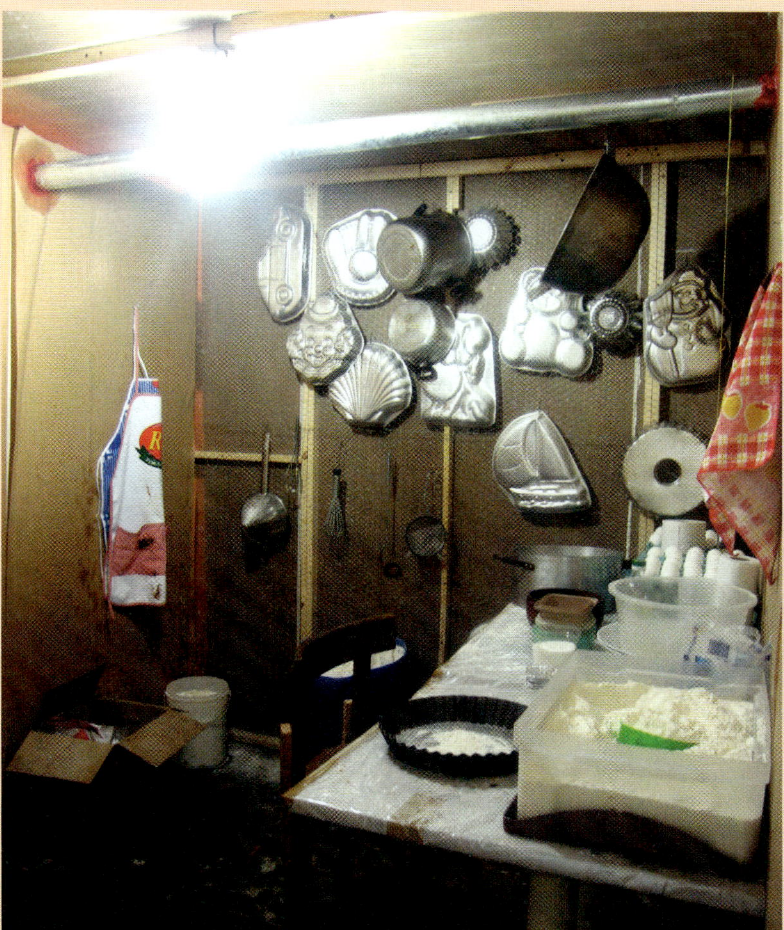

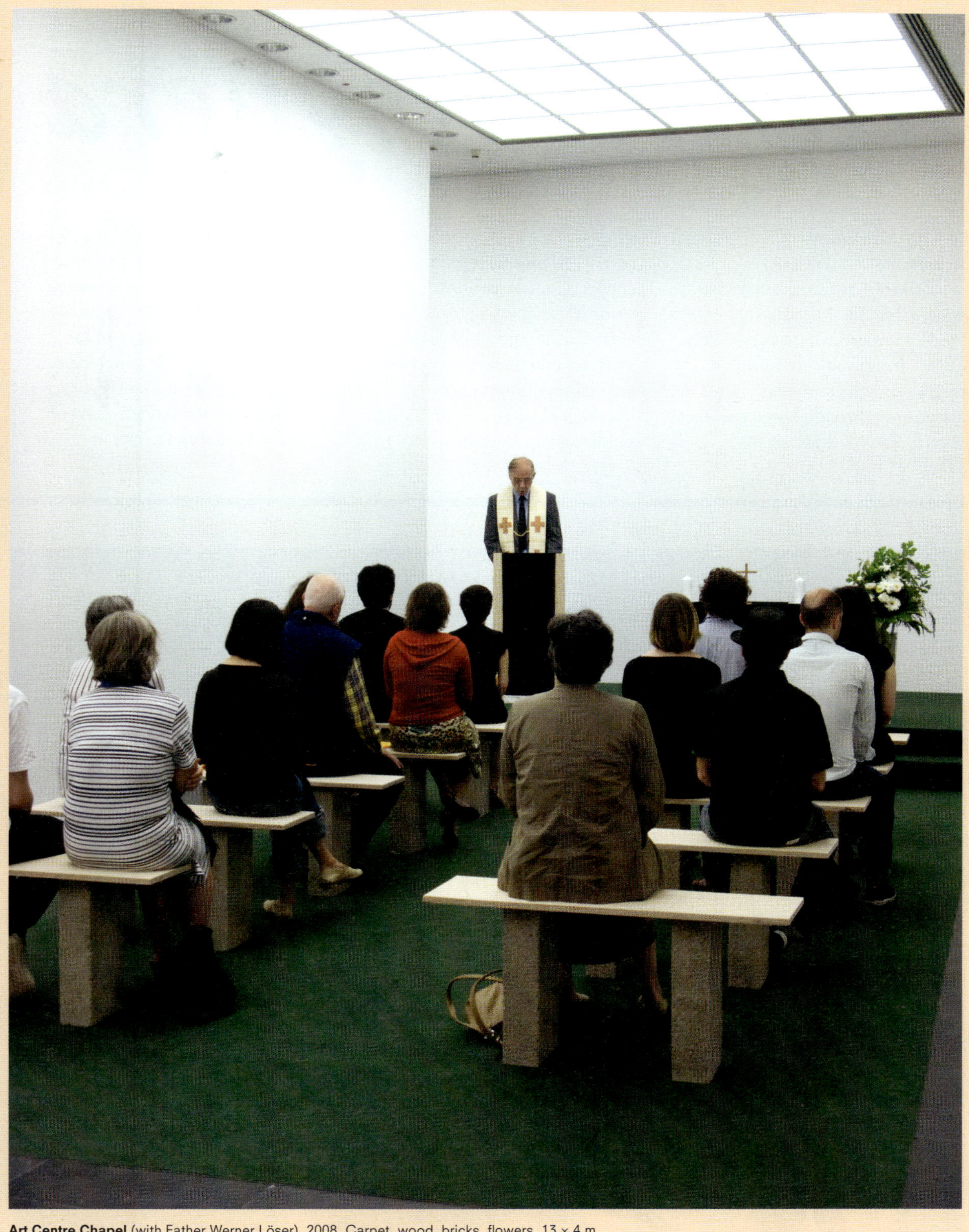

Art Centre Chapel (with Father Werner Löser), 2008. Carpet, wood, bricks, flowers. 13 × 4 m

Function with an unusual degree of ambiguity and humour

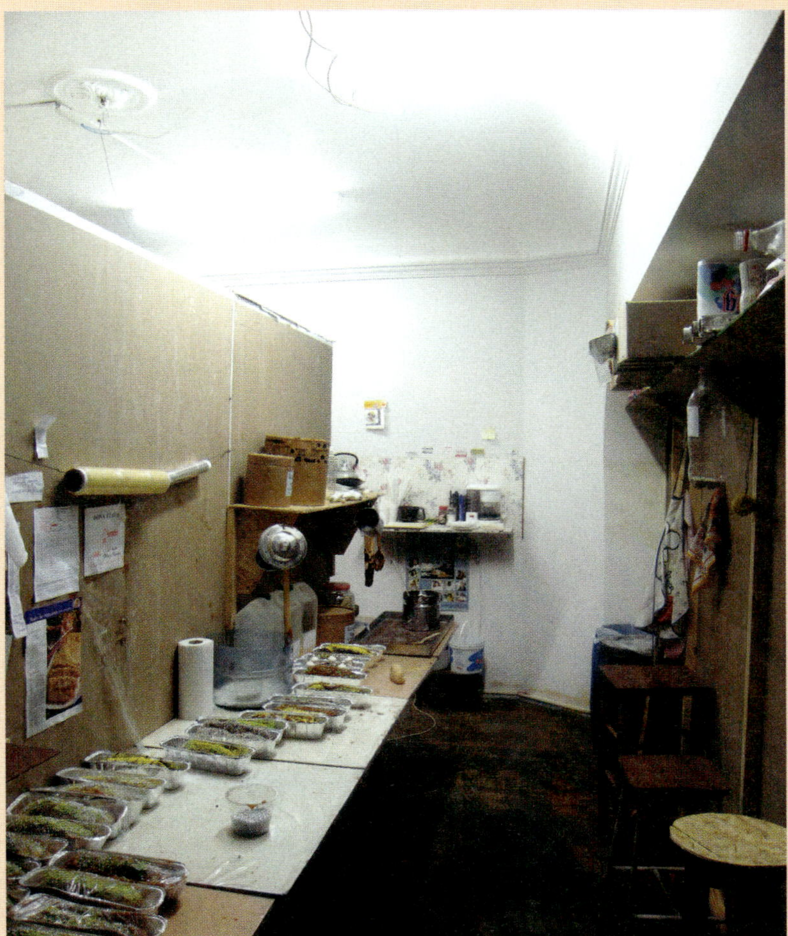

Fabricantes Unidos, 2008. Illegal pudding factory with assembly line created on the first floor of Commercial Galleria La Dulce in the Once neighbourhood, Buenos Aires. 60 × 60 × 60 m

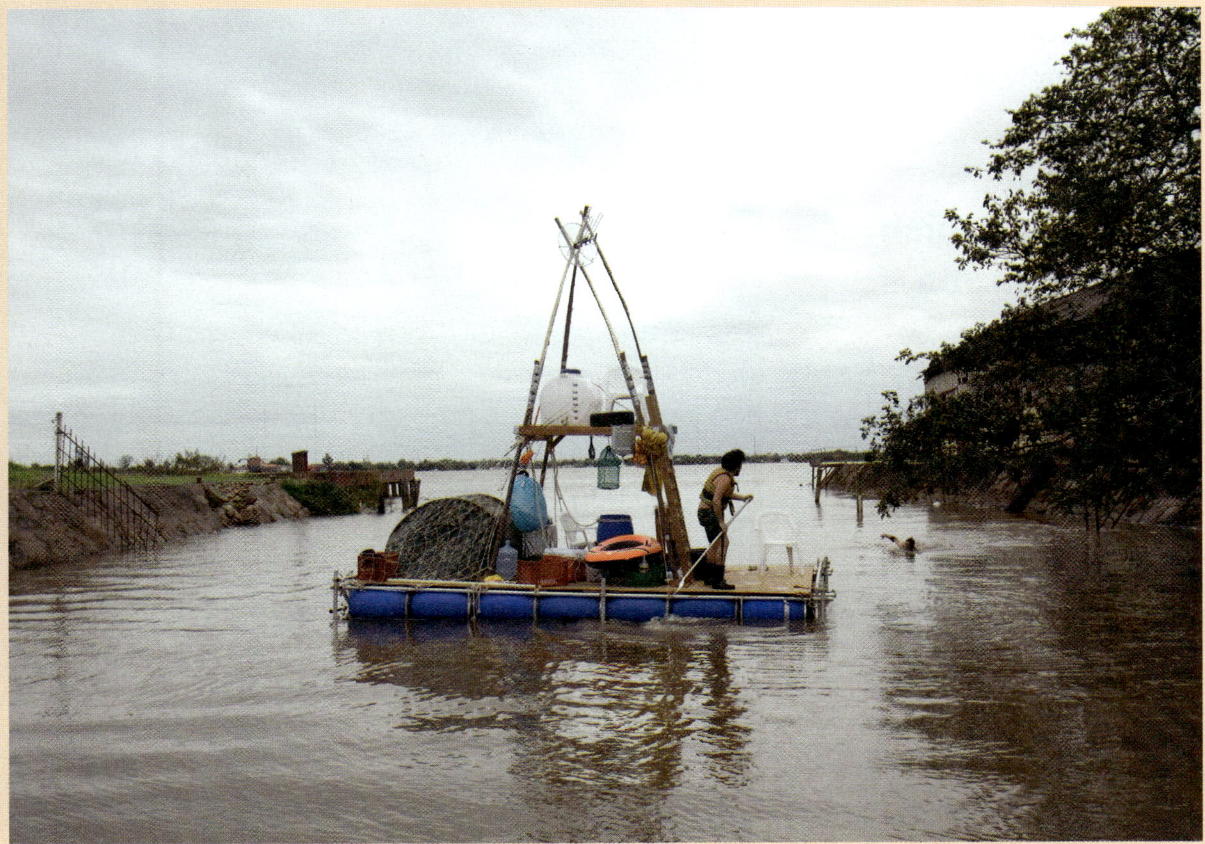

Self–sufficient water purifying station (with biologist Bernardo Lacer), 2009. Performance. Water tank, inverse osmosis water filter, wood, tent, plywood, aluminium structure, kitchen, bananas, plastic pipes, plastic chairs, lifeboat, antenna, chickens, electric generator. 6 × 3 × 4.5 m

Miguel Noguera

Representation without reproduction is the most concise way to describe Miguel Noguera's work. His performances, which he calls 'Ultrashows', are based on the way in which mental images are created through language and speech. Each Ultrashow is nourished by a long process of collecting ideas, notions, expressions and sentences from everyday life. To achieve this, the artist becomes a listening device, paying attention to the ways in which ideas take form in the public sphere — in bar and telephone conversations, instant messaging, television, literature, radio programmes, taxis and buses. All are collected in his impressive archive of notebooks, which operate as a storyboard, illustrating the last ten years of everyday life in the city of Barcelona. From these notebooks he selects and constructs the outline for each Ultrashow, normally a page containing ten to fifteen ideas.

Noguera is by no means a comedian, and even less a purveyor of cynical or ironic subject matter. However, he is fascinated by the way in which the non-spectacular and commonplace, when combined through certain means, open up a brand new world of mental images whose surprising absurdity cannot fail to make you laugh.

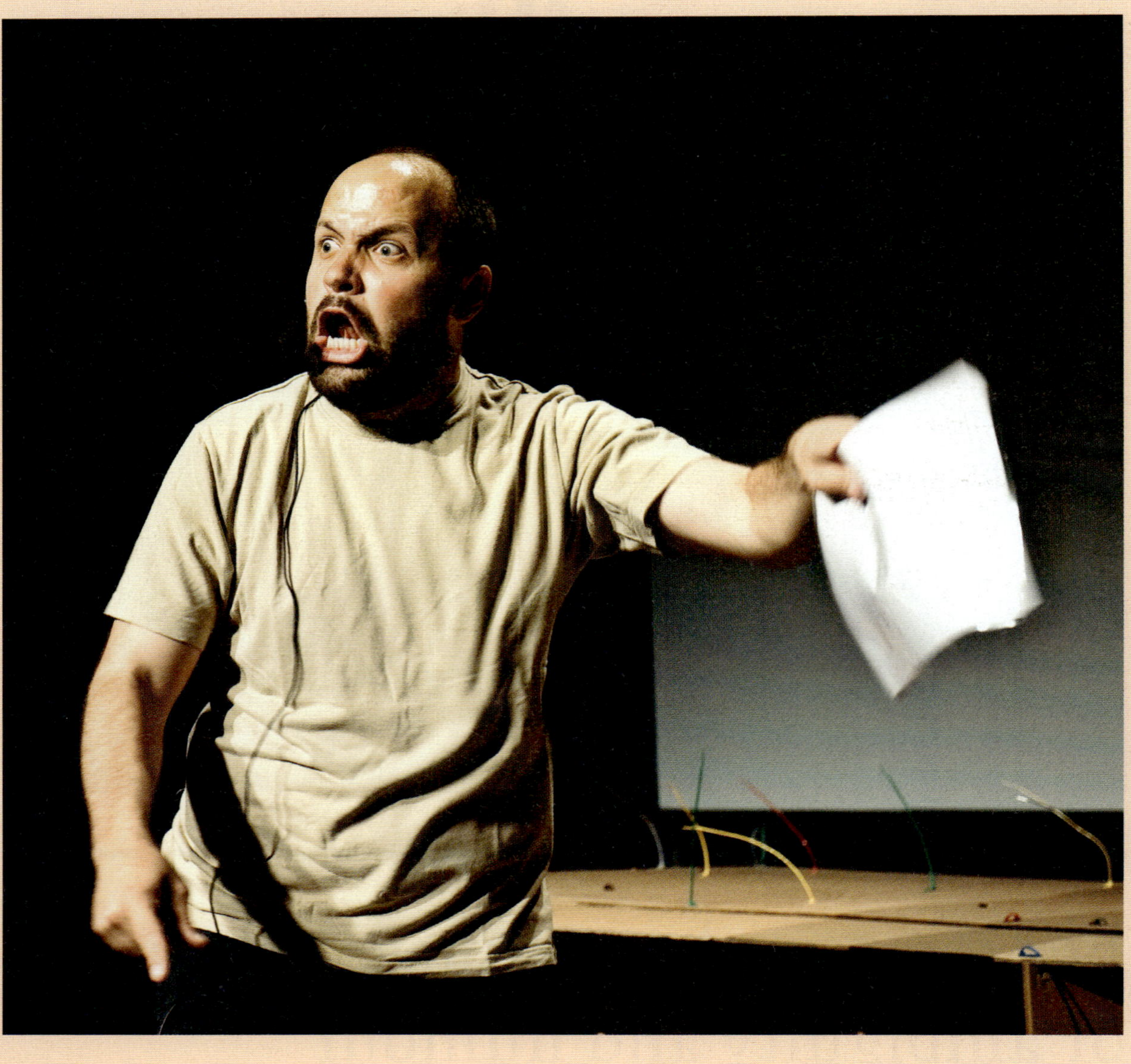

The artist becomes a listening device

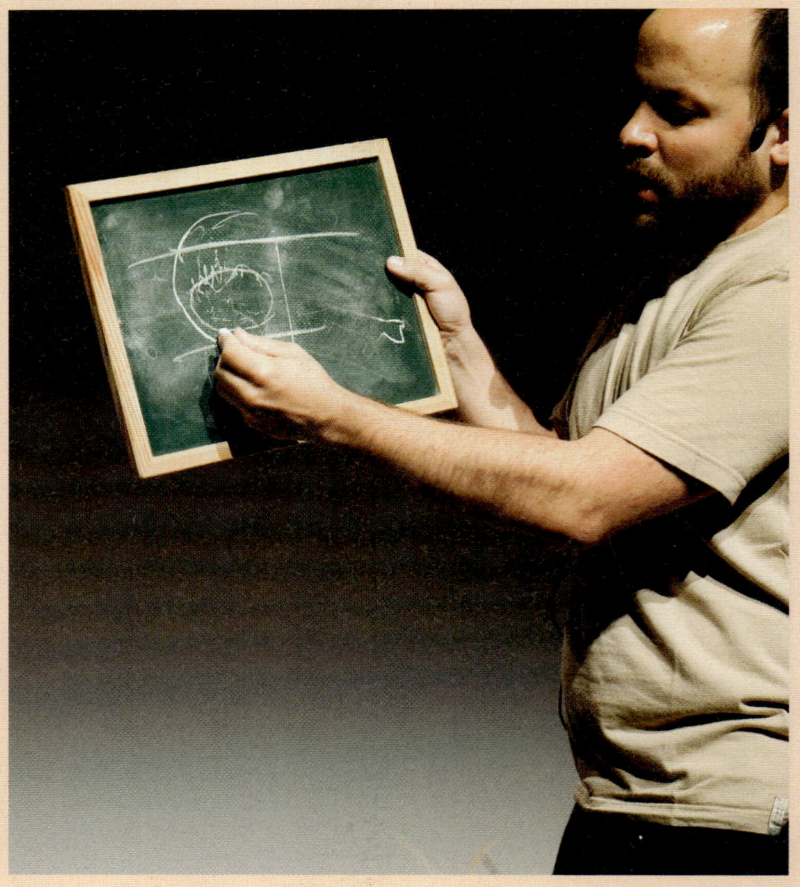

His performances, which he calls 'Ultrashows', are based on the way in which mental images are created through language and speech.

The Ultrashows are very simple productions in which the artist presents a monologue to a small audience with the help of illustrative diagrams. With a sophisticated economy of words, he describes uncomplicated events with great precision. In one performance, for example, he asks the audience to imagine receiving a surprise Christmas gift box of Kiehls, an American brand of natural cosmetics that until recently were not available in Spain.

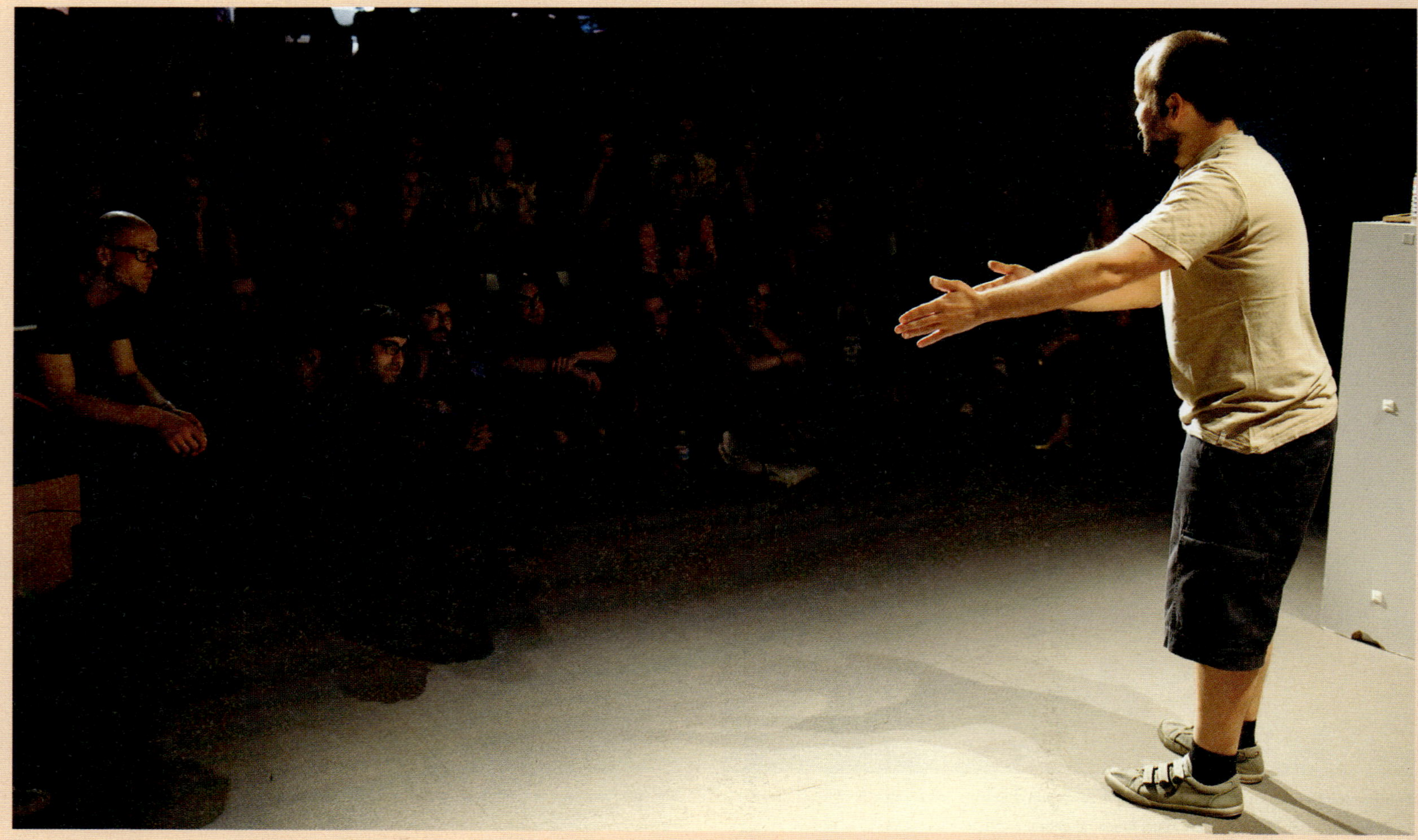

Ultrashow Against Amstetten Monster 1, 2009. Photo documentation of a performance

Illustrating the last ten years of everyday life in Barcelona

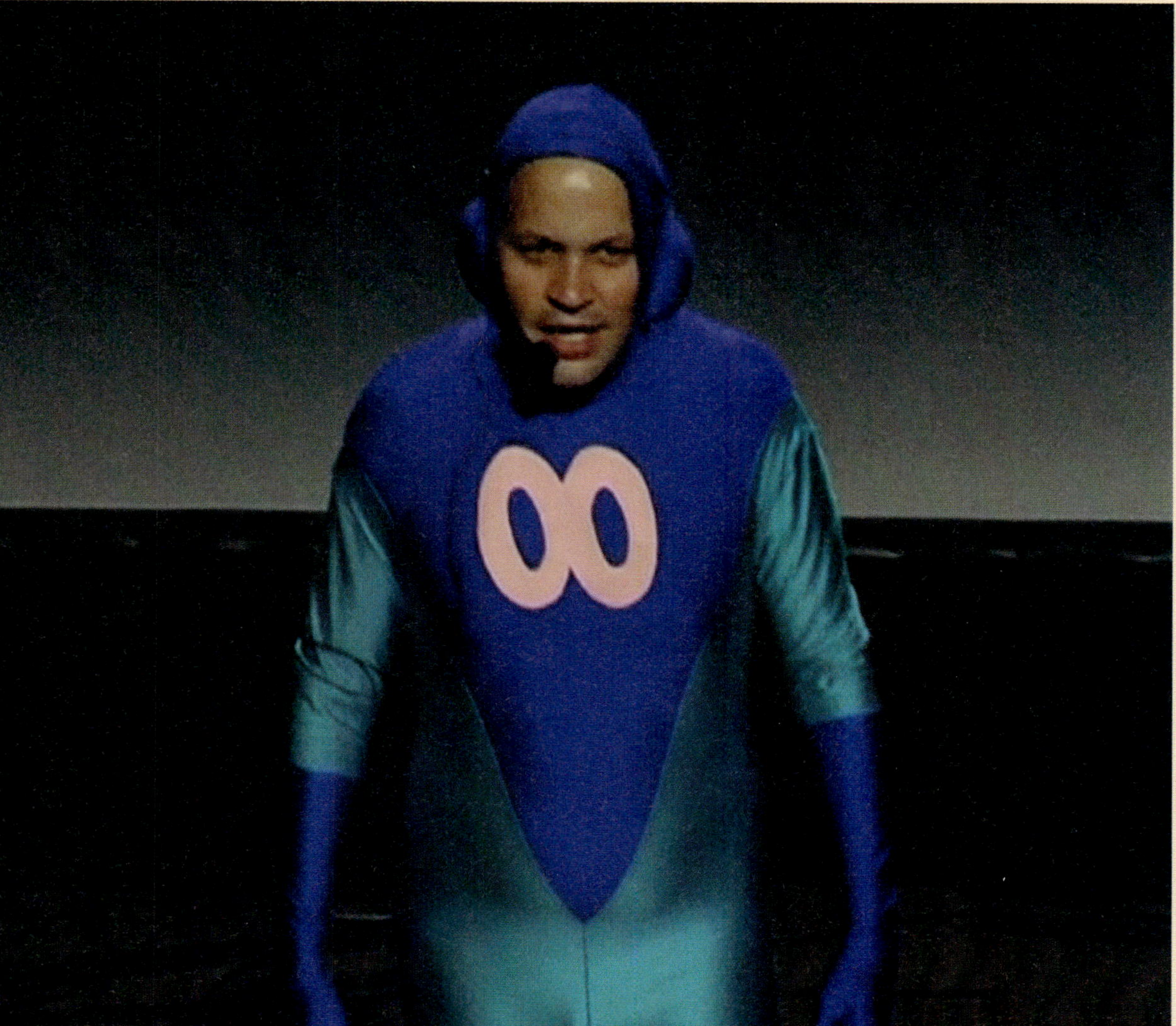

Ultrashow Against Amstetten Monster II, 2009. Video documentation of a performance. 1 hour, 20 min.

Sophisticated economy of words

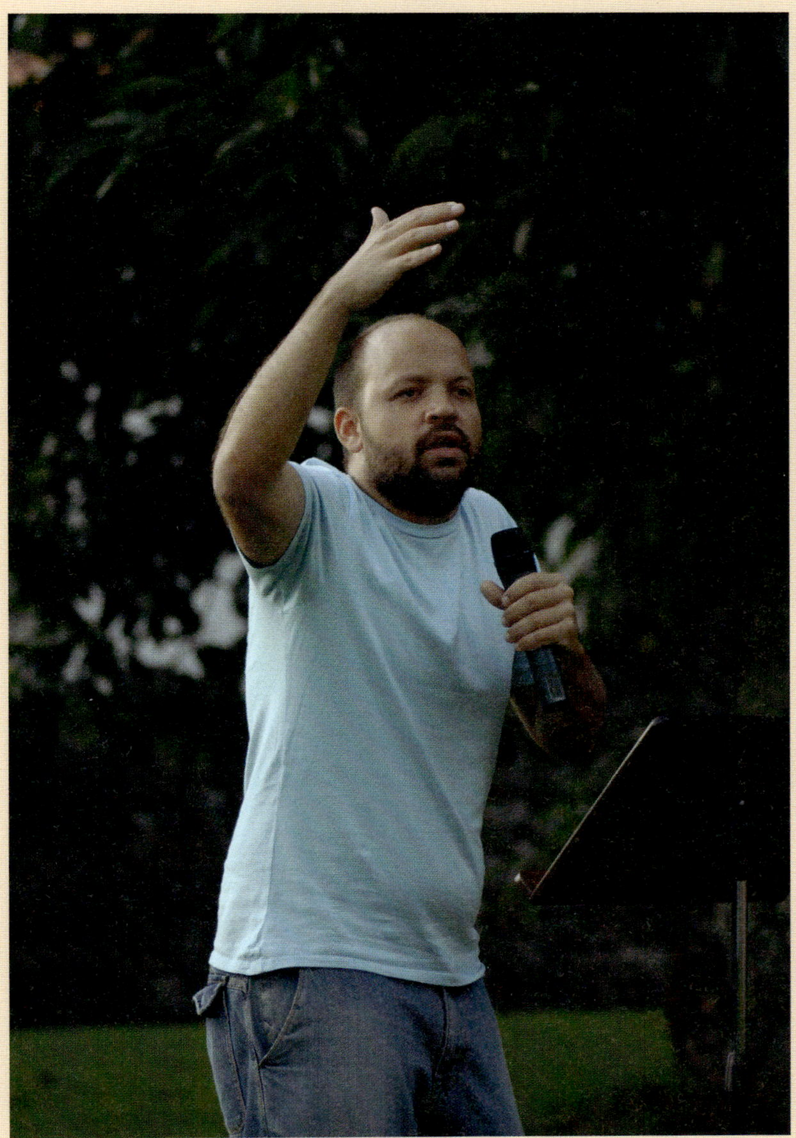

Ultrashow Jesús Mariñas, 2008. Photo documentation of a performance

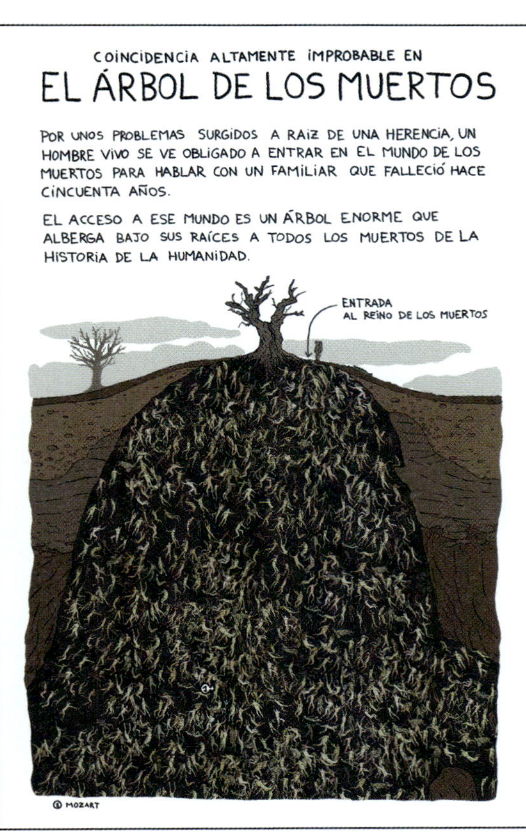

Hervir un Oso (Boiling a Bear) (with Jonathan Millán), 2010. Book, 105 pages. 24 × 17 cm

They arrive, you open up one of the charming glossy boxes, where the products are immersed in a beautiful potpourri of dried leaves and winter flowers, and there, in the middle of the box, you discover a tiny man. The perfect human, rendered on an incredibly small scale, is dead. What do you do? Should you call the police? He is a man, after all, no matter how small, and he is dead, possibly murdered. But would it be too absurd to make the call?

Memory and scale play an important role in Noguera's method of articulating paradoxical situations. The limited number of people in the audience at a specific time and space form a microcosm of the much larger community that has anonymously shaped the language he employs. Through his rational-irrational games, Noguera helps us to understand the place we occupy in the world and how we live. We may laugh, but his performances are not only funny: they also inspire our curiosity and provoke in us the desire for a further reading of the real.

Olivia Plender

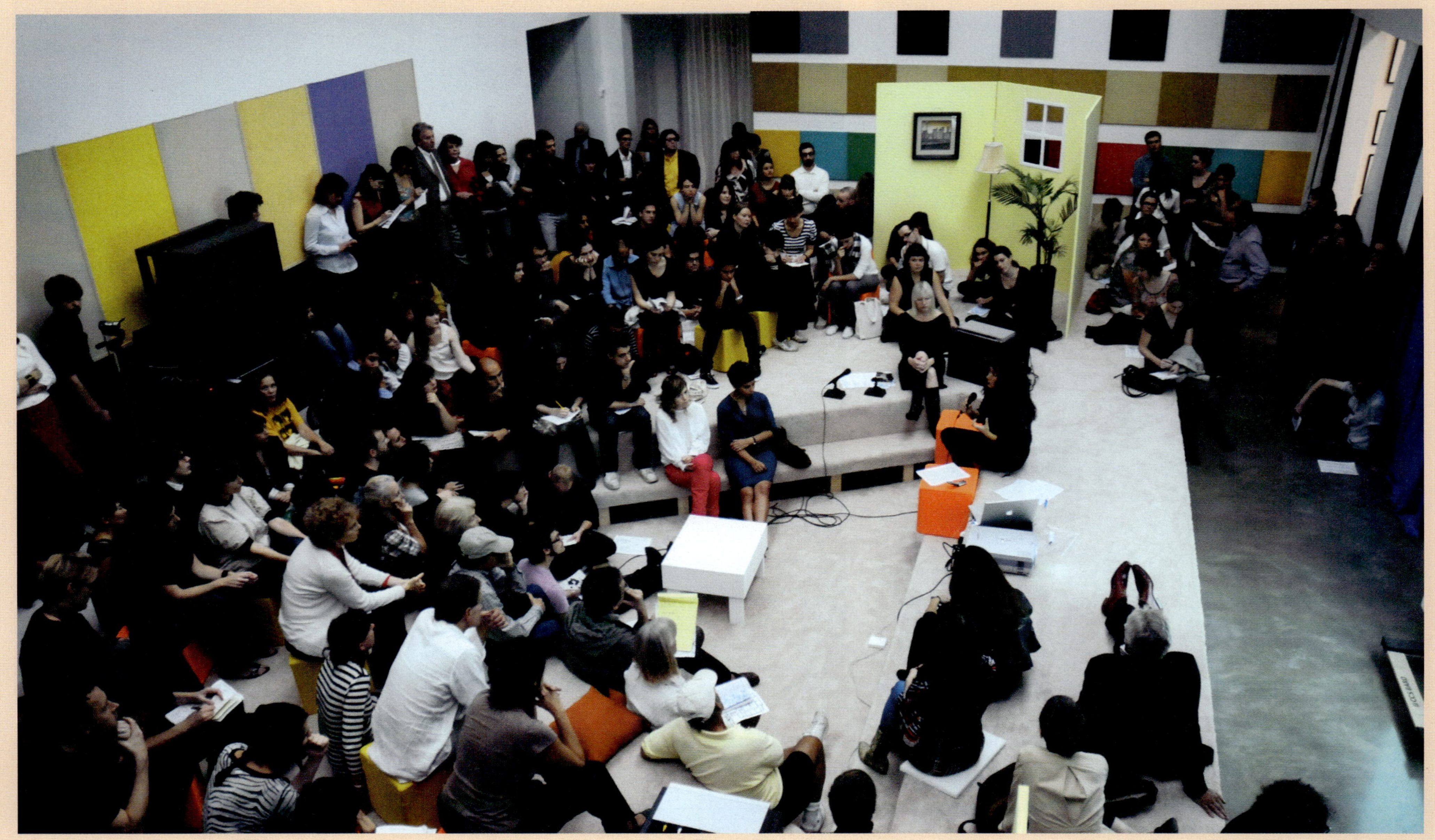

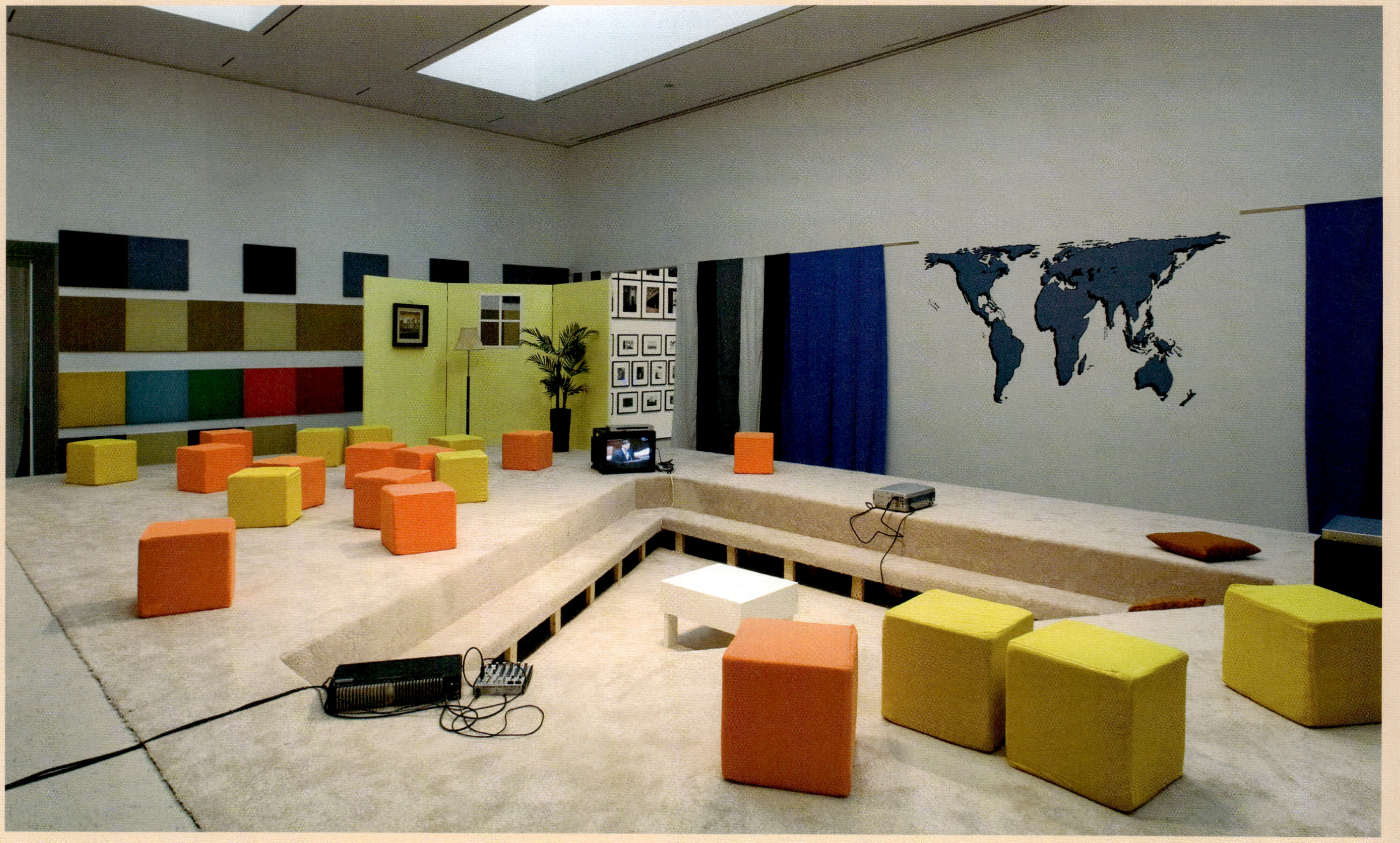

Newsroom, 2008. Site–specific installation. Dimensions variable

Olivia Plender's work successfully reinvents the formats through which art is traditionally displayed and circulated, not only in her overall working temperament but in her very choice of media. Her Wikipedia page reminds us that she is 'best known for a project entitled *The Masterpiece* (2002–present), an epic hand-drawn comic book about the life of a fictional artist in 1960s London'. Referencing the late Övyind Fahlström, Plender uses the comic book as a less predictable, more secular mode of dissemination for her work. Rendered in pencil on paper, the *Masterpiece* series reflects her complex and conflicting approach to Romanticism and the archetypes of art production, telling the sad and mysterious tale of a tortured painter in 1960s London.

However just as she chooses the comic as a format, she grapples with exhibitions themselves as a medium, using museological reconstructions and set designs as her artistic means. Her 2007 exhibition *Information, Education, Entertainment* , whose title referred to a BBC maxim, emulated a TV studio as a setting. But the idea was to evoke the mass media not so much as a topic and an ambience, but as a foil through which to revisit the figure of the artist, both in mainstream representation and in the self-understanding of the professional field itself (where ideas of the

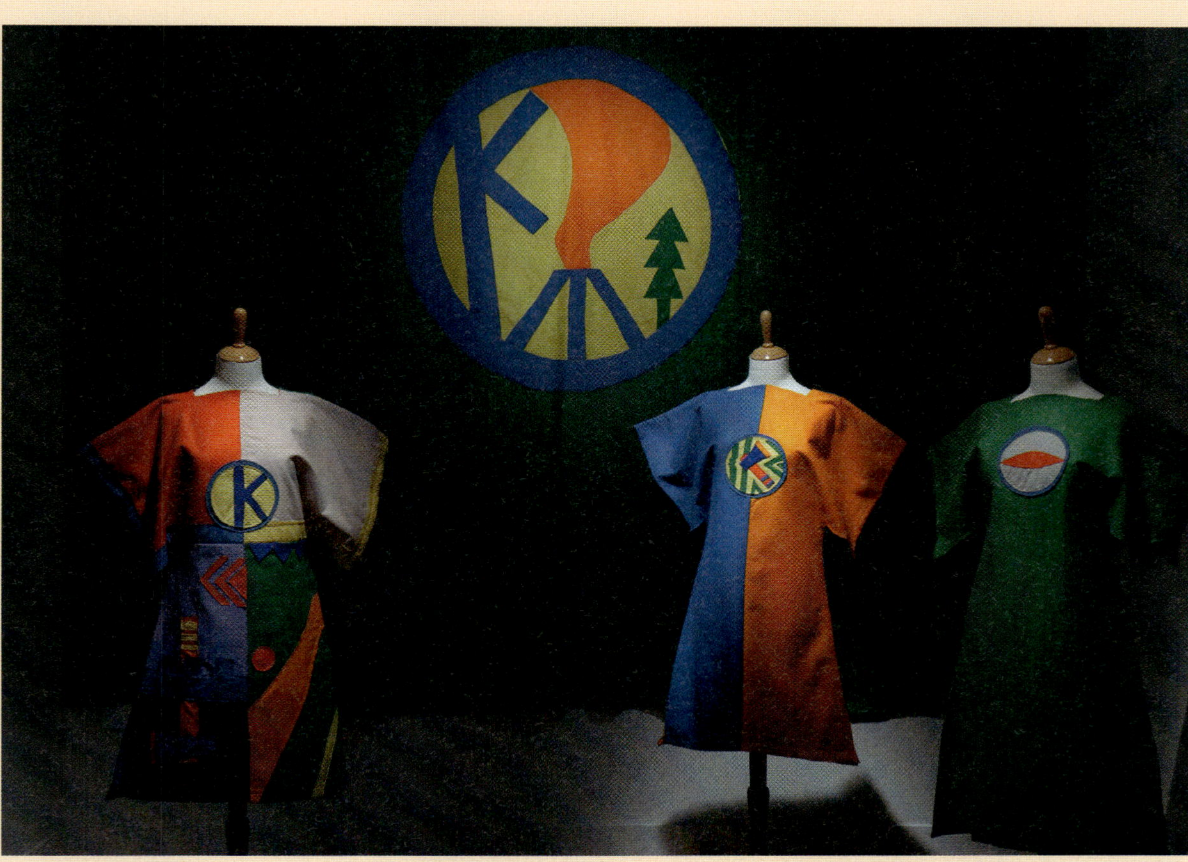

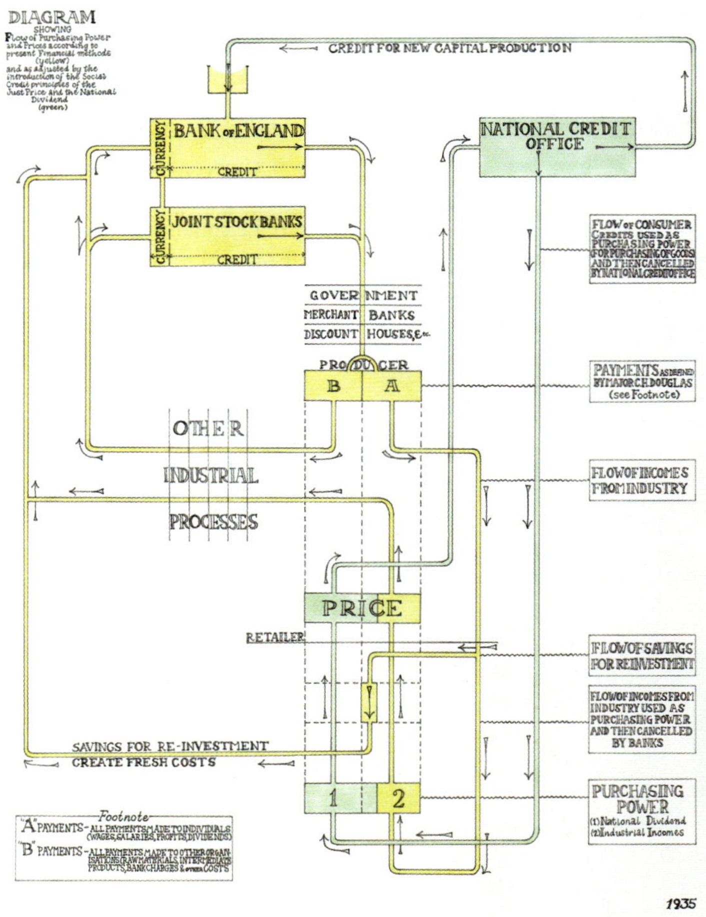

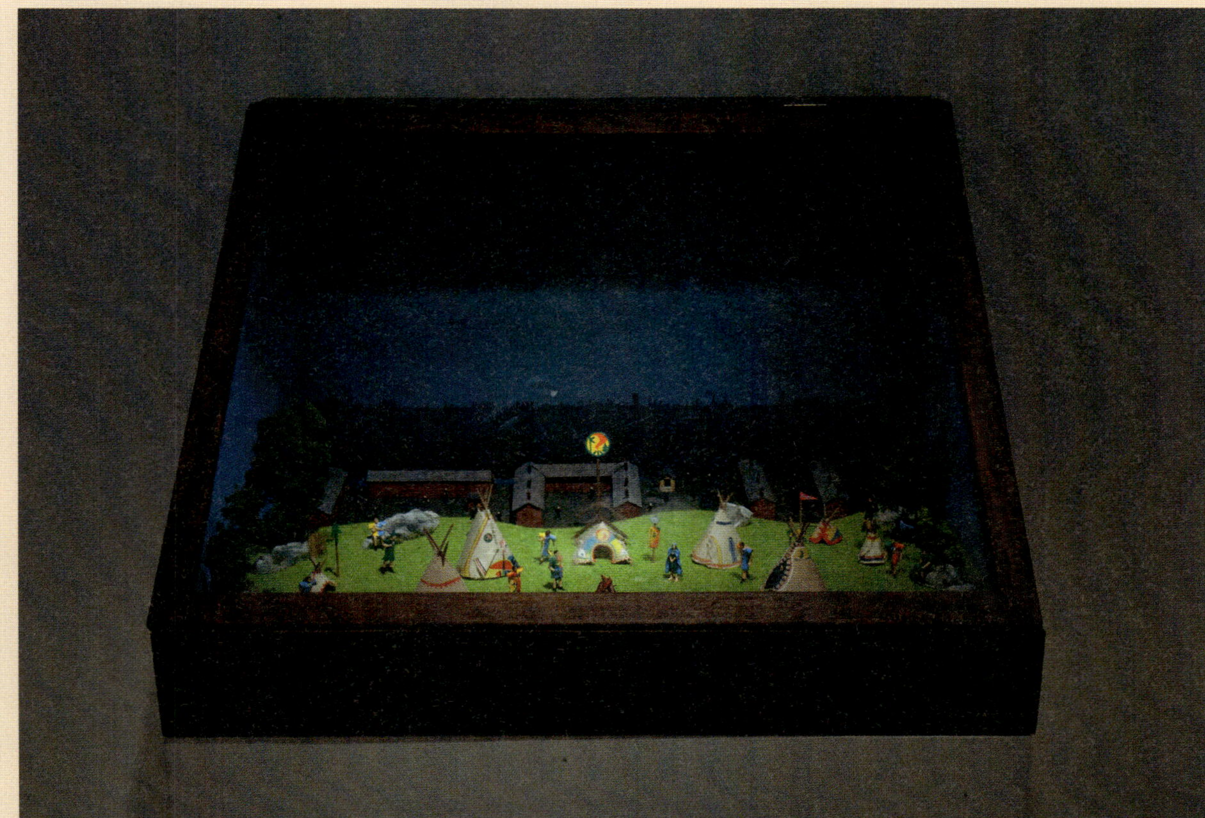

Machine Shall be the Slave of Man, but We Will Not Slave for the Machine, 2009. Mixed–media installation including diorama, fabric costumes, banner, work station, video, ink on paper drawing. Dimensions variable

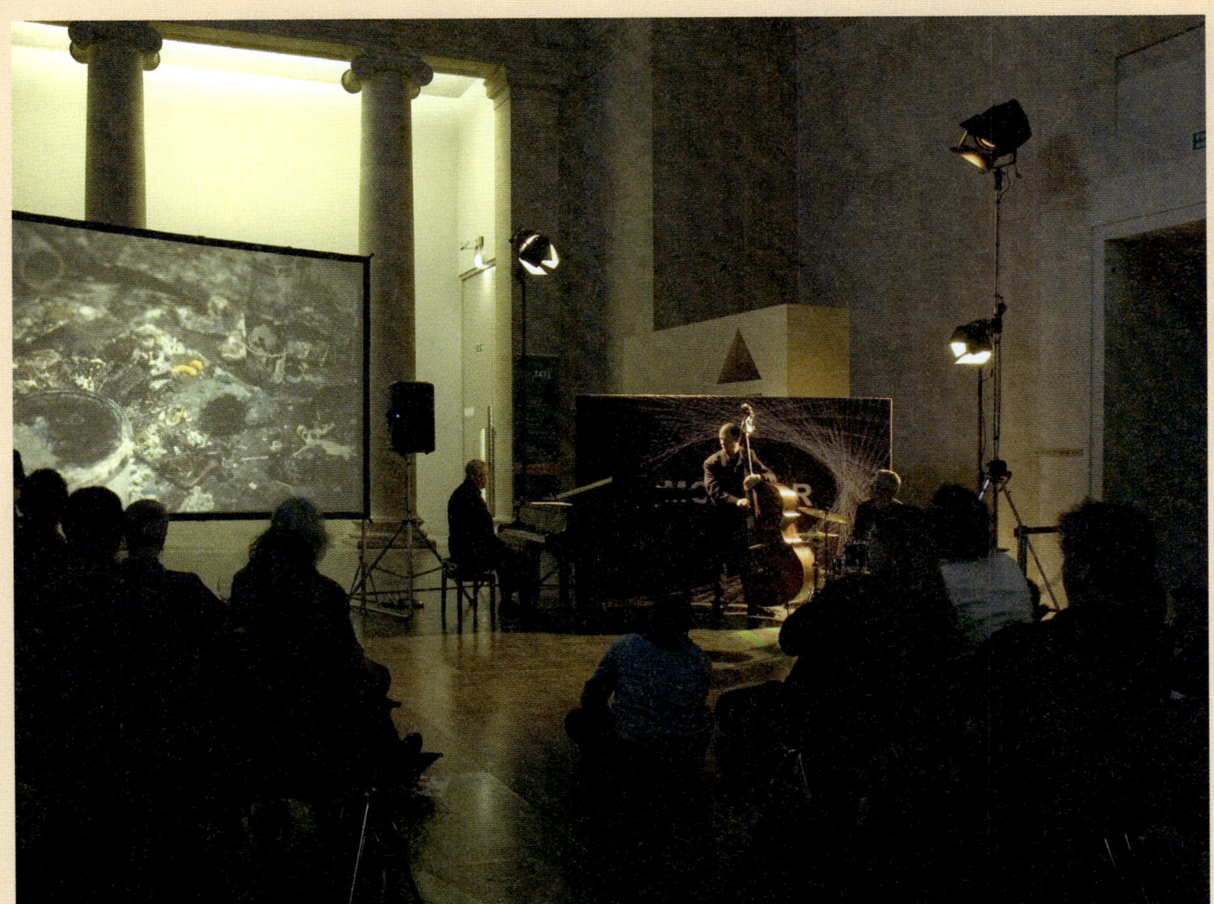

Monitor, 2006. Performance. Tate Triennial, Tate Britain, London

Plender grapples with exhibitions themselves as a medium

informative, educational and entertaining are prevalent indeed). Similarly, a previous exhibition, 'The Medium and Daybreak', held in Manchester in 2005, shrewdly addressed the overlaps between art production and spiritualism, conspiracy and the occult. Meanwhile, a project from 2008 commissioned for the show 'The Greenroom: Reconsidering the Documentary and Contemporary Art' was, in curator Maria Lind's words, a 'project-in-progress' which continued developing throughout the exhibition period.

Plender's installation formed the very nucleus of the exhibition, creating a stage for seminars, lectures, screenings, performances and panels. This setting not only was visually consummate but also effortlessly and smoothly bestowed a more reflexive spin on the show as a whole without recourse to unnecessary theory-mongering. By highlighting in a deadpan manner an unusual projector at the same time as the film it projected, for example, Plender achieved her aim simply with a scenographic nod or two.

Michael Portnoy

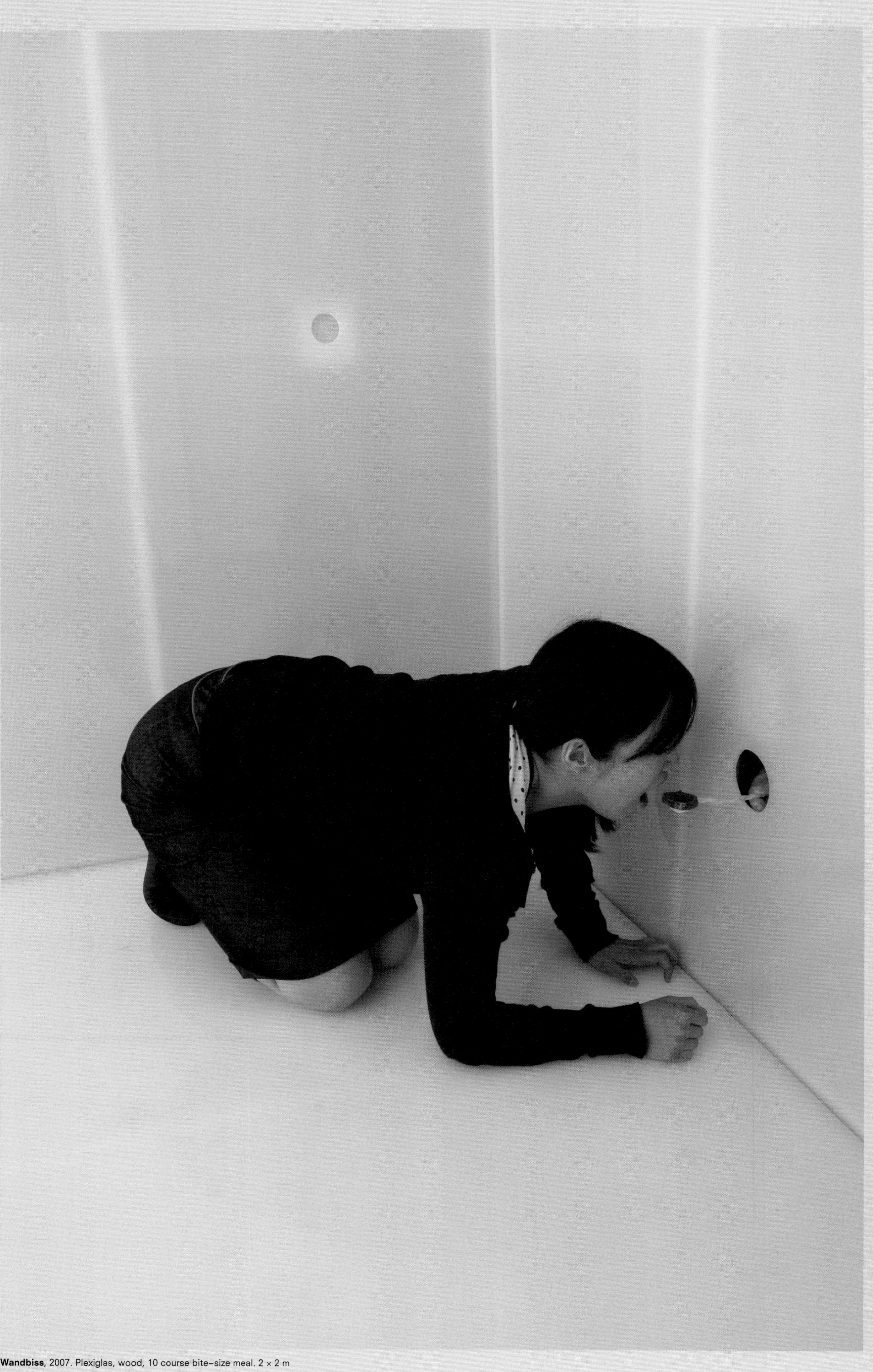

Wandbiss, 2007. Plexiglas, wood, 10 course bite–size meal. 2 × 2 m

Relational Stalinism

Michael Portnoy works not only
as an artist but also as a
choreographer and a musician,
often devising unexpected places
where his various disciplines can
meet. He often creates
collaborative performances, such
as in *The K Sound* (2006), where
a series of experimental jokes
were enacted by a diverse cast of
performers, dancers and actors in
tightly choreographed scenes.

In the *Dudion Levers*
(2008), he collaborated with
engineer and amateur malacologist
Oliver Sudden to devise *The
Instrument*, which comprises two
elements: a 'Microphone' (in
the form of a giant pair of walnut
clogs, which ascend into a kind
of scimitar), and a 'Cooker'.
Portnoy chooses three objects and
places them inside the Cooker to
form the basis of a new work, then
proceeds to sing about this project
into the Microphone. In the artist's
words, the apparatus trans-
figures his song into a medley of
'orchestral instruments,
synthesizers, drums, guitars (based
on the pitch, intonation and many
other variables) and this song
is inscribed upon the assemblage
of objects in mother of pearl
graphic notation'.

Portnoy likes to call his
take on interaction with the
audience 'Relational Stalinism':
participation without the
populism, involvement without
the moral double standards. In
sum, the fashionable promise that
an artwork might offer a
democratic magic, transforming
inter-relational codes into
something nicer, is abandoned in
favour of a clarification of the
artist's imperious role as producer
and performer vis à vis the
spectators. In *Wandbiss* (2007),
patrons were on their knees within
a cramped space, craning and
contorting as they tried to bite
morsels of haute cuisine served
on edible skewers erratically
protruding from the walls. On
another occasion (*Casino Ilinx*,
2008), participants, who were
hand-picked exclusively by the
artist, engaged in vertiginous
games within a casino ambience
involving terrifying sculptural
props made of engraved sheep
bones, quilted maple veneer,
vibrant industrial felt and
lacquered Brahmin-Glagolitic
fonts. In *Filzzungeungewiss*
(2008) Portnoy continuously

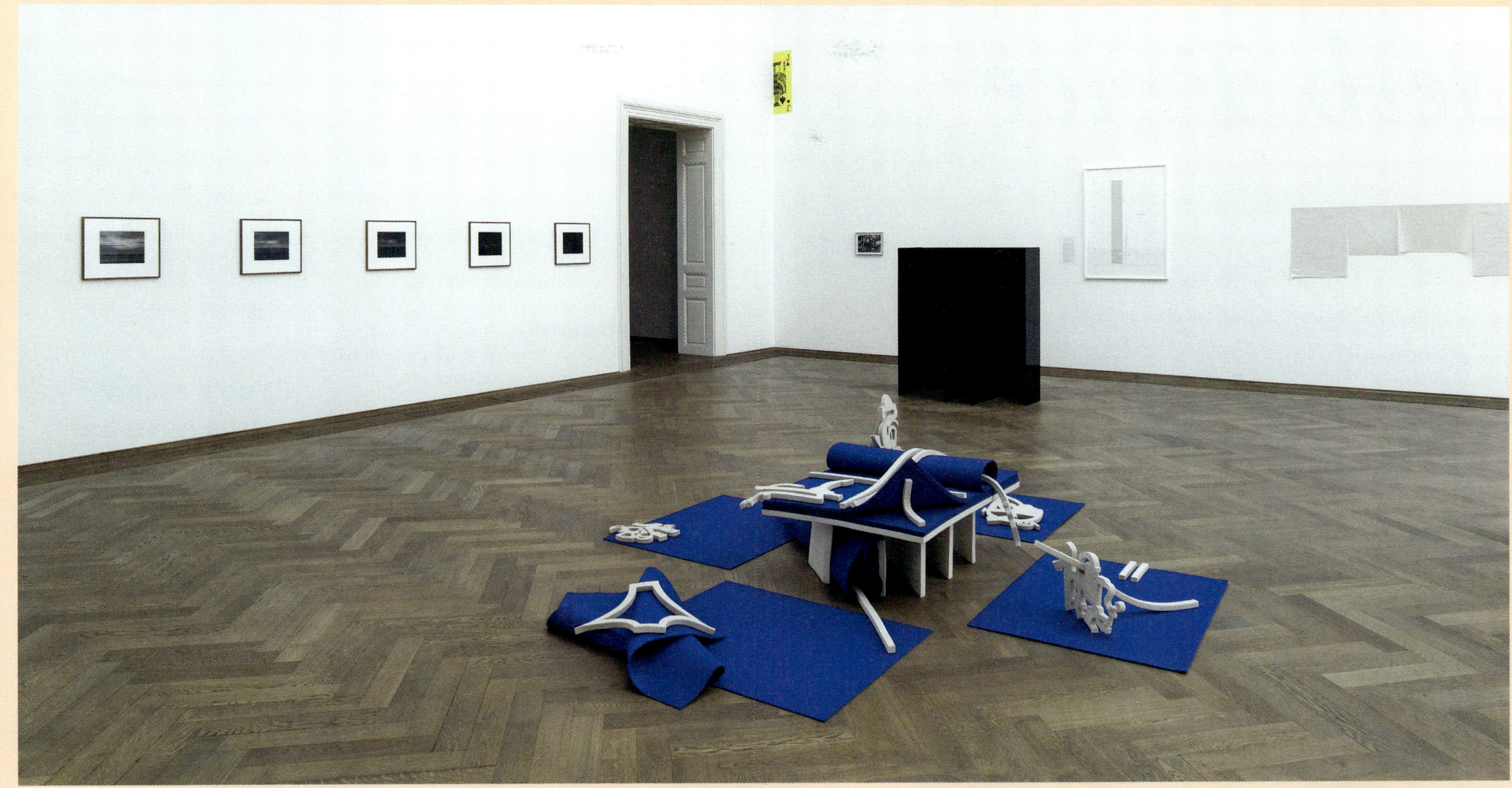

Filzzungeungewiss, 2008. Felt. 34 × 275 × 284 cm

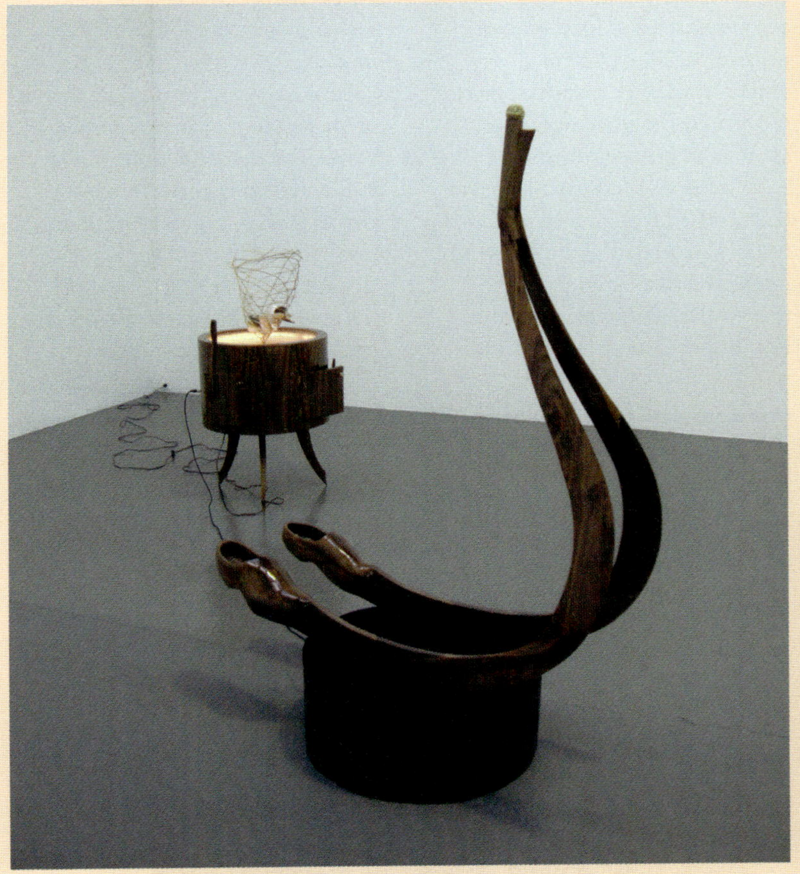

The Instrument, 2008. Microphone, American black walnut, electronics. 178 × 81 × 152 cm. **Microphone**, 2008. American black walnut, electronics. 178 × 81 × 152 cm. **Cooker**, 2008. American black walnut, copper, gold leaf, felt, mother–of–pearl shells, machinery, electronics. 102 × 117 × 102 cm

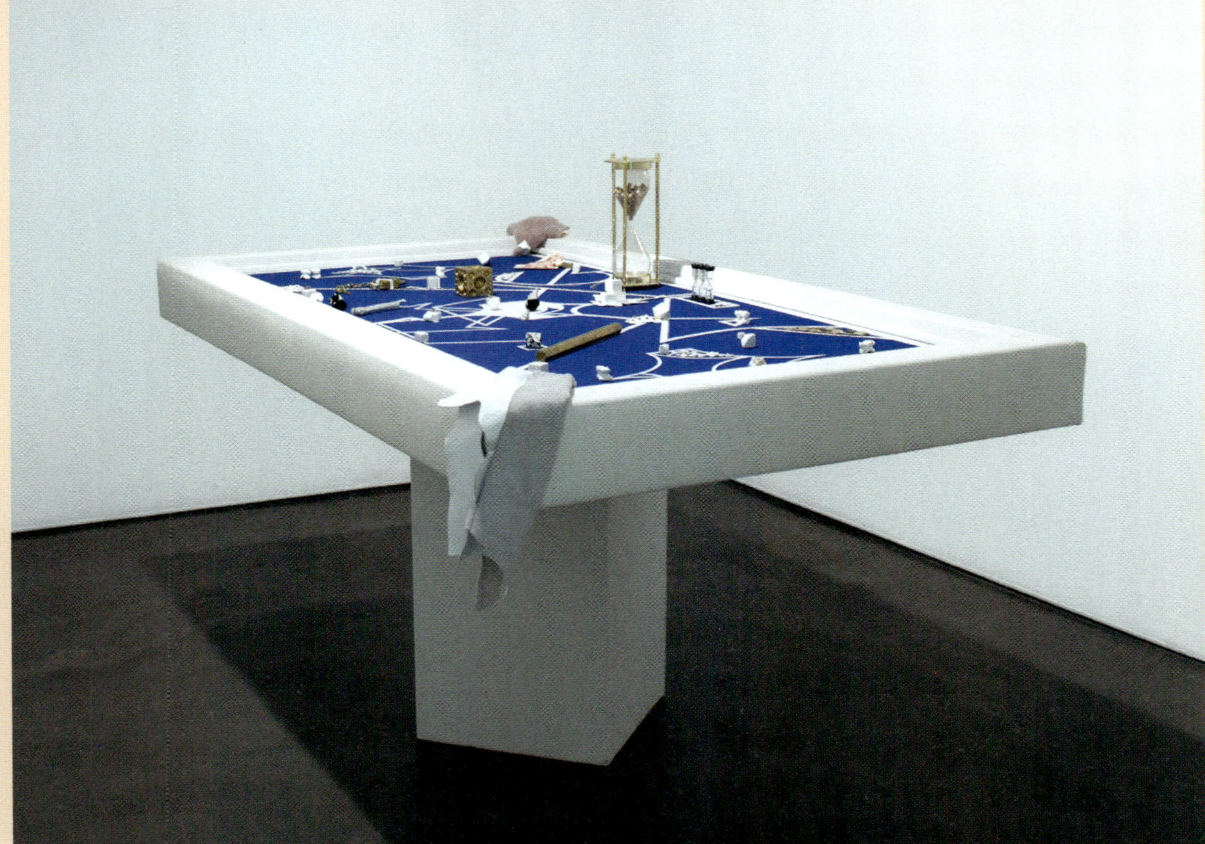

Talus, 2007. Dye sublimated felt, wood, brass, silver, engraved sheep ankle bones, painted and burnt die, mother–of–pearl shells, leather, 50 kapeek notes. 90 × 107 × 198 cm

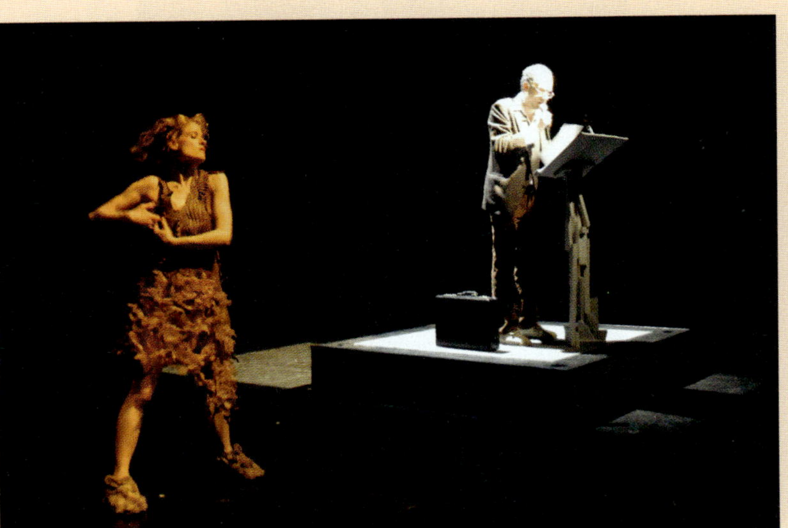

The K Sound, 2006. Performance

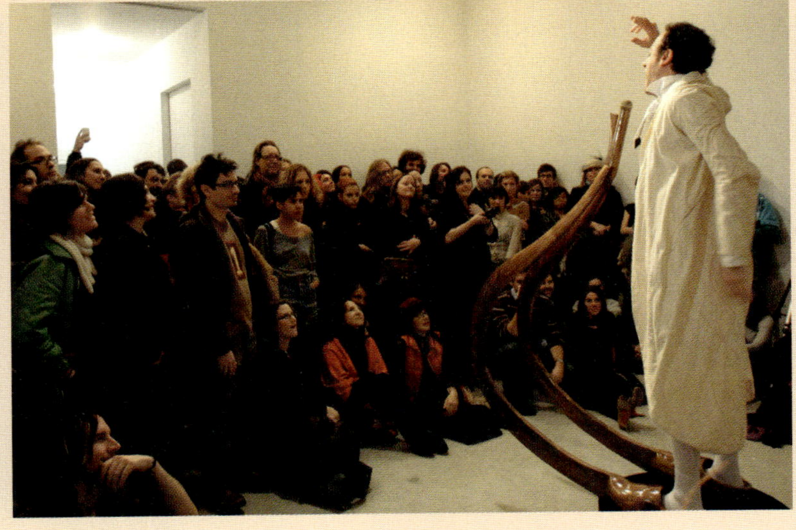

The Dudion Levers, 2008. Performance

reinvented the complicated rules as he went along: 'Drop the two. Now hold it. Necessary's are in-between. 10 on the table. Re-release the table to complete.' In *A Seminar in Sublingual Carnage — The 33 Holdmusic Variations* (2008), unsuspecting figures of the Art Review Power 100 and CEOs of waste management companies were called up before a live audience and fed elaborate stories connecting the two industries then told to hold for seveal minutes while Portnoy sang smooth jazz 'hold' music.

Seth Price

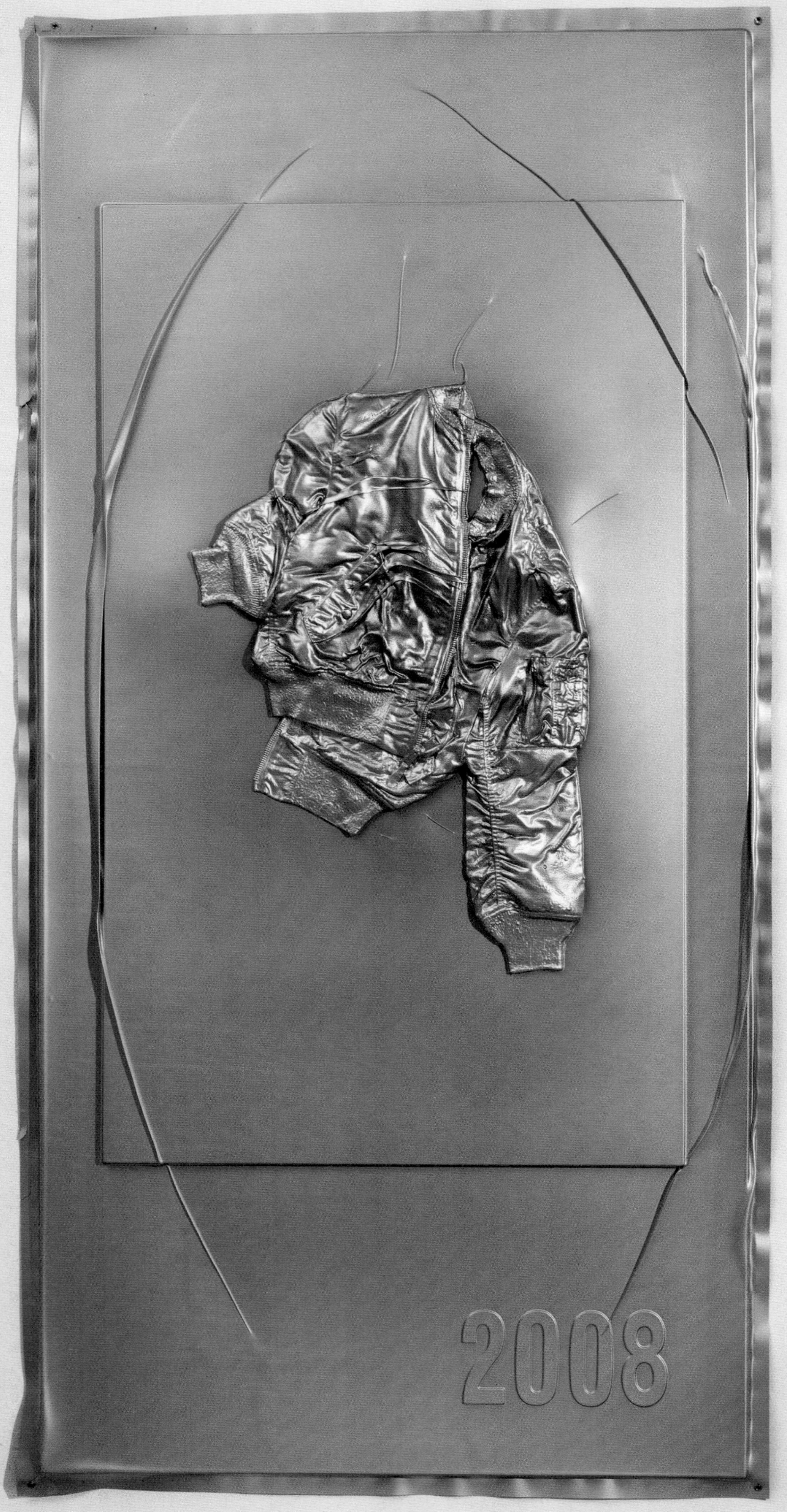

Seth Price's multivalent artistic practice fluctuates between video, installation, sculpture, painting, music, internet projects, performance lectures and writing. Underlying these disparate efforts is an interest in various modes of production and the ways in which 'products' — whether art or consumer objects — accrue multiple meanings through distinct mechanisms of valuation and distribution. Price creates his works using found and pirated elements, unearthed primarily by trawling the unfathomable depths of the internet. His chosen materials contain references to popular culture and well-known artworks of the not-so-distant past. He then uses digital tools to transform the appropriated material into something entirely different. The final works alternate between those that are available for free on the internet (videos, music compilations and writings), to those that may surface in a mass-consumer market for a modest price (a packaged CD or vinyl record), to expensive objects specifically designed for gallery spaces and private collections.

Price's recent works have been crafted from materials more usually associated with industrial mass production and packaging than with traditional art media. For instance, some have been made out of long sheaths of transparent Mylar, on to which Price has printed fragments of barely recognizable images, whose

> **Price's recent works have been crafted from materials more associated with industrial mass production and packaging than with traditional art media**

references range from distressing media images to snippets of famous works from art history. Another series comprises plastic vacuum-sealed forms (made out of high-impact polystyrene) hang in the gallery like wall reliefs. The shapes of the cast items range from vintage bomber jackets and knots of ropes to isolated body parts. In these works, a now rather old-fashioned material used for packaging is elevated to an artwork, in which the material characteristics become part of the work's commentary.

Untitled, 2008. Vacuum-formed high impact polystyrene. 244 × 122 cm

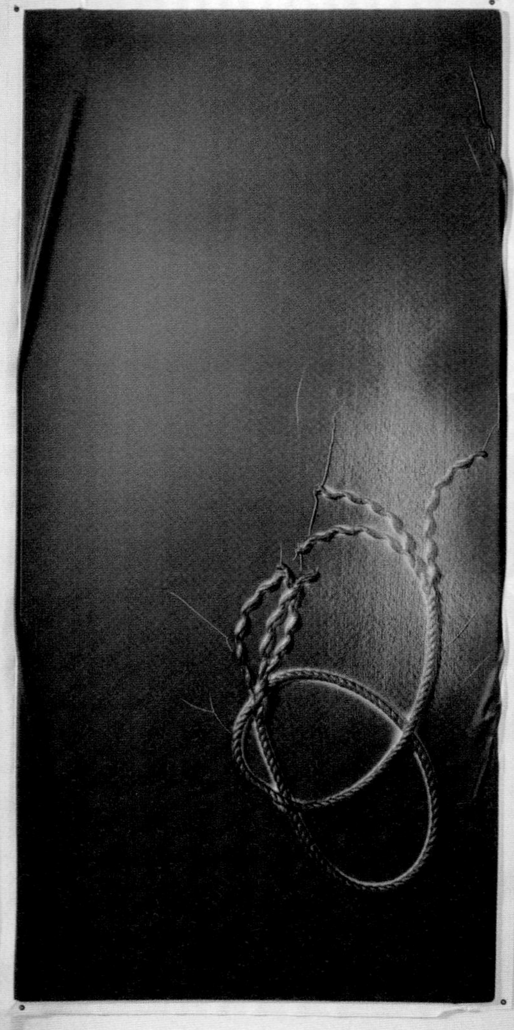

Untitled, 2009. UV-cured inkjet on high-impact polystyrene vacuum-formed over ropes. 244 × 122 cm

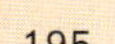

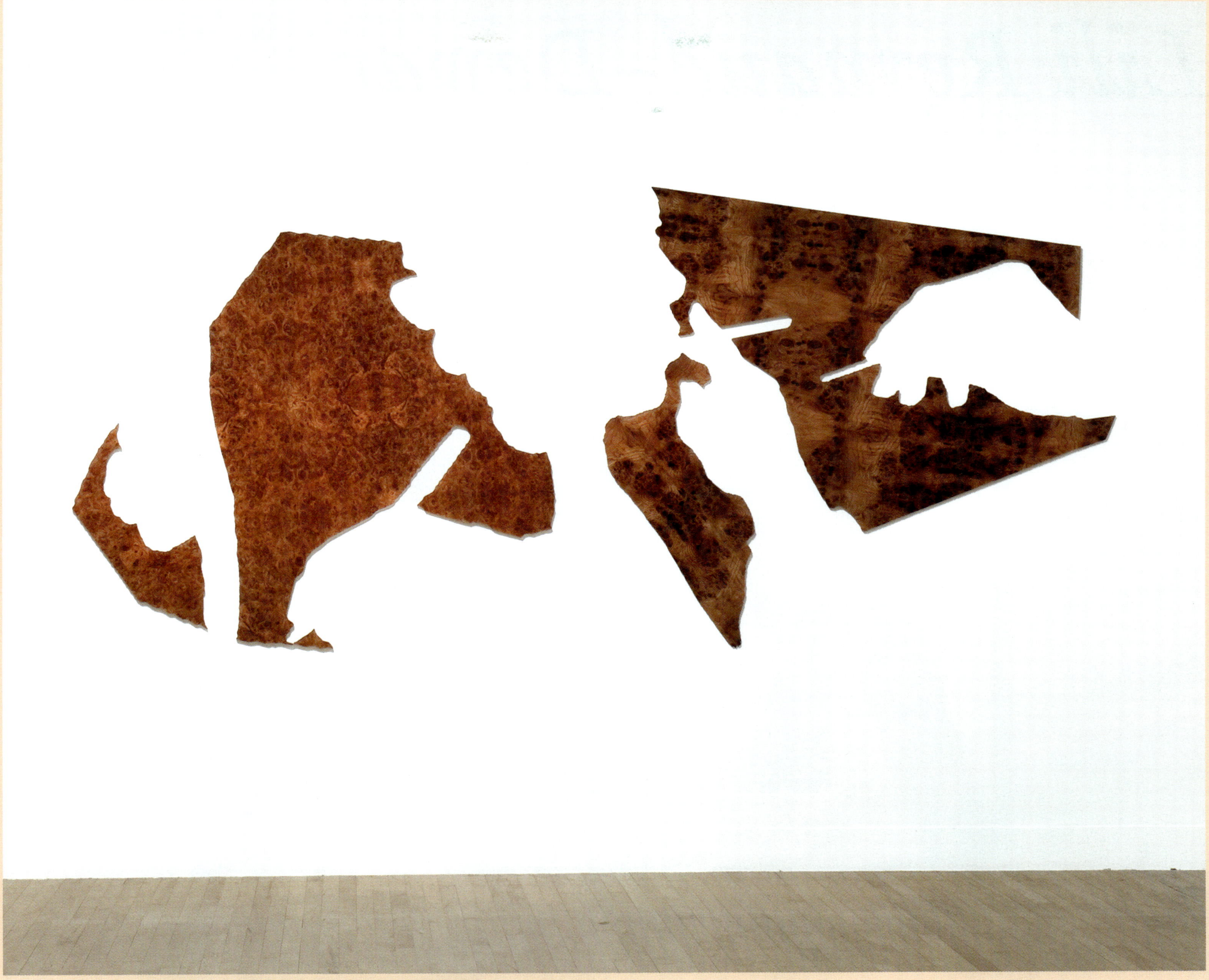

Untitled, 2008. Burled Carpathian elm, burled olive ash, diamond acrylic. 4 parts. Overall 165 × 457 cm

Reflexive model

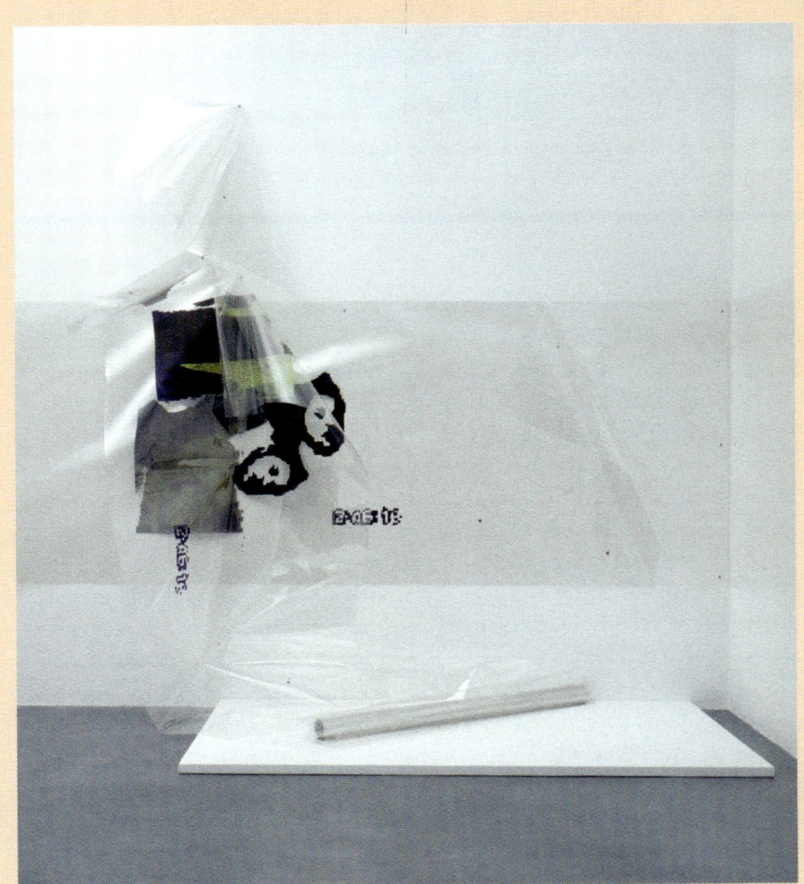

Hostage Video Still, 2006. Sign ink on polyester film, eyelets. Dimensions variable

By contrast, the *Silhouette* series, begun in 2008, exudes an austere elegance. These wall-bound works, which are made from luxurious wood-veneer panels covered in acrylic plastic, exist in a middle realm between painting and sculpture. Reversing the typical figure-ground relationship, the silhouettes of the representational imagery are described by the negative white spaces outlined by the object. The images depict basic human interactions, such as one person lighting another's cigarette, one person feeding another, two people toasting glasses or kissing. This tactic of optical reversal is also utilized in *Untitled* (2008), a series Price refers to as the 'Gold Keys'. These works were derived from a found internet gesture of one hand dropping a key into another and are executed in an industrial material, Dibond, which is generally used for mounting photographs.

In both cases, instantly recognizable forms have been generated by image files downloaded from the internet and then transformed into more streamlined, abstracted, yet physical versions of an earlier data set. Both series also focus on an instance of social exchange or communication. And, although the results look mass-produced, they are in fact unique, playing with notions of originality and origin. Most significant is the role of the viewer in these works. Price creates a situation that necessitates the viewer's own projection of meaning on to the work in order for any recognizable image to coalesce. The subject matter is paradoxically both absent and present: the physical fragments placed on the walls delimit a missing presence that the eye can only discern when 'not seeing' the physical structure on the wall.

Price's reflexive model of art-making is indicative of conditions today wherein notions of 'value' and 'meaning' circulating through systems of art and culture are continually in flux and redefined by new possibilities enabled by digital technologies and the internet. Destabilizing our understanding of what constitutes the original and the copy, the real and the virtual, Price's works perpetually manipulate that which

Destabilizing our understanding of what constitutes the original and the copy, the real and the virtual, Price's works perpetually manipulate that which already exists

already exists, and it is through his interactions with the past that his works start to articulate new relations for the future between consumption, production and distribution.

Lili Reynaud-Dewar

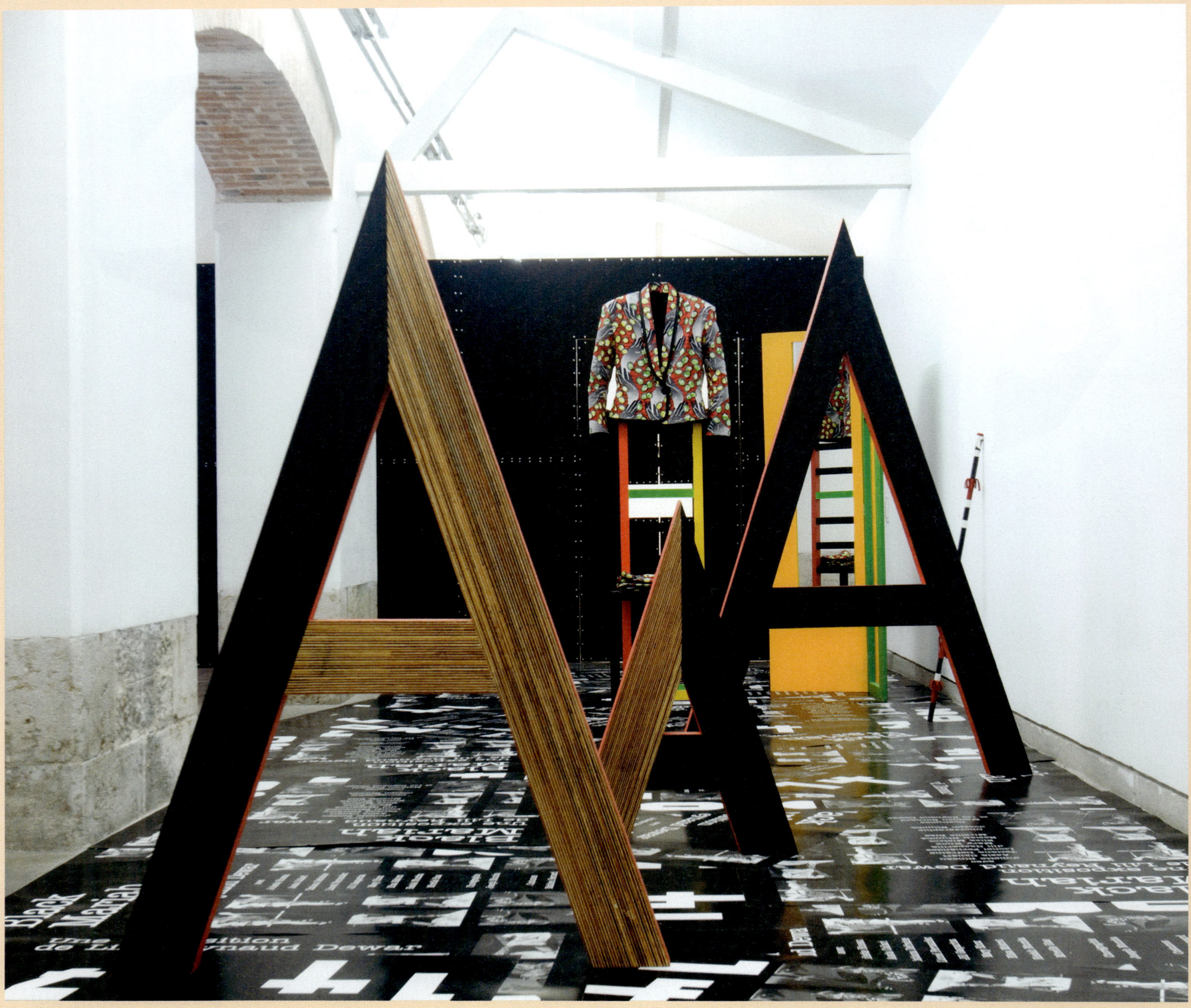

Black Mariah (The Woman's performance objects), 2009. Fabric costume with jacket and trousers, wooden screen with paint and mirrors, painted wooden chair, leather and wood stick, three painted wood As, performance documentation on DVD. Dimensions variable

Qualities of ritual

A sculptor whose works also involve performance, typography, design and music, Lili Reynaud-Dewar has adopted a decidedly anti-mainstream stance as an artist. Her practice can be described as experimental-revolutionary or avant-garde, in that it proposes a radically new language of images, words and bodily movements

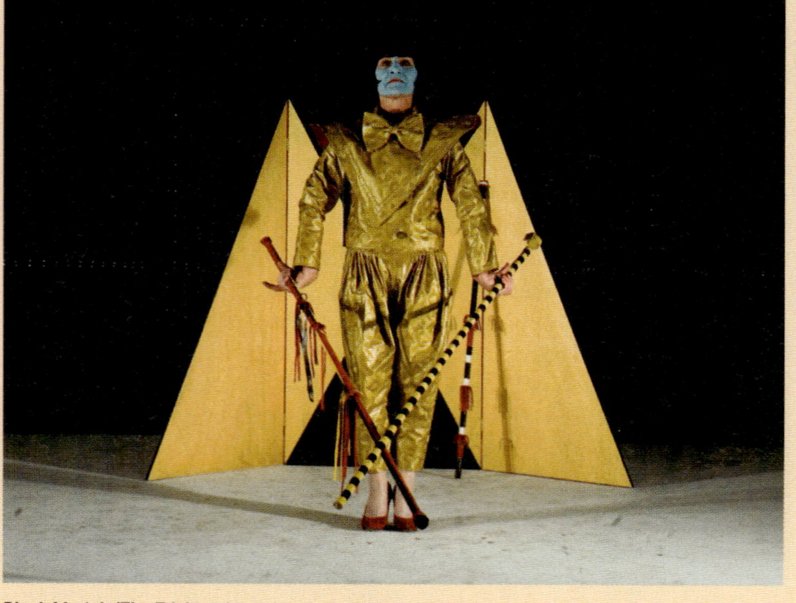

Black Mariah (The Trickster's performance films), 2009. Performance documentation on DVD

instead of justifying an existing one. A voracious reader and habitual collector of cultural scraps — pictures, texts, statements and attitudes that can be salvaged as tools in the process of political emancipation and the liberation of consciousness — Reynaud-Dewar takes her political and aesthetic inspiration from various sources that favour eclecticism, exception and excessive behaviour rather than accepting the rule of universal order based on rational principles that bears down heavily on Western European culture.

Reynaud-Dewar's performances are characterized by their ritualistic qualities. *The Race/ La Razza/La Corsa* at Galleria Civica d'Arte Contemporanea in Siracusa, Sicily (2008), consisted of long, hypnotizing sequences of movements made by a (white) female and (black) male performer in a setting that had a centrepiece of an altar-like bed designed by the artist, accompanied by a wild live guitar improvisation. In other performances such as *Power Structures, Rituals, & Sexuality of the European Short-Hand Typists* (2008), the actors are often almost immobilized, controlled, placed in a fixed position, reduced to performing only one function or activity at a time. 'I position the characters as I might place objects,

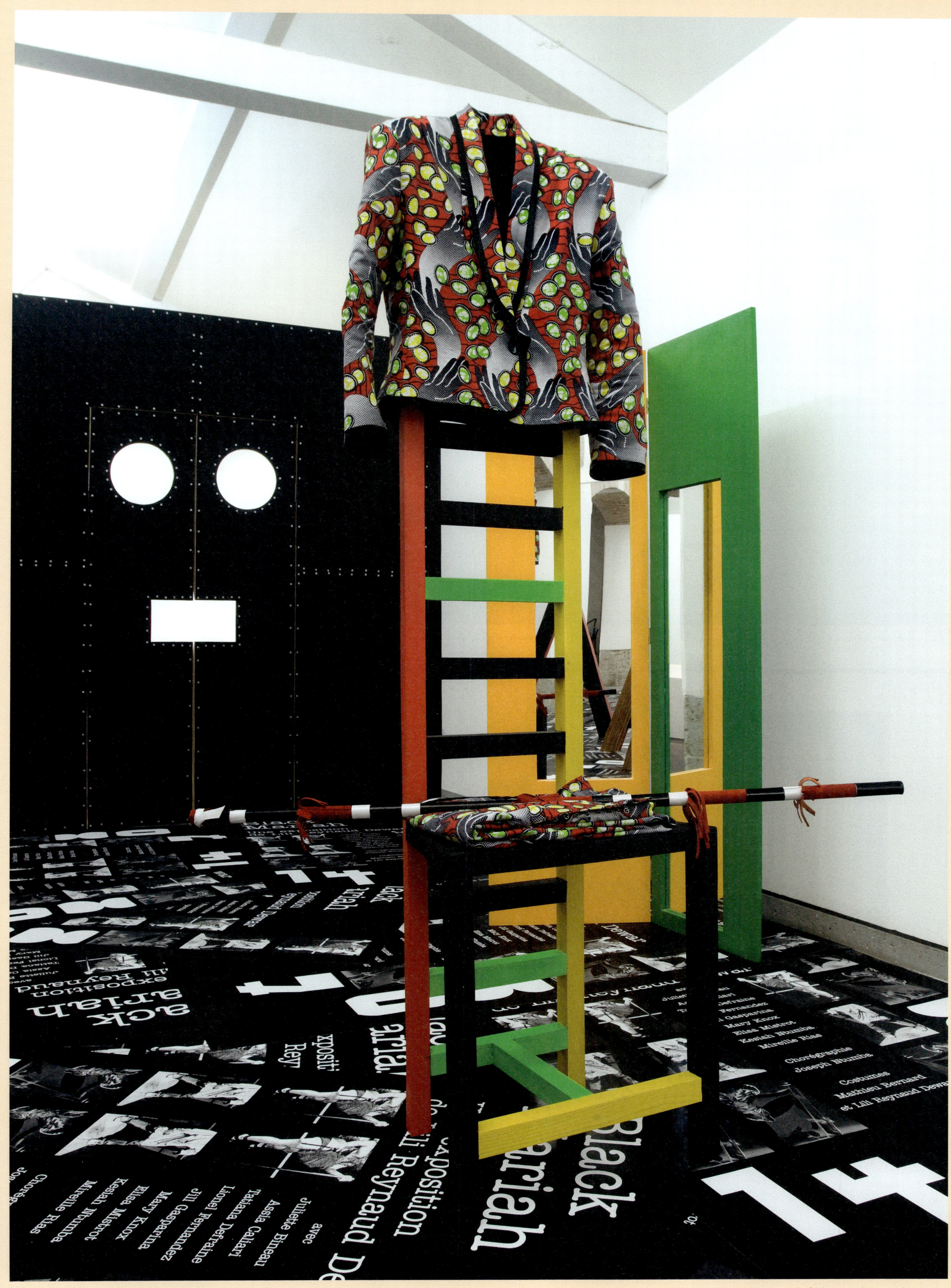

Black Mariah (The Woman's performance objects) (detail), 2009. Fabric costume with jacket and trousers, wooden screen with paint and mirrors, painted wooden chair, leather and wood stick, three painted wood As. Performance documentation on DVD. Dimensions variable

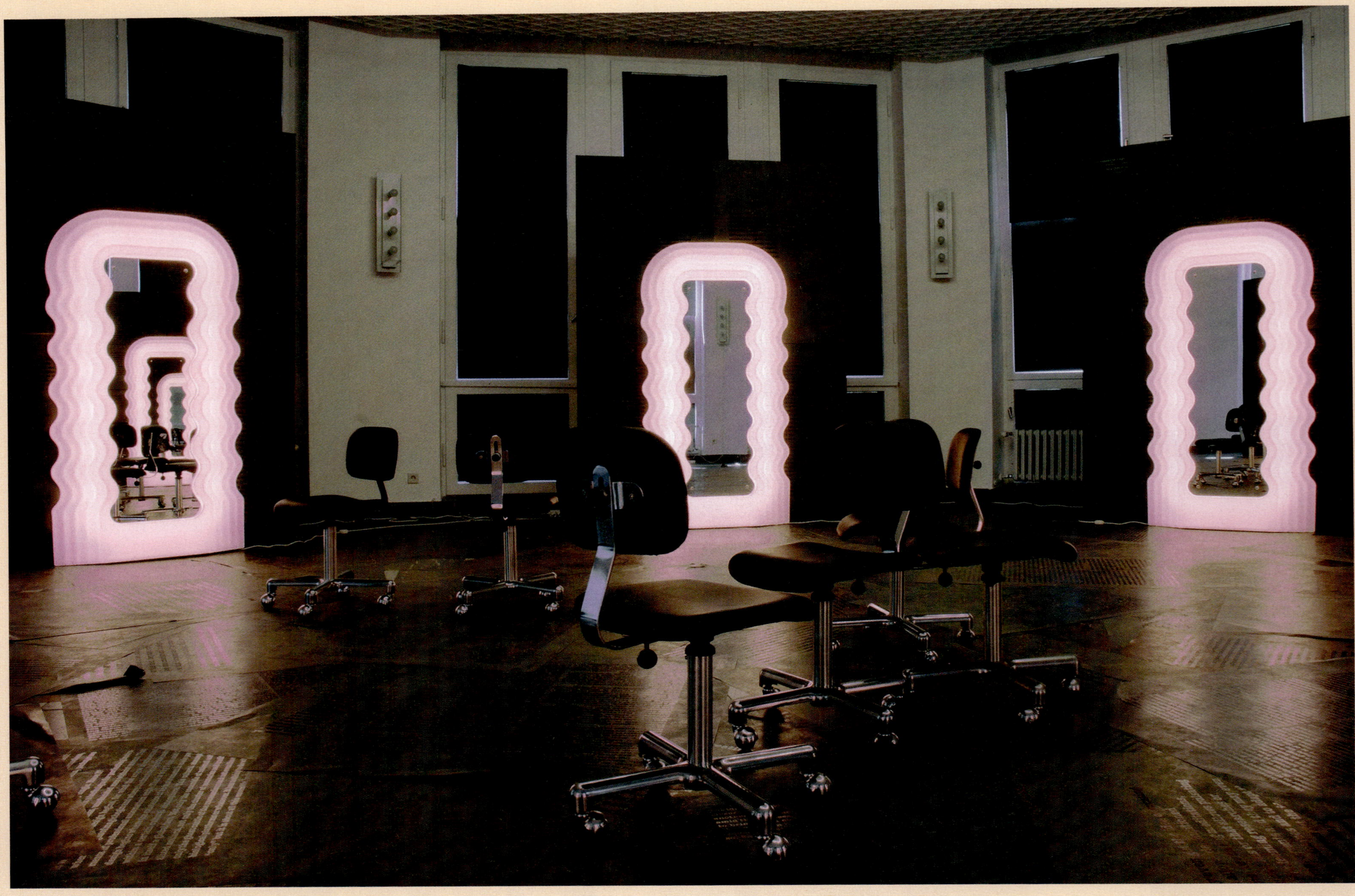

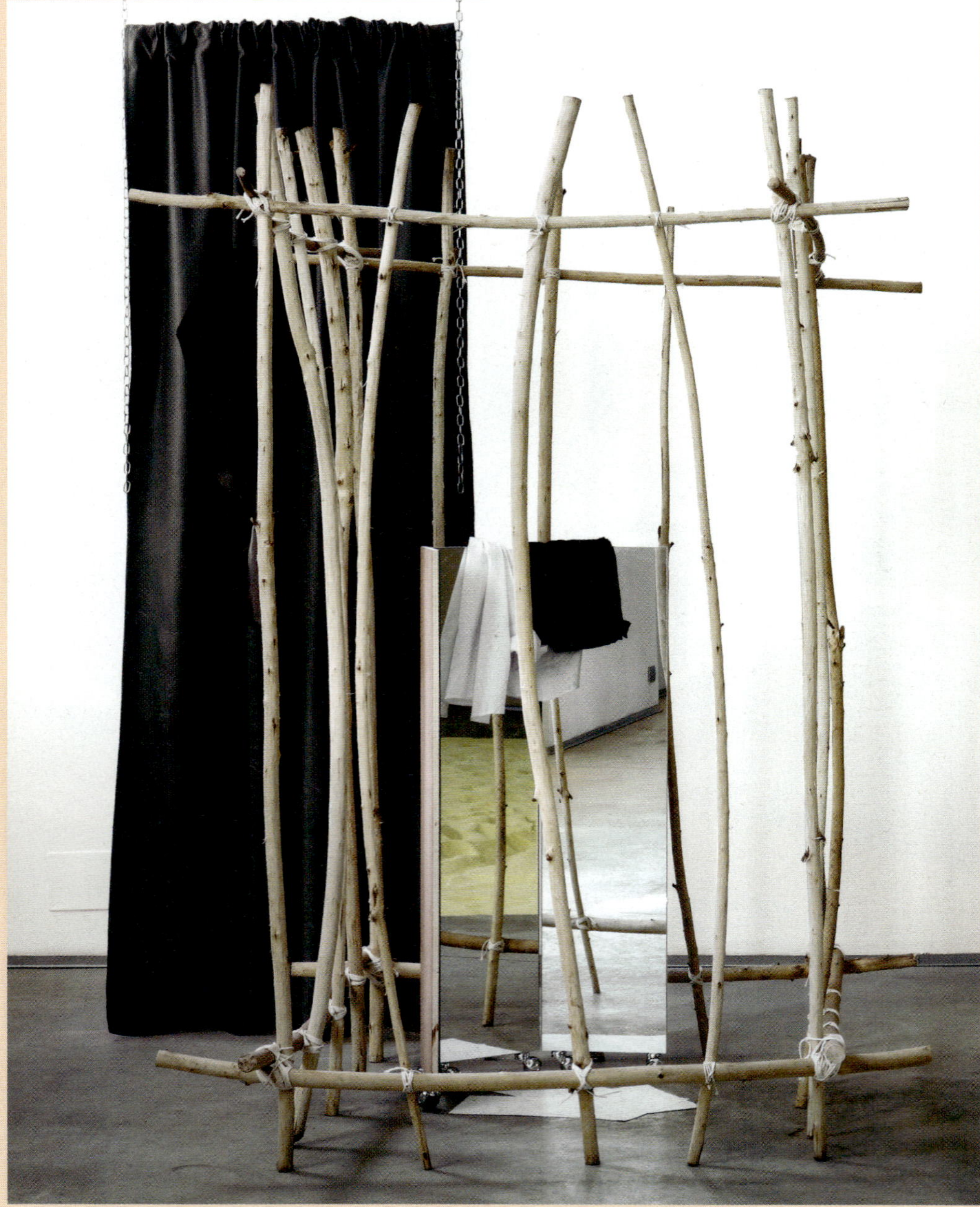

In every room there is the ghost of sex, 2008. Several sets of 12 screenprints, works by Ettore Sotsass, performance by Mary Knox and Lionel Fernandez. Dimensions variable

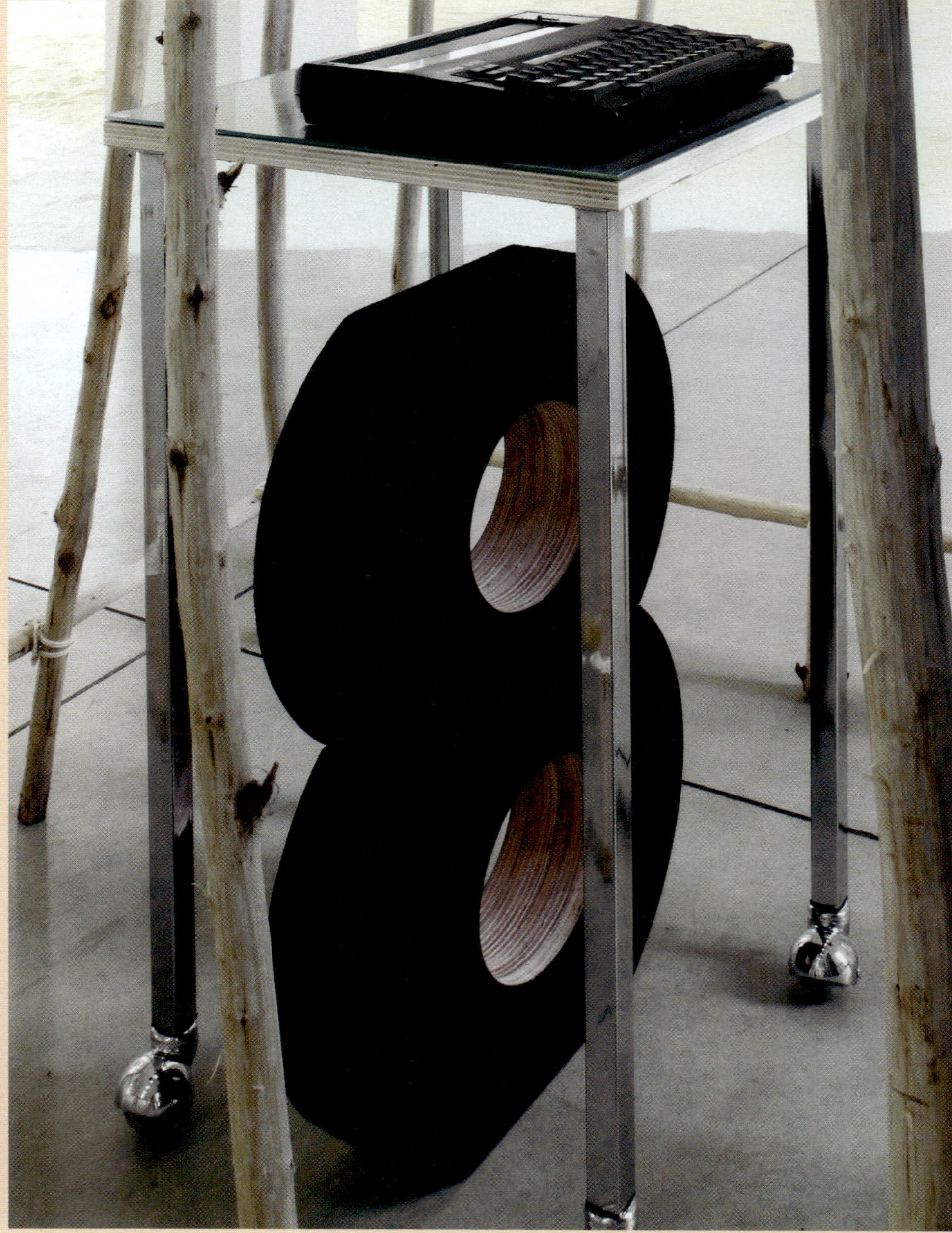

The Power Structures, Rituals & Sexuality of the European Shorthand Typists (Indoor version) (detail), 2009. Wood, fabric, mirror, metal, handmade suit, white shirt, paper. 220 × 160 × 160 cm

The Power Structures, Rituals and Sexuality of the European Shorthand Typists (Indoor version) (detail), 2009. Wood, fabric, mirror, metal, handmade suit, white shirt, paper. 220 × 160 × 160 cm

A deconstruction of dominant discourses of racial and gender identity animate her work

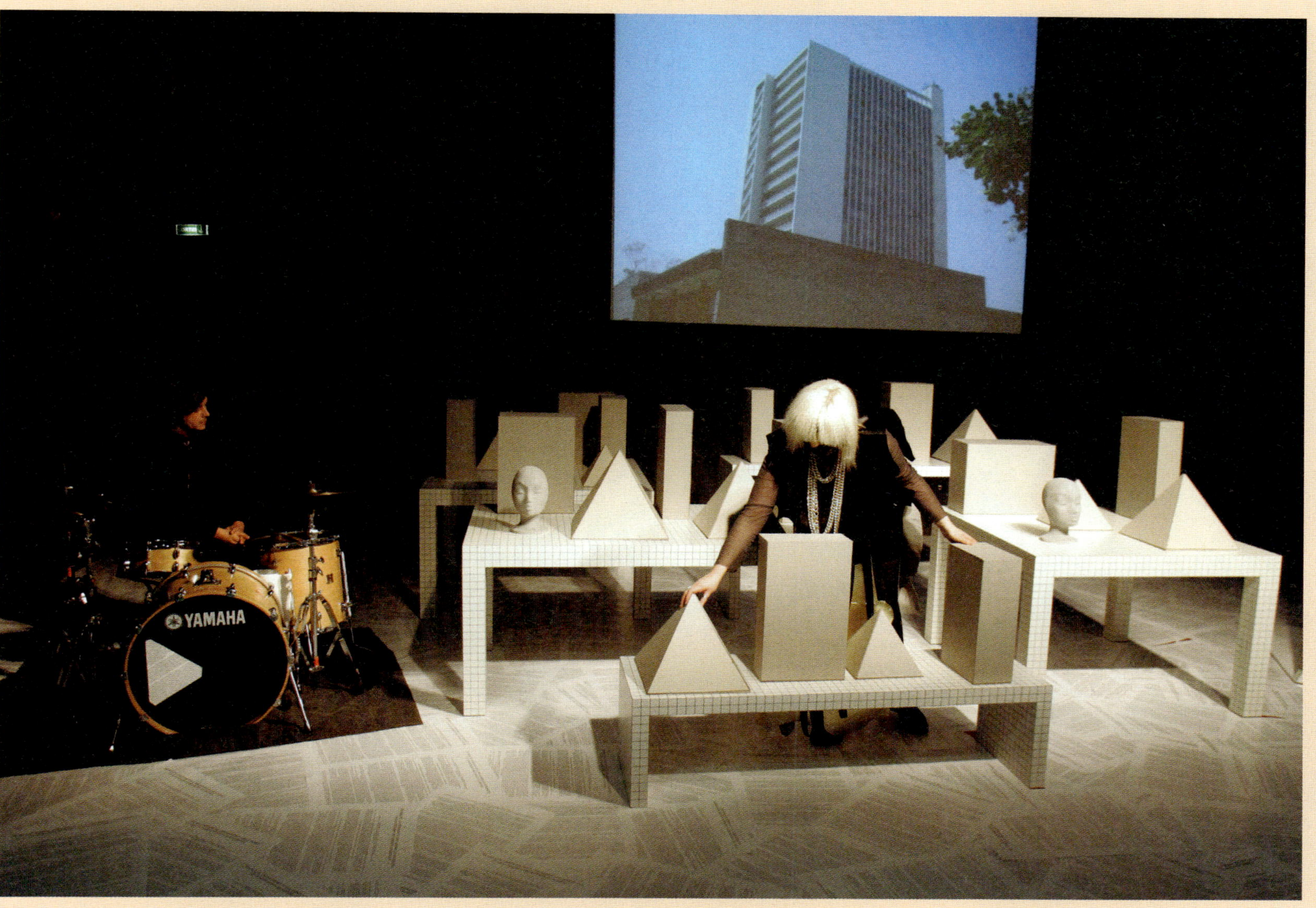

In Reality, Is The Sphinx an Annex of the Monument, or the Monument an Annex of the Sphinx?, 2008. Posters, mirror, drumkit, leather costume, chains, cardboard models, Quaderna tables from the Misura M series by Superstudio, video projection. Performance with Xavier Chabellard and Mary Knox

to the point that one could say that the girls are painted and the objects wearing too much makeup', comments the artist. Simple acts, such as reading texts aloud, painting one's face in different colours, wearing costumes, posing with props, playing instruments, walking, staring at the audience or looking away, gain an almost totemic quality through their frontal, often symmetrical staging.

Departing from her own cultural background as a young female French artist, Reynaud-Dewar uses odd historical dramatis personae as 'types' cast to signify specific ideas of political and social resistance. Several apparently unrelated figures and movements comprise the heterogeneous field of her interests. These include Peter Berlin, the gay icon and porn actor of 1970s and 1980s New York and Berlin; the designer and thinker Ettore Sottsass who defined the 'new international style' with the Memphis Group in the 1980s and whose work Reynaud-Dewar explored in her curated project *In every room there is the ghost of sex* as at the 2008 Berlin Biennial; or the visionary African-American musician and political activist Sun Ra, who claimed that Black Americans were an 'angel race' from Saturn and whose message exerted an enormous influence on music and the visual arts.

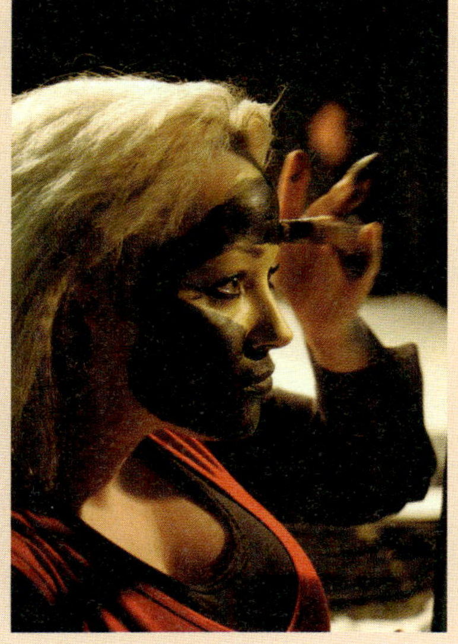

The Race/La Razza/La Corsa (detail), 2008. Wood, mirror, paint, leather, fabric, silkscreen poster. Performance with Mary Knox, Jean–Marie Racon & Lionel Fernandez. Dimensions variable

Reynaud-Dewar employs these bizarre role models and mythologies to perform a contemporary critique of stereotyped ideas of gender, power and sexuality. The concept of 'creolization', the notion of exceptionalism and a deconstruction of dominant discourses of racial and gender identity animate her work. The artist sides with displaced, uprooted peoples, focusing on the emblematic, quasi-mythical exponents who provide them with a powerful voice.

In Reality, Is The Sphinx an Annex of the Monument, or the Monument an Annex of the Sphinx?, 2008. Performance documentation on DVD. 22 min. 34 sec.

Robin Rhode

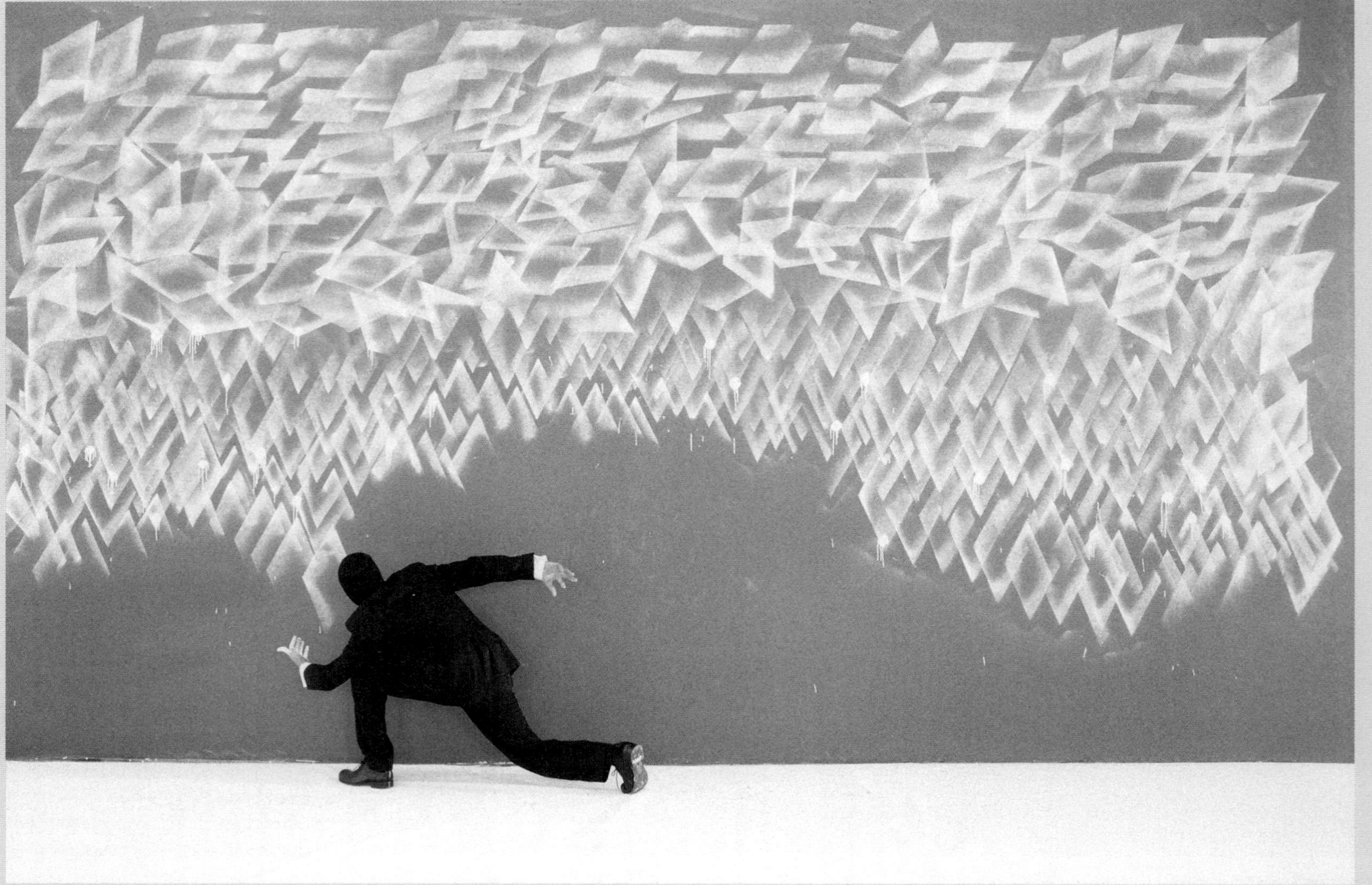

Graffiti

Robin Rhode combines graffiti staged in the street with performances utilizing the body as an expressive medium, and captures the results in photographs and film. His ephemeral drawings, rendered in the simple materials used for graffiti — a stick of chalk, spray paint, charcoal — come to life as props in performances, evoking with voluble vividness the realities of urban life and memories of his native land.

Born in Cape Town and then moving to Johannesburg, Rhode studied art, then film. Since 2002, he has been based in Berlin, but for this artist whose personal experience connects directly to his work, the land and history of South Africa remain the platform for his creativity and his chief source of inspiration.

Referring to the difficult political experiences endured by his country, he notes that 'the culture has always used humour to deal

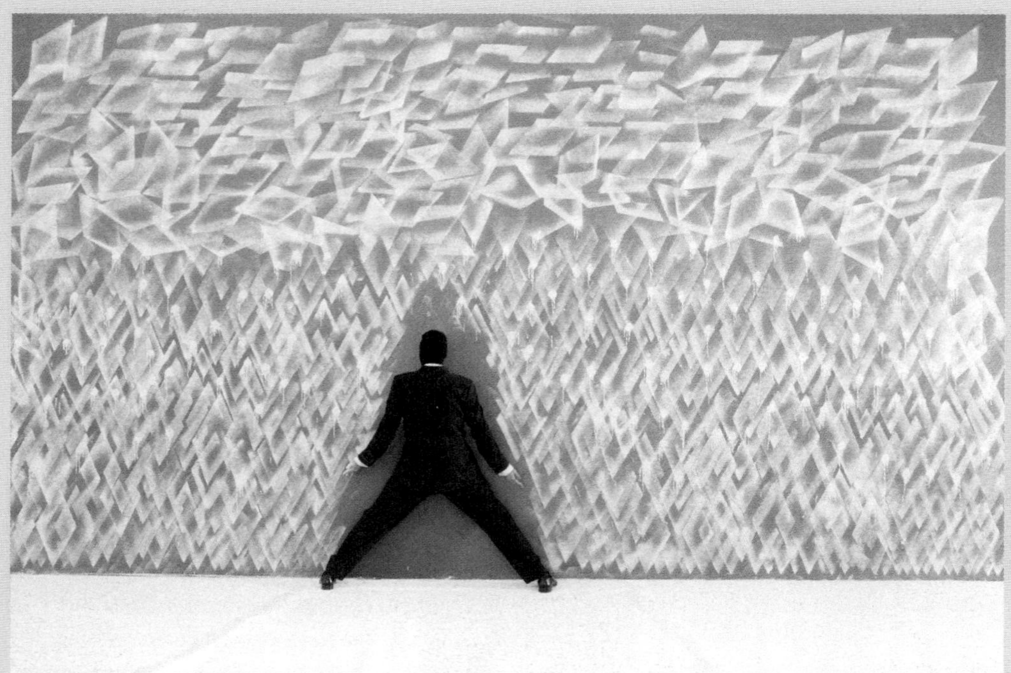

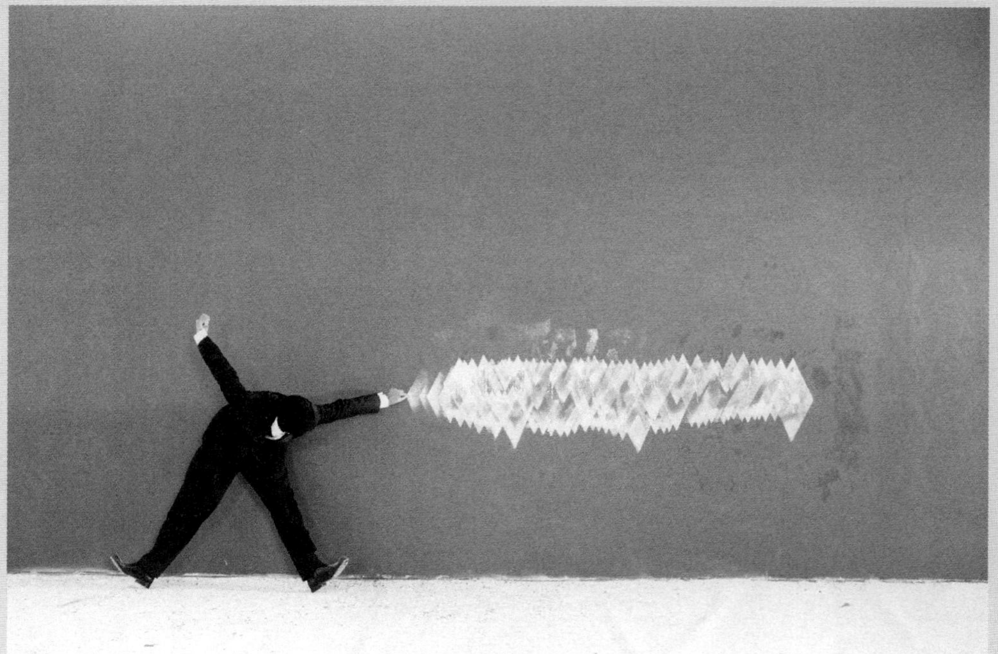

Promenade, 2008. 3 of 36 C–prints face–mounted with Plexiglas on aluminium panels. Each 36 × 53 cm

with this kind of trauma' and accordingly mixes in healthy doses of mischievous wit when passing comment on his own identity as coloured, addressing matters of mixed-race heritage, or other political issues. An example is *Stone Flag* (2004), in which bricks are arranged to look like a flag; the comical notion of waving the almost immovable standard demonstrates the difficulty of controlling individuals, despite political pressure to mould a uniform identity — like bricks of a regular size — under a single flag.

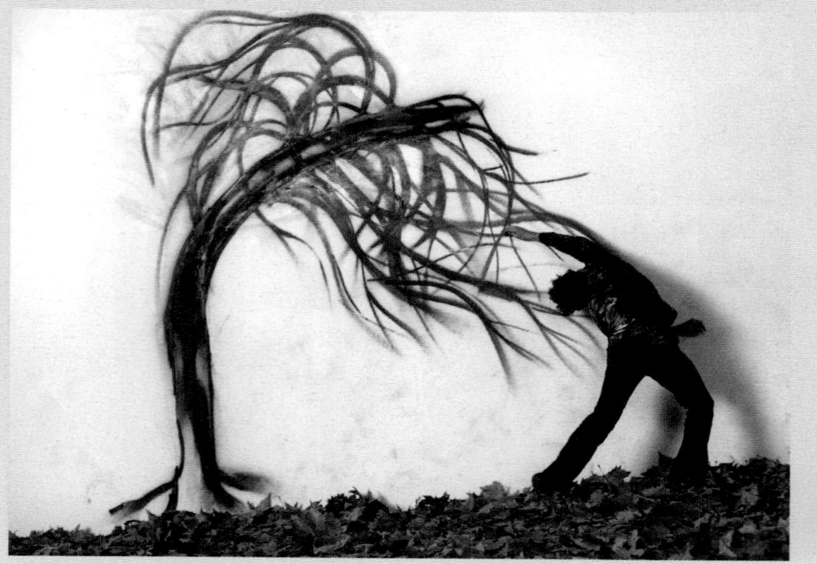

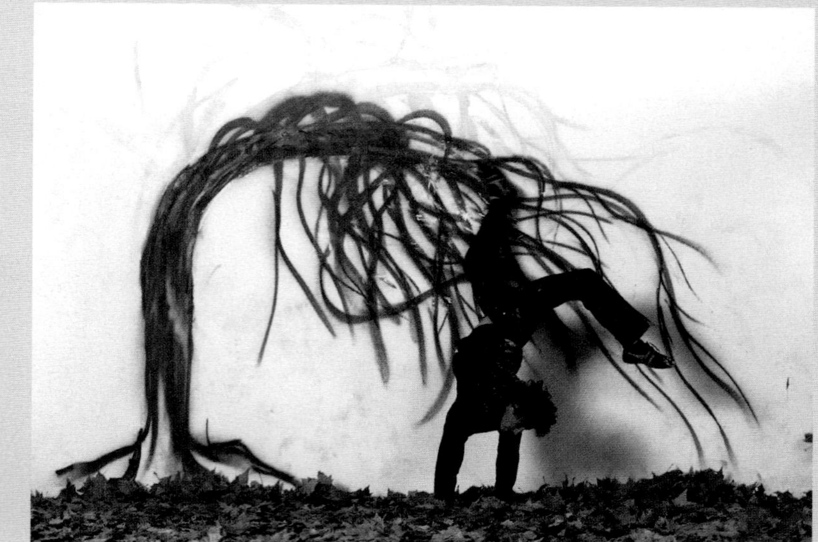

The Storyteller, 2006. 16 mm film transferred to video. 12 min. 50 sec.

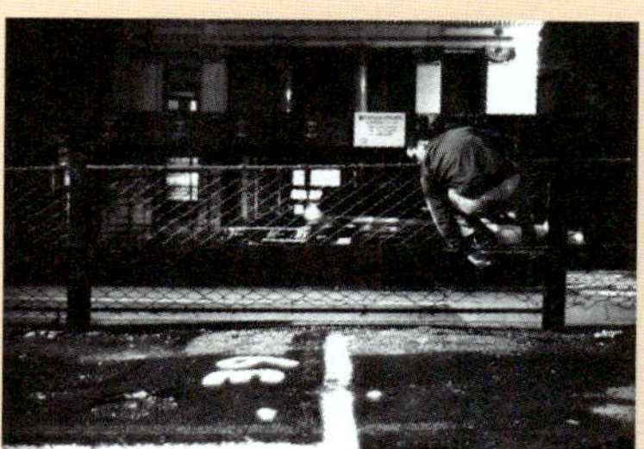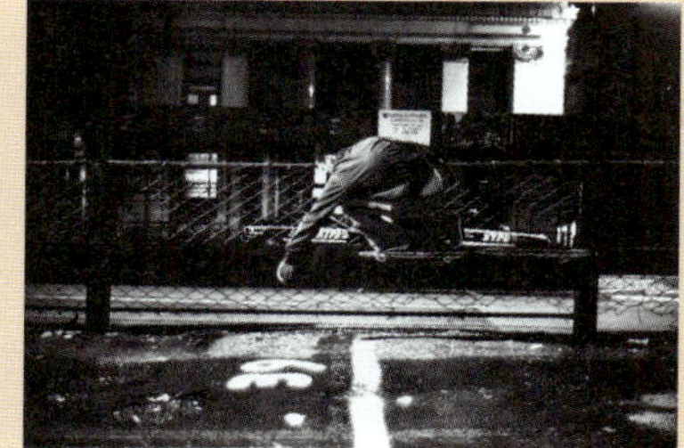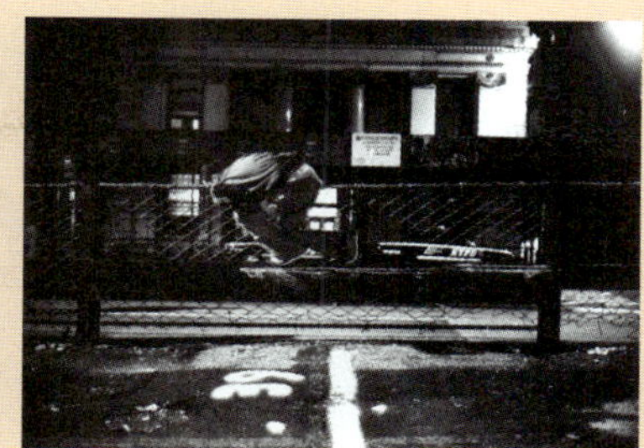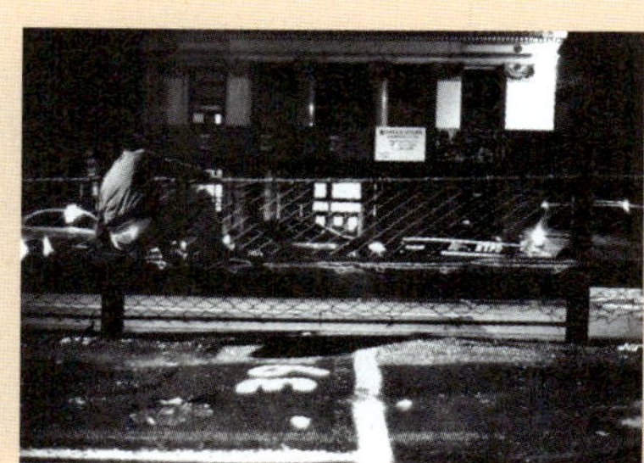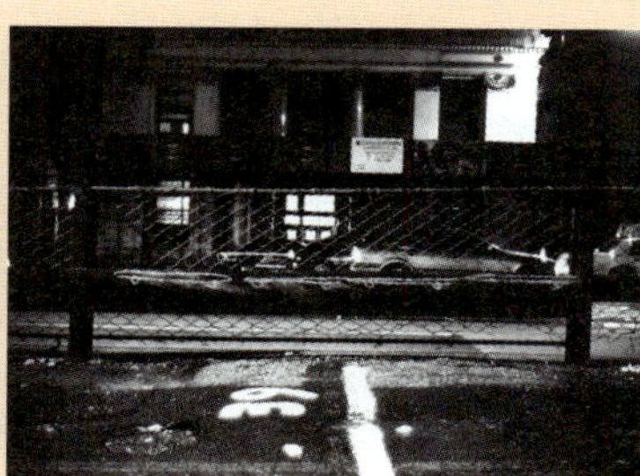

Night Boarding, 2004. 6 gelatin silver prints face–mounted with Plexiglas on aluminum panels. Each 40 × 27 cm

Rhode also has much to say about lessons he has learned from the street, youth culture and tricks for survival. In *Night Boarding* (2004) he uses stop-motion photography akin to Eadward Muybridge's filmic sequences to capture himself apparently jumping a wire fence on a skateboard drawn in chalk. For Rhode, who lends vibrant visual expression to the tension and pace of city life, the streets are at once a canvas and a backdrop.

As an artist who has left his home country and now roams the globe, he responds to streetscapes encountered on his travels; the resulting works may be seen as an attempt to view the whole world in equivalent terms, through the common language of contemporary urban culture.

Since 2005, Rhode's works have taken a more lyrical turn, in revisiting fine art techniques encompassing monotone paintings and calligraphy. Still more recently he has extended his practice to include collaborations with professional composers, musicians and dancers. Whereas previously he would simply turn up in public spaces for improvised happenings without first requiring an audience, now his works are more choreographed in nature. In *Pictures Reframed* (2009), for example, a two-year collaboration with the Norwegian pianist Leif Ove Andsnes, several of Rhode's videos create an installation surrounding the stage.

In the spirit of graffiti artists like Keith Haring and Jean-Michel Basquiat, Rhode embeds himself in public spaces, pushing the boundaries of art through popular culture and interdisciplinary collaborations. Occupying the space where an ever-expanding world and local singularity are experienced simultaneously, he links the street and a place for art, performance and the visual arts, to create innovative new spaces of expression.

Tricks for survival

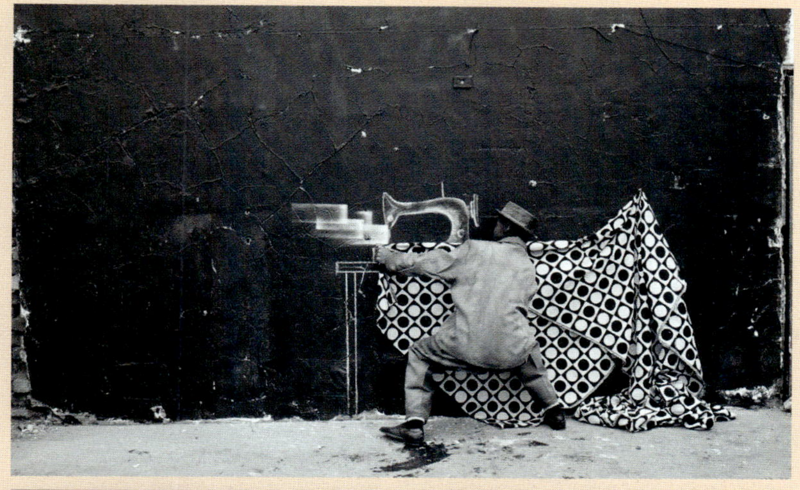

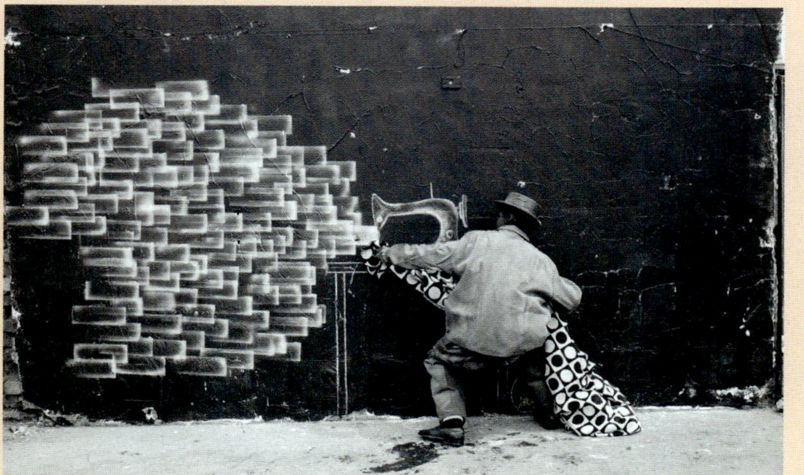

Brick Face (detail), 2008. 20 digital pigment prints mounted on 4-ply museum board. Each 46 × 74 cm

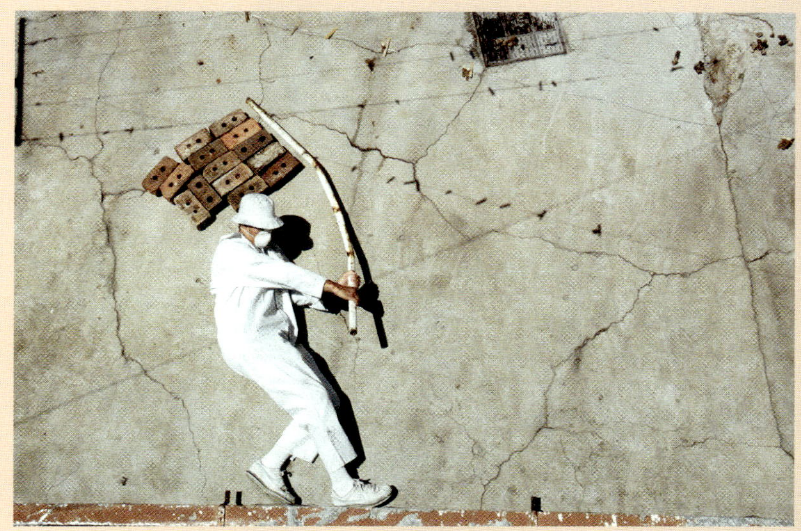

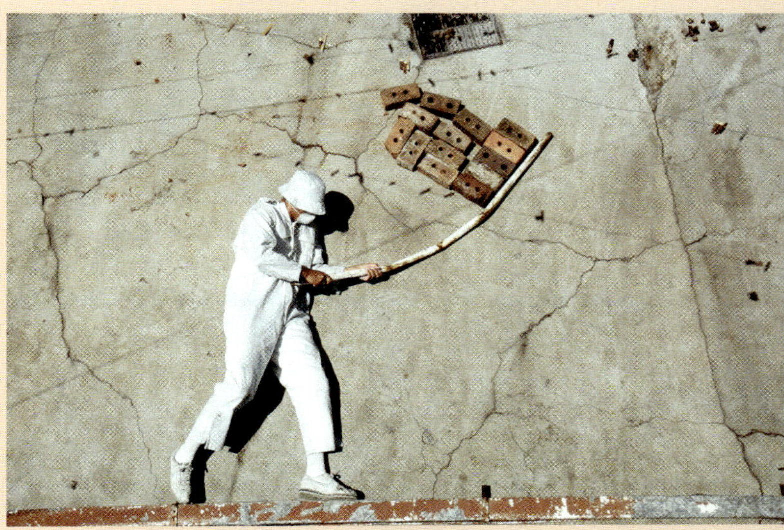

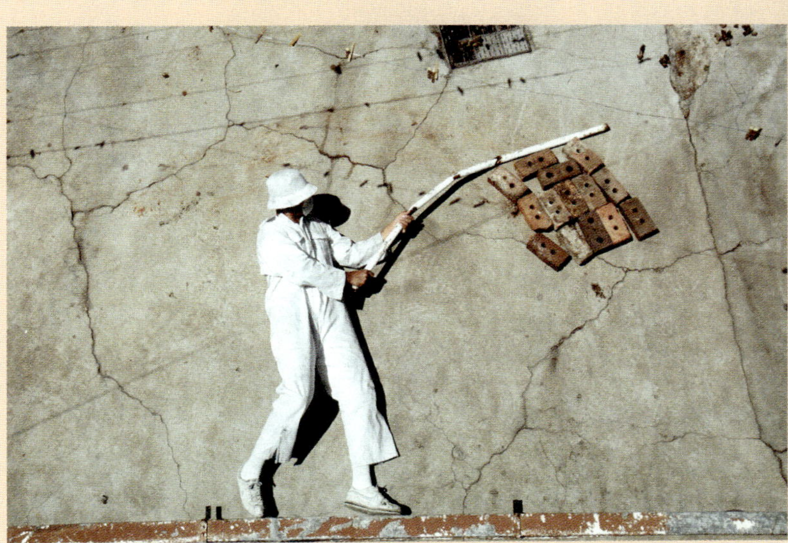

Stone Flag, 2004. 3 of 9 C–prints face–mounted with Plexiglas on aluminum panels. Each 31 × 46 cm

Tension and pace of city life

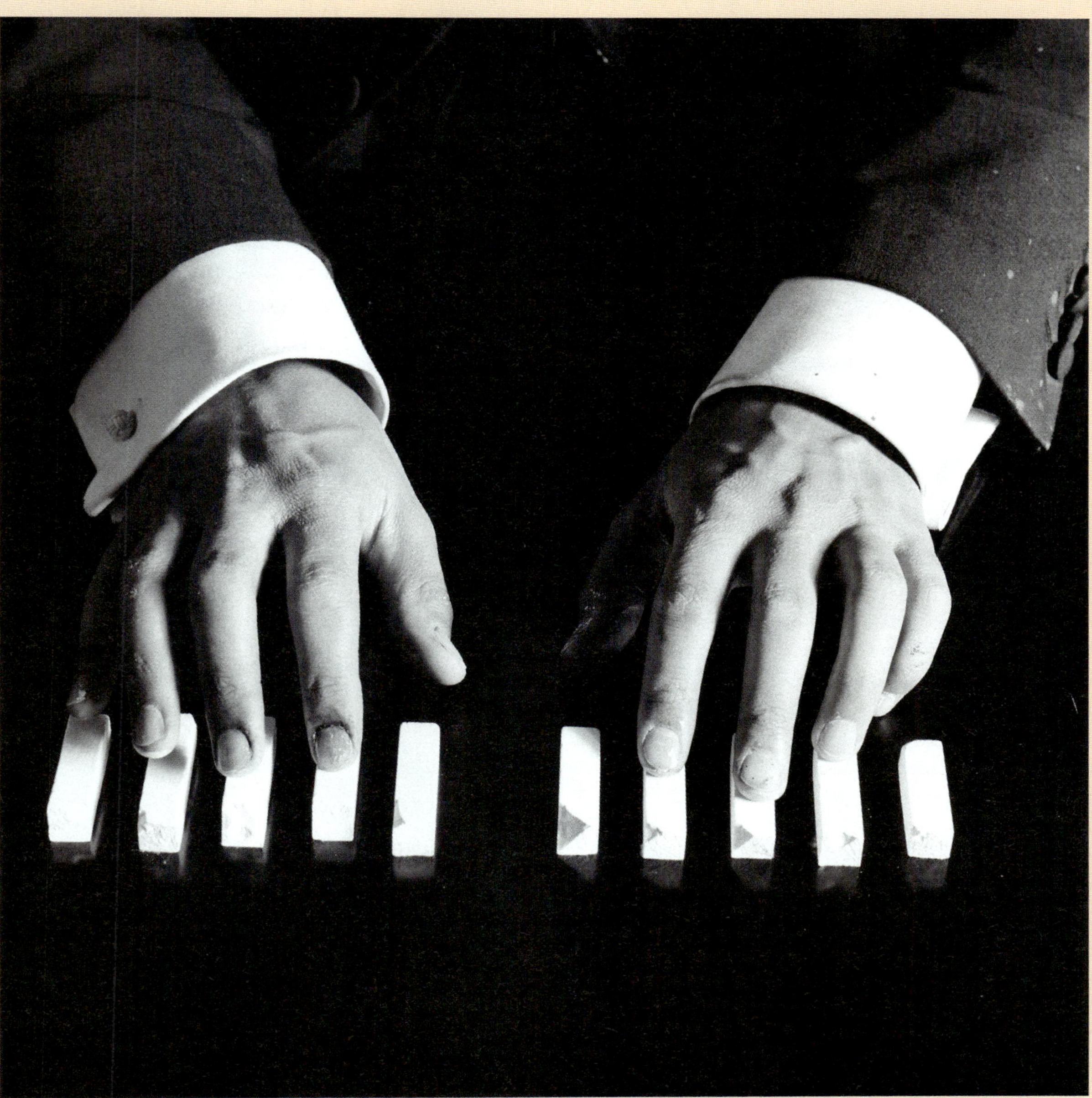

Keys, 2008. Black and white pigment print. 119 × 119 cm

Stephen G. Rhodes

Stephen G. Rhodes's obsession with the complex blurring of myth, fantasy and history has its origins in a film that his teachers would show when they had time to kill at primary school. The 1962 short film *An Occurrence at Owl Creek Bridge* is an adaptation of the American author Ambrose Bierce's 1890 short story of the same name. As a Confederate sympathizer during the American Civil War is about to be hung, the rope breaks and he escapes, only to realize shortly afterwards that his liberation was simply a fantasy. Rhodes was deeply affected by this film, which became the basis of his work *Recurrency* (2007), an elaborate sculptural installation that includes a makeshift gallows, lengths of rope and a three-

History is stuttering

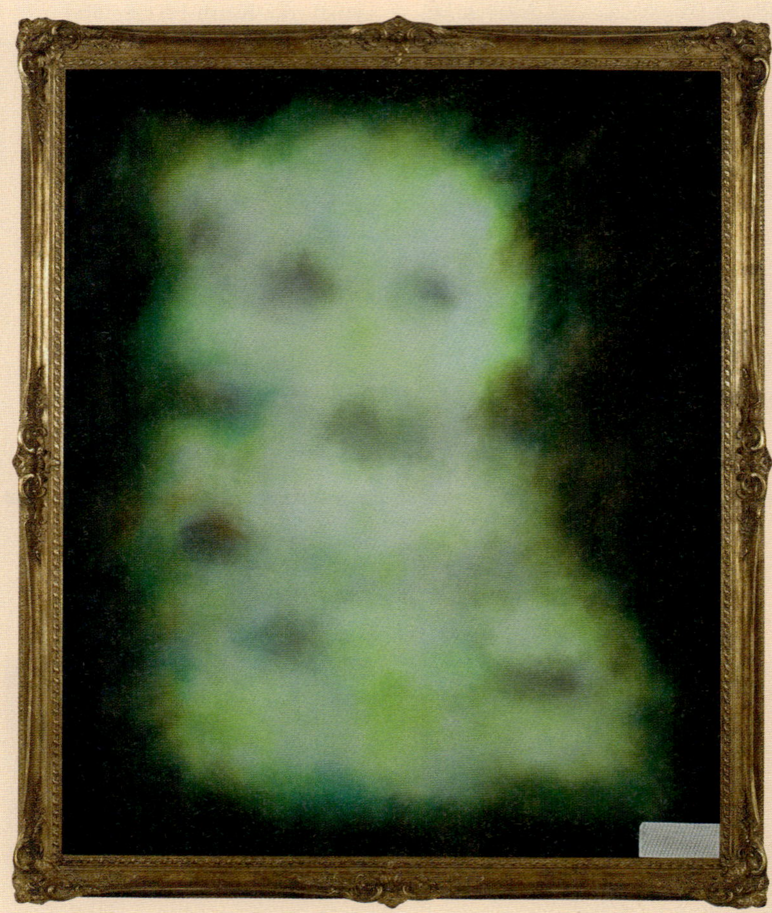

Vacant Portrait 21, 2008. Oil and collage on canvas, frame. 183 × 156 cm

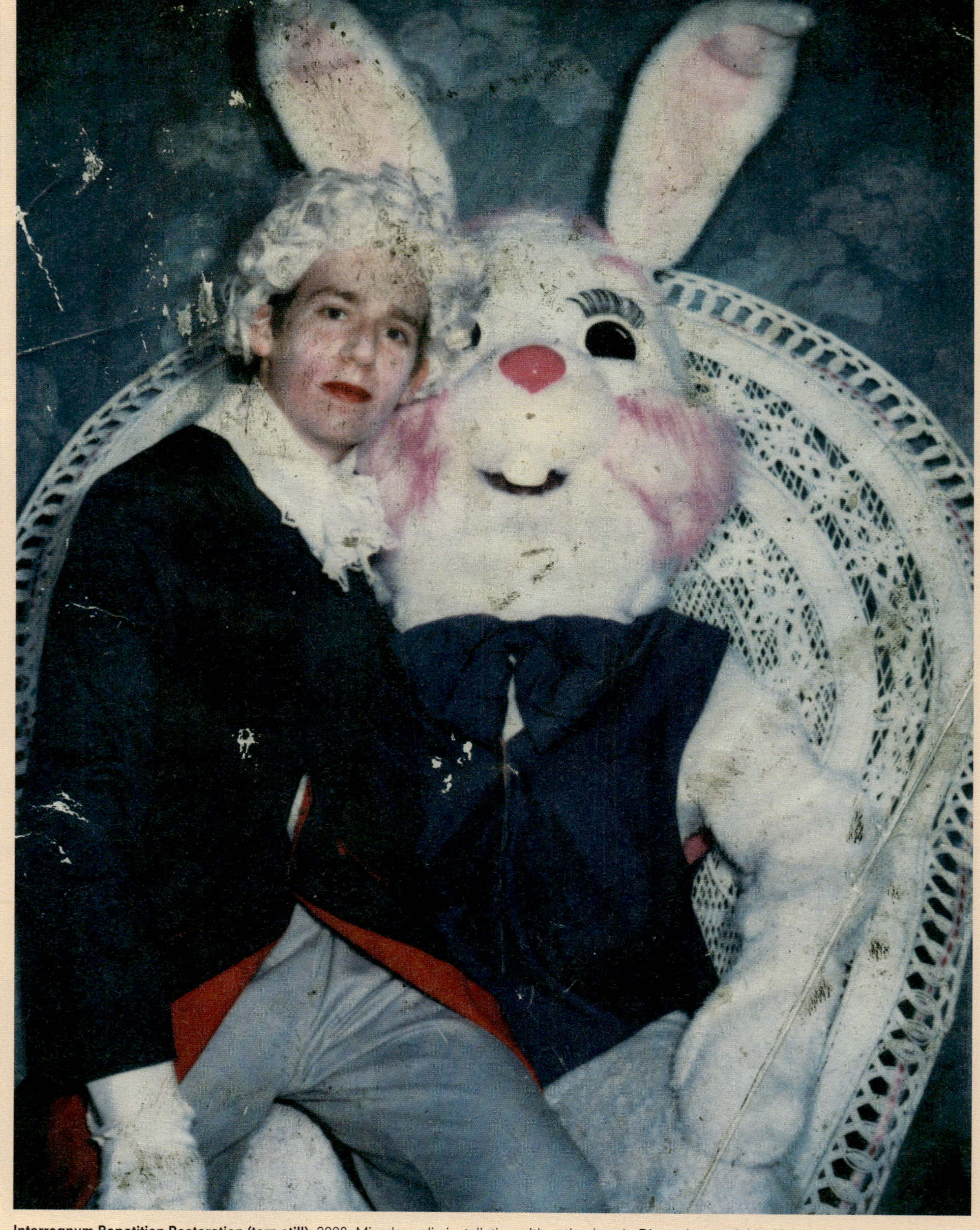

Interregnum Repetition Restoration (torn still), 2008. Mixed–media installation with voting booth. Dimensions variable. Video. 2 min. 8 sec.

Personal and collective memory

channel video offering various interpretations of Bierce's original story. In Rhodes' installation, the story loops and repeats itself over and over again as if history is stuttering.

Working in a wide range of media from video and sculpture to drawing and painting, Rhodes has been particularly fascinated with the cultural politics involved in the telling and revision of American history as it collides with fantasies and myths generated by personal and collective memory. In another installation, *There is No Bear Bear Ladder* (2009), the artist takes on the Disneyfication of history in his

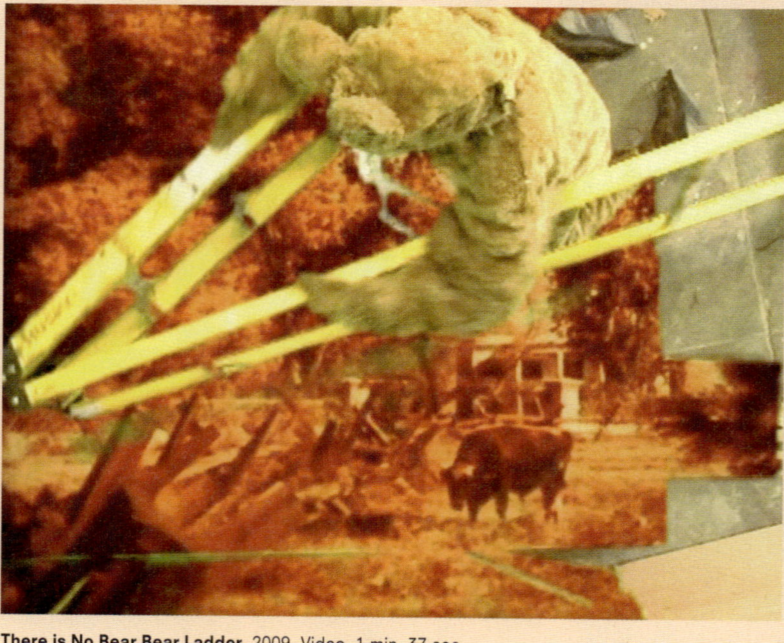

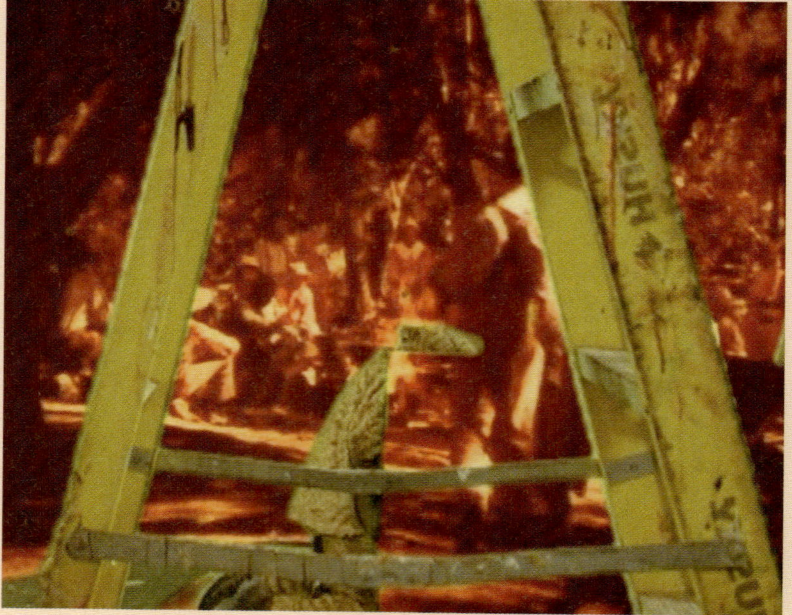

There is No Bear Bear Ladder, 2009. Video. 1 min. 37 sec.

Questionable attempt at history-telling

reconstruction, or rather subversion, of the 1946 animated Disney film *The Song of the South*, a movie that shamelessly deployed racist caricatures. Amidst a room littered with green-painted plywood panels and a ladder, we see a video projection of the artist dressed in a well-worn bear costume as he performs a series of manic exercises, or perhaps comic pratfalls, in front of projected footage of the Disney film. Ballroom music from Stanley Kubrick's film *The Shining*, as well as the title's evocation of Gertrude Stein's phrase 'there is no there there', foreground the problematic

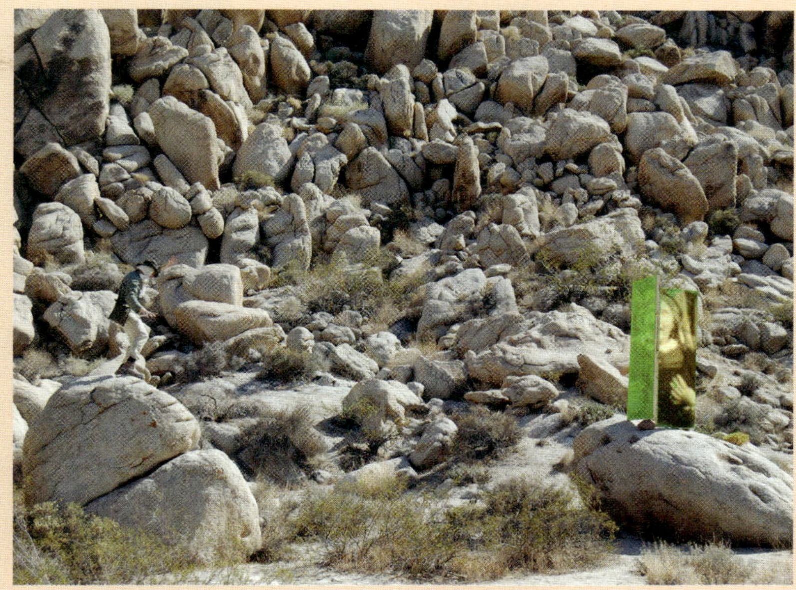

Reconstruction or Something, 2009. Video. Length variable

nature of this bit of Disney mythmaking by pushing it to a darkly absurd level.

The statement 'there is no there there' is an apt description for the blurring of history, memory and myth that Rhodes investigates in his work. This finds an allegorical outlet in his *Vacant Portraits*, a series of ghostly oil paintings that offer erased versions of nineteenth-century portraiture. More akin to the 'spirit' or 'aura' photographs of that era, these works speak to the sense of uncertainty and loss associated with the vagaries of memory, as opposed to the certainty offered by the purported exactitude of the historical method.

We see a further iteration of Rhodes' fascination with this

Psychedelic and anachronisitc quality

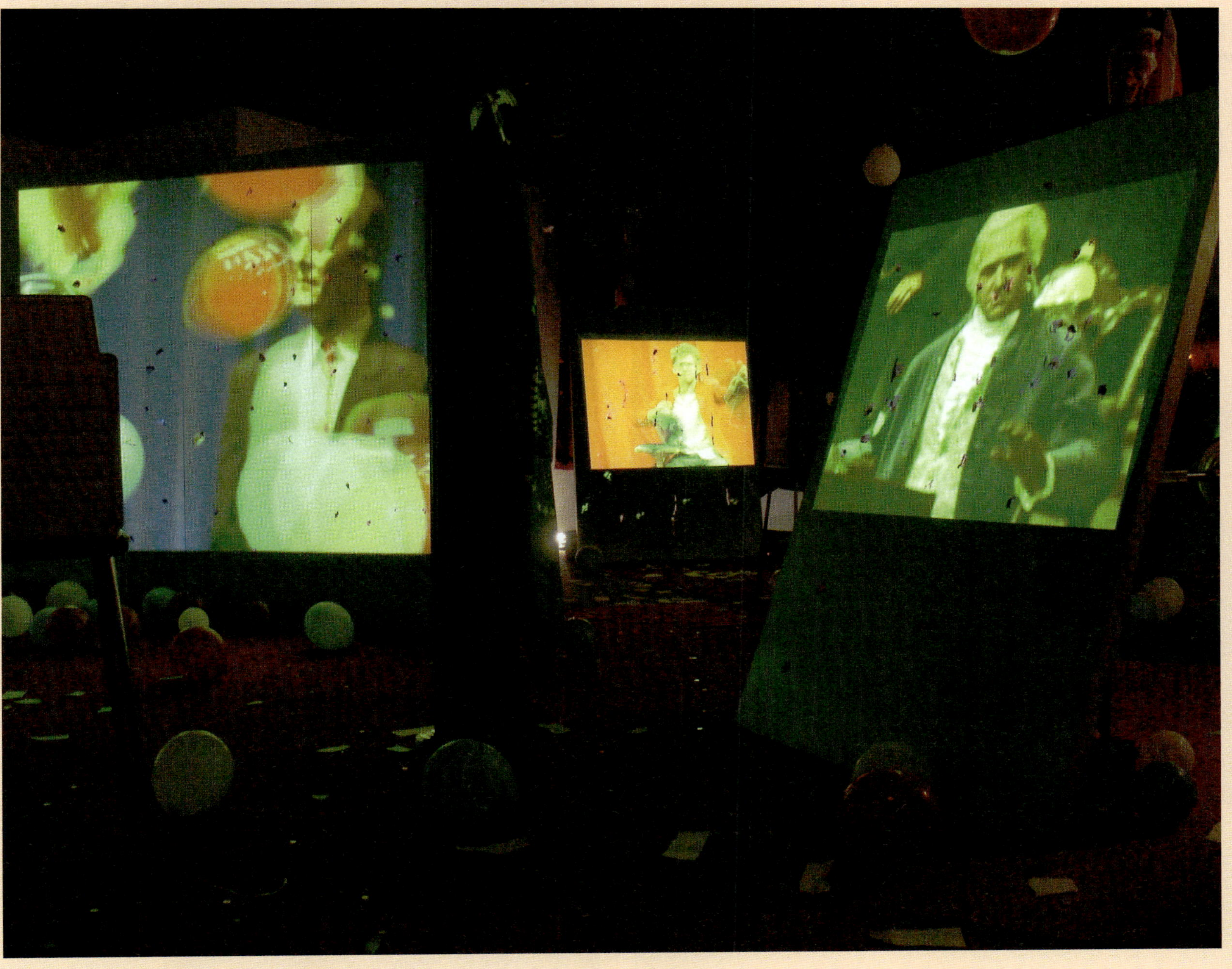

Working in a wide range of media from video and sculpture to drawing and painting, Rhodes has been particularly fascinated with the cultural politics involved in the telling and revision of American history as it collides with fantasies and myths generated by personal and collective memory

blurring in his installation *Interregnum Repetition Restoration* (2008), which takes as its point of departure another questionable attempt at history-telling in the form of the Hall of Presidents at Disney World. As Rhodes puts it, 'to be ushered into the Hall of Presidents is to descend into he realm of paranoia' as silent animatronic versions of all the American presidents convene around a speechifying Abraham Lincoln.

Rhodes' installation highlights the psychedelic and anachronistic quality of this congress of robotic leaders, projecting altered images of the Hall of Presidents in a back-lot Oval office. Filtered through his own acerbic take on American history, Rhodes's work both embraces and questions the blurring of reality and fantasy that is at the heart of both historiography and storytelling.

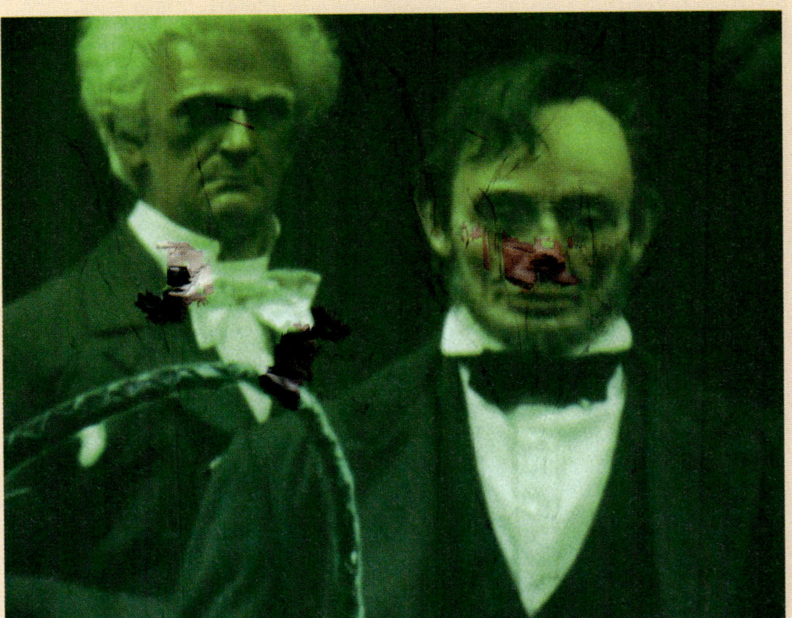

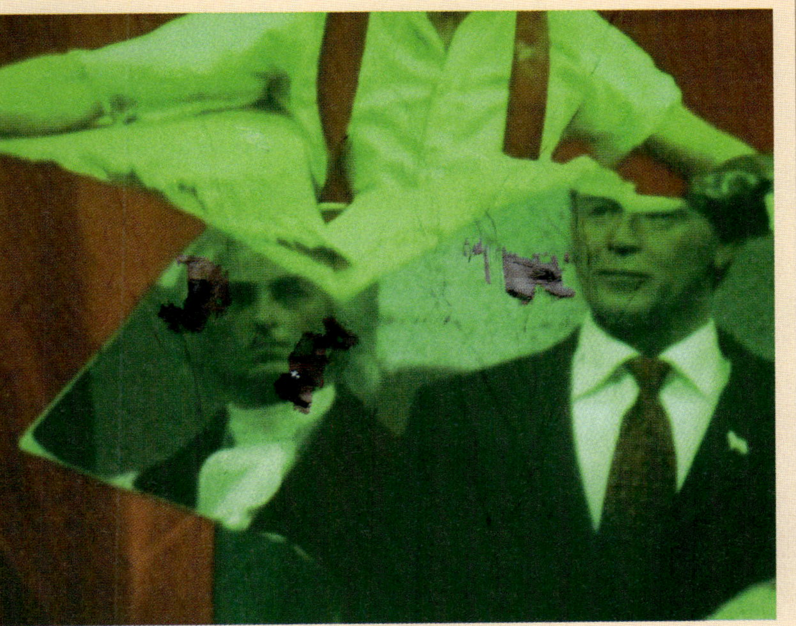

Interregnum Repetition Restoration (Whipped Lincoln), 2008. Mixed-media installation with voting booth. Dimensions variable. Video. 2 min. 8 sec.

Noguchi Rika

Noguchi Rika has always regarded her own experiences and the act of taking pictures as equal. Since her debut, for which she learned to dive in order to photograph a diver, her tranquil photographs have belied a very physical practice.

She has certainly seen a great deal of the planet: from sacred peak to ocean floor, from snow-covered mountains to extreme desert conditions, then beyond blue skies to the sun, stars and space. Rika's photographs are devoid of special effects or manipulation of any sort; they are never products of the studio.

She directs her camera wherever sunlight (or moonlight) falls, complying with the properties of photography as a medium to capture the 'truth' of her subjects. In this she is unmistakably following a documentary tradition. But while not photographing anything special, she manages to present a world like none we've ever seen.

Having turned her focus and imagination to space for the series *Rocket Hill* (2001–present), featuring the launch pad at the Tanegashima Space Center, in *I Dreamt of Flying* (2003)

Rika photographed the launch of a hand-made rocket of her own. Made from the pages of a calendar, it flies through a blue sky and heads for the heavens. The sky is suffused with light, like a vision of a hopeful future. In *I Dreamt of Flying 2* (2009), the scene has changed to that of glowing galaxies in the inky black of space. Rika declines to explain the source of the glistening light in the photographs, but the idea that the tiny rocket has traversed the earth's atmosphere and is now drifting in space runs throughout the series.

Drifting in space

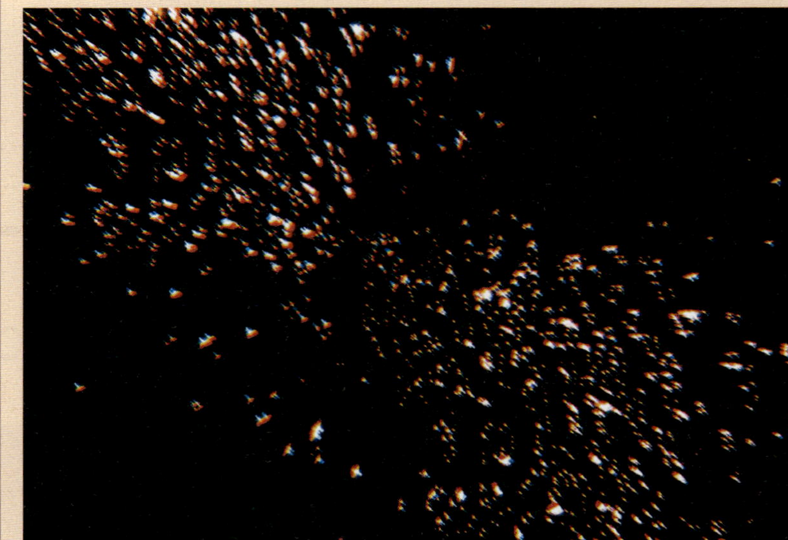

I Dreamt of Flying 2 #6, 2009. C–print. 125 × 188 cm

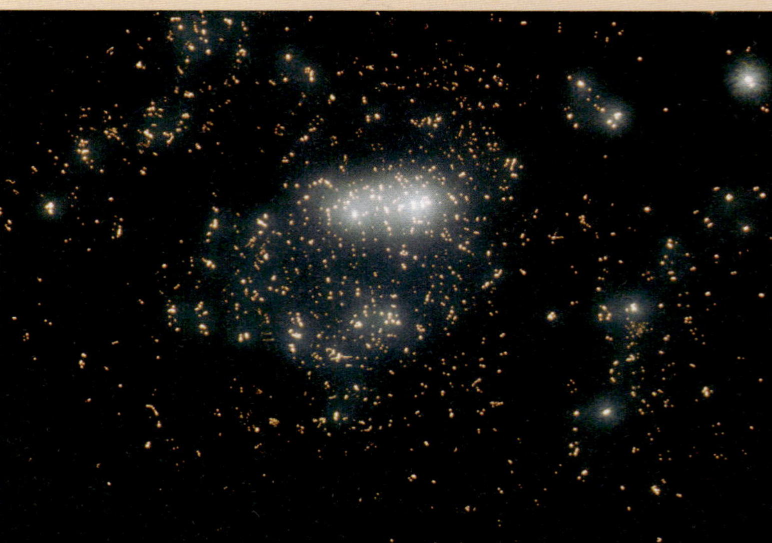

I Dreamt of Flying 2, #1, 2009. C–print. 125 × 188 cm

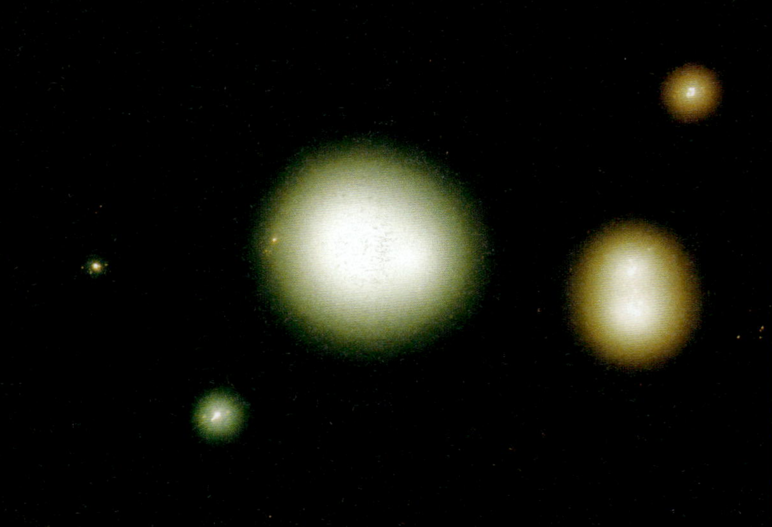

I Dreamt of Flying 2, #4, 2009. C–print. 100 × 150 cm

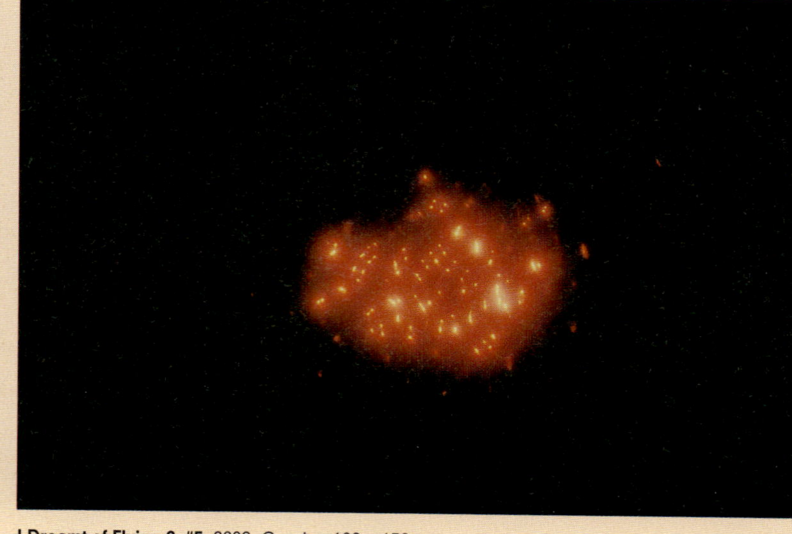

I Dreamt of Flying 2, #5, 2009. C–print. 100 × 150 cm

A documentary tradition

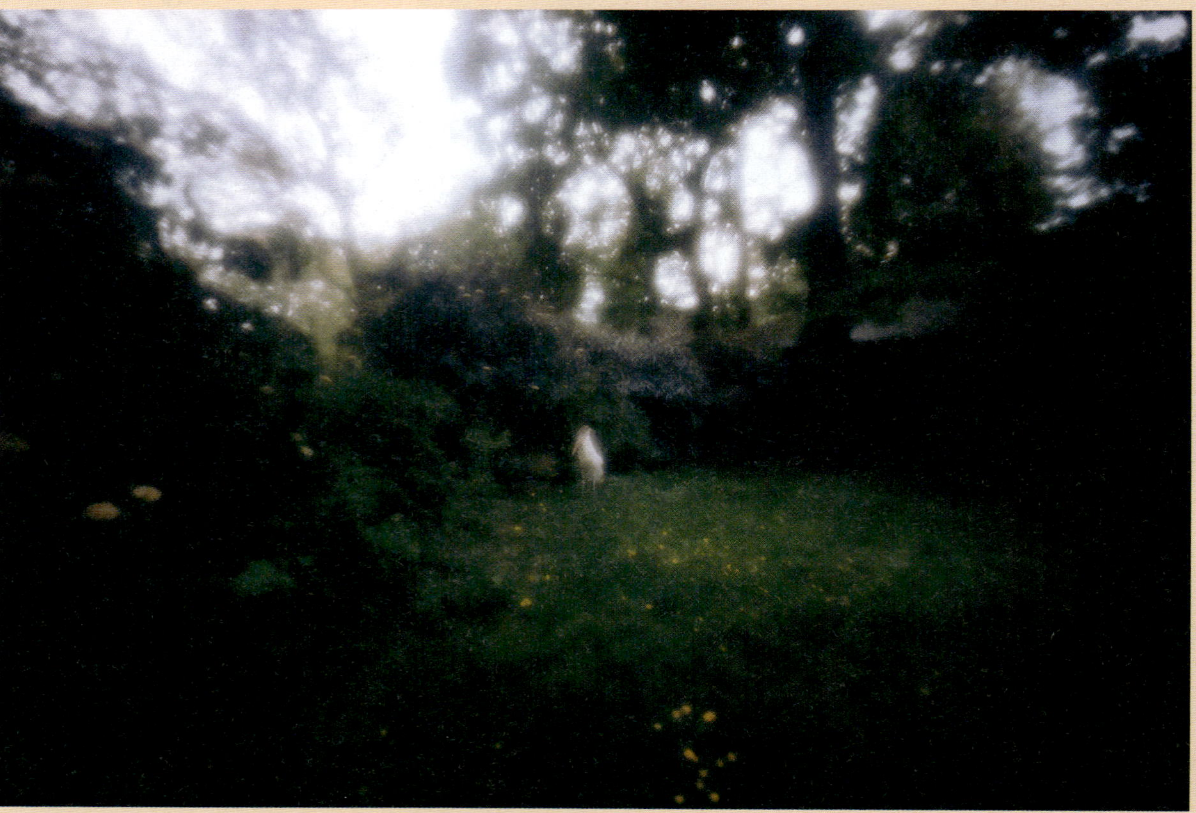

Marabu #1, 2005. C–print. 50 × 75 cm

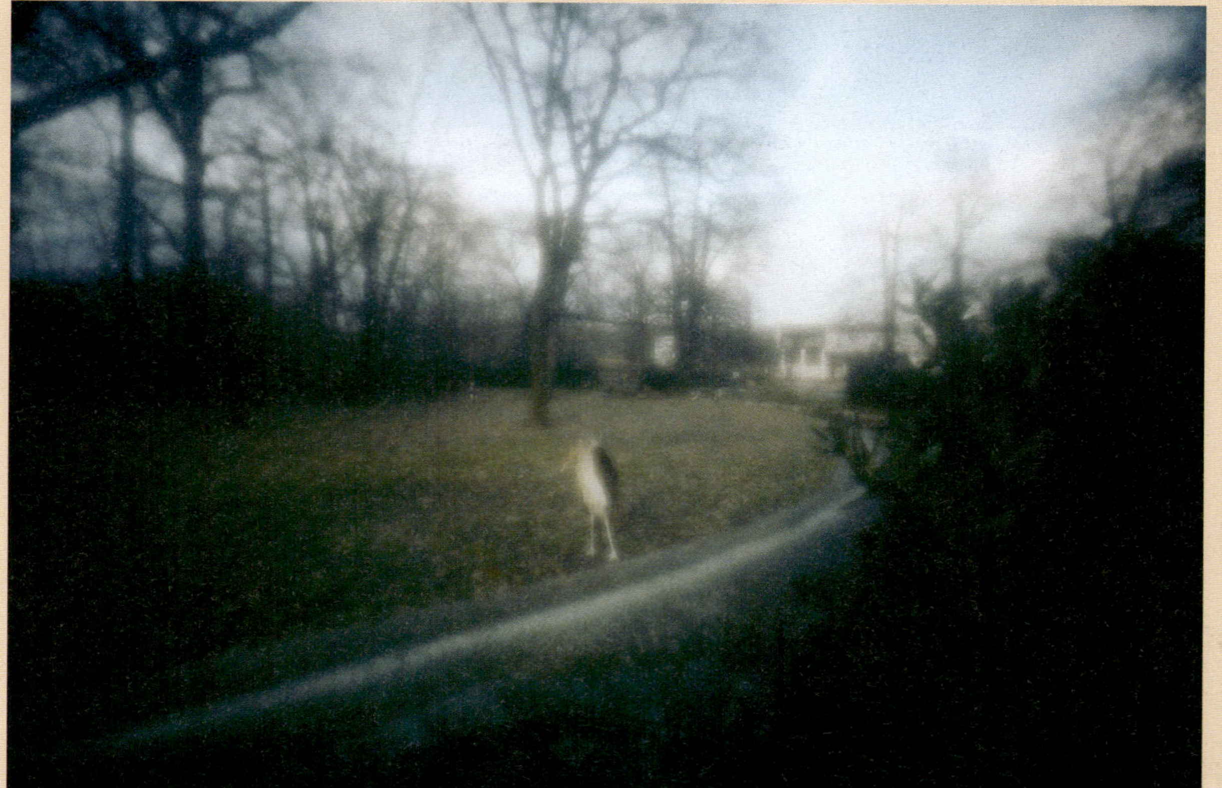

Marabu #14, 2005. C–print. 50 × 75cm

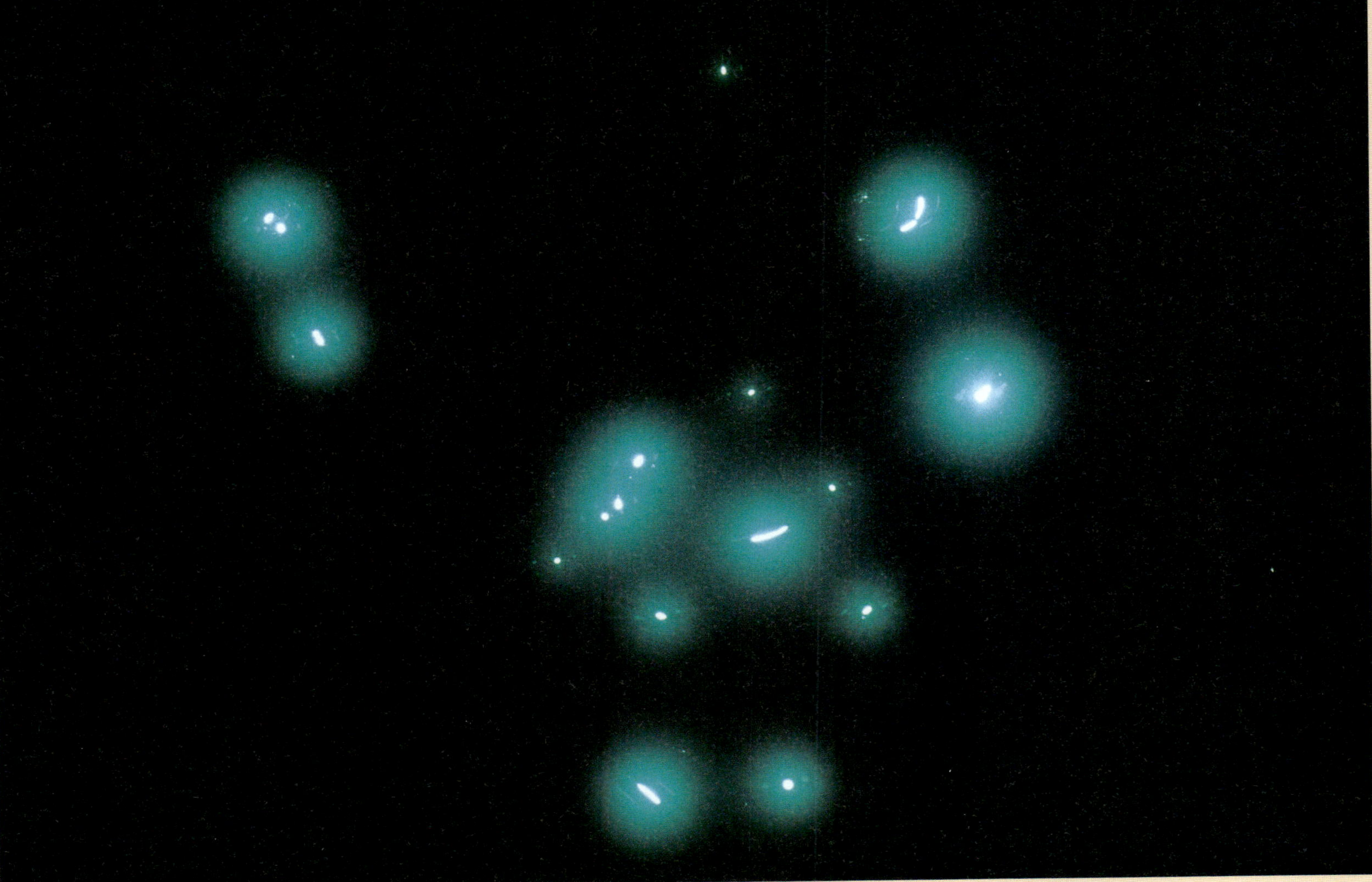

I Dreamt of Flying, #1, 2003. C–print. 96 × 120 cm

I Dreamt of Flying 2, #2, 2009. C–print. 100 × 150 cm

**She directs
her camera
wherever sunlight
(or moonlight)
falls, complying
with the
properties of
photography as
a medium
to capture the
'truth' of
her subjects.**

Rika continues her experiments in photographing light in her series *The Sun* (2005 – present), in which she uses a pinhole camera to photograph the sun in various locations, shooting so that its light is directed straight into the camera box and captured there. These works, divorced from any emotion, personal or narrative

The Sun

element, seem akin to scientific records. At the same time, the strong light that radiates from behind trees or through a window and renders contours of obejcts vague, gives these works the look of paintings, recalling the attempts of the nineteenth-century Impressionists to capture light outdoors in two dimensions.

When Rika turns her camera to people and animals she maintains an objective distance from her subject. *In the Desert* (2006–07), a series of photo-graphs captured by the artist while at the Sharjah Biennial, features racing camels tied together in the desert, as well as the people who raise them, offering glimpses of their everyday lives. And while desert and camels may be a hackneyed combination, Rika refrains from casting an exotic veil over the scenes, preferring to reflect an eye-opening wonder and freshness. The purity of her own eye is a miracle of sorts.

At a time when we know there are no utopias, Rika's photographs, like rays of light piercing a suffocating space, offer a presentiment that there are worlds out there still invisible to us, no matter how wide we open our eyes.

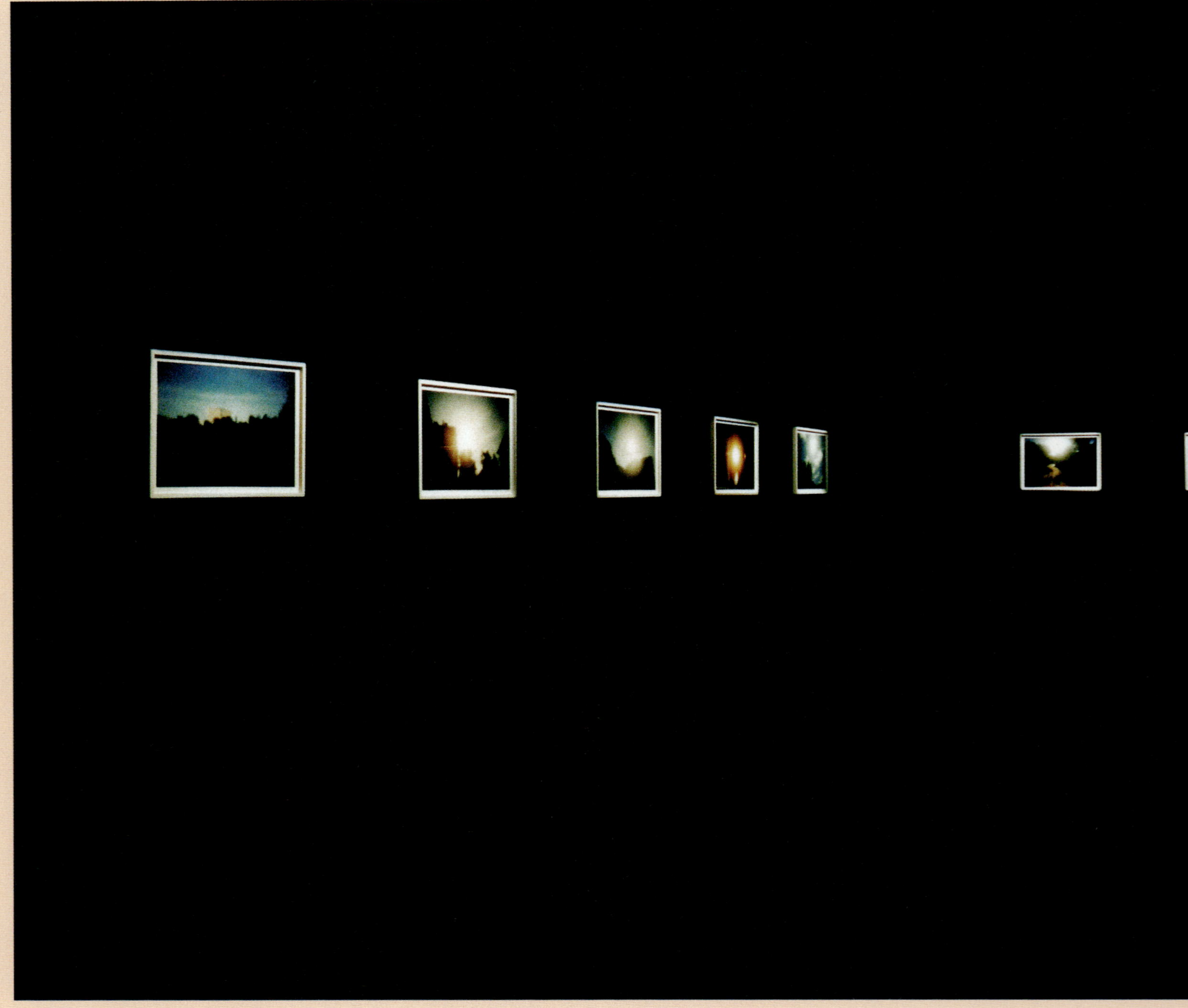

The Sun, 2005–08. 36 C–prints. Each 40 × 60 cm

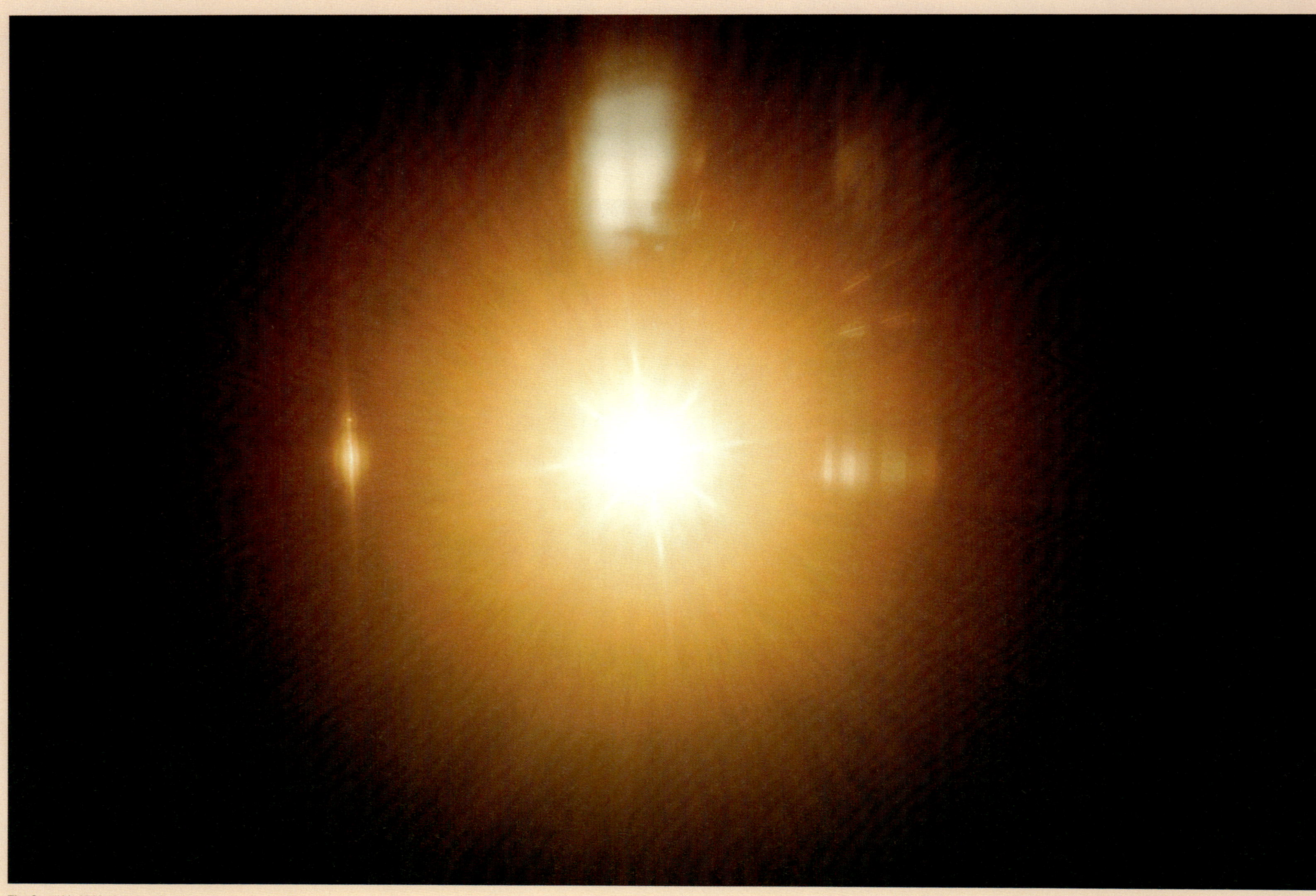

The Sun #11, 2006. C–print. 40 × 60 cm

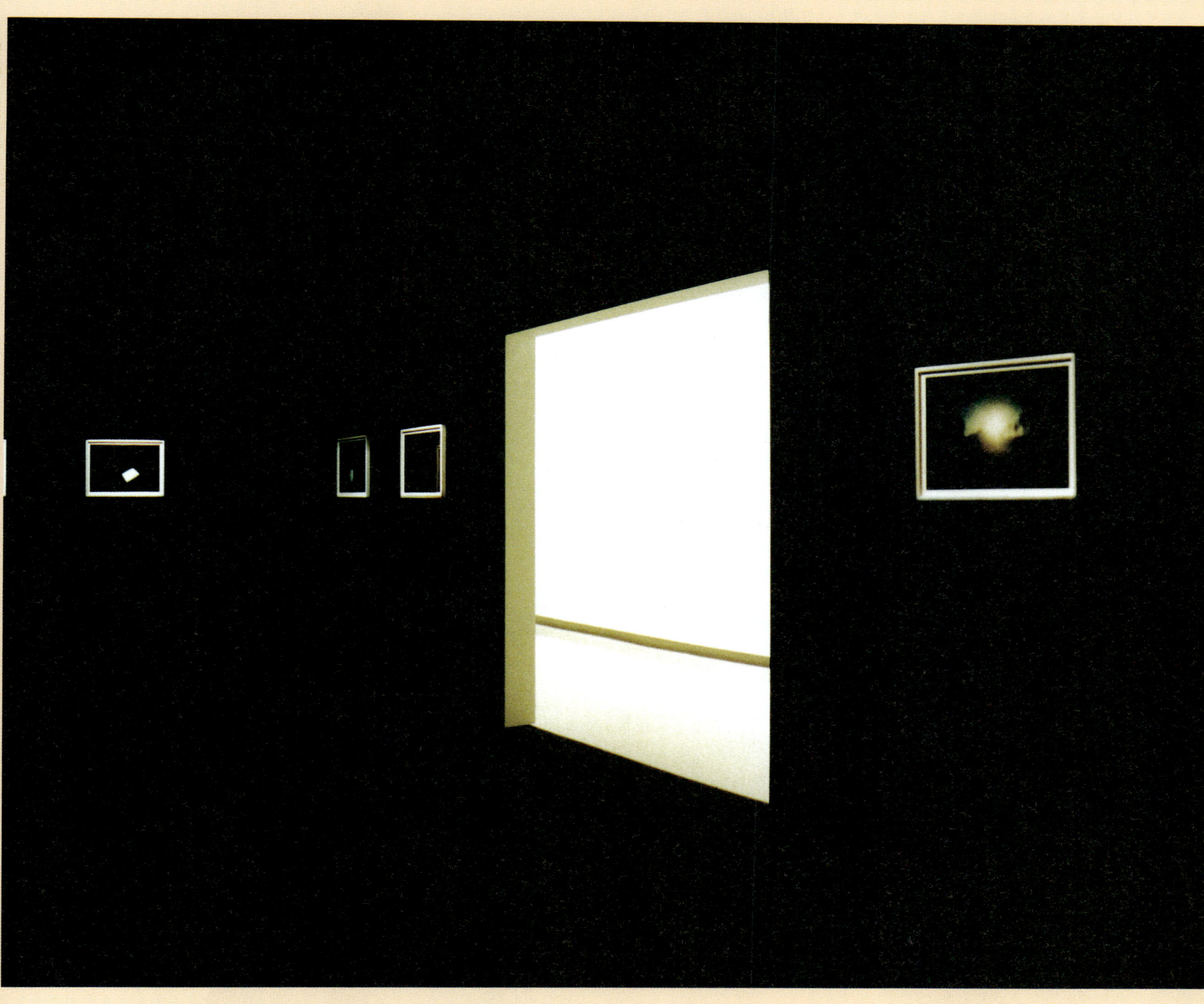

At a time when we know there are no utopias, Rika's photographs, like rays of light piercing a suffocating space, offer a presentiment that there are worlds out there still invisible to us, no matter how wide we open our eyes

The Sun #23, 2008. C–print. 40 × 60 cm

Aïda Ruilova

It is said that because the passage of time is inexplicable in words, grasping it is only possible (and even then, only indirectly) through images. Yet the 'motion picture', that medium seemingly with the most potential to express duration and temporal shifts, rarely tells us much about time per se. In a film, we might see a child age, seasons change or people die, but rarely do we feel that time has passed in a visceral sense. The paradox of Aïda Ruilova's videos is that while they often clock in at less than a minute and show little representation of time's passage or narrative progression, their abrupt editing, fractured sense of cinematic advancement and recurrent use of repetition make time and duration lived and felt. The American artist's videos might thus be as much *about* time as they are about their overt subject matter.

In Ruilova's works, single figures are often caught thrashing around or tap-tap-tapping their acrylic nails in claustrophobic spaces (corridors, stairwells, basements), feverishly performing acts somewhere between the macabre, the insane and the erotic. The result is what curator Ralph Rugoff has called 'a depraved kind of slapstick'. Yet almost nothing of the explicitly or graphically macabre, insane or erotic is actually shown. Instead, the uniquely visceral expression of time and mood is constructed in and between the montage.

Ruilova's use of extreme angles, abrupt camerawork and frequent jump cuts come out of the B-movie heritage that inspires her.

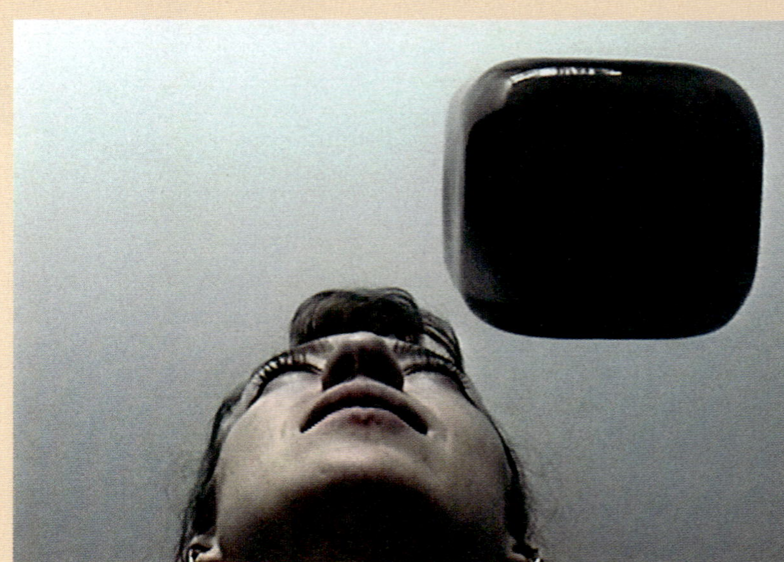

Duration and temporal shifts

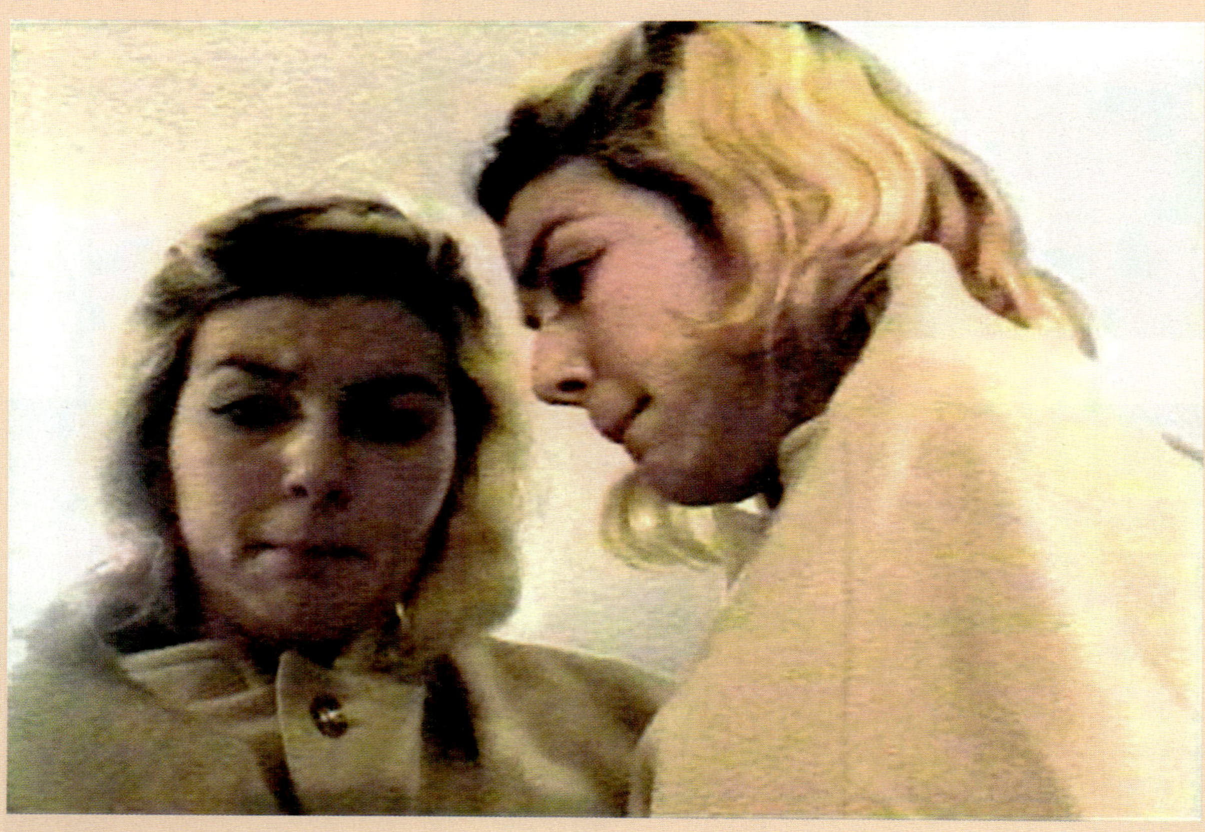

Beat & Perv, 1999. Video. 1 min. 25 sec.

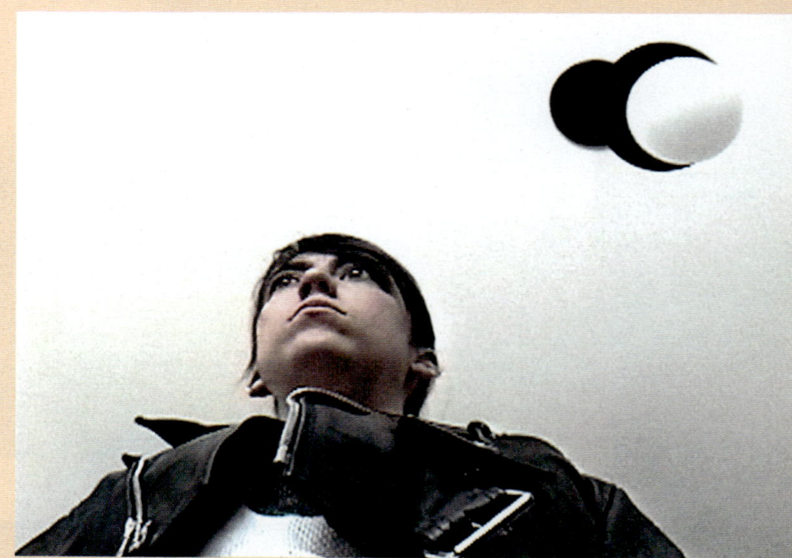

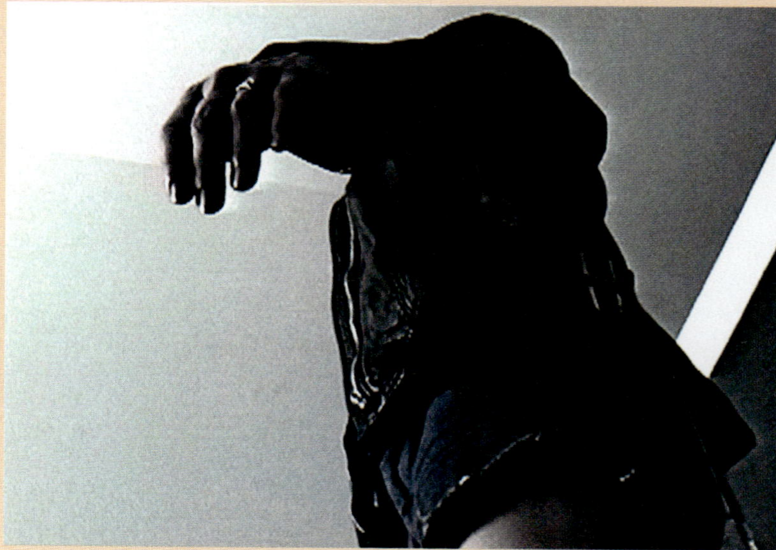

Uh Oh, 2004. Video. 19 sec.

A sense of hurried time

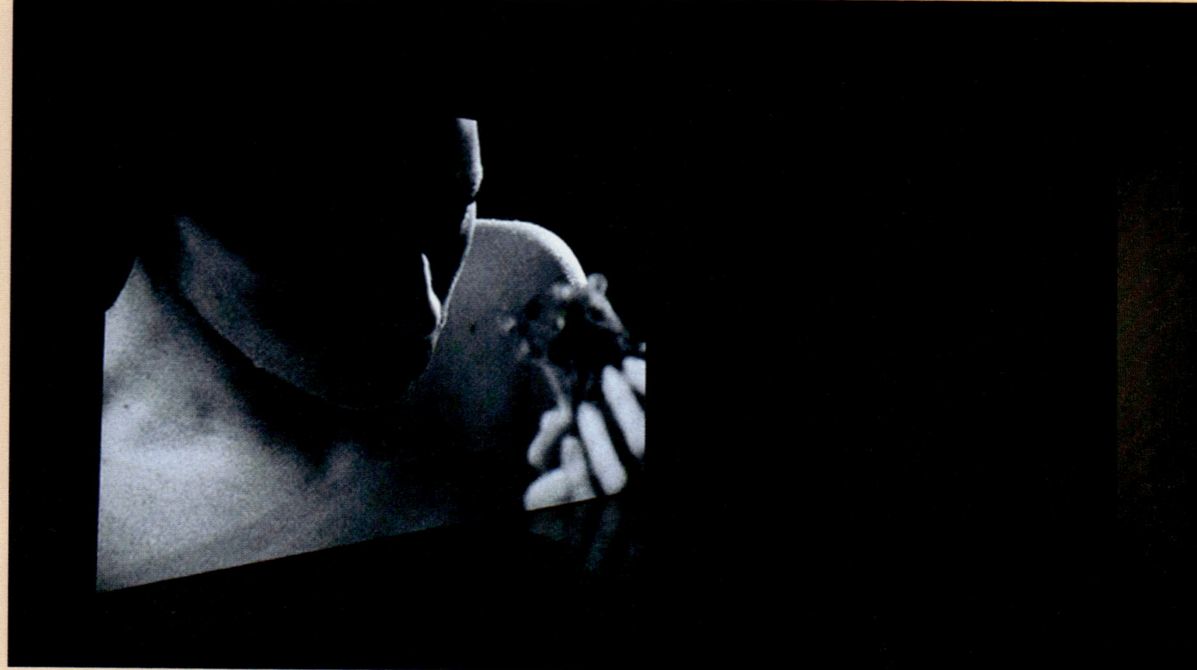

Two–Timers, 2008. Black and white 16 mm film with sound. 2 min. 40 sec.

Whereas some artists manipulate video so as to make the result resemble or function like its more expensive cousin, celluloid film, Ruilova's earliest experiments suggest that she was instead wilfully exploring the trash-aesthetic of video. Still, for all its cheapness, there is always something aesthetically ravishing in the result, where muted colours and oblique angles create moments of gorgeous abstraction. The way Ruilova makes a bruised face in *Beat & Perv* (1999) look strangely pleasing, or a man with his mouth held open in *The Stun* (2000) look like a Francis Bacon painting is indeed, stunning.

'Frenetic' is the adjective most often used to describe her work. Implicit in this is a sense of hurried time. The violence that Ruilova wreaks on both the idea of a stable image and any conventional sequential flow contributes to the frenzied angst of her films. Her use of repetition, whereby she choppily inserts single images back into the mix, equally gives them their epileptic air. Through it all, sound is as important as the image, with each of the cacophonic soundtracks orchestrated by Ruilova, a classically trained musician and

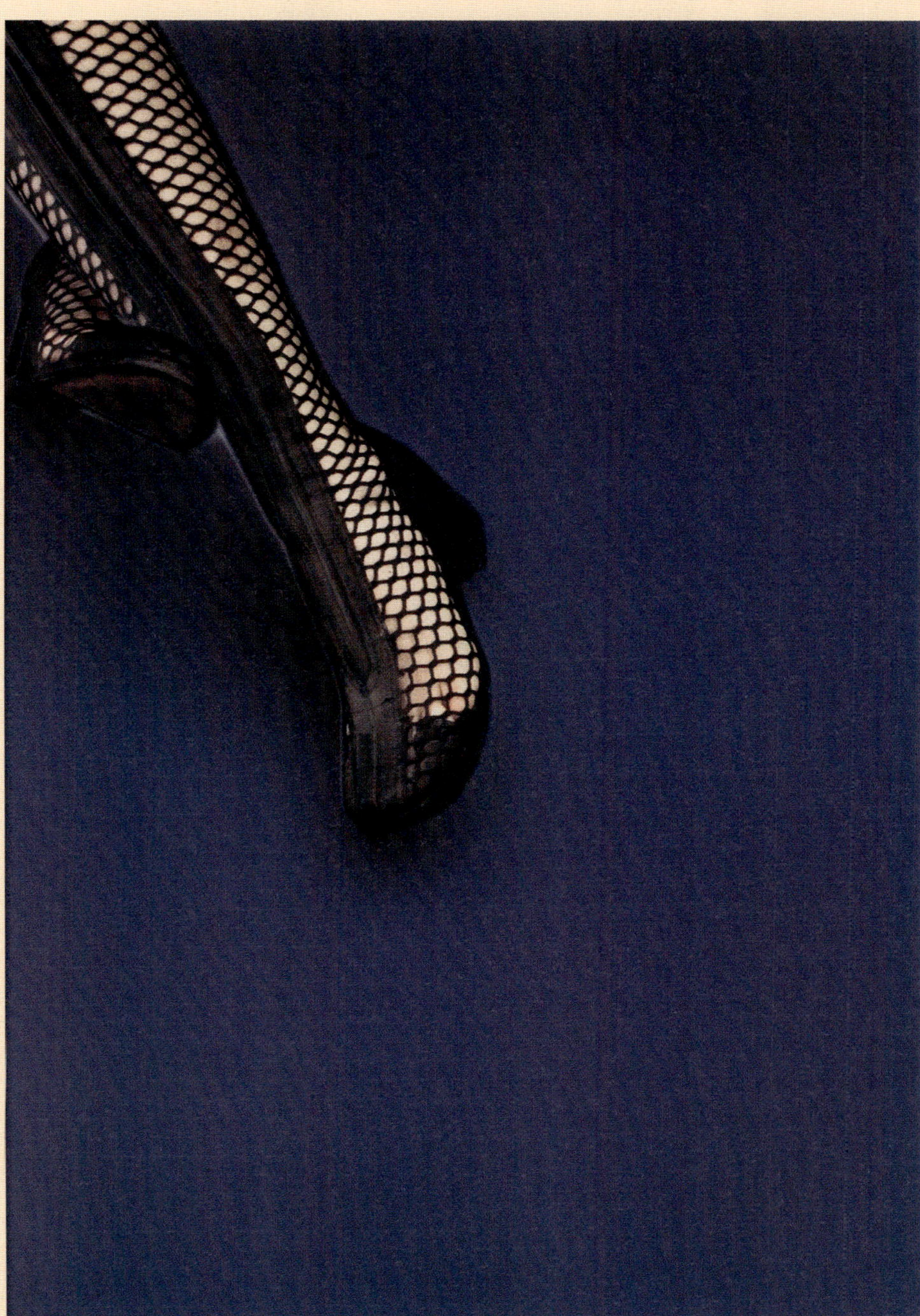

A–Z, Legs in the corner, 2008. C–print relief. 70 × 50 cm

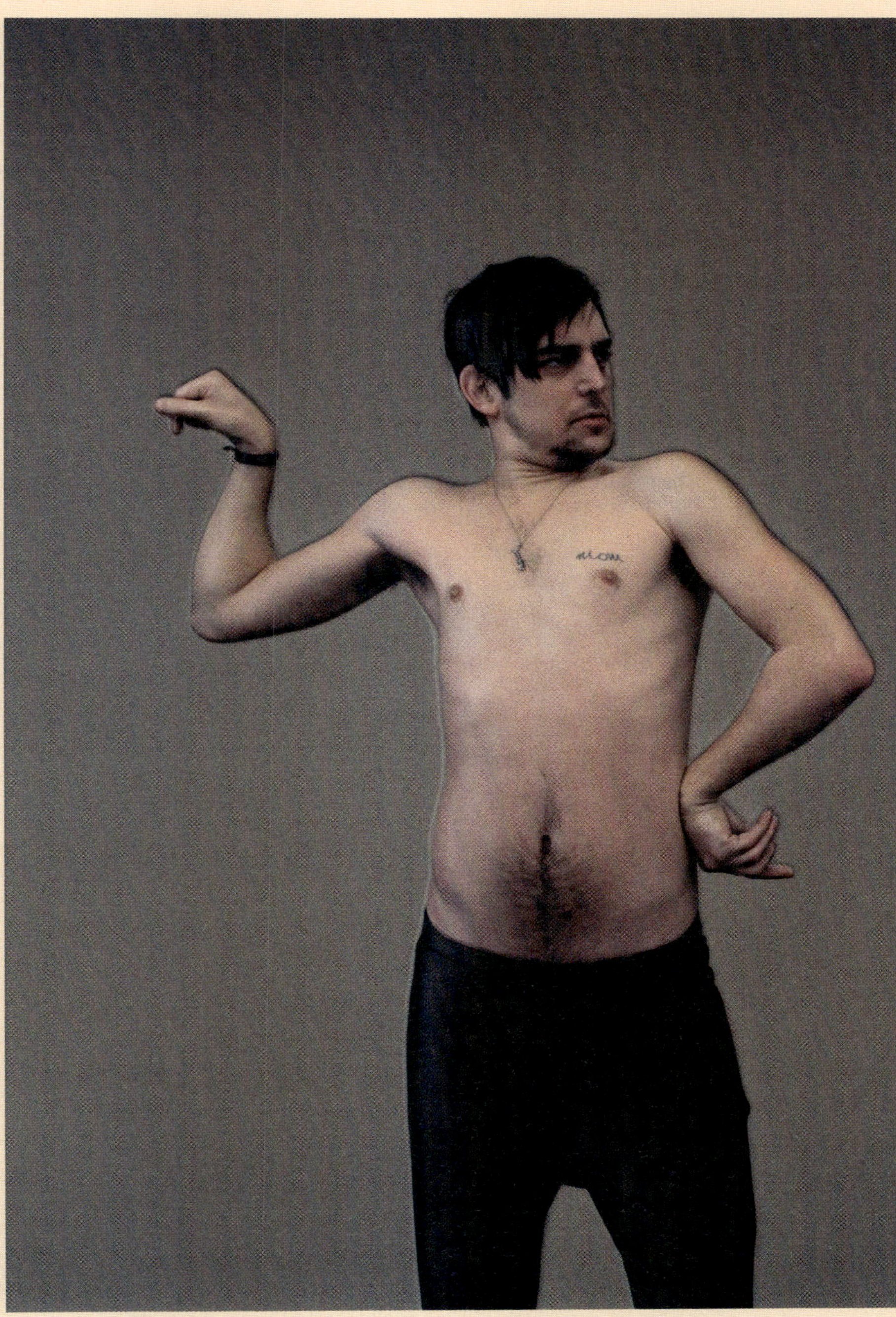

A–Z, God's a guy with a mom tattoo, 2008. C–print relief. 70 × 50 cm

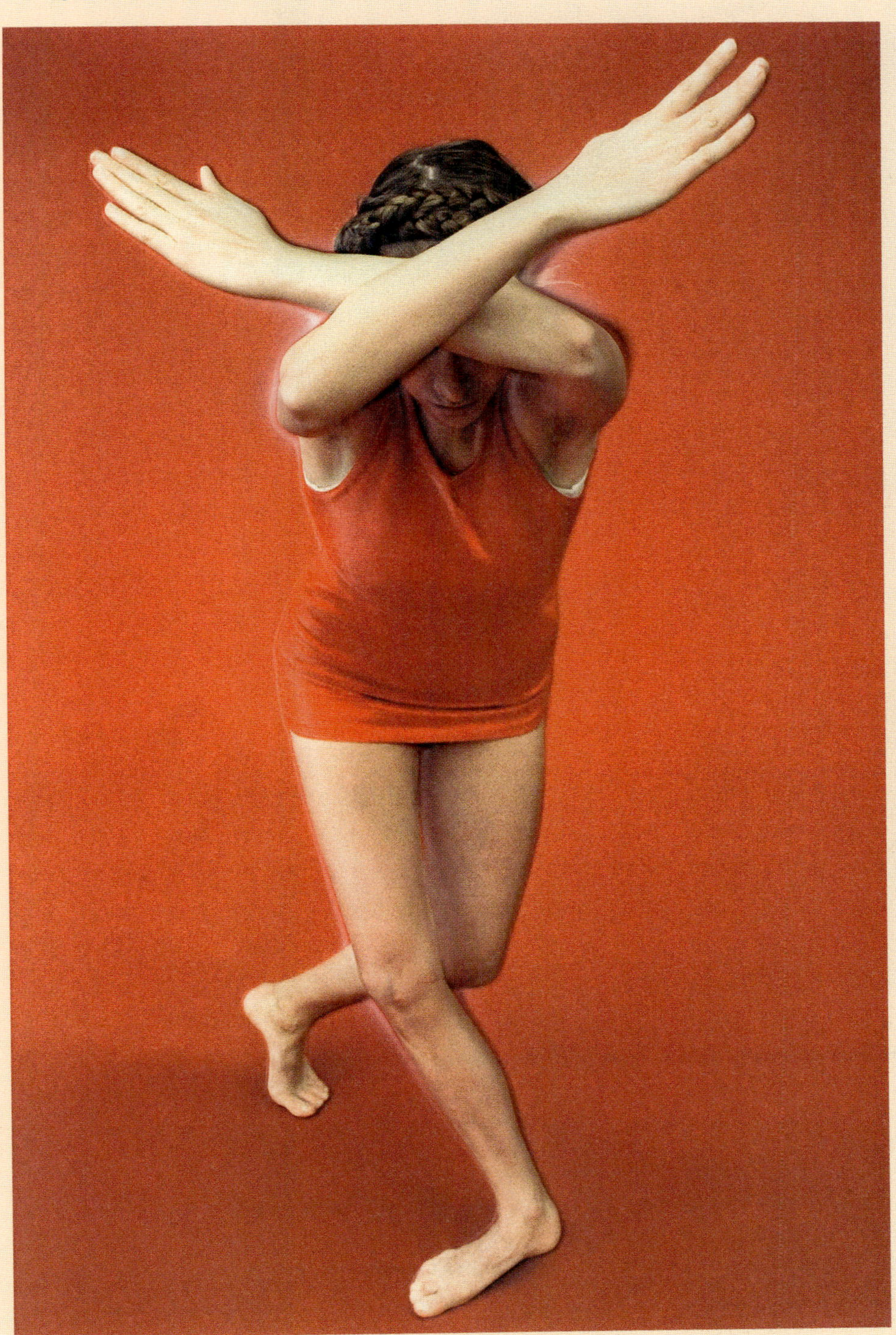

A–Z, X, 2008. C–print relief. 70 × 50 cm

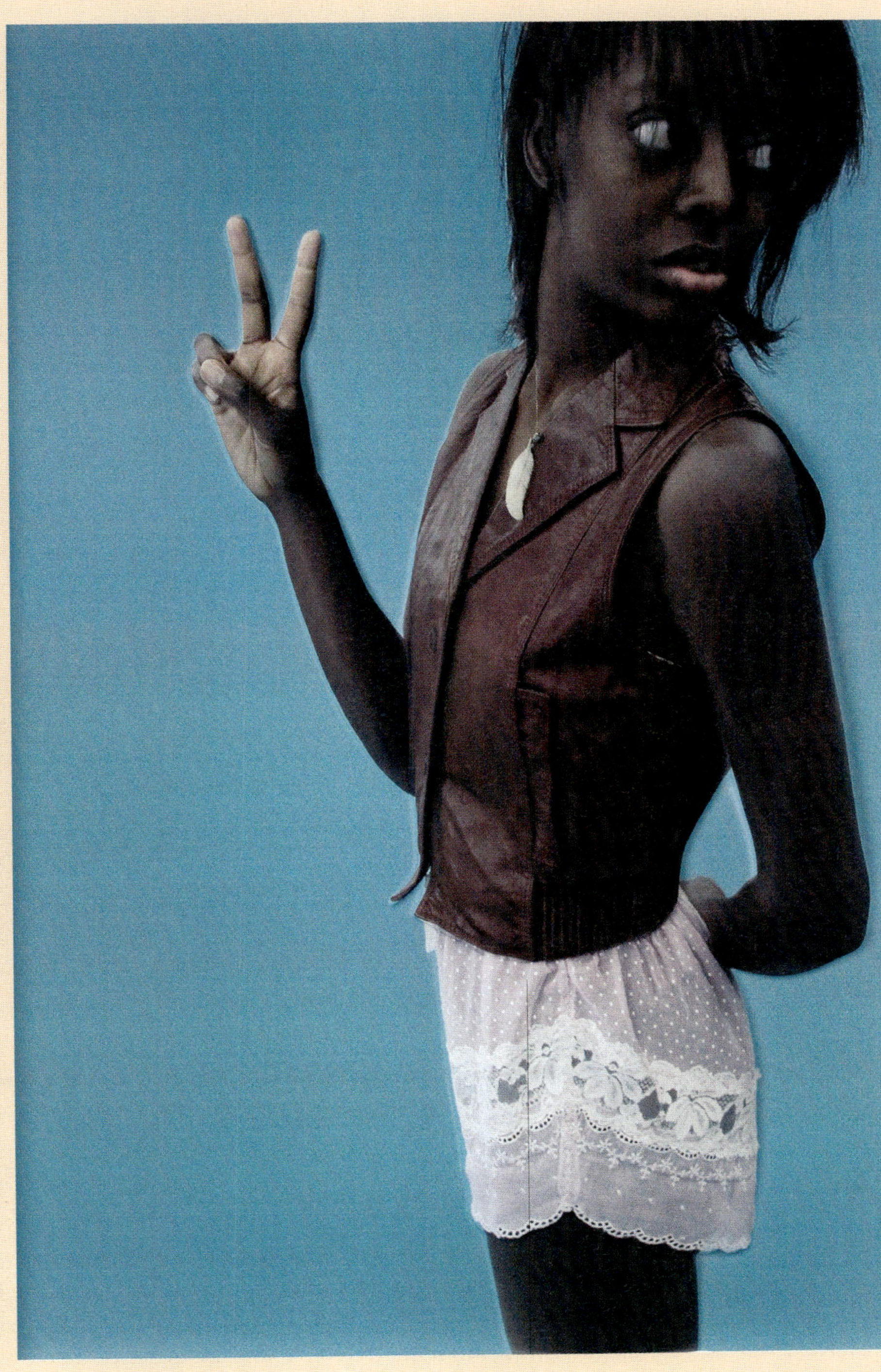

A–Z, Peace, 2008. C–print relief. 70 × 50 cm

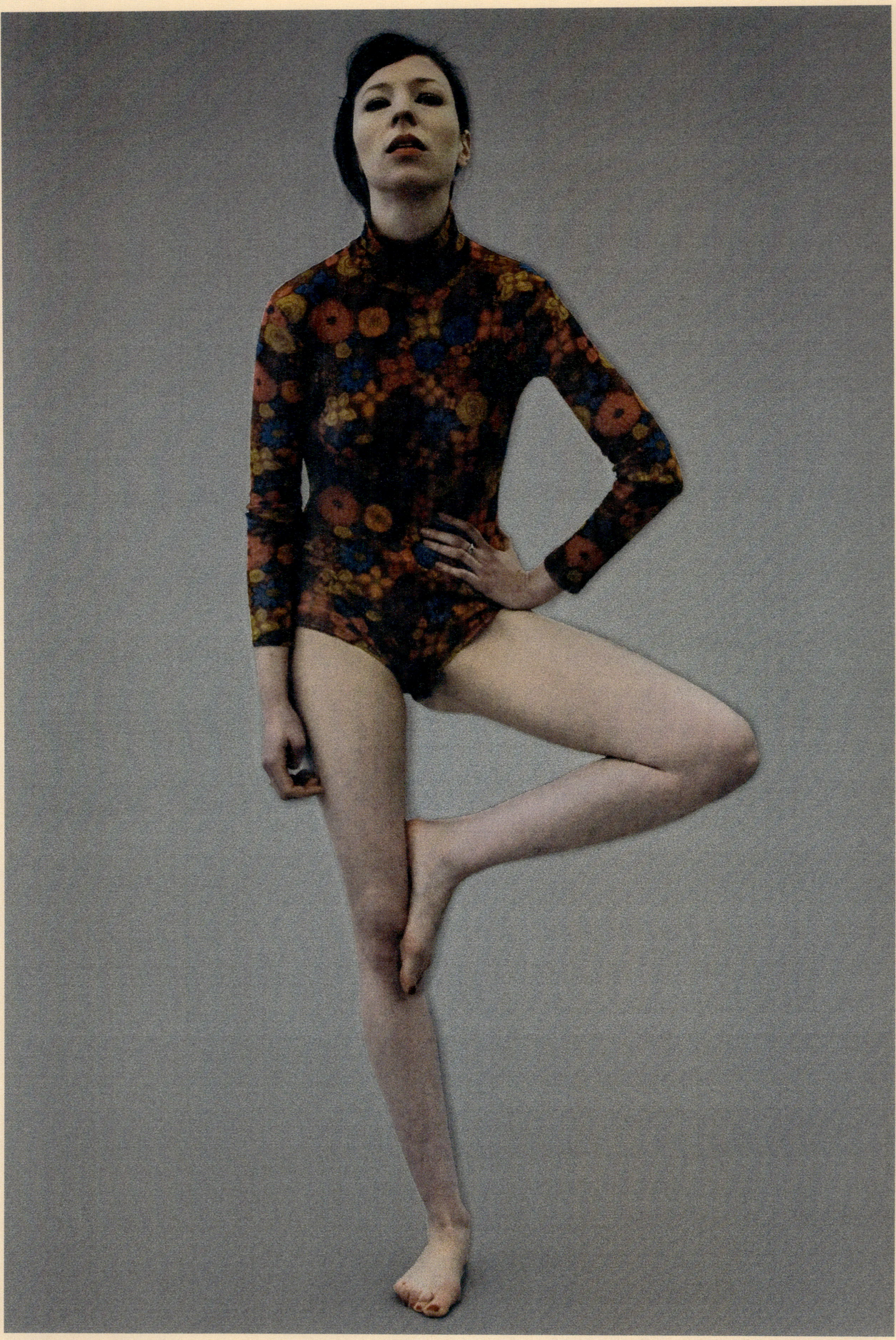

A–Z, B, 2008. C–print relief. 70 × 50 cm

a former member of a noise band. For many of her films, the title, a short duo-syllabic utterance, such as *Uh Oh* (2004) or *Alright* (2005) is grunted, moaned or muttered in the films themselves — repeatedly, of course.

Ruilova's *Life Like* (2006), her first film to run for more than a minute in length, includes excerpts from the 1970s soft-core horror films of Jean Rollin mixed with views of a young woman writhing and crying on the filmmaker's now-aged, prostrate body. Playing on the implied eroticism and menace of her mentor's vampire films, this and Ruilova's more recent projects exude an altogether different sense of confidence. Take, for example, *Two-Timers* (2008), in richly saturated black and white, in which a woman recites a poem to a rat as they both wallow in a moonlit pond. No matter how seemingly sophisticated her means, Ruilova's sense of dark foreboding, repetition and very particular sense of time remain.

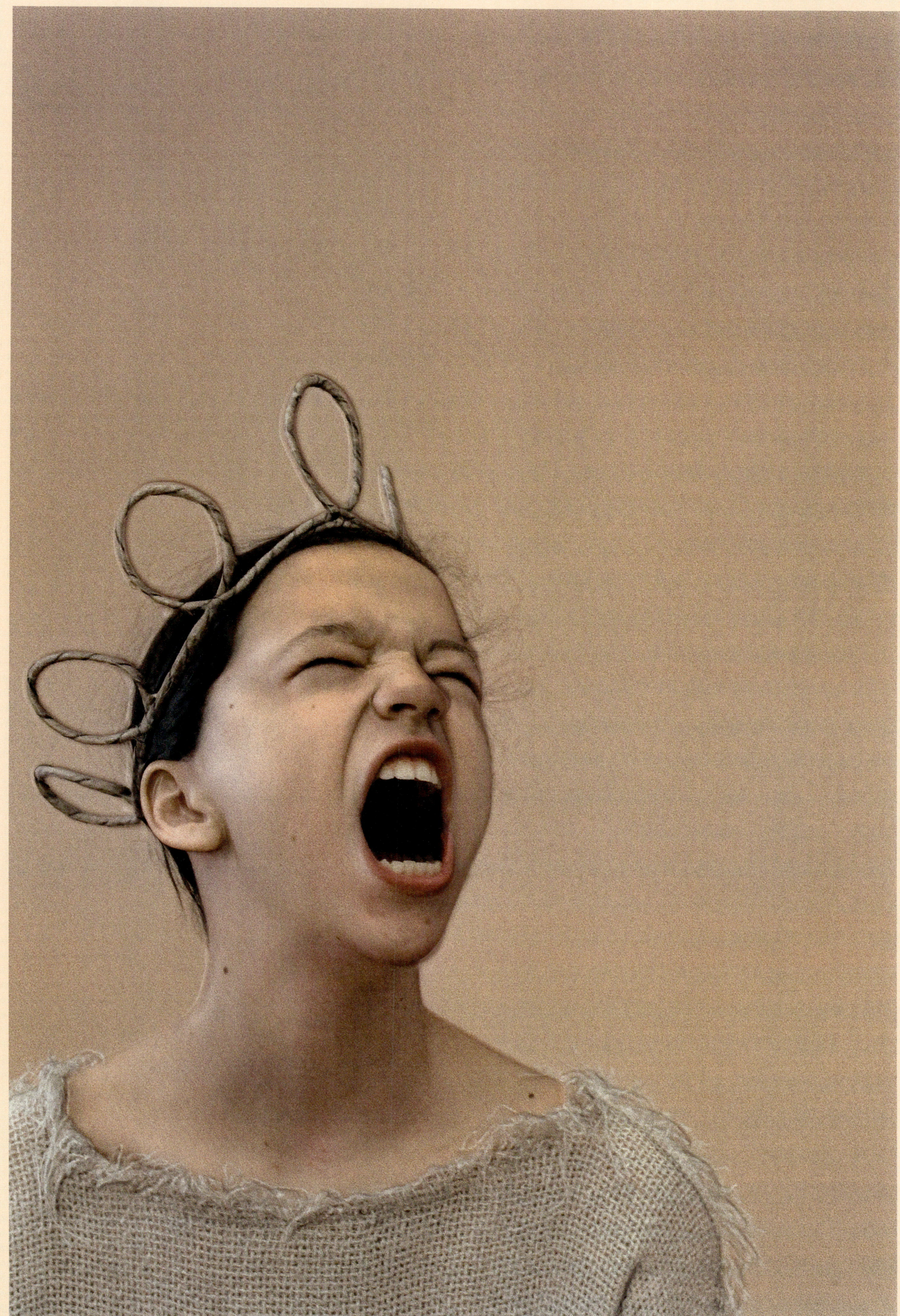

A–Z, The passion of Joan, 2008. C–print relief. 70 × 50 cm

Tomas Saraceno

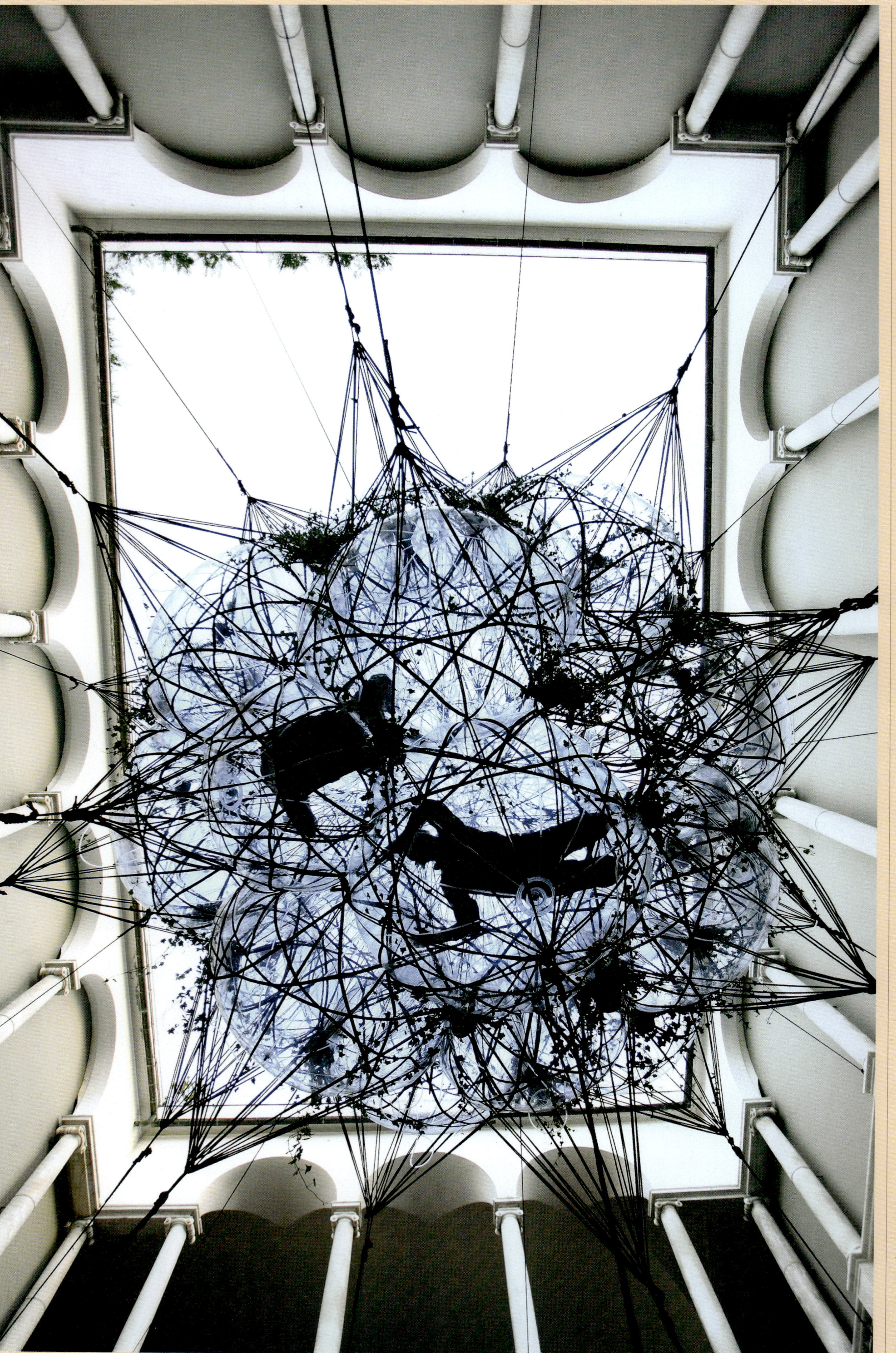

Biosphere MW32/Flying Garden/Air–Port–City, 2007. 12 elliptical pillows. Each 128 × 75cm. 20 elliptical pillows. Each 170 × 100 cm. Webbing, tillandsia plants. Dimensions variable. Sharjah Biennial, 2007

The poetics and politics of space lie at the heart of Tomas Saraceno's artistic practice. Originally trained as an architect, this Argentina-born, Germany-based artist navigates an intellectual territory that crosses the disciplinary boundaries of art, architecture, engineering, physics, aeronautics, biology and urban planning. Revelations from all of these fields are brought to bear by the artist in his investigation of issues of sustainability, nomadism, indeterminacy and the coalescence of communities across traditional geo-political boundaries. Finding inspiration in the geodesic domes of Richard Buckminster Fuller and the utopian architectural visions of the Archigram group (he was a student of one of its core members, Peter Cook), Saraceno practices a kind of 'science friction', whereby the utopian elements of artistic fantasy come into productive collision with the real world of hard science.

Many of Saraceno's works can be seen as attempts to elaborate on his ongoing theoretical architectonic project *Air Port City* (2001 – present), in which the artist envisions creating mile-long geodesic balloons that would be ecologically self-sustaining and would negate the stultifying effects of national boundaries. Over the last few years, this vision has been manifested by the artist in the form of sculptures and installations that take the inflatable sphere as their foundational form. In works such as *Biosphere MW32/Flying Garden/Air-Port City* (2007), Saraceno materializes an organic Fulleresque architectural entity that takes as its basic building blocks inflatable plastic spheres and stretched elastic supports. Floating within the space of the gallery like some sort of symbiotic architectural lichen, this inherently provisional work becomes an inhabitable platform for human beings and plants. Crucial to this sculpture and many of Saraceno's other works is his inclusion of plants from the genus Tillandsia, amongst which is included Spanish moss, a self-sufficient organism that does not need soil since it can take its necessary nutrients directly from the air. These plants form a metaphor for the artist's visions of freedom and self-sufficiency.

Saraceno's interest in self-sustaining biospheres extends to the cosmos itself, as could be seen in his contribution to the 2009 Venice Biennale. In his immersive installation *Galaxies forming along filaments, like droplets along the strands of a spider's web* (2009) he metaphorically lurched from the macro to the micro and back again with his labyrinthine latticework of spheres and elastic filaments. Condensing and falling apart at the

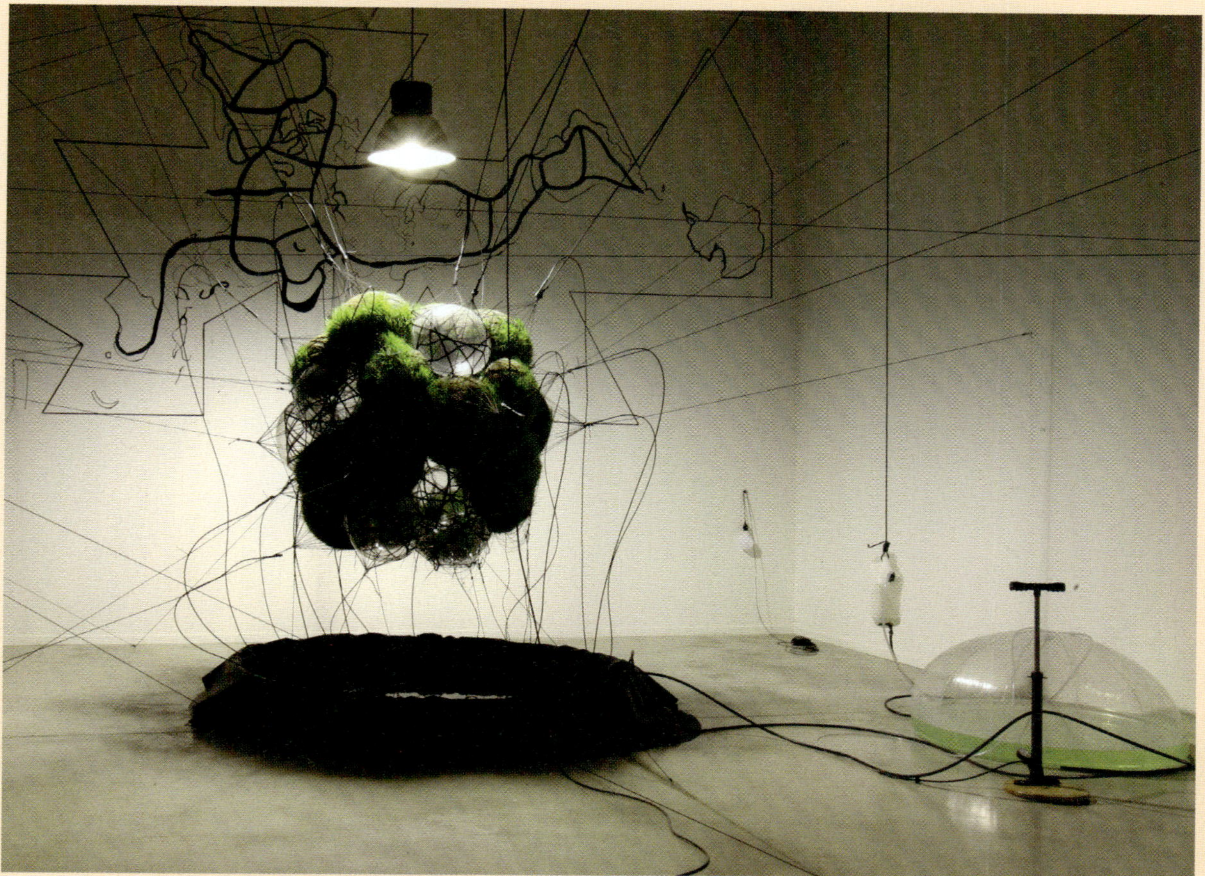

same time, these forms had to be negotiated by visitors, who climbed in and through the work as if they were navigating an astrophysical cluster of galactic globes clusters, or the elegant biomorphic designs of a spider's web. Other works such as *Poetic Cosmos of the Breath* (2007) totally envelop the viewer in a precarious inflatable foil 'shelter' with a structural support system based on the movement of air. In the end, it is this immersive quality of Saraceno's work that gives it such a human dimension. However, his is a conception of 'immersion' in an expanded field that challenges the boundaries not only between art and science, but also among the organic and the synthetic, the poetic and the practical, and the anchored and the unmoored.

Galaxies forming along filaments, like droplets along the strands of a spiders web

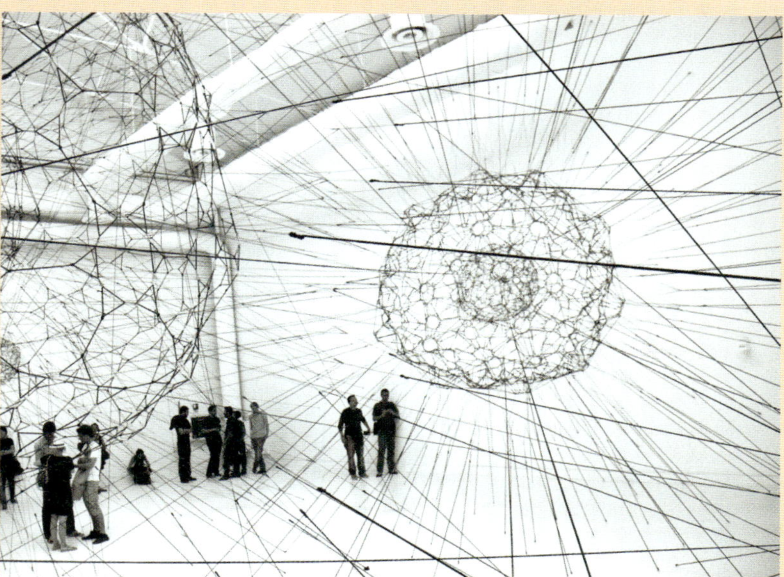

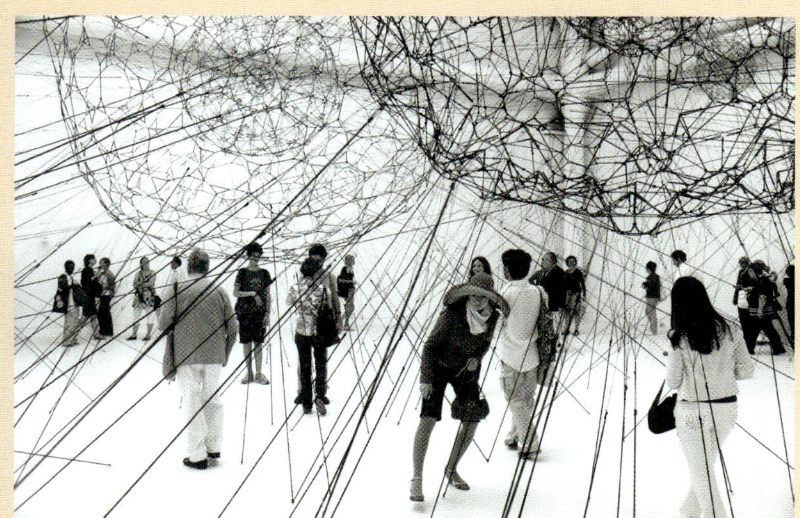

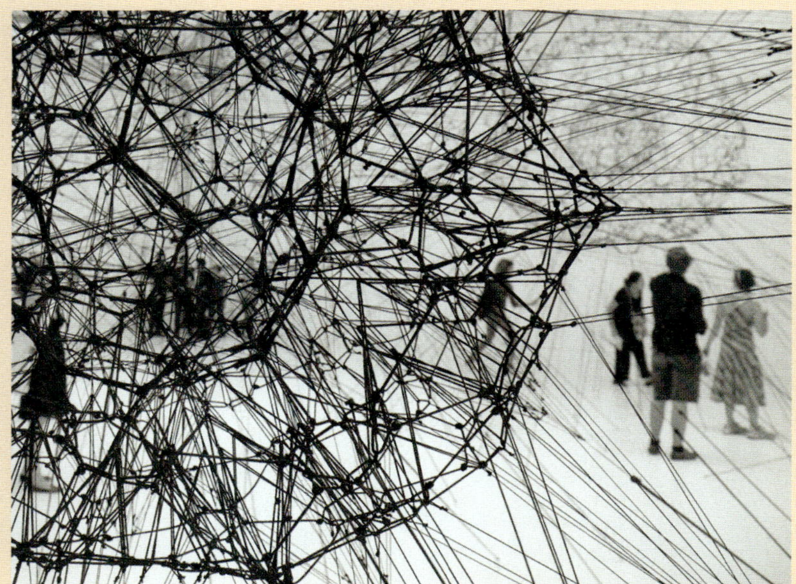

2SW/Stay Green/Flying Garden/Air–Port–City, 2007–09. Pillows filled with pressurized air, webbing, black felt, grass, flexible solar panels, electrical cables, battery, solar pump, water supply system, pool. Diameter 490 cm. Lyon Biennial, 2007

Galaxies forming along filaments, like droplets along the strands of a spider's web, 2009. Elastic cords, Dimensions variable. Venice Biennale, 2009

          Tomas Saraceno — Frankfurt, Germany

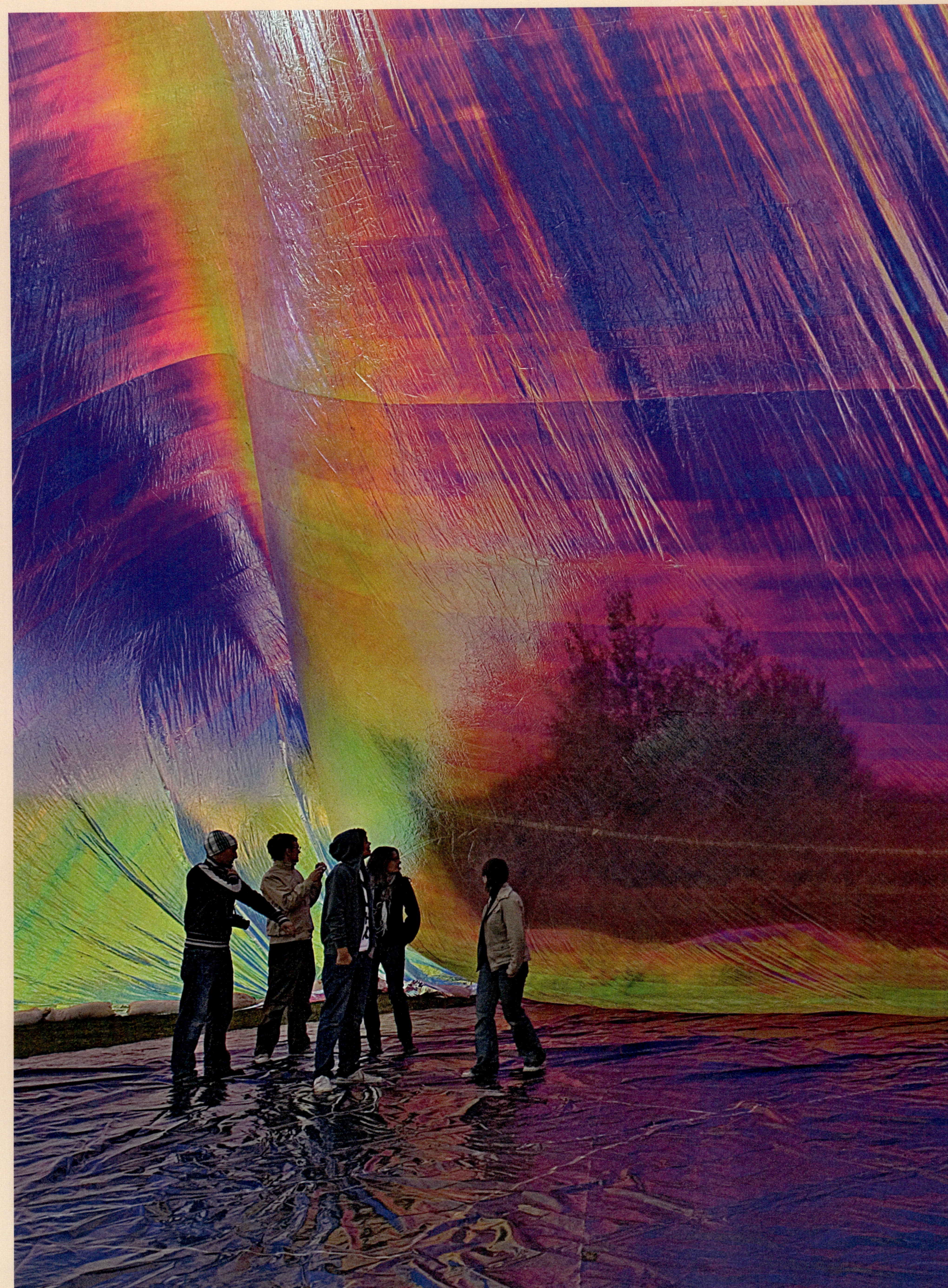

Untitled, 2007. Iridescent foil, air. Dimensions variable. 'Air Show', Gunpowder Park, London.

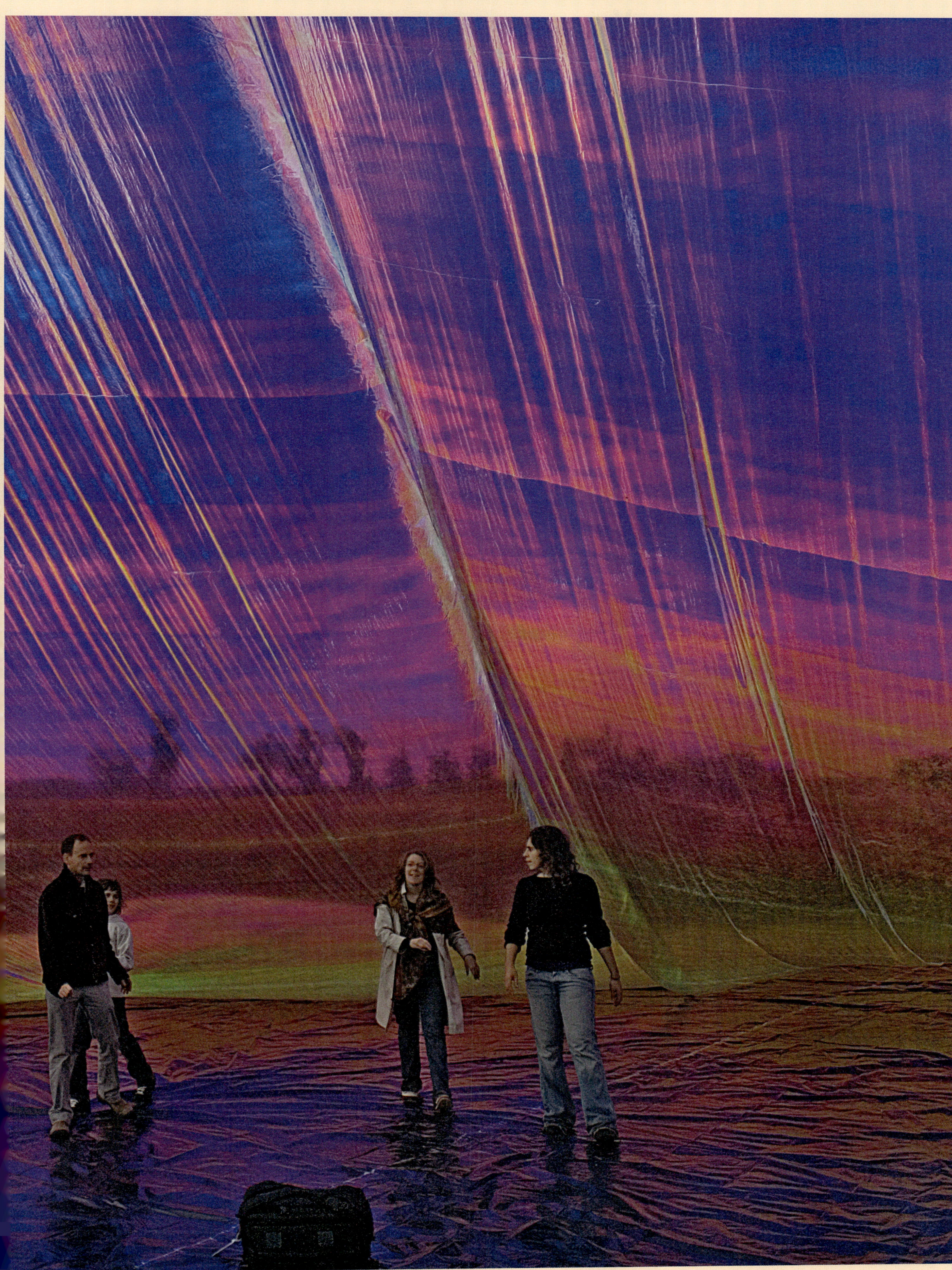

Katerina Šedá

Katerina Šedá's projects are always collaborative, bordering on coercive, in nature. In the majority of the large-scale works she has made in the past few years, she has put a great deal of time and energy into negotiating with, and securing the participation of, large groups of people from her native village in the Czech Republic, or from neighbouring villages. Šedá's work might be termed 'applied conceptualism': taking the rule-games of 1960s and 1970s art (whether On Kawara's mail art, Yvonne Rainer's minimalist choreography, or the near-invisible street actions of Jiri Kovanda, who taught Šedá) and using them to sculpt action and interaction in real life. Each work sets up a situation in which the participants are subject to certain kinds of regulation, and in the process become party to new kinds of reciprocity.

Šedá's childhood experience of living under communism is often invoked in discussions of her work, but despite these explorations of communality, she does not appear to be nostalgic for its way of life. Yet that does not mean that she is satisfied with the current state of things. From *It Doesn't Matter* (2005), a project made in collaboration with her late grandmother Jana Šedá to rouse her from the depression of bereavement, to *Over and Over* (2008), in which she persuaded her neighbours to construct means for climbing over their garden fences, creating a circuit through the private land of the entire village, Šedá explores both societal and familial bonds, and how they might be challenged or reinvented.

In *For Every Dog a Different Master* (shown at Documenta 12) Šedá created an action involving the inhabitants of a high-rise housing complex in nearby Nová Líšeň that is typical of late twentieth-century architectural atomization. Residents in the

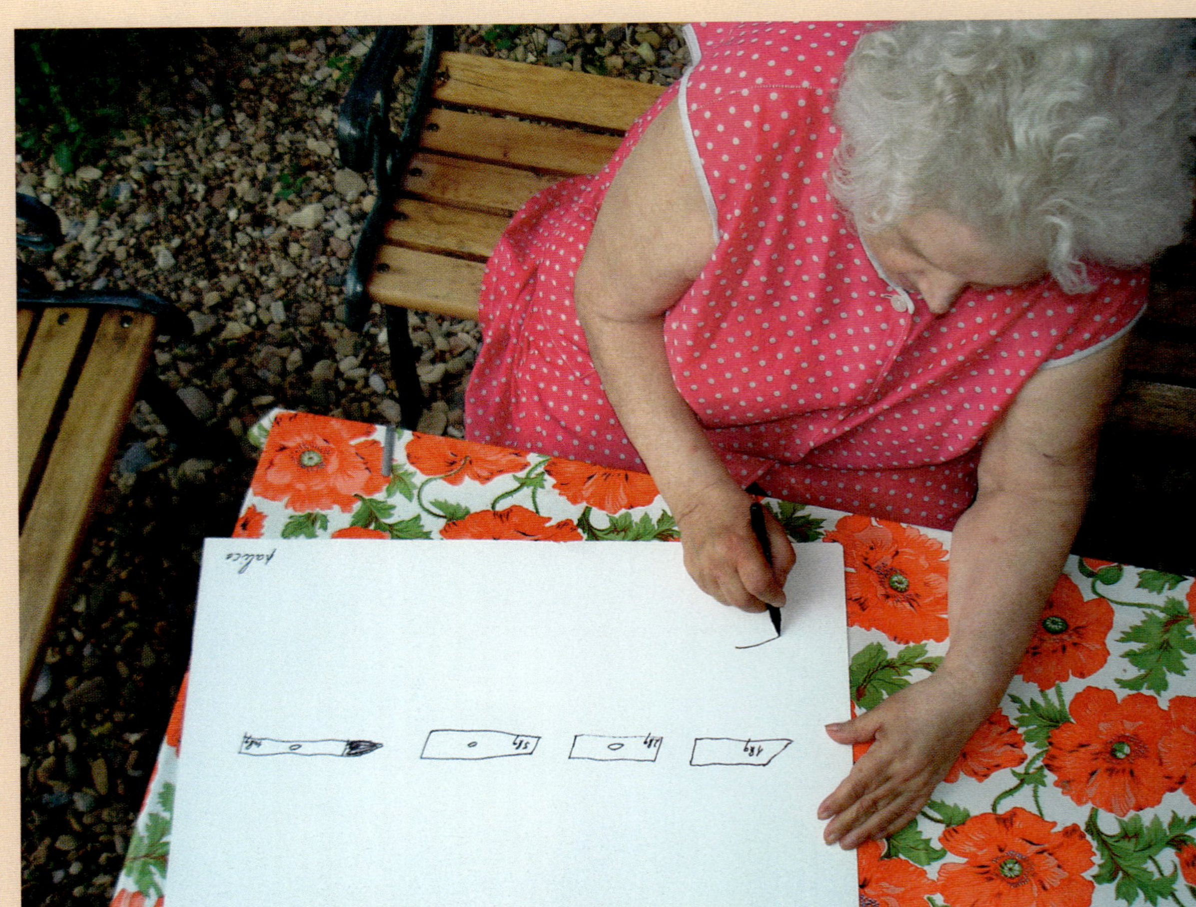

It Doesn't Matter, 2005–07. Colour photograph. 30 × 40 cm

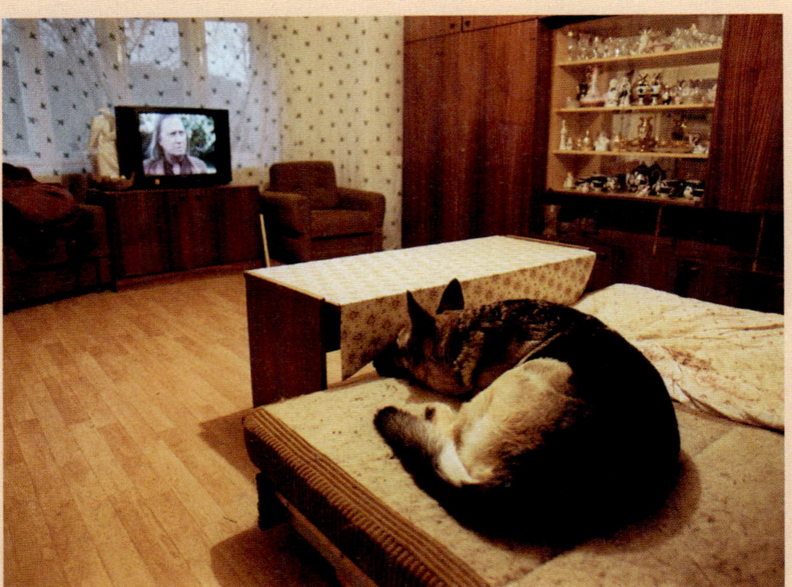

Her Mistress's Everything, 2008. Colour photograph. 60 × 40 cm

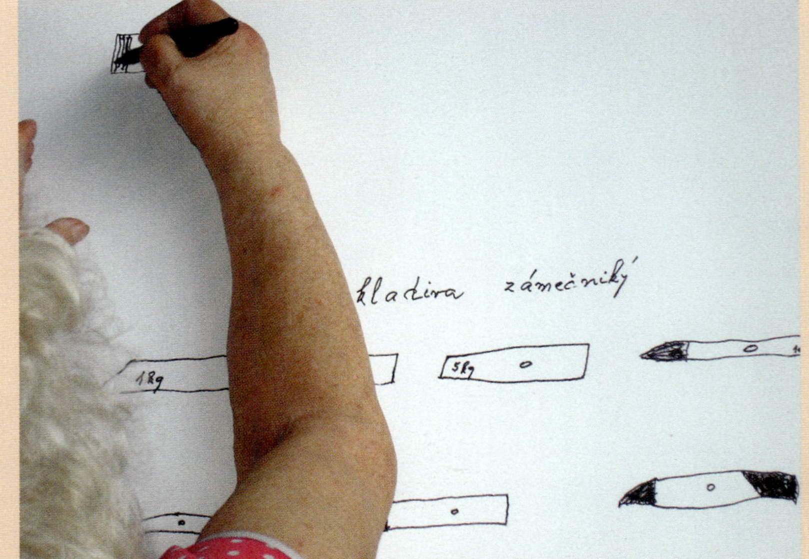

It Doesn't Matter, 2005–07. Colour photograph. 30 × 40 cm

> **Šedá's childhood experience of living under Communism is often invoked in discussions of her work, but despite these explorations of communality, she does not appear nostalgic for its way of life.**

Realist representation

blocks had moved from smaller villages where they had regularly seen a network of neighbours, and were living in relative isolation. Šedá designed and had printed a shirt that featured an image of the housing blocks and then paired the addresses of the over 1,000 inhabitants from different parts of the block, sending hand-written envelopes containing the shirts to each one, so that it appeared they had sent them to each other. Šedá then observed the resulting interaction as people began, in her words, to 'see one another'. A month later, the artist invited the residents to her exhibition at a local gallery. The invitation card stated that the exhibition's subject was Nová Líšeň, and a significant number of its residents showed up. The following month Šedá sent another letter to the residents explaining the project's intentions and asking for comments. Although many residents expressed their gratitude, several gave critical repsonses, accusing the artist of being naive and intrusive. Šedá considers the feedback an essential part of the project. The transformations and revelations that occur in her work are perhaps aimed at creating a form of realist representation, rather than being utopian in character.

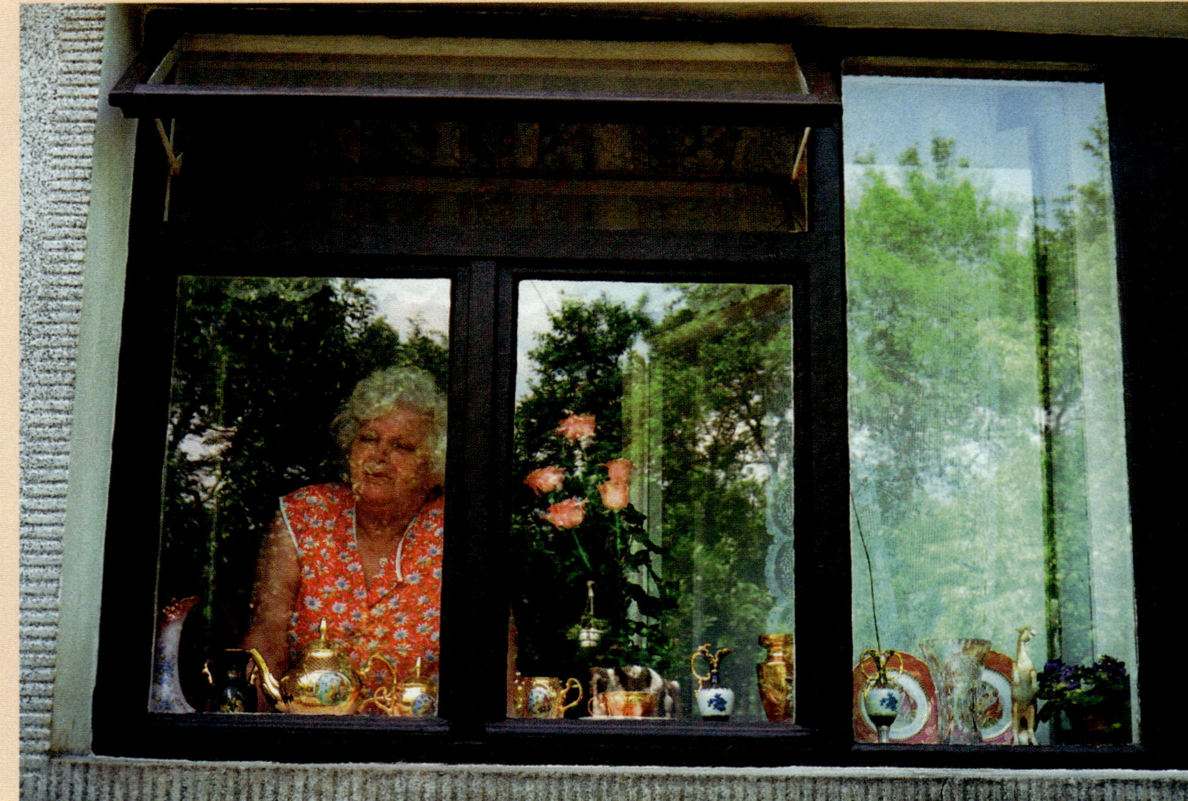

Window Exhibition, 2001. Colour photograph. 130 × 180 cm

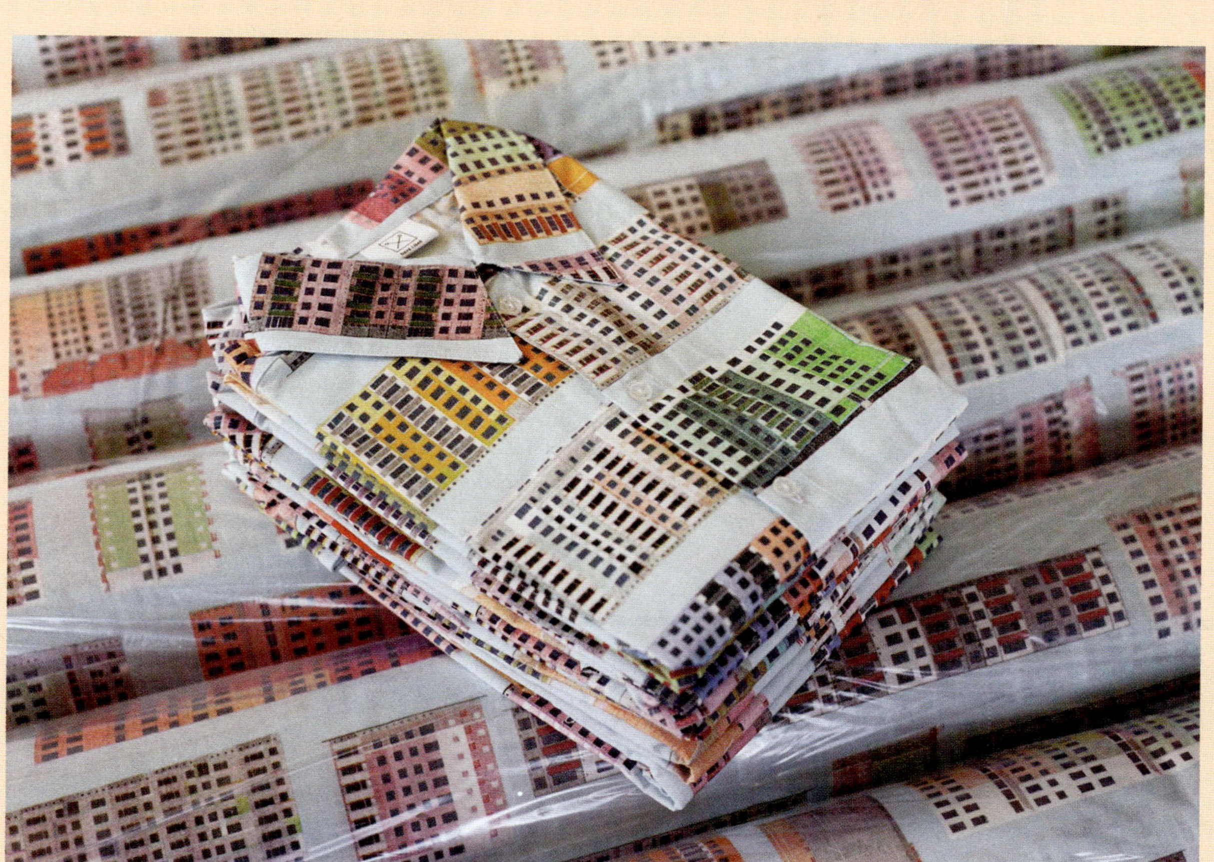

For Every Dog a Different Master, 2007. Fabric, shirts. Dimensions variable

Transformations and revelations

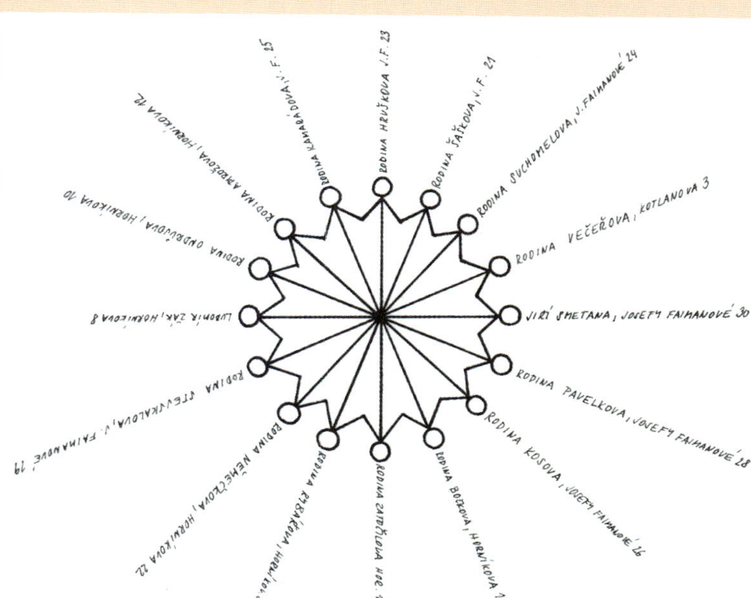

For Every Dog a Different Master, 2007. Ink on paper. 21 × 30 cm

Societal and family bonds

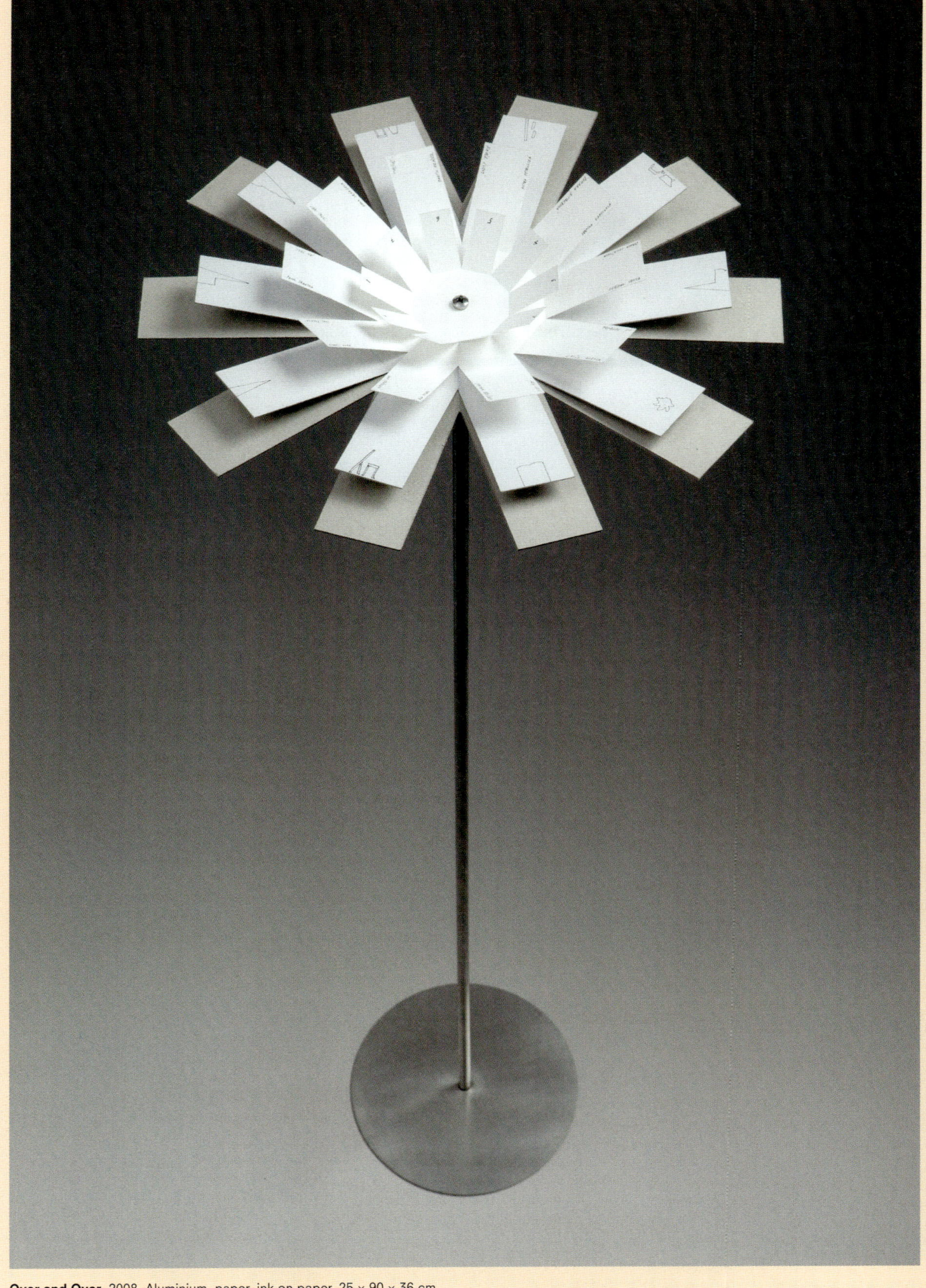

Over and Over, 2008. Aluminium, paper, ink on paper. 25 × 90 × 36 cm

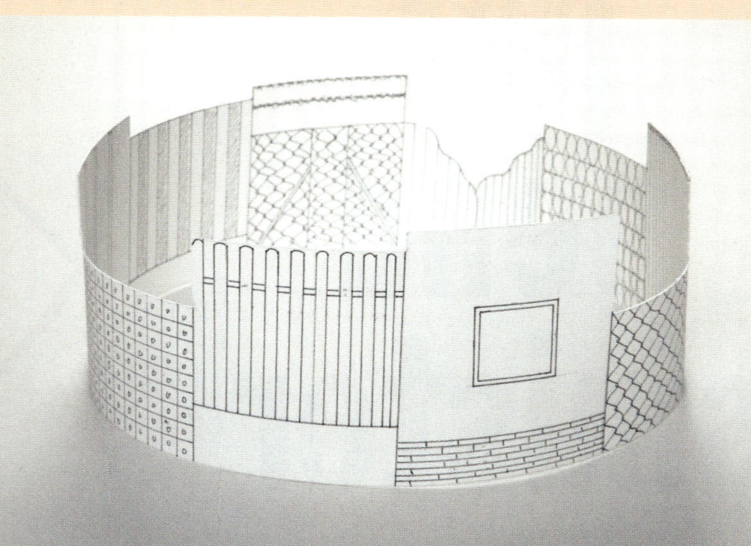

Over and Over, 2008. Ink on paper. Diameter 15 cm

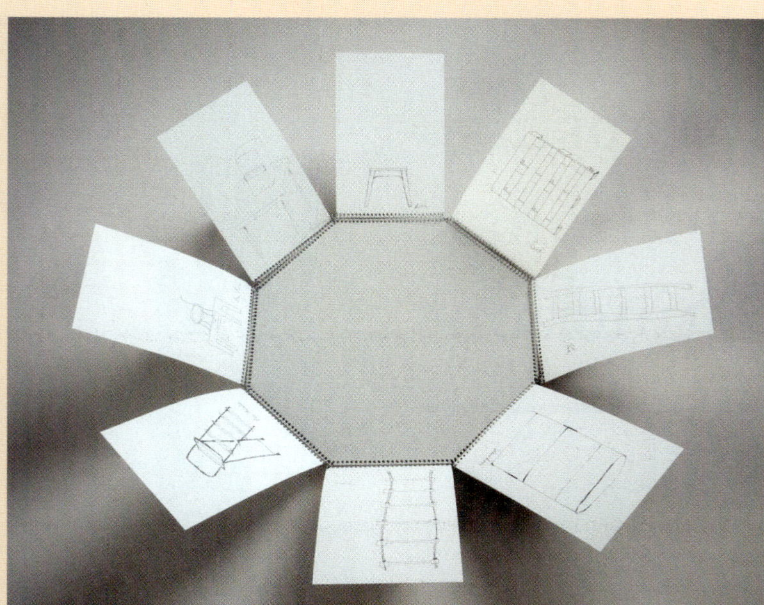

Over and Over, 2008. Aluminium, paper, ink on paper. Diameter 33 cm

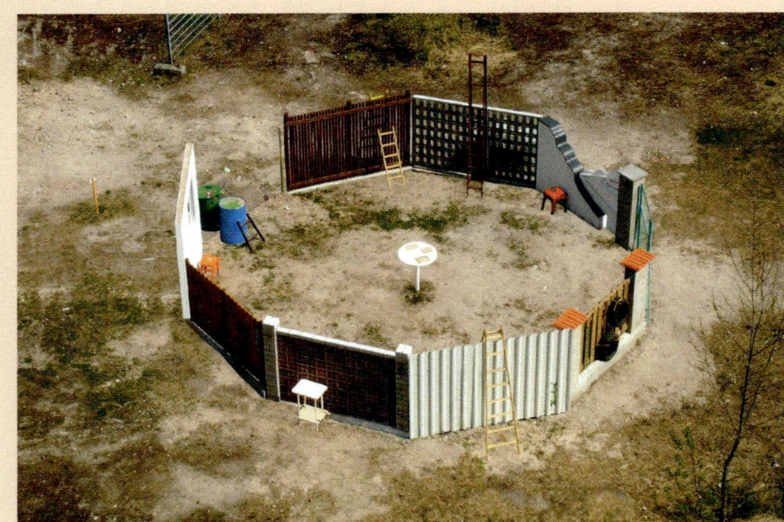

Over and Over, 2008. Wood, concrete, glass, aluminium brick, iron. Diameter 10 m

David Reinfurt — New York, NY, USA & **Stuart Bailey** — Los Angeles, CA, USA

Dexter Sinister

A small, low-ceilinged basement workshop on New York's Lower East Side serves as the office/studio/workshop and sometimes bookshop for Dexter Sinister, the compound name of David Reinfurt and Stuart Bailey. Together,

Reinfurt and Bailey have been exploring contemporary publishing since 2006 by utilizing print-on-demand, inexpensive local presses and alternative distribution strategies while collapsing the traditional distinctions between

editor, designer, producer, publisher and distributor.

In 2005, Reinfurt and Bailey were in charge of producing all the graphic-design material for Manifesta 6. At that time, they developed the name Dexter

Sinister and a crest consisting of a heraldic device: a plain shield with a diagonal line running from the top right corner to bottom left edge — in Latin *dexter* and *sinister*, respectively. When Manifesta 6 failed to materialize, they decided

to relocate to New York and took the name and crest with them.

In 2007 Dexter Sinister was invited by the Centre d'Art Contemporain in Geneva to participate in a group exhibition on design and utopia entitled

(party) per bend sinister

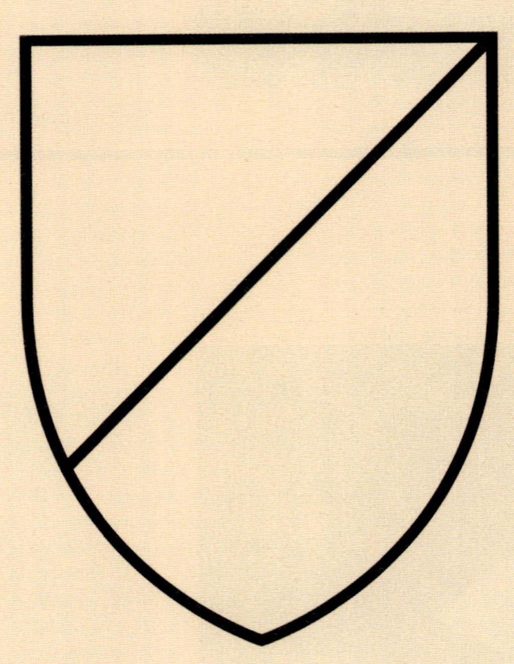

Dexister Sinister crest, 2006

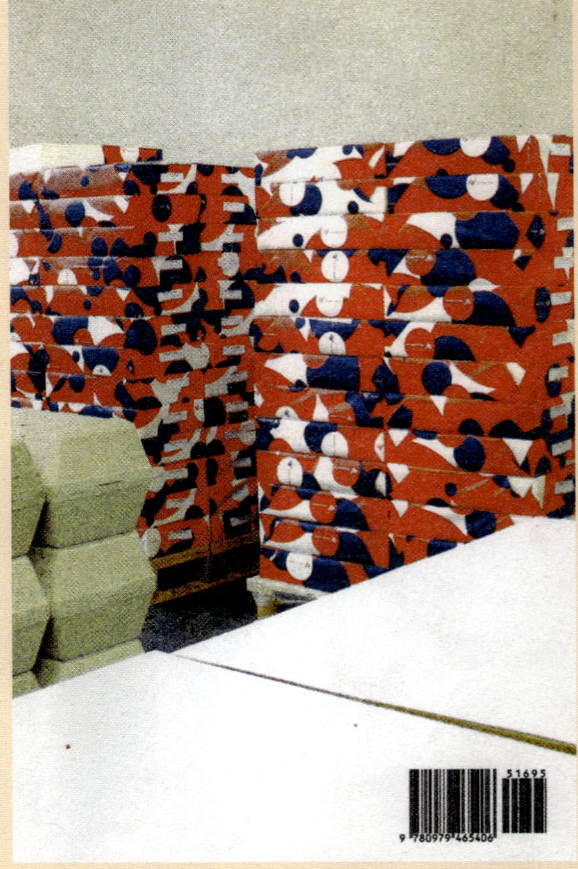

Dot Dot Dot 15

Dot Dot Dot 15 (cover), 2007. Stencil-printed publication. 104 pages. 235 × 165 cm

Collapsing traditional distinctions

'Wouldn't it Be Nice …'. They decided to produce — from start to finish — a copy of their house journal, *Dot Dot Dot*. In two weeks the journal was written, designed, edited and printed in the museum, and eventually copies were shipped back to New York for distribution.

During the 2008 Whitney Biennial, Dexter Sinister took up residence for almost a month in the Commander's Room at the 7th Regiment Armory and responded to the exhibition by releasing a series of communiqués through multiple modes of distribution. This material was then archived in *True Mirror Microfiche* (2008), which then generated a projected microfiche lecture performance with many participants.

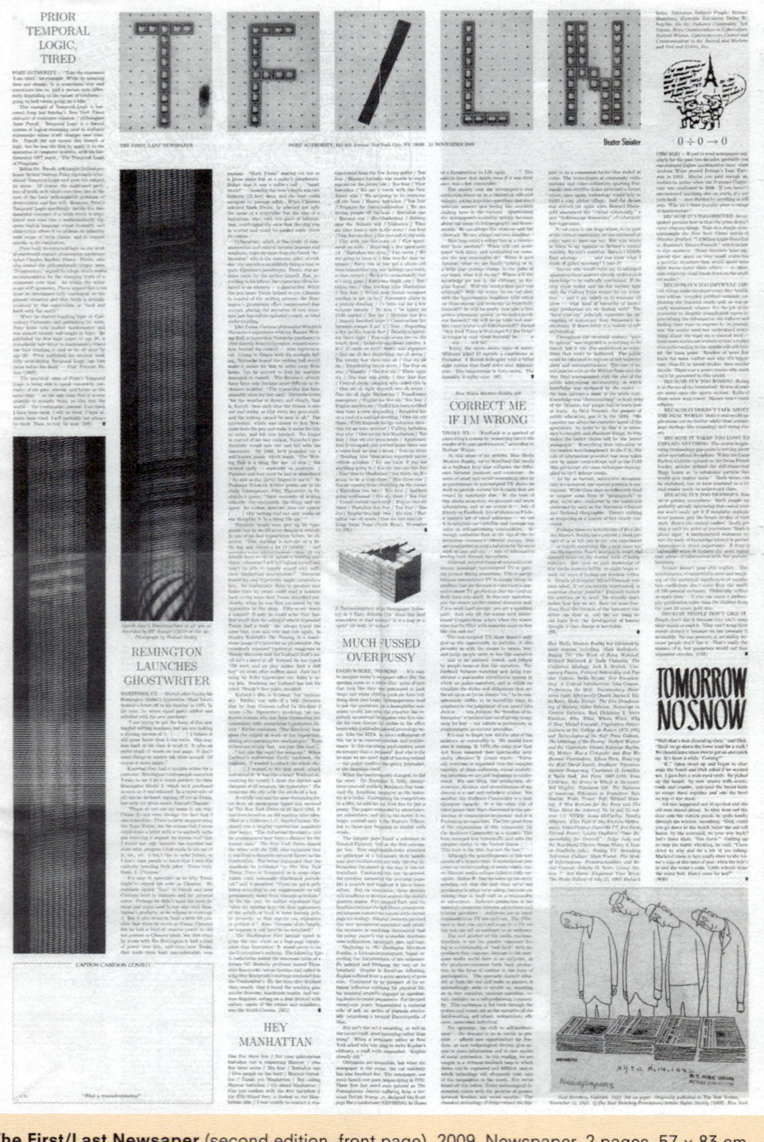

The First/Last Newsaper (second edition, front page), 2009. Newspaper. 2 pages. 57 × 83 cm

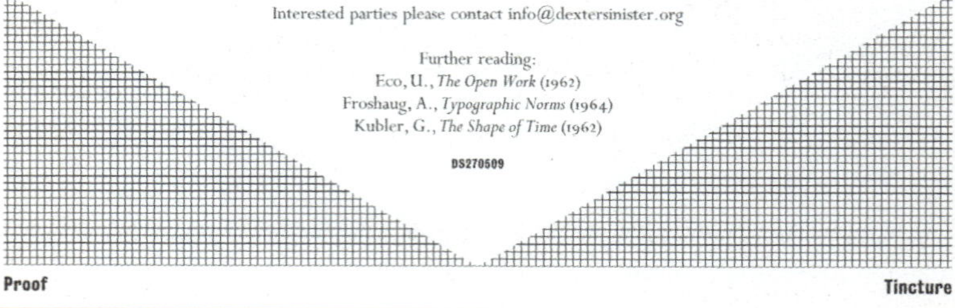

Black Whisky, 2009. PDF announcement/bond/label. Dimensions variable

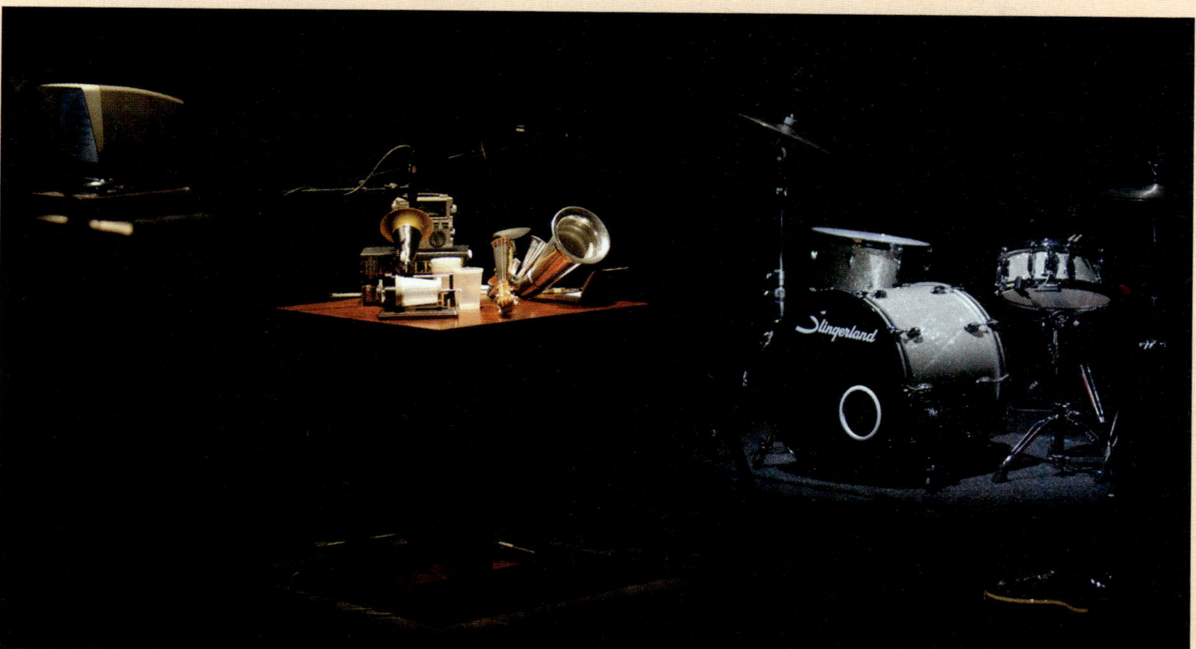

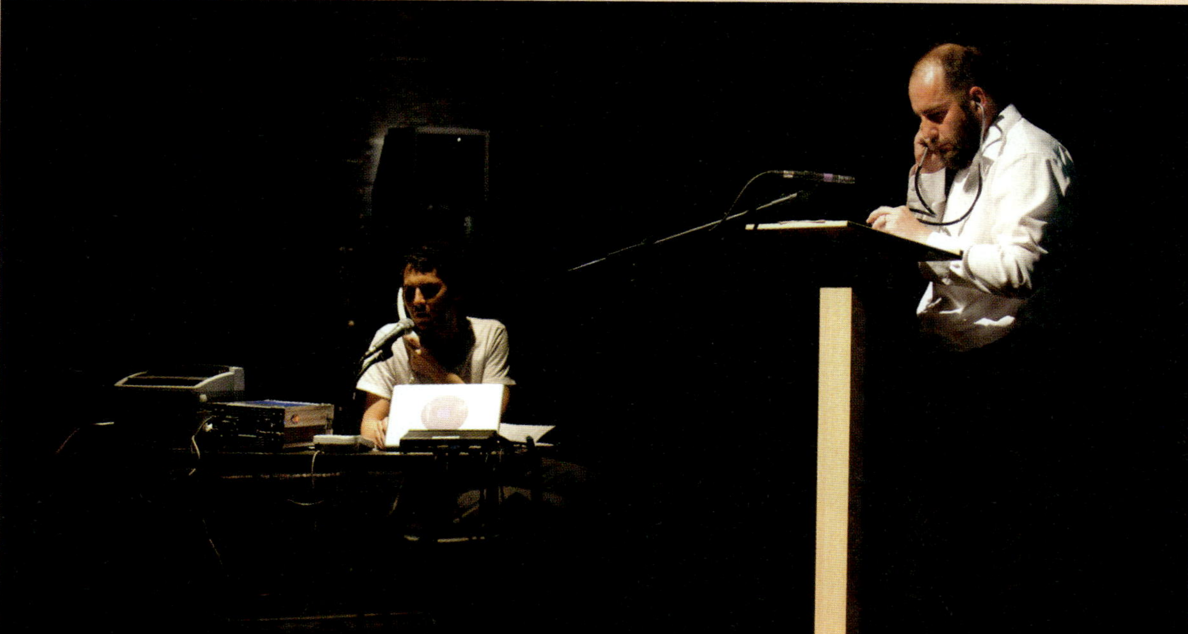

Multiple modes of distribution

For Performa 09, Dexter Sinister produced six issues of *The First/Last Newspaper* (2009) in a broadsheet format, at a time when print journalism is in decline, if not obsolescence. They occupied a workshop space within the Port Authority Bus Terminal, opposite the *New York Times* building, transforming it in order to produce and distribute the paper. Visitors could wander in and out, watching the editing process and taking away issues of the publication, which included reprints of articles from a variety of sources as well as contributions from various artists, critics and curators, including Shannon Ebner, Will Holder, Anthony Huberman, Seth Price, Dana Vajda and Jan Verwoert. Three thousand copies of each issue were distributed via the Performa network by hand and on six 'street readers' placed in public spaces such as the Bus Terminal and the Cooper Union School of Art.

Dexter Sinister has a distinctive and highly developed online presence. They list an inventory for sale, share a 'library' of downloadable PDFs and have a clearly organized archive of all the material produced for the 2008 Whitney Biennial. Ultimately

Ultimately Dexter Sinister is interested in projects that fall outside traditional categories and that cannot be identified as art or some other recognizable form

Dexter Sinister is interested in projects that fall outside traditional categories and that cannot be identified as art or some other recognizable form. Through their works, the duo continue to respond to the unique requirements of individual projects in a sophisticated and unexpected way.

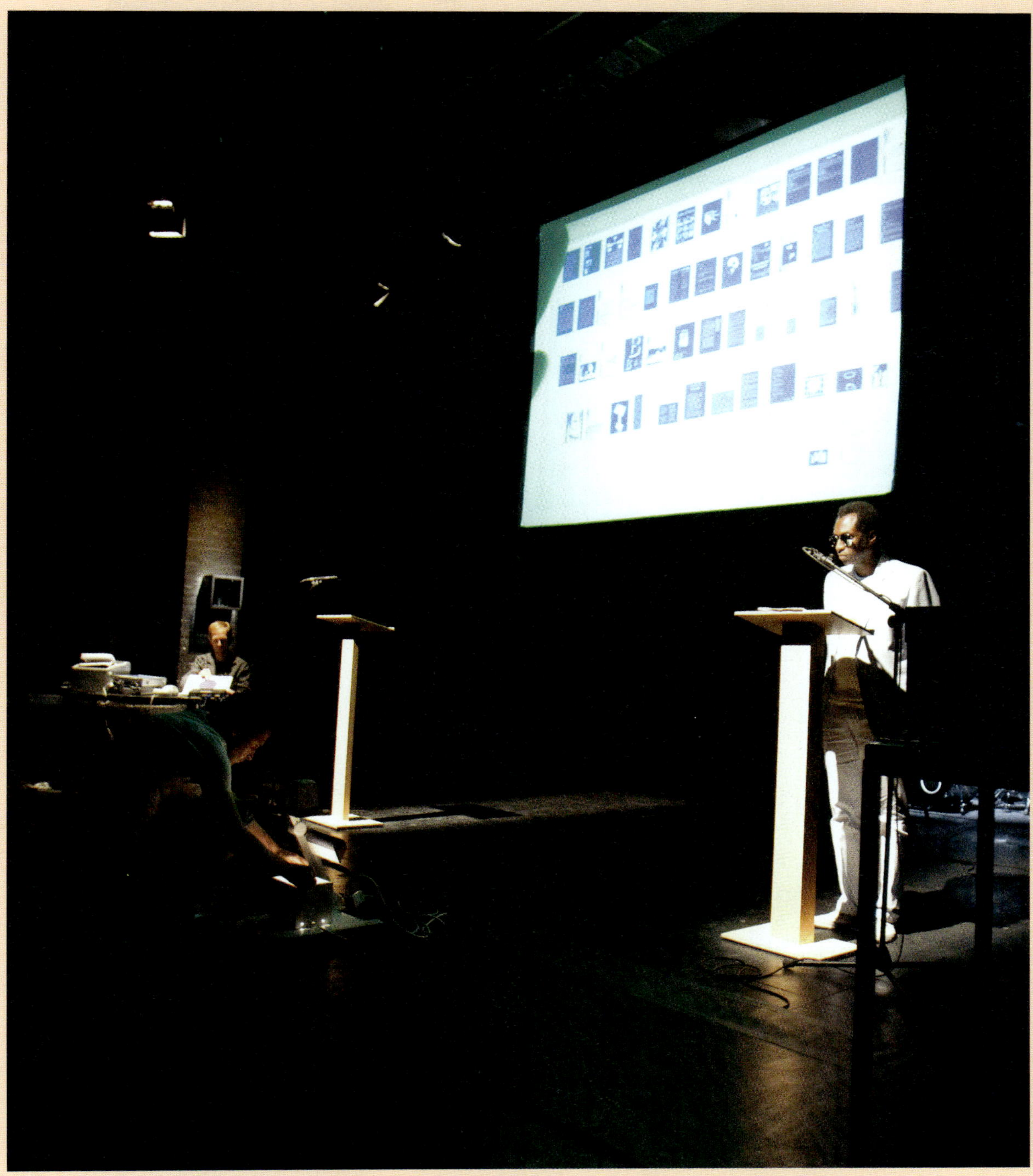

True Mirror Microfiche, 2009. Performance. Institute of Contemporary Arts, London

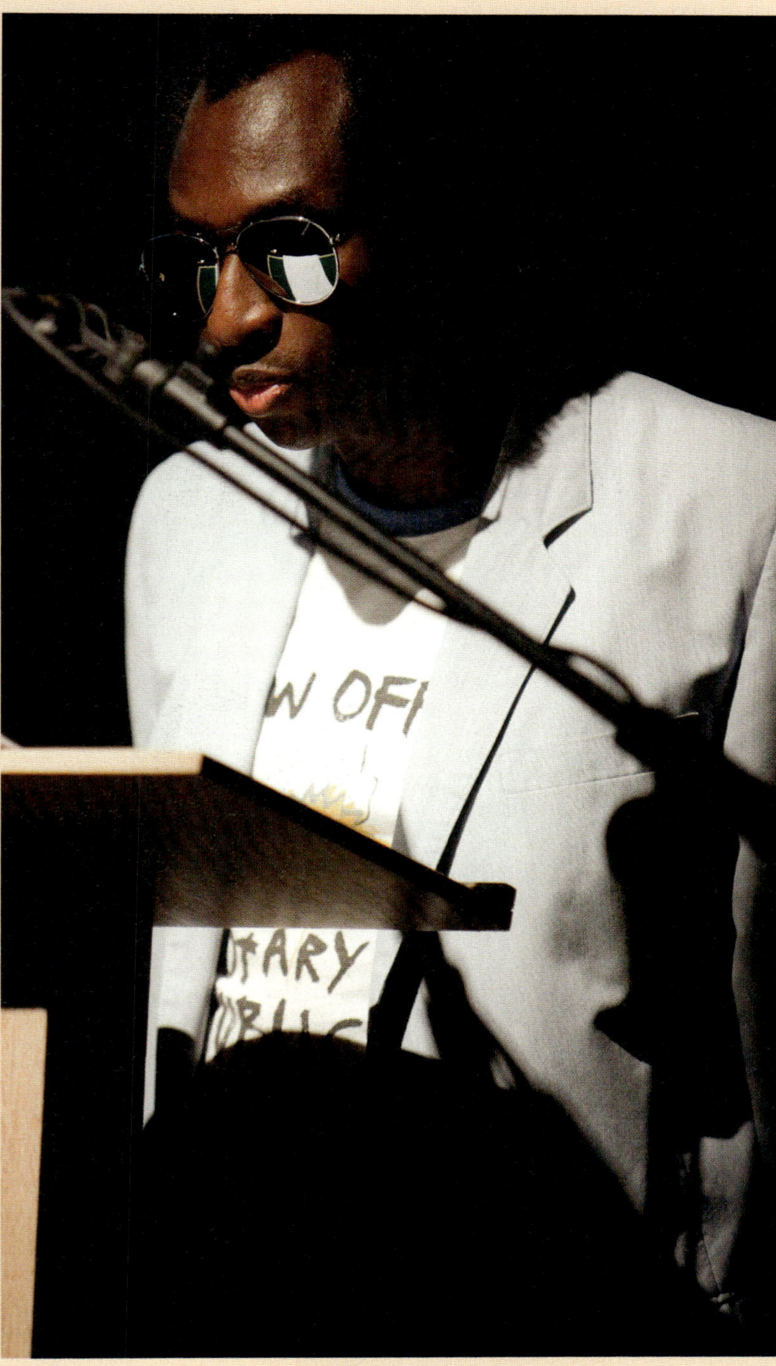

Reena Spaulings

Reena Spaulings is an artist, film-maker, gallerist, curator and musician, as well as a commodity. She is the protagonist of a novel that describes her varied and exotic life. However, at the same she undermines the traditional currency of the artist's signature brand or style, establishing herself as a collective project with only a fictionally singular identity, underwritten by a proliferation of narratives and artistic positions.

In 2004, the Bernadette Corporation — an artist's collective established in the early 1990s, imagined as a fictional company (a latter day Art Club 2000 perhaps) — invented Spaulings via the novel that bears her name. Bernadette Corporation invited writers such as the artist Jutta Koether and actor/poet Jim Fletcher to plot out the main storyline and then, inspired by the Hollywood studio screenwriting system, assigned multiple authors (up to 150 in total) to work on different parts of the text. As Emily Pethick observes in Frieze magazine, the resulting book is 'a summation of multiple experiences of, and perspectives on, its main subject, New York City, seen through the eyes of its central protagonist, Reena Spaulings'. Spaulings herself is depicted as 'a continually morphing, interconnected, social, sexual being who moves through the city as it

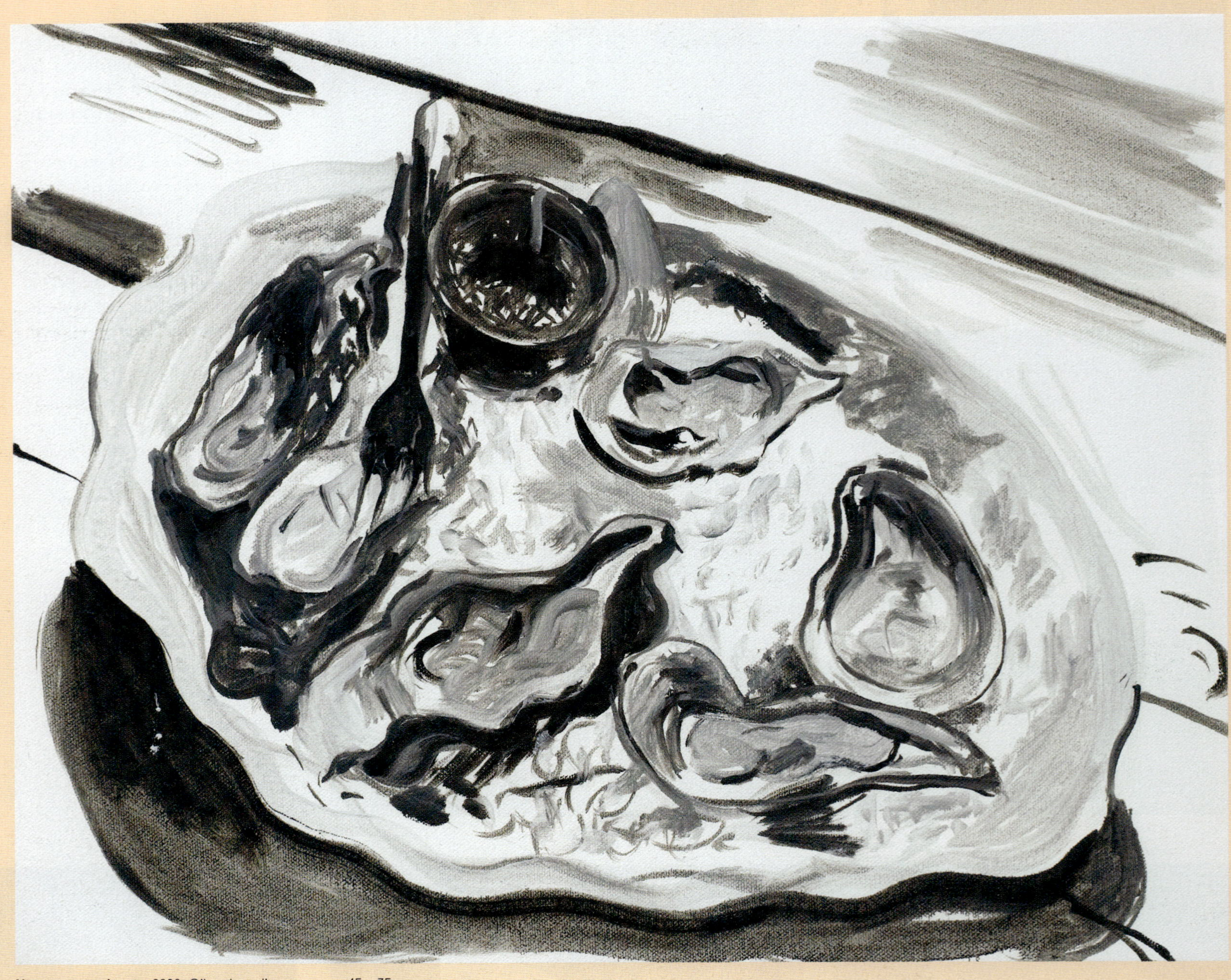

Nature morte vivante, 2008. Oil and acrylic on canvas. 45 × 35 cm

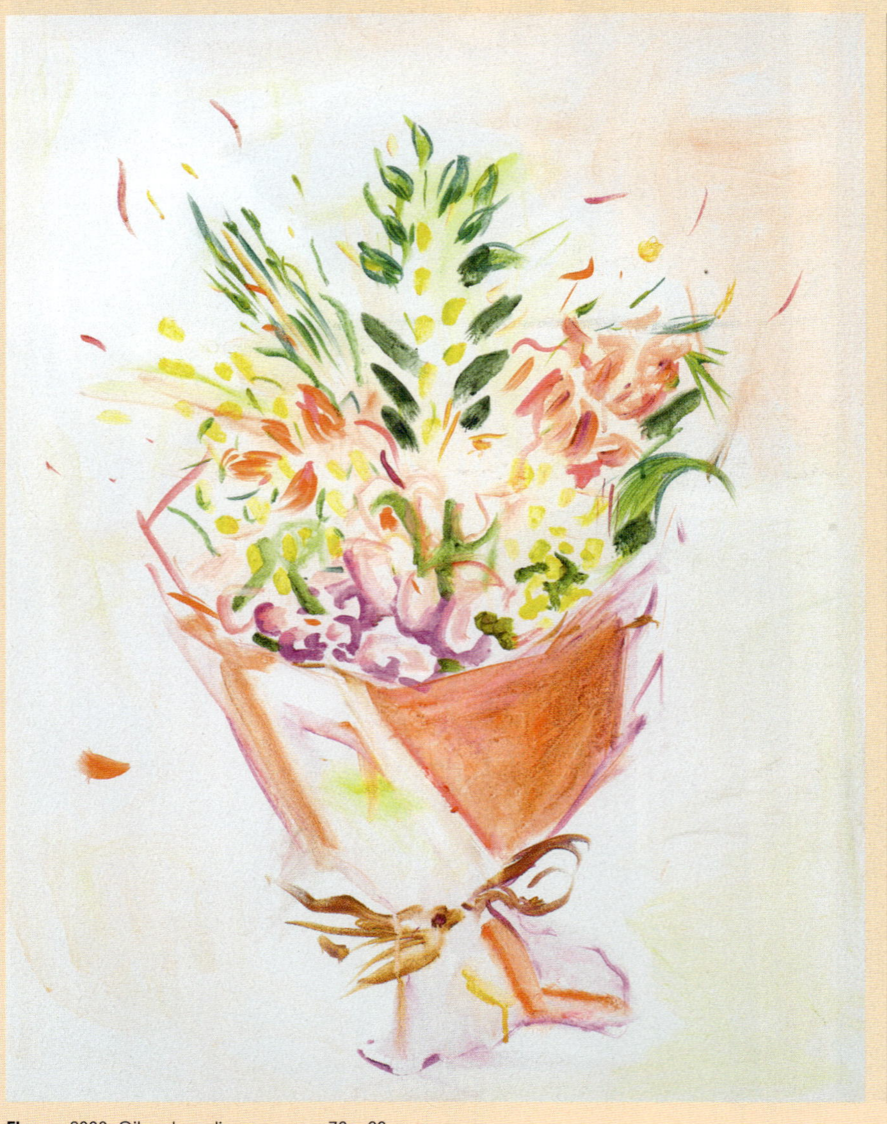

Flower, 2008. Oil and acrylic on canvas. 76 × 60 cm

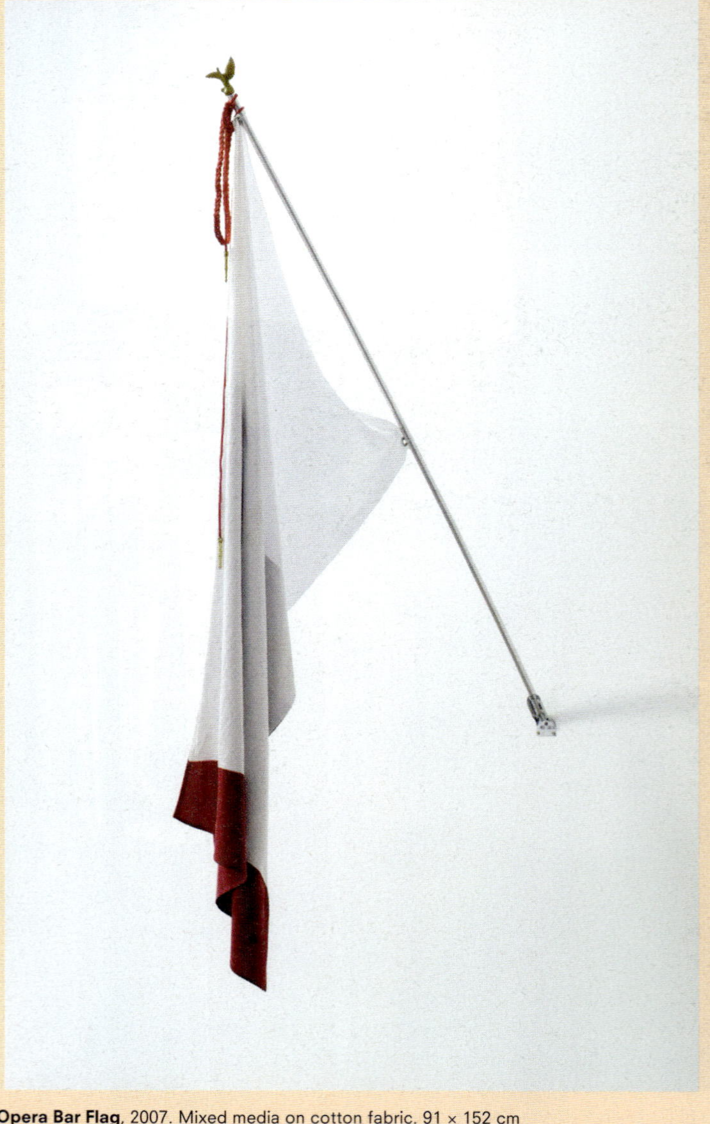

Opera Bar Flag, 2007. Mixed media on cotton fabric. 91 × 152 cm

shapes her subjectivity; her body is an open, receptive, shared space, frequently coerced by others, "a site for things to take place".'

In real life, as it were, Spaulings is also a facilitator of events. Her gallery — Reena Spaulings Fine Art — plays host to exhibitions by artist peers including Claire Fontaine, Merlin Carpenter, Josephine Pryde and Seth Price. She also makes artworks of her own and is represented by the gallery Sutton Lane in London and Paris. As well as paintings and sculpture, Spaulings has made a series of untitled flag sculptures from a variety of found or appropriated materials that deliberately obfuscate their traditional signification of loyalty to an idea or state by claiming occupancy in different contexts. Evolving a new-millennial attitude of evolved 'subversive complicity' (Craig Owens's term for postmodern artists grappling with their role in the art market during the 1980s), Spaulings challenges the idea that she is able to take an authentically critical position vis-a-vis the markets and art circuits in which she operates. For 'Pop Life' at Tate Modern in 2009, Spaulings

Personal mythology

presented an intervention that connected the café and shop spaces with the last room of the exhibition (featuring Takashi Murakami), which comprised a flag piece, in combination with walls paper with slogans taken from a recent Merlin Carpenter exhibition at the Simon Lee Gallery. The slogans — resembling spontaneous graffiti but in fact ready-printed in strips — proclaimed 'lame' critical phrases such as 'Banks are Bad', or 'Kunst = Kapital', 'Destroy Neo-liberal' and 'Stop Art'. Spaulings' fictional identity, underwritten by collective, ever-shifting anonymity and her faux-radical position, combine to challenge the art world's continued appetite for the figure of the artist to wrap personal mythology and radicality into a saleable package.

Undermining the traditional currency of the artist's signature brand or style, she is at the same time a collective project with only a fictionally singular identity, underwritten by a proliferation of narratives and artistic positions

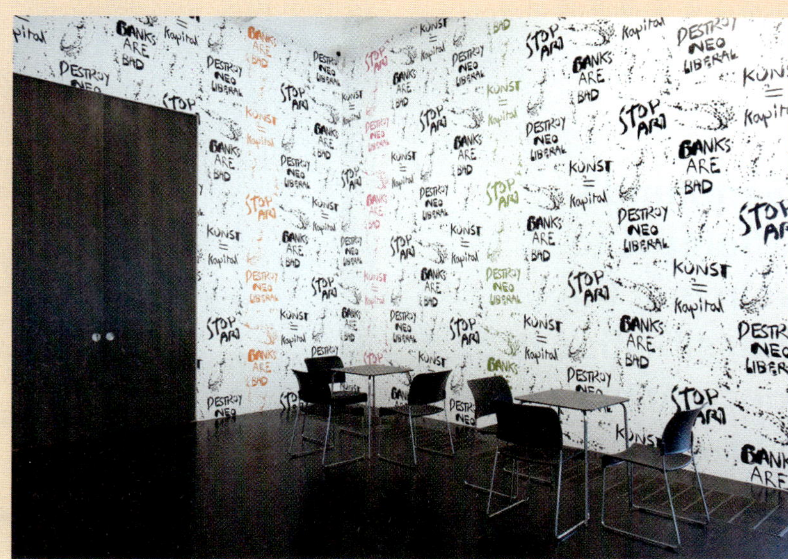

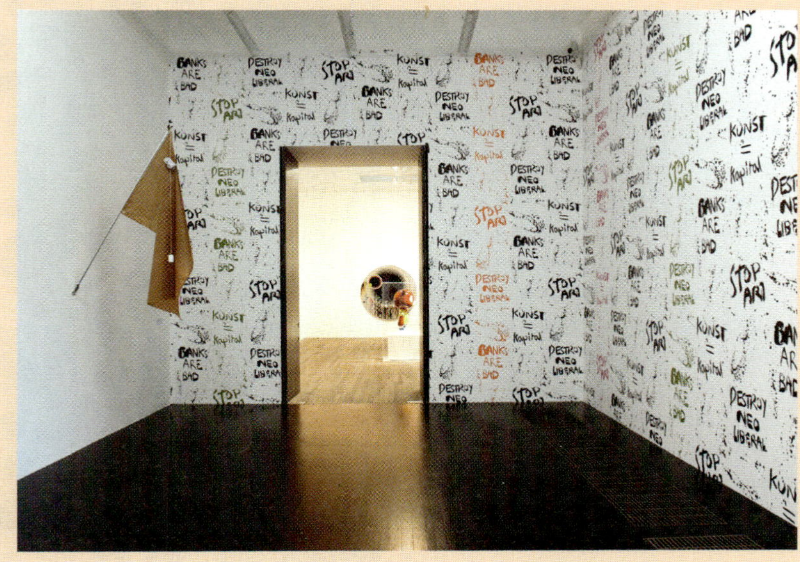

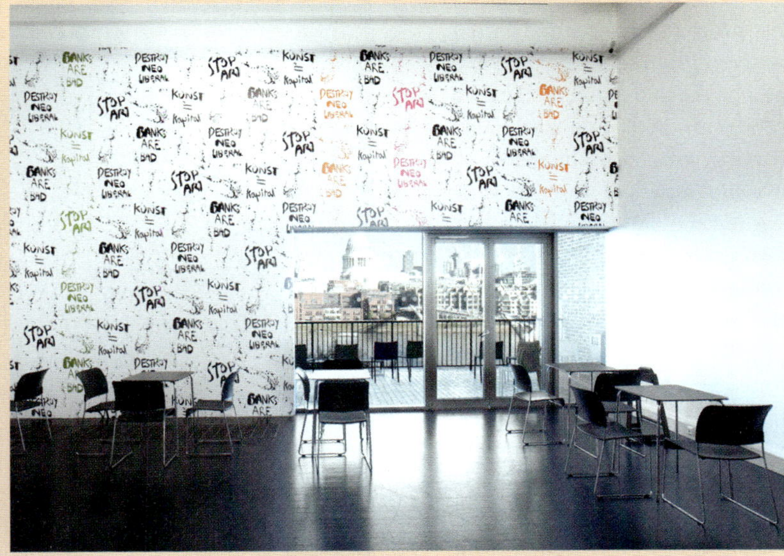

Wallpaper (after Merlin Carpenter), 2009. Ink on paper. Dimensions variable. Installation view, 'Pop Life', Tate Modern, London, 2009

Drone Rack, 2008. Postcard rack, postcards with images of unmanned aerial drones. 190 × 34 × 34 cm

Fia Stina Sandlund

Back in 2001, the feminist collective Unfucked Pussy, consisting of Fia-Stina Sandlund and Joanna Rytel, jumped up on stage during the Miss Sweden contest, holding up a banner with the word Gubbselm (Male Phlegm) on it; their action attracted so much negative media attention that the contest flopped economically. Later in 2005, a swimwear designer who goes by the name Bikini King, or Panos Papadopoulous, bought the rights to the Miss Sweden competition, only to put it on hold and contact Sandlund for 'advice' in regards to the future of the contest – making persistent telephone calls and appearances on live TV. Ultimately Papadopoulous didn't take Sandlund's advice of cancelling the contest entirely, but rather started the 'New Miss

Sandlund's attempts to reinvent the possibilities of documenting and narrating her work are just as important as the ideas that inform it

Sweden', a version that he thought was more politically correct, although the contest became even more of a flop. Swedish feminism is famous for its astonishing across-the-board achievements, so you would be forgiven for assuming that newer generations of women artists might be tempted to kick back and settle down into apolitical smugness or macha reactionism. But it appears that Sandlund has never even come close to generational stereotypes of that kind.

As refreshingly antagonistic as it is marvellously deadpan, her project has succeeded entirely without gratuitous sloganeering and has been documented by way of various media and materials, leading, in 2006, to the video *Mythos, Logos and Miss Understanding* and the radio documentary *My Business with the Bikini King —* a tragedy of mistaken identity in thirteen acts for Swedish Radio.

Sandlund's attempts to reinvent the possibilities of documenting and narrating her work are just as important as the ideas that inform it. *If you are the rebel, I will be decent*, for example, was performed during late 2006 in theatres throughout

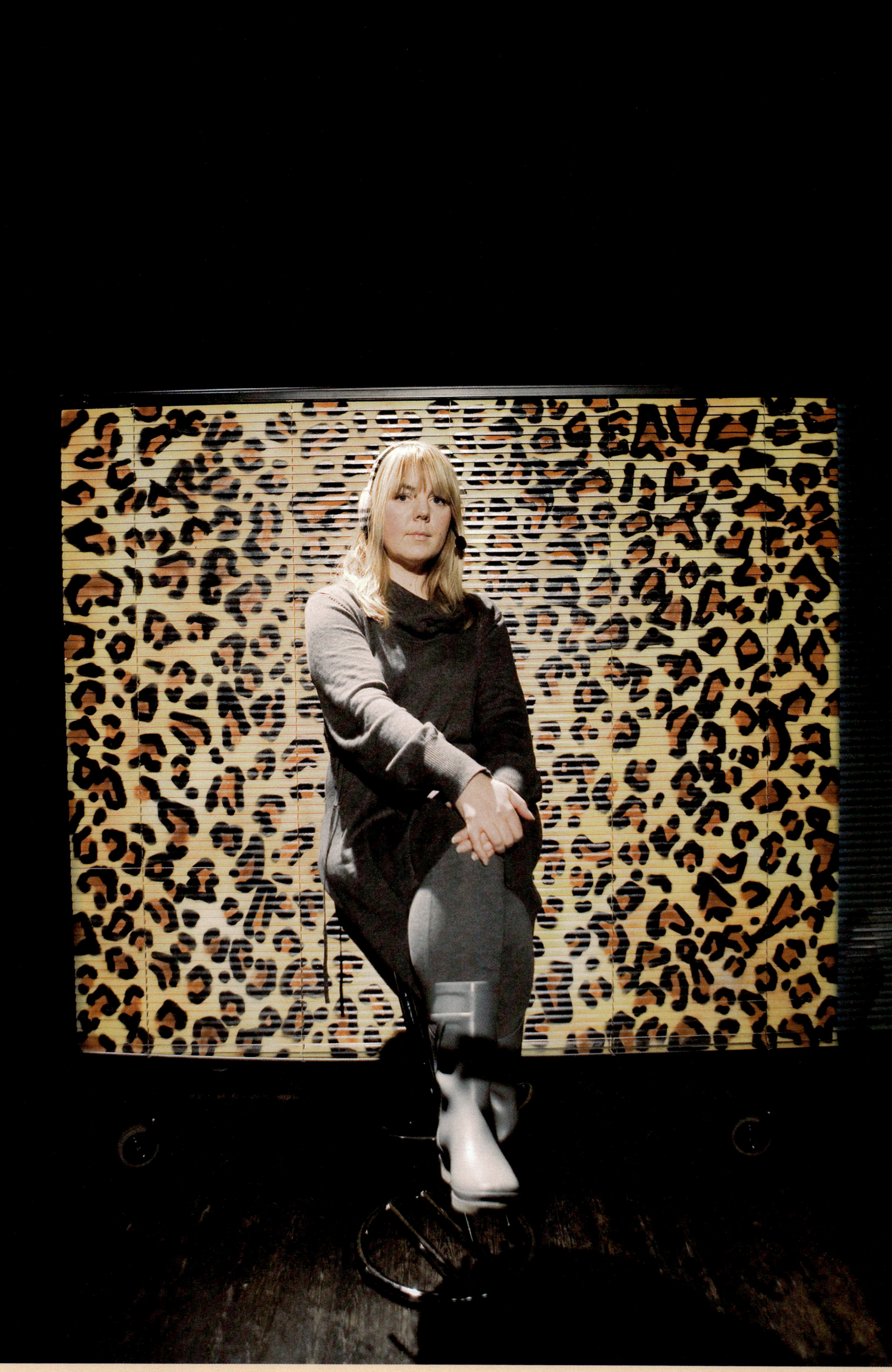

If you are the rebel, I will be decent, 2006. Performance

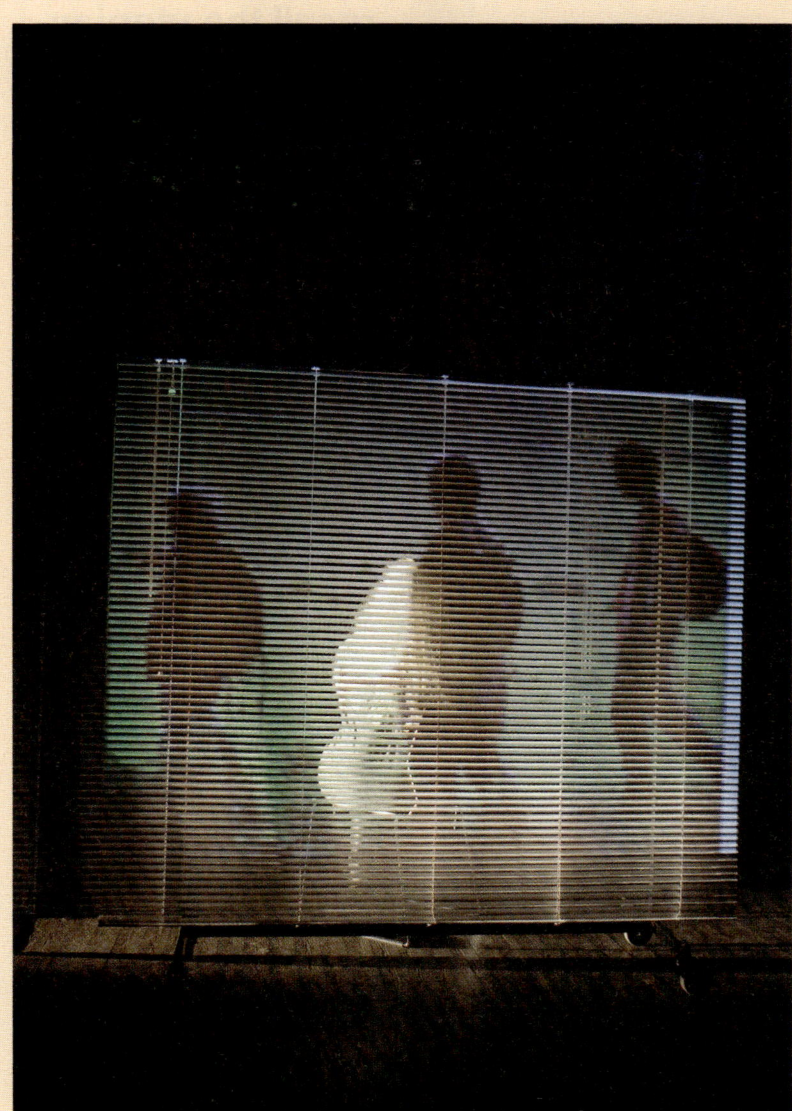

If you are the rebel, I will be decent, 2006. Performance

Radicalism that is self-aware

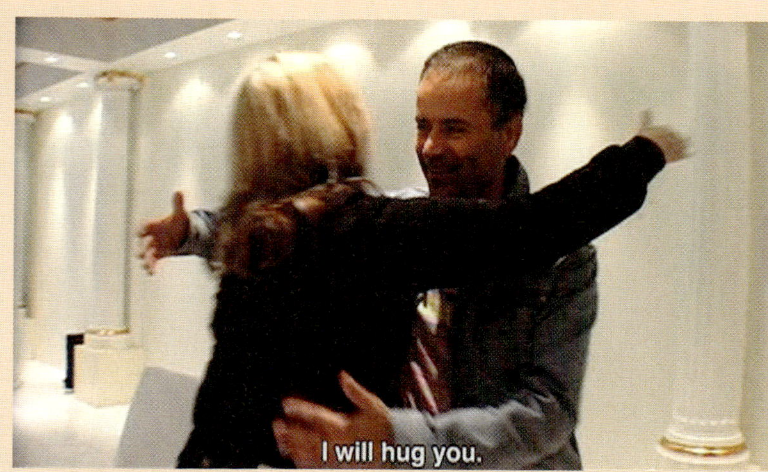

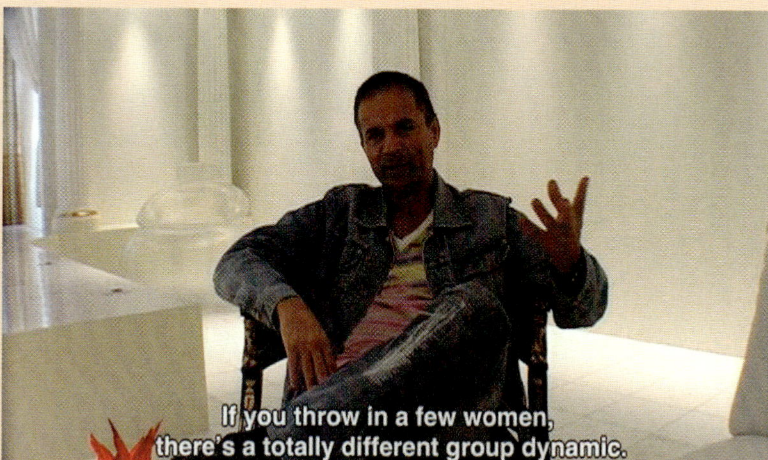

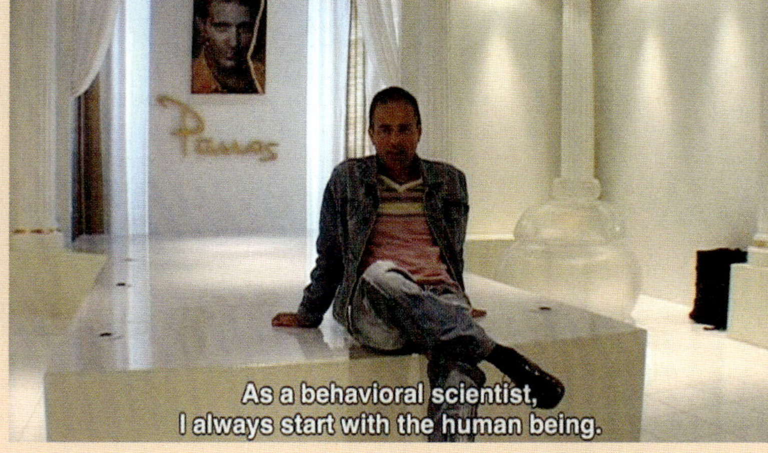

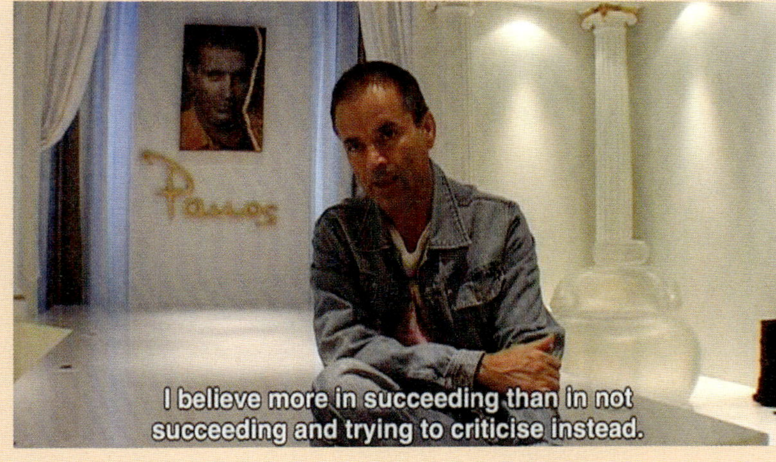

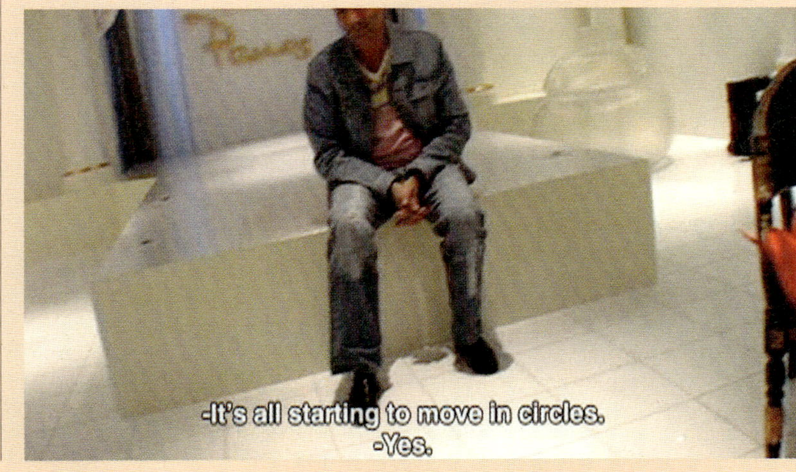

Mythos, Logos and Miss Understanding, 2006. Video. 22 min.

Sweden. This performance was in three acts, each one showing an encounter between Sandlund and an interlocutor from the worlds of art, activism or the media, with the conversations accompanied by a backdrop of shifting soundtracks and projections.

Perhaps more traditionally 'protest-activist' in orientation was *One More Monument*, produced for the 2007 'Agorafolly' exhibition in Brussels. A nine-square metre flagstone of Swedish black granite, it bore the inscription: 'In honour of the future victims of Swedish-made weapons'. The polished granite reflected two nearby monuments of more traditional, bellicose character, complete with flags, cannons and cherubs. All of which was marvelously rendered in Sandlund's monument itself, making it just as portentous. There's much to be said for a radicalism that is self-aware enough to do entirely without sanctimonious elements but brusque enough to be effective nonetheless. Sandlund's work is a case in point.

If you are the rebel, I will be decent, 2006. Performance

Katja Strunz

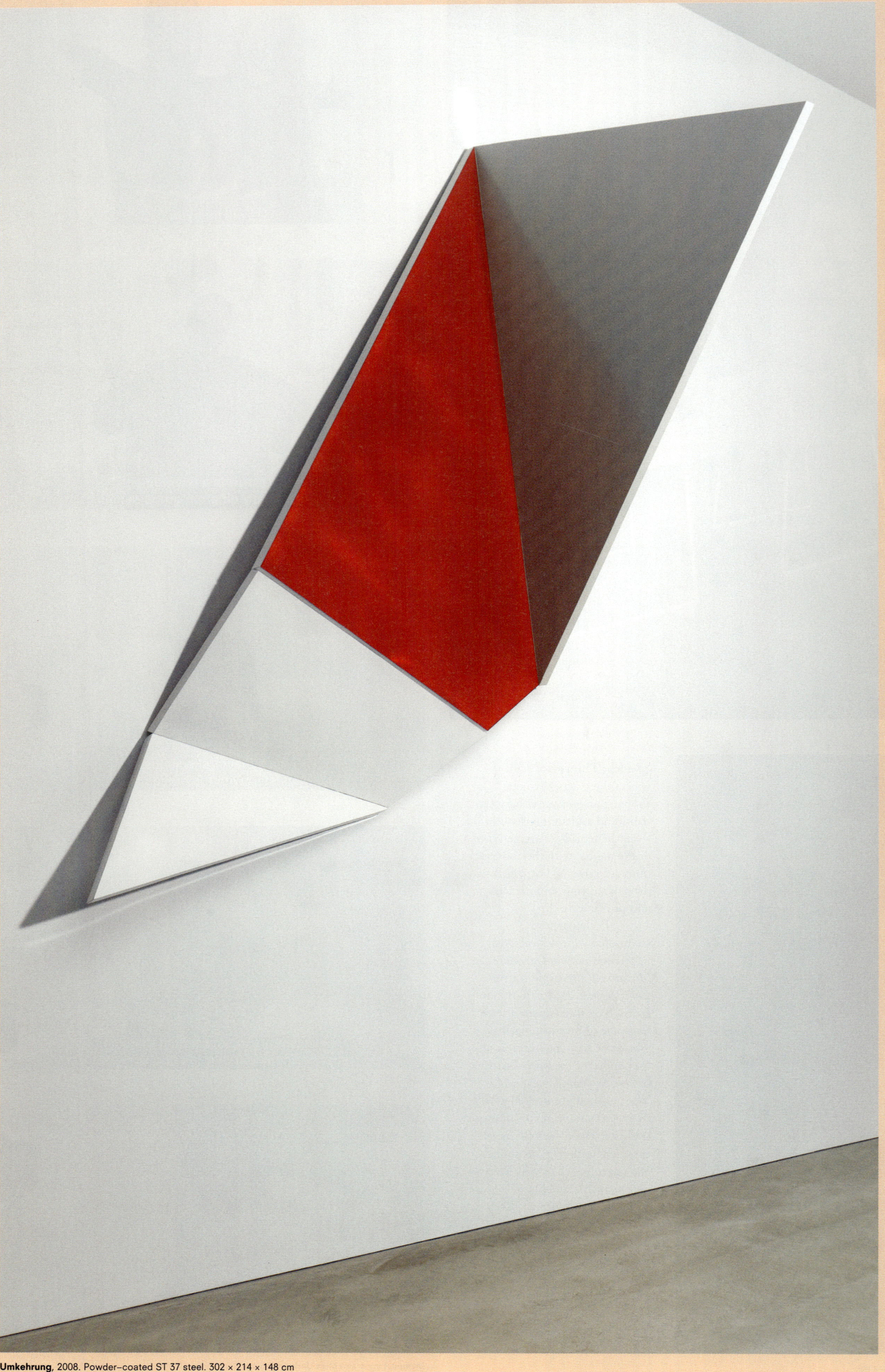

Umkehrung, 2008. Powder–coated ST 37 steel. 302 × 214 × 148 cm

Katja Strunz's sculptures and installations — made from recycled metal, salvaged wood, found photographs and yellowed book pages — invoke a dialogue with history and the past's continued impact in the present day. Throughout Strunz's work, angular, hard-edged abstract forms conjure up disparate art-historical phantoms, ranging from the early twentieth-century Futurists and Constructivists to the latter-century Minimalists and post-Minimalists.

The artist often manipulates a signature inventory of dynamic, undulating shapes that typically appear as modestly scaled sculptures in shades of black, rusted brown and grey sheet metal. They articulate complex topographies of crisp, triangulated folds, as if the intractable steel has miraculously yielded to her will like paper origami. Gathered

Gathered together in clusters, the sculptures appear anachronistic in a retro-futuristic kind of way. Their sharp creases, shifting axes and streamlined thrusts recall the utopian geometries of El Lissitsky and a sense of dynamism reminiscent of the Futurists.

together in clusters, the sculptures appear anachronistic in a retro-futuristic way. Their sharp creases, shifting axes and streamlined thrusts recall the utopian geometries of El Lissitzky and a sense of dynamism reminiscent of the Futurists. At the same time, the rhythmic progression of closely interrelated dimensional forms appears equally conversant with works by Robert Smithson, whose crystalline, faceted wall structures have directly influenced Strunz. However, in contrast to Smithson's analytic, geometrical formal sequencing, Strunz offers organic, unpredictable permutations. More music than mathematics, more soul than science, her structures proceed like a sonata's themes and variations, generating patterns more easily intuited than concretely described.

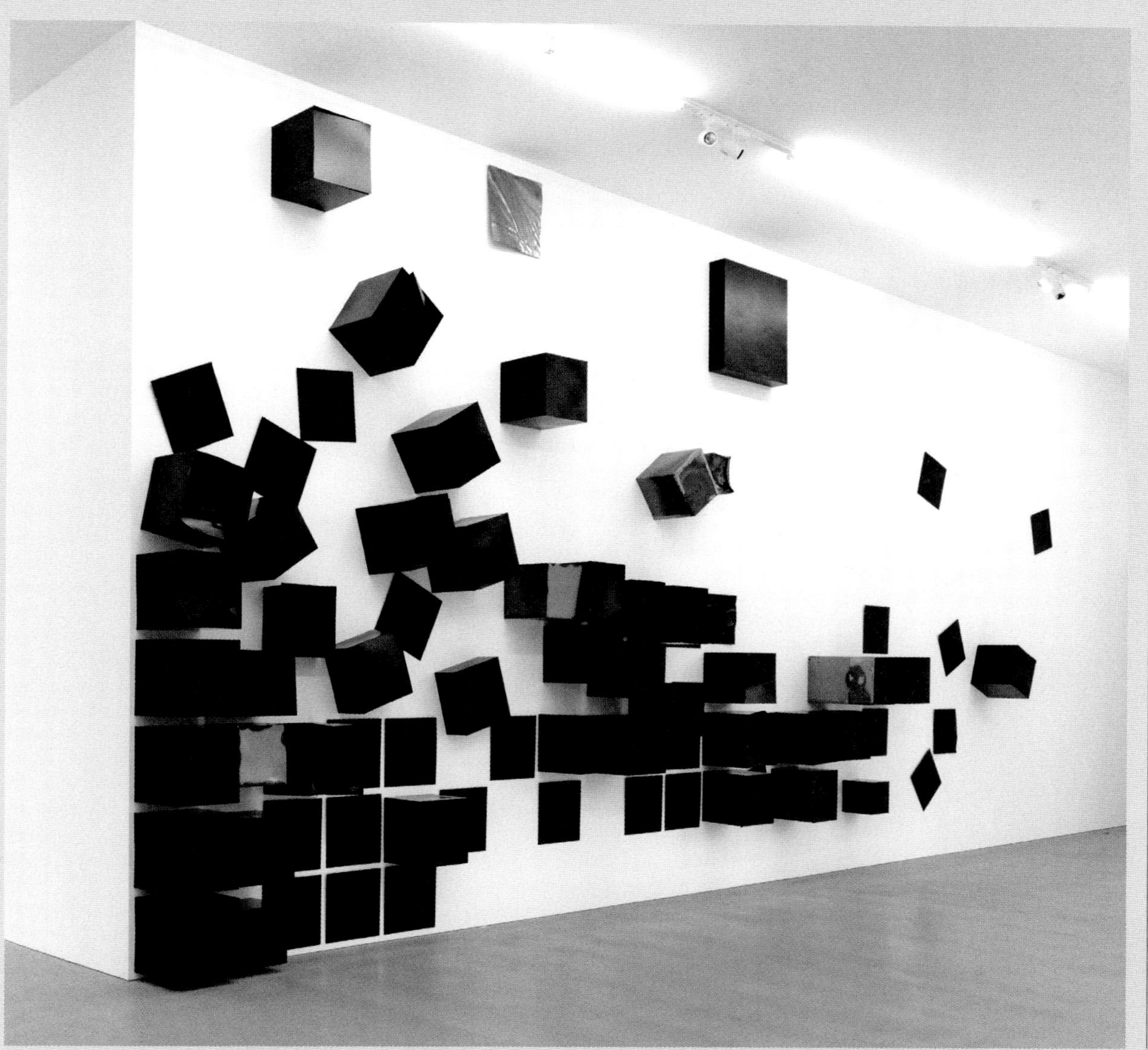

Memory Wall (Part II), 2008. Powder coated ST 37 steel, bronze. 550 × 1200 × 45 cm

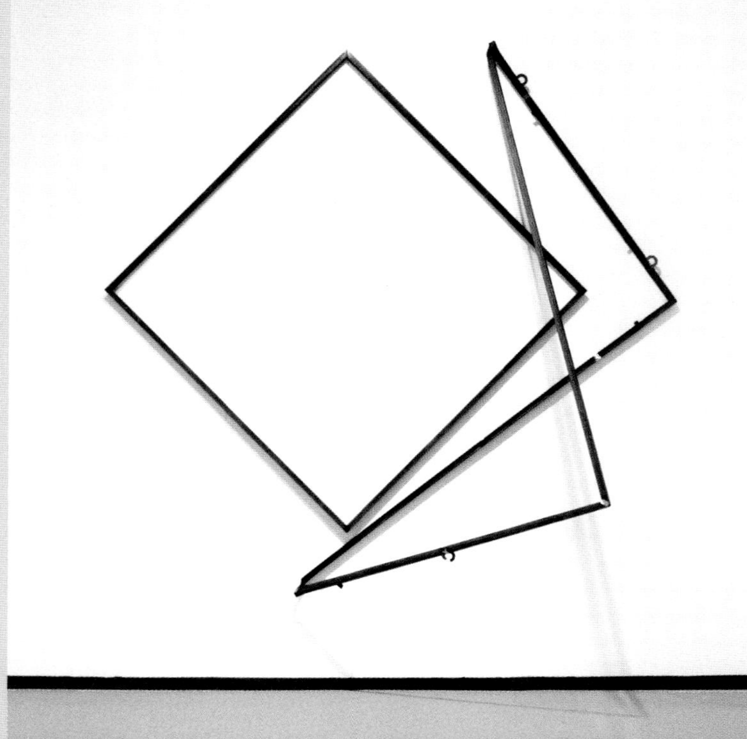

Sepulchral visions of bygone eras

Mirrors against Identity, 2008. Waxed ST 37 steel. 332 × 360 × 98 cm

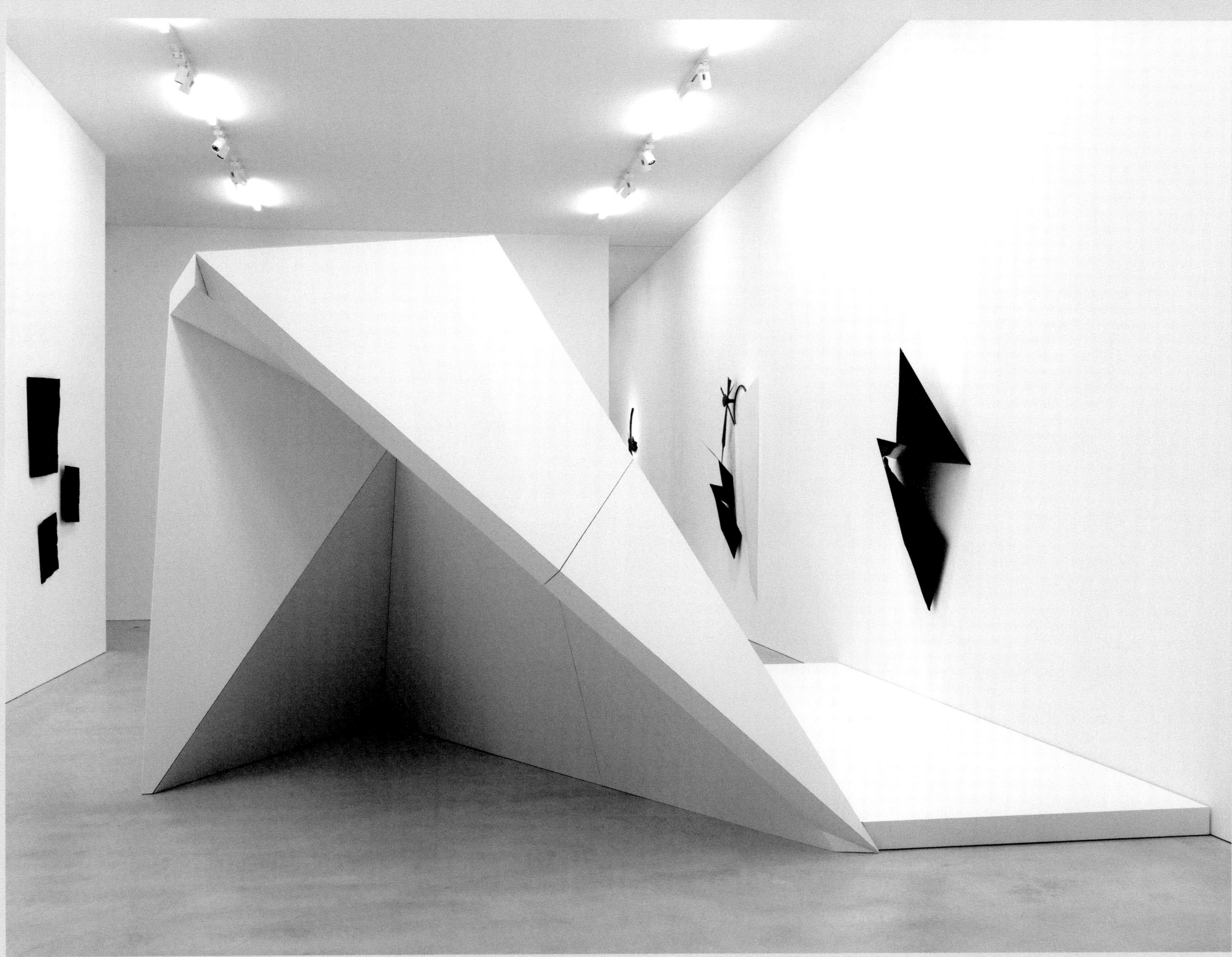

Der müde Traum, 2008. Wood, paint. 330 × 550 × 550 cm

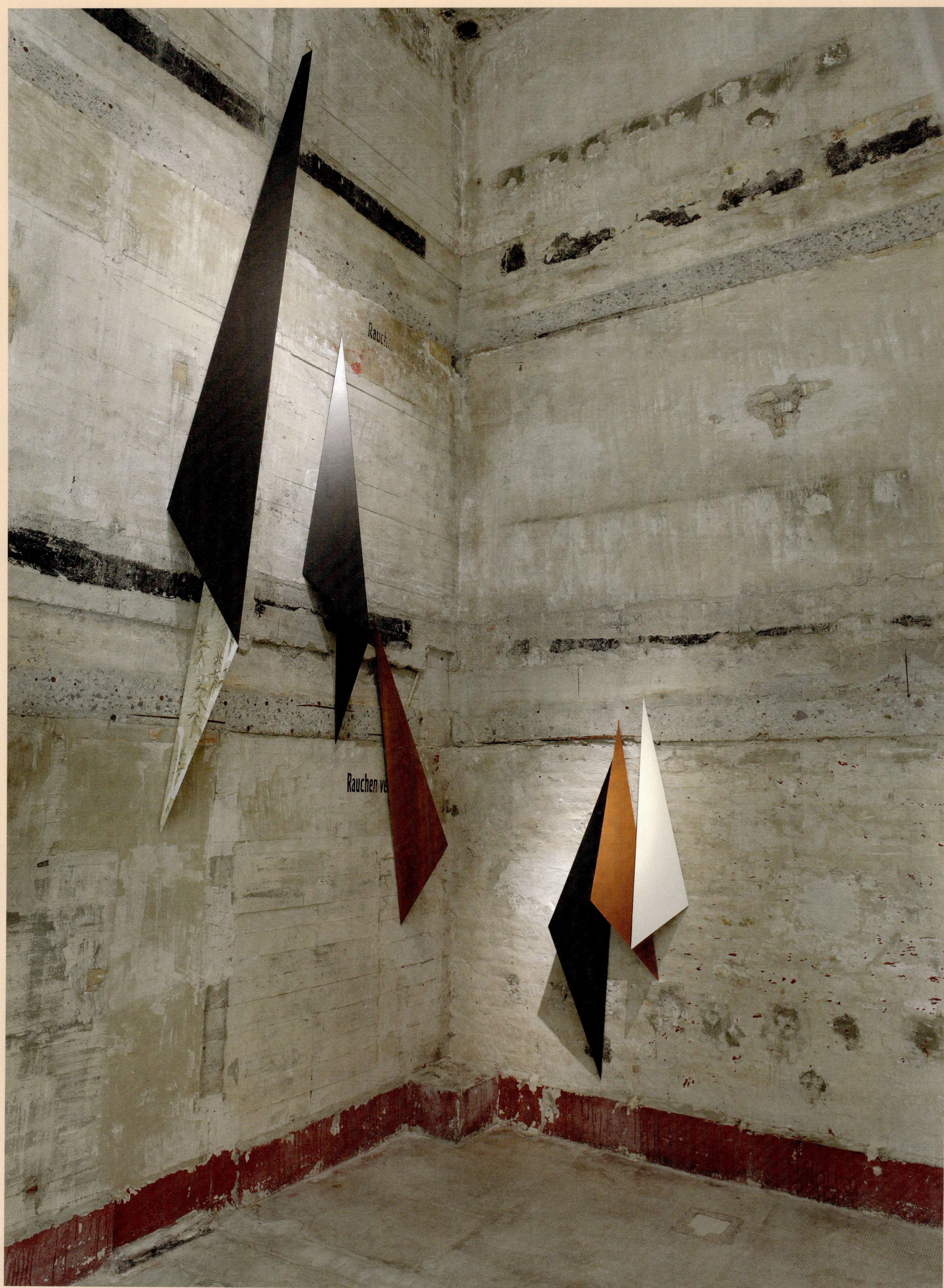

Zeittraum (detail), 2004. Wood, steel, wallpaper, paint, glass. Dimensions variable

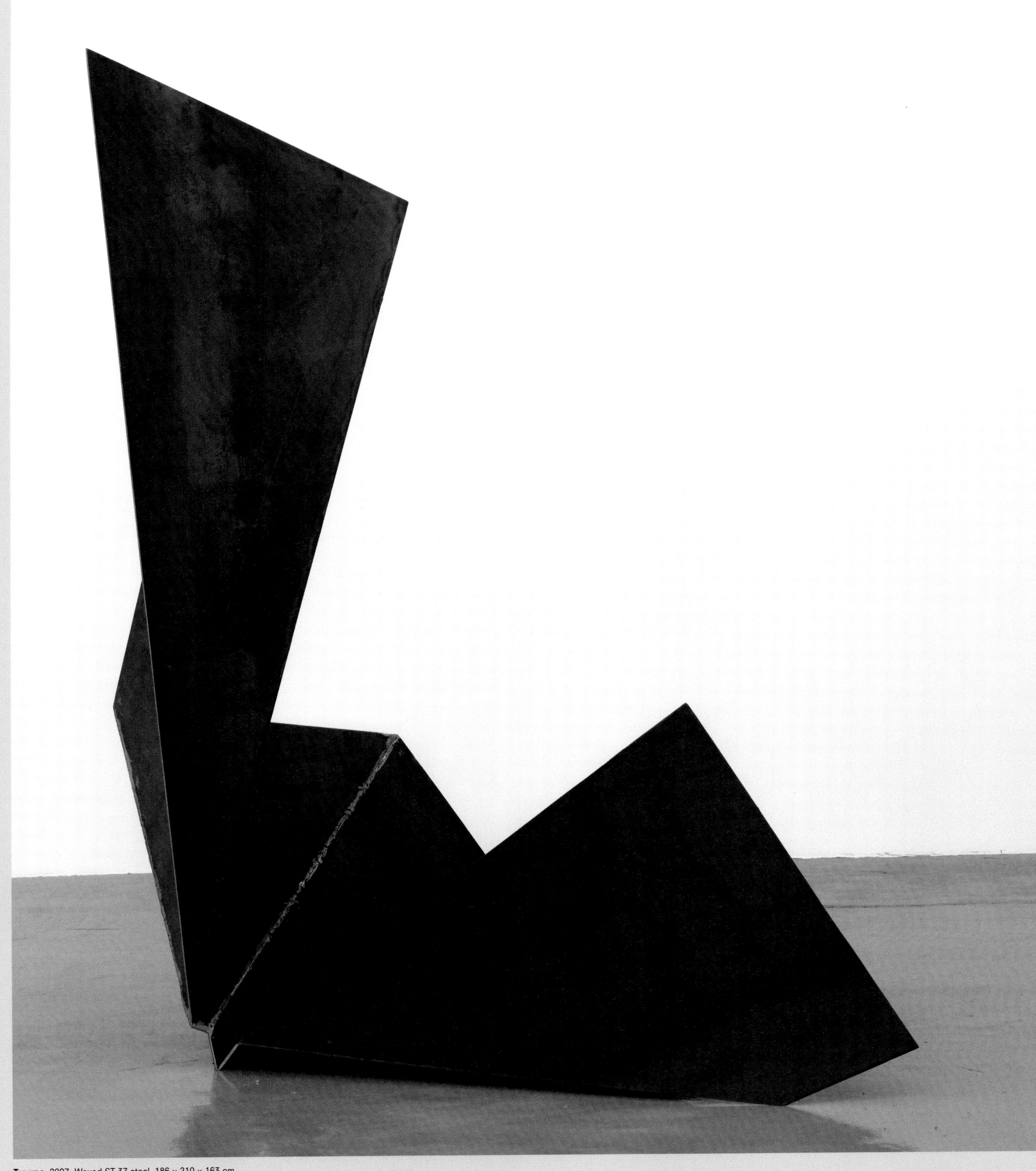

Trauma, 2007. Waxed ST 37 steel. 186 × 210 × 163 cm

Strunz's sculptural components can be peculiar trapezoids or unruly triangles, or constellations of cube-like forms that cling, lean, hover and creep along the floors and climb up the walls of a gallery space. Despite their material rigidity, her irregular geometries imbue the works with uncanny, biomorphic qualities — as if they have only momentarily frozen into abstract shapes and will come back to life when your back is turned. The elements, however literally static, activate a friction between the indeterminate and the structured that creates an illusory sense of movement within the gallery space, which operates almost as a surrogate representation of time. Strunz's pairing of recycled materials and citations of art-historical precedents maps out a morphological chronology — one that refers not only to the passage of time, but also to the non-linear, haphazard way in which we experience memories.

Relays between past and present are apparent everywhere in Strunz's work. Like archaeological relics, the decrepit qualities of many works evoke sepulchral visions of bygone industrial eras, as well as fragments of a failed Minimalist monument. Without cynicism or irony, she traces the lineage of classic modernism and its aftermath, while acknowledging its contradictions. Originality and invention are anachronistic concepts; only variable repetitions within extant possibilities remain viable. This observation plays out in the expressive narrative embedded in her abstract, formalist work. Her approach to history is in itself appealingly antiquated. In her reclamation of past or forgotten art-making practices to produce new styles, she shares nineteenth-century Romantic and Gothic notions of decay and resurrection, which both propose that within such ruins lies the potential for positive transformation.

Tadasu Takamine

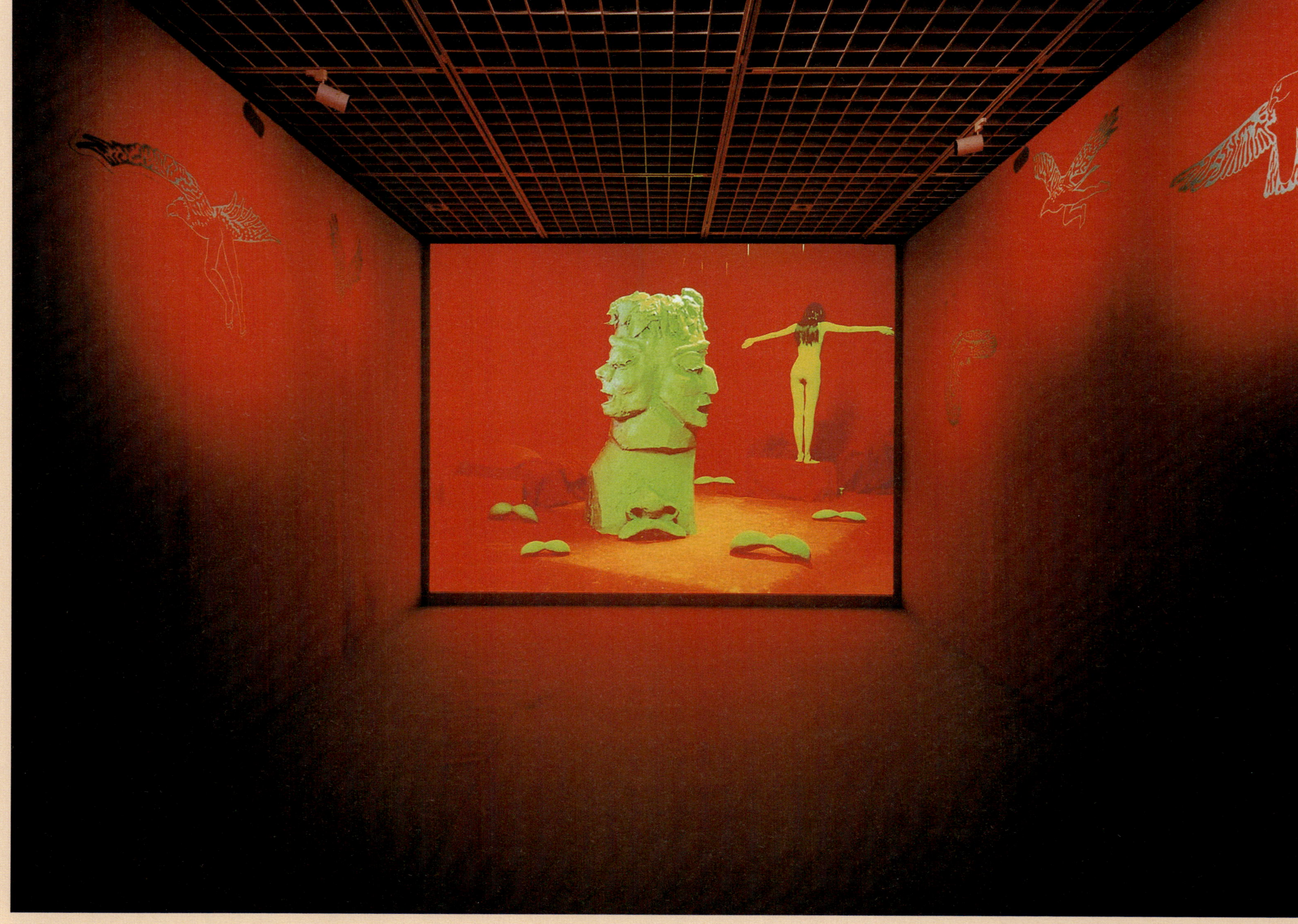

God Bless America, 2002. Oil clay installation. 12 × 6 × 4.5 m. Video. 8 min.

Imagine the whole from the fragments

Tadasu Takamine's diverse artistic practice — encompassing video, installation, performance and stage-production work — invariably possesses at its heart a corporeal presence. In a move reflecting his interest in improvisation, during the early 1990s he began making live performances, whose speed and spontaneity were diametrically opposing to the lacquer art he had studied at university. Between 1993 and 1997 he served as a performer for Dumb Type, a group offering a radical Japanese take on gender and queer issues, incorporating video and media art in their stage sets. It was during this period that his command of physical expression blossomed.

God Bless America (2002), a striking example of Takamine's talent as a visual artist, could be described as a work of video-performance that captures to dramatic effect the day-to-day existence of the artist, and the creative process. Here he documents his life for eighteen days, at a pace of one minute per frame, the process of battling two tons of clay to make a giant head singing 'God Bless America'. A fixed camera records Takamine actually living on site — eating, drinking, working, sleeping and having sex. The patriotic American tune playing throughout served as a question mark directed at the great power in the post-9/11 climate, a challenge to its insidiously egotistical, conveniently broad interpretation of justice and freedom. The work's self-reverential, comical condition is a statement that, to Takamine, creation is everyday work, and in the everyday there is creation.

Kagoshima Esperanto (2005) is a theatrical installation in which fragments of the dialect of Kagoshima dialect — Kagoshima being the artist's home region — and the international language Esperanto are projected on the walls and floor of a vast dark space resembling ruins, covered in ten tons of soil and dotted with a jumble of found objects. Urging viewers to imagine the whole from the fragments, the work connects the local and the global on an equal footing in a metaphor for modern life, in which we all grope for individual presence.

Orchestras (2008), a collaboration with the musician Yoshihide Otomo, takes the form of a multi-layered combination of sound and light, courtesy of diverse sound sources ranging from professional performers to amateur humming. Discarded household goods suspended from every inch of the ceiling bring vividly to life the memories and existence of things. Meanwhile, in *Big Stop-Gardening of Anger* (2008), Takamine makes props from items found in a demolished house, to be not only seen but sensed at the invitation of a blind tour guide.

Takamine queries the act of looking that is fundamental to visual art, and attempts to summon up physical perceptions that one might call primitive. His attachment to discarded things is not only due to championing environmental sustainability, but is the outcome of a challenge that he posed himself concerning the fundamental nature of creating art: that it should not necessarily mean fabricating or processin g things.

Takamine's projects for stage also encompass a wide range of collaborations: with the choreographer/dancer Jo Kanamori in *Black Ice* (2004), an amateur performance by art-school students in *Motto Darwin* (2005), and a joint performance featuring Japanese and Thai dancers in *Melody Cup* (2009). All the performances are engaged in processes aimed at understanding others with different backgrounds and values, and incorporating social and political themes into the works.

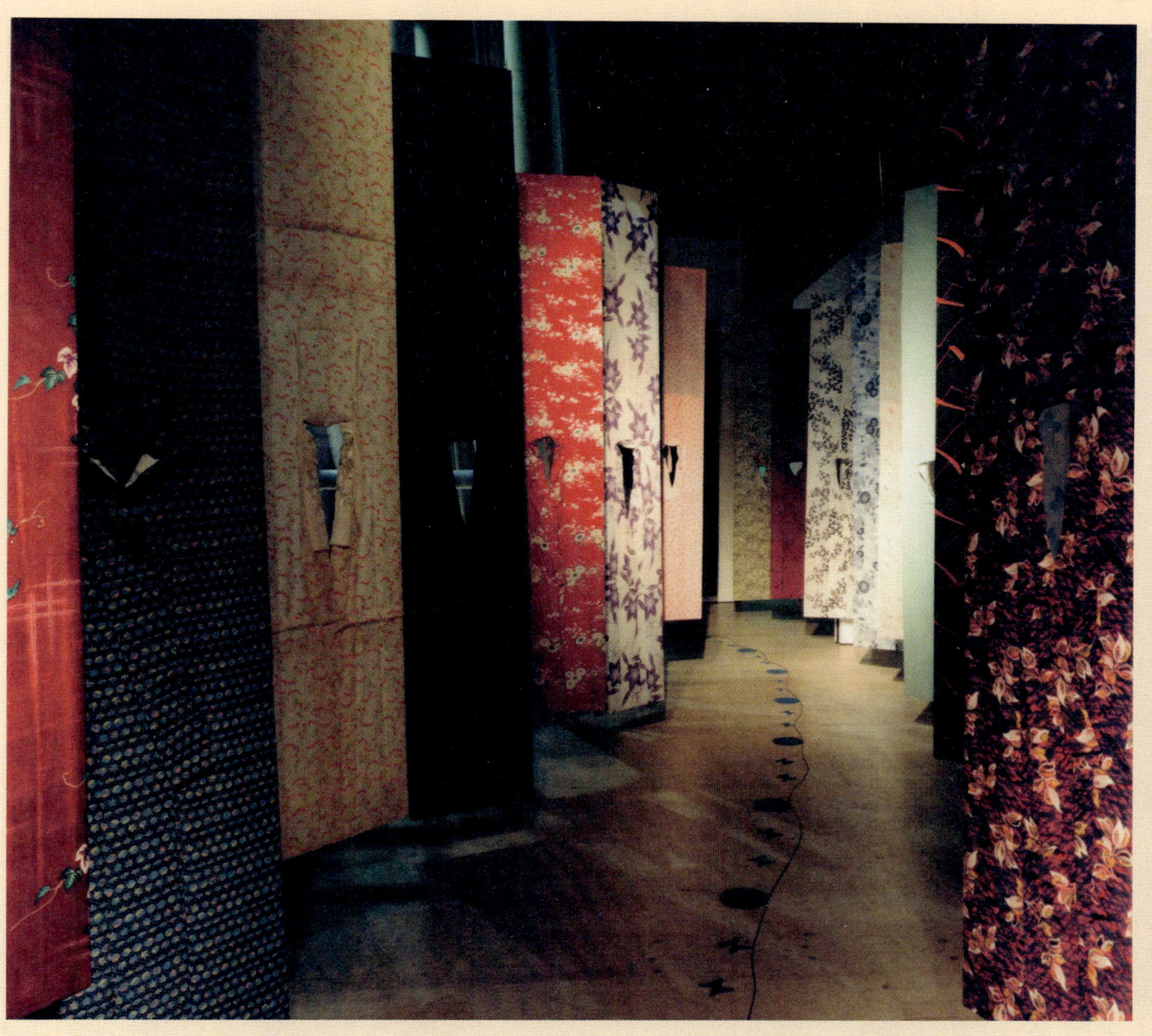

Big Stop–Gardening of Anger, 2008. Waste wood, clay, kimono, blanket, bicycle, water pump, fan, Braille, stuffed animals, LED, OHP, video projectors, moving light, interactive systems, speakers, blind attendant. 32 × 20 × 4.2 m

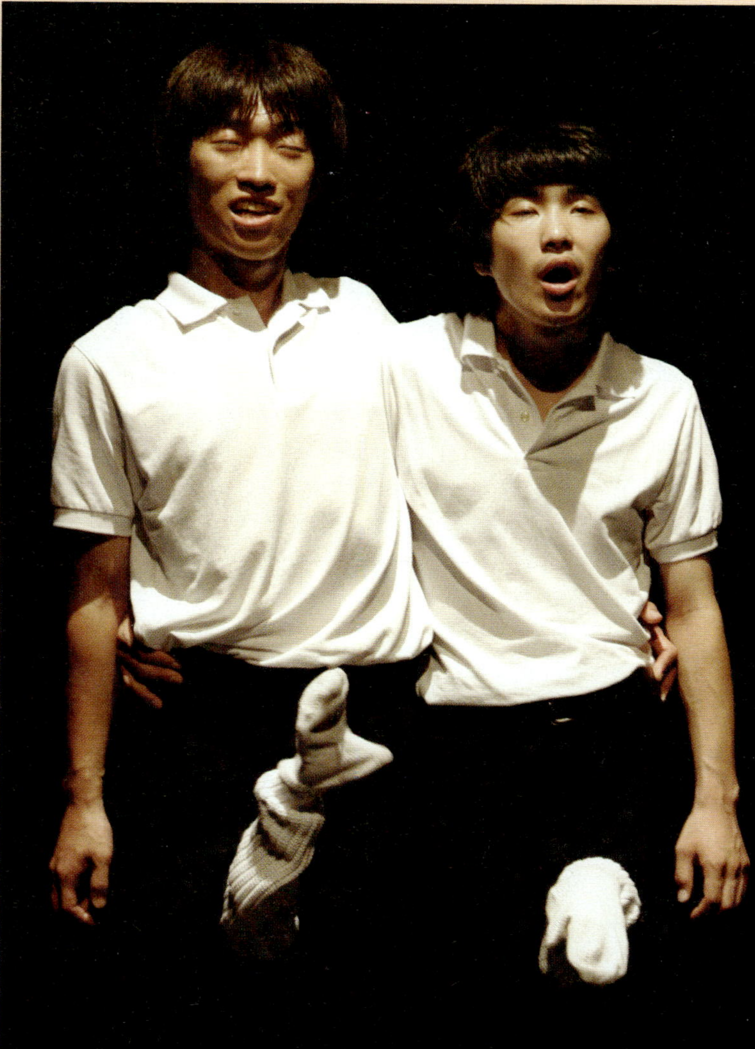

Motto Darwin, 2005. Performance. 85 min.

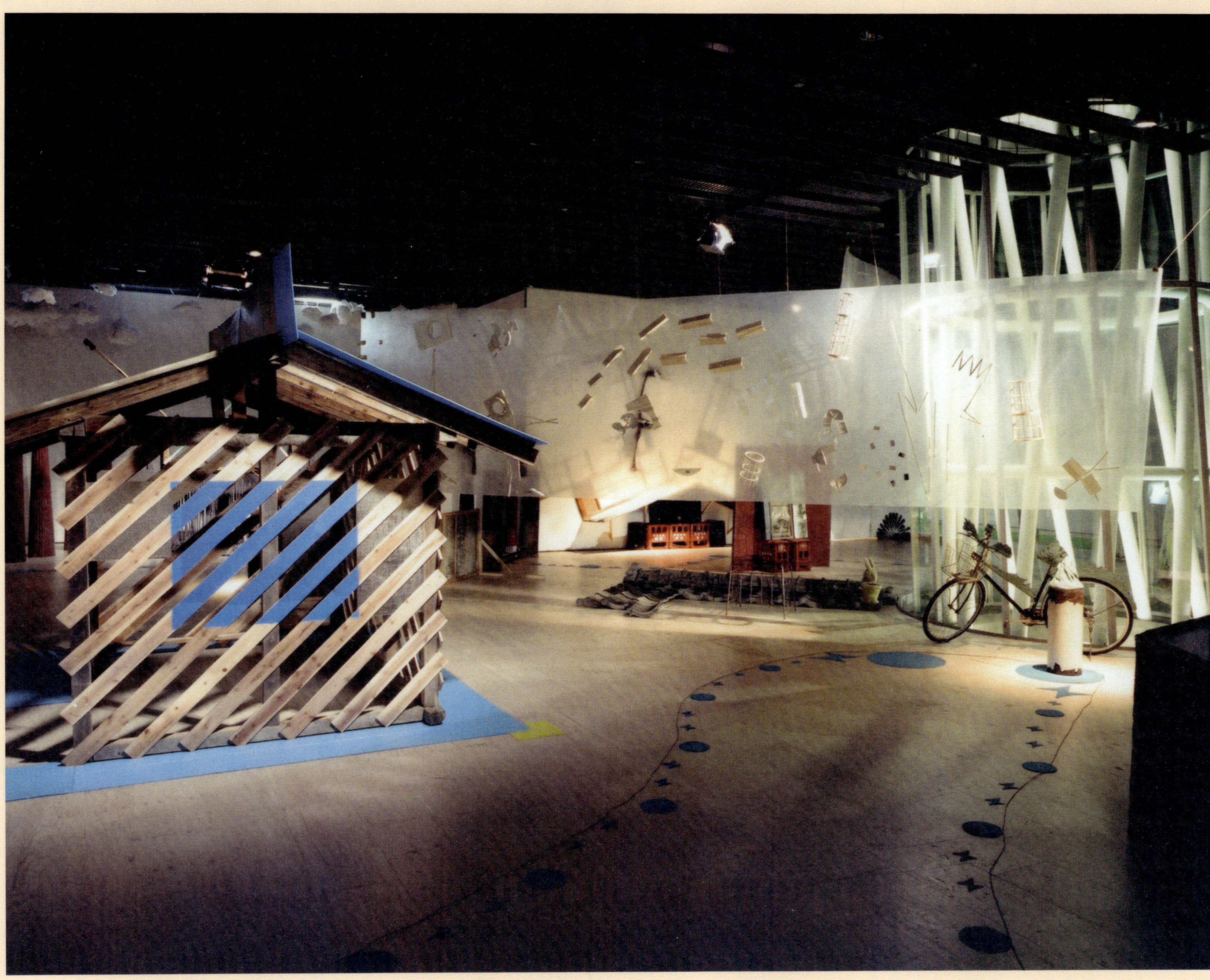

Big Stop–Gardening of Anger, 2008. Waste wood, clay, kimono, blanket, bicycle, water pump, fan, Braille, stuffed animals, LED, OHP, video projectors, moving light, interactive systems, speakers, blind attendant. 32 × 20 × 4.2 m

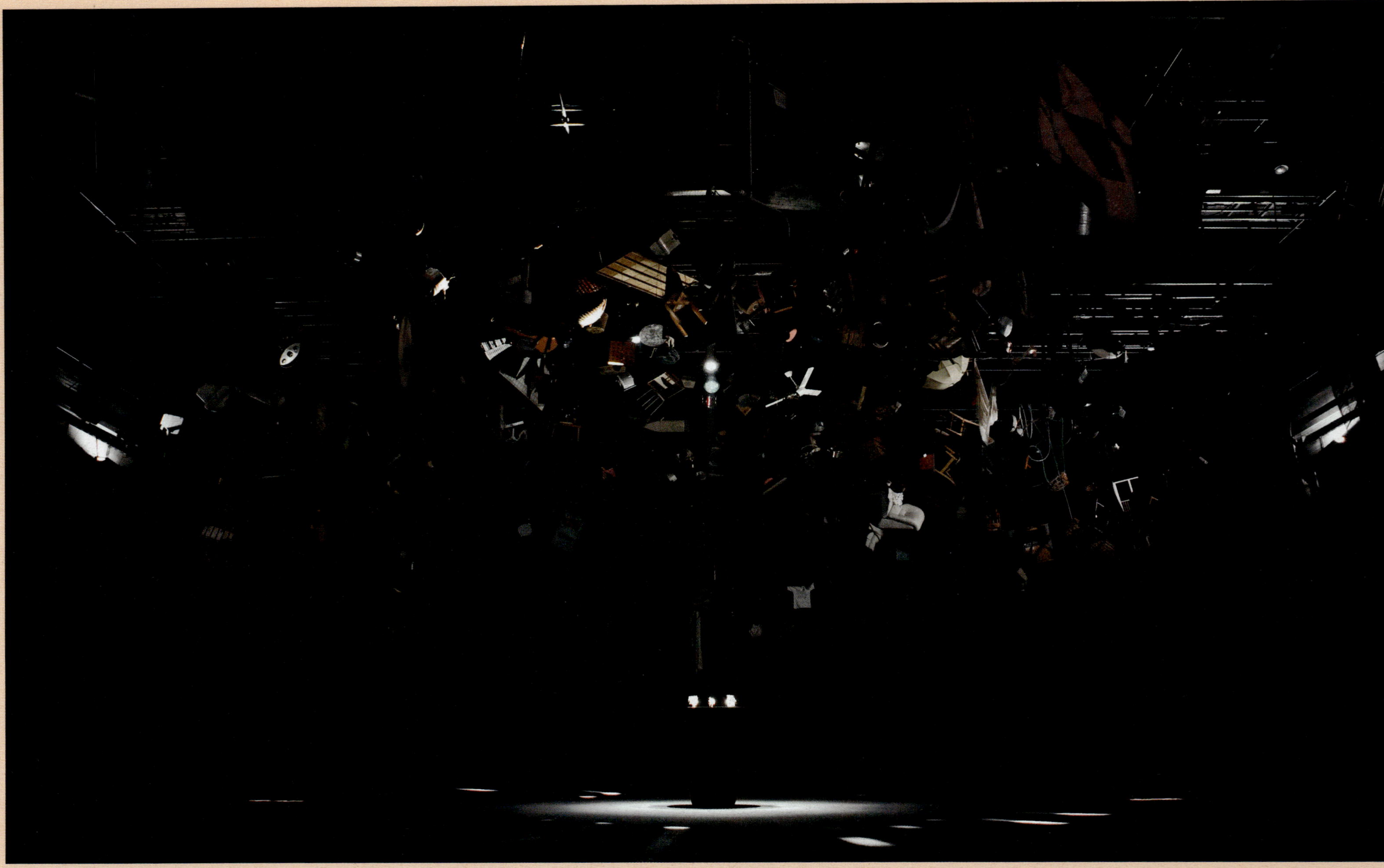

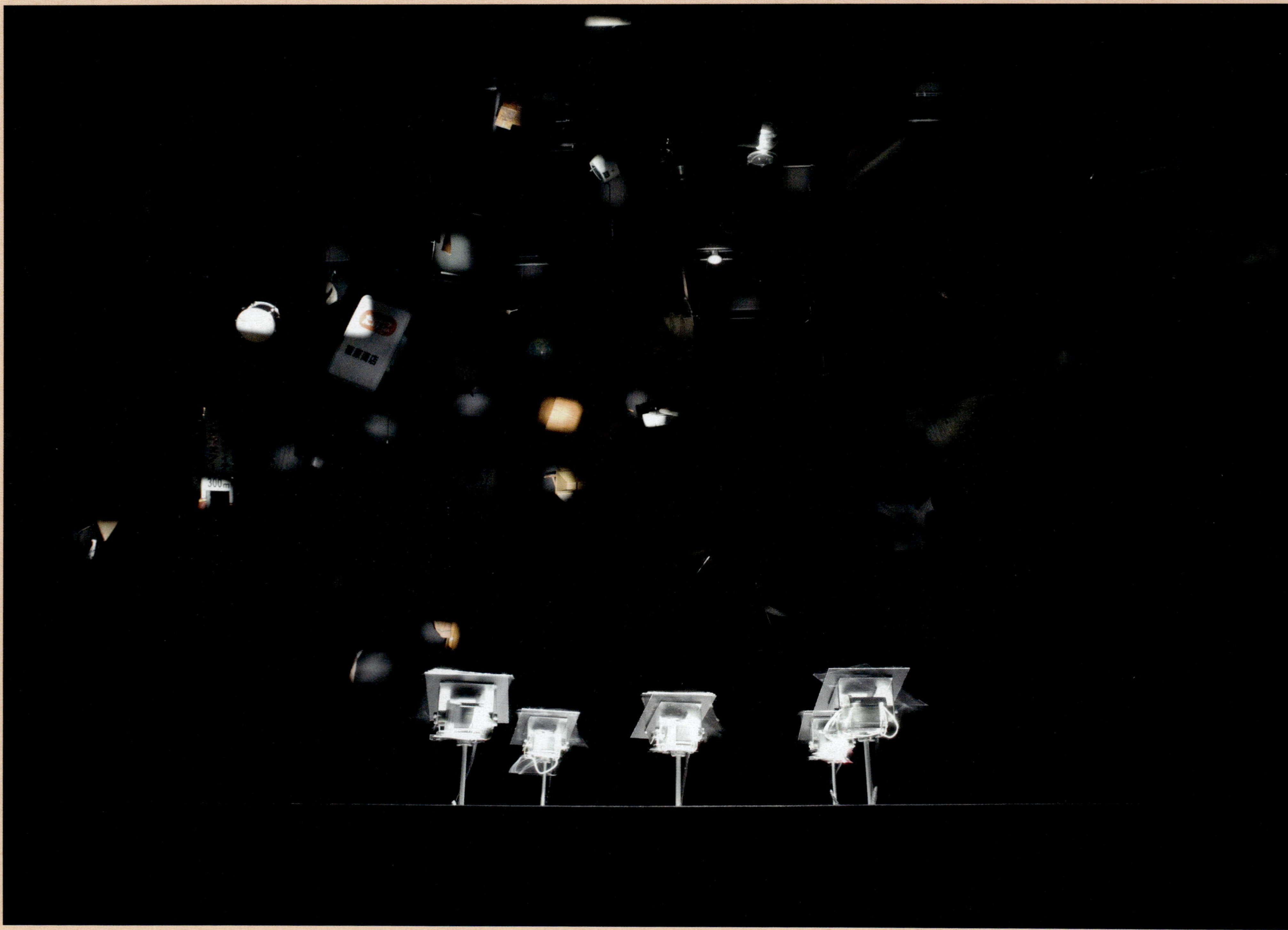

Orchestras (with Yoshihide Otomo), 2008. Waste objects, mirrors, motor control device, spotlights, strobe, computers, speakers. 40 × 20 × 15 m

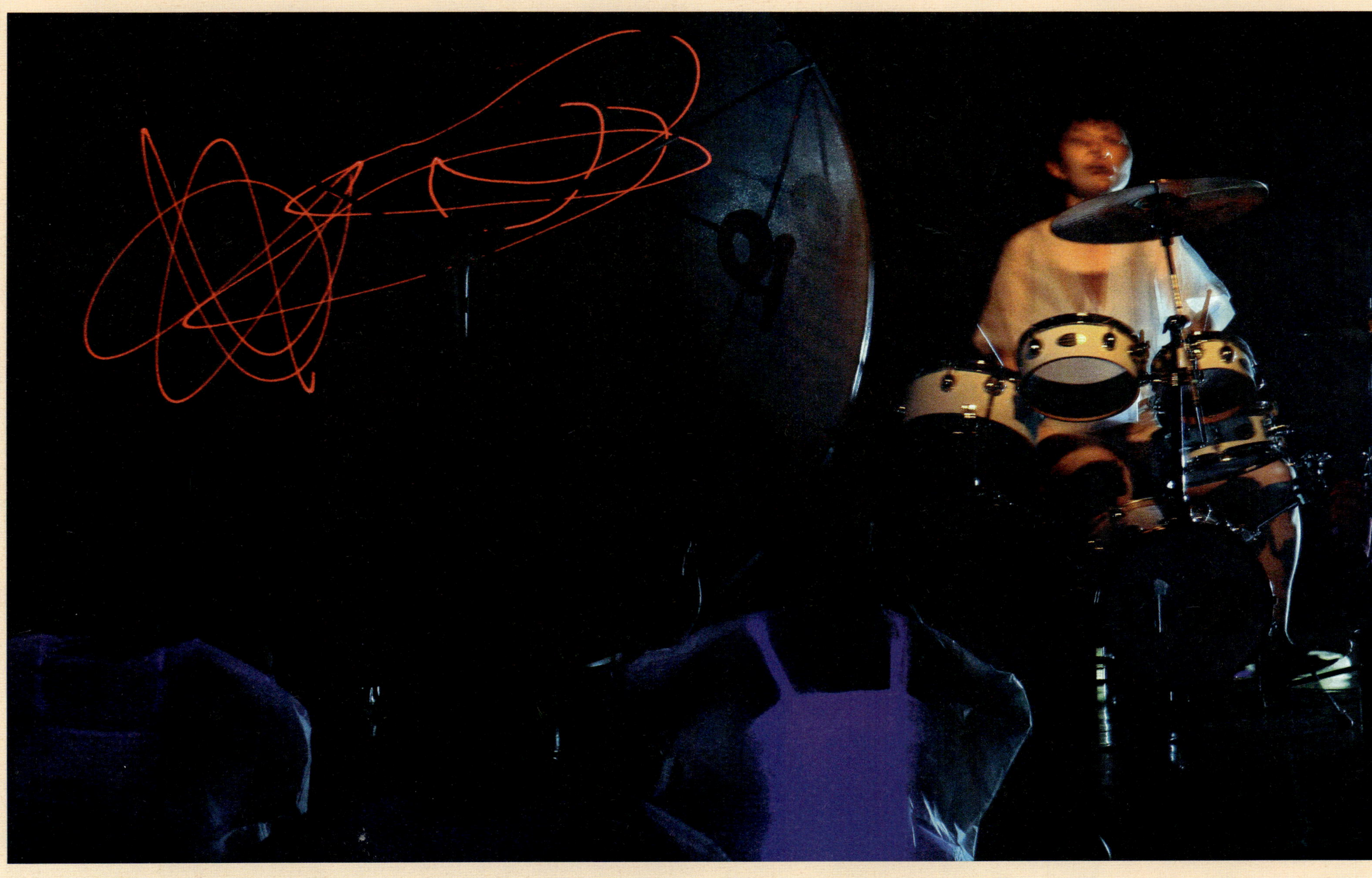

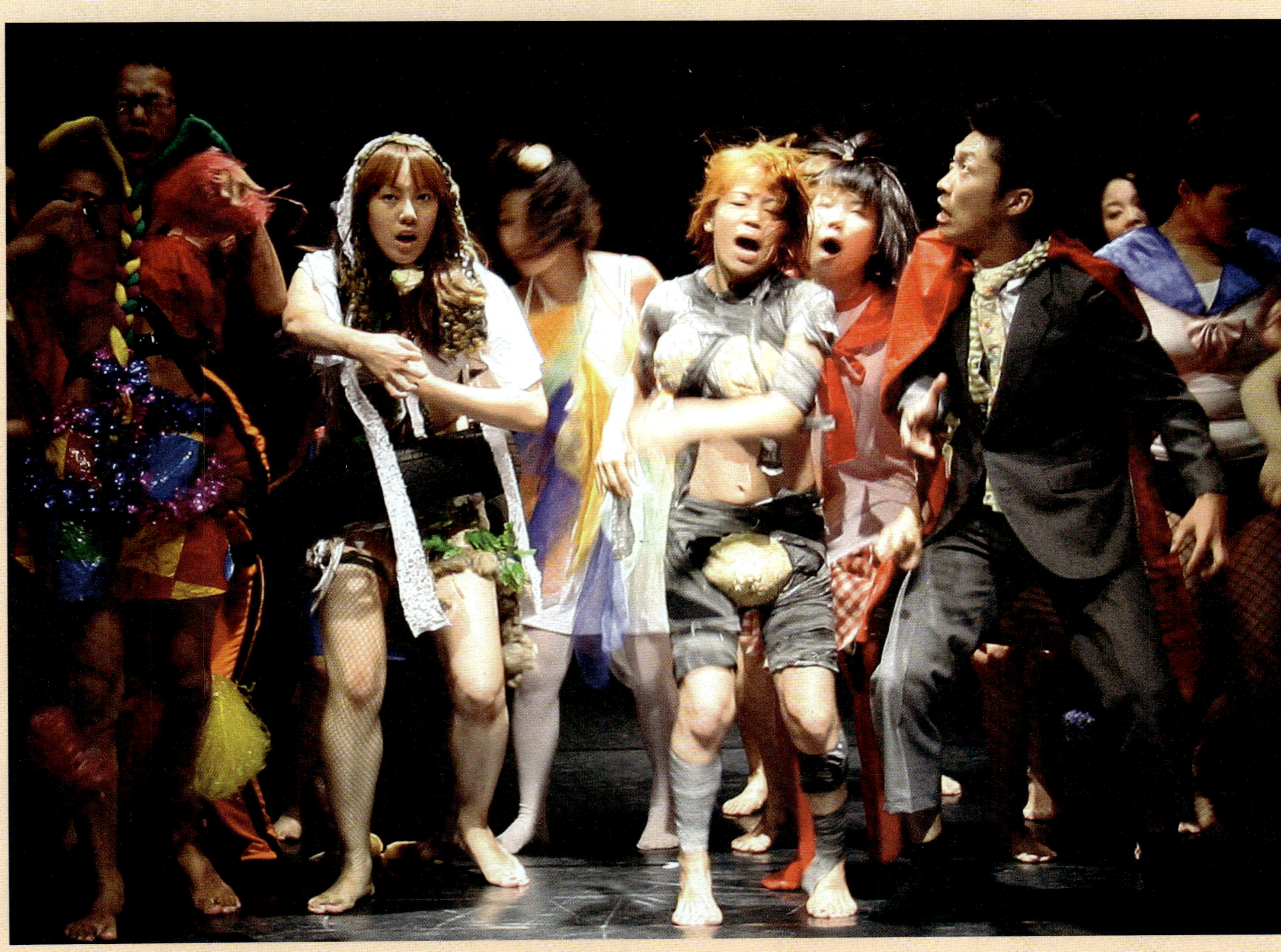

Life ... it's reversible, 2007. Performance. 90 min

Ron Terada

Ron Terada belongs to a younger generation of artists working in Vancouver, for whom the city's reputation as a centre for photoconceptualism is taken as given. The myth of the Vancouver school comes in for gentle teasing in *Entering City of Vancouver* (2002), which Terada asked the city's public-works department to realize as a highway sign. Displayed in his Vancouver gallery's window, it self-consciously and reflexively points to the marketing of the local artistic scene and its magnified self-image. Somewhat ironically, however, it has since become an earnest emblem of Vancouver when included in international group exhibitions. That ambivalence, the uneasy balance between critique and promotion, may be said to be the characteristic tenor of Terada's engaging body of recent work.

Much of Terada's work has taken the form of signage, most often mimicking the appearance of pre-existing displays. Sometimes, this has displayed the character of an in-joke, as in *Big Star* (2003), a neon sign that simultaneously appropriates the logo of the under-recognized 1970s power pop band of the same name and refers in tongue-in-cheek fashion to Terada's own status in the art world.

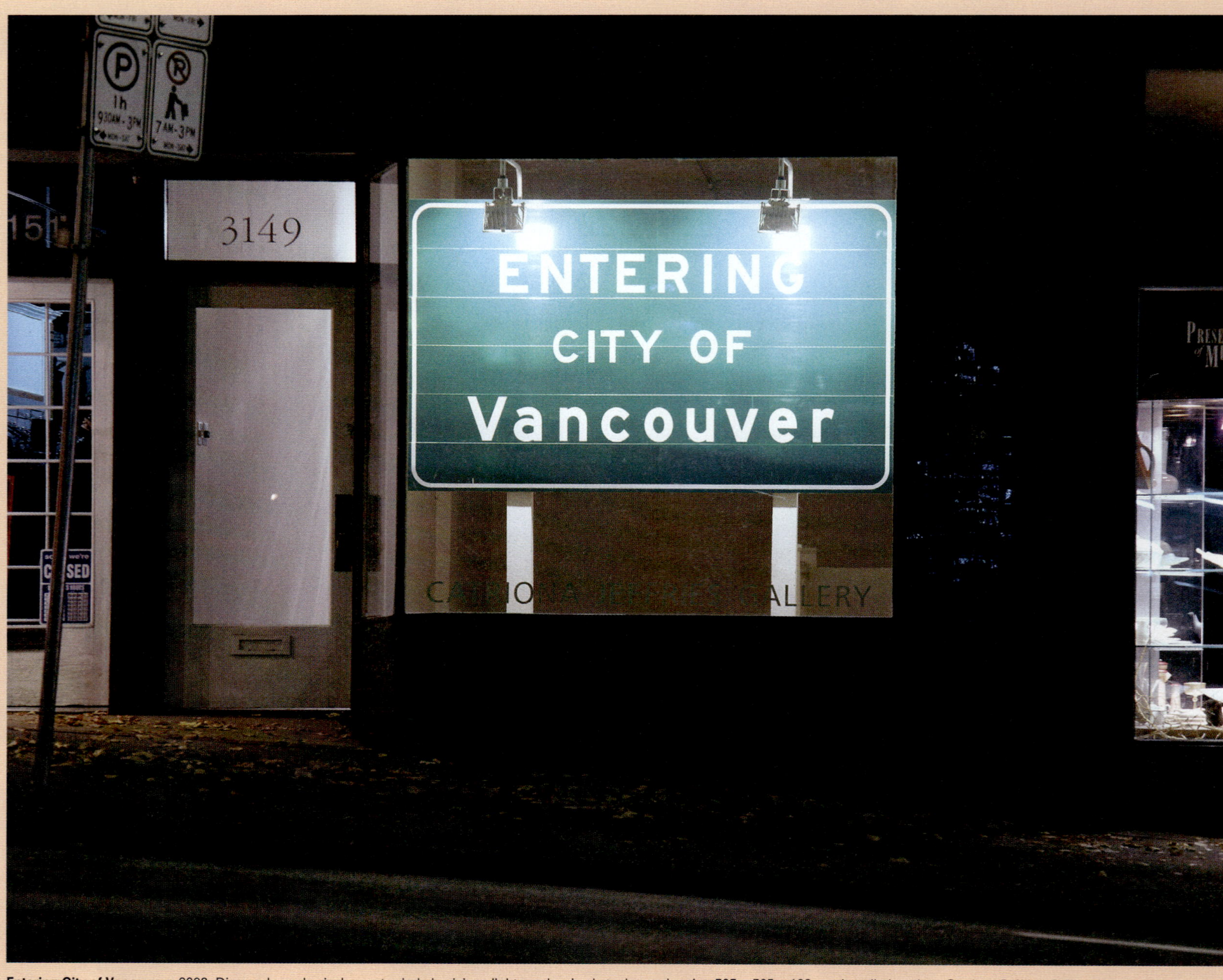

Entering City of Vancouver, 2002. Diamond–grade vinyl on extruded aluminium, lights, galvanized steel, wood, paint. 305 × 305 × 122 cm. Installation view, Catriona Jeffries Gallery, Vancouver

Between critique and promotion

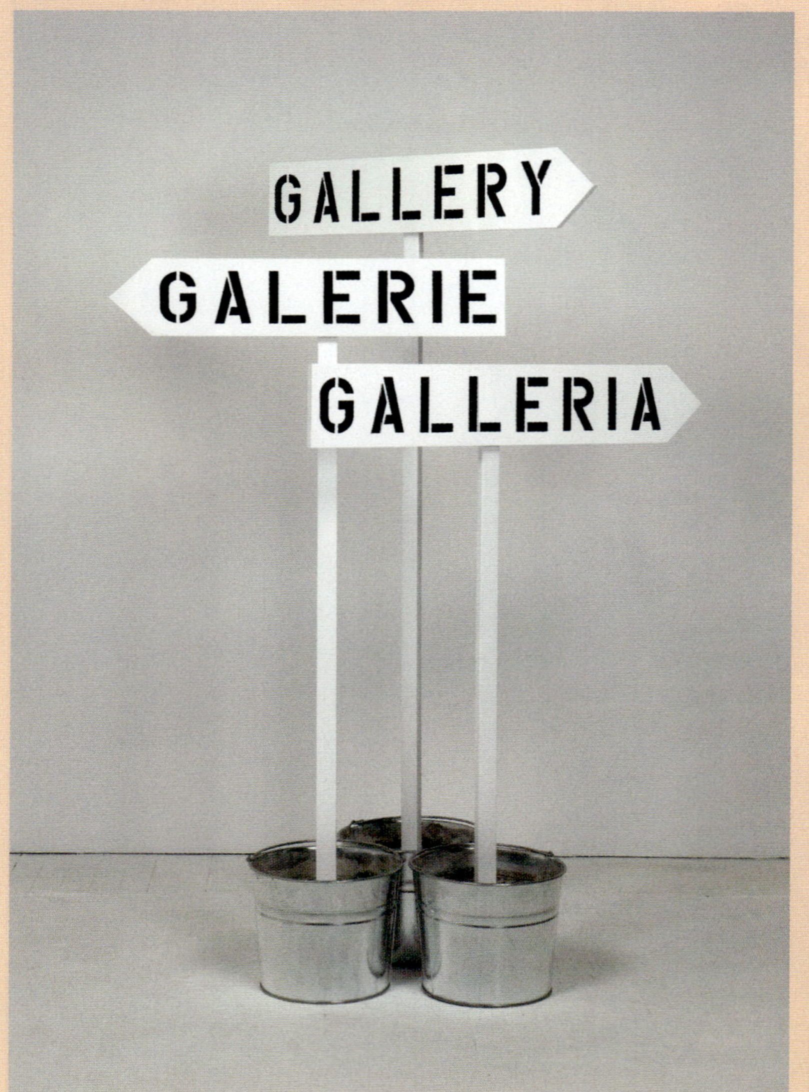

Gallery, Galerie, Galleria, 2010. Paint, wood, concrete, aluminium buckets. Approx. 81 × 112 × 48 cm

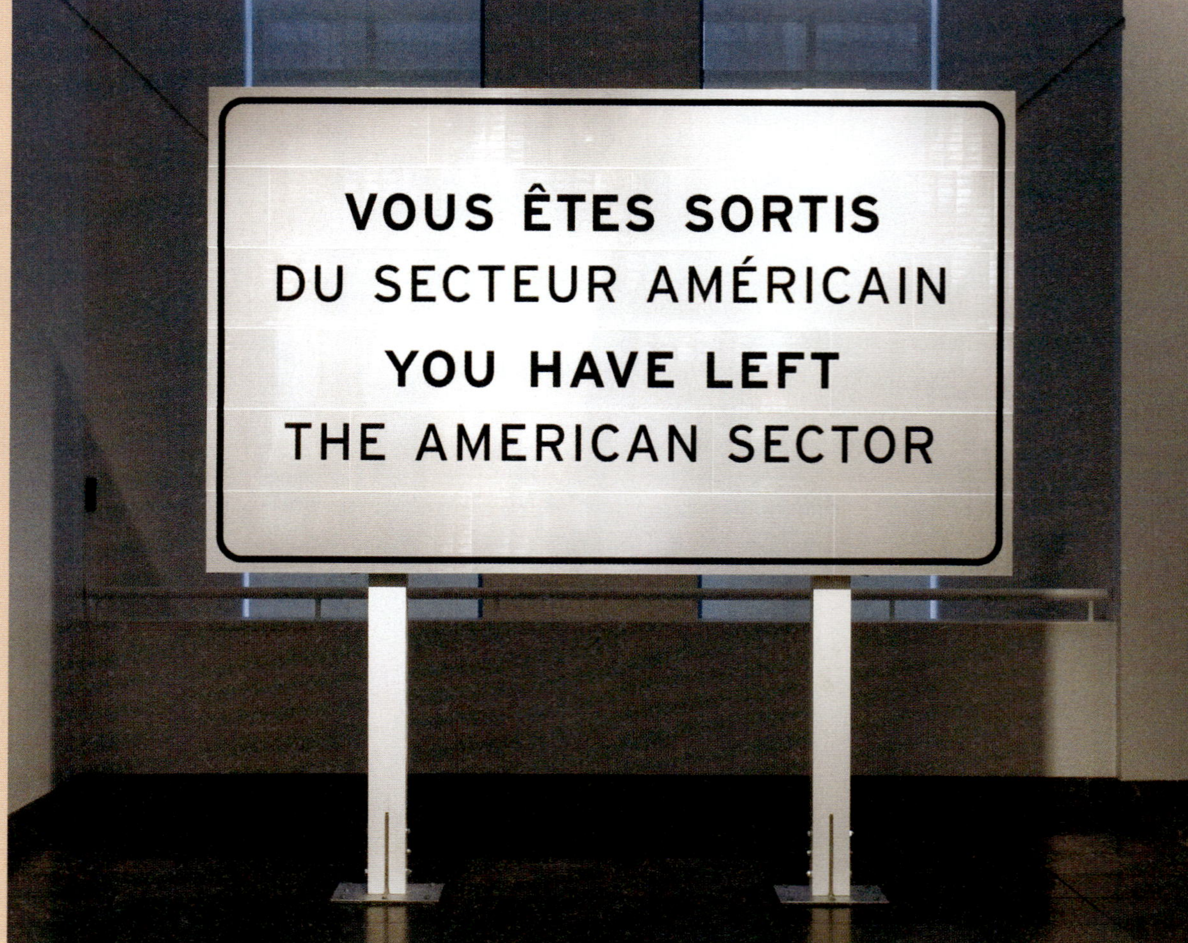

You Have Left the American Sector, 2006. Diamond–grade vinyl on extruded aluminium, galvanized steel, wood, paint. 305 × 305 × 25 cm

Terada has often been attracted to stories of failure and underestimation, which he has taken up in ironic self-identification, most recently in *Jack* (2009), his new series of paintings that pay homage to the late Jack Goldstein through stencilled quotations from his autobiography. But other signs have a more resolutely public character, such as *Stay Away From Lonely Places* (2005), a large white neon sign commissioned by the Ikon Gallery in Birmingham that broadcast its melancholy message over a rundown area of the city. *You Have Left the American Sector* (2005), like the Vancouver billboard, assumes the form of an official display of information, with a message in French and English that echoes the wording of Checkpoint Charlie, the Cold War crossing between West and East Berlin. It was, however, sited along that other contested border, the one separating Canada and the United States. A commission of the Art Gallery of Windsor, just across from Detroit, it was removed soon after its unveiling under orders from a municipal government worried about provoking the ire of its neighbour to the south.

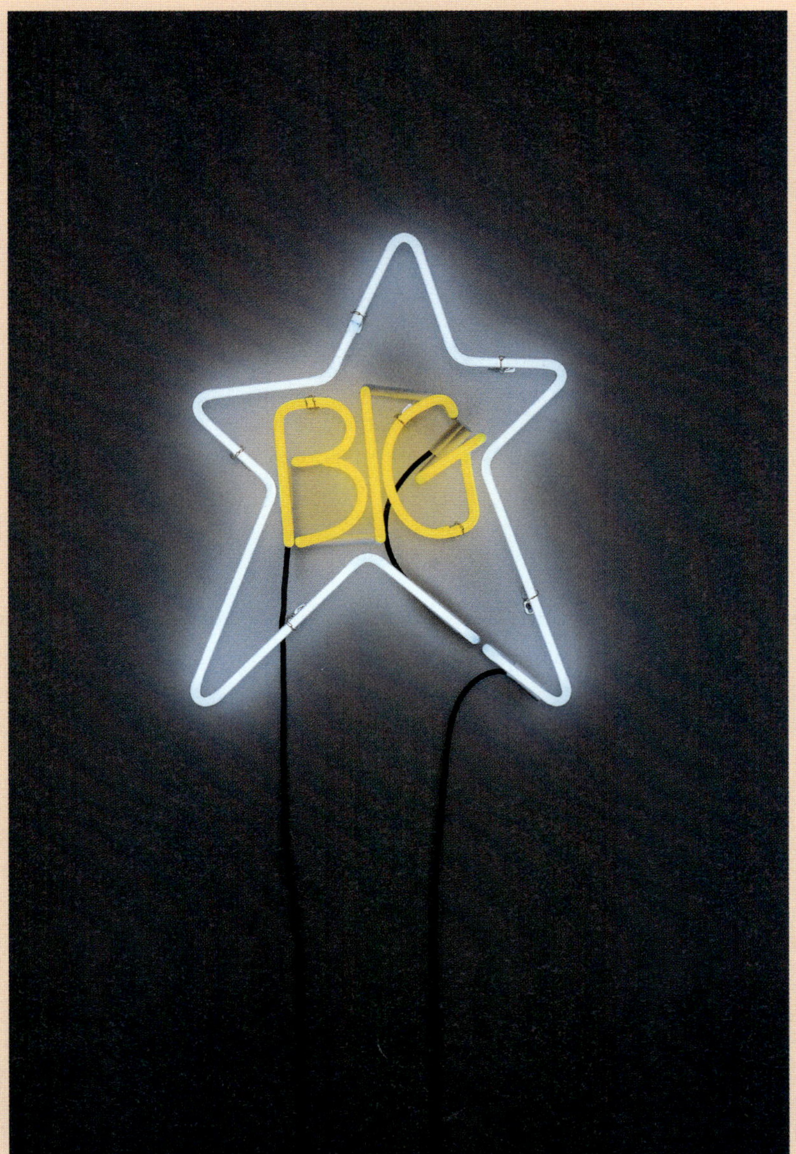

Big Star, 2003. Gold and white neon. Approx. 58 × 46 cm

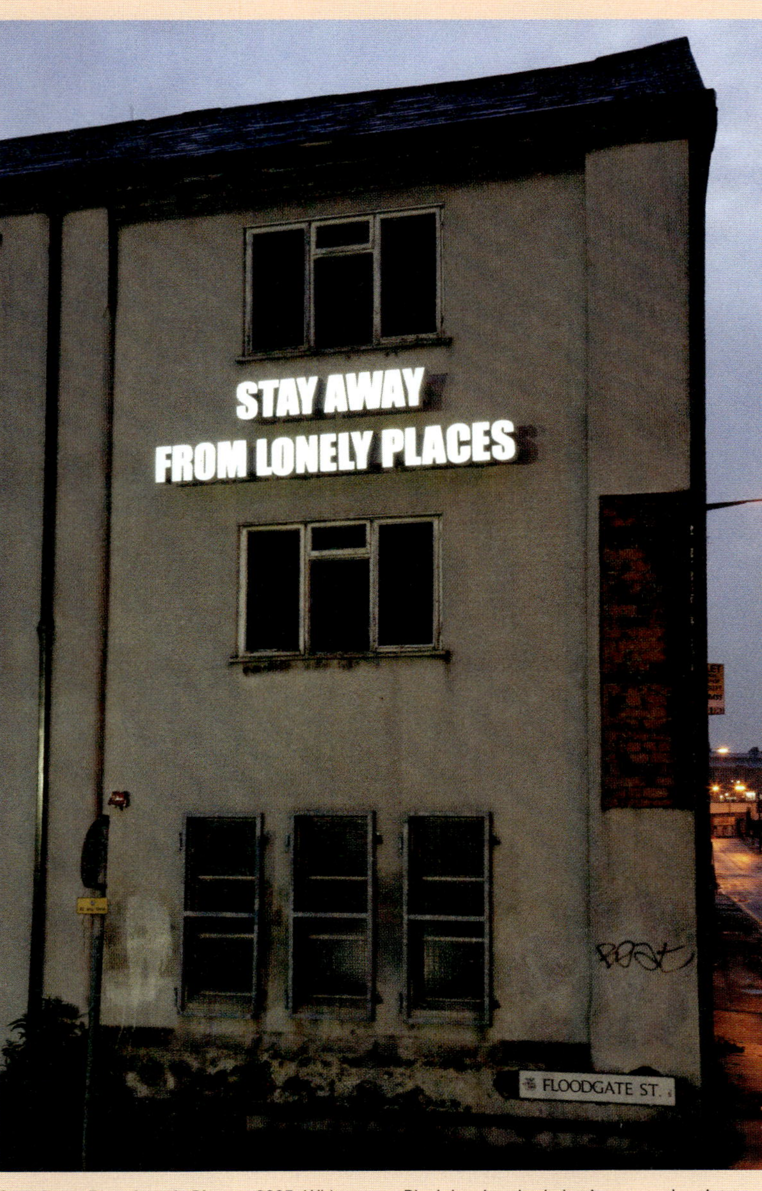

Stay Away From Lonely Places, 2005. White neon, Plexiglas, brushed aluminum, steel, paint 97 × 323 × 28 cm. Installation view, Birmingham, 2006

Separating homage from parody

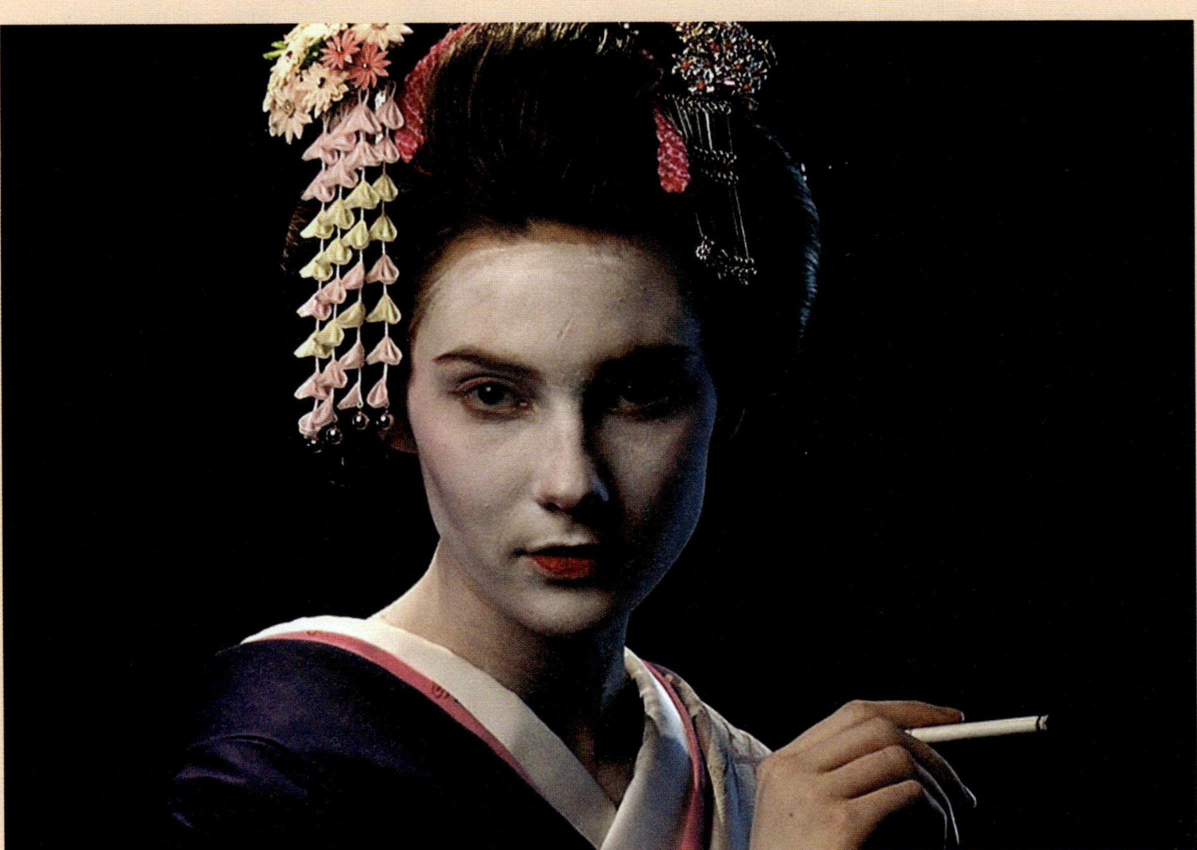

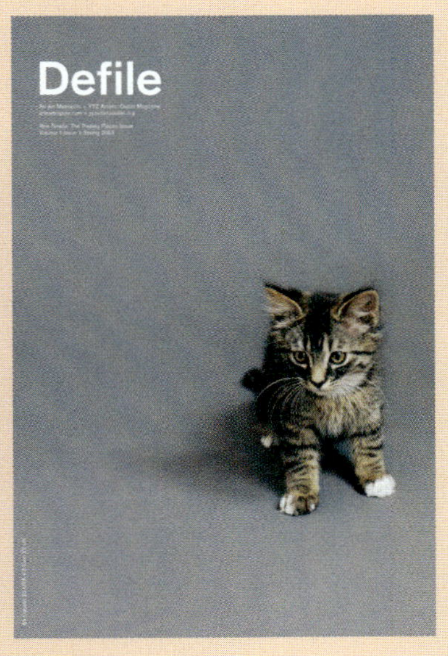

Defile Magazine, 2003. Magazine without articles, composed of only advertisement exchanges with national and international art magazines. 52 pages, colour, offset print on paper. 28 × 20 cm

Peripheral framing devices

Other works engage with the institutions of contemporary art through close attention to peripheral framing devices. When he was invited to make a solo show at the Contemporary Art Gallery in Vancouver, Terada sold wall space to various patrons and sponsors, whose names were displayed as the only visual component of the show, while their donations went towards the production of *Catalogue* (2003), a hardcover publication that, in a sense, was the exhibition. That same year he undertook a magazine project entitled *Defile* (2003), which swapped advertising space with prominent art magazines: they advertised *Defile* within their pages, while Terada's magazine consisted only of advertisements drawn from their issues.

Even works that seem to articulate quite separate concerns generally include this self-reflexive aspect. The video projection *Voight-Kampff* (2008), which shows three Caucasian women in geisha-like outfits popping pills, smoking and drinking, is ostensibly a reference to the electronic billboards and polygraph-like machines in the 1982 film *Blade Runner*, which detect whether an individual is human or replicant.

Perhaps this is an allusion to the kinds of neo-Orientalism endemic to the racially mixed milieu of a Pacific Rim city like Vancouver, but it is likely that once again Terada is calling our attention to the infinitesi-mally small line separating homage from parody in any act of mimetic appropriation.

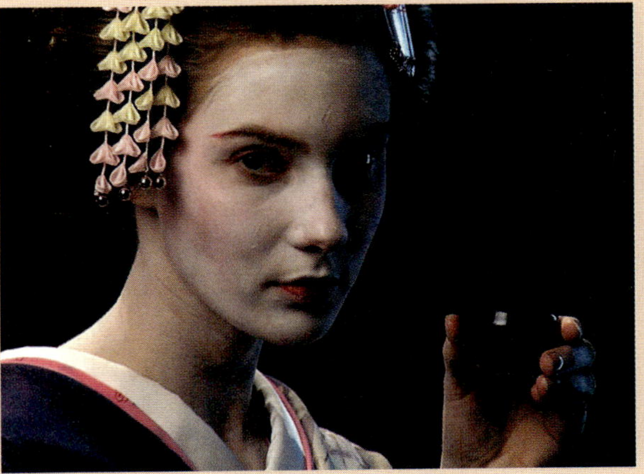

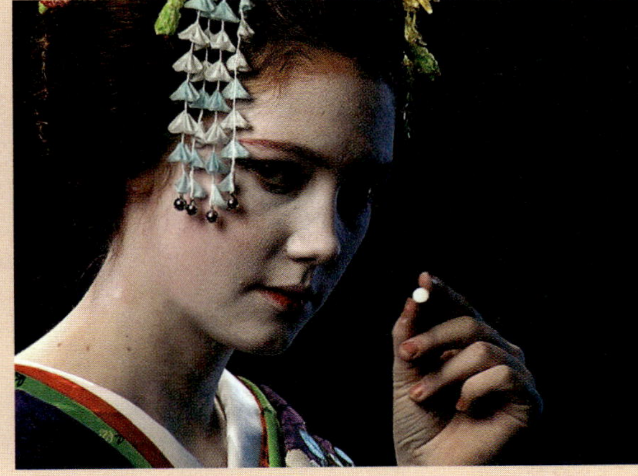

Voight-Kampff, 2008. Silent video. 1 min. 30 sec. loop

Yuken Teruya

McDonald's, Krispy Kream, Dunkin' Donuts: those familiar paper bags from ubiquitous fast-food joints would usually be scrunched up along with their paper serviettes and tossed unceremoniously into the bin, but in the hands of Yuken Teruya, they become precious objects.

For his ongoing project *Notice-Forest*, Teruya meticulously cut and folded a paper bag into a tree to recreate a tiny scene from nature. As well as bags from mass market food providers, he uses shopping bags from luxury brands such as Louis Vuitton, Tiffany's and Hermes. In the enclosed confines of these bags from corporations that manufacture for global consumption, Teruya restores a delicate piece of the natural world. These fragile works convey the artist's interpretation of landscape painting and the diorama, prompting recollections that paper was once a tree. The opposing forces of mass consumerism and nature cohabit within them, yet they are not mere social criticism, but lyrical expressions of survival through recycling the disposable.

Teruya's birthplace of Okinawa was placed under American military rule after World War II, and governed directly by the Unite States up to its return to Japan in 1972.

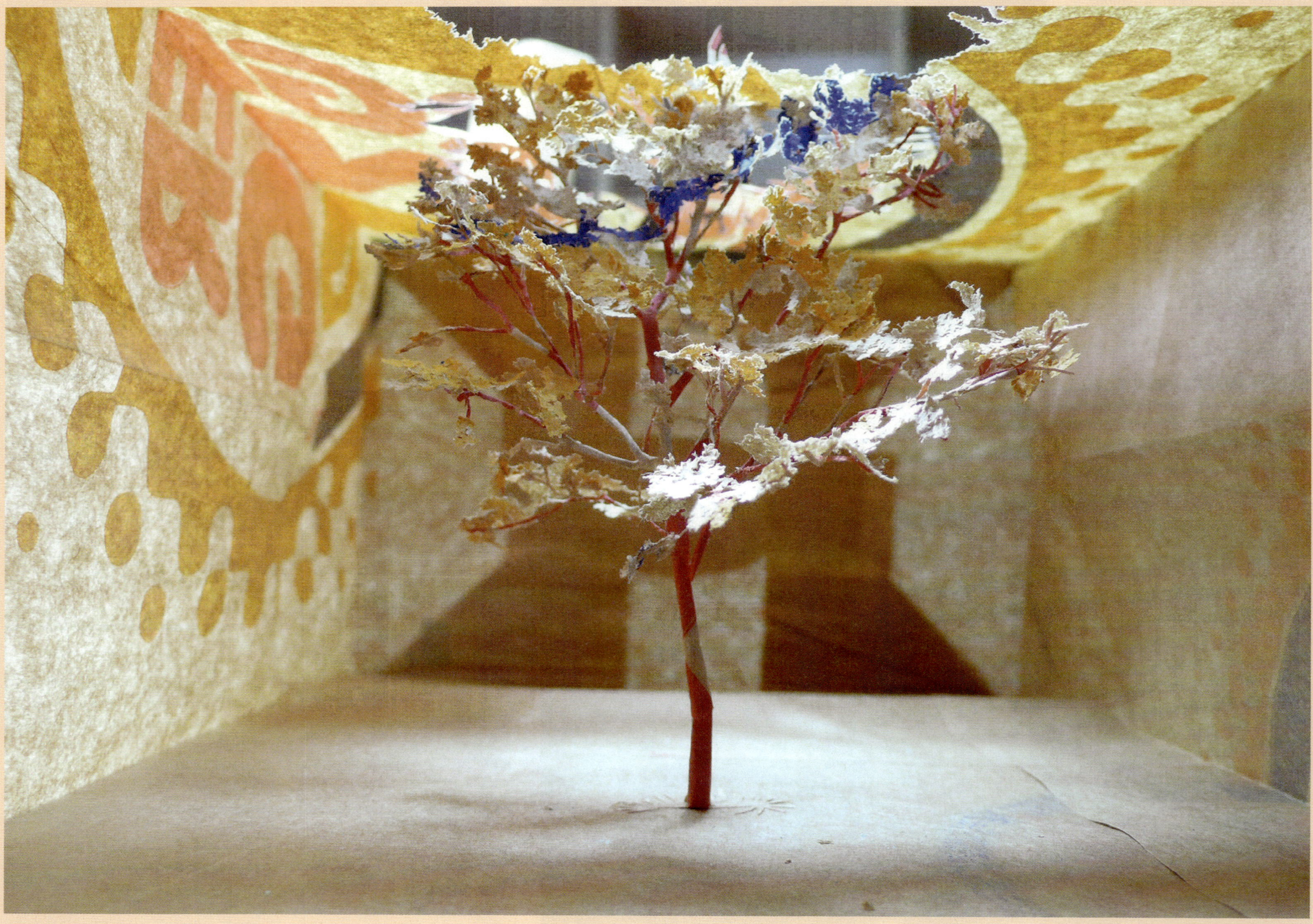

Notice–Forest (Burger King), 2005. Paper shopping bag, glue. Dimensions variable

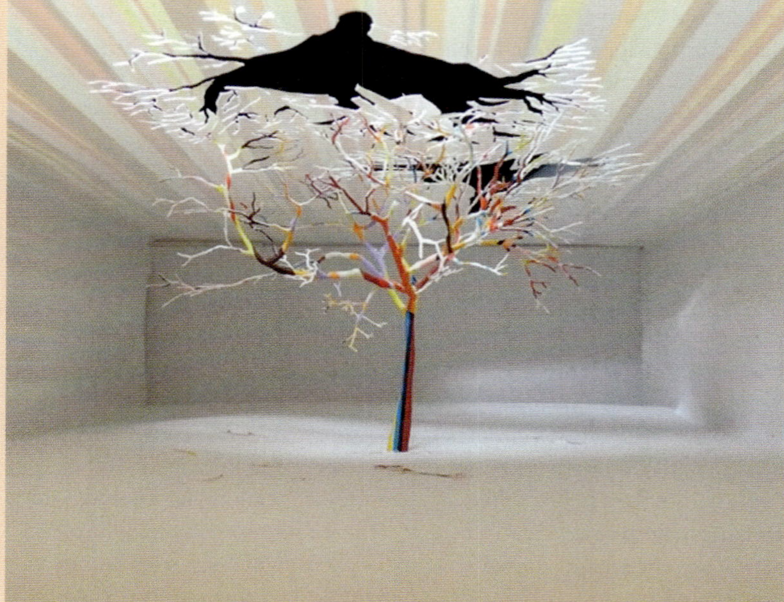

Notice–Forest (Paul Smith), 2005. Paper shopping bag, glue. Dimensions variable

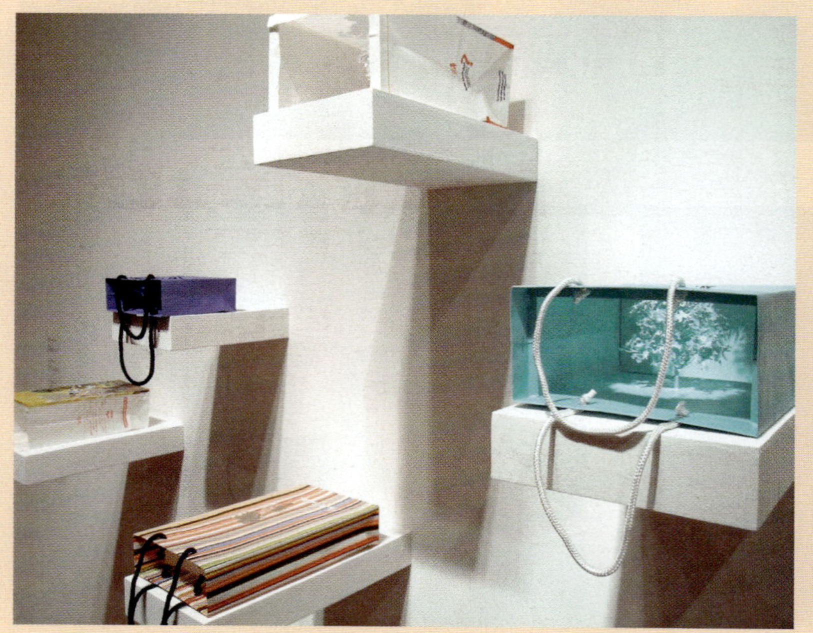

Notice–Forest, 2005. 7 paper shopping bags, glue. Dimensions variable

Okinawa still accounts for more than seventy percent of the US base presence in Japan, and has almost singlehandedly borne the brunt of issues surrounding the US-Japan security treaty. As a child of a place where indifference to politics is impossible, Teruya initially made works that were dominated by this perspective. *You-1, You-1* (2008), for example, is a kimono that he made using the traditional Okinawan dyeing technique of bingata, imprinting the area's history on the design through motifs such as fighter planes and paratroopers amid the traditional flowers and trees.

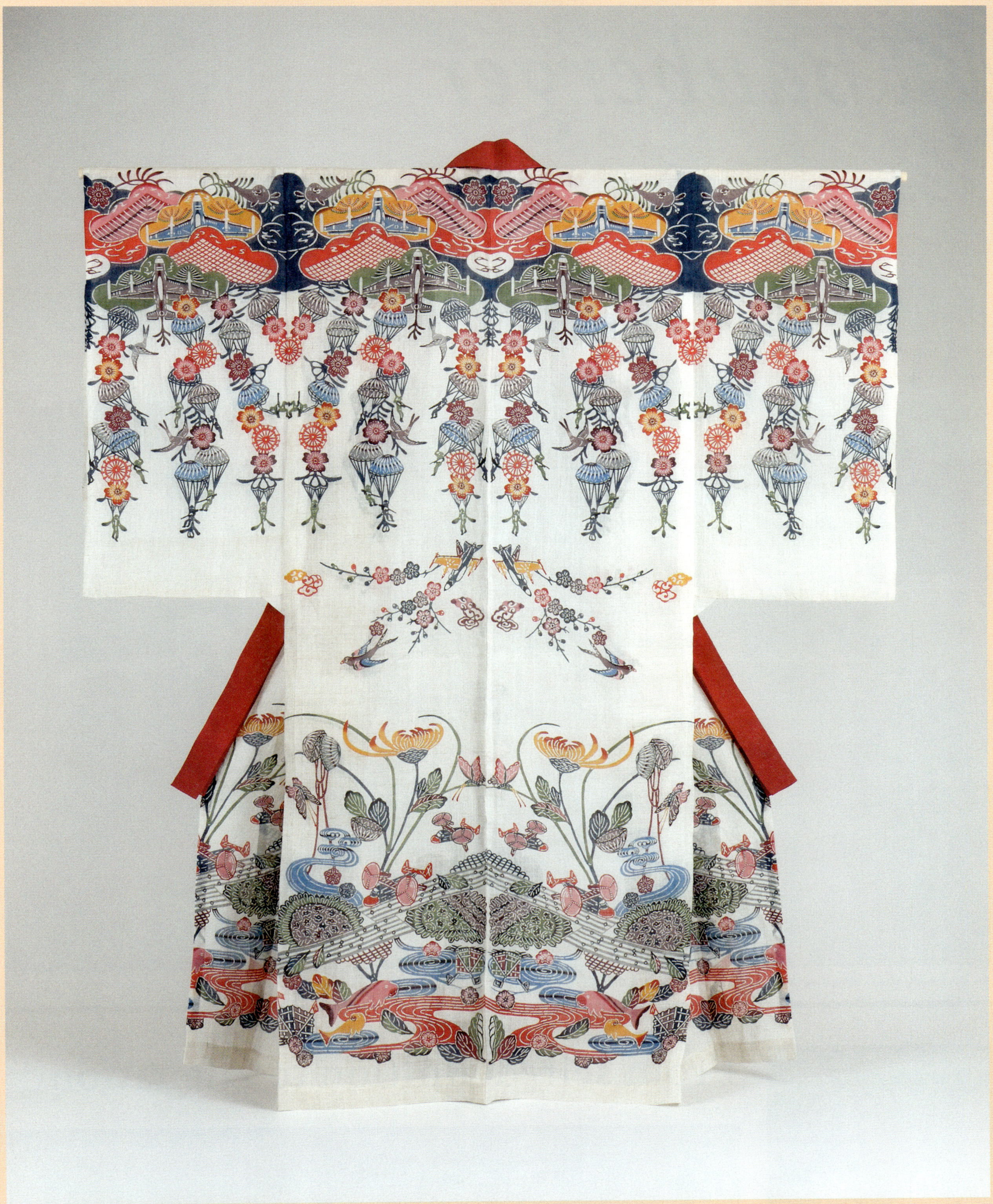

Cross-cultural hybrid

Now, as just one of many immigrants from different backgrounds living in New York, Teruya lends the political references in his work poetic visualization through his delicate handiwork, grounded in a profound awareness of history and identity from the standpoint of the cross-cultural hybrid.

In *Free Fish* (2007), a site-specific work for the Asia Society in New York, Teruya took an ancient Ming jar decorated with red carp from the collection and surrounded it with plastic bags of a similar colour, of the type commonly found in Chinatown. From the gently fluttering bags he cut out silhouettes of small fish, a design that linked the creative powers that produced the exquisite piece of craftsmanship hundreds of years ago and the creative vitality of contemporary Chinese immigrants.

Earn lots of money, No need to write any letters, just send home the money first (2008) is Teruya's first installation with a video component. When the Hispanic residents of his neighbourhood in Brooklyn broke open a fire hydrant to cool off in the sweltering heat, Teruya launched origami boats flying tiny national flags on the water that pooled and flowed along the side of the road. Invoking emigrant ships setting sail for a new life in a land of plenty, the work also recalled through its title the exhortations to those leaving Okinawa for distant lands.

Teruya's works are charming, but never cloying, and consistently express his powerful sense of mission as an artist: to acquire greater humanity by questioning the logic of the strong from the perspective of the weak.

You–I, You–I, 2008. Linen, colour pigment. 152 × 162 × 30 cm

Lyrical expressions

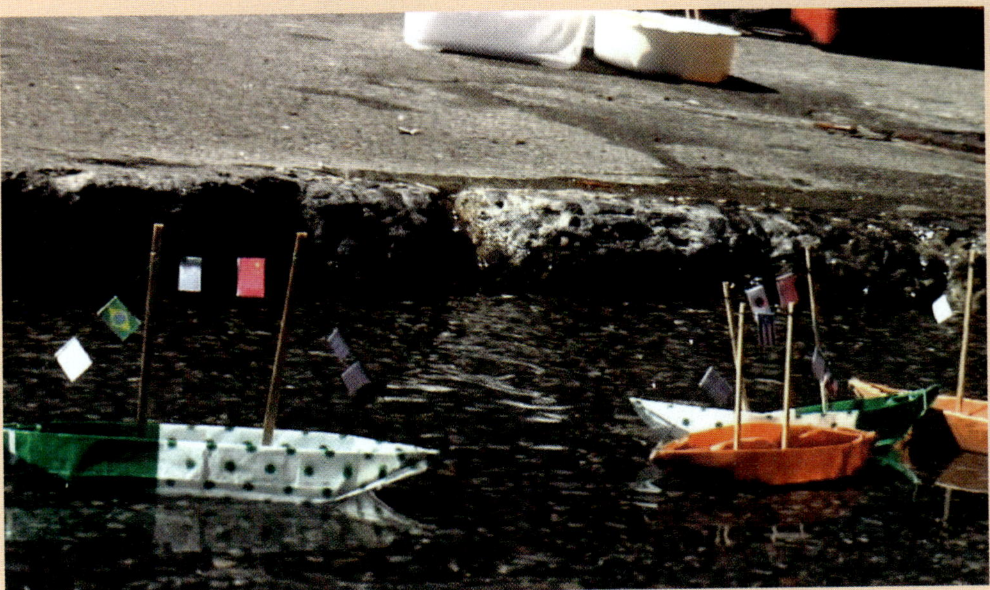

Earn lots of money, No need to write any letters, just send home the money first, 2008. Video.

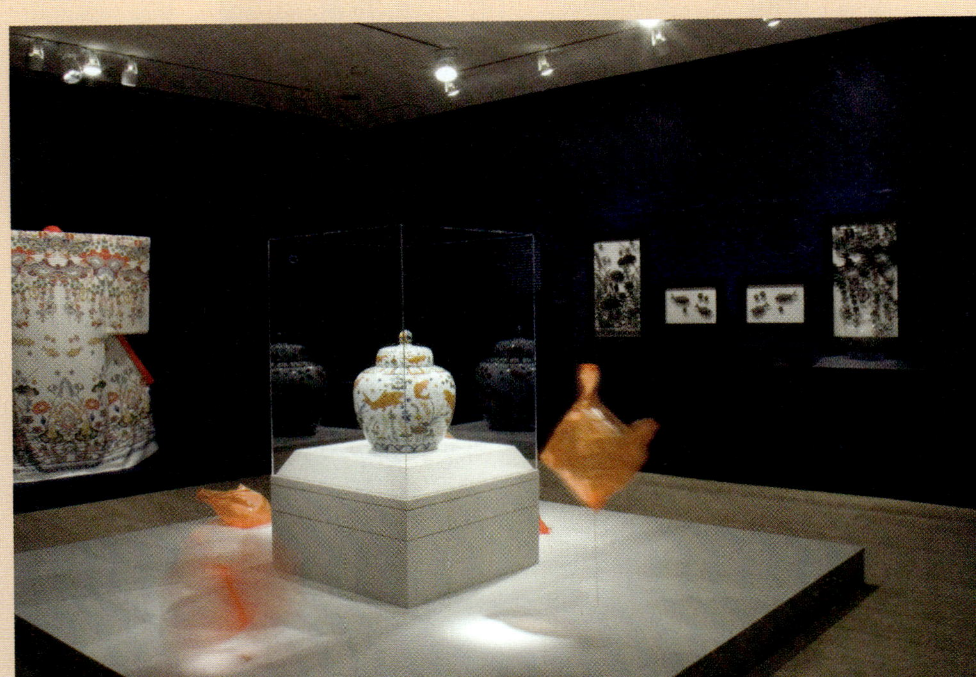

Free Fish, 2007. Ming vase, plastic bags. Dimensions variable

Althea Thauberger

Althea Thauberger collaborates with distinct groups and communities: she has worked with teenage girl singer-songwriters, San Diego military wives, male youths in the German civil service, Canadian tree planters and members of the Laddin linguistic minority in the Dolomites. After undertaking short- or long-term research with each group, she creates a work that permits members some means of self-expression and visibility, which ranges from self-definition to alienation. Her work takes one of several forms: performance, photography, film, video, audio recording and books.

For *Songstress* (2002), Thauberger worked with teenage girls to produce their songs as music videos. The artist shot the videos in outdoor settings in British Columbia and the songs are full of clichéd, if heartfelt emotion. As is often the case in Thauberger's projects, the spectator tends to feel uncomfortable, embarrassed for the girls.

The large colour photomural *The Art of Seeing Without Being Seen* (2007) portrays Canadian troops performing a surveillance exercise on a military base near Chilliwack, north of Vancouver, while training for deployment in Afghanistan. The work was installed at the Arts

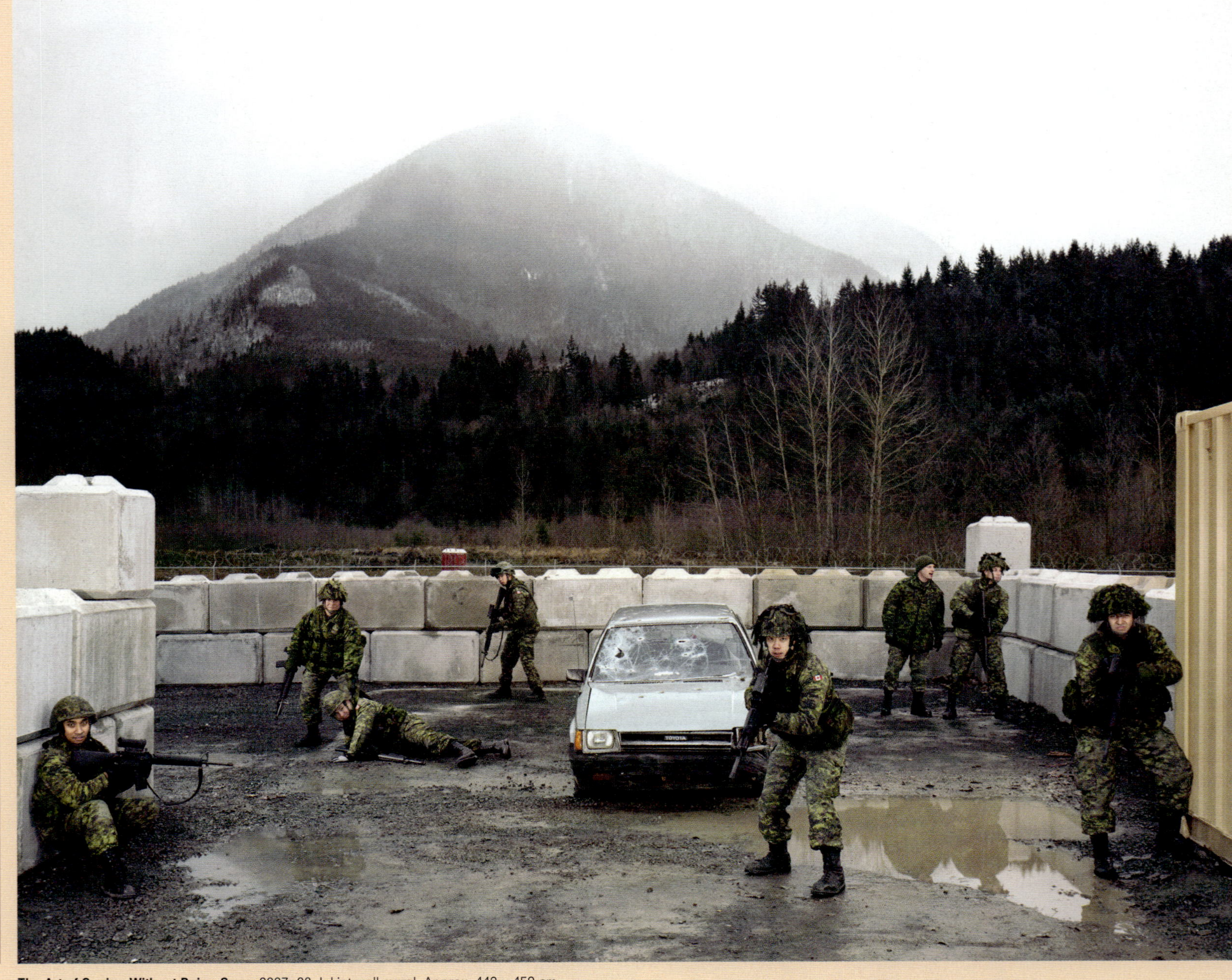

The Art of Seeing Without Being Seen, 2007–08. Inkjet wall mural. Approx. 442 × 459 cm

From self-definition to alienation

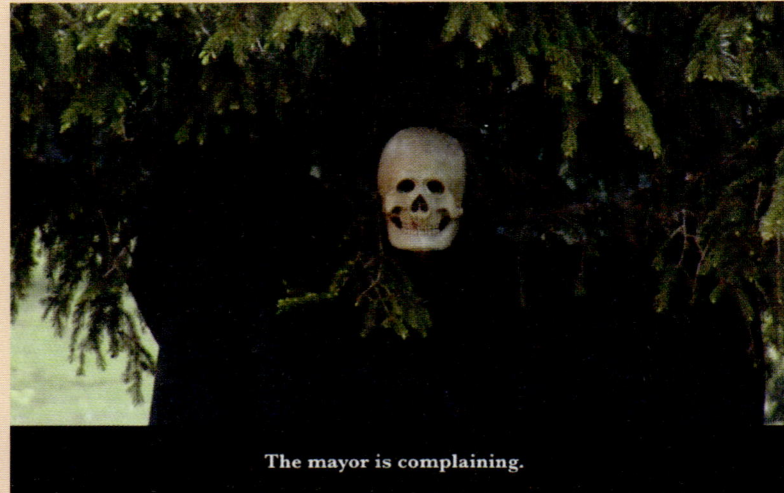

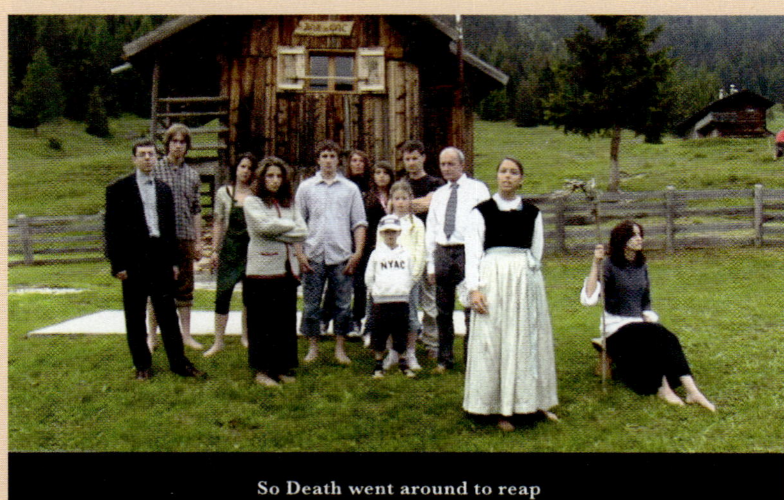

La mort e la miseria, 2009. HD video. 6 min. 20 sec.

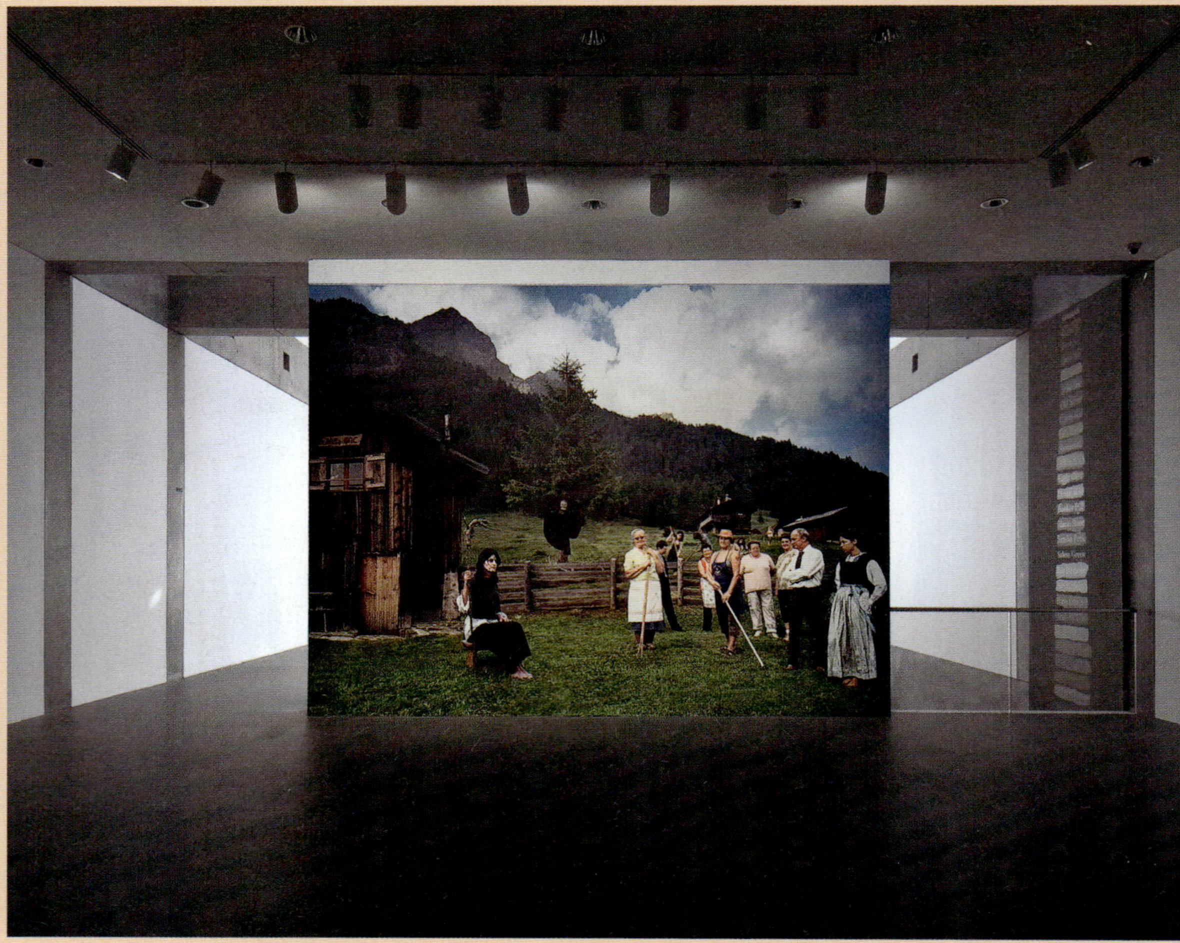

La mort e la miseria, 2009. Inkjet wall mural. Approx. 419 × 572 cm

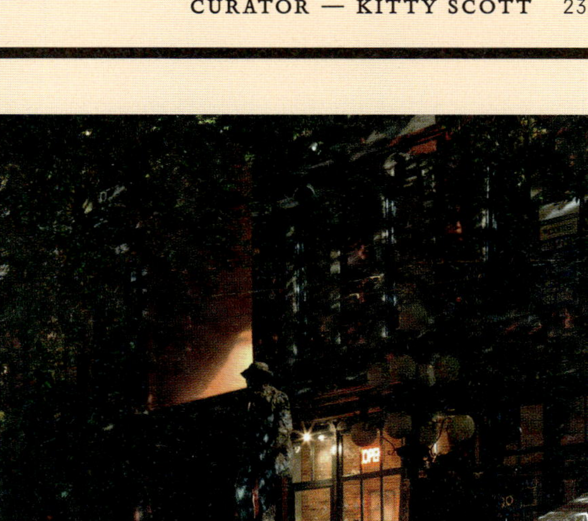

Performers repeated quotidian actions, speeches and scripted conversations

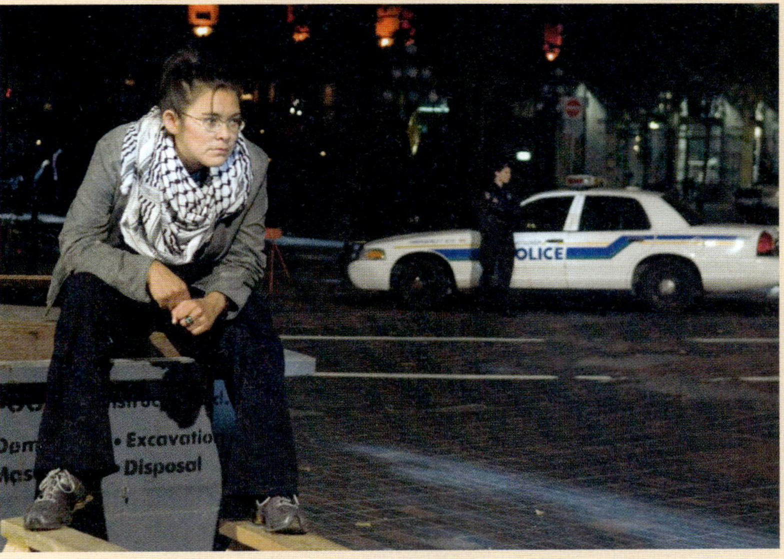

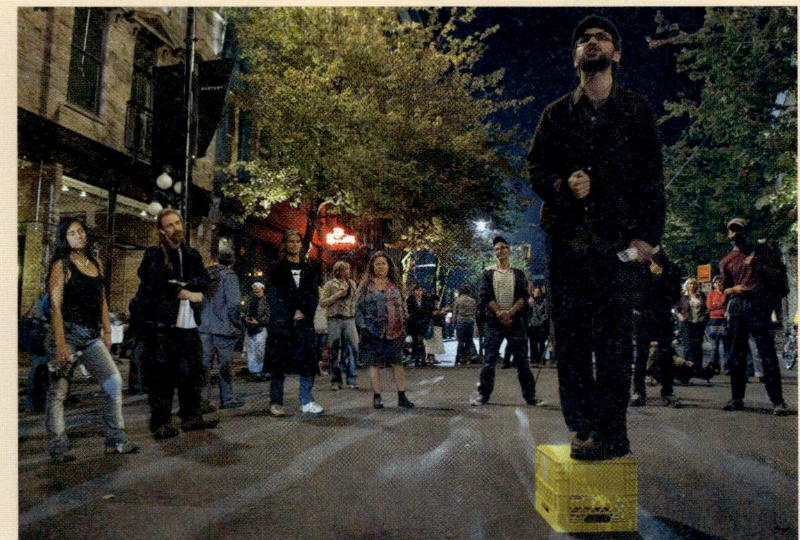

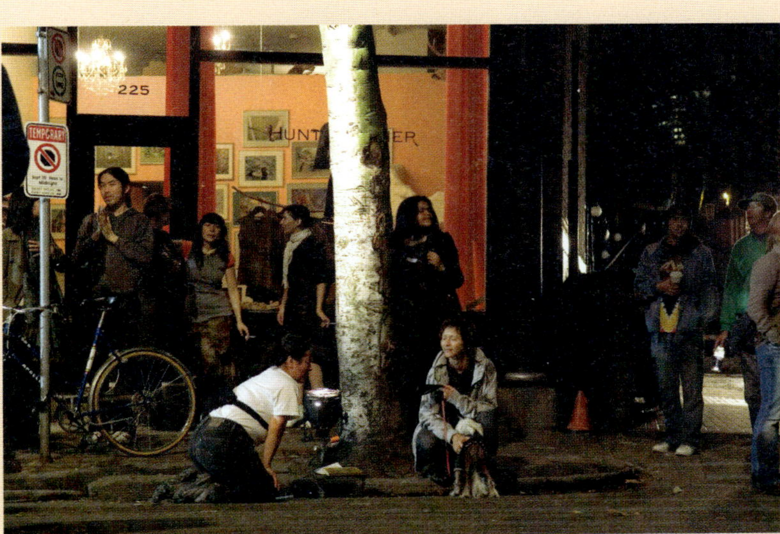

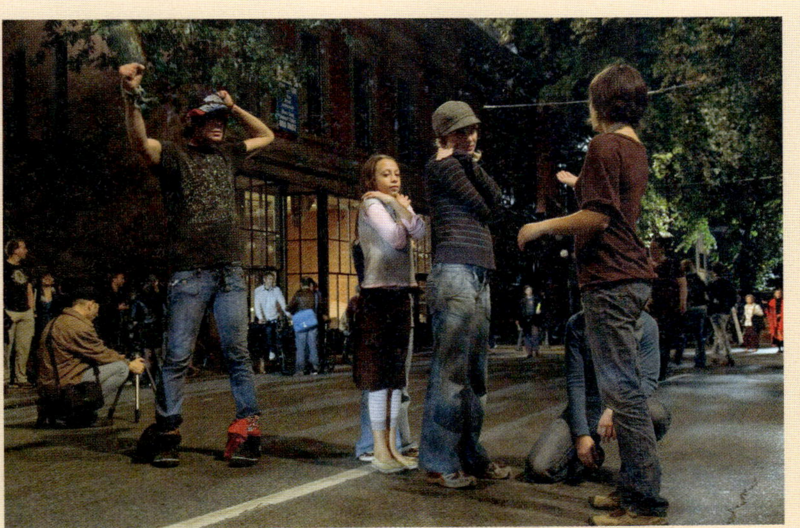

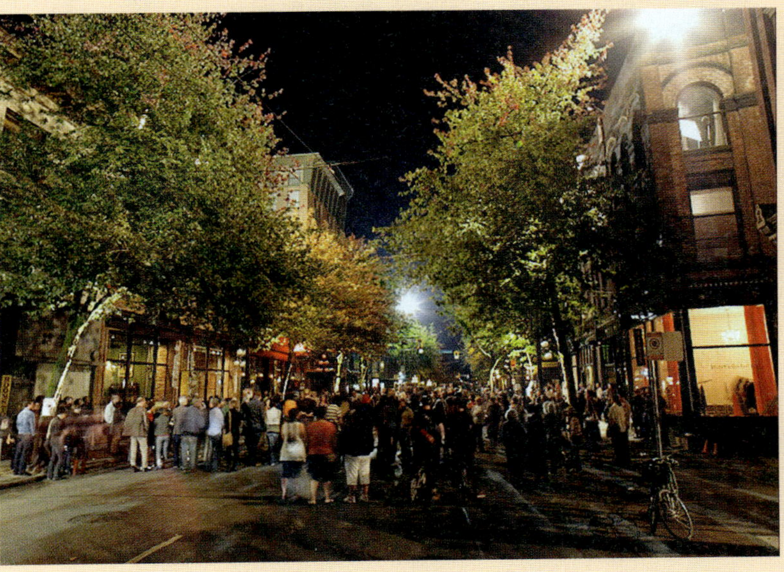

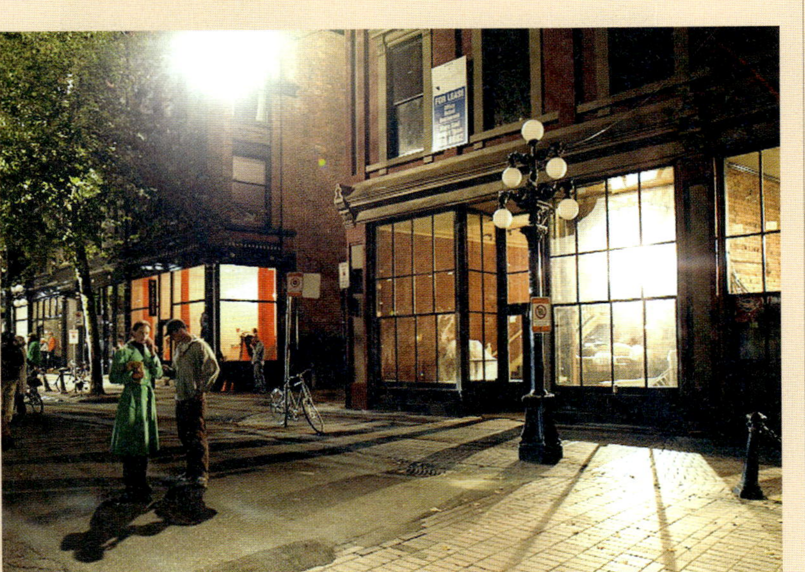

Carrall Street, 2009. Documentation of public street event. 200 Block of Carrall Street, Vancouver, 30 September, 2008.

Library on the University of British Columbia campus, where it elicited a lively debate around the subject of war.

Made for Manifesta 7, *La Mort e la Miseria* (2008), depicts the ethnic and linguistic minority of Laddin speakers, who once lived in an isolated part of the Fassa Valley in northern Italy. The group, originally subsistence farmers, has seen a massive transformation in their way of living. Its members have endured cycles of oppression, the trauma of wars and fascism, and are now experiencing a vibrant tourist economy. Thauberger's collaboration resulted in a video of a performance of a traditional myth. The story tells of how the old woman Poverty refuses Death, whom she traps in a tree; thus both Death and Poverty live on in the valley.

Carrall Street (2008) was a three-hour site-specific performance that started in the early evening on a downtown eastside Vancouver block that is a nexus of social, economic, political and cultural forces due to the overwhelming presence of poverty and drugs in an area that is undergoing revitalization and gentrification. For the duration of the project, Thauberger flooded the street with film lights, something familiar to residents since many movies are shot in the neighbourhood. To prepare for the evening, Thauberger collaborated with many diverse local communities, individuals and organizations staging performances on Carrall Street and in the surrounding alleyways and bars. During the event, these activities blurred with those of engaged spectators and passersby. Performers repeated quotidian actions, speeches and scripted conversations, while local residents, who are often ushered off other film sets, continued to act freely. While *Carrall Street* generated much criticism, most agree that this was a rare opportunity for the neighbourhood to be itself, since in most films the downtown eastside is made to stand in for another city.

Jos de Gruyter &
Harald Thys

If by 'emerging' artists we mean the mix of promise and presence evident in an artist's budding visibility in the art world, then the term applies perhaps nowhere more appropriately than to Jos de Gruyter and Harald Thys, despite the fact that the duo has been quietly making films for nearly twenty years. Their particular brand of tragicomic cinematic autism, at once wholly idiosyncratic and decidedly Belgian in its darkness, has been an art insiders' cult secret until relatively recently, when their critically acclaimed presence at several biennials and solo projects finally brought them wider international attention.

The duo's practice combines films with photographic works, sculpture and occasional performances, each element united in a persistent exploration of the underbelly of human behaviour and its unspoken power relations.

The duo's practice combines films with photographic works, sculpture and occasional performances, each element united in a persistent exploration of the underbelly of human behaviour and its unspoken power relations. Theirs is a theatre of cruelty in which robots, objects and an odd-ball cast of bullies, perverts, indeterminate furry beasts and deranged workers inhabit a world that is by turns slapstick and desolate. Almost no one speaks in their films, at least not naturally or easily; grunting often represents the alienation and powerlessness of these human puppets. They are played by non-professional actors, extended family members and even people culled from a local pub, whom the filmmakers place in banal but claustrophobic spaces with almost all indication of time and place effaced.

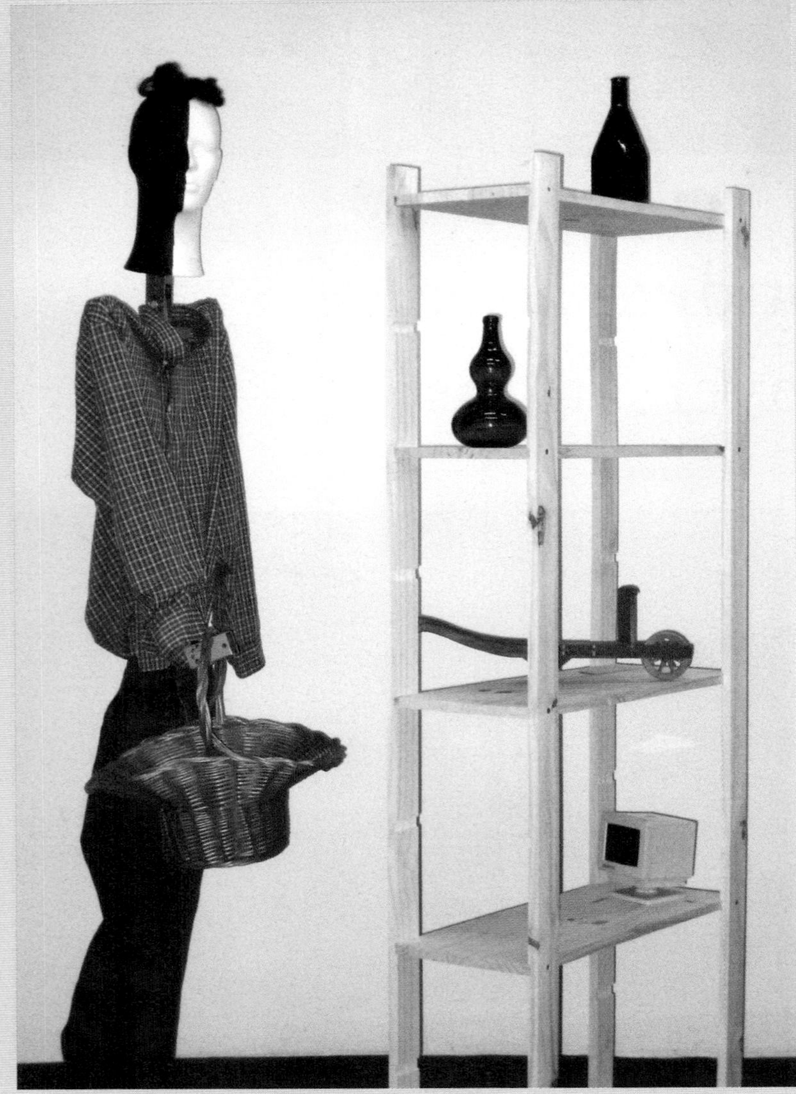
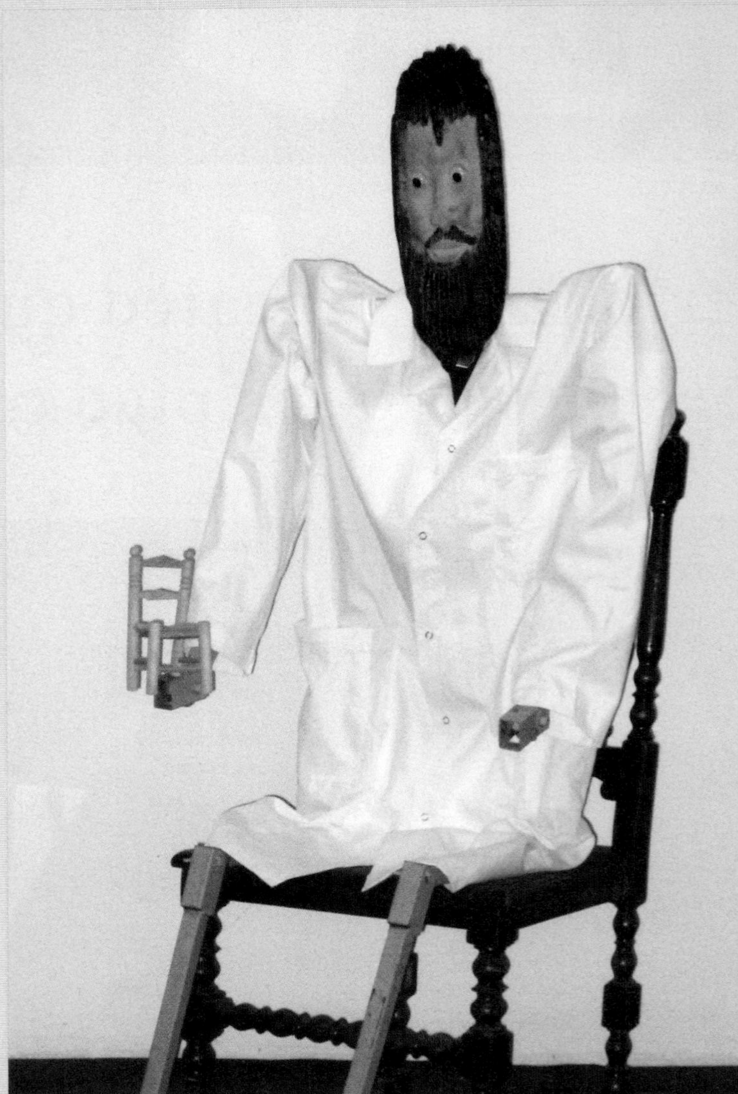
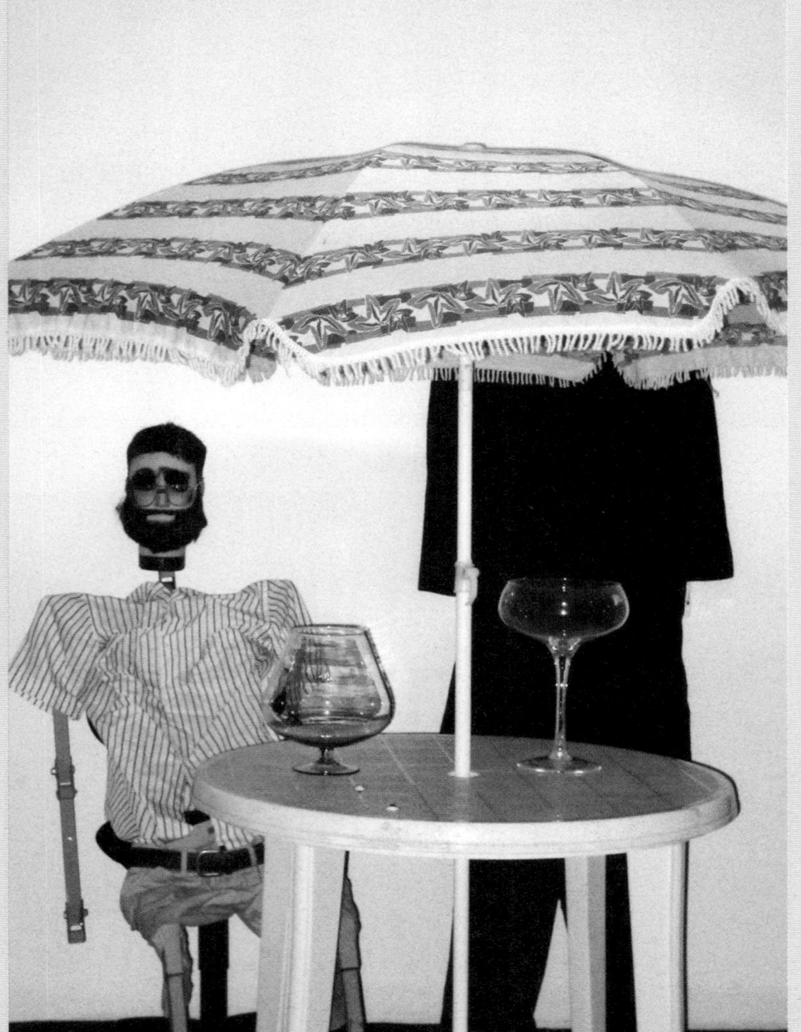
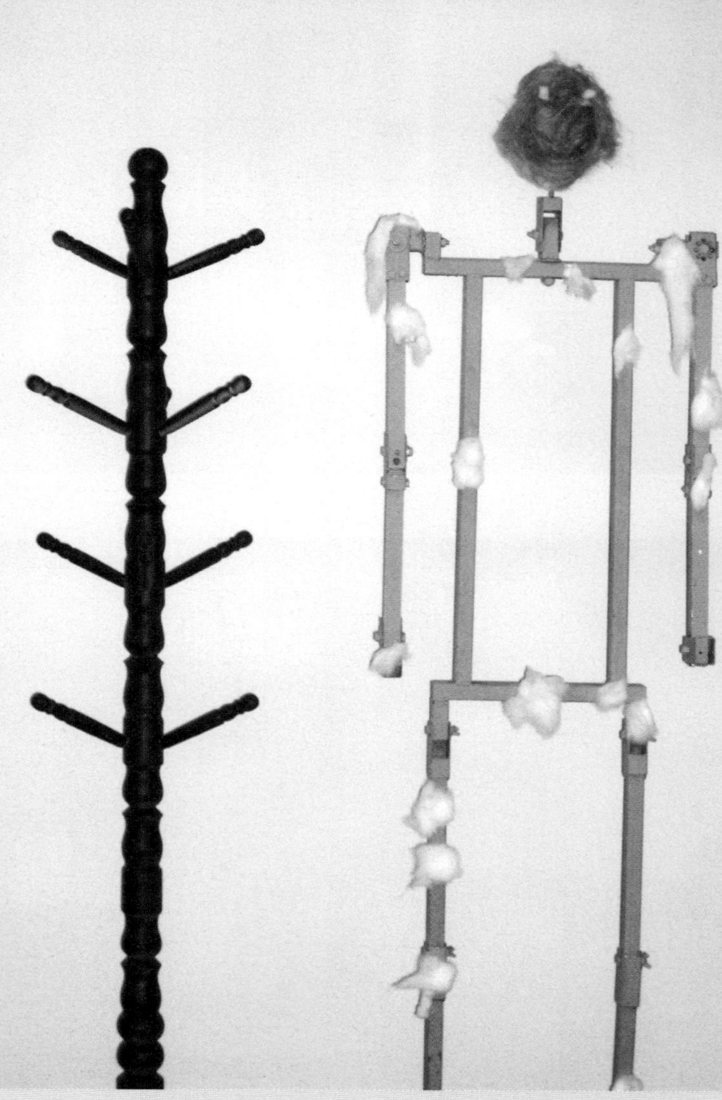

Untitled, 2009. 4 black and white photographs mounted on MDF. Each 119 × 84 cm

The capacity to derange

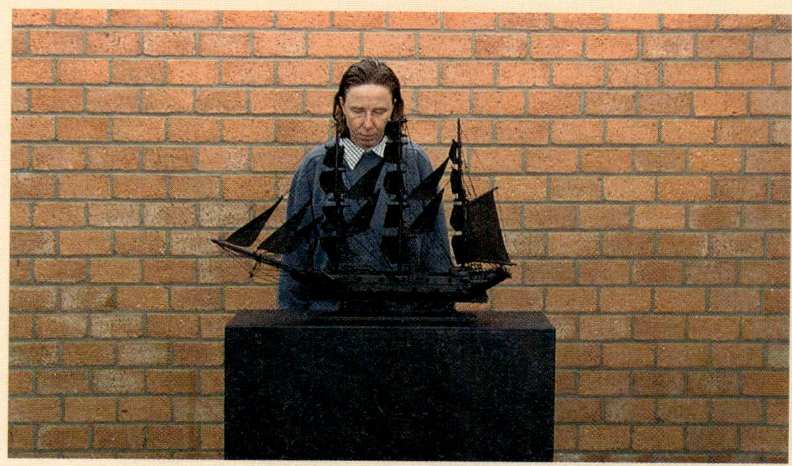

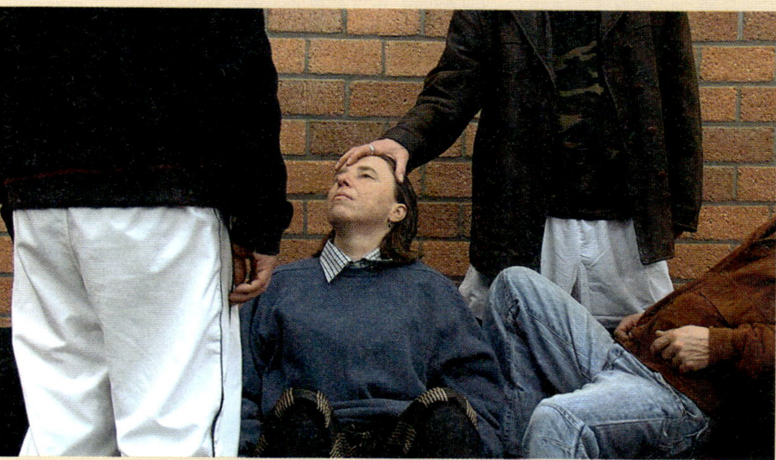

The Frigate, 2008. Video. 19 min.

The strength of their projects lies not only in the way in which de Gruyter and Thys corral their actors to perform with a painful-to-watch awkwardness, seemingly interminable bouts of staring, and little or no spoken language, but also in the duo's apparent disregard for the conventions of 'good form', mastery and hipness that permeate so much of today's contemporary art. One could cite their excruciating long takes, lack of any narrative structure, recurrent desynchronization of sound and image, or their use of hopelessly outdated organ music and cheap 1980s video effects. Despite their disavowal of so many of the unspoken rules of contemporary art filmmaking, there is nothing slapdash or accidental about the results.

Where could such a bizarre vision of the world (and of art) come from? When asked, they reveal a motley of disparate influences: the glazed gazes of psychiatric patients dressed up for amateur theatre productions (photographs of which Thys purloined from a clinic's archive while working there), the rigid

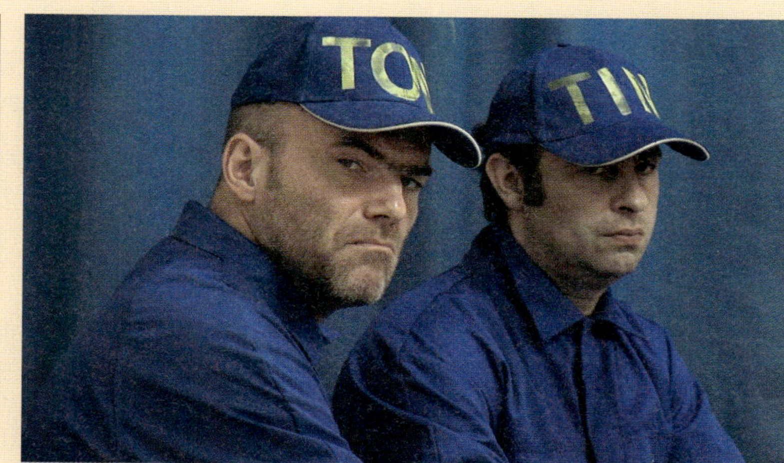

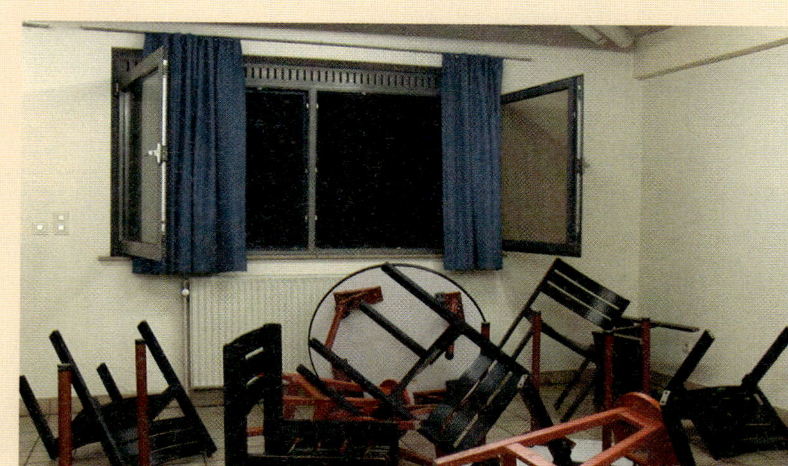

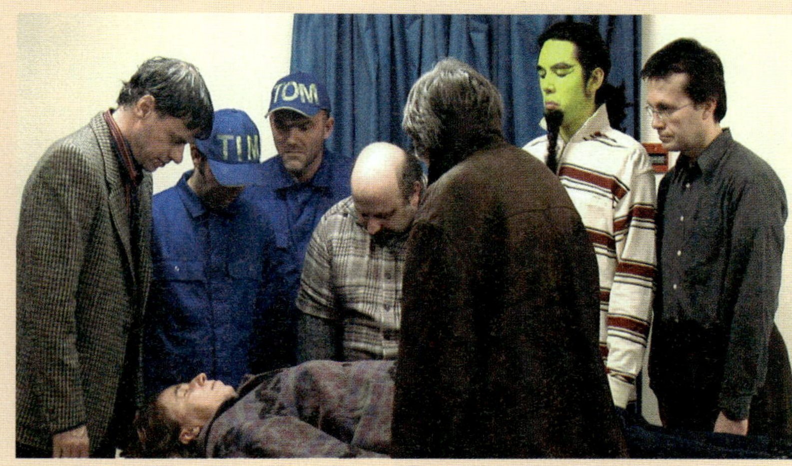

Ten Weyngaert, 2007. Video. 26 min.

Lack of any narrative structure

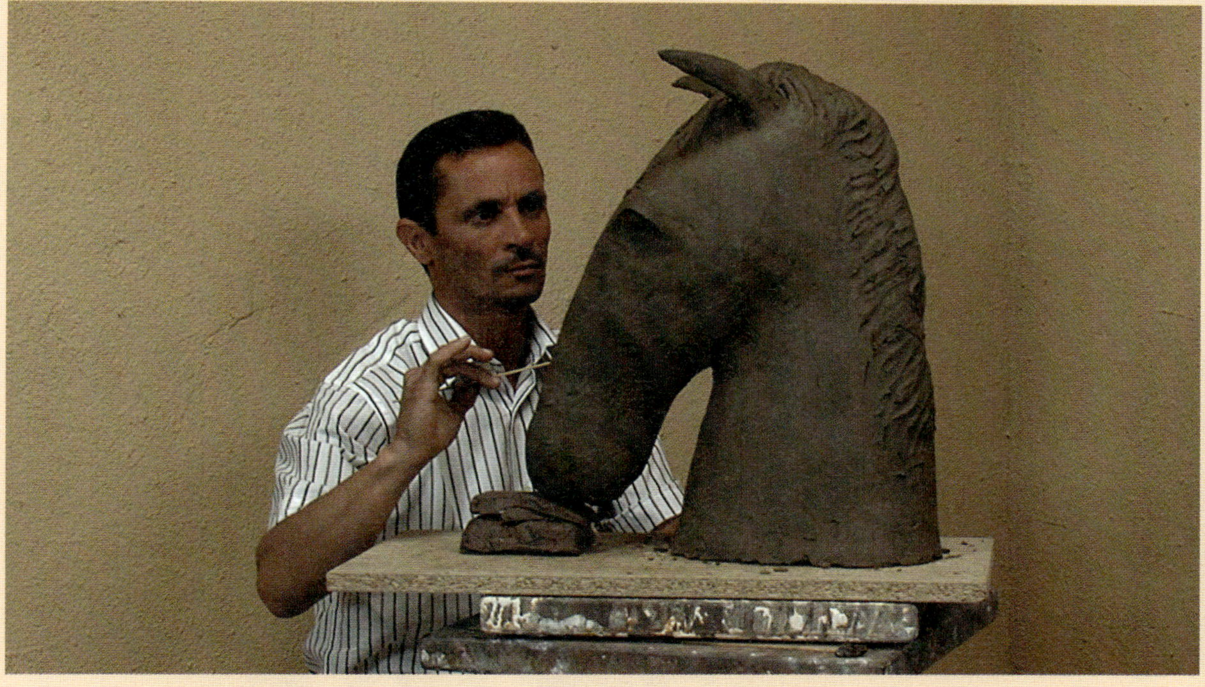

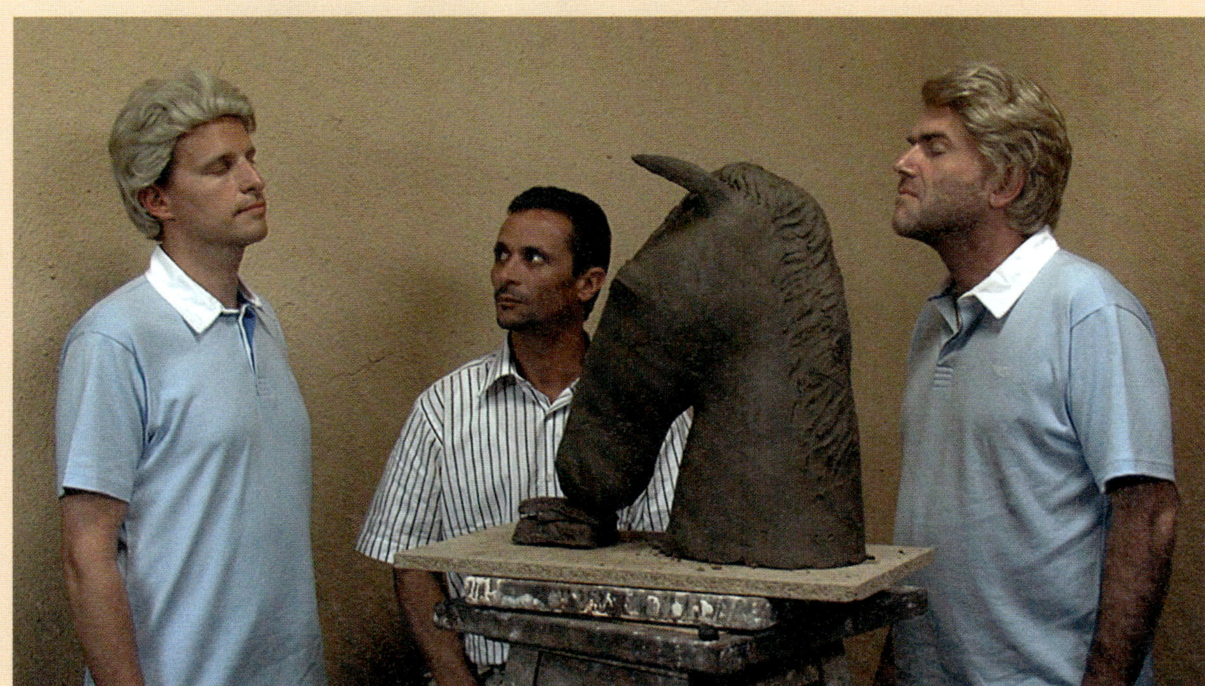

Der Schlamm von Branst, 2008. Video. 20 min.

formalism of Pier Paolo Pasolini's films, the strangeness of Hieronymus Bosch's world, nineteenth-century engravings of public torture, or the documentary material, recorded over many years, of the public spaces and quotidian life in the small, bleak Flemish towns in which they grew up.

Their film *The Frigate* (2007) depicts a group of recreation-centre misfits, obsessed with a model of a black frigate and with the sole female in the room. It was presented at the 2008 Berlin Biennial in a dank, brick-lined cellar to which the artists added heavy self-closing metal doors, enhancing the strange oppressiveness of the work. The result could not be called cinema. Nor was it theatre, despite the recurrent tableaux vivants presented in the film. Nor was it your typical contemporary art installation. For if the dramas of de Gruyter and Thys consistently present a suffocating *huit clos*, their attention to the site of viewing makes the actual experience of their work all the more discomforting. After twenty years of collaborative practice, the uneasiness they court contributes to an oeuvre with the capacity to derange, while maintaining a freshness that gives the impression that these artists have only just begun.

Ryan Trecartin

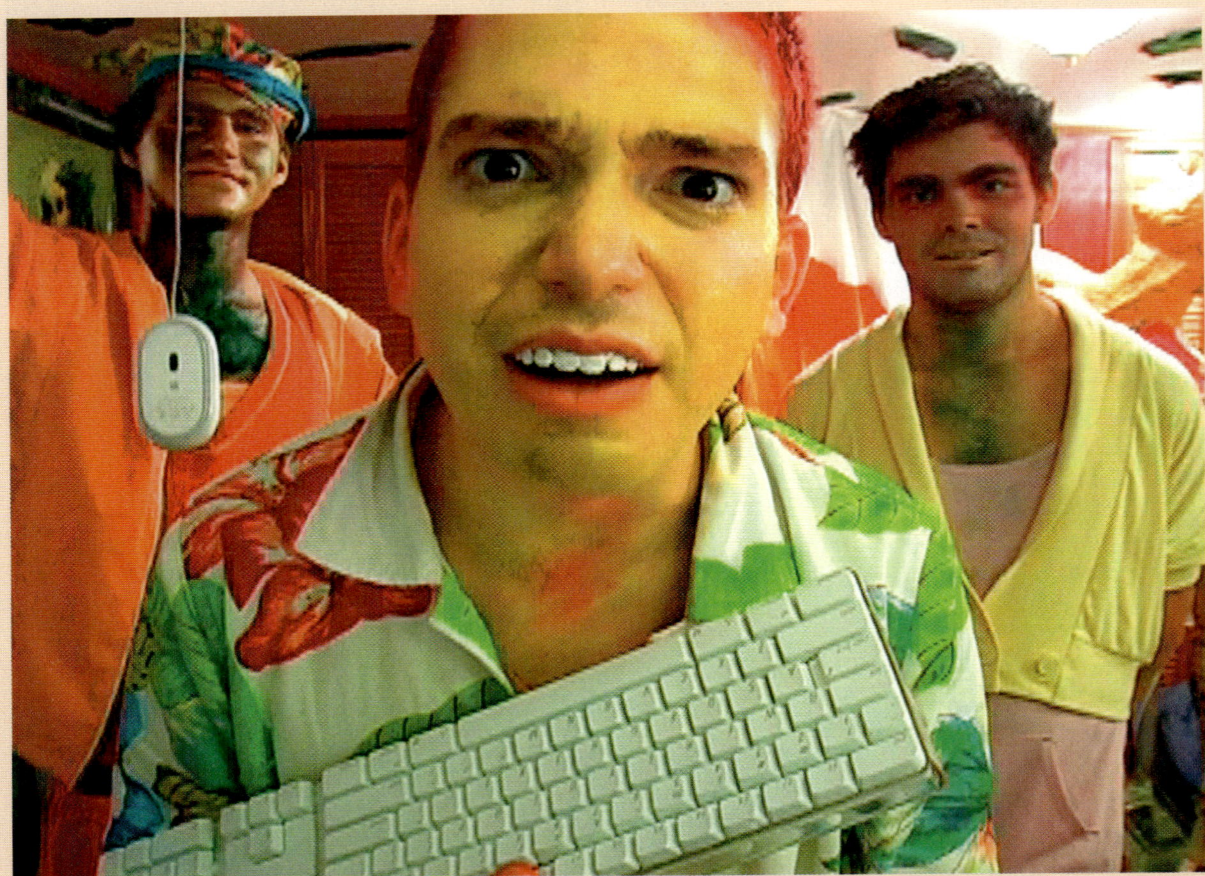

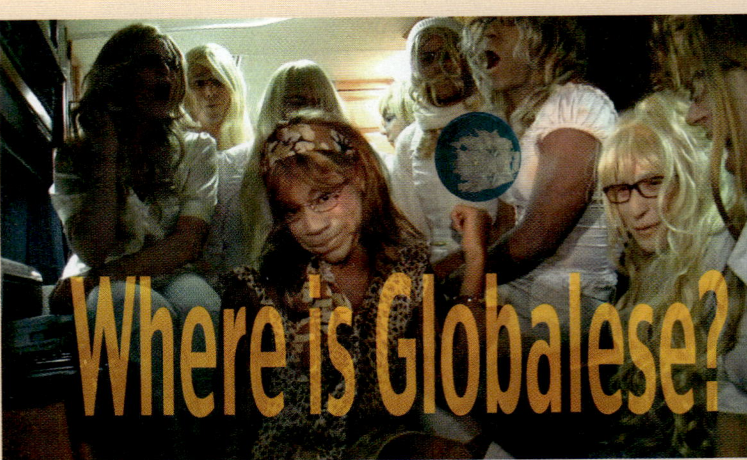

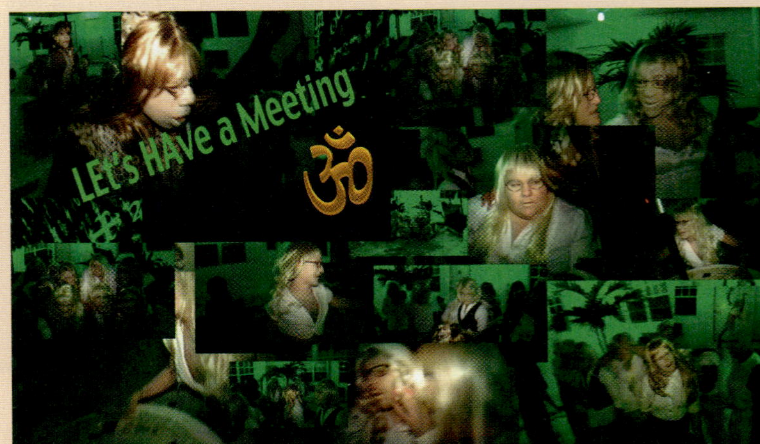

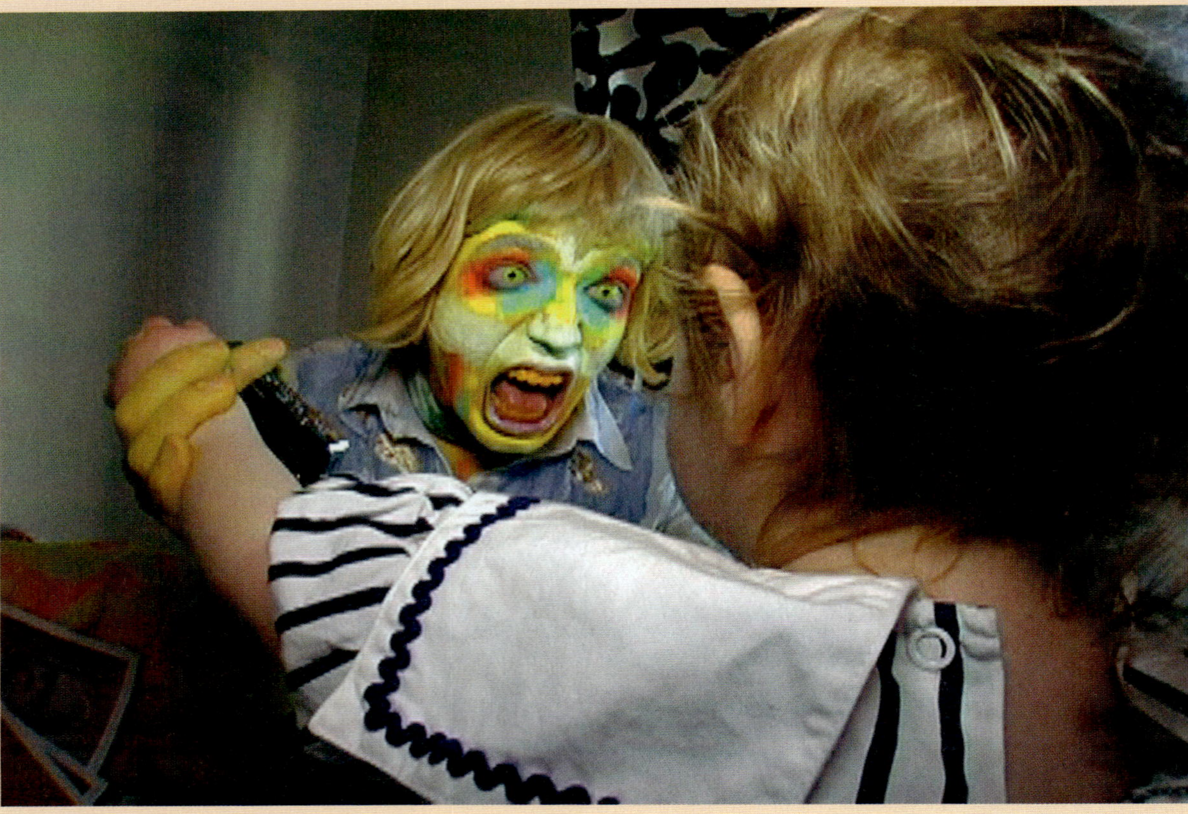

I–Be Area, 2007. Video. 1 hour. 48 min.

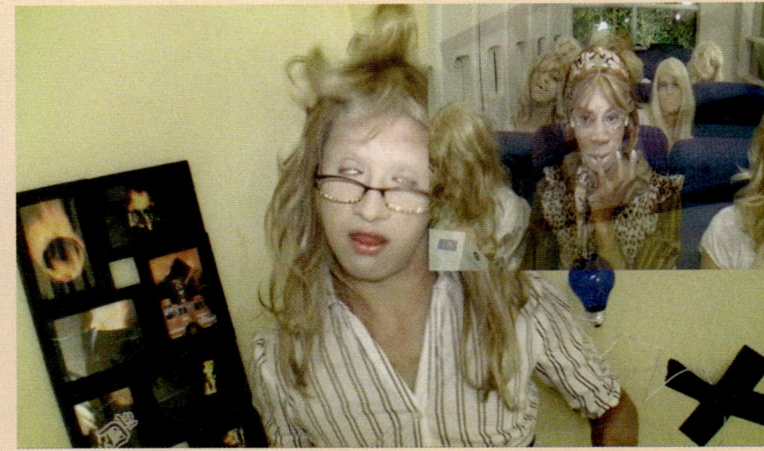

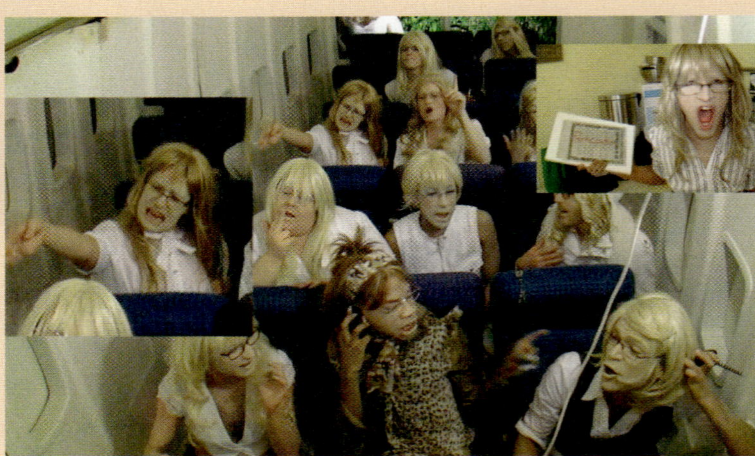

'There are so many things to be... And, I don't want to be any of them', exclaims a character in Ryan Trecartin's video *I-Be Area* (2007). The artist takes up this mantra in his works, proposing parallel realms that envision new ways of 'being' in the real and virtual worlds. Trecartin's brand of frenzied anarchy depicts a glorious technicolor universe of characters who find themselves intertwined in complex, melodramatic scenarios which are a cross between personal webcam revelations and the surveillance feeds of televised reality shows. His work explores a dizzying array of identity issues through dualities of connection and isolation, abandonment and belonging, individuality and conformity and ultimately, family and friendship.

Trecartin writes, directs, produces and usually stars in his work, alongside a group of collaborators and friends. His DIY aesthetic resembles an acid-fuelled joy ride through the internet, filled with psychedelic colours, rapid jump cuts, startling digital effects, windows-within-windows of imagery, and eccentric soundtracks — all of which reflect his upbringing as part of an ADD, YouTube generation and his shared sensibility with artists such as Paper Rad and the campy 1980s

Trecartin's intuitive merging of video, digital technologies, television, performance and installation elements subverts conventions of behaviour, family structures and sexual identities.

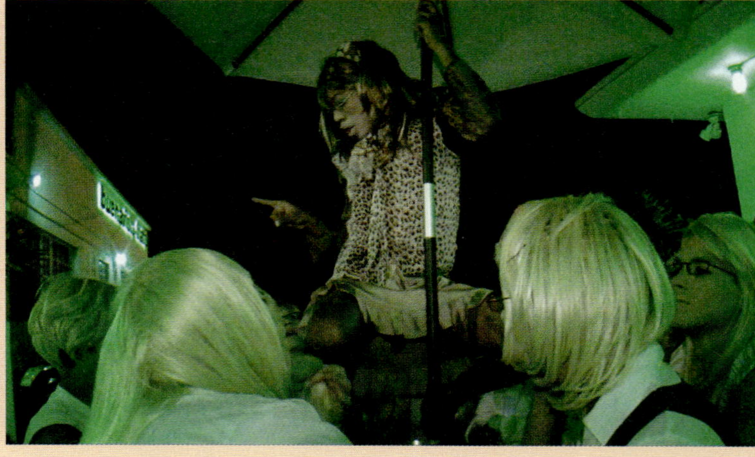

K–Corea INC. K (Section A), 2009. HD video. 31 min. 20 sec.

video of Tom Rubnitz. While Trecartin himself cites among his influences the films of Pedro Almodóvar, it is hard not to think of experimental filmmakers such as Jack Smith, John Waters and Kenneth Anger as important precursors. In *A Family Finds Entertainment* (2004) Trecartin performs alongside his friends, playing the lead role of Skippy, a hapless gay teenager with slightly psychopathic tendencies. After locking himself in the bathroom with a knife, he is rejected by his family, and then meets a documentary filmmaker who wants to make a movie about him, only to be suddenly run over and killed by a car. However, he is subsequently (and inadvertently) brought back to life by the music of his friends. The video is filled with mundane suburban scenes of college-age youth hanging out and partying, alternating with trippy montage sequences of floating internet imagery.

Complex melodramatic scenarios

Contrasting concepts of connection

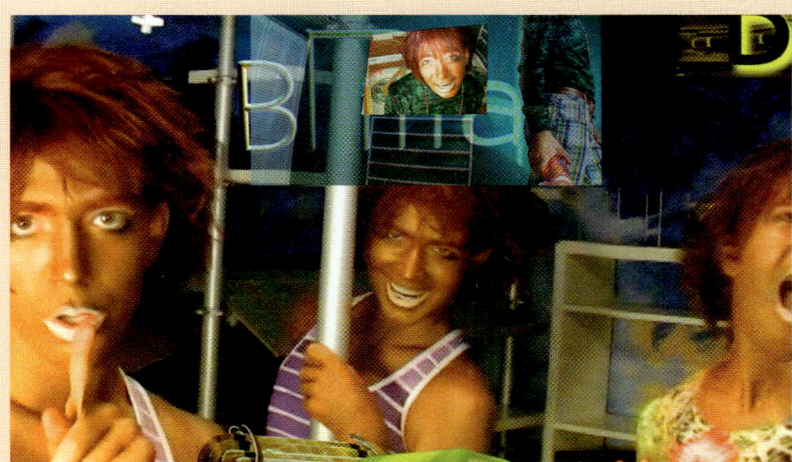

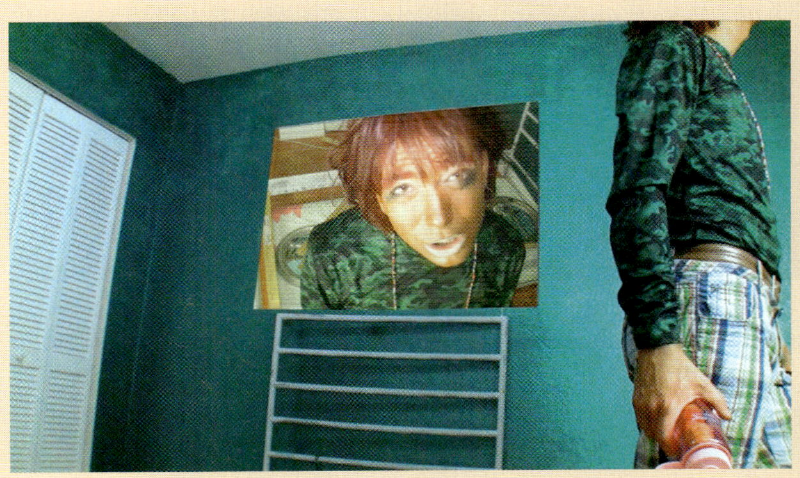

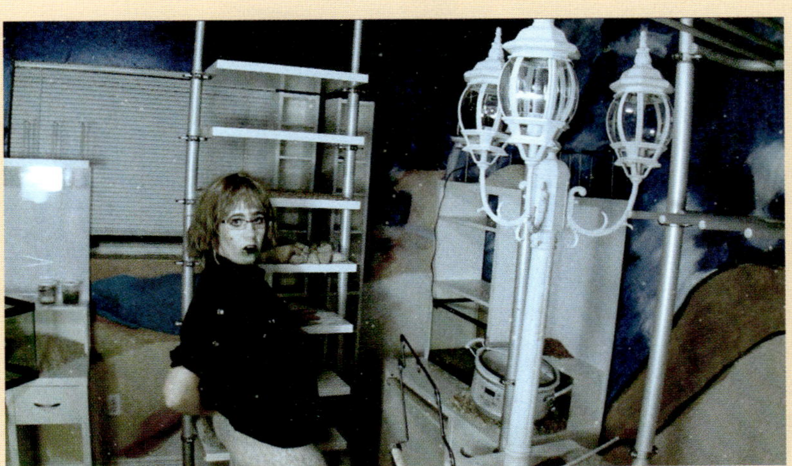

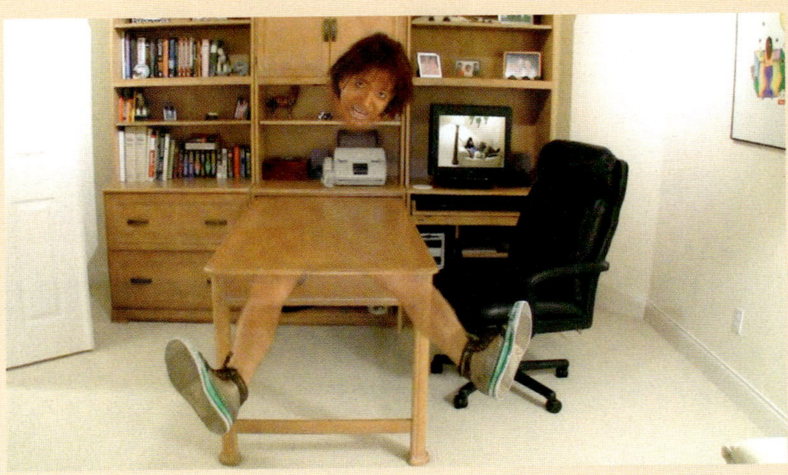

Sibling Topics (Section A), 2009. HD video. 50 min.

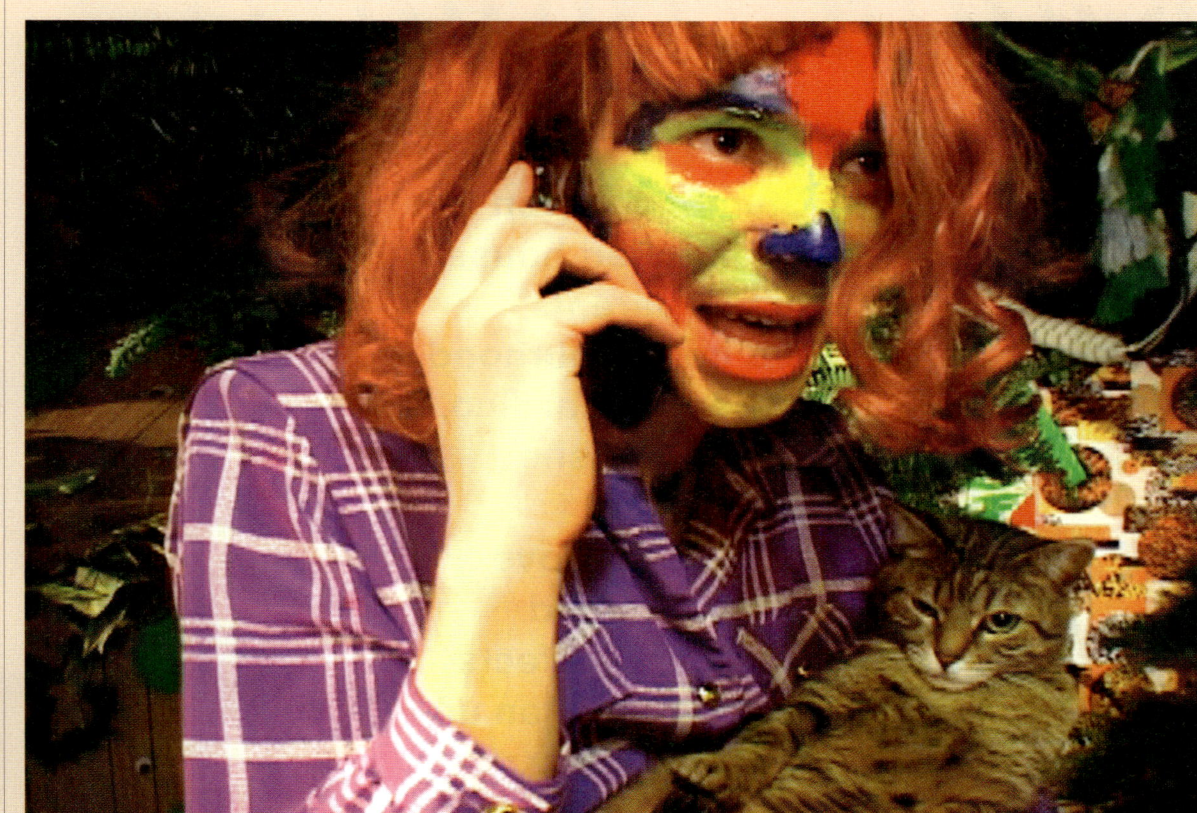

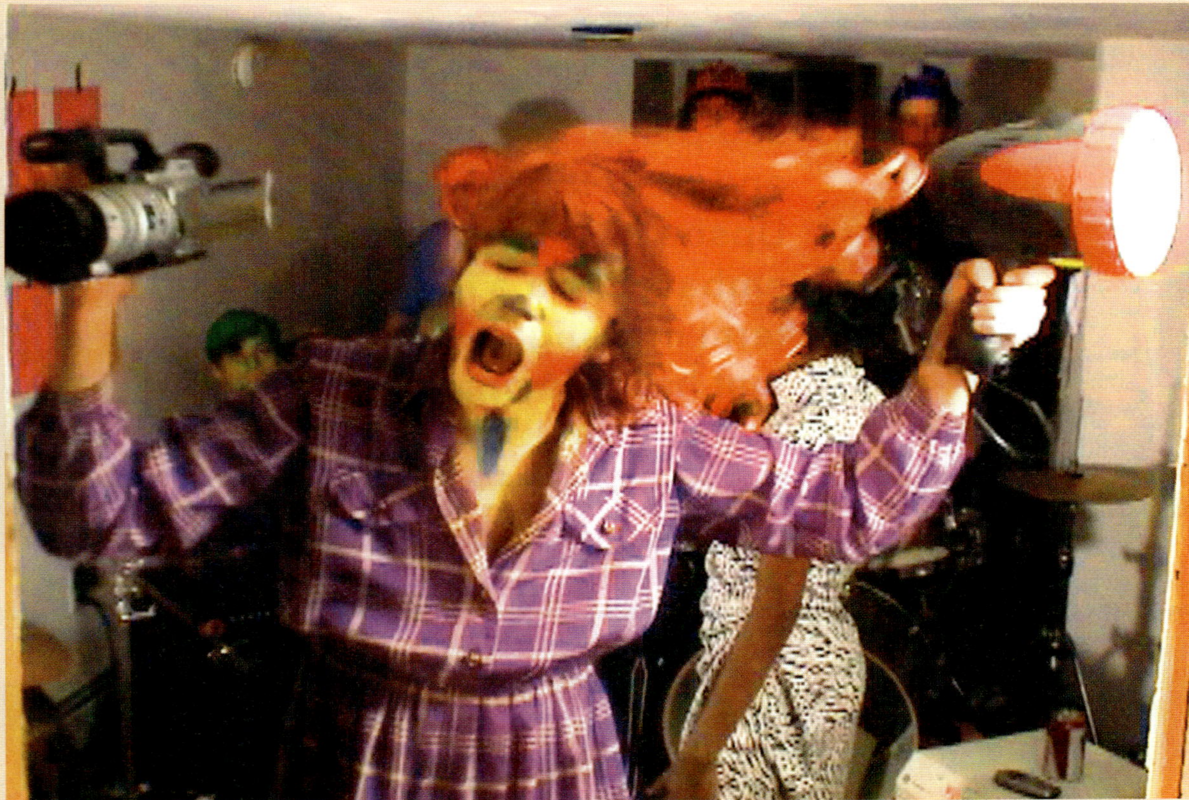

A Family Finds Entertainment, 2004. Video. 41 min. 12 sec.

While seemingly improvised, the dialogue is actually carefully edited and scripted, filled with exchanges that recall rapid-fire online chat relays or text messages. Faces and bodies are painted in surreal hues, voices are digitally altered, strange accents are adopted, further diffusing our understanding of who and what we are watching.

Similar themes of finding community resurface in *I-Be Area* (2007), in which Trecartin stars as I-Be II, a clone who seeks to gain a greater sense of self, purpose and belonging. Trecartin and his cast of volatile, creatively cross-dressing friends, siblings and clones alternate between addressing the camera directly and clamouring for attention amongst themselves as they compete with one another in various parental and child-like roles, indulging in techno-babble, power struggles, moody tantrums and hedonistic partying.

Constructed in a non-linear way, the video's narrative is comprised of mini-episodes that address ideas of individuality, parenthood, adoption and family.

In his work *K-CoreaINC.K (Section A)* (2009) Trecartin shifts from the model of family-as-business to business-as-family in a manic send-up of global corporate culture which explores ideas of power, competition, exploitation, conformity and personal freedom. The characters are primarily women, played almost indistinguishably by actors of both sexes, with everyone donning a corporate uniform of blond wigs, white-powdered faces and drab casual attire. Hysteria and juvenile bad behaviour are the order of the day as corporate 'leaders' plot world take-overs and market domination in an interminable meeting/party that takes place in multiple locations.

Trecartin's intuitive merging of video, digital technologies, television, performance and installation elements subverts conventions of behaviour, family structures and sexual identities. They offer up in their stead new understandings of contemporary existence in which boundaries between real and virtual life are constantly in flux, and notions of sexuality and identity are shape-shifting pluralities. His inscrutable, highly personal and intricate narratives speak to a new-millennial generation's collective understanding of social aesthetics and culture, which taps into the ever-expanding possibilities of digital technologies as tools for achieving new concepts of self-creation and self-empowerment. As Trecartin announces in *I-Be Area*: 'The world is starting over … starting NOW.'

Kaari Upson

Kaari Upson has spent the last few years practising a unique type of aesthetic forensic archaeology. A native Californian who now lives and works in Los Angeles, Upson has been involved in what she calls the *Larry Project*, an ongoing multi-media and inter-disciplinary work that has its origins in a chance occurrence that took place while the artist was still in graduate school at the California Institute of the Arts. Stumbling upon an abandoned house in her parents' old neighbourhood in San Bernardino, California, she discovered a treasure trove of abandoned personal artefacts belonging to an unknown man, including diaries, photographs, letters and so on. Through drawing, painting, sculpture, video and performance, Upson has embarked on a long-term investigation that has attempted to discover the essence of her anonymous subject. In so doing, she takes us through the looking glass into a world where her artistic obsession to reconstruct a profile of this man has become conflated with her fantasies of who he might actually be.

Pursuing her investigation with an obsessive ferocity worthy of the filmmaker Werner Herzog, Upson has subjected her found artefacts to all sorts of analyses ranging from

Stumbling upon an abandoned house in her parents' old neighbourhood in San Bernardino, California, she discovered a treasure trove of abandoned personal artifacts belonging to an un-known man, including diaries, photographs, letters and so on. Through drawing, painting, sculpture, video and performance, Upson has embarked on a long-term investigation that has attempted to discover the essence of her anonymous subject.

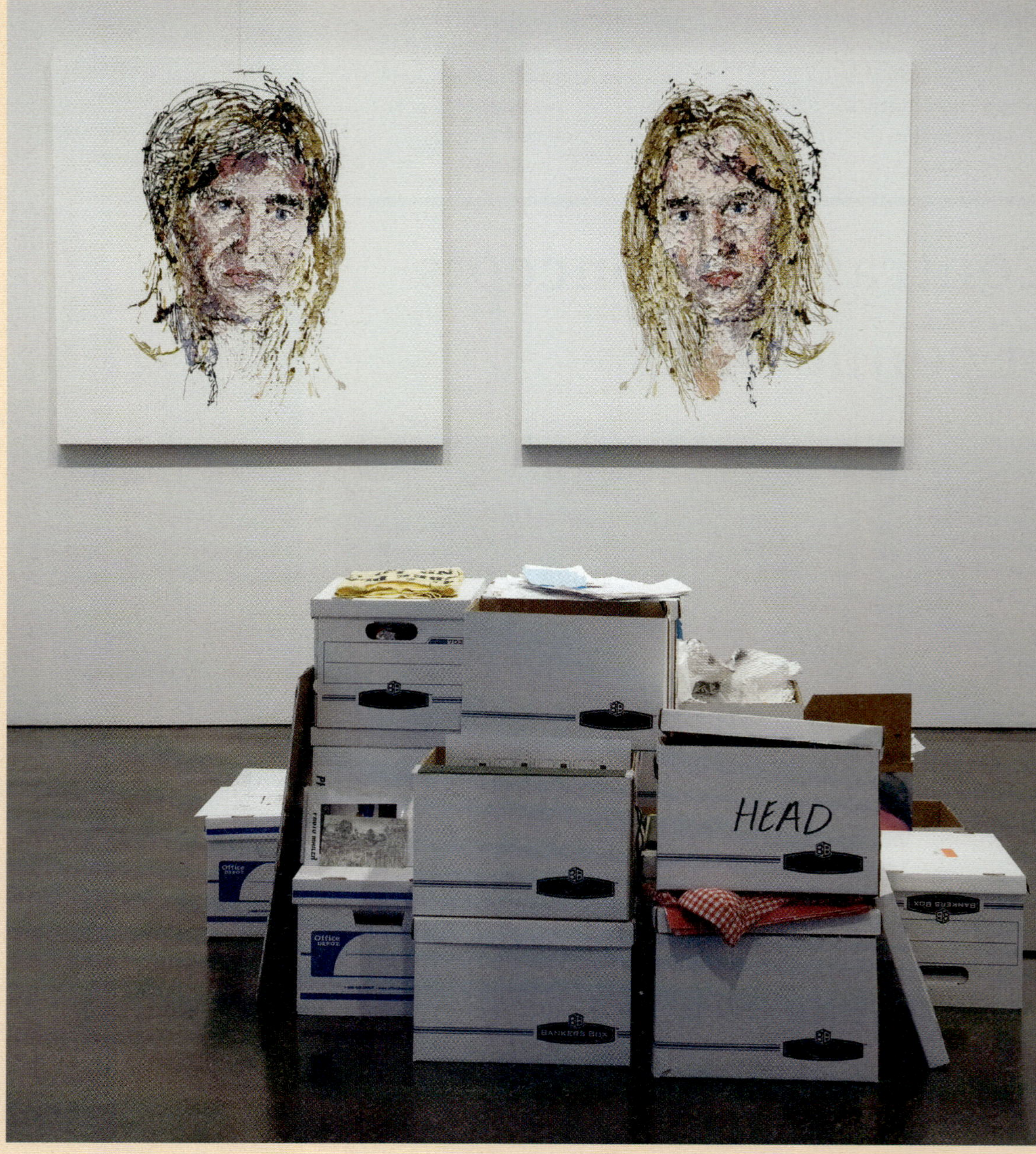

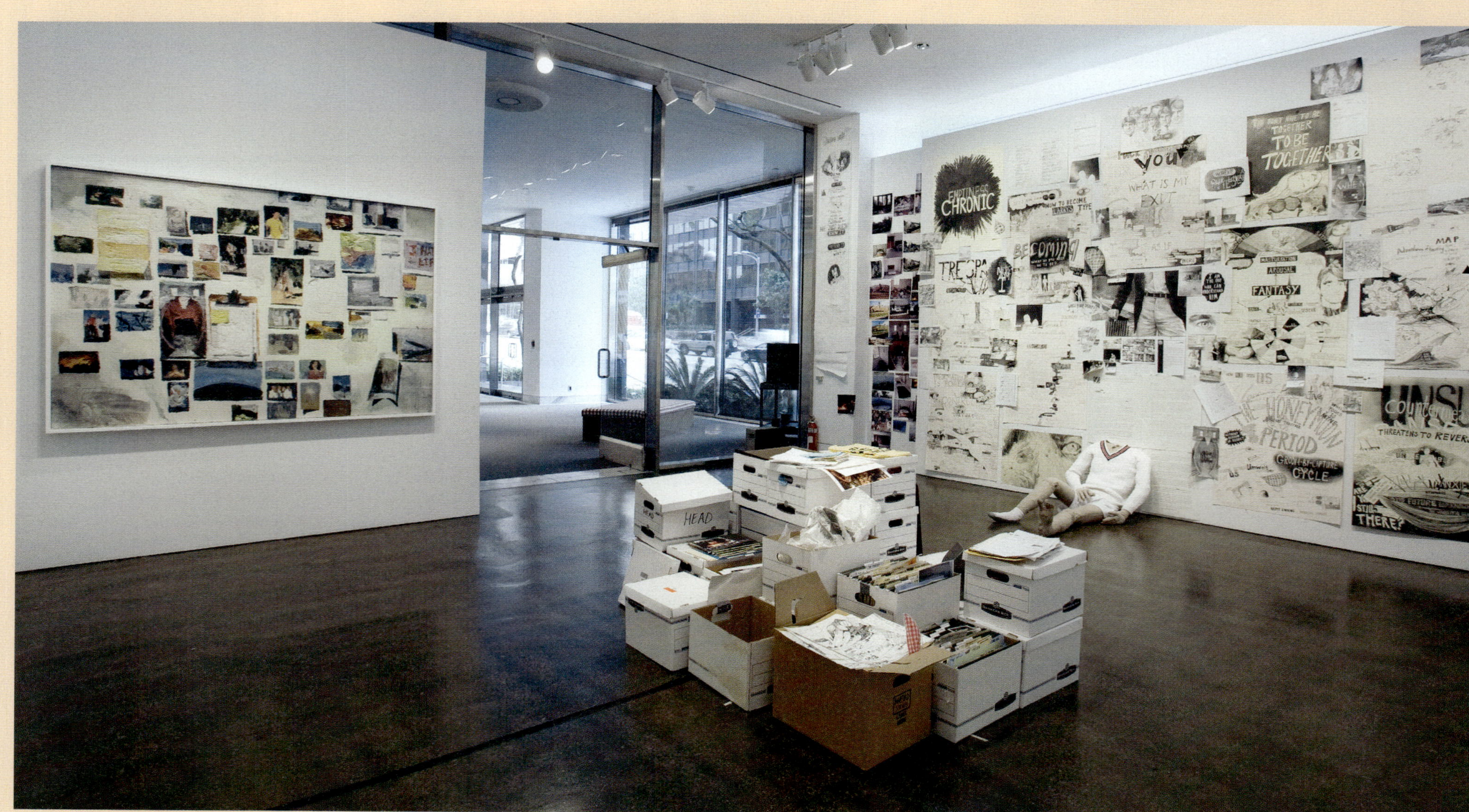

The Larry Project, 2007. Mixed-media installation. Dimensions variable

Obsessive ferocity

the objectively scientific to non-traditional alternative procedures. Using astrological readings, fingerprint and handwriting analysis, as well as straightforward internet research, Upson attempted to compose a portrait of a late-1970s New Age playboy whose interests include astrology, self-improvement ideologies, Frisbee and Hugh Hefner. As the artist progressed further into her research, reality and fantasy became blurred, and she found that the project had become as much about her own desire to construct a fictional life for a man that she never met as it was about 'Larry'. The result of this first chapter of her research was an installation that included quasi-taxonomic displays of Larry's photographs, Upson's innumerable graphite drawings that moved from the objectively forensic to the pathologically obsessive, as well as a hand-sewn doll that stood in as a doppelganger for the man. In the process, the obsessive quality of her own quest became clearer and she began to over-identify with her subject, who became her imaginary lover, her son, her brother and her father all at once.

One of the most striking elements of Upson's investigation is her series of 'kiss paintings', in which she paints a heavily-

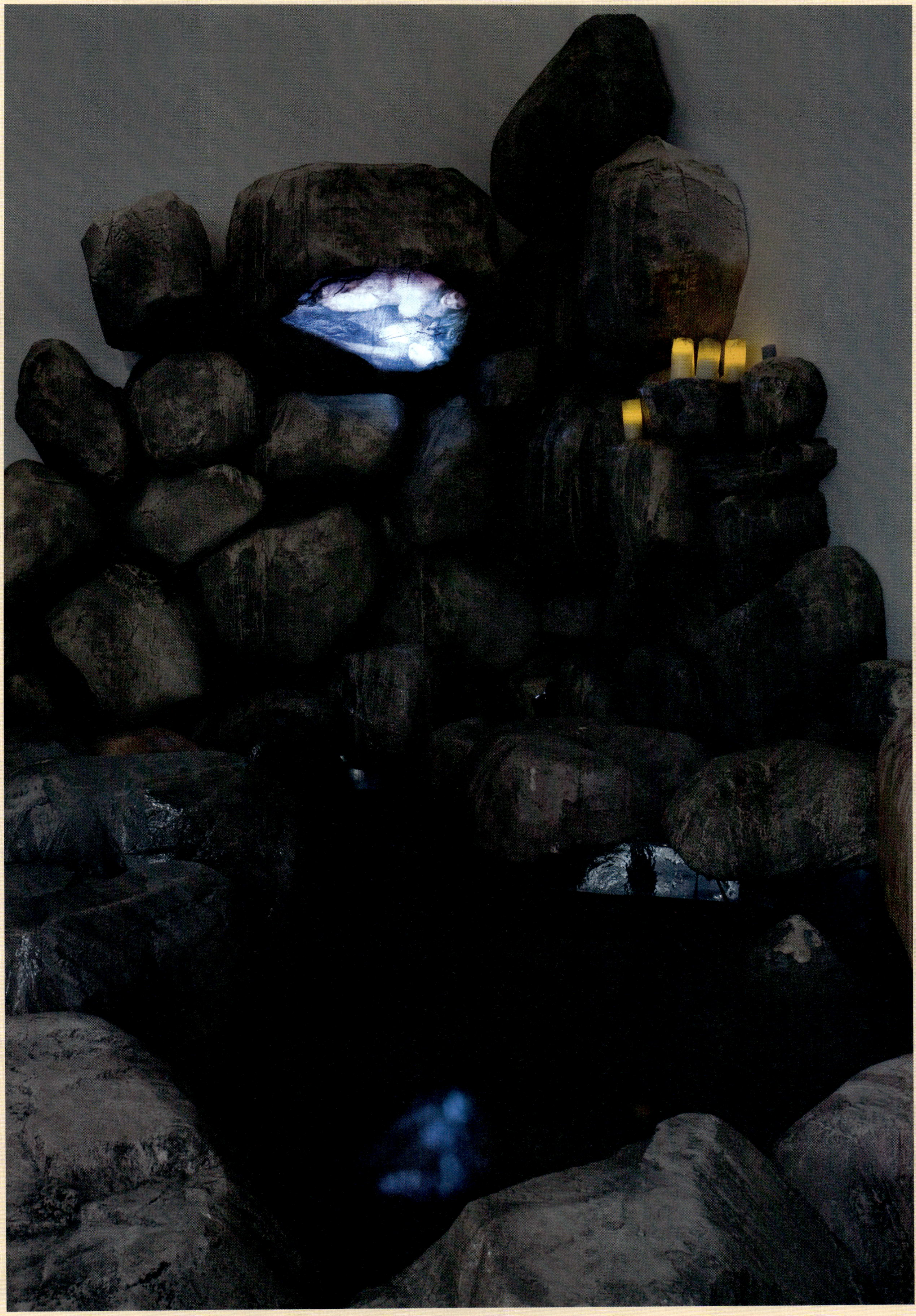

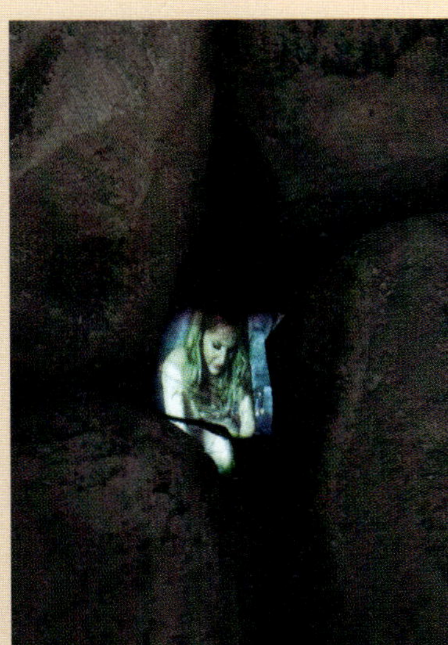

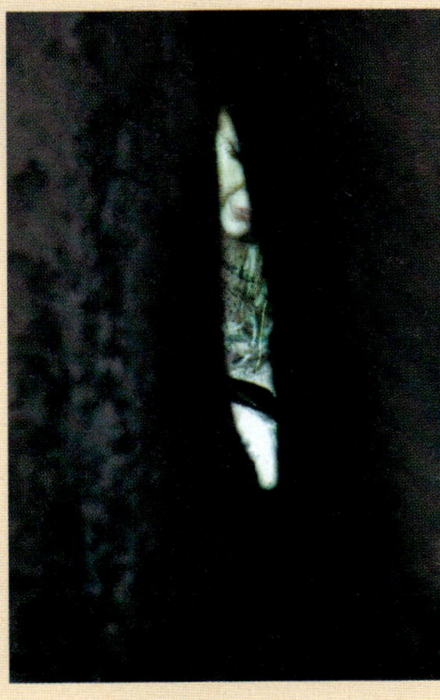

The Grotto, 2008–09. Mixed–media installation with video projections. Dimensions variable

The Grotto, 2008–09. Mixed–media installation with video projections. Dimensions variable

impastoed portrait of Larry as well as her own self-portrait and then smashes their still-wet surfaces together in a violent kiss. Once pulled apart, this painterly embrace leaves us with a grotesque diptych, a kind of fucked-up police composite sketch of a relationship gone badly wrong, rather than a prospective portrait of an unknown criminal perpetrator.

In her research, Upson learned that Larry had over the last thirty years been a frequent visitor to the infamous Playboy Mansion in Los Angeles, with its iconic grotto. She subsequently decided to construct her own fantasy interpretation of The Grotto (2008–09) as an attempt to exorcise her possession by Larry. Never having been to the Playboy Mansion, Upson created a mythological version of the grotto in which she showed her own videos, exploring her self-obliteration by this project in the form of lurid psycho-sexual narratives. As she conintues to pursue the *Larry Project*, one wonders if she is a stalker, an ethically challenged crime-scene investigator or a spurned imaginary lover. In the end, *The Larry Project* is more about our own desire and tragic inability to truly know someone than it is about the search for any one person.

Kostis Velonis

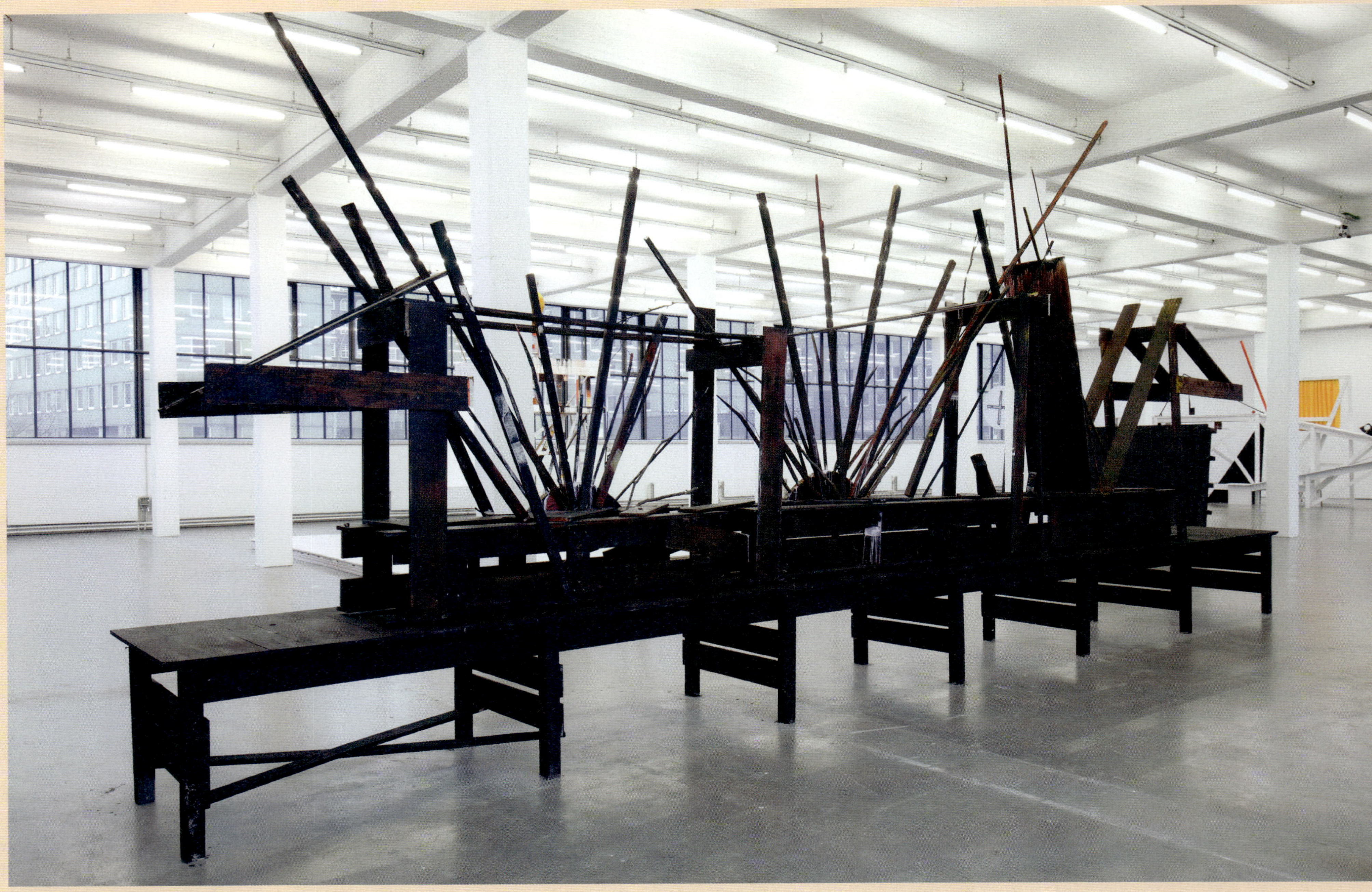

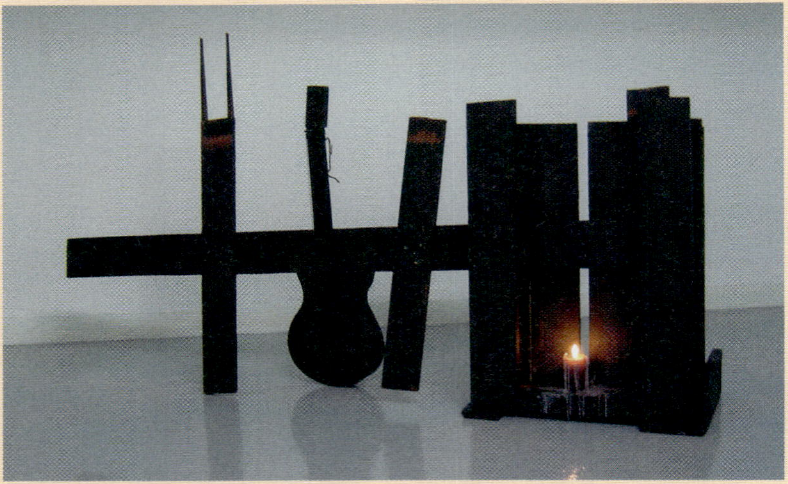

Endless Construction (Victory over the Sun), 2009. Wood, acrylic, plywood. Approx. 1000 × 400 × 90 cm

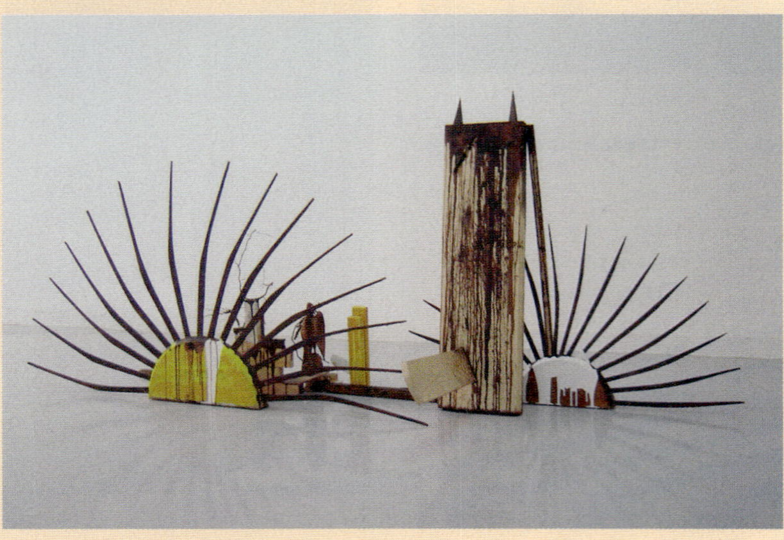

Dirty Country Boy, 2004. Wood, acrylic, guitar, candle. 94 × 170 × 40 cm

Day is Done, Nothing's Gonna Harm Me, 2005. Wood, acrylic, plywood. Approx. 200 × 45 × 100 cm

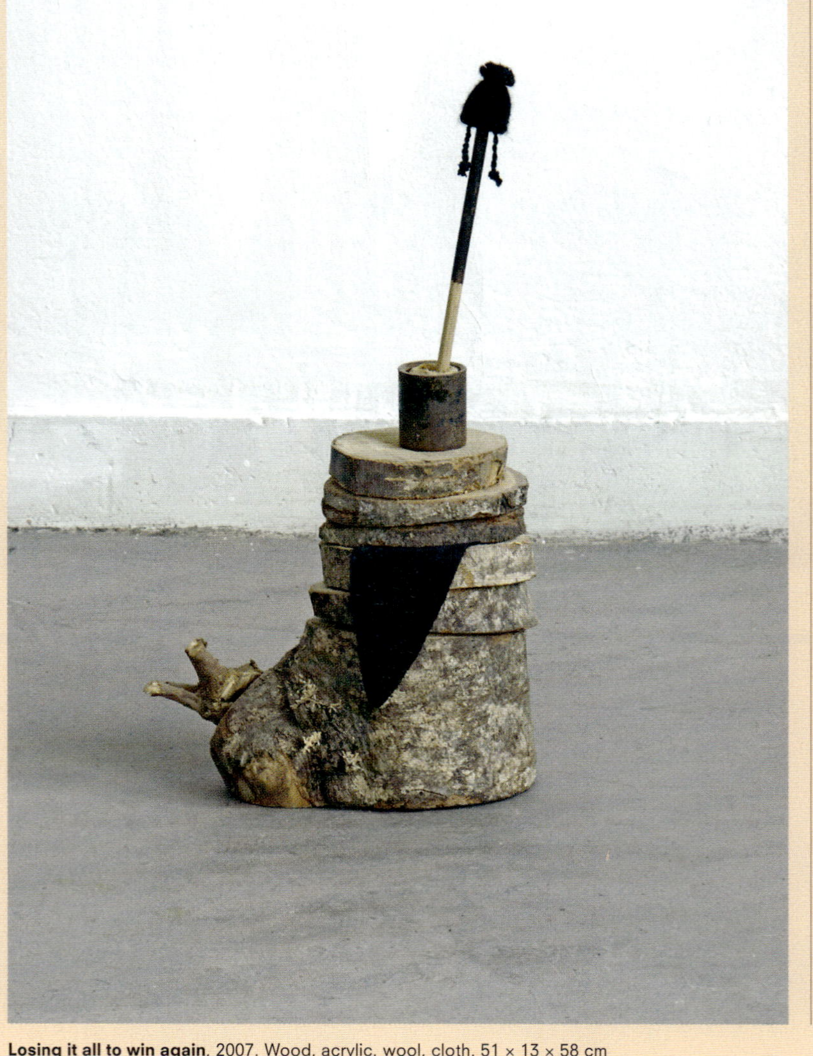

Losing it all to win again, 2007. Wood, acrylic, wool, cloth. 51 × 13 × 58 cm

Kostis Velonis's wooden sculptures speak of different ways of presenting and interpreting form, about the role objects play in a given historical and political context, and how a sculpture constructs or excludes a space for the autobiographical content. His works may be modest in terms of their construction and material, which give them an almost humble presence, but they have prominent personalities. In *Dirty Country Boy* (2004), for example, a roughly made guitar leans on a palisade-like wooden structure. A lit candle inside the vaulted space of the sculpture evokes an eerie character; the small light in the middle of the piece brings together the simple elements into a kind of handmade memorial.

Velonis's sculptures have some of the qualities of a manifesto. They are all built to a clear architectural plan, and their structures and materials create a sense of being derived from other objects and from previous works. It is as if Velonis has developed his own reading of the history of sculpture, a sort of private dictionary that he has re-assembled

The collision of many interpretations of an inherited past

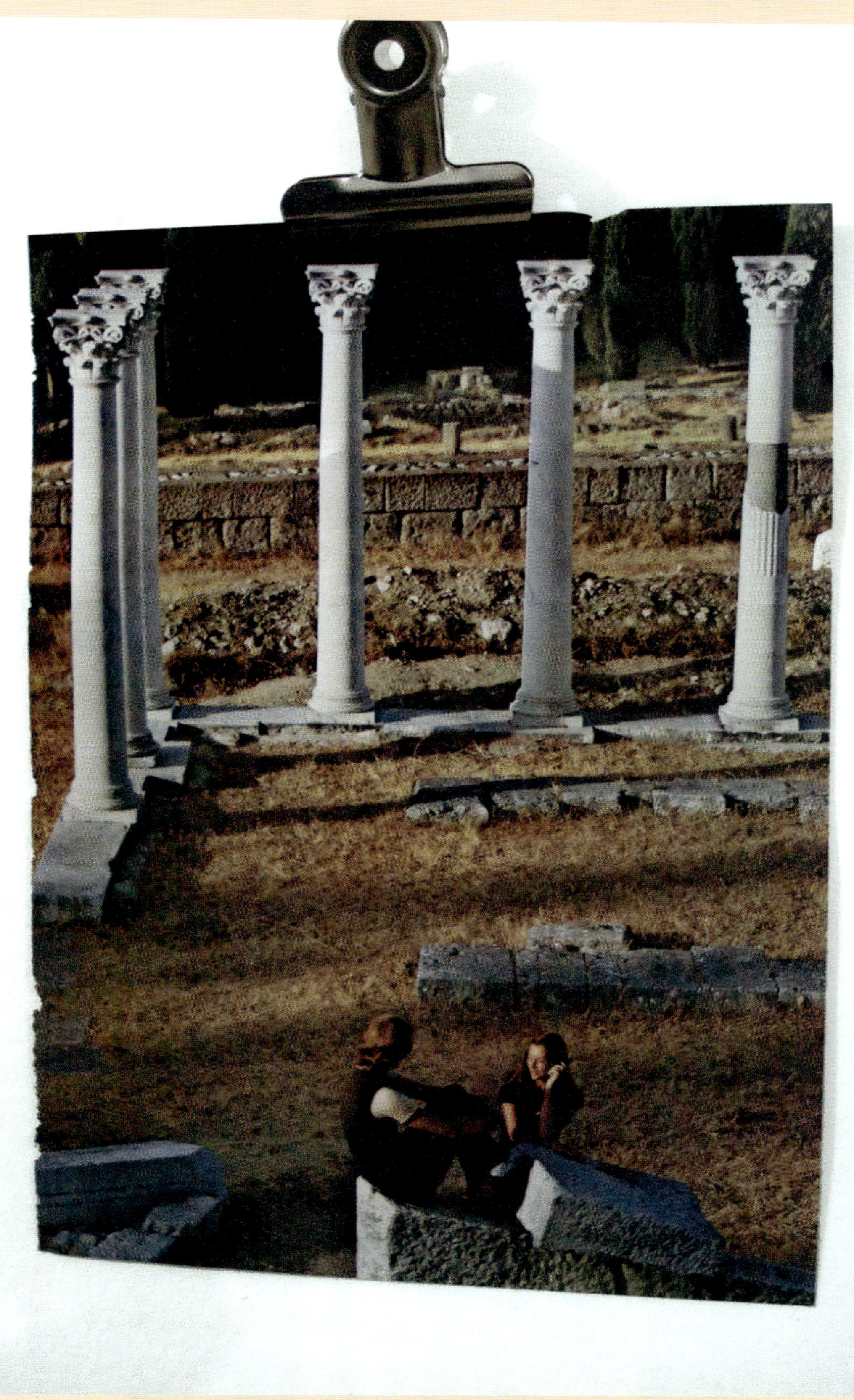

How one can think freely in the shadow of a temple, 2010. Slide projection. Dimensions variable

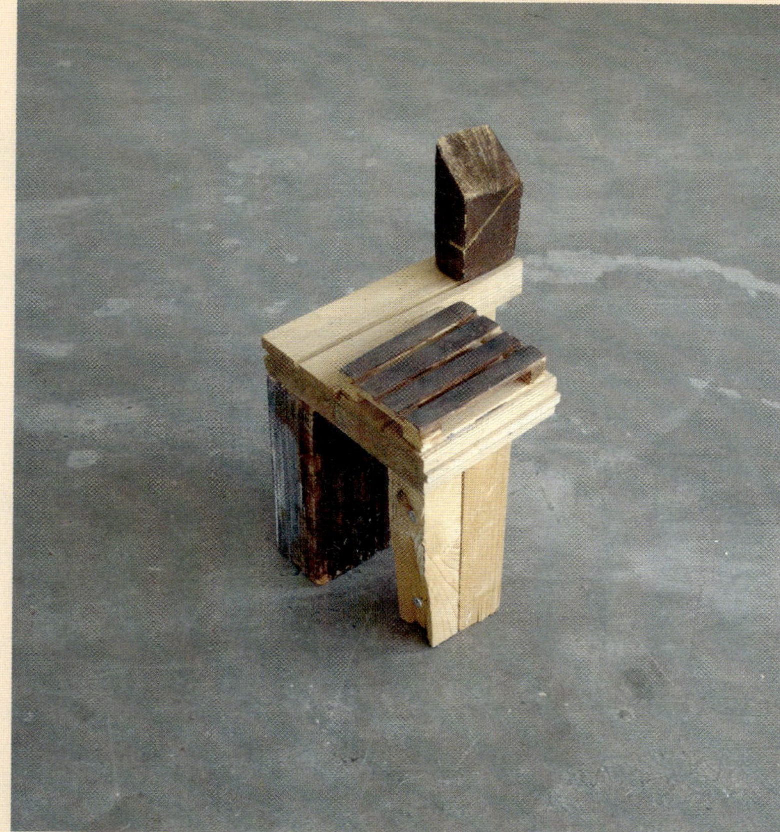

Working Class Discourse, 2010. Wood, brick, acrylic. 20 × 30 × 34 cm

A private dictionary

again in every work of art.

From Russian Constructivism to the Bauhaus and the radical movements of 1968, Velonis takes up the grand narratives and edifices of ideas, carrying them over into sub-narratives of personal struggles, passion and solitude. *Working Class Discourse* (2009) is a very small construction made of wood, brick and acrylic. Inspired by Russian Constructivism, the piece seems to embody the remains of a more eloquent discourse, which makes us reflect on history, on what we actually know of it and the very place we are reading it from. Literary figures like Don Quixote serve as models for melancholy heroes amidst lost dreams of revolution, as in the slide projection *How one can think freely*

in the shadow of a temple (2009).

Velonis's pieces appear humble and serene, but display an uncanny calmness marked by the many practices from which they emerge, such as his own art historical interpretations and his fascination for certain literary classics. His sculptural work involves a process of infinite translation. No single mind is responsible for the definitive form of a piece; it is the result of the collision of many interpretations of an inherited past, which co-exists with the here and now. The flow of different sculptural languages in the work creates an awareness of the lack of correspondence between the sources and the result, between the choice of materials and their meaning or the role they play.

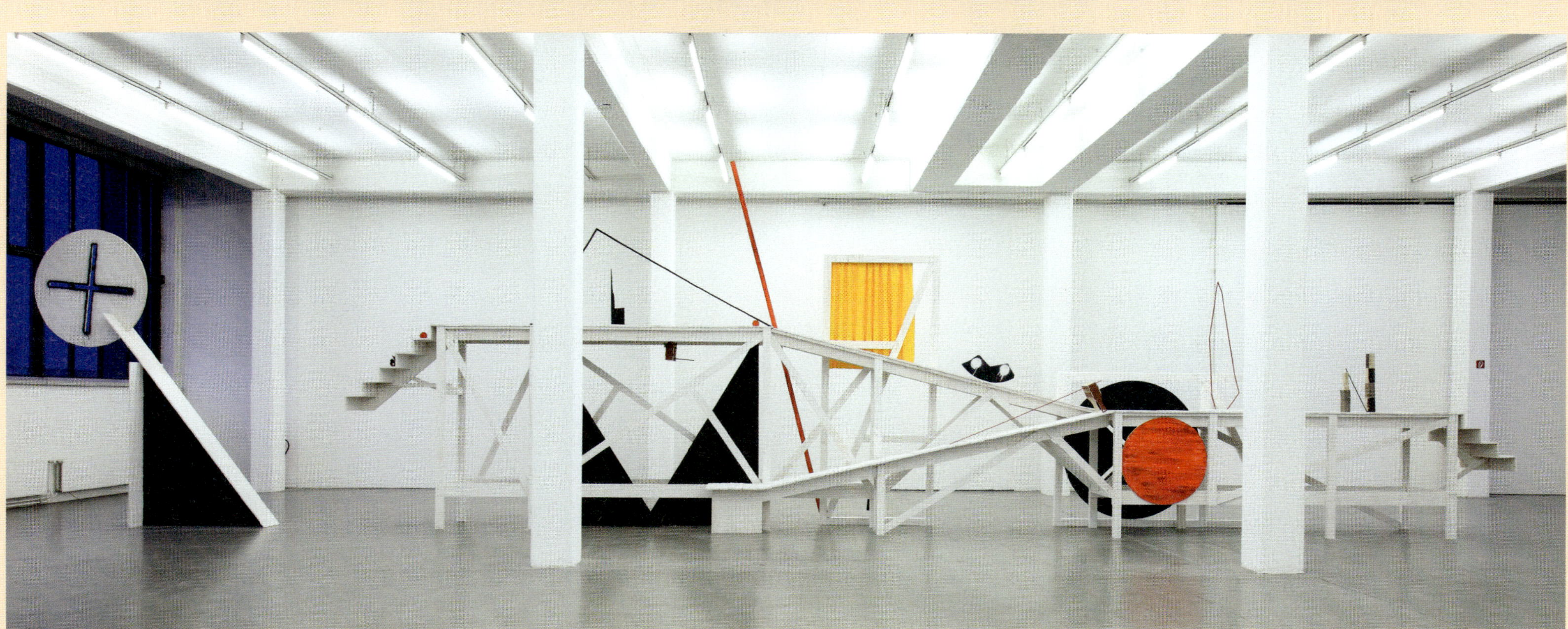

Gaining socialism while losing your wife (after Popova's set construction for 'Le Cocu magnifique', 1922), 2009. Wood, MDF, plywood, acrylic, fabric, metal, pot with flowers. 4.5 × 9.2 × 17 m

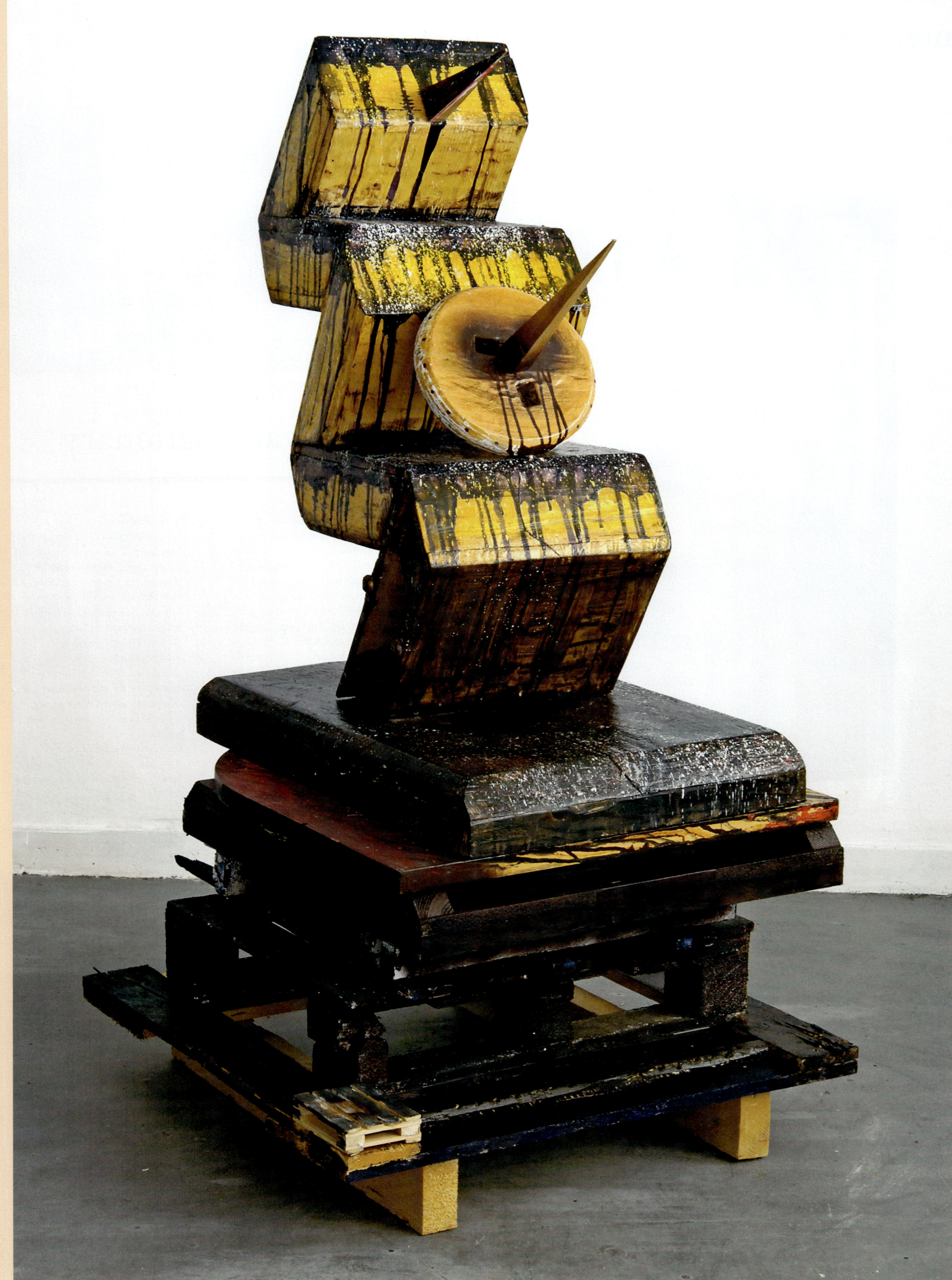

Brancusi was a Hippie Carpenter or the Physical Condition of Mockery Through Space, 2008. Wood, acrylic, varnish. 175 × 80 × 70 cm

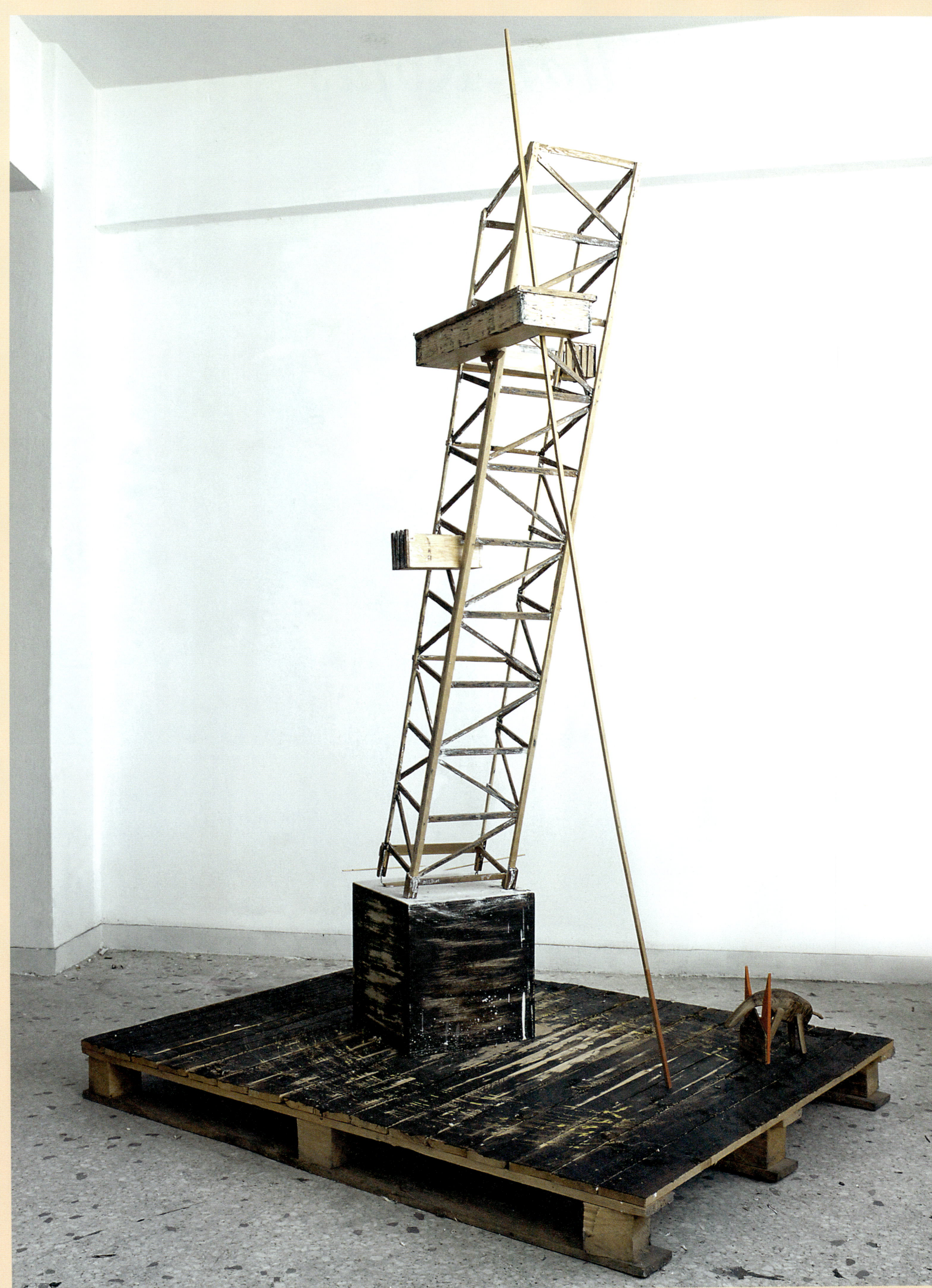

Sancho Panza in front of Lenin's Tribune, 2006. Acrylic, wood, plywood. 190 × 190 × 170 cm

Adrián Villar Rojas

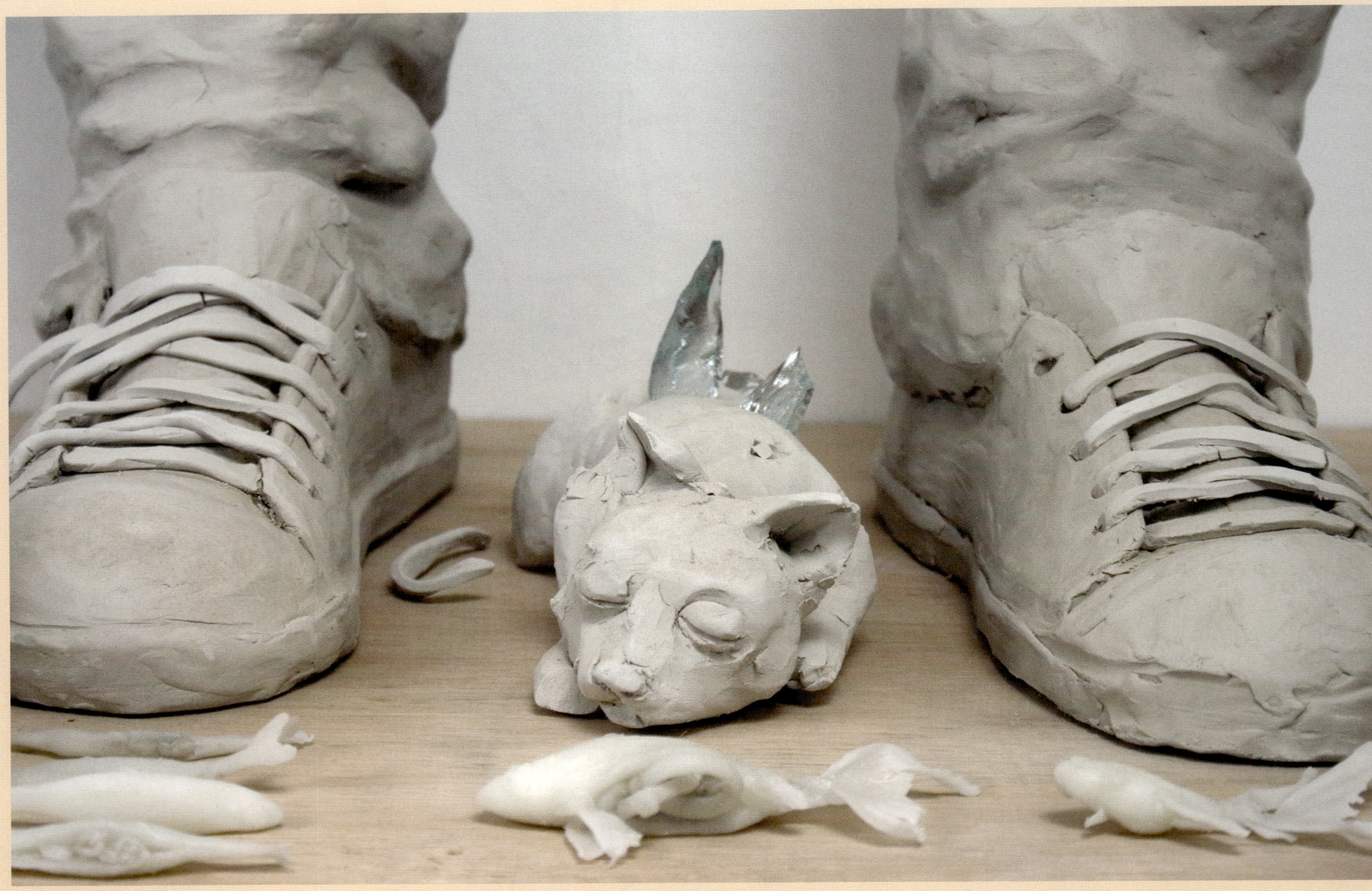

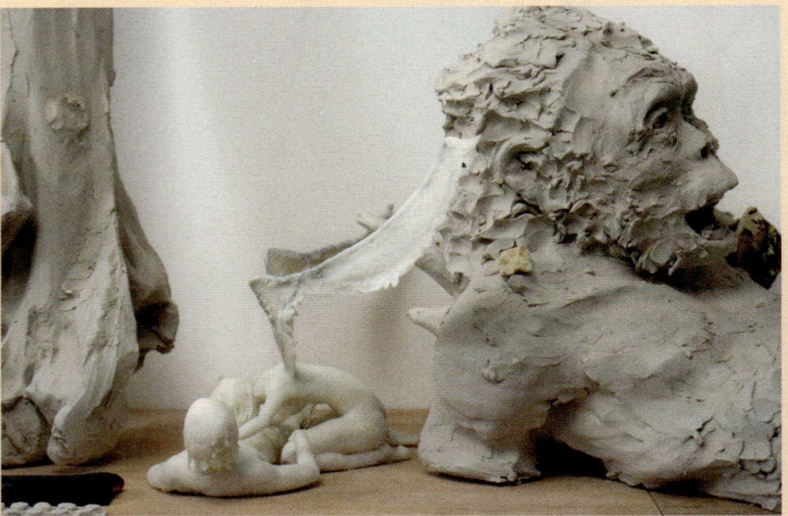

Lo que el fuego me trajo, 2008. Bricks, cement, lime, sand, demolition rubbish, wood, water tanks, iron gallow brackets, clay, cold porcelain, mirror, glass, soap, sea shells, windshield, Ford Escort hood, pins, stickers. 10.9 × 9.5 × 2.2 m

'I'd like emotional flesh in my work. Enough with cool form! I'd like to show each square centimetre of sadness, develop it in a world woven out of infinite and exasperated relations.' This statement by the young artist Adrián Villar Rojas crystallizes the intensity and romanticism of his world. Two works, made between 2008 and 2009, expose his ambitious and expansive style in their own different ways.

Lo que el fuego me trajo (What fire brought me, 2008), formed an installation which took up the entire space of a gallery. The floor was covered with broken bricks, which gave the impression that one was entering the room after an explosion; shelves holding hundreds of unpainted, half-destroyed clay figures extended across the walls. An enormous mirror installed on one of the walls distorted the setting so that it appeared to be expanded, thus producing a disorientating, asphyxiating effect. Huge brick chimneys and water tanks were placed in the middle of the space next to a statue of David and other sculptural pieces standing around the detritus.

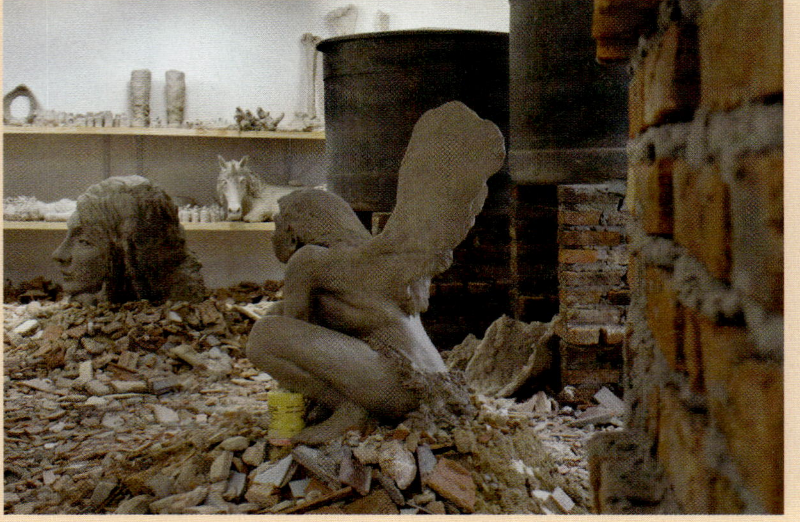

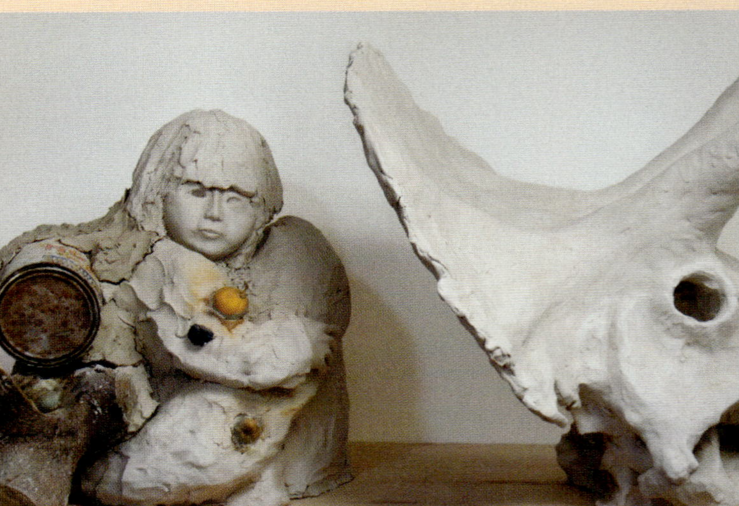

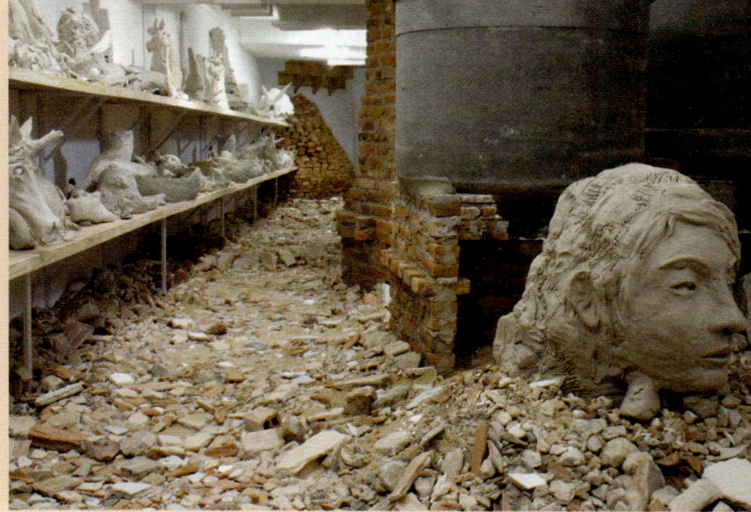

Remainders of my life, aged 1000 years

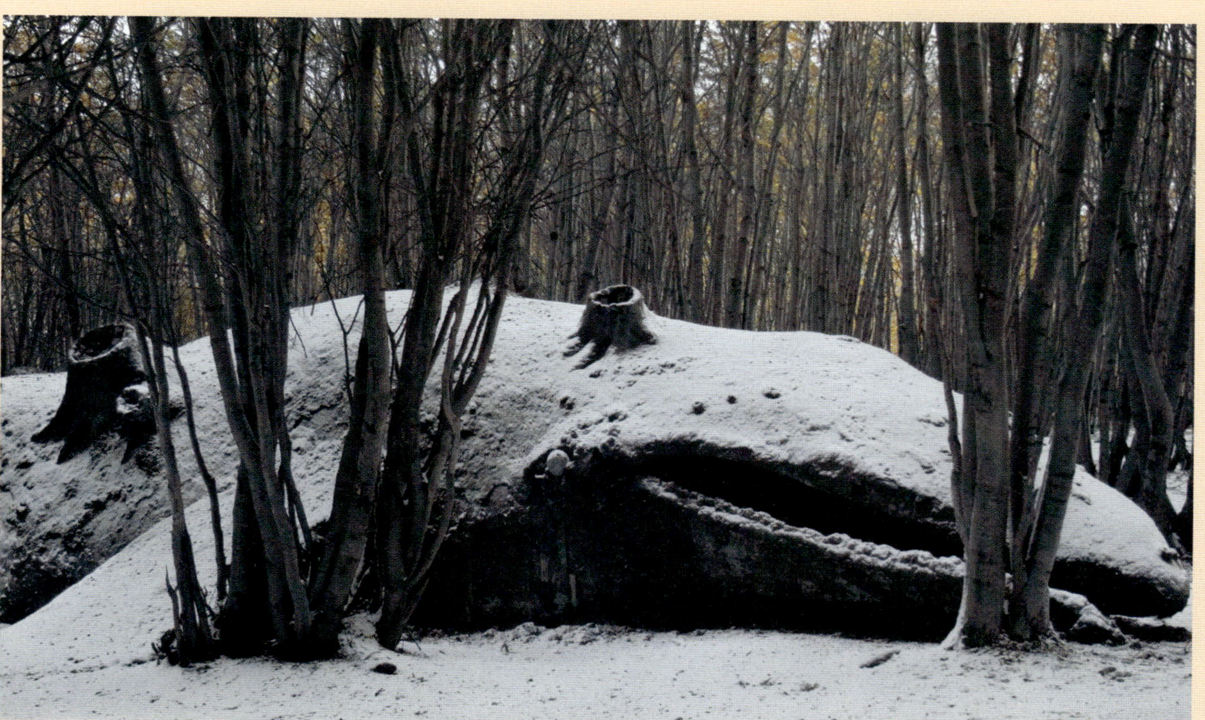

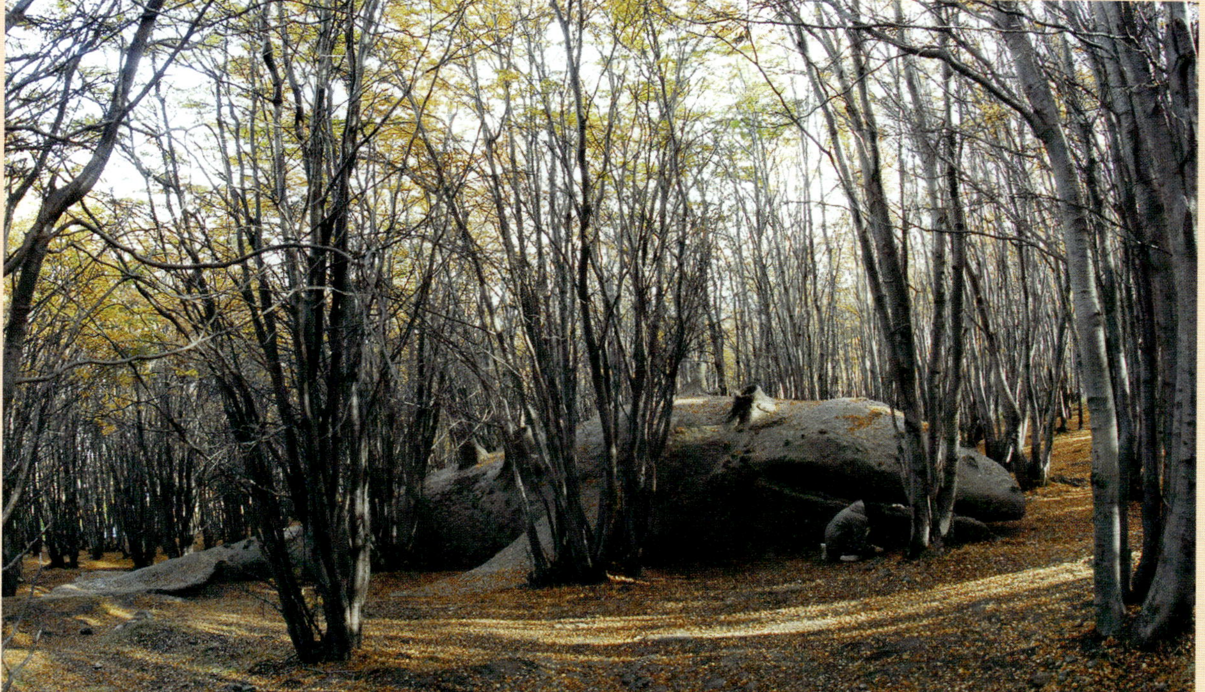

The whole scene was grey, dusty, at once harsh and fragile, triggering uncomfortable feelings of claustrophobia and hostility.

The chaotic appearance of the work contrasted its precise planning, creating a tension between the artisanal and the conceptual. Despite the hundreds of hours that were spent in moulding the clay pieces, the impression given was of a few fundamental gestures: a ceramics museum, a rug made out of rubbish, the occupation of the space with chimneys and tanks, and the doubling of the space through a mirror. A collapse of temporalities was triggered by the constant swing between the present, the future and the ancestral past suggested by the mythological figures (including dinosaurs and fossils) on the museum shelves, contemporary objects such as an iPod made out of clay, and images of Kurt Cobain and even of the artist's parents' dead bodies, all covered with the same patina of dust. 'Remainders of my life, aged 1000 years', according to Villar Rojas, the set-up represented both a moment of origin and a posthumous moment, the unearthing of geological layers.

This same fiction of time could be felt in front of the enormous whale that Villar Rojas built in the middle of a forest for the Biennial of the End of the World (2009). *Mi familia muerta* (My dead family, 2009), a titanic construction at twenty-seven metres in length, four metres in width and three metres in height, was camouflaged into the landscape thanks to the weather—snow covered its body as it covers a rock—and every day it became more real. Made out of clay, the work, Villar Rojas points out, 'was created to be devoured, destroyed and reintegrated into the landscape in the same way that a dead organic body would be. It's all about constructing a ruin, an abandoned moment … something whose life is only a day or a week long but that appears to be hundreds of years of age.' In contrast to his previous installation, which was overwhelming both as a whole and in its hundreds of objects and details, this work operated through a single image and the effect of its scale. It was a monument to a massive, languid and ancestral animal, abandoned by water and preserved in the landscape thanks to an unknown fantastic force, and, given work's title, the scene became even more uncanny.

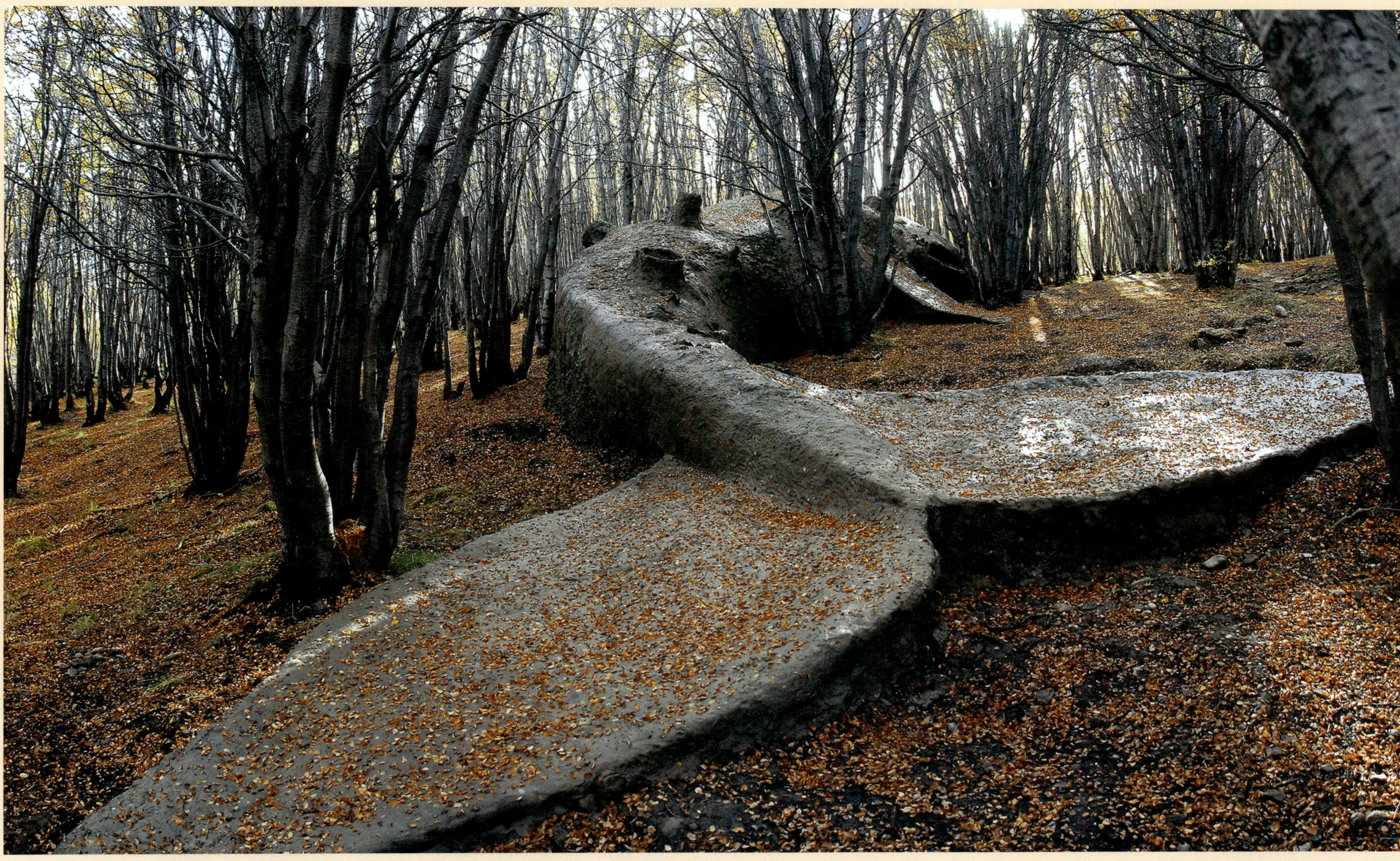

Mi familia muerta, 2009. Wood, rocks, clay. 3 × 27 × 4 m. Installation, Biennial of the End of the World, Ushuaia, Argentina

Danh Vo

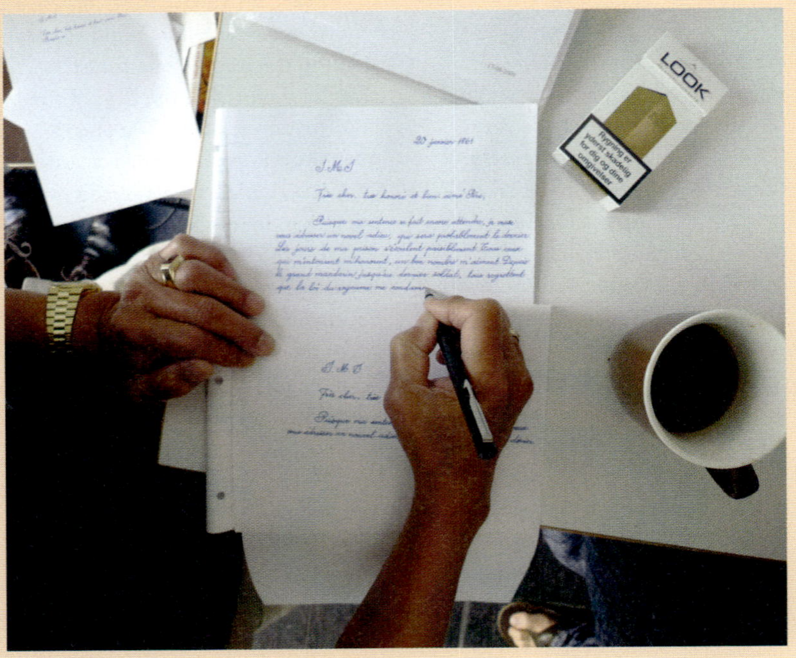

An elderly man living in Copenhagen might at this very moment be copying the last letter that a certain nineteenth-century French missionary penned to his father just before being decapitated in Vietnam. The able copyist, who writes out the lines in elegant calligraphy, is the father of Danish-Vietnamese artist Danh Vo; his task is to make a series of multiples, *Untitled* (2009), whose edition number will be defined after his death. That the purchaser of the newly handwritten letter has paid for something that doesn't exactly reproduce the visual particularities of the original (which Vo senior has never seen), and yet looks every bit like *an* original (and,

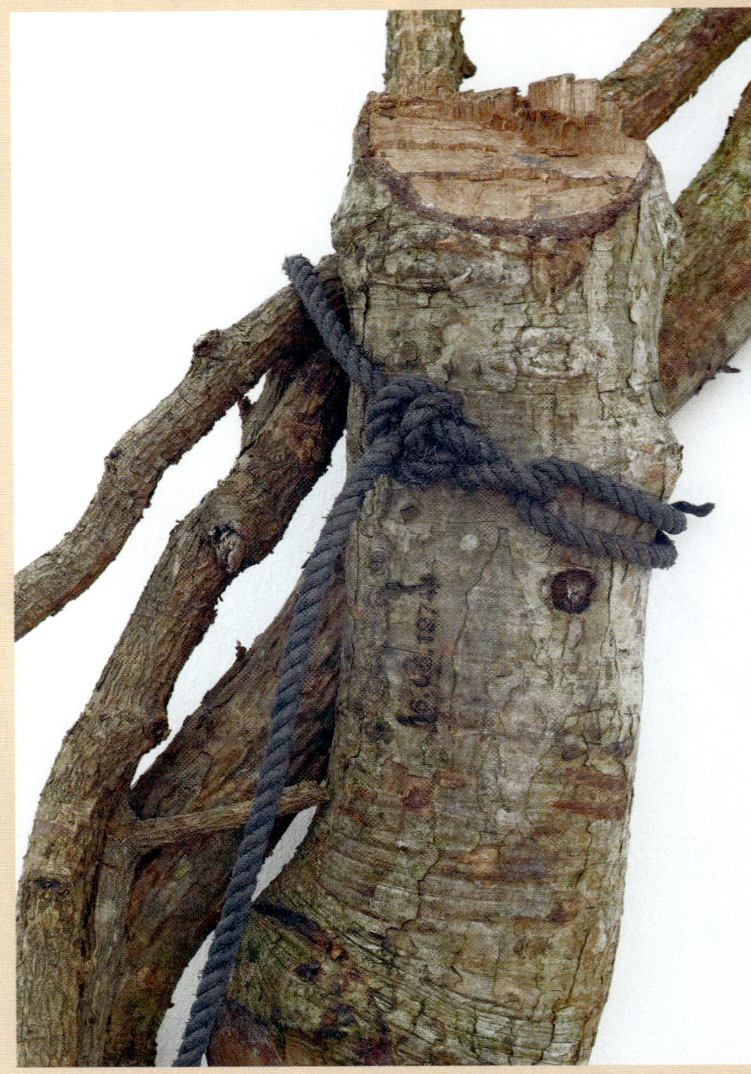

16.06.1974 (detail), 2009. Branches from the tree in An Thoi, Vietnam used as a marker for the lost grave of the artist's brother. Dimensions variable

20 janvier 1861.

J. M. J

Très cher, très honoré et bien-aimé Père,

Puisque ma sentence se fait encore attendre, je veux vous adresser un nouvel adieu, qui sera probablement le dernier. Les jours de ma prison s'écoulent paisiblement. Tous ceux qui m'entourent m'honorent, un bon nombre m'aiment. Depuis le grand mandarin jusqu'au dernier soldat, tous regrettent que la loi du royaume me condamne à la mort. Je n'ai point eu à endurer de tortures, comme beaucoup de mes frères. Un léger coup de sabre séperera ma tête, comme une fleur printanière que le Maître du jardin cueille pour son plaisir. Nous sommes tous des fleurs plantées sur cette terre que Dieu cueille en son temps, un peu plus tôt, un peu plus tard. Autre est la rose empourprée, autre le lys virginal, autre l'humble violette. Tâchons tous de plaire, selon le parfum ou l'éclat qui nous sont donnés, au souverain Seigneur et Maître.

Je vous souhaite, cher Père, une longue, paisible et vertueuse vieillesse. Portez doucement la croix de cette vie, à la suite de Jésus, jusqu'au calvaire d'un heureux trépas. Père et fils se reverront au paradis. Moi, petit éphémère, je m'en vais le premier. Adieu.

Votre très dévoué et respectueux fils,

J. Théophane Vénard

m. s.

Untitled, 2009. Farewell letter from the French missionary J. Théophane Vénard to his father; each edition hand-copied by the artist's father, after whose death the edition number will be defined.

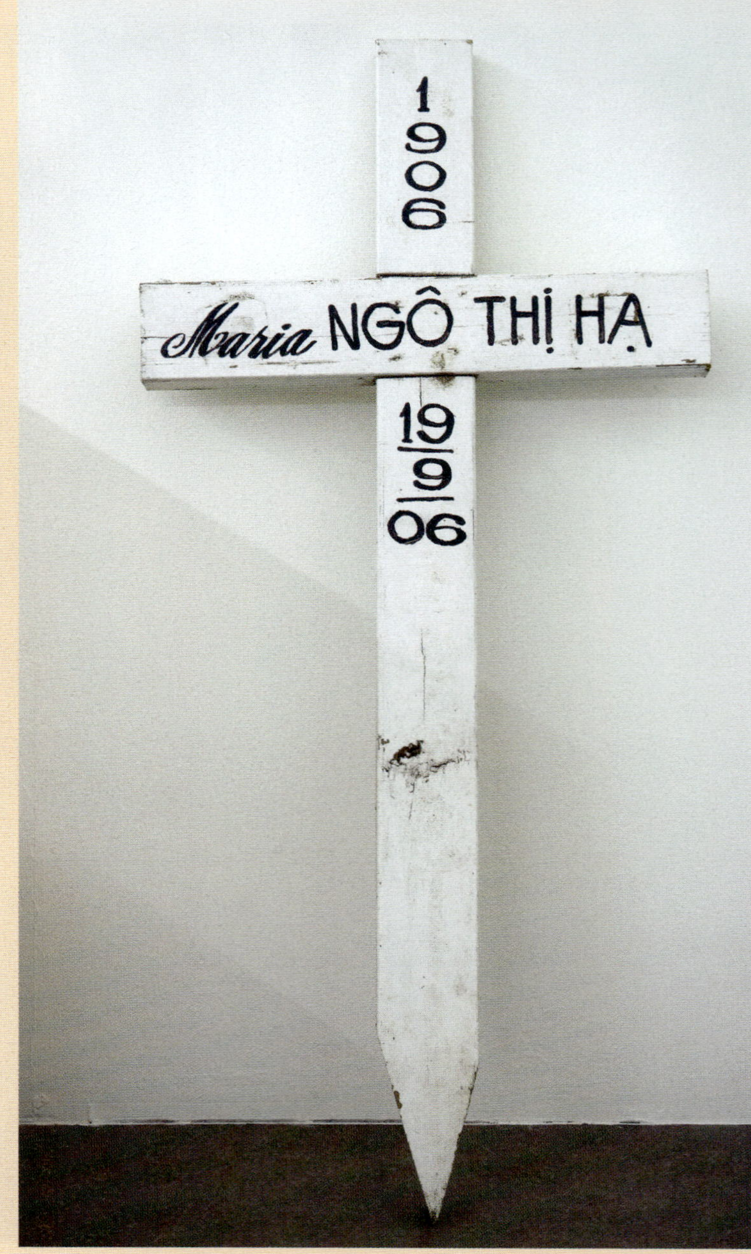

Ngo Thi Ha, 2008. Temporary grave marker. Dimensions variable

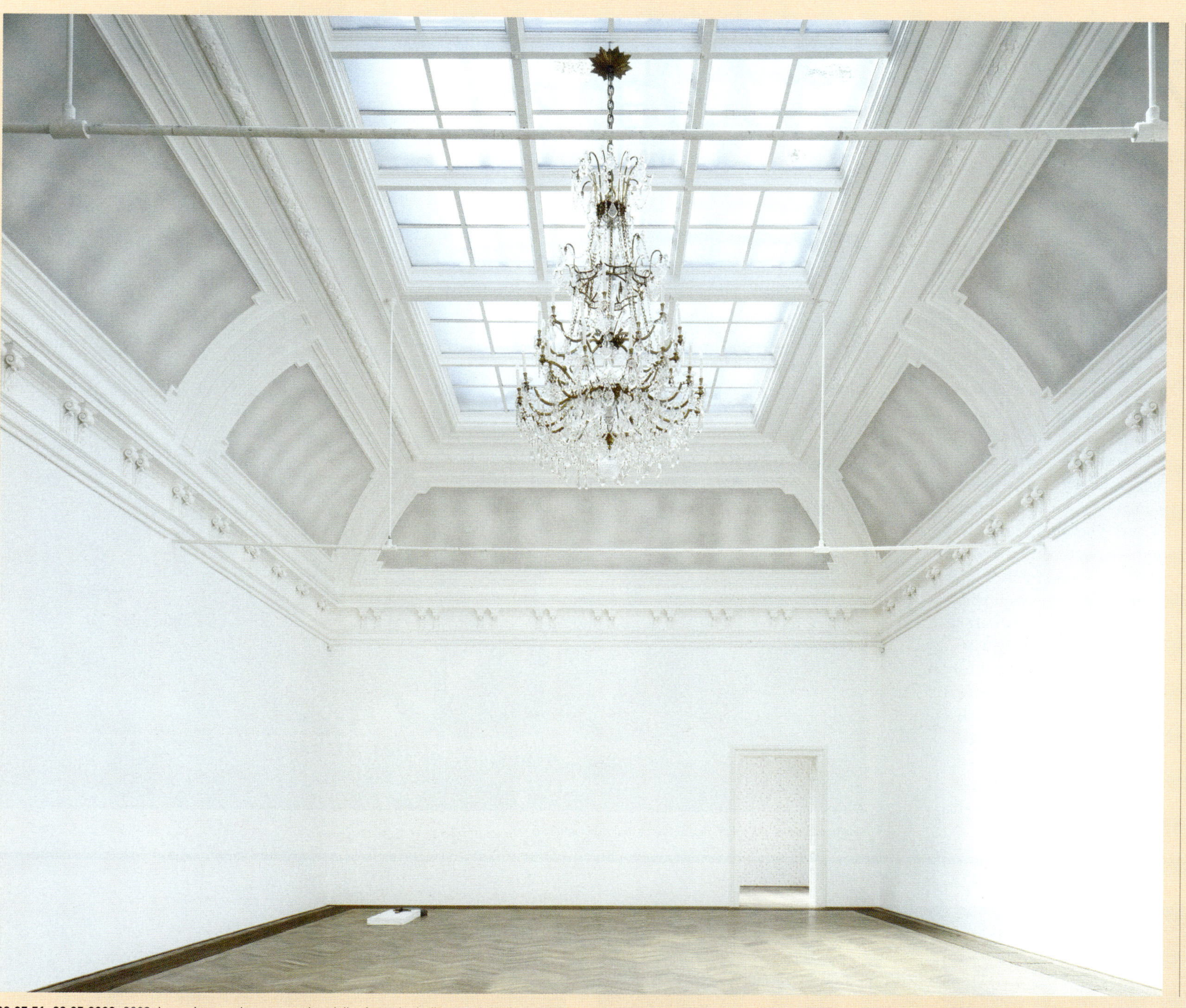

08:03:51, 28.05.2009, 2009. Late nineteenth–century chandelier from the ballroom of the former Hotel Majestic, Avenue Klèber, Paris. **Tombstone for Nguyen Thi Ty**, 2009. Marble, granite, bronze and wood relief. Dimensions variable

in a sense, actually is), is not important to the artist. What is important is that the buyer is paying for the manual labour involved in producing that ambiguously auratic copy-as-multiple — a letter originally written by someone else, remade by the artist's father and yet decisively belonging to Vo's artistic oeuvre.

This work contains the fulcrums of much of what Vo's work is about: the potential dubiousness of authenticity, the unmistakeable allure of originality, the tenuous nature of identity, the translation of the personal into an abstract form, the legacy of colonialism, and finally, but no less importantly, the legal and economic transactions that make up quotidian life. Such issues manifest themselves everywhere in the artist's practice, from his art-school graduation project in which members of his family made all his decisions (aesthetic and administrative) to his ongoing project to marry and then quickly divorce various individuals who have inspired him, leaving behind only a legal paper trail. They are also present in the artist's use of found and appropriated objects, such as his *Oma Totem* (2009), made from the actual washing machine, refrigerator, television and wooden crucifix given to his grandmother by the Immigrant Relief Program and the Catholic Church upon her arrival in Germany. Later, Vo made a piece intimately related to this work

(*Tombstone for Nguyen Thi Ty*, 2009), a marble replication of those same domestic appliances to serve as a marble tombstone for his now-dead grandmother.

'Is history *true?*', I once asked the artist. 'No, it's messy', was his reply. So it is. Perhaps Vo's background has made this all the more so, given the twists of fate and questions of identity encapsulated in his immigration to Denmark, which has become the repeated fodder for narratives about him. He was four when his family attempted to escape by boat from Vietnam to the United States and was instead picked up by a Danish tanker obliged to bring the refugees to safety. An entanglement of the personal and the visual is ever present in his artworks. Yet it would be a profound misconception to see his oeuvre as mere autobiography. Even the wooden cross that provisionally marked his grandmother's grave, and that the artist, after months of reflection, began to see as a hermetic sculpture, *Ngo Thi Ha* (2008), could become so only once it seemed that it could exist as an abstraction. His work at once invites and resists personal or historical readings to reach the degree zero of the object, subverting along the way common understandings of 'private' and 'public' and the relation of these notions to each other.

Twists of fate and questions of identity

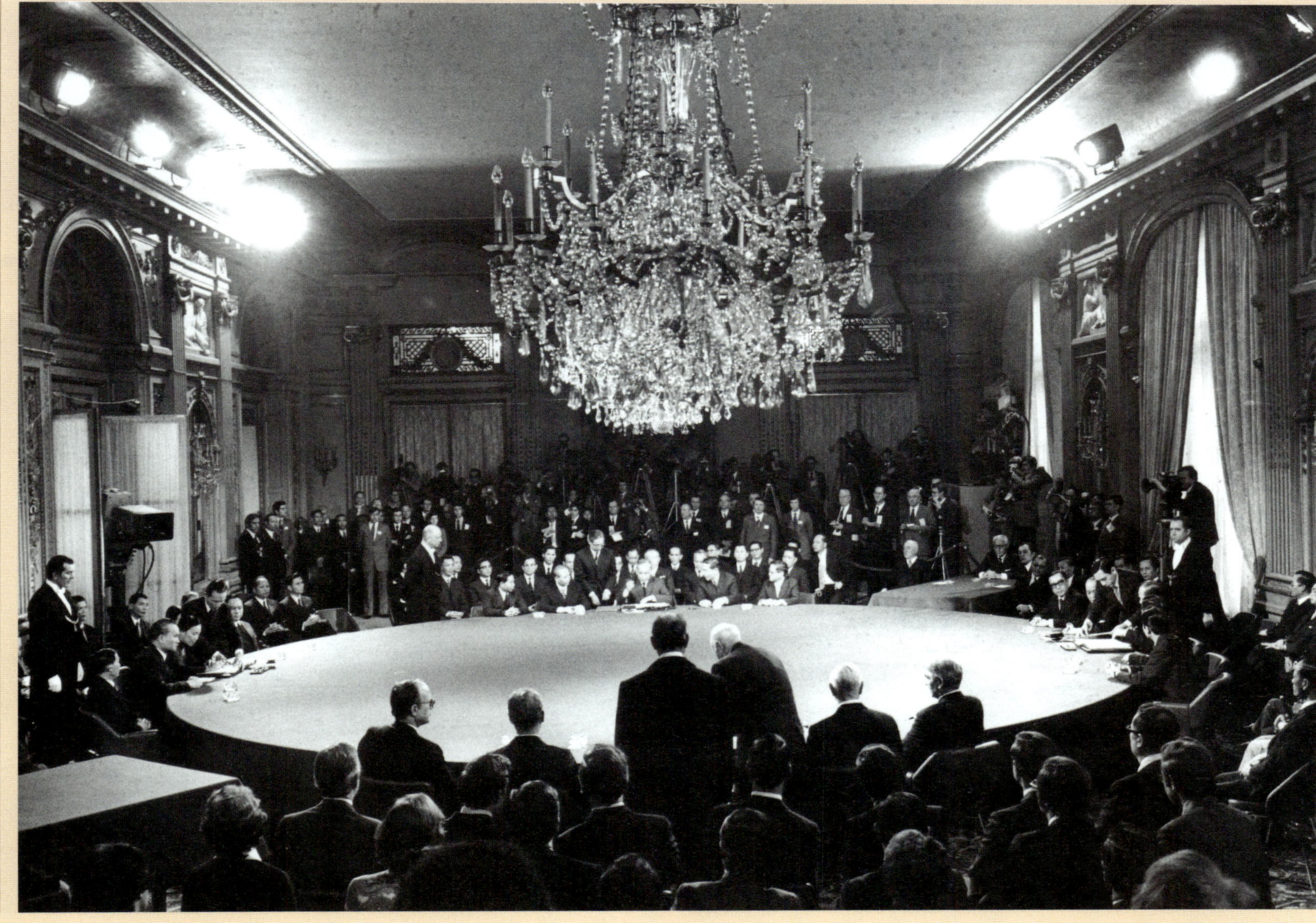

Untitled, 2009. Newspaper clipping, 26 × 17 cm

Tris Vonna-Michell

Tris Vonna-Michell once declared that he wanted his artworks to be able to 'mutate', even after being sold. The fact that a piece, de facto and unquestionably, remains forever fixed bothered him. This is hardly surprising, since his attempt to construct a work of art in which there is an inherent volatility corresponds with the larger concerns of his practice: the flux and fragility of both the spoken word and history.

Vonna-Michell is, before anything else, a storyteller. For several years now, he has read aloud his home-cooked narratives which mix fact and fiction, the concrete and the chance-derived, the plausible and the improbable. Performed without spectacular fanfare, the tales nevertheless entail a speed of delivery (breathless, rapid-fire), accent (implacably British) and gesture (a combination of pacing and swiftly repeated but controlled hand motions) that are entirely his own, as are his choice of topics and the circuitous route he takes to get to them.

Yet regardless of the explicit subject matter to which he turns (a crumbling post-industrial Detroit, a forgotten 1980s film, a defunct music scene, secret tunnels in Germany, three similarly named men, buildings ruined by aerial bombings, his family's move to Southend), the actual focus is always and inescapably history and the ways in which— of necessity and by definition— it tells and hides, constructs and, ultimately, lies. Perhaps fittingly, then, Vonna-Michell's version of history (one part research, one part memory and one part misunderstanding) is accompanied by slide-projected or printed and paper-clipped images that

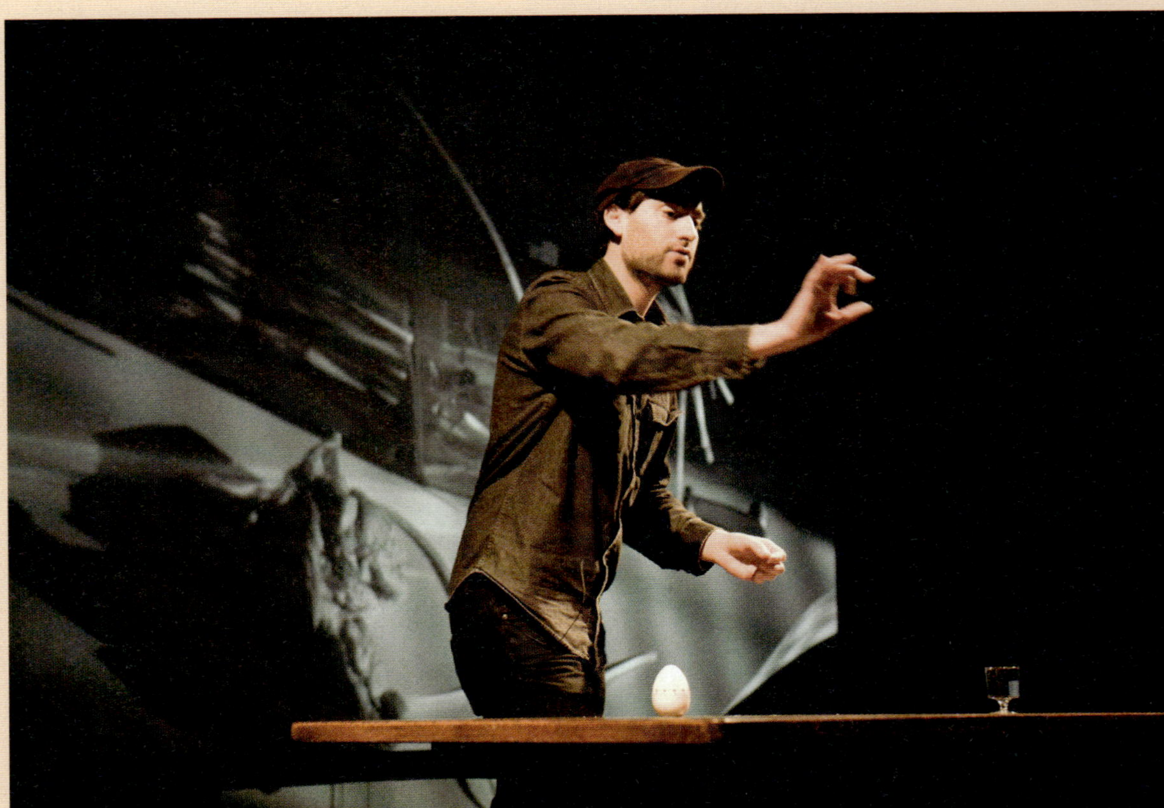

Finding Chopin, 2005–09. Performance. Duration variable

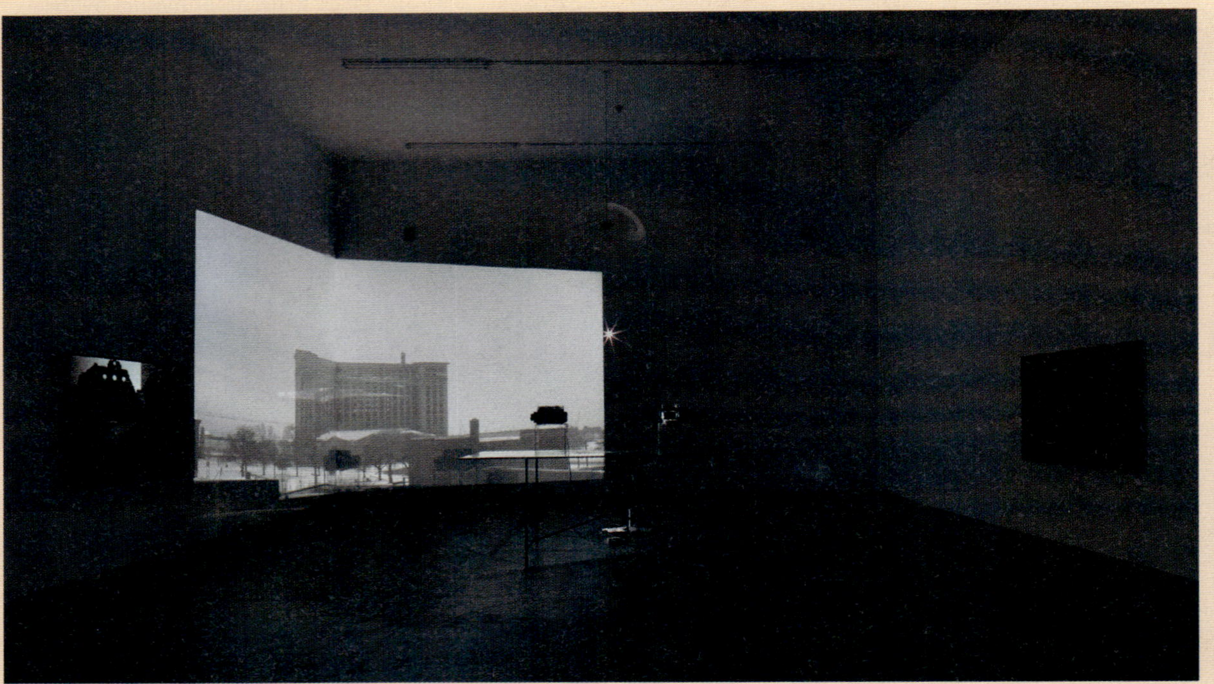

Seizure, 2007–08. Mixed–media installation. Dimensions variable

Oral collages

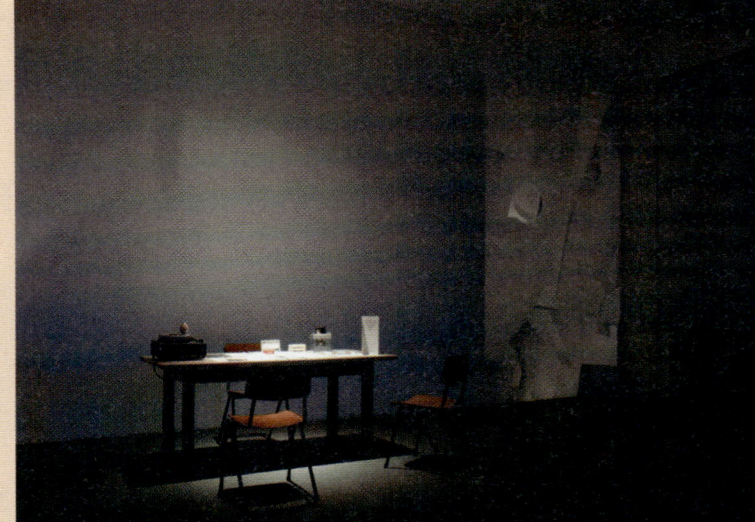

Down the Rabbit–Hole, 2006–07. Mixed–media installation. Dimensions variable

Makeshift ensembles of obsolete technologies

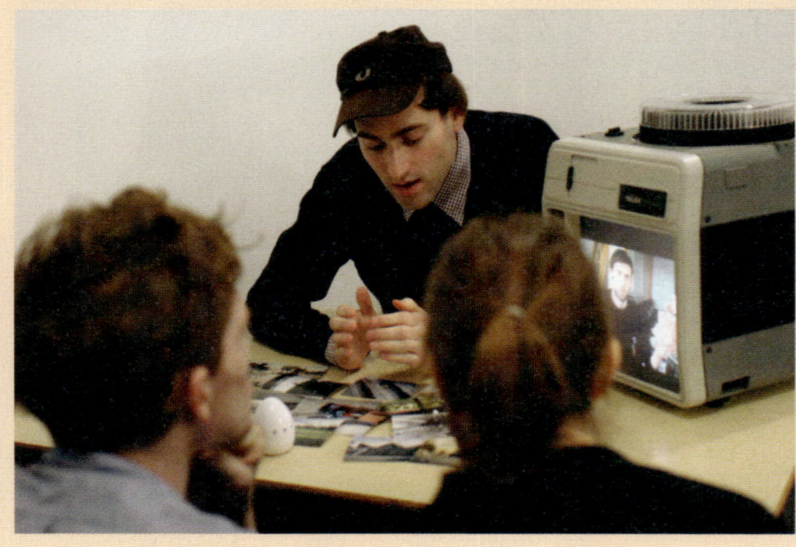

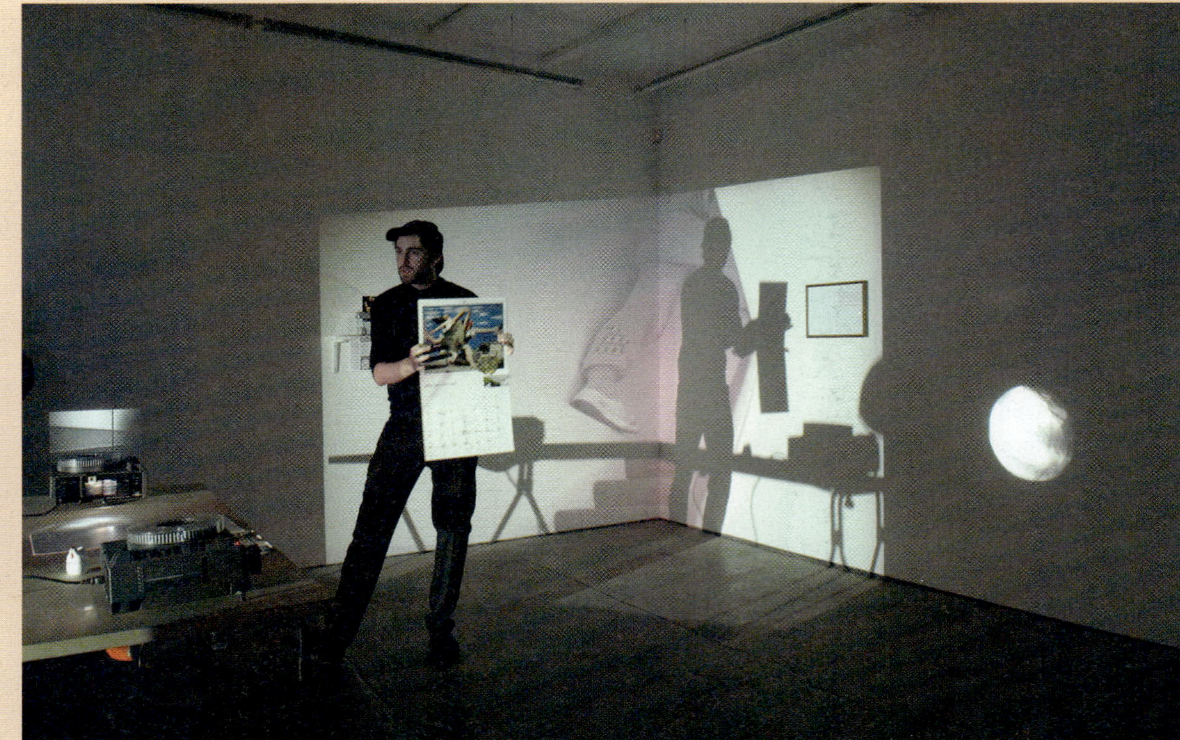

Tall Tales and Short Stories, 2007. Mixed–media installation and performance. Dimensions variable

neither act as proper documents nor certify the artist's presence in this or that place; they are instead images that are intended to be 'unhinged', as the former student of photography puts it, by the narratives that accompany them. This unhinging comes in part through repetition. The same image can appear in various contexts, in relation to different spoken words, or photographed and then rephoto-graphed, so that any sense of finality or fixity is lost. In this way, the images operate like Vonna-Michell's oral collages, as they are constantly revisited and spoken anew.

The German Stasi archives, for instance, and the so-called 'puzzlers' hired to piece together shredded documents have, for years now, been fodder for a variety of different vocal reveries and installations, ranging from

Vonna Michell is a storyteller. For several years now, he has read aloud his home-cooked narratives that mix fact and fiction, the concrete and the chance-derived, the plausible and the improbable

Hahn / Huhn (2003 – present) to *Down the Rabbit-Hole* (2006 – 07). Vonna-Michell's search for the avant-garde sound poet Henri

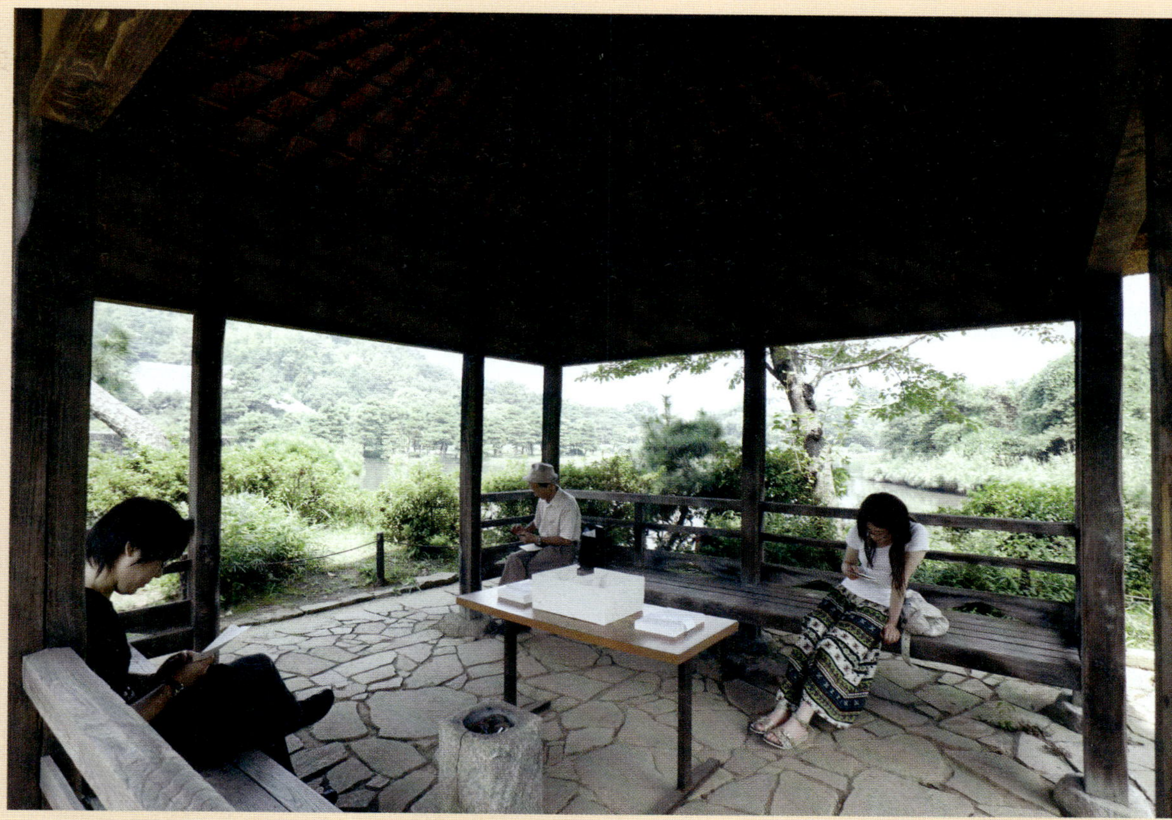

Wasteful Illuminations, 2008. Mixed–media installation. Dimensions variable

Vocal reveries and installations

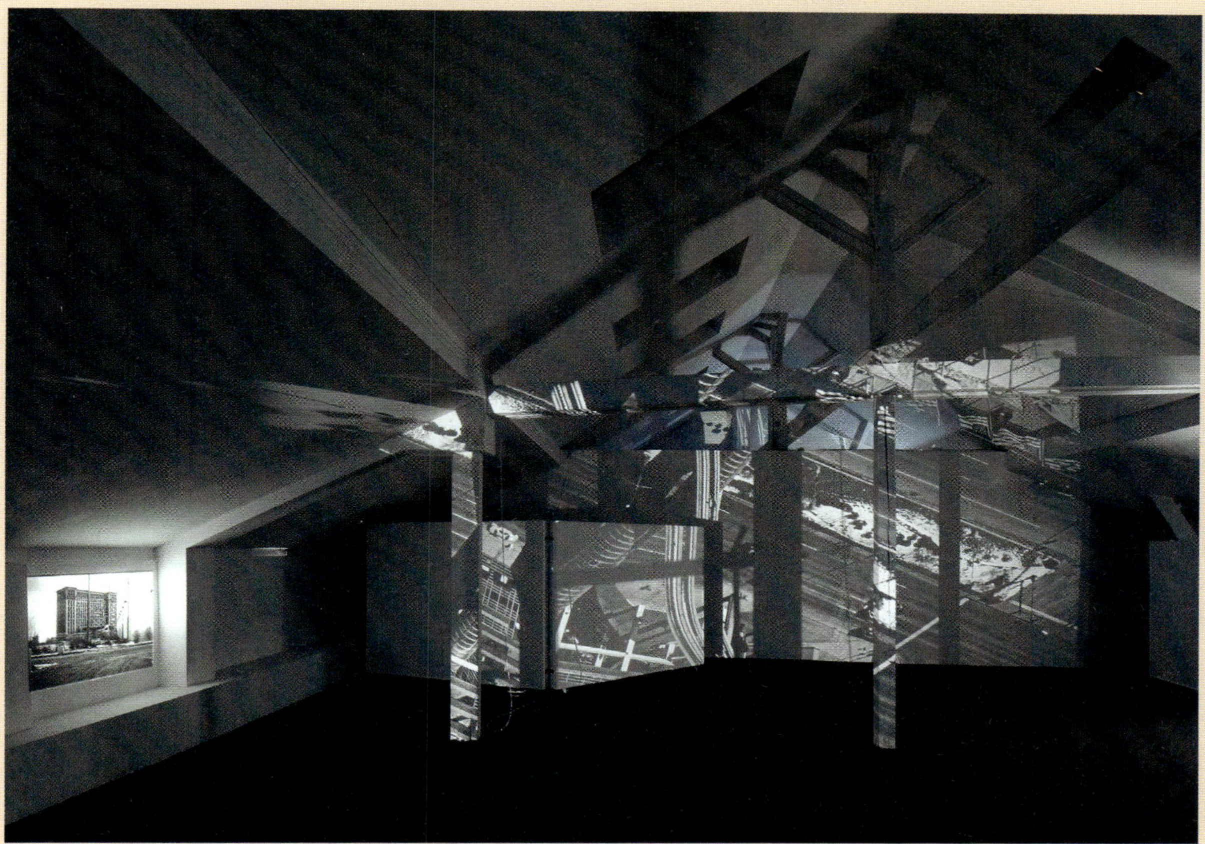

Studio A, 2008. Mixed–media installation. Dimensions variable

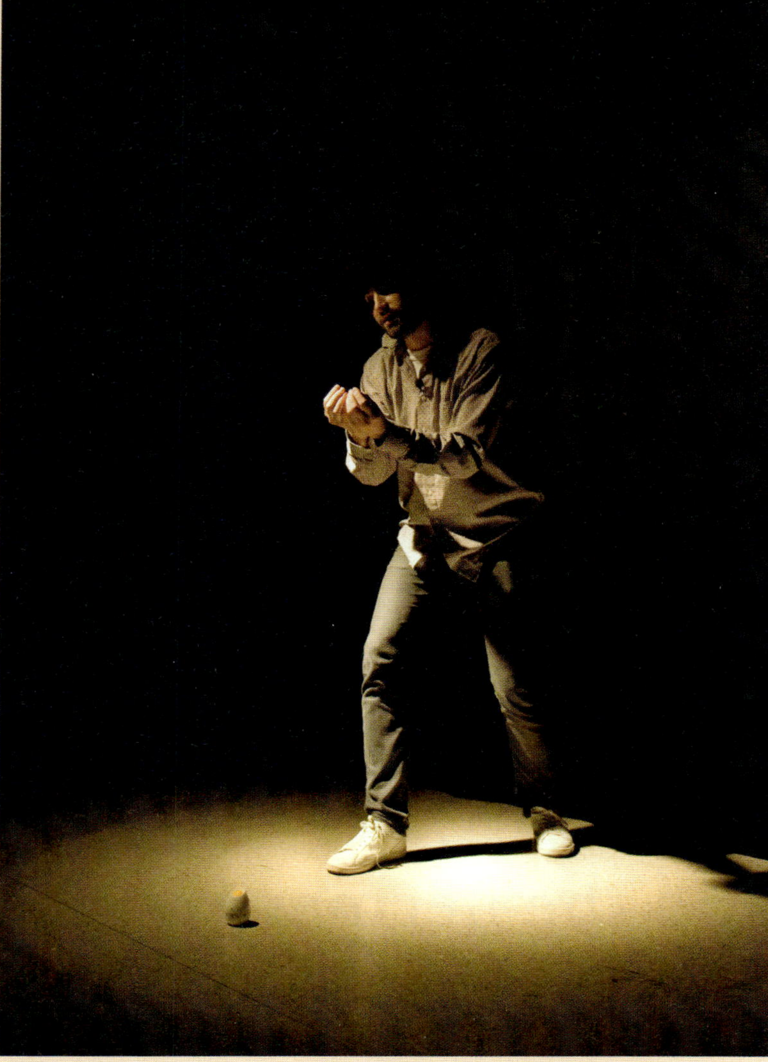

Hahn/Huhn, 2003–present. Performance. Duration variable

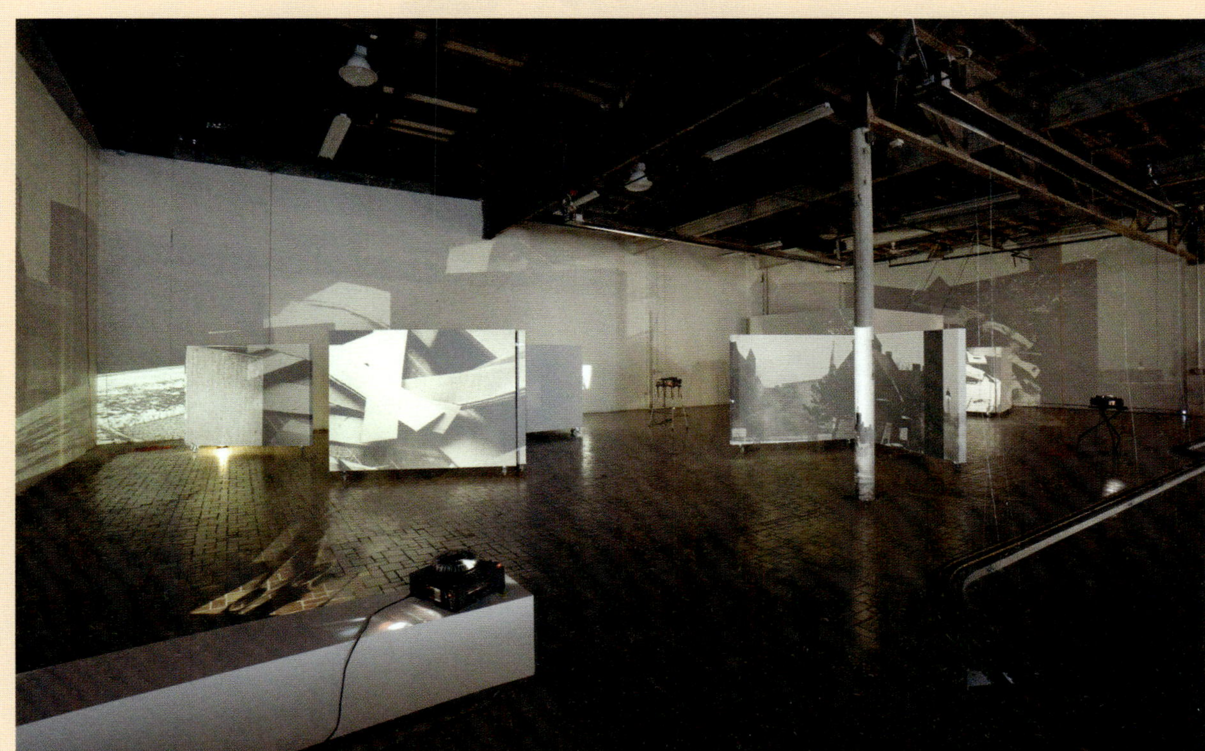

Auto–Reverse, 2009. Mixed–media installation. Dimensions variable

Chopin also resulted in several years of performances and installations (whose culmination, *Finding Chopin: Endnotes* 2005–09, the artist warned, might not be an end at all). The installations that emerge from these are makeshift ensembles which were composed of obsolete technologies (cassette recorders, turntables, slide projectors), mundane detritus (forlorn photo-copies, toothpicks, cartons of quail eggs, plastic kitchen timers) and fragile architectures, either evoked (a crumbling Detroit, Kurt Schwitter's *Merzbau*, Vincent Van Gogh's skewed vision of his bedroom) or literally serving as the supports for his objects (temporary partitions, wall panels on wheels, tables on trestle legs).

However scrappy or unstable, these are concretely material things, and their arrangement is always carefully considered — extremely formal, even. Yet precisely when Vonna-Michell's work appears at its most material, the permanence of his installations is undercut by the fact that he often disassembles and recycles the elements into a new project. He seems, for the moment at least, to be constructing a rare thing: an oeuvre as fugitive and unsettled as memory, passing time, or even the spoken word.

Claude Wampler

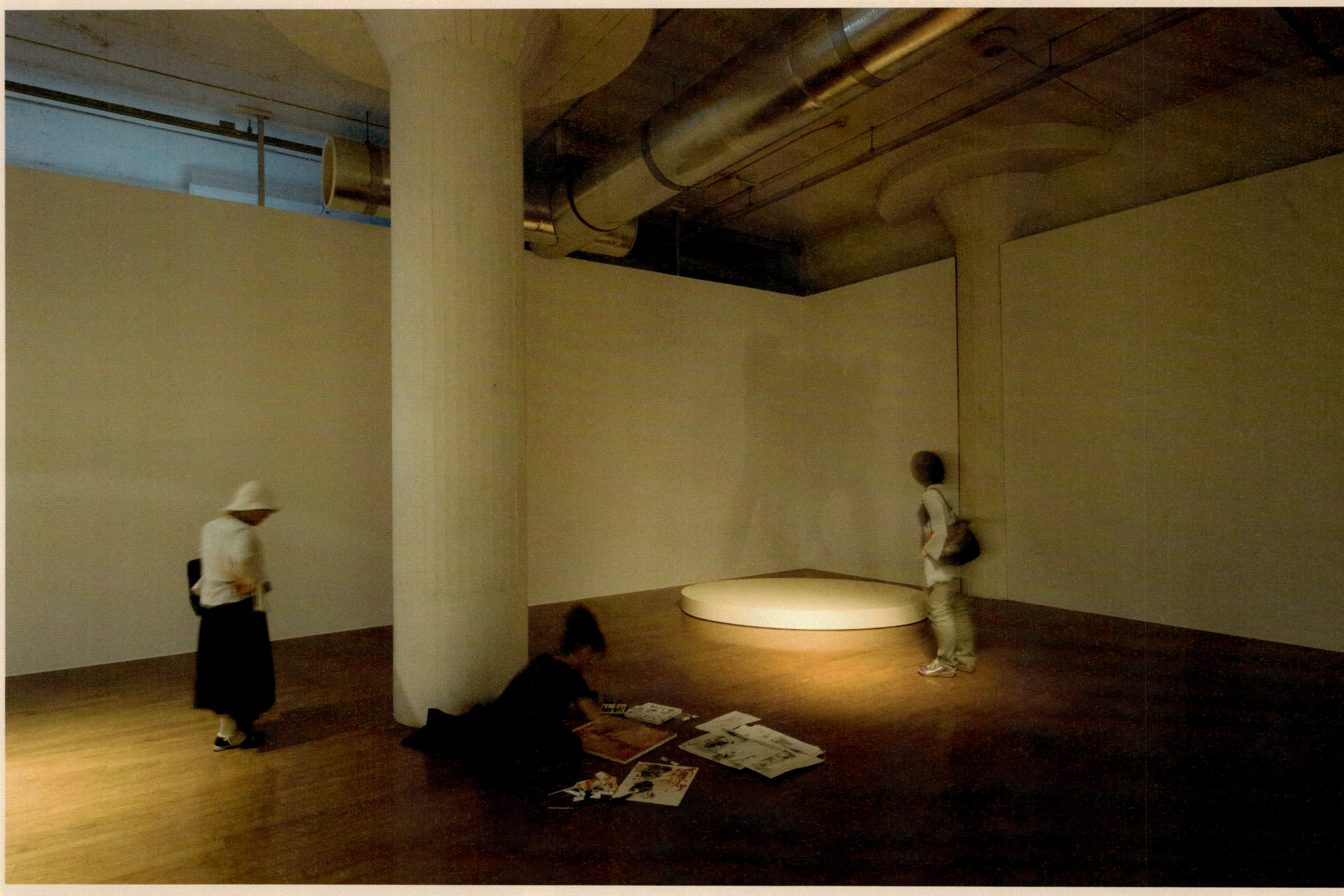

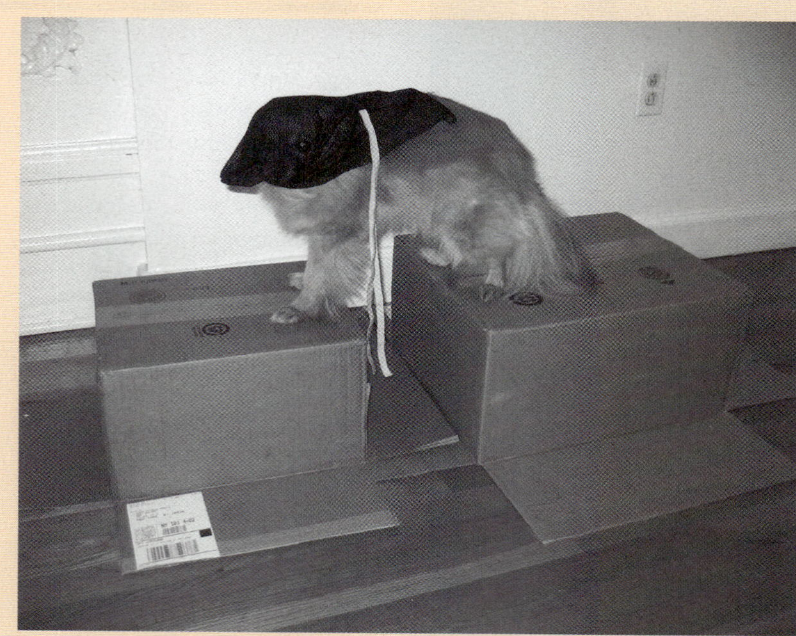

Untitled sculpture (LARGE-SCALE FLEXIBLE & SEXY SELF-CANNIBALIZING NAKED VAMPIRE), 2008. Steel, fibreglass, enamel paint, wax, synthetic hair, rubber, wood, cotton fabric. 366 × 183 × 122 cm

Hopelessly softcore imaginary and the hermeneutics of wishful thinking

Little critical attention is paid to the mnemonic particularities of artworks, and yet the afterlife that a piece enjoys in the remembrance of the beholder, beyond the physical encounter, is obviously key. This is particularly so in the fleeting, overloaded context of large group shows, where little has changed since the days of the Paris Salon, which famously crammed as many works as possible into a given space. The main difference between today's exhibitions and those of the nineteenth century is that the names of curators are often seen as more important than those of the artists. The best you can hope for is a chance encounter with an artwork that stands apart.

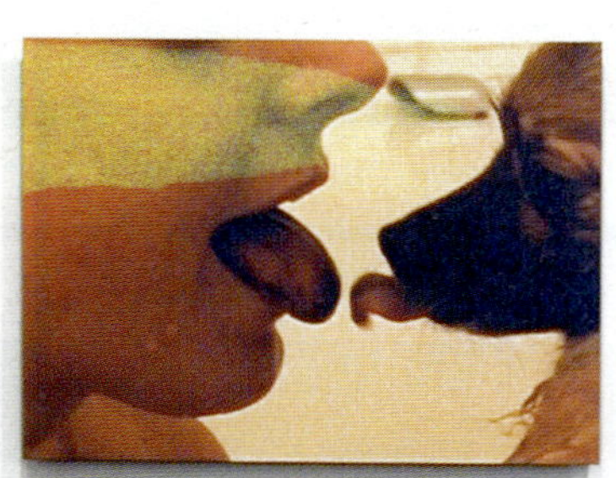

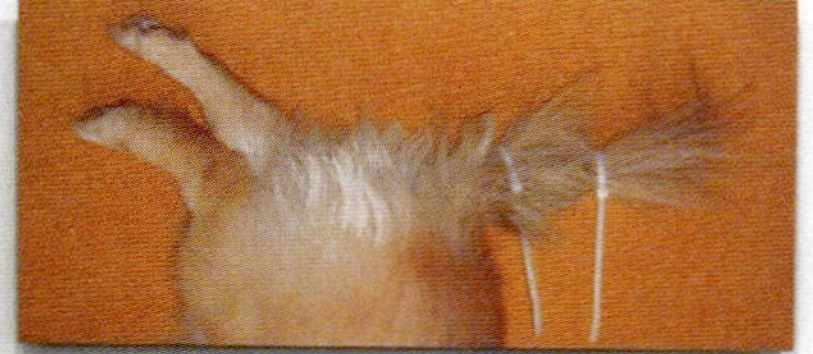

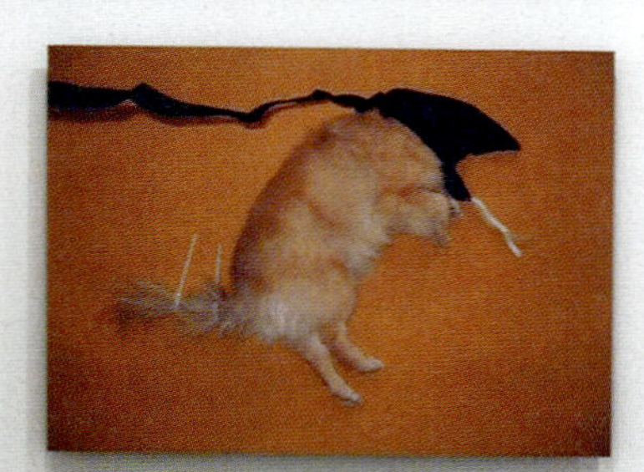

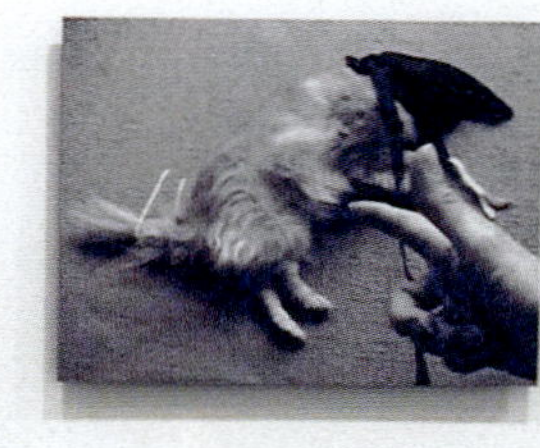

A hooded pomeranian appears to have been left standing on boxes, 2005. Black and white photograph. 122 × 81cm

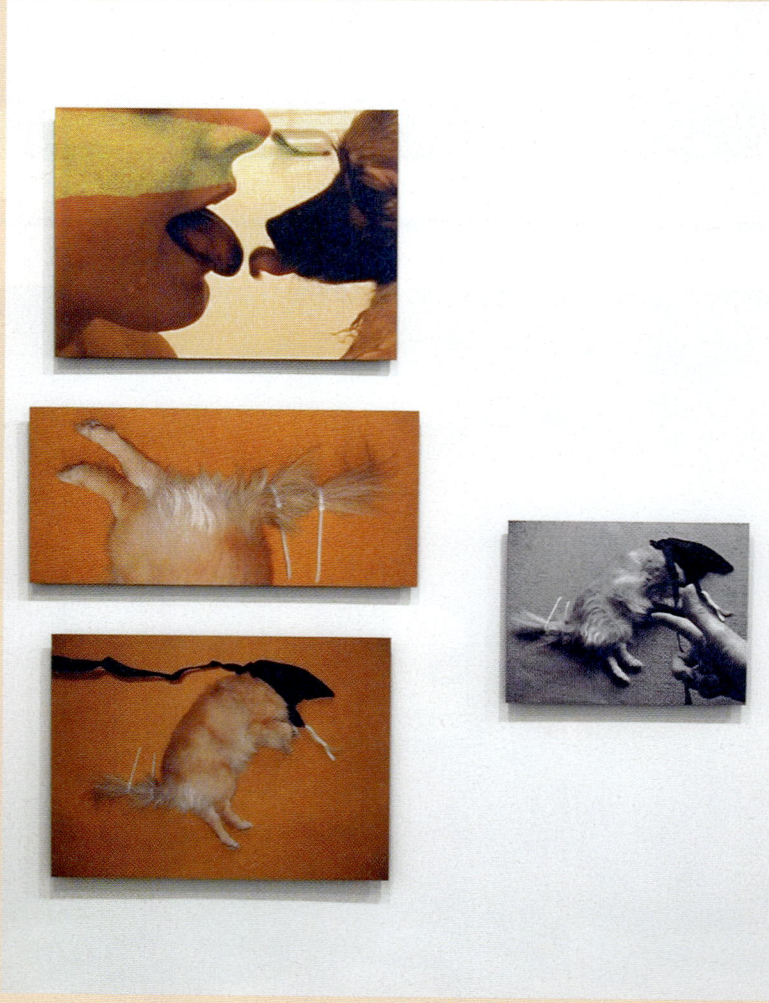

Cake Shoot and Abu Poms 1–3, 2005. Black and white photograph. 51 × 38 cm.
3 digital C–prints. 71 × 51cm, 81 × 37 cm, 71 × 51cm

Flexible, self-cannibalizing vampirical power

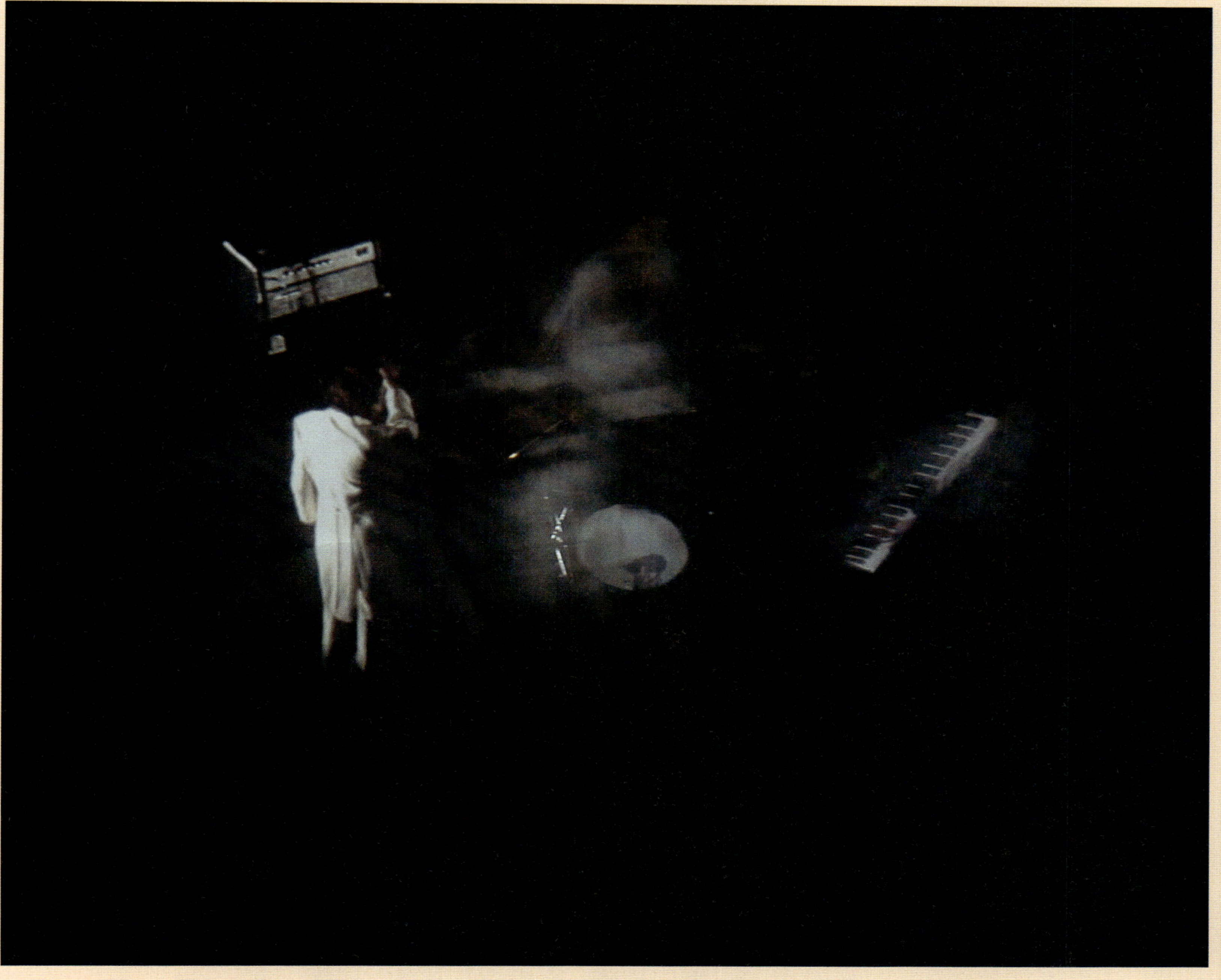

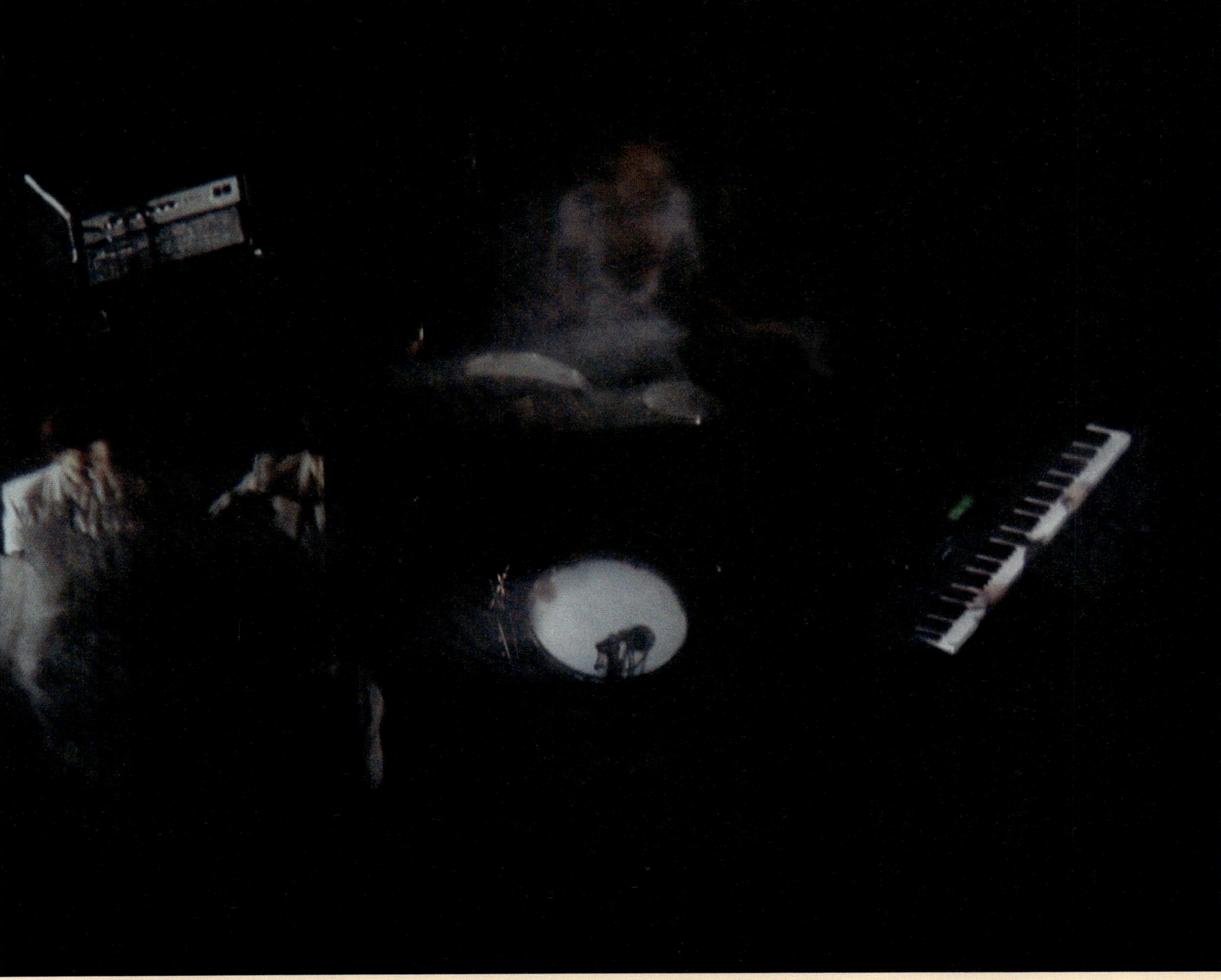

PERFORMANCE (career ender), 2008. Performance. Approx. 75 min.

By this I do not mean the adventure of fresh discovery, nor the visual caffeine that overcomes exhibition fatigue, but a longevity that lingers, haunts and hangs around for reasons that you cannot necessarily identify. At the 2008 Yokohama Triennial, I came across such a work — a shadow on the wall that at first seemed to be the silhouette of something sci-fi and menacing, but at second glance appeared to be something more or less traditionally beaux-arts. It was hard to discern, for there was no source object to be seen, just a young woman sitting on the floor, energetically drawing the empty scene before her. As I recall the situation a year later, she was hunched over her sketchbook in a way that would have required a slightly obtrusive approach to determine whether it was the shadow or an imagined signifier that she was sketching. I have deliberately avoided clarification even now, at the time of writing, and as I conjure Wampler's *Untitled sculpture (LARGE-SCALE FLEXIBLE & SEXY SELF-CANNIBALIZING NAKED VAMPIRE)* (2008) in my mind's eye, it resembles an expressionist ghoul, although I recall being struck by a more restrained ambiguity at the time. The woman on the floor, it now seems, was a fetching Japanese teen in school uniform, yet I do remember thinking she was a typically anonymous MFA student. The merging of historical precedents, a hopelessly softcore imaginary and the hermeneutics of wishful thinking at play in this work exemplify the way in which sign and signifier, material and audience, institution and situation can merge in Wampler's work, which generally revisits the relationship between live performance and the art object through all possible media.

An earlier piece, -~~PERFORMANCE~~ *(career ender)* (2007) presented at Portland's Time Based Art Festival, began with footage of a band's rehearsal, projected for a live audience through a confusing haze of holograms and smoke machines, until the band eventually took to the stage to play the song they had been rehearsing. The audience included planted collaborators who danced, heckled or otherwise manipulated the atmosphere in the room. A reviewer argued that Wampler seemed 'interested in more than the Cageian notion of recognizing ambient experience as an inseparable part of live performance. She seeks total control over the experience.' A blogger, on the other hand, appreciated the resulting 'sweet chaos' and 'for once at a theatre, having absolutely no fucking idea what was going on'. To me it seems that the attempt to simultaneously heighten and relinquish control over the experience drives Wampler's work which gives it its flexible, self-cannibalizing vampirical power to haunt and persist in the viewer's mind.

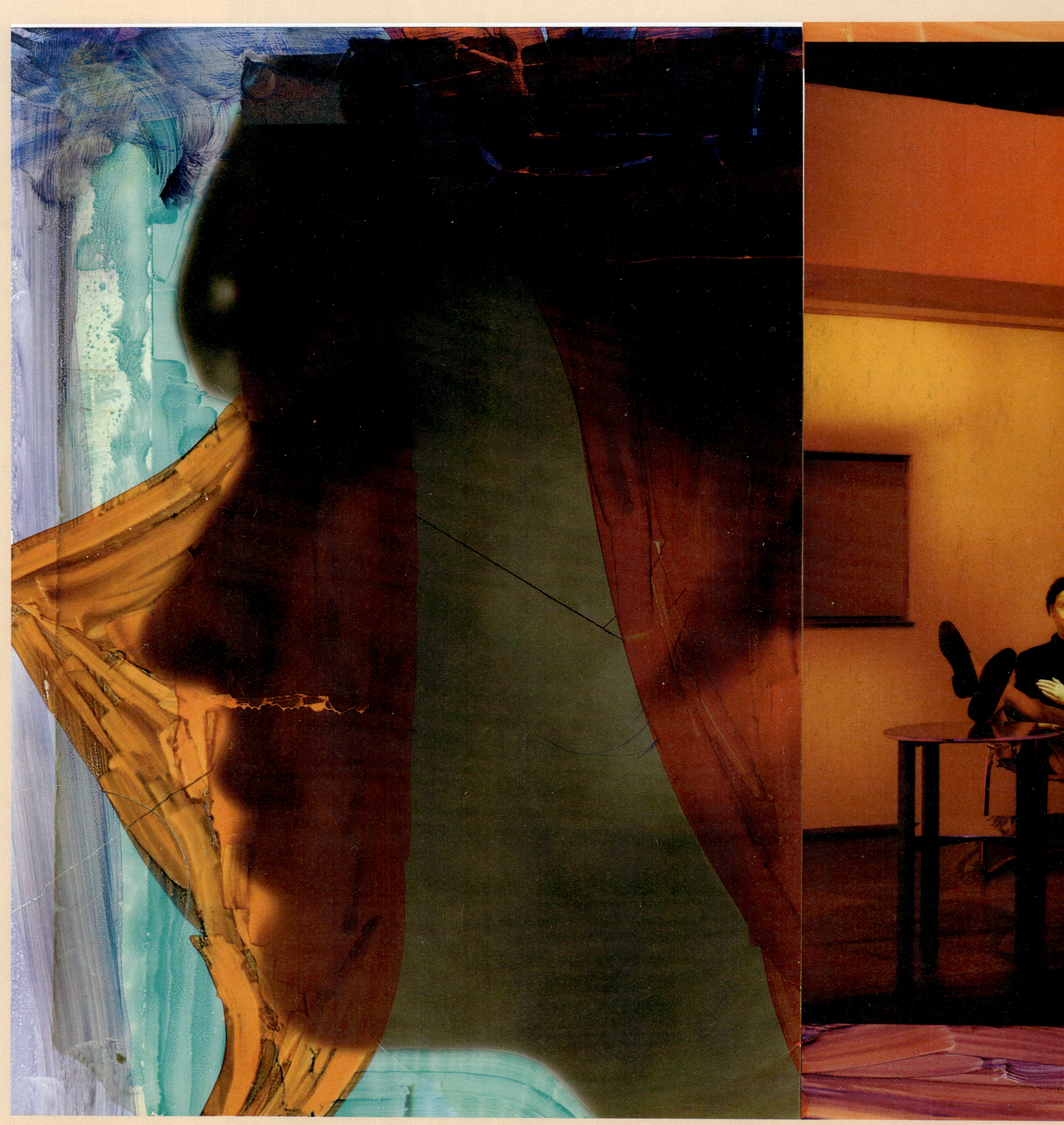

Calling over, 2007. Collage, felt pen, ballpoint pen on photograph. 15 × 36 cm

Effects of the uncanny

Much has been made of the personal history of Georgia-born Berlin-based artist Andro Wekua. The mood of melancholia that characterizes his work has been attributed to the fact he suffered a family tragedy and was forced to flee Georgia after the fall of the Soviet Union when he was a child. The artist, however, resists this attempt to reduce his work to a personal narrative of trauma and loss. In his haunting films, paintings, drawings, collages, prints, installations and sculptural tableaux there is more exploration of the mechanisms of myth, the vagaries of memory and the psychological effects of the uncanny than there is of autobiography and individual history.

An overarching concern at the heart of Wekua's work is the principle of collage. Using photocopies, photographs and his own prints, he appropriates images from the flow of media circulating through our world in both the present and the past. Images of landscapes, architectural interiors, children and women

Andro Wekua

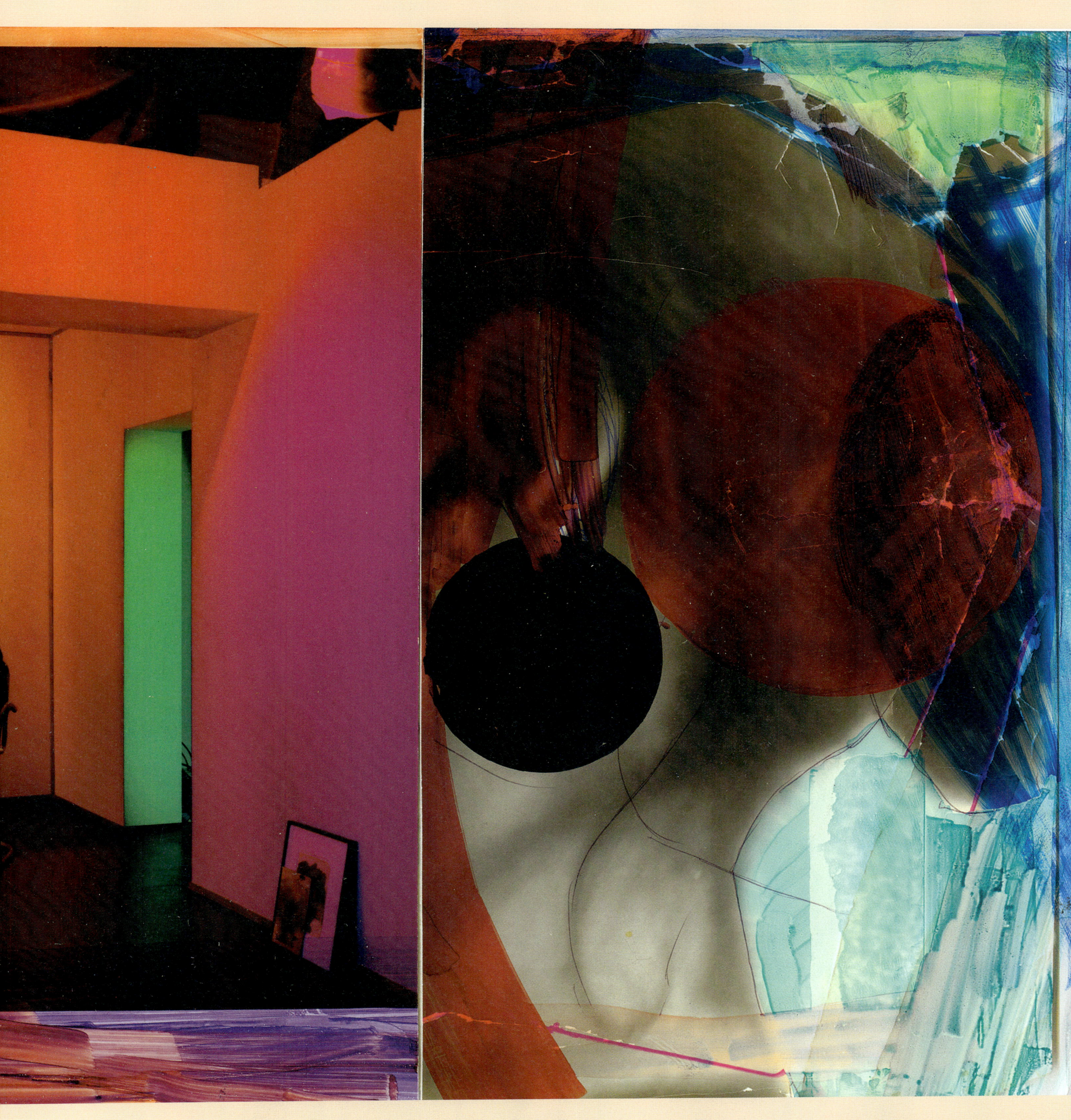

from fashion magazines are layered with sombre paints and inks. There is something anachronistic about these works, as if time (and memory) has been frozen in a kind of kaleidoscopic amber generated by the over-saturated colours of the artist's felt-tip pens. Collage is itself a parallel activity to the mechanism of memory and dreams in which images collide with one another in both our conscious and unconscious minds as we try to construct narratives that make sense of our personal experiences and everyday lives in the modern world. These works are therefore as much a result of Wekua's attempt to understand his own environment as they are a subtle commentary on the tenuous and fragmentary nature of memory.

This particular reading of the collage aesthetic flows from his works on paper to his sculptures in which forlorn solitary wax figures, often boys and girls, inhabit vitrines, sit behind desks or slouch in chairs. In *Wait to Wait, Part 1* (2006), for example, an adolescent boy dressed only in a white shi[rt] moves slowly back and forth in a rocking chair placed on a bri[ck] platform and surrounded by a Plexiglas vitrine. As with man[y] of Wekua's figures, the boy's fa[ce] is painted out, affecting a kind of metaphorical erasure of ide[ntity]

Flow of history

that makes these works a screen for the projection of our own hopes and fears, dreams and nightmares. As we can see in *Get out of my room* (2006), in which a similarly dressed young man sits with his feet on a table, his eyes painted closed, Wekua's figures are often blind and mute, bearing witness to the flow of history from their perches without fully participating in those events. Are they victims or simply witnesses? The title of a more recent work, *God is Dead but Not the Girl* (2008), suggests an answer to this question. In this work Wekua presents us with a young girl in a tennis dress, slouching in a chair inside a Plexiglas room with her arms crossed in an expression of youthful ennui or defiance. God might be dead, but not this girl. Life goes on in a world where tragedy and comedy are now inseparable. Wekua's sculptures are not the historical figures and celebrities of Madame Tussaud's waxworks. They are rather his own Oracles of Delphi, soothsayers in a world where history has been displaced by memory and fact had been usurped by allegorical stories.

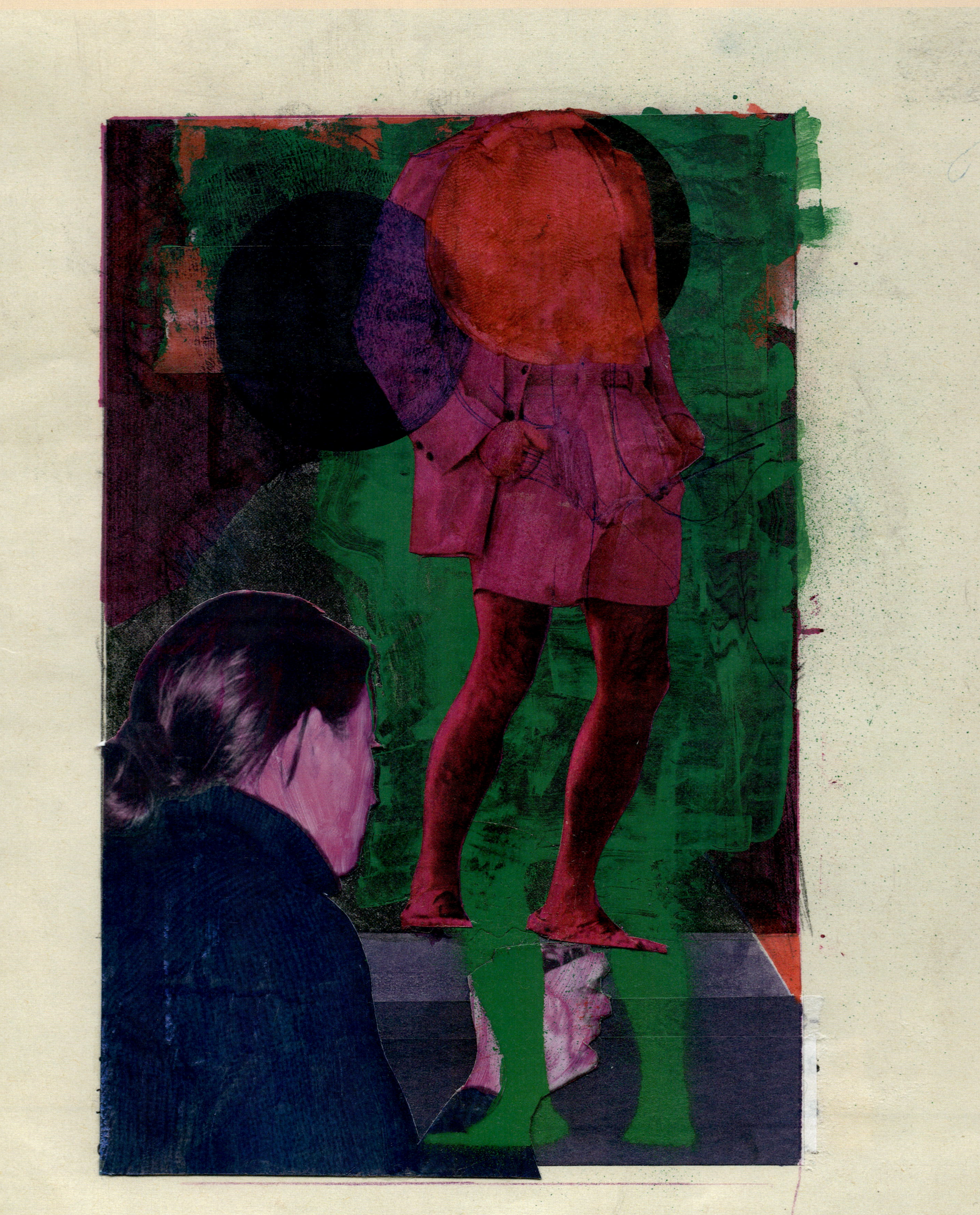

Circle Smile, 2007. Collage, felt pen, colour pen, lacquer spray, pencil, ballpoint pen on paper and photograph. 23 × 18 cm

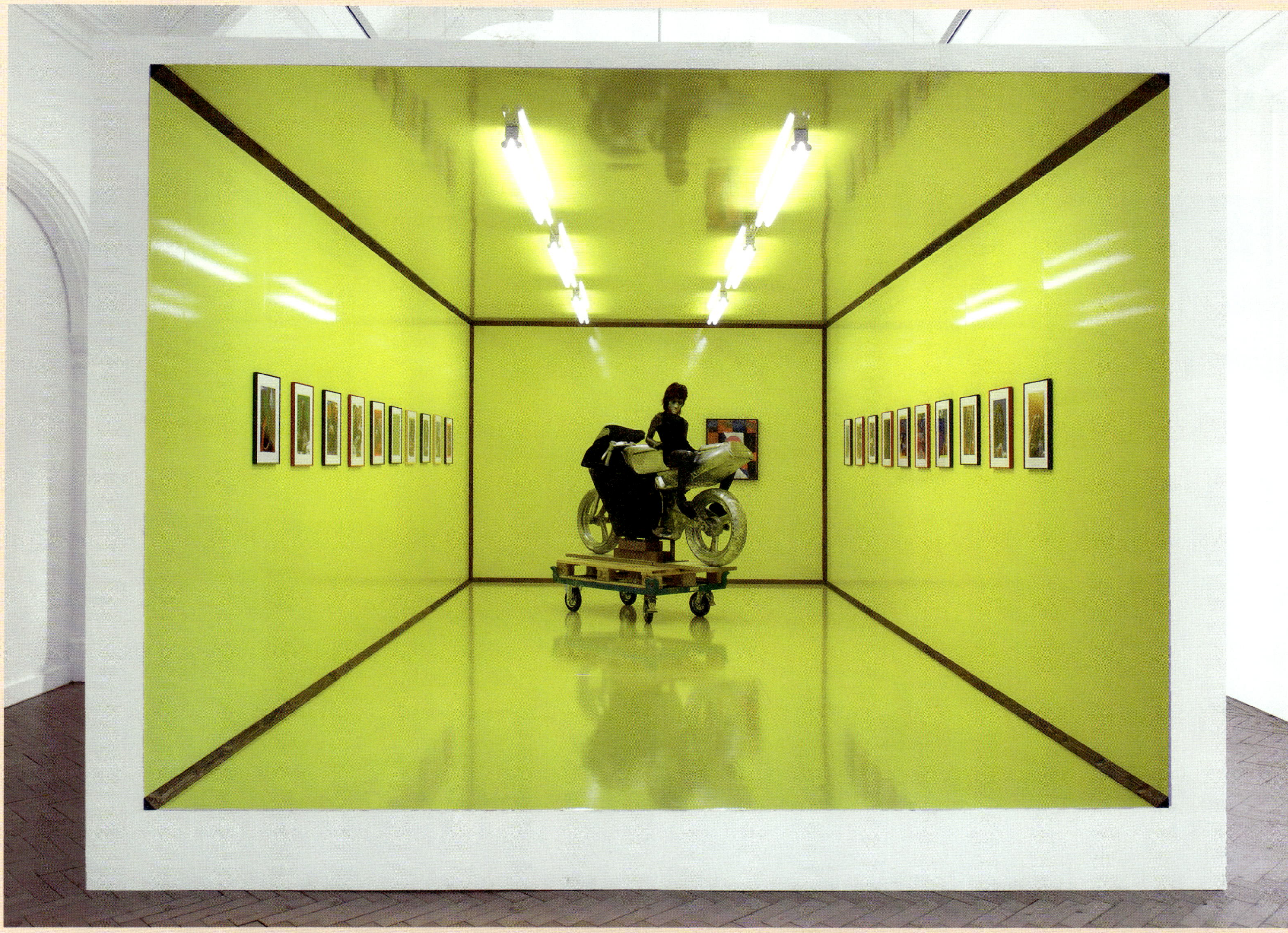

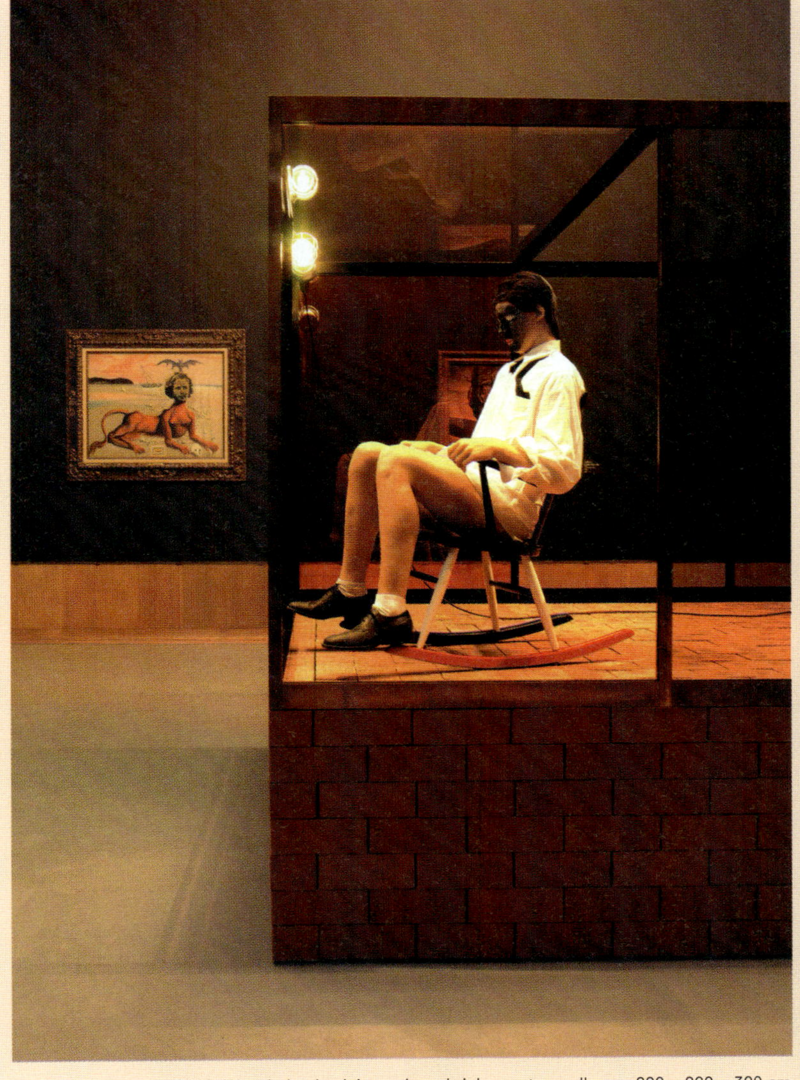

My Bike and your swamp (6 p.m.), 2008. Black polyurethane rubber, wax, aluminium, wood, cloth, artificial hair, 1 painting, 20 collages. Overall 202 × 86 × 186 cm

Tenuous and fragmentary nature of memory

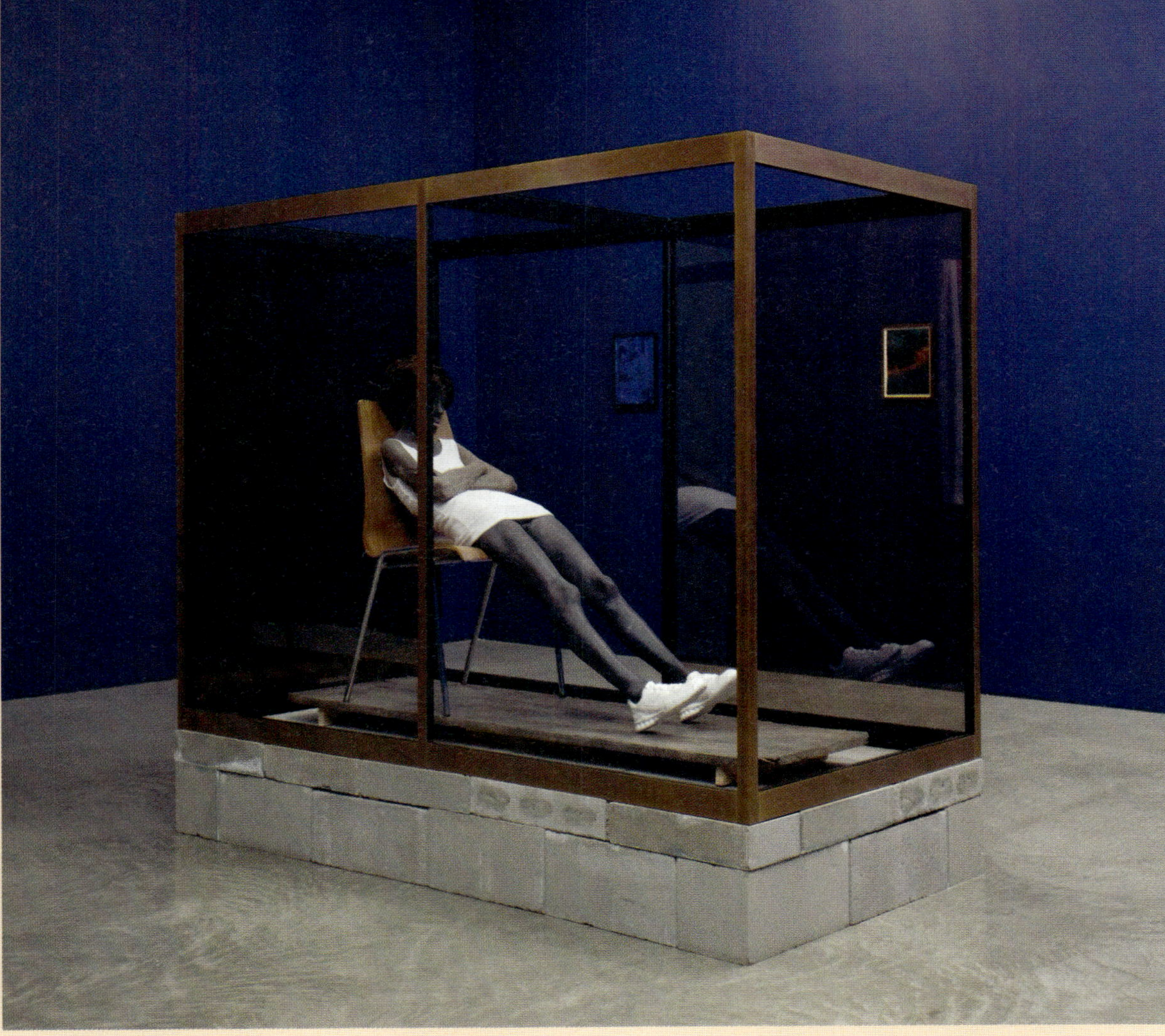

Wait to Wait, Part 1, 2006. Wax, hair, aluminium, glass, bricks, motor, collages. 220 × 200 × 300 cm

God is Dead but Not the Girl, 2008. Wax, hair, aluminium, coloured Plexiglas, brass, bricks. 150 × 203 × 103

Xijing Men

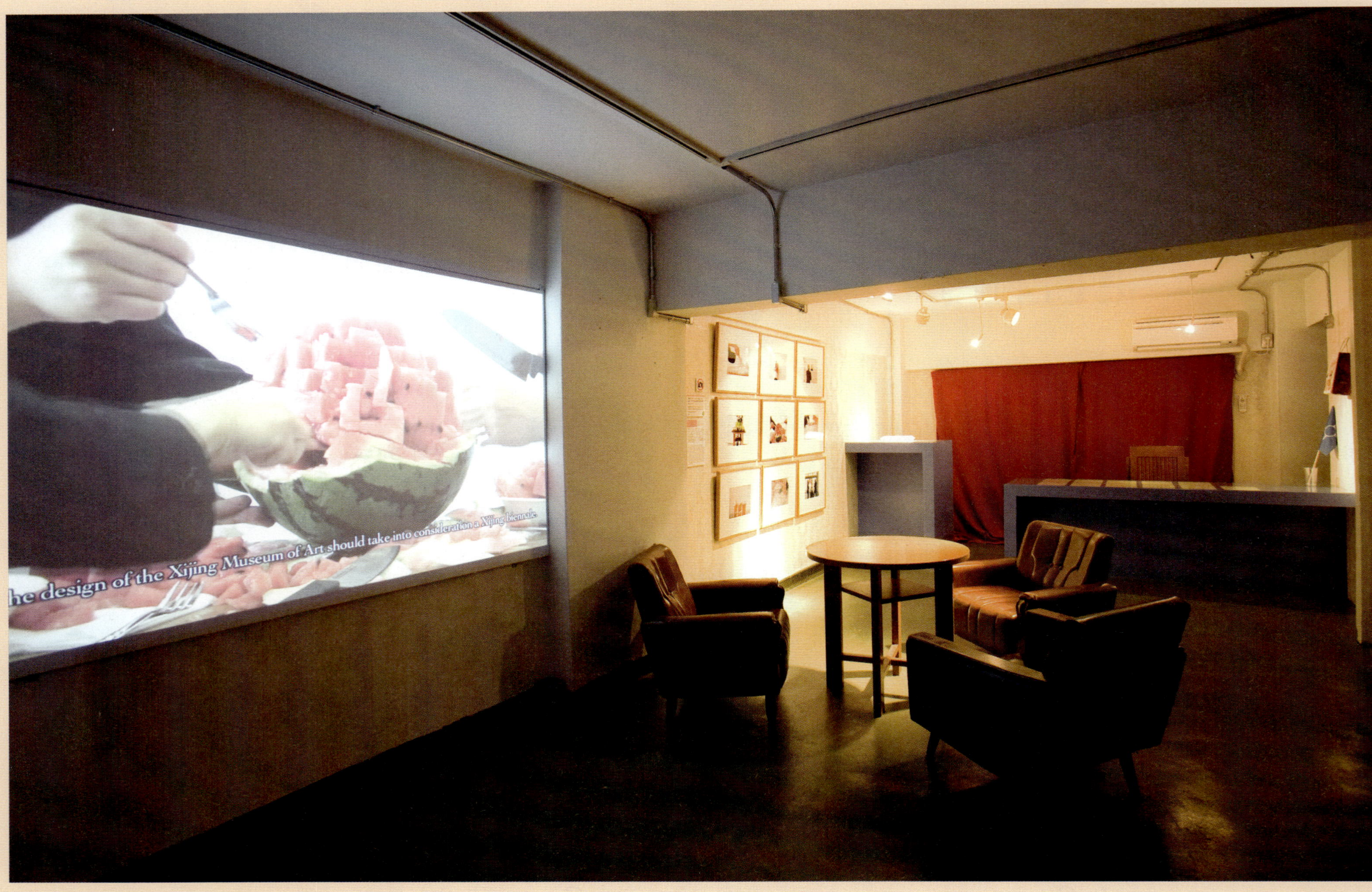

Xijing Project Chapter 4: I love Xijing — Daily Life of Xijing President 2009. Video, 9 photographs, furniture, paper bag, mirror, tissues. Dimensions variable

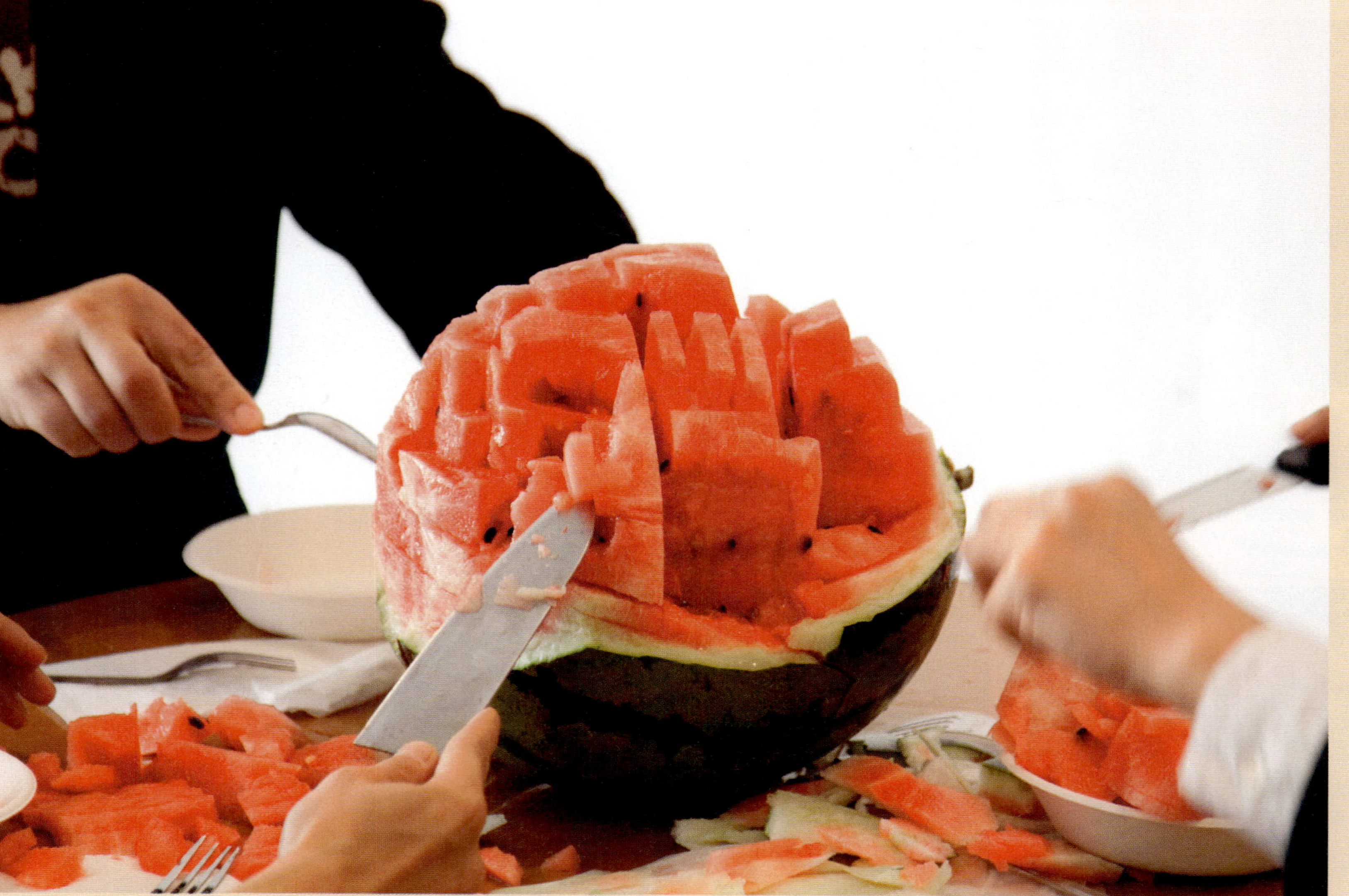

Xijing Project Chapter 4: I love Xijing — Daily Life of Xijing President (detail), 2009. Video, 9 photographs, furniture, paper bag, mirror, tissues. Dimensions variable

The brisk boom in international biennials starting in the second half of the 1990s offered artists in Asia various opportunities to exhibit their work in the global arena. For artists pursuing their practice in their local areas, this new-found mobility led in turn to a host of fresh encounters and networks, as well as a greater comprehension of cultural differences and similarities. Xijing Men, formed in 2007, is an artists' group consisting of Chen Shaoxiong (b. 1962, China), Gimhonsok (b. 1964, Korea) and Tsuyoshi Ozawa (b. 1965, Japan), all of whom boast prolific individual careers. Not only pursuing their unconventional and high-profile practices in their own countries, they are also regulars at international exhibitions and comrades-in-art from Asia, their shared home.

Xijing means 'western capital' and refers to a non-existent, imaginary metropolis, as opposed to the three actual cities of Beijing, whose Chinese characters mean 'northern capital', Nanjing, the 'southern capital', and Tokyo, the 'eastern capital'. Works by Xijing Men challenge concepts and notions of nation and ethnicity,

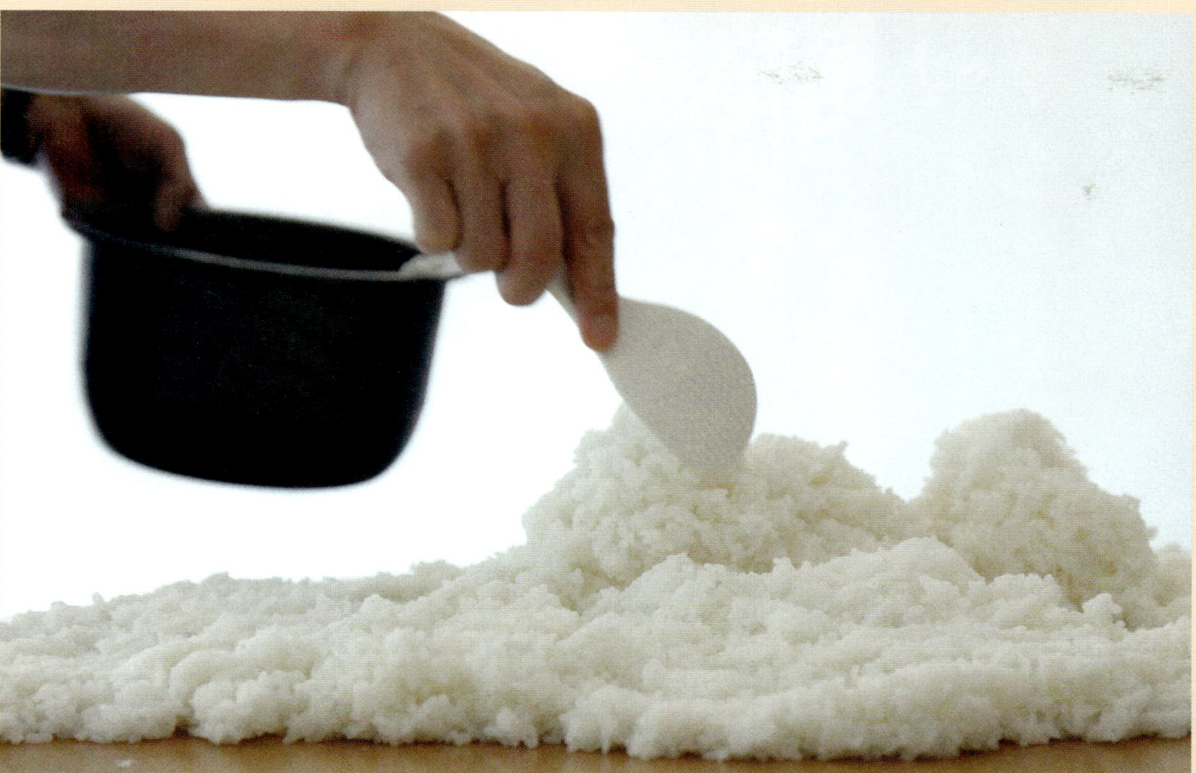

Expand the potential for creativity and communication

highlighting with humour the problems of rigid political frameworks, and exploring possible alternatives, all through the device of this imaginary nation-state.

Sharing a sense of unease about the stereotypical view of ethnicity and region as arbitrary determinants of how people perceive culture and artists, and at a time when the visibility of artists in Asia and platforms for their work are growing, this trio of different nationalities speaking different languages formed a unit to propose a new vision for a nation. By extension they offered a perspective transcending ethnicity, as well as new possibilities for expression, through upbeat collaborations reminiscent of jolly summer-camp activities.

This has resulted in humorous works that simultaneously make serious statements about politics and society. Since the artists speak different native languages, communication among the three consists in large measure of guesswork, but through mutual understanding based on trust, tolerance and common experience — miraculously, and always peacefully — things go forward. Sharing a Dadaesque avant-garde spirit, by interposing their bodies in physical performances Xijing Men refuse to confine their exploration to the abstract, preferring to pose real, life-size questions.

One of their projects, entitled *Xijing Olympics* was staged in 2008 to coincide with the Beijing Olympics. Here, the trio — the only participants — competed in seventeen events that took serious sporting tests and modified them in bizarre and nonsensical ways to create hilarious contests which included 'tickle fencing' and 'watermelon football' to name just two.

Another feature of Xijing Men is their willingness to invite others to join them in the creation of collaborative art spaces; for example, in places to which they have been invited to exhibit, such as Seoul and Liverpool, they gave local puppeteers scenarios to stage. Rather than being paeans to a utopian ideal, such symbiotic projects significantly expand the potential for creativity and communication. These amusing intellectual diversions highlight real problems from multiple perspectives, and open up possible new approaches to these problems through individual art practice.

Xijing Project Chapter 4: I love Xijing — Daily Life of Xijing President (detail), 2009. Video, 9 photographs, furniture, paper bag, mirror, tissues. Dimensions variable

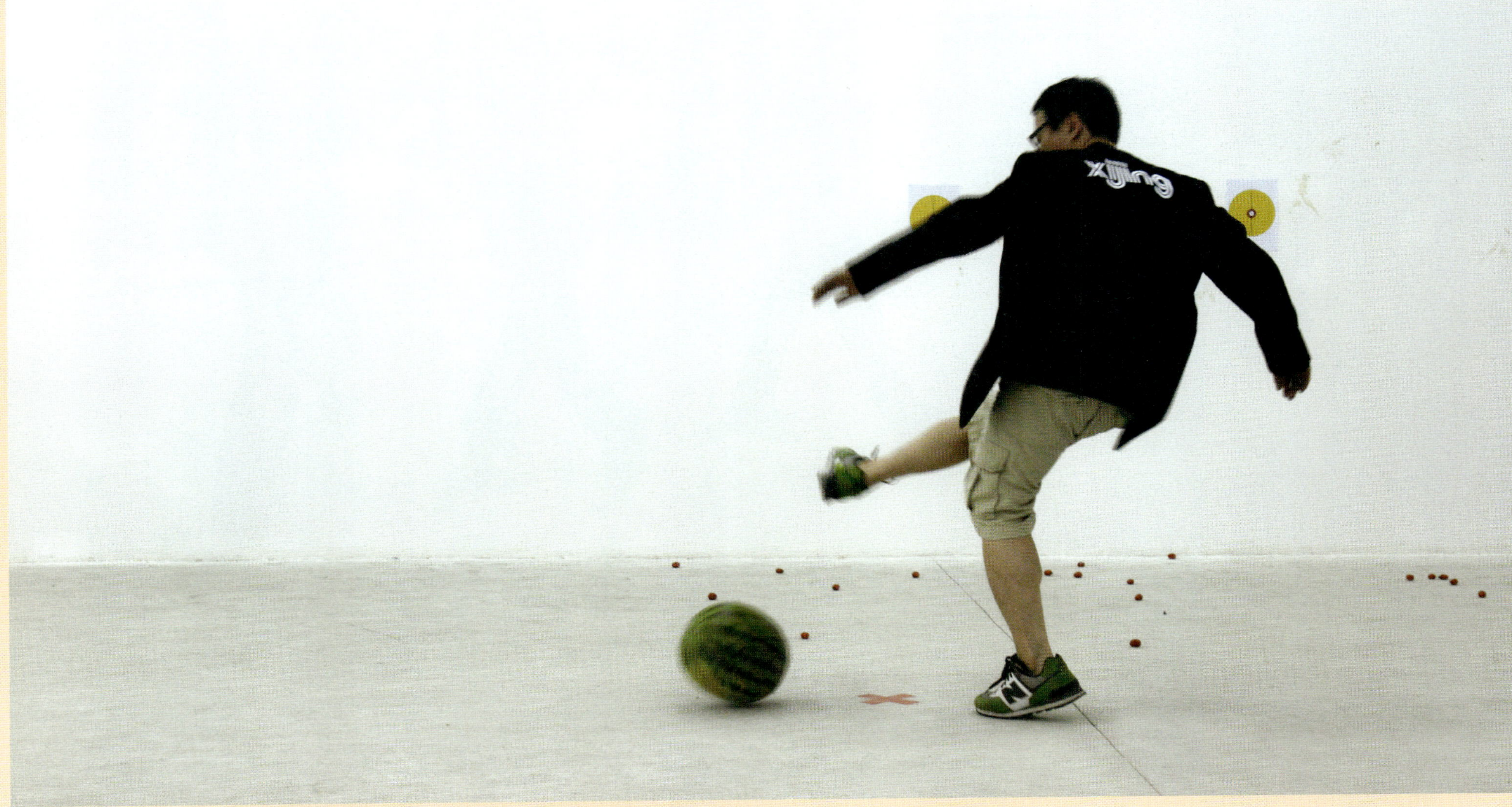

Xijing Project Chapter 3: Welcome to Xijing — Xijing Olympics, 2008. Video, 17 photographs, mixed media including flag, suit, bicycle, boxing gloves, rubbish bin, bread, bat. Dimensions variable

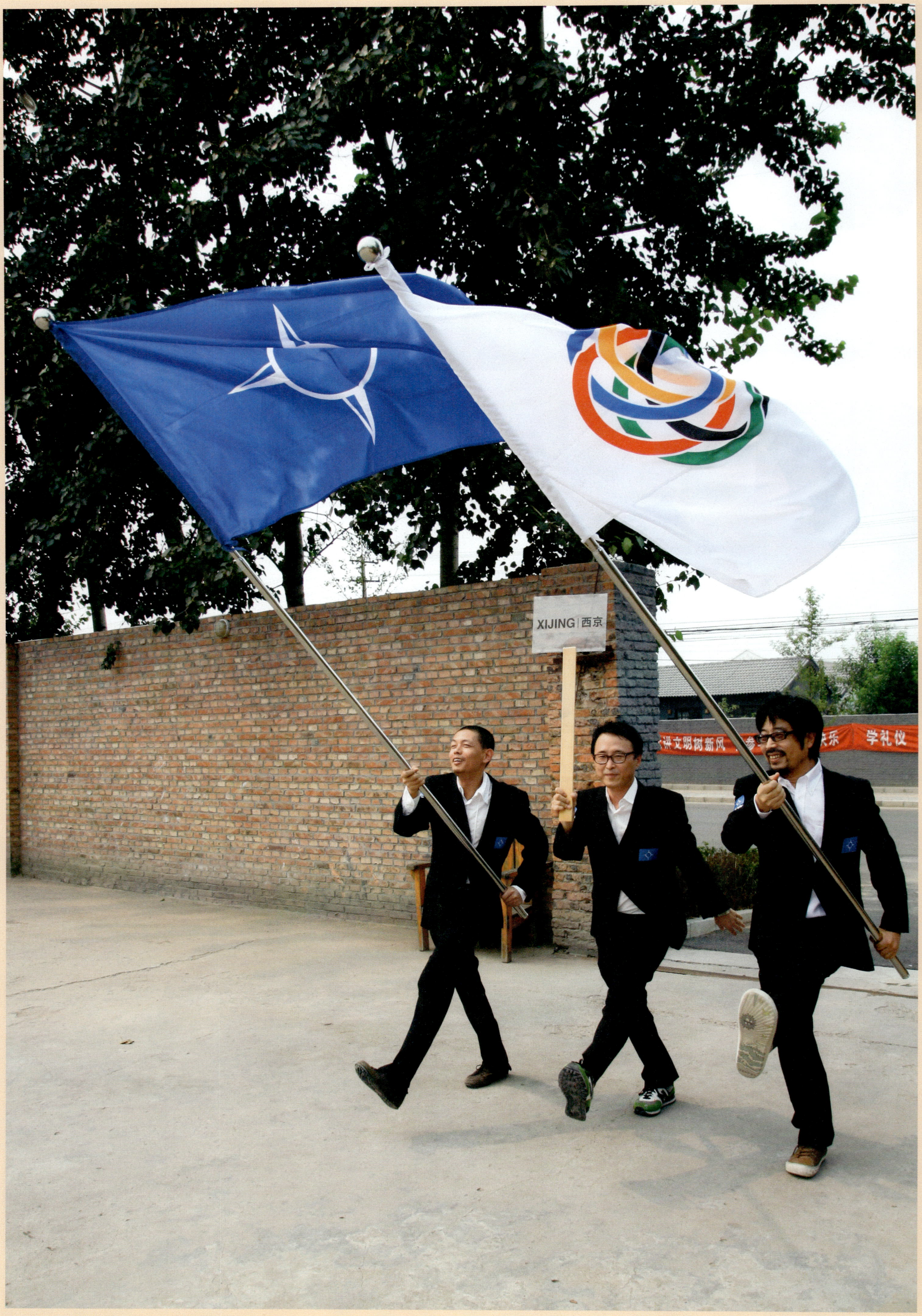

Xijing Project Chapter 3: Welcome to Xijing — Xijing Olympics, 2008. Video, 17 photographs, mixed media including flag, suit, bicycle, boxing gloves, rubbish bin, bread, bat. Dimensions variable

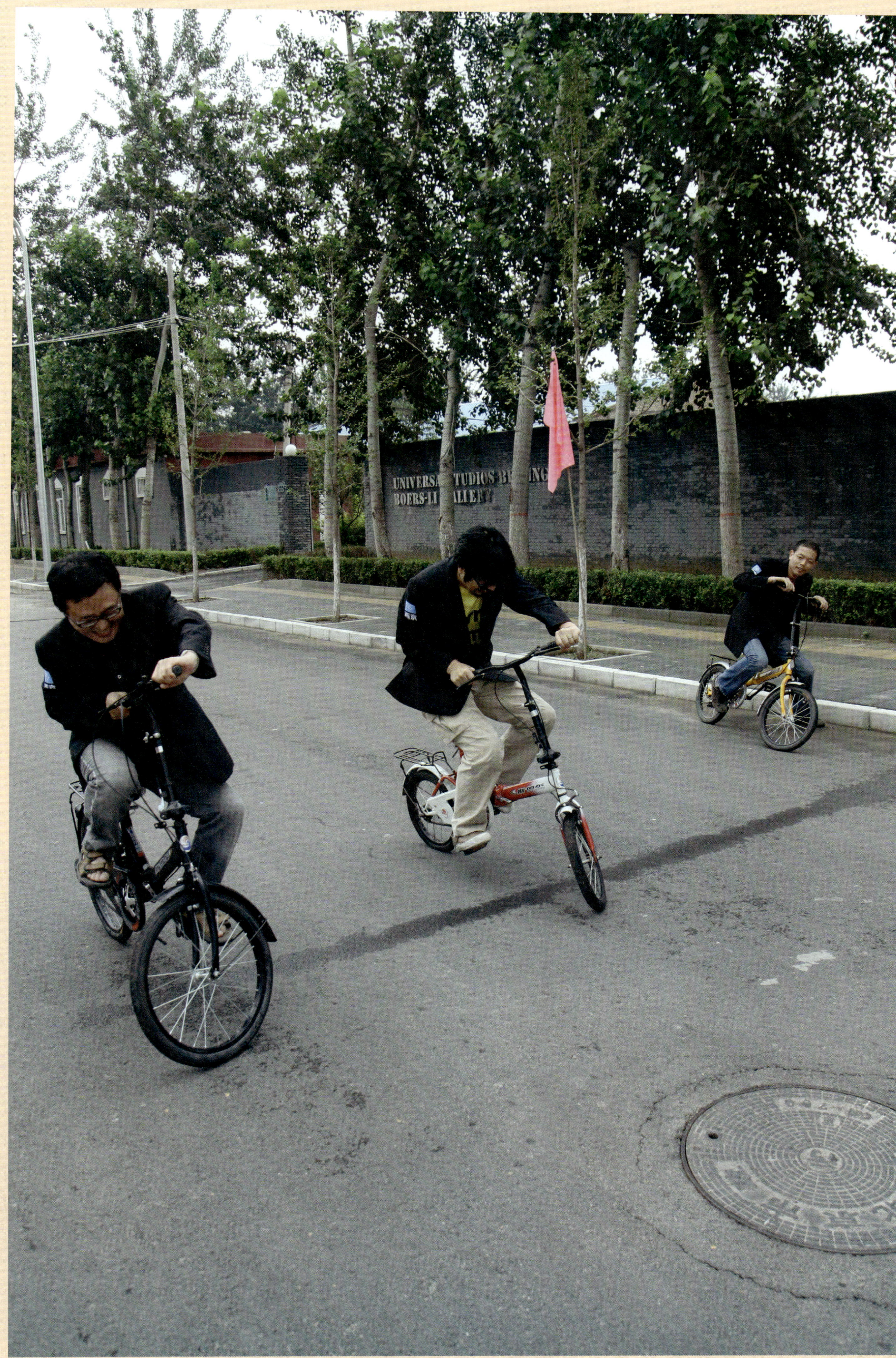

Xijing Project Chapter 3: Welcome to Xijing — Xijing Olympics, 2008. Video, 17 photographs, mixed media including flag, suit, bicycle, boxing gloves, rubbish bin, bread, bat. Dimensions variable

Haegue Yang

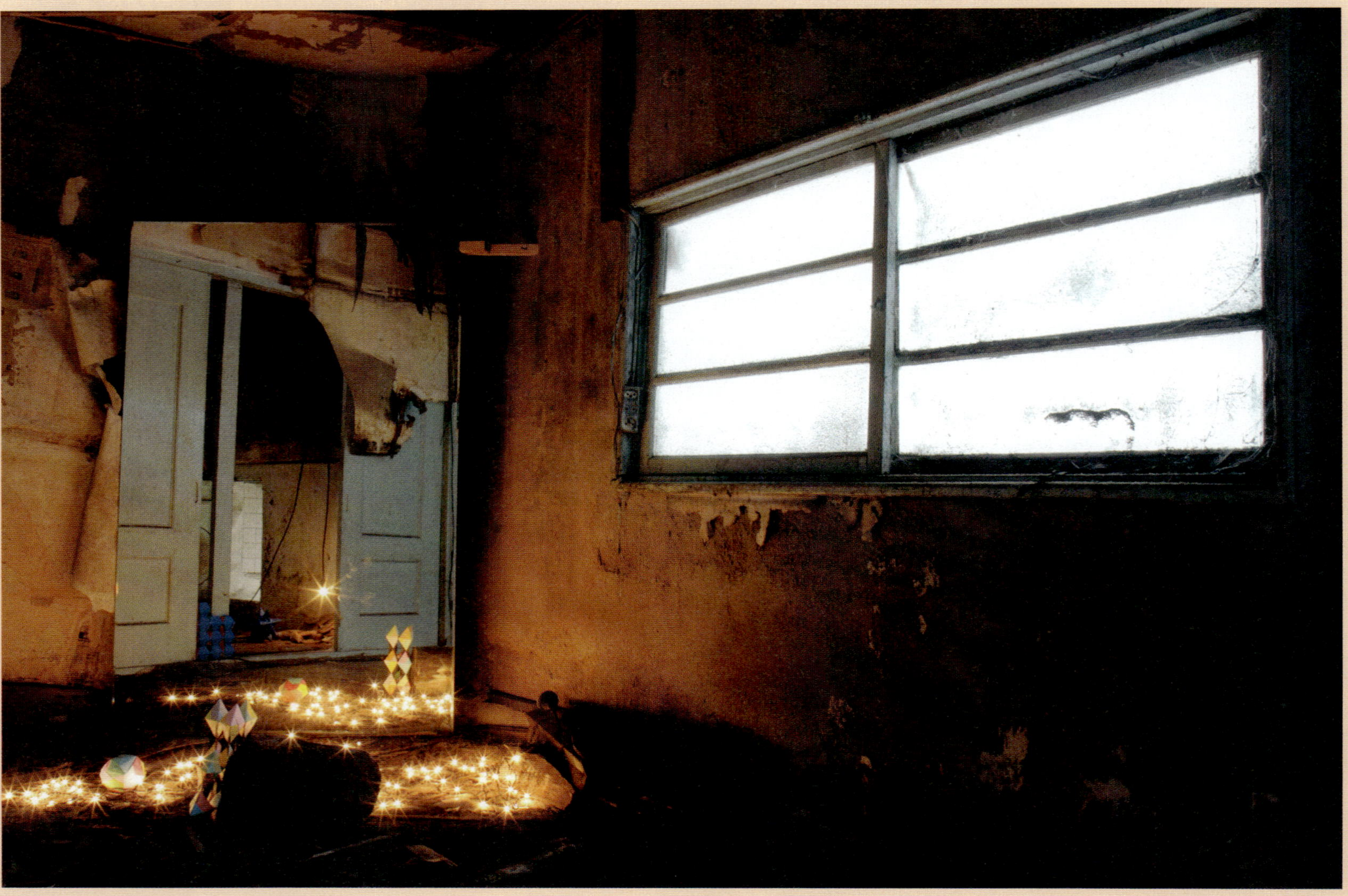

Sadong 30, 2006. Hanging light bulbs, strobe lights, light chain, mirror, origami objects, drying rack wrapped in fabric, fan, viewing terrace, cooler filled with bottles of mineral water, chrysanthemums and garden balsams, wood bench, wall clock, glow–in–the–dark paint, wood piles, spray paint. Dimensions variable

As evidenced by her sculptures and installations, the artist Haegue Yang might be perceived as a choreographer of bodies, objects and space. In these works, she puts on display a precarious provisionality that is as much a metaphor for the fragility of the human condition as it is an apt description of her signature choice of everyday commercially available materials such as Venetian blinds, electric fans and lighting apparatuses.

Living and working in Berlin and Seoul, Yang has emphasized the transitory 'placelessness' of her work. This sensibility was on prominent display in her site-specific installation *Sadong 30* (2006), a hallucinatory and revelatory intervention in an abandoned, decrepit house in an industrial zone of Incheon, South Korea. Invited by the artist to travel to a nondescript sector of this port city, one found that she had colonized this small, crumbling domestic house with strings of lights, geometric origami forms, mirrors and other discrete objects.

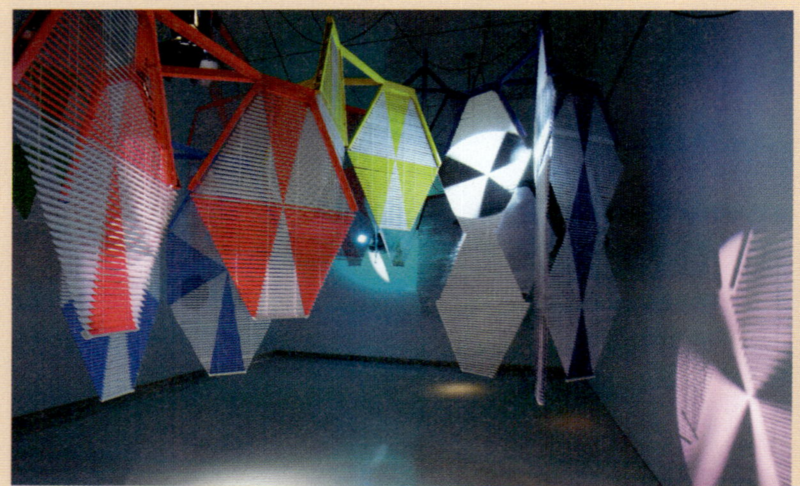

Three Kinds, 2008. Aluminium venetian blinds, moving spotlights, floodlights. Dimensions variable

Provisional and permeable spaces that offer a sense of privacy

Upon entering, one was taken on a voyage in space as well as in time, where the contradiction between the entropy at work in the building's decay and its original function as an inhabited dwelling was held at least temporarily in abeyance by her poetic sculptural interventions. Time stood still in this uninhabited non-place as the phenomenological ghosts of its past were brought into dialogue with the people whom the artist encouraged to visit the site.

It is the body of the viewer that often completes Yang's work and thereby gives it a phenomenological dimension. In her gallery-based installations such as *Three Kinds* (2008), *Yearning Melancholy Red* (2008) and *Series of Vulnerable Arrangements — Voice and Wind* (2009), her installation at the Korean Pavilion for the 53rd Venice Biennale, she makes another kind of architectural intervention altogether. Dividing the rooms that these works inhabit with carefully determined installations of Venetian blinds, Yang creates provisional and porous spaces that offer a sense of privacy as well as the possibility of open communication through the osmotic quality of their alternately monochromatic or multi-hued membranes. When combined with other elements such as robotic

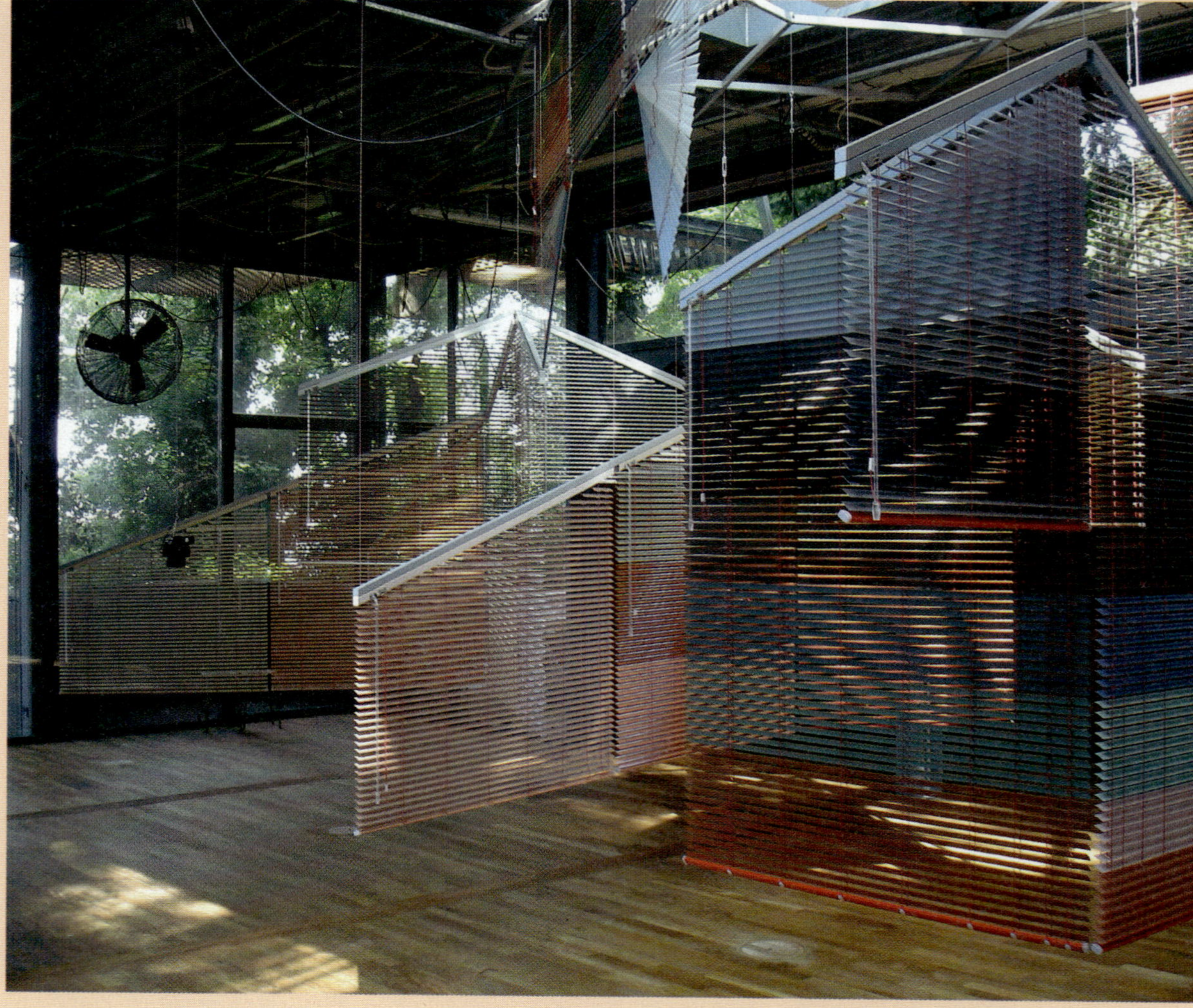

Series of Vulnerable Arrangements — Voice and Wind, 2009. Aluminium Venetian blinds, aluminium frame, industrial electric fan, wind machine, scen emitters (Buddha Temple, Musty, Fresh Cut Grass, Earth, Rainforest, Ocean Mist). Dimensions variable

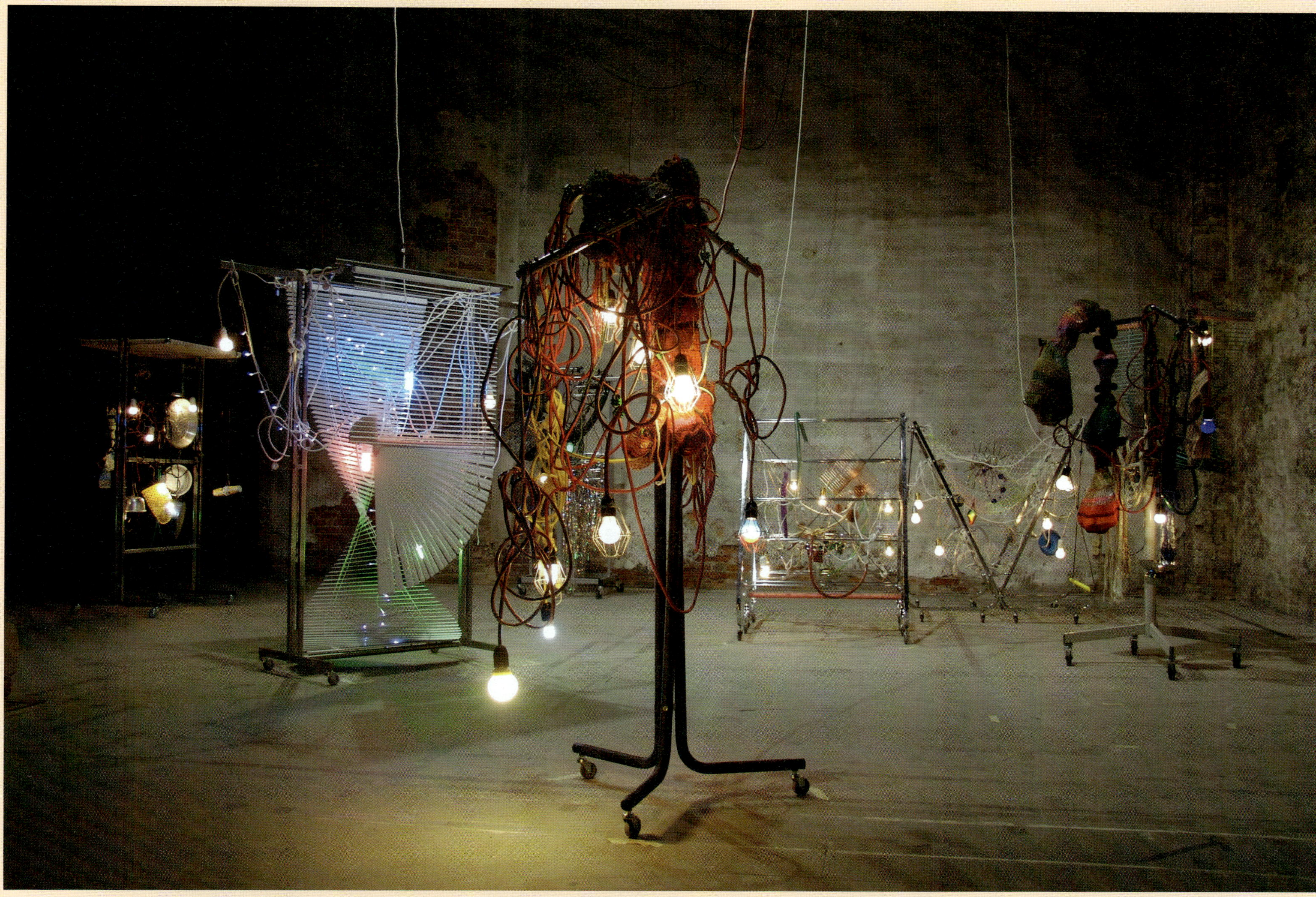

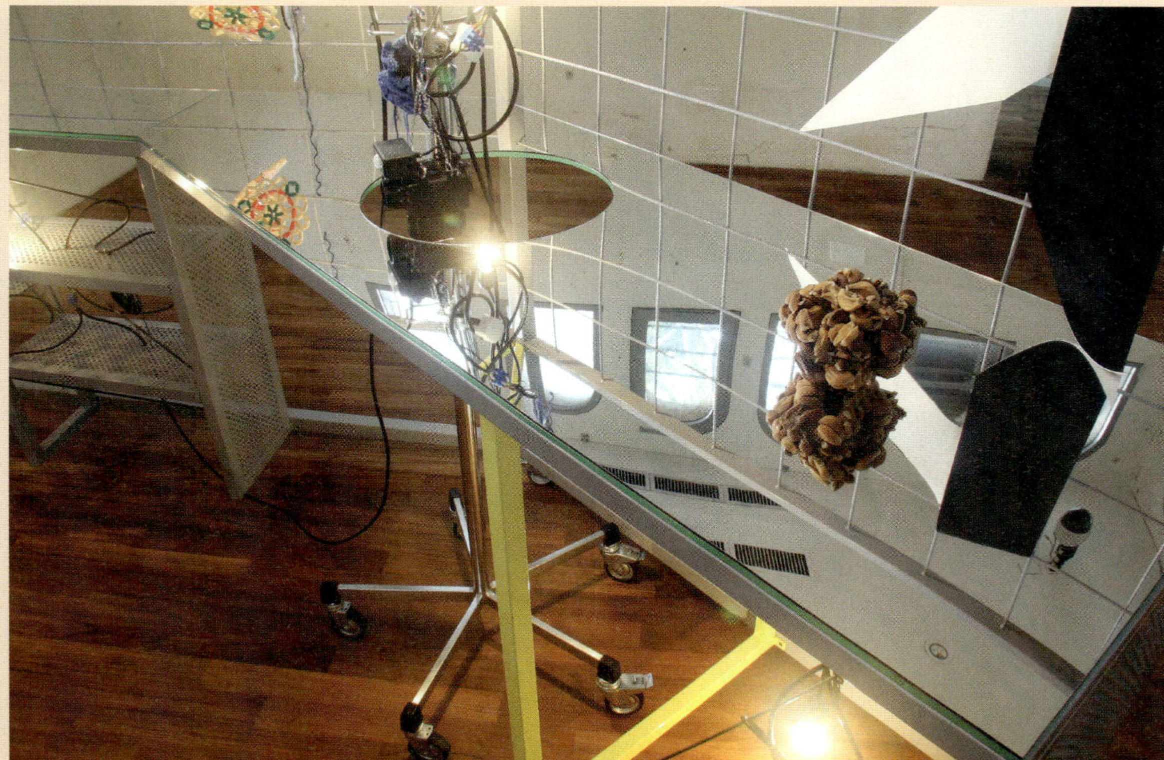

Series of Vulnerable Arrangements — Domestics of Community, 2009. Seven light sculptures. Clothing and shoe racks on casters, light bulbs, cable, knitting yarn, rope, socks, hammock net, aluminium Venetian blinds, stainless–steel strainer, paint grill, fish grill, plastic tube, plastic packages, plastic funnel, tin, buttons, metal ring, metal sponge, silver tinsel, mardi gras trinkets, toy spring, garden supply, seashells. Dimensions variable

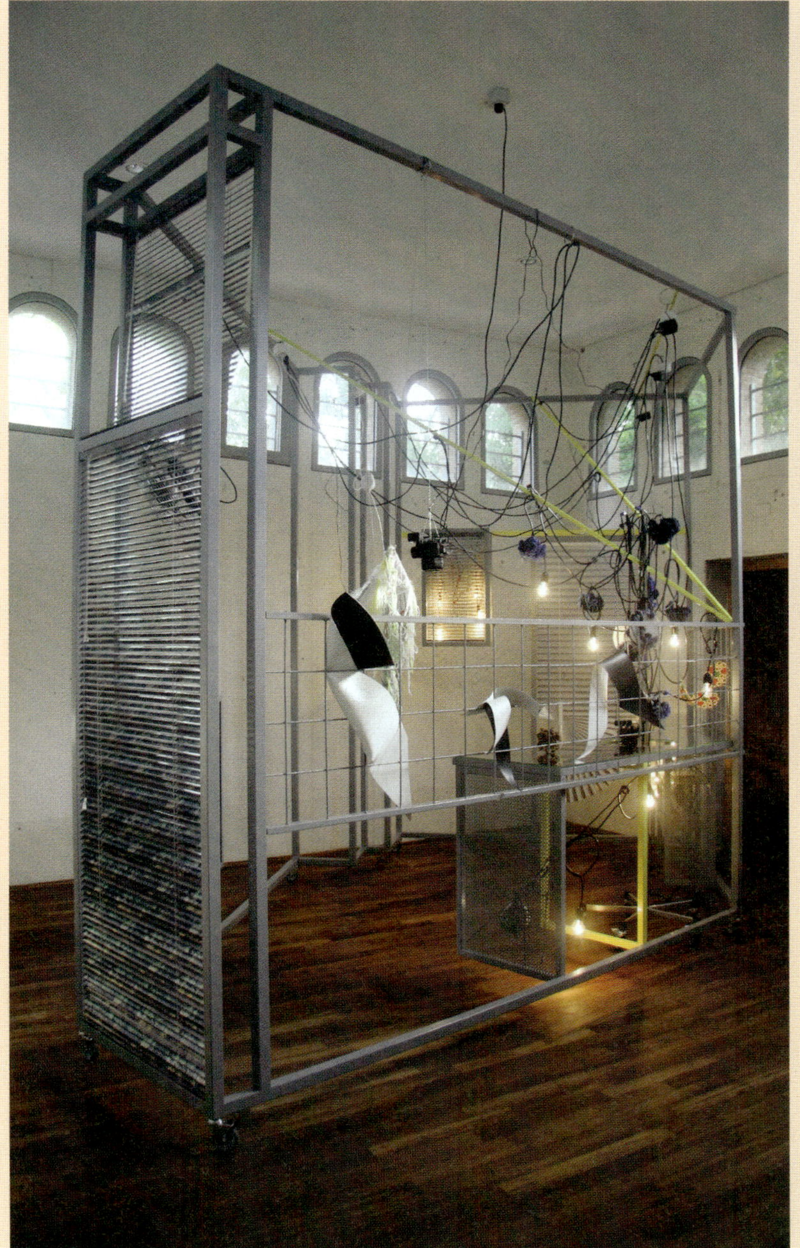

Sallim, 2009. Steel frame, perforated metal plate, casters, aluminium Venetian blinds, knitting yarn, acrylic mirror, IV stand, light bulbs, cable, electric fan, timer, garlic, dishes, hot pad, scent emitters (Curry, Fresh Brewed Coffee, French Bread, Hot Apple Pie, Vomit, Dinosaur Dung). 250 × 420 × 310 cm

theatrical lights, electric fans and metres of hanging electrical cords, they become sculptural constellations that beckon the viewer to inhabit them. The result is a phenomenological choreography of bodies and blinds in which we become dancers in the dark, pulled in by the gravity of Yang's system of objects.

There is a strange kind of existential optimism at play in these works, an abstracted, uniquely human sensibility. In other works, such as her light sculptures *Series of Vulnerable Arrangements — Seven Basel Lights* (2007) and *Temporary Belgrade Lights* (2007), the sculptures themselves take on the character

of portraits of bodies. By hanging strings of multi-coloured lights, origami, tinsel and other objects from a series of rolling medical stands for IV fluids, Yang creates her own surrogate dancers. As in *Sadong* 30, these figures exude a spectral quality in which time stands still, only to be activated by our interaction with them.

10
Sources

Tell Me
Guy de Cointet

The White Album
Joan Didion

1Q84
Haruki Murakami

Film trilogy:
Rapado
Silvia Prieto
Los Guantes Mágicos
Martín Rejtman

Inside the White Cube:
The Ideology of the
Gallery Space
Brian O'Doherty

Six Years:
The Dematerialization
of the Art Object from
1966 to 1972
Lucy Lippard

Flaming Creatures
Jack Smith

Studio of Henryk
Stażewski and Edward
Krasiński, Warsaw

Monkey Island
Mike Kelley

Commissioned Paintings
John Baldessari

Guy de Cointet

Tell Me

(1979)

Guy de Cointet (1934–83) was a French artist based in Los Angeles. His plays and printmaking projects — texts broken down into their visual components — are defined by his particular interest in language. He was keenly aware of the imprecision of language, and intrigued by our ability to glean meaning quickly from ambiguous uses of words, open to many interpretations. His plays — of which he wrote around twenty — are an attempt to transform the language experience into a visual one through establishing a precise relationship between the props, the elements that constitute the stage, the actors and the language they use. In this way, he shows the irremediable figurativeness of human language: that seeing and reading are two interchangeable activities. Words become images in the same way that objects and actors become words. The endless availability of the system of language and its many permutations of condensation and displacement lie at the core of his image-word theatre. The viewer witnesses a curious spectacle that consists of the evanescence and dilution of meaning which shifts towards a gestural automatism.

Cointet summarised the plot of his play Tell Me (1979) as follows: 'Northern California, October 1979. It's late afternoon at Mary's. Her house is situated on the bank of the Sacramento River, in that stretch of the river which is as beautiful as the Danube between Yvvs and Melk, east of Vienna. A few miles away is the town of Courtland, a Chinese settlement for many years, where the famous Dr. Sun Yat Sen lived for a time in exile. After her day's work, Mary is home planning to spend the evening with some of her best friends: Michael, Olive and, hopefully, the elusive Mark.'

The way these young women behave, talking and listening

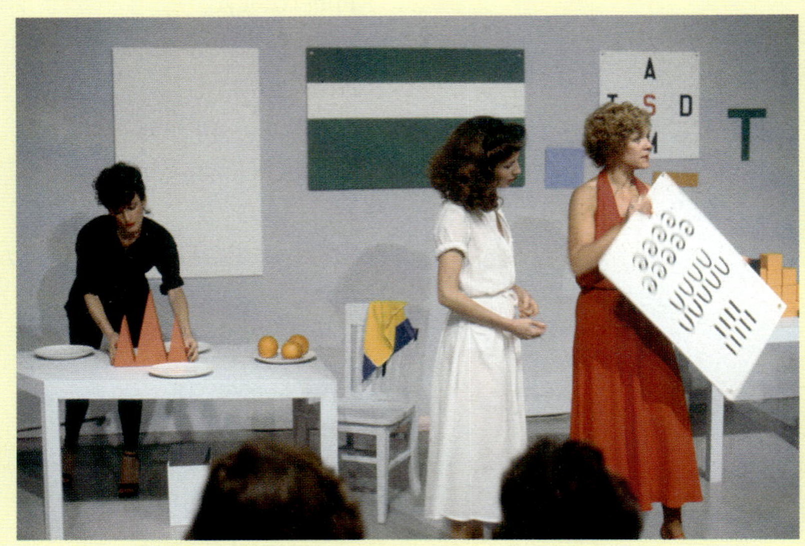

1

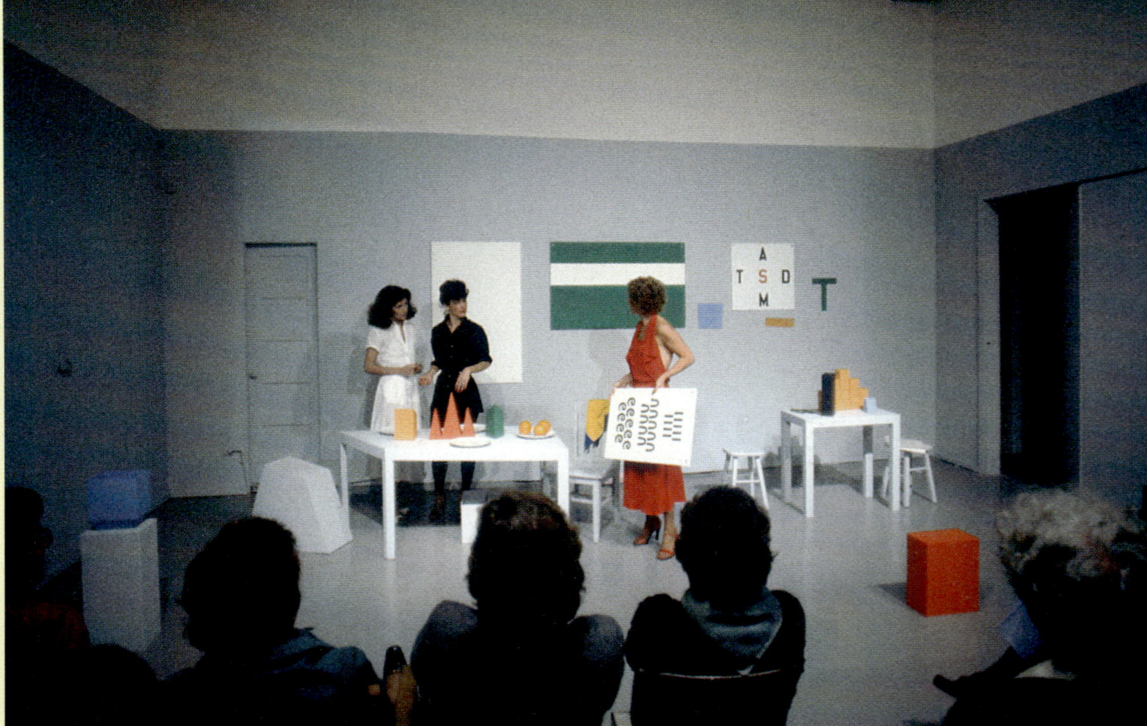

2

1, 2 & **3** — Guy de Cointet
Tell Me, 1979. Performance view.
Rosamund Felsen Gallery,
Los Angeles, 1979. Performers:
Denise Domergue, Helen Mendez
Berlant, Jane Zingale

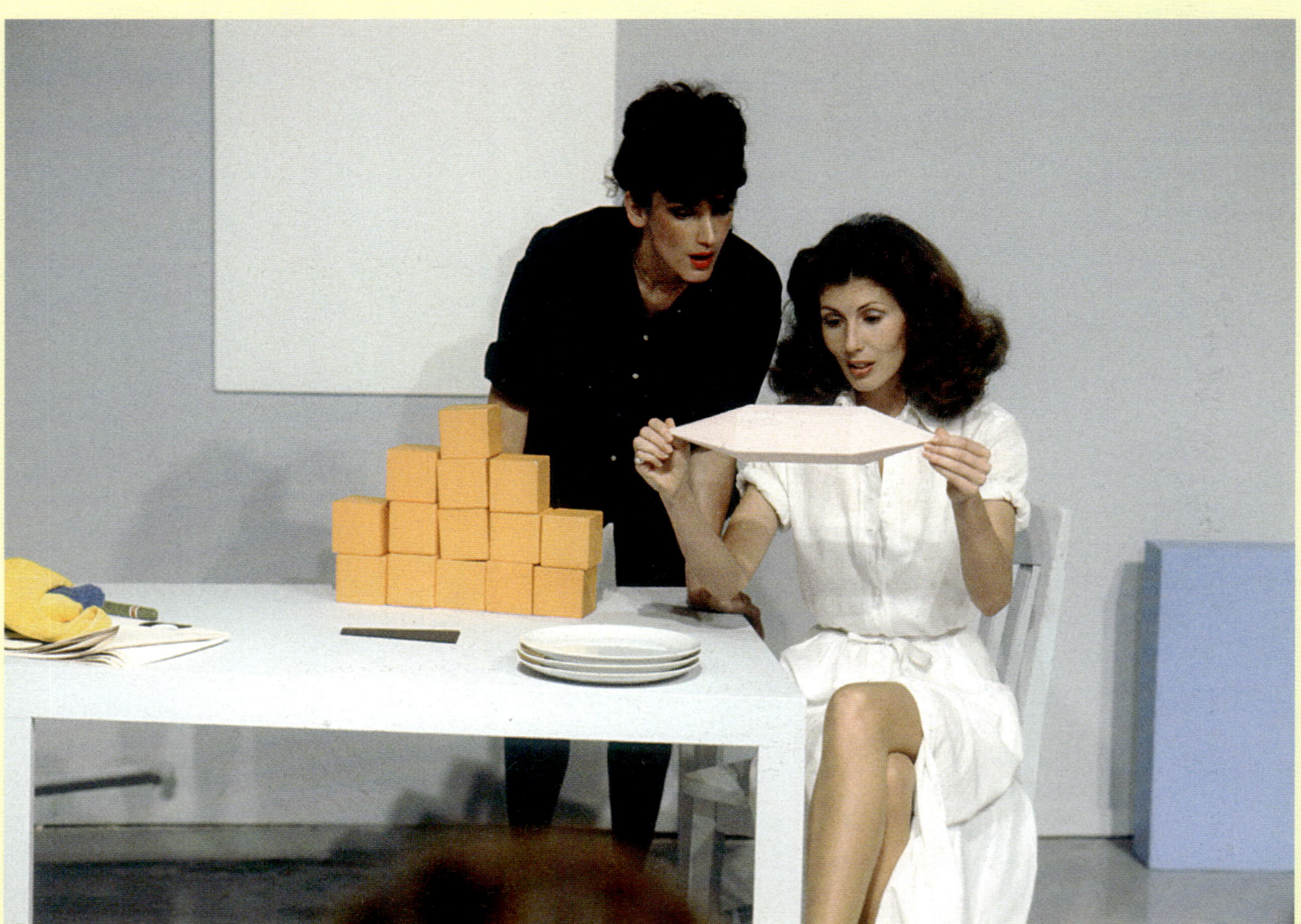

3

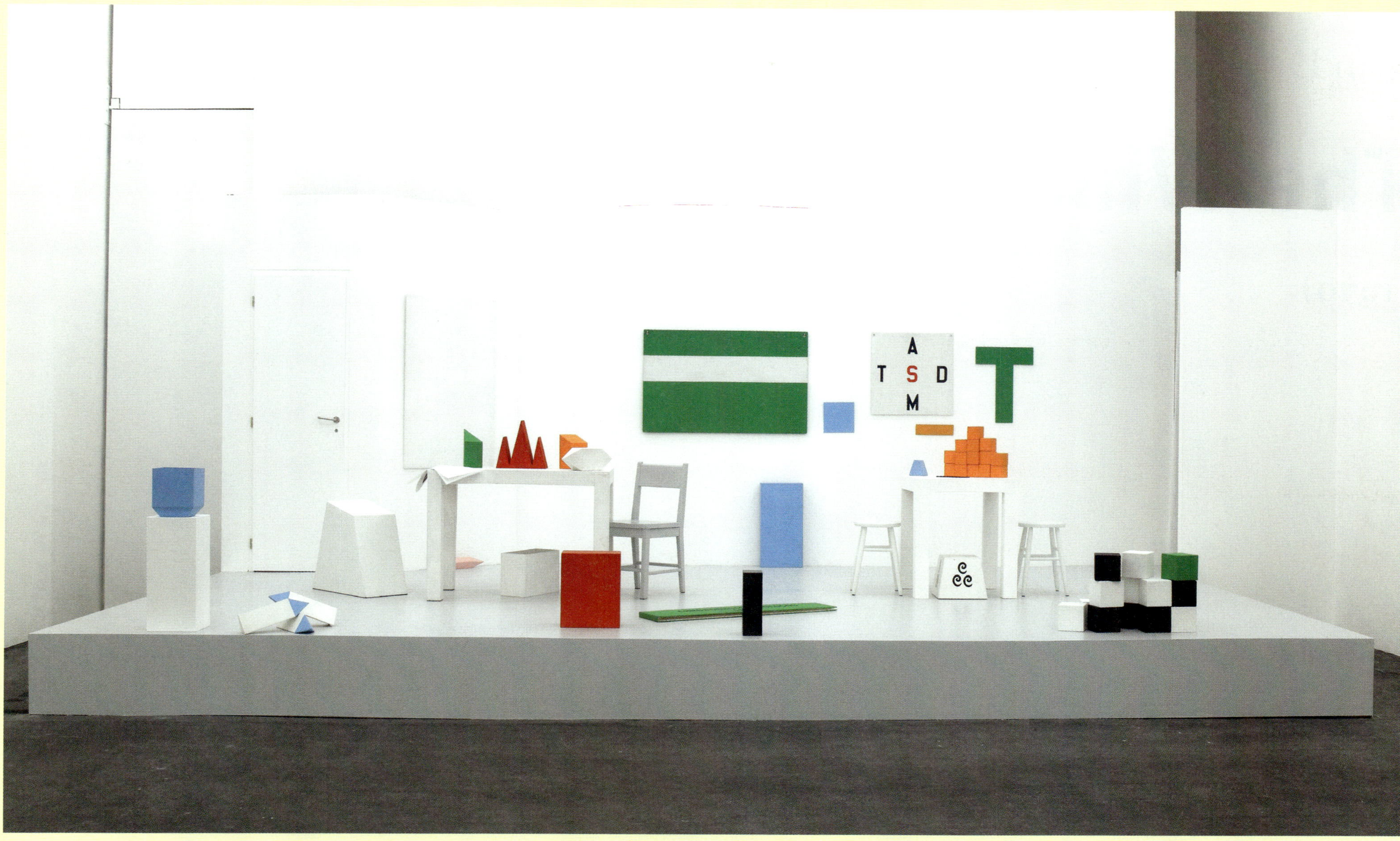

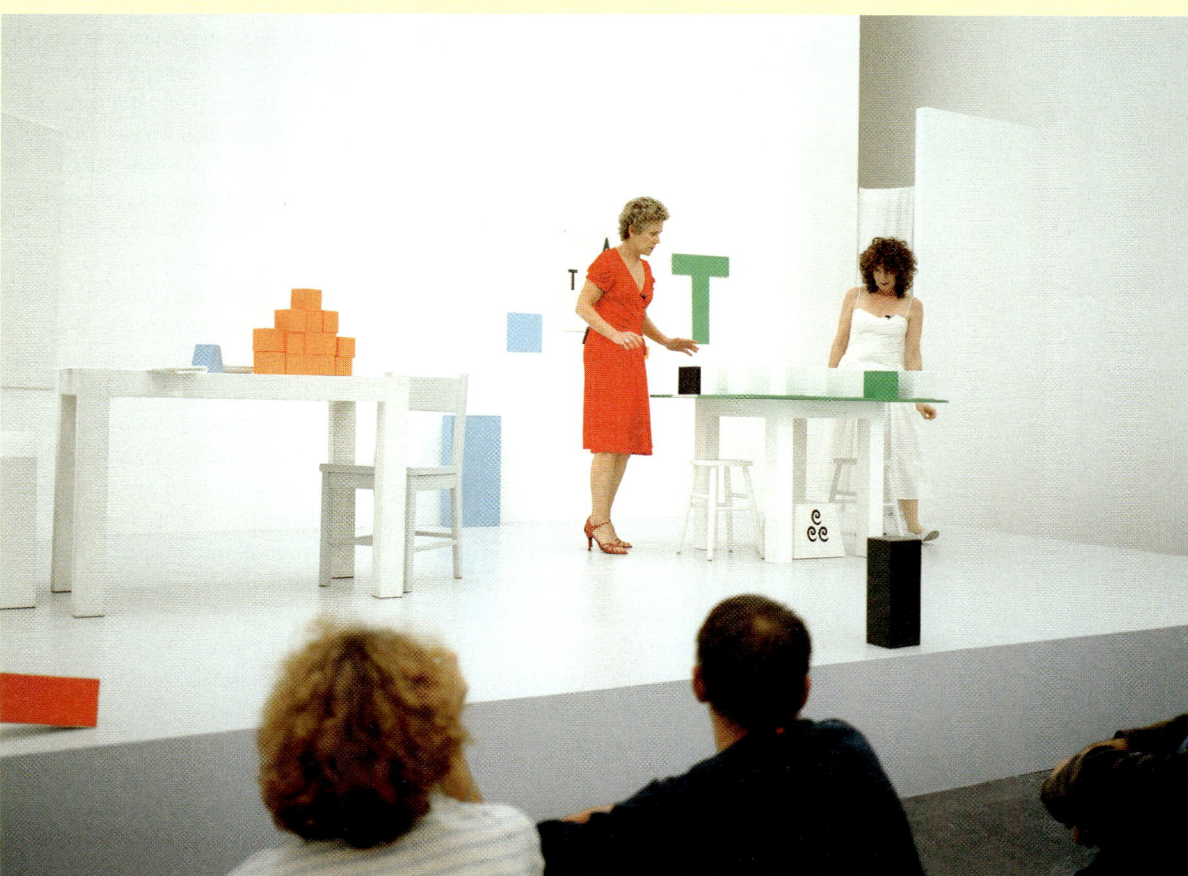

4

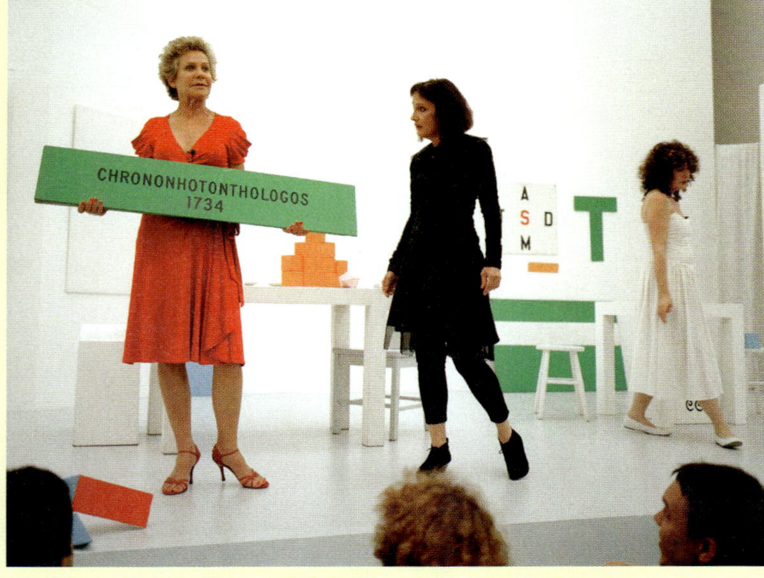

6

5

4 — Guy de Cointet
Tell Me, 1979. Set. Acrylic on wood and
cardboard, various objects. Dimensions
variable. Collection Musée National d'Art
Moderne, Centre Pompidou, Paris

5 & 6 — Guy de Cointet
Tell Me, 1979. Performance view, Centre
Régional d'Art Contemporain Languedoc-
Roussillon, Sète, France, 17 November
2006. Performers: Denise Domergue, Helen
Mendez Berlant, Jane Zingale. Director:
Bob Wilhite

to each other, how they see and
perceive their surroundings interests
me. One of these days, I believe,
I'm going to drive up North and pay
a visit to Mary. '

As the play unfolds, the three
women, speaking in a conversational
language that directly references
soap operas, engage with the
brightly coloured abstract forms
and furniture that comprise the set.
As they misuse and misname
objects, the process of naming and
recognition is subverted; the
abstracted forms become blank
decoys with uses that mutate within
the dialogue of the play. This trait is
fundamental to understanding

Cointet's work, his aversion to allegory,
symbolism or any literary form of
concealing meaning, and his creation
of scenarios where the emphasis
on surface and space expresses his
understanding of meaning as
something irredeemably elusive.

Tell Me was first staged at
the Rosamund Felson Gallery in
Los Angeles and has since been recreated twice (Tate Modern,
London, 2006; Centre Régional d'Art
Contemporain Languedoc-
Roussillon, Sète, France, 2006). For
these re-stagings the original
actresses (Denise Domergue, Jane
Zingale and Helen Mendez Berlant)
performed the play, more than twenty

years after its inception. What
is striking about these re-creations
is how contemporary the work
still seems, as well as Cointet's clear
influence on other Los Angeles-
based artists, such as Mike Kelley,
Allen Ruppersberg, Larry Bell, Eric
Orr and Paul McCarthy.

Cointet's plays go beyond
any form of visual poetry, refusing
to engage in logical discourse
or analytical commentary in
a similar manner to concrete poetry.
Exploring the way in which the
social sphere determines our
personal emotions, feelings and
moods, his work is ultimately about
performing the imagination.

Joan Didion

The White Album

(1979)

Joan Didion
The White Album, 1979.
Simon & Shuster, New York
222 pages

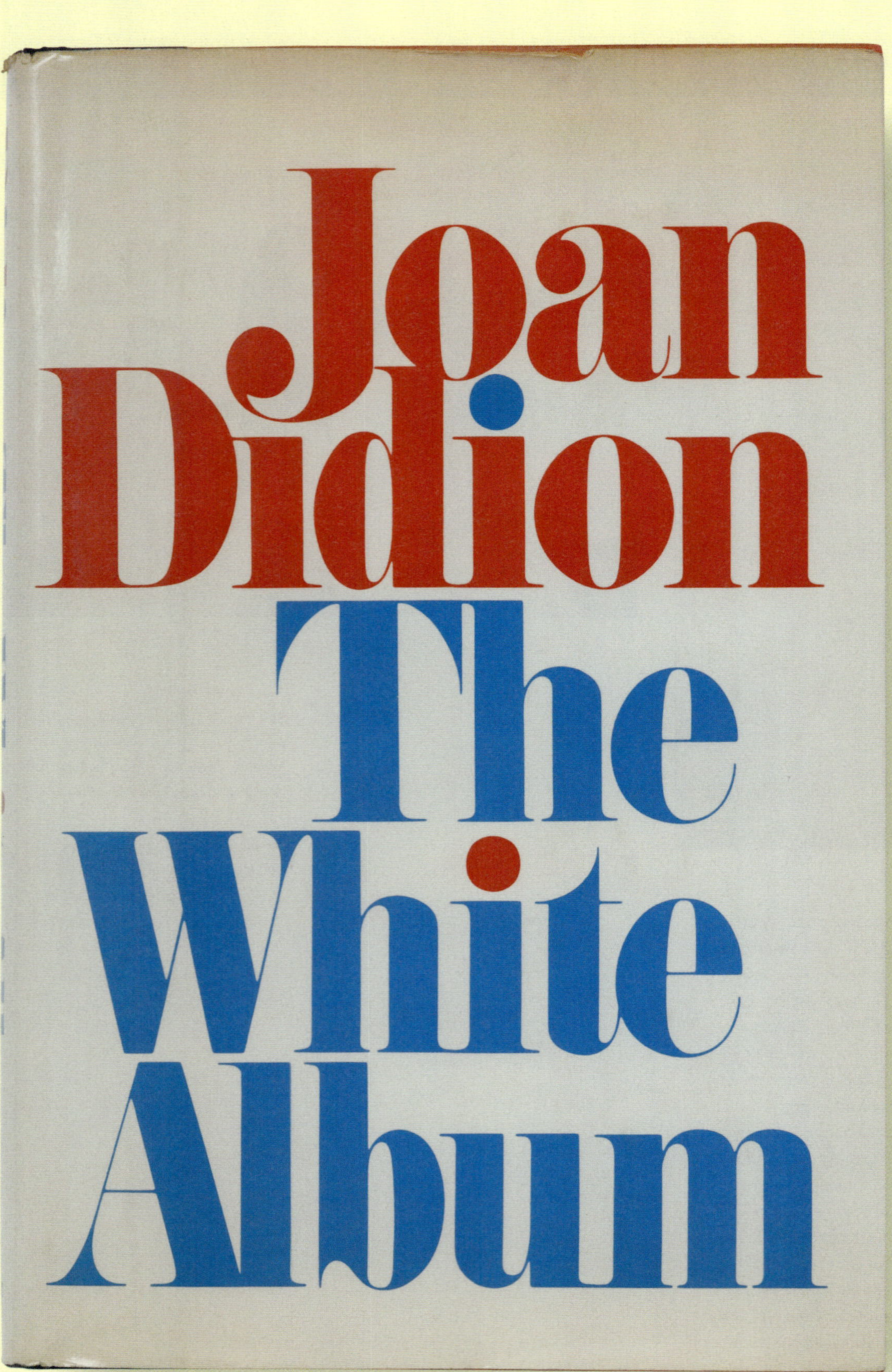

'Driving a Budget Rent-A-Car between Sacramento and San Francisco one rainy morning in November of 1968 I kept the radio on very loud. On this occasion I kept the radio on very loud not to find out what time it was but in an effort to erase six words from my mind, six words which had no significance for me but which seemed that year to signal the onset of anxiety or fright. The words, a line from Ezra Pound's "In a Station of the Metro", were these: Petals on a wet black bough. The radio played "Wichita Lineman" and "I Heard it on the Grapevine". Petals on a wet black bough. Somewhere between the Yolo Causeway and Vallejo it also occurred to me that the fright on this particular morning was going to present itself as an inability to drive the Budget Rent-A-Car across the Carquinas Bridge. The Wichita Lineman was still on the job. 'I closed my eyes and drove across the Carquinas Bridge, because I had appointments, because I was working, because I had promised to watch the revolution being made at San Francisco State College and because there was no place in Vallejo to turn in a Budget Rent-A-Car and because nothing on my mind was in the script as I remembered it'.

Begun in 1968 and written over a period of ten years, Joan Didion's epoch-defining essay 'The White Album' narrates Didion's personal meditation on the unravelling of the 1960s in an attempt to make sense of the world that she inhabited. In this lead essay of her collection of the same name, Didion takes us down a psycho-cultural rabbit hole on a kaleidoscopic journey from the Hollywood music studio where The Doors recorded their nihilistic odes to Eros and Thanatos, to interviews with Black Panther Party leaders Huey Newton and Eldridge Cleaver [in] Oakland, and finally to the death of the 1960s, as embodied in the August 1969 Manson murders in the Hollywood Hills. Shifting between bouts of paranoia and moments of utter clarity, Didion was experiencing personally and professionally the cultural aftershocks of some epistemic seismic event whose contours were impossible to make out clearly. 'We tell ourselves stories in order to live,' she begins. She then goes on to document poetically the fracturing of those stories as well as her own psyche, while qualifying that opening mantra by stating that 'nothing on my mind was in the script as I remembered it'. Didion bore witness to the crumbling of an edifice that defined an era and bode nothing but uncertainty.

The script that is our historical narrative always seems to shift under our feet. Didion understood this on a personal and a meta-historical level. It is her clarity about the inherently unstable mechanics of history that makes this essay as relevant now as the day on which it was written. If we fast-forward some forty years, we also find ourselves driving across a metaphorical bridge into an uncertain future laced with unspeakable anxiety. Strangely enough, 9/11 now seems almost unbelievably far away, as do the twin disasters of Abu Ghraib and Hurricane Katrina. We are currently entering the hangover of the Bush years, where the decline of empire is obscured by the historical white noise that seems to be leaking out of our television screens. How do we negotiate this metaphorical drive across Didion's bridge into a disquieting landscape? Didion's answer: 'We tell ourselves stories in order to live.' Isn't that what art is all about?

Haruki Murakami

1Q84

(2009)

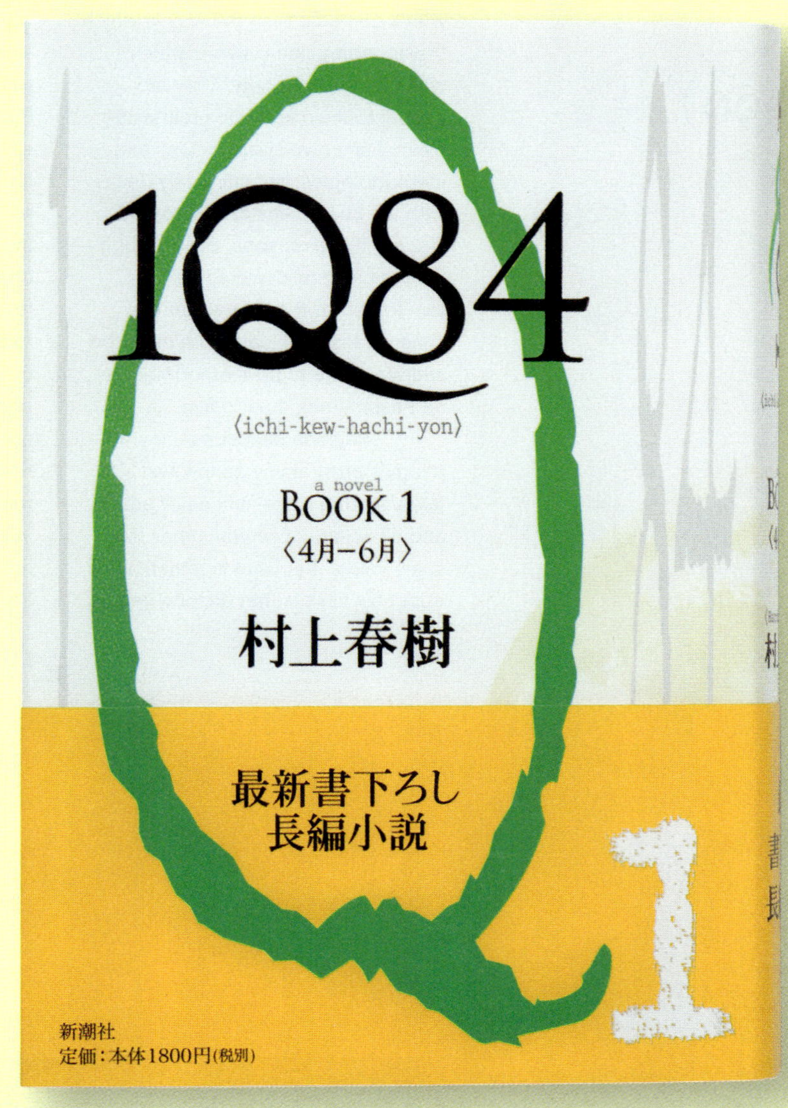

Haruki Murakami
IQ84, 2009. Book 1
Shinchosha Publishers, Tokyo
554 pages

IQ84, 2009. Book 2
Shinchosha Publishers, Tokyo
501 pages

Defying the chilly winds of recession, Haruki Murakami's latest novel 1Q84 (pronounced ichi-kew-hachi-yon, Japanese for 1984) is selling like hotcakes. Although not even six months have passed since the book's release, Korean and Chinese translations are already on shelves.

As the title suggests, inspiration for Murakami's work came from George Orwell's novel, penned a year before his death in 1949 and set in the near future. The dystopian world of 1984 is Orwell's satirical vision of a sterile imaginary future stripped of all humanity, a metaphor for Stalin's Russia. Sixty years on, Murakami's 1Q84 takes the opposite tack, reflecting on memories of an imaginary past and unearthing the seeds of a nightmarish and violent historical truth.

The story is rendered in Murakami's signature style, the playing out in turn of two apparently unrelated narratives, a warp and weft that gradually interweave. A female sports instructor with the alter ego of a professional killer, and a prep-school maths tutor who aspires to be a writer: these two individuals leading solitary lives in different worlds become enmeshed in a incident caused by a mysterious organization, and step into an alternative reality, a mysterious imaginary past in a world with two moons.

Underpinning the novel — which strives to eliminate the boundary between reality and fiction — are the themes of religion and terrorism, the fanatical zeal of human beings and their destructive impulses. Taking as his model Japan's Aum Shinrikyo cult, which carried out indiscriminate poison-gas attacks on the Tokyo underground in 1995, he pens a tale reflecting the uncertainties of our age which moves through 9/11, the Iraq War, global warming and environmental destruction, the economic meltdown and other world events over the past decade.

The realm of Murakami's novels — a worldview coloured by political disillusionment, the stagnation and frustrations of a mature capitalist society, and cosmopolitan cultural transgressiveness — inspires and resonates with artists who project the present through the different medium of visual art. Some critics have identified the sense of déjà vu pervading Murakami's works as emerging from his innumerable literary antecedents, and this approach coincides with the techniques of today's artists, who reference countless forms of expression in every possible permutation of their work.

Twenty years have passed since Murakami was introduced to the world with the publication in English of his third novel A Wild Sheep Chase in 1989. His books are now available in almost forty languages. He also translates American literature by the likes of F. Scott Fitzgerald, Raymond Carver and Raymond Chandler into Japanese, and contributes essays to publications such as the New Yorker. He has an encyclopedic knowledge of music, having run a jazz café before embarking seriously on his writing career, and he frequently deals with Hollywood films in his work. This vocabulary of popular culture makes him a poster child for urban culture in a global age. Writing in his native Japanese, however, he remains a surprisingly local figure, who describes his native culture from an objective viewpoint. Thus Murakami is a pioneering model of an artist who, in a late-capitalist world, approaches the global and the local on equal terms.

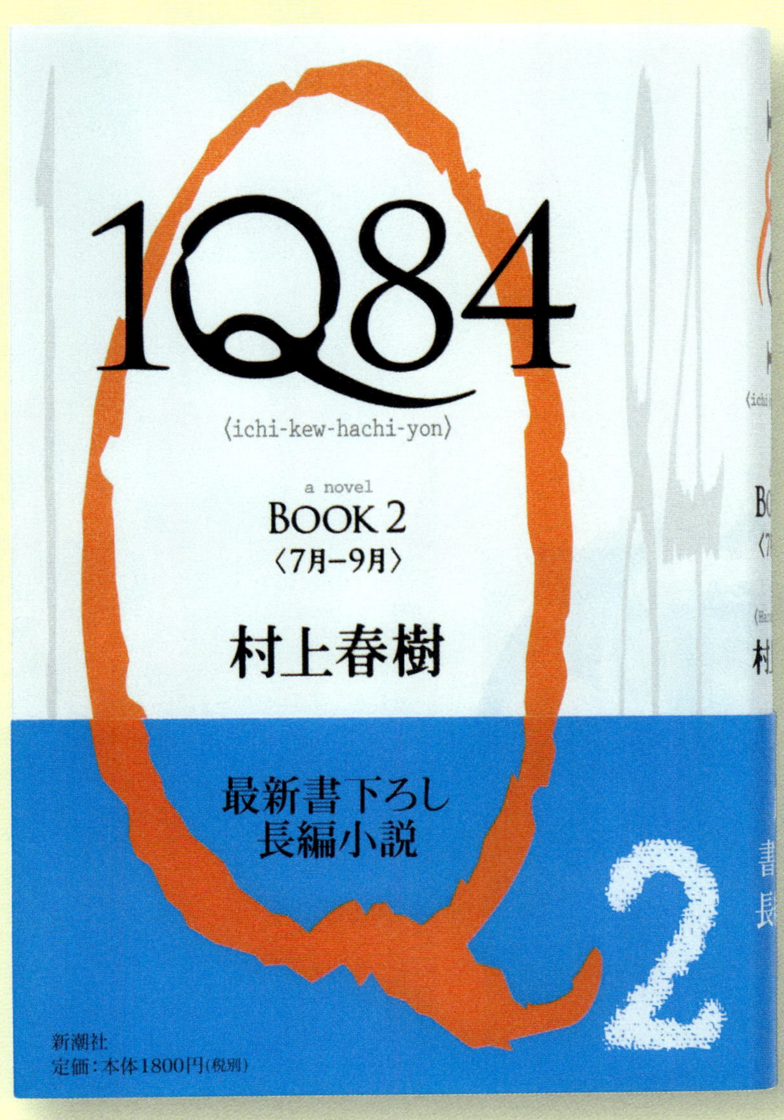

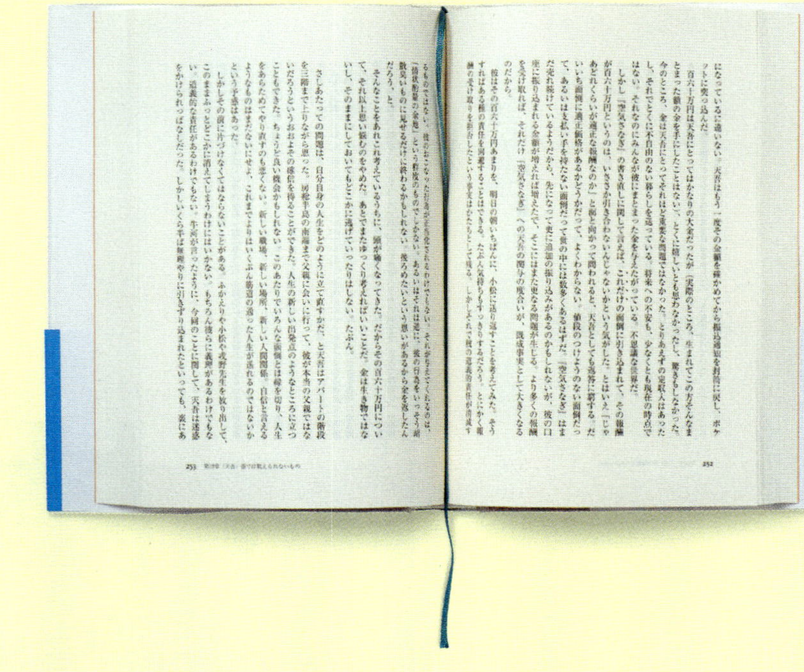

Martín Rejtman

Film Trilogy:

Rapado (1992)
Silvia Prieto (1999)
Los Guantes Mágicos (2003)

Martín Rejtman's film-based work fulfils what I see as some aspirational wishes of contemporary art practice; his film trilogy Rapado (Shaved Off, 1992), Silvia Prieto (1999) and Los Guantes Mágicos (The Magic Gloves, 2003) stands as a model of perspicacious observation of context, experimentation and eccentricity.

These films could only have been made in his home city, Buenos Aires, yet they are as non-folkloric as one could imagine. They document with a comedic tone the way in which the economy dominates the life of cities on the periphery. They are conceptual works, which follow the filmmaker's own specific rules and methodologies, but ultimately deal with the absurdities of day-to-day life. For these reasons, even though Rejtman is considered to be the 'father' of the New Argentine Cinema, his work can more easily be seen to relate to art methodologies and aspirations than to film.

Rejtman describes the trilogy's programme as follows: 'All takes are the same, just as all actors and all objects. Everything has the same value.' But what is remarkable about his films is that despite being radical in their constitution, they are neither analytical nor pretentious. They are funny and full of casual gags; as they move forward the artificiality of their construction and their dialogues dilutes into a general oddness that is suddenly unveiled as a new kind of naturalism.

Rapado is the story of a teenager whose motorcycle is stolen and who shaves his head, Silvia Prieto the tale of a young woman who decides to change her life on her twenty-seventh birthday, while Los Guantes Mágicos is about an embittered forty-year-old man who tries financial entrepreneurship. But plot is the least important element in Rejtman's films; even if hundreds of things happen, there is no overall dramatic structure. Instead, he works by negating his characters' introspection, and as a result also their expressionism, to the point where the objectivism cultivated by the amount of photography that preceded their creation is taken to the extreme. Feelings appear in strange ways; romantic relationships are formed in a practically automatic manner, and if someone is sad they simply cry unstoppably, as if suffering

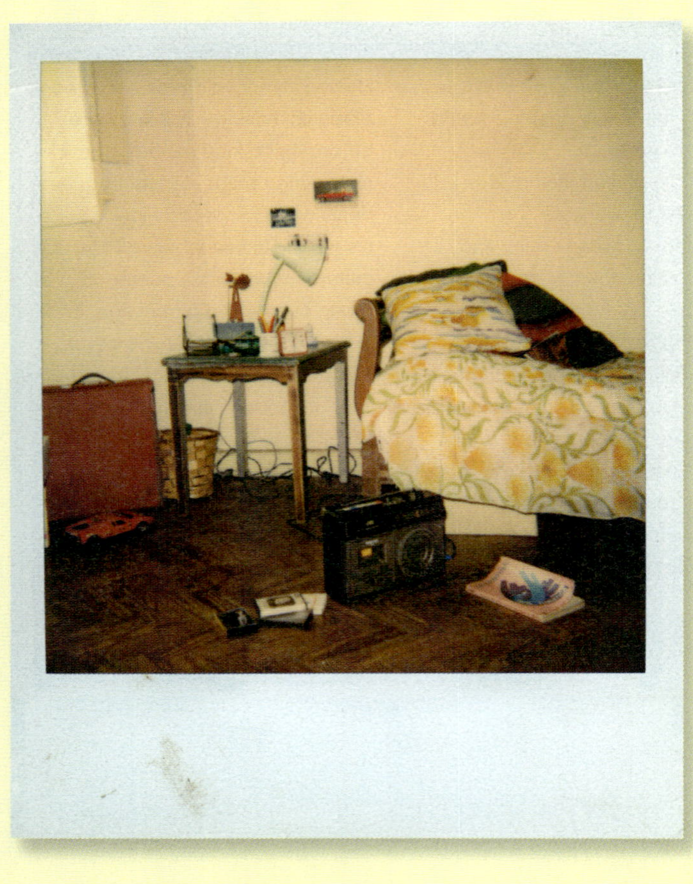

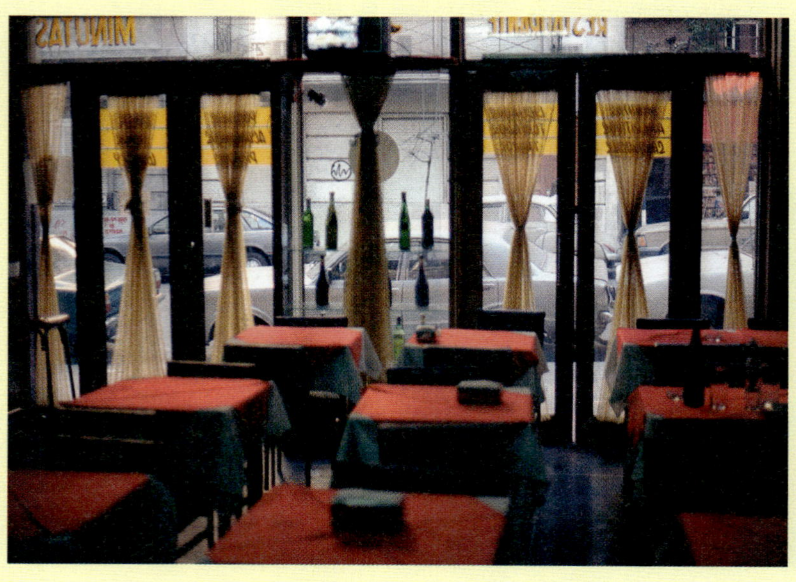

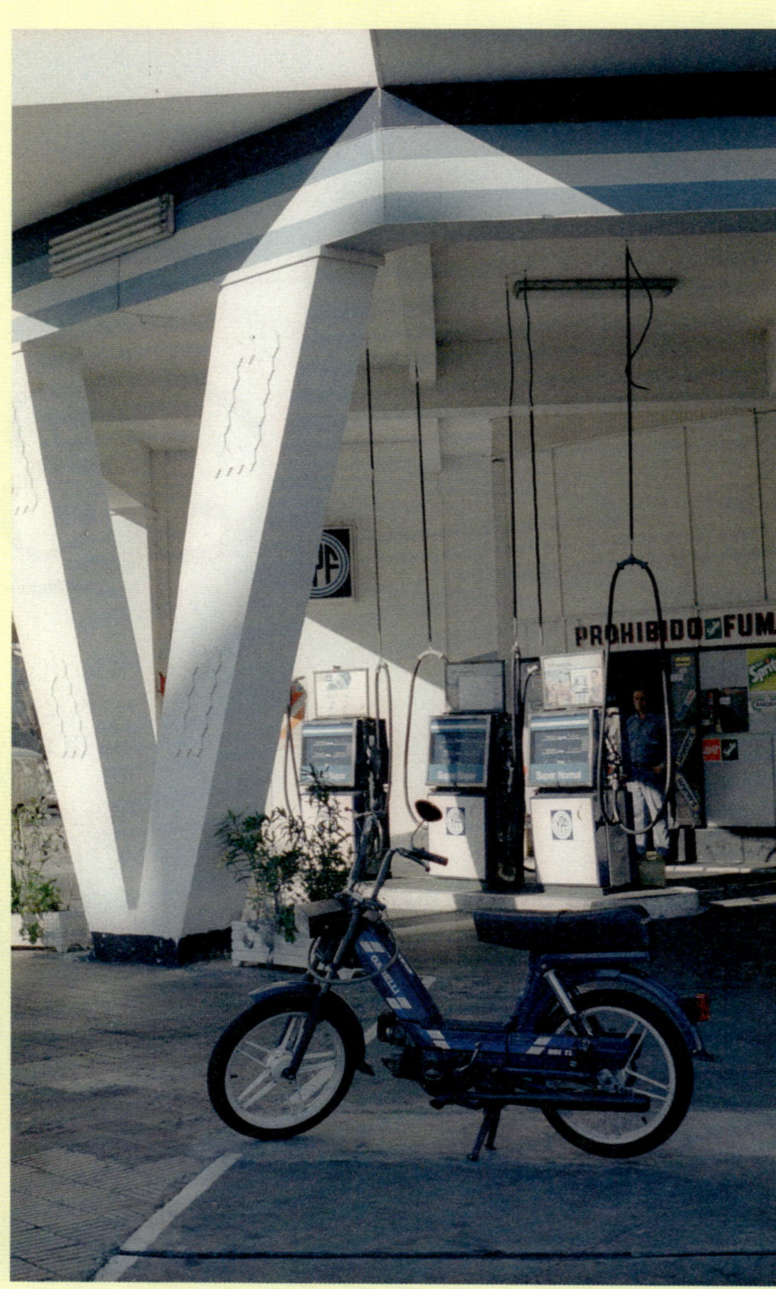

Martín Rejtman
Location–scouting photographs
1990

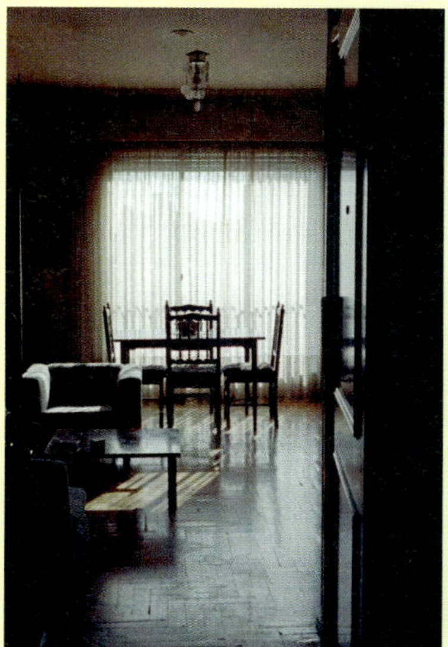

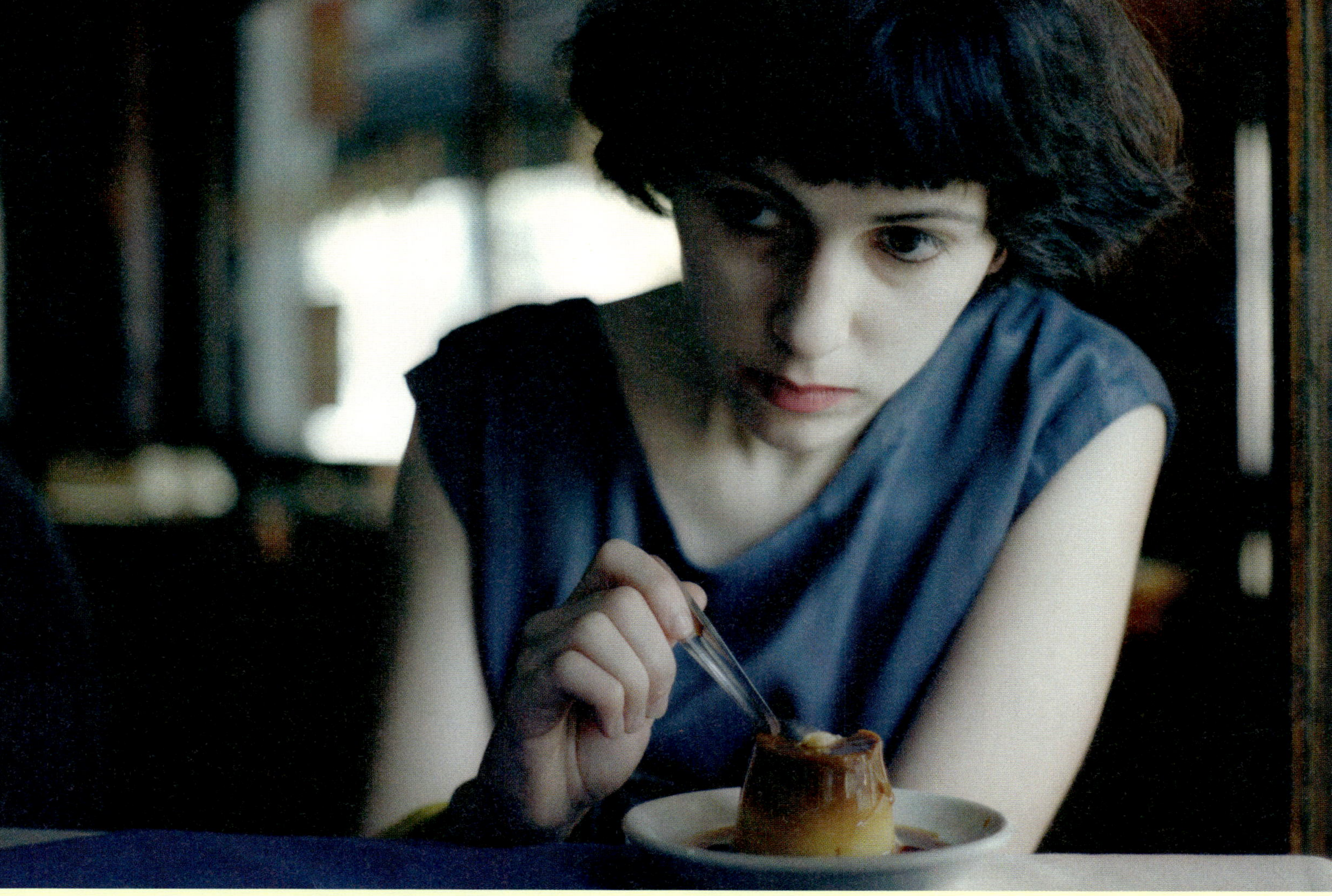

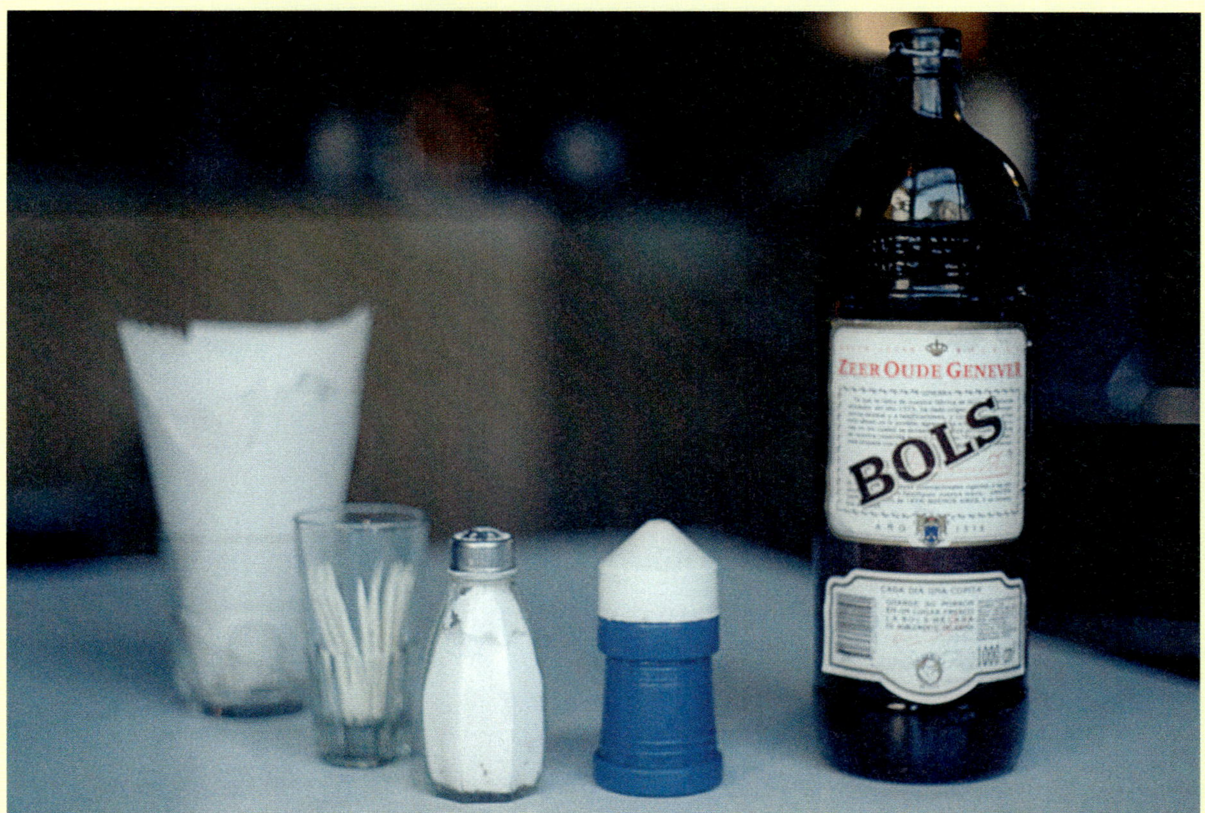

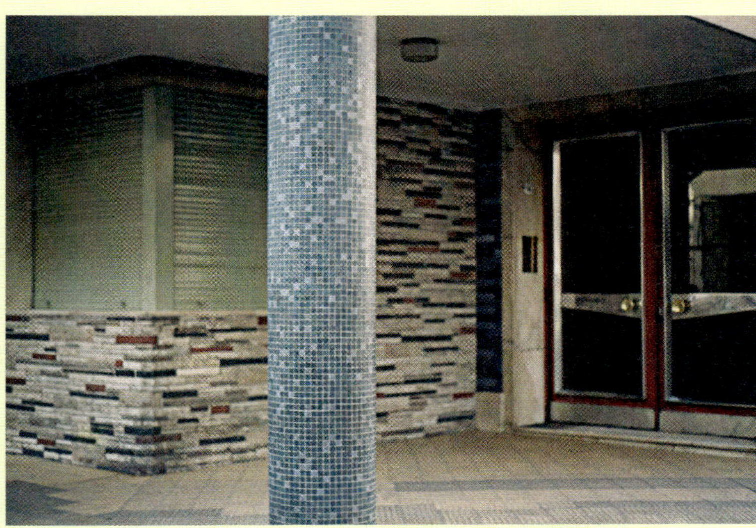

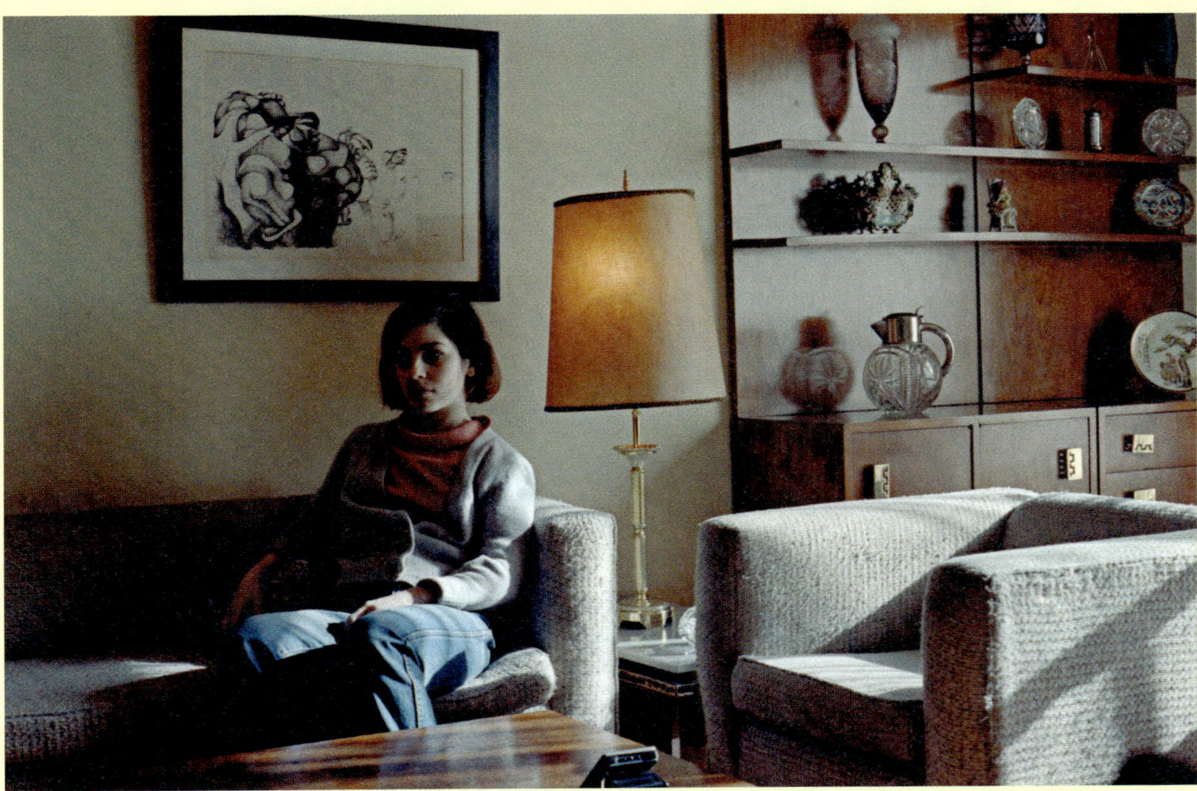

from an allergy. There's something robotic, even under-acted, in these characters, who operate as if propelled by accidental circumstance and chains of coincidences rather than by profound decisions. This emotional constraint is also affirmed on a visual level. If house interiors are shown, they are situated in a specific time and space (Argentina in the 1990s), but they are treated in a timeless way, with many old things intermixed with the contemporary.

The characters also appear to be ageless. In the same way, information about class and background is flattened, and everything seems to share an unrealistic middle ground.

The austerity of Rejtman's realms, in which people and things circulate in a state of permanent disaffected exchange, proposes an almost socialist alternative, absurd but practical, to consumption and the dominating prerogatives of autonomy and progress.

Brian O'Doherty

Inside the White Cube

(1976)

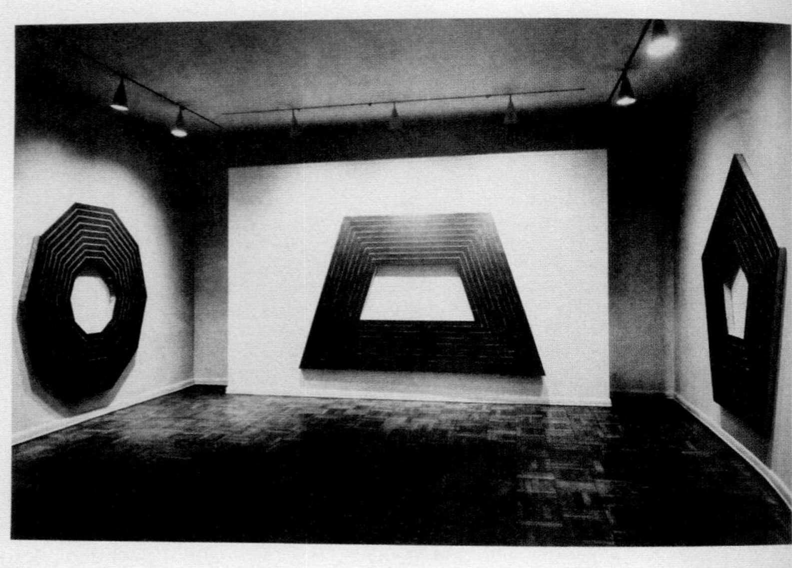

Inside the
White Cube

The Ideology
of the Gallery Space

Expanded Edition

by Brian O'Doherty

Begun when many of the artists in this book were still in their infancy, the series of articles gathered in Brian O'Doherty's Inside the White Cube: The Ideology of the Gallery Space has enjoyed a remarkable renaissance. O'Doherty, an artist himself (working under the name of Patrick Ireland), analyzed in these texts the aesthetic, historic and ideological implications of the exhibition space with an acuteness that, more than thirty years on, has yet to be rivalled. The author coined the now familiar term 'white cube' to describe the ubiquitous spare, white, modernist space for art, ensuring that it could no longer be claimed as 'neutral'.

'Notes on the Gallery Space', the first of the articles, appeared in the pages of Artforum in 1976, followed by two other essays later that same year. Its impact was immediate and widespread. Fiercely debated, the essays were written at a time when some of the most precursive writing about contemporary art and theory was emerging from the pens of artists (notably Dan Graham, Donald Judd, Martha Rosler and Robert Smithson). O'Doherty's acute and prescient eye is striking; his essays remain as relevant today as they were in their own time. He spoke about a norm in the display of artworks that, regardless of its half-century-long dominance, had not yet been theorized or even put into question. His feat was to treat historically a phenomenon that had found no proper place in a history of art built for so long on the analysis of autonomous objects. The result has lead to a seismic shift in thinking about the importance of the exhibition, both as an historical phenomenon and as an ideological device. If it is today understood that art history could be, perhaps even should be, rewritten as a history of art exhibitions, it is in large part thanks to these essays. That the discipline of art history is still being shaken by the implications of one artist's writing stands as an empowering testimony to the fact that an artist can not only be the producer of objects, but also of critical reflections about the apparatus in which his or her production circulates.

Our contemporary period is now the beneficiary of O'Doherty's insistence that the exhibition is a complex and study-worthy construct. No mere inconsequential envelope nor seat of pure visuality, it is a device of presentation as much as it is a machine for the control of bodies, the disciplining of citizens, the organization of perception, a public sphere, an articulation of politics, a cultural object and an ideological tool (one that is masculine, Western and as white as its walls). The way in which an exhibition begins and ends its 'story', the juxtapositions it constructs, the aesthetic and other conditions it offers, the discursive arguments it brings forth — all of these potentially shift the way in which its contents might be understood by the public, shaping the meaning and reception of an oeuvre, which is to say, nothing less than the construction of history. An awareness of this is the legacy that Inside the White Cube has left — to artists, curators and exhibition visitors alike.

Brian O'Doherty
Inside the White Cube: The Ideology of the Gallery Space, 1986
University of California Press, Berkeley and Los Angeles. 113 pages

Now a participant in, rather than a passive support for the art, the wall became the locus of contending ideologies; and every new development had to come equipped with an attitude toward it. (Gene Davis' exhibition of micro-pictures surrounded by oodles of space is a good joke about this.) Once the wall became an esthetic force, it modified anything shown on it. The wall, the context of the art, had become rich in a content it subtly donated to the art. It is now impossible to paint up an exhibition without surveying the space like a health inspector, taking into account the esthetics of the wall which will inevitably "artify" the work in a way that frequently diffuses its intentions. Most of us now "read" the hanging as we would chew gum – unconsciously and from habit. The wall's esthetic potency received a final impetus from a realization that, in retrospect, has all the authority of historical inevitability: the easel picture didn't have to be rectangular.

Stella's early shaped canvasses bent or cut the edge according to the demands of the internal logic that generated them. (Here Michael Fried's distinction between inductive and deductive structure remains one of the few practical hand tools added to the critic's black bag.) The result powerfully activated the wall; the eye frequently went searching tangentially for the wall's limits. Stella's show of striped U-, T-, and L-shaped canvasses at Castelli in 1960 "developed" every bit of the wall, floor to ceiling, corner to corner. Flatness, edge, format, and wall had an unprecedented dialogue in that small, uptown Castelli space. As they were presented, the works hovered between an ensemble effect and independence. The hanging there was as revolutionary as the paintings; since the hanging was part of the esthetic, it evolved simultaneously with the pictures. The breaking of the rectangle formally confirmed the wall's autonomy, altering for good the concept of the gallery space. Some of the mystique of the shallow picture plane (one of the three major forces that altered the gallery space) had been transferred to the context of art.

This result brings us back again to that archetypal installation shot – the suave extensions of the space, the pristine clarity, the pictures laid out in a row like expensive bungalows. Color Field

Frank Stella, installation view, 1964,
courtesy Leo Castelli Gallery, New York

Lucy Lippard

Six Years: The Dematerialization of the Art Object from 1966 to 1972

(1973)

Published in 1973, Six Years: The Dematerialization of the Art Object from 1966 to 1972 is a must-read for everyone interested in the histo[ry] of Conceptual art. The cover clearly states the book's purpose a[nd] method in a large, easy-to-read Helvetica font.

In this way, the book itself becomes an example of the art tha[t] is championing. Dedicated to Sol LeWitt, indexed by Carl Andre, and assisted by various other notab[le] practioners including Germano Celant, Charlotte Gault, Konrad Fischer, Ursula Meyer and Seth Siegelaub, Six Years is cleanly designed and easy to dip into for periods of concentrated attention.

I first remember coming across this compilation in the 1980s when I was studying art history in Montreal. At that time, I had not be[en] exposed to much Conceptual art and I experienced a sense of wond[er] and excitement with respect to the broad range of activities listed that could be understood as art. A 1969 entry reads, 'February, Düsseldorf: Joseph Beuys accepts full responsibility for any snowfall from

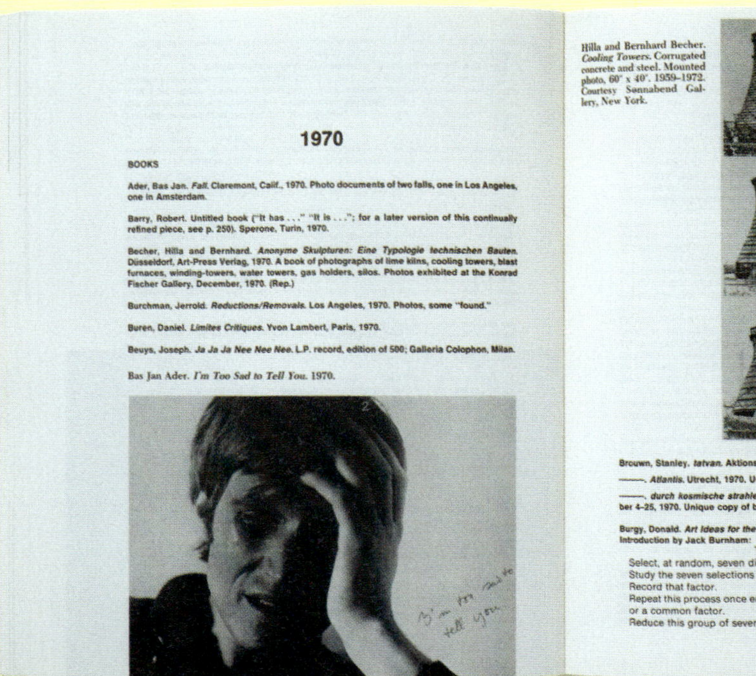

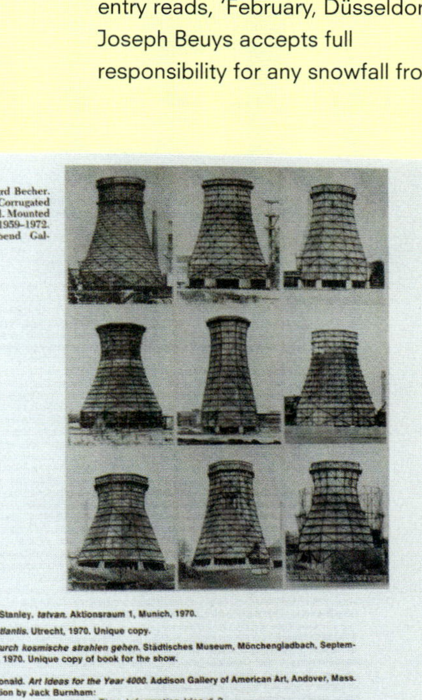

Six Years: The dematerialization of the art object from 1966 to 1972: a cross-reference book of information on some esthetic boundaries: consisting of a bibliography into which are inserted a fragmented text, art works, documents, interviews, and symposia, arranged chronologically and focused on so-called conceptual or information or idea art with mentions of such vaguely designated areas as minimal, anti-form, systems, earth, or process art, occurring now in the Americas, Europe, England, Australia, and Asia (with occasional political overtones), edited and annotated by Lucy R. Lippard.

February 15 to 20.' How can you help but smile a little here? Mention is made of Rafael Ferrer's Three Leaf Pieces, which appeared unexpectedly at various New York Gallery locations in 1968. A beautiful photograph at the top of the same page depicts leaves in the gritty industrial stairwell of Leo Castelli's warehouse. Opposite, two black and white landscape photographs by the N.E. Thing Co. (Iain and Ingrid Baxter) document their snow pieces on Mount Seymour in British Columbia.

Thinking back to this initial foray into the text, I remember I felt some sort of relief. Canada, the country in which I was living, did not seem to figure much in the other readings I had completed for my contemporary art courses. However,

Lippard's pages revealed new information about the Nova Scotia College of Art and Design, Vancouver Art Gallery, Edmonton Art Gallery and artists Gerald Ferguson, Jeff Wall, Ian Wallace, N.E. Thing Co., as well as the author's Vancouver exhibition 955,000 (1970) and Wall's booklet Landscape Manual (1970), produced by the Fine Arts Gallery at the University of British Columbia.

On opening the book recently I was struck by all of its different kinds of landscape images. There are Alice Aycock's contact sheets filled with clouds. We see Ulrich Rückriem using a hammer to mark a circle in the earth. Sigmar Polke's last name forms a constellation in a starry night sky. Robert Smithson's Asphalt Rundown (1969) is sublime, as is Michael Heizer's Double Negative (1969).

Lucy Lippard
Six Years: The Dematerialization of the Art Object from 1966 to 1972, 1973. Praeger, New York
272 pages

Jack Smith

Flaming Creatures

(1962–63)

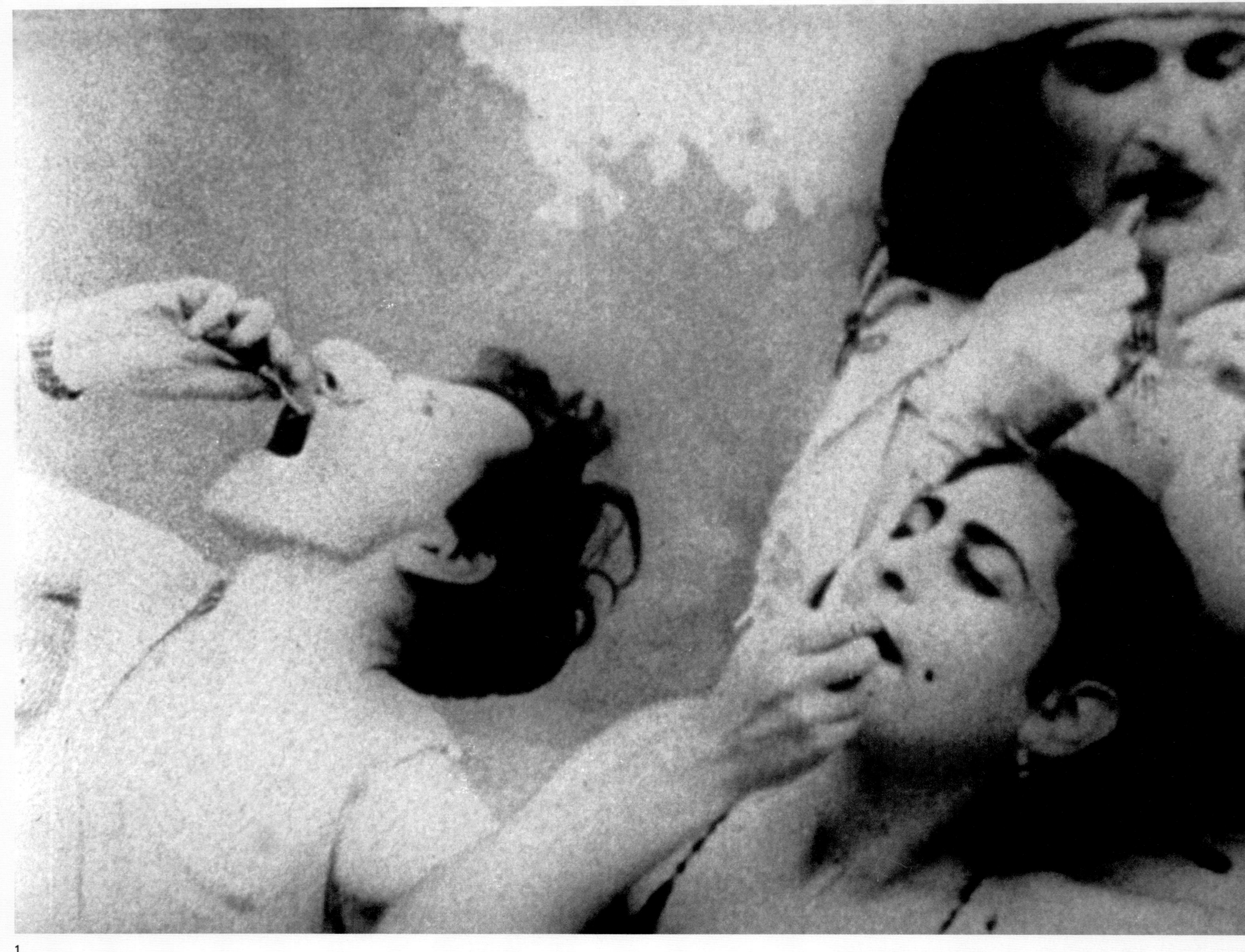

1

The late Jack Smith was one of the most influential and charismatic figures to emerge in the mid-1960s in the cross-over worlds of experimental theatre, underground film and performance art, and by far his most influential, best-known (and notorious) work was his film Flaming Creatures (1962–63). Produced early in his two-decade-long career, Flaming Creatures is a titillating, non-narrative, 42-minute, black and white film that guides us through a disorientating cavalcade of unrestrained eroticism blended with campy elements of over-the-top humorous flamboyance.

Shot on the rooftop of an old movie theatre in the Lower East Side of New York with an assortment of friends and other artists, Smith's fantastical scenes present a meandering, visually luxurious pageant. A harem-like cast of characters or 'creatures', young men and women scantily dressed — and cross-dressing — in Arabian, Spanish-Moroccan and vampire costumes with caked-on make-up and dripping in costume jewels move amidst equally atmospheric sets made up of sheer gauzy fabrics, patterned textiles, swinging glass lanterns and multitudes of white lilies. The cinematic tableaux shift from orgiastic escapades of flashing, groping and writhing, to Mardi-Gras-like sequences and dance numbers recalling the early entertainment spectacles of Busby Berkeley.

Flaming Creatures's aesthetic reflects Smith's love of Hollywood movies from the 1930s and 1940s and that era's popular interest in the 'exotic' as represented at that time by Arab and Middle Eastern cultures. The film was paradigmatic of Smith's visionary style of filming and editing in abstract and impressionistic ways and reveals his inventiveness when working within his low-budget constraints.

1 & 2 — Jack Smith
Flaming Creatures, 1963.
Black and white film with
sound. 45 min.

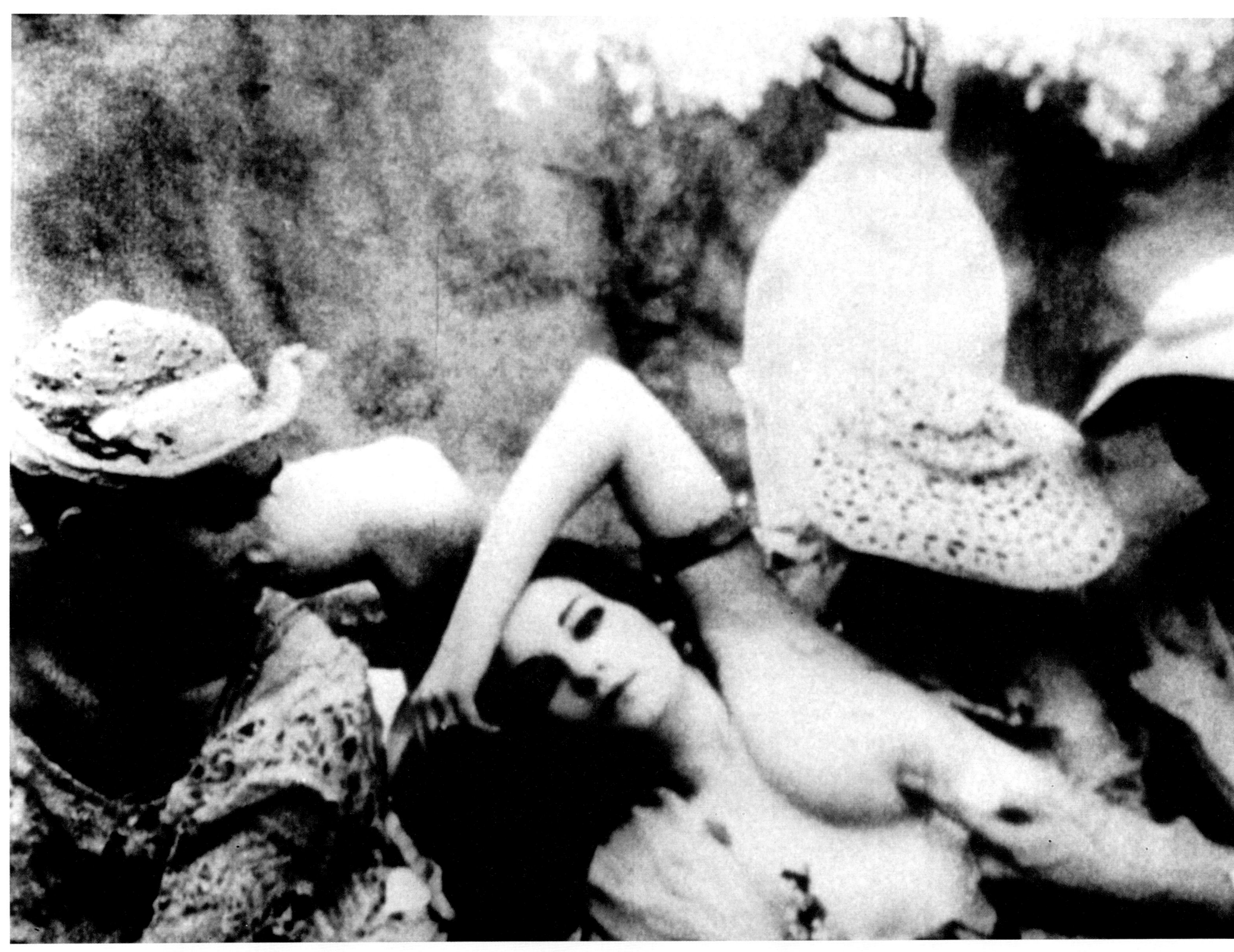

2

Shot on outdated film stock to reduce costs, many parts of the film look dramatically overexposed and burnt out, adding an elusive, ghostly and surreal quality. The shaky, hand-held filming technique recalls an amateur home-movie, but Smith took this limitation and turned it to his advantage through his dramatically unconventional framing and cropping of figures.

Considered both ground-breaking and taboo at the time of its release, Flaming Creatures provoked a public response that was almost as theatrical as the film itself. It was banned soon after its release in New York in 1964 for its explicit sexual content. (The attack on the work was part-and-parcel of censoring measures against films with gay content, which in turn were an element of a broader bureaucratic curtailment of gay culture at that time.) But it was also immediately recognized among Smith's artistic peers and many critics of the day as a key work of avant-garde film and performance. Not only did it influence a slew of other of filmmakers, photographers and performance artists of Smith's own generation, such as Andy Warhol, but it also inspired those after him, including Richard Foreman, Robert Wilson Susan Sontage, Jonas Mekas and John Waters, to name only a few.

Flaming Creatures is a testament to Smith's particular sense of innovative, low-tech filmic experimentation. Moreover, its DIY resourcefulness combined with its decadent humour, camp performan style and uninhibited gay sexuality amounted to a celebration of a new way of being in the world and of being an artist. The film summed up and presaged, a working philosoph to which many artists of a younger generation now adhere: if the worl you want does not exist, then inven it for yourself.

Studio of

Henryk Stażewski and Edward Krasiński, Warsaw

The studio formerly belonging to Henryk Stażewski (1894–1988) and Edward Krasiński (1925–2004) occupies a flat on the eleventh floor of a typical Communist-era housing block in Warsaw. From the windows and adjoining large terrace one has an almost unobstructed panoramic view of the new office towers built during the last decade, the Old Town reconstructed in the 1950s, bridges across the Vistula River, post-war housing in the vast area east of the Old Town where the Warsaw Ghetto was located during World War II, and the East-West Highway that connects the workers' district Praga on the right bank with the Old Town. These surroundings constituted the working environment of two artists — Stażewski, a prominent artist of the Polish Constructivist avant-garde who lived there from 1963 with the painter Mewa Lunkiewicz and her husband Jan Rogoyski, and Krasiński, who was invited to share the studio and living space in the early 1970s. Krasiński continued to live and work there after Stażewski passed away in 1988, until his own death in 2004. Three years later—at the instigation of Krasiński's former wife Anka Ptaszkowska, his daughter Paulina Krasińska and the Foksal Gallery Foundation—a pavilion designed by BAR Architects and Marcin Kwietowicz was built on the terrace as an extension of the studio to host exhibitions of visiting artists and seminars. The studio has been kept intact, save for some urgently needed repairs, and is at present available for study and private viewing by appointment.

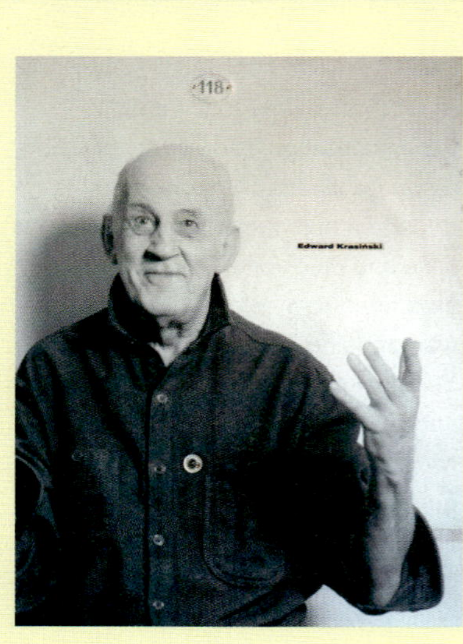

1

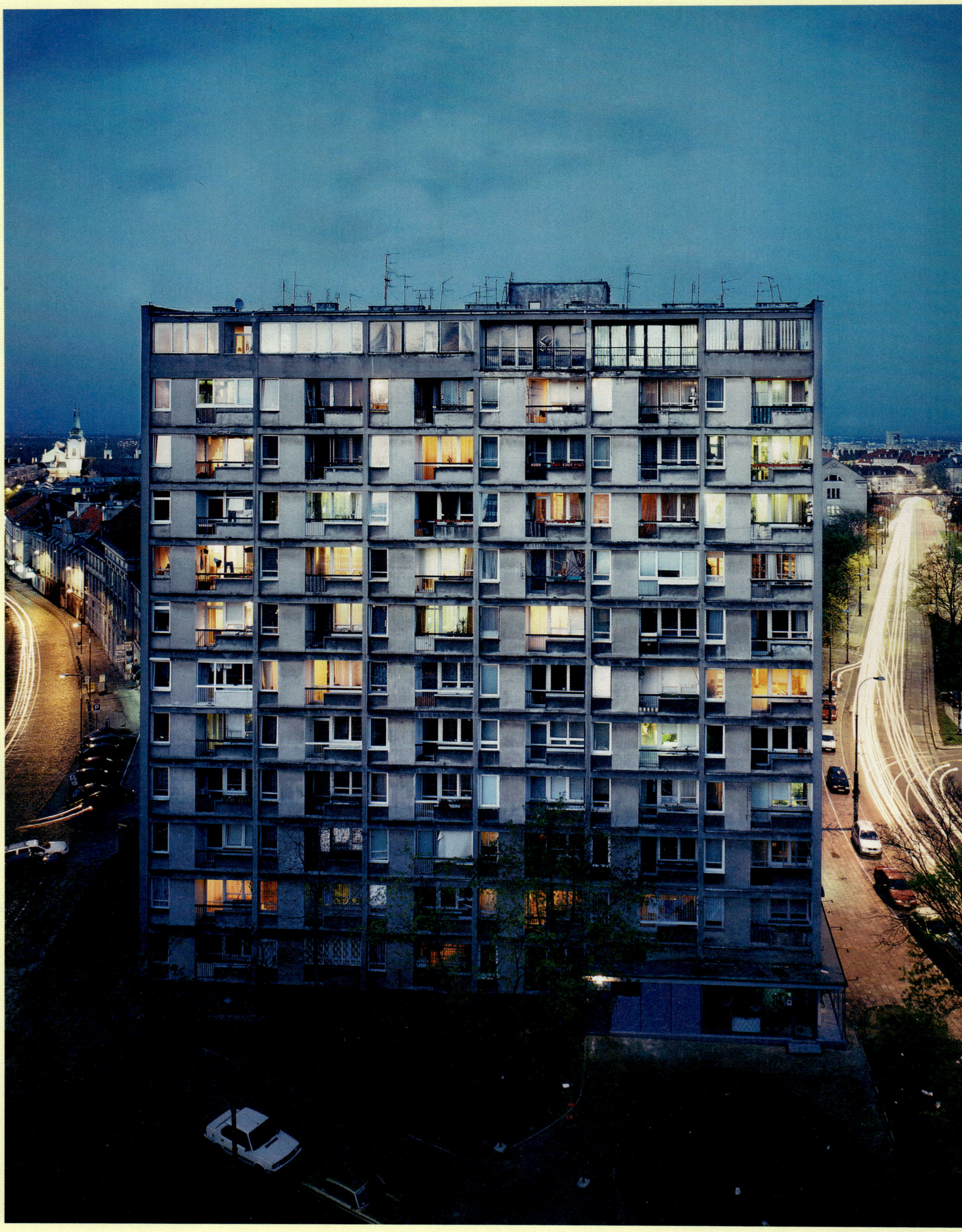

2

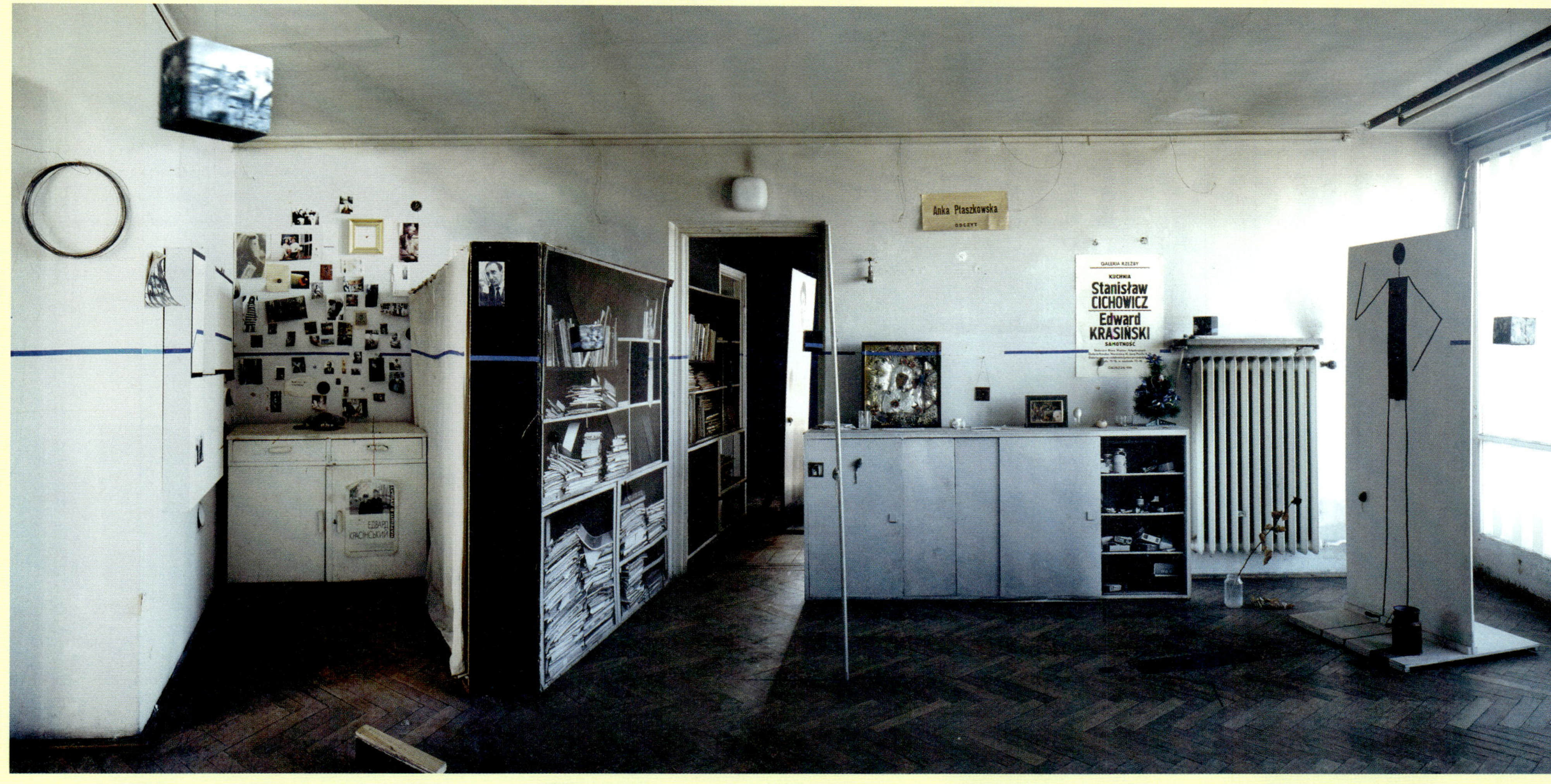

3

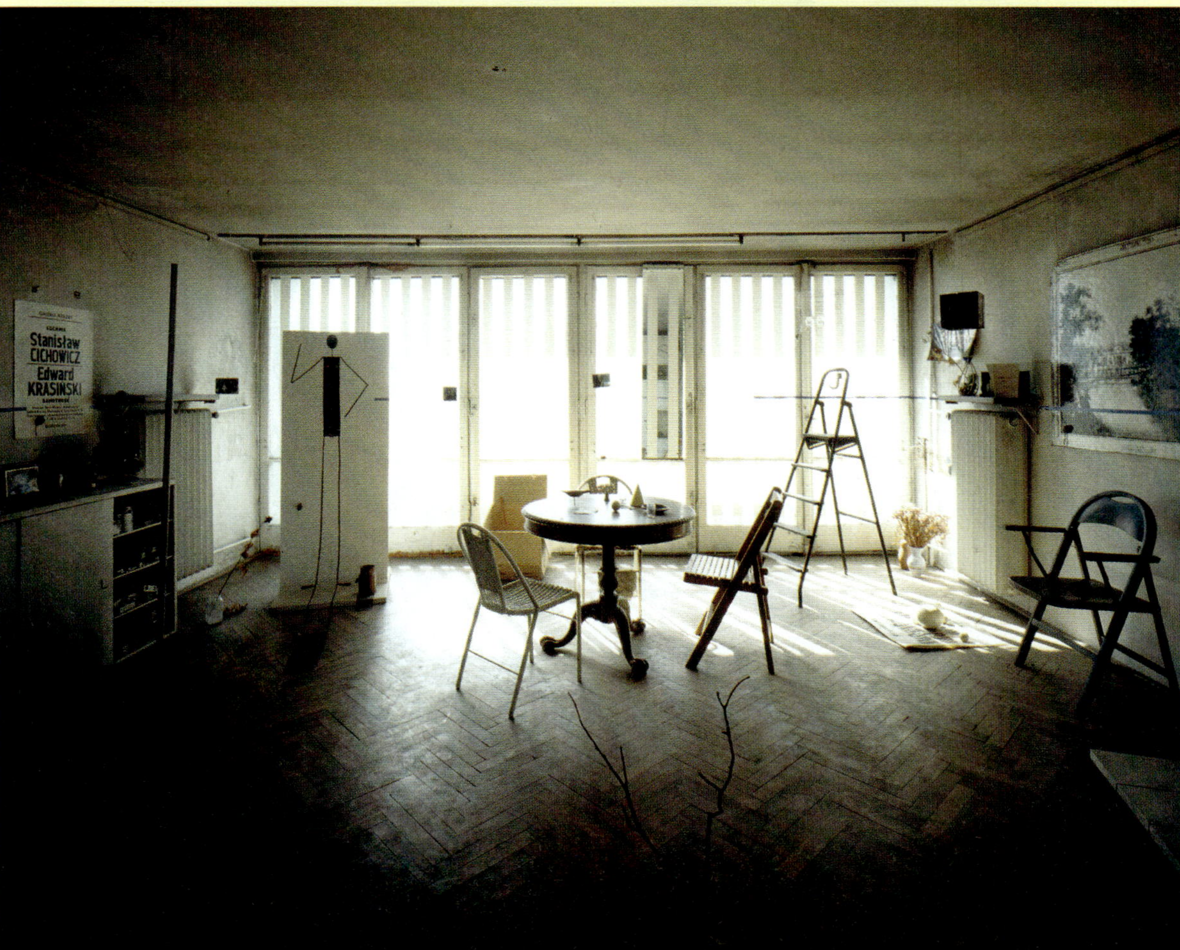

4

1 — Life-size photo of Edward
Krasiński mounted on the door to the
studio, 2004

2 — Building exterior
2004

3, 4 & **5** — Studio interior
2004

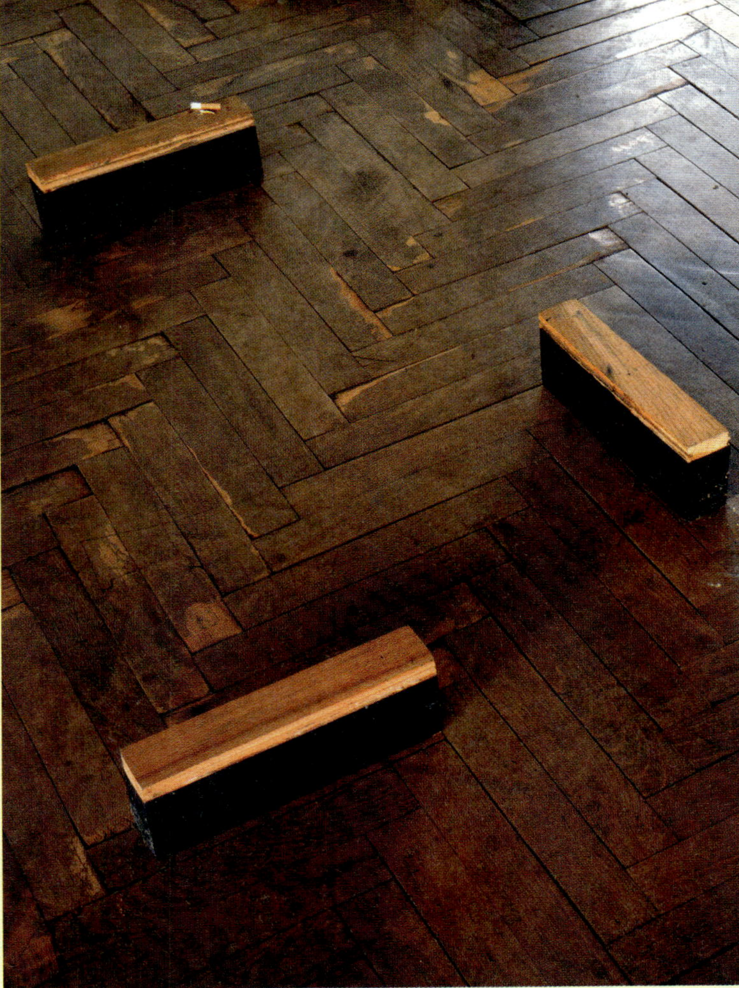

5

It consists of two modestly sized rooms — salon and atelier — and a corridor with kitchen and bathrooms. Each space was carefully, if casually, arranged by Krasiński, featuring his own works, objets trouvés and works by other artists, including Daniel Buren's vertical stripes applied on the windows in 1974 and 1994, private photographs and documents, furniture transformed into art objects, photographs of parts of the studio that Krasiński used in the exhibition 'Hommage à Stażewski' at Foksal Gallery in 1989 and last but not least, the strip of blue adhesive tape that marks the walls of the studio at a constant height of 130 cm — Krasiński's trademark medium since 1969.

When Stażewski and Krasiński were living together in the studio, they would receive numerous guests — they befriended artists, writers and thinkers, but also occasional random visitors — and the studio was an important meeting point for the Warsaw art milieu over three decades. Later for Krasiński alone, it became the locus of his own work. Since he hated the concept of 'work', he felt most comfortable in the ambiguous situation of the studio where he also lived, embodying the precarious balance between art and everyday life.

Krasiński decidedly broke with the production of art objects in favour of 'making things visible'. He once declared, 'I'm through with art. There's no point in exhibiting pictures. My last exhibition didn't have any pictures in it. It's a bit of snobbery on the part of the artist to put pictures as objects of adoration in people's faces. I make spaces, walls and circumstances visible that would be otherwise unremarkable or lifeless.'

Mike Kelley

Monkey Island

(1982–83)

1 — **Monkey Island**, 1983.
Mixed-media installation
Dimensions variable. Installation view,
Rosamund Felsen Gallery, Los Angeles

2 — **Monkey Island
(Los Angeles Zoo #1),** 1982–83.
Black and white photograph
28 × 35 cm

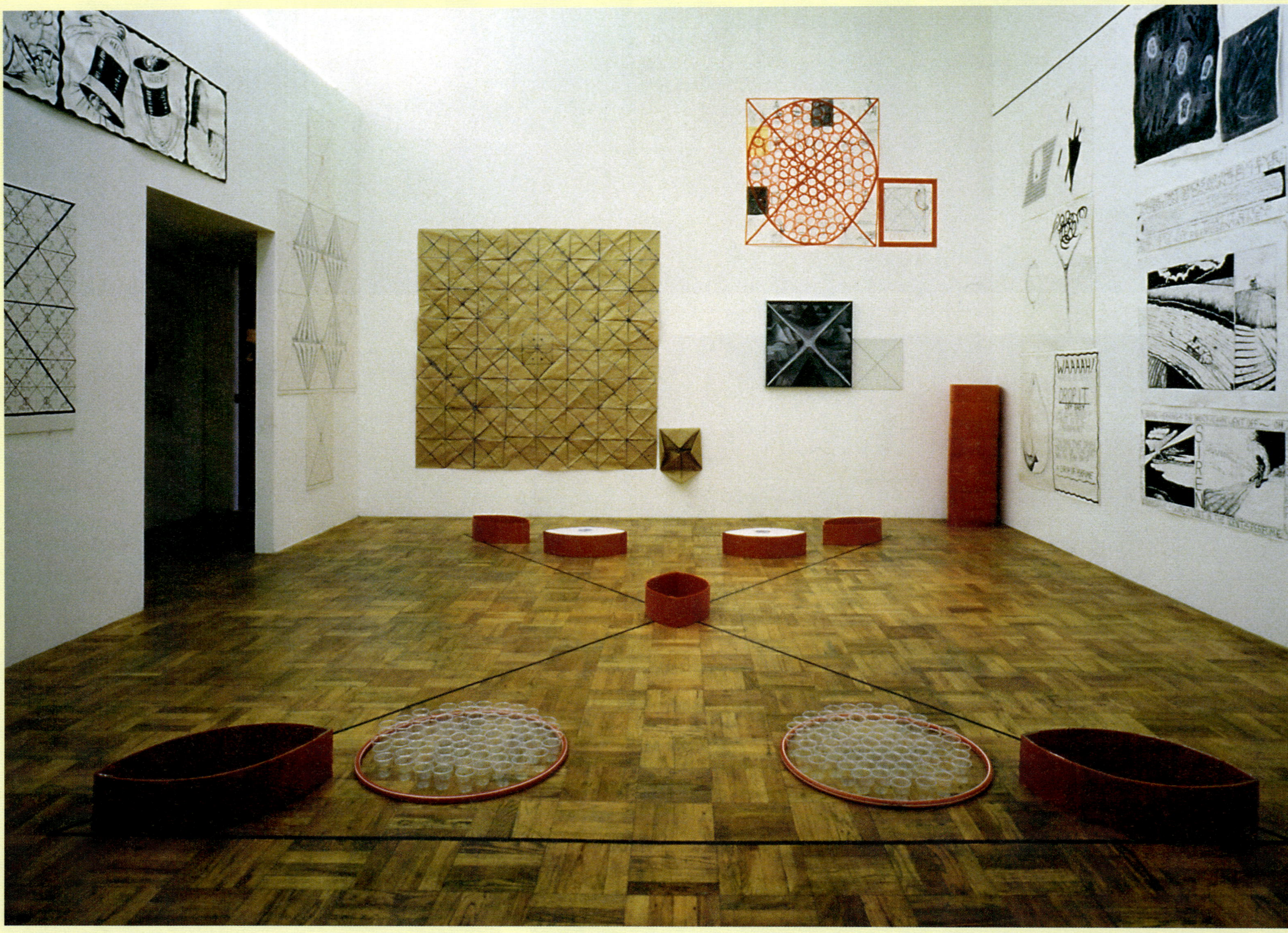

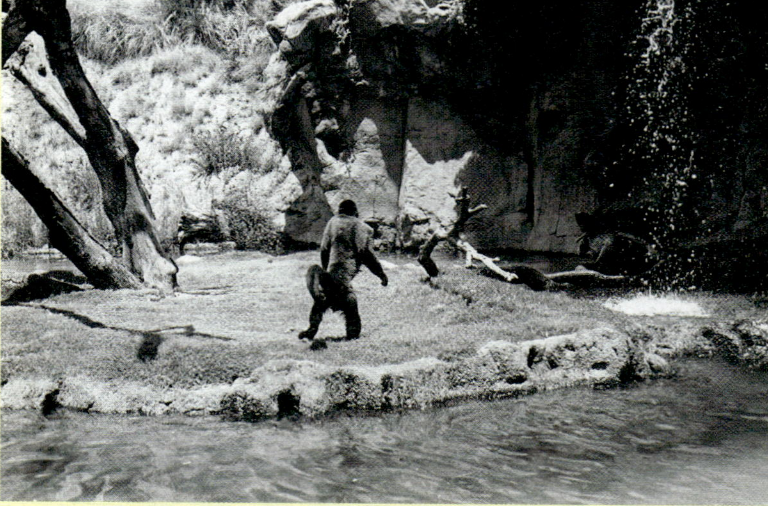

1

Mike Kelley's multifaceted installation and performance Monkey Island (1982–83) marked a transgressive shift in the critical understanding of the relationship between art, performance and cultural ritual. It brought the implied theatricality of 1960s Minimalist sculpture by Robert Morris or Donald Judd into the 1980s by literally incorporating theatre into an investigation of sculptural and pictorial representation. Linking together obsessive, large-scale drawings and minimal objects, this animal allegory was described by Robert L. Pincus as 'the geographical heart of Kelley's fictional universe', in which 'everything is determined by the existence of a tormenting lust'. Typical of Kelley's approach to probing language and images from an abject perspective, forms that resemble clean-cut Constructivist design are inflected with a base undercurrent, with fictional primates occupying relationships to art normally designated for the human spectator.

The critic Michael Duncan wrote, 'In Monkey Island […] Kelley plays with the metaphorical implications of an X-shaped […] diagram [marked out on the floor of the space], that stands for the relation of the viewer to the illusionistic space in a perspectival painting. Throughout the course of the performance and project, Kelley variously interprets this hourglass shape as a symbol of bilateral division, as a map, as a diagram of the human body, as an imaginary landscape and as an overlay of the mind.'

2

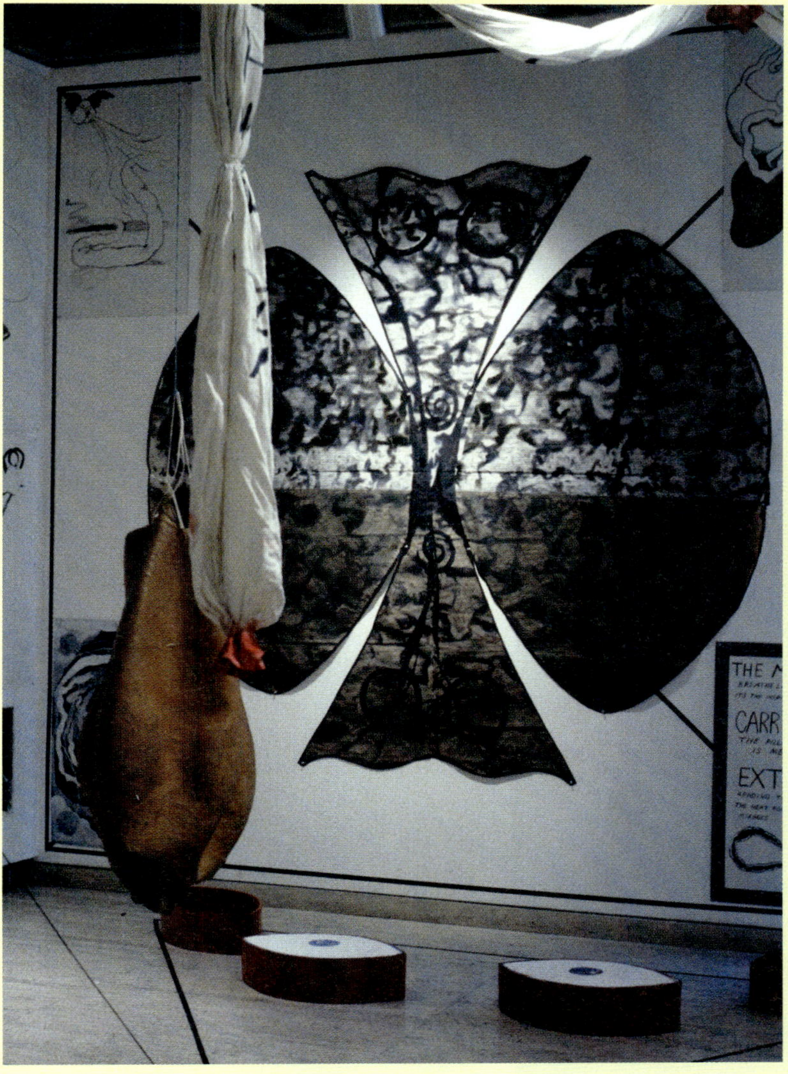

3

Monkey Island was
partly informed by Harry Harlow's
experiments in the Primate
Laboratory in the University of
Wisconsin in the 1950s and 1960s.
Harlow created an 'open field'
playroom in which he could conduct
experiments exploring primate
affection and social bonding in order
to reflect on human psychology.
Kelley has described his impression
of this 'test room' as an equivalent to
the way in which our own aesthetic
culture has evolved. The artist noted
that Harlow's 'highly melodramatic
and psychological theatre' was '
not such a great leap [from] Martha
Graham's dance work', a
choreographic aesthetic that was
linked to the idea of the 'primitive'.

In Monkey Island, we see
Kelley 'detourn' forms associated
with the 'progressive' twentieth-
century modernist project, dragging
its utopian constructions back to
service a primal insistence on
drawing and sculpture's ability to
prompt narrative fiction.

Monkey Island's combination
of drawing, sculpture, theory, and
ritual prefigured Kelley's persistent
attempts in subsequent work
to negotiate relationships between
individual subjectivity and cultural
behaviour, through its repressions
and absences. This early experiment
in conflating physical and
representational space makes literal
sense of his attitude to sculpture as
'props for verbalization'.

Kelley's approach was
informed by the early influence of
West Coast Conceptualism, notably
the works of John Baldessari
and Douglas Huebler, with whom he

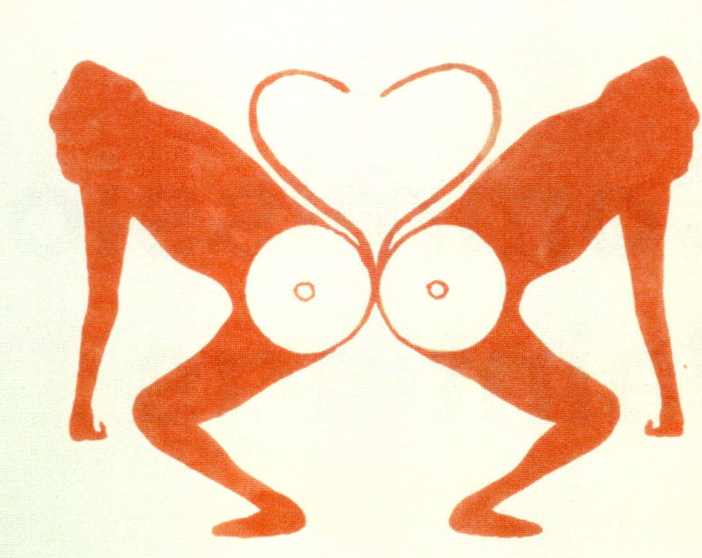

4

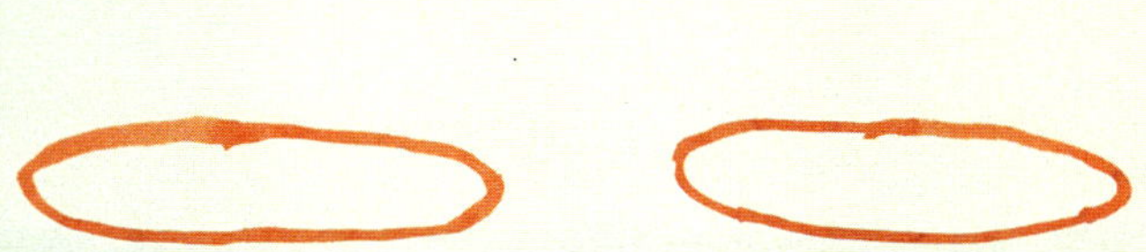

5

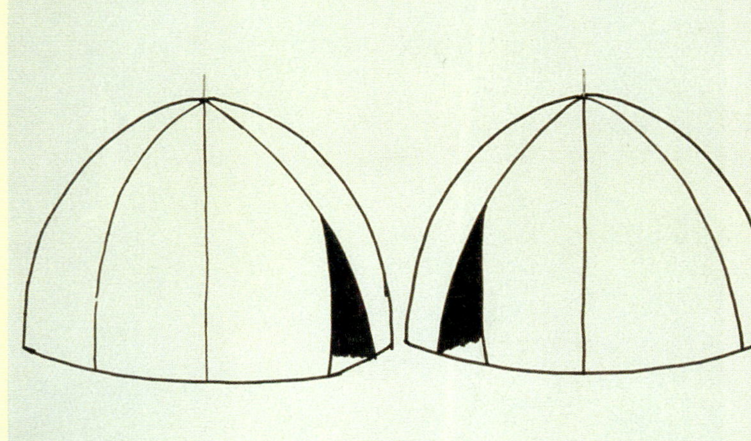

6

3 — Mike Kelley
Private Symbol: Social Metaphor,
1984. Mixed-media installation.
Dimensions variable.
Installation view, Sydney Biennial
1984.

4 — Mike Kelley
Symmetrical Sets (Ass Insect),
1982–83. Mercurochrome on paper.
46 × 61 cm

5 — Mike Kelley
Symmetrical Sets (Red Reefs),
1982–83. Mercurochrome on paper.
46 × 61 cm

6 — Mike Kelley
Symmetrical Sets (Two Tents),
1982–83. Marker on paper.
46 × 61 cm

7 — Mike Kelley
Symmetrical Sets (Two Buttocks),
1982–83. Marker and acrylic on
paper. 46 × 61 cm

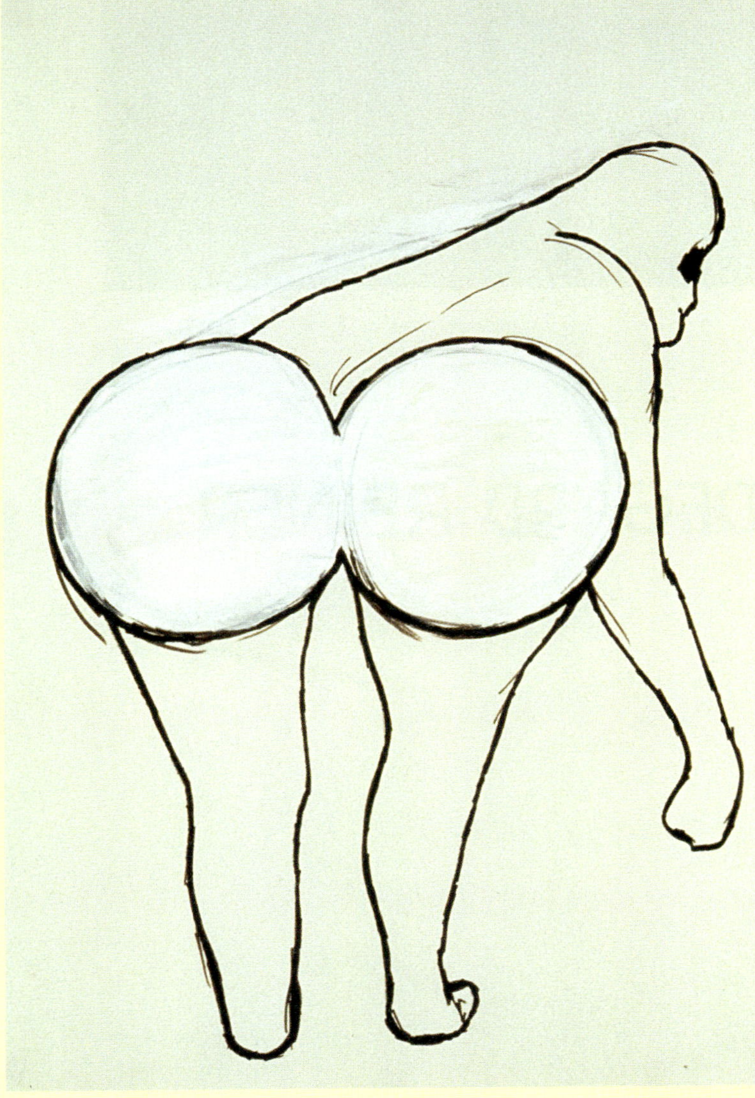

7

studied, through the radical
performances of the Vienna
Actionists (in particular, Otto Muehl),
melded with his everyday experience
of American popular culture.
These influences combined to forge
what has been described as a
'conceptual vernacular'.

Kelley's vernacular is
philosophical, regressive, trashy,
entertaining and abject in equal
measure, drawing energy and
influence from sources as varied as
psychoanalytic theory, folk-craft
practices and drag-punk band The
Cockettes. The work that Guy de
Cointet made in Los Angeles in the
1970s, and of Matt Mullican in the
1970s and 1980s, are also
acknowledged as influences by the
artist, in particular, their respective
investigations into language,

association and context, and how
they dramatize ways in which
inanimate objects might become
invested with subjectivity
via language.

Monkey Island brought
Kelley's experiments in performanc
together with his sculptural
practice. The ideas it contains wer
expanded in his 1985 work Plato's
Cave, Lincoln's Profile, Rothko's
Chapel and also inform his influenc
stuffed-animal sculptures of the ea
1990s. The linking of objects, text
and live presence through
fictionalized narrative evident in th
early work continues to provide
momentum for the current generat
of artists who, like Kelley, give equ
weight in their work to language,
sound and the movement of objec
in an agitated field of representati

John Baldessari

Commissioned Paintings

(1969)

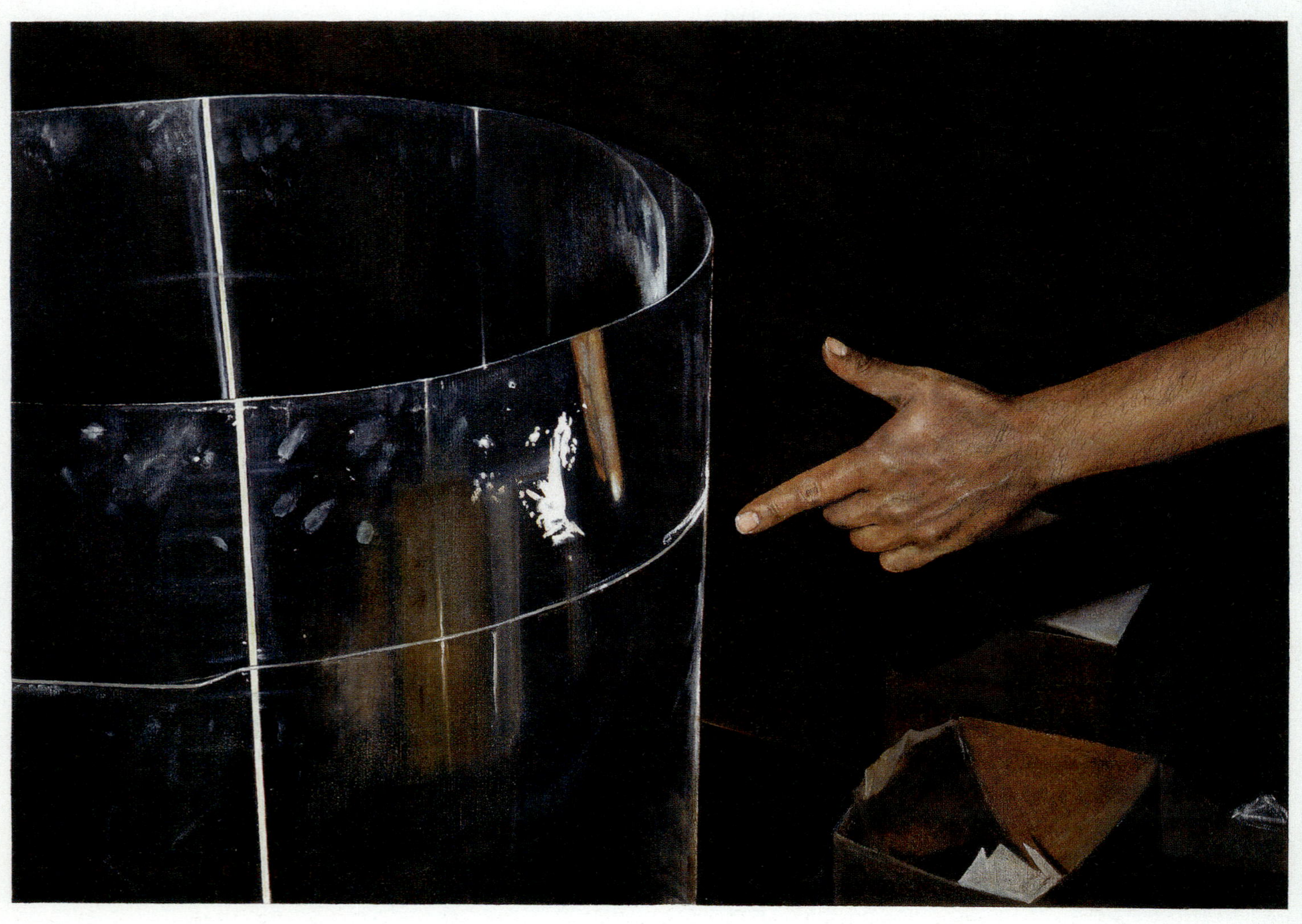

In 1969 John Baldesarri commissioned twelve amateur artists to make photorealist paintings of a hand pointing at everyday banalities. He was referring to a statement made by painter Al Held, who proclaimed that all Conceptual art was 'just pointing at things'. In Commissioned Paintings an emergent artist engages in high-conceptual satire, without clarifying whether the joke is on Held or on the nameless amateurs who lent the work a low-brow edge. The relationships between pointer and 'bepointed', motive and action, are more convoluted than they appear.

For Creamier, curators are invited to point out 'emerging' artists, which, in Baldessari's heyday, we may have called 'cutting edge' or, a century ago, 'avant-garde'. Today's concept of 'emerging' is more innocuous by comparison. But the term is not necessarily condescending. The literary scholar Wlad Godzich, when discussing postcolonial writing, uses the term 'emergent' as borrowed from botany, where it refers to newly discovered fauna. Importantly, an emergent plant is interesting not by virtue of novelty alone, but in terms of redefining what the taxonomy had offered hitherto. So in the best of cases, the emergent is what redefines the classificatory scheme at large.

If you accept this admittedly somewhat grandiose definition, it becomes difficult to pinpoint a 'key creative work' of 'significant influence' on the emerging generation. In terms of subject matter, the only common ground among my 'emergentista' is that their work is reflexive of conditions of production within the art world — including, indeed, its classificatory systems. That said, the different reflexivities betray different shades of political and aesthetic engagement. But even in simple terms of generation, the differences between the selected artists are considerable. So by way of a source work, I have attempted to reflect a more genuine common ground — that of my own decision-making process. What if we saw the Creamier hit parade as an example of art writing, not merely a shopping list for kingmakers, but a case of mediation in and of itself? Discussions of criticism and its death, demise and decrepitude rarely venture beyond the exhibition review and the catalogue essay. What to make of the blogs, the mainstream reportage, the scenes and herds, the vernissageTV and indeed the many examples of Top Ten brokerage that equally constitute critical parts of the food chain? Creamier offers a strong example of the prime contemporar[y] function of criticism: 'pointing'. It matters not whether you slander [or] praise, as critic Boris Groys likes to say; the mere act of pointing ou[t is] key. Groys believes that critics clo[the] the bepointed in a 'textual bikini', bashfully pre-empting any discursi[ve] nudity. With Creamier, however, we do no such thing. It is pointing[,] pure and simple, marvellously unapologetic and refreshingly raw[.]

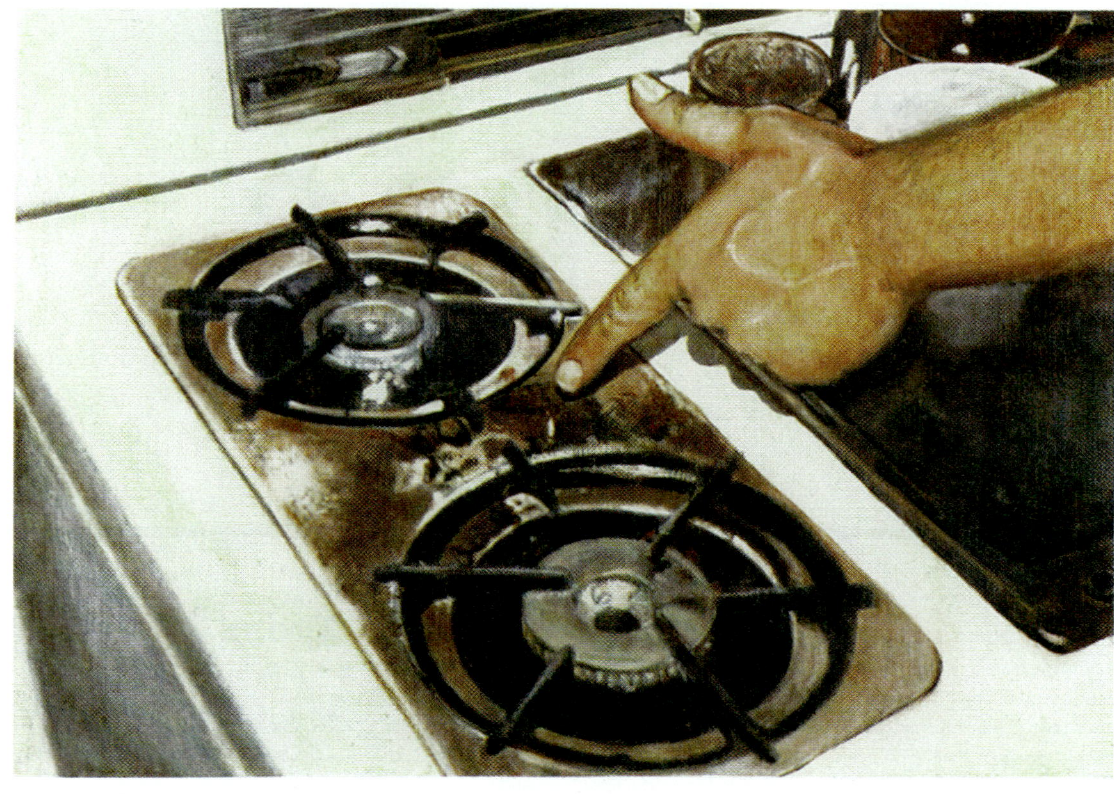

A PAINTING BY JANE MOORE

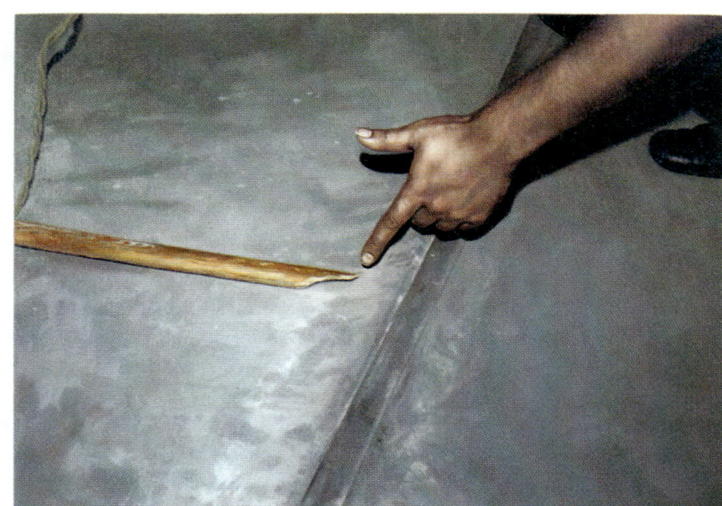

A PAINTING BY PAT NELSON

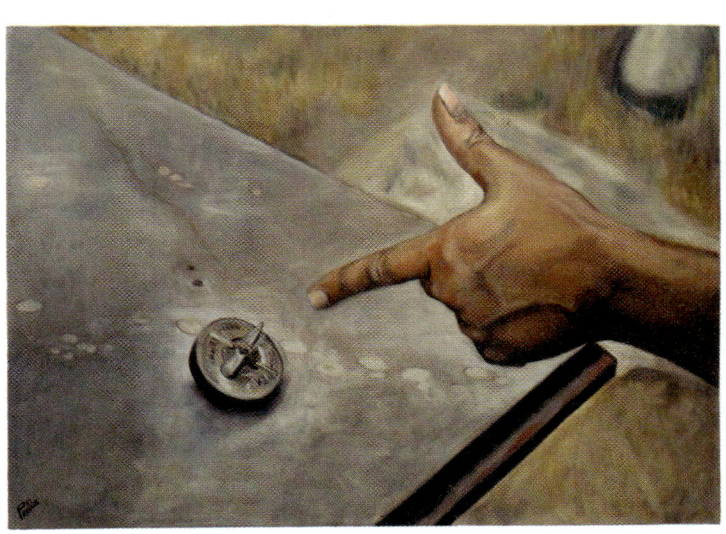

A PAINTING BY PAT PERDUE

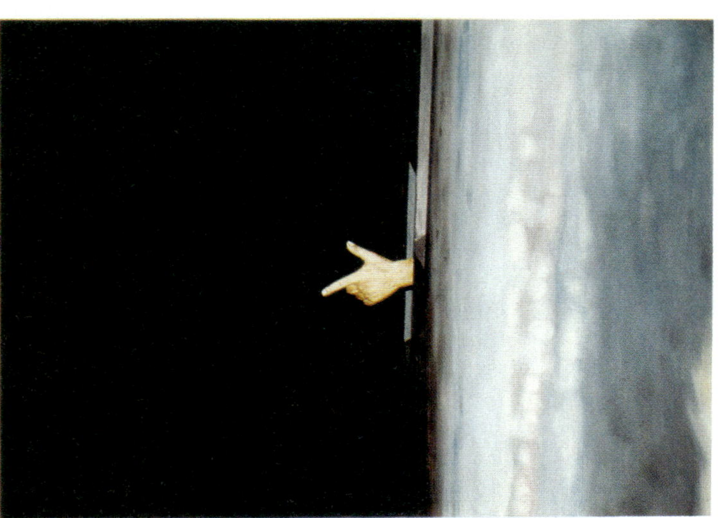

A PAINTING BY PATRICK X. NIDORF O.S.A.

1 — John Baldessari
Commissioned Painting:
A Painting by Hildegard Reiner, 1969.
Acrylic and oil on canvas
150 × 116 cm

2 — John Baldessari
Commissioned Painting:
A Painting by Jane Moore, 1969.
Acrylic and oil on canvas
150 × 116 cm

3 — John Baldessari
Commissioned Painting:
A Painting by Pat Nelson, 1969.
Acrylic and oil on canvas
150 × 116 cm

4 — John Baldessari
Commissioned Painting:
A Painting by Pat Perdue, 1969.
Acrylic and oil on canvas
150 × 116 cm

5 — John Baldessari
Commissioned Painting:
A Painting by Patrick X. Nidorf O.S.A.,
1969. Acrylic and oil on canvas
150 × 116 cm

Curator Biographies

Elena Filipovic

Elena Filipovic is Associate Curator at Wiels Centre d'Art Contemporain, Brussels. With Adam Szymczyk she co-curated the 5th Berlin Biennial, 'When Things Cast No Shadow' (2008), and with Barbara Vanderlinden she co-edited The Manifesta Decade: Debates on Contemporary Art Exhibitions and Biennials in Post-Wall Europe (2006).

Recent exhibitions include 'Marcel Duchamp: A Work That Is Not a Work of Art' at the Museu de Arte Moderna, São Paulo, and the Fundación Proa, Buenos Aires (2008–09), and 'Felix Gonzalez-Torres: Specific Objects without Specific Form' at Wiels, Brussels; Fondation Beyeler, Basel; and the Museum für Moderne Kunst, Frankfurt (2010–11).

She is Tutor of Theory and Exhibition History at De Appel postgraduate curatorial training program and advisor at the Rijksakademie in Amsterdam. She is currently guest curator of the Satellite programme of emerging artists at Jeu de Paume, Paris (2009–11).

Douglas Fogle

Douglas Fogle is Deputy Director, Exhibition and Programs and Chief Curator at the Hammer Museum in Los Angeles. From 2005 to 2009 he was Curator of Contemporary Art at the Carnegie Museum of Art in Pittsburgh, where he organized the 55th Carnegie International, 'Life on Mars', in 2008.

Prior to that he spent eleven years as a curator in the Visual Arts Department of the Walker Art Center in Minneapolis, where his exhibitions included 'Painting at the Edge of the World' (2001), 'The Last Picture Show: Artists Using Photography 1960–1982' (2003), 'Andy Warhol/Supernova: Stars, Deaths, and Disasters 1962–1964' (2005) and solo exhibitions by Catherine Opie and Julie Mehretu. Also a writer, he has published widely in exhibition catalogues and in such journals as Artforum, Frieze and Parkett.

Yukie Kamiya

Yukie Kamiya is Chief Curator at the Hiroshima City Museum of Contemporary Art and a visiting lecturer at Waseda University, Tokyo. From 2003 to 2006 she was Associate Curator and later Adjunct Curator at the New Museum of Contemporary Art, New York. Kamiya has curated a number of international exhibitions, including 'Under Construction', which toured various countries in Asia from 2001 to 2003, and 'Thermocline of Art' at ZKM, Karlsruhe (2007), for which she was a contributing curator. She has curated monographic exhibitions with artists such as Cai Guo-Qiang (2008) and Tsuyoshi Ozawa (2009) at Hiroshima MOCA and has contributed to many catalogues and periodicals, including Asahi Newspaper, Afterall and Art Asia Pacific.

Inés Katzenstein

Inés Katzenstein is Director of the Art Department at the Universidad Torcuato Di Tella in Buenos Aires, Argentina. From 2004 to 2008 she was Curator at Malba Colección Costantini, Buenos Aires, where she curated projects by Carlos Amorales, Fabian Marcaccio and David Lamelas and supervised the selection and acquisition of works for the contemporary art collection.

She was curator of the Argentina Pavilion at the 2007 Venice Biennale, presenting a project by Guillermo Kuitca, and co-curator of the Bienal de Mercosur in 2007, where she presented projects by Leopoldo Estol and M7red. Among her many books, she edited Listen, Here, Now!! Argentine Art of the Sixties: Writings of the Avant-Garde (2004), published by The Museum of Modern Art, New York.

Chus Martínez

Chus Martínez is Chief Curator at the Museu d'Art Contemporani, Barcelona (MACBA). Between 2001and 2005 she was Artistic Director of Sala Rekalde, Bilbao,

and from 2005 to 2008 Director of the Frankfurter Kunstverein, where she founded a residency program and curated a series of group shows, including 'Whenever It Starts It Is the Right Time' (2007) and 'Pensée Sauvage: On Freedom' (2007).

She curated the first retrospective of the Lithuanian artist and filmmaker Deimantas Narkevicius (Museo Nacional Centro de Arte Reina Sofía, 2008) and the first retrospective exhibition of Thomas Bayrle (MACBA, 2009). She is Associate Curator of the 2010 São Paulo Biennial and a visiting lecturer at the Royal College of Art, London, and the Universidad Autónoma de Barcelona. As a writer she has contributed to Artforum, Flash Art and other journals.

Kitty Scott

Kitty Scott is Director of Visual Arts at The Banff Centre, Canada. Previously she was Chief Curator at the Serpentine Gallery, London, and Curator of Contemporary Art at the National Gallery of Canada, Ottawa. Scott has curated exhibitions of artists such as Francis Alÿs, Janet Cardiff, Peter Doig and Ron Terada.

In 2008 she organized the curatorial symposium Trade Secrets: Education/ Collection/History at The Banff Centre and edited the forthcoming publication Raising Frankenstein: Curatorial Education and its Discontents. She is Visiting Professor for the Curatorial Practice programme at the California College of the Arts, San Francisco.

Debra Singer

Debra Singer is Executive Director and Chief Curator of The Kitchen, New York. Prior to her appointment at The Kitchen in 2004, Singer was Curator at the Whitney Museum of American Art, where she co-curated the 2004 and 2002 Whitney Biennials as well as solo exhibitions by Tom Burr, Helen Mirra, Jennifer Pastor and Paul Pfeiffer, among others. During her seven years at the Whitney, she was the

museum's primary performance curator, producing live music, dance, theater, literary and performance art events. At The Kitchen, she has organized projects with Edgar Arceneaux, Tracy and the Plastics, Walid Raad/The Atlas Group and Alix Pearlstein, as well as the 2009 group exhibition, 'Besides, With, Against, and Yet: Abstraction and The Readymade Gesture'. She has also written for many periodicals, including Artforum and Parkett.

Adam Szymczyk

Adam Szymcyk is Director and Chief Curator at Kunsthalle Basel, where he has organized solo exhibitions with artists such as Tomma Abts, Gustav Metzger, Ahlam Shibli, Lee Lozano and Danh Vo as well as the group show 'Report on Probability' (2009). With Elena Filipovic he co-curated the 5th Berlin Biennial, 'When things cast no shadow' (2008). In 1997 he co-founded the Foksal Gallery Foundation in Warsaw and was Curator there until 2002. He is also a member of the board of the Museum of Modern Art, Warsaw.

Catherine Wood

Catherine Wood is Curator of Contemporary Art and Performance at Tate Modern, London. In 2009, she co-curated the exhibition 'Pop Life: Art in a Material World' with Jack Bankowsky and Alison Gingeras and commissioned a re-make of Robert Morris' 1971 Tate Gallery installation, 'Bodyspacemotionthings'. She co-curated 'The World as a Stage' with Jessica Morgan in 2007 and programmed a series of performances by artists including Marc Chaimowicz, Liam Gillick and Spartacus Chetwynd for the 2006 Tate Triennial.

She has produced live projects at Tate Modern with Keren Cytter, Mark Leckey, Joan Jonas, Pablo Bronstein and Tino Sehgal. She is the author of Yvonne Rainer: The Mind is a Muscle (Afterall/ MIT Press, 2007) and has written regularly for many periodicals including Afterall, Artforum and Parkett.

Tirdad Zolghadr

Tirdad Zolghadr is an independent writer and curator based in Berlin. He writes regularly for Frieze and teaches at the Center for Curatorial Studies, Bard College, Annandale-on-Hudson, New York. As a curator Zolghadr organized the national pavilion of the United Arab Emirates at the 2009 Venice Biennale and the long-term project 'Lapdogs of the Bourgeoisie' (with Nav Haq, 2007–08). Zolghadr is a curatorial advisor to the Artist Pension Trust and the Guggenheim Abu Dhabi, and is Editor at large for Cabinet. His first novel, Softcore, was published 2007 (Telegram Books, with translations in German, Italian, French). He is currently writing his second novel, Top Ten.

Artist Biographies

Gabriel Acevedo Velarde

Born 1976, Lima, Peru. Lives Mexico City, Mexico. **Selected solo exhibitions: 2010** Modern Art Museum of Fort Worth TX, USA **2009** Maribel López Gallery, Berlin • Museo de Arte Carrillo Gil, Mexico City **2008** Y Gallery, New York • Galeria Leme, São Paulo **2006** Galeria OMR, Mexico City **Selected group exhibitions: 2009** 'Restraint/Contrainte: New Media Art Practices from Brazil and Peru', Oboro and Maison de la Culture Marie-Uguay, Montreal • Mercosul Biennial, Porto Alegre, Brazil • 'Juntos Acordaron Adelantar el Oscurecer', Centro de Cultura Sa Nostra, Palma de Mallorca, Spain **2008** Guangzhou Triennial • 'Contraditório: Panorama da Arte Brasileira', Sala de Exposiciones, Alcalá 31, Madrid **2007** '10°00 S / 76°00 W', Galeria Leme, São Paulo • 'Geopolíticas de la Animación', Centro Andaluz de Arte Contemporáneo, Seville • 'En Perfecto Desorden', Museo de Arte Reina Sofía, Madrid **Selected bibliography: 2009** Cuauhtémoc Medina, 'Los daminificados de la utopía', Reforma, Mar **2008** Patricia Esquivias and Manuela Moscoso (eds.), 'Juntos Acordaron', Adelantar el Oscurecer, Centro de Cultura Sa Nostra **2007** Jacob Fabricius (ed.), Acceso Directo, GPB04, Geneva **2006** Cuauhtémoc Medina, 'Edición y Manualidad', Reforma, May

Nevin Aladag

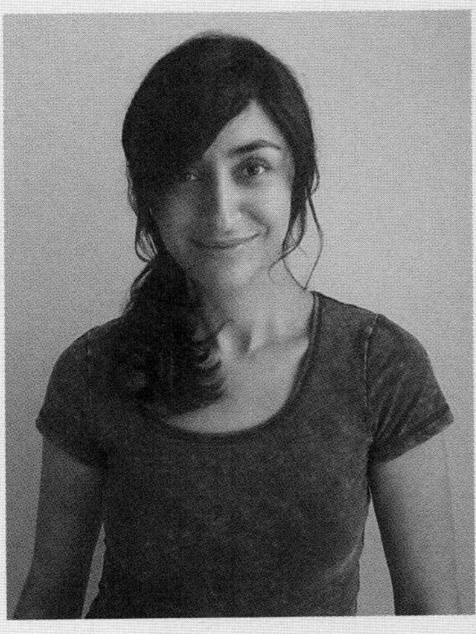

Born 1972, Van, Turkey. Lives Berlin, Germany. **Selected solo exhibitions: 2008** Outlet, Istanbul **2007** Gitte Weise Galerie, Berlin **2007** Kunsthalle Palazzo Liesthal, Switzerland **2006** Hebbel am Ufer, Berlin **2003** Künstlerhaus Bethanien, Berlin **Selected group exhibitions: 2009** 'The Jerusalem Syndrom', Al-Ma'mal Foundation for Contemporary Art, Jerusalem • 'Scorpio's Garden', Temporäre Kunsthalle Berlin • Istanbul Biennal • 'Reading the City', Open e v+a, Limerick City Gallery of Art, Ireland • 'Biennale Cuvée 09', O.K. Centrum für Gegenwartskunst, Linz, Austria **2008** Taipei Biennial • 'U-Turn', Quadrennial for Contemporary Art, Copenhagen **Selected bibliography: 2009** What, How and for Whom (WHW), What keeps mankind alive? 11th Istanbul Biennial, IKSV, Istanbul • Angelika Nollert and Yilmaz Dziewior, Reading the City, open ev+a, Gandon Editions, Limerick **2008** Anke Hoffmann, Shifting Identities, Kunsthaus Zürich; JRP Ringier, Zurich **2007** Marius Babias and René Block, Die Balkan Triologie, Silke Schreiber Editions, Munich **2006** Harald Fricke, 'Best of 2006: Nevin Aladag', Artforum, Dec

Can Altay

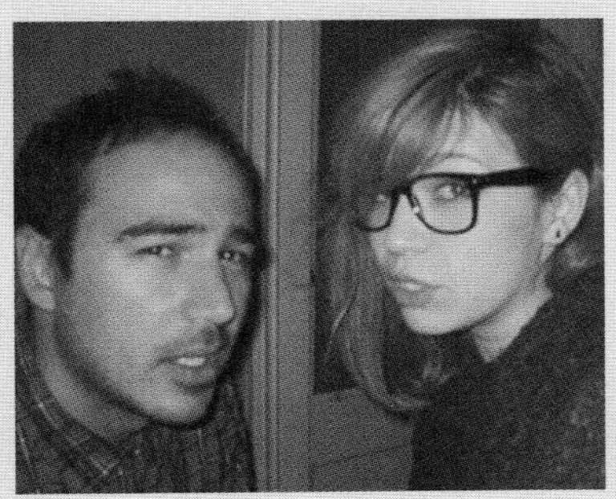

Born 1975, Ankara, Turkey. Lives Ankara, Turkey. **Selected solo exhibitions: 2008** Künstlerhaus Bethanien, Berlin **2007** Spike Island, Bristol **2006** The Abstract Cabinet at Sala Rekalde, Bilbao **Selected group exhibitions: 2009** 'There is No Audience', Montehermoso, Vitorio-Gasteiz, Spain • 'A Fantasy for Alann Kaprow', Contemporary Image Collective, Cairo **2008** Gwangju Biennial • 'New Ends Old Beginnings', Bluecoat, Liverpool **2006** 'How to Build a Universe That Doesn't Fall Apart Two Days Later', CCA Wattis Institute, San Francisco • Busan Biennial **Selected bibliography: 2009** Jeremiah Day and Helen Westgeest, 'We're papermen' he said, self-published, Istanbul **2008** Can Altay and D. Altay, 'Counter-Spatialization (of Power) (in Istanbul)', Urban Makers: Parallel Narratives on Grassroots Structures and Tensions, B_Books, Berlin • Valeria Schulte-Fischedick, 'Niche Communities', Be, no. 15 **2005** Will Bradley, 'Can Altay', Frieze, Summer

Armando Andrade Tudela

Born 1975, Lima, Peru. Lives Berlin, Germany. **Selected solo exhibitions: 2010** Museu d' Art Contemporani de Barcelona • Fonds Régional d'Art Contemporain Bourgogne, Dijon **2009** Deutscher Akademischer Austausch Dienst, Berlin • Ikon Gallery, Birmingham • Frankfurter Kunstverein • Kunsthalle Basel **2007** Annet Gelink Gallery, Amsterdam **Selected group exhibitions: 2009** 'Panorama da Arte Brasileira', Museu de Arte Moderno, São Paulo • 'Warsaw Under Construction', Museum of Modern Art, Warsaw • 'Modernologies', Museu d'Art Contemporani de Barcelona • 'Yellow and Green', Museum für Moderne Kunst, Frankfurt **2008** 'Autour de Max Bill', Centre Culturel Suisse, Paris • 'Neutre Intense', La Maison Populaire, Paris • 'Brave New Worlds', Walker Art Center, Minneapolis **2007** Lyon Biennial

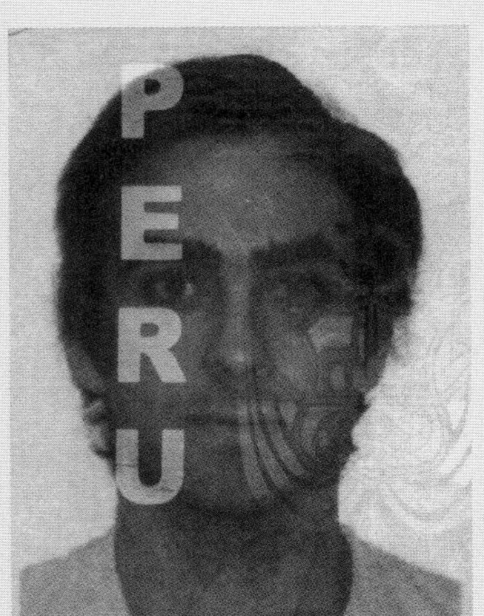

Selected bibliography: 2007 Doryun Chong and Yasmin Raymond, Brave New Worlds, Walker Art Center, Minneapolis **2006** Tania Kovats (ed.), The Drawing Book, Black Dog, London • Mark Godfrey, 'Armando Andrade Tudela', Vitamin Ph: New Perspectives in Photography, Phaidon, London • Lisette Lagnado and Adriano Pedrosa (eds.), 27 Bienal de São Paulo: Como Viver Junto, Fundacao Bienal, São Paulo • Dan Fox, 'Armando Andrade Tudela', Frieze, Oct

Ibon Aranberri

Born 1970, Itziar, Spain. Lives Bilbao, Spain. **Selected solo exhibitions: 2008** Frankfurter Kunstverein **2007** Kunsthalle Basel **2007** Galería Pepe Cobo, Madrid **2005** Iaspis Project Room, Stockholm **2005** Galerie Isabella Bortolozzi, Berlin **Selected group exhibitions: 2009** 'A Space on the Side of the Road', Röda Sten, Gothenburg, Sweden **2008** Sydney Biennial • 'The Martian Museum of Terrestrial Art', Barbican Art Gallery, London **2007** Documenta 12, Kassel • 'The Routines of Resistance', Standard Gallery, Oslo **2006** 'Fantom', Charlottenborg Exhibition Hall, Copenhagen • 'Several ways out', Unge Kunstneres Samfund, Oslo **2005** 'Cork Caucus', National Sculpture Factory, Cork, Ireland • 'Be what you want but stay where you are', Witte de With, Rotterdam **Selected bibliography: 2007** Juan Antonio Alvarez Reyes, 'Ibon Aranberri: On communitarian identity and its fragility', Arte Contexto, no.16 • Barnaby Drabble, 'Integration', Metropolis, no.6 • Pip Day, 'The Logic of Stories'; Peio Aguirre, 'Ibon Aranberri: Footprints', Afterall, no.14 • Eva Scharrer, 'Ibon Aranberri, Integration', Artforum, Dec • Jaio Miren, 'Los pasos de una liturgia ascensional', La Vanguardia — Culturas, no. 259

Tonico Lemos Auad

Born 1968, Belém, Brasil. Lives London, UK. **Selected solo exhibitions: 2009** Stephen Friedman Gallery, London **2008** CRG Gallery, New York **2007** Galeria Luisa Strina, São Paulo, Brazil

Aspen Art Museum, CO, USA **Selected group exhibitions: 2009** 'Textiles: Art a[nd] the Social Fabric', Museum van Hedendaagse Kunst Antwerpen, Antwe[rpen]

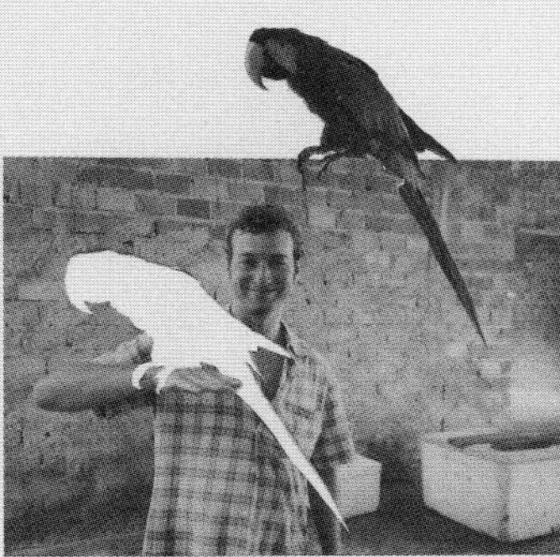

'The Subject IS you', Weatherspoon Ar[t] Museum at University of North Carolina [at] Greensboro • 'Grau Zero', Paço das A[rtes,] São Paulo • 'Family Jewels', Galerie Chantal Crousel, Paris **2008** 'This is no[t] Void', Galeria Luisa Strina, São Paulo • 'Blooming: Brazil-Japan Where You A[re]', Toyota Municipal Art Museum, Japan • 'Wall Rockets: Contemporary Artists and Ed Ruscha', Flag Art Foundation, N[ew] York; Albright Knox, Buffalo **Selected bibliography: 2009** Chris Fite-Wassilak, 'Tonico Lemos Auad', Flash Art, May-J[une] **2007** Alex Farquharson, Andrea Schliek[er] and Heidi Zuckerman Jacobson, Tonico Lemos Auad, Aspen Art Museum

Lisa Anne Auerbach

Born 1967, Ann Arbour, MI, USA. Lives Los Angeles, CA, USA.

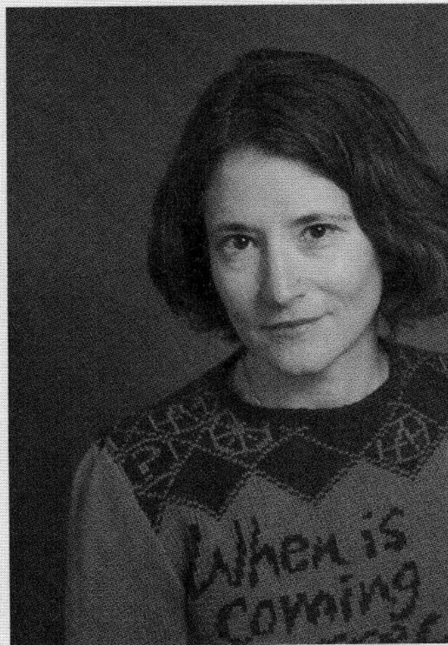

Selected solo exhibitions: 2009
Nottingham Contemporary, UK • University of Michigan Museum of Art, Ann Arbor **2008** Aspen Art Museum, CO, USA • Printed Matter, New York **2007** David Patton Los Angeles **Selected group exhibitions: 2009** 'Nine Lives', Hammer Museum, Los Angeles • 'Prescriptions', Acme Gallery, Los Angeles **2008** 'Cottage Industry', Baltimore Contemporary Museum • 'Make You Notice', San Francisco Arts Commission Gallery **2007** 'Words Fail Me', Museum of Contemporary Art Detroit **2006** 'Open Walls 2', White Columns, New York • 'Street Signs and Solar Ovens: Social Craft in Los Angeles', Craft and Folk Art Museum, Los Angeles **Selected bibliography: 2009** Patricia Zohn, 'Culture Zohn: Lisa Anne Auerbach and Jenny Holzer: Art Meets Politics Over Words', Huffington Post, 13 Mar • Ali Subotnick, Nine Lives: Visionary Artists from LA, Hammer Museum, Los Angeles **2008** Andrew Berardini, 'Lisa Anne Auerbach: Auerbachtoberfest', Art Review, Jan **2007** Sabrina Gschwandtner, KnitKnit: Profiles and Projects from Knitting's New Wave, Stewart, Tabori & Chang, New York

Sven Augustijnen

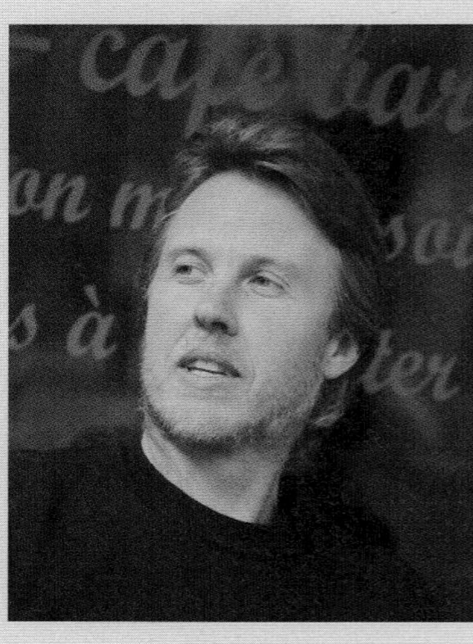

Born 1970, Mechelen, Belgium. Lives Brussels, Belgium. **Selected solo exhibitions: 2008** Jan Mot, Brussels **2007** Jan Mot, Brussels **Selected group exhibitions: 2009** 'The State of Things', Bozar, Brussels • 'Report On Probability', Kunsthalle Basel • 'A Story Of The Image', Shanghai Art Museum; National Museum, Singapore • 'Stutter', Tate Modern, London **2008** 'Weder Entweder Noch Oder', Wurttembergischer Kunstverein, Stuttgart • 'Peripheral Vision and Collective Body', Museion, Bolzano • 'A Portrait of the Artist as a Researcher 2.0', Beursschouwburg, Brussels **2007** 'A Story of the Image: Visual Art as Visual Culture', Museum van Hedendaagse Kunst Antwerpen, Antwerp • 'Tanzen, Sehen: The Provocation of the Media in the Dialogue of Dance and Fine Art', Museum für Gegenwartskunst Siegen, Germany; Centro Andaluz de Arte Contemporáneo, Seville **Selected bibliography: 2009** Cathleen Chaffee, 'Les Demoiselles de Bruxelles: A "Philosophical Brothel"', Newspaper Jan Mot, Jan **2008** Lieven Van den Abeele, 'De man met de camera: Sven Augustijnen', Ons Erfdeel, Apr • Dirk De Wit and Anne Judong (eds.), Arts Flanders 08 Compilation Box, Flemish Institute for Visual, Audiovisual and Media Art, Ghent **2007** Jan Verwoert, 'The Practical Surrealism of Power', A Prior, no. 14 • Raimundas Malasauskas, 'Royal Itineraries', Dot Dot Dot, no. 13 **2006** Raimundas Malasauskas, 'Koninklijke Routes: Een Interview Met Sven Augustijnen', Metropolis M, Jun-Jul

Alexandra Bachzetsis

Born 1974, Zurich, Switzerland. Lives Zurich, Switzerland. **Selected solo exhibitions: 2008** Kunsthalle Basel **2007** Perla Mode Message Salon (with Julia Born), Zurich **2006** De Appel, Amsterdam **2005** Juliette Jongma Gallery, Amsterdam **2004** Etablissement d'en face (with Danai Anesiadou), Brussels

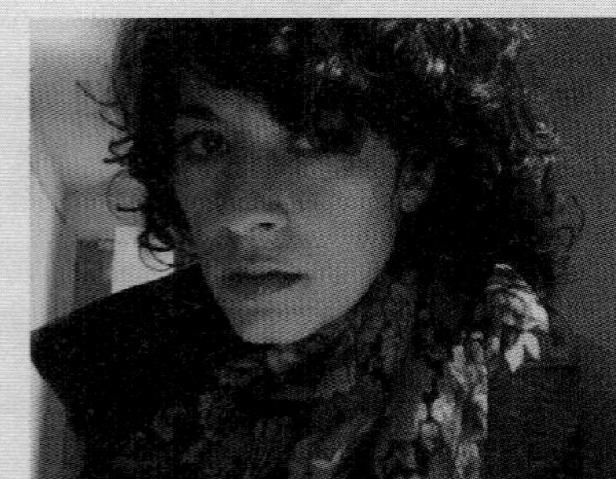

Selected group exhibitions: 2009 'Quick, Quick, Slow: Text, Image and Time', Museu Colecçao Berardo and ExperimentaDesign, Lisbon • 'Something Raw: International Dance and Performance Festival', Brakke Grond, Flemish Cultural Centre, Amsterdam • 'The Swiss Cube', Instituto Svizzero, Rome **2008** 'Aurum', CentrePasquArt, Biel • 'Word Event', Kunsthalle Basel • Berlin Biennial • 'Shifting Identities', Kunsthaus Zürich • 'Forms of Inquiry: The Architecture of Critical Graphic Design' Architectural Association School of Architecture, London **2007** 'If I Can't Dance, I Don't Want To Be Part Of Your Revolution', Festival aan de Werf, Utrecht; De Appel, Amsterdam • 'The Weasel', South London Gallery **Selected bibliography: 2009** Eva Scharrer, 'Alexandra Bachzetsis: Kunsthalle Basel', Artforum, Feb **2008** Miriam Glass, 'Getanzte Klischees', Basler Zeitung, Kulturmagazin, 17 Nov • 'Ursula Haas, 'Kraftvolle Auseinandersetzung mit gemachter Weiblichkeit', Basellandschaftliche Zeitung, 25 Oct • Dieter Roelstraete, 'Gold', Shifting Identities, Kunsthaus Zurich **2007** Maxine Kopsa, 'Oversexed and underfucked: Alexandra Bachzetsis's Dance Performances', Metropolis M, no. 2 • Dominic Eichler, 'Act', Frieze, Mar • 'Felizitas Ammann, 'Explosive Mischung', Tages-Anzeiger, 12 May • Benjamin Chaix, 'Qu'on se la danse', La Tribune de Genève, 24 Jul • Anne Davier, 'L'amour comme il se zappe', Journal de l'adc, Sep-Dec

Nairy Baghramian

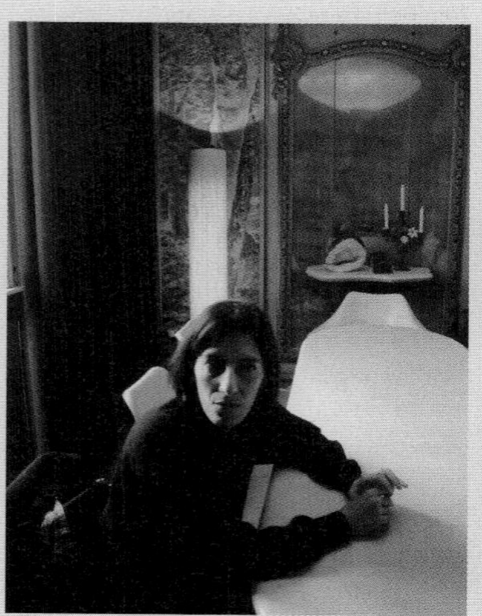

Born 1971, Isfahan, Iran. Lives Berlin, Germany. **Selected solo exhibitions: 2009** Studio Voltaire **2008** Kunstverein Aachen, Germany; Staatliche Kunsthalle Baden-Baden • Schinkel Pavillon (with Janette Laverrière), Berlin Biennial **2007** Kunstverein Nürnberg, Nuremberg **2006** Kunsthalle Basel **Selected group exhibitions: 2009** 'Monument und Utopie', Steierischer Herbst, Graz • 'Gespins', Museum Abteiberg, Moenchengladbach • 'Depression', Marres, Maastricht • 'Entre deux actes (Loge de comédienne)', Staatliche Kunsthalle Baden-Baden • 'Looking is Political', Kunsthalle Bergen, Norway **2008** '…In the Cherished Company of Others', Museum of Modern Art, Oostende, Belgium; De Appel Arts Centre, Amsterdam • 'Draw a Straight Line and Follow it', Tate Modern, London **2007** 'Devotee', Cabinet, London • Skulptur Projekte Münster **Selected bibliography: 2009** Catrin Lorch, 'Nairy Baghramian', Artforum, Jan • Dominic Eichler, 'Nairy Baghramian', Mousse, Summer **2008** Dominic Eichler, Karola Grässlin & André Rothmann, The Walker's Day Off, Staatliche Kunsthalle Baden-Baden; Walther König, Cologne **2008** Juliane Rebentisch, 'Im Glaushaus', Texte Zur Kunst, May **2007** Manfred Herms, 'Nairy Baghramian: Deserted frames, whispery voices; marquees, mirrors and steel earrings', Frieze, May

Dave Hullfish Bailey

Born 1963, Denver, CO, USA. Lives Los Angeles, CA, USA. **Selected solo exhibitions: 2009** The Suburban, Chicago • David Pestorius Projects, Brisbane **2008** Mesler & Hug, Los Angeles **2007** Casco, Utrecht **2006** Centre d'Art Santa Mónica, Barcelona • Secession, Vienna **Selected group exhibitions: 2009** 'For the blind man in the dark looking for the black cat that isn't there', Culturgest, Lisbon; De Appel, Amsterdam; Museum of Contemporary Art, Detroit; Institute of Contemporary Arts, London; Contemporary Art Museum St Louis **2009** 'Dave Hullfish Bailey & Nils Norman: Surrounded by Squares', Raven Row, London **2007** Lyon Biennial **2006** 'Turrbal-Jagera: The University of Queensland Art Projects 2006', University Art Museum, Brisbane **Selected bibliography: 2009** Sarah Lehrer-Graiwer, 'Dave Hullfish Bailey', Artforum, Feb **2008** Lars Bang Larsen and Jan Tumlir, What's Left, Casco, Utrecht; Sternberg, Berlin and New York **2007** Catherine Chevalier, 'Dave Hullfish Bailey: Queensland University, Brisbane', Frog, no. 5 **2006** Emily Pethick and Susanne Neuberger, Elevator, Secession, Vienna

Anna Barham

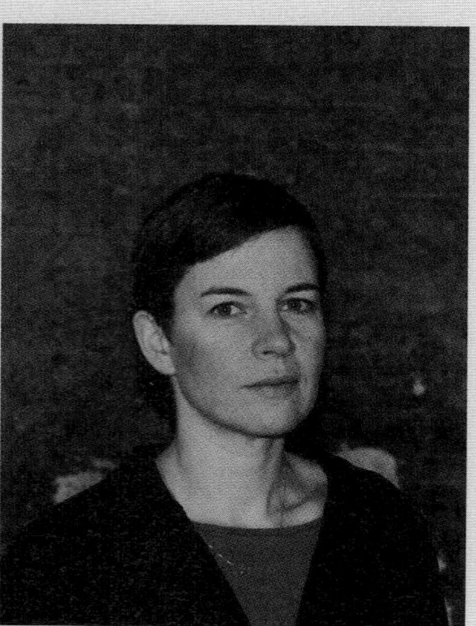

Born 1974, Sutton Coldfield, UK. Lives London, UK. **Selected solo exhibitions: 2009** Port Eliot, Cornwall (with Institute of Contemporary Arts, London) • Arcade, London **2007** Four, Dublin **2005** Irish Museum of Modern Art, Dublin. **Selected group exhibitions: 2009** 'Stutter', Tate Modern, London • 'Poor. Old. Tired. Horse.', Institute of Contemporary Arts, London • 'Free Radicals', Arcade, London **2008** 'Travelogue', One in the Other, London • 'On Your Marks', Pippy Houldsworth, London **2007** 'Like Leaves', Tanya Bonakdar Gallery, New York • 'Lost Tongues Rediscovered', Stroom, The Hague **Selected bibliography: 2010** Anna Barham, Return To Leptis Magna, self-published **2009** Charlotte Bonham-Carter and Mark Sladen, 'Anna Barham', Roland, Institute of Contemporary Arts, London

Walead Beshty

Born 1976, London, UK. Lives Los Angeles, CA, USA. **Selected solo exhibitions: 2009** Thomas Dane Gallery, London • The Hirshhorn Museum and Sculpture Garden, Washington, DC • The University of Michigan Museum of Art, Ann Arbor • LAXART, Los Angeles • Wallspace, New York **2008** Galerie Rodolphe Janssen, Brussels Hammer Museum, Los Angeles **Selected group exhibitions: 2009** 'New Photography 2009', The Museum of Modern Art, New York • 'Walead Beshty, Kelly Walker, Christopher Williams', China Art Objects Galleries, Los Angeles • Tate Triennial, London • 'The Space of the Work and the Place of the Object', SculptureCenter, New York • 'The Photographic Object: Between sculpture and photography', Photographer's Gallery, London. **2008** Whitney Biennial, New York • 'Now You See It', Aspen Art Museum, CO, USA • 'Objects of Value, Miami Art Museum • 'Signs of the Times', Whitney Museum of American Art, New York

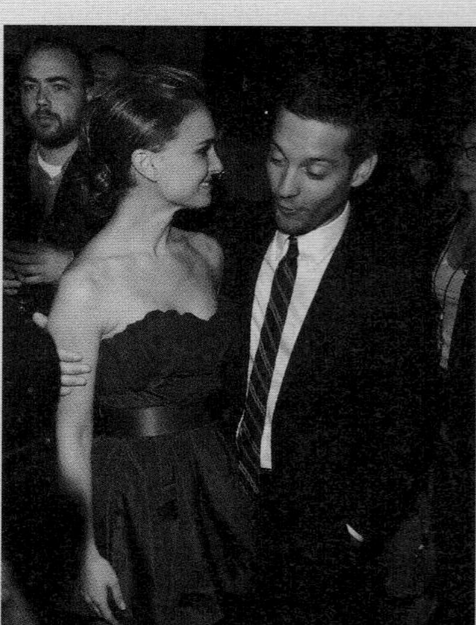

'The Sickness of the Hunt', Musée d'Art Moderne et d'Art Contemporain, Nice • 'Word Event (After George Brecht)', Kunsthalle Basel • 'Meanwhile in Baghdad', Renaissance Society, Chicago **Selected bibliography: 2009** Susan Bright, The Self-Portrait in Contemporary Art, Thames & Hudson, London • Colin Davies and Monika Parrinder (eds.), Limited Language — Rewriting Design, Birkhauser, Basel • Hamza Walker and Brian Sholis, Walead Beshty: American Passages, LAXART Books, Los Angeles • 'Walead Beshty and Eileen Quinlan in Conversation', Bomb Magazine, Sep • 'Roundtable Discussion on Abstraction and Photography with Christopher Bedford, Walead Beshty, Liz Deschenes and Eileen Quinlan', Frieze, Sep • Steve Pulimood, 'Popular Mechanics: Walead Beshty', Art in America, Apr • 'The Pier Conversation: Walead Beshty and Olivier Mosset', Mousse, Summer

Cezary Bodzianowski

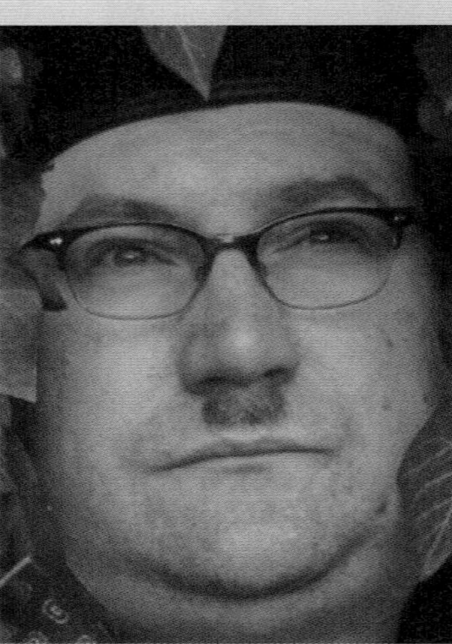

Born 1966, Szczecin, Poland. Lives Lodz, Poland. **Selected solo exhibitions: 2008** Gesellschaft für Aktuelle Kunst Bremen, Germany **2005** Gedächtnis Neue Kunsthalle, St Gallen • Kölnischer Kunstverein, Cologne • Centre Pompidou, Paris

Selected group exhibitions: 2008 'Nos Cambiamos de Domicilio', Kurimanzutto, Mexico City • 'Delusive orders', Muzeum Sztuki w Łodzi, Poland; Städtisches Museum Abteiberg, Moenchengladbach, Germany • Berlin Biennial • 'The World as a Stage', Tate Modern, London; Institute of Contemporary Art, Boston **Selected bibliography: 2009** Cezary Bodzianowski, Sababa, Centre for Contenporary Art, Tel Aviv **2008** Jannet de Vries, Maybe, Gesellschaft für Aktuelle Kunst, Bremen • Adam Szymczyk, 'Please Use Stairs', Flash Art, Mar-Apr **2003** Lars Bang Larsen and Joanna Mytkowska, Cezary Bodzianowski, Foksal Gallery Foundation, Warsaw; Revolver, Frankfurt

Pablo Bronstein

Born 1977, Buenos Aires, Argentina. Lives London, UK. **Selected solo exhibitions: 2010** Tate Britain, London **2009** Metropolitan Museum of Art, New York • 'Farm Building' (permanent installation), Grizedale Arts, Cumbria, UK **2008** Franco Noero, Turin • Herald Street, London **2007** Städtisch Galerie im Lenachhaus und Kunstbau Luisenstrasse, Munich **Selected group exhibitions:**

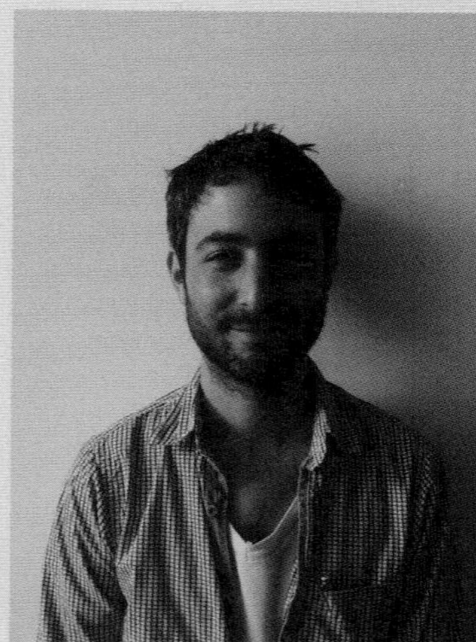

2010 Bucharest Biennial • 'Choreographing You', Hayward Gallery, London 2009 'Characters, Figures and Signs: Choreography as "Doing" and "Saying"', Tate Modern, London • 'Staging the Phenomenal Character', Tracy Williams Ltd, New York 2008 'La Petite Histoire', Kunstraum Niederoesterreich, Vienna • 'That Beautiful Pale Face is my Fate (for Lord Byron)', Nottingham Contemporary 2007 Peforma 07, New York • 'You Have Not Been Honest', Museo d'Arte Contemporanea Donnaregina, Naples Selected bibliography: 2009 Nicholas Cullinan, 'Pablo Bronstein: Galleria Franco Noero', Artforum, Feb 2008 Jan Verwoert, 'Metaphors that Move the Body', Metropolis M, Feb-Mar • Pablo Bronstein, Ornamental Designs, Walther König, Cologne • Pablo Bronstein, Postmodern Architecture in London, Walther König, Cologne 2007 Cornelia Gockel, 'Pablo Bronstein', Kunstforum, May-Jun

Tom Burr

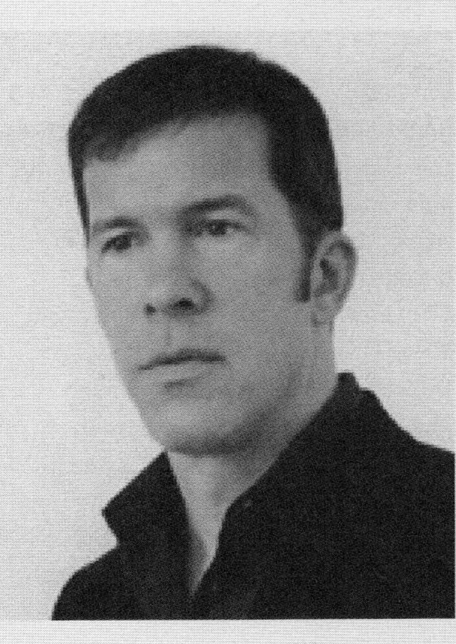

Born 1963 New Haven, CT, USA • Lives New York, NY, USA. Selected solo exhibitions 2009 Städtische Galerie im Lenbachhaus und Kunstbau, Munich; Kunstmuseum Basel • Museum für Gegenwartskunst, Basel (with Monica Bonvincini(• Stuart Shave/Modern Art, London • Bortolami Gallery, New York 2008 Franco Noero, Turin • Sculpture Center, New York • Galerie Almine Rech, Paris 2007 Schinkel Pavillon, Berlin • Secession, Vienna Selected group exhibitions: 2009 'The World is Yours', Louisiana Museum of Modern Art, Denmark 2008 'A Season in Brussels', Galerie eu at Dépendance, Brussels • 'A New High in Getting Low', John Connelly Presents, New York • 'Abstract America', Saatchi Gallery, London 2007 'Walk!', Kunstraum Kreuzberg/Bethanien, Berlin • 'Oh Girl, It's a Boy!', Munich Kunstverein • 'Body Politicx', Witte de With, Rotterdam • 'The Happiness of Objects', Sculpture Center, New York • 'Unmonumental', New Museum, New York • 'Pale Carnage', Arnolfini, Bristol; Dundee Contemporary Arts, UK Selected bibliography: 2009 Melissa Gronlund, 'Tom Burr', Vitamin 3-D: New Perspectives in Sculpture and Installation, Phaidon Press, London • Tom Burr, Tom Burr, Städtische Galerie im Lenbachhaus und Kunstbau München; Kunstmuseum Basel Museum für Gegenwartskunst 2008 Tom Burr, 'Questionnaire', Frieze, Jun-Aug • Francesco Vezzoli, 'Tom Burr', Mousse, Mar. • Joshua Decter, 'Tom Burr Talks About Addict-Love', Artforum, Feb 2007 George Baker, 'The Other Side of the Wall', October, Spring • Richard Flood, Massimiliano Gioni, Laura Hoptman, Unmonumental, Phaidon, London

Gerard Byrne

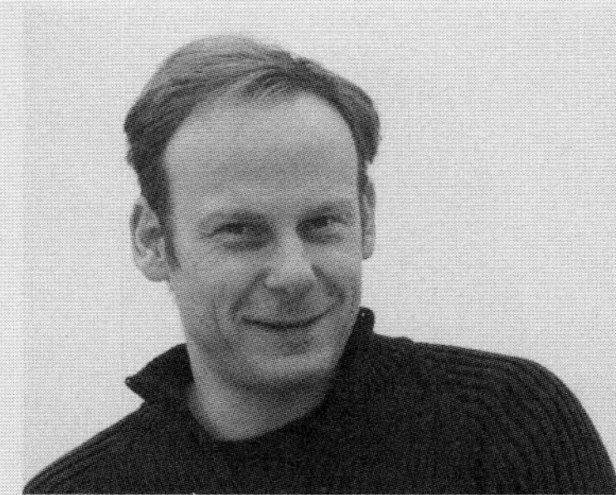

Born 1969, Dublin, Ireland. Lives Dublin, Ireland. Selected solo exhibitions: 2009 Lisson Gallery, London 2008 Institute of Contemporary Art, Boston • Statens Museum for Kunst, Copenhagen 2007 Contemporary Art Centre, Vilnius • Charles H. Scott Gallery, Vancouver • Venice Biennale • Kunstverein für die Rheinlande und Westfalen, Düsseldorf • Lisson Gallery, London Selected group exhibitions: 2009 'Little Theatre of Gestures', Kunstmuseum Basel; Malmö Konsthall • 'The New Monumentality', Henry Moore Institute, Leeds, 'Slow Movement', Kunsthalle Bern 2008 Sydney Biennial • Gwangju Biennial • Turin Triennial 2007 Lyon Biennal • 'The Art of Failure', Kunsthaus Basel Selected bibliography: 2008 Barbara Clausen and Marianne Torp, Related Works, Statens Museum for Kunst, Copenhagen 2007 Mark Godfrey, Vanessa Joan Müller, Lytle Shaw, Catherine Wood, The Present Tense through the Ages, Charles H. Scott Gallery, Vancouver; Farmleigh Gallery, Dublin; Kunstverein für die Rheinlande und Westfalen, Düsseldorf; Lisson Gallery, London, Models Arts and Niland Gallery, Sligo 2005 Emily Pethick, '1984 and Beyond', If I can't Dance… Episode 1, Rotterdam

Duncan Campbell

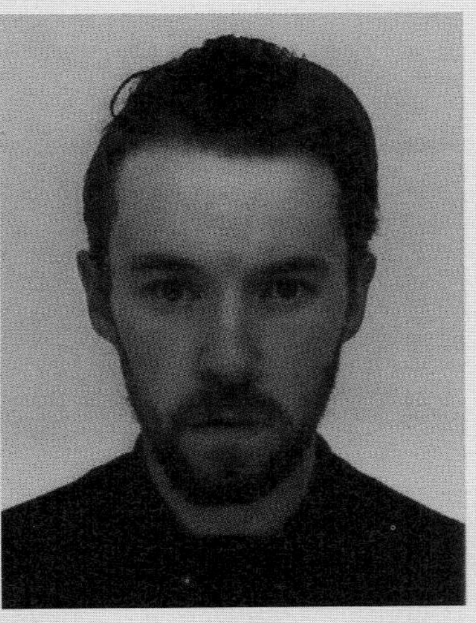

Born 1972, Dublin, Ireland. Lives Glasgow, UK. Selected solo exhibitions: 2010 Chisenhale Gallery, London 2009 Museum Moderner Kunst Stiftung, Vienna • List Visual Arts Center, Massachusetts Institute of Technology, Cambridge, MA • Ludlow 38, New York • Kunstverein München, Munich • Scottish National Gallery of Modern Art, Edinburgh 2008 Hotel, London • Institute of Contemporary Arts, London Selected group exhibitions: 2009 'Border Crossings: Current Art and Modernism in the 21st Century', Kunstmuseum Wolfsburg 2008 'After October', Elizabeth Dee Gallery, New York • 'Rictus Grin', Broadway 1602, New York 2007 'You Have Not Been Honest', Museo d'Arte Donnaregina, Naples 2006 'Art Now', Tate Britain, London Selected bibliography: 2009 Daniel Jewesbury, Duncan Campbell, Museum Moderner Kunst Stiftung Ludwig Wien, Vienna • Toby Maier, 'Duncan Campbell' Mousse, Apr-May • Mary Brodbin, 'Bernadette', Socialist Review, Jan 2008 Stuart Comer, 'Best of 2008', Artforum, Dec • Duncan Campbell, 'Life in Film', Frieze, Oct • Ken Neil, 'Telling Stories', Map Magazine, Fall • Martin Herbert, 'Focus: Duncan Campbell', Frieze, Apr

Bonnie Camplin

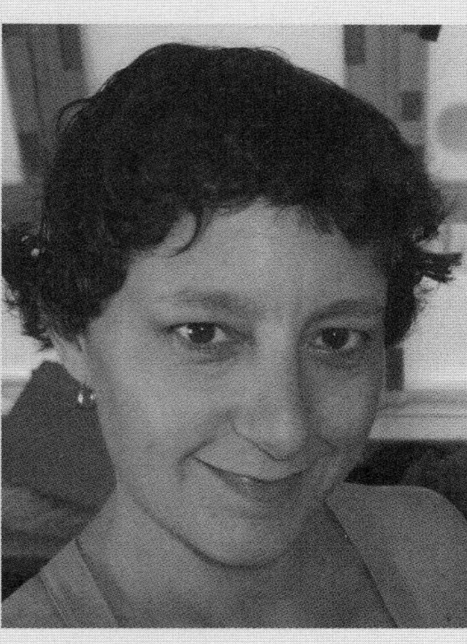

Born 1970, London, UK. Lives London, UK. Selected solo exhibitions and performances: 2009 Michael Benevento, Los Angeles • Chisenhale Gallery, London 2008 Lightbox, Tate Britain, London • Galerie Cinzia Friedländer, Berlin • 'Usher We (Down There)' (with Paulina Olowska), Saturday Live Performance, Tate Modern, London 2007 Cabinet, London • 'A like Akarova' (with Paulina Olowska), Wiels, Brussels • 'Salty Water/ What of Salty Water' (with Paulina Olowska), Portikus, Frankfurt Selected group exhibitions: 2008 Turin Triennial 2007 'Strange Things Permit Themselves the Luxury of Occuring', Camden Arts Centre, London • 'UBS Drawing Collection', Tate Modern London 2006 'Special Afflictions by Roy Harryhozen', The Artist's Cinema, Frieze Art Fair, London Selected bibliography: 2008 Barry Schwabsky, 'Reviews: Bonnie Camplin', Artforum, Dec 2007 Catherine Wood, 'Openings: Bonnie Camplin', Artforum, Nov • 'Bonnie Camplin in Coversation with Catherine Wood', Untitled, spring 2006 Andrew Hunt, 'A séance for people yet to come', The New Art, Rachmaninoffs Books, London 2004 Mark Beasley, 'Bonnie Camplin', Frieze, Jun-Aug

Nina Canell

Born 1979, Växjö, Sweden. Lives Berlin, Germany. Selected solo exhibitions: 2010 Museum Moderner Kunst Stiftung Ludwig, Vienna • Konrad Fischer Galerie, Düsseldorf 2009 Hamburg Kunstverein • Neuer Aachener Kunstverein, Aachen Douglas Hyde Gallery, Dublin 2008 Galerie Barbara Wien, Berlin • Institute of Contemporary Arts, London • Mother's Tankstation, Dublin

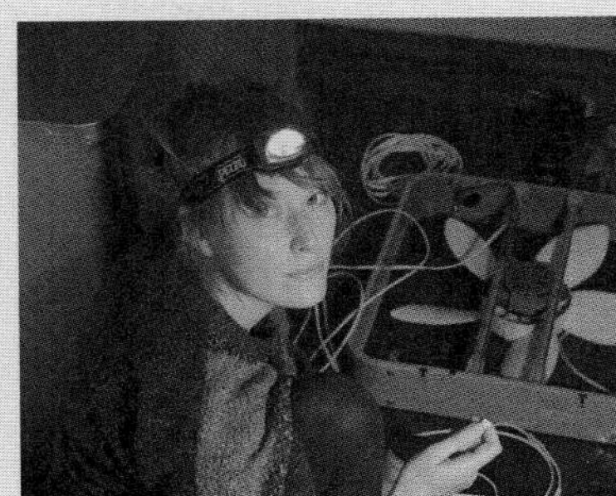

Selected group exhibitions: 2010 Liverpool Biennial • 'The Inner Life of Things', Frankfurter Kunstverein, Frankfurt 2009 'The Actuality of the Idea', Stuart Shave/Modern Art, London • 'All That Is Solid Melts into Air', Museum van Hedendaagse Kunst Antwerpen, Antwerp • 'Nina Canell, Aleana Egan, Marzena Nowak', Konrad Fischer Galerie, Düsseldorf 2008 Gwangju Biennial • Manifesta 7, Rovereto • 'Auto-Stop', Malmö Konsthall Selected bibliography: 2009 Lauren Cornell, Massimiliano Gioni and Laura Hoptman (eds.), Younger Than Jesus: Artist Directory, Phaidon, London • Chris Sharp, 'Nina Canell', Map Magazine, Spring • Isobel Harbison, 'Nina Canell', Nought to Sixty, Institute of Contemporary Arts, London 2008 Hyunjin Kim, Movement, Contingency, Community, Darun Books • Martin Herbert, 'Nina Canell', Modern Painters, Dec 2007 Georgina Jackson, Arpeggio Book, Model Arts & Niland Gallery

Alejandro Cesarco

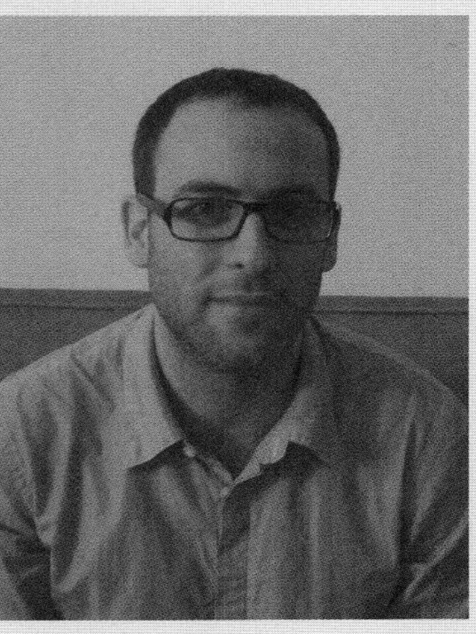

Born 1975, Montevideo, Uruguay. Lives New York, NY, USA. Selected solo exhibitions: 2010 Artpace, San Antonio, TX, USA 2009 Murray Guy, New York • Tanya Leighton Gallery, Berlin • Charles H. Scott Gallery, Emily Carr University, Vancouver • Turtle Point Press, New York 2008 Murray Guy, New York • New Langton Arts, San Francisco 2007 'Retrospective' (with John Baldessari), Murray Guy, New York Selected group exhibitions: 2009 'A Sensed Pertubation', Murray Guy, New York • 'Rubber Sheets', C.R.E.A.M. Projects, Brooklyn • 'Just What are they Saying...', Jonathan Ferrara Gallery, New Orleans • Poli/Graphica Triennial, San Juan, Puerto Rico 2008 'September Show', Tanya Leighton, Berlin • 'Power Structure', Andrew Roth, New York • 'Salon of the Revolution', HDLU/Mestrovic Pavilion, Zagreb Selected bibliography: 2009 Nicolas Guagnini, 'Alejandro Cesarco', Bomb, Winter • Hans Ulrich Obrist, 'Just an Artist with More Experience', Hans Ulrich Obrist, John Baldessari: The Conversation Series #18, Walther König, Cologne 2008 David Coggins, 'John Baldessari and Alejandro Cesarco at Murray Guy', Art in America, Jun-Jul • Tim Griffin, 'Notes on Jokes', Artforum, Jan

Paul Chan

Born 1973, Hong Kong. Lives New York, NY, USA. Selected solo exhibitions: 2009 Renaissance Society, Chicago • Greene Naftali Gallery, New York 2008 Carpenter Center for the Visual Arts, Harvard University, Cambridge, MA, USA 2007 Serpentine Gallery, London • New Museum, New Yor[k] • Stedelijk Museum, Amsterdam • Western Front, Vancouver Selected gro[up] exhibitions: 2009 Venice Biennale • 'The Quick and the Dead', Walker Art Center, Minneapolis

2008 'Betwixt', Magasin 3 Stockholm Konsthall • 'The Art of the Real', Kunstmuseum aan Zee, Oostende, Belgiu[m] • Turin Triennial • 'That Was Then...This Is Now', P.S.1 Contemporary Art Center, Ne[w] York • 'Traces du Sacré'. Centre Pompid[ou] Paris • Sydney Biennial • 'The Cinema Eff[ect] Illusion, Reality and the Moving Image', Hirshhorn Museum, Washington, DC 200[7] Istanbul Biennial • 'Art in America: 300 Yea[rs] of Innovation', National Art Museum of China, Beijing; Shanghai Museum of Contemporary Art Selected bibliograph[y] 2008 Maurizio Cattelan and Paul Chan, 'Some Things Just Stick In Your Mind', Flash Art, Oct • George Baker and Paul Chan, 'An Interview with Paul Chan', October, Winter • Nancy Spector, 'The Colour of Money', Frieze, Jan-Feb 2007 Daniel Birnbaum, Chronology, Sternberg, Berlin and New York • Tim Griffin, 'Waiting for Godot', Artforum, Dec • Caroline Chiu, 'Paul Chan', Art Asia Pacific, Winter • Paul Chan and Jay Saunders, 'A Dialogue about the Movin[g] Image', Lyon Biennial: The History of a Decade That Has Not Been Named, JRP Ringier, Zurich • Paul Chan, The Shadow[s] and Her Wanda, Serpentine Gallery, London; Watlher König, Cologne

Rosa Chancho

Founded 2006 by Mumi, Julieta García Vázquez, Tomás Lerner, Javier Villa and Osías Yanov. Selected solo exhibition[s] 2008 South Limit, arteBA, Buenos Aires • Appetite Gallery, Buenos Aires 2007 Centro Cultural de España en Buenos Aires • Mitlag's Residence, Buenos Aires 2006 Museo de Arte Contemporáneo de Rosario • Rosa Chancho Gallery, Buenos Aires Selected group exhibitions: 2009 'Gospel Choir', Daniel Abate Gallery, Buenos Aires 2006 'Opening', Estudio Abierto, Buenos Aires Selected bibliography: 2009 Rosa Chancho, 'Poéticas Contemporáneas', Ramona, n[o.] 90 2008 Valeria González, Contemporar[y] Argentine Art: Artist by Artist, Papers Editores, Buenos Aires • Claudio Iglesia[s] 'Rosa Chancho, fuga hacia adelante', Planta, no. 4 • Eva Grinstein, 'Argentin[a] Generation 2000: Building community together', Artecontexto, no. 18 2007 Tamara Stuby, 'Buenos Aires: Ros[a] Chancho', Contemporary, Mar

Spartacus Chetwyn[d]

Born 1973, London, UK. Lives London, [UK] Selected solo exhibitions: 2008 Mass[imo] de Carlo, Milan

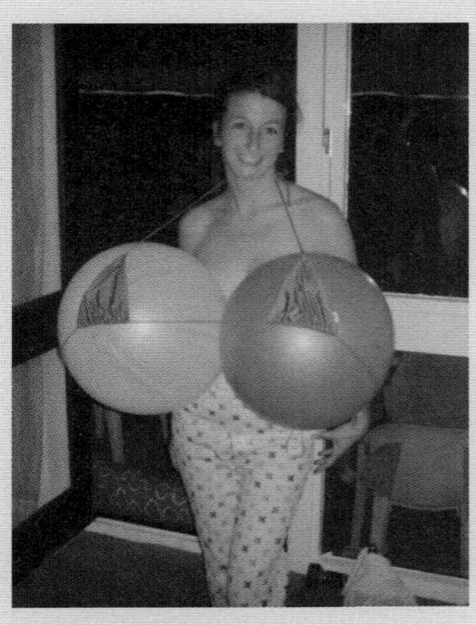

2007 Migros Museum, Zurich
2005 Gasworks, London **Selected group exhibitions: 2009** Tate Triennial, London
2008 'Help! I'm trapped in a Muzuzah Factory', Le Consortium, Dijon • 'Martian Museum of Terrestrial Art', Barbican Art Gallery, London • 'Don't Play with Dead Thing', Villa Arson, France • 'The Skat Players', Vilma Gold, London **2007** 'The Call of the Wild', Collective Gallery, Edinburgh • 'A Comedy of Errors', Artspace, Sydney • 'The Perfect Man Show', White Columns, New York. **Selected performances: 2010** 'Money', Witte de With, Rotterdam **2009** 'Alright!', Giti Nourbakhsch, Berlin **2008** 'Helmut Newton Ladies Nights', Royal Academy, London • 'Yo-Yos', South East London Cultural Centre • 'Jabba the Hutt's Reading Group', Vilma Gold, London • 'The Snail Race', Massimo De Carlo, Milan **2007** 'The Shark Arm Case –1935', Artspace, Sydney • 'Plumbing Pipe...1...2...3', Creative Time, New York • 'The Humanzee Theatre Company – Presents Giotto's Play', Migros Museum, Zurich • 'Sparky Chatroom's Film Club', Studio Voltaire, London **Selected bibliography: 2009** Nicolas Bourriaud, Altermodern: Tate Triennial, Tate Publishing, London • Spartacus Chetwynd, 'Questionnaire', Frieze, Jan-Feb **2008** Francesco Manacorda, Martian Museum of Terrestrial Art, Barbican Art Gallery, London **2007** Raphael Gygax and Heike Munder, Spartacus Chetwynd, JRP Ringier, Zurich

Chto Delat

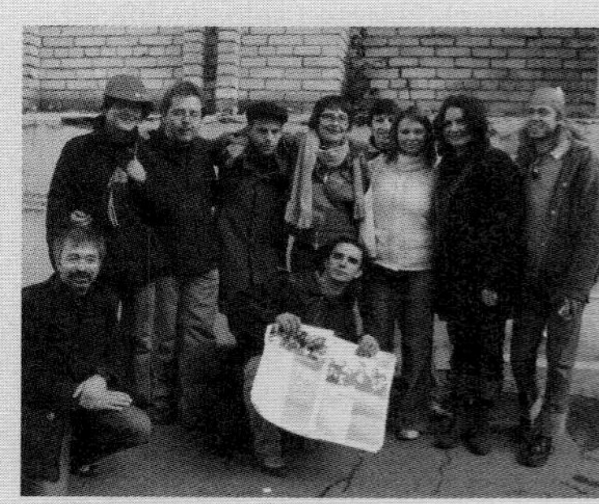

Founded 2003, St Petersburg, Russia, by Olga Egorova/Tsaplya (artist, St Petersburg), Artiom Magun (philosopher, St Petersburg), Nikolai Oleinikov (artist, Moscow), Natalia Pershina/Glucklya (artist, St Petersburg), Alexei Penzin (philosopher, Moscow), David Riff (art critic, Moscow), Alexander Skidan (poet, critic, Petersburg), Oxana Timofeeva (philosopher, Moscow) and Dmitry Vilensky (artist, St Petersburg). **Selected exhibitions: 2009** Istanbul Biennial • 'Plug in Nr. 51: Activist Club', Van Abbemuseum, Eindhoven, Netherlands **2008** 'Artist-Citzen', October Salon, Belgrade **2007** 'Societe Anonyme', Le Plateau, Paris **2006** 'La Normalidad/Ex Argentina', Palacio Nacional de las Artes, Buenos Aires **2005** 'Collective Creativity', Kunsthalle Fridericianum, Kassel

Selected bibliography: 2009 Dmitry Vilensky, 'Interview with Gerald Raunig', Afterall, no. 19 • David Riff and Dmitry Vilensky, 'From Communism to Commons?', Third Text, no. 99 **2008** 'Dmitry Vilensky interviewed by Lolita Jablonskiene: Spaces for Art, Political Learning and Subjectivation', Printed Project, no. 10 **2007** David Riff, 'It's all about people: A Self-Education in Post-Soviet Space', Documenta 12 Magazine **2006** Dmitri Vilensky and David Riff , 'Chto Delat — Angry Sandwich People or: In Praise of Dialectics', Springerin, no. 3

Anne Collier

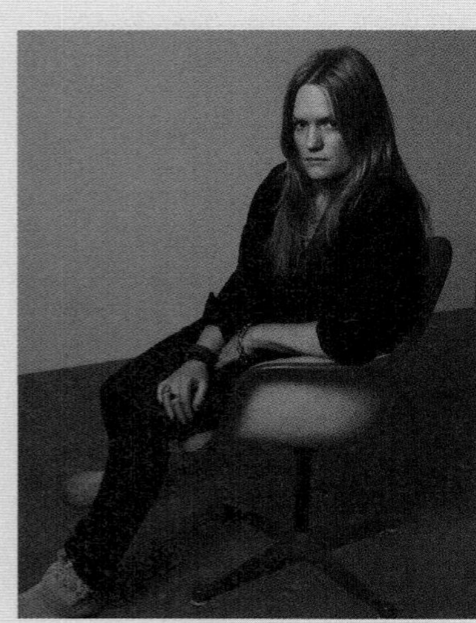

Born 1960, Los Angeles, CA, USA. Lives New York, NY USA. **Selected solo exhibitions: 2009** Art Pace, San Antonio, TX, USA • Giti Nourbakhsch, Berlin **2008** Bonner Kunstverein, Bonn • Anton Kern Gallery, New York • Presentation House, Vancouver • Marc Foxx, Los Angeles **2007** Corvi-Mora, London **Selected group exhibitions: 2009** 'The Secret Life of Objects', Midway Contemporary Art, Minneapolis • 'Revolver', Coco Kunstverein, Vienna • 'To Be Determined', Andrew Kreps Gallery, New York **2008** 'Unknown Passengers', Aspen Art Museum, CO, USA • 'Dispersion', Institute of Contemporary Arts, London • 'Records Played Backwards', Modern Institute, Glasgow **2007** 'Two Years', Whitney Museum of American Art, New York **Selected bibliography: 2009** Daniel Baumann, 'Getting Controlled and Lost', Spike, Summer **2008** Jan Verwoert, 'So How Come You Want To Know', Anne Collier, Presentation House, Vancouver **2008** J. J. Charlesworth, 'Anne Collier', Art Review, Feb **2006** Brian Dillon, 'Anne Collier', Frieze, Mar

Keren Cytter

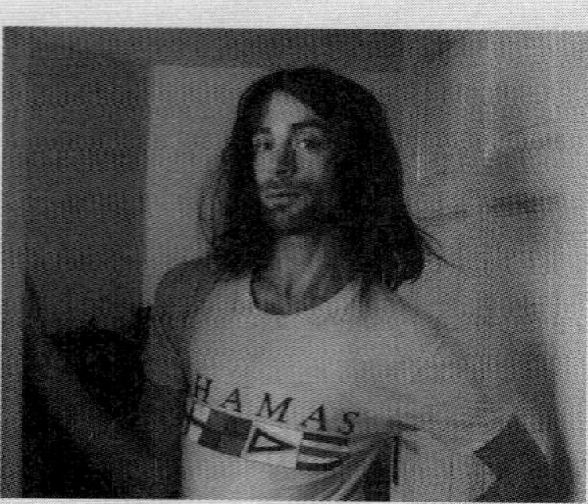

Born 1977 in Tel Aviv, Israel. Lives Berlin, Germany. **Selected solo exhibitions: 2009** Le Plateau, Paris • History in the Making, Tate Modern, London • Noga Gallery of Contemporary Art, Tel Aviv • Center for Contemporary Art, Kitakyushu

2008 Centro Huarte de Arte Contemporáneo, Huarte, Spain • Witte de With, Rotterdam **2007** Stuk Kunstcentrum, Leuven, Belgium • Museum Moderner Kunst Stiftung Ludwig, Vienna • Cubitt, London **Selected group exhibitions: 2009** Venice Biennale • 'Nationalgalerie Prize for Young Art', Hamburger Bahnhof, Berlin • 'The Generational: Younger Than Jesus', New Museum, New York **2008** 'Television Delivers People', Whitney Museum of American Art, New York • Manifesta 7, Trentino, Italy • Yokohama Triennial • 'Concepts of Love', Kölnischer Kunstverein **2007** Lyon Biennial • Moscow Biennial • 'There have to be many and they do(n't) need to be reconciled with one another', Kunstverein Braunschweig, Germany • 'Depiction Perversion Repulsion Obsession', Witte de With, Rotterdam **Selected bibliography: 2009** Keren Cytter, The Amazing True Story of Mosche Klinberg – A Media Star, Onestar Press • Lauren Cornell, Massimiliano Gioni and Laura Hoptman (eds.), Younger Than Jesus: Artist Directory, Phaidon, London **2008** Keren Cytter, The seven most exciting hours of Mr. Trier's life in twenty-four chapters, Witte de With, Rotterdam; STUK Kunstcentrum; Sternberg, Berlin and New York **2006** Barry Schwabsky, 'On Keren Cytter', Artforum, Oct • Diedrich Diederichsen and Avi Pitchon, Keren Cytter: I was the good and he was the bad and the ugly, KW, Berlin; Revolver, Frankfurt

Kate Davis

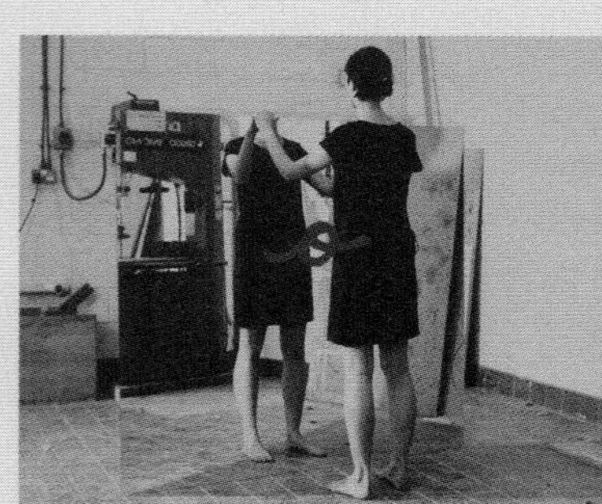

Born 1977, Wellington, New Zealand. Lives Glasgow, UK. **Selected solo exhibitions: 2010** 'The Long Loch: How Do We Go On From Here?' (with Faith Wilding), Centre for Contemporary Arts, Glasgow **2008** Sorcha Dallas, Glasgow **2007** Tate Britain, London • Galerie Kamm, Berlin **Selected group exhibitions: 2010** Art Sheffield, UK **2009** 'The End of the Line: Attitudes in Drawing', Hayward Gallery, London • 'Two or Three Things I Know about Her', Four Gallery, Dublin • 'Das Gespinst (Die Sammlung Schürmann zu Besuch im Museum Abteiberg)', Stadtisches Museum Abteiberg, Monchengladbach • 'Time after Time', Galerie Kamm, Berlin • 'When the Mood Strikes: The Collection of Wilfried and Yannicke Cooreman', Museum Dhondt-Dhaenens, Belgium **2008** 'The Object is the Mirror (Part II)', Wilkinson Gallery, London **2007** 'Like Leaves', Tanya Bonakdar Gallery, New York. **Selected bibliography: 2009** Isla Leaver-Yap, 'Eva Hesse: Present Tense', Map Magazine, Oct **2008** Lauren Cornell, Massimiliano Gioni and Laura Hoptman (eds.), Younger Than Jesus: Artist Directory, Phaidon, London • Sherman Sam, Insider: invented drawing, Sorcha Dallas, Glasgow • Moira Jeffrey, 'Review', Scotland on Sunday, Aug **2007** John Calcutt, 'Could We? I am Asking', Map Magazine, Jun **2005** Sarah Lowndes, 'Kate Davis', Frieze, May

Thea Djordjadze

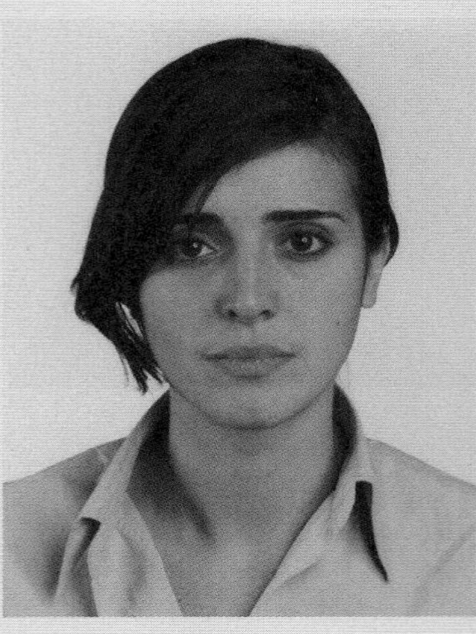

Born 1971, Tbilisi, Georgia. Lives Cologne, Germany. **Selected solo exhibitions: 2009** Micky Shubert, Berlin • Sprüth Magers, Berlin • Kunsthalle Basel • De Garage, Mechelen, Netherlands **2008** Kunstverein Nürnberg, Nuremberg • Sprüth Magers, Cologne **2007** Studio Voltaire, London • Micky Schubert, Berlin **Selected group exhibitions: 2009** 'Your Gold Teeth II', Marianne Boesky, New York • 'Remote Memories', Kai 10, Düsseldorf • 'In May (After October)', Gallery TPW, Toronto **2008** 'After October', Elizabeth Dee, New York • 'Transformational Grammars', Francesca Kaufmann, Milan • 'On Interchange', Museum Kurhaus, Kleve, Germany • 'Martian Museum of Terrestrial Art', Barbican Art Gallery, London • Berlin Biennial **2007** Lyon Biennial **Selected bibliography: 2009** Quinn Latimer, 'Thea Djordjadze', Frieze, Aug • Melissa Gronlund, 'Thea Djordjadze', Vitamin 3-D: New Perspectives in Sculpture and Installation, Phaidon, London **2008** Lilian Haberer and Regina Barunke, On Interchange, Museum Kurhaus, Kleve • Kathleen Rahn, Mark von Schlegell, Nora Schultz and Catherine Wood, Thea Djordjadze, Verlag für moderne Kunst Nürnberg, Nuremberg • Niklas Maak, 'Was hinter der Faust haust', Frankfurter Allgemeine Zeitung, 5 Apr

Nathalie Djurberg

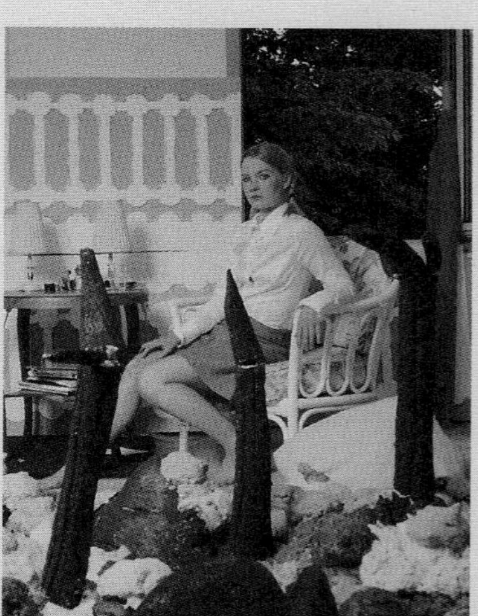

Born 1978, Lysekil, Sweden. Lives Berlin, Germany. **Selected solo exhibitions: 2009** Fondazione Prada, Milan • Frye Art Museum, Seattle **2008** OMA Prada Transformer, Seoul • Hammer Museum, Los Angeles **2007** Kunsthalle Winterthur, Switzerland • Kunsthalle Wien, Vienna **2005** Moderna Museet, Stockholm **Selected group exhibitions: 2009** Venice Biennale • 'Eclipse: Art in a Dark Age', Moderna Museet, Stockholm **2008** 'After Nature', New Museum, New York **2006** 'Into Me/Out of Me', P.S.1, New York; KW, Berlin; Museo d'Arte Contemporanea, Rome •

Berlin Biennial **Selected bibliography: 2008** Germano Celant, Nathalie Djurberg: Turn Into Me, Fondazione Prada, Milan • Hans Werner Holzwarth, 'Nathalie Djurberg', Art Now: Volume 3, Taschen, Cologne **2007** Gerald Matt and Angela Stief, Nathalie Djurberg: Denn es ist schön zu leben, Kunsthalle Wien; Verlag für Moderne Kunst Nürnberg, Nuremberg

Matías Duville

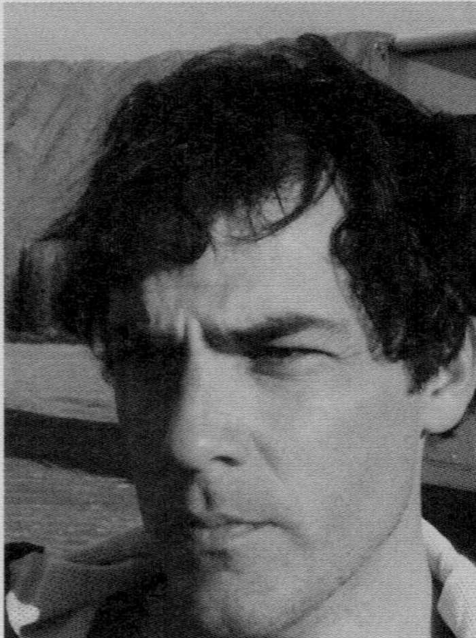

Born 1974, Buenos Aires, Argentina. Lives Buenos Aires, Argentina. **Selected solo exhibitions: 2009** Distrito 4 Gallery, Madrid **2008** Alberto Sendros Gallery, Buenos Aires **2007** Museo de Arte Contemporáneo de Castilla y León, Spain **2006** Galeria Baró Cruz, São Paulo **2005** Museo de Arte Contemporáneo de Rosario, Argentina **Selected group exhibitions: 2009** 'Huesped Colección MUSAC', Museo de Bellas Artes, Buenos Aires • 'Argentina Hoy', Centro Cultural Banco do Brasil, São Paulo • 'Destructivo Arte', Centro Cultural Borges, Buenos Aires **2008** 'Narrative/Non-Narrative': Contemporary Artists from the CIFO Program', Scope, Miami • 'Bosque', Centro Cultural de España, Buenos Aires **2007** 'Signos de existencias', Museo de Art Contemporáneo de Santiago de Chile • 'Transatlántica 9669', Sala de esta, Seville, Spain **Selected bibliography: 2008** María Gainza, 'Reviews: Matias Duville', Artforum, Mar • Eva Grinstein, 'Matías Duville', Artecontexto, no. 17 **2007** Jorge Macchi and Victoria Noorthoorn, Matías Duville: Obras 2000–2007, Galeria Alberto Sendros, Buenos Aires

Shannon Ebner

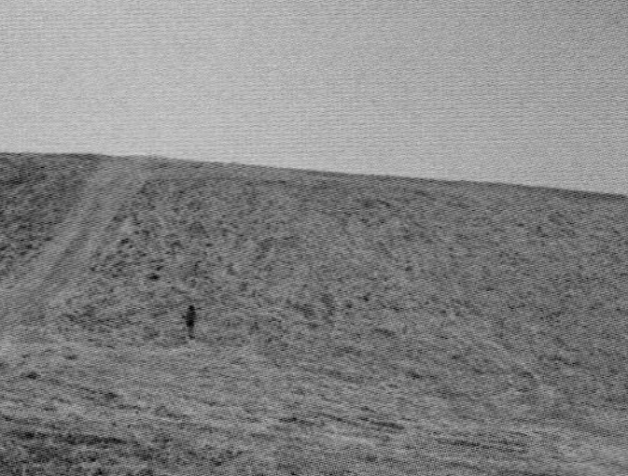

Born 1971, Englewood, NJ, USA. Lives Los Angeles, CA, USA. **Selected solo exhibitions: 2010** Altman-Siegal Gallery, San Francisco **2009** Wallspace, New York **2007** P.S.1, New York **2005** Wallspace, New York **Selected group exhibitions: 2009** 'Saints and Sinners', Rose Art Museum, Brandeis University, Waltham, MA, USA **2008** 'Imaginary Thing', Aspen Art Museum, CO, USA • 'Untitled (Vicarious)', Gagosian Gallery, New York

'Not So Subtle Subtitle', Casey Kaplan, New York • Whitney Biennial **2007** 'Learn to Read', Tate Modern, London **Selected bibliography: 2010** Christy Lange, 'No End in Sight', <u>Frieze</u>, Mar **2009** Shannon Ebner, <u>The Sun as Error</u>, Los Angeles County Museum of Art **2008** Elizabeth Schambelan, 'Whitney Biennial', <u>Artforum</u>, Summer **2007** Matthew Higgs, 'Best of 2007', <u>Artforum</u>, Dec • Dan Torop, 'Shannon Ebner', <u>Modern Painters</u>, Summer • Lisa Turvey, 'Words Words Words: Photographs by Shannon Ebner', <u>Aperture</u>, Summer **2005** Peter Eleey, 'Shannon Ebner', <u>Frieze</u>, Jul-Aug

Sherif El Azma

Born 1975, Manchester, UK. Lives Cairo, Egypt. **Selected solo exhibitions: 2008** Townhouse, Cairo **Selected group exhibitions: 2009** 'Pictorial Mappings of Islam and Modernity', Martin-Gropius-Bau, Berlin **2007** 'Occidentalism: Contemporary Artists From Egypt', Hotel Suisse, Cairo **2005** Venice Biennale **2004** 'Contemporary Arab Representations: CAIRO', Palacio de los Condes de Gabia, Granada, Spain **Selected bibliography: 2009** Kaelen Wilson-Goldie, 'Sherif El-Azma', <u>Bidoun</u>, no. 17

Haris Epaminonda

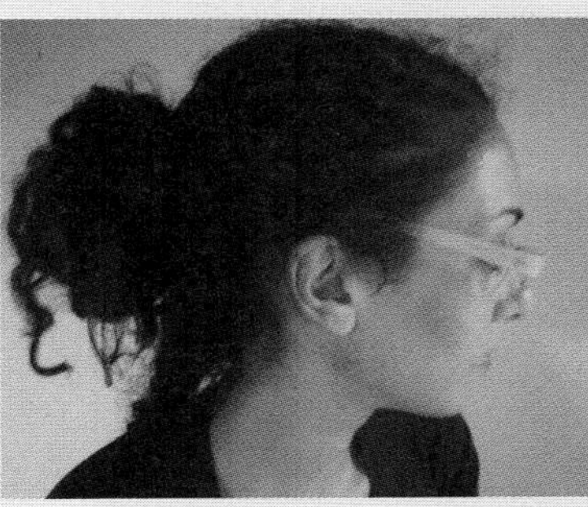

Born 1980, Nicosia, Cyprus. Lives Berlin, Germany. **Selected solo exhibitions: 2009** Rodeo, Istanbul • Malmö Konsthall, Sweden • BolteLang, Zurich (with Daniel Gustav Cramer) • Moufflon bookshop, Nicosia **2008** Circus, Berlin • Künstlerhaus Bethanien, Berlin **2007** Cyprus Pavilion, Venice Biennale **Selected group exhibitions: 2009** 'Taj Mahal Travellers', Nordenhake Gallery, Stockholm • Athens Biennial • 'Green Light', Laura Bartlett, London • 'Solaris', Giò Marconi, Milan • 'Deste Prize', Deste Foundation at Cycladic Museum, Athens • 'The Happy Interval', Tulips and Roses, Vilnius • 'The Generational: Younger Than Jesus', New Museum, New York **2008** 'If Tomorrow Never Comes', Rodeo, Istanbul • 'A Rictus Grin', Broadway 1062, New York • 'Fare una Scenata/Making a Scene', Fondazione Morra Greco, Naples, • 'Past-Forward', Zabludowicz Art Projects, London • Berlin Biennial **2007** 'Her(his)tory', Museum of Cycladic Art, Athens Thessaloniki Biennial **Selected bibliography: 2009** Isla Leaver-Yap, 'Images In Search Of Lost Time', <u>Map Magazine</u>, Summer • Lauren Cornell, Massimiliano Gioni and Laura Hoptman (eds.), <u>Younger Than Jesus: Artist Directory</u>, Phaidon, London **2008** Ozge Ersoy, 'A Principle of Assumptions', <u>Bidoun</u>, Fall • Sonia Campagnola, 'Artists at Work: Haris Epaminonda', <u>Afterall Online</u>, 7 Oct • Jörg Heiser, 'Aufgepasst: Das Ist Gute Kunst', <u>Das Magazin</u>, no. 22 **2007** James Quandt, 'Best of 2007', <u>Artforum</u>, Dec • Cristina Travaglini, 'Haris Epaminonda', <u>Mousse</u>

Patricia Esquivias

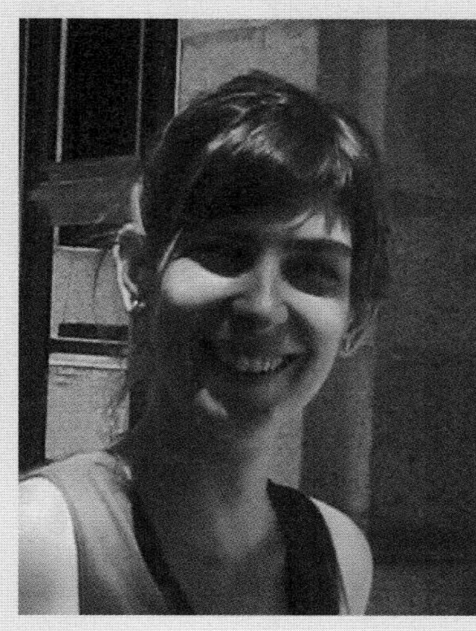

Born 1979, Caracas, Venezuela. Lives Madrid, Spain. **Selected solo exhibitions: 2009** Museo Nacional Centro de Arte Reina Sofía, Madrid • Midway Contemporary Art, Minneapolis **2008** Murray Guy, New York • White Columns, New York **2007** Maisterravalbuena Galería, Madrid **2006** DF Arte Contemporanea, Santiago de Compostela • Playspace, San Francisco **Selected group exhibitions: 2009** 'Report on Probability', Kunsthalle Basel • 'The Generational: Younger Than Jesus', New Museum, New York • 'Wrinkles in Time', Instituto Valencia de Arte Moderna, Spain 'Monuments to Transformation', City Gallery Prague **2008** Berlin Biennial • 'Beyond Paradise', Stedelijk Museum Bureau, Amsterdam **Selected bibliography: 2009** Gene McHugh, 'The Generational: Younger Than Jesus', <u>Artforum</u>, Summer **2008** Yasmine Van Pee, 'Bending the Word', <u>Modern Painters</u>, Dec • Elena Filipovic and Adam Szymczyk (eds.), <u>5th Berlin Biennale for Contemporary Art: When Things Cast No Shadow</u>, KW, Berlin; JRP Ringier, Zurich

Leopoldo Estol

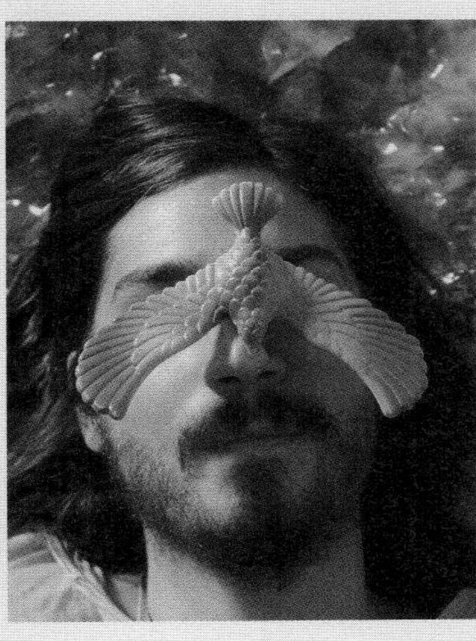

Born 1981, Buenos Aires, Argentina. Lives Buenos Aires, Argentina. **Selected exhibitions: 2009** 'Talismán se busca', Galeria Ruth Benzacar, Buenos Aires **2008** 'Recuerdos del Futuro' (with Juan Roman Diosque), Espacio La Punta, Tucuman, Argentina • 'Banda Escuchar', Galería Alberto Sendros, Buenos Aires • 'La mañana del mundo', Galeria Ruth Benzacar, Buenos Aires **2007** Mercosur Bienal, Porto Alegre, Brazil • 'Mi primera escultura', Museo de Arte Moderno, Buenos Aires **Selected bibliography: 2009** Andrea Giunta, 'Poscrisis': Arte Argentino Despues de 2001, Siglo Veintiuno, Guatamala **2008** Daniel Molina, 'La máquina de sentido', <u>Diario La Nación</u>, 12 Apr • Anne Ellegood, '6th Mercosur Biennial', <u>Artforum</u>, Mar

2007 Mariano Mayer, 'Arte Acumulación', <u>NEO2</u>, Nov **2005** Maria Gainza, 'Actividades Prácticas', <u>Radar</u>, 13 Nov

Roe Ethridge

Born 1969, Miami, FL, USA. Lives New York, NY, USA. **Selected solo exhibitions: 2009** Gladstone Gallery, Brussels • Rat Hole Gallery, Tokyo **2008** Andrew Kreps Gallery, New York • Sutton Lane, Paris **2007** Mai 36 Galerie, Zurich • Medium, St Barthélemy • Greengrassi, London **Selected group exhibitions: 2009** 'ICA Collection: In the Making', Institute of Contemporary Art, Boston • 'Phot(o)bjects', Presentation House Gallery, Vancouver • 'The Living and the Dead', Gavin Brown's Enterprise, New York • 'Collecting History: Highlighting Recent Acquisitions', Museum of Contemporary Art, Los Angeles **2008** 'Photographers on Photography: Reflections on the Medium since 1960' Metropolitan Museum of Art, New York **2007** 'Artists in and Out of Cologne', Henry Art Gallery, Seattle **Selected bibliography: 2009** Skye Sherwin, 'Roe Ethridge', <u>Art Review</u>, Apr • Roe Ethridge, <u>Farewell Horse</u>, Rat Hole Gallery, Tokyo **2008** John Zinsser, 'Roe Ethridge', <u>Flash Art</u>, Nov-Dec • Suzanne Hudsun, 'Roe Ethridge', <u>Artforum</u>, Nov **2007** Brian Sholis, 'Roe Ethridge', <u>Vitamin Ph: New Perspectives in Photography</u>, Phaidon, London

Geoffrey Farmer

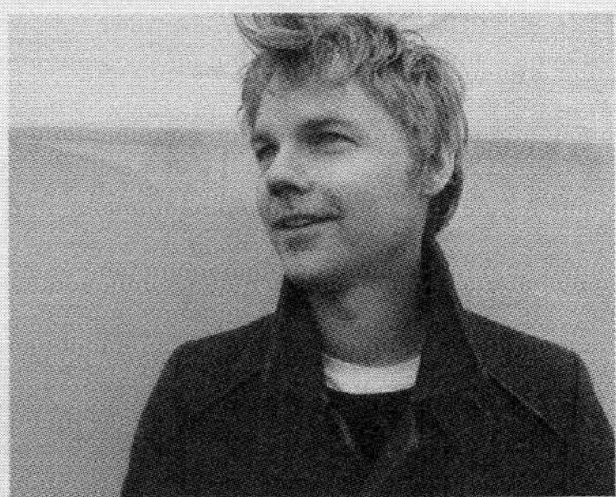

Born 1967, Eagle Island, Canada. Lives Vancouver, Canada. **Selected solo exhibitions: 2010** Catriona Jeffries Gallery, Vancouver **2008** Witte de With, Rotterdam • Musée d'Art Contemporain de Montréal **2007** Spacex, Exeter • The Drawing Room, London **Selected group exhibitions: 2010** 'Conversation Pieces: A Chamber Play – Act III, Climax', Johnen Galerie, Berlin **2009** 'Nuit Blanche', Toronto • 'Le chant de la carpe', Parc St Leger, Pougues-les-Eaux, France • 'Loaded', Catriona Jeffries Gallery, Vancouver • 'Nomads', National Gallery of Canada, Ottawa **2008** 'The Human Arc', Tramway, Glasgow • Brussels Biennial • 'Caught in the Act: Viewer as Performer', National Gallery of Canada, Ottawa • 'Don't Come In, Be Merciful', Johnen + Schöttle, Cologne • Sydney Biennial **Selected bibliography: 2009** Andrew Bonacina, 'Geoffrey Farmer', <u>Vitamin 3-D: New Perspectives in Sculpture and Installation</u>, Phaidon, London **2008** Anne-Marie Ninacs, <u>Caught in the Act: The Viewer as Performer</u>, National Gallery of Canada, Ottawa • Thierry Davila, Vanessa Desclaux and Diedrich Diederichsen, <u>Geoffrey Farmer</u>, Witte de With, Rotterdam • Pierre Landry, Jessica Morgan and Scott Watson, <u>Geoffrey Farmer</u>, Musée d'Art

Contemporain de Montreal • Dan Adler, 'Geoffrey Farmer: Musée d'Art Contemporain de Montréal', <u>Artforum</u>, Sep **2007** Andrew Bonacina, 'Entrepreneur Alone Returning Back to Sculptural Form', <u>Uovo</u>, no. 13

Claire Fontaine

Founded by Fulvia Carnevale and James Thornhill, 2004, Paris, France. **Selected solo exhibitions: 2009** Aspen Art Museum, CO, USA • Reena Spaulings Fine Art, New York • CCA Wattis Institute for Contemporary Arts, San Francisco • Galeria T293, Naples **2008** Maison Descartes, Institut Français des Pays-Bas, Amsterdam • Contemporary Art Museum St Louis • Kubus, Städtische Galerie im Lenbachhaus und Kunstbau, Munich • Schinkel Pavillon, Berlin • Witte de With, Rotterdam • The Kitchen, New York **Selected group exhibitions: 2009** 'Audio, Video, Disco', Kunsthalle Zürich • 'Shifting Identities', Contemporary Art Centre, Vilnius • 'Getting Even, Oppositions & Dialogues', Kunstverein Hannover • 'The Making of Art', Schirn Kunsthalle, Frankfurt • 'Untitled (Take the Money and Run)', De Appel, Amsterdam • 'Living Together: Estrategias para la convivencia', Museo de Arte Contemporánea de Vigo, Spain • 'Mamõyguara opá mamõ pupé: Panorama da Arte Brasileira', Museu de Moderna Arte de São Paulo, • 'Pivot Points 3', Museum Of Contemporary Art, North Miami • 'Contemplating the Void: Interventions in the Guggenheim Museum', Solomon R. Guggenheim Museum, New York • 'Dance in My Experience', Kunstverein Düsseldorf **Selected bibliography: 2009** Christian Höller, 'Claire Fontaine: Recessions', <u>Springerin</u>, Jul • Paul B. Franklin, 'Claire Fontaine', <u>Art in America</u>, Mar • Fabio Cypriano, 'This is not a void', <u>Frieze</u>, Apr • Bart va der Heide, 'In life there is no purity, only struggle: An interview with Claire Fontaine', <u>Metropolis M</u>, Feb-Mar • Jennifer Allen, 'Readymade Women', <u>Mousse</u>, Dec-Jan • Lauren Cornell, Massimiliano Gioni and Laura Hoptman (eds.), <u>Younger Than Jesus: Artist Directory</u>, Phaidon, London

Zachary Formwalt

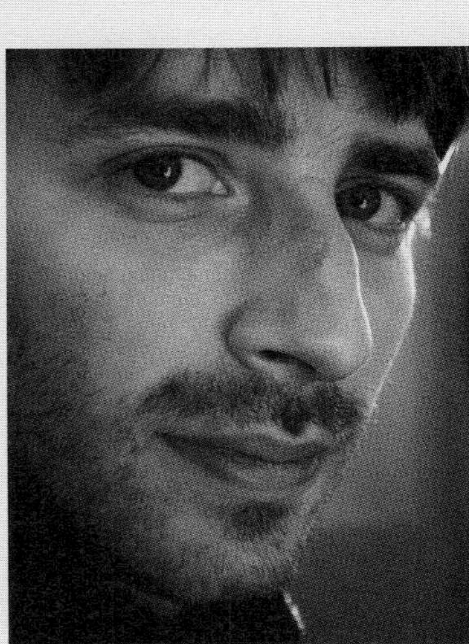

Born 1979, Albany, GA, USA. Lives Amsterdam, Netherlands. **Selected solo exhibitions: 2009** Kunsthalle Basel **2005** Rooseum Centre for Contemporary Art, Malmo **Selected group exhibitions: 2009** 'That was Yesterday: A Screen Programme about 'Value', Arnolfini, Bristol **2008** 'DIS-EASE', Iziko South African

National Gallery, Cape Town, and Bar Gallery, Durban, South Africa • 'RijksakademieOPEN', Rijksakademie, Amsterdam **2005** 'We are the State', T Site Rooseum Center for Contempora Art, Malmo **Selected bibliography: 2009** Daniel Morgenthaler, 'Fotografie der Ökonomie: Zachary Formwalt's Bllder des Marktes in der Kunsthalle', <u>Basler Zeitung</u>, 7 Sep

Cyprien Gaillard

Born 1980, Paris, France. Lives Paris, France. **Selected solo exhibitions: 2010** Hirshhorn Museum and Sculpture Garden, Washington, DC • Wexner Centre for the Arts, Columbus, OH, U **2009** Museo de Arte Contemporáneo Castilla y León, Spain • Fonds Région d'Art Contemporain Champagne Ardenne, Reims, France • Kunsthalle Fridericianum, Kassel, Germany • Stro Den Haag, The Hague, Netherlands **20** SMS Contemporanea, Siena, Italy • Hayward Gallery, London • Centre d'a Contemporain de Brétigny, Brétigny su Orge, France • Centre d'art Les Eglise Chelles, France **Selected group exhibitions: 2009** 'Warsaw Under Construction', Museum of Modern Art Warsaw • Performa 09, New York • 'Vi Art Replay', Institute of Contemporary Philadelphia • 'Actual Fears 2', Centre d'art Neuchâtel, France • 'Modernism a Ruin: An Archaeology of the Present Generali Foundation, Vienna • 'Summertime; or, Close-ups on Places We've (Never) Been: An Exhibition of F and Video Works', San Francisco Art Institute • 'The Generational: Younger Than Jesus', New Museum, New York 'Sounds and Visions: Art Film and Vide from Europe', Tel Aviv Museum of Art, Israel **2008** 'Sudden White', Royal Academy of Arts, London • 'La consistence du visible', Fondation Rica Paris • Busan Biennial • 'Degrees of Remove: Landscape and Affect', Sculpture Center, New York **Selected bibliography: 2010** Jonathan Griffin, 'New Romantic', <u>Frieze</u>, Apr **2009** Catherine Wood, 'Cyprien Gaillard', <u>Artforum</u>, Feb **2008** Lauren Cornell, Massimiliano Gioni and Laura Hoptma (eds.), <u>Younger Than Jesus: Artist Directory</u>, Phaidon, London • Joanna Fiduccia, 'Recycling The Ruin <u>Map Magazine</u>, Winter • Payam Sharif 'Flattened History: A Conversation with Cyprien Gaillard', <u>Metropolis M</u>, Oct-Nov • Vivian Rehberg, 'Prospecti Cinema', <u>Frieze</u>, May • Skye Sherwin, 'Building, Dwelling, Thinking', <u>Art Revi</u> Apr **2007** Edoardo Bonaspetti, 'Cyprien Gaillard', <u>Mousse</u>, Summer • Lillian Davies, 'Cyprien Gaillard', <u>UOVO</u>, no.13

Mario Garcia Torr

Born 1975, Monclova, Coahuila, Mexico. Lives Los Angeles, CA, USA. **Selected solo exhibitions: 2009** Jan Mot, Brussels • University of California, Berkeley Art Museum and Pacific Film Archive, California • Jeu de Paume, Pa • Taka Ishi Gallery, Tokyo • Espai 13, Fundació Joao Miró, Barcelona **2008** Proyectos Monclova, Mexico • Kunsth Zürich • White Cube, London **2007** Stedelijk Museum, Amsterdam **Selecte group exhibitions: 2008** 41 Salón Nacionál de Artistas, Cali, Colombia

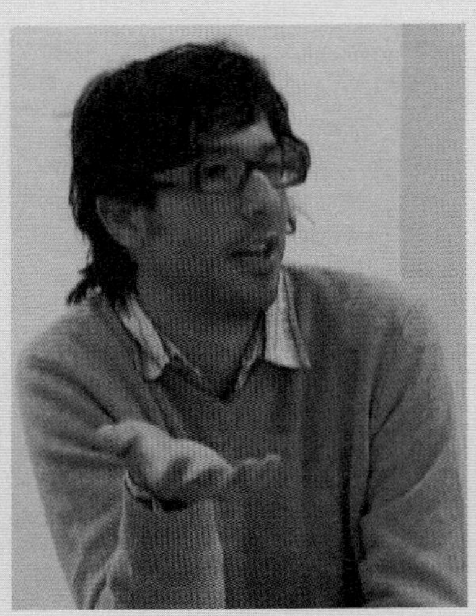

Yokohama Triennial • Panama Biennial, Panama City **2007** Venice Biennale • Baltic Triennial, Vilnius **Selected bibliography: 2008** Eva Scharrer, 'Animating the Void', Modern Painters, Mar **2007** Magali Arriola, 'Fragments of History', Spike, no. 12 • Catherine Lorch, 'Mario Garcia Torres', Frieze, Sep • Craig Burnett, 'Secrets and Lies', Art Review, no.15

Shilpa Gupta

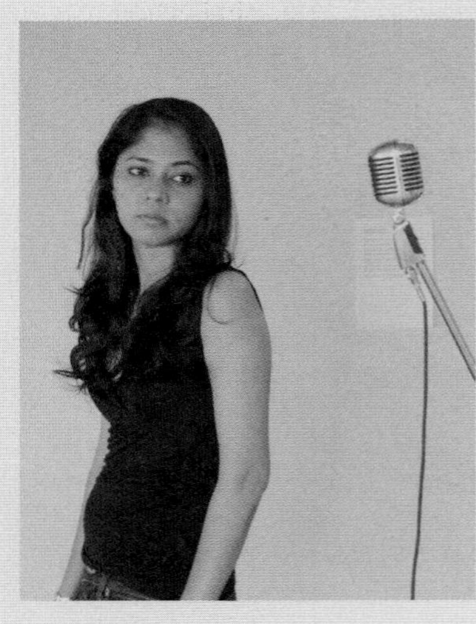

Born 1976, Mumbai, India. Lives Mumbai, India. **Selected solo exhibitions: 2010** Contemporary Arts Center, Cincinatti **2009** Yvon Lambert, Paris • Vadehra Gallery, New Delhi • Galleria Continua, San Gimignano • La Laboratoire, Paris **2008** Galerie Volker Diehl and BodhiBerlin, Berlin **2007** Apeejay Media Gallery, New Delhi • Sakshi Gallery, Mumbai **Selected group exhibitions: 2010** Auckland Biennial, New Zealand **2009** Lyon Biennial • 'The World is Yours', Louisiana Museum of Modern Art, Humlebaek, Denmark • 'Everyday Miracles', San Francisco Art Institute; REDCAT, Los Angeles • 'Rotating Views Number 1', Astrup Fearnley Museum of Modern Art, Oslo • 'The Generational: Younger than Jesus', New Museum, New York **2008** Yokohama Triennial, Japan • Gwangju Biennial, Korea • 'Indian Highway', Serpentine Gallery, London **Selected bibliography: 2009** Mahzarin Banaji, Kaushik Bhowmick, Noam Chomsky, Caroline Naphegyi and Sandhini Poddar, While I Sleep: Shilpa Gupta, Le Laboratoire, Paris **2008** Nancy Adajania, Shaheen Merali, Hans Ulrich Obrist and Julia Peyton-Jones, BlindStars StarsBlind: Shilpa Gupta, Kehrer, Heidelberg

Lasse Schmidt Hansen

Born 1978 Albertslund, Denmark. Lives Berlin, Germany.

Selected solo exhibitions: 2009 Art 3, Valence, France • Kunstverein für die Rheinlande und Westfalen, Düsseldorf **2008** Galerie Reinhard Hauff, Stuttgart **2007** Aktualisierungsraum, Hamburg • Heidelberger Kunstverein, Germany **2006** Croynielsen, Berlin • Ritter&Staiff, Frankfurt • Peles Empire, London • KBH Kunsthal, Copenhagen

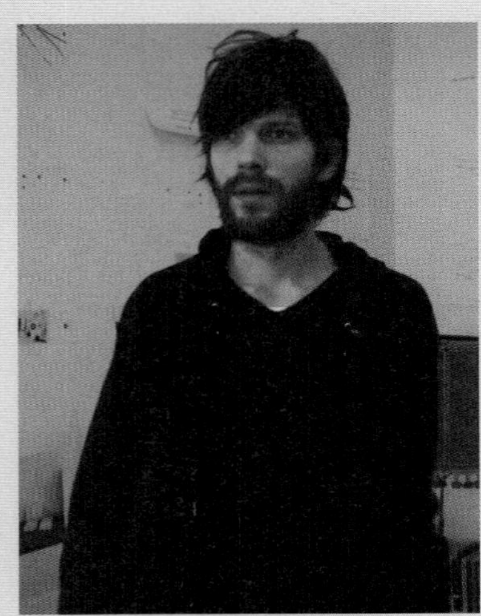

Selected group exhibitions: 2009 'Drawing Sculpture', Daimler Contemporary, Berlin • Athens Biennial • 'Working Title: Archive', Muzeum Sztuki, Lodz, Poland • 'Art Without Audience', De Fabriek, Eindhoven, Netherlands • 'RAiR#1', RAiR, Rotterdam **2008** 'Weisses Lächeln', Croynielsen, Berlin • '+10', Columbus Art Foundation, Leipzig **2007** 'Empty Frames', Hermes und der Pfau, Stuttgart • 'Die Blaue Blume', Grazer Kunstverein • 'Bling', Galleri Michael Andersen, Copenhagen • 'About the Possibility of a Sculpture', Galerie Reinhard Hauff, Stuttgart • 'Whenever It Starts It Is the Right Time', Frankfurter Kunstverein, • 'Aspen 12', Neue Alte Brücke, Frankfurt **Selected bibliography: 2009** Lars Bang Larsen, 'Indiscretions of a Bureaucratic Galactico: Will and Forms of Organisation in Lasse Schmidt Hansen's Work', Working Title Archive #2, Muzeum Sztuki, Lodz • Arnaud-Pierre Fourtané, 'More and Less', Kaiserin-Magazine, no. 6 **2007** Anne Kathrine Eriksen, 'Lasse Schmidt Hansen', Ny Dansk Kunst 07, Kopenhagen Publishing

Leslie Hewitt

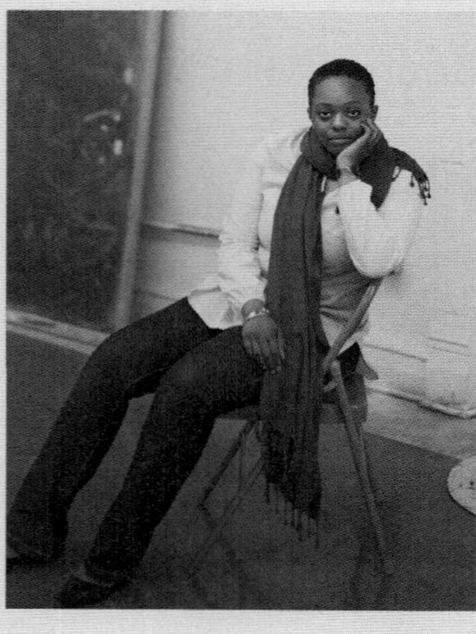

Born 1977, Saint Albans, NY, USA. Lives New York, NY, USA. **Selected solo exhibitions: 2009** 'Clough-Hanson Gallery', Rhodes College, Memphis, TN • 'The Everyday', Hessel Museum of Art at Bard College, Annandale-on-Hudson, NY, USA **2007** 'It's Just a Feeling…', D'Amelio Terras, New York • 'Replica of a Lost Original', Artists Space, New York **2006** 'Make it Plain', LAXART, Los Angeles **Selected group exhibitions: 2009** '30 Seconds Off an Inch', Studio Museum

---

in Harlem, New York • 'New Photography 2009', The Museum of Modern Art, New York • 'The Everyday', Hessel Museum of Art at Bard College, Annandale-on-Hudson, NY, USA **2008** 'After 1968: Contemporary Artists and the Civil Rights Legacy', National Museum of African American History and Culture, Washington, DC; High Museum of Art, Atlanta • Whitney Biennial **2007** 'Replica of a Lost Original', Artists Space, New York • 'Alabama', Office Baroque Gallery, Antwerp • 'Nexus Texas', Contemporary Arts Museum Houston **Selected bibliography: 2009** Alex Klein, 'Why Photography Now', Words Without Pictures, Los Angeles County Museum of Art **2008** Lauren Cornell, Massimiliano Gioni and Laura Hoptman (eds.), Younger Than Jesus: Artist Directory, Phaidon, London • Wendy Koenig, 'After 1968: Contemporay Artists and the Civil Rights Legacy', Art Papers, Sep-Oct • Jeffrey D. Grove, After 1968: Contemporary Artists and The Civil Rights Legacy, High Museum of Art, Atlanta **2007** Andrea Scott, 'Art in Review: Leslie Hewitt', The New York Times, 23 Feb

Richard Hughes

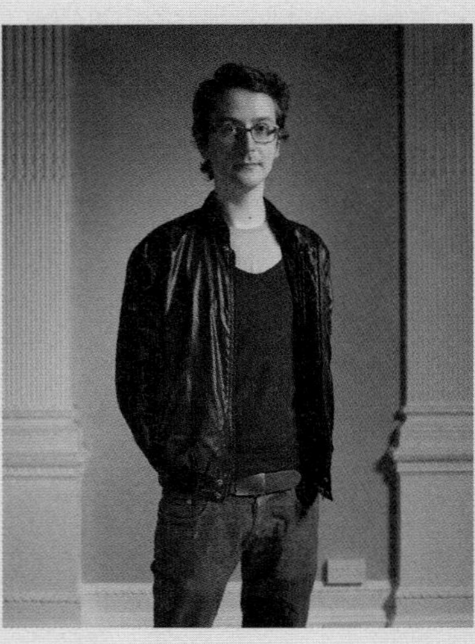

Born 1974, Birmingham, UK. Lives London, UK. **Selected solo exhibitions: 2008** Sadie Coles HQ, London • The Modern Institute, Glasgow **2007** Anton Kern Gallery, New York **2006** Tate Britain, London **Selected group exhibitions: 2009** 'Trying to Cope with Things that Aren't Human (Part 1)', Cell Project Space, London • 'Tonite', The Modern Institute, Glasgow **2008** Carnegie International, Pittsburgh • 'Variable Capital', Bluecoat Gallery, Liverpool • 'Living London', 176, London • 'All Inclusive: A Tourist World', Schirn Kunsthalle, Frankfurt **2007** 'The Zabludowicz Collection', Baltic, Gateshead • 're-dis-play ', Kunstverein Heidelberg, Germany **Selected bibliography: 2008** Morgan Falconer, 'Richard Hughes', Art Review, Mar **2007** Gair Boase, 'Richard Hughes', Keep On Onnin': Contemporary Art at Tate Britain, Tate Publishing, London **2006** Andrew Hunt and Neil Mulholland, 'British Art (does it) Show?', Frieze, Jan-Feb

Jamie Isenstein

Born 1975, Portland, OR, USA. Lives New York, NY, USA. **Selected solo exhibitions: 2010** Andrew Kreps Gallery, New York • Michael Benevento Gallery, Los Angels **2007** Andrew Kreps Gallery, New York • Hammer Museum, Los Angeles **2006** Galerie Giti Nourbakhsch and Meyer Riegger Gallery, Berlin

---

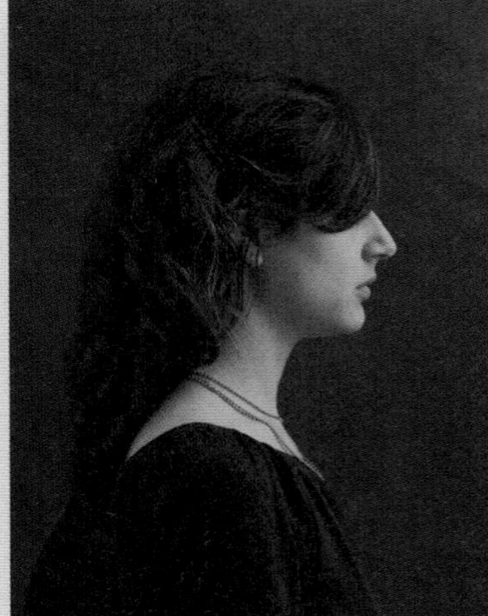

Selected group exhibitions: 2009 'One Minute More', The Kitchen, New York • 'Regift', Swiss Institute, New York • 'Marina Abramovic Presents', Whitworth Art Gallery, Manchester International Festival **2008** 'Funny Not Funny', Bellwether Gallery, New York • 'Tales of the Grotesque', Karma International, Zurich • 'Thanks for Coming!!', Michael Benevento, Los Angeles • 'Second Thoughts', Hessel Museum at Bard College, Annandale-on-Hudson, NY, USA **Selected bibliography: 2009** Gianni Jetzer, (ed.), Regift, Swiss Institute, New York **2008** Gianni Jetzer, Tales of the Grotesque, Karma International, Zurich • Piper Marchall, 'The Way to Egress: Jamie Isenstein', Art Papers, Sep-Oct **2007** Ali Subotnick, Hammer Projects: Jamie Isenstein, Hammer Museum, Los Angeles • Roberta Smith, 'Jamie Isenstein', The New York Times, 12 Oct • Tyler Coburn, 'Sleight of Hand', Art Review, Sep

Jackson Pollock Bar

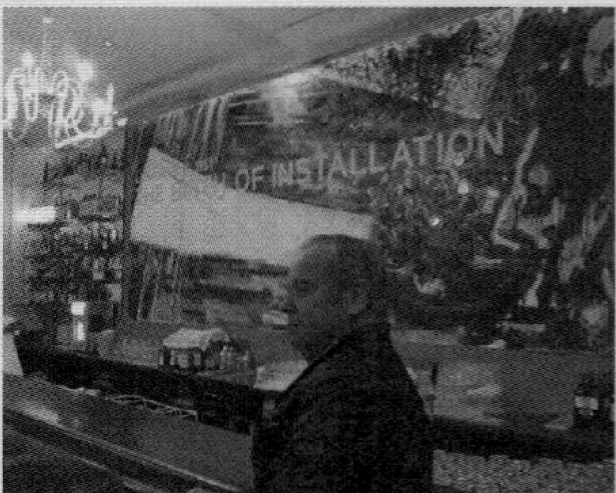

Founded 1994 by Christian Matthiessen. Based in Freiburg, Germany. **Selected exhibitions: 2009** 'Opening', UAE Pavilion, Venice Biennale • 'Picasso/Braque 1989', Gallery 400, University of Chicago • 'Art & Language Interview with Mayo Thompson', Art Institute of Chicago **2008** 'Utopia Station 2003', Zentrum für Kunst und Medientechnologie, Karlsruhe • 'Art & Language Sings a Song', Zentrum für Kunst und Medientechnologie, Karlsruhe **2007** 'Art & Language's Theses on Feuerbach installed in the Style of the Jackson Pollock Bar', unitednationsplaza, Berlin **2006** 'Institutional Critique as Institution', Association of Art Historians Annual Conference, Leeds **Selected bibliography: 2009** Thomas Crow, 'Acting the Part', Artforum, Sep **2007** Tirdad Zolghadr, 'Critical Karaoke', Modern Painters, Oct **2001** Charles Harrison, Conceptual Art and Painting, MIT, Cambridge, MA and London, UK

Izumi Kato

Born 1969, Shimane, Japan. Lives Tokyo, Japan. **Selected solo exhibitions:**

2008 Ueno Royal Museum Gallery, Tokyo **2007** Arataniurano, Tokyo • Takahashi Collection, Tokyo **2005** Scai the Bathhouse, Tokyo **2004** Murata & Friends, Berlin **Selected group exhibitions: 2010** 'Garden of Painting: Japanese Art of the 00s', National Museum of Art, Osaka **2009** 'Neoteny Japan: From Takahashi Collection', Ueno Royal Museum, Tokyo • 'Dorodoro Doron: The Uncanny World in Folk and Contemporary Art in Asia', Hiroshima City Museum of Contemporary Art **2008** 'Forwards 08: Daimler Awards for Contemporary Art from Germany, Japan, South Africa and the USA', Daimler Contemporary, Berlin • 'Kankai Pavilion Opening Exhibition: Beyond Time, Beyond Space', Hara Museum ARC, Gunma, Japan **2007** Venice Biennale • 'Painting as Forest: Artist as Thinker', Okazaki Mindscape Museum, Aichi, Japan • 'MOT Annual 2007: From a World as Large as Life', Museum of Contemporary Art, Tokyo

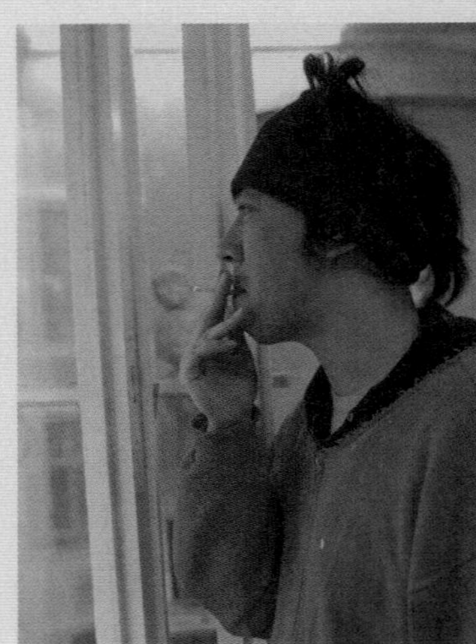

Selected bibliography: 2008 'Interview with Izumi Kato', Foundation Art-en-Ciel, Jul **2007** Francesca Pietropaolo, Venice Biennale: Think with the Senses Feel with the Mind, Rizzoli, New York **2004** Tamaki Saito, 'Pioneers on the Frontier: Izumi Kato', Bijutsu Techo, Jun **2004** Kenji Kubota, Lonely Planet, Art Tower Mito, Ibaraki, Japan

Janice Kerbel

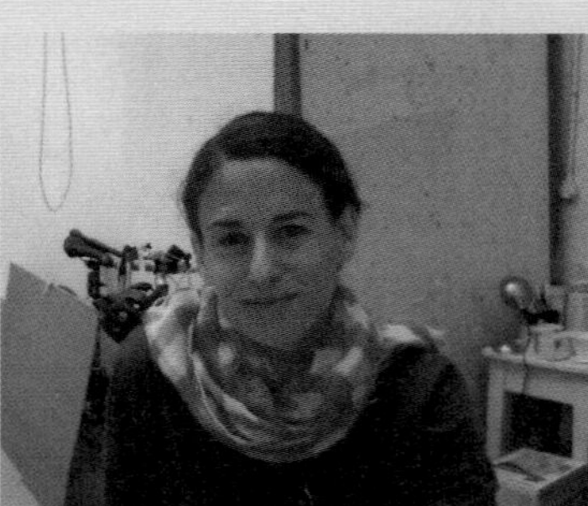

Born 1969, Toronto, Canada. Lives London, UK. **Selected solo exhibitions: 2010** Tate Britain, London • Chisenhale Gallery, London **2009** i8 Gallery, Reykjavik • Greengrassi, London **2008** European Kunsthalle, Cologne **Selected group exhibitions: 2009** 'Poor. Old. Tired. Horse', Institute of Contemporary Arts, London • 'Magic Show', UAD, Derby; Grundy Art Gallery, Blackpool; Tullie House Museum and Art Gallery, Carlisle; Chapter, Cardiff; Pump House Gallery, London **2008** 'Janice Kerbel, Silke Otto Knapp, Allen Ruppersberg', Galerie Karin Günther, Hamburg • 'Acclimation', Villa Arson, Nice • 'See History', Kunsthalle Kiel • 'Typed', Sadie Coles HQ, London • 'True Romance', Kusthalle Wien, Vienna **2007** Montreal Biennial **Selected bibliography: 2009** Ed Krcma, 'Janice Kerbel, Art in America, Nov **2008** Janice Kerbel, 'Ideal Syllabus', Frieze, Oct

Ian Hunt, 'Sheffield 08: Yes, No and Other Options', Art Monthly, Apr **2007** Janice Kerbel, Deadstar: A Ghost town, Locus+, Newcastle **2006** Mark Godfrey, 'Janice Kerbel', Artforum, Jan • Sally O'Reilly, 'Nick Silver', Frieze, Dec

Hassan Khan

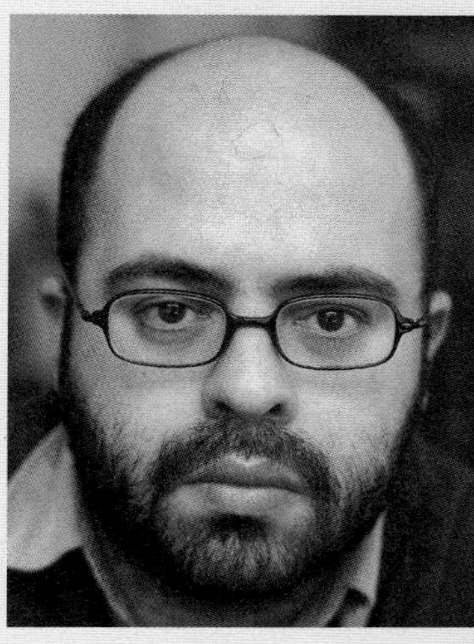

Born 1975, Cairo, Egypt. Lives Cairo, Egypt. **Selected solo exhibitions: 2010** Kunsthalle St Gallen, Switzerland **2008** Uqbar, Berlin **2007** Le Plateau, Paris **2006** Gasworks, London **Selected group exhibitions: 2010** Manifesta 8, Murcia, Spain **2009** 'Lap Dogs of the Bourgeoisie', Arnolfini, Bristol **2008** Yokohama Biennial, Japan • Gwangju Biennial, Korea **2006** Seville Biennial **Selected bibliography: 2010** Edit Molnar, 'Dialogue with Hassan Khan', Arab Studies Journal, Spring **2009** Hassan Khan, Nine Lessons Learned from Sherif El Azma, Contemporary Image Collective, Cairo **2009** Omnia El-Shakry, 'The Hidden Location: Art and Politics in the work of Hassan Khan', Third Text Asia, Spring **2007** 'Based in Cairo: An Interview with Hassan Khan', Local Folk, Apr **2006** Regine Basha, 'Transmission Fixation', Art Papers, Nov-Dec

Yuki Kimura

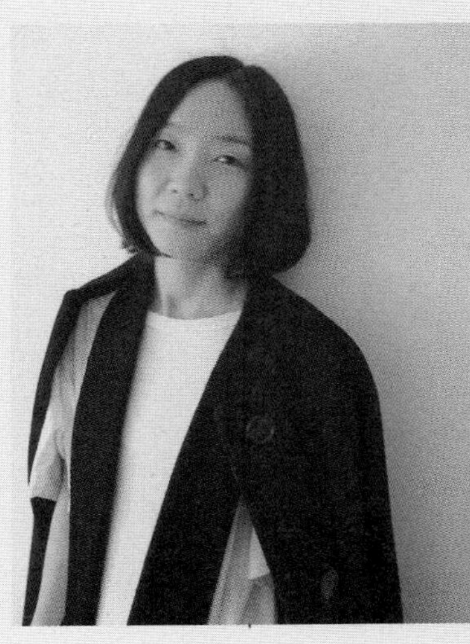

Born 1971, Kyoto, Japan. Lives Kyoto, Japan. **Selected solo exhibitions: 2009** Taka Ishii Gallery, Tokyo **2008** Daiwa Press Viewing Room, Hiroshima **2007** Kodama Gallery, Osaka **2005** Taka Ishii Gallery, Tokyo **Selected group exhibitions: 2009** 'Circle of Friends', Vacant, Tokyo • 'Incidental Affairs: Contemporary Art of Transient States', Suntory Museum, Osaka **2008** 'Yoshihide Otomo ENSEMBLES', Yamaguchi Center for Arts and Media, Japan • 'Mellow Fever', La Galerie des Galeries, Paris

2007 'Love? Letter', Asahi Beer Oyamazaki Villa Museum, Kyoto • 'Imaginary Chuya: Chuya's Words as Image', Yamaguchi Center, Japan • 'Slow Tech', Museum of Contemporary Art, Taipei **2005** 'Set', Taka Ishii Gallery, Tokyo • 'Ignore your perspective', Kodama Gallery, Tokyo **Selected bibliography: 2009** Andrew Maerkle, 'Yuki Kimura', Frieze, Nov-Dec **2008** Hiroyasu Yamauchi, 'Female Photographers Now', Perikan Sha **2007** Yuki Kimura, Pictures of a Man, Taka Ishii Gallery, Tokyo • Yukihiro Hirayoshi, Rept!, The Japan Foundation **2006** Minoru Shimizu, 'The Thinking Eye: Yuki Kimura's New Works', You May Attend the Party Where Strange Customs Prevail, Taka Ishii Gallery, Tokyo

Ragnar Kjartansson

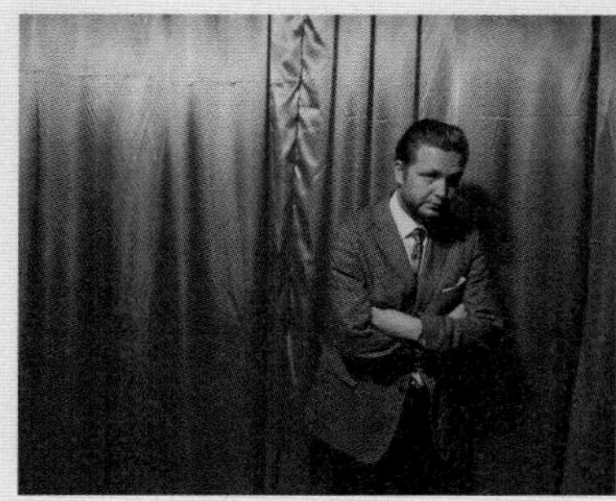

Born 1976, Reykjavik, Iceland. Lives Reykjavik, Iceland. **Selected solo exhibitions: 2009** Icelandic Pavilion, Venice Biennale **2007** 'Repeat Performances: Roni Horn and Ragnar Kjartansson', Centre for Curatorial Studies, Bard College, Annandale-on-Hudson, NY, USA • 508 West 25th Street, New York • The Living Art Museum, Iceland • i8 Gallery, Reykjavik, Iceland • Galleria Crespi, Milan **2006** Galerie Adler, Frankfurt **Selected group exhibitions: 2008** Turin Triennial • Manifesta 8, Roverto, Italy • 'Pleinairism', i8 Gallery, Reykjavik • 'It's Not Your Fault: Art from Iceland', Luhring Augustine Gallery, New York • 'Iceland on the Edge', Reykjavik Art Museum **2006** 'Momentum', Moss, Norway • 'Pakkhús Postulanna', Listasafn Reykjavikur, Iceland **Selected bibliography: 2009** Jeff Byles, 'Ragnar Kjartansson: What do you do with a drunken painter?' Modern Painters, May • Nicholas Cullinan, '2nd Turin Triennial', Artforum, Mar • Randy Kennedy, 'Another Day in Venice, Another Pose Struck, Another Portrait Painted', The New York Times, 7 Sep • Ragnar Kjartansson, The End, Hatje Cantz, Ostfildern • Lilly Wei, 'Ragnar Kjartansson: The Beginning of "The End"', Art in America, Jun-Jul **2008** Caroline Corbetto, 'Everyone is Decadent These Days', Mousse, Oct-Nov • Lara Kristin Lentini, 'It's Not Your Fault: Art from Iceland', Art Papers, Nov-Dec

Friedrich Kunath

Born 1974, Chemnitz, Germany. Lives Los Angeles, CA, USA. **Selected solo exhibitions: 2009** BQ, Berlin • Kunsthalle Baden-Baden, Germany • Kunstverein Hannover, Germany **2008** Aspen Art Museum, CO, USA • Blum & Poe, Los Angeles **2007** Andrea Rosen Gallery, New York **Selected group exhibitions: 2009** 'Play', Galeria Monica de Cardenas, Milan

2008 'The Eternal Flame', Kunsthaus Baselland • Carnegie International, Pittsburgh • 'Gravity in Art', Telic Arts Exchange, Los Angeles • 'Informed by Function', Lehman College Art Gallery, New York **2007** 'Blind Date', Magazzino d'Arte Moderna, Rome • 'Dream and Trauma: Works from the Dakis Joannou Collection', Museum Moderner Kunst Stiftung Ludwig, Vienna • 'Learn to Read', Tate Modern, London

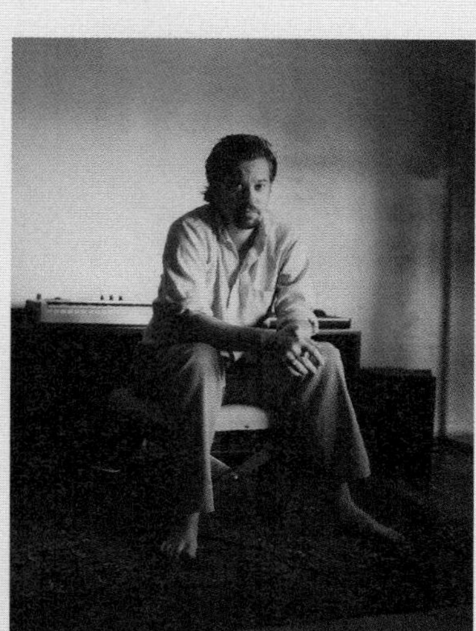

Selected bibliography: 2009 Andrew Beradini, 'Review: Friedrich Kunath', Art Review, Jan **2008** Marina Cashdan, 'Cruz Control', Whitewall, Winter • Morgan Falconer, 'Friedrich Kunath', Frieze, Jan-Feb • Douglas Fogle, Life on Mars: 55th Carnegie International, Carnegie Museum of Art, Pittsburgh • Heidi Zuckerman Jacobson, 'History with a Twist', Aspen Magazine, Summer **2007** Noemi Smolik, 'Friedrich Kunath', Artforum, Sep • Friedrich Kunath, Ausstellungskatalog, BQ, Cologne

Ignacio Lang

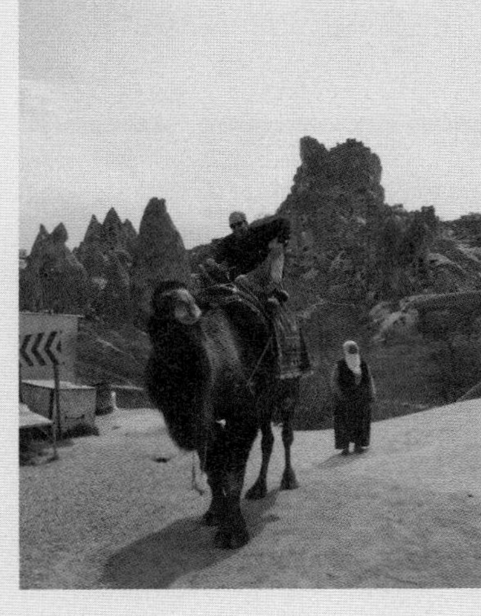

Born 1975, San Juan, Puerto Rico. Lives New York, NY, USA. **Selected solo exhibitions: 2004** Art in General, New York **2001** Ortra Islas, ARCO, Madrid **2000** Fundació Joan Miró, Barcelona **Selected group exhibitions: 2009** 'It Won't Stop Until We Talk', Dvir Gallery, Tel Aviv • 'Fellows', Frost Art Museum, Miami **2008** 'Autopsia de lo Invisible', Museo de Arte Latinoamericano de Buenos Aires **2006** 'Biennale Cuvée', OK Centrum für Gegenwartskunst, Linz **2005** 'Day Labour', P.S.1, New York • Baltic Triennial, Contemporary Art Centre, Vilnius • '33 ½', Institute of Contemporary Arts, London **Selected bibliography: 2009** Jennifer Allora and Guillermo Calzadilla, 'Future Greats: Ignacio Lang', Art Review, Mar **2008** Alicia de Arteaga, 'Los Ojos Abiertos', La Nacion, 8 Mar **2006** Liutauras Psibilskis, 'IX Baltic Triennial of International Art', Artforum, Feb **2005** Roberta Smith, 'Day Labor', The New York Times, 11 Nov

Valentina Liernur

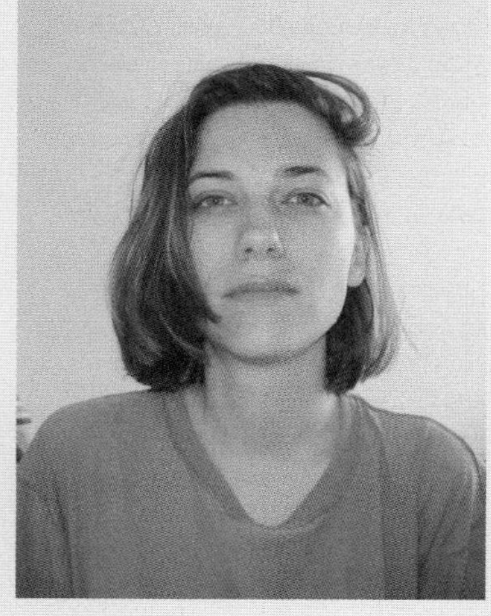

Born 1978, Buenos Aires, Argentina. Lives Buenos Aires, Argentina. **Selected solo exhibitions: 2009** Frankfurter Kunstverein **2008** Colegio Goethe, Buenos Aires **2007** Appetite Arte Contemporáneo, Buenos Aires • Blast, Rosario **2006** Galería Ruth Benzacar, Buenos Aires **Selected group exhibitions: 2009** 'Flüchtige Zeiten', Westfälischer Kunstverein, Munster • 'El Dorado', Planta Alta Galería, Asunción, Paraguay **2008** 'Sink the boat before it sails', Basis, Frankfurt **2008** 'Aquello que finalmente uno cree que no es tan determinante que los demas sepan sobre las propias ideas', Limite Sud/South Limit, Buenos Aires **2007** 'Muestra por un día', Déborah Pruden Galería, Buenos Aires **Selected bibliography: 2008** Claudio Iglesias, 'Solo los chicos', RADAR Página 12, 22 Jun • Mariano Mayer, 'Performances', Revista Neo, 2 Apr **2007** Javier Villa, 'Volver a pintar', ADN La Nación, 22 Sep **2006** Claudio Iglesias, 'Para pupilas exquisitas no hay sermón que valga', Revista Ramona, Jun **2006** Mariano Pigni, 'El Bar Roma de Liernur y Pruden', Revista El niño Stanton, Dec

Kalup Linzy

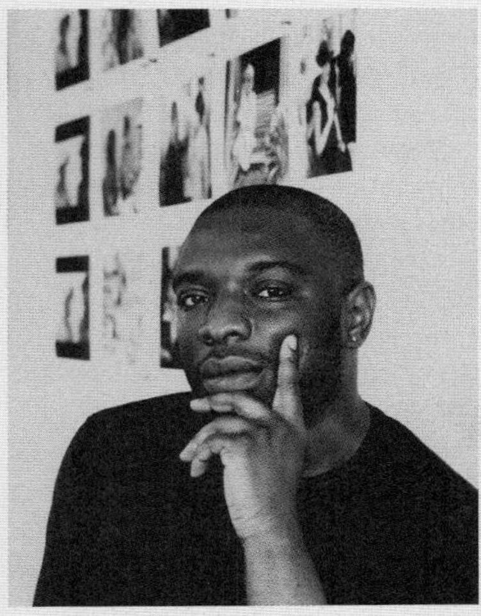

Born 1977, Stuckey, FL, USA. Lives New York, NY, USA. **Selected solo exhibitions: 2009** Taxter & Spengemann, New York • The Breeder, Athens • Studio Museum in Harlem, New York **2008** Moore Space, Miami **2007** Taxter & Spengemann, New York • LAXART, Los Angeles **Selected group exhibitions: 2009** ICP Triennial of Photography and Video, International Centre of Photography, New York • Athens Biennial • 'This is Killing Me', Massachusetts Museum of Contemporary Art, North Adams **2008** '30 Americans', Rubell Family Collection, Miami • Prospect 1, New Orleans • 'Disguise: The Art of Attracting and Deflecting Attention', Michael Stevenson Gallery, Cape Town

'Whatever is Whatever', Hydra School Project, Hydra, Greece • 'Laughing in a Foreign Language', Hayward Gallery, London **2007** 'Television Delivers People', Whitney Museum of American Art, New York • El Salvador Biennial • 'Playback', Musée d'Art Moderne de la Ville de Paris **Selected bibliography: 2009** Morgan Falconer, 'Kalup Linzy at Studio Museum in Harlem', Art Review, Summer • Karen Rosenberg, 'Video Art as Video Art: Glimpses of an Alter Ego Trip', The New York Times, 16 Apr • Thomas Lax, If It Don't Fit, Studio Museum Harlem, New York • Steven Stern, 'Kalup Linzy', Frieze, Apr **2008** Nick Stillman, 'Kalup Linzy', Bomb, Summer • Lauren Cornell, Massimiliano Gioni and Laura Hoptman (eds.), Younger Than Jesus Artist Directory, Phaidon, London **2007** Debra Singer, 'First Takes: Debra Singer on Kalup Linzy', Artforum, Jan

Hilary Lloyd

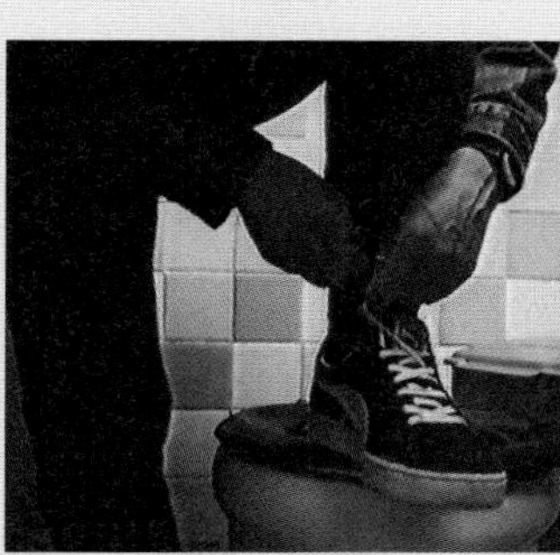

Born 1964, Halifax, UK. Lives London, UK. **Selected solo exhibitions: 2010** Raven Row, London **2009** Tramway, Glasgow • Le Consortium, Dijon **2006** Kunstverein München, Munich **Selected group exhibitions: 2009** 'Little Theatre of Gestures', Kunstmuseum Basel and Museum für Gegenwartskunst Basel **2008** 'Dispersion', Institute of Contemporary Arts, London **2007** 'Die Blaue Blume', Grazer Kunstverein, Graz, Austria • Lyon Biennial **Selected bibliography: 2009** Amna Malik, Sarah Lucas: Au Naturel, Afterall Books, London **2008** David Barrett, 'Hilary Lloyd', Art Monthly, Oct • Jan Verwoert, 'Body Language' Frieze, Oct **2001** Jan Verwoert, 'TV eye on you', Afterall, Issue 3

Maria Loboda

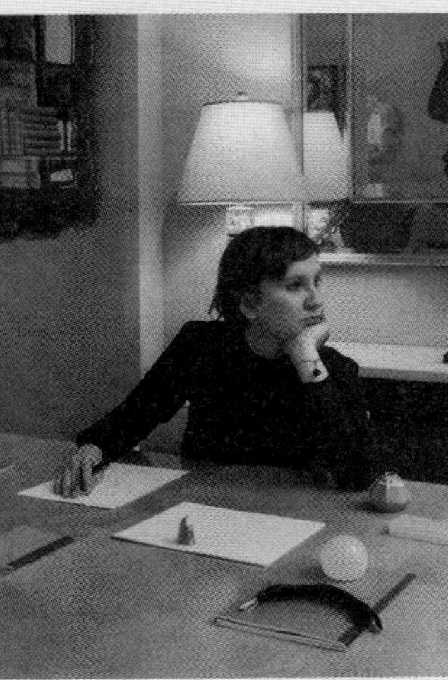

Born 1979, Krakow, Poland. Lives Berlin, Germany. **Selected solo exhibitions: 2010** Kunsthalle Bielefeld, Germany **2009** Galerie Schleicher+Lange, Paris **2006** Ritter & Staiff, Frankfurt **Selected group exhibitions: 2010** 'Maria Loboda and Lasse Schmidt Hansen', IMO, Copenhagen

2009 'Euphoria Left the Room', Scion Installation, Los Angeles • 'The Object of the Attack', David Roberts Art Foundation, London • 'The Long Dark', Manchester International • Athens Biennial • 'From the Corner of the Eye: The Extra-infra-ordinary', Galerie Schleicher+Lange, Paris **2008** 'Great Transformation: ART and Tactical Magic', Museo d'Arte Contemporanea, Vigo, Spain **Selected bibliography: 2009** Chus Martínez and Paul Simon Richards, The Apartment, Dresdner Bank, Frankfurt **2008** Katja Schroeder, The Great Transformation, Frankfurter Kunstverein; Museo de Arte Contemporanea de Vigo • Lars Bang Larsen, 'Transcendental Pop', Reading Room, Auckland Art Gallery, Toi o Tamaki, New Zealand • Ferdinand Ahm Krag (ed.), 'Once advances only by means of abstractions, but one finds rest only in the image', Site Magazine, no.11 • Lauren Cornell, Massimiliano Gioni and Laura Hoptman (eds.), Younger Than Jesus: Artist Directory, Phaidon, London **2007** Chus Martínez, Whenever It Starts Is the Right Time, Frankfurter Kunstverein

Renata Lucas

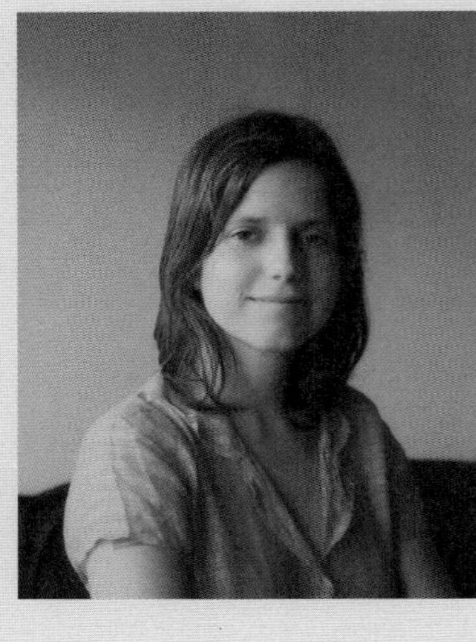

Born 1971, Ribeirão Preto, Brazil. Lives São Paulo, Brazil. **Selected solo exhibitions: 2007** Gasworks, London • REDCAT, Los Angeles **2006** Galeria Millan Antonio, São Paulo **Selected group exhibitions: 2009** Venice Biennale • 'Tiempo como material, Colección MACBA: Nuevas incorporaciones', Museu d'Art Contemporani de Barcelona • 'Biennale Cuvée', OK Center for Contemporary Art, Linz, Austria • San Juan Triennial **2008** Sydney Biennial • Yokohama Triennial **2007** 'The World as a Stage', Tate Modern, London; Institute of Contemporary Art, Boston **Selected bibliography: 2009** Daniel Birnbaum and Jochen Volz, Making Worlds, Venice Biennale **2008** Eva Fabris, 'Manipulating Architecture', Mousse, Jan • Sérgio Martins, 'Mi propio suelo para pisar', Dardo, Feb **2007** Clara Kim, Adriano Pedrosa and Lynn Zelevansky, Renata Lucas, REDCAT, Los Angeles • Jessica Morgan and Catherine Wood, The World as a Stage, Tate Publishing, London • Christoper Bedford, 'Renata Lucas', Artforum, Nov • Lisette Lagnado, 'Turning So Many Corners', Frieze, May

Goshka Macuga

Born 1967, Warsaw, Poland. Lives London, UK. **Selected solo exhibitions: 2010** Institute of Contemporary Art, Boston **2009** Whitechapel Art Gallery, London • Kunsthalle Basel

2008 Galerie Rüdiger Schöttle, Munich **2007** Tate Britain **Selected group exhibitions: 2009** 'The Dark Monarch: Magic and Modernity in British Art', Tate St Ives, UK • 'Textiles Art and the Social Fabric', Museum van Hedendaagse Kunst Antwerpen, Antwerp • Venice Biennale • 'Modern Ruins', Kate MacGarry, London **2008** 'That Beautiful Pale Face Is My Fate (For Lord Byron)', Nottingham Contemporary, UK • 'The Great Transformation: Art and Tactical Magic', Frankfurter Kunstverein; Museo de Arte Contemporanea de Vigo, Spain **Selected bibliography: 2009** Eva Scharrer, 'Goshka Macuga: Kunsthalle Basel', Modern Painters, May • Tom Lubbock, 'East Meets Best', The Independent, 3 Apr • Adrian Searle, 'Whitechapel Gallery Reopens with Picasso and Anthrax', The Guardian, 31 Mar • Grant Watson, 'Friendship of the Peoples: On the work of Goshka Macuga', Afterall, Spring

Rubens Mano

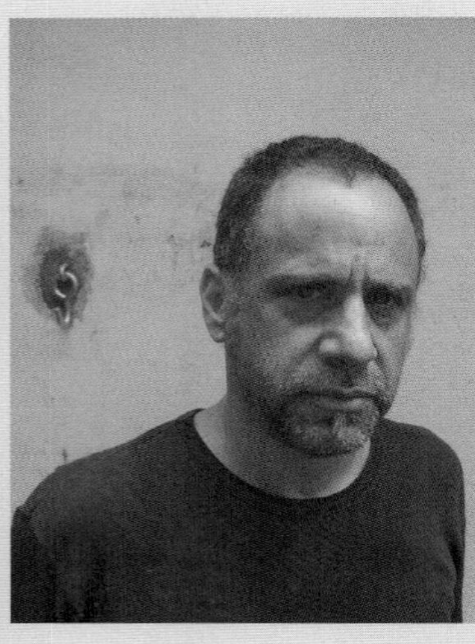

Born 1960, São Paulo, Brazil. Lives São Paulo, Brazil. **Selected solo exhibitions: 2008** Galeria Casa Triângulo, São Paulo • Projeto Octógono, São Paulo **Selected group exhibitions: 2009** 'The Sky Within my House', Museo de Bellas Artes, Córdoba, Spain **2008** São Paulo Biennial • 'When Lives Become Form', Museum of Contemporary Art, Tokyo • 'Espaços Reversíveis', Museu Cruz e Souza, Florianópolis, Brazil **2006** '10 Defining Experiments', Cisneros Fontanals Art Foundation, Miami **Selected bibliography: 2008** Camila Belchior, 'Rubens Mano', ArtNexus, Dec-Feb • Ivo Mesquita, Rubens Mano: Contemplaçã Suspensa, Projeto Octógono Arte Contemporânea, Pinacoteca do Estado, São Paulo **2007** Osvaldo Sánchez, 'Rubens Mano', 100 Artistas Latinoamericanos/100 Latin American Artists, Exit Publicaciones, Madrid **2004** Laymert Garcia Does Santos, 'Un art de l'espace et de sa production', Parachute, Oct-Dec

Josephie Meckseper

Born 1964, Lilienthal, Germany. Lives New York, NY, USA. **Selected solo exhibitions: 2009** Ausstellungshalle zeitgenössische Kunst, Münster • Indianapolis Museum of Art • Glenn Horowitz Bookseller, New York (with John McWhinnie) • Nottingham Contemporary, UK • Blaffer Gallery, Art Museum of the University of Houston • Migros Museum für Gegenwartskunst, Zurich

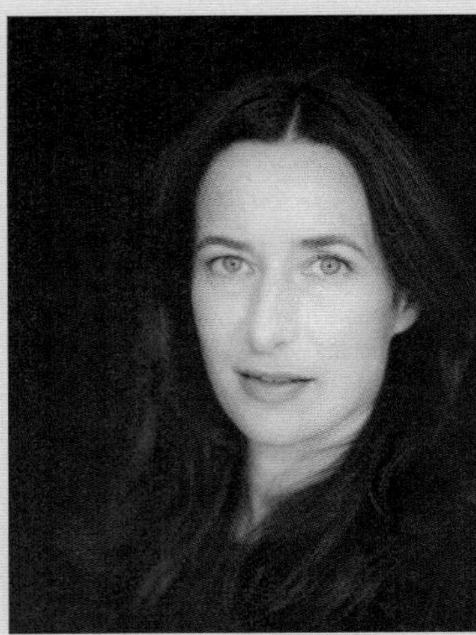

2008 The Museum of Modern Art, New York (with Mikhael Subotzky) • Gesellschaft für Aktuelle Kunst, Bremen • Colette, Paris **2007** Kunstmuseum Stuttgart **Selected group exhibitions: 2009** 'Dance in My Experience', Kunstverein für die Rheinlande und Westfalen, Düsseldorf • 'Morality', Witte de With, Rotterdam • '1989: End of History or Beginning of the Future? Comments on a Paradigm Shift', Kunsthalle Wien, Vienna **2008** Prospect 1, New Orleans • 'Business As Usual', Museum of Contemporary Art Detroit • 'That Was Then… This is Now', P.S.1, New York **2007** 'Brave New Worlds', Walker Art Center, Minneapolis • 'Resistance Is', Whitney Museum of American Art, New York • Moscow Biennial **Selected bibliography: 2009** Rachel Hooper, Sylvère Lotringer and Heike Munder, Josephine Meckseper, JRP Ringier, Zurich • Sylvère Lotringer, Vitamin 3-D: New Perspectives in Sculpture and Installation, Phaidon, London **2008** Sylvère Lotringer, Gabriele Mackert and Mona Schieren, Quelle International, Josephine Meckseper, Gesellschaft für Aktuelle Kunst, Bremen **2007** Okwui Enwezor, Christian Hoeller and Marion Ackermann, Josephine Meckseper, Hatje Cantz, Ostfildern **2006** Sylvère Lotringer, The Josephine Meckseper Catalogue No. 2, Sternberg, Berlin and New York

Miguel Mitlag

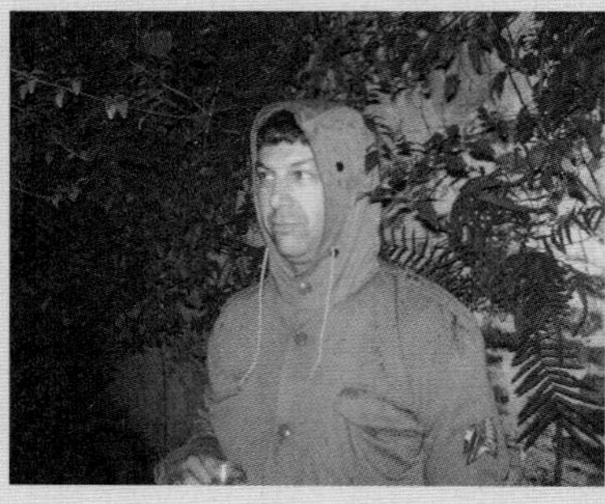

Born 1969, Buenos Aires, Argentina. Lives Buenos Aires, Argentina. **Selected solo exhibitions: 2009** Braga Menéndez, Buenos Aires **2008** Koal Gallery, Berlin **2007** Museo de Arte Latinoamericano de Buenos Aires **2006** Braga Menéndez, Buenos Aires • ArteBA-Petrobas, Buenos Aires **Selected group exhibitions: 2009** 'Escuelismo', Museo de Arte Latinoamericano de Buenos Aires • 'Vamos', Galería Nueveochenta, Bogota **2007** 'Expansive Link', Diverse Works, Houston, TX **2004–06** 'Civilizacion y Barbarie: Contemporanean Argentinean', Espacio Cultural Renato Russo, Brasilia; Museo de Arte Modern Carlos Merida, Guatemala; Museo del Canal Interceanico, Panama; Museo Nacional de Arte Contemporáneo, Santiago de Chile; Museo Sofia Imber, Caracas; Museo de Arte Contemporáneo de Rosario, Argentina

2005 'Folk: Pedraza, Mitlag, Navarro', Daniel Abate Galeria, Buenos Aires **Selected bibliography: 2007** Maria Gainza, 'Miguel Mitlag', Artforum, Nov

Anna Molska

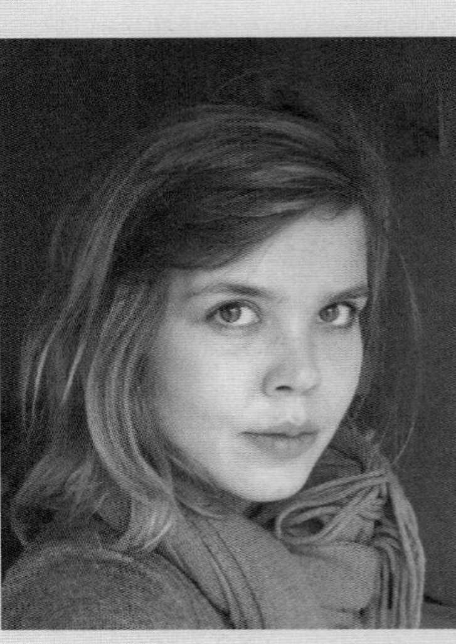

Born 1983, Prudnik, Poland. Lives Warsaw, Poland. **Selected solo exhibitions: 2009** 'Completed' (with Wojtek Bakowski), Kunstverein Freiburg, Germany • Broadway1602, New York, USA • Foksal Gallery Foundation, Warsaw, Poland **2008** Galeria Arsenal, Bialystok, Poland **Selected group exhibitions: 2009** 'Views', National Gallery of Art, Warsaw • 'Report on Probability', Kunsthalle Basel • 'The Generational: Younger Than Jesus', New Museum, New York **2008** 'Ain't No Sorry', Museum of Modern Art, Warsaw • Berlin Biennial **2007** 'Samsung Art Master 4', Centre for Contemporary Art, Ujazdowski Castle, Warsaw **Selected bibliography: 2009** Karol Sienkiewicz, 'G Point and Thereabouts', Spojrzenia/Views, Zacheta National Gallery of Art, Warsaw • Quinn Latimer, 'Report on Probability', Frieze, Oct • Lauren Cornell, Massimiliano Gioni and Laura Hoptman (eds.), Younger Than Jesus: Artist Directory, Phaidon, London **2008** Elena Filipovic and Adam Szymczyk, 'Anna Molska', 5th Berlin Biennale for Contemporary Art: When Things Cast No Shadow, KW, Berlin; JRP Ringier, Zurich • Tomasz Fudala, 'The Builders of the World in Anna Molska's Films', Artforum, Sep

Matthew Monahan

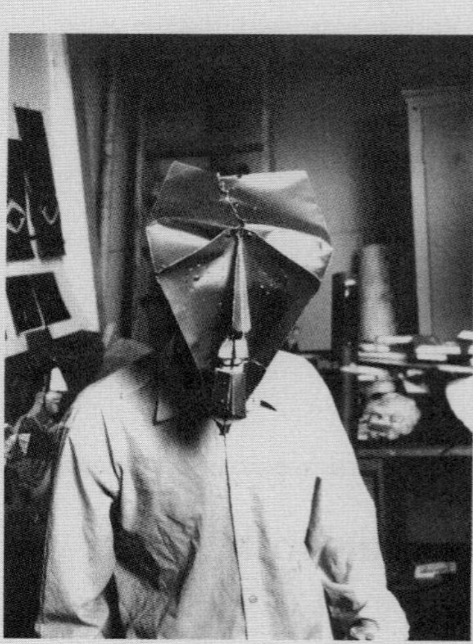

Born 1972, Eureka, CA, USA. Lives Los Angeles, CA, USA. **Selected solo exhibitions: 2009** Stuart Shave/Modern Art, London **2008** Anton Kern Gallery, New York **2007** Los Angeles Museum of Contemporary Art, Los Angeles • Douglas Hyde Gallery, Dublin

Selected group exhibitions: 2008 'Sphinxx', Stuart Shave/Modern Art, London • Carnegie International, Pittsburgh • 'Martian Museum of Terrestrial Art', Barbican Art Gallery, London • 'Sonsbeek Sculpture Exhibition', Sonsbeek Park, Arnhem, Netherlands **2007** 'Unmonumental' New Museum, New York • 'Eden's Edge: Fifteen LA Artists', Hammer Museum, Los Angeles • 'Red Eye: Los Angeles Artists from the Rubell Family Collection', Hammer Museum, Los Angeles **2006** Whitney Biennial, New York **Selected bibliography: 2009** Laura Hoptman, 'Matthew Monahan', Vitamin 3-D: New Perspectives in Sculpture and Installation, Phaidon, London **2008** Roberta Smith, 'An Alien Sighting on Planet Pittsburgh', The New York Times, 9 May **2007** Malik Gaines, 'Under the Volcano: History and What We Make of the Work of Matthew Monahan', Modern Painters, Oct • Jonathan Griffin, 'Back to Eden's Edge', Frieze, Oct • Andrew Beradini, 'MOCA Focus: Matthew Monahan', Art Review, Oct • Richard Flood, Massimiliano Gioni, Laura Hoptman Unmonumental, Phaidon, London

Melvin Moti

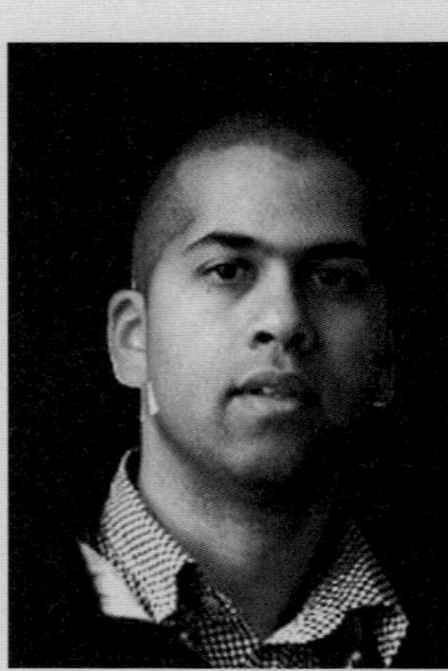

Born 1977, Rotterdam, Netherlands. Lives New York, NY, USA, and Rotterdam, Netherlands. **Selected solo exhibitions: 2010** Fondazione Galleria Civica, Trento • Wiels, Brussels **2008** Museum fur Moderne Kunst, Frankfurt • Fonds Régional d'Art Contemporain Champagne Reims **2007** Artspeak, Vancouver • Stedelijk Museum, Amsterdam • Kunstlerhaus Bethanien, Berlin **Selected group exhibitions: 2009** 'Lisson Presents #5', Lisson Gallery, London • 'Paper Exhibition', Artists Space, New York • 'The Immediate Future', Lund Konsthal, Sweden • 'Score & Script', Contemporar Arts Centre New Orleans **2008** 'Draw a Straight Line and Follow it', Tate Modern, London • 'Artist Module', Palais de Tokyo, Paris • 'Legend', Chamarande, France • 'Santal Family', Museum van Hedendaagse Kunst, Antwerp • Berlin Biennial **2007** 'Against Time', Bonniers Konsthall, Stockholm • 'Playback', Musée d'Art Moderne de la Ville de Paris • 'Infinite Island', Brooklyn Museum, New York • 'Pure Self Expression', Kölnischer Kunstverein Cologne • 'Double Movement: Migration Aesthetics', Murcia Spain • Moscow Biennial **Selected bibliography: 2009** John Menick, 'Minor Histories: A Conversation with Melvin Moti', Art in America, May • Andrea Lissoni, 'The Magical Bucket', Mousse, Feb • Melvin Moti, 'Miamalism', Retrospect, Artspeak, Vancouver **2008** Melvin Moti, 'Fast Asleep', Santhal Family Museum van Hedendaagse Kunst, Antwerp **2007** Melvin Moti, 'Brown is White', Metropolis, Jun

Martijn van Nieuwenhuyzen, 'Interview with Melvin Moti', Stedelijk Museum Magazine, Oct • Maria Hlavajova, 'Interview with Melvin Moti', Citizens and Subjects, Dutch Pavilion, Venice Biennale, Les Presses du Réel, Dijon

Museum of American Art

Founded 2004, Berlin, Germany. **Selected solo exhibitions: 2009** Halle fur Kunst, Luneburg, Germany **2008** Galerie Oberwelt, Stuttgart **2007** Kunsthaus Dresden • Galerija Nova, Zagreb **2006** Museum of Contemporary Art, Belgrade **Selected group exhibitions: 2009** Istanbul Biennial **2008** 'MoMA', Museumsbauhutte, Werkbundarchiv-Museum der Dinge, Berlin **2007** Lyon Biennial **2006** 'What is Modern Art?', Kunsthaus Bethanien, Berlin **2005** Venice Biennale **Selected bibliography: 2009** El Lissitzky and Alexander Dorner, 'Kabinett d. Abstrakten: Original and Facsimile', Displayer, no. 3 **2007** Tirdad Zolghadr, 'Museum of American Art', The History of a Decade That Has Not Yet Been Named, Lyon Biennial **2006** Inke Arns and Walter Benjamin, What is Modern Art?, Museum of American Art, Berlin • Inke Arns, 'Le MoAA à Berlin', Art Press, Aug.

Rosalind Nashashibi

Born 1973, Croydon, UK. Lives London, UK. **Selected solo exhibitions**: **2009** Institute of Contemporary Arts, London • Bergen Kunsthall • Projects in Art and Theory, Cologne • Kunstlerhaus Stuttgart **2008** Presentation House, Vancouver • Professional Gallery, Ontario College of Art and Design, Toronto **2007** Berkeley Art Museum, CA • Tate Britain, London • Chisenhale Gallery, London

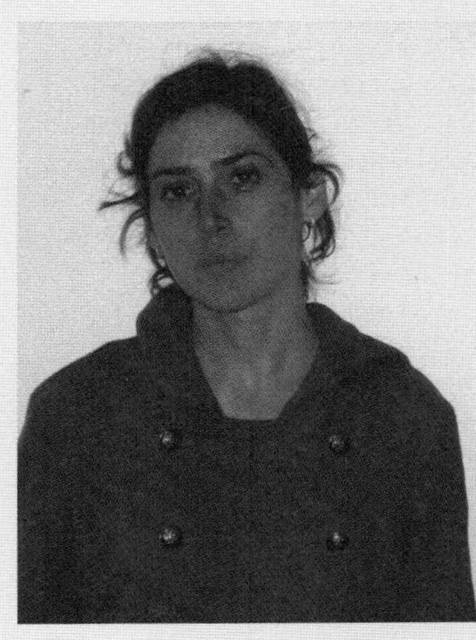

Selected group exhibitions: 2009 'Running Time: Artist Films in Scotland 1960 to Now', Dean Gallery, Edinburgh • 'Sculpture of the Space Age', David Roberts Art Foundation, London • 'Horizontale Durchlässigkeiten: Rosalind Nashashibi, Elodie Pong, Haegue Yang', Gebert Stiftung für Kultur, Altefabrik, Switzerland • 'space_revised 1: Friendly Takeovers', Gesellschaft Für Aktuelle Kunst, Bremen • 'Flicker', British Council, Damascus, Syria **2008** Manifesta 7, Trento • 'Éclats de frontiers, nouvelles acquisitions', Fonds Regional d'Art Contemporain Paca, Marseille • 'She doesn't think so but she's dressed for the h-bomb', Tate Modern, London

2007 'Winter Palace', De Ateliers, Amsterdam • 'MACBA In Frankfurt', Frankfurter Kunstverein • Scottish Pavilion, Venice Biennale • 'Pensée Sauvage: On Freedom', Frankfurter Kunstverein; Ursula Blickle Foundation, Kraichtal **Selected bibliography: 2009** Martin Herbert and Dieter Roelstraete, Rosalind Nashashibi, Institute of Contemporary Arts, London • Claire Denis, Anselm Franke, Martin Herbert, Mark Leckey, G. Ch. Lichtenberg, Thomas Mann, Jonas Mekas, Pier Paolo Pasolini and Marcel Proust, Roland, Institute of Contemporary Arts, London **2008** Rosalind Nashashibi, Proximity Machine, Scottish Arts Council; Arts Council England; Bookworks, London • Chus Martínez, Pensée Sauvage: On Freedom, Frankfurter Kunstverein

Eduardo Navarro

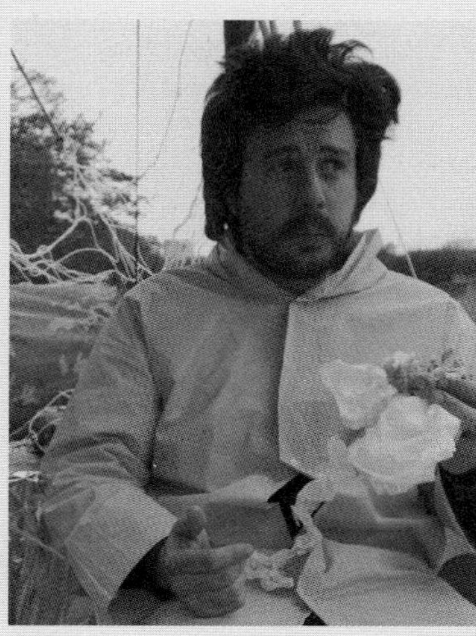

Born 1979, Buenos Aires, Argentina. Lives Buenos Aires, Argentina. **Selected solo exhibitions: 2008** Frederieke Taylor Gallery, New York • Daniel Abate Galleria, Buenos Aires **2007** Balin House Projects, London **2006** Blanton Museum, Austin, TX, USA **2004** Belleza y Felicidad, Buenos Aires **Selected group exhibitions: 2009** Mercosur Biennial, Porto Alegre, Brazil • 'Reading the City', Limerick, Ireland **2008** 'The Great Transformation: Art and Tactical Magic', Frankfurter Kunstverein **2007** 'Beginning with a Bang: From Confrontation to Intimacy' Americas Society, New York **2004–06** 'Civilizacion y Barbarie: Contemporanean Argentinean', Espacio Cultural Renato Russo, Brasilia; Museo de Arte Modern Carlos Merida, Guatemala; Museo del Canal Interceanico, Panama; Museo Nacional de Arte Contemporaneo, Santiago de Chile; Museo Sofia Imber, Caracas; Museo de Arte Contemporáneo de Rosario, Argentina **Selected bibliography: 2008** Brigitte Weingart, 'The Great Trasformation: Art and Tactical Magic', Artforum, May • Santiago Garcia Navarro, 'Exposiciones del Mundo/Fabricantes Unidos', Exit Expres, no. 36 **2007** Ken Johnson, 'Roars of Argentina's Past, Murmurs of Its Present', The New York Times, 14 Dec **2006** Meredith Mendelssohn, 'Young Artist to watch', Art News, Nov

Miguel Noguera

Born 1979, Las Palmas de Gran Canaria, Spain. Lives Barcelona, Spain. **Selected solo exhibitions: 2009** Museo de Arte Contemporáneo de Barcelona **2008** Centro Galego de Arte Contemporánea, Spain **2007** Museo de Arte Contemporáneo de Castilla y León, Spain **2006** Centre d'Art Santa Mònica, Spain

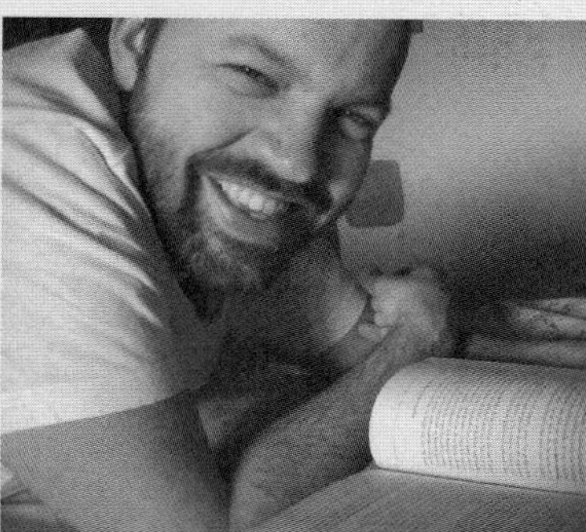

Selected group exhibitions: 2009 'The Malady of Writing', Museo de Arte Contemporáneo de Barcelona **2008** Musica Ex Machina Festival, Bilbao **2005** 'Genres, Deferred Stories', Obra Social Caja, Madrid **Selected bibliography: 2010** Miguel Noguera and Jonathan Millán, Boiling a Bear, Belleza Infinita, Bilbao **2009** Ignacio Vidal-Folch, 'La idea de que...', El País, 2 Jun

Olivia Plender

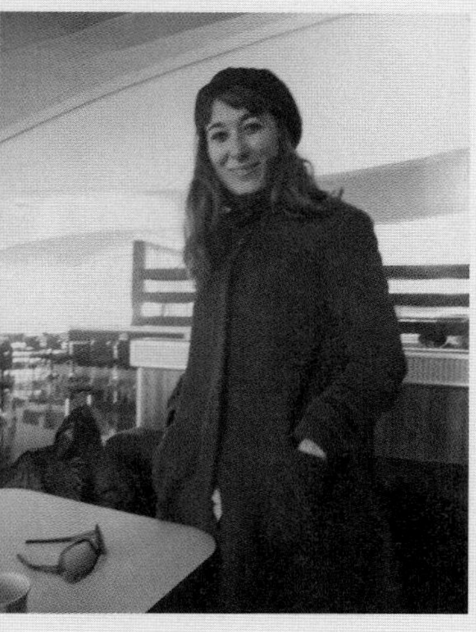

Born 1977, London, UK. Lives London, UK. **Selected solo exhibitions: 2009** Gasworks, London • Kiosk, Ghent, Belgium **2008** Art in General, New York **2007** Marabou Parken Annex, Stockholm **2006** Frankfurter Kunstverein **Selected group exhibitions: 2009** Tate Triennial, London • 'The Malady of Writing', Museu d'Art Contemporani de Barcelona • 'Critical Applause' (performance lecture with Robert Leckie), Centre for Contemporary Arts, Glasgow • 'Notes from the Living Dead Museum', Living Art Museum, Reykjavik • 'Practical Truths', Castlefield Gallery, Manchester **2008** 'The Greenroom: Reconsidering the Documentary and Contemporary Art', Hessel Museum of Art, Bard College, Annandale-on-Hudson, NY, USA • 'Algulnas Negras', Centro Cultural, São Paolo • 'The Great Transformation', Frankfurter Kunstverein; Museo de Arte Contemporánea de Vigo, Spain • 'Not Quite How I Remember It', Power Plant, Toronto • 'Bending the Word, Berkeley Art Museum and Pacific Film Archive, California • 'Moot Points: Exercises in Self-Organisation, Discourse and Collaboration', Transmission Gallery, Glasgow **Selected bibliography: 2009** Olivia Plender, 'Bouvard et Pécuchet', A Prior, no. 19 • Nicolas Bourriaud, Altermodern: Tate Triennial, Tate Publishing, London • Robert Stasinski 'Olivia Plender: I'll Give you Television', Flash Art, Jul-Sep • Melissa Gronlund, 'Olivia Plender', Frieze, Jun **2008** Olivia Plender, Bring Back Robin Hood: Notes on an Imagined Community, Transmission Gallery, Glasgow • Olivia Plender, Spirit Swindlers, University of California Press, Berkeley • Maria Lind and Hito Steyerl (eds.) The Greenroom: Reconsidering the Documentary and Contemporary Art, Sternberg, Berlin and New York • Chus

Martínez, The Great Transformation, Veenman, Rotterdam Helena Reckitt, Not Quite How I Remember It, Power Plant, Toronto • Lauren Cornell, Massimiliano Gioni and Laura Hoptman (eds.), Younger Than Jesus: Artist Directory, Phaidon, London **2007** Olivia Plender, A Stellar Key to the Summerland, Bookworks, London

Michael Portnoy

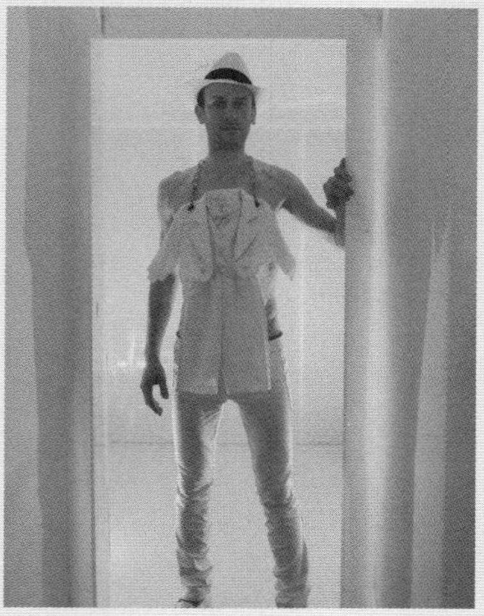

Born 1971, Washington, DC, USA. Lives New York, NY, USA. **Selected solo exhibitions and performances: 2009** 'On se bat toujours quelque part: The Dudion Levers', Le Confort Moderne, Poitiers, France **2008** 'The Dudion Levers', Martos Gallery, New York • 'Lend a Polt in the Put', Ibid Projects, London • 'Casino Ilinx', Sculpture Center, New York **2007** 'Seminar in Subliminal Carnage: The 33 Holdmusic Variations', Performa 07, The Swiss Institute, New York • 'Talus', Dexter Sinister, New York • 'The Gutsongs of Xar', Tensta Konsthall, Stockholm • 'Piano Destruction Party', Session, New York **Selected group exhibitions: 2009** Performa 09 • 'Bloodsport: The Illusion of Abstract Gambling', ReMap 2, Athens • 'Strip/stripe', Emily Harvey Foundation, New York • 'Paper Exhibition', Artists Space, New York **2008** 'A Choreographed Exhibition', La Ferme du Buisson, Noisiel, France • 'One of These Things is Not Like the Other Things', 1/9 Unosunove, Rome • 'Word Event', Kunsthalle Basel **2007** 'A Choreographed Exhibition', Kunsthalle St Gallen, Switzerland • 'Speak Easy: Reading on the Rocks', Sculpture Center, New York • Moscow Biennial • **Selected bibliography: 2009** Maxine Kopsa, 'I did not have relational asthmatics with that woman, although I did cough in her lemongrass soup', Metropolis M, Oct • '600 Words with Michael Portnoy', Art in America, Aug **2008** Nick Currie, 'Satirizing Luxury', The New York Times, 11 Jul • Adrian Dannatt, 'Sculptor Breaks the Bank', Art Newspaper, 1 Jun

Seth Price

Born 1973, East Jerusalem. Lives New York, NY, USA. **Selected solo exhibitions: 2010** Capitain Petzel, Berlin • Isabella Bortolozzi, Berlin **2009** Reena Spaulings Fine Art, New York • Museo d'Arte Moderna di Bologna **2008** Kunsthalle Zurich • Kölnischer Kunstverein, Cologne • Friedrich Petzel Gallery, New York • Institute of Contemporary Arts, London **2007** Modern Art Oxford (with Kelley Walker) • Galerie Gisela

Capitain, Cologne.

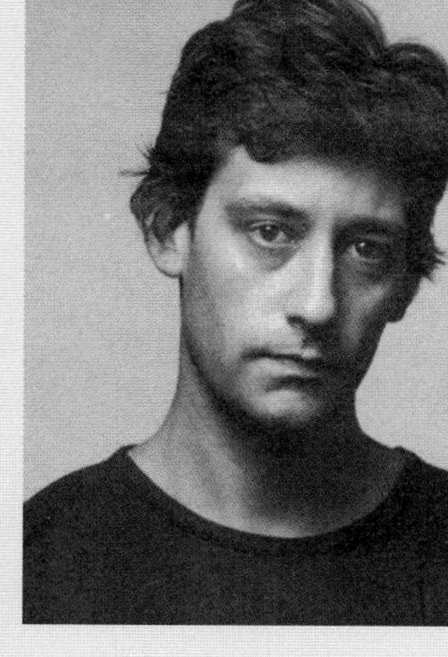

Selected group exhibitions: 2009 'Looking Back: The White Columns Annual', White Columns, New York • 'Chinese Box', Overduin and Kite, Los Angeles • 'Playground', Micro Onde and Quartier, Paris • 'A Guest + a Host = A Ghost', Deste Foundation, Athens • Tate Triennial, London **2008** 'Kunst In Heim', Capitain Petzel Gallery, Berlin • Whitney Biennial, New York • 'Ghost in the Machine', Kunstnernes Hus, Oslo **2007** 'Transactions', Blanton Museum of Art, TX, USA • 'Conditions of Display', The Moore Space, Miami, and Locust Projects, Miami • 'A Fair Show: Slang Cool Orthodoxy', Massimo de Carlo, Milan • Lyon Biennial • 'Freelance Stenographer' (with Kelley Walker), The Kitchen, New York **Selected bibliography: 2009** Guido Molinari, 'Sarah Morris / Seth Price', Flash Art, Sep • Tim Griffin, 'The Personal Effects of Seth Price', Artforum, Summer **2008** Jack Bankowsky, 'Best of 2008: Seth Price, Kunsthalle Zürich', Artforum, Dec • Seth Price, 'Poems', Tank, Dec • Susanne Saether, 'Ghost in the Machine: Probing the States In-Between', Ghost in the Machine, Kunstnernes Hus, Oslo • Polly Staple, 'The Producer', Frieze, Oct • Skye Sherwin, 'Seth Price: The End of Meaning', Art Review, Jun • Suzanne Hudson, 'Seth Price, Whitney Biennial, Whitney Museum of American Art, New York • Elizabeth Schambelan, 'Seth Price', Artforum, May **2007** Andrew Viliani, 'Seth Price: What Is It?', Lyon Biennial: The History of a Decade That Has Not Yet Been Named, JRP Ringier, Zurich

Lili Reynaud-Dewar

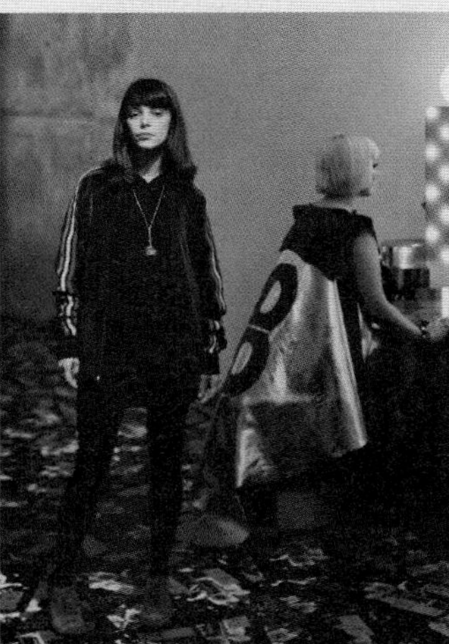

Born 1975, Nantes, France. Lives Paris, France. **Selected solo exhibitions: 2010** Fonds Régional d'Art Contemporain Champagne Ardennes, Reims, France **2009** Mary Mary, Glasgow • Centre d'Art, Parc Saint-Leger, Pougues les Eaux, France **2008** Centre d'Arts Plastiques Contemporains, Bordeaux • Fonds Régional d'Art Contemporain Bordeaux

Galleria Civica d'Arte Contemporanea Montevergini di Siracusa, Italy **Selected group exhibitions:** **2010** 'Morality', Witte de With, Rotterdam **2009** 'La Suite', Air de Paris, Paris • 'The Pursuit of Pleasure', Barriera Fundazione, Turin • 'Je n'étais pas qu'une simple chimère', Saidye Bronfman Centre for the Arts, Montreal • 'Elles@centrepompidou', Centre Pompidou, Paris •'Kerhaus-Abschied von Stabilen Wanden', Westfalische Kunstverein, Münster • 'Les Formes Féminines', Triangle Galerie de la Friche Belle de Mai, Marseille • 'Revolver', Coco Kunstverein, Vienna • 'Latifa Echakhch/Lili Reynaud-Dewar', Karma International at James Fuentes, New York **2008** 'Prix Ricard', Fondation d'entreprise Ricard, Paris • Berlin Biennial **Selected bibliography: 2009** Joanna Fiduccia, 'Power Structures, Pantomimes and Parodies', Map Magazine, Nov • Clare Moulène, 'Lili Reynaud-Dewar', Artforum, Jun. • Céline Kopp, 'Lili Reynaud-Dewar', Vitamin 3-D: New Perspectives in Sculpture and Installation, Phaidon, London • Katie Kitamura, 'Latifa Echakhch and Lili Reynaud-Dewar', Frieze, May **2008** Nicolas Bourriaud, La consistance du visible: 10ème prix de la fondation Ricard, Fondation d'entreprise Ricard, Paris

Robin Rhode

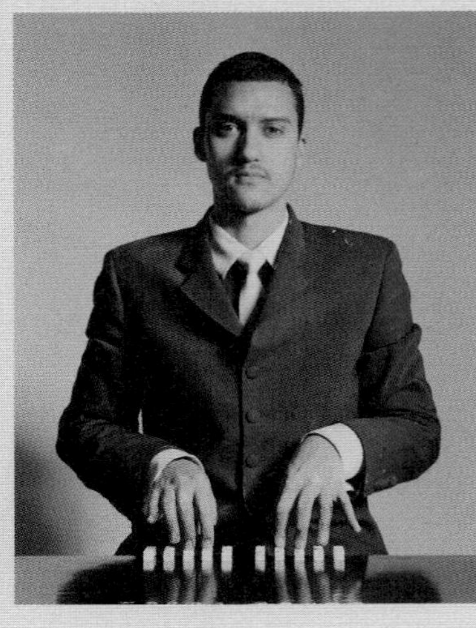

Born 1976, Cape Town, South Africa. Lives Berlin, Germany. **Selected solo exhibitions: 2010** Los Angeles County Museum of Art **2009** Wexner Center for the Arts, Columbus, OH, USA **2008** Hayward Gallery, London • White Cube, London • Tucci Russo, Turin **2007** Haus der Kunst, Munich **Selected group exhibitions: 2010** 'Choreographing You: Fifty years of Art and Dance', Hamburger Kunsthalle, Hamburg; Hayward Gallery, London **2009** 'Dada South', Iziko South African National Gallery, Cape Town • '30 Seconds Off an Inch', Studio Museum in Harlem, New York • 'Intimate Geographies', Fundación Marcelino Botín, Santander, Spain • 'The Moving Image: Scan to Screen, Pixel to Projection, Part I', Orange County Museum of Art, Newport Beach, CA, USA **2008** Prospect 1, New Orleans • 'Currents: Recent Acquisitions', Hirshhorn Museum, Washington • 'Street Level: Mark Bradford, William Cordova and Robin Rhode', Institute of Contemporary Art, Boston **Selected bibliography: 2009** Catharina Manchanda (ed.), Catch Air, Wexner Center for the Arts, Columbus, OH, USA **2008** Stephanie Rosenthal (ed.), Who Saw Who, Hayward Publishing, London • Linda Yee (ed.), Street Art, Street Life, Aperture, New York; Bronx Museum of the Arts, New York **2007** Stephanie Rosenthal (ed.), Robin Rhode: Walk Off, Haus der Kunst, Munich; Hatje Cantz, Ostfildern

Stephen G. Rhodes

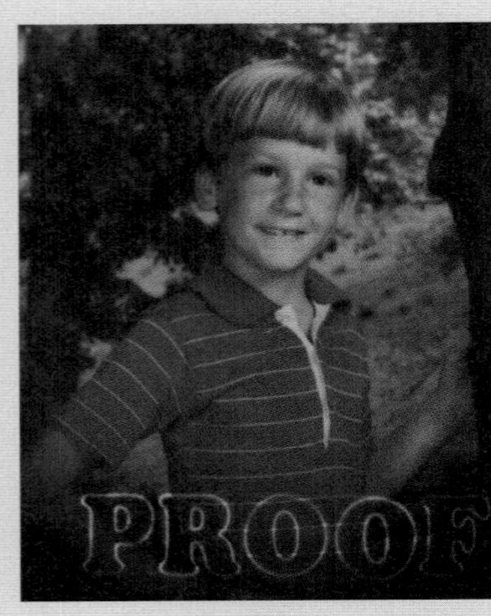

Born 1977, Houston, TX, USA. Lives Los Angeles, CA, USA. **Selected solo exhibitions: 2009** Vilma Gold, London • Isabella Bortolozzi, Berlin • Misako & Rosen, Tokyo **2007** Overduin and Kite, Los Angeles • Guild & Greyshkul, New York **Selected group exhibitions: 2009** 'On From Here', Guild & Greyshkul, New York • 'Abstract America: New Painting and Sculpture', Saatchi Gallery, London • 'Second Nature: The Valentine-Adelson Collection', Hammer Museum, Los Angeles, • 'The Generational: Younger than Jesus', New Museum, New York **2008** Prospect 1, New Orleans • 'KABUL 3000 Love Among the Cabbages', Zero, Milan • 'Nobody Puts Baby in a Corner', Isabella Bortolozzi, Berlin • 'Self-Portrait,' James Fuentes Gallery, New York **2007** 'Post Rose: Artists In and Out of the Hazard Park Complex', Galerie Christian Nagel, Berlin • 'USA Today,' State Hermitage Museum, St Petersburg • 'Between Two Deaths', Zentrum für Kunst und Medientechnologie, Karlsruhe **Selected bibliography: 2009** Gigiotto Del Vecchio, 'An American De-Mithology', Mousse, Jan • Elizabeth Schambelan, 'Being There', Artforum, Jan • Lauren Cornell, Massimiliano Gioni and Laura Hoptman (eds.), Younger Than Jesus: Artist Directory, Phaidon, London **2008** Roberta Smith, 'Kaleidoscopic Biennial for a Scarred City', The New York Times, 3 Nov **2007** Michael Ned Holte, 'Stephen G. Rhodes', Artforum, Dec • Catherine Taft, 'Stephen G. Rhodes', Modern Painters, Nov • Andrew Berardini, 'Stephen G. Rhodes: Ruined Dualisms', ArtReview, Nov • Aram Moshayedi, 'Stephen G. Rhodes at Overduin and Kite', Afterall Online, 30 Oct

Noguchi Rika

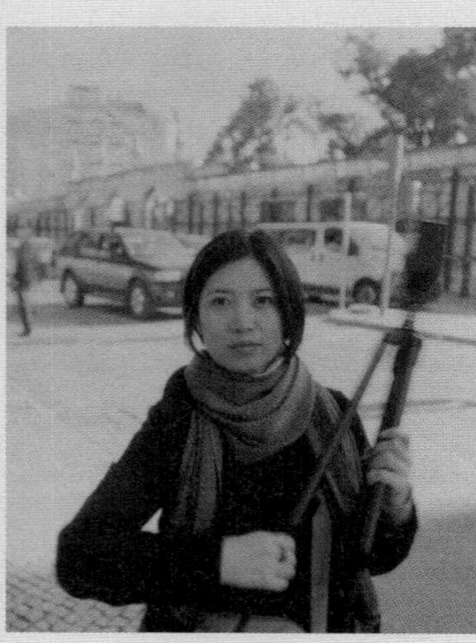

Born 1971 Saitama, Japan. Lives Berlin, Germany. **Selected solo exhibitions: 2009** D'Amelio Terras, New York **2007** Gallery Koyanagi, Tokyo **2006** DAAD Gallery, Berlin **2004** Ikon Gallery, Birmingham **2004** Hara Museum of Contemporary Art, Tokyo

Selected group exhibitions: 2009 'The Light: Matsumoto Yoko and Noguchi Rika', National Art Centre, Tokyo **2008** Carnegie International, Pittsburgh **2007** 'Brave New Worlds', Walker Art Center, Minneapolis • Sharjah Biennial • 'The Door into Summer: The Age of Micropop', Mito, Ibaraki, Japan **Selected bibliography: 2009** Minami Yusuke, 'Noguchi Rika: Photographs that Transcend the Speed of Light', The Light: Matsumoto Yoko and Noguchi Rika, National Art Center, Tokyo **2007** Midori Matsui, 'Noguchi Rika', The Door into Summer: The Age of Micropop, Art Tower Mito • Doryun Chong, 'The Quiet Awe of Noguchi Rika', Brave New Worlds, Walker Art Center, Minneapolis **2006** Tetsuya Ozaki, 'Noguchi Rika', Vitamin Ph: New Perspectives in Photography, Phaidon, London **2004** Atsuo Yasuda and Jonathan Watkins, The Planet: Noguchi Rika, Hara Museum of Contemporary Art; Ikon Gallery, Birmingham

Aïda Ruilova

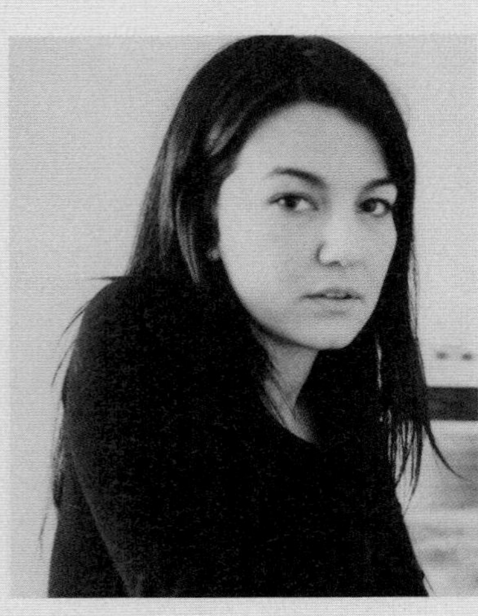

Born 1974, Wheeling, WV, USA. Lives New York, NY, USA. **Selected solo exhibitions: 2009** Museum of Contemporary Art Cleveland • Contemporary Art Center New Orleans • Hammer Museum, Los Angeles **2008** Contemporary Art Museum St Louis • Sketch Gallery, London • Aspen Art Museum, CO, USA • Galerie Guido W. Baudach, Berlin **2007** The Kitchen, New York • Salon 94, New York **Selected group exhibitions: 2008** 'Slightly Unbalanced', Chicago Cultural Center; Huntington Museum of Art, Huntington, WV, USA • 'Paul & Lulu', Hiliard University Art Museum, Lafayette, LA, USA • 'Sympathy for the Devil', Museum of Contemporary Art, Miami; Museum of Contemporary Art, Montreal; Museum of Contemporary Art, Chicago **2007** 'Exhibitionism', Hessel Museum, Bard College, Annandale-on-Hudson, NY, USA • 'Fantastisk FilmFestival', Lund, Sweden • 'Between 2 Deaths', Zentrum für Kunst und Medientechnologie, Karlsruhe • Moscow Biennial • 'Pale Carnage', Arnolfini, Bristol; Dundee Contemporary Art Center, UK • 'Köln Show 2', European Kunsthalle, Cologne • 'Pensée Sauvage: On Freedom', Ursula Bllickle Foundation, Karlsruhe; Frankfurter Kunstverein **Selected bibliography: 2008** Adam E. Mendelsohn, 'Special Focus: Reviews Marathon, New York', ArtReview, Feb **2007** Jerry Saltz, 'The Year in Art', New York Magazine, Dec • Holland Cotter, 'An Upbeat Moment for a Downtrodden Area', The New York Times, 1 Dec • Claudia La Rocco, 'As Conceptual Art Evolves, One Mission Is Unchanged: Keep Expanding the Possibilities', The New York Times, 22 Nov **2006** Roberta Smith, 'The Berlin Biennial', The New York Times, 7 May • Gean Moreno, 'Aïda Ruilova', Contemporary, Feb

Tomas Saraceno

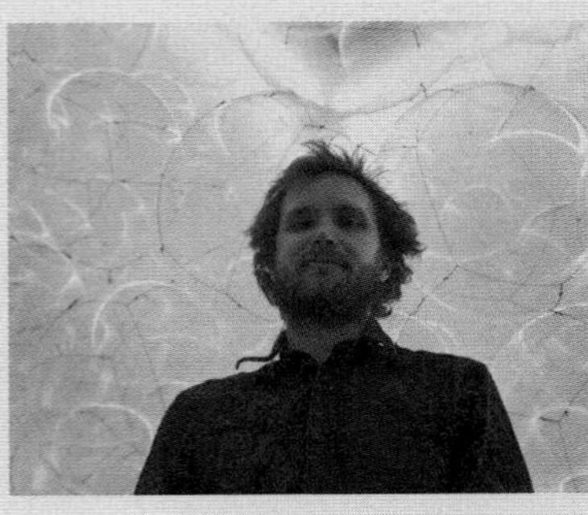

Born 1973, Tucuman, Argentina. Lives Frankfurt, Germany. **Selected solo exhibitions: 2009** Walker Art Center, Minneapolis • Musée d'Art Moderne Grand-Duc Jean, Luxembourg • Statens Museum for Kunst, Copenhagen **2008** Tanya Bonakdar Gallery, New York **2007** De Vleeshal, Middelburg, Netherlands **2007** Berkeley Art Museum, CA, USA **2006** Portikus (with Marjetica Potrc), Frankfurt **Selected group exhibitions: 2009** Venice Biennale • 'Radical Nature', Barbican Art Gallery, London **2008** 'Psycho Buldings: Artists and Architecture', Hayward Gallery, London • 'Sonsbeek 2008: Grandeur', Arnhem, Netherlands • 'Experiment Marathon Reykjavik', Reykjavik Art Museum **2007** Lyon Biennial • Sharjah Biennial **Selected bibliography: 2009** Jonathan Porritt, Francesco Manacorda and T. J. Demos, Radical Nature. Art and Architecture for a Changing Planet 1969–2009, Barbican Art Gallery, London • Sally O'Reilly, 'Tomas Saraceno', Vitamin 3-D: New Perspectives in Sculpture and Installation, Phaidon, London **2008** Kristin M. Jones, 'Tomas Saraceno', Frieze, summer **2007** Luca Cerizza, 'Temporary Communities', Tema Celeste, no. 119

Katerina Šedá

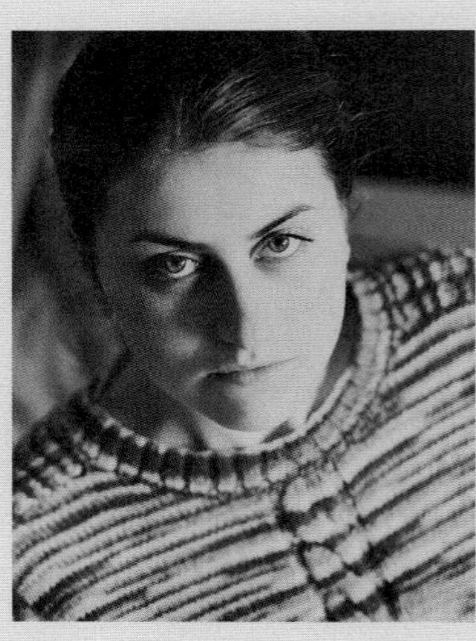

Born 1977, Brno, Czech Republic. Lives Brno and Prague, Czech Republic. **Selected solo exhibitions: 2008** The Renaissance Society, Chicago • La Box, Bourges, France **2007** Galerie im Taxispalais, Innsbruck, Austria • Index, Stockholm • Czech Center, New York **2006** Modern Art Oxford, UK **Selected group exhibitions: 2009** Lyon Biennial, France • 'The Generational: Younger Than Jesus', New Museum, New York **2008** Manifesta 7, Bolzano, Italy • Berlin Biennial • 'Social Diagrams', Künstlerhaus Stuttgart, Germany **2007** Documenta 12, Kassel • 'Stalking with Stories: The Pioneers of the Immemorable', Apexart, New York **Selected bibliography: 2009** Valentina Bucco, 'Katerina Šedá', Temporale, no. 68/69 • Lauren Cornell, Massimiliano Gioni and Laura Hoptman (eds.), Younger Than Jesus: Artist Directory, Phaidon, London **2008** Karel Cisa, 'Life is Elsewhere', Flash Art, Nov-Feb

Martin Herbert, 'Katerina Šedá', Artforum, Nov **2007** Amanda Church, 'Art Therapy: Talking with Czech artist Katerina Seda about her grandmother', Art on Paper, May

Dexter Sinister

Founded in New York in 2006 by David Reinfurt (born 1971 Chapel Hill, NC; lives New York, NY) and Stuart Bailey (born 1973 York, UK; lives Los Angeles, CA, USA.) **Selected solo exhibitions: 2009** Contemporary Art Museum St Louis **2008** New Langton Arts, San Francisco • Nice & Fit Gallery, Berlin **Selected group exhibitions: 2009** 'Talk Show', Institute of Contemporary Arts, London • 'Paper Exhibition', Artists Space, New York **2008** 'Moot Points', Transmission Gallery, Glasgow • 'Word Event', Kunsthalle Basel • Whitney Biennial, New York **2007** 'Wouldn't It Be Nice …', Centre d'Art Contemporain, Geneva • 'On the Future of Art School', Store Gallery, London **Selected bibliography: 2009** Dexter Sinister, Portable Document Format, Sternberg, Berlin and New York **2009** Eric Fredricksen and Dexter Sinister, 'Re: The Serving Library', Fillip, Fall **2008** Adam Kleinman, 'Dexter Sinister', Bomb, Spring **2007** Anthony Huberman, 'Out of Circulation', Artforum, Apr

Reena Spaulings

Founded in 2004 by John Kelsey and Emily Sundblad. **Selected solo exhibitions: 2009** Sutton Lane, Brussels **2008** Contemporary Art Museum St Louis • Galerie Chantal Crousel, Paris **2007** Kunsthalle Zurich **2006** Sutton Lane, London • Galerie Chantal Crousel, Paris **Selected group exhibitions: 2009** 'Here Is Every: Four Decades of Contemporary Art', The Museum of Modern Art, New York • 'Pop Life', Tate Modern, London • 'It's Not Me. It's You' Andrew Kreps Gallery, New York • 'Sonic Youth etc: Sensational Fix', Kunsthalle Düsseldorf; Malmö Konsthall; Museion Bolzano, Italy **2008** 'Painting: Now and Forever, Part II', Greene Naftali and Matthew Marks, New York • 'L'argent', Le Plateau, Paris • 'Some Neighbors', Kunstverein München • 'Records played backwards', The Modern Institute, Glasgow • 'One Season in Hell', MD 72, Berlin **2007** 'Terrible Video', Kunsthalle Zurich • 'Someone Else with My Fingerprints', Galerie Chantal Crousel • 'Make Your Own Life', Museum of Contemporary Art, Miami; Henry Art Gallery, Seattle • 'Uncertain States of America;, CCA Ujazdowski Castle, Warsaw, Poland **Selected bibliography: 2009** Beatrice Gross, 'Le retour de la mort de l'auteur', Double, Spring-Summer • Michel Gauthier, 'Néo-conceptuels: la redistribution des roles', Artpress, Apr **2008** Benjamin Thorel, 'Reena Spaulings', Flash Art, Oct • Violaine Boutet de Monvel, 'Reena Spaulings: Courbet Your Enthusiasm', Art Review, Oct • Yates Mckee, 'Besprechungen', Texte Zur Kunst, Dec **2007** Magali Arriola, 'Otra de vaqueros', Spike, Dec • Anthony Huberman, 'Toaster's Choice', Modern Painters, Dec • Bettina Funcke, 'Displaced Struggles', Artforum, Mar • Cameron Irving, 'Reena Spaulings', Untitiled, Spring

Fia Stina Sandlund

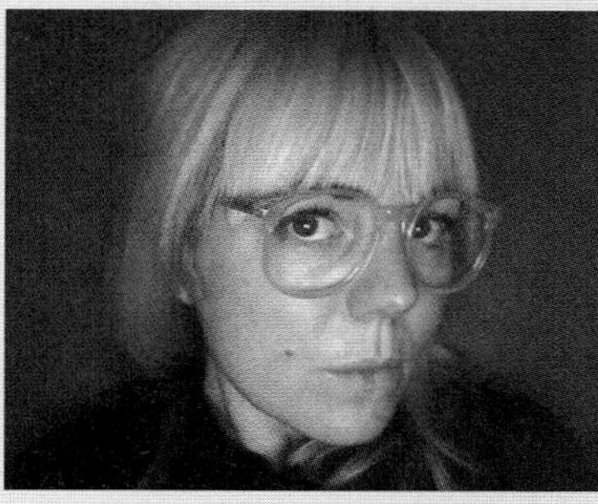

Born 1973, Stockholm, Sweden. Lives New York, NY, USA **Selected solo exhibitions and performances: 2009** 'INTERIOR: A CAFE IN VENICE-DAY. Julie in an interview about the movie', Gervasuti Foundation, Venice **2006** 'If you are the rebel, I will be decent', various locations, Sweden **2005** 'Blind Date' (with Lars Nittve), Gallery AK28, Stockholm **Selected group exhibitions: 2008** 'Revolution, I Love You', Centre of Contemporary Art, Thessaloniki; Trafó Gallery, Budapest; International Project Space. Birmingham **2007** Gothenburg Biennial • 'Agorafolly', Europalia, Brussels **2006** 'The Moderna exhibition 2006', Moderna Museet, Stockholm • 'Capital (It Fails Us Now)', Kunstihoone, Tallinn; Unge Kunstneres Samfund, Oslo **Selected bibliography: 2009** Cecilia Widenheim (ed.), Voice Over: On Staging and Performative Strategies in Contemporary Art, IASPIS, Stockholm; Sternberg, Berlin and New York **2007** Tirdad Zolghadr, 'Tough Love', Frieze, Mar • Sinziana Ravini, 'Konst som en form av motstånd', Göteborgs-Posten, 13 Jul

Katja Strunz

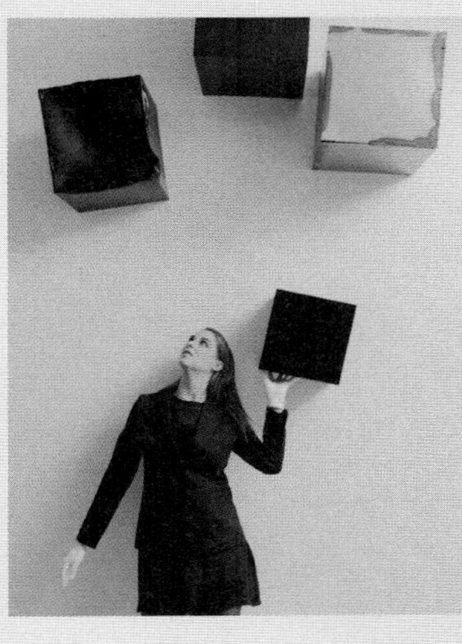

Born 1970, Ottweiler, Germany. Lives Berlin, Germany. **Selected solo exhibitions: 2009** Camden Arts Centre, London • Mount Stuart Gallery, UK **2008** Contemporary Fine Arts, Berlin **2007** Artpace, San Antonio, TX, USA **2006** Museum Haus Esters, Krefeld **Selected group exhibitions: 2009** 'Elles@ centrepompidou', Centre Pompidou, Paris **2008** Carnegie International, Pittsburgh • 'So ist es und anders', Museum Abteiberg, Moenchengladbach, Germany **2007** 'Delusive Orders', Muzeum Sztuki, Lodz, Poland **2005** 'Ars Ziva 04/05: Zeit/ Time', Kunstverein für die Rheinlande & Westfalen, Düsseldorf; Zacheta National Gallery of Art, Warsaw **Selected bibliography: 2009** Christy Lange, 'Katja Strunz', Vitamin 3-D: New Perspectives in Sculpture and Installation, Phaidon, London • Charlotte Klonk, 'In the studio: Katja Strunz, Standing with One's Back to Utopia', Tate etc., Spring **2008** Heather Pesanti, 'Katja Strunz', Life on Mars: 55th Carnegie International, Carnegie

Museum of Art, Pittsburgh **2007** Suzanne Hudson and Lutz Niethammer, Katja Strunz, Walther König, Cologne

Tadasu Takamine

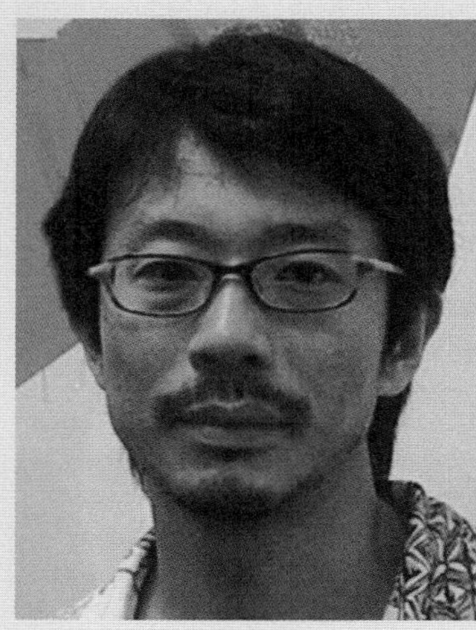

Born 1968, Kagoshima, Japan. Lives Shiga, Japan. **Selected solo exhibitions: 2008** Mediatheque, Miyagi, Japan • Arataniurano, Tokyo **2007** AD&A gallery, Osaka **2006** Gertrude Contemporary Art Space, Melbourne **Selected group exhibitions: 2009** 'I Believe: Contemporary Art in Japan', Museum of Modern Art, Toyama, Japan **2008** 'The Demon of Comparisons: A Project by Electric Palm Tree', Stedelijk Museum Bureau, Amsterdam **2007** 'Beautiful New World: Contemporary Visual Culture from Japan', Guangdong Museum of Art, Guangzhou, China • 'Tomorrow', Kumho Museum, Seoul **2006** 'Aestetics /Dietetics', Galleria d'Arte Moderna e Contemporanea, Bergamo, Italy **2005** Yokohama Triennial **Selected bibliography: 2008** Tadasu Takamine, A Lover from Korea, Kawade Shobo Shinsha, Tokyo

Ron Terada

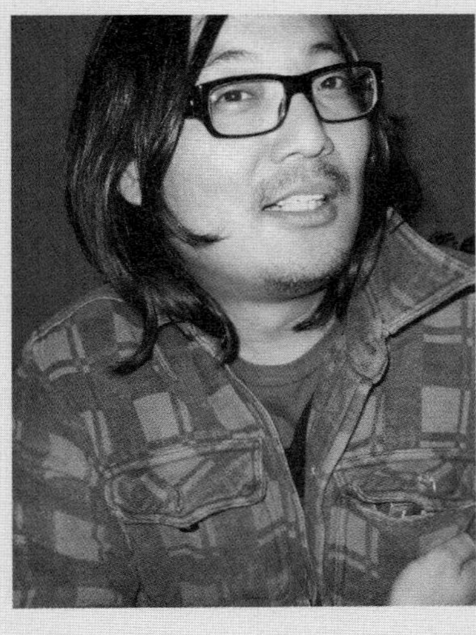

Born 1969, Vancouver, Canada. Lives Vancouver, Canada. **Selected solo exhibitions: 2010** Walter Phillips Gallery, Banff Centre, Canada • Ikon, Birmingham **2008** Catriona Jeffries Gallery, Vancouver **2006** Eastside, Birmingham **2005** Art Gallery of Windsor, Canada **Selected group exhibitions: 2009** 'Morality', Witte de With Center for Contemporary Art, Rotterdam **2008** 'Tractatus Logico-Catalogicus', Vox, Montreal • Christchurch Biennial, New Zealand • 'The Store', Tulips & Roses, Vilnius • 'Signals in the Dark: Art in the Shadow of War', Blackwood Gallery, University of Toronto at Mississauga **2007** 'Sobey Art Award', Art Gallery of Nova Scotia, Halifax

'Words Fail Me', Museum of Contemporary Art, Detroit • 'For Sale', Cristina Guerra Contemporary Art, Lisbon • 'The Idea of North', Isabella Bortolozzi Galerie, Berlin **2006** 'The Show Will Be Open When The Show Will Be Closed', Kadist Art Foundation, Paris • 'Concrete Language', Contemporary Art Gallery, Vancouver • Shanghai Biennial **Selected bibliography: 2010** Cliff Lauson, 'The Idea of a Vancouver Artist', Ron Terada: Who I Think I Am, Ikon, Birmingham; Walter Phillips Gallery, Banff Centre; Justina M Barnicke Gallery, Hart House, Toronto **2009** Adam Carr, 'Trading Places: The Story of Defile', Ciel Variable, No. 83 **2008** Jon Bywater, 'Ron Terada', SCAPE Christchurch Biennial, Christchurch, New Zealand • Christopher Mooney, 'Ron Terada', Art Review, Jul-Aug **2007** Doreen Mende, 'The Idea of North', C Magazine, no. 94 • Helga Pakasaar, 'Ron Terada', Sobey Art Award 2007, Art Gallery of Nova Scotia, Halifax

Yuken Teruya

Born 1973, Okinawa, Japan. Lives New York, NY, USA. **Selected solo exhibitions: 2010** Josee Bienvenu Gallery, New York **2009** Gallery Okinawa, Japan **2007** Murata and Friends Gallery, Berlin • Asia Society, New York • Shoshana Wayne Gallery, Santa Monica, CA, USA **2006** Asahi Art Festival, Japan • Hiroshima City Museum of Contemporary Art, Japan **Selected group exhibitions: 2009** 'The Book Borrowers: Contemporary Artists Transforming the Book', Bellevue Arts Museum, Seattle • 'Migration and Expression', Okinawa Prefectural Art Museum, Japan • 'Hundred Stories about Love', 21st Century Museum of Contemporary • Art, Kanazawa, Japan **2008** 'Okinawa Prismed', National Museum of Modern Art, Tokyo • 'Second Life!', Museum of Arts & Design, New York • 'Wall Rockets', Arts FLAG Foundation, New York **2007** 'Milk Crown and Mushroom Cloud', David Castillo Gallery, New York • 'Making a Home: Japanese Contemporary Artists in New York', Japan Society, New York • 'The Shapes of Space', Solomon R. Guggenheim Museum, New York **Selected bibliography: 2008** Scarlet Cheng, 'Paper Work? Bring It On', Los Angeles Times, 26 Oct • Roberta Smith, 'Using Old Materials to Put A New Face on A Museum', The New York Times, 26 Sep **2007** Craig Adcock and Terri Lindbloom, Running Around the Pool: Contemporary Drawing, Museum of Fine Arts, Florida State University • Emily Talbot, 'Art: Yuken Teruya', Time Out New York, 15 Mar **2006** Greg Cook, 'Crafty', Boston Phoenix, 29 Sep

Althea Thauberger

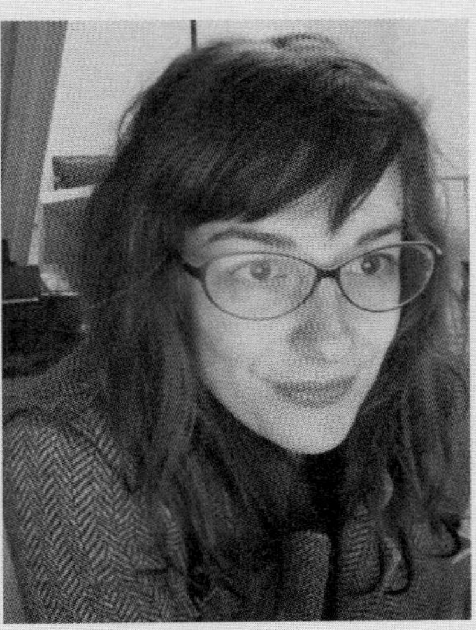

Born 1970, Saskatoon, Canada. Lives Vancouver, Canada. **Selected solo exhibitions: 2008** Dunlop Art Gallery, Regina, Canada **2007** John Connelly Presents, New York • Basis voor actuele kunst, Utrecht **2006** Künstlerhaus Bethanien, Berlin **Selected group exhibitions: 2008** 'Nomads', National Gallery of Canada, Ottawa • Manifesta 7, Trento, Italy • Guangzhou Triennial, China • 'Exponential Future', Morris and Helen Belkin Gallery at University of British Columbia, Vancouver **2007** 'Imagine Action', Lisson Gallery, London • 'Place of the Transcommon', Institute of Visual Arts at University of Wisconsin, Milwaukee • 'Utopian Mirage', Vassar College Art Gallery, Poughkeepsie, NY **2006** 'The Peninsula', Singapore History Museum • 'Canada Dreaming', Wolfsburg Kunstverein, Germany **Selected bibliography: 2008** Brian Skar, 'Strange Manifestations', Artnet, Aug **2007** Emily Hall, 'Althea Thauberger at John Connelly Presents', Artforum, Summer • Wim Peeters, 'Althea Thauberger', Contemporary, no. 89 • Rosemary Heather, 'The Consternation Effect', Canadian Art, Spring **2006** Emily Vey Duke, 'Althea Thauberger: Experimentalism is Dead. Long Live the Internet', C Magazine, Fall

Harald Thys & Jos De Gruyter

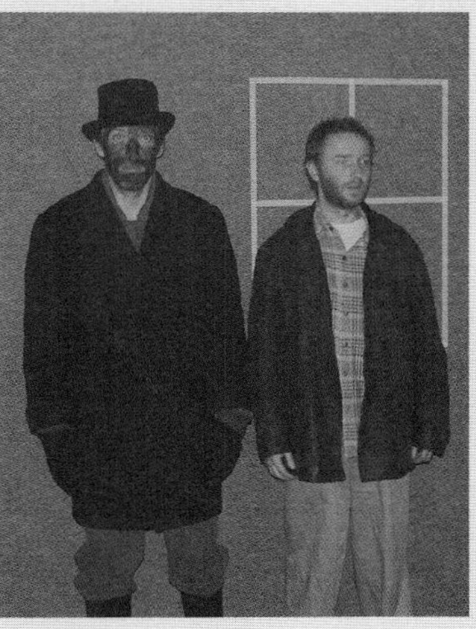

Born 1965, Geel, Belgium. Born 1966, Wilrijk Belgium. Live Brussels, Belgium. **Selected solo exhibitions: 2009** Dépendance, Brussels **2008** Galerie Isabella Bortolozzi, Berlin **2007** Le Plateau, Paris (with François Curlet) • Museum van Hedendaagse Kunst Antwerpen, Antwerp • Artspeak, Vancouver **Selected group exhibitions: 2010** 'La Ricarda', Museu d'Art Contemporani de Barcelona **2008** Manifesta 7, Trento, Italy • Berlin Biennial **2007** Ellen de Bruijne Projects, Amsterdam • Carlier Gebauer, Berlin • 'The Go Between', De Appel, Amsterdam • 'La Ricarda', Casa Gomis, La Ricarda Estate, Spain **Selected bibliography: 2008** Elena Filipovic and Adam Szymczyk (eds.), 5th Berlin Biennale for Contemporary Art: When Things Cast No Shadow, KW, Berlin; JRP Ringier, Zurich **2005** Dieter Roelstraete, 'Dieter Roelstraete ponders the work of Jos de Gruyter and Harald Thys', A Prior, no. 11

Ryan Trecartin

Born 1981, Webster, TX, USA. Lives Philadelphia, PA, USA. **Selected solo exhibitions: 2010** Power Plant,

Toronto **2009** Kunsthalle Wien, Vienna **2008** Hammer Museum, Los Angeles • Wexner Center for the Arts, Columbus **2007** Elizabeth Dee Gallery, New York **Selected group exhibitions: 2010** 'Virtuoso Illusion: Cross Dressing and the New Media Avant-Garde', List Visual Arts Center, MIT, Cambridge, USA **2009** '100 Years', P.S.1, New York • 'Number Three: Here and Now', Julia Stoschek Foundation, Düsseldorf • 'The Jack Wolgin International Competition in the Fine Arts', Tyler School of Art at Temple University, Philadelphia • 'Installations II: Video from the Guggenheim Collections', Guggenheim Museum, Bilbao • 'The Generational: Younger than Jesus', New Museum, New York **Selected bibliography: 2009** Wayne Koestenbaum, 'Situation Hacker', Artforum, Summer • Lauren Cornell, Massimiliano Gioni and Laura Hoptman (eds.), Younger Than Jesus: Artist Directory, Phaidon, London • Randy Kennedy, 'High, Nonlinear Reality, and Welcome to It', The New York Times, 1 Feb **2008** Holland Cotter, 'Video Art Thinks Big: That's Showbiz', The New York Times, 6 Jan

Kaari Upson

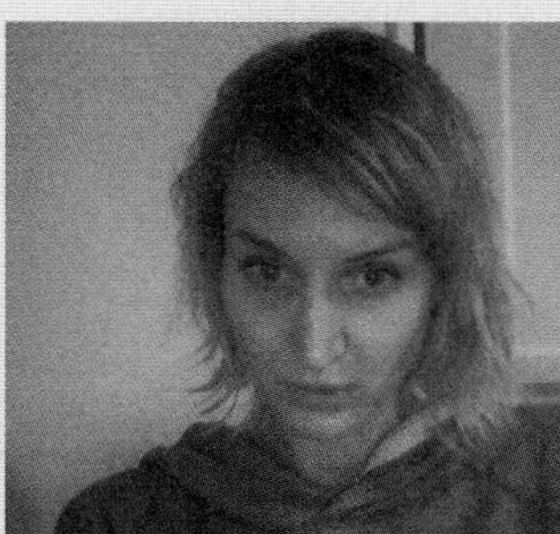

Born 1972, San Bernardino, CA, USA. Lives Los Angeles, CA, USA. **Selected solo exhibitions: 2009** Maccarone, New York **2007** Hammer Museum, Los Angeles • D301 Gallery at California Institute of the Arts, Valencia **2006** L-Shape Gallery at California Institute of the Arts, Valencia **Selected group exhibitions: 2009** 'Wood', Maccarone, New York • 'Berlino – Los Angeles, A Tale of Two (Other) Cities', Massimo di Carlo, Milan • 'Chinese Box', Overduin and Kite, Los Angeles • 'Nine Lives: Visionary Artists from L.A.', Hammer Museum, Los Angeles **2008** 'Sack of Bones', Peres Projects, Los Angeles • 'Pretty Ugly', Gavin Brown's Enterprise, Maccarone, New York **2007** 'Internal Mechanisms', High Energy Constructs, Los Angeles • 'For Ever, 915 Mateo, Los Angeles **Selected bibliography: 2009** Jan Tumlir, 'Nine Lives: Visionary Artists from L.A.', Artforum, Summer • Ali Subotnick, Nine Lives: Visionary Artists from L.A., Hammer Museum, Los Angeles • Sarah Lehrer-Graiwer, 'Artists from L.A.', Artforum, Jan **2008** Maxwell Williams, 'Meet Larry', Tokion, Spring • Irene Lacher, 'Chinese Box', Obsession', Los Angeles Times, 3 Jan • Michael Ned Holte, 'Kaari Upson', Artforum, Feb

Kostis Velonis

Born 1968, Athens, Greece. Lives Athens, Greece. **Selected solo exhibitions: 2010** Monitor Gallery, Rome • Galerie Dana Charkasi , Vienna • National Museum of Contemporary, Athens **2009** Kunstverein Hamburg

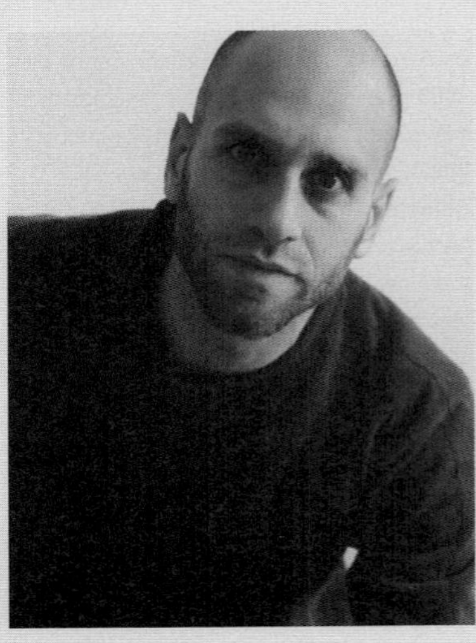

2008 Monitor Gallery, Rome •
Fine Arts Academy, Sarajevo **2007**
Z. Athanassiadou, Salonica • BQ Gallery,
Cologne **Selected group exhibitions:
2009** Athens Biennial • 'Vlassis Caniaris:
In Contrapunto', National Bank
of Greece Cultural Foundation, Athens
• 'Naughtiness', Beltsios Collection,
Amphilochia. Greece • 'Mediterranean',
Palazzo Rospigliosi, Rome **2008** Brussels
Biennial • 'Collage, Cut, Paste', State
Museum of Contemporary Art, Salonica
• 'Athensville', Helexpo, Athens
2007 Lyon Biennial • 'In Present Tense',
National Museum of Contemporary
Art, Athens **Selected bibliography:
2008** Florian Waldvogel, About Apollonian
Beauty, Futura, Athens • Marina
Fokidis and Augustine Zenakos, Craft
Consciousness Is a Class
Consciousness, Futura, Athens **2007**
Nicolaus Schafhausen and Renske
Janssen, Changing Roles, Witte de With,
Rotterdam **2006** Xenia Kalpaktsoglou,
'Bauhaus is not our House', Annual
Review of Design+Art, no. 37

Adrián Villar Rojas

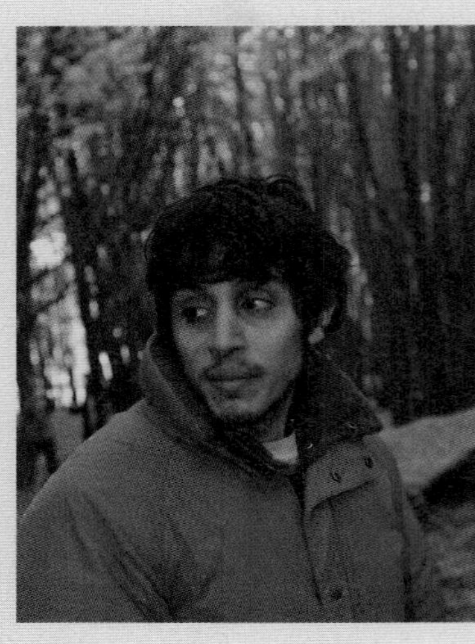

Born 1980, Rosario, Argentina. Lives
Buenos Aires, Argentina. **Selected
solo exhibitions: 2008** Ruth Benzacar
Galería de Arte, Buenos Aires
2007 Belleza y Felicidad, Buenos Aires
• Ciclo Contemporáneo del Centro
Cultural Borges, Buenos Aires **2006**
Galería del Poste Centro Cultural Ricardo
Rojas, Buenos Aires **2005** Centro Cultural
Alianza Francesca; Ruth Benzacar Galería
de Arte, Buenos Aires **Selected group
exhibitions: 2009** 'Moby Dick',
CCA Wattis Institute, San Francisco •
'Panorama del Arte Brasilero', Museo
de Arte Modern de São Paulo •
Cuenca Biennial, Ecuador • 'Intemperie:
Bienal del Fin del Mundo', Ushuaia,
Argentina • Poli/Gráfica Triennial, San
Juan, Puerto Rico **2008** 'Nuevas
incorporaciones', Museo de Arte
Contemporá de Rosario, Argentina
Selected bibliography: 2009
Inés Katzenstein, 'Arte y sentimento,
sobre "Lo que el fuego me trajo"

'de Adrián Villar Rojas', Otra Parte, no. 17 •
María Gainza, 'Adrián Villar Rojas: Lo que
el fuego me trajo', Artforum, Mar **2008** Ana
María Battistozzi, 'Un Artista en Duelo',
Ñ Clarín, May **2007** Eva Grinstein, 'Diario
Intimo 3D', Artecontexto, Madrid, no 15

Danh Vo

Born 1975, Vung Tau, Vietnam. Lives
Berlin, Germany. **Selected solo
exhibitions: 2010** Artists Space, New York
2009 Kunsthalle Basel • Daniel Buchholz,
Colgone • Kadist Art Foundation, Paris

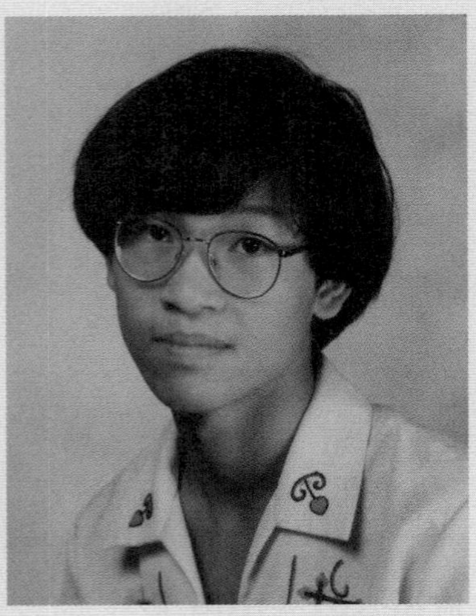

**Selected group exhibitions:
2010** Berlin Biennial **2009** 'Morality II: From
Love to Legal', Witte de With, Rotterdam
• 'Quodlibet II', Daniel Buchholz,
Cologne **Selected bibliography: 2010**
Luigi Fassi, 'Terra Incognita: The Art
of Danh Vo'; Tim Griffin; '1000 Words:
Danh Vo' Artforum, Feb **2009** Danh Vo
and Julie Ault, Where the Lions Are,
Kunsthalle Basel • Francesca Pagliuca, 'No
Way Out', Mousse, no. 17

Tris Vonna-Michell

Born 1982, Rochford, UK. Lives Southend-
on-Sea, UK. **Selected solo exhibitions:
2009** Jeu de Paume, Paris • X-Initiative,
New York • Kunsthalle Zürich • Galleria
d'Arte Moderna e Contemporanea
di Bergamo **2007** Kunstverein
Braunschweig • Witte de With, Rotterdam
Selected group exhibitions: 2009
'The Generational: Younger than Jesus',
New Museum, New York • 'The Front
Room', Contemporary Art Museum,
St Louis • 'I Repeat Myself When Under
Stress', Museum of Contemporary Art,
Detroit • Tate Triennial, London
2008 'Ars Viva 08/09: Inszenierung /
Mise en scene', Museum Abteiberg,
Moenchengladbach, Germany •
Yokohama Triennial • Berlin Biennial

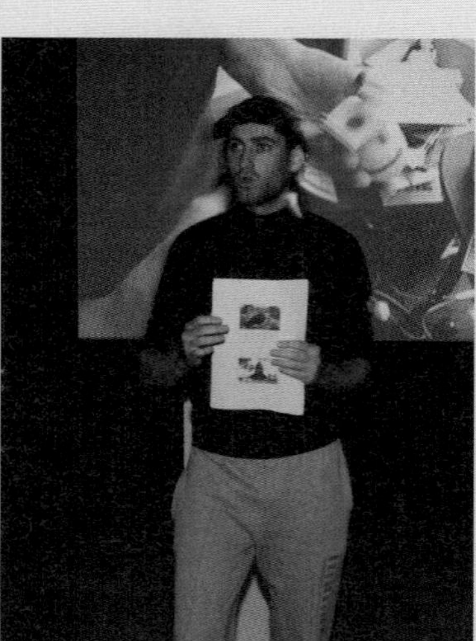

Selected bibliography: 2009 Nicolas
Bourriaud, Altermodern: Tate Triennial,
Tate Publishing, London• Lauren Cornell,
Massimiliano Gioni and Laura Hoptman
(eds.), Younger Than Jesus: Artist Directory,
Phaidon, London • Catrin Lorch, Ars Viva
08/09, Kulturkreis der deutshen Wirtschaft
im BDI e.V. **2008** Elena Filipovic and Adam
Szymczyk (eds.), 5th Berlin Biennale for
Contemporary Art: When Things Cast No
Shadow, KW, Berlin; JRP Ringier, Zurich

Claude Wampler

Born 1966, Pottstown, PA, USA. Lives New
York, NY, USA. **Selected solo exhibition:
2008** Forde Espace d'Art Contemporain,
Geneva • Walker Art Center, Minneapolis
2007 Portland Institute for Contemporary
Art, OR, USA • Diverse Works Arts Space,
Houston, TX, USA **2006** The Kitchen, New
York • Monkeytown, New York **Selected
group exhibitions: 2008** Yokohama
Triennial **2007** 'What we do is sercret',
Blancpain Art Contemporain, Geneva •
'Evacuation', Museum van Hedendaagse
Kunst Antwerpen, Antwerp • 'BloodBath
&Beyond' (with Christian Holstad and Ryan
Schaefer), Hiromi Yoshii Gallery, Tokyo
• 'Plastic', Cabinet des Estampes, Geneva
• 'Melvins', The Mandrake, Los Angeles
2006 'Domino', Air de Paris, Paris

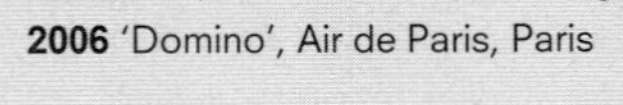

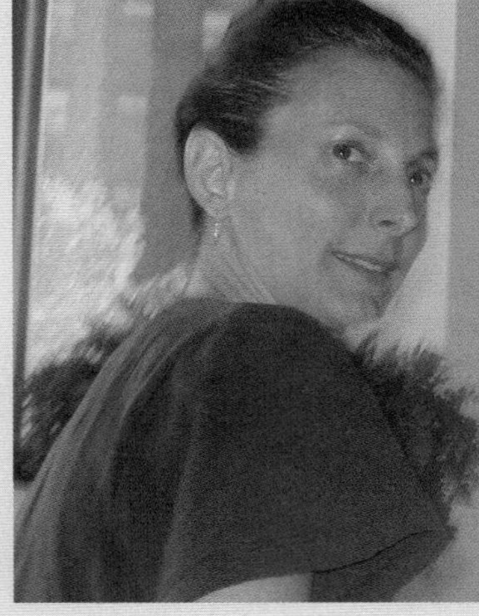

Selected bibliography: 2009 Patricia
Reed, 'Claude Wampler: Staging Shadows
Without Source, C Magazine, Spring **2008**
Christy DeSmith, 'Claude Wampler: What
Just Happened?', The Rake, 28 Jan •
Rohan Preston, 'Claude Wampler,
Disappointing Yet Interesting', Star
Tribune, 25 Jan **2007** Kelly Klaasmeyer,
'Claude Wampler', Houston Press, 22 Nov
• Trajal Harell, 'Claude Wampler: Interview',
Movement Research #31, Aug **2006** Gia
Kourlas, 'Maybe Some Spontaneity Can
Happen', The New York Times, 10 Sep

Andro Wekua

Born 1977, Sochumi, Georgia. Lives Berlin,
Germany, and Zurich, Switzerland.
Selected solo exhibitions: 2009 Wiels,
Brussels • Museion, Bozen, Italy **2008**
Camden Arts Centre, London • Hallen
Haarlem, Netherlands • Le Magasin,
Grenoble • Gladstone Gallery, New York
2007 Galerie Peter Kilchmann, Zurich •
Museum Boijmans van Beuningen,
Rotterdam **Selected group exhibitions:
2009** 'Le Sang d'un Poète', Estuaire Nantes,
Saint-Nazaire, France • 'A Guest + A Host
= A Ghost', Deste Foundation, Athens
2008 'Modern Modern', Chelsea Art
Museum, New York • Busan Biennial •
'Shifting Identities', Kunsthaus Zürich •
Carnegie International, Pittsburgh

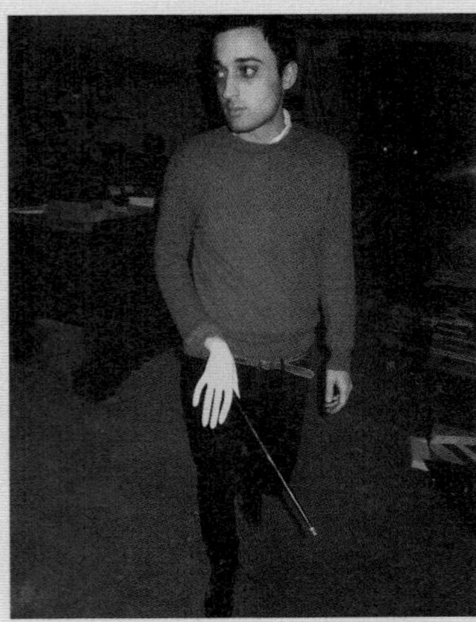

2007 'Everyday is Saturday', Tbilisi Centre
for Contemporary Art, Georgia •
'Works in Ceramic', Gladstone Gallery,
New York **2006** Berlin Biennial **Selected
bibliography: 2009** Boris Groys and
Andro Wekua, Wait to Wait, Christoph
Keller Editions, Zurich • Andro Wekua,
Workshop Report, Museion Bozen; Wiels,
Brussels; Walther Köenig, Cologne •
Lauren Cornell, Massimiliano Gioni and
Laura Hoptman (eds.), Younger Than Jesus:
Artist Directory, Phaidon, London **2008**
Daniel Baumann and Andro Wekua,
Sunset. I Love the Horizon, Le Magasin,
Grenoble • Andro Wekua, Lady Luck,
Gladstone Gallery, New York, JRP Ringier,
Zurich **2006** Dieter Schwarz and Rein
Wolfs, If there ever was one, Kunstmuseum
Winterthur; JRP Ringier, Zurich

Xijing Men

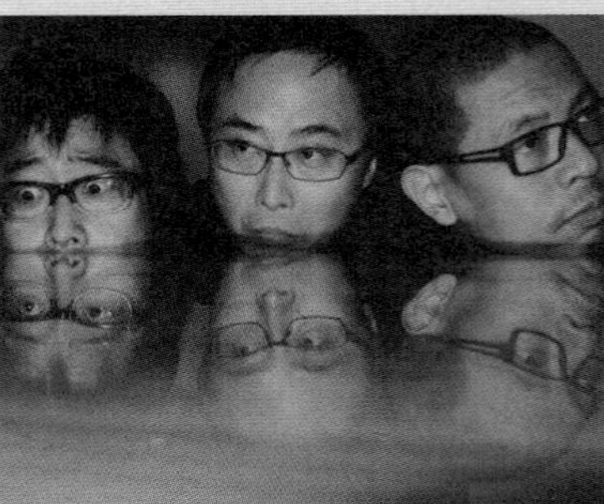

Founded 2007 by Tsuyoshi Ozawa (born
1965, Japan), Gimhonsok (born 1964,
Korea) and Chen Shaoxiong (born 1962,
China). **Selected solo exhibitions: 2008**
'Xijing Olympics: An Exhibition by the Xijing
Men Collective', Bores-Li Gallery, Beijing
Selected group exhibitions: 2009 Lyon
Biennial • Fukuoka Asian Art Triennial •
'The first stop on the super highway', Nam
June Paik Art Center, Seoul **2008** 'Too Early
for Vacation: 32nd Annual Exhibition
of Visual Art', Limerick City Gallery of Art,
Ireland • Nanjing Triennial, China •
'Platform Seoul 2008', Kukje Gallery, Seoul
• 'The Fifth Floor', Tate Liverpool, UK
2007 'Beautiful New World: Contemporary
Culture from Japan', Long March Project,
B.T.A.P., Inter Arts Center, Beijing; Guandong
Museum of Art, Guangzhou • 'Tomorrow ',
Artsonje Centre, Seoul **Selected
bibliography: 2009** Pauline J. Yao, 'A
Game Played Without Rules Has No Losers',
e-Flux Journal, no. 7 • Peter Gorschluter,
The Fifth Floor: Ideas Taking Space,
Liverpool University Press • Hou Hanru et
al., 10th Lyon Biennale: The Spectacle of
the Everyday, Les Presses du Réel, Dijon

Haegue Yang

Born 1971, Seoul, Korea. Lives Berlin,
Germany and Seoul, Korea.

Selected solo exhibitions: 2009 Walker
Art Center, Minneapolis • Korean Pavilion,
Venice Biennale **2008** Sala Rekalde, Bilbao
• Portikus, Frankfurt • Cubitt, London
2007 Haubrokshows, Berlin • Galerie
Barbara Wien, Berlin **Selected group
exhibitions: 2009** 'Sequelism. Episode 3:
Possible, Probable or Preferable Futures',
Arnolfini, Bristol, UK • 'Your Bright Future:
12 Contemporary Artists from Korea', Los
Angeles County Museum of Art; Museum
of Fine Arts, Houston **2008** Turin Triennial /
Carnegie International, Carnegie Museum
of Art, Pittsburgh • 'Whose History',
Hamburger Kunstverein **2007** 'Brave New
Worlds', Walker Art Center, Minneapolis
• 'Feminist Legacies and Potentials in
Contemporary Art Practice', Museum van
Hedendaagse Kunst Antwerpen, Antwerp

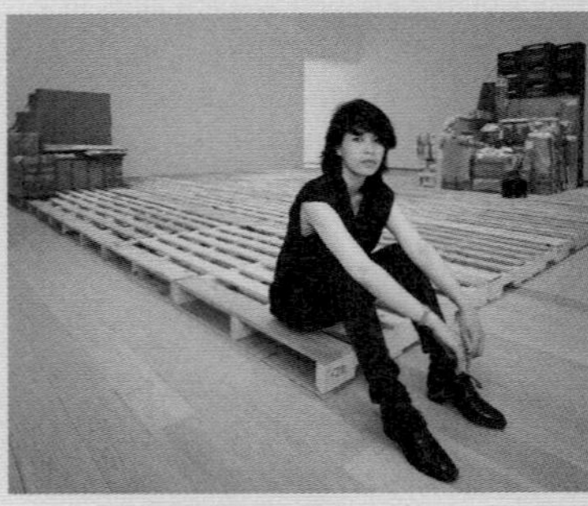

Selected bibliography: 2009 Eungie
Joo (ed.), Haegue Yang: Condensation,
Arts Council Korea, Seoul; Wiens, Berlin
• Melanie Ohnemus (ed.), Haegue Yang:
Siblings and Twins, Portikus, Frankfurt
• Yasmil Raymond, 'Haegue Yang', Domus
Feb • Leire Vergara (ed.), Haegue Yang:
Symmetric Inequality, REDCAT,
Los Angeles; Sala Rekalde, Bilbao • Emily
Pethic, 'Haegue Yang', Vitamin 3-D: New
Perspectives in Sculpture and Installation,
Phaidon, London **2007** Binna Choi (ed.),
Haegue Yang: Community of Absence,
Basis voor Actuele Kunst, Utrecht;
Revolver, Frankfurt • Hyunjin Kim (ed.),
Haegue Yang: Sadong 30, Wiens, Berlin

The publishers are grateful to the 100 artists and 10 curators

We would also like to thank the following: Galerie Air de Paris, Paris; Andersen-s Contemporary, Copenhagen and Berlin; Andrea Rosen Gallery, New York; Andrew Kreps Gallery, New York; Anton Kern Gallery, New York; Arataniurano, Tokyo; Arndt & Partner, Berlin; Arratia, Beer, Berlin; John Baldessari; Galerie Barbara Wien, Berlin; Berlin Biennial for Contemporary Art; Montse Bernal; Blum & Poe, Los Angeles; BQ, Berlin; Cabinet Gallery, London; Carl Freedman Gallery, London; Carnegie Museum of Art, Pittsburgh; Catriona Jeffries Gallery, Vancouver; Galerie Chantal Crousel, Paris; Contemporary Fine Arts, Berlin; CRG Gallery, New York; Croy/Nielsen, Berlin; Dépendance, Brussels; Distrito 4 Gallery, Madrid; Doggerfisher, Edinburgh; Dvir Gallery, Tel Aviv; Elizabeth Dee, New York; Estate of Guy de Cointet; Foksal Gallery Foundation, Warsaw; Galerie Gabriele Senn, Vienna; Hiroshima City Museum of Contemporary Art; Hiroshima Symphony Orchestra; Galleri i8, Reykjavik; Ibid Projects, London; Ikon Gallery, Birmingham; Institute of Contemporary Arts, London; Isabella Bortolozzi, Berlin; Kate MacGarry, London; Mike Kelley; Kukje Gallery, Seoul; Kunsthalle Basel; Lisson Gallery, London; Luhring Augustine, New York; Galeria Luisa Strina, São Paulo; Martos Gallery, New York; Mary Mary, Glasgow; Galleria Massimo De Carlo, Milan; Galerie Micky Schubert, Berlin; Mother's Tankstation, Dublin; Museum van Hedendaagse Kunst Antwerpen; Galerie Neu, Berlin; Edward Park; Perry Rubenstein Gallery, New York; Peter Kilchmann, Zurich; Pilar Corrias, London; Pinksummer Contemporary Art, Genoa; Karishma Rafferty; Reena Spaulings Fine Art, New York; Galerie Reinhard Hauff, Stuttgart; Martin Rejtman; Sadie Coles HQ, London; Galerie Schleicher+Lange, Paris; SculptureCenter, New York; Sprüth Magers, Berlin, London; Stephen Friedman Gallery, London; Tanya Bonakdar, New York; Tate, London; Taxter & Spengemann, New York; Tensta Konsthall, Stockholm; Tucci Russo Studio per l'Arte Contemporanea, Torre Pellice; Uli Ziemons, Institut für Film und Videokunst e.V. Berlin; Vancouver Art Gallery; VG Bild-Kunst, Bonn; Wallspace Gallery, New York; Warburg Institute, London; Yokohama Triennial; Ylva Ogland and Rodrigo Mallea Lira, Konst2; Yvon Lambert, Paris; Galleria Zero, Milan

Photographers
A Database; Ketuta Alexi; Stefan Altenburger; Laleper Aytek; Carla Barbero; Tomas Barry; Jan Bauer; Peter Bellamy; Hans Berg; Juan Biderman; Hannes Böck; Bernd Borchardt; Polly Braden; A. Burger; Jun Hui Byun; Luca Campigotto; Pattara Chanruechachai; Monica Chojnicka; Pierluigi Cipelli; Alessandro Coco; David Cottridge; Sam Drake; Marc Domage; Martin Eberle; James Ewing; Guillermo Faivovich; Edouard Fraipon; Julia Fuchs; Julian Gastelo; Hugo Glendinning; Nicolas Goldberg; Milutin Gubash; Wolfgang Günzel; Serge Hasenböhler; Lucas Heavy; Ignacio Iasparra; Yasushi Ichikawa; Imamura Kaoru; Andy Keate; Chris Kendall; Daniel Kiblisky; Keizo Kioku; Daenam Kim; Florian Kleinefenn; Viktor Kolibàl; Asier Larraza; Nadine Lawson & Sebastian Bruno; Marcus J Leith; Tom Little; Jason Mandella; Ryuichi Maruo; Scott Massey; Aubrey Maye; Stefan Meier; Jacopo Menzani; Norbert Miguletz; Stephan Minx; Christian McDonald; Fredrik Nilsen; Jorge Porcel de Peralta; Wilfried Petzi; Rafael Pinho; Karl Rabe; Stefan Maria Rother; Rokma; Stephen Rowe; Paolo Mussat Sator; Jason Schmidt; Elfie Semotan; Shimabuku; Toshihiro Shimizu; Studio Schaub; Lothar Schnepf; Andy Stagg; Lee Stalsworth; Mikiya Takimoto; Tate Photography; Serkan Taycan; Akiko Tominaga; Wolfgang Träger; Tom Van Eynde; Eva Vermandel; Uwe Walter; Carl Warner; Ikuhiro Watanabe; Stuart Whipps; Joshua White; José Luis López de Zubiria

Translators
Texts by Inés Katzenstein translated from Spanish by Lupe Núñez-Fernández.
Texts by Yukie Kamiya translated from Japanese by Pamela Miki.

Phaidon Press Limited
Regent's Wharf
All Saints Street
London N1 9PA

Phaidon Press Inc.
180 Varick Street
New York, NY 10014

www.phaidon.com

First published 2010
© 2010 Phaidon Press Limited
All works © the artists

ISBN 9 78 0 7148 5683 4

A CIP catalogue record of this book is available from the British Library

Designed by Sonya Dyakova

Printed in Italy

Acknowledgements

Murakami's exhibition @ MURAKAMI, Brooklyn Museum, New York, 2008, 2008. Tablecloth mounted on stretcher. 305 × 305 cm

PHAIDO